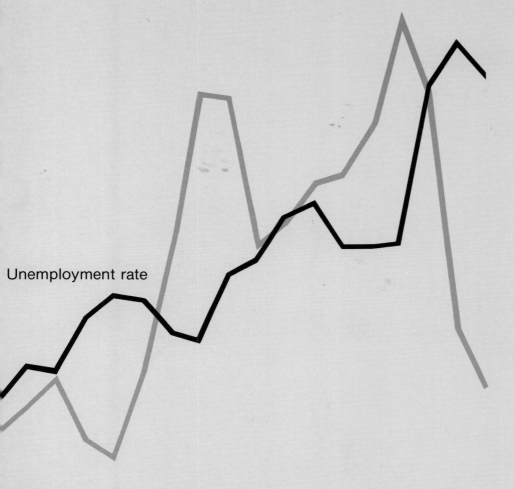

Unemployment rate

nflation rate

1970   1975   1980   1984

ar

ECONOMICS

Principles and Policy　　Canadian Edition

William J. Baumol
New York University
and
Princeton University

Alan S. Blinder
Princeton University

William M. Scarth
McMaster University

Academic Press Canada
Toronto

To my three children,
Ellen, Daniel,
and now Sabrina
W.J.B.

For William, who loves to read
and Scott, who loves to write
A.S.B.

To Brian, David
and the memory of Michael
W.M.S.

Copyright © 1985 by Academic Press Canada
55 Barber Greene Road, Don Mills, Ontario, M3C 2A1

Canadian Cataloguing in Publication Data

Baumol, William J.
    Economics, principles and policy

Includes index.
ISBN 0-7747-3042-0.

1. Economics.   I. Blinder, Alan, S.   II. Scarth,
William M., 1946–   III. Title.

HB171.5.B322 1985   330   C85-098462-9

ISBN: 0-7747-3042-0

90 89 88 87 86 85   BP 1 2 3 4 5 6

Printed in Canada

Cover photograph features Gold Maple Leaf bullion coins struck by the Royal Canadian Mint, Ottawa. Courtesy of Royal Canadian Mint.

Preface

For decades, the "principles of economics" book has been expected to codify the entire discipline of economics. In recent years, this has become increasingly difficult, but also more imperative. The explosion of economic knowledge has made it impossible to put all of economics between two covers. But at the same time, more and more public policy issues either are basically economic in nature or involve important economic considerations. Intelligent citizens can no longer afford to be innocent of economics.

This dilemma has guided the preparation of this book in two ways. First, we have studiously avoided the encyclopaedic approach and abandoned the fiction, so popular among textbook writers, that literally everything is of the utmost importance. Second, we have tried to highlight those important ideas that are likely to be of lasting significance—principles that you will want to remember long after the course is over because they offer insights that are far from obvious, because they are of practical importance, and because they are widely misunderstood by intelligent laymen. A dozen of the most important of these ideas have been selected as **12 Ideas for Beyond the Final Exam** and are called to your attention when they occur through the use of the book's logo. ▣

All modern economics textbooks abound with "real-world" examples, but we have tried to go beyond this, to elevate the examples to pre-eminence. For in our view, the policy issue or everyday economic problem ought to lead the student naturally to the economic principle, not the other way around. For this reason, many chapters start with a real policy issue or a practical problem that may seem puzzling or paradoxical to non-economists, and then proceed to describe the economic analysis required to remove the mystery. In doing this, we have tried to utilize technical jargon and diagrams only where there is a clear need, never for their own sake.

Still, economics is a somewhat technical subject and, except for a few rather light chapters, this is a book for the desk, not for the bed. We have, however, made strenuous efforts to simplify the technical level of the discussion as much as we could without sacrificing content. Fortunately, almost every important idea in economics can be explained in plain English, and this is how we have tried to explain them. Yet, even while reducing the technical difficulty of the book, we have incorporated some elements of economic analysis that have traditionally been left out of introductory books but that are really too important to omit.

Foremost among these is our extensive treatment of prices and inflation in Parts Two and Three. For years, textbooks devoted many chapters to unrealistic, but presumably simpler, economic models in which prices never rose. The original American edition of this book was the first introductory text to put inflation into the story from the very beginning, rather than as an afterthought—a practice we maintain and expand in this first Canadian edition.

Another example is our treatment of how the market mechanism is able, under ideal circumstances, to allocate society's resources in the most efficient manner possible. Many introductory texts, thinking the topic too difficult for beginning students, give little more than some general hints about this important result. We offer a genuine proof and an extensive discussion of precisely what the result does—and does not—imply about the efficiency of real-world market economies.

Microeconomics

The discussion of microeconomics is organized around a central theme that we believe deals with the most significant lessons to be learned in an introductory economics course: what a market system does well, and what it does poorly.

Part One introduces this central theme and some of the fundamental ideas of economics (such as scarcity, opportunity cost, markets, and prices). Then Part Four acquaints students with the central analytical tools of microeconomics and uses them to explain how both consumers (Chapters 20 and 21) and producers (Chapters 22 and 23) make decisions that best serve their own interests. Part Five examines how these decisions interact in the marketplace, and provides an extensive examination of the virtues and vices of free markets. The early chapters of Part Five (Chapters 25 and 26) extol the remarkable accomplishments of an idealized system of markets, while the later chapters (Chapters 27 to 29) discuss some of the market system's principal failings. In this way, Part Five sets the stage for Parts Six and Seven, in which we discuss where, why, and how the government intervenes in the economy.

The policy-oriented chapters examine new developments in regulation (Chapter 30), competition laws (Chapter 31), environmental problems (Chapter 34), energy (Chapter 35), and income distribution issues (Chapters 36, 37, and 38). Criteria for judging whether taxes are good or bad are developed in Chapter 33.

The material on comparative advantage and tariff policy is not left tucked away at the end of the book, but is fully integrated within the core of the microeconomic analysis. Since the legal approaches to limiting market power (that is, regulation and competition laws) have met with rather limited success, it is stressed that tariff cuts can be used to make Canadian markets contestable. Thus, tariff policy (Chapter 32) is introduced as one among several instruments for stimulating competition. Of course, the gains from international trade do not depend solely on Canada's small domestic markets and any incomplete exploitation of the economies of large-scale production. Thus the principle of comparative advantage in the standard situation of constant costs is fully explained in Chapter 32.

Macroeconomics

Students are invariably interested in learning enough macroeconomics within an introductory course to enable them to make sense of (or at least evaluate) such things as major statements by the Governor of the Bank of Canada. This is simply not possible without an analysis that stresses the cost-increasing effects of a falling Canadian dollar, which requires an integrated analysis of aggregate demand *and* supply. We do not ask the student to make do with a fixed-price macroeconomic analysis; aggregate supply and demand are used from the outset.

The macroeconomic section of the book starts with a brief history of macroeconomic events in Canada and an initial use of the aggregate-demand-and-supply curves (Chapter 5). There follows a full discussion of the costs associated with unemployment and inflation (Chapter 6), and the development of multiplier theory, fiscal policy, and supply-side economics (Chapters 7 through 11). The effects of personal income tax changes, sales tax policy, and corporate tax concessions are thoroughly examined.

Chapter 12 introduces financial considerations and explains the money supply and the chartered banking system. The study of central banking that follows (Chapter 13) stresses that pegging the exchange rate forces the Bank of Canada to conduct "open-market operations" in the foreign-exchange market, in just the same way that it does in domestic bond markets when initiating monetary policy. The nature of the foreign-exchange market is explained at this stage, and monetary and exchange-rate policy are discussed simultaneously. The chapter ends with a full discussion of a public statement issued by the Governor of the Bank of Canada concerning the viability of an independent interest-rate policy for Canada.

The following two chapters integrate the fiscal and monetary/exchange-rate policy analyses. Chapter 14 considers the Monetarist–Keynesian debate from a closed-economy viewpoint, while Chapter 15 analyses the relative effectiveness of monetary and fiscal policies under alternative exchange-rate regimes for a small open economy like Canada's. Several policy episodes (such as the Trudeau government's attempt to use monetary policy under fixed exchange rates, and the Diefenbaker government's need to rely on fiscal policy under floating exchange rates) are used to illustrate the direct importance of the economic analysis. Further issues concerning exchange rates, the balance of payments, and the history of the international monetary system are discussed in Chapter 16.

Chapters 17 through 19 represent the remaining parts of the core macro-economic section of the book. Each deals with a central issue that is both highly topical, and of enduring importance. Chapter 17 discusses the question "Are large government budget deficits bad?"; Chapter 18 asks "What is the nature of the trade-off between inflation and unemployment?"; and Chapter 19 considers the question "Should the government have an active stabilization policy at all?".

Some twenty years of lag in the growth rate of Canadian productivity behind that of a substantial number of European and Far Eastern countries has elicited concern about the consequences for Canadian competitiveness. Our belief that Canadian productivity performance will continue to be a major concern of policy-makers has prompted us to include an entire chapter on this subject. Chapter 39 describes the pertinent facts, examines some of the explanations that have been offered, analyses the consequences of a protracted lag in productivity growth, and discusses some of the productivity stimulation policies that have been proposed. To make room in curricula for this chapter on productivity, we have combined economic growth and the problems of the less-developed countries into a single chapter (Chapter 40).

Studying Principles of Economics

Most courses will begin with Part One, where we have touched most of the traditional bases while keeping the introductory materials briefer than in most texts. Courses dealing with macroeconomic theory and policy in the first term will proceed next to Parts Two and Three, while courses commencing with micro-economics will skip to Part Four. Either sort of course may make use of some of the chapters in Parts Seven and Eight.

Whatever the nature of your course, we would like to offer one suggestion. Unlike some of the other courses you may be taking, principles of economics is cumulative—each week's lesson builds on what you have learned before. You will save yourself a lot of frustration (and also a lot of work) if you keep up on a week-to-week basis. To help you do this, there is a chapter summary, a list of important terms and concepts, and a selection of discussion questions to help you review at the end of each chapter. In addition to these aids, many students will find the *Study Guide*, designed specifically to accompany this text, helpful as a self-testing and diagnostic device. When you encounter difficulties in the *Study Guide*, you will know which sections of the text you need to review.

Note to the Instructor

The ordering of chapters in the book is based on courses that treat macroeconomics before microeconomics. The macroeconomic analysis is found in Parts Two and Three. The core micro materials occupy Parts Four through Seven, in an order chosen to emphasize the central theme: the working of markets. Parts Eight and Nine contain an assortment of topics that you will use or omit at your discretion. There seems to us no obvious "order" in which to treat these chapters.

Two topics in microeconomics that students find difficult in a first course are the connection between profit maximization and the marginal revenue (MR) = marginal cost (MC) condition, and the choice of cost-minimizing input proportions for the production process. In the book we have dealt with each of these in a special way designed to facilitate the students' grasp of the material.

For marginal analysis of profit maximization (Chapter 23), we have invented the concept of marginal profit, defined as MR minus MC, which connects directly with the slope of the hill-shaped curve of profits. It becomes clear to the student why, if marginal profit is either positive or negative, one must be on one of the sides of the hill rather than its summit. Only if marginal profit is zero, i.e., MR = MC, can the firm possibly be at the highest point of the hill. It thus becomes clear why the firm is better off if *marginal* profit is zero than if it is positive, a point that students often find difficult to grasp at first.

The chapter on cost-minimizing input choice (Chapter 22) is divided into two parts. In the earlier part it is assumed that the quantities of all of the firm's inputs except one are fixed. We then explain just how the quantity of that input can be chosen, and the connection between that choice and the firm's costs is examined thoroughly. Only after the student has had the opportunity to master the principles of the single input choice do we turn to multi-input production and the simultaneous choice of the quantities of several inputs. The two parts of the chapter are written so that the first can be studied quite independently of the second. Thus, the instructor who wants to postpone or leave out the multi-input case can do so without causing complications or leaving inconvenient gaps.

Regarding macroeconomics, we have found that a few instructors are reluctant to use aggregate-supply-and-demand analysis in the introductory course. But there are several important advantages to doing so: It is the most natural vehicle for explaining stagflation; it is already very popular in intermediate macro courses, and is fast becoming the standard paradigm within which even sophisticated research issues are being discussed; and it helps integrate the macro and micro portions of the principles text, so that students no longer feel that these are two different subjects. Finally, as noted above, we simply cannot make sense of newspaper reports on such topics as the cost-increasing effects of a falling Canadian dollar without this analysis.

In trying to improve the book from one edition to the next, we will rely heavily on our own experiences as teachers. But our experience using the book is small compared to that of the community of instructors who will be using it. If you encounter problems, or have suggestions for improving the book, we urge you to let us know by writing to Bill Scarth in care of Academic Press Canada, University and Professional Department, 55 Barber Greene Road, Don Mills, Ontario, M3C 2A1. Such letters are invaluable, and we are glad to receive them, even if they are critical.

With Thanks

Finally, and with great pleasure, we turn to the customary acknowledgments of indebtedness. Some of these have been accumulating now through two American editions of the book. The many American instructors whose comments were invaluable in planning this edition have been individually listed in the third American edition. Friends and colleagues who have made helpful suggestions directly for this Canadian edition include: John Burbidge, Martin Dooley, Jim Johnson, Wayne Lewchuk, Les Robb, and Byron Spencer of McMaster University, Doug Burgess of Burgess–Graham Securities, Michael Hare of the University of Toronto, and Brian Scarfe of the University of Alberta. We are particularly indebted to Don Dawson of McMaster University, who provided thorough and invaluable input for the chapters on industrial organization.

The book you hold in your hand was not done by us alone. The staff of Academic Press Canada, including Darlene Zeleney, Keith Thompson, Howard Davidson, and Byron Wall, worked hard and well to turn our manuscript into the book you see. Valuable services were contributed by Greg Ioannou, Ingrid Philipp Cook, Beverley Beetham Endersby, Joyce Wilson, and Jack Steiner. We appreciate all their efforts, and thank Darlene in particular for her tireless and most effective assistance.

And finally, there are our wives, Hilda Baumol, Madeline Blinder, and Kathy Scarth. They have helped in so many ways. Their patience, good judgment, and love have made everything go more smoothly than we had any right to expect. We salute them.

William J. Baumol
Alan S. Blinder
William M. Scarth

The Parts of the Book

Contents

PART II
Essentials of Macroeconomics: Aggregate Supply and Aggregate Demand   71

5 Macroeconomics and Microeconomics 73

6 Unemployment and Inflation: The Twin Evils of Macroeconomics   87

9 Changes on the Demand Side: Multiplier Analysis   161

10 Supply-Side Equilibrium: Unemployment *and* Inflation?   173

13 Central Banking and Monetary Policy

243

14 Stabilization Policy: Without International Capital Flows

265

15 Stabilization Policy: With International Capital Flows

287

23 The Common Sense of Business Decisions: Outputs and Prices   451

Appendix: The Relationships Among Total, Average, and Marginal Data   467

PART V
The Market System: Virtues and Vices   471

24 Firms in Reality: The Corporation and the Stock Market   473

28 Between Competition and Monopoly   539

29 Shortcomings of the Market Mechanism and Government Attempts to Remedy Them   557

PART VI
The Government and the Economy   575

30 Limiting Market Power: Regulation of Industry   577

31 Limiting Market Power: Competition Policy 597

32 Limiting Market Power: Tariff Policy 615

PART VIII
Alternative Economic Systems 813

41 Comparative Economic Systems: What Are the Choices?   815

42 Dissenting Opinions: Conservative, Moderate, and Radical   839

I

What Is Economics All About?

What Is Economics?

Why does public discussion
of economic policy so often
show the abysmal ignorance
of the participants? Why do I
so often want to cry at what
public figures, the press, and
television commentators say
about economic affairs?
ROBERT M. SOLOW

Economics is a broad-ranging discipline, both in the questions it asks and in the methods it uses to seek answers. Many definitions of economics have been proposed, but we prefer to avoid any attempt to define the discipline in a single sentence or paragraph. Instead, this chapter will introduce you to economics by letting the subject matter speak for itself.

The first part of this chapter is intended to give you some idea of the types of problems that can be approached through economic analysis and the kinds of solutions that economic principles suggest. By the time you finish this course, we can promise you a better understanding of some of the nation's and the world's most pressing problems and of some approaches to solving these problems. This is the real payoff from studying economics.

The second part briefly introduces the methods of economic inquiry and the tools that economists use. These are tools you may find useful in your life as a citizen, consumer, and worker after the course is over.

Ideas for Beyond the Final Exam

As university professors, we realize it is inevitable that you will forget much of what you learn in this course—perhaps with a sense of relief—very soon after the final exam. There is not much point bemoaning this fact; elephants may never forget, but people do. Nevertheless, there are a number of economic ideas that are important enough for you to remember well beyond the final exam. You will want to remember them because they offer insights into the workings of the economy, because their significance is enduring, and because you will have shortchanged your own education if you forget them as soon as the course is over.

To help you pick out a few of these crucial ideas, we have selected 12 of them from among the many contained in this book. Some bear on important policy issues that often appear in the newspapers and that may have relevance to your own future decisions. Others point out common misunderstandings that occur among even the most thoughtful lay observers. As the quotation that opens this chapter suggests, many learned judges, politicians, business leaders, and university administrators who failed to understand or misused these economic principles could have made far wiser decisions than they did.

Each of the **12 Ideas for Beyond the Final Exam** will be discussed in depth as it occurs in the course of the book; you should not expect to understand these ideas fully after reading this first chapter. None the less, we think it useful to sketch them briefly here both to introduce you to economics and to provide a selective preview of what is to come.

We have organized our 12 Ideas into three groups. The first four are encountered in courses that specialize in *macroeconomics* (the study of the national economy). The next two concern a topic that is particularly important to Canada—international trade. The last six are covered in courses that specialize in *microeconomics* (the study of the price system). All of these topics will appear in a full-year course.

IDEA 1: The Trade-Off Between Inflation and Unemployment

At the start of this decade, Canadian policy-makers waged all-out war on inflation. The war was won: Inflation was reduced dramatically. But casualties were heavy: The national unemployment rate, which averaged 6.8 percent during the 1970s, averaged a stunning 11.5 percent in 1982 and 1983.

Economists maintain that this conjunction of events was no coincidence. Owing to features of our economy that we will study in Parts Two and Three, there is an agonizing *trade-off between inflation and unemployment*, meaning that most policies that bring down inflation also cause unemployment to rise.

Since this trade-off poses the fundamental dilemma of national economic policy, we will devote all of Chapter 18 to examining it in detail. And we shall also consider some suggestions for escaping from the trade-off, such as supply-side economics (Chapter 11) and wage–price controls (Chapter 19).

IDEA 2: The Illusion of High Interest Rates

Is it more costly to borrow money at 5 percent interest or at 13 percent interest? That would appear to be an easy question to answer, even without a course in economics. But, in fact, it is not. An example will show why.

Around 1960, banks were lending money to home buyers at annual interest rates of about 5 percent. Twenty years later, these rates had risen to 13 percent. Yet economists maintain that it was actually cheaper to borrow in 1980 than in 1960. Why? Because inflation in 1980 was running at about 10 percent per year and at only about 1 percent in 1960.

What does inflation have to do with interest rates? Consider the position of a person who lends $100 for one year at a rate of 13 percent interest when the inflation rate is at 10 percent. At the end of the year the lender gets back his $100 plus $13 interest. But over that same year, because of inflation, he loses $10 *in terms of what his money can buy*. That is, in terms of *purchasing power*, the lender gains only $3 on his $100 loan, or 3 percent.

Now consider someone who lends $100 at 5 percent interest when prices are rising only 1 percent a year. This lender gets back the original $100 plus $5 in interest and loses only $1 in purchasing power from inflation—for a net gain of $4, or a 4 percent return on his loan.

As we will learn in Chapter 6, the failure to understand this principle has caused troubles for our tax laws, and in Chapter 17 we will see that it has even led to misunderstanding of the size and nature of the government budget deficit.

IDEA 3: The Consequences of Budget Deficits

Large federal budget deficits have been much in the news in recent years, as have proposals to cut the deficit.

The conflicting claims and counterclaims that have marked the debate over budget deficits are bound to confuse the layman. Some critics claim that deficits hold dire consequences—including higher interest rates, more inflation, a stagnant economy, and an irksome burden on future generations of Canadians. Others deny these charges.

Who is right? Are deficits really malign or benign influences on our economy? The answers, economists insist, are so complicated that the only correct short answer is: It all depends. The precise factors on which the answers depend, and the reasons why, are sufficiently important that they merit an entire chapter of this book (Chapter 17). There we will learn that a budget deficit may be sound or unsound policy, depending on its size and on the reasons for its existence. However, whether or not the deficit represents sound policy, if it is generally believed to be unsound, its existence limits the government's ability to undertake new policies.

IDEA 4: Productivity Is Everything in the Long Run

In Geneva a worker in a watch factory now turns out almost exactly one hundred times as many mechanical watches per year as his ancestor did three centuries earlier. The **productivity** of labour (output per worker hour) in cotton production has probably gone up more than a thousandfold in two hundred years. It is estimated that production per hour of labour in manufacturing in the United States has gone up about seven times in the past century. This means the average American can enjoy about seven times as much clothing, housewares, and luxury goods as were available to a typical inhabitant of the United States one hundred years before. Similar data is not available for Canada, but we know that similar increases in living standards have taken place.

Economic issues such as inflation, unemployment, and monopoly are important to us all and will receive great attention in this book. But in the long run nothing has as great an effect on our material well-being and the amounts society can afford to spend on hospitals, schools, and social amenities as the rate of growth of productivity. Chapter 39 points out that, because productivity compounds like the interest on savings in a bank, what appears to be a small increase in productivity growth can have a huge effect on a country's standard of living over a long period of time. Since 1800, for example, U.S. productivity is estimated to have grown only a bit more than 1.5 percent a year on the average. But that was enough to increase the output of manufactured goods per person about twenty times—a truly incredible amount.*

IDEA 5: Mutual Gains from Voluntary Exchange

One of the most fundamental ideas of economics is that in a **voluntary exchange** both parties must gain something, or at least expect to gain something. Otherwise, why would they both agree to the exchange? This principle may seem self-evident, and it probably is. Yet it is amazing how often it is ignored in practice.

For example, it was widely believed for centuries that governments should interfere with international trade because one country's gain from a swap must be the other country's loss (see Chapter 32). Analogously, some people feel instinctively that if Mr. A profits handsomely from a deal with Mr. B, then Mr. B must have been exploited. Laws sometimes prohibit mutually beneficial exchanges between buyers and sellers—as when rental housing units are eliminated because the rent is "too high" (Chapter 4), or when a willing worker cannot be hired because the wage rate is "too low" (Chapter 37).

*Unfortunately data are not available to make similar calculations for Canada.

In every one of these cases, and in many more, well-intentioned but misguided reasoning blocks the mutual gains that arise from voluntary exchange—and thereby interferes with one of the most basic functions of an economic system (see Chapter 3).

IDEA 6: The Surprising Principle of Comparative Advantage

The Japanese economy produces many products that Canadians buy in huge quantities—including cars, TV sets, cameras, and electronic equipment. Canadian manufacturers have complained about the competition and demanded protection against the flood of imports that, in their view, threatens Canadian standards of living. Is this view justified?

Economists think not. But what if a combination of higher productivity and lower wages were to permit Japan to produce *everything* more cheaply than we could? Would it not then be true that Canadians would have no work and that our nation would be impoverished?

A remarkable result, called the **law of comparative advantage**, shows that even in this extreme case the two nations should still trade and that each can gain as a result! We will explain this principle fully in Chapter 32, where we will also note some potentially valid arguments in favour of protecting domestic industry. But for now a simple parable will make the reason clear.

Suppose Sam grows up on a farm and is a whiz at ploughing, but he is also a successful country singer and gets paid $2000 a performance at hotels and nightclubs. Should Sam refuse some singing engagements to leave time for ploughing? Of course not. Instead he should hire Alfie, a much less efficient farmer, to plough for him. Sam is the better farmer, but he earns so much more by specializing in singing that it pays him to leave the farming to Alfie. Alfie, though a poorer farmer than Sam, is an even worse singer. Thus Alfie earns a living by specializing in the job at which he at least has a *comparative* advantage (his farming is not quite as bad as his singing), and both Alfie and Sam gain. The same is true of two countries. Even if one of them is more efficient at everything, both countries can gain by producing the things they do best *comparatively*.

IDEA 7: Attempts to Repeal the Laws of Supply and Demand: The Market Strikes Back

When a commodity is in short supply, its price naturally tends to rise. Sometimes disgruntled consumers badger politicians into "solving" the problem by imposing a legal ceiling on the price. Similarly, when supplies are abundant—say, when fine weather produces extraordinarily abundant crops—prices tend to fall. This, naturally, makes suppliers unhappy, and they often succeed in getting legislation enacted that prohibits low prices by imposing price floors. But such attempts to repeal the laws of supply and demand usually backfire and sometimes produce results virtually the opposite of those that were intended.

Where rent controls are adopted to protect tenants, housing grows scarce because the law makes it unprofitable to build and maintain apartments. When minimum-wage legislation is enacted to protect marginal workers, marginal jobs disappear. Price floors are placed under agricultural products and surpluses pile up. History provides spectacular examples of the way in which free markets strike back at attempts to interfere with the way they would otherwise work. For example, when the armies of Spain surrounded Antwerp in 1584, hoping to starve the city into submission to King Phillip's harsh rule, profiteers kept Antwerp going by smuggling food and supplies through enemy lines. However, when the city fathers adopted price controls to end these "unconscionable" profits, supplies suddenly dried up and the city soon surrendered.

As we will see in Chapter 4 and elsewhere in this book, such consequences of interference with the price mechanism are no accident. They follow inevitably from the way free markets work. Despite the many examples from history, many policy-makers still call for interference with the price mechanism. A common example in the early 1980s has been the suggestion that our government should preclude residents from buying stocks and bonds from other countries, so that our interest rates can remain lower than those in the United States.

IDEA 8: Externalities: A Shortcoming of the Market Cured by Market Methods

Markets are very efficient in producing the goods that consumers want in the quantities in which they are desired. They do so by offering large financial rewards to those who respond to what consumers want to buy and who make these products available economically. Similarly, the market mechanism minimizes waste and inefficiency by causing inefficient producers to lose money.

This system works out very well as long as an exchange between a seller and a buyer affects only those two parties. But often an economic transaction affects uninvolved third parties. Examples abound: The utility that supplies electricity to your home also produces soot that discolours your curtains and pollutants that despoil the air and even affect your health; after a farmer sprays his crops with toxic pesticides, the poison may seep into the ground water and affect the health of neighbouring communities.

Such social costs—called **externalities** because they affect parties *external* to the economic transaction that causes them—escape the control of the market mechanism, as we will learn in Chapter 29. There is no financial incentive that motivates the polluter to minimize the damage he does. The electric company and the farmer do not include environmental damage in their cost calculations. As a consequence, it pays firms to make their products as cheaply as possible, disregarding externalities that may damage the quality of life.

Yet, as we will learn in Chapters 29 and 34, there is a way for the government to use the market mechanism to control undesirable externalities. If the public utility and the farmer are charged for the harm they cause to the public, just as they are charged when they use tangible resources such as coal and fertilizer, then they will have an incentive to cut down as much as possible on the amount of pollution they generate. Thus, in this case, economists believe that market methods are often the best way to cure one of the market's most important shortcomings.

IDEA 9: Rational Choice and True Economic Costs

Despite dramatic improvements in our standard of living since the industrial revolution, we have not come anywhere near a state of unlimited abundance, and so we must constantly make choices. If you purchase a new house, you may not be able to afford to eat at expensive restaurants as often as you used to. If a firm decides to retool its factories, it may have to postpone plans for new executive offices. If a government expands its road networks, it may be forced to reduce its outlays on school buildings.

Economists say that the true costs of such decisions are not the number of dollars spent on the house, the new equipment, or the roads, but rather *the value of what must be given up in order to acquire the item*—the restaurant meals, the new executive offices, and the new schools. These are called **opportunity costs** because they represent the *opportunities* the individual, firm, or government must forego to make the desired expenditure. Economists maintain that opportunity costs must be considered in the decision-making process if rational choices are to be made (see Chapter 3).

The costs of a university or college education provide a vivid example that is probably close to the hearts of all students reading this book. How much do you think it *costs* to go to university? Most likely you would answer this question by adding together your expenditures on tuition, room and board, books, and the like, and then deducting any scholarship funds you may receive. Economists would not. They would first want to know how much you could be earning if you were not attending university. This may sound like an irrelevant question, but because you give up these earnings by attending university, they must be added to your tuition bill as a cost of your education. Nor would economists accept the university's bill for room and board as a measure of your living costs. They would want to know by how much this exceeds what it would have cost you to live at home, and only this extra cost would be counted as an expense. On balance, a university or college education probably costs more than you think.

IDEA 10: The Importance of Marginal Analysis

Many pages in this book will be spent explaining, and extolling the virtues of, a type of decision-making process called **marginal analysis** (see especially Chapters 20–23), which can best be illustrated by an example.

Suppose that an airline is told by its accountants that the full cost of transporting one passenger from Montreal to Edmonton is $350. Can the airline profit by offering a reduced rate of $250 to students who fly on a standby basis? The surprising answer is: Probably yes. The reason is that most of the $350 cost per passenger must be paid whether the plane carries 20 passengers or 120 passengers. Marginal analysis says that full costs—which include costs of maintenance, landing rights, ground crews, and so on—are irrelevant to the decision at hand. The only costs that are relevant in deciding whether to carry standby passengers for reduced rates are the extra costs of writing and processing additional tickets, the food and beverages these passengers consume, the additional fuel required, and so on. These costs are called **marginal costs**, and they are probably quite small in this instance. Any passenger who pays the airline more than its marginal cost will add something to the company's profit, so it probably is more profitable to let the students ride for the reduced fare than to fly the plane with some empty seats.

There are many real cases in which decision-makers, not understanding marginal analysis, have rejected advantageous possibilities like the reduced fare in our hypothetical example. These people were misled by calculating in terms of *average* rather than *marginal* cost figures—an error that can be quite costly.

IDEA 11: The Cost Disease of the Service Sector

There is a distressing phenomenon occurring throughout the industrialized world. Many community services have apparently been growing poorer—fewer postal deliveries, larger classes in public schools, less reliable garbage pickups—while the public is paying more and more for them. Indeed, the costs have risen substantially and consistently faster than has the rate of inflation. A natural response is to attribute the problem to political corruption and government inefficiency. But this is certainly not the whole story.

As we shall see in Chapter 29, one of the major causes of the problem is economic. And it has nothing to do with corruption or inefficiency of public employees; rather, it has to do with the dazzling growth in efficiency of private manufacturing industries! Because technological improvements make workers more productive in manufacturing, wages rise. And they rise not only for the manufacturing workers but also for postal workers, teachers, and other public employees. But here technology is not easily changed; since it still takes one person to drive a postal truck and one teacher to teach a class, the cost of these services is forced to rise.

The same sort of cost disease affects other services like medical care, university teaching, restaurant cooking, retailing, and automobile repairs. And it explains why their prices have often gone up far faster than the general inflation rate.

This is important to understand not because it excuses the financial record of our governments, but because an understanding of the problem suggests what we should expect the future to bring and, perhaps, indicates what policies should be advocated to correct it.

IDEA 12: Increasing Output May Require Sacrificing Equality

Many people favour tax cuts (which are discussed in detail in Chapter 11) to spur productivity and efficiency by providing greater incentives for working, saving, and investing.

Yet, there is at least one problem with this approach—known as supply-side economics. In order to provide stronger incentives for success in the economic game, the gaps between the "winners" and the "losers" must necessarily be widened. For it is these gaps, after all, that provide the incentives to work harder, to save more, and to invest productively.

However, some observers feel that the unequal distribution of income in our society is unjust, that it is inequitable for the super rich to sail yachts and give expensive parties while poor people live in slums and eat inadequate diets. People who hold this view are disturbed by the fact that supply-side tax cuts are quite likely to make the distribution of income even more unequal than it already is.

This example illustrates a genuine and pervasive dilemma. There is often a *trade-off* between the *size* of a nation's output and the degree of *equality* with which that output is distributed. As illustrated by the example of supply-side tax cuts, programs that increase production often breed inequality. And, as we will see in Chapter 38, many policies designed to divide the proverbial economic pie more equally inadvertently cause the size of the pie to shrink.

Epilogue

These, then, are a dozen of the more fundamental concepts to be found in this book—ideas that we hope you will retain **Beyond the Final Exam**. Do not try to learn them perfectly right now, for you will hear much more about each as the book progresses. Instead, keep them in mind as you read—we will point them out to you as they occur by the use of the book's logo ▨ —and look back over this list at the end of the course. You may be amazed to see how natural, or even obvious, they will seem then.

Inside the Economist's Tool Kit

Now that you have some idea of the kinds of issues economists deal with, you should know something about how they grapple with these problems. Economics has something of a split personality. Clearly the most rigorous of the social sciences, it nevertheless looks decidedly more "social" than "scientific" when compared with physics. Economists strive to be humanists and scientists simultaneously.

What Economists Do

An economist is, by necessity, a jack of several trades and master of none. Economists borrow modes of investigation from numerous fields, adjusting each to fit the particular problems posed by economic events. Usefulness, not methodological purity, is the criterion for including a technique in the economist's tool kit.

Mathematical reasoning is used extensively in economics, but so is historical study. And neither looks quite the same as when practised by a mathematician or a historian. Statistical inference, too, plays an important role in economic inquiry, but economists have had to modify standard statistical procedures to fit the kinds of data they deal with. In 1926, John Maynard Keynes, the great British economist, summed up the many faces of economic inquiry in a statement that still rings true today:

The master-economist ... must understand symbols and speak in words. He must contemplate the particular in terms of the general, and touch abstract and concrete in the same flight of thought. He must study the present in the light of the past for the purposes of the future. No part of man's nature or his institutions must lie entirely outside his regard. He must be purposeful and disinterested in a simultaneous mood; as aloof and incorruptible as an artist, yet sometimes as near the earth as a politician.[1]

Economics is more easily distinguished by the types of *problems* it addresses than by the investigative *techniques* it employs to study them. An introductory course in economics cannot make you an economist, but it should help you approach social problems from a pragmatic and dispassionate point of view. Answers to all society's problems will not be found in this book. But you should learn how to pose questions in ways that will help produce answers that are both useful and illuminating.

The Need for Abstraction

Some students find economics unduly abstract and "unrealistic." The stylized world envisioned by economic theory seems only a distant cousin to the world they see around them. There is an old joke about three people—a chemist, a physicist, and an economist—stranded on an isolated island with an ample supply of canned food but no implements to open the cans. In debating what to do, the chemist suggested lighting a fire under the cans, thus expanding their contents and causing the cans to burst. The physicist doubted that this would work. He advocated building a catapult with which they could smash the cans against some nearby boulders. Then they turned to the economist for his suggestion. He thought for a moment and announced his solution: "Let's assume we have a can opener."

Economists *do* make unrealistic assumptions, and you will encounter many of them in the pages that follow. But this propensity to abstract from reality results from the incredible complexity of the real world, not from any fondness economists have for sounding absurd.

Compare the chemist's task of explaining the interactions of compounds in a

---

[1] As quoted by Robert Heilbroner in *The Worldly Philosophers*, revised edition (New York: Simon and Schuster, 1972), page 250.

chemical reaction with the economist's task of explaining the interactions of people in an economy. Are molecules ever motivated by greed or altruism, by envy or ambition? Do they ever emulate other molecules? Do forecasts about them ever influence their behaviour? People, of course, do all these things, and many, many more. It is therefore immeasurably more difficult to predict human behaviour than it is to predict chemical reactions. If economists tried to keep track of every aspect of human behaviour, they could surely never hope to understand the nature of the economy. Thus:

Abstraction from unimportant details is necessary to understand the functioning of anything as complex as the economy.

To appreciate why the economist **abstracts** from details, put yourself in the following hypothetical situation. You have just arrived, for the first time in your life, in Vancouver. You are now at the Burnaby General Hospital. This is the point marked *A* in Figures 1–1 and 1–2, which are alternative maps of part of Vancouver. You want to drive to the Vancouver General Hospital, marked *B* on each map. Which map would you find more useful? You will notice that Map 1 (Figure 1–1) has the full details of the Vancouver road system. Consequently, it requires a major effort to read it. In contrast, Map 2 (Figure 1–2) omits many minor roads so that the major arteries stand out more clearly.

Most strangers to the city would prefer Map 2. With its guidance they are likely to find the Vancouver General in a reasonable amount of time, even though a slightly shorter route might have been found by careful calculation and planning using Map 1. Map 2 seems to *abstract* successfully from a lot of confusing details while retaining the essential aspects of the city's geography. Economic theories strive to do the same thing.

Abstraction means ignoring many details in order to focus on the most important factors in a problem.

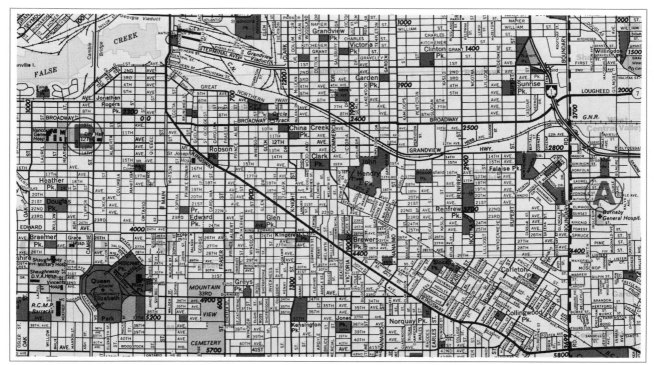

Figure 1–1: Map 1

Map 1 gives complete details of the road system of Vancouver. If you are like most people, you will find it hard to read and not very useful for figuring out how to get from the Burnaby General Hospital (point *A*) to the Vancouver General Hospital (point *B*). For this purpose, the map carries far too much detail, though for some other purposes (for example, locating some very small street in Vancouver) it may be the best map available.

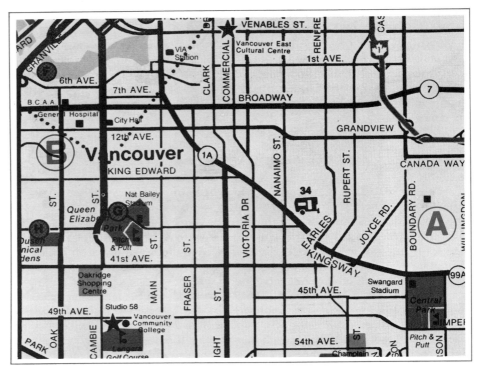

Figure 1-2: Map 2

Map 2 shows a very different perspective of Vancouver. Minor roads are eliminated—we might say, *assumed away*—in order to present a clearer picture of where the major arteries go. As a result of this simplification, several ways of getting from the Burnaby General Hospital (point *A*) to the Vancouver General (point *B*) stand out clearly. For example, we can get on Broadway or the Kingsway and drive west. While we might find a shorter route by poring over the details of Map 1, most of us will feel more comfortable with Map 2.

Figure 1-3: Map 3

Map 3 strips away still more details of the Vancouver road system. In fact, only major roads remain. This map may be useful for passing through the city or getting around it, but it will not help the tourist who wants to see the sights of Vancouver. For this purpose, too many details are missing.

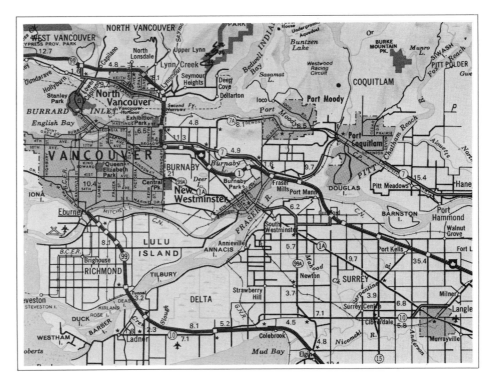

Map 3 (Figure 1–3), which shows little more than the major routes that pass through the greater Vancouver area, illustrates a danger of which all theorists must beware. Armed only with the information provided on this map, you might never find the Vancouver General. Instead of a useful idealization of the Vancouver road network, the map-makers have produced a map that is oversimplified for our purpose. Too much has been assumed away. Of course, this map was never intended to be used as a guide to the Vancouver General, which brings us to a very important point:

There is no such thing as one "right" degree of abstraction for all analytic purposes. The optimal degree of abstraction depends on the objective of the analysis. A model that is a gross oversimplification for one purpose may be needlessly complicated for another.

Economists are constantly treading the thin line between Map 2 and Map 3, between useful generalization about complex issues and gross distortions of the pertinent facts. How can they tell when they have abstracted from reality just enough? There is no objective answer to this question, which is why applied economics is as much art as science. One of the factors distinguishing good economics from bad economics is the degree to which analysts are able to find the factors that constitute the equivalent of Map 2 (rather than Maps 1 or 3) for the problem at hand. It is not always easy to do, as the following examples illustrate.

The Distribution of Income

Suppose you are interested in learning why different people have different incomes, why some are fabulously rich while others are pathetically poor. People differ in many ways, too many to enumerate, much less to study. The economist ignores most of these details in order to focus on a few important facts. The colour of a person's hair or eyes probably is not important to the problem at hand, but the colour of his skin certainly is. Height and weight may not matter, but his parents' bank balance may. Proceeding in this way, we pare Map 1 down to the manageable dimensions of Map 2. But there is a danger of going too far. To make it easy to analyze a problem we can end up stripping away some of its most crucial features.

The Determination of National Income

Suppose we want to know what factors determine the size of the output of the whole economy. Since the volume of goods and services turned out by the whole economy is affected by literally millions of decisions by investors, business managers, employees, government officials, and others, a complete enumeration of all the factors determining the nation's output clearly makes analysis unworkable (Map 1). Abstraction is necessary. We must prune the list to manageable size. Part Two of this book explains how economists do this; that is, how they draw up a Map 2 of the nation's output. Several shortcuts to this process have been proposed, but in the opinion of their critics, they have proved on inspection to be like Map 3.

The Role of Economic Theory

A person "can stare stupidly at phenomena; but in the absence of imagination they will not connect themselves together in any rational way." These words of the renowned American philosopher–scientist C. S. Peirce succinctly express the crucial role of theory in scientific inquiry and help explain why economists are so enamoured of it. To the economist or the physical scientist, the word *theory* does not mean what it does in common speech. In scientific usage, a theory is *not* an untested assertion of alleged fact. The statement that saccharine causes cancer is not a theory, it is a *hypothesis* that will either prove to be true or false after the right sorts of experiments have been completed.

A **theory** is a deliberate
simplification of factual
relationships whose purpose
is to explain how those
relationships work.

Instead, a **theory** is a deliberate simplification (abstraction) of factual relationships that attempts to explain how those relationships work. In other words, it is an *explanation* of the mechanism behind observed phenomena. For example, astronomers' data describe the paths of the planets, and gravity forms the basis of theories that are intended to explain these data. Similarly, economists have data suggesting that government policies can affect the degree of a country's prosperity. Keynesian theory (which will be discussed in Parts Two and Three) seeks to describe and explain these relationships.

To economists, theorizing is not a luxury but a necessity. Economic theory provides a logical structure for organizing and analyzing economic data. It proceeds deductively from assumptions to conclusions—which can later be tested against data. Without theory, economists could only "stare stupidly" at the world. With theory, they can attempt to understand it.

People who have never studied economics often draw a false distinction between *theory* and *practical policy*. Politicians are particularly guilty of this, scoffing at abstract economic theory as something that is best ignored by "practical" policy-makers. The irony of these statements is that:

It is precisely the concern for policy that makes economic theory so necessary and important.

If there were no possibility of changing the economy through public policy, economics might be a historical and descriptive discipline, asking, for example, What happened in Canada during the Great Depression of the 1930s? or How is it that industrial pollution got to be so serious in the 1960s?

But deep concern about public policy forces economists to go beyond such historical and descriptive questions. To analyze policy options, they are forced to deal with possibilities that have not actually occurred. For example, to learn how to prevent depressions, they must investigate whether the Great Depression could have been avoided by more astute government policies. Or to determine what environmental programs will be most effective, they must examine what might happen to pollution in the 1980s if government placed taxes on industrial waste discharges and automobile emissions. As Peirce pointed out, not even a lifetime of ogling at real-world data will answer such questions.

Indeed, the facts can sometimes be highly misleading. Statistics often indicate that two variables behave very similarly: Whenever one rises so does the other, and they also both go down simultaneously. But this **correlation** between the data does not prove that either of these variables *causes* the other. For example, in rainy weather, people tend to drive their cars more slowly, and there are also more traffic accidents. But this correlation does not mean that slow driving causes accidents. Rather, both phenomena can be attributed to a common underlying factor (more rain) that leads both to more accidents and to slower driving. Thus, just looking at the degree of correlation (the degree of similarity) between the behaviour of two sets of statistics (like accidents and driving speeds) may not tell us much about cause and effect. We need to use theory as part of the analysis.

Two variables are said to be
correlated if they tend to
go up or down together. But
correlation need not imply
causation.

Because most economic issues hinge on some question of cause and effect, only a combination of theoretical reasoning and data analysis can hope to provide solutions. Simply observing a correlation between data is not enough. We must understand how, if at all, different government policies will lead to a lower unemployment rate or how a tax on emissions will reduce pollution.

What Is an Economic "Model"?

Economists use *models* to describe such cause-and-effect relationships. The notion of a "model" is familiar enough to children, and economists (in common with other scientists) use the term in much the same way that children do.

A child's model automobile or airplane looks and operates much like the real thing, but it is much smaller and much simpler, and so it is much easier to manipulate and understand. Engineers for General Motors and Boeing also build models of cars and planes. While their models are far bigger and much more elaborate than a child's toy, they use them for much the same purposes: to observe the workings of these vehicles "up close," to experiment with them in order to see how they might behave under different circumstances ("What happens if I do this?"). From these experiments, they make educated guesses as to how the real-life version will perform. Often these guesses prove uncannily accurate, as exemplified by the success of the Boeing 747. But sometimes they are wide of the mark: The chronic mechanical problems of General Motors' Corvair prompted Ralph Nader's acclaimed book *Unsafe at Any Speed*, which helped launch the consumer movement.

Economists use **models** for similar purposes and with similarly mixed results. A. W. Phillips, the famous engineer-turned-economist who discovered the "Phillips curve" (discussed in Chapter 18), was talented enough to construct a working model of the determination of national income in a simple economy, using coloured water flowing through pipes. For years this contraption, depicted in Figure 1–4, graced the basement of the London School of Economics. However, most economists lack Phillips's manual dexterity, so economic models are generally built with paper and pencil rather than with hammer and nails.

An economic **model** is a simplified, small-scale version of some aspect of the economy. Economic models are often expressed in equations, by graphs, or in words.

Because many of the models used in this book are depicted in diagrams, we explain the construction and use of various types of graphs in the next chapter. But sometimes economic models are expressed only in words. The statement "Business people produce the level of output that maximizes their profits" is the basis for a behavioural model whose consequences are explored in some detail in Parts Four through Seven. Don't be put off by seemingly abstract models. Think of them as useful road maps, and remember how hard it would be to find your way around Vancouver without one.

The Concept of "Rational" Behaviour

Many economic models rest on a fundamental assumption: namely, that the decision-maker—be it a consumer or a business firm—behaves "rationally." What do we mean by *rational* behaviour?

The late Professor A. W. Phillips, while teaching at the London School of Economics in the early 1950s, built this machine to illustrate Keynesian theory. This is the same theory that we will explain with words and diagrams later in this book; but Phillips's background as an engineer enabled him to depict the theory with the help of tubes, valves, and pumps. Because economists are not very good plumbers, few of them try to build models of this sort; most rely on paper and pencil instead. But the two sorts of models fulfill precisely the same role. They simplify reality in order to make it understandable.

Figure 1–4
THE PHILLIPS MACHINE

First, we do not use the phrase as a term of approval. It is not necessarily "better" to be rational than to be irrational. Some people usually behave rationally and some do not. This is simply a fact, and we are not concerned with judging the virtues of either behaviour.

Rationality is defined in economics as characterizing those decisions that are most effective in helping the decision-maker achieve his own objectives, whatever they may be. The objectives themselves (unless they are self-contradictory) are never considered either rational or irrational.

Second, and perhaps more important, we use the term **rationality** to characterize *means* rather than *ends*. Rational behaviour is behaviour that is well designed to achieve the desired ends, whatever those ends may be. It is neither more nor less rational to want a pistachio ice-cream cone than to want a mushroom pizza. But once the consumer decides that he wants either the ice cream or the pizza, it is irrational for him to go to the shoe-repair shop for it.

Reasons for Disagreements: Imperfect Information and Value Judgments

"If all the earth's economists were laid end to end, they could not reach an agreement," or so the saying goes. If economics is a scientific discipline, why do economists seem to quarrel so much? Politicians and reporters are fond of pointing out that economists can generally be found arguing both sides of every issue of public policy. Physicists, on the other hand, do not debate whether the earth revolves around the sun or vice versa.

The question reflects a misunderstanding of the nature of science. First of all, the apparently extreme disagreement is attributable in part to the greater visibility of economic discussions. As a matter of fact, physicists formerly did argue over whether the earth revolves around the sun, often with rather grim results for themselves. (Economists, fortunately, are not often burned at the stake!) Nowadays, physicists argue about "black holes," the existence of certain subatomic particles, and other esoteric phenomena. These arguments often go unnoticed by the public because most of us do not understand what they are talking about. In contrast, everyone is eager to join economic debates over inflation, unemployment, pollution, and almost everything else. Because economics is a *social* science, its disputes are aired in public, and almost everyone is personally concerned with the subject matter. Anyone who has ever bought or sold anything, it seems, fancies himself an amateur economist.

Second, there is a much greater area of agreement among economists than most people think. Virtually all economists, regardless of their politics, agree that taxing polluters is one of the best ways to protect the environment (see Chapters 29 and 34), that a negative income tax is superior to most alternative antipoverty programs (see Chapter 38), that free trade among nations is preferable to the erection of barriers through tariffs and quotas (see Chapter 32). The list could go on and on. It is probably true that the issues about which economists agree *far* exceed the subjects on which they disagree.

Third, many of the disputes among economists are not disputes at all. Economists, like everyone else, come in all political persuasions: conservative, middle-of-the-road, liberal, radical. Each may hold a different view of what is best for society, and so may have a different opinion on what is the "right" solution to any problem of public policy. Public policy issues can rarely be decided on purely scientific and "objective" grounds.

While economists can contribute the best theoretical and factual knowledge there is on a particular issue, the final decision on policy questions often rests either on information that is not currently available, or on tastes and ethical opinions about which people differ (the things we call "value judgments"), or on both.

To illustrate why pure scientific analysis often does not lead to a policy conclusion, consider the following problems.

Taxing Industrial Wastes

As you will learn in Chapter 34, the proper tax to levy on industrial wastes depends on quantitative estimates both of the harm done by the pollutant and the costs of pollution abatement. For most waste products, these numbers are not yet known, although knowledge is accumulating rapidly. So a lack of complete information makes it difficult to formulate a concrete policy proposal.

Inflation and Unemployment

Government policies that succeed in shortening a recession are virtually certain to cause higher inflation for a while. Using tools that we will describe in Parts Two and Three, many economists believe they can even measure how much more inflation the economy will suffer as the price of fighting a recession. Is it worth it? An economist cannot answer this any more than a nuclear physicist could have determined whether dropping the atomic bomb on Hiroshima was a good idea. The decision rests on value judgments about the moral trade-off between inflation and unemployment, judgments that can be made only by the citizenry through its elected officials.

These examples underscore something we said earlier in this chapter: Economics cannot provide all the answers, but it can teach you how to ask the right questions. By the time you finish studying this book, you should have a good understanding of when the right course of action turns on disputed facts, when on value judgments, and when on some combination of the two.

The Economist's Odd Vocabulary

George Bernard Shaw once remarked that America and England are two nations separated by a common language. Much of the same might be said of economists and other people, for economists often assign peculiar meanings to familiar words. Here are two examples; you will find many others later on.

1. **Cost** We have already mentioned that when economists speak of "costs" they are normally referring to **opportunity costs**. Accountants, on the other hand, almost always measure costs as only direct monetary expenses involved in any activity. Thus, in calculating the costs of the same activity, the accountant and the economist may arrive at two very different results, as the example of the costs of going to university illustrated. Accountants and economists are indeed divided by a common language.

> The **opportunity cost** of some decision is the value of the next-best alternative which you have to give up because of that decision (for example, working instead of going to school).

2. **Money** Most people work for money, or so they think. Again, the economist disagrees. He will insist that people work to earn *income*, which often happens to be paid—for reasons of convenience—in the form of *money*. What is the difference? To the economist *money* refers to the amount of cash and bank-account balances you own at any particular moment. Your holdings of money change frequently, often several times in a single day. But *income* refers to the rate at which you earn money over time. A worker would answer the question "What is your income?" by saying "$10,000 a year," or "$200 a week," or something like that. Income probably changes much less frequently than holdings of money, perhaps only once a year. The distinction between money and income is important, and it will occupy our attention in Part Three.

The economist, it would appear, is much like Humpty Dumpty in *Alice in Wonderland* who said imperiously, "When I use a word it means just what I choose it to mean—neither more nor less." Why such obstinacy? Because economists need a *scientific jargon*, just as other scientists do. Any dictionary will testify to the fact that most words in any language have a multiplicity of meanings. Scientists must be more precise than that. And, rather than conjure up entirely new words, as natural scientists frequently do, economists take ordinary words and give them slightly special meanings.

One wag pointed out that Canada has two groups whose members steadfastly refuse to speak English: *separatists* and *economists*. Who, though, would prefer that we say "phlogiston" instead of "cost" or "nutches" instead of "money"?

Summary

1. To help you get the most out of your first course in economics, we have devised a list of *12 important ideas* that you will want to remember *Beyond the Final Exam*. Here we list them, very briefly, indicating where each idea occurs in the book.

   1) Most government policies that reduce inflation are likely to intensify the unemployment problem, and vice versa. (Chapter 18)
   2) Interest rates that appear very high may actually be very low if they are accompanied by rapid inflation. (Chapter 6)
   3) Budget deficits may or may not be advisable, depending on circumstances. (Chapter 17)
   4) In the long run, productivity is almost the only thing that matters for a nation's material well-being. (Chapter 39)
   5) In a voluntary exchange, both parties must expect to benefit. (Chapter 3 and 32)
   6) Two nations can gain from international trade, even if one is more efficient at making everything. (Chapter 32)
   7) Lawmakers who try to repeal the "law" of supply and demand are liable to open a Pandora's box of troubles they never expected. (Chapter 4)
   8) Externalities cause the market mechanism to misfire, but this defect of the market can be remedied by market-oriented policies. (Chapters 29 and 34)
   9) To make a rational decision, the opportunity cost of an action must be measured, because only this calculation will tell the decision-maker what he has given up. (Chapter 3)

   10) Rational decisions often require the use of marginal analysis to isolate the costs and benefits of a particular decision. (Chapter 23)
   11) The operation of free markets is likely to lead to rising prices for public and private services. (Chapter 29)
   12) Most policies that equalize income exact a cost by reducing the nation's output. (Chapter 38)

2. Economics is a discipline that uses a variety of approaches, some of them scientific and others humanistic, to address important social questions.

3. Because of the great complexity of human behaviour, the economist is forced to abstract from many details, make generalizations that he knows are not quite true, and organize what knowledge he has according to some theoretical structure.

4. Correlation need not imply causation.

5. Economists use simplified models to understand the real world and predict its behaviour, much as a child uses a model railway to learn how trains work.

6. While these models, if skillfully constructed, can illuminate important economic problems, they rarely can answer the questions that policy-makers are confronted with. For this purpose, value judgments are needed, and the economist is no better equipped to make them than is anyone else.

7. A course in economics seeks to teach the student how to formulate the right questions, questions that point to the value judgments or unknown pieces of data that must be obtained in order to make an intelligent decision. It does not try to provide all the answers.

Concepts for Review

Voluntary exchange	Correlation versus causation	Marginal analysis
Comparative advantage	Model	Marginal costs
Productivity	Rationality	Abstraction and generalization
Externalities	Opportunity cost	Theory

Questions for Discussion

1. Think about how you would construct a "model" of how your university is governed. Which officers and administrators would you include and exclude from your model if the objective were
   a. to explain how decisions on tuition payments are made?
   b. to explain the quality of the football team?
   Relate this to the map example in the chapter.

2. Relate the process of "abstraction" to the way you take notes in a lecture. Why do you not try to transcribe every word the lecturer utters? Why do you not just write down the title of the lecture and stop there? How do you decide, roughly speaking, on the correct amount of detail?

3. Explain why a government policy-maker cannot afford to ignore economic theory.

The Use and Misuse of Graphs

Everything should be made
as simple as possible, but not
more so.
ALBERT EINSTEIN

In the preceding chapter we pointed out that economic models frequently appear as diagrams. And if you flip through the pages of this book you will see that indeed they are used quite often. Because many of you may not be familiar with diagrams, this chapter explains how some of the simple graphs used by economists are constructed and how they are to be interpreted.

Most readers of this book eventually will encounter graphs quite frequently in everyday life. If you become a doctor, you will see graphs depicting trends in costs of medical care as well as graphs recording the behaviour of patients' vital functions. If you are concerned about social problems, you will have to read graphs depicting changes in ethnic composition of the population of a city or those relating frequency of conviction for a felony to family income. If you work for a large corporation, you will encounter graphs of sales, profits, and the like. Graphs appear almost daily in the financial pages of the newspaper.

Graphs are invaluable because of the large quantity of data they can display and because of the way they facilitate the interpretation and analysis of the data. They enable the eye to take in at a glance important statistical relationships that would be far less apparent from lengthy prose descriptions or long lists of numbers. It is therefore worth the effort needed to learn how data can be portrayed in graphs. At the very least, you will want to learn to avoid the serious errors into which one can easily be led by graphs that are misleading or distorted.

In this chapter we show, first, how to read a graph that depicts a relationship between two variables. Second, we define the term *slope* and describe how it is measured and interpreted. Third, we explain how the behaviour of three variables can be shown on a two-dimensional graph. Fourth, we discuss how misinterpretation is avoided by adjusting many economic graphs to accommodate changes in the purchasing power of the dollar, in the population of the nation, and in other pertinent developments. And finally, we examine several other common ways in which graphs can be misleading if not drawn and interpreted with care.

Graphs Used in Economic Analysis*

Two-Variable Diagrams

Much of the economic analysis to be found in this and other books requires that we keep track of two variables simultaneously. For example, in studying the operation of markets, we will want to keep one eye on the price of a commodity and the other on the quantity that is bought and sold.

For this reason, economists frequently find it useful to display real or imaginary figures in a *two-dimensional graph*, which simultaneously represents the behaviour of two economic variables. The numerical value of one variable is measured along the bottom of the graph (called the *horizontal axis*), starting from the **origin** (the point labelled "0"), and the numerical value of the other is measured along the side of the graph (called the *vertical axis*), also starting from the origin.

Figure 2–1 is a typical graph used in economic analysis; it depicts a *demand curve*, represented by the heavy coloured line. The diagram shows the price of natural gas on the vertical axis and the quantity of gas that people want to buy on the horizontal axis. (Demand curves will be studied in detail in Chapter 4.)

Economic diagrams are generally read as one reads latitudes and longitudes on a map. On the demand curve in Figure 2–1, the point marked *a* represents a hypothetical combination of price and quantity demanded in Halifax. By drawing a horizontal line leftward from that point to the vertical axis, we learn that the average price for gas in Halifax is $30 per thousand cubic metres. By dropping a line straight down to the horizontal axis, we find that 80 million cubic metres are wanted by consumers at this price. The other points on the graph give similar information. For example, point *b* indicates that if natural gas in Halifax costs only $20 per thousand cubic metres, quantity demanded would be higher—it would reach 120 million cubic metres.

*Students who have a nodding acquaintance with geometry and feel quite comfortable with graphs can safely skip the first sections of this chapter and proceed directly to the second part, which begins on page 26.

The lower left-hand corner of a graph where the two axes meet is called the **origin**. Both variables are equal to zero at the origin.

Figure 2–1
A DEMAND CURVE FOR NATURAL GAS IN HALIFAX

This demand curve shows the relationship between the price of natural gas and the quantity of it that will be demanded. For example, the point labelled *a* indicates that at a price of $30 per thousand cubic metres (point *P*), the quantity demanded will be 80 million cubic metres (point *Q*).

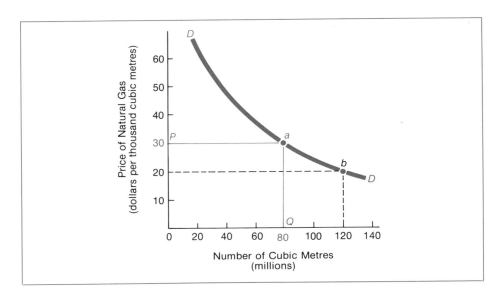

Notice that information about price and quantity is *all* we can learn from the diagram. The demand curve will not tell us about the kinds of people who live in Halifax, the size of their homes, or the condition of their furnaces. It tells us the price and the quantity demanded at that price—no more, no less.

A diagram abstracts from many details, some of which may be quite interesting, in order to focus on the two variables of primary interest—in this case, the price of natural gas and the amount of gas that is demanded at each price. All the diagrams used in this book share this basic feature. They cannot tell the reader the "whole story" any more than a map's latitude and longitude figures for a particular city can make someone an authority on that city.

The Definition and Measurement of Slope

One of the most important features of the diagrams used by economists is the rapidity with which the line, or curve, being sketched runs uphill or downhill as we move to the right. The demand curve in Figure 2–1 clearly slopes downhill (the price falls) as we follow it to the right (that is, as more gas is demanded because of the lower price). In such instances we say that *the curve has a negative slope, or is negatively sloped, because one variable falls as the other one rises.*

The **slope of a straight line** is the ratio of the vertical change to the corresponding horizontal change as we move to the right along the line, or as it is often said, the ratio of the "rise" over the "run."

The four panels of Figure 2–2 show all the possible slopes for a straight-line relationship between two unnamed variables called Y (measured along the vertical axis) and X (measured along the horizontal axis). Figure 2–2(a) shows a negative slope, much like our demand curve. Figure 2–2(b) shows a positive slope, because variable Y rises (we go uphill) as variable X rises (we move to the right). Figure 2–2(c) shows a *zero* slope, where the value of Y is the same irrespective of the value of X. Figure 2–2(d) shows an *infinite* slope, meaning that the value of X is the same, irrespective of the value of Y.

Slope is a numerical concept, not just a qualitative one. The two panels of Figure 2–3 show two positively sloped straight lines with different slopes. The line in Figure 2–3(b) is clearly steeper. But by how much? The labels should help you compute the answer. In Figure 2–3(a) a horizontal movement, *AB*, of 10 units (13 – 3) corresponds to a vertical movement, *BC*, of 1 unit (9 – 8). So the slope is

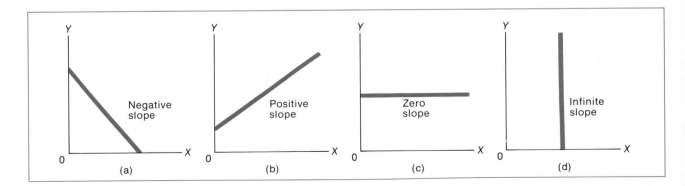

Figure 2–2
DIFFERENT TYPES OF SLOPE OF A STRAIGHT-LINE GRAPH
In Figure 2–2(a), the curve goes downward as we read from left to right, so we say it has a negative slope. The slopes in the other figures can be interpreted similarly.

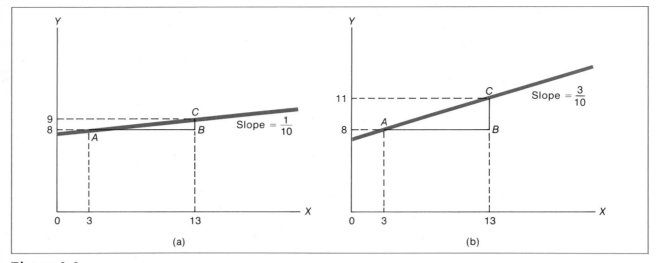

Figure 2–3

HOW TO MEASURE SLOPE

Slope indicates how much the graph rises per unit move from left to right. Thus, in Figure 2-3(b), as we go from point A to point B, we go 13 – 3 = 10 units to the right. But in that interval, the graph rises from the height of point B to the height of point C, that is, it rises 3 units. Consequently, the slope of the line is $BC/AB = 3/10$.

$BC/AB = \frac{1}{10}$. In Figure 2–3(b), the same horizontal movement of 10 units corresponds to a vertical movement of 3 units (11 – 8). So the slope is $\frac{3}{10}$, which is larger.

The slope of any particular straight line is the same no matter where on that line we choose to measure it. That is why we can pick any horizontal distance, *AB*, and the corresponding slope triangle, *ABC*, to measure slope. But this is not true of lines that are curved.

Curved lines also have slopes, but the numerical value of the slope is different at every point.

The four panels of Figure 2–4 provide some examples of **slopes of curved lines**. The curve in Figure 2–4(a) has a negative slope everywhere, while the curve in Figure 2–4(b) has a positive slope everywhere. But these are not the only possibilities. In Figure 2–4(c) we encounter a curve that has a positive slope at first but a negative slope later on. Figure 2–4(d) shows the opposite case: a negative slope followed by a positive slope.

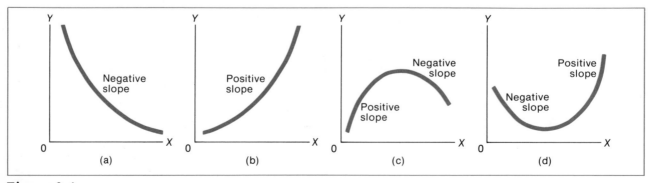

Figure 2–4

BEHAVIOUR OF SLOPES IN CURVED GRAPHS

As Figures 2-4(c) and 2-4(d) indicate, where a graph is not a straight line it may have a slope that starts off as positive but that becomes negative farther to the right, or vice versa.

It is possible to measure the slope of a smooth curved line numerically *at any particular point*. This is done by drawing a *straight* line that *touches*, but does not *cut*, the curve at the point in question. Such a line is called a **tangent to the curve**.

The slope of a curved line at a particular point is the slope of the straight line that is tangent to the curve at that point.

In Figure 2–5 we have constructed tangents to a curve at two points. Line *tt* is tangent at point *C*, and line *TT* is tangent at point *F*. We can measure the slope of the curve at these two points by applying the definition. The calculation for point *C*, then, is the following:

$$\text{Slope at point } C = \text{Slope of line } tt = \frac{\text{Distance } BC}{\text{Distance } AB}$$
$$= \frac{6-2}{10-0} = \frac{4}{10} = +0.4.$$

A similar calculation yields the slope of the curve at point *F*, which, as we can see from Figure 2–5, must be smaller:

$$\text{Slope at Point } F = \text{Slope of line } TT = \frac{14-9}{50-0} = \frac{5}{50} = +0.1.$$

EXERCISE
Show that the slope of the curve at point *D* is between + 0.1 and + 0.4.

What would happen if we tried to apply this graphical technique to the high point in Figure 2–4(c) or to the low point in Figure 2–4(d)? Take a ruler and try it. The tangents that you construct should be horizontal, meaning that they should have a slope of exactly zero. It is always true that where the slope of a smooth curve changes from positive to negative, or vice versa, there will be at least a single point with a zero slope.

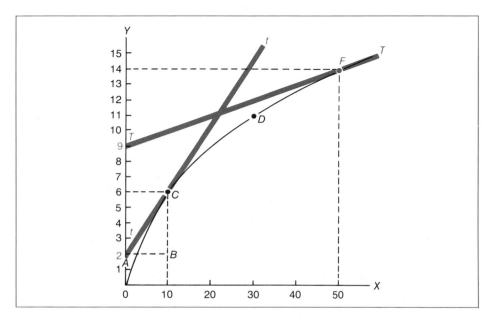

Figure 2–5
HOW TO MEASURE SLOPE AT A POINT ON A CURVED GRAPH

To find the slope at point *F*, draw the line *TT*, which is tangent to the curve at point *F*; then measure the slope of the straight-line tangent *TT* as in Figure 2–3. The slope of the tangent is the same as the slope of the curve at point *F*.

Curves that have the shape of a hill, such as Figure 2–4(c), have a zero slope at their *highest* point. Curves that have the shape of a valley, such as Figure 2–4(d), have a zero slope at their *lowest* point.

Rays Through the Origin and 45° Lines

The point at which a straight line cuts the vertical (Y) axis is called the *Y-intercept*. For example, the Y-intercept of line *tt* in Figure 2–5 is 2, while the Y-intercept of line *TT* is 9. Lines whose Y-intercept is zero have so many special uses that they have been given a special name, a **ray through the origin**, or a **ray**.

Figure 2–6 contains three rays through the origin, and the slope of each is indicated in the diagram. The ray in the centre—whose slope is 1—is particularly useful in many economic applications because it marks off points where X and Y are equal (as long as X and Y are measured in the same units). For example, at point A we have X = 3 and Y = 3, at point B, X = 4 and Y = 4, and a similar relation holds at any other point on that ray.

How do we know that this is always true for a ray whose slope is 1? If we start from the origin (where both X and Y are zero) and the slope of the ray is 1, we know from the definition of slope that:

$$\text{Slope} = \frac{\text{Vertical change}}{\text{Horizontal change}} = 1.$$

This implies that the vertical change and the horizontal change are always equal, so the two variables must always remain equal.

Rays through the origin with a slope of 1 are called **45° lines** because they form an angle of 45° with the horizontal axis. If a point representing some data is above the 45° line, we know that the value of Y exceeds the value of X. Conversely, whenever we find a point below the 45° line, we know that X is larger than Y.

[1]The definition assumes that both variables are measured in the same units.

A straight line emanating from the origin, or zero point on a graph, is called a **ray through the origin** or, sometimes, just a **ray**.

A **45° line** is a ray through the origin with a slope of +1. It marks off points where the variables measured on each axis have equal values.[1]

Figure 2–6
RAYS THROUGH THE ORIGIN

Rays are straight lines drawn through the zero point on the graph (*the origin*). Three rays with different slopes are shown. The middle ray, the one with slope = + 1, has two properties that make it particularly useful in economics: (1) it makes a 45° angle with either axis, and (2) any point on that ray (for example, point A) is exactly equal in distance from the horizontal and vertical axes (length DA = length CA). So if the items measured on the two axes are in equal units, then at any point on that ray, such as A, the number on the X-axis (the abscissa) will be the same as the number on the Y-axis (the ordinate).

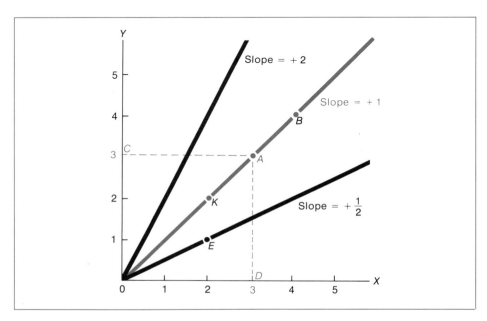

Squeezing Three Dimensions into Two: Contour Maps

Sometimes, because a problem involves more than two variables, two dimensions just are not enough, which is unfortunate since paper is only two dimensional. When we study the decision-making process of a business firm, for example, we may want to keep track simultaneously of three variables: how much labour it employs, how much machinery it uses, and how much output it creates.

Luckily, there is a well-known device for collapsing three dimensions into two, namely a *contour map*. Figure 2–7 is a contour map of Mont Tremblant, near Montreal. On several of the irregularly shaped "rings" we find a number indicating the height above sea level at that particular spot on the mountain. Thus, unlike the more usual sort of map, which gives only latitudes and longitudes, this contour map exhibits three pieces of information about each point: latitude, longitude, and altitude.

Figure 2–8 looks more like the contour maps encountered in economics. It shows how some third variable, called Z (think of it as a firm's output, for example), varies as we change either variable X (think of it as a firm's employment) or variable Y (think of it as the use of a firm's machines). Just like the map of Mont Tremblant, any point on the diagram conveys three pieces of data. At point A, we can read off the values of X and Y in the conventional way (X is 30 and Y is 40), and we can also note the value of Z by checking to see on which contour line point A falls. (It is on the $Z = 20$ contour.) So point A is able to tell us that 30 hours of labour and 40 hours of machine time produces 20 units of output.

While most of the analyses presented in this book will be based on the simpler two-variable diagrams, contour maps will find their applications, especially in the appendixes to Chapters 20 and 22.

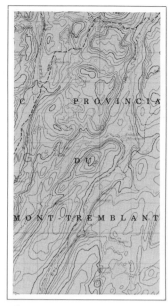

Figure 2-7

A GEOGRAPHIC CONTOUR MAP

All points on any particular contour line represent geographic locations that are at the same height above sea level.

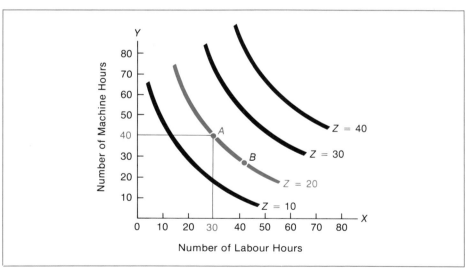

Figure 2-8

AN ECONOMIC CONTOUR MAP

In this contour map, all points on a given contour line represent different combinations of labour and capital capable of producing a given output. For example, all points on the curve $Z = 20$ represent input combinations that can produce 20 units of output. Point A on that line means that the 20 units of output can be produced using 30 labour hours and 40 machine hours. Economists call such maps *production indifference maps*.

Perils in the Interpretation of Graphs

The preceding materials contain just about all you will need in order to understand the simple graphics used in economic models. We turn now to the second objective of this chapter: to show how statistical data are portrayed on graphs and some of the pitfalls to watch out for.

The Interpretation of Growth Trends

A **time-series graph** depicts how a variable changes over time.

Probably the most common form of graph in empirical economics is a year-by-year (or perhaps a month-by-month) depiction of the behaviour of some economic variable—the profits of a particular corporation, or its annual sales, or the number of persons unemployed in the Canadian economy, or some measure of consumer prices. For example, Figure 2–9 is this sort of **time-series graph** showing the month-by-month unemployment rate in Canada from 1967 to 1984. It shows that the percentage of the labour force that was jobless was relatively low during the late 1960s and particularly high since the late 1970s. Time-series graphs are a type of two-variable diagram in which time is always the variable measured along the horizontal axis.

Such graphs can be quite illuminating, offering an instant visual grasp of the course of the relevant events. *However, if misused, such graphs are very dangerous.* They can easily mislead persons who are not experienced in dealing with them. Perhaps even more dangerous are the misinterpretations perpetuated accidentally and unintentionally by people who draw graphs without sufficient care and who may innocently mislead themselves as well as others.

A fine example of this latter occurrence is illustrated in Figure 2–10. Many people felt that there was a "cultural boom" underway in the period after World War II that led to an explosion in the demand for tickets to all sorts of artistic performances. This boom, it was thought, accounted for the rapidly rising prices of theatre tickets. Figure 2–10 shows a time-series graph that formed the basis for this allegation. The growth in spending for theatre tickets certainly looks impressive; expenditures rose about 1250 percent from 1929 to 1982.

But there is less to this graph than meets the eye—much less. Most of the spectacular growth in spending on theatre admissions was a reflection of three rather banal facts. First, there were many more North Americans alive in 1982

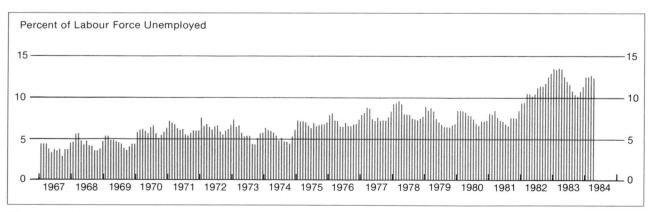

Figure 2–9
TIME-SERIES GRAPH
This graph shows the percentage of the labour force that was unemployed in each of the months indicated, from January 1967 through April 1984.

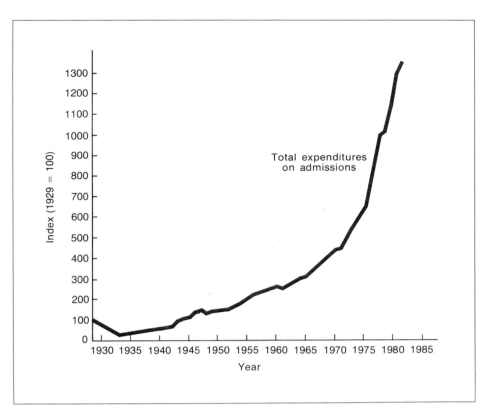

Figure 2-10
INDEX OF EXPENDITURES
ON ADMISSIONS TO
ARTISTIC PERFORMANCES
This graph, showing expenditures
on admissions to artistic
performances, seems to indicate
that since about 1932 North
Americans have become much
more interested in attending the
performing arts.
SOURCE: *Survey of Current Business*,
July issues, various years; and
Economic Report of the President,
Washington, D.C.: U.S. Government
Printing Office, various years.

than in 1929, so spending *per person* rose by much less than Figure 2-10 suggests. Second, the price of almost everything, not just theatre tickets, was higher in 1982 than in 1929. In fact, average prices were more than five times their 1929 levels. Third, the average citizen was richer in 1982 than in 1929, and consequently was more inclined to spend money on everything—not just on cultural activities.

All three of these factors can be accounted for by expressing spending on theatre admissions as a *fraction* of total consumer income. The results of this "correction" are shown in Figure 2-11. The explosive growth suggested by the uncorrected data really amounts to a decline in the share of income that the average North American spent on theatre tickets—from about 15 cents out of each $100 in 1929 to only 8 cents in 1982! How misleading it can be to simply "look at the facts." There is a general lesson to be learned from this example:

The facts, as portrayed in a time-series graph, most assuredly do not "speak for themselves." Because almost everything grows in a growing economy, one must use judgment in interpreting growth trends. Depending on what kind of data are being analyzed, it may be essential to correct for population growth, for rising prices, for rising incomes, or for all three.[2]

Distorting Trends by Choice of the Time Period

In addition to possible misinterpretations of growth trends, users of statistical data must be on guard for distortions of trends caused by unskillfully chosen first and last periods for the graph. This is best explained by an example.

---

[2]For a full discussion of how to use a "price index" to correct for rising prices, see the appendix to Chapter 6.

Figure 2-11
APPEARANCE AND REALITY IN ARTS EXPENDITURE

The curve in black shows correctly that the number of *dollars* spent on the arts rose dramatically since 1932. But because of inflation, a dollar in 1982 was worth much less than in 1929, and there were many more North Americans in the later year, who were also wealthier on the average. After correction for inflation, population changes, and so on, the black line is transformed into the coloured line, showing that in 1982 an average citizen actually spent less of his purchasing power on the arts than in 1929.
SOURCE: *Survey of Current Business*, July issues, various years; and *Economic Report of the President*, Washington D.C.: U.S. Government Printing Office, various years.

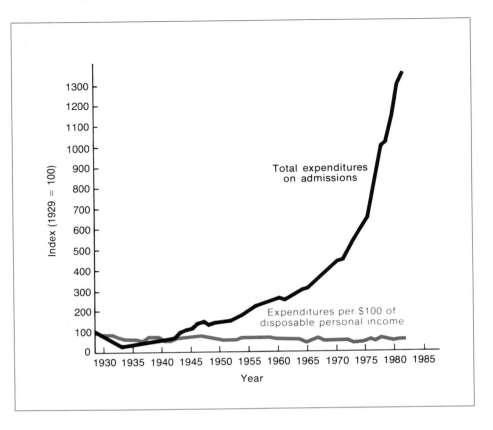

Figures 2-12 and 2-13 show the behaviour of average stock-market prices (the Dow-Jones Index in the United States) over the periods 1929-32 and 1973-75. They both display a clear downhill movement and would suggest to anyone who does not have other information that stocks are a terrible investment.

However, an unscrupulous seller of stocks could use the same set of stock-market statistics to tell exactly the opposite story by carefully selecting another group of years. Figure 2-14 shows the behaviour of average stock prices from 1940 through 1965. The persistence and size of the increase is quite dramatic. Stocks now look like a rather good investment.

An even longer and less biased period gives a less distorted picture (Figure 2-15). It indicates that investment in stocks are sometimes profitable and other times unprofitable.

The deliberate or inadvertent distortion resulting from an unfortunate or unscrupulous choice of time period for a graph must constantly be watched for.

There are no rules that can give absolute protection from this difficulty, but several precautions can be helpful.

1. Make sure the first date shown on the graph is not an exceptionally high or low point. In comparison with 1929, a year of unusually high stock-market prices, the years immediately following are bound to give the impression of a downward trend.

2. For the same reason, make sure the graph does not end in a year that is extraordinarily high or low (although this may be unavoidable if the graph simply ends with figures that are as up-to-date as possible).

Figure 2-12
STOCK PRICES, 1929-1932

This graph seems to show that stock-market prices generally go down.

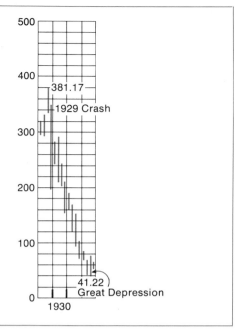

381.17
— 1929 Crash

41.22
Great Depression

1930

Figure 2-13
STOCK PRICES, 1973-1975

This figure also seems to show that stock prices generally fall.

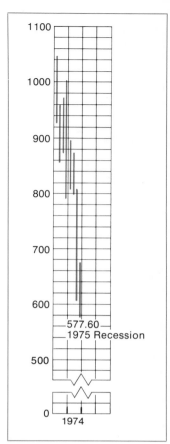

577.60
— 1975 Recession

1974

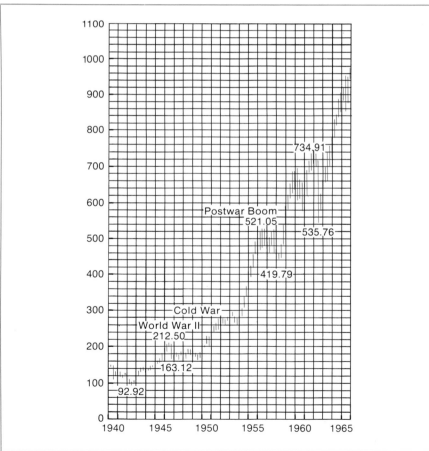

734.91

Postwar Boom
521.05   535.76

419.79

Cold War
World War II
212.50

163.12

92.92

Figure 2-14
STOCK PRICES, 1940-1965

This graph seems to indicate that the value of stocks is on a never-ending climb.

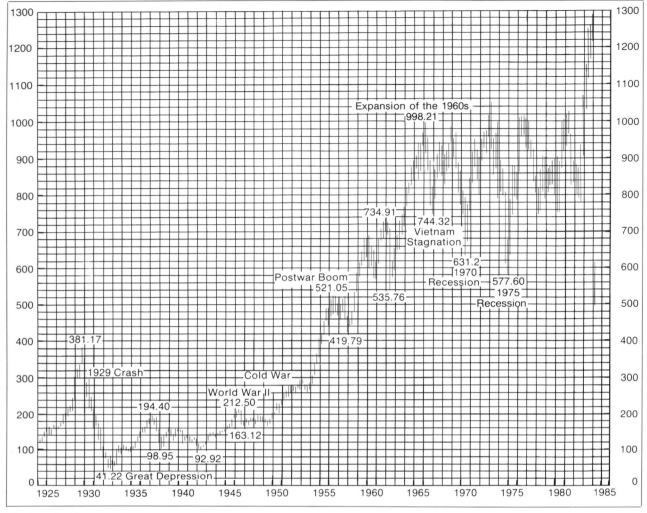

Figure 2-15
THE FULL HISTORY OF STOCK PRICES, 1925-1984
Here we see that stock prices have lots of ups and downs, though they have risen quite a bit on the average.

3. Make sure that (in the absence of some special justification) the graph does not depict only a very brief period, which can be easily atypical.

Dangers of Omitting the Origin

Frequently, the value of an economic variable described on a graph does not fall anywhere near zero during the period under consideration. For example, the prime lending rate offered by Canadian banks rose during the first half of 1984 from 11 to 13 percent. This means that a graph representing the behaviour of interest rates in 1984 would have a good deal of wasted space between the horizontal axis of the graph, where the interest rate is zero, and the level of the graph representing an 11 percent interest rate. In that area there are simply no data to plot. It is therefore tempting simply to eliminate this wasted space by beginning the graph just below the 11 percent interest-rate level. This was done by *Maclean's* in a recent issue, as reproduced in our Figure 2–16.

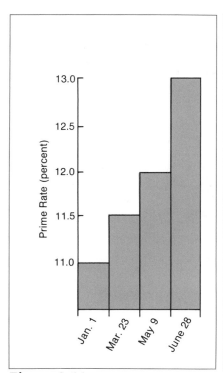

Figure 2-16
A GRAPH SHOWING
OMISSION OF THE ORIGIN
A hasty glance at this figure
seems to show that interest rates
tripled during the first half of 1984.

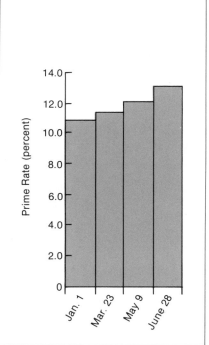

Figure 2-17
INTEREST-RATE FIGURES
INCLUDING POINT OF
ORIGIN
Adding the point of zero interest
rate to the previous graph shows
that the rise in the interest rate
was in fact not so enormous as
Figure 2-16 suggests.

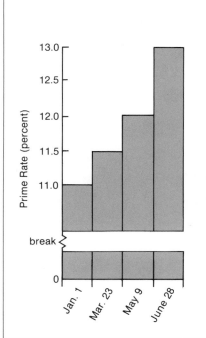

Figure 2-18
A BREAK IN A GRAPH
An alternative way of warning the
reader that the zero point has
been left out is to put a break in
the graph, as illustrated here.

What is wrong with the drawing? The answer is that it vastly exaggerates the size of the increase in the interest rate that is depicted. It makes it look like the interest rate trebled. The more informative graph, which includes the origin as well as the "wasted space" in between, is shown in Figure 2-17. Note how this alternative presentation puts matters into perspective.

Omitting the origin in a graph is dangerous because it always exaggerates the magnitudes of the changes that have taken place.

Sometimes, it is true, the inclusion of the full graph would waste so much space that it is undesirable to include it. In that case, a good practice is to put a very clear warning on the graph to remind the reader that some space has been omitted. Figure 2-18 shows one way of doing so.

Unreliability of Steepness and Choice of Units

The last problem we will consider has consequences very similar to the one we have just discussed. The problem is that we can never trust the impression we get from the steepness of an economic graph. A graph of stock-market prices that moves uphill sharply (has a large positive slope) appears to suggest that prices are rising rapidly, while another graph in which the rate of climb is much slower seems to imply that prices are going up sluggishly. Yet, depending on how one draws the graph, exactly the same statistics can produce a graph that is rising very quickly or very slowly.

The reason for this possibility is that in economics there are no fixed units of measurement. Coal production can be measured in pounds, hundredweight (hundreds of pounds), or in tons. Prices can be measured in cents, dollars, or millions of dollars. Time can be measured in days, months, or years. Any of these choices is perfectly legitimate, but it makes all the difference to the rapidity with which a graph using the resulting figures rises or falls.

An example will bring out the point. Suppose that we have the following (imaginary) figures on daily coal production from a mine, which we measure both in hundredweight and in tons (remembering that 1 ton = 20 hundredweight):

YEAR	PRODUCTION IN TONS	PRODUCTION IN HUNDREDWEIGHT
1975	5000	100,000
1980	5050	101,000
1985	5090	101,800

Look at Figures 2–19(a) and 2–19(b), one graph showing the figures in tons and the other showing the figures in hundredweight. The line looks quite flat in Figure 2–19(a) but quite steep in Figure 2–19(b).

Unfortunately, we cannot solve the problem by agreeing always to stick to the same measurement units. Pounds may be the right unit for measuring demand

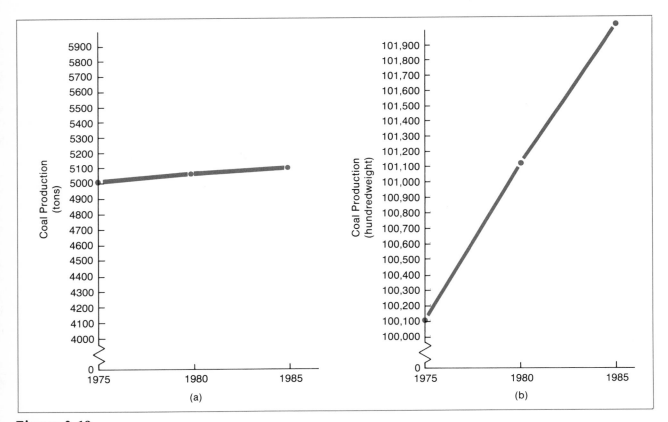

Figure 2-19

SLOPE DEPENDS ON UNITS OF MEASUREMENT

(a) Coal production is measured in tons, and production seems to be rising very slowly. (b) Production is measured in hundredweight (hundred-pound units), so the same facts now seem to say that production is rising spectacularly.

for beef, but they will not do in measuring demand for cloth or for coal. A penny may be the right monetary unit for postage stamps, but it is not a very convenient unit for the cost of airplanes or automobiles.

A change in units of measurement stretches or compresses the axis on which the information is represented, which automatically changes the slope of a graph. Therefore we must never place much faith in the apparent implications of the slope of an ordinary graph in economics.

Later, in Chapter 21 on demand analysis, we will encounter a useful approach economists have adopted to deal with this problem. Instead of calculating changes in "absolute" terms—like tons of coal—they use as their common unit the *percentage* increase. By using percentages rather than absolute figures the problem can be avoided. The reason is simple. If we look at our hypothetical figures on coal production again, we see that no matter whether we measure the increase in output from 1975 to 1980 in tons (from 5000 to 5050) or in hundredweight (from 100,000 to 101,000), the *percentage* increase has been the same. Fifty is 1 percent of 5000, and 1000 is 1 percent of 100,000. Since a change in units affects both the numbers *proportionately*, the result is a washout—it does not do anything to the percentage calculation.

Summary

1. Because graphs are used so often to portray economic models, it is important for students to acquire some understanding of their construction and use. Fortunately, the graphics used in economics are usually not very complex.

2. Most economic models are depicted in two-variable diagrams. We read data from these diagrams just as we read the latitude and longitude on a map: each point represents the values of two variables at the same time.

3. In a few instances, three variables must be shown at once. In these cases, economists use contour maps, which, as the name suggests, show "latitude," "longitude," and "altitude" all at the same time.

4. Often, the most important property of a line or curve drawn on a diagram will be its slope, which is defined as the ratio of the "rise" over the "run," or the vertical change divided by the horizontal change. Curves that go uphill as we move to the right have positive slopes, while curves that go downhill have negative slopes.

5. By definition, a straight line has the same slope wherever we choose to measure it. The slope of a curved line changes, but the slope at any point on the curve can be calculated by measuring the slope of a straight line tangent to the curve at that point.

6. A time-series graph is a particular type of two-variable diagram that is useful in depicting statistical data. Time is measured along the horizontal axis, and some variable of interest is measured along the vertical axis.

7. While time-series graphs are invaluable in helping us condense a great deal of information in a single picture, they can be quite misleading if they are not drawn and interpreted with care. For example, growth trends can be exaggerated by inappropriate choice of units of measurement or by failure to correct for some obvious source of growth (such as rising population). Omitting the origin can make the ups and downs in a time series appear much more extreme than they actually are. Or, by a clever choice of the starting and ending points for the graphs, the same data can be made to tell very different stories. Readers of such graphs—and this includes anyone who ever reads a newspaper—must be on guard for problems like these or they may find themselves misled by "the facts."

Concepts for Review

Two-variable diagram
Horizontal and vertical axes
Origin (of a graph)
Slope of a straight (or curved) line

Negative, positive, zero, and infinite
 slope
Tangent to the curve
Y-intercept

Ray through the origin, or ray
45° line
Contour map
Time-series graph

Questions for Discussion

1. Look for a graph in your local newspaper, on the financial page or elsewhere. What does the graph try to show? Is someone trying to convince you of something with this graph? Check to see if the graph is distorted in any of the ways mentioned in this chapter.

2. Portray the following hypothetical data on a two-variable diagram:

ENROLLMENT DATA:
UNIVERSITY OF NOWHERE

ACADEMIC YEAR	TOTAL ENROLLMENT	ENROLLMENT IN ECONOMICS COURSES
1980–1981	3000	300
1981–1982	3100	325
1982–1983	3200	350
1983–1984	3300	375
1984–1985	3400	400

Measure the slope of the resulting line, and explain what this number means.

3. From Figure 2–5, calculate the slope of the curve at point D.

4. From Figure 2–6, determine the values of X and Y at point K and at point E. What do you conclude?

5. From Figure 2–8, interpret the economic meaning of points A and B. What do the two points have in common? What is the difference in their economic interpretation?

6. Suppose that between 1984 and 1985 expenditures on dog food rose from $35 million to $70 million and that the price of dog food doubled. What do these facts imply about the popularity of dog food?

7. Suppose that between 1975 and 1985 the population of North America went up 10 percent and that the number of people attending professional wrestling matches rose from 3,000,000 to 3,100,000. What do these facts imply about the growth in popularity of professional wrestling?

The Economic Problem

3

Our necessities are few but
our wants are endless.
INSCRIPTION FOUND IN A
FORTUNE COOKIE

This chapter examines a subject that many economists consider to be *the* fundamental issue of economics: the fact that since virtually no resource is available in unlimited supply, people must consequently make decisions consistent with their limited means. A wild-eyed materialist may dream of a world in which everyone owns a yacht and five automobiles, but the earth almost certainly lacks the resources needed to make that dream come true. The scarcity of resources, both natural and man-made, makes it vital that we stretch our limited resources as far as possible.

This chapter introduces a way to describe the choices available to decision-makers, given the resources at their command. The same sort of analysis, based on the concept of *opportunity cost*, will be shown to apply to the decisions of business firms, of governments, and of society as a whole. Many of the most basic ideas of economics—such as *efficiency, division of labour, exchange*, and the *role of markets*—are introduced here for the first time. In particular, we will see that a market system can, if it is functioning properly, promote the efficient use of society's resources without intervention by government planners. Finally, this chapter introduces a broad question that constitutes the central theme of this text: What does the market do well and what does it do poorly?

The "Indispensable Necessity" Syndrome

Governments at all levels were forced to tighten their belts sharply in the early 1980s. Economic recession cut into tax revenues. Also, federal government grants to provinces and provincial grants to municipalities were reduced.

Budget cuts forced politicians and administrators to make some hard decisions over which services to cut. As they struggled with these decisions, they learned to their dismay that their constituents often were unwilling to accept *any* reductions. Mayors who proposed closing a fire station or a hospital were confronted by demonstrators decrying the proposed cutback as a "false economy" and describing the fire station or hospital as "indispensable." Groups marched to the B.C. legislative building to oppose Premier Bennett's budget cuts. University administrators found that suggestions to eliminate poorly attended courses, cut library hours, or restrict access to the Xerox machine all too frequently were met with the cry that each of these was *absolutely* essential.

Yet, regrettable as it is to have to give up any of these good things, reduced budgets mean that *something* must go. If everyone reacts by declaring *everything* to be indispensable, the decision-maker is in the dark and is likely to end up making cuts that are bad for everyone. When the budget must be reduced, it is critical to determine which cuts are likely to prove *least damaging* to the people affected.

It is nonsense to assign top priority to everything. No one can afford everything. An optimal decision is one that chooses the most desirable alternative *among the possibilities that the available resources permit.*

Scarcity, Choice, and Opportunity Cost

One of the basic themes of economics is that the resources of decision-makers, no matter how large they may be, are always limited, and that as a result everyone has some hard decisions to make. Even Philip II, of Spanish Armada fame and one of the most richly endowed kings of history, frequently had to cope with rebellion on the part of his troops, whom he was often unable to pay or to supply with even the most basic provisions.

But far more fundamental than the scarcity of funds is the scarcity of physical resources. The supply of fuel, for example, has never been limitless, and a real scarcity of fuel would force us to make some hard choices. We might have to keep our homes cooler in winter and warmer in summer, live closer to our jobs, or give up such fuel-using conveniences as dishwashers. While energy is the most widely discussed scarcity these days, the general principle of scarcity applies to all the earth's resources—iron, copper, uranium, and so on.

Even goods that can be produced are in limited supply because their production requires fuel, labour, and other scarce resources. Wheat and rice can be grown. But nations have none the less suffered famines because the land, labour, fertilizer, and water needed to grow these crops were unavailable. We can increase our output of cars, but the increased use of labour, steel, and fuel in auto production will mean that something else, perhaps the production of refrigerators, will have to be cut back. This all adds up to the following fundamental principle of economics, one we will encounter again and again in this text.

Virtually all resources are scarce, meaning that humanity has less of them than it would like. So choices must be made among a *limited* set of possibilities, in full recognition of the inescapable fact that a decision to have more of one thing means we must give up some of another thing.

In fact, one popular definition of economics is the "study of how best to use limited means in the pursuit of unlimited ends." While this definition, like any short statement, cannot possibly cover the sweep of the entire discipline, it does convey the flavour of the type of problem that is the economist's stock in trade.

The Principle of Opportunity Cost

Economics examines the options left open to households, business firms, governments, and entire societies by the limited resources at their command; and it studies the logic of how **rational decisions** can be made from among the competing alternatives. One overriding principle governs this logic—a principle we have already introduced in Chapter 1 as one of the **12 Ideas for Beyond the Final Exam**. With limited resources, a decision to have more of something is simultaneously a decision to have less of something else. Hence, the relevant *cost* of any decision is its **opportunity cost**—the value of the next best alternative that is given up. Rational decision-making, be it in industry, government, or households, must be based on opportunity-cost calculations.

To illustrate opportunity cost, we can continue the example in which production of additional cars requires the production of fewer refrigerators. While the production of a car may cost $7000 per vehicle, or some other money amount, its real cost to society is the refrigerators it must forgo to get an additional car. If the labour, steel, and fuel needed to make a car are sufficient to make eight refrigerators, we say that the opportunity cost of a car is eight refrigerators. The principle of opportunity cost is of such general applicability that we devote most of this chapter to it.

Opportunity Cost and Money Cost

Since we live in a market economy where (almost) everything "has its price," students often wonder about the connection between the opportunity cost of an item and its market price. What we just said seems to divorce the two concepts. We stressed that the true cost of a car is not its market price but the value of the other things (like refrigerators) that could have been made instead. This *opportunity cost* is the true sacrifice the economy must incur to get a car.

But isn't the opportunity cost of a car related to its money cost? The answer is that the two are often very closely tied because of the way a market economy sets the prices of the steel and electricity that go into the production of cars. Steel is valuable because it can be used to make other goods. If the items that steel can make are themselves valuable, the price of steel will be high. But if the goods that steel can make have very little value, the price of steel will be low. Thus, if a car has a high opportunity cost, then a well-functioning price system will assign high prices to the resources that are needed to produce cars, and therefore a car will also command a high price. In sum:

If the market is functioning well, goods that have high opportunity costs will tend to have high money costs, and goods whose opportunity costs are low will tend to have low money costs.

Yet it would be a mistake to treat opportunity costs and explicit monetary costs as identical. For one thing, there are times when the market does *not* function well, and hence does not assign prices that accurately reflect opportunity costs. Many such examples will be encountered in this book, especially in Chapters 29 and 34.

Moreover, some valuable items may not bear explicit price tags at all. We have already encountered one example of this in Chapter 1, where we contrasted the opportunity cost of going to university with the explicit money cost. We learned that one important item typically omitted from the money-cost calculation is the value of the student's time; that is, the wages he or she could have earned by working instead of attending university. These forgone wages, which are given up by students in order to acquire an education, are part of the opportunity cost of a university education just as surely as are tuition payments.

Other common examples are goods and services that are given away "free." You incur no explicit monetary cost to acquire such an item. But you may have to pay implicitly by waiting in line. If so, you incur an opportunity cost equal to the value of the next best use of your time.

Scarcity and Choice for a Single Firm

The nature of opportunity cost is perhaps clearest in the case of a single business firm that produces two outputs from a fixed supply of inputs. Given the existing technology and the limited resources at its disposal, the more of one good the firm produces the less of the other it will be able to produce. And unless management carries out an explicit comparison of the available choices, weighing the desirabil-

A **rational decision** is one that best serves the objective of the decision-maker, whatever that objective may be. The term "rational" connotes neither approval nor disapproval of the objective itself.

The **opportunity cost** of any decision is the forgone value of the next best alternative that is not chosen.

ity of each against the others, it is unlikely that it will make rational production decisions.

Consider the example of a farmer whose available supplies of land, machinery, labour, and fertilizer are capable of producing the various combinations of soybeans and wheat listed in Table 3–1. Obviously, the more land and other resources he devotes to production of soybeans, the less wheat he will be able to produce. Table 3–1 indicates, for example, that if he produces only soybeans, he can harvest 40,000 bushels. But, when soybean production is reduced to only 30,000 bushels, the farmer can also grow 38,000 bushels of wheat. Thus the opportunity cost of obtaining 38,000 bushels of wheat is 10,000 fewer bushels of soybeans. Or put the other way around, the opportunity cost of 10,000 bushels of soybeans is 38,000 bushels of wheat. The other numbers in Table 3–1 have similar interpretations.

Table 3-1
PRODUCTION POSSIBILITIES OPEN TO A FARMER

BUSHELS OF SOYBEANS	BUSHELS OF WHEAT	LABEL IN FIGURE 3-1
40,000	0	A
30,000	38,000	B
20,000	52,000	C
10,000	60,000	D
0	65,000	E

Figure 3–1 is a graphical representation of this same information. Point *A* corresponds to the first line of Table 3–1, point *B* to the second line, and so on. Curves like *AE* will appear frequently in this book; they are called **production possibilities frontiers**. Any point *on or below* the production possibilities frontier is attainable. Points above the frontier cannot be achieved with the available resources and technology.

The production possibilities frontier always slopes downward to the right. Why? Because resources are limited. The farmer can *increase* his wheat production (move to the right in Figure 3–1) only by devoting more of his land and labour to growing wheat, meaning that he must simultaneously *reduce* his soybean produc-

A **production possibilities frontier** shows the different combinations of various goods that a producer can turn out, given the available resources and existing technology.

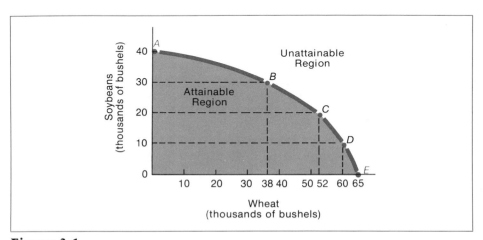

Figure 3-1
PRODUCTION POSSIBILITIES FRONTIER FOR PRODUCTION BY A SINGLE FIRM
With a given set of inputs, the firm can produce only those output combinations given by points in the shaded area. The production possibilities frontier, *AE*, is not a straight line but one that curves more and more as it nears the axes. That is, when the firm specializes in only one product, those inputs that are especially adapted to the production of the other good lose at least part of their productivity.

tion (move downward) because less of his land and labour remains available for growing soybeans.

Notice that in addition to having a negative slope, our production possibilities frontier, curve AE, has another characteristic—it is "bowed outward." Let us consider a little more carefully what this curvature means.

Suppose our farmer is initially producing only soybeans, so that he uses for this purpose even land that is much more suitable for wheat cultivation (point A). Now suppose he decides to switch some of his land from soybean production into wheat production. Which part of his land will he switch? Obviously, if he is sensible, he will use the part best suited to wheat growing. If he shifts to point B, soybean production falls from 40,000 bushels to 30,000 bushels as wheat production rises from zero to 38,000. A sacrifice of only 10,000 bushels of soybeans "buys" 38,000 bushels of wheat.

Imagine now that the farmer wants to produce still more wheat. Figure 3–1 tells us that the sacrifice of an additional 10,000 bushels of soybeans (from 30,000 down to 20,000) will yield only 14,000 more bushels of wheat (see Point C). Why? The main reason is that inputs tend to be specialized. As we noted, at point A the farmer was using resources for soybean production that were much more suitable for growing wheat. Consequently, their productivity in soybeans was relatively low, and when they were switched into wheat production the yield was very high. But this cannot continue forever. As more wheat is produced, the farmer must utilize land and machinery that are better suited to producing soybeans and less well-suited to producing wheat. This is why the first 10,000 bushels of soybeans forgone "buys" the farmer 38,000 bushels of wheat while the second 10,000 bushels of soybeans "buys" him only 14,000 bushels of wheat. Figure 3–1 and Table 3–1 show that these returns continue to decline as wheat production expands: the next 10,000-bushel reduction in soybean production yields only 8000 bushels of additional wheat, and so on.

We can now see that the *slope* of the production possibilities frontier represents graphically the concept of *opportunity cost*. Between points C and B, for example, the opportunity cost of acquiring 10,000 additional bushels of soybeans is 14,000 bushels of forgone wheat, and between points B and A, the opportunity cost of 10,000 bushels of soybeans is 38,000 bushels of forgone wheat. In general, as we move upward to the left along the production possibilities frontier (toward more soybeans and less wheat), the opportunity cost of soybeans in terms of wheat increases. Or, putting the same thing differently, as we move downward to the right, the opportunity cost of acquiring wheat by giving up soybeans increases.

The Principle of Increasing Costs

We have just described a very general phenomenon, which is applicable well beyond farming. The **principle of increasing costs** states that as the production of one good expands, the opportunity cost of producing another unit of this good generally increases.

This principle is not a universal fact; there can be exceptions to it. But it does seem to be a technological regularity that applies to a wide range of economic activities. As our example of the farmer suggests, the principle of increasing costs is based on the fact that resources tend to be specialized, at least in part, so that some of their productivity is lost when they are transferred from doing what they are relatively good at doing to what they are relatively bad at doing. In terms of diagrams like Figure 3–1, the principle simply asserts that the production possibilities frontier is bowed outward.

Perhaps the best way to understand this idea is to contrast it with a case in which there are no specialized resources. Figure 3–2 depicts a production possibilities frontier for producing black shoes and brown shoes. Because the labour and capital used to produce black shoes are just as good at producing brown shoes, the

The **principle of increasing costs** states that as the production of one good expands, the opportunity cost of producing another unit generally increases.

Resources that produce black
shoes are just as good at
producing brown shoes. So there
is no loss of productivity when
black-shoe production is
decreased in order to increase
brown-shoe production. For
example, if the firm moves from
point A to point B, black-shoe
output falls by 10,000 pairs and
brown-shoe output rises by 10,000
pairs. The same would be true if it
moved from point B to point C or
from point C to point D. The
production possibilities frontier is
therefore a straight line.

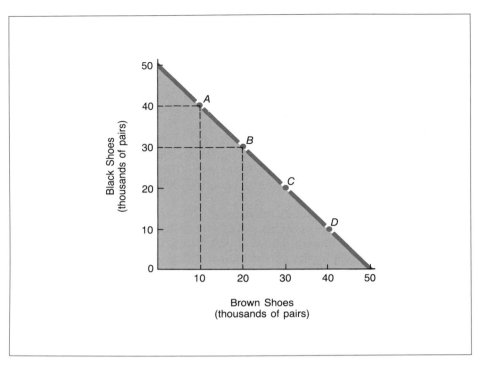

frontier is a straight line. If the firm cuts back its production of black shoes by 10,000 pairs, it always gets 10,000 additional pairs of brown shoes. No productivity is lost in the switch because resources are not specialized.

Scarcity and Choice for the Entire Society

Like an individual firm, the entire economy is also constrained by its limited resources and technology. If society wants more aircraft and tanks, it will have to give up some boats and automobiles. If it wants to build more factories and stores, it will have to build fewer homes and sports arenas. In general:

The position and shape of the production possibilities frontier that constrains the choices of the economy are determined by the economy's physical resources, its skills and technology, its willingness to work, and its investments in factories, research, and innovation.

Since the debate over acid rain has been so active in recent years, let us illustrate the nature of society's choices by the example of choosing between clean air and manufactured goods. Just like a single firm, the economy as a whole has a production possibilities frontier for these items determined by its technology and the available resources of land, labour, capital, and raw materials. This production possibilities frontier may look like curve BC in Figure 3–3.

If most workers are employed at factories, coal mines, and refineries, the production of manufactured goods will be large but the availability of clean air will be small. If resources are transferred from the mines and factories to emission treatment operations, the mix of output can be shifted toward cleaner air at some sacrifice of manufactured goods (the move from D to E). However, something is likely to be lost in the transfer process—some of the machines and chemicals that helped produce the manufactured goods will not help in the emission treatment operations. As summarized in the principle of increasing costs, physical resources tend to be specialized, so the production possibilities frontier probably curves downward and toward the axes.

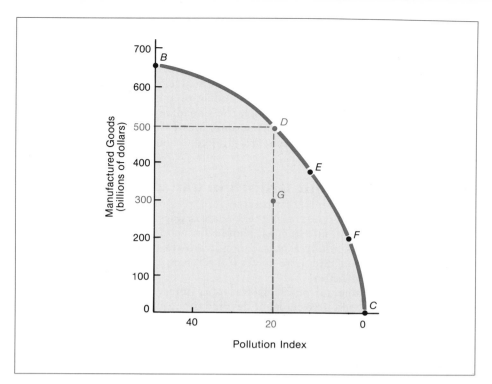

Figure 3-3
THE PRODUCTION
POSSIBILITIES FRONTIER
FOR THE ENTIRE ECONOMY
This production possibilities
frontier is curved because
resources are not perfectly
transferable from goods
production to emission treatment
operations. The limits on available
resources place a ceiling, C, on
the availability of clean air (a
reading of zero on the pollution
index), and a ceiling, B, on the
output of manufactured goods.

We may even reach a point where the only resources left are items that are not very useful outside of factories. In that case, even a very large additional sacrifice of goods yields very little cleaner air. That is the meaning of the steep segment, FC, on the frontier. At point C the air is only slightly cleaner than at F, even though at C goods production has been given up entirely.

The downward slope of society's production possibilities frontier implies that hard choices must be made. Our nation's pollution problems can be solved only by decreasing material consumption, not by rhetoric nor by wishing it so. The curvature of the production possibilities frontier implies that, as emission treatment increases, it becomes progressively more expensive to "buy" cleaner air by sacrificing manufactured goods.

Scarcity and Choice Elsewhere in the Economy

We have stressed that limited resources force hard choices upon business managers and society as a whole. But the same type of choices arise elsewhere—in households, in universities, in nonprofit organizations, and in the government.

The nature of opportunity cost is perhaps most obvious for a household that must decide how to divide its income among the goods and services that compete for the family's trade. If the Higgins family buys an expensive new car, they may be forced to cut back sharply on their other purchases. This does not make it unwise to buy the car. But it does make it unwise to buy the car until the full implications of the purchase for the family's overall budget are considered. If the Higgins family are to use their limited resources most effectively, they must explicitly acknowledge that the opportunity costs of the car are, say, a shorter vacation and making do with the old TV set.

Even a rich and powerful government like that of the United States or the

Soviet Union must cope with the limitations implied by scarce resources. The necessity for choice imposed on the government by its limited budget is similar in character to the problems faced by business firms and households. For the goods and services it buys from others, a government has to prepare a budget similar to that of a very large household. For the items it produces itself—education, police protection, libraries, and so on—it faces a production possibilities frontier much like that of a business firm. Even though the Canadian government spent over $100 billion in 1984, some of the most acrimonious parliamentary debates were over how to allocate the government's limited resources among competing programs.

Application: Economic Growth in Canada and Japan

Among the economic choices that any society must make, there is one very important choice that illustrates well the concept of opportunity cost. This choice is embodied in the question "How fast should the economy grow?"[1] At first, the question may seem ridiculous. Since economic growth means, roughly, that the average citizen has more and more goods and services, is it not self-evident that faster growth is always better?

Again, the fundamental problem of scarcity intervenes. Economies do not grow by magic. Scarce resources must be devoted to the process of growth. Cement and steel that could be used to make swimming pools and stadiums must be diverted to build more machinery and factories. Wood that could be made into furniture and skis must be used for hammers and ladders instead. Grain that could be eaten must be ploughed back into the soil to increase future yields. By deciding how large a quantity of resources to devote to future needs rather than to current consumption, society in effect *chooses* (within limits) how fast it will grow.

An **investment good** is an item that is used to produce other goods and services in the future, rather than being consumed today.

Figure 3–4 illustrates the nature of the choice by depicting production possibilities frontiers for goods that are consumed today (like food and electricity) versus **investment goods** that provide for future consumption (like grocery stores and generating plants) for two different societies.

Figure 3–4(a) depicts a society like Canada's that devotes a relatively small quantity of resources to growth, preferring current consumption instead. It chooses a point like A on this year's production possibilities frontier, FF. At A, consumption is relatively high and investment is relatively low, so the production possibilities frontier shifts only to GG next year. Figure 3–4(b) depicts a society much more enamoured of growth, like Japan's. It selects a point like B, on its production possibilities frontier, ff. At B, consumption is much lower and investment is much higher; so its production possibilities frontier moves all the way to gg by next year. Japan grows faster than Canada, but the more rapid growth has a price—an *opportunity cost*. The Japanese must give up some of the current consumption that Canadians enjoy.

An economy grows by giving up some current consumption and investing instead for the future. The more it invests, the faster will its production possibilities frontier shift outward over time.

The Concept of Efficiency

So far in our discussion of scarcity and choice, we have assumed that either the single firm or the whole economy always operates *on* its production possibilities frontier rather than *below it.* In other words, we have tacitly assumed that, whatever it decides to do, the firm or economy does so *efficiently.* An efficient economy utilizes all of its available resources, and produces the maximum amount

[1]Economic growth will be studied in detail in Chapter 40.

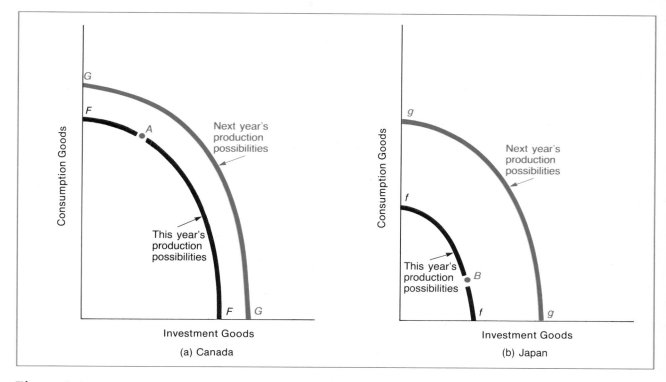

Figure 3-4

GROWTH IN TWO ECONOMIES

Growth shifts the production possibilities frontiers *FF* and *ff* (black) outward to the frontiers *GG* and *g g* (blue), meaning that each economy can produce more of both goods than it could before. If the shift in both economies occurs in the same period of time, then the Japanese economy (b) is growing faster than the Canadian economy (a) because the outward shift in (b) is much greater than the one in (a).

of output that its technology permits.[2] Economists define *efficiency* as the absence of waste.

To see why any point on the economy's production possibilities frontier in Figure 3–3 represents an efficient decision, suppose for a moment that society has decided to settle for air with a purity level of 20. According to the production possibilities frontier, if this level of clean air is to be attained, then the maximum amount of manufactured goods that can be made is $500 billion (point *D* in Figure 3–3). The economy is, therefore, operating efficiently if it actually produces $500 billion worth of goods rather than some smaller amount, such as $300 billion (as at point *G*). Point *D* is efficient while point *G* is not.

Note that the concept of efficiency does not tell us which point on the production possibilities frontier is *best*; it only tells us that no point that is *not* on the frontier can be best, because any such point represents wasted resources. For example, should society ever find itself at point *G*, the necessity of making hard choices would (temporarily) disappear. It would be possible to increase both the production of goods *and* air purity by moving to a point such as *E*.

Why, then, would an economy ever find itself at a point below its production possibilities frontier? There are a number of ways in which resources are wasted in real life. The most important of them, unemployment, is an issue that will take up a substantial part of this book (especially in Parts Two and Three). When many workers are unemployed, the economy finds itself at a point like *G*, below the frontier, because by putting the unemployed to work in both manufacturing and emission treatment jobs the economy could produce more goods and have cleaner air. The economy would then move from point *G* to the right (cleaner air) and

[2]A more formal definition of *efficiency* is offered in Chapter 26, page 517.

upward (more goods) toward a point like *E* on the production possibilities frontier. Only when no resources are wasted by unemployment or misuse is the economy *on* the frontier.

Analogous problems occur in the firm. For example, if a firm uses fertilizer wastefully, it will end up at a point *inside* its production possibilities frontier. It will not be operating efficiently.

The Three Co-ordination Tasks of Any Economy

In deciding how to use its scarce resources, society must somehow make three sorts of decisions. First, as we have just emphasized, it must figure out **how to utilize its resources efficiently**; that is, it must find a way to get *on* its production possibilities frontier. Second, it must decide **what combination of goods to produce**—how many goods versus cleaner air and so on; that is, it must select one specific point on the production possibilities frontier. Finally, it must decide **how much of each good to distribute to each person**, doing it in a sensible way so that meat does not go to vegetarians and wine to teetotallers.

Certainly, each of these decisions could be made by a central planner who told people how to produce, what to produce, and what to consume.[3] But many of the decisions can also be made without central direction, through a system of prices and markets. Let us consider each task in turn.

Specialization, Division of Labour, and Exchange

Efficiency in production is one of the three basic tasks. Many features of society contribute to efficiency; others interfere with it. While different societies pursue the goal of economic efficiency in different ways, one source of efficiency is so fundamental that we must single it out for special attention: the tremendous gains in productivity that stem from **specialization** and the consequent **division of labour**.

Division of labour means breaking up a task into a number of smaller, more specialized tasks so that each worker can become more adept at his or her particular job.

Adam Smith, the founder of modern economics, first marvelled at this mainspring of efficiency and productivity on a visit to a pin factory. In a famous passage near the beginning of his monumental book *The Wealth of Nations* [1776], he described what he saw:

One man draws out the wire, another straightens it, a third cuts it, a fourth points it, a fifth grinds it at the top for receiving the head; to make the head requires two or three distinct operations; to put it on is a peculiar business, to whiten the pins is another; it is even a trade by itself to put them into the paper....[4]

Smith observed that by dividing the work to be done in this way, each worker became quite skilled in his particular specialty, and the productivity of the group of workers as a whole was enhanced enormously. As Smith related it:

I have seen a small manufactory of this kind where ten men only were employed.... Those ten persons ... could make among them upwards of forty-eight thousand pins in a day.... But if they had all wrought separately and independently, ... they

---

[3]Central planning will be considered in some detail in Chapter 41.
[4]Adam Smith, *The Wealth of Nations* (New York: Random House, Modern Library Edition, 1937), page 4.

certainly could not each of them have made twenty, perhaps not one pin in a day. . . .[5]

In other words, through the miracle of division of labour and specialization, ten workers accomplished what would otherwise have required thousands. This was the secret of the Industrial Revolution, which helped lift humanity out of the abject poverty that had for so long been its lot.

But specialization created a problem. With division of labour, people no longer produced only what they wanted to consume themselves. The workers in the pin factory had no use for the thousands of pins they produced each day; they wanted to trade them for things like food, clothing, and shelter. Specialization thus made it necessary to have some mechanism by which workers producing pins could **exchange** their wares with workers producing such things as cloth and potatoes.

Without a system of exchange, the productivity miracle achieved by the division of labour would have done society little good. With it, standards of living rose enormously. As we observed in Chapter 1:

Mutual Gains from Voluntary Exchange

Unless there is deception or misunderstanding of the facts, a voluntary exchange between two parties must make both parties better off. Even though no additional goods are produced by the act of trading, the welfare of society is increased because each individual acquires goods that are more suited to his needs and tastes. This simple but fundamental precept of economics is one of our **12 Ideas for Beyond the Final Exam**.

While goods can be traded for other goods, a system of exchange works better when everyone agrees to use some common item (such as pieces of paper) for buying and selling goods and services. Enter *money*. Then workers in pin factories, for example, can be paid in money rather than in pins, and they can use this money to purchase cloth and potatoes. Textile workers and farmers can do the same.

These two principles—specialization and exchange (assisted by money)—working in tandem led to a vast improvement in the well-being of mankind. This process of specialization and exchange is extended when a country's citizens trade with those living in other countries. Indeed it can be shown that even if the citizens in one country are more efficient at producing *everything* than are the citizens in the other country, *both* countries benefit from specializing and trading. We explain this *principle of comparative advantage* fully in Chapter 32. We show there that a country can obtain points *beyond* its own production possibilities curve, by engaging in foreign trade.

Markets, Prices, and the Three Co-ordination Tasks

We have emphasized above that the two important principles—specialization and exchange—have led to a vast improvement in material welfare. But what forces induce workers to join together so that the fruits of the division of labour can be enjoyed? And what forces establish a smoothly functioning system of exchange so that each person can acquire what he or she wants to consume? One alternative is to have a central authority telling people what to do. But Adam Smith explained and extolled another way of organizing and co-ordinating economic activity—the use of markets and prices.

Smith noted that people were very good at pursuing their own self-interest,

---

[5]Ibid., page 5.

Biographical Note: Adam Smith (1723-1790)

Adam Smith, who was to become the leading advocate of freedom of international trade, was born the son of a customs official in 1723 and ended his career in the well-paid post of collector of customs for Scotland. He received an excellent education at Glasgow College, where, for the first time, some lectures were being given in English rather than Latin. A fellowship to Oxford University followed, and for six years he studied there mostly by himself, since, at that time, teaching at Oxford was virtually nonexistent.

After completing his studies, Smith was appointed professor of logic at Glasgow College and, later, professor of moral philosophy, a field which then included economics as one of its branches. Fortunately, he was a popular lecturer because, in those days, a professor's pay in Glasgow depended on the number of students who chose to attend his lectures. At Glasgow, Smith was responsible for helping young James Watt find a job as an instrument maker. Watt later invented the steam engine, so in this and many other respects, Smith was present virtually at the birth of the Industrial Revolution, whose prophet he was destined to become.

After thirteen years at Glasgow, Smith accepted a highly paid post as a tutor to a young Scottish nobleman with whom he spent several years in France, a customary way of educating nobles in the eighteenth century. Primarily because he was bored during these years in France, Smith began working on *The Wealth of Nations*. Several years after his return to England, in 1776, the book was published and rapidly achieved popularity.

The Wealth of Nations contains many brilliantly written passages. It was one of the first systematic treatises in economics, contributing to both theoretical and factual knowledge about the subject. Among the main points made in the book are the importance for a nation's prosperity of freedom of trade and the division of labour permitted by more widespread markets; the dangers of governmental protection of monopolies and imposition of tariffs; and the superiority of self-interest—the instrument of the "invisible hand"—over altruism as a means of improving the economy's service to the general public.

The British government was grateful for the ideas for new tax legislation Smith proposed, and to show its appreciation appointed him to the lucrative sinecure of collector of customs, which, together with the lifetime pension awarded him by his former pupil, left him very well off financially, although he eventually gave away most of his money to charitable causes.

In the eighteenth century, the intellectual world was small, and among the many people with whom Smith was acquainted were David Hume, Samuel Johnson, James Boswell, Benjamin Franklin, and Jean Jacques Rousseau. Smith got along well with everyone except Samuel Johnson, who was noted for his dislike of Scots. Smith was absent-minded and apparently timid with women, being visibly embarrassed by the public attention of the eminent ladies of Paris during his visits there. He never married, and lived with his mother most of his life. When he died, the Edinburgh newspapers recalled only that when Smith was four years old he was kidnapped by gypsies. But thanks to his writings, he is remembered for a good deal more than that.

---

and that a *market system* was a very good way to harness this self-interest. As he put it, with pretty clear religious overtones, in doing what is best for themselves, people are "led by an invisible hand" to promote the economic well-being of society.

Since we live in a market economy, the outlines of the process by which the invisible hand works are familiar to all of us.[6] Firms are encouraged by the profit motive to use inputs efficiently. Valuable resources (like energy) will command high prices, thus causing producers to economize on their use. The price system also guides firms' output decisions, and hence those of society. A rise in the price

[6]This topic is studied in detail in Chapter 26.

of wheat, for example, will persuade farmers to produce more wheat and fewer soybeans. Finally, a price system determines who gets what goods through a series of voluntary exchanges. Workers with valuable skills and owners of scarce resources will be able to sell what they have at attractive prices. With the incomes they earn, they can then purchase the goods and services they want most, within the limits of their budgets.

This, in broad terms, is how a market economy solves the three basic problems facing any society: how to produce any given combination of goods efficiently, how to select an appropriate combination of goods, and how to distribute these goods sensibly among the people. As we proceed through the following chapters, you will learn much more about these issues. You will see that they constitute the central theme that permeates not only this text, but the work of economists in general. As you progress through the book, keep in mind the following two questions: **What does the market do well and what does it do poorly?** There are plenty of answers to both questions. As you will learn in coming chapters:

1. Society has many important goals. Some of them, such as producing goods and services with maximum efficiency (minimum waste), can in certain circumstances be achieved extraordinarily well by letting markets operate more or less freely.

2. Free markets will not, however, achieve all of society's goals. For example, as we will see in Part Two, they often have trouble keeping unemployment and inflation low. And there are even some goals—such as protection of the environment—for which the unfettered operation of markets may be positively harmful.

3. But even in cases where the market does not perform at all well, there may be ways of harnessing the power of the market mechanism to remedy its own deficiencies, as you will learn particularly in Parts Three and Six.

Radicalism, Conservatism, and the Market Mechanism

Since economic debates often have political and ideological overtones, we think it important to close this chapter by stressing that the central theme that we have just outlined is neither a defence of nor an attack upon the capitalist system. Nor is it a "right-wing" position. One does not have to be a conservative to recognize that the market mechanism can be a helpful instrument for the pursuit of economic goals. A number of socialist countries, including Yugoslavia and Hungary, have openly and deliberately organized parts of their economies along market lines, and the People's Republic of China is now moving in that direction.

The point is not to confuse means and ends in deciding on how much to rely on market forces. Radicals and conservatives surely have different goals, and they may also differ in the means they advocate to pursue these goals. But means should be chosen on the basis of how effective they are in achieving the adopted goals, not on some ideological prejudgments.

For example, radicals may assign a much higher priority to pollution control than conservatives do. Consequently, radicals may favour very strict controls even if such controls cut into business profits; conservatives may prefer things the other way around. Nevertheless, each side may want to use the market mechanism to achieve its goals. Indeed, each side may conclude that, should it lose the political struggle and the other side's position be adopted, less damage will be done to its own goals if market methods are used.

Certainly, there are economic problems with which the market cannot deal. Indeed, we have just noted that the market is the *source* of a number of significant problems. But the evidence leads economists to believe that many economic problems are best handled by market techniques. The analysis in this book is intended to help you identify the strengths and weaknesses of the market mechanism. Forget the slogans you have heard—whether from the Left or from the Right—and make up your own mind after you have read this book.

Summary

1. Supplies of all resources are limited. Because resources are scarce, a rational decision is one that chooses the best alternative among the options that are possible with the available resources.

2. It is irrational to assign highest priority to everything. No one can afford everything, and so hard choices must be made.

3. With limited resources, if we decide to obtain more of one item, we must give up some of another item. What we give up is called the *opportunity cost* of what we get; this is the true cost of any decision. The concept of opportunity cost is one of the **12 Ideas for Beyond the Final Exam**.

4. When the market is functioning effectively, firms are led to use resources efficiently and to produce the things that consumers want most. In such cases, opportunity costs and money costs (prices) correspond closely. When the market performs poorly, or when important items of cost do not get price tags, opportunity costs and money costs can be quite different.

5. A firm's production possibilities frontier shows the combinations of goods the firm can produce with a given quantity of resources, given the state of technology. The frontier usually is not a straight line but is bowed outward because resources tend to be specialized.

6. The principle of increasing costs states that as the production of one good expands, the opportunity cost of producing another unit of this good generally increases.

7. The economy as a whole has a production possibilities frontier whose position is determined by its technology and by the available resources of land, labour, capital, and raw materials.

8. If a firm or an economy ends up at a point below its production possibilities frontier, it is using its resources inefficiently or wastefully. This is what happens, for example, when there is unemployment.

9. Economic growth means there is an outward shift in the economy's production possibilities frontier. The faster the growth, the faster this shift will occur. But growth requires a sacrifice of current consumption and this is its opportunity cost.

10. Efficiency is defined by economists as the absence of waste. It is achieved primarily by gains in productivity brought about through specialization, division of labour, and a system of exchange.

11. If an exchange is voluntary, both parties must benefit even though no new goods are produced. This is another of the **12 Ideas for Beyond the Final Exam**.

12. Every economic system must find a way to answer three basic questions: How can goods be produced most efficiently? How much of each good should be produced? How should goods be distributed?

13. The market system works very well in solving some of society's basic problems, but it fails to remedy others and may, indeed, create some of its own. Where and how it succeeds and fails constitute the theme of this book and characterize the work of economists in general.

Concepts for Review

Scarcity
Choice
Opportunity cost
Production possibilities frontier

Principle of increasing costs
Investment goods
Efficiency
Specialization

Division of labour
Exchange
Market system
Three co-ordination tasks

Questions for Discussion

1. Discuss the resource limitations that affect:
   a. the poorest person on earth
   b. the richest person on earth
   c. a firm in Switzerland
   d. a government agency in China
   e. the population of the world

2. If you were president of your university, what would you change if your budget were cut by 5 percent? By 20 percent? By 50 percent?

3. If you were to drop out of university, what things would change in your life? What, then, is the opportunity cost of your education?

4. A person rents a house for which he pays the landlord $5000 a year and keeps money in a bank account that pays 9 percent interest a year. The house is offered for sale at $70,000. Is this a good deal for the potential buyer? Where does opportunity cost enter the picture?

5. Construct graphically the production possibilities frontier for Lower Atlantis given in the table at the top of the next column.

   Does the principle of increasing cost hold in Lower Atlantis?

PRODUCTION POSSIBILITIES FOR LOWER ATLANTIS, 1986

SOUFFLÉS (millions)	COMPUTERS (thousands)
75	0
60	12
45	22
30	30
15	36
0	40

6. Consider two alternatives for Lower Atlantis in the year 1986. In case (a) its inhabitants eat 60 million soufflés and build only 12,000 computers. In case (b) the population eats only 15 million soufflés but builds 36,000 computers. Which case will lead to a more generous production possibilities frontier for Atlantis in 1987? (*Note*: In Atlantis, computers are used for cooking soufflés.)

7. Mel's Sports Shop sells two brands of tennis balls. Brand X costs Mel $1.50 per can, and Brand Y costs Mel $2 per can. Draw Mel's production possibilities frontier if he has $60 to spend on tennis balls. Why is it not "bowed out"?

Supply and Demand: An Initial Look

Reformers have the idea that
change can be achieved by
brute sanity.
GEORGE BERNARD SHAW

If the issues of scarcity, choice, and co-ordination constitute the basic *problem* of economics, then the mechanism of supply and demand is its basic investigative tool. Whether your course concentrates on macroeconomics or microeconomics, you will find that the so-called law of supply and demand is the fundamental tool of economic analysis. Supply and demand analysis is used in this book to study issues seemingly as diverse as inflation and unemployment, the international value of the dollar, government regulation of business, and protection of the environment. So careful study of this chapter will pay rich dividends.

The chapter describes the rudiments of supply and demand analysis in steps. We begin with demand, then add supply, and finally put the two sides together. *Supply and demand curves*—graphs that relate price to quantity supplied and quantity demanded, respectively—are explained and used to show how prices and quantities are determined in a free market. Influences that shift either the demand curve or the supply curve are catalogued briefly. And the analysis is used to explain why housing prices in Calgary and Edmonton rose so dramatically following the "energy crisis" in the 1970s, and why the home-computer industry has grown so fast.

One major theme of this chapter is that governments around the globe and throughout recorded history have attempted to tamper with the price mechanism. We will see that these bouts with Adam Smith's invisible hand often have produced undesired side effects that surprised and dismayed the authorities. And we will show that many of these unfortunate effects were no accidents but were inherent consequences of interfering with the operation of free markets. The invisible hand fights back!

Finally, a word of caution. This chapter makes heavy use of graphs such as those described in Chapter 2. If you encounter difficulties with these graphs, we suggest you review pages 19–34.

Fighting the Invisible Hand

Adam Smith was a great admirer of the price system. He marvelled at its intricacies and extolled its accomplishments. Many people since Smith's time have shared his enthusiasm; but many others have not. His contemporaries in the American colonies, for example, were often unhappy with the prices produced by free markets and thought they could do better by legislative decree. And there have been countless other instances in which the public's sense of justice was outraged by the prices charged on the open market, particularly when the sellers of the expensive items did not enjoy great popularity—landlords, moneylenders, and oil companies are good examples.

Attempts to control interest rates (which may be thought of as the price of borrowing money) go back hundreds of years before the birth of Christ, at least to the code of laws compiled under Hammurabi in Babylonia about 1800 B.C. Our historical legacy also includes a rather long list of price ceilings on foods and other products imposed in the reign of Diocletian, emperor of the declining Roman Empire. More recently, Canadians have been offered the "protection" of a variety of price controls. Ceilings have been placed on prices of some items (such as energy) to protect buyers, while floors have been placed under prices of other items (such as farm products) to protect sellers. Many if not most of these measures were adopted in response to popular opinion, and there is a great outcry whenever it is proposed that any one of them be weakened or eliminated.

Yet, somehow, everything such regulation touches seems to end up in even greater disarray than it was before. Despite rent controls, rents in Vancouver and Toronto have considerably more than doubled in the last ten years. Despite laws against ticket "scalping," tickets for popular shows and sports events sell at tremendous premiums. Surplus agricultural products have had to be destroyed or stored indefinitely. The list could go on.

Still, legislators continue to turn to controls whenever the economy does not work to their satisfaction. The 1970s and 1980s have seen a return to rent controls in many Canadian cities, the Anti-Inflation Board and the "6 and 5" program for wage restraint in the public sector, a web of controls over energy prices, and the continued use of agricultural price support schemes.

Interferences with the "Law" of Supply and Demand

Public opinion frequently encourages legislative attempts to "repeal the law of supply and demand" by controlling prices. The consequences usually are quite unfortunate, exacting heavy costs from the general public and often aggravating the problem the legislation was intended to cure. This is another of the **12 Ideas for Beyond the Final Exam**, and it will occupy our attention throughout this chapter.

To understand what goes wrong when markets are tampered with, we must first learn how they operate when they are unfettered. This chapter takes a first step in that direction by studying the machinery of supply and demand. Then, at the end of the chapter, we return to the issue of price controls, illustrating the problems that can arise by case studies of rent controls and price supports for milk.

We begin our analysis on the demand side of the market.

Demand and Quantity Demanded

Non-economists are apt to think of consumer demands as fixed amounts. For example, when the production of a new type of machine tool is proposed, management asks "What is its market potential? How many will we be able to sell?" Similarly, government bureaus conduct studies to determine how many engineers will be "required" in succeeding years.

Economists respond that such questions are not well posed—that there is no *single* number that describes the information required. Rather, they say, the "market potential" for machine tools or the number of engineers that will be "required" depends on a great number of things, *including the price that will be charged for each.*

Price Controls
in the Eighteenth Century

The following excerpts illustrate the unfortunate results that have followed from two of the many attempts to override market forces with legislation that have occurred over the years. In these examples, price ceilings made it unprofitable for suppliers to operate, so that scarcities and lost jobs were the unintended by-products.

The French Revolution

During the twenty months between May 1793 and December 1794, the Revolutionary Government of the new French Republic tried almost every experiment in wage and price controls which has been attempted before or since. . . .

. . . [The] first Law of the Maximum, as it was called, provided that the price of grain and flour in each district of France should be the average of local market prices which were in effect from January to May 1793. . . .

. . . By the summer of 1794, demands were coming from all over the country for the immediate repeal of the Law. In some towns in the South the people were so badly fed that they were collapsing in the streets from lack of nourishment. The department of the Nord complained bitterly that their shortages all began just after the passage of the by now hated Law of the Maximum. "Before that time," they wrote to the Convention in Paris, "our markets were supplied, but as soon as we fixed the price of wheat and rye we saw no more of those grains. The other kinds not subject to the maximum were the only ones brought in. The deputies of the Convention ordered us to fix a maximum for all grains. We obeyed and henceforth grain of every sort disappeared from the markets. What is the inference? This, that the establish-ment of a maximum brings famine in the midst of abundance. What is the remedy? Abolish the maximum."

. . . When Robespierre and his colleagues were being carried through the streets of Paris on their way to their executions, the mob jeered their last insult: "There goes the dirty Maximum."

Early Canada—Louisbourg

During 1750 rules were made as to the price that must be charged for fresh cod fish. It was, by this order, explicitly forbidden for fishermen to refuse to sell their fish at the posted price provided only that the buyer was solvent. To appreciate the serious nature of this law, it is necessary to remember that the bulk of New France's wealth was derived from the cod fishery. Of course, from time to time this regulation led to desperate circumstances for the fishermen and there is some reason to believe that it was responsible for the decline in the fishery in that area of New France.

SOURCE: Robert L. Schuettinger, "The Historical Record: A Survey of Wage and Price Controls over Fifty Centuries," in *Tax-Based Incomes Policies—A Cure for Inflation?* edited by M. Walker (Vancouver: The Fraser Institute, 1982), pages 67, 73–76.

The **quantity demanded** of any product normally depends on its price. Quantity demanded also has a number of other determinants, including population size, consumer incomes, tastes, and the prices of other products.

Because of the central role of prices in a market economy, we begin our study of demand by focusing on the relationship between quantity demanded and price. Shortly, we will bring the other determinants of quantity demanded back into the picture.

Consider, as an example, the quantity of milk demanded. Almost everyone purchases at least some milk. However, if the price of milk is very high, its "market potential" may be very small. People will find ways to get along with less milk, perhaps by switching to tea or coffee. If the price declines, people will be encouraged to drink more milk. They may give their children larger portions or switch away from juices and sodas. Thus:

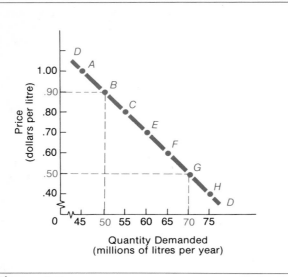

Figure 4-1
DEMAND CURVE FOR MILK
This curve shows the relation between price and quantity demanded. To sell 70 million litres per year, the price must be only 50¢ (point G).
If, instead, price is 90¢ only 50 million litres will be demanded (point B). To sell more milk, the price must be reduced. That is what the
negative slope of the demand curve means.

Table 4-1
DEMAND SCHEDULE FOR MILK

PRICE (dollars per litre)	QUANTITY DEMANDED (millions of litres per year)	LABEL IN FIGURE 4-1
1.00	45	A
0.90	50	B
0.80	55	C
0.70	60	E
0.60	65	F
0.50	70	G
0.40	75	H

There is no *one* demand figure for milk, for machine tools, or for engineers. Rather there is a series of alternative quantities demanded, each corresponding to a different price.

A **demand schedule** is a table showing how the quantity demanded of some product during a specified period of time changes as the price of that product changes, holding all other determinants of quantity demanded constant.

The Demand Schedule

Table 4-1 displays this information for milk in what we call a **demand schedule**. It shows the quantity of milk that will be demanded in a year at each possible price ranging from $1 to 40¢ per litre. We see, for example, that at a relatively low price, like 50¢ per litre, customers wish to purchase 70 million litres per year. But if the price were to rise to, say, 90¢ per litre, quantity demanded would fall to 50 million litres.

Common sense tells us why this should be so.[1] First, as prices rise, some customers will reduce their consumption of milk. Second, higher prices will induce some customers to drop out of the market entirely—for example, by switching to soda or juice. On both counts, quantity demanded will decline as the price rises.

As the price of an item rises, the quantity demanded normally falls. As the price falls, the quantity demanded normally rises.

A **demand curve** is a graph showing how the quantity demanded of some product during a specified period of time will change as the price of that product changes, holding all other determinants of quantity demanded constant.

The Demand Curve

The information contained in Table 4-1 can be summarized in a graph, which we call a **demand curve**, displayed in Figure 4-1. Each point in the graph corresponds to a line in the table. For example, point B corresponds to the second line in the table, indicating that at a price of 90¢ per litre, 50 million litres per year will be demanded. Since the quantity demanded declines as the price increases, the demand curve has a negative slope.[2]

Notice the last phrase in the definitions of the demand schedule and the demand curve: "holding all other determinants of quantity demanded constant." These "other things" include consumer incomes and preferences, the prices of

[1]This common-sense answer is examined more fully in Chapter 20.
[2]If you need to review the concept of *slope*, refer back to Chapter 2, especially pages 21–24.

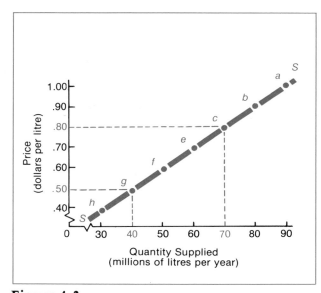

Table 4-2
SUPPLY SCHEDULE FOR MILK

PRICE (dollars per litre)	QUANTITY SUPPLIED (millions of litres per year)	LABEL IN FIGURE 4-2
1.00	90	a
0.90	80	b
0.80	70	c
0.70	60	e
0.60	50	f
0.50	40	g
0.40	30	h

Figure 4-2
SUPPLY CURVE FOR MILK
This curve shows the relation between the price of milk and the quantity supplied. To stimulate a greater quantity supplied, price must be increased. That is the meaning of the positive slope of the supply curve.

soda and orange juice, and perhaps even advertising by the dairy association. We will examine the influences of these factors later in the chapter. First, however, let's look at the supply side of the market.

Supply and Quantity Supplied

Like quantity demanded, the quantity of milk that is supplied by dairy farmers is not a fixed number but also depends on many things. Obviously, if there are more dairy farms, or larger ones, we expect more milk to be supplied. Or if bad weather deprives the cows of their feed, they may give less milk. As before, however, let's turn our attention first to the relationship between *quantity supplied* and one of its major determinants—the price of milk.

Economists generally suppose that a higher price calls forth a greater quantity supplied. Why? Remember our analysis of the principle of increasing cost in Chapter 3 (page 39). According to that principle, as more of any farmer's (or the nation's) resources are devoted to milk production, the cost of obtaining another litre of milk increases. Farmers will therefore find it profitable to raise milk production only if they can sell the milk at a higher price—high enough to cover the higher costs involved.

Looked at the other way around, we have just concluded that higher prices normally will be required to persuade farmers to raise milk production. This idea is quite general and applies to the supply of most goods and services.[3] As long as suppliers want to make profits, and the principle of increasing costs holds:

As the price of an item rises, the quantity supplied normally rises. As the price falls, the quantity supplied normally falls.

The Supply Schedule and the Supply Curve
The relationship between the price of milk and its quantity supplied is recorded in Table 4-2, which we call a **supply schedule**. The table shows that a low price

A **supply schedule** is a table showing how the quantity supplied of some product during a specified period of time changes as the price of that product changes, holding all other determinants of quantity supplied constant.

[3]This analysis is carried out in much greater detail in Chapters 22 and 23.

A **supply curve** is a graph showing how the quantity supplied of some product during a specified period of time will change as the price of that product changes, holding all other determinants of quantity supplied constant.

like 50¢ per litre will induce suppliers to provide only 40 million litres, while a higher price, like 80¢ will induce them to provide much more—70 million litres.

As you might have guessed, when information like this is plotted on a graph, it is called a **supply curve**. Figure 4–2 is the supply curve corresponding to the supply schedule in Table 4–2. It slopes upward because quantity supplied is higher when price is higher.

Notice again the same phrase in the definition: "holding all other determinants of quantity supplied constant." We will return to these "other determinants" a bit later. But first we are ready to put demand and supply together.

Equilibrium of Supply and Demand

To analyse how price is determined in a free market, we must compare the desires of consumers (demand) with the desires of producers (supply) and see whether the two sets of plans are consistent. Table 4–3 and Figure 4–3 are designed to help us do this.

Table 4–3 brings together the demand schedule from Table 4–1 and the supply schedule from Table 4–2. Similarly, Figure 4–3 puts together the demand curve from Figure 4–1 and the supply curve from Figure 4–2 on a single graph. Such a graphic device is called a **supply-demand diagram**, and we will encounter many of them in this book. Notice that, for reasons already discussed, the demand curve has a negative slope and the supply curve has a positive slope. Most supply-demand diagrams are drawn with slopes like these.

There is only one point in Figure 4–3, point E, at which the supply curve and the demand curve intersect. At the price corresponding to point E, which is 70¢ per litre, the quantity supplied is equal to the quantity demanded. At a lower price, such as 50¢, only 40 million litres of milk will be supplied (point g) whereas 70 million litres will be demanded (point G). Thus, quantity demanded will exceed quantity supplied. There will be a **shortage** equal to 70 – 40 = 30 million litres.

A **shortage** is an excess of quantity demanded over quantity supplied. When there is a shortage, buyers cannot purchase the quantities they desire.

A **surplus** is an excess of quantity supplied over quantity demanded. When there is a surplus, sellers cannot sell the quantities they desire to supply.

An **equilibrium** is a situation in which there are no inherent forces that produce change. Changes away from an equilibrium position will occur only as a result of "outside events" that disturb the status quo.

Alternatively, at a higher price, such as $1, quantity supplied will be 90 million litres (point a) while quantity demanded will be only 45 million (point A). Quantity supplied will exceed quantity demanded, so there will be a **surplus** equal to 90 – 45 = 45 million litres.

Since 70¢ is the price at which quantity supplied and quantity demanded are equal, we say that 70¢ per litre is the **equilibrium price** in this market. Similarly, 60 million litres per year is the **equilibrium quantity** of milk.

The term "equilibrium" merits a little explanation, since it arises so frequently in economic analysis. An **equilibrium** is a situation in which there are no inherent forces that produce change; that is, a situation that does not contain the seeds of its own destruction. Think, for example, of a pendulum at rest at its centre point. If no outside force (such as a person's hand) comes to push it, the pendulum will remain where it is; it is in *equilibrium*.

But, if someone gives the pendulum a shove, its equilibrium will be disturbed and it will start to move upward. When it reaches the top of its arc, the pendulum will, for an instant, be at rest again. But this is not an equilibrium position. A force known as gravity will pull the pendulum downward, and thereafter its motion from side to side will be governed by gravity and friction. Eventually, we know, the pendulum must return to the point at which it started, which is its only equilibrium position. At any other point inherent forces will cause the pendulum to move.

The concept of equilibrium in economics is similar and can be illustrated by our supply and demand example. Why is no price other than 70¢ an equilibrium price in Table 4–3 or Figure 4–3? What forces will change any other price?

Consider first a low price like 50¢, at which quantity demanded (70 million) exceeds quantity supplied (40 million). If the price were this low, there would be many frustrated customers unable to purchase the quantities they desire. They

Table 4-3

DETERMINATION OF THE EQUILIBRIUM PRICE AND QUANTITY OF MILK

PRICE (dollars per litre)	QUANTITY DEMANDED	QUANTITY SUPPLIED	SURPLUS OR SHORTAGE?	PRICE WILL:
	(millions of litres per year)			
1.00	45	90	Surplus	Fall
0.90	50	80	Surplus	Fall
0.80	55	70	Surplus	Fall
0.70	60	60	Neither	Remain the same
0.60	65	50	Shortage	Rise
0.50	70	40	Shortage	Rise
0.40	75	30	Shortage	Rise

would compete with one another for the available milk. Some would offer more than the prevailing price and, as customers tried to outbid one another, the market price would be forced up. In other words, a price below the equilibrium price cannot persist in a free market because a shortage sets in motion powerful economic forces that push price upward.

Similar forces operate if the market price is *above* the equilibrium price. If, for example, the price should settle at $1, Table 4–3 tells us that quantity supplied (90 million) would far exceed quantity demanded (45 million). Sellers would be unable to sell their desired quantities of milk at the prevailing price, and some would find it in their interest to undercut their competitors by reducing price. This process of competitive price-cutting would continue as long as the surplus persisted, that is, as long as quantity supplied exceeded quantity demanded. Thus, a price above the equilibrium price cannot persist indefinitely.

We are left with only one conclusion. The price 70¢ per litre and the quantity 60 million litres is the only price-quantity combination that does not sow the seeds of its own destruction. It is the only *equilibrium*. Any lower price must rise, and any higher price must fall. It is as if natural economic forces place a magnet at point E that attracts the market just like gravity attracts the pendulum.

The analogy to a pendulum is worth pursuing further. Most pendulums are more frequently in motion than at rest. However, unless they are repeatedly buffeted by outside forces (which, of course, is exactly what happens to pendulums used in clocks), pendulums gradually return to their resting points. The same is

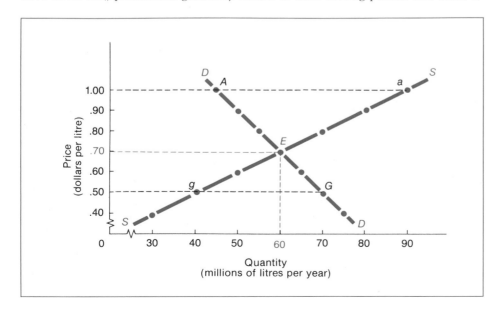

Figure 4-3

SUPPLY-DEMAND EQUILIBRIUM

In a free market, price and quantity are determined by the intersection of the supply curve and the demand curve. In this example, the equilibrium price is 70¢ and the equilibrium quantity is 60 million litres of milk per year. Any other price is inconsistent with equilibrium. For example, at a price of 50¢, quantity demanded is 70 million litres (point C), while quantity supplied is only 40 million litres (point g), so that price will be driven up by the unsatisfied demand.

true of price and quantity in a free market. Markets are not always in equilibrium, but, if they are not interfered with, we have good reason to believe that they normally are *moving toward equilibrium*.

In principle, in a free market the forces of supply and demand are capable of selecting an equilibrium price and an equilibrium quantity toward which, in practice, we may expect actual price and actual quantity to gravitate.

The last interesting aspect of the analogy concerns the "outside forces" of which we have spoken. A pendulum that is being blown by the wind or pushed by a hand does not remain in equilibrium. Similarly, many outside forces can disturb a market equilibrium. A frost in Florida will disturb equilibrium in the market for oranges. A strike by miners will disturb equilibrium in the market for coal.

Many of these outside influences actually *change the equilibrium price and quantity* by shifting either the supply curve or the demand curve. If you look again at Figure 4-3, you can see clearly that any event that causes *either* the demand curve *or* the supply curve to shift will also cause the equilibrium price and quantity to change. Such events constitute the "other things" that we held constant in our definitions of supply and demand curves. We are now ready to analyse how these outside forces affect the equilibrium of supply and demand, beginning on the demand side.

Shifts of the Demand Curve

Returning to our example of milk, we noted earlier that the quantity of milk demanded is probably influenced by a variety of things other than the price of milk. Changes in population, consumer income, and the prices of alternative beverages such as soda and orange juice presumably cause changes in the quantity of milk demanded, even if the price of milk is unchanged.

Since the demand curve for milk depicts only the relationship between the quantity of milk demanded and the price of milk, holding all other factors constant, a change in any of these other factors produces a *shift of the entire demand curve*. That is:

A change in the price of a good produces a **movement along a fixed demand curve**. By contrast, a change in any other variable that influences quantity demanded produces a **shift of the demand curve**. If consumers want to buy *more* at any given price than they wanted previously, the demand curve shifts to the right (or outward). If they desire less at any given price, the demand curve shifts to the left (or inward).

To make this general principle more concrete and to show some of its many applications, let us consider some specific examples.

1. **Consumer incomes.**   If incomes increase, consumers may purchase more of many foods, including milk, even if the price of milk remains the same. That is, *increases in income normally shift demand curves outward to the right*, as depicted in Figure 4-4(a). In this example, the quantity demanded at the old equilibrium price of 70¢ increases from 60 million litres per year (point E on demand curve D_0D_0) to 75 million (point R on demand curve D_1D_1). We know that 70¢ is no longer the equilibrium price, since at this price quantity demanded (75 million) exceeds quantity supplied (60 million). To restore equilibrium, price will have to rise. The diagram shows the new equilibrium at point T, where the price is 80¢ per litre and the quantity (demanded and supplied) is 70 million litres per year. This illustrates a general result.

Any factor that causes the demand curve to shift outward to the right, and does not affect the supply curve, will raise the equilibrium price and the equilibrium quantity.[4]

Everything works in reverse if consumer incomes fall. Figure 4–4(b) depicts a leftward (inward) shift of the demand curve that results from a decline in consumer incomes. For example, the quantity demanded at the previous equilibrium price (70¢) falls from 60 million litres (point E) to 45 million (point L on demand curve D_2D_2). At the initial price, quantity supplied must begin to fall. The new equilibrium will eventually be established at point M, where the price is 60¢ and both quantity demanded and quantity supplied are 50 million. In general:

Any factor that shifts the demand curve inward to the left and does not affect the supply curve will lower both the equilibrium price and the equilibrium quantity.

2. **Population.**   Population growth should affect quantity demanded in more or less the same way as increases in consumer incomes. A larger population will presumably wish to consume more milk, even if the price of milk is unchanged, thus shifting the entire demand curve to the right as in Figure 4–4(a). The equilibrium price and quantity both rise. Similarly, a decrease in population should shift the demand curve for milk to the left, as in Figure 4–4(b), causing equilibrium price and quantity to fall.

3. **Consumer preferences.**   If the dairy industry mounts a successful advertising campaign extolling the benefits of drinking milk, families may decide to raise their quantities demanded. This would shift the entire demand curve for

[4]This statement, like many others in the text, assumes that the demand curve is downward-sloping and the supply curve is upward-sloping.

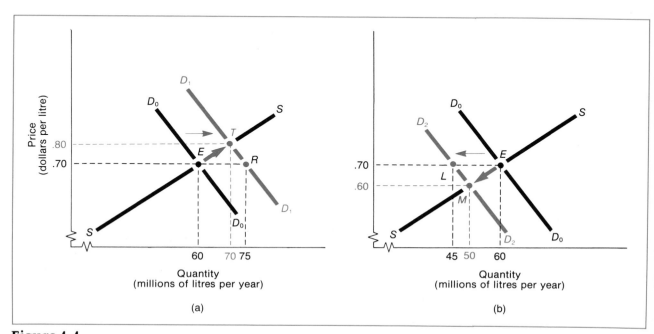

Figure 4-4
THE EFFECTS OF SHIFTS OF THE DEMAND CURVE
A shift of the demand curve will change the equilibrium price and quantity in a free market. In part (a), the demand curve shifts outward from D_0D_0 to D_1D_1. As a result, equilibrium moves from point E to point T; both price and quantity rise. In part (b), the demand curve shifts inward from D_0D_0 to D_2D_2, and equilibrium moves from point E to point M; both price and quantity fall.

milk to the right, as in Figure 4-4(a). Alternatively, a medical report on the dangers of high cholesterol may persuade consumers to drink less milk, thereby shifting the demand curve inward, as in Figure 4-4(b).

Again, these are quite general phenomena. *If consumer preferences shift in favour of a particular item, that item's demand curve will shift outward to the right, causing both price and quantity to rise [Figure 4-4(a)]. Conversely, if consumer preferences shift against a particular item, that item's demand curve will shift inward to the left, causing price and quantity to fall [Figure 4-4(b)].*

4. ***Prices and availability of related goods.*** Because soda, orange juice, and coffee are popular drinks that compete with milk, a change in the price of any of these beverages can be expected to shift the demand curve for milk. If any of these alternative drinks become cheaper, some consumers will switch away from milk. Thus the demand curve for milk will shift to the left, as in Figure 4-4(b). The introduction of an entirely new beverage—like coconut milk—can be expected to have a similar effect.

But other price changes shift the demand curve for milk in the opposite direction. For example, suppose that cookies, a commodity that goes well with milk, become less expensive. This may induce some consumers to drink more milk and thus shift the demand curve for milk to the right as in Figure 4-4(a).

Common sense normally will tell us in which direction a price change for a related good will shift the demand curve for a good in question. *Increases in the prices of goods that are substitutes for the good in question (as soda is for milk) move the demand curve to the right, thus raising both the equilibrium price and quantity. Increases in the prices of goods that are normally used together with the good in question (such as cookies and milk) shift the demand curve to the left, thus lowering both the equilibrium price and the quantity.*

Application: Housing Prices in Calgary and Edmonton During the Energy Crisis

While the preceding list does not exhaust the possible influences on quantity demanded, enough has been said to indicate the principles involved. Let us therefore turn to a concrete example.

In 1973, the Organization of Petroleum Exporting Countries (OPEC) quadrupled its selling price of oil. This led to a dramatic increase in the demand for oil from other sources, such as Western Canada. The resulting boom in the energy-related industries in Alberta meant that the demand for homes in Calgary and Edmonton in particular soared, as did housing prices and rents. Average housing prices in these cities rose from $30,000 in 1973 to about $90,000 in 1980, and there was a construction boom in both cities.

Our supply and demand diagram makes it easy to interpret these events. The boom in the energy industries caused a sharp rightward shift of the demand curve for houses in Calgary and Edmonton. As Figure 4-5 shows, we expect such a shift to raise housing prices and to increase the number of homes. This is precisely what happened. After 1980, however, the world recession and certain aspects of the National Energy Program led to a decline in the energy industries in Alberta. This means that the demand curve in Figure 4-5 shifted back to the left, and it is therefore no surprise that housing prices declined in Calgary and Edmonton during the 1980s, and that housing construction halted.

Shifts of the Supply Curve

Like quantity demanded, the quantity supplied on a market typically responds to a great number of influences other than price. The weather, the cost of feed, the number and size of dairy farms, and a variety of other factors all influence how much milk will be brought to market. Since the supply curve depicts only the relationship between the price of milk and the quantity of milk demanded, holding

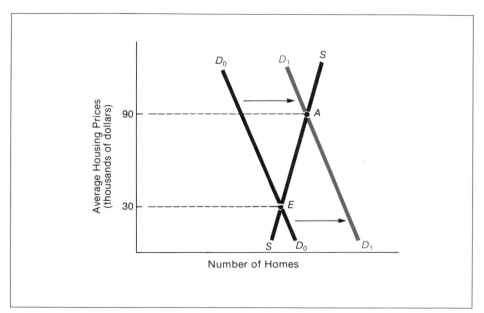

Figure 4-5
THE EFFECT OF THE
ENERGY CRISIS ON
HOUSING PRICES IN
CALGARY AND EDMONTON
The energy crisis of the 1970s
caused a rightward shift of the
demand curve for houses in
Calgary and Edmonton, from D_0D_0
to D_1D_1. As a consequence, the
market equilibrium point shifted
from E to A. Price and quantity
both increased.

all other factors constant, a change in any of these other factors will cause the entire supply curve to shift. That is:

A change in the price of the good causes a **movement along a fixed supply curve**. But price is not the only influence on quantity supplied. And, if any of these other influences changes, **the entire supply curve shifts**.

Let us consider what some of these other factors are, and how they shift the supply curve.

1. **Size of the industry.**   We begin with the most obvious factor. If more farmers enter the milk industry, the quantity supplied at any given price probably will increase. For example, if each farm provides 60,000 litres of milk per year when the price is 70¢ per litre, then 1000 farmers provide 60 million litres and 1300 farmers provide 78 million. Thus, the more firms that are attracted to the industry, the greater will be the quantity of milk supplied at any given price and, hence, the farther to the right will be the supply curve.

Figure 4-6(a) illustrates the effect of an expansion of the industry from 1000 farms to 1300 farms—a rightward shift of the supply curve from S_0S_0 to S_1S_1. Notice that at the initial price of 70¢, the quantity supplied after the shift is 78 million litres (point I on supply curve S_1S_1), which exceeds the quantity demanded of 60 million (point E on supply curve S_0S_0). We can see in the graph that the price of 70¢ is too high to be the equilibrium price; so price must fall. The diagram shows the new equilibrium at point J, where the price is 60¢ per litre and the quantity is 65 million litres. The general point is that:

Any factor that shifts the supply curve outward to the right, and does not affect the demand curve, will lower the equilibrium price and raise the equilibrium quantity.

This must *always* be true if the industry's demand curve has a negative slope because the greater quantity supplied can be sold only if price is decreased to induce customers to buy more.[5]

---

[5]Graphically, whenever a positively sloped curve shifts to the right, its intersection point with a negatively sloping curve must always move lower (just try drawing it yourself).

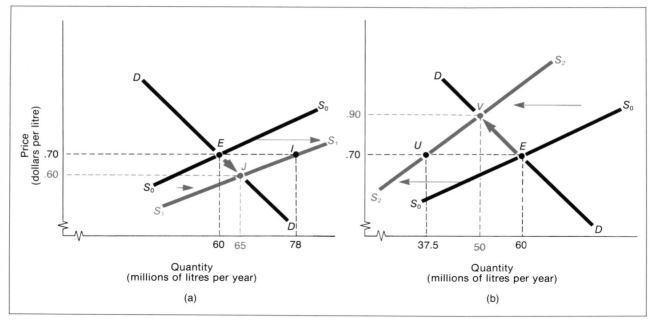

Figure 4-6
EFFECTS OF SHIFTS OF THE SUPPLY CURVE

A shift of the supply curve will change the equilibrium price and quantity in a market. In part (a), the supply curve shifts outward to the right, from S_0S_0 to S_1S_1. As a result, equilibrium moves from point E to point J; price falls as quantity increases. Part (b) illustrates the opposite case—an inward shift of the supply curve from S_0S_0 to S_2S_2. Equilibrium moves from point E to point V, which means that price rises as quantity falls.

Figure 4-6(b) illustrates the opposite case: a contraction of the industry from 1000 farms to 625 farms. The supply curve shifts inward to the left and equilibrium moves from point E to point V, where price is 90¢ and quantity is 50 million litres. In general:

Any factor that shifts the supply curve inward to the left, and does not affect the demand curve, will raise the equilibrium price and reduce the equilibrium quantity.

Even if no farmers enter or leave the industry, results like those depicted in Figure 4-6 can be produced by expansion or contraction of the existing farms. If farms get larger by adding more land, expanding the herds, and so on, the supply curve shifts to the right as in Figure 4-6(a). If farms get smaller, the supply curve shifts to the left, as in Figure 4-6(b).

2. **Technological progress.** Another influence that shifts supply curves is technological change. Suppose someone discovers that cows give more milk if Mozart is played during milking. Then, at any given price of milk, farmers will be able to provide a larger quantity of output; that is, the supply curve will shift outward to the right, as in Figure 4-6(a). This, again, illustrates a quite general influence that applies to most industries: *cost-reducing technological progress shifts the supply curve outward to the right.* Thus, as Figure 4-6(a) shows, the usual consequences of technological progress are lower prices and greater output.

3. **Prices of inputs.** Input price changes also shift supply curves. Suppose that farm workers become unionized and win a raise. Farmers will have to pay higher wages and consequently will no longer be able to provide 60 million litres of milk profitably at a price of 70¢ per litre [point E in Figure 4-6(b)].

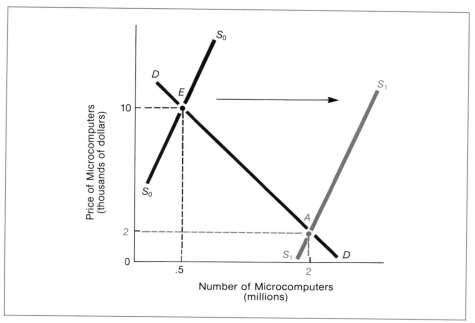

Figure 4-7
TECHNOLOGICAL CHANGE
AND THE COMPUTER
MARKET
The invention of the microchip, and subsequent improvements in microchip technology, caused the supply curve of minicomputers to shift outward to the right—moving from $S_0 S_0$ to $S_1 S_1$. Consequently, equilibrium shifted from point E to point A. The price of microcomputers fell from \$10,000 to \$2000, and the quantity increased from 0.5 million to 2 million per year.

Perhaps they will provide only 37.5 million (point U on supply curve $S_2 S_2$). This example illustrates that *increases in the prices of inputs that suppliers must buy will shift the supply curve inward to the left.*

4. **Prices of related outputs.**   Dairy farms produce more than milk. If cheese prices rise sharply, farmers may decide to use some raw milk to make cheese, thereby reducing the quantity of milk supplied. On a supply–demand diagram, the supply curve would shift inward, as in Figure 4-6(b).

Similar phenomena occur in other industries, and sometimes the effect goes in the opposite direction. For example, suppose the price of beef goes up, which increases the quantity of meat supplied. That, in turn, will cause a rise in the number of cowhides supplied at any given price of leather. Thus, a rise in the price of beef will lead to a rightward shift in the supply curve of leather. In general: *A change in the price of one good produced by a multiproduct industry may be expected to shift the supply curves of all the other goods produced by that industry.*

Application: A Computer in Every Home?

Only about a decade ago, no one owned a home computer. Now there are millions in North America, and enthusiasts look toward the day when computers will be as commonplace as television sets. What happened to bring the computer from the laboratory into the home? Did people suddenly develop a craving for computers?

Hardly. What actually happened is that scientists in the early 1970s invented the microchip—a major breakthrough that drastically reduced both the size of computers and, more important, the cost of manufacturing them. Within a few years, microcomputers were in commercial production. And microchip technology continued to improve throughout the 1970s and 1980s, leading to ever smaller, better, and cheaper computers. Today, for a few hundred dollars you can buy a desktop machine whose computing powers rival those of the giant computers of the early 1960s.

In terms of our supply and demand diagrams, the rapid technological progress in computer manufacturing shifted the supply curve dramatically to the right. As Figure 4-7 shows, a large outward shift of the supply curve should bring down the equilibrium price and increase the equilibrium quantity—which is just what happened in the computer industry. The figure calls attention to the fact that consumers naturally buy more computers as the price of computers falls (a *movement along* demand curve *DD* from *E* to *A*), even if the demand curve does not *shift*.

Restraining the Market Mechanism: Price Ceilings

As we have noted already, lawmakers and rulers have often been dissatisfied with the outcomes of the operation of the market system. All through the ages, legislators have done battle with the invisible hand. Sometimes, rather than trying to make adjustments in the workings of the market, governments have sought to raise or to lower the prices of specific commodities by decree. In many of these cases, the feeling of those in authority was that the prices set by the market mechanism were, in some sense, immorally low or immorally high. Penalties were therefore imposed on anyone offering the commodities in question at prices lower or higher than those determined by the authorities.

But the market has proven itself a formidable foe that strongly resists attempts to circumvent its workings. In case after case where legal ceilings on prices are imposed, virtually the same set of consequences ensues:

1. A persistent shortage develops of the items whose prices are controlled. Queuing, direct rationing, or any of a variety of other devices, usually inefficient and unpleasant, have to be substituted for the distribution process provided by the price mechanism. *Example*: U.S. price controls on gasoline led to long lines at service stations in 1979.

2. An illegal or "black" market often arises to supply the commodity. There are usually some individuals who are willing to take the risks involved in meeting unsatisfied demands illegally, if legal means will not do the job. *Example*: Although it is illegal in most places, ticket "scalping" occurs at most popular sporting events.

3. The prices charged on the black market are almost certainly higher than those that would prevail in a free market. After all, black marketeers expect compensation for the risk of being caught and punished. *Example*: Goods that are illegally smuggled into a country are normally quite expensive.

4. In each case, a substantial portion of the price falls into the hands of the black-market supplier instead of going to those who produce the good or who perform the service. *Example*: A constant complaint in the series of hearings that have marked the history of theatre-ticket price controls in New York City has been that the "ice" (the illegal excess charge) falls into the hands of ticket scalpers rather than going to those who invested in, produced, or acted in the play.

These points and others are best illustrated by considering a concrete example of price ceilings.

Case Studies:
(1) Rent Controls in New York City

New York is the only major city in North America that has had rent controls continuously since World War II. The objective of rent control is, of course, to protect the consumer from high rents. But most economists believe that rent control does not help the cities or their inhabitants and that, in the long run, it makes almost everyone worse off. Let's use supply–demand analysis to see what actually happens.

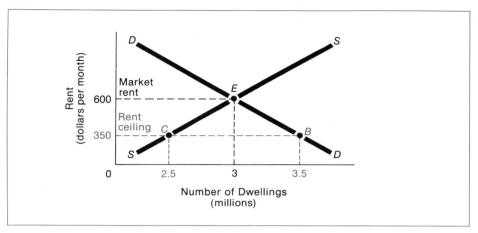

Figure 4-8
SUPPLY-DEMAND
DIAGRAM FOR HOUSING
When market forces are permitted
to set rents, the quantity of
dwellings supplied will equal the
quantity demanded. But when a
rent ceiling forces rent below the
market level, the number of
dwellings supplied (point C) will be
less than the number demanded
(point B). Thus, rent ceilings
induce housing shortages.

Figure 4-8 is a supply-demand diagram for rental units in New York. Curve *DD* is the demand curve and curve *SS* is the supply curve. Without controls, equilibrium would be at point *E*, where rents average $600 per month and 3 million units are occupied. Effective rent controls must set a ceiling price below the equilibrium price of $600, because otherwise the rent level would simply settle at the point determined by market forces. But with a low rent ceiling, such as, say, $350, the quantity of housing demanded will be 3.5 million (point *B*) while the quantity supplied will be only 2.5 million (point *C*).

The diagram shows a shortage of 1 million apartments. This theoretical concept of a "shortage" shows up in New York City as an abnormally low vacancy rate—typically about half the national urban average.

As we expect, rent controls have spawned a lively black market in New York. The black market works to raise the effective price of rent-controlled apartments in many ways, including bribes, "key money" paid to move up on the waiting list and requiring prospective tenants to purchase worthless furniture at inflated prices.

According to the diagram, rent controls reduce the quantity supplied from 3 million to 2.5 million apartments. What do we see in New York? First, some property owners, discouraged by the low rents, have converted apartment buildings into office space or other uses. Second, some apartments have not been maintained adequately. After all, rent controls create a shortage which makes even dilapidated apartments easy to rent. Third, some landlords have actually abandoned their buildings rather than pay rising tax and fuel bills. These abandoned buildings rapidly become eyesores and eventually pose threats to public health and safety.

With all these problems, why do rent controls persist in New York City? And why are some other cities moving in the same direction? Part of the explanation is that many people simply do not understand the problems that rent controls cause. Another part is that landlords are unpopular politically. But a third, and important, part of the explanation is that not everyone is hurt by rent controls, and those who benefit from controls fight hard to preserve them. In New York, for example, many tenants pay rents that are only a fraction of what their apartments would fetch on the open market.

This last point illustrates another very general phenomenon:

Virtually every price ceiling or floor creates a class of people with a vested interest in preserving the regulations because they benefit from them. These people naturally use their political influence to protect their gains, which is one reason why it is so hard to eliminate price ceilings or floors.

(2) Rent Controls in Ontario

The effects of rent control in New York and in several European cities have prompted Swedish economist Assar Lindbeck to quip: "In fact, next to bombing, rent control seems in many cases to be the most efficient technique so far known for destroying cities..." [6]

Despite this evidence, rent control was introduced in Ontario in 1975. Again, the evidence on the impact of the controls illustrates the power of basic supply and demand analysis. Both apartment vacancy rates and the rate of apartment construction starts declined. Cities were not "destroyed" however, and one reason is that provincial-government subsidies for apartment construction were increased dramatically. In a study of rent controls in Toronto, it is reported that the proportion of apartment starts which depended on government support increased from 13 percent in 1974 to 91 percent in 1977.[7]

Restraining the Market Mechanism: Price Floors

Interferences with the market mechanism are not always designed to keep prices low. Agricultural price supports and minimum wages are two notable examples in which the law keeps prices *above* free-market levels. Price floors are typically accompanied by a standard set of symptoms:

1. A surplus develops as some sellers cannot find buyers. *Example:* The minimum-wage law helps create high unemployment among teenagers.[8]

2. Where goods, rather than services, are involved, the surplus creates a problem of disposal. Something must be done about the excess of quantity supplied over quantity demanded. *Example:* The government has often been forced to purchase, and then store, large amounts of surplus agricultural commodities.

3. To get around the regulations, sellers may offer discounts in disguised—and often unwanted—forms. *Example:* When transatlantic air fares were more heavily regulated, airlines offered bargains on the land portions of package holidays to the U.K. that were often not fully used.

Once again, a specific example is useful.

A Case Study: Milk-Price Supports

Perhaps you have seen news items about farmers having to throw away surplus eggs, milk, or other agricultural products. The surpluses are by-products of various government programs designed to raise the incomes of farmers. For many products, a price higher than the equilibrium price is maintained through the provincial marketing boards, which stipulate production limits for each farmer. For other products, a high price is maintained because the government buys up any output that the market does not absorb at the higher price.

One example is the Canadian Dairy Commission, established in 1966. One of its purposes is to stabilize the price of dairy products at a high enough level to permit reasonable incomes to be earned by all existing dairy farmers. Generally, this involves a support price well above the free-market level, so a surplus develops, as indicated in Figure 4–9. To maintain the price above the free-market level, the government must buy the surplus milk and other dairy products. But this creates a problem. Milk is so highly perishable that it must be turned into cheese or butter or dried milk before it can be stored. Buying and storing these products is costly,

---

[6]Assar Lindbeck, *The Political Economy of the New Left: An Outsider's View*, Second Edition (New York: Harper & Row, 1977), page 39.

[7]Basil A. Kalymon, "Apartment Shortages and Rent Control", in *Rent Control: Myths and Realities*, edited by W. Block and E. Olsen (Vancouver: The Fraser Institute, 1981), page 241.

[8]This subject is dealt with more fully in Chapter 37.

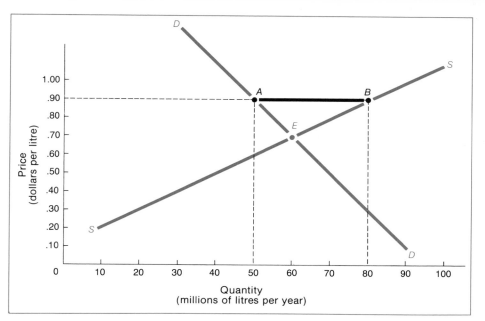

Figure 4-9
PRICE SUPPORTS FOR MILK
In this diagram, which repeats the supply and demand curves from Figure 4-3, the support price for milk (90¢ per litre) is above the equilibrium price (70¢). Quantity supplied is 80 million litres per year (point B), while quantity demanded is only 50 million (point A). To keep the price at 90¢, the government must buy 30 million litres of milk per year and store it as cheese or milk powder, or dispose of it.

so often the products are simply disposed of. Similar problems have developed in the United States and in Europe. One solution to the surplus wine that has resulted from price-support programs in Europe has been to convert it to automobile fuel (gasohol), at much expense to the taxpayer.

This analysis does not imply that individual farm incomes should be lower than they are. It simply shows how the basic forces of supply and demand lead to inefficiencies under the current methods for maintaining farm incomes.

Fixed Exchange Rates

One of the most common prices to be set by government policy is the international value of the Canadian dollar, known as the **exchange rate**. The federal government often stands ready to buy or sell quantities of foreign currencies in whatever amounts that are required to stabilize the price of the Canadian dollar. For example, for a period during 1984, the government tried to keep the value of the Canadian dollar from falling below a price of 75 cents (U.S.). They tried to maintain this price floor by trading currencies in the foreign exchange market. Whenever private traders who desired U.S. dollars or other foreign currencies could not find a trader who would give up Canadian dollars at this price (exchange rate), the Canadian authorities would buy up the otherwise unwanted Canadian currency. The authorities did this by selling off part of their foreign currency reserves. Thus the foreign exchange rate can be fixed in precisely the same manner as in the milk-price supports discussed above. The only difference is that there are no direct storage costs for holding inventories of foreign currencies. Because of this, and because a fluctuating value of the Canadian dollar is often thought to deter foreign trade, this price is heavily managed and sometimes absolutely fixed.

The **exchange rate** states the price at which one currency can be bought in terms of another currency.

Unfortunately, we must wait until Chapters 15 and 16 to assess the costs and benefits of this form of market intervention. It turns out that it very much determines which government policies the Minister of Finance can or cannot use to fight unemployment and inflation.

A Can of Worms

Our two major case studies—rent controls and milk-price supports—illustrate some of the major side effects of price floors and ceilings but barely hint at others.

And there are yet more difficulties that we have not even mentioned. For the market mechanism is a tough bird that imposes suitable retribution on those who seek to circumvent it by legislative decree. Here is a partial list of other problems that may arise when prices are controlled.

Favouritism and Corruption

When price ceilings create a shortage, someone must decide who gets the limited quantity that is available. This can lead to political favouritism, to corruption in government, or even to discrimination along racial or religious lines.

Unenforceability

Attempts to control prices are almost certain to fail in industries with numerous suppliers, simply because the regulating agency must monitor the behaviour of so many sellers. Some ways will be found to evade or to violate the law, and something akin to the free-market price will generally re-emerge. But there is a difference: since the evasion mechanism, whatever its form, will have some operating costs, those costs must be borne by someone. That someone will be the consumer.

Auxiliary Restrictions

Fears that a system of price controls will break down invariably lead to regulations designed to shore up the shaky edifice. Consumers may be told when and from whom they are permitted to buy. The powers of the police and the courts may be used to prevent the entry of new suppliers. Occasionally, an intricate system of market subdivision is imposed, giving each class of firms its protected category of operations in which others are not permitted to compete. Milk-marketing orders are one good example. Laws banning conversion of rent-controlled apartments to condominiums are another.

Limitation of Volume of Transactions

To the extent that controls succeed in affecting prices, they can be expected to reduce the volume of transactions. Curiously, this is true whether the regulated price is above or below the free market's equilibrium price. If it is set above the equilibrium price, quantity demanded will be below the equilibrium quantity. On the other hand, if the imposed price is set below the free-market level, quantity supplied will be cut down. Since sales volume cannot exceed either the quantity supplied or the quantity demanded, a reduction in the volume of transactions (and hence employment) is likely to result.

Encouragement of Inefficiency

A price that is above the equilibrium level permits the survival of less-efficient firms whose high operating costs would doom them in an unrestricted market. This invitation to continued inefficiency becomes even more serious if entry of new suppliers is prevented as part of the program of enforcement of price regulations. (This is why deregulation of the airline industry in the United States led to a painful "shake out" of the weaker companies in the early 1980s.) Moreover, with the penalties for inefficiency severely restricted, the motivation for continued economy of operation by any firm is reduced.

Misallocation of Resources

Departures from free-market prices are likely to produce misuse of the economy's resources because the connection between production costs and prices is broken. For example, shippers use trucks or barges over routes where the resource cost of rail transportation is lower because artificial restrictions impose floors on railway rates. In addition, just as more complex locks lead to more sophisticated burglary tools, more complex regulations lead to the use of yet more resources for their avoidance. New jobs are created for executives, lawyers, and economists. It may well be conjectured that at least some of the expensive services of these professionals could have been used more productively elsewhere.

Economists put it this way. Free markets are capable of dealing with the three basic co-ordination tasks outlined in Chapter 3: deciding *what* to produce, *how* to produce it, and *to whom* the goods should be distributed. Price controls throw a monkey wrench into the market mechanism. Though the market is surely not flawless, and government interferences often have praiseworthy goals, good intentions are not enough. Any government that sets out to repair what it sees as a defect in the market mechanism must take care lest it cause serious damage elsewhere. As a prominent economist once quipped, societies that are too willing to interfere with the operation of free markets soon find that the invisible hand is nowhere to be seen.

Summary

1. The quantity of a product that is demanded is not a fixed number. Rather, quantity demanded depends on such factors as the price of the product, consumer incomes, and the prices of other products.

2. The relationship between quantity demanded and price, holding all other things constant, can be displayed graphically on a demand curve.

3. For most products, the higher the price, the lower the quantity demanded. So the demand curve usually has a negative slope.

4. The quantity of a product that is supplied also depends on its price and many other influences. A supply curve is a graphical representation of the relationship between quantity supplied and price, holding all other influences constant.

5. For most products, the supply curve has a positive slope, meaning that higher prices call forth greater quantities supplied.

6. A market is said to be in equilibrium when quantity supplied is equal to quantity demanded. The equilibrium price and quantity are shown by the point on a graph where the supply and demand curves intersect. In a free market, price and quantity will tend to gravitate to this point.

7. A change in quantity demanded that is caused by a change in the price of the good is represented by a movement along a fixed demand curve. A change in quantity demanded that is caused by a change in any other determinant of quantity demanded is represented by a shift of the demand curve.

8. This same distinction applies to the supply curve: Changes in price lead to movements along a fixed supply curve; changes in other determinants of quantity supplied lead to shifts of the whole supply curve.

9. Changes in consumer incomes, tastes, technology, prices of competing products, and many other influences cause shifts in either the demand curve or the supply curve and produce changes in price and quantity that can be determined from supply–demand diagrams.

10. An attempt by government regulations to force prices below or above their equilibrium levels is likely to lead to shortages or surpluses, black markets in which goods are sold at illegal prices, and to a variety of other problems. This is one of the **12 Ideas for Beyond the Final Exam**.

Concepts for Review

Demand schedule	Shortage	Shifts in vs. movements along
Demand curve	Surplus	supply and demand curves
Supply schedule	Equilibrium price and quantity	Price ceiling
Supply curve	Equilibrium	Price floor
Supply–demand diagram		Exchange rate

Questions for Discussion

1. How often do you go to the movies? Would you go less often if a ticket cost twice as much? Distinguish between your demand curve for movie tickets and your "quantity demanded" at the current price.

2. What would you expect to be the shape of a demand curve:

a. for a type of medicine that means life or death for a patient?

b. for the gasoline sold by Sam's gas station, which is surrounded by many other gas stations?

3. The following are the assumed supply and demand schedules for transistor radios:

DEMAND SCHEDULE		SUPPLY SCHEDULE	
PRICE (dollars)	QUANTITY DEMANDED	PRICE (dollars)	QUANTITY SUPPLIED
30	70,000	30	120,000
25	80,000	25	110,000
20	90,000	20	90,000
15	100,000	15	60,000
10	110,000	10	0

a. Plot the supply and demand curves and indicate the equilibrium price and quantity.

b. What effect will an increase in the price of copper wire (a production input) have on the equilibrium price and quantity of transistor radios, assuming all other things remain constant? Explain your answer with the help of a diagram.

c. What effect will a decrease in the price of television sets (a substitute commodity) have on the equilibrium price and quantity of transistor radios, assuming again that all other things are held constant? Use a diagram in your answer.

4. Assume that the supply and demand schedules for wheat are the following:

PRICE (dollars)	QUANTITY DEMANDED (millions of bushels)	QUANTITY SUPPLIED (millions of bushels)
6	13	20
4	17	17
2	21	16

a. Suppose that the government sets a floor under the price of wheat at $6. What is greater, the quantity demanded or the quantity supplied? What will be the effect on the wheat market?

b. Now assume that the government abolishes the minimum price for wheat. What will happen to the price and the quantity of wheat consumed?

c. Now assume that the government sets a ceiling on the price of wheat at $2. What would be the effect on the wheat market?

5. Show how the following demand curves are likely to shift in response to the indicated changes:

a. The effect on the demand curve for boots when snowfall increases.

b. The effect on the demand curve for tea when coffee prices fall.

c. The effect on the demand curve for tea when sugar prices fall.

6. Discuss the likely effects of:

a. rent ceilings on the supply of apartments.

b. minimum wages on the demand for teenage workers.

Use supply-demand diagrams to show what may happen in each case.

7. Drinking water is costly to supply. Draw a supply-demand diagram showing how much water would be bought if water were supplied by a private industry controlled by supply and demand. In the same diagram show how much will be consumed if water is supplied by a city government at zero charge. What do you conclude from these results about areas of the country in which water is in short supply?

8. On page 68 it is claimed that either price floors or price ceilings reduce the actual quantity exchanged in a market. Use a diagram, or diagrams, to support this conclusion, and explain the common sense behind it.

9. The same rightward shift of the demand curve may produce a very small or a very large increase in quantity, depending on the slope of the supply curve. Explain with diagrams.

10. (More difficult.) Consider the market for milk discussed in this chapter (Tables 4–1 through 4–3 and Figures 4–1 through 4–3). Suppose the government decides to fight kidney stones by levying a tax of 30¢ per litre on sales of milk. Follow these steps to analyse the effects of the tax:

a. Construct the new supply curve (to replace Table 4–2) that relates quantity supplied to the price consumers pay. (*Hint*: Before the tax, when consumers paid 70¢, farmers supplied 60 million litres. With a 30¢ tax, when consumers pay 70¢ farmers will receive only 40¢. Table 4–2 tells us they will provide only 30 million litres at this price. This is one point on the new supply curve. The rest of the curve can be constructed in the same way.)

b. Graph the new supply curve constructed in part (a) on the supply-demand diagram depicted in Figure 4–3. What are the new equilibrium price and quantity?

c. Does the tax succeed in its goal of reducing the consumption of milk?

d. How much does the equilibrium price increase? Is the price rise greater than, equal to, or less than the 30¢ tax?

e. Who actually pays the tax, consumers or producers? (This may be a good question to discuss in class.)

II

Essentials of Macroeconomics: Aggregate Supply and Aggregate Demand

Macroeconomics and Microeconomics

Where the telescope ends,
the microscope begins.
Which of the two has the
grander view?

VICTOR HUGO

Economics traditionally has been divided into two fields: microeconomics and macroeconomics. These rather inelegant words are derived from the Greek—"micro" means something small and "macro" means something large. Although they were not specifically described as such, the basic notions and subject matter of **microeconomics** were introduced in Chapters 3 and 4. This chapter does the same for **macroeconomics**.

We begin the chapter by investigating the dividing line between microeconomics and macroeconomics: How do the two parts of the discipline differ and why? Next, we stress that while the *questions* studied by macroeconomists differ from those addressed by microeconomists, the underlying *tools* each group uses are almost the same. Supply and demand provide the basic organizing framework for constructing macroeconomic models, just as they do for microeconomic models. Third, we define some important macroeconomic concepts, like recession, inflation, and gross national product. Fourth, we look briefly at the broad sweep of Canadian economic history to obtain some evaluation of the prevalence and seriousness of the macroeconomic problems of recession and inflation. And, finally, we preview what is to come in subsequent chapters by introducing the notion of government management of the economy.

Drawing a Line Between Macroeconomics and Microeconomics

In microeconomics *we study the behaviour of individual decision-making units.* The dairy farmers and consumers of Chapter 4 are individual decision-making units. How do they decide what courses of action are in their own best interests? How are these millions of decisions co-ordinated by the market mechanism, and with what consequences? Questions like these are the substance of microeconomics and are taken up in Parts Four through Seven.

Although Plato and Aristotle might wince at the abuse of their language, microeconomics applies to the decisions of some astonishingly large units. Exxon and the American Telephone and Telegraph Company, for instance, have annual sales that exceed the total production of many nations. Yet an American economist who studies the pricing policies of AT&T is a microeconomist, whereas someone who studies inflation in Trinidad and Tobago is a macroeconomist. So the micro versus macro distinction in economics is certainly not predicated solely on size.

What, then, is the basis for this time-honoured distinction? Whereas micro-economics focuses on the decisions of individual units (no matter how large), *macroeconomics concentrates on the behaviour of entire economies* (no matter how small). Rather than looking at the price and output decisions of a single company, macroeconomists study the overall price level, unemployment rate, and other things that we call *economic aggregates*.

Aggregation and Macroeconomics

What is an "economic aggregate"? Nothing but an *abstraction* that people find convenient in describing some salient feature of economic life. For example, while we observe the prices of butter, telephone calls, and movie tickets every day, we never observe "the price level." Yet many people (not only economists) find it both meaningful and natural to speak of "the cost of living"—so natural, in fact that Statistics Canada's monthly attempts at measuring it are widely publicized by the news media.

Among the most important of these abstract notions is the concept of *national product*, which represents the total production of a nation's economy. The process by which real objects like hairpins, baseballs, cigarettes, and theatre tickets get combined into an abstraction called national product is called **aggregation**, and it is one of the foundations of macroeconomics. We can illustrate it by a simple example.

Imagine a nation called Agraria, whose economy is far simpler than the Canadian economy: Business firms in Agraria produce nothing but foodstuffs to sell to consumers. Rather than deal separately with all the markets for pizzas, candy bars, hamburgers, and so on, macroeconomists group them all into a single abstract "market for output." Thus, when macroeconomists in Agraria announce that output in Agraria rose 10 percent this year, are they referring to more potatoes or hot dogs, more soybeans or green peppers? The answer is: They do not care! In the aggregate measures of macroeconomics, output is output, no matter what form it takes.

Amalgamating many markets into one means that distinctions among different products are ignored. Can we really believe that no one cares whether the national output of Agraria consists of $800,000 worth of pickles and $200,000 worth of ravioli rather than $500,000 each of lettuce and tomatoes? Surely this is too much to swallow. Macroeconomists clearly do not believe that no one cares; instead, they rest the case for aggregation on two foundations.

1. While the *composition* of demand and supply in the various markets may be terribly interesting and important for *some* purposes (such as how income is distributed and what kinds of diets the citizens enjoy or endure), it may be of little consequence for the economy-wide issues of inflation and unemployment—the issues that concern macroeconomists.

2. During economic fluctuations, markets tend to move in unison. When demand in the economy rises, there is more demand for potatoes *and* tomatoes, more demand for artichokes *and* pickles, more demand for ravioli *and* hot dogs.

Though there are exceptions to these two principles, both seem serviceable enough as approximations. In fact, if they were not, there would be no discipline called macroeconomics, and this book would be only half as long as it is. (Lest this cause you a twinge of regret, bear in mind that unemployment and inflation would be far more difficult to control without macroeconomics, and that would be even more regrettable.)

Aggregation means combining many individual markets into one overall market.

The Line of Demarcation Revisited

These two principles—that markets normally move together and that the composition of demand and supply may be unimportant for some purposes—enable us to draw a different kind of dividing line between the territories of microeconomics and macroeconomics.

In macroeconomics, we typically assume that most details of resource allocation and income distribution are of secondary importance to the study of the overall rates of inflation and unemployment.

In microeconomics, we typically ignore inflation and unemployment and focus instead on how individual markets allocate resources and distribute income.

To use a well-worn metaphor, the macroeconomist analyses the determination of the size of the economic "pie," paying scant attention to what is inside it or to how it gets divided among the dinner guests. A microeconomist, on the other hand, assumes that the pie is of the right size and shape and frets over its ingredients and its division. If you have ever baked or eaten a pie, you will realize that either approach alone is a trifle myopic.

In some chapters of this book (especially in Parts Two and Three), macroeconomic issues are discussed as if they could be divorced from questions of resource allocation and income distribution. In other chapters (especially in Parts Four through Seven), microeconomic problems are investigated with scarcely a word about overall inflation and unemployment. This is done solely for the sake of pedagogical clarity. In reality, the crucial interconnection between macroeconomics and microeconomics is always with us. There is, after all, only one economy.

Supply and Demand in Macroeconomics

Some students reading this book will be taking a course that concentrates on macroeconomics while others will be studying microeconomics. The discussion of supply and demand in Chapter 4 serves as an invaluable introduction to both fields because the basic apparatus of supply and demand is just as important in macroeconomics as it is in microeconomics.

Figure 5–1 shows two diagrams that should look familiar from Chapter 4. In Figure 5–1(a), there is a downward-sloping demand curve, labelled DD, and an upward-sloping supply curve, labelled SS. The axes labelled "Price" and "Quantity" do not specify what commodity they refer to because this is a multipurpose diagram. To start on familiar terrain, first imagine that this is a picture of the market for milk, so the price axis measures the price of milk while the quantity axis measures the quantity of milk demanded and supplied. As we know, if there are no interferences with the operation of a free market, equilibrium will be at point E with a price P_0 and a quantity of output Q_0.

Next, suppose something happens to shift the demand curve outward. For example, we learned in Chapter 4 that an increase in consumer incomes might do this. Figure 5–1(b) shows this shift as a rightward movement of the demand curve from $D_0 D_0$ to $D_1 D_1$. Equilibrium has shifted from E to A, so both price and output have risen.

Now let us reinterpret Figure 5–1 as representing an abstract market for "national product." This is one of those abstractions—an economic aggregate—that we described earlier. No one has ever seen, touched, smelled, or eaten a "unit of national product," but these are the kinds of abstractions upon which macroeconomic analysis is built. Consistent with this reinterpretation, think of the price measured on the vertical axis as being another abstraction—the overall price index, or "cost of living."[1] Then curve DD in Figure 5–1(a) is called an **aggregate-demand curve**, and curve SS is called an **aggregate-supply curve**.

The **aggregate-demand curve** shows the quantity of national product that is demanded at each possible value of the price level.

The **aggregate-supply curve** shows the quantity of national product that is supplied at each possible value of the price level.

[1]The appendix to Chapter 6 explains how such price indexes are calculated.

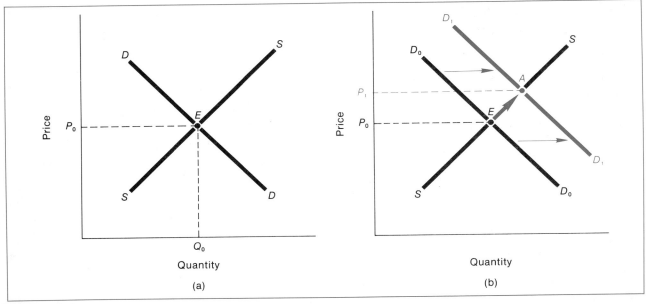

Figure 5-1
TWO INTERPRETATIONS OF A SHIFT IN THE DEMAND CURVE
Part (a) shows an equilibrium at point *E*, where demand curve *DD* intersects supply curve *SS*. Part (b) shows how this equilibrium moves from point *E* to point *A* if the demand curve moves outward. If this graph represents the market for milk as it did in the previous chapter, then it shows an increase in the price of milk. But if the graph represents the aggregate market for "national product," then it shows inflation—a rise in the general price level.

Inflation refers to a sustained *increase* in the general price level.

With this reinterpretation, Figure 5-1(b) can depict the macroeconomic problem of **inflation**. We see from the figure that the outward shift of the aggregate-demand curve, whatever its cause, pushes the price level up from P_0 to P_1. If aggregate demand keeps shifting out month after month, the economy will suffer from inflation, that is, a sustained increase in the general price level.

The other principal problems of macroeconomics, recession and unemployment, also can be illustrated on a supply–demand diagram, this time by shifting the demand curve in the opposite direction. Figure 5-2 repeats the supply and demand curves of Figure 5-1(a) and in addition depicts a leftward shift of the aggregate-demand curve from D_0D_0 to D_2D_2. Equilibrium now moves from point *E* to point *B* so that national product (total output) declines from Q_0 to Q_2. This is what we normally mean by a **recession**.

A **recession** is a period of time during which the total output of the economy declines.

Gross National Product

Gross national product (GNP) is the sum of the money values of all final goods and services produced by the economy during a specified period of time, usually one year.

The economy's total output, we have just seen, is one of the major variables of concern to macroeconomists. While there are several ways to measure it, the most popular choice undoubtedly is the **gross national product**, a term you have probably encountered in the news media. The gross national product, or "GNP" for short, is the most comprehensive measure of the output of all the factories, offices, and shops in the Canadian economy. Specifically, it is the sum of the money values of all final goods and services produced within the year.

Several features of this definition need to be underscored.[2] First, you will notice that:

We add up the *money values* of things.

[2]Certain exceptions to the definition, which are not important here, are noted in the appendix to Chapter 7, especially on pages 133–34.

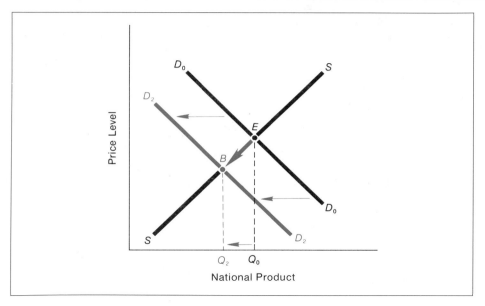

Figure 5-2

AN ECONOMY SLIPPING
INTO A RECESSION

In this aggregate supply–demand diagram, there is an initial equilibrium at point E, where demand curve D_0D_0 intersects supply curve SS. When the demand curve falls from D_0D_0 to D_2D_2, equilibrium moves to point B, and output falls from Q_0 to Q_2.

The GNP consists of a bewildering variety of goods and services: mousetraps and computers, bologna and caviar, ballet performances and rock concerts, cars and textbooks. How are we to combine all of these into a single number? To an economist, the natural way to do this is first to convert every good and service into *money* terms. If we want to add 10 apples and 20 oranges, we first ask: How much *money* does each cost? If apples cost 20¢ and oranges cost 25¢, then the apples count for $2 and the oranges for $5, so the sum is $7 worth of "output." The market *price* of each good or service is used as an indicator of its *value* to society simply because *someone* is willing to pay that much money for it.

This decision raises the question of what prices to use in valuing the different outputs. The official data offer two choices. First, we can value each good and service at the price at which it was actually sold during the year. If we do this, the resulting measure is called **nominal GNP**, or *money GNP*, or *GNP in current dollars*. This seems like a perfectly sensible choice. But as a measure of output, it has one serious drawback: nominal GNP rises when prices rise, even if there is no increase in actual production. For example, if hamburgers cost $1 this year but cost only 75¢ last year, then 100 hamburgers will contribute $100 to this year's nominal GNP but only $75 to last year's. But 100 hamburgers are still 100 hamburgers—output has not grown.

For this reason, government statisticians have devised an alternative measure that corrects for inflation by valuing all goods and services at some fixed set of prices. (Currently, the prices of 1971 are used.) For example, if the hamburgers were valued at 75¢ each in both years, $75 worth of hamburger output would be included in GNP in each year. When we treat every output in this way, we obtain the **real GNP** or *GNP in constant dollars*. The news media often refer to it as "GNP corrected for inflation." Throughout most of this book, and certainly when we are discussing the nation's output, it is the real GNP that we shall be concerned with. The distinction between nominal and real GNP leads us to a working definition of a *recession* as a period in which *real* GNP declines. For example, between 1981 and 1982, nominal GNP rose from $339 billion to $357 billion; but real GNP *fell* from $136 billion to $130 billion.

The next important aspect of the definition of GNP is that:

Nominal GNP is calculated by valuing all outputs at current prices.

Real GNP is calculated by valuing all outputs at the prices that prevailed in some agreed-upon year (currently 1971). Therefore, real GNP is a far better measure of changes in national production.

The GNP for a particular year includes only goods and services produced during that year. Sales of items produced in previous years are explicitly excluded.

For example, suppose you buy a perfectly beautiful 1974 Plymouth next week and are overjoyed by your purchase. The national-income statistician will not share your glee because she already counted your car in the GNP in 1974 when it was first produced and sold; the car will never be counted again. The same holds true of houses. An old house (unlike an old car) often will sell for more than its purchasers originally paid, yet the resale value of the house does not count in the GNP since it was already counted in the year it was built. For the same reason, transactions on the stock market and other exchanges of existing assets are not included in the GNP.

Final goods and services are those that are purchased by their ultimate users.

An **intermediate good** is a good purchased for resale or for use in producing another good.

Third, you will note the use of the phrase **final goods and services** in the definition. The adjective "final" is the key word here. For example, when a supermarket buys milk from a farmer, the transaction is not included in the GNP because the supermarket does not want the milk for itself. It buys milk only for resale to consumers. Only when the milk is sold to consumers is it considered a final product. When the supermarket buys it, economists consider it an **intermediate good**. The GNP does not include sales of intermediate goods or services.

Finally, although the definition does not state this explicitly:

For the most part, only goods and services that pass through organized markets count in the GNP.

This, of course, excludes many economic activities. For example, illegal activities are not included in the GNP. Thus, illegal gambling services are not in the GNP, but the costs of running the many official lotteries are. The definition reflects the statisticians' confession that they could not hope to measure the value of many of

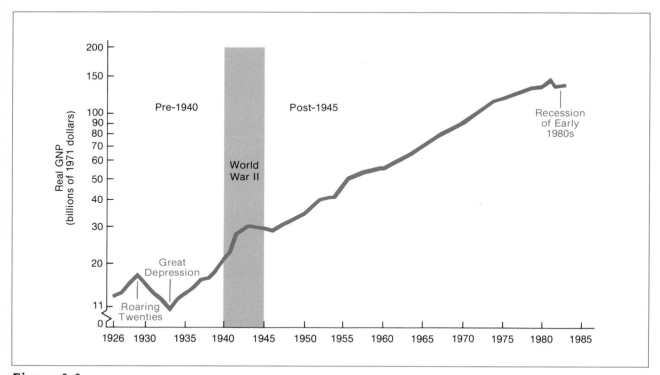

Figure 5-3

REAL GROSS NATIONAL PRODUCT OF CANADA, 1926–1983

This time-series chart displays the behaviour of real gross national production in Canada from 1926 to 1983. (Here real GNP is measured in 1971 prices.) The Great Depression (1929–33) stands out vividly. The years during World War II are shaded. Does the line look smoother to the right of this shaded area? Notice that the vertical axis is calibrated by what is called a "ratio scale." This means, for example, that the distance between 1000 and 100 is the same as the distance between 100 and 10.

SOURCE: Historical Statistics of Canada, and Statistics Canada.

the economy's most important activities, such as housework, do-it-yourself repairs, and leisure time. While these are certainly economic activities that result in currently produced goods or services, they all lack that important measuring rod—a price.

This omission results in certain oddities. For example, suppose that each of two neighbouring families hires the other to clean house, generously paying $1000 a week for the services. Each family can easily afford such generosity since it collects an identical salary from its neighbour. Nothing real changes, but GNP goes up by about $100,000 a year. If this example seems foolish, consider the potential effect of the women's movement on the GNP. Presumably, more and more housework is being done by hired men and women (and thus channelled through the market) and less and less is being done by unpaid housewives. Thus more housework is being included in the GNP. Billions of dollars may be added to the GNP in this way.

The Economy on a Roller Coaster

Having defined several of the basic concepts of macroeconomics, let us breathe some life into them by perusing the economic history of Canada. Figures 5–3 and 5–4 provide a capsule summary of this history since 1926. Figure 5–3 charts the behaviour of real GNP over a period of almost sixty years. The pronounced upward slope of the line indicates that the main feature has been economic growth. But the figure also shows that recessions—periods during which the real GNP decreased—have occurred. The ups and downs that are evident in Figure 5–3 are often referred to as *business cycles*.

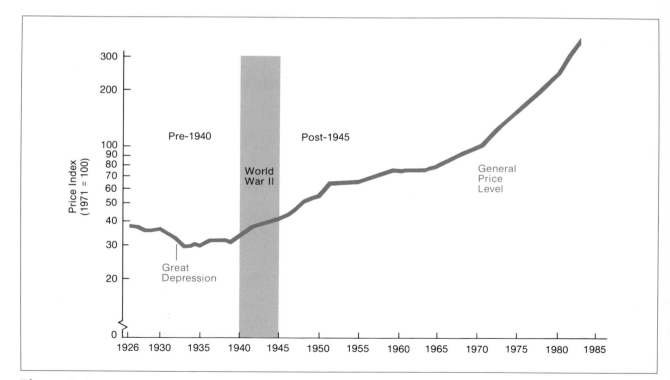

Figure 5-4
THE PRICE LEVEL IN CANADA, 1926–1983
This time-series chart portrays the behaviour of the Canadian price level from 1926 to 1983. (The specific price index used is called the *GNP deflator* and it is defined as the ratio of nominal GNP divided by real GNP.) Once again, the vertical axis has a ratio scale, and the World War II years are shaded. The difference between the 1926–40 period and the 1946–83 period is quite pronounced.
SOURCE: Historical Statistics of Canada, and Statistics Canada.

The history of the price level (Figure 5–4) displays a broadly similar pattern, but one that differs in some important respects. Prices also have been generally rising—that is, inflation has been much more common than deflation—but there have been two exceptions: stable prices during the 1920s and later 1930s, and the falling prices of the early 1930s (the Great Depression).

The following exercise may be enlightening. Cover the portions of Figures 5–3 and 5–4 that deal with the period beginning in 1940, the portions to the right of the shaded area in each figure. The picture that emerges is of an economy on a roller coaster. In Figure 5–3, the ups and downs around the underlying growth trend are quite pronounced. In Figure 5–4 we see periods of both inflation and **deflation**, with hardly any upward trend at all. Indeed, prices at the eve of World War II were lower than they were in the mid-1920s.

Deflation refers to a sustained *decrease* in the general price level.

Now do the reverse. Cover the data prior to 1946 and look only at the postwar period. There is, indeed, a difference. The upward trend in real GNP predominates more, and business cycles are much less severe. While perfection has not been achieved, things do look much better. When we turn to the price level, however, things look rather worse. Gone is any period of falling prices that occurred before World War II, even periods of reasonable price stability are rather rare.

This quick inspection of the data suggests that something has happened. The Canadian economy behaved differently in 1946–83 than it did before World War II. Many economists attribute this shift in the economy's behaviour to lessons the government has learned about managing the economy—lessons that we will be learning in Part Three. When you look at the pre-1940 data, you are looking at an unmanaged economy that went through booms and recessions for "natural" economic reasons. The government did little about either. When you examine the post-1945 data, on the other hand, you are looking at an economy that has been increasingly managed by government policy—sometimes successfully and sometimes unsuccessfully. While the recessions are less severe, a cost seems to have been exacted: The economy appears to be more inflation-prone than it was in the more distant past.

The Great Depression of the 1930s

As you look at these graphs, the Great Depression of the 1930s is bound to catch your eye. The decline in economic activity from 1929 to 1933 (see Figure 5–3) was the most severe in our nation's history, and the rapid deflation (see Figure 5–4) was most unusual. The Depression is but a dim memory now, but those who lived through it will never forget it.

While statistics usually conceal the true drama of economic events, this is not so of the Great Depression—they stand here as a bitter testimony to its severity. From its 1929 high to its 1933 low, the production of goods and services dropped 30 percent and the price level fell 18.5 percent. Business investment almost ceased entirely. The unemployment rate rose ominously to 20 percent in 1933. From the data alone, one can virtually conjure up pictures of soup lines, beggars on street corners, closed factories, and homeless families. (See the boxed insert on the next page.)

The Great Depression was a worldwide event; no country was spared its ravages. This traumatic episode literally changed the history of many nations. In Germany, it facilitated the ascendancy of the Nazi party. In the United States, it enabled Franklin Roosevelt's Democratic party to engineer one of the most dramatic political realignments in history and to push through a host of political and economic reforms.

The worldwide depression also caused a much-needed revolution in the thinking of economists. Up until the 1930s, the prevailing economic theory held that a capitalist economy, while it occasionally misbehaved, had a "natural"

Ten Lost Years

During the worst years of the Great Depression, about 25 percent of Canadian families were forced onto "relief." The loss of work for city dwellers was compounded by the loss of work for farmers due to dust, drought, and grasshoppers. The Canadian government provided rent for cheap, overcrowded accommodation and money for food (about $10 to $15 per month for a family). These desperate times have been described by Canadian author Barry Broadfoot in his *Ten Lost Years*. The quotation and picture below are from his moving descriptions.

For the men who had been taught that their main goal was to be a good family provider, the depression was a degrading time. Sometimes relief officers added to the humiliation by withdrawing liquor permits. Some families were too proud to go on relief, and the starving children stayed home from school so people would not know they had no shoes.

With so much hunger in the family, older sons and depressed fathers became transients, so those remaining at home would have more food and room to sleep. They would pick fruit, harvest crops, and hop a train, hoping to find work elsewhere. Thousands of men were riding back and forth across the country on top of trains or in boxcars. The men lived in "hobo jungles" on the edge of large cities, where they built small shacks and tents from old boards, cardboard, and blankets.

The government worried that the unemployed might start a revolution, so they started relief camps far from the cities, and ran them in a military fashion. The government felt this was a practical solution to the problem, and the men were clothed and fed. However, many men felt they had been forced to the camps and that they worked under slave conditions.

You've got to realize this, in the relief camps of the Thirties we weren't treated as humans. We weren't treated as animals, either, and I've always thought we

A relief camp scene near Ottawa.

were just statistics written into some big ledger in Ottawa. I was 18 and had come out west from Brantford because there was no work for a young fellow in that part of Ontario. . . .

I headed for Vancouver where at least I wouldn't freeze to death, but we were harassed there and kicked around and so I joined up for a relief camp.

It was one of several up the old Hope-Princeton Trail, made up of board and canvas tents, and buildings they called cabooses where we slept. There was about 150 of us in this one, guys as young as 16 and up to 35 or 45, I should guess, and the thing was, we were all single and no jobs, stony broke and no future and the politicians considered us as dangerous. Their thinking was that if we were isolated then we wouldn't be hanging around vacant lots and jungles listening to Communist trouble-makers.

SOURCE: Excerpts from *Ten Lost Years, 1929–1939* by Barry Broadfoot. Copyright © 1973 by Barry Broadfoot. Reprinted by permission of Doubleday & Company, Inc.

tendency to cure recessions or inflations by itself. The roller coaster bounced around but did not normally run off the tracks.

This optimistic view was not confined to academia. It characterized the views of most politicians (certainly including Prime Minister William Lyon McKenzie King) and business leaders as well.

The stubbornness of the Great Depression shook almost everyone's faith in the ability of the economy to right itself. In Cambridge, England, this questioning attitude led John Maynard Keynes, one of the world's most respected economists to write *The General Theory of Employment, Interest, and Money* (1936). Probably the most important book in economics of the twentieth century, it carried a rather revolutionary message. Keynes discarded the notion that the economy always gravitated toward high levels of employment, replacing it with the assertion that—if a pessimistic outlook led business firms and consumers to curtail their spending plans—the economy might be condemned to stagnation for years.

While this doleful prognosis sounded all too realistic at the time, Keynes closed his book on a hopeful note, for he showed how government actions might prod the economy out of its depressed state. The lessons he taught the world then are the lessons we shall be learning in Part Two. They show how governments can manage their economies so that recessions will not turn into depressions and depressions will not last as long as the Great Depression. While Keynes was working on *The General Theory*, he wrote his friend George Bernard Shaw that, "I believe myself to be writing a book on economic theory which will largely revolutionize ... the way the world thinks about economic problems." In many ways, he was right.

From World War II to the 1970s

The Great Depression finally ended when the country engaged in war at the end of the 1930s. With total spending at extraordinarily high levels during the war, mostly because of government expenditures, the economy boomed and the unemployment rate fell to less than 2 percent.

Wartime spending of this magnitude usually leads to inflation, but much of the potential inflation during World War II was contained by price controls. With prices held below the levels at which quantity supplied equalled quantity demanded, many goods had to be rationed, and shortages of consumer goods were quite common. All of this ended with a burst of inflation when controls were lifted after the war.

The period from the end of the war until the early 1960s resembled an earlier period of growth with recessions before 1929. The main difference was that the recessions between 1945 and 1965 were noticeably shorter and less severe than their prewar counterparts. Moderate but persistent inflation also became a fact of life. This period of sustained growth, reasonably low unemployment, and non-accelerating inflation was thought by many to be the result of "The New Economics," a term the media created for the policy of economic management prescribed by Keynes in the 1930s. For a while it looked as if we could avoid both unemployment and inflation. But the optimistic verdicts were premature in both cases.

Inflation was the first problem to crop up, beginning in about 1965. Its major cause, as it had been so many times in the past, was high levels of wartime spending—this time for the Vietnam War by the United States. Demand for Canadian goods was very high during this period partly because of record-level exports to the United States, and partly because we followed a fixed exchange-rate policy. By not letting the international value of the Canadian dollar rise, our government blocked a major route by which demands for our exports could have been held in check.

The Great Stagflation, 1973–1980

In October 1973, things began to get much worse for the oil-importing nations of the world. The war between Israel and the Arab nations led to an embargo on oil shipments to several Western countries and then to a quadrupling of the price of oil by the Organization of Petroleum Exporting Countries (OPEC).

While staggering price increases for oil and other energy resources were principal components of the inflation of this period, they were not the only ones. Continued poor harvests in 1974 in many parts of the globe kept world food prices rising rapidly. Prices of other raw materials also skyrocketed. Naturally, these higher costs of fuel and other materials soon were reflected in the prices of manufactured goods.

For these reasons, the inflation rate in the United States soared to above 12 percent during 1974. Meanwhile, the U.S. economy was slipping into its longest and most severe recession since the 1930s. Real GNP fell by about 5 percent between late 1973 and early 1975, and the unemployment rate almost doubled. Thus, both the twin evils of macroeconomics—inflation and unemployment—were unusually virulent in 1974 and 1975. Indeed, a new term—**stagflation**—was coined to refer to the simultaneous occurrence of economic *stag*nation and rapid in*flation* in the United States.

Canada suffered less unemployment and more inflation than the United States during the mid-1970s for two reasons. The Canadian government cushioned the recession that would have followed from the large drop in export sales to the United States by policies that stimulated demand. Second, the government did not allow the Canadian consumer price of oil to increase to world levels. Nevertheless, the stimulation of the general demand for goods was sufficient to cause inflation to rise dramatically in Canada.

The price of oil began to "misbehave" again in 1979 when the revolution that deposed the Shah of Iran caused a disruption in the flow of Iranian oil, thus sparking chaos in the world oil market. In a series of price increases, OPEC more than doubled the price of its oil during 1979. The consequences of OPEC's actions were similar to those of 1973–75: stagflation returned. By 1980, the Canadian unemployment rate was 7.5 percent, and the inflation rate was over 10 percent.

Disinflation in the Early 1980s

Disinflation is the process of reducing inflation.

During the early 1980s, Canada followed Margaret Thatcher's and Ronald Reagan's contractionary high interest-rate policies to curb inflation. The policy worked but at a tremendous cost. Inflation fell to 5.8 percent in 1983 (the lowest value since 1972), but unemployment soared to 11.9 percent in 1983 (over twice what it was in 1973).

The Problem of Macroeconomic Stabilization

This brief look at the historical record shows that our economy has not generally produced a steady pattern of growth without inflation. Rather, it has been buffeted by periodic bouts of unemployment or inflation, and sometimes has been plagued by both. Also, the discussion involved numerous references to the fact that government policies contributed to our macroeconomic performance (both good and bad). Let us now commence a more formal discussion of this connection.

We can provide a preliminary analysis of **stabilization policy**, the name given to government programs designed to prevent or shorten recessions and to counteract inflation, by using the basic tools of aggregate-supply and aggregate-demand analysis. To facilitate this, we have reproduced as Figures 5–5 and 5–6 two of the diagrams found earlier in this chapter [Figures 5–1(b) and 5–2], but we now give them slightly different interpretations.

Stabilization policy is the name given to government programs designed to prevent or shorten recessions and to counteract inflation (that is, to *stabilize* prices).

Figure 5–5 gives a simplified view of government policy to fight unemployment. We suppose that, in the absence of government intervention, the economy would reach an equilibrium at point E, where demand curve D_0D_0 crosses supply curve SS. Now, if the output corresponding to point E is so low that many workers are unemployed, *the government can reduce unemployment by increasing aggregate demand*. In the diagram, this action shifts the demand curve to D_1D_1, causing equilibrium to move to point A. In general:

Recessions and unemployment are often caused by insufficient aggregate demand. When this is so, government policies that augment demand—such as increases in government spending—can be an effective way to increase output and reduce unemployment.

Figure 5-5
STABILIZATION POLICY TO
FIGHT UNEMPLOYMENT
This diagram duplicates Figure
5-1(b), but here we assume that
point E—the intersection of
demand curve D_0D_0 and supply
curve SS—corresponds to high
unemployment. With the kind of
policy tools that we will study in
later chapters, the government can
shift the aggregate-demand curve
outward to D_1D_1. This would raise
output and lower unemployment.

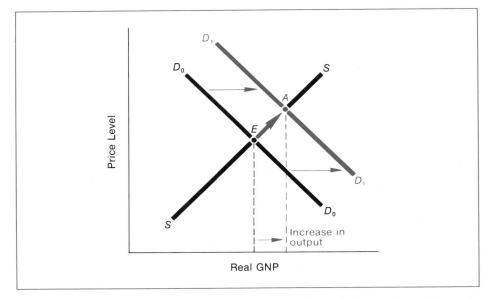

The opposite type of demand management is often called for when inflation is the main macroeconomic problem. Figure 5-6 illustrates this case. Here again, point E, the intersection of demand curve D_0D_0 and supply curve SS, is the equilibrium that would be reached in the absence of government policy. But now we suppose that the price level corresponding to point E is considered "too high," meaning that the *change* in the price level from the previous period to this one would be too rapid if the economy moved to point E. A government program that reduces demand from D_0D_0 to D_2D_2 (for example, a reduction in government spending) can keep prices down and thereby reduce inflation. Thus:

Inflation is frequently caused by aggregate demand racing ahead too fast. When this is the case, government policies that reduce aggregate demand can be effective anti-inflationary devices.

This, in brief, summarizes the job of stabilization policy. When demand behaviour is the source of economic instability, the government can limit both recession and inflation by managing aggregate demand, pushing it ahead when it

Figure 5-6
STABILIZATION POLICY TO
FIGHT INFLATION
This diagram duplicates Figure
5-2, but here we assume that
point E—the equilibrium the
economy would attain without
government intervention—
represents high inflation (that is,
the price level corresponding to
point E is far above last year's
price level). By using its policy
instruments to shift the aggregate-
demand curve inward to D_2D_2, the
government can keep this year's
price level lower than it would
otherwise have been; in other
words, the government can reduce
inflation.

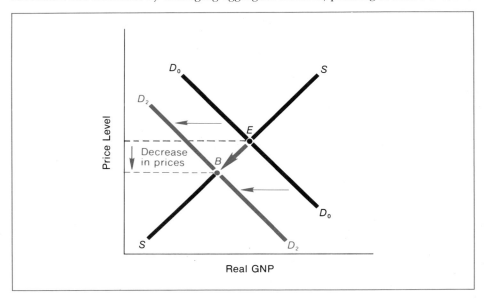

would otherwise lag, and restraining it when it would otherwise grow too quickly.

Sound simple? It's not. In reality, managing aggregate demand is a lot more complicated than shifting around lines on graphs with pencil and paper. We will spend several chapters examining the methods of demand management and learning why these methods do not always lead to the results that policy-makers hope for.

One problem is that the economy is sometimes plagued by both unemployment and inflation *at the same time*. In this case, the tools of demand management, even if wielded with great precision, are simply not up to the task. In Part Three we will see why demand management is not enough and study some suggestions for dealing with unemployment and inflation at the same time.

Summary

1. Microeconomics studies the decisions of individuals and firms, how these decisions interact, and how they influence the allocation of society's resources and the distribution of income. Macroeconomics looks at the behaviour of entire economies and studies the pressing social problems of inflation and unemployment.

2. While their respective subject matters differ greatly, the basic tools of microeconomics and macroeconomics are virtually identical. Both rely on the supply and demand analysis introduced in Chapter 4.

3. Macroeconomic models use abstract concepts like "the price level" and "national product" that are derived by amalgamating many different markets into one. This process is known as aggregation; it should not be taken literally but should be viewed as a useful approximation.

4. The best specific measure of the abstract concept "national product" is the gross national product (GNP), which is obtained by adding up the money values of all final goods and services produced in a given year. These outputs can be evaluated at current market prices (to get nominal GNP), or the prices of some previous year (to get real GNP). Neither intermediate goods nor transactions that take place outside organized markets are included in GNP.

5. Canada's economic history is one of growth punctuated by periodic recessions; that is, periods in which real GNP declined. While the distant past included some periods of falling prices (deflation), more recent history shows only rising prices (inflation).

6. The Great Depression of the 1930s was the worst in our country's history. It had profound effects both on our nation and on other countries throughout the world and led also to a revolution in economic thinking, thanks to the work of John Maynard Keynes.

7. From World War II to the early 1970s, the Canadian economy exhibited much steadier growth than it had in the past. Many observers attribute this to the implementation of the economic policies that Keynes suggested. At the same time, however, the price level seems only to rise, never to fall, in the modern economy. The economy seems to have become more "inflation prone."

8. Since the mid-1970s, the Canadian economy has suffered through several serious recessions. At the same time, inflation has been unusually virulent. This unhappy combination of economic stagnation with rapid inflation was nicknamed "stagflation."

9. One major cause of inflation is that aggregate demand may grow more quickly than aggregate supply. In such a case, a government policy that reduces aggregate demand may be able to check the inflation.

10. Similarly, recessions often occur because aggregate demand grows too slowly. In this case, a government policy that stimulates demand may be an effective way to fight the recession.

Concepts for Review

Microeconomics

Macroeconomics

National product

Aggregation

Aggregate-demand and aggregate-
    supply curves

Inflation

Deflation

Recession

Gross national product (GNP)

Nominal versus real GNP

Final goods and services

Intermediate goods

Stagflation

Disinflation

Stabilization policy

Questions for Discussion

1. Which of the following problems are likely to be studied by a microeconomist and which by a macroeconomist?
   a. The allocation of a university's limited budget.
   b. Why the Great Depression lasted so long.
   c. Why Japan's economy grows faster than the United States' economy, while Britain's grows slower.
   d. Why General Motors sells more cars than Ford Motor Company.
2. You probably use "aggregates" quite frequently in everyday discussions. Try to think of some examples. (Here is one: Have you ever said, "The student body at this school generally …."? What, precisely, did you mean?)
3. Use an aggregate supply–demand diagram to study what would happen to an economy in which the aggregate-supply curve never moved while the aggregate-demand curve shifted outward year after year.
4. Try asking a friend who has not studied economics in which year he or she thinks prices were higher: 1928 or 1940? (You can find the correct answer by referring to Figure 5–4.) Most people your age think that prices have always risen. Why do you think they have this opinion?
5. When were the two worst recessions of the past 60 years?
6. Which of the following transactions are included in the gross national product, and by how much does each raise GNP?
   a. Smith pays a carpenter $4000 to build a garage.
   b. Smith purchases $1000 worth of lumber and materials and builds himself a garage, which is worth $4000.
   c. Smith goes to the woods, cuts down a tree, and uses the wood to build himself a garage that is worth $4000.
   d. The Jones family sells its old house to the Reynolds family for $80,000. The Joneses then buy a newly constructed house from a builder for $130,000.
   e. Your university purchases a used computer from another university, paying $500,000.
   f. Your university purchases a new computer from IBM, paying $1 million.
   g. You lose $100 in a Las Vegas casino.
   h. You lose $100 in the stock market.

Unemployment and Inflation: The Twin Evils of Macroeconomics

Nothing so weakens
governments as inflation.
J. K. GALBRAITH

When men are employed they
are best contented.
BENJAMIN FRANKLIN

Among the many trials faced by Odysseus, the hero of Homer's *Odyssey*, one of the most difficult was to steer his fragile boat through a narrow strait. On one side lay the rock of the monster Scylla, which threatened to break his craft into pieces, and on the other was the menacing whirlpool of Charybdis. The makers of national economic policy face a similarly difficult task in trying to chart a middle course between the Scylla of unemployment and the Charybdis of inflation. If they steer the economy far from the rocks of unemployment, they run the risk of being swept up in the swift currents of inflation. But if they maintain a safe distance from inflation, they may smash against the rocks of unemployment.

In Part Three we will explain how economic planners attempt to strike a balance between high employment and low inflation, why these goals cannot be attained with machinelike precision, and why improvement on one front generally spells deterioration on the other. A great deal of attention will be paid to the *causes* of inflation and unemployment.

But before getting involved in such important issues of theory and policy, we pause in this chapter to take a rather close look at the twin evils themselves: Why is it that a rise in unemployment is generally considered bad news? Why is inflation so loudly deplored? Can we measure the costs of unemployment and inflation? The answers to some of these questions may at first seem obvious, but we will see that there is more to them than meets the eye.

The chapter is divided into two parts. In the first part we deal with unemployment. After a few words on the human costs of high unemployment, we explain how government statisticians measure unemployment and consider how the concept of "full employment" can be defined. We turn next to our country's system of unemployment insurance, and we conclude by investigating—and quantifying—the economic losses associated with unemployment.

In the second part of the chapter we turn to inflation. We begin by exploding some persistent myths about inflation, myths that help explain why inflation is so universally deplored. But the costs of inflation are not all mythical. The first real cost we consider is how and why inflation redistributes income and wealth from one group of people to another. Next, we learn how certain laws cause inflation to have heavy economic costs that could be avoided if the laws were written differently. This leads us to one of our **12 Ideas for Beyond the Final Exam** mentioned in Chapter 1. We shall see that it is the failure to understand the effect of inflation on interest rates that explains the existence of some of these laws and accounts for these costs of inflation. Finally, we define and analyse the difference between creeping and galloping inflation and explode another myth about inflation: the myth that creeping inflation always leads to galloping inflation. In an appendix, we explain how inflation is measured.

The Costs of Unemployment

The human costs of unemployment are probably sufficiently obvious. Years ago, loss of a job meant not only enforced idleness and a catastrophic drop in income, it often led to hunger, cold, ill health, and even death. This is the way one unemployed worker during the Great Depression described his family's plight in a mournful letter to his political representative:

I have six little children to take care of. I have been out of work for over a year and a half. Am back almost thirteen months and the landlord says if I don't pay up before the 1 of 1932 out I must go, and where am I to go in the cold winter with my children! If you can help me please for God's sake and the children's sakes and like please do what you can and send me some help, will you, I cannot find any work. I am willing to take any kind of work if I could get it now. Thanksgiving dinner was black coffee and bread and was very glad to get it. My wife is in the hospital now. We have no shoes to were [sic]; no clothes hardly. Oh what will I do I sure will thank you.[1]

Nowadays, unemployment does not have such dire consequences for most families, although it still holds these terrors for some. Part of the sting has been taken out of temporary unemployment by our system of unemployment insurance (discussed below), and there are other social-welfare programs to support the incomes of the poor (see Chapter 38). Yet most families still do suffer a painful loss of income when their breadwinner becomes unemployed.

Even families that are well protected by unemployment compensation suffer when joblessness strikes. Ours is a work-oriented society. A man's "place" has always been in the office or factory or shop, and lately this has become increasingly true for women as well. A worker forced into idleness by a recession endures a psychological cost that is no less real for our inability to measure it. Enforced joblessness is a demoralizing mental burden on the unemployed worker. High unemployment leads to a higher incidence of psychological disorders, divorces, suicides, and the like. (See the boxed insert on the next page.)

Nor are the costs only psychological. Accumulated work experience is a valuable asset. When forced into idleness, workers not only cease accumulating experience, but lengthy periods of unemployment may make them "rusty," and thus less productive when they are reemployed. Short periods of unemployment exact different kinds of costs. A record of steady employment is important in applying for a new job, and a worker who has frequently been laid off will lack this record of reliability.

It is important to realize that these costs, whether large or small in total, are distributed most unevenly across the population. At the bottom of the severe recession of 1981–84, the **unemployment rate** among all workers was 12.5 percent. This is a shockingly big increase from the 7.5 percent figure for 1981. It is also important to note that the 1983 situation was even worse for certain groups. For example, the unemployment rate in Newfoundland was 19 percent, and the unemployment rate among those 15 to 24 years old was 23 percent.

The **unemployment rate** is the number of unemployed people, expressed as a percentage of the **labour force**.

The **labour force** is the number of people employed or seeking employment.

[1]From *Brother, Can You Spare a Dime! The Great Depression 1929–1933*, by Milton Meltzer, page 103. Copyright© 1969 by Milton Meltzer. Reprinted by permission of Alfred A. Knopf, Inc.

Health, Crime, and Unemployment: Evidence from a U.S. Study

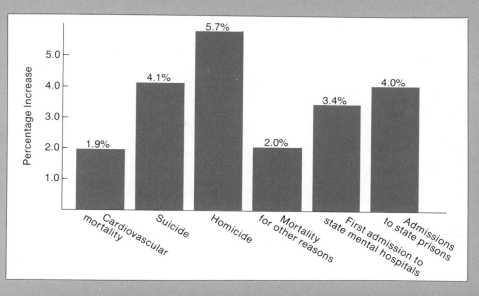

The social costs of unemployment are by no means limited to narrow economic losses such as reduced incomes and output. It is widely believed, for example, that high unemployment breeds crime, mental anxiety, and ill health. A study by a researcher at Johns Hopkins University documented the strong statistical association between unemployment and various measures of mental and physical health and criminal aggression.

Using these statistical relationships, it has been estimated how many more cases of various maladies the United States would have if the unemployment rate over a six-year period were one percentage point higher than it actually was. The results are summarized in the accompanying bar chart. For example, such a rise in unemployment would be expected to lead to about 2 percent more deaths from heart disease. The other figures in the chart have similar interpretations.

In looking at these numbers, it should be kept in mind that while the study found a high correlation between unemployment and the various maladies, it does not necessarily imply that unemployment was the *cause* of these ills. Still, the figures are dramatic enough to suggest that there is a real link between unemployment and ill health.

SOURCE: M. Harvey Brenner, "Influence of the Social Environment on Psychopathology: The Historical Perspectives" in James E. Barrett *et al* eds., *Stress and Mental Disorder* (New York: Raven Press, 1979).

Counting the Unemployed: The Official Statistics

Statistics Canada is responsible for measuring unemployment. How do they do it? How accurate are their measurements?

Statistics Canada's basic method for counting the unemployed is quite direct: it asks people. Specifically, a survey of 56,000 households is conducted each month. The sample is designed to represent all persons 15 years of age and over residing in Canada, with the exception of the following: full-time members of the armed forces, inmates of institutions, residents of the Yukon and Northwest Territories, and those living on Indian reserves. The census-taker asks several questions about the employment status of each member of the household. On the basis of these answers, each person is categorized as being *employed, unemployed,* or *not in the labour force.*

The first category is simplest to define. It includes everybody currently working at a job, including part-time workers. Although some part-time workers work less than a full week because they choose to, others do so only because they cannot find a suitable full-time job. Nevertheless, these workers are not considered "unemployed," though many would consider them "underemployed."

The second category is a bit trickier. For those not currently working, Statistics Canada first determines whether they are temporarily laid off from a job to which they expect to return. If so, they are counted as unemployed. The remaining workers are asked whether they actively sought work during the previous week. If they did, they are also counted as unemployed. But if they did not, they are classified as not in the labour force; that is, since they failed to look for a job they are not considered unemployed.

A **discouraged worker** is an unemployed person who gives up looking for work, and is therefore no longer counted as part of the labour force.

This seems a reasonable way to draw the distinction—after all, we would not want to count all university students who work during the summer months as unemployed between September and May. Yet, there is a problem: Research has shown that many unemployed workers give up looking for jobs after a time. These so-called **discouraged workers** are victims of poor job prospects, just like the officially unemployed. Ironically, when they give up hope, the official unemployment statistics decline! Some critics have therefore argued that an estimate should be made of the number of discouraged workers and that these people should be added to the roles of the unemployed.

Statistics Canada has made an effort to estimate the number of discouraged workers by periodically conducting a much more detailed survey. The results of the recent survey are discussed in the accompanying newspaper article on the opposite page.

Involuntary part-time work, loss of overtime or shortened work hours, and discouraged workers are all examples of "hidden" or "disguised" unemployment. And those who are concerned about these phenomena argue that we should include them in the official unemployment rate because, if we do not, the magnitude of the problem will be *underestimated*.

There is, however, an opposing school of thought that argues that the official unemployment rate really *overestimates* the unemployment problem. First, they argue, the unemployment rate of 1985 is not directly comparable to the unemployment rate of, say, 1955 because the composition of the labour force has changed dramatically over these years. Specifically, a larger fraction of all workers are young and female today than was the case 30 years ago. These groups have always had higher rates of unemployment than adult males. Therefore, even if adult men, adult women, and teenagers each had the *same* unemployment rates in 1985 that they had in 1955, the unemployment rate for the entire population would have been higher in 1985 than in 1955.[2] Second, they argue, to count as unemployed, a person need only *say* that he is looking for work, even if he is not really interested in finding a job. No one knows to what extent the unemployment problem is overstated on account of this, but some think that it may be considerable.

Types of Unemployment

Frictional unemployment is unemployment that is due to the normal workings of the labour market. It includes people who are temporarily between jobs because they are moving or changing occupations, or for similar reasons.

Providing jobs for those willing to work is one principal goal of macroeconomic policy. How are we to define this goal? One clearly *incorrect* answer would be "a zero measured unemployment rate." Ours is a dynamic and highly mobile economy. Households move from one province to another. Individuals quit jobs to look for better positions or to "retool" for more attractive occupations. These phenomena, and many more, produce some minimal amount of unemployment—people who literally are *between* jobs. Economists call this the level of **frictional unemployment**.

[2]If you do not understand why, consider the following analogy. Suppose your university class contains a mixture of "A" students and "C" students. If, between your first year and your final year, more "C" students enter the class as transfers from other universities, your class's overall average grade will decline even if every student earns the same grades in the final year that he or she did in first year.

Many Jobless Missed in Statscan's Survey of the Unemployed

When Statistics Canada reported that more than a million people were unemployed in December, the official announcement sent shockwaves through the country.

But the one million mark was probably surpassed some months ago, because the labour force survey fails to count a significant number of the jobless as unemployed.

Statscan conducts a monthly survey . . . and . . . based on this sampling . . . defines the employed as all people who worked one hour or more during the reference week of the survey.

There were 1,599,000 people in December who were working part-time (defined as less than 30 hours a week). The part-time labour force represented 15 percent of the total employment figure. . . .

Statscan reported in its December survey that 266,000 part-time workers wanted full-time work, and social planners thus consider these people underemployed.

The part-time labour force worked an average of less than 20 hours a week in December, compared with about 40 hours for full-time employees. Critics of the survey method argue, therefore, that half of the 266,000 underemployed should be added to the unemployment figure to more accurately reflect the lack of full employment opportunities.

In addition, Statscan defines the unemployed as all those who were without jobs but were actively seeking work in the reference week. But the agency also acknowledges that substantial numbers of people were not counted as unemployed because they failed to satisfy the job-search criterion.

A special survey conducted by Statscan in March last year revealed that 339,000 people wanted work even though they were not officially counted as unemployed because they had not been actively looking for work.

Slightly more than 100,000 of these people said they were not looking for work because they believed no work was available. Other reasons given included illness and waiting for a job recall. Depending on various interpretations of the data, the inclusion of the hidden unemployed in the official jobless figures would significantly raise the unemployment levels.

The labour force survey also fails to reflect the high unemployment levels in the Northwest Territories and the Yukon and on Indian reserves. Statscan officials say it would be too costly and difficult to extend the survey's coverage to these areas. . . .

SOURCE: Abridged article from *The Globe and Mail*, Toronto, February 1, 1982, page 4.

The critical distinguishing feature of frictional unemployment is that it is short-lived. A frictionally unemployed person has every reason to expect to find a new job soon. People tend to think of frictional unemployment as irreducible, but that is not the case. During World War II, for example, unemployment in this country fell below 2 percent—substantially below the frictional level. Frictional unemployment is "irreducible" only in the sense that—under normal circumstances—it is socially undesirable to reduce it.

Geographical and occupational mobility play important roles in our market economy—enabling people to search for better jobs. Similarly, waste is avoided by allowing inefficient firms, or firms producing items no longer desired by consumers, to be replaced by new firms. Inhibition of either of these phenomena must hamper the workings of the market economy. But, if these adjustment mechanisms are allowed to operate, there will always be some temporarily unemployed workers looking for jobs just as there will always be some firms with unfilled positions looking for workers. This is the genesis of frictional unemployment.

Structural unemployment refers to workers who have lost their jobs because they have been displaced by automation, because their skills are no longer in demand, or for similar reasons.

Cyclical unemployment is the portion of unemployment that is attributable to a decline in the economy's total production. Cyclical unemployment rises during recessions and falls as prosperity is restored.

A second type of unemployment is often difficult to distinguish from frictional unemployment, but it has very different implications. **Structural unemployment** arises when jobs are eliminated by changes in the structure of the economy, such as automation or permanent changes in demand. The crucial difference between frictional and structural unemployment is that, unlike a frictionally unemployed worker, a structurally unemployed worker cannot realistically be considered "between jobs." Instead, he may find his skills and experience unwanted in the changing economy in which he lives. He is thus faced with either a prolonged period of unemployment or the necessity of making a major change in his occupation. For older workers in particular, this may be difficult.

The remaining type of unemployment, **cyclical unemployment**, will occupy our attention most in this book. Cyclical unemployment arises when the overall level of economic activity declines. Whenever the unemployment rate rises ominously or falls precipitously, the data are almost certainly reflecting changes in cyclical unemployment.

What Is "Full Employment"?

After World War II, the Canadian federal government committed itself to pursue a policy of full employment. In the White Paper of April 1945 it was stated that "the government will be prepared, in periods when unemployment threatens, to incur deficits and increases in the national debt resulting from its employment and income policy." The government has consistently followed this part of their plan, but follow through has been less obvious on the other part of their plan: "In periods of buoyant employment and income, budget plans will call for surpluses." Part of the reason for this excess of budget deficits over surpluses over the years is that the government seems to be constantly optimistic about what "full employment" is.

During the prosperous years of the late 1940s and early 1950s, unemployment rates were consistently below 4 percent, dropping as low as 2.2 percent in 1947. This led the Economic Council of Canada (formed in the early 1960s) to select 3 percent as a definition of full employment. By this it was meant that 3 percent was the normal level of frictional unemployment in Canada. However, as Figure 6–1 shows, the unemployment rate has never fallen below 3.5 percent since 1956. As a result, economists now feel that the 3 percent target is unrealistic, and most now define full employment as involving a 6.5 or 7 percent unemployment rate.

There are several reasons for this upward adjustment. First, there is the changed composition of the labour force that we discussed above. The big growth in those wanting work has been among females and the young, while the rapid growth in job vacancies since the mid-1970s has been in the processing, fabricating, and extractive fields (occupations that traditionally have employed males in the 25–54 age bracket). Estimates show that about one-half of the increase in the "floor" unemployment rate shown in Figure 6–1 is due to this mismatching difficulty and other related structural factors. Another reason for this rise is the increased generosity of the unemployment-insurance legislation that took effect in 1971. These changes have reduced an individual's incentive to get himself off the unemployment rolls. Why work if unemployment benefits and other programs provide an income nearly as large as the salary one could earn on the job? This lack of work incentives made low unemployment harder to achieve. Finally, many economists have claimed that substantial increases in the minimum-wage levels during the 1970s have made it harder to employ teenagers and other workers whose productivity was low. If, for example, their productivity was exceeded by the legal minimum wage, who would hire them?[3]

[3]For a full discussion of minimum-wage laws, including their effect on unemployment, see Chapter 37.

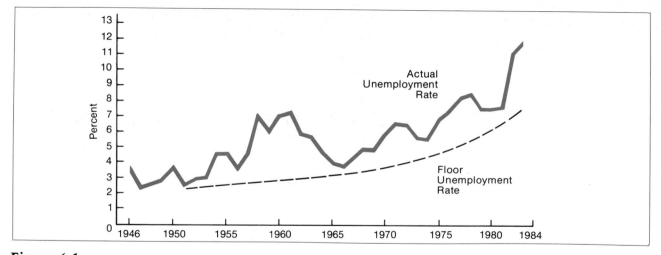

Figure 6-1

UNEMPLOYMENT RATE IN CANADA SINCE WORLD WAR II

The unemployment rate has risen dramatically since the war, but not all of this increase is cyclical unemployment. Cyclical unemployment was high in the recessions of 1958-62, 1970-71, 1977-78, and the early 1980s. The increase in the floor unemployment rate is due to structural factors such as demographic changes (the baby boom and increased labour-force participation of females) and certain institutional changes (the unemployment-insurance provisions).

SOURCE: Statistics Canada

While there is disagreement about whether "full" employment should be defined as slightly more or less than the 6.5 to 7 percent range, there is no argument about whether a significant amount of cyclical unemployment exists in the 1980s.

Unemployment Insurance: The Invaluable Cushion

A surprising feature of the recession of the early 1980s was the equanimity with which the electorate tolerated high unemployment rates. One major reason for this was our system of **unemployment insurance**.

One of the most valuable pieces of legislation to emerge from the trauma of the Great Depression was the Unemployment Insurance Act of 1941. It established a system whereby employers, employees, and the federal government would share the burden of financing the unemployment benefits. The federal government required the consent of all provinces to amend the BNA Act to permit the introduction of this legislation, which formerly came under provincial jurisdiction. Thanks to this system, many—but, as we shall see, not all—Canadian workers need never experience the complete loss of income that so many suffered during the 1930s.

The benefits paid to an unemployed worker are set at 60 percent of his or her average weekly insurable earnings. These payments are taxable, but the individual can earn up to 25 percent of his benefits through part-time or temporary work, without having his benefits reduced. There is a two-week waiting period following unemployment before benefits are paid. Though a 40 percent drop in earnings poses problems, especially if there are no other earners in the family, families covered by unemployment insurance simply do not go hungry when they lose their jobs, and they are only rarely dispossessed from their homes.

Who is eligible to receive these benefits? Precise qualifications vary from region to region, but some stipulations apply quite generally.

1. *Only experienced workers qualify.* The amount of experience necessary to establish eligibility varies between 10 and 14 weeks of work (depending on

the unemployment rate in the region). This means that persons just joining the labour force (for instance, new graduates of high schools, universities, or community colleges) or reentering after a protracted absence (such as women resuming work after many years of child rearing) are not eligible.

2. **Job quitters must wait longer.** With certain exceptions, people who quit their last jobs must wait several extra weeks to collect benefits.

3. **You must be looking for work to qualify.** People unwilling or unable to work cannot receive unemployment benefits, and a recipient of benefits must conduct an active search for employment.

4. **Benefits can run up to 50 weeks.** This time limit depends on one's employment history, and the unemployment rate of both the country and region.

Over the years, the government has extended the unemployment-insurance program. In 1971 several new groups were included, such as: seasonally unemployed fishermen, pregnant women (with sufficient work experience), those on extended sickness, and those attending retraining programs. Since 1977, the insurance fund has been administered in tandem with Canada Employment Centres, so that claimants have more convenient access to job and retraining information and to counselling. Also since 1977, some unemployment-insurance funds have been used to keep people working rather than to compensate them for not working. There have been a series of job-sharing plans. For example, if all employees work four days a week instead of five, the company pays the wages for four days and the insurance fund pays wages for the fifth day.

The importance of unemployment insurance to the unemployed is obvious. But there are also significant benefits to citizens who never become unemployed. During recession years many billions of dollars are paid out in unemployment benefits, and since recipients probably spend most of their benefits, unemployment insurance limits the severity of recessions by providing additional purchasing power when and where it is most needed.

The unemployment-insurance system is one of several "cushions" that have been built into our economy since the 1930s to prevent the possibility of another Great Depression. By giving the money to those who become unemployed, the system helps prop up aggregate demand during recessions.

While the Canadian economy is now probably "depression proof," this should not be a cause for too much rejoicing, for the recession of the early 1980s has demonstrated that we are very far from being "recession proof."

The Economic Costs of High Unemployment

The fact that unemployment insurance and other social-welfare programs replace a significant fraction of lost income has led some skeptics to claim that unemployment is no longer a serious problem. But the fact is that:

Unemployment insurance is just what the name says—an *insurance* program. And insurance can never prevent a catastrophe from occurring; it can only *spread the costs* of a catastrophe among many people instead of letting them all fall on the shoulders of those few unfortunate souls whom it affects directly.

Fire insurance is an example. If you are covered by fire insurance and your house burns down, you will probably suffer only a small financial loss because the insurance company will pay most of the expenses. Where does it get the money? It cannot create it out of thin air. Rather, it must have collected the funds from the many other families who purchased insurance but did not suffer any fire damages. Thus, one family's loss of perhaps $75,000 is covered by the insurance payments of 300 families each paying $250 a year. In this way, the costs of the catastrophe are spread among hundreds of families, and in the process, made much more bearable.

But despite the insurance, the family whose house is destroyed by fire suffers anguish and inconvenience. No insurance policy can eliminate this. Furthermore, society loses a valuable resource—a house. It will take a great deal of wood, cement, nails, paint, and labour to replace the burnt-out home. *An insurance policy cannot insure society against losses of real resources.*

The case is precisely the same with insurance against unemployment. All workers and employers pay for the insurance policy by a tax that the government levies on wages and salaries. With the funds so collected, the government compensates the victims of unemployment. Thus, instead of letting the costs of unemployment fall entirely on the minority of workers who are out of work, the system of payroll taxes and unemployment benefits *spreads* the costs over the entire population. But it does not eliminate the basic economic cost.

When the economy does not generate enough jobs to employ all those who are willing to work, a valuable resource is lost. Potential goods and services that might have been enjoyed by consumers are lost forever. This is the real economic cost of high unemployment, and no insurance plan can eliminate it.

And these costs are by no means negligible. Table 6-1 summarizes the idleness of workers and machines, and the resulting loss of national output, for some of the years of lowest economic activity in recent decades. The first column lists the unemployment rate, and thus measures unused labour resources. The second lists the percentage of industrial capacity that Canadian manufacturers were actually using, and thus indicates the extent of unused plant and equipment. And the third column shows how much more output (real GNP) could have been produced if these labour and capital resources had been fully employed.

Table 6-1

THE ECONOMIC COSTS OF HIGH UNEMPLOYMENT

YEAR	UNEMPLOYMENT RATE (percent)	CAPACITY UTILIZATION RATE (percent)	PERCENTAGE OF REAL GNP LOST DUE TO IDLE RESOURCES
1961	7.1	72	6.3
1971	6.4	80	2.6
1977	8.1	80	2.8
1983	11.9	67	6.4

SOURCES: Statistics Canada, and Figure 6-1.

While these years are extreme examples, the inability to utilize all of the nation's available resources has been a recurrent problem for our economy. The blue line in Figure 6-2 shows the actual real GNP in Canada from 1960 to 1983, while the black line shows the real GNP we *could have* produced if "full employment" had been maintained. This last statement defines a concept called **potential GNP**. As our previous discussion of full employment pointed out, it *is* possible to push employment beyond its normal full-employment level. This occurs whenever the unemployment rate dips below the "full-employment unemployment rate"—a rate now thought to be 6.5 or 7 percent. Consequently, it *is* possible for actual GNP to exceed potential GNP. Figure 6-2 shows several instances where this happened. But it also shows that, more typically, actual GNP falls short of potential GNP. The total shortfall of actual GNP below potential GNP since 1960 provides some startling information.

Potential gross national product is the real GNP the economy would produce if its labour and other resources were fully employed.

Figure 6-2

ACTUAL AND POTENTIAL
GNP IN CANADA, 1960–1983
This chart compares the growth of
actual GNP (blue line) with that of
potential GNP (black line). There
have been three lengthy periods
during which real GNP remained
below its potential (1960–64,
1969–72, and 1975 to the present),
but only two brief periods during
which GNP was above potential
(1965–66 and 1973–74).
SOURCE: Economic Council of
Canada, *Annual Review* (1979),
updated by the authors.

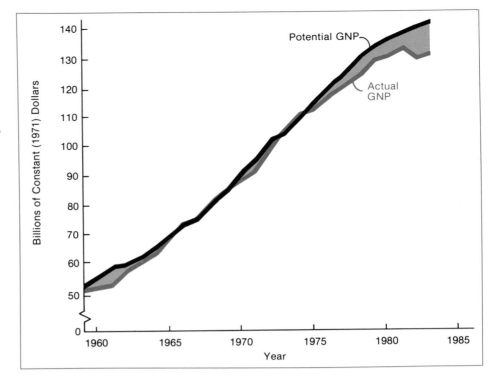

The cumulative gap between actual and potential GNP over the years 1960–83 (all evaluated in 1971 prices), which is shown by the shaded area in Figure 6–2, is an astounding $48 billion. At 1983 levels of output, this loss in output as a result of unemployment would be just over four months' worth of production. And there is no way to redeem these losses. The labour wasted in 1982 cannot be utilized in 1986.

Those who argue that unemployment is nothing to worry about today because of unemployment insurance, or because unemployment is concentrated among certain kinds of workers (such as teenagers), or because many unemployed workers become reemployed within a few weeks, should ponder Figure 6–2. Is the loss of this much output really no cause for worry? Would these optimists react the same way if the government collected a fraction of the output of every factory in Canada and dumped it into the sea? Waste is waste no matter who ultimately pays the cost.

The Costs of Inflation

Both the human and the economic costs of inflation are less obvious than the costs of unemployment. But this does not necessarily make them any less real, for if one thing is crystal clear about inflation, it is that people do not like it.

Public-opinion polls consistently show that inflation ranks high on people's list of major national problems, sometimes ahead of unemployment. Surveys also find that inflation, like unemployment, causes a deterioration in consumers' sense of well-being—it makes people unhappy. Why?

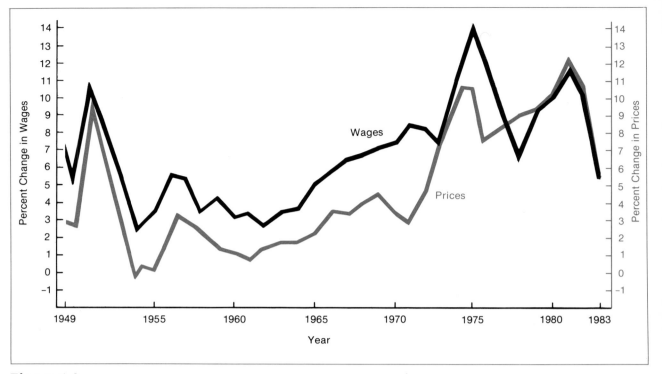

Figure 6–3

RATES OF CHANGE OF WAGES AND PRICES IN CANADA, 1949–1983

This chart compares the rate of price inflation (blue line) with the rate of growth of nominal wages in the postwar period. The patterns are clearly quite similar, with wages and prices normally accelerating or decelerating together. Notice that the traditional gap between wage increases and price increases has not prevailed in recent years.

SOURCE: Statistics Canada. The price index is the Consumer Price Index, and the wage series is average weekly wages and salaries (industrial composite).

Inflation: The Myth and the Reality

At first, the question may seem ridiculous. During times of inflation, people must keep paying higher prices for the same quantities of goods and services they had before. So more and more income is needed just to maintain the same standard of living. Is it not obvious that this erosion of **purchasing power**—that is, the decline in what money will buy—makes everyone worse off?

This would indeed be the case were it not for one very significant fact. The wages people earn are also prices—prices for labour services. During a period of inflation, wages also rise and, in fact, the average wage typically rises more or less in step with prices. Thus, contrary to popular myth, workers as a group are not usually victimized by inflation.

The purchasing power of wages is not systematically eroded by inflation. Sometimes wages rise faster than prices, and sometimes prices rise faster than wages. The fact is that in the long run wages tend to outstrip prices as new capital equipment and innovation increase output per worker.

Figure 6–3 illustrates this simple fact. The blue line shows the annual rate of increase of consumer prices in Canada for each year since 1949 while the black line shows the annual rate of wage increases. Generally, wages rise faster than prices, reflecting the steady advance of technology and of labour productivity. So the black line is usually above the blue line. The years from 1973 to 1983 stand out as an unusual period in which wages often did not rise faster than prices. This

The **purchasing power** of a given sum of money is the volume of goods and services it will buy.

single fact goes a long way toward explaining why people have been so dissatisfied with economic performance since the mid-1970s.

The feature of Figure 6-3 that virtually jumps off the page is the way the two lines dance together. Wages normally rise rapidly when prices rise rapidly, and rise slowly when prices rise slowly. But you should not draw any hasty conclusions from this association. We cannot, for example, learn from this figure whether rising prices cause rising wages or whether rising wages cause rising prices. Remember the warnings given in Chapter 1 about trying to infer causation just by looking at data. But analysing cause and effect is not our purpose right now. We merely want to explode the myth that inflation inevitably robs workers of their wages.

Why is this myth so widespread? Imagine a world without inflation in which wages are rising 2 percent a year because of the increasing productivity of labour. Now imagine that, all of a sudden, inflation sets in and prices start rising 5 percent a year but that nothing else changes. Figure 6-3 suggests that, with perhaps a small delay, wage increases will accelerate to 2 percent plus 5 percent, or 7 percent a year.

Will workers view this change with equanimity? Probably not. To each worker, the 7 percent wage increase will be seen as something he earned by the sweat of his brow. In his view, he *deserves* every penny of his 7 percent raise. And, in a sense, he is right because "the sweat of his brow" earned him a 2 percent increment in purchasing power that, when the inflation rate is 5 percent, can only be achieved by increasing his wages by a total of 7 percent. An economist would divide the wage increase in the following way:

REASON FOR WAGE INCREASE	AMOUNT
Higher productivity	2%
Compensation for higher prices	5%
Total	7%

"Sure, you're raising my allowance. But am I actually gaining any purchasing power?"

An item's **relative price** is its price in terms of some other item, rather than in terms of dollars.

But the worker will probably keep score differently. Feeling that he earned the entire 7 percent by his own merits, he will view inflation as having "robbed" him of 5 percent of his just deserts. The higher the rate of inflation, the more of his raise the worker will feel robbed of.

Of course, nothing could be farther from the truth. Basically, the economic system is rewarding the worker with *the same 2 percent increment for higher productivity regardless of the rate of inflation.* The "evils of inflation" are often exaggerated because of a failure to understand this mechanism.

A second reason for misunderstanding the effects of inflation is that people are in the habit of thinking in terms of the number of dollars it takes to buy something rather than in the terms of the *purchasing power* of these dollars. For example, if inflation doubles both prices and wages, workers will have to labour exactly the same amount of time as before to earn the price of a loaf of bread. But because they now pay $1 a loaf instead of 50¢, they feel that the price of bread is scandalously high. In fact, nothing has really changed; but people remain stuck with an outmoded idea of what bread *should* cost.

A third misperception results from failure to distinguish between a *rise in the general price level* and a change in **relative prices**, that is, a rise in the price of one commodity relative to that of another. To see the distinction most clearly, imagine first a *pure inflation* in which *every* price rises by 10 percent during the year, so that relative prices do not change. Table 6-2 gives an example in which movie tickets go up from $4 to $4.40, candy bars from 50¢ to 55¢, and automobiles from $8000 to $8800. After the inflation, just as before, it will still take 8 candy bars to buy a movie ticket, 2000 movie tickets to buy a car, and so on. A person

Table 6–2			
ITEM	LAST YEAR'S PRICE	THIS YEAR'S PRICE	PERCENT INCREASE
Candy bar	$ 0.50	$ 0.55	10
Movie ticket	4.00	4.40	10
Automobile	8000.00	8800.00	10

Table 6–3			
ITEM	LAST YEAR'S PRICE	THIS YEAR'S PRICE	PERCENT INCREASE
Candy bar	$ 0.50	$ 0.50	0
Movie ticket	4.00	5.00	25
Automobile	8000.00	8400.00	5

who manufactures candy bars in order to purchase movie tickets is neither helped nor harmed by the inflation. Neither is a car dealer with a sweet tooth.

But real inflation is not like this. When there is 10 percent general inflation—meaning that the "average price" rises by 10 percent[4]—some prices may jump 20 percent or more while others actually fall. Suppose that, instead of the price increases shown in Table 6–2, prices rise as shown in Table 6–3. Movie prices go up by 25 percent, but candy prices do not change. Surely, candy manufacturers who love movies will be disgruntled because it now costs 10 candy bars instead of 8 to get into the theatre. They will blame inflation for raising the price of movie tickets, even though their real problem stems from the *increase in the price of movies relative to candy*. (They would have been hurt just as much if movie tickets had remained at $4 while the price of candy fell to 40¢.)

Since car prices have risen by only 5 percent, theatre owners in need of new cars will be delighted by the fact that an auto now costs only 1680 movie admissions (just as they would have cheered if car prices had fallen to $6720 while movie tickets remained at $4). However, they are unlikely to attribute their good fortune to inflation—as indeed they should not. What has actually happened is that *cars became cheaper relative to movies*.

Because real-world inflation proceeds at *uneven* rates, relative prices are constantly changing. There are gainers and losers, just as some would gain and others lose if relative prices changed without any general inflation. Inflation, however, gets a bad name because losers often blame inflation for their misfortune while gainers rarely credit inflation for their good luck. Alas, nobody loves inflation.

These three kinds of misconceptions may go a long way toward explaining why respondents to public-opinion polls consistently list inflation as a major national issue, and why higher inflation rates depress consumers.

Inflation does not systematically erode the purchasing power of wages. Nor does it lead to "unfair" prices. Nor is it usually to blame when some goods become more expensive relative to others.

But not all the costs of inflation are mythical. Let us now turn to some of the real costs.

Inflation as a Redistributor of Income and Wealth

We have just seen that the *average* person is neither helped nor harmed by inflation. But almost no one is exactly average! Some persons gain from inflation and others lose. It is hard to say anything more systematic than this about the effects of inflation on particular prices and wages.

But inflation does have systematic effects on the distribution of income and wealth. Senior citizens trying to scrape by on pensions or other fixed incomes

[4]The way statisticians figure out "average" price increases is discussed in the appendix to this chapter.

suffer badly from inflation. Since they earn no wages, it is little solace to them that wages are keeping pace with prices. Their private pension incomes tend not to.[5]

This example actually illustrates a much more general problem. We can think of pensioners as people who "lend" money to an organization (the pension fund) when they are young in order to be "paid back" with interest when they are old. Because of the rise in the price level during the intervening years, the unfortunate pensioners get paid back in less valuable dollars than those they originally loaned. In general:

Those who lend money are usually victimized by inflation.

While lenders lose heavily, borrowers do quite well. For example, homeowners who borrowed money from banks in the form of mortgages back in the 1950s, when interest rates were 3 or 4 percent, gained enormously from the surprisingly virulent inflation of the late 1960s and 1970s. They paid back dollars of much lower value than those that they borrowed. And the same is true of other borrowers.

Borrowers usually gain from inflation.

Since the redistribution caused by inflation generally benefits borrowers at the expense of lenders, and since both lenders and borrowers can be found at every income level, we must conclude that:

Inflation does not always steal from the rich to aid the poor, nor does it always do the reverse.

Why, then, is the redistribution caused by inflation so widely condemned? Because its victims are selected capriciously. Nobody legislates this redistribution. Nobody enters into it voluntarily. The gainers do not earn their spoils, and the losers do not deserve their fate. Moreover, there have been particular classes of people whom inflation has systematically robbed of purchasing power year after year—old-age pensioners, people who have saved money and "loaned" it to banks, and workers on long-term contracts or those whose wages and salaries do not adjust easily for some other reason. Even if people "on the average" suffer no damage from inflation, that offers little consolation to those who are hurt by it persistently and systematically. This is the fundamental indictment of inflation.

Inflation redistributes income in an arbitrary way that distorts society's distribution of income. The actual income distribution should reflect the interplay of the operation of free markets and the deliberate efforts of government to alter the distribution. Inflation interferes with and distorts this process.

Real Versus Nominal Interest Rates

But wait. Must inflation always rob lenders to bestow gifts upon borrowers? If both parties see inflation coming, won't lenders demand that borrowers pay a higher interest rate as compensation for the coming inflation? Indeed they will. For this reason, economists draw a conceptual distinction between inflation that is *expected* and inflation that comes as a surprise.

What happens when inflation is fully expected by both parties? Suppose Diamond Jim wants to borrow $1000 from Scrooge, and both agree that, in the absence of inflation, which erodes the value of money, a fair rate of interest would

[5]This is not true, for example, for Canada's Old Age Security plan. These benefits are financed out of tax revenues rather than directly through accumulated savings, and benefit levels are generally increased to compensate recipients for changes in the price level. For further discussion of Canada's pension provisions, see Chapter 33.

be 4 percent on a one-year loan. This means that Diamond Jim would pay back $1040 at the end of the year for the privilege of having $1000 now.

If both expect prices to increase by 6 percent, Scrooge may reason as follows: "If Diamond Jim pays me back $1040 a year from today, that money will buy less than what $1000 buys today. Thus I'll really be *paying him* to borrow from me! I'm no philanthropist. Why don't I charge him 10 percent instead? Then he'll pay back $1100 at the end of the year. With prices 6 percent higher, this will buy roughly what $1040 is worth today. So I'll get the same 4 percent increase in purchasing power that we would have agreed on in the absence of inflation, and won't be any worse off. That's the least I'll accept."

Diamond Jim may follow a similar chain of logic. "With no inflation, I was willing to pay $1040 a year from now for the privilege of having $1000 today, and Scrooge was willing to lend it. He'd be crazy to do the same with a 6 percent inflation. He'll want to charge me more. How much should I pay? If I offer to him $1100 a year from now, that will have roughly the same purchasing power as $1040 today, so I won't be any worse off. That's the most I'll pay."

This kind of thinking will lead Scrooge and Diamond Jim to write a contract with a 10 percent interest rate—4 percent as the increase in purchasing power that Diamond Jim pays to Scrooge and 6 percent as compensation for the expected inflation. Then, if the expected 6 percent inflation actually materializes, neither party will have been made better or worse off than was expected at the time the contract was signed.[6]

This example illustrates a very general principle. The 4 percent increase in purchasing power that Diamond Jim agrees to hand over to Scrooge is called the **real rate of interest**. And the 10 percent contractual interest charge that Diamond Jim and Scrooge write into the loan agreement is called the **nominal rate of interest**. The nominal rate of interest is arrived at by adding the **expected rate of inflation** to the real rate of interest. Expected inflation is added to compensate the lender for the loss in purchasing power that he is expected to suffer as a result of inflation. Because of this:

Inflation that is accurately predicted need not redistribute income between borrowers and lenders. If the *expected* rate of inflation that is embodied in the nominal interest rate closely approximates the *actual* rate of inflation, no one gains and no one loses. However, to the extent that expectations prove incorrect, inflation will still redistribute income.

It need hardly be pointed out that errors in predicting the rate of inflation are the norm, not the exception. Published forecasts bear witness to the fact that economists have great difficulty in predicting the rate of inflation. The task is no easier for businesses, consumers, and banks. This is one reason why inflation is so widely condemned as unfair and undesirable. It sets up a guessing game that no one likes.

> The **real rate of interest** is the percentage increase in purchasing power that the borrower pays to the lender for the privilege of borrowing. It indicates the increased ability to purchase goods and services that the lender earns.
>
> The **nominal rate of interest** is the percentage by which the money the borrower pays back exceeds the money that he borrowed, making no adjustment for any fall in the purchasing power of this money that results from inflation.

Inflation and the Tax System

So inflation imposes costs on society because it is hard to predict. But there are other costs of inflation, perhaps even more serious, that arise from high inflation, even when inflation is predicted accurately. These costs stem from the fact that our taxation system was designed for an inflation-free economy; and these laws may malfunction when inflation is high.

Our tax law does not recognize the distinction between nominal and real interest rates. The law simply taxes nominal interest regardless of how much real

[6]EXERCISE: Who gains and who loses if the inflation turns out to be only 4 percent instead of the 6 percent that Scrooge and Diamond Jim expected? What if the inflation rate is 8 percent?

Table 6-4

INFLATION AND THE TAXATION OF INTEREST INCOME

(1)	(2)	(3)	(4)	(5)	(6)	(7)	(8)	(9)
INFLATION RATE (percent)	NOMINAL INTEREST RATE (percent)	INTEREST INCOME (dollars)	LOSS OF PURCHASING POWER DUE TO INFLATION (dollars)	REAL INTEREST INCOME (dollars)	TAXES PAID (dollars)	REAL INCOME AFTER TAX	(as a percentage of $1000 loan)	EFFECTIVE RATE OF TAXATION (percent)
						(dollars)		
0	4	40	0	40	20	20	2	50
6	10	100	60	40	50	-10	-1	125

interest it represents. As a result, strange things happen when there is high inflation. Our example of Scrooge's loan to Diamond Jim will illustrate the problem.

The top line of Table 6-4 shows how taxation affects the loan agreement where there is no inflation and the nominal and real interest rates are both at 4 percent. Scrooge earns $40 in nominal interest income (column 3). Since there is no inflation, this also represents $40 in real interest income (column 5). If Scrooge pays 50 percent of his income in taxes, his tax bill rises by $20 (column 6), leaving him with $20 after tax (column 7). This $20 amounts to 2 percent of the $1000 originally loaned (column 8). Because his $20 tax payment is half of his $40 in real interest income, Scrooge's effective tax rate is 50 percent (column 9), just as Parliament intended.

Now let's consider the same transaction when the inflation rate is 6 percent and Scrooge and Diamond Jim settle on a 10 percent nominal interest rate. Scrooge collects $100 in interest (column 3). But, with 6 percent inflation, the purchasing power of the $1000 he lends declines by $60 (column 4). Thus his real interest income is again $40 (column 5). However, assuming that Scrooge has already used up his $1000 interest income-tax exemption, the tax collector taxes the $100 nominal interest income, not the $40 real interest income, so Scrooge must pay $50 (50 percent of $100) in taxes (column 6). As we can see in column 7, his after-tax real income on the loan is –$10. Or, putting the same point a different way, the effective real after-tax interest rate he earns is –1 percent! As column 9 shows, the effective tax rate on Scrooge's real interest income is 125 percent, far larger than the 50 percent rate intended by Parliament.

So a tax system that works well at zero inflation misfires at 6 percent inflation because it taxes nominal, rather than real, interest. This little example illustrates a general, and very serious, problem:

Because it fails to recognize the distinction between nominal and real interest rate, our tax system levies high, and presumably unintended, tax rates on interest income when there is high inflation. And similar problems arise in the taxation of dividends, corporate profits, and other items.[7] Many economists feel that these high tax rates discourage saving, lending, and investing, and that high inflation therefore retards economic growth. Thus, there are major costs of inflation that are not purely redistributive.

[7]A particularly serious problem arises in the taxation of capital gains. Capital gains are the difference between the price at which one sells an asset and the price at which one bought it. In Canada, capital gains are taxed at one-half of their actual values, without any adjustment for changes in their purchasing power resulting from inflation. An example will bring out the point. Between 1971 and 1980 the price level doubled, approximately. Consider a piece of land that was purchased for $50,000 in 1971 and sold for $75,000 in 1980. The owner would have lost purchasing power in the transaction because 75,000 1980 dollars purchased less than 50,000 1971 dollars. Yet, since the tax authorities do not correct for inflation, the owner will be forced to pay tax on $12,500 as though there had been a profit rather than a loss.

Why do inappropriate tax laws stay on the books so long? One reason is a general lack of understanding of the difference between real and nominal interest rates. People seem not to understand that it is normally the *real* rate of interest that matters in an economic transaction because only that rate reveals how much borrowers pay (and lenders receive) *in terms of the goods and services which that money can buy.* They think about the high nominal rates caused by inflation, even if these rates correspond to very low real interest rates. Here are some other examples that may help you appreciate how widespread and important this interest-rate illusion is.

Regulation of Public Utilities

During the early 1960s, when the rate of inflation averaged about 1.5 percent a year, interest rates on high-grade corporate bonds hovered around 5 percent, yielding a real rate of interest about 3.5 percent. Regulated public utilities were permitted to earn profits at rates that exceeded 3.5 percent, since the utilities were able to afford borrowing funds at this rate. There were few public complaints suggesting that there was anything scandalous about such earning rates.

Yet during 1980 when the rate of inflation rose above 10 percent and corporate interest rates rose to 13 percent (implying a slightly lower real interest rate than earlier), there were many complaints. Regulated utilities, which asked the regulatory agencies to permit them a nominal rate of return closer to 13 percent so that they could afford to borrow the money needed to serve expanding public demand, found that their requests were considered exorbitant by the commissions and by the general public.

Record Profit Rates

Amazingly, even business managers were subject to the same form of illusion. Often they were taken aback by the notion that their investors actually lost out (earned a negative *real* rate of return) when the company was earning a 10 percent nominal profit. The managers noted that 10 percent was the company's highest earnings rate in recent history; but with inflation at 12 percent, it turned out that in real terms it was in fact the firm's lowest.

Monetary Policy

Throughout the first half of the 1970s, Western governments increased their countries' money supplies at record rates, because they thought credit must be made more available to lower the apparent high borrowing costs. But it was only nominal, not real, interest rates that were high. Real interest rates had never been lower. The extra money simply worsened the inflation and widened the gap between the real and nominal interest rates.

Thus, failure to understand that high *nominal* interest rates can signify very low *real* interest rates has been known to impoverish savers during a period of inflation. It has made profits appear high when they were really low, and it has led to major mistakes in the formation of monetary policy.

The Illusion of High Interest Rates

The difference between real and nominal interest (and profit) rates, and the fact that the real rate matters most in terms of economic effects while the nominal rate is politically significant, are matters that are of the utmost importance and yet are understood by very few people, including many persons who make public-policy decisions in these areas.

This concept is one of the **12 Ideas for Beyond the Final Exam**, and if you remember it ten years from now, you will truly have gotten a great deal out of studying economics.

Indexation of the Personal Income-Tax System

Some reforms have occurred. Since 1975, the authorities have properly separated the real and nominal interest rates in all discussions of their monetary policies. Also, in 1973, the federal government indexed the major provisions in the personal income-tax system.

Without indexing, inflation generates increasingly larger amounts of government revenue without any change in tax rates. One reason for the increase in revenue is that the deductions allowed on the tax form decline as a proportion of income in an inflationary situation, so that a larger proportion of income is subject to tax. The other reason for the unintended increase in revenues is that individuals are pushed into successively higher income-tax brackets as nominal incomes rise due to inflation. Thus, even if wages rise as rapidly as prices, people's real *after-tax* incomes fall.

The case for indexing rests generally on two arguments. One argument is that, in the absence of indexing, a greater share of national income flows automatically to the government with inflation, and it is felt by many that decisions about the division of resources between the public and private sectors should be made explicitly by legislation rather than by the amount of inflation in the economy. The second argument is that indexing will improve the equity or fairness of the personal income tax. Without indexing, inflation erodes the value of the allowed income-tax deductions, so that many low-income individuals are brought on to the tax rolls as inflation raises their incomes in nominal terms above the cut-off level provided by exemptions and deductions. Indexing the personal income tax for inflation reduces this as well as other inequities.

The Canadian indexing system works as follows: The limits on each income bracket and the value of the exemptions are multiplied annually by a factor that represents the amount of inflation during the past year. An illustration may make this more clear. The exemption for a taxpayer was $1600 and the tax rate was 19 percent for taxable income between $1000 and $2000 in Canada in 1973. If prices had risen 10 percent in 1973, the value of the exemption would have increased to $1760, and taxable income between $1100 and $2200 would have been taxed at a rate of 19 percent in 1974. (The actual inflation adjustment factor for 1974 was 6.6 percent.) Since indexing has been in operation, the basic exemption for a single taxpayer has risen from $1600 in 1973 to $3770 for the 1983 tax year.

Indexing, along with the government's refusal to explicitly raise tax rates or cut expenditures, has been a major factor contributing toward the large budget deficits. Partly because of this, and partly to advertise its restraint program in the early 1980s, the government limited the indexing factor to a maximum of 6 percent and 5 percent for the 1983 and 1984 tax years.

Other Costs of Inflation

Another cost of inflation is that rapidly changing prices make it risky to enter into long-term contracts. In an extremely severe inflation, the "long term" may be only a few days. But even moderate inflation can have remarkable effects on long-term loans. Suppose a corporation wants to borrow $1 million to finance the purchase of some new equipment and needs the loan for 20 years. If the inflation rate averages 8 percent over this period, the $1 million it repays at the end of 20 years will be worth only $214,548 in today's purchasing power. If inflation averages 4 percent instead, it will be worth $456,387. Lending or borrowing for this long a period is obviously a big gamble. With the stakes this high, the outcome may be that neither lenders nor borrowers want to get involved in long-term contracts. But without long-term loans, business investment becomes impossible. The economy stagnates.

Inflation also makes life difficult for the shopper. You probably have a group of stores that you habitually patronize because you know they generally carry the items you want to buy at (roughly) the prices you want to pay. This knowledge saves you a great deal of time and energy. But when prices are changing rapidly, your list becomes obsolete very quickly. You return to your favourite clothing store only to find that the price of jeans has risen drastically. Should you buy? Should you shop around at other stores? Will they have also raised their prices? And business firms have precisely the same problem with their suppliers. Rising prices force them to shop around more than they are accustomed to, which imposes costs on the firms and, more generally, reduces the efficiency of the whole economy.

Shopping costs may sound frivolous and unimportant, but they are not. The late Arthur Okun, who chaired the Council of Economic Advisers under U.S. President Johnson, suggested an ingenious mental exercise that illustrates the importance of shopping costs. Ask yourself the following question: How much would you have to be paid to promise never again to buy anything from any of the stores you have patronized in the past? When you ponder this for a while, you realize the great value of having normal places to shop. Inflation takes some of this value away.

Creeping Versus Galloping Inflation

The preceding litany of costs of inflation alerts us to one very important fact: *predictable inflation is far less burdensome than is unpredictable inflation.* When will inflation be most predictable? When it proceeds year after year at more or less the same rate. Thus the *variability of the inflation rate* is a crucial factor. Inflation of 6 percent a year for three consecutive years will exact far lower social costs than inflation that is 8 percent in the first year, zero in the second, and 10 percent in the third. In general:

Steady inflation is much more predictable than variable inflation and therefore has much smaller social and economic costs.

But the *average level of the inflation rate* is also important. Partly because of the incomplete indexing provisions in taxes and the interest rate illusions mentioned above, and partly because of the more rapid breakdown in normal customer relationships that we have just mentioned, a steady inflation of 8 percent a year is more damaging than a steady inflation of 3 percent a year.

Economists distinguish between **creeping inflation** and **galloping inflation** partly on their average level and partly on their variability. Under creeping inflation, prices rise for a long time at a moderate and fairly steady rate. Postwar Sweden provides a good example. During the 13-year period from 1954 to 1967, prices climbed a total of 64 percent (compared with only 33 percent in Canada), for an average annual inflation rate of 3.9 percent. And the pace of inflation was remarkably steady, rarely dropping below 2.5 percent or rising above 5 percent.

Galloping inflation refers to inflation that proceeds at an exceptionally high rate, perhaps for only a relatively brief period. Galloping inflation is generally characterized by accelerating rates of inflation so that the rate of inflation is higher this month than it was last month.

Germany after World War I suffered through one of the more severe inflations in history. Wholesale prices increased over 140 percent in 1921 and a colossal 4100 percent during 1922. At this point, what had been very serious galloping inflation simply got out of control. Between December 1922 and November 1923, when a hard-nosed reform finally broke the inflationary spiral, wholesale prices in Germany increased by almost 100 million percent! But even this experience was dwarfed by the great Hungarian inflation of 1945–46, the greatest inflation of them all. For a period of one year, the rate of inflation averaged about 20,000

Creeping inflation refers to inflation that proceeds for a long time at a moderate and fairly steady pace.

Galloping inflation refers to inflation that proceeds at an exceptionally high rate, perhaps for only a relatively brief period.

These children in Germany during the hyperinflation of the 1920s are building a pyramid with cash, worth no more than the sand or sticks used by children elsewhere.

percent *per month*. And in the final month, the price level skyrocketed 42 quadrillion percent!

While the distinction between creeping and galloping inflation is a quantitative one, we refrained from putting any specific numbers into the definitions. This is because different societies at different points in time have very different conceptions about what rate constitutes creeping inflation and what rate constitutes galloping inflation. For example, in Canada today, annual rates of inflation in the 3 to 7 percent range are generally considered to be "creeping," while rates in the 25 to 30 percent range would surely be construed as "galloping." In most Latin American countries, however, inflation consistently in the 25 to 30 percent range is viewed as "creeping." And in the Canada of the 1950s a 7 percent annual inflation might have been branded "galloping."

The Costs of Creeping Versus Galloping Inflation

If you review the costs of inflation that have been discussed in this chapter, you will see why the distinction between creeping and galloping inflation is so fundamental. Many economists feel we can live reasonably well, indeed can prosper, in an environment of creeping inflation. No one feels we can survive very well under galloping inflation.

Under creeping inflation, the rate at which prices rise is relatively easy to predict and to take into account in setting interest rates. Under galloping inflation, where prices are rising at ever-increasing rates, this is very difficult, and perhaps impossible, to accomplish. The potential redistributions become monumental, and as a result, lending and borrowing may cease entirely.

Any inflation makes it difficult to write long-term contracts. With creeping inflation, the "long term" may be 20 years, or 10 years, or 5. But with galloping inflation, the "long term" may be measured in weeks or even hours. Restaurant prices may change before you finish your dessert. Railway fares may go up while you are in the middle of your journey. When it is impossible to enter into contracts of any duration longer than a few minutes, economic activity becomes paralysed. We conclude that:

The horrors of galloping inflation either are absent in creeping inflation or are present in such muted forms that they can scarcely be considered horrors.

Creeping Inflation Does Not Necessarily Lead to Galloping Inflation

We noted earlier that inflation is surrounded by a mythology that bears precious little relation to reality. It seems appropriate to conclude this chapter by disposing of one particularly persistent myth: that creeping inflation invariably leads to galloping inflation.

There is neither statistical evidence nor theoretical support for the myth that creeping inflation leads to galloping inflation. To be sure, creeping inflation sometimes accelerates. But at other times it slows down.

Galloping inflation has only occurred when the government has printed incredible amounts of money, usually to finance wartime expenditures.

In the German inflation of 1923, the government finally found that its printing presses could not produce enough paper money to keep pace with the exploding prices. Not that it did not try. By the end of the inflation, the *daily* output of currency was over 400 quadrillion marks! The Hungarian authorities in 1945–46 tried even harder. The average growth rate of the money supply was more than 12,000 percent *per month*. Needless to say, these are not the kinds of inflation problems that are likely to face Canada in the foreseeable future.

But this should not be interpreted to imply there is nothing wrong with creeping inflation. Much of this chapter has been spent analysing the very real costs of inflation, no matter how slow. A case against even moderate inflation can indeed be built, but it does not help this case to shout foolish slogans like "Creeping inflation always leads to galloping inflation." Fortunately, it is simply not true.

Summary

1. Unemployment exacts heavy financial and psychological costs from those who are its victims, costs that are borne quite unevenly by different groups in the population.
2. Unemployment is measured by a government survey. Some critics claim that the survey methods understate the unemployment problem, while others contend that the methods overstate the problem.
3. Frictional unemployment arises when people are between jobs for normal reasons. Thus, most frictional unemployment is acceptable.
4. Structural unemployment is due to shifts in the pattern of demand or to technological change that results in certain skills becoming obsolete.
5. Cyclical unemployment is the portion of unemployment that rises in recessions and falls when the economy booms.
6. In 1945, the federal government committed itself to limiting unemployment to the frictional variety. However, it set no numerical goals.
7. During the 1950s and 1960s, most economists regarded cyclical unemployment as anything above 3.5 percent. Now, with increased structural problems, most economists regard cyclical unemployment as about 6.5 percent.
8. Unemployment insurance replaces about sixty percent of the lost income of unemployed persons who are insured. But not all the unemployed are covered by insurance, and no insurance program can bring back the lost output that could have been produced had these people been working.
9. In recent decades, the Canadian economy typically has produced less output than it could have were it operating at full employment. This shortfall has been particularly large since the mid-1970s.

10. People have many misconceptions about inflation. For example, many people believe that inflation systematically erodes the purchasing power of wages, are appalled by rising prices even when wages are rising just as fast, and blame inflation for any unfavourable changes in relative prices. All of these are myths.
11. Other costs of inflation are very real indeed. For example, inflation often redistributes income from lenders to borrowers.
12. This redistribution can be eliminated by adding the expected rate of inflation to the interest rate, but expectations often prove to be quite inaccurate.
13. The real rate of interest is the nominal rate of interest minus the expected rate of inflation.
14. Since the real rate of interest indicates the command over real resources that the borrower surrenders to the lender, it is of primary economic importance.
15. Yet public attention often is riveted on nominal rates of interest, and this confusion can lead to costly policy mistakes when high inflation converts high nominal interest rates into very low real interest rates. This is one of the **12 Ideas for Beyond the Final Exam**.
16. Despite indexing of the basic personal income-tax system in 1973, our tax system levies very heavy taxes on interest income when inflation is high, since nominal, not real, interest income is taxed.
17. Creeping inflation, which proceeds at moderate and fairly predictable rates year after year, carries far lower social costs than galloping inflation, which proceeds at high and variable rates.
18. The notion that creeping inflation inevitably leads to galloping inflation is a myth with no foundation in economic theory and no basis in historical fact.

Concepts for Review

Unemployment rate	Full employment	Real rate of interest
Labour force	Unemployment insurance	Nominal rate of interest
Discouraged workers	Potential GNP	Expected rate of inflation
Frictional unemployment	Purchasing power	Indexed taxes
Structural unemployment	Relative prices	Creeping inflation
Cyclical unemployment	Redistribution by inflation	Galloping inflation

Questions for Discussion

1. Why is it not as terrible to become unemployed nowadays as it was during the Great Depression?
2. "Since unemployed workers receive unemployment benefits and other benefits that make up for most of their lost wages, unemployment is no longer a social problem." Comment.
3. Using what you learned about aggregate demand and aggregate supply in Chapter 5, try to explain why the Canadian economy has failed so frequently to produce up to its potential. (You will learn more about this question in later chapters, so don't worry if you find the question difficult now.)
4. Do you think that Statistics Canada overestimates or underestimates the number of people that are unemployed? Why?
5. Why is it so difficult to define "full employment"? What unemployment rate should the government be shooting for today?
6. Show why each of the following complaints is based on a misunderstanding about inflation:
   a. "Inflation must be stopped because it robs workers of their purchasing power."
   b. "Inflation is a terrible social disease. It leads to unconscionably high prices for basic necessities."
   c. "Inflation makes it impossible for working people to afford many of the things they were hoping to buy."
   d. "Inflation must be stopped today, for if we do not stop it, it will surely accelerate to ruinously high rates and lead to disaster."
7. What is the *real interest rate* paid on a loan bearing 18 percent nominal interest per year, if the rate of inflation is:
   a. zero
   b. 2 percent
   c. 7 percent
   d. 12 percent
   e. 19 percent
8. Suppose you agree to lend money to your friend on the day you both enter university, at what you both expect to be a zero *real* rate of interest. Payment is to be made at graduation, with interest at a fixed *nominal* rate. If inflation proves to be *lower* during your four years in university than what you both had expected, who will gain and who will lose?
9. You have lived with inflation all your life. Think about the costs that inflation has imposed on you personally. How do these costs relate to the material in this chapter?
10. Add a third line to Table 6–4 showing what would happen if the inflation rate went to 12 percent and the real interest rate remained 4 percent.

Appendix

How Statisticians Measure Inflation

Index Numbers for Inflation

Inflation is generally measured by the change in some index of the general price level. For example, between 1973 and 1983, the Consumer Price Index (CPI), which stood at 100 in 1981, rose from 47.6 to 117.2, an increase of 146 percent. The meaning of the *change* is clear enough. But what is the meaning of the 47.6 figure for 1973 and the 117.2 figure for 1983?

These numbers are **index numbers**; each expresses the cost of a market basket of goods *relative to its cost in some "base" period*. Since the CPI uses 1981 as its base period, the CPI of 117.2 for 1983 means that it cost $117.20 in 1983 to purchase the same basket of goods and services that cost $100 in 1981.

Now, the particular basket of consumer goods and services under scrutiny really did not cost $100 in 1981. When constructing index numbers, it is conventional to set the index at 100 in the base year. How is this conventional figure used in obtaining index numbers for other years? Very simply. Suppose the budget needed to buy the roughly 400 items included in the CPI was $500 per month in 1981 and $586 per month in 1983. Then the index is defined by the following rule:

$$\frac{\text{CPI in 1983}}{\text{CPI in 1981}} =$$

$$\frac{\text{Cost of the 400-item market basket in 1983}}{\text{Cost of the 400-item market basket in 1981}}$$

Since the CPI in 1981 is set at 100:

$$\frac{\text{CPI in 1983}}{100} = \frac{\$586}{\$500} = 1.172$$

or

$$\text{CPI in 1983} = 117.2.$$

Exactly the same sort of equation enables us to calculate the CPI in any other year. We have the rule:

CPI in given year =

$$\frac{\text{Cost of market basket in given year}}{\text{Cost of market basket in base year}} \times 100.$$

Of course, not every combination of consumer goods that cost $500 in 1981 rose to $586 by 1983. For example, a colour TV set that cost $500 in 1981 might have sold for $450 in 1983, but a $500 insurance bill in 1981 might have ballooned to $700. Since no two families buy precisely the same bundle of goods and services, no two families suffer precisely the same increase in their cost of living unless all prices rise at the same rate. Economists refer to this phenomenon as the **index number problem**.

When relative prices are changing, there is no such thing as a "perfect price index" that is correct for every consumer. Any statistical index will understate the increase in the cost of living for some families and overstate it for others. At best, the index can represent the situation of an "average" family.

The Consumer Price Index

The most closely watched price index is surely the **Consumer Price Index**, which is calculated and announced each month by Statistics Canada. When you read in the newspaper or see on television that the "cost of living" rose by 0.8 percent last month, chances are the reporter is referring to the CPI.

The CPI is measured by pricing the items on a list representative of a typical urban household budget. To know what items to include and in what amounts, Statistics Canada conducts an extensive survey of spending habits roughly twice every decade (the last one was in 1978). This means that the *same* bundle of goods and services is used as a standard for several years, whether or not spending habits change.[8]

[8]Economists call this a *base-period weight index* because the relative importance it attaches to each price depends on how much money consumers actually chose to spend on it during the base period.

The 1978 family expenditure survey examined the spending patterns of Canadians living in the 64 urban communities of 30,000 people or more. In addition to the overall CPI, a separate one is published for each of the 15 major cities within this group.

A simple example will help us understand how the CPI is constructed. Imagine that university students purchase only three items—hamburgers, jeans, and movie tickets—and that we want to devise a cost-of-living index (call it SPI, for "student price index") for them. First we would conduct a survey of spending habits in the base year (suppose it is 1973). Table 6–5 represents the hypothetical results. You will note that the frugal students of that day spent only $50 per month: $28 on hamburgers, $12 on jeans, and $10 on movies.

Table 6–5
RESULTS OF STUDENT EXPENDITURE SURVEY, 1973

ITEM	AVERAGE PRICE	AVERAGE QUANTITY PURCHASED PER MONTH	AVERAGE EXPENDITURE PER MONTH
Hamburger	$ 0.40	70	$28
Jeans	12.00	1	12
Movie ticket	2.50	4	10
			Total $50

Table 6–6
PRICES IN 1985

ITEM	PRICE	PERCENTAGE INCREASE OVER 1973
Hamburger	$ 1	150
Jeans	15	25
Movie ticket	4	60

Table 6–6 presents hypothetical prices of these same three items in 1985. Each price has risen by a different amount, ranging from only 25 percent for jeans to 150 percent for hamburgers. By how much has the SPI risen? Pricing the 1973 student budget at 1985 prices, we find that what once cost $50 now costs $101, as the following calculation shows:

COST OF 1973 STUDENT BUDGET IN 1985 PRICES	
70 hamburgers at $1	$70
1 pair of jeans at $15	15
4 movie tickets at $4	16
Total	$101

Thus the SPI, based on 1973 = 100, is

$$\text{SPI} = \frac{\text{Cost of budget in 1985}}{\text{Cost of budget in 1973}} = \frac{\$101}{\$50} \times 100 = 202.$$

So the SPI in 1985 stands at 202, meaning that a student's cost of living has increased 102 percent over the 12 years.

How to Use a Price Index to "Deflate" Monetary Figures

One of the most common uses of price indexes is in the comparison of monetary figures relating to two different points in time. The problem is that, if there has been inflation, the dollar is not a good measuring rod because it is worth less now that it was in the past.

Here is a simple example. Suppose that the average student spent $50 per month in 1973, and that this monthly spending figure had grown to $90 per month in 1985. If there was an outcry that students had become spendthrifts, how would you answer the charge?

The obvious answer is that a dollar in 1985 does not buy what it did in 1973. Specifically, our SPI shows us that it takes $2.02 in 1985 to purchase what $1 would purchase in 1973. To compare the spending habits of students in the two years, we must divide the 1985 spending figure by 2.02. Specifically, *real* spending per student in 1985 (where "real" is defined by 1973 dollars) is:

$$\text{Real spending in 1985} = \frac{\text{Nominal spending in 1985}}{\text{Price index of 1985}}$$

Thus,

$$\text{Real spending in 1985} = \frac{\$90}{2.02} = \$44.55.$$

In sum, this calculation shows that, despite appearances to the contrary, the change in nominal spending from $50 to $90 actually represented a *decrease* in real spending.

This calculation procedure is called **deflating by a price index**, and it serves to translate non-comparable monetary figures into more directly comparable real figures.

Deflating is the process of finding the real value of some monetary magnitude by dividing by some appropriate price index.

The GNP Deflator

In macroeconomics, one of the most important of the monetary magnitudes that we have to deflate is the nominal gross national product (GNP). The price index used to do this is called the **GNP deflator**. Our general principle for deflating a nominal magnitude tells us just how to go from nominal GNP to real GNP:

$$\text{Real GNP} = \frac{\text{Nominal GNP}}{\text{GNP deflator}} \times 100.$$

As with the CPI, the 100 simply serves to establish the base of the index as 100, rather than 1.00.

Economists often consider the GNP deflator to be a better measure of overall inflation in the economy than the Consumer Price Index. The main reason for this is that the two price indexes are based on different market baskets. As already mentioned, the CPI is based on the budget of a typical urban family. By contrast, the GNP deflator is constructed from a market basket that includes *every* item in the GNP—that is, every final good and service produced by the economy. Thus, in addition to prices of consumer goods, the GNP deflator includes the prices of airplanes, lathes, and other goods purchased by business. It also includes government services. For this reason, the measures of inflation that these two indexes give are rarely the same. Usually their disagreements are minor, but sometimes they can be quite substantial.

Summary

1. Inflation is measured by the percentage increase in an index number of prices, which shows how the cost of some basket of goods has changed over a period of time.
2. Since relative prices are changing all the time, and since all families purchase different items, no price index can represent precisely the change in the cost of living for every family.
3. The Consumer Price Index (CPI) tries to measure the cost of living for an "average" urban household by pricing a "typical" market basket every month.
4. Price indexes like the CPI can be used to *deflate* monetary figures to make them more comparable. This amounts to dividing the monetary magnitude by the appropriate price index.
5. The GNP deflator is a better measure of economy-wide inflation than is the CPI because it includes the price of every good and service in the economy.

Concepts for Review

Index number
Index number problem
Consumer Price Index

Deflating by a price index
GNP deflator

Questions for Discussion

1. Just below you will find nominal GNP and the GNP deflator for 1963, 1973, and 1983.
a. Compute real GNP for each year.
b. Compute the percentage change in nominal and real GNP from 1963 to 1973, and from 1973 to 1983.
c. Compute the percentage change in the GNP deflator over these two periods.

	GNP STATISTICS		
	1963	1973	1983
Nominal GNP (billions of dollars)	45.9	123.5	388.6
GNP deflator	74.6	114.6	290.0

2. Fill in the blanks in the following table of GNP statistics.

YEAR	1981	1982	1983
Nominal GNP	339.0		388.6
Real GNP	136.1	130.1	
GNP deflator		274.2	290.0

3. Use the following data to compute the University Price Index for 1984, using the base 1972=100.

ITEM	PRICE IN 1972	QUANTITY PER MONTH IN 1972	PRICE IN 1984
Button-down shirts	$10	1	$20
Loafers	25	1	45
Sneakers	10	3	15
Textbooks	12	12	22
Jeans	12	3	36
Restaurant meals	5	11	10

4. (More difficult.) The example in the appendix showed that the Student Price Index (SPI) rose by 102 percent from 1973 to 1985. You can understand the meaning of this better if you:
a. Use Table 6–5 to compute the fraction of total spending accounted for by each of the three items in 1973. Call these the "expenditure weights."
b. Compute the weighted average of the percentage increases of the three prices shown in Table 6–6, using the expenditure weights you have just computed.
c. You should get 102 percent as your answer. This shows that "inflation," as measured by the SPI, is a weighted average of the percentage price increases of all the items that are included in the index.

Income and Spending: The Powerful Consumer

Men are disposed, as a rule
and on the average, to
increase their consumption
as their income increases,
but not by as much as the
increase in their income.

JOHN MAYNARD KEYNES

In Chapter 5 we saw how the strength of aggregate demand influences the performance of the economy. When aggregate demand is growing briskly, the economy is likely to be booming, though it may also be having trouble with inflation. Similarly, when aggregate demand stagnates, a recession is likely to follow.

This chapter begins our detailed study of the *determination* of aggregate demand. In this and the next few chapters, we will learn why the *aggregate-demand curve* of Chapter 5 has a negative slope and how the government can *manage* aggregate demand. Since consumer spending accounts for over 60 percent of total demand, it is natural to begin with the consumer. The following chapters will bring investment spending, government spending, foreign spending, and the supply side of the economy into the picture.

We start the chapter with some definitions of alternative concepts of economic activity—distinguishing carefully among total *spending* (aggregate demand), total *output*, and total *income*. Next, we turn to the interactions among these three concepts, using a convenient pictorial device that shows how they are all interrelated. Then we note that government attempts to influence consumer spending have sometimes succeeded and sometimes failed, and we pose the question: Why?

The bulk of this chapter is devoted to this question. To answer it, we first describe the important relationship between consumer income and consumer spending, and we use this relationship to show how government policies have worked when they have been successful. Then we discuss some complications that arise from the fact that consumer income, though crucial, is not the only factor governing consumer spending. One of these complications gives us the first of several reasons why the aggregate-demand curve slopes downward. Another holds the clue to why the government's income-tax policies have sometimes failed to influence consumer spending as expected. Also, the analysis explains why the Canadian federal government has tried to arrange sales-tax changes to avoid the problems associated with income-tax policy.

Aggregate Demand, National Product, and National Income

Aggregate demand is the total amount that all consumers, business firms, government agencies, and foreigners are willing to spend on final goods and services.

Consumer expenditure, symbolized by the letter C, is the total amount spent by consumers on newly produced goods and services (excluding purchases of new homes, which are considered investment goods).

Investment spending, symbolized by the letter I, is the sum of the expenditures of business firms on new plant, equipment, and inventories, plus the expenditures of households on new homes. Financial "investments" are not included, nor are resales of existing physical assets.

Government purchases, symbolized by the letter G, refers to all the goods (such as airplanes and paper clips) and services (such as school teaching and police protection) purchased by all levels of government. It does not include government **transfer payments** to individuals (such as welfare benefits), nor transfer payments from one level of government to another.

Net exports, symbolized by $X - IM$, is the excess of foreign expenditures on our products over our purchases of their goods (Canadian exports minus Canadian imports).

We begin with some definitions. We have already introduced the concept of **gross national product** as the standard measure of the total output of the economy.[1]

For the most part, goods are produced in a market economy only if they can be sold. **Aggregate demand**, another concept encountered in Chapter 5, is the total amount that all consumers, business firms, government agencies, and foreigners wish to spend on all final goods and services. Many factors enter into the determination of aggregate quantity demanded, including price level, consumer incomes, various government policies, and the level of foreign incomes. We can understand the nature of aggregate demand best if we break it up into its major components.

Consumer expenditure ("**consumption**" for short) is simply the total demand for all consumer goods and services. This is the focus of the current chapter, and we shall represent it by the letter **C**.

Investment spending, which we represent by the letter **I**, is the amount that firms spend on factories, machinery, and the like, plus the amount that families spend on new homes. Notice that this is a very different usage of the word "investment" from that which is found in common parlance. Most people speak of "investing" in the stock market or in a bank account. This kind of "investment" merely swaps one form of financial asset (such as money) for another form (such as a share of stock). When economists speak of "investment," they mean instead the purchase of some *new physical asset*, like a drill press or an oil rig or a home. It is only this kind of investment that leads directly to additional demand for newly produced goods in the economy.

Another major component of aggregate demand is **government purchases** of goods and services; that is, things like paper, typewriters, airplanes, ships, and labour that are bought by all levels of government—federal, provincial, and municipal. We use the letter **G** to denote this variable.

Finally, the last major component of aggregate demand is **net exports**. This consists of exports, which we represent by the letter **X**, and imports, which we denote by **IM**. Exports are the sum of all expenditures by foreigners on Canadian-produced final goods (such as wheat, fish, and snowmobiles) and services (such as transportation, hotel, and restaurant services purchased by foreigners while vacationing in Canada). Canadian expenditures on imports from other countries must be subtracted when calculating total demand for domestic production, since the spending by households, firms, and governments include their expenditures on the products from other countries.

Given all these abbreviations, we have the following shorthand definition of aggregate demand.

Aggregate demand is the sum $C + I + G + X - IM$.

The last concept we need is a measure of the total *income* of all the individuals in the economy. There are two versions of this: one for before-tax incomes, called **national income**, and one for after-tax incomes, called **disposable income**.[2] The term "disposable income" is meant to be descriptive: it tells us how many dollars consumers actually have available to spend or to save. Because it plays such a prominent role in this chapter, we shall need an abbreviation for it as well; we call it **DI**.

---

[1] See Chapter 5, pages 76–79.

[2] More detailed information on these and other concepts is provided in an appendix to this chapter.

The Circular Flow of Spending, Production, and Income

Enough definitions. How do these three concepts—national product, aggregate demand, and national income—interact in a market economy? We can answer this best with a rather elaborate diagram (Figure 7–1). For obvious reasons, Figure 7–1 is called a **circular flow diagram**. It depicts a large circular tube in which a fluid is circulating in a clockwise direction. There are several breaks in the tube where either some of the fluid leaks out or additional fluid is injected in.

Let us examine this system beginning on the far left. Here, at point 1 on the circle, we find consumers. Disposable income (*DI*) is flowing into them, and two things are flowing out: consumption (*C*), which stays in the circular flow, and saving (*S*), which "leaks out." This just says that consumers normally spend less than they earn and save the balance. The "leakage" to savings, of course, does not disappear, but flows into the financial system. We postpone a consideration of what happens there until Chapter 12.

The upper loop of the circular flow represents expenditures, and as we move clockwise to point 2, we encounter the first "injection" into the flow: investment spending (*I*). The diagram shows this as coming from "investors"—a group that includes both business firms and consumers who buy new homes.[3] As the circular flow moves beyond point 2, it is bigger than it was before. Total spending has increased from *C* to *C* + *I*.

---

[3] You are reminded of the specific definition of investment on the preceding page.

National income is the sum of the incomes of all the individuals in the economy earned in the forms of wages, interest, rents, and profits. It is calculated before any deductions are taken for income taxes.

Disposable income is the sum of the incomes of all the individuals in the economy after all taxes have been deducted.

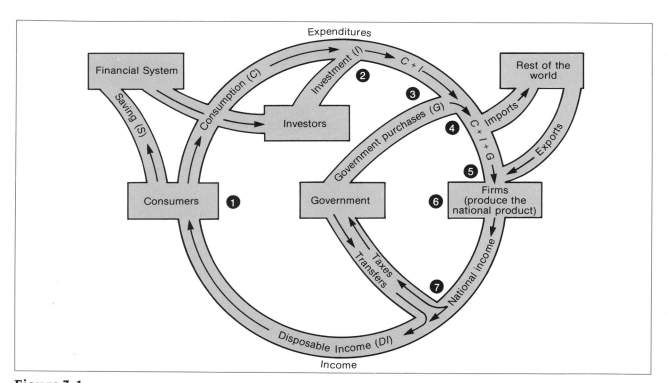

Figure 7–1
THE CIRCULAR FLOW OF EXPENDITURE AND INCOME
The upper half of this circular flow diagram depicts the flow of expenditures on goods and services that comes from consumers (point 1), investors (point 2), government (point 3), and foreigners (point 5), and goes to the firms that produce the output (point 6). Some of the expenditures are spent on imports (point 4), and so never reach domestically operating firms. The lower half of the diagram indicates how the income paid out by firms (point 6) flows to consumers (point 1), after some is siphoned off by the government in the form of taxes and part of this is replaced by transfer payments (point 7).

At point 3 there is yet another injection. The government adds its demand for goods and services (G) to those of consumers and investors (C + I). At point 4 there is another leakage, which allows some of the demands for goods and services to flow out to foreign producers. Demand for Canadian products is less than the total expenditures of households, firms, and governments by the amount of these imports. At point 5 there is the final injection—exports. Thus, by the time we have passed point 5 and have added in the foreign purchases, we have accumulated the full amount of aggregate demand, C + I + G + X – IM.

The circular flow diagram shows this aggregate demand for goods and services arriving at the business firms, located at point 6 on the extreme right of the diagram. Responding to this demand, firms produce the national product. As the circular flow emerges from the firms, however, we have renamed it *national income*. Why? Because, except for some complications explained in the appendix:

National income and national product must be equal.

Why is this the case? When a firm produces and sells $100 worth of output, it pays most of the proceeds to its workers, to people who have lent it money, and to the landlord who owns the property on which it is located. All of these payments are *income* to some individuals. But what about the rest? Suppose, for example, that the wages, interest, and rent that the firm pays add up to $90, while its output is $100. What happens to the remaining $10? The answer is that the owners of the firm receive it as *profits*. But these owners are also citizens of the country, so their incomes count in national income, too. Thus, when we add up all the wages, interest, rents, *and profits* in the economy to obtain the national income, we must arrive at the value of the national output.

A slight complication occurs when some of the firms are foreign-owned, as is the case in Canada. In this case, some of the profits earned in Canada add to another country's national income, not ours. This is partly compensated for by the fact that some Canadians earn profits by being part owners of firms that operate outside Canada. To allow for these activities, we could complicate our circular flow diagram with an additional leakage and injection between points 6 and 7. The leakage is incomes paid to foreigners operating within Canada, and the injection is incomes received by Canadians operating elsewhere. These flows do not exactly cancel off, so national product and national income are not exactly equal. National product is called *gross domestic product* (GDP), and national income is called GNP. We have followed the convention of ignoring the difference between these two aggregates for two reasons. First, we wish to keep the circular flow diagram simplified; second, the cyclical swings in GNP and GDP are virtually identical, as can be seen in Figure 7–2. Employment variations depend on these cyclical swings, not on the absolute level of either GNP or GDP.

The lower loop of the circular flow diagram traces the flow of income by showing national income leaving the firms and heading for consumers. But there is a detour along the way. At point 7, the government does two things. First, it siphons off a portion of the national income in the form of taxes. Second, it adds back government **transfer payments** to individuals, like disability compensation and government pension benefits, which are sums of money that certain individuals receive as *grants* from the government rather than as payments for services rendered to employers.

When taxes are subtracted from GNP, and transfer payments are added, we obtain disposable income.[4]

$$DI = \text{GNP} - \text{Taxes} + \text{Transfer payments.}$$

Disposable income flows unimpeded to consumers at point 1, and the cycle repeats.

Transfer payments are sums of money that certain individuals receive as *grants* from the government rather than as payments for services rendered to employers.

[4] This equation omits a few minor details, which are explained in an appendix to this chapter.

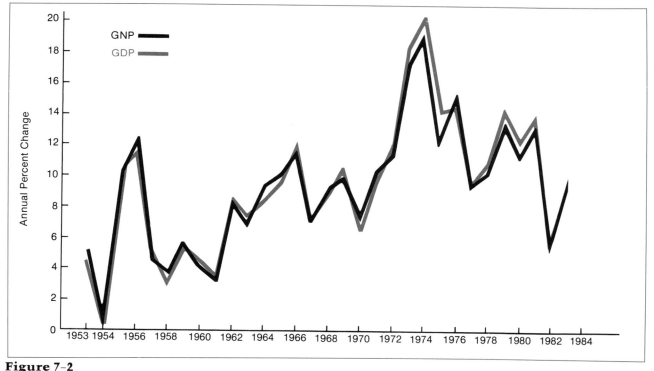

Figure 7-2

THE CLOSE RELATIONSHIP BETWEEN GDP AND GNP

GNP is the total income of Canadian factors of production, wherever they are employed. GDP is the total amount of employment-creating economic activity that actually takes place within Canada. For stabilization policy, we are concerned only with the cyclical swings in national income and production. The figure shows that the swings in nominal GNP and GDP are virtually identical.
SOURCE: Statistics Canada.

Figure 7–1 raises several complicated questions. Although we pose them here, we will not try to answer them at this early stage. The answers will be made clear in subsequent chapters.

1. Is the output that the firms produce at point 6 (the GNP) equal to aggregate demand? If so, what makes these two quantities equal? If not, what happens?

2. Is the flow of spending and income growing larger or smaller as we move clockwise around the circle, and why?

Chapter 8 provides the answers to questions 1 and 2.

3. Are the government's accounts in balance, so that what flows in at point 7 (taxes minus transfers) is equal to what flows out at point 3 (government purchases)? What happens if they are not?

This important question is first addressed in Chapter 11 and then recurs many times, especially in Chapter 17, which discusses budget deficits.

We cannot discuss these issues profitably now because first we must understand what goes on at point 1 (where consumers make decisions) and point 2 (where investors make decisions). We turn next, therefore, to the determinants of consumer spending.

Demand Management and the Powerful Consumer

As we suggested in Chapter 5, the government sometimes wants to shift the aggregate-demand curve. There are a number of ways in which it can try to do so.

One direct approach is to alter its own spending (*G*), becoming extravagant when private demand is weak and miserly when private demand is strong. But the government can also take a more indirect route by using taxes and other policy tools to influence *private* spending decisions.

A government desiring to change private spending can concentrate its energies on consumer spending (*C*), on investment spending (*I*), or on net exports (*X* – *IM*). At various times in our history, the Canadian government has elected to pursue one of these courses of action. Their favourite target has been firms' investment spending, which they try to manipulate with variations in the corporate tax system. We discuss these in Chapter 11. For the present, we discuss attempts to alter household consumption and consider some illuminating policy experiments that were tried in the United States. Also, we describe the Canadian government's attempt to benefit from this U.S. experience.

While there are many things it can do to alter consumer spending, the government's principal weapon is the personal income tax. Any reduction in personal taxes leaves consumers with more disposable income to spend. Any increase in taxes leaves them with less. The linkage from taxes to disposable income to consumer spending seems direct and unmistakable, and, in a certain sense, it is. But a look at the history of some major U.S. tax changes aimed at altering *C* is sobering. The varying degrees of success both of the measures themselves and of the predictions of their effects explain why economic research into the relationship between taxes and consumption continues.

Case 1: The U.S. Income-Tax Reduction of 1964

The year 1964 was a good one for economists. For years economists had been proclaiming that a cut in personal taxes would be an excellent way to stimulate a stagnating economy. But the plea fell on deaf ears until President John F. Kennedy was persuaded of the basic logic of the argument. Under his successor, Lyndon B. Johnson, the U.S. Congress reduced personal taxes by about 18 percent. The legislation was designed to spur consumer spending, and it succeeded admirably. Consumers reacted just about as the textbooks of the day predicted, the economic situation improved rapidly and markedly, and economists smiled knowingly.

Case 2: The U.S. Income-Tax Increase of 1968

The euphoria of 1964 was both unwarranted and short-lived. In 1968–69, the United States learned—the hard way—that economists did not have all the answers. Largely because of the massive defense spending associated with the Vietnam War, the macroeconomic problem confronting the United States in 1966–68 was precisely the opposite of that in 1964: too much demand rather than too little. It appeared logical, then, to prescribe the opposite medicine, and economists were quick to suggest an increase in personal income taxes to force consumers to spend less.

After a considerable delay, President Johnson recommended a temporary tax increase and Congress enacted a 10 percent rise in personal tax payments (calling it a "surcharge"). However, this attempt to cut aggregate demand by reducing *C* enjoyed only modest success. While consumer spending probably was below what it would have been in the absence of the surcharge, it was substantially above what the 1964 experience had led economists to predict.

Case 3: The U.S. Income-Tax Reduction of 1975

The next major change in U.S. tax laws for stabilization purposes also met with partial success at best. In the spring of 1975, as the American economy neared the bottom of what was then its worst postwar recession, President Gerald R. Ford and the Congress agreed on a double-edged tax cut to spur consumer spending. First, they returned to each taxpayer part of the taxes paid in 1974. Second, they reduced income-tax rates for the balance of 1975. However, consumers confounded the wishes of the president and Congress by saving a good deal of their rebates rather than spending them.

What went wrong in 1968 and 1975 that had not gone wrong in 1964? This chapter will attempt to provide some answers. We begin by exploring the important relationship between consumer income and consumer spending, more or less retracing the chain of logic that led American economists to the right conclusion in 1964. Once this is accomplished, we turn to some of the complications that made things go awry in 1968 and 1975.

Case 4: The Canadian Sales-Tax Reduction of 1978

At the end of this chapter, we describe how the Canadian federal government tried to avoid the problems encountered by the Americans, by relying on *sales-tax* changes rather than *personal income-tax* policies, in their 1978 budget.

Consumer Spending and Income: The Important Relationship

An economist interested in predicting how consumer spending will respond to a change in personal income-tax payments must first ask how C is related to disposable income; for an increase in taxes is a decrease in after-tax income, and a reduction in taxes is an increase in after-tax income. This section, therefore, will examine what we know about the response of consumer spending to a change in disposable income.

Figure 7–3 depicts the historical paths of C and DI for Canada since 1926. The association is obviously rather close and certainly suggests that consumption will rise whenever disposable income does and fall whenever income falls. The difference between the two lines is personal saving. Notice how little saving consumers did during the Great Depression of the 1930s, where the two lines are very close together, and how much more they did during World War II, when many consumer goods were either unavailable or rationed so there was little on which to spend money. The only puzzling feature of Figure 7–3 is the apparent bulge in savings that has occurred in the last ten years. The main reason for this is the inflation in this period. When there is no sustained inflation, real and nominal interest rates coincide, so that households do not need to save any of their interest earnings to keep the real value of their bonds and shares constant. With a sustained inflation, however, much of the received nominal interest rate is the inflation premium, and *all* of this part of interest must be saved just to keep real asset holdings constant. (Real asset holdings can be constant only if nominal holdings of bonds and stocks increase as rapidly as the inflation rate.) To be comparable with the earlier (non-inflationary) periods, then, the consumption expenditure series for the last ten years should be adjusted for the gap that has emerged between the real and nominal interest rates.

There is a mirror image of this overstatement of household savings in inflationary times. The *dis*saving by the other sectors (firms and governments) is overstated in the standard data by the same amount and for the same reason. We return to this point when discussing the size of the government budget deficit in Chapter 17. This discussion represents another application of the important **12 Ideas for Beyond the Final Exam**: the difference between nominal and real interest.

Of course, knowing that consumer expenditures, C, will move in the same direction as disposable income, *DI*, is not enough for policy planners. They need to know *how much* one will go up when the other rises a given amount. Figure 7-4 presents the same data that we saw in Figure 7-3 but in a way designed to help answer the "how much" question.

Economists call such pictures **scatter diagrams**, and they are very useful in predicting how one economic variable (in this case, consumer spending) will change in response to a change in another economic variable (in this case, disposable income). Each dot in the diagram represents the data on *C* and *DI* corresponding to a particular year. For example, the point labelled "1970" shows that real consumer expenditures in 1970 were $51.5 billion (which we read off the vertical axis), while real disposable incomes amounted to $55.3 billion (which we read off the horizontal axis). Similarly, each year from 1926 to 1983 is represented by its own dot in Figure 7-4.

How can such a diagram assist the fiscal policy planner? Imagine that you are an American economist in 1963 and you must decide whether to recommend to the government a tax cut of $5 billion, $10 billion, or $15 billion. (It has already

A **scatter diagram** is a graph showing the relationship between two variables (such as consumption and disposable income). Each year is represented by a point in the diagram. The co-ordinates of each year's point show the values of the two variables in that year.

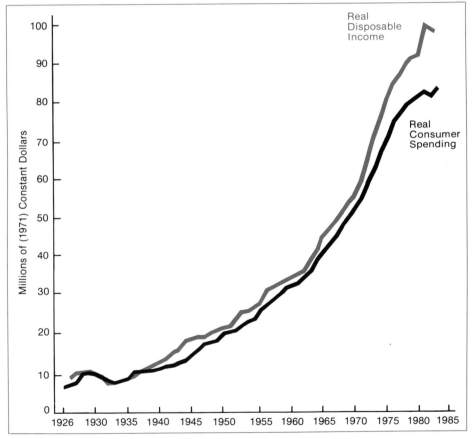

Figure 7-3

CONSUMER SPENDING AND DISPOSABLE INCOME IN CANADA SINCE 1926

This time-series chart shows the behaviour of consumer spending and disposable income in Canada since 1926. The correspondence between the two variables is remarkably close. The distance between the two lines represents measured consumer saving, which was quite small during the Great Depression of the 1930s, quite large during World War II, and quite large in the last ten years. This recent bulge in savings is largely due to a measurement problem that is based on the large inflation premium that has become incorporated within nominal interest rates.
SOURCE: Statistics Canada.

been decided that a cut smaller than $5 billion is not worth the legislative effort and that a cut of more than $15 billion is politically not feasible.) You have forecasts of what consumer expenditures are expected to be if taxes are not reduced. This, plus other forecasts of investment, government spending, and net exports has led you to conclude that aggregate demand in 1964 will be insufficient if taxes are not reduced. To assist you, the pre-1964 scatter diagram for the United States is given in Figure 7–5. With no more training in economics than you have right now, what would you do?

One rough-and-ready approach is to get a ruler, set it down on Figure 7–5, and sketch a straight line that comes as close as possible to hitting all the points. Try that now. You will not be able to hit each point exactly, but you will find that you can come remarkably close. The line you have just drawn summarizes, in a very rough way, the consumption–income relationship that is the focus of this chapter. We see at once that it confirms something we might have guessed—that a rise in income is associated with a rise in consumer spending. The slope of the line is certainly positive.

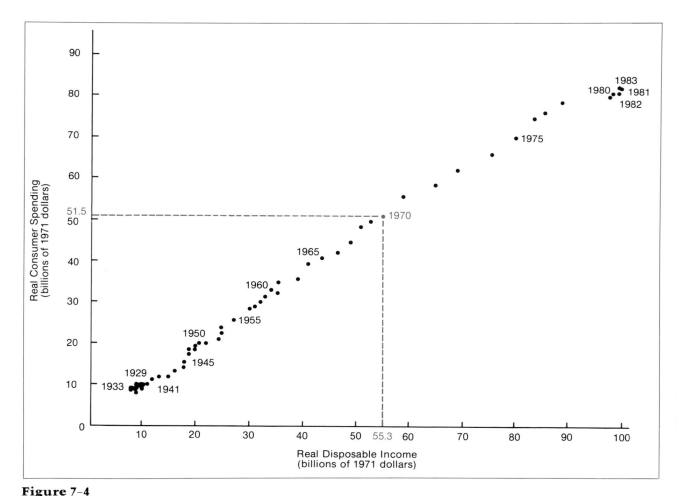

Figure 7–4

SCATTER DIAGRAM OF CONSUMER SPENDING AND DISPOSABLE INCOME IN CANADA, 1926–1983
This diagram shows the same data as depicted in Figure 7–3 but in a different manner. Each point on the diagram represents the data for both consumer spending and disposable income during a particular year. For example, the point labelled "1970" indicates that in that year consumer spending was $51.5 billion while disposable income was $55.3 billion. Diagrams like this one are called "scatter diagrams."

Figure 7-5

SCATTER DIAGRAM OF
CONSUMER SPENDING AND
DISPOSABLE INCOME IN THE
UNITED STATES, 1947–1963
This scatter diagram indicates the
information that policy planners
might have used in deciding upon
the size of the 1964 income-tax
cut in the United States.

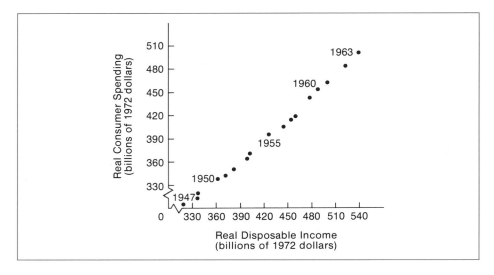

The slope of your line is very important.[5] That line has been drawn into Figure 7-6, and we note that its slope is:

$$\text{Slope} = \frac{\text{Vertical change}}{\text{Horizontal change}} = \frac{\$90\text{ billion}}{\$100\text{ billion}} = 0.90.$$

Since the horizontal change involved in the move from *A* to *B* represents a rise in disposable income of \$100 billion (from \$420 billion to \$520 billion), and the corresponding vertical change represents the associated \$90 billion rise in consumer spending (from \$390 billion to \$480 billion), the slope of the line indicates how spending responds to changes in disposable income. In this case, we see that each additional \$1 of income leads to 90¢ of additional spending.

In terms of the policy issue of 1964, this line can therefore help provide an answer to the question: How much more consumer spending will be induced by tax cuts of \$5 billion, \$10 billion, or \$15 billion if the effects are similar to those observed in the past? First, we need to keep in mind that each dollar of tax cut increases disposable income by \$1. Then we apply Figure 7-6's finding that each additional dollar of disposable income increases consumer spending by 90¢, and

[5] To review the concept of *slope*, turn back to pages 21–24.

Figure 7-6

SCATTER DIAGRAM OF
CONSUMER SPENDING AND
DISPOSABLE INCOME IN THE
UNITED STATES, 1947–1963
This diagram is the same as
Figure 7-5 except for the addition
of a straight line that comes about
as close as possible to fitting all
the data points.

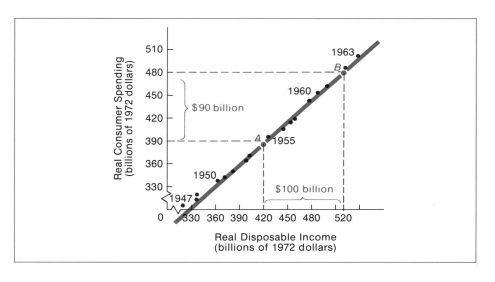

Table 7-1

CONSUMPTION AND INCOME IN MACROLAND

YEAR	(1) CONSUMPTION, C (billions of dollars)	(2) DISPOSABLE INCOME, DI (billions of dollars)	(3) MARGINAL PROPENSITY TO CONSUME, MPC
1980	170	200	
1981	210	250	0.8
1982	250	300	0.8
1983	290	350	0.8
1984	330	400	0.8
1985	370	450	0.8

conclude that proposed tax cuts of $5 billion, $10 billion, or $15 billion would be expected to increase consumer spending by $4.5 billion, $9 billion, and $13.5 billion, respectively. Similar questions addressed by U.S. economists in 1964 led to a decision to cut taxes by about $9 billion.

Later in this and other chapters, we will encounter several reasons why this procedure, while basically valid, must be used with great caution.

The Consumption Function and the Marginal Propensity to Consume

It has been said that economics is just systematized common sense. Let us, then, try to organize and generalize what has been a completely intuitive discussion thus far. One thing we have learned is that there is a close and apparently reliable relationship between consumer spending, C, and disposable income, DI. Economists call this relationship the **consumption function**.

A second fact we have picked up from these figures is that the slope of the consumption function is fairly constant. We infer this from the fact that the straight line in Figure 7–6 comes close to touching every point. If the slope of the consumption function had changed a lot, it would not be possible to do so well with a single straight line. Because of its importance in such applications as the tax-cut example, economists have given a special name to this slope—the **marginal propensity to consume**, or MPC for short. The MPC tells us how many more dollars consumers will spend if disposable income rises by $1 billion.

The MPC is best illustrated by an example, and for this purpose we turn away from both Canadian and U.S. data for a moment and look at the consumption and income data of a hypothetical country called Macroland (see Table 7–1). The data for Macroland resemble those for Canada and the United States, except that in Macroland, C and DI figures happen to be nice round numbers, which facilitates computation.

Columns 1 and 2 of Table 7–1 show annual consumer expenditure and disposable income from 1980 to 1985. These two columns constitute Macroland's consumption function and are plotted in Figure 7–7. Column 3 in the table shows the marginal propensity to consume (MPC), which is the slope of the line in Figure 7–7; it is derived from the first two columns. We can see that between 1982 and 1983, DI rose by $50 billion (from $300 billion to $350 billion) while C rose by $40 billion (from $250 billion to $290 billion). Thus the MPC was:

$$\frac{\text{Change in consumption}}{\text{Change in disposable income}} = \frac{\$40 \text{ billion}}{\$50 \text{ billion}} = 0.80.$$

As you can easily verify, the MPC between any other pair of years in Macroland was also 0.80.

The **consumption function** is the relationship between total consumer expenditure and total disposable income in the economy holding all other determinants of consumer spending constant.

The **marginal propensity to consume** (or MPC for short) is the ratio of the change in consumption to the change in disposable income that produces the change in consumption. On a graph, it appears as the slope of the consumption function.

MPC =

Change in consumption

Change in disposable income that produces the change in consumption

Figure 7-7

THE CONSUMPTION FUNCTION OF MACROLAND
This diagram is similar to Figure 7-6, except that it applies to a hypothetical (and blissfully simple!) economy called Macroland. As can be seen, a straight-line consumption function passes through every point exactly. The slope of this line is 0.8, which is the marginal propensity to consume in Macroland.

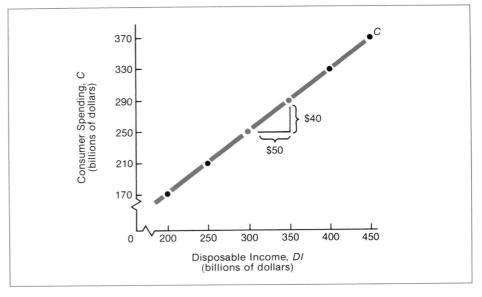

This explains why the slope of the line in Figure 7-6 was so crucial in estimating the effect of a tax cut. Since the slope is the MPC, it tells us how much *additional* spending will be induced by each dollar *change* in disposable income. For each $1 of tax cut, economists expect consumption to rise by $1 times the marginal propensity to consume. Thus:

To estimate the *initial* effect of a tax cut on consumer spending, economists must first estimate the MPC and then multiply the amount of the tax cut by the estimated MPC. But since they never know the true MPC with certainty, this prediction is always subject to some margin of error.[6]

In 1963, for example, economists multiplied the anticipated $9 billion tax cut by the estimated MPC of 0.90 and concluded that consumer spending would initially rise by about $8 billion. Their estimate seems to have been remarkably accurate.

Movements Along Versus Shifts of the Consumption Function

Unfortunately, this sort of calculation does not always yield such precise results. Among the most important reasons for this is that the consumption function does not always stand still; sometimes it shifts.

You will recall from Chapter 4 the important distinction between a *movement along* a demand curve and a *shift* of the curve.

A demand curve depicts the relationship between quantity demanded and only *one* of its many determinants—price. Thus, a change in price causes a movement *along* the demand curve, but a change in any other factor that influences quantity demanded causes a *shift of the entire demand curve*.

Because consumer spending is influenced by factors other than disposable income, a similar distinction is vital to understanding real-world consumption functions. A change in disposable income leads to a **movement along the consumption function**, because the consumption function depicts the relationship between *C* and *DI*. This is what we have been considering in the last

---

[6] The word "initial" in the first sentence is an important one. Later chapters explain why the effects discussed in this chapter are only the beginning of the story.

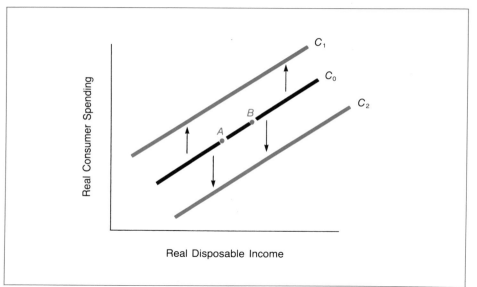

Figure 7-8
SHIFTS OF THE CONSUMPTION FUNCTION
An increase in disposable income causes a movement along a fixed consumption function, such as the movement from point A to point B on consumption function C_0. But a change in any other determinant of consumer spending will cause the whole consumption function to shift upward (consumption function C_1) or downward (consumption function C_2).

two sections. But consumption also has other determinants. And a change in any of these "other determinants" of consumer spending will **shift the entire consumption function**, as indicated in Figure 7–8. These unexpected shifts account for many of the errors in forecasting consumption. To summarize:

Any change in disposable income moves us *along* a given consumption function. But a change in any of the other variables that influence consumption results in a *shift* of the entire consumption schedule (see Figure 7–8).

Let us now list some of these "other variables" that can shift the consumption function.

Other Determinants of Consumer Spending

Recent Past Incomes
One factor is simple *inertia*, the fact that households normally take some time to adjust to changes in their economic circumstances. If income rises at an extraordinary pace—as in an economic boom—consumer spending does not surge ahead as fast as income. You can understand why by considering a close-to-home example. Unless you continue on to graduate study, your income will register a very sharp increase when you graduate from university and get a job. See how long it takes until your spending habits have caught up. The same process works in reverse. At the onset of a recession, consumers normally try to maintain their customary spending levels despite losses of income.

Wealth
A second factor affecting consumption is consumers' *wealth*, which is a source of demand in addition to income. Wealth and income are different things. A wealthy person may currently have very little *income*. Similarly, a high-income individual who spends all he earns will not accumulate wealth. To appreciate the importance of the distinction, consider two consumers, both earning $25,000 this year. One of them has $50,000 in the bank, while the other has no assets at all. Who do you think will spend more this year? Presumably the one with the big bank account.

The general point is that current income is not the only source of funds that households have; they can also finance spending by withdrawals from their bank accounts or by cashing in other forms of wealth. A stock-market boom may therefore raise the consumption function (see the shift from C_0 to C_1 in Figure 7–8), while a collapse of stock prices may lower it (see the shift from C_0 to C_2).

The Price Level

A **money fixed asset** is an asset with a face value fixed in terms of dollars, such as money itself, government bonds, and corporate bonds.

A good deal of consumer wealth is held in forms whose values are fixed in money terms. Money itself is the most obvious example of this, but government bonds, savings accounts, and corporate bonds are all assets with fixed face values in money terms. The purchasing power of any **money fixed asset** obviously declines whenever the price level rises, which means that the asset can buy less. For example, if the price level rises by 10 percent, a $1000 government bond will buy about 10 percent less than it could when prices were lower. Consequently:

Higher overall prices, by eroding the purchasing power of consumer wealth, decrease the demand for goods and services.

This is no trivial matter. It has been estimated that the total volume of money fixed assets in Canada is around $100 billion, so that each 1 percent rise in the price level reduces the purchasing power of consumer wealth by about $1 billion, a tidy sum. The process, of course, operates equally well in reverse. A decline in the price level increases the purchasing power of money fixed assets. So:

Lower overall prices, by enhancing the purchasing power of consumer wealth, increase the demand for goods and services. For these reasons a change in the price level will shift the entire consumption function. Specifically:

A higher price level leads to lower real wealth and therefore to less spending *at any given level of real income.* Thus, a higher price level leads to a lower consumption function (such as C_2 in Figure 7–8). Conversely, a lower price level leads to a higher consumption function (such as C_1 in Figure 7–8).

Students are often confused on this point, so it is worth repeating that the depressing effect of the price level on consumer spending works through real *wealth*, not real *income*. The consumption function is a relationship between *real* consumer income and *real* consumer spending. Thus any decline in real income, regardless of its cause, moves the economy *leftward along a fixed consumption function*; it does not shift the consumption function.[7] By contrast, any decline in *real wealth* will *shift the whole consumption function downward*, meaning that there is less spending at any given level of real income.

The Inflation Rate

Prices may be high and rising slowly, or they may be low but rising rapidly. Therefore, the depressing effect of a high *price level* on real consumer spending must be distinguished from any effect on spending of the *rate of inflation* (that is, the rate at which prices are rising).

Conclusions about the effect of the inflation rate on spending are more complicated. In the past, economists believed that high rates of inflation caused consumers to spend more to "beat" the inflation. That is, people were thought to purchase goods ahead of their needs in order to avoid the higher prices that loomed on the horizon. But behaviour during the inflationary period since 1974 shows that consumer spending was actually unusually low. We explained this on page 119 in terms of the inflation premium that gets embedded in nominal interest rates during inflationary times.

---

[7] This is true even if a rise in the price level lies behind the decline in real income. However, wages and prices normally move together, so there is no reason to expect real wages to fall when the price level rises.

To keep our model economy simplified, we ignore these complications and assume that the position of the consumption function is influenced by the *price level*, but not by the *inflation rate*.

Expectations of Future Incomes

It will hardly be considered earth shattering to suggest that consumers' expectations about future income may affect their spending in important ways. This final determinant of consumer spending turns out to hold the key to answering the question we posed earlier. Why did the U.S. tax policy that succeeded so well in 1964 fail to alter consumer spending as much in 1968 and 1975?

Why U.S. Income-Tax Policy Failed in 1968 and 1975

To understand how expectations of future incomes affect current consumer expenditures, consider the abbreviated life histories of three consumers given in Table 7–2. The reason for giving our three imaginary individuals such odd names will be apparent shortly.

The consumer named "No Change" earned $100 in each of the four years considered in the table. The consumer named "Temporary Rise" earned $100 in three of the four years but had a good year in 1975. The consumer named "Permanent Rise" enjoyed a permanent rise in income in 1975 and was clearly the richest.

Table 7–2

INCOMES OF THREE CONSUMERS

| | INCOMES IN EACH YEAR | | | | TOTAL |
CONSUMER	1974	1975	1976	1977	INCOME
No Change	100	100	100	100	400
Temporary Rise	100	120	100	100	420
Permanent Rise	100	120	120	120	460

Now let us use our common sense to figure out how much each of these consumers might have spent in 1975. Temporary Rise and Permanent Rise had the same income that year. Do you think they spent the same amount? Not if they had some ability to foresee their future incomes, because Permanent Rise was richer in the long run.

Now compare No Change and Temporary Rise. Temporary Rise had 20 percent higher income in 1975 ($120 versus $100) but only 5 percent more over the entire four-year period ($420 versus $400). Do you think her spending was closer to 20 percent above No Change's or closer to 5 percent above it? Most people guess the latter.

The point of this example is that it is reasonable for consumers to decide on their *current* consumption spending by looking at their *long-run* income prospects. This should not be a shocking idea to most university students. How many of you are spending only what you earn this year? Probably not very many. And this is not because you are all foolish spendthrifts. On the contrary, you are rational planners. Knowing that your university education gives you a reasonable expectation of future income prospects much greater than those you now have, you are no doubt spending with that in mind.

Now what does all this have to do with the failure of the 1975 income-tax rebate in the United States? Imagine that the three rows in Table 7–2 now represent the entire economy under three different government policies. Recall that 1975 was the year of the rebate. The first row (No Change) shows the unchanged path of disposable income if no tax cut was enacted. The second (Temporary Rise) shows an increase in disposable income attributable to a tax cut *for one year only*. The bottom row (Permanent Rise) shows a policy that increases *DI* in *every future year* by cutting taxes permanently in 1975. Which of the two lower rows do you imagine would have generated more consumer spending in 1975? The bottom row (Permanent Rise), of course. What we have concluded, then, is this:

Permanent cuts in income taxes cause greater increases in consumer spending than do temporary cuts of equal magnitude.

The application of this analysis to the case of the 1975 tax cut is immediate. About half the cut was a refund of some of the 1974 taxes that had already been paid. These rebates were clearly one-time increases in income like that experienced by Temporary Rise in Table 7–2. No future income was affected. The remaining cuts came in the form of special reduced tax rates announced to apply in 1975 *only*, and thus might reasonably have been expected to be temporary as well. Since the 1975 tax-cut package had little effect on expected future incomes, it is not surprising that its impact on consumer spending was rather mild.

Much the same situation prevailed in 1968, when the U.S. Congress enacted a temporary 10 percent increase in income taxes to help finance the Vietnam War. Consumers considered the resulting decrease in their disposable income as only a *temporary* loss and did not curtail their spending as much as government officials had hoped. The general lesson is:

A permanent increase in income taxes provides a greater deterrent to consumer spending than does a temporary increase of equal magnitude.

We have, then, what appears to be a general principle, backed up both by historical evidence and common sense. Permanent changes in income taxes have a more significant impact on consumer spending than do temporary changes.

Though it may now seem obvious, this is not a lesson you would have learned from the introductory textbooks of 1968; it is one that was learned the hard way, through bitter experience. The tax surcharge of 1968 was meant to slow down inflation. Yet consumer prices rose faster in 1968 than they had in 1967, and faster in 1969 than in 1968. The tax reductions of 1975 were meant to halt a precipitous downswing in economic activity. It was subsequently learned that the recession had bottomed out, of its own accord, before the cuts became effective, and the recovery in consumer spending was far from spectacular.

The Canadian Sales-Tax Reduction of 1978

A sales-tax change does not affect consumption by changing household incomes. Instead, alterations in sales taxes change the relative price of buying a good now versus in the future. Indeed, the more *temporary* a sales-tax change is, the more *effective* it is.

For example, if a sales tax is cut for a six-month period, and households know that this is temporary, they probably will accelerate some purchases to fit within the six-month period. However, if they expect that the lower price will apply indefinitely, they may respond more sluggishly, so less spending is transferred to the recession period. This suggests that temporary sales-tax changes should be far more effective measures for managing aggregate demand than temporary income-tax changes.

Unfortunately, there is an important implementation problem that stems from our constitution. The retail sales tax is a provincial government instrument in Canada, while aggregate demand management is a federal government responsibility. The federal government does control the manufacturers' sales tax, which is levied at the wholesale level, but this tax raises relatively little revenue.

The federal government's Budget of 1978 represented an attempt to overcome this implementation problem (and it therefore illustrates the government's appreciation of the lessons we have learned from the U.S. experience with temporary income-tax changes). The federal government transferred some of its personal income-tax revenue to the provinces in return for a specified temporary sales-tax cut by the provinces. A full agreement was reached with all provinces except Alberta and Quebec. Alberta was excluded because there is no sales tax there. The Quebec government decided that political points could be scored by refusing to agree to the deal and by publicly decrying the meddling in provincial matters by the federal government. After two months of intense political wrangling, the federal government just paid all Quebec taxpayers directly an income-tax rebate of either $85 or the person's federal tax payable (whichever was less). This episode has made federal–provincial co-operation on sales-tax policy unlikely in the near future—which is unfortunate, in light of the lessons of this chapter.

The Predictability of Consumer Behaviour

We have now learned enough to see why the economist's problem in predicting how consumers will react to an increase or decrease in taxes is not quite as simple as suggested earlier in this chapter.

The principal problem seems to be anticipating how taxpayers will view any changes in the income-tax law. If the government *says* that an income-tax cut is permanent, will consumers *believe* it and increase their spending accordingly? Perhaps not, if the government has a history of raising taxes after promising to keep them low. Similarly, when (as in 1968 in the United States) the government explicitly announces that an income-tax increase is temporary, will consumers always believe this? Or might they greet such an announcement with a hefty dose of skepticism? This is quite possible if there is a long history of "temporary" tax increases that stayed on the books indefinitely.

Thus the effectiveness of any *future* tax-policy move may well depend on the government's *past* track record. A government that repeatedly uses a succession of so-called "permanent" income-tax cuts and income-tax increases for short-run stabilization purposes may find consumers beginning to ignore the tax changes entirely. The story of the boy who cried wolf is not yet required reading for fiscal policy planners, but it probably should be recommended.

Nor is this the only problem. Economists may underestimate or overestimate the degree of inertia in consumer behaviour. Their predictions may fail to take adequate account of large and rapid accumulations of wealth (as happened immediately after World War II, when consumption forecasts were notoriously low) or of sizable losses of wealth (such as the drastic decline in the stock market in 1973–75, when consumption forecasts were too high). Poor forecasts of future prices may lead consumption forecasts astray. And there are further hazards that we have not even mentioned here. Economic predictions are inexact, and predictions of consumption illustrate this well.

There is much more that can be said about the determinants of consumption, but it is best to leave the rest to more advanced courses. For we are now ready to apply our knowledge of the consumption function to the construction of the first model of the whole economy. While it is true that income determines consumption, the consumption function in turn helps to determine the level of income. If that sounds like circular reasoning, read the next chapter!

Summary

1. Aggregate demand is the total amount of goods and services that consumers, businesses, government units, and foreigners are willing to purchase. It can be expressed as the sum $C + I + G + X - IM$ where C is consumer spending, I is investment spending, G is government purchases, and $X - IM$ is exports minus imports.

2. Economists reserve the term "investment" to refer to purchases of newly produced factories, machinery, and homes.

3. National product is the total output of final goods and services of the economy. It is most commonly measured by the gross national product (GNP).

4. National income is the sum of the before-tax wages, interest, rents, and profits earned by all individuals in the economy. If we ignore incomes earned in other countries, and foreign-owned factors of production operating here, national income must by necessity be equal to national product.

5. Disposable income is the sum of the incomes of all individuals in the economy, after taxes and transfers, and is the chief determinant of consumer expenditure.

6. All of these concepts, and others, can be depicted in a circular flow diagram that shows expenditures from all four sources flowing into business firms and national income flowing out.

7. The government often has tried to manipulate aggregate demand by influencing private expenditure decisions.

8. The close relationship between consumer spending (C) and disposable income (DI) is called the consumption function. Its slope, which is used to predict the change in consumption that will be caused by a change in income taxes, is called the marginal propensity to consume (MPC).

9. Changes in disposable income move us along a given consumption function. Changes in any of the other variables that affect C will shift the entire consumption function. Among the most important of these other variables are total consumer wealth, the price level, and expected future incomes.

10. Because consumers hold so many money fixed assets, they lose out when prices rise, which leads them to reduce their spending. This decline in consumer demand when prices rise helps explain why the aggregate-demand curve slopes downward.

11. Future income prospects help explain why U.S. tax policy did not affect consumption as much as was hoped in 1968 and 1975. This is because the 1968 tax increase and the 1975 tax cut were both temporary, and therefore left future incomes unaffected. By contrast, the U.S. tax cut of 1964 was "permanent," and affected future as well as current incomes. It is no surprise, then, that the 1964 actions had stronger effects on spending than did the 1968 or 1975 actions.

12. Temporary sales-tax changes affect consumption by changing the ratio of current to future prices, and therefore their impact does not depend on any change in people's permanent income position. However, the retail sales tax is a provincial matter in Canada, while aggregate-demand management is a federal responsibility.

Concepts for Review

Aggregate demand	National income (GNP)	Marginal propensity to consume (MPC)
Consumer expenditure (C)	Gross domestic product (GDP)	
Investment spending (I)	Disposable income (DI)	Movements along versus shifts of the consumption function
Government purchases (G)	Circular flow diagram	
Exports (X)	Transfer payments	Money fixed assets
Imports (IM)	Scatter diagram	Temporary versus permanent tax changes
$C + I + G + X - IM$	Consumption function	

Questions for Discussion

1. What are the four components of aggregate demand? Which of these is the largest?

2. What is the difference between "investment" as the term is used by most people and "investment" as defined by an economist? Which of the following acts constitute "investment" according to the economist's definition?

   a. General Motors constructs a new assembly line.

   b. You buy 100 shares of General Motors stock.

   c. A small steel company goes bankrupt, and Stelco purchases its factory and equipment.

   d. Your family buys a newly constructed home from a developer.

   e. Your family buys an older home from another family. (*Hint*: Are any *new* products demanded by this action?)

3. What would the circular flow diagram (Figure 7–1, page 115) look like in an economy with no government? Draw one for yourself.
4. The marginal propensity to consume (MPC) for the nation as a whole is roughly 0.90. Explain in words what this means. What is your personal MPC?
5. Look at the scatter diagram in Figure 7–4 (page 121). What does it tell you about what was going on in this country in the years 1942–45?
6. What is a "consumption function," and why is it a useful device for government economists planning a tax cut?
7. On a piece of graph paper, construct the consumption function for Simpleland from the following data:

YEAR	CONSUMER SPENDING	DISPOSABLE INCOME
1981	110	100
1982	155	150
1983	200	200
1984	245	250
1985	290	300

What is the MPC?

8. In which direction will the consumption function for Simpleland shift if the price level rises? Show this on your graph.
9. Explain why permanent income-tax cuts are likely to lead to bigger increases in consumer spending than are temporary income-tax cuts.

Appendix A
The Saving Function and the Marginal Propensity to Save

There is an alternative way of looking at the relationships we have discussed in this chapter. Disposable income that is not spent must be saved. Therefore we can examine the effect of income on *saving* as well as its effect on consumer *spending*.

To see how saving appears on the consumption function diagram, we have repeated the consumption function of Macroland (see Figure 7–7) in Figure 7–9 and added a 45° line. You will recall that a 45° line marks those points where the distances along the horizontal and vertical axes are equal. (If you wish to review, see page 24.) Since the consumption schedule is below the 45° line, the figure shows that consumer spending is less than income, so some is being *saved*.

To find the amount of saving at each level of income, we need only read the vertical distance from the consumption function up to the 45° line. For example, when income is $400 billion, saving is the distance AB, or $70 billion.

There is also a more direct way to find saving. Table 7–3 repeats the consumption and disposable income data for Macroland from Table 7–1 (page 123). Then, in column 3, we compute the difference between disposable income and consumption, which gives us **aggregate saving**.

Aggregate saving is the difference between disposable income and consumer expenditure. In symbols, $S = DI - C$.

The subtraction is exactly what we showed graphically in Figure 7–9. Columns 2 and 3 of Table

7–3 constitute what economists call the **saving function**.

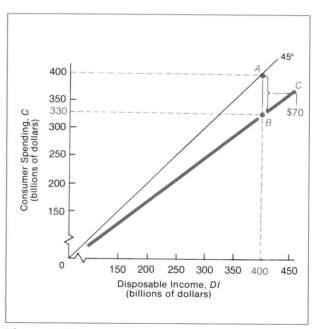

Figure 7–9
THE CONSUMPTION FUNCTION OF MACROLAND
The consumption function of Macroland, which we encountered in Figure 7–7 (page 124), is repeated here, and a 45° line is added for convenience. Since consumption and saving must always add up to disposable income, the vertical distance between the two lines represents saving. For example, points A and B indicate that when disposable income is $400 billion, saving is $70 billion.

Table 7-3

SAVING IN MACROLAND

YEAR	(1) CONSUMPTION, C	(2) DISPOSABLE INCOME, DI	(3) SAVING, S	(4) MARGINAL PROPENSITY TO SAVE, MPS
1980	170	200	30	0.2
1981	210	250	40	0.2
1982	250	300	50	0.2
1983	290	350	60	0.2
1984	330	400	70	0.2
1985	370	450	80	

The **saving function** is the schedule relating total consumer saving to total disposable income in the economy, holding other determinants of saving constant.

These data are portrayed in Figure 7–10, which is constructed from the numbers in Table 7–3. It could equally well have been constructed as the difference between the 45° line and the C line in Figure 7–9. (Because saving is so much less than consumption, we have stretched the scale of the vertical axis considerably.) Points A and B correspond to the same points in Figure 7–9. When the consumption function is a straight line, and thus has a constant slope, the same will be true of the saving function. In Figure 7–10, we show this slope as the ratio of distance EB to distance DE or $40 billion/$200 billion = 0.2. Economists call this slope the **marginal propensity to save**.

The **marginal propensity to save** (or MPS) is the slope of the saving function. It tells us how much more consumers will save if disposable income rises by one unit.

You may have noticed that the MPS is 0.2 while the MPC for Macroland is 0.8. They add up to 1, and not by accident. Since the portion of each additional dollar of disposable income that is not spent must be saved, the MPC and the MPS always add up to 1. It is a simple fact of accounting.

The MPC and the MPS always add up to 1, meaning that an additional dollar of income must be divided between consumption and saving. In symbols:

$$MPC + MPS = 1.$$

This enables us to compute either one of them from the other.

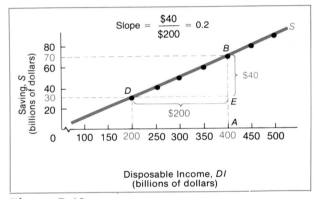

Figure 7–10

THE SAVING FUNCTION OF MACROLAND

The saving function of Macroland, depicted here, can be constructed either from the data in Table 7–3 or from Figure 7–9. This is because when we plot saving against disposable income (as we do here), we are also plotting the difference between consumption and disposable income (the vertical distance between line C and the 45° line in Figure 7–9) against disposable income.

Summary

1. Instead of studying the consumption function, it is possible to study the same data by looking at the saving function, which is defined as the relationship between disposable income and consumer saving.

2. Since consumer saving is merely the difference between disposable income and consumer expenditure, everything we have learned about the consumption function applies to the saving function.

3. The amount of additional saving caused by a growth of $1 in disposable income is called the marginal propensity to save, or MPS.

4. Since each additional $1 of disposable income is either spent or saved, the MPC and the MPS must always add up to 1. Thus, knowledge of one implies knowledge of the other.

Concepts for Review

Aggregate saving
Saving function
Marginal propensity to save (MPS)

Questions for Discussion

1. Look at the circular flow diagram in Figure 7–1 (page 115). Where does the saving function enter the picture?
2. Take the data from Simpleland in Question 7 on page 131 and use them to construct a saving function for Simpleland on a piece of graph paper.

3. (More difficult.) If taxes are cut *temporarily* and consumer spending does not increase much, what must happen to consumer saving?

Appendix B
National Income Accounting

The type of macroeconomic analysis presented in this book dates from the publication of John Maynard Keynes's *The General Theory of Employment, Interest, and Money* in 1936. But at that time there was really no way to test Keynes's theories because the necessary data did not exist. It took some years for the theoretical notions used by Keynes to find concrete expression in real-world data. The system of measurement devised for this purpose is called **national income accounting**.

The development of this system of accounts ranks as a great achievement in applied economics, perhaps as important in its own right as Keynes's theoretical work. For without it the practical value of Keynesian analysis would be severely limited. Many men and women spent long hours wrestling with the numerous difficult conceptual questions that arose in translating the theory into numbers, but they had one acknowledged leader: Professor Simon Kuznets of Harvard University, who, in 1971, was awarded the Nobel Prize in Economics for his contributions to economic measurement techniques. Along the way some more-or-less arbitrary decisions and conventions had to be made. You may not agree with all of them, but the accounting framework that was devised is eminently serviceable, though, inevitably, it has some limitations that must be understood.

Defining GNP: Exceptions to the Rules

We first encountered the concept of **gross national product** (GNP) in Chapter 5.

Gross national product (GNP) is the sum of the money values of all final goods and services produced by domestically owned factors of production during a specified period of time, usually one year.

However, the definition of GNP given there, and repeated above for your convenience, has certain exceptions we have not yet noted. Three major exceptions are discussed here.

First, the treatment of government output involves a minor departure from the principle of using market prices. Outputs of private industries are sold on markets, so their prices are observed. But "outputs" of government offices are not sold; indeed, it is sometimes even difficult to define what those outputs are. Lacking prices for outputs, national income accountants fall back on the only prices they have: prices for the inputs from which the outputs are produced. Thus:

Government outputs are valued at the cost of the inputs needed to produce them.

This means, for example, that if a clerk at the Department of Transportation and Communications earns $8 an hour and spends one-half hour torturing you with explanations of why you cannot get a driver's licence, that particular government "service" is considered as being worth $4, and will increase GNP by that amount.

Second, some goods that are not actually sold on markets during the year are none the less counted in that year's GNP. These are the goods that are produced during the year but not sold; that is, goods that firms stockpile as *inventories*. Goods that are added to inventories are part of the GNP even though they do not pass through markets.

National income statisticians treat inventories as if they were "bought" by the firms that produced them, even though this "purchase" never takes place.

Finally, the treatment of investment goods runs slightly counter to the rule that only final goods are to be counted. In a broad sense, factories, generators, machine tools, and the like might be considered as intermediate goods. After all, their owners want them only for use in producing other goods, not for any innate value that they possess. But this would present a real problem, for factories and machines normally are never sold to consumers. So when would we count them in GNP? National income statisticians avoid this problem by defining investment goods as final products demanded by the firms that buy them.

Now that we have a complete definition of just what the GNP is, let us turn to the problem of actually measuring it. National income accountants have devised three ways to perform this task, and we consider each of them in turn.

GNP as the Sum of Final Goods and Services

The first way to measure GNP seems to be the most natural, since it follows so directly from the circular flow diagram in this chapter. It also turns out to be the most useful definition from the point of view of macroeconomics. We simply add up the final demands of all consumers, business firms, the government and foreigners. Using the symbols C, I, G, X, and IM as we did in the text, we have:

$$GNP = C + I + G + X - IM.$$

The I that appears in the actual Canadian national accounts is called **gross private domestic investment**. The word "gross" will be explained presently. "Private" indicates that government investment is considered part of G, and "domestic" just means that machinery sold by Canadian firms to foreign companies is included in exports. Gross private domestic investment in Canada has three components: business investment in plant and equipment, residential construction (home building),[8] and inventory investment. We repeat again that *only* these three things

are **investment** in national income accounting terminology.

As defined in the national income accounts, **investment** includes only newly produced goods, such as machinery, factories, and new homes. It does not include exchanges of existing assets.

In common parlance, all sorts of activities that are not part of the GNP are often called "investment." People are said to "invest" in the stock market when they purchase shares. Or wealthy individuals "invest" in works of art. But since transactions like these merely exchange one type of asset (money) for another (stock or art works), they are not included in the GNP.

The symbol G, for government purchases, represents the *volume of current goods and services purchased by all levels of government*. Thus, anything the government pays to its employees is counted in G, as are its purchases of paper, pencils, airplanes, bombs, typewriters, and so forth.

Very few citizens realize that *most of what the federal government spends its money on is not for purchases of goods and services*. Instead, it is on **transfer payments**—literally, giving away money—either to individuals or to other levels of government.

The importance of the conceptual distinction lies in the fact that G represents the part of the national product that government uses up for its own purposes—to pay for armies, bureaucrats, paper, and ink—whereas transfer payments merely represent shuffling of purchasing power from one group of citizens to another group. Except for the administrators needed to run the programs, real economic resources are not used up in this process. In adding up the nation's total output as the sum of $C + I + G + X - IM$, we are summing the shares of GNP that are used up by consumers, investors, governments, and foreigners, respectively. Since transfer payments merely give someone the capability to spend on C, it is logical to exclude them from our definition of G, including in C only the portion of these transfer payments that is spent. If we included them in G, the same spending would get counted twice: once in G and then again in C.

Table 7–4 shows the GNP for 1983 computed as the sum of $C + I + G + X - IM$.

GNP as the Sum of All Factor Payments

There is another way to count up the GNP—*by adding up all the incomes in the economy*. Let's see how this method handles some typical transactions. Suppose Canadian General Electric sells a generator to Ontario

---

[8] Thus purchases of new homes are considered part of I rather than part of C.

Table 7–4

GROSS NATIONAL PRODUCT IN 1983 AS THE SUM OF FINAL DEMANDS

ITEM		AMOUNT (billions of dollars)
Personal consumption expenditures (C)		229.0
Gross private domestic investment (I)		64.5
Government purchase of goods and services (G)		94.5
Net exports (X–IM)		0.7
exports (X)	108.2	
imports (IM)	107.5	
Gross national product (Y)		388.7

SOURCE: Statistics Canada

Hydro for a price of $1 million. The first method of calculating GNP simply counts the $1 million as part of *I*. The second method asks: What incomes resulted from the production of this generator? The answer might be something like this:

Wages of C.G.E. employees	$400,000
Interest to bondholders	$50,000
Rentals of buildings	$50,000
Profits of C.G.E. stockholders	$100,000.

The total is $600,000. The remaining $400,000 is accounted for by inputs that C.G.E. purchased from other companies: steel, circuitry, tubing, rubber, and so on.

But if we traced this $400,000 back further, we would find that it is accounted for by the wages, interest, and rentals paid by these other companies, *plus* their profits, *plus* their purchases from other firms. In fact, for *every* firm in the economy, there is an accounting identity that says:

$$\text{Revenues from sales} = \left\{ \begin{array}{l} \text{Wages paid +} \\ \text{Interest paid +} \\ \text{Rentals paid +} \\ \text{Profits earned +} \\ \text{Purchases from} \\ \text{other firms.} \end{array} \right.$$

Why must this always be true? Because profits are the balancing item; they are what is *left over* after the firm has made all its other payments. In fact, this accounting identity is really just the definition of profits: sales revenue less all costs of production.

Now apply this accounting identity to *all the firms in the economy*. Total purchases from other firms are precisely what we call *intermediate goods*. What, then, do we get if we subtract these intermediate transactions from both sides of the equation?

$$\left. \begin{array}{l} \text{Revenues from sales} \\ \text{minus} \\ \text{Purchases from} \\ \text{other firms} \end{array} \right\} = \left\{ \begin{array}{l} \text{Wages paid +} \\ \text{Interest paid +} \\ \text{Rentals paid +} \\ \text{Profits earned.} \end{array} \right.$$

On the right-hand side, we have the sum of all factor incomes: payments to labour, land, and capital. On the left-hand side, we have total sales minus sales of intermediate goods. This means that we have only sales of *final* goods, which is precisely our definition of GNP. Thus, the accounting identity for the entire economy can be rewritten as:

GNP = Wages + Interest + Rents + Profits,

and this gives national income accountants another way to measure the GNP.

Table 7–5 shows 1983's GNP measured by the sum of all incomes. Once again, a few details have been omitted in our discussion. The sum of wages, interest, rents, and profits actually adds up to only $299 billion (whereas GNP was $388.7 billion). We call this sum the **national income** because it is the sum of all factor payments. But the actual selling prices of goods include another category of income

Table 7–5

GROSS NATIONAL PRODUCT IN 1983 AS THE SUM OF INCOMES

ITEM	AMOUNT (billions of dollars)
Wages, salaries, and supplementary labour income	219.8
plus	
Interest and miscellaneous investment income	30.4
plus	
Rents and net income of farmers and unincorporated business	16.5
plus	
Corporation profits before profits taxes	32.3
equals	
National income	299.0
plus	
Indirect business taxes (less subsidies) and miscellaneous items	42.7
equals	
Net national product	341.7
plus	
Depreciation	47.0
equals	
Gross national product	388.7

SOURCE: Statistics Canada

that we have ignored so far: sales taxes, excise taxes, and the like. National income statisticians call these *indirect business taxes*, and when we add these to national income we obtain the **net national product (NNP)**.

Now we are almost at the GNP. The only difference between GNP and NNP is **depreciation** of the nation's capital stock.

Depreciation is the value of the portion of the nation's capital equipment that is used up within the year. It tells us how much output is needed just to keep the economy's capital stock intact.

The difference between "gross" and "net" simply refers to whether depreciation is included or excluded. We add depreciation to NNP to get GNP. Thus, GNP is a measure of all final output taking no account of the capital used up in the process (and therefore in need of replacement). NNP deducts the required replacements to arrive at a *net* production figure.

From a conceptual point of view, most economists feel that NNP is a more meaningful indicator of the economy's output than GNP. After all, the depreciation component of GNP represents the output that is needed just to repair and replace worn out factories and machines; it is not available for anybody to consume.[9] So NNP seems to be a better measure of well-being than GNP. But, alas, GNP is much easier to measure because depreciation is a particularly tricky item. (What fraction of his tractor did Farmer Jones "use up" last year? How much did Montreal's Olympic Stadium depreciate during 1984?) Since the sum of expenditure method of calculation can be used for it, most economists feel that GNP is measured more accurately than is NNP. For this reason, most economic models are based on GNP.

In Table 7–5 you can hardly help noticing the preponderant share of employee compensation in total national income—75 percent. Labour is by far the most important factor of production. Corporate profits before tax account for 11 percent of national income (8 percent of GNP), perhaps less than the public thinks. If, by some magic stroke, we could eliminate all corporate profits without upsetting the performance of the economy, the average worker would get a raise of about 14 percent!

GNP as the Sum of Values Added

We come now to the third, and final, way to measure the GNP. But before we explain this method, we must introduce a new concept, called **value added**.

[9] If it is used for consumption, the capital stock will decline, and the nation will wind up poorer than before.

The **value added** by a firm is its revenue from selling a product minus the amounts paid for goods and services purchased from other firms.

The intuitive sense of the concept is clear: If a firm buys some inputs from other firms, does something to them, and sells the resulting product for a price higher than it paid for the inputs, we say that the firm has "added value" to the product. If we sum up the values added in this way by all the firms in the economy, we must get the total value of all final products. Thus:

GNP can be measured as the sum of the values added by all firms.

To verify that this is so, look back at the first accounting identity on page 135. The left-hand side of this equation, sales revenue minus purchases from other firms, is just what we mean by the firm's value added. Thus:

Value added = Wages + Interest + Rents + Profits.

Since the second method we gave for measuring GNP is to add up wages, interest, rents, and profits, we see that the value-added approach must also yield the same answer.

The value-added concept is particularly useful in avoiding double counting. Often it is hard to distinguish intermediate goods from final goods. Paint bought by a painter, for example, is an intermediate good. But paint bought by a do-it-yourselfer is a final good. What happens, then, if the professional painter has some paint left over and uses it to refurbish his own garage? The intermediate good becomes a final good. You can see that the line between intermediate goods and final goods is a fuzzy one in practice.

If we measure GNP by the sum of values added, however, it is not necessary to make such subtle distinctions. In this method, *every* purchase of a new good or service counts, but we do not count the entire selling price, only the part that represents value added.

To illustrate this idea, consider the data in Table 7–6 and how they would affect GNP as the sum of final products. Our example begins when a farmer who grows soybeans sells them to a mill for $3 a bushel. This transaction does *not* count in the GNP, because the miller does not purchase the soybeans for his own use. The miller then grinds up the soybeans and sells the resulting bag of soy meal to a factory that produces soy sauce. The miller receives $4, but GNP still has not increased because the ground beans are also an intermediate product. Next, the factory turns the beans into soy sauce, which it sells to your favorite Chinese restaurant for $8. Still no effect on

Table 7-6

AN ILLUSTRATION OF FINAL AND INTERMEDIATE GOODS

ITEM	SELLER	BUYER	PRICE
Bushel of soybeans	Farmer	Miller	$ 3
Bag of soy meal	Miller	Factory	4
Bottle of soy sauce	Factory	Restaurant	8
Bottle of soy sauce used as seasoning	Restaurant	Consumers	10
		Total:	$25
		Addendum: Contribution to GNP:	$10

GNP. But then the big moment arrives: The restaurant sells the sauce to you and other customers as a part of your meals, and you eat it. At this point, the $10 worth of soy sauce becomes a final product and is included in the GNP.

What is the logic of this procedure? Transactions in intermediate goods also have value. So why do we not count these along with transactions in final goods? The reason is that we are interested in measuring the economy's new output, and if we counted all the intermediate goods, we would be double or triple counting by including an item each time it changed hands. We would get an exaggerated impression of the amount of job-creating economic activity that is actually going on.

Look again at Table 7-6, which summarizes the four transactions in the life of the soybeans. As we have just noted, only the last transaction counts in the GNP. So all of this activity raises GNP by $10. If we had also counted the three intermediate transactions (farmer to miller, miller to factory, factory to restaurant), we would have come up with $25—two and one-half times too much.

Why is it too much? The reason is straightforward. Neither the miller nor the factory owner nor the restauranteur value the product we have been considering *for its own sake*. Only the customers who eat the final product (the soy sauce) have had an increase in their material well-being. So only this last transaction counts in the GNP. However, as we shall now see, value-added calculations enable us to come up

with the right answer ($10) by counting only part of each transaction. The basic idea is to count at each step only the contribution to the value of the ultimate final product that is made at that step, excluding the values of items produced at earlier steps.

Ignoring the minor items (such as fertilizer) that the farmer purchases from others, the entire $3 selling price of the bushel of soybeans is new output produced by the farmer; that is, the whole $3 is value added. The miller then grinds the beans and sells them for $4. He has added $4 – $3 = $1 to the value of the beans. When the factory turns this soy meal into soy sauce and sells it for $8, it has added $8 – $4 = $4 more in value. And finally, when the restaurant sells it to hungry customers for $10, a further $2 of value is added.

Table 7-7 shows this chain of creation of value added by appending another column to Table 7-6. We see that the total value added by all four firms is $10, exactly the same as the restaurant's selling price. This is as it must be, for only the restaurant sells the soybeans as a final product.

Alternative Measures of the Income of the Nation

Economists use the term *national income* in two different ways. The most common usage is as a general term indicating the size of the income of the nation as a whole, without being very specific as to exactly how this income is to be measured. This is the sense in

Table 7-7

AN ILLUSTRATION OF VALUE ADDED

ITEM	SELLER	BUYER	PRICE	VALUE ADDED
Bushel of soybeans	Farmer	Miller	$ 3	$ 3
Bag of soy meal	Miller	Factory	4	1
Bottle of soy sauce	Factory	Restaurant	8	4
Bottle of soy sauce used as seasoning	Restaurant	Consumers	10	2
		Totals:	$25	$10

Addendum: Contribution to GNP
Final products $10
Sum of values added $10

which the term "national income" is used in this book. The second, and much more precise, use of the term refers to a very specific concept in national income accounting, which we encountered in Table 7–5 on page 135.

Aside from this formal definition of national income, what other accounting concept might be used to measure the total income of the nation? The first and most obvious candidate is the GNP itself. We noted earlier that GNP correlates very well with GDP, and so is a good measure of employment-creating production activity in the nation. However, the GNP has several drawbacks as a measure of income. First, it includes some output that represents income to no one—output that simply replaces worn out machinery and buildings (depreciation). When we deduct this depreciation, we obtain the net national product (NNP), as shown in Figure 7–11. Second, because of sales taxes and related items (indirect business taxes), part of the price paid for each good and service does not represent the income of any individual. When we deduct these indirect business taxes from NNP, we arrive at the formal definition of national income (refer again to Figure 7–11). Both of these accounting concepts have already been described.

There are, however, two other measures of income. **Personal income** is meant to be a better measure of the income that actually accrues to indi-viduals. It is obtained from national income by *subtracting* corporate profits taxes, retained earnings, and payroll taxes (because these items are never received by individuals) and then *adding in* transfer payments to individuals (because these sources of income are not part of the wages, interest, rents, or profits that constitute the national income). As Figure 7–11 suggests, this adding and subtracting normally results in a number that is rather close to national income. Finally, if we subtract personal income taxes from personal income, we obtain **disposable income**.

Among all the concepts of the nation's income depicted in Figure 7–11, only two are used frequently in the construction of models of the economy: gross national product (GNP) and disposable income (DI). Since the models presented in this book ignore depreciation and indirect business taxes, GNP is basically identical to national income (see Figure 7–11). Similarly, if we ignore retained earnings, GNP and DI differ only by the amounts of taxes and transfers (again, see Figure 7–11).

Limitations of the GNP: What GNP Is Not

Having seen in some detail what the GNP *is*, it is worth pausing to expand upon what it *is not*. In particular:

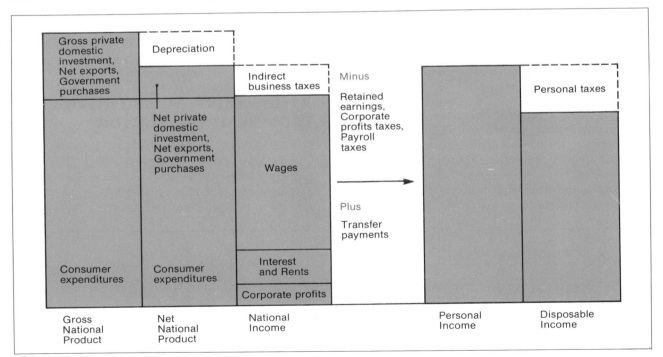

Figure 7–11

ALTERNATIVE MEASURES OF THE INCOME OF THE NATION

This bar chart indicates the relationships among the five alternative measures of the total income of the nation, starting with the largest and most comprehensive measure (GNP) and ranging down to the measure that most closely approximates the spendable income of consumers (disposable income).

Gross national product is not a measure of the nation's economic well-being.

Here are several reasons why:

1. *Only market activity is included in GNP.* Work done by housewives and do-it-your-selfers certainly contributes to the nation's well-being, but it is not measured in the GNP because it has no price tag.

An important implication of this exclusion is seen when we try to compare the GNPs of developed and less developed countries. Canadian students are always incredulous to learn that the per-capita GNP of the poorest African countries is less than $200 a year. Surely, no one could survive in Canada on $4 a week. How can Africans do it? One part of the answer, of course, is that these people are incredibly poor. We shall study their plight in Chapter 40. But another part of the answer is that:

International GNP comparisons are vastly misleading when the two countries differ greatly in the fraction of economic activity that each conducts in organized markets.

This fraction is relatively large in Canada and relatively small in the less developed countries, so when we compare their respective measured GNPs we are not comparing the same economic activities at all. Many things that get counted in the Canadian GNP are not counted in the GNPs of less developed nations. So it is ludicrous to think that these people, poor as they are, survive on what to Canadians would amount to $4 a week.

2. *GNP places no value on leisure.* As a country gets richer, one of the things that happens is that its citizens take more and more leisure time. The steady decrease in the length of the typical workweek in Canada is sufficient evidence for this. This means that the gap is steadily widening between official GNP and some truer measure of national well-being that would include the value of leisure time. For this reason, growth in GNP systematically *understates* the growth in national well-being. But there are also

reasons why the GNP *overstates* how well off we are; we consider these next.

3. *"Bads" as well as "goods" get counted in GNP.* Suppose there is a natural disaster—as when the Ocean Ranger oil-drilling rig sank off the coast of Newfoundland in 1982. Surely the well-being of the nation was diminished by this catastrophe. Much expensive equipment was lost, and of course, many people were killed. Yet the disaster may well have caused GNP to rise. Replacing the machinery added to I; extra government spending for relief, searches, and legal investigations all added to G. Yet no one would think that the nation was better off for its higher GNP.

Wars represent an extreme example of this. Mobilization for outright war always causes a country's GNP to rise rapidly. But men called into the army could be producing civilian output. Factories needed to produce armaments could instead be making cars, washing machines, and televisions. A country at war is surely worse off than a country at peace, but this fact will not be reflected in its GNP accounts.

4. *Ecological costs are not netted out of the GNP.* Many of the activities in a modern industrial economy that produce goods and services also have undesirable side effects on the environment. Automobiles provide enjoyment and a means of transportation, but they also despoil the atmosphere. Factories pollute rivers and lakes while manufacturing valuable commodities. Almost everything seems to produce garbage, which creates the problem of what to do with it. None of these ecological costs are deducted from the GNP in an effort to give us a truer measure of the *net* increase in economic welfare that our economy produces. Is this foolishness? Not if we remember the job that national income statisticians are trying to do: They are measuring the economic activity conducted through organized markets not national welfare. Our main interest in the GNP stems from its being a measure of the amount of job-creating economic activity that is taking place. Thus, the fact that it is not intended to measure well-being is not a serious limitation.

Summary

1. Gross national product (GNP) is the sum of the money values of all final goods and services produced during a year and sold on organized markets. There are, however, certain exceptions to this definition.
2. One way to measure the GNP is to add up the final demands of consumers, investors, governments, and foreigners: GNP = $C + I + G + X - IM$.
3. A second way to measure the GNP is to start with all

the factor payments—wages, interest, rents, and profits—that constitute the national income, and then add indirect business taxes and depreciation.
4. A third way to measure the GNP is to sum up the values added by every firm in the economy (and then once again add indirect business taxes and depreciation).
5. Except for possible bookkeeping and statistical errors,

all three methods must give the same answer.

6. The GNP is meant to be a measure of the *production* of the economy, not of the increase in its *well-being*. For example, the GNP places no value on housework and other do-it-yourself activities, nor on leisure time.

On the other hand, even commodities that might be considered as "bads" rather than "goods" are counted in the GNP (for example, activities that harm the environment).

Concepts for Review

National income accounting	Transfer payments	Depreciation
Gross national product (GNP)	Net exports	Value added
Inventories	National income	Personal income
Gross private domestic investment	Net national product (NNP)	Disposable income
Government purchases		

Questions for Discussion

1. Which of the following transactions are included in the gross national product, and by how much does each raise GNP?
   a. You buy a new car, paying $6000.
   b. You buy a used car, paying $2000.
   c. IBM builds a $40 million factory to make computers.
   d. An unemployed worker receives a government check for $300 in unemployment compensation.
   e. General Motors builds 1000 Cadillacs at a cost of $14,000 each. Unable to sell them, it holds them as inventories.
   f. Mr. Black and Mr. Blue, each out for a Sunday drive, have a collision in which their cars are destroyed. Black and Blue each hire a lawyer to sue the other, paying the lawyers $2000 each for services rendered. The judge throws the case out of court.
   g. You sell a $200 painting to your roommate.

2. Explain the difference between final goods and intermediate goods. Why is it sometimes difficult to apply this distinction in practice? In this regard, why is the concept of value added useful?

3. Explain the difference between government spending and government purchases of goods and services (G). Which is larger?

4. Explain why national income and gross national product would be exactly equal if there were no depreciation and no indirect business taxes.

5. Give some reasons why the gross national product is not a suitable measure of the well-being of the nation. (Have you noticed newspaper accounts in which journalists seem to use GNP for this purpose?)

6. The following is a complete description of all economic activity in Trivialand for the year 1984. Draw up versions of Tables 7–4 and 7–5 for Trivialand showing GNP computed in two different ways.
   a. There are thousands of farmers but only two big business firms in Trivialand: Specific Motors (an auto company) and Super Duper (a chain of food markets). There is no government and no depreciation.

   b. Specific Motors produced 1000 small cars, which they sold at $6000 each, and 100 trucks, which they sold at $8000 each. Consumers bought 800 of the cars, and the remaining 200 cars were exported to the United States. Super Duper bought all the trucks.
   c. Sales at Super Duper markets amounted to $14 million, all of it sold to consumers.
   d. All the farmers in Trivialand are self-employed and sell all their wares to Super Duper.
   e. The costs incurred by all the businesses were as follows:

	SPECIFIC MOTORS	SUPER DUPER	FARMERS
Wages	$3,800,000	$4,500,000	0
Interest	100,000	200,000	700,000
Rent	200,000	1,000,000	2,000,000
Purchases of food	0	7,000,000	0

7. (More difficult.) Now complicate Trivialand in the following ways and answer the same questions. In addition, calculate national income, personal income, and disposable income.
   a. The government bought 50 cars, leaving only 150 cars for export. In addition, the government spent $800,000 on wages for soldiers and made $1,200,000 in transfer payments.
   b. Depreciation for the year amounted to $600,000 for Specific Motors and $200,000 for Super Duper. (The farmers had no depreciation.)
   c. The government levied sales taxes amounting to $500,000 on Specific Motors and $200,000 on Super Duper (none on farmers). In addition, the government levied a 10 percent income tax on all wages, interest, and rental income.
   d. In addition to the food and cars mentioned in Question 6, consumers in Trivialand imported 500 computers from Canada at $2000 each.

Demand-Side Equilibrium: Unemployment or Inflation?

Investment ... is a flighty
bird, which needs to be
controlled.
J.R. HICKS

As we learned in Chapter 5, the interaction of aggregate demand and aggregate supply determines whether the economy will stagnate or prosper, and whether our resources of labour and capital will be fully employed or unemployed. This is the first of eight chapters devoted to studying this important process.

A simplified model of aggregate demand is constructed in Chapters 8 and 9, and the supply side is added in Chapter 10. This first model of the economy teaches us much about the causes of unemployment and inflation, but it is too simple to deal with policy issues because the government and the financial system are largely ignored. Chapters 11–14 remedy these omissions, thereby making it possible to study how government policies affect unemployment and inflation. By Chapter 15 we will have provided a model that is capable of dealing with a wide variety of policy issues.

In Chapter 7 we examined the largest component of aggregate demand, which is consumer expenditure (C); here, we turn our attention first to the most volatile component, investment (I), and discuss its determinants and the reasons why investment spending is so variable and so difficult to predict.[1] Then, rather than waiting for a full discussion of the other components of aggregate demand, government purchases (G), and net exports (X – IM), we construct an abbreviated model of the determination of national income based only on the C and I components. We use this model to provide a preliminary description of how the state of aggregate demand influences the level of the gross national product and to consider a question of great importance to policy-makers: Can the economy be expected to achieve full employment of its resources if the government does not intervene?

[1] We repeat the warning given in the previous chapter about the meaning of the word *investment*. It *includes* spending by businesses and individuals on *newly produced* factories, machinery, and houses. But it *excludes* sales of *used* industrial plants, equipment, and homes, and it *also excludes* purely financial transactions, such as the purchase of stocks and bonds.

The Extreme Variability of Investment

The first thing to be said about investment spending is that it is extraordinarily variable.

Unlike consumer spending, which follows movements in disposable income with great (though not perfect) reliability, investment spending swings from high to low levels with annoying rapidity. During recessions, for example, the decline in investment generally constitutes the greatest part of the total drop in real GNP, despite the fact that investment is a much smaller portion of GNP than is consumption. What accounts for these movements of investment demand?

Business Confidence and Expectations About the Future

While many factors influence business people's desires to invest, Keynes himself laid great stress on the *state of business confidence*, which in turn depends on *expectations about the future*.

While it is tricky to measure, it does seem obvious that businesses will build more factories and purchase more new machines when their expectations are optimistic. Conversely, their investment plans will be very cautious if the economic outlook appears bleak. Keynes pointed out that psychological perceptions like these are subject to abrupt shifts, so that fluctuations in investment can be a major cause of instability in aggregate demand. Thus, we see the logic in Hicks's analogy to a "flighty bird."

Unfortunately, neither economists nor, for that matter, psychologists have any very good ideas about how to *measure*—much less how to *control*—business confidence. Therefore, economists usually focus on several more objective determinants of investment—determinants that are easy to quantify and more easily influenced by government policy.

The Rate of Interest

The interest rate is the determinant of investment that is perhaps most extensively discussed by economists. A good deal of business investment is financed by borrowing, and the interest rate indicates how much firms must pay for that privilege. The higher the interest rate, the more costly it is to borrow. Some investment projects that look profitable at an interest rate of 7 percent will look disastrous if the firm has to pay 12 percent. Thus:

The amount that businesses will want to invest depends on the real interest rate they have to pay on their borrowings. The lower the real rate of interest, the more investment spending there will be.

In Chapter 13 we will study in some detail how the government can influence the rate of interest. Since interest rates affect investment, policy-makers have a handle on aggregate demand—a handle they do not hesitate to use. The point is that, unlike business confidence, interest rates are visible and manipulable, at least for short periods. Therefore, even if investment responds much more dramatically to changes in confidence than to changes in interest rates, interest rates attract more attention as a potential instrument of government policy.

The State of Demand and Capacity Utilization

There will be a strong incentive to invest when firms find that demand is pressing against their capacity. Under these circumstances, firms are very likely to feel that new factories and machinery can be employed profitably. By contrast, if there is a great deal of spare capacity (unused machinery, empty factories, and so on), business managers will not find investment attractive even if interest rates are very low.

The Growth of Demand

Since it takes a substantial amount of time to order machinery or to build a factory, investment plans are made with an eye on the future. Even when pressures on current capacity are not particularly severe, a firm experiencing rapid growth in sales is likely to start investing *now* so that it will have adequate capacity when it is needed in the future. In addition, briskly growing sales are likely to make business people more optimistic. Conversely, slow growth of output will discourage investment.

We can summarize these last two points by saying that:

High levels of sales in relation to available capacity and rapid economic growth create an atmosphere favourable to investment. On the other hand, low levels of sales and slow growth are likely to discourage investment.

Government stabilization policy thus has another handle on investment spending, for by stimulating aggregate demand it can induce business firms to invest more, though the precise amount may be hard to predict.

Tax Provisions

The government has still another important way to influence investment spending—by altering various provisions of the tax law. For example, the tax law sets maximum **depreciation allowances**, which govern how firms may deduct the costs of investment from their taxable income. In many of the federal government budgets in the last 20 years, the government has made these allowances more generous in a variety of ways. The idea was simple. More generous depreciation allowances lead to bigger tax deductions, and hence smaller tax bills, for firms that invest. This enhances the profitability of investment, and so should encourage more investment. We examine the effectiveness of these tax breaks, and their implications for the distribution of income, in Chapter 11. For now, we simply summarize:

Depreciation allowances are tax deductions that businesses may claim when they spend money on investment goods.

The tax law gives the government several ways to influence business spending on investment goods. But its control is imperfect. Investment remains a "flighty bird."

A Simplified Circular Flow

Let us now put consumption and investment together and see how they interact, using as our organizing framework the circular flow diagram introduced in the last chapter. For this purpose, we simplify the circular flow somewhat by leaving out the government and the foreign sector.

There are two reasons for doing this. The first is pedagogical: The workings of the model are much clearer if we strip away some of its complications. But there is a much more important reason. One of the crucial questions surrounding government attempts to stabilize the economy is whether the economy would *automatically* gravitate toward full employment if the government simply left it alone. We can study this issue best by imagining an economy that has no government, so that all the aggregate demand comes from the private sector. This is just what we do in this chapter.

Look now at Figure 8-1, which is the same as Figure 7-1 of the last chapter except that the government and foreign sectors have been omitted. The first thing you may notice is that, with the government and foreigners out of the picture, there is no longer any leakage out of the national income for taxes (nor are there transfer payments) and imports, so there is no important difference between national income and disposable income. Second, there is no government or foreign component of total spending; instead, spending is represented by the sum $C + I$.

The Meaning of Equilibrium GNP

We can use Figure 8–1 to begin the construction of a simple model of the determination of national income. A first step is to understand what we mean by "equilibrium income."

As was explained in the last chapter, national *product* and national *income* must, of necessity, be equal. But the same cannot automatically be said of total *spending*. Look again at Figure 8–1 and imagine that, for some reason, the total expenditures (*C + I*) that are being made at point 3 are greater than the output that is being produced by the business firms at point 4.

Two things may happen in such a situation. Since consumers and firms together are buying (in the forms of *C* and *I*) more than firms are producing, business firms are being forced to take goods out of their warehouses to meet customer demands. Thus, inventory stocks must be falling. These inventory reductions are a signal to retailers of a need to increase their orders, and to manufacturers of a need to step up their production. Consequently, production is likely to rise. At some later date, if there is evidence that the high level of aggregate demand is not just a temporary aberration, either manufacturers or retailers (or both) may also respond to the buoyant sales performances by raising their prices. Economists therefore say that neither output nor the price level is in **equilibrium** when aggregate demand exceeds the current rate of production.

It is clear from the definition of equilibrium that the economy cannot be in equilibrium when aggregate demand exceeds production, for the falling inventories demonstrate to firms that their production and pricing decisions were not quite

Equilibrium refers to a situation in which consumers and firms have no incentive to change their behaviour. They are content to continue with things as they are.

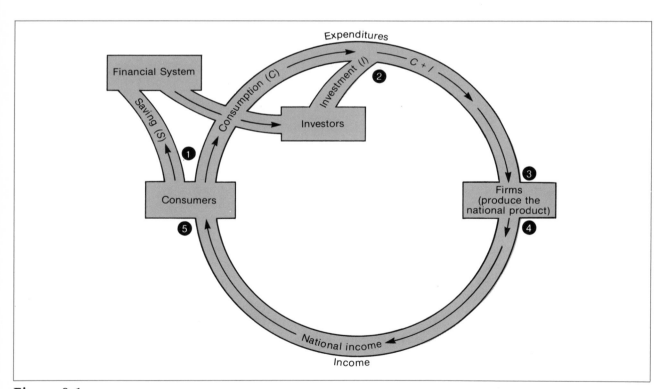

Figure 8–1
A SIMPLIFIED CIRCULAR FLOW
Here we show a simplified version of the circular flow of income and expenditures that we introduced in Chapter 7. The simplification amounts to shutting off the pipes leading into and out of the government and the rest of the world. Thus, this circular flow represents an economy with no government or foreign sector. Notice that aggregate demand now has only two components (consumer spending and investment spending) and that the entire national income flows to consumers without taxation.

appropriate. Thus, since we normally use GNP to measure output:

The equilibrium level of GNP cannot be one at which aggregate demand exceeds output because firms will notice that inventory stocks are being depleted. They may first decide to increase production sufficiently to meet the higher demand. Later they may decide to raise prices as well.

Now imagine the other case, in which the flow of aggregate demand reaching firms falls short of current production. Some output cannot be sold and winds up as additions to inventories. The inventory pile-up acts as a signal to firms that at least one of their decisions was wrong. Once again, they will probably react first by cutting back on production, causing the GNP to fall. If the imbalance persists, they may also lower prices in order to stimulate sales. But they certainly will not be happy with things as they are. Thus:

The equilibrium level of GNP cannot be one at which aggregate demand is less than output because firms will not allow inventories to continue to pile up. They may decide to decrease production, or they may decide to cut prices in order to stimulate a demand. Normally, firms are reluctant to cut prices until they are quite certain that the low level of demand is not a temporary phenomenon. So they rely more heavily on reductions in output.

Equilibrium on the Demand Side of the Economy

You may have noticed that we have now determined, through a process of elimination, the level of national income and product that is consistent with peoples' desires to spend. We have reasoned that whenever GNP is below total spending $(C + I)$, the GNP will rise; and that whenever GNP is above $C + I$, the GNP will fall. Equilibrium can only occur, then, when there is just enough spending to absorb the current level of production. Under such circumstances, producers conclude that their price and output decisions are correct, and they have no incentive to change them. We conclude that:

The **equilibrium level of GNP on the demand side** is the one at which total spending equals production. In such a situation, firms find their inventories remaining at desired levels; so there is no incentive to change output or prices.

The simple circular flow diagram, then, has helped us to understand the concept of the equilibrium level of GNP and also how the economy is driven toward it. It leaves unanswered, however, three important questions.

1. How large is the equilibrium level of GNP?
2. Will the economy suffer from unemployment, inflation, or both?
3. Is the equilibrium level of GNP on the demand side also consistent with firms' desires to produce? That is, is it also an equilibrium on the *supply* side?

The first two questions will occupy our attention in this chapter; the third question is reserved for Chapter 10.

Constructing the Expenditure Schedule

Our first objective is to determine precisely the equilibrium level of GNP and to see what factors it depends upon. To make the analysis more concrete, we turn to

Table 8-1

TOTAL EXPENDITURE IN MACROLAND (billions of dollars)

(1) INCOME (Y)	(2) CONSUMPTION (C)	(3) INVESTMENT (I)	(4) TOTAL EXPENDITURE ($C + I$)
200	170	70	240
250	210	70	280
300	250	70	320
350	290	70	360
400	330	70	400
450	370	70	440
500	410	70	480
550	450	70	520
600	490	70	560

This table illustrates the derivation of the expenditure schedule, which is shaded in blue. It is derived from the consumption schedule, columns 1 and 2, and from the investment schedule, columns 1 and 3, by simple addition. This is because total spending is the sum $C + I$.

a numerical example. Specifically, we examine the relationship between aggregate demand and GNP in Macroland, the hypothetical economy that was introduced in the last chapter.

Columns 1 and 2 of Table 8-1 incorporate the consumption function of Macroland that we first encountered in Table 7-1. They show how consumer spending, C, depends on national income, which we now begin to symbolize by the letter Y. However, one thing has changed here. The consumption function in Chapter 7 related C to *disposable* income (DI), whereas the consumption function in Table 8-1 relates C to *national* income (Y).This change is legitimate because, in this chapter, we have eliminated the government and the foreign sector from the picture. With no taxes and no transfer payments, there is no difference between DI and Y. Because (as we showed in Chapter 7) national income must equal national product, Y can be used to represent either income or output.

Column 3 provides the other component of aggregate demand, I, through the simplifying assumption that investment spending is $70 billion in Macroland, regardless of the level of GNP. By adding together the second and third columns, we calculate $C + I$, or total expenditure, which is displayed in column 4. Columns 1 and 4, shaded in blue, show how total expenditure depends on income in Macroland. We call this the **expenditure schedule**.

Figure 8-2 shows the construction of the expenditure schedule graphically. The line labelled C is the consumption function of Macroland and simply duplicates Figure 7-7 of the last chapter, except that Y, not DI, appears on the horizontal axis. It plots on a graph the numbers given in columns 1 and 2 of Table 8-1. The line labelled $C + I$ in the diagram depicts the total expenditure schedule that we have just derived by plotting the data in columns 1 and 4 of the table. That is, at each level of GNP measured along the horizontal axis, the height of the $C + I$ line indicates the sum of consumption plus investment.

The difference between the two lines, therefore, is investment. In the diagram, the lines are parallel; that is, the distance between them is always the same. This distance is $70 billion—the volume of investment assumed in the example. If investment were not always $70 billion, the two lines would either move closer together (at income levels at which investment was below $70 billion) or grow farther apart (at income levels at which investment was above $70 billion). For example, our list of determinants of investment spending suggested that I might be larger at higher levels of GNP. Because of this added investment—which is called **induced investment**—the resulting $C + I$ schedule would have a steeper slope than the C schedule.

An **expenditure schedule** shows how total spending varies with the level of national income (GNP).

Induced investment is investment that rises when GNP rises and falls when GNP falls.

Table 8-2

THE DETERMINATION OF EQUILIBRIUM OUTPUT

(1) OUTPUT (*Y*) (billions of dollars)	(2) TOTAL SPENDING (*C + I*) (billions of dollars)	(3) BALANCE OF SPENDING AND OUTPUT	(4) INVENTORIES ARE:	(5) PRODUCERS WILL RESPOND BY:
200	240	Spending exceeds output	Falling	Producing more
250	280	Spending exceeds output	Falling	Producing more
300	320	Spending exceeds output	Falling	Producing more
350	360	Spending exceeds output	Falling	Producing more
400	400	Spending equals output	Constant	Not changing production
450	440	Output exceeds spending	Rising	Producing less
500	480	Output exceeds spending	Rising	Producing less
550	520	Output exceeds spending	Rising	Producing less
600	560	Output exceeds spending	Rising	Producing less

Columns 1 and 2 are the expenditure schedule derived in the previous table. The remaining columns explain how the equilibrium level of national income can be derived from these data. For example, reading across the first row we see that when GNP is $200 billion, total spending is $240 billion. Thus spending exceeds production (by $40 billion), so that inventories must be falling. Producers are likely to respond to this drop in inventory stocks by raising their rate of production. The other rows are read similarly, and together they show that only $400 billion can be the equilibrium level of GNP. This is the only output level that firms will not want to change.

The Mechanics of Income Determination

We are now ready to determine the equilibrium level of GNP in Macroland. Look first at Table 8–2, which presents the logic of our circular flow argument in tabular form. The first two columns of this table reproduce the expenditure schedule that was constructed in Table 8-1. The other columns explain the process by which equilibrium is approached. Let us see why a GNP of $400 billion must be the equilibrium level.

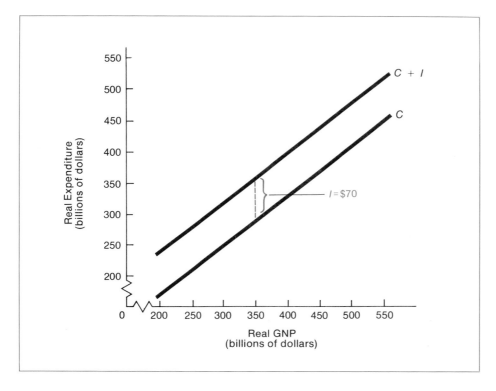

Figure 8-2

CONSTRUCTION OF THE EXPENDITURE SCHEDULE
This figure shows in a diagram what Table 8-1 showed numerically—the construction of a total expenditure schedule from its components. Line *C* is the consumption function that we first encountered in Figure 7-7, except that GNP, not disposable income, is measured along the horizontal axis. Line *C + I* is the expenditure schedule and is obtained by adding investment (assumed always to be $70 billion in this example) to the consumption function.

Consider first any output level below \$400 billion. For example, at output level Y = \$350 billion, total expenditure is \$360 billion (column 2), which is \$10 billion more than production. With spending greater than output (column 3), inventories will be falling (column 4). As the table suggests, this will be a signal to producers to raise their output (column 5). Clearly, then, no output level below Y = \$400 billion can be an equilibrium. Output is too low.

A similar line of reasoning can eliminate any output level above \$400 billion. Consider, for example, Y = \$450 billion. The table shows that total spending would be \$440 billion if national income were \$450 billion. So \$10 billion of the GNP would go unsold. This would raise producers' inventory stocks and signal them that their rate of production is too high.

Just as we concluded from our circular flow diagram, then, equilibrium will be achieved only when total spending $(C + I)$ is equal to GNP (Y). In symbols, our condition for equilibrium GNP is:

$$C + I = Y.$$

The table shows that this occurs only at a GNP of \$400 billion. This, then, must be the equilibrium level of GNP.

Figure 8–3 shows this same conclusion graphically, by adding a 45° line to Figure 8–2. Why a 45° line? Recall that a 45° line marks all points on a graph at which the value of the variable measured on the horizontal axis is equal to the value of the variable measured on the vertical axis. In this convenient graph of the expenditure schedule, gross national product (Y) is measured on the horizontal axis and total expenditure $(C + I)$ is measured on the vertical axis. So the 45° line shows all the points at which output and spending are equal: that is, where $Y = C + I$. The 45° line therefore displays all the points at which the economy *can possibly* be at equilibrium.

Figure 8–3

INCOME–EXPENDITURE DIAGRAM

This figure adds a 45° line—which marks off points where expenditure and output are equal—to Figure 8-2. Since the condition for equilibrium GNP is that expenditure and output must be equal, this line can be used to determine the equilibrium level of GNP. In this example, equilibrium is at point E, where GNP is \$400 billion—precisely as we found in Table 8-2.

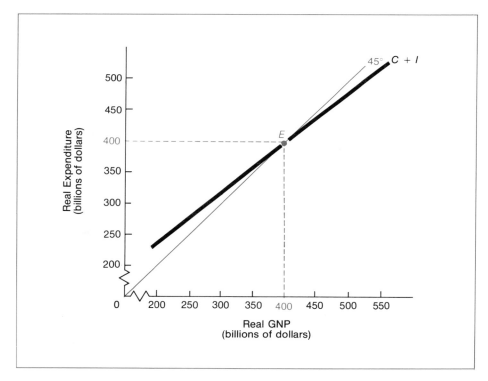

Now we must compare these potential equilibrium points with the actual combinations of spending and output that the economy can attain, given the behaviour of consumers and investors. That behaviour, as we have seen, is described by the $C + I$ line in Figure 8-3, which shows how total expenditure varies as income changes. Thus, the economy will *always* be on the $C + I$ line; only points on the $C + I$ line are consistent with the spending plans of consumers and investors. Similarly, *if* the economy is in equilibrium, it *must* be on the 45° line. As Figure 8-3 shows, these two requirements together imply that the only viable equilibrium is at point E, where the $C + I$ line intersects the 45° line. Only this point is consistent both with equilibrium and with the actual desires to consume and invest.

Notice that to the left of the equilibrium point, E, the $C + I$ line lies above the 45° line. This means that total spending exceeds total output, as we have already noted in words and with numbers. The opposite is true to the right of equilibrium point E; here, spending falls short of output.

Diagrams like this one will recur so frequently in this and the next several chapters that it will be convenient to have a name for them. Let us, therefore, call them **income-expenditure diagrams** since they show how expenditures vary with income. Sometimes we shall also refer to them simply as **45° line diagrams.**

The Aggregate-Demand Curve

Chapter 5 sketched a framework for macroeconomic analysis by introducing aggregate-demand and aggregate-supply curves that relate aggregate quantities demanded and supplied to the price level. Yet the price level has not even been mentioned so far in our discussion of equilibrium. It is now time to remedy this omission, for only by explicit analysis of the determination of the price level will we be able to deal with important issues relating to inflation.

Fortunately, no further mechanical apparatus is required. The price level can be brought into our income-expenditure analysis by recalling something we learned in the last chapter: At any given level of real income, higher prices lead to lower real consumer spending. The reason, you will recall, is that consumers own many assets whose values are fixed in money terms, and which therefore lose purchasing power when prices rise.[2] With real wealth lower, consumers spend less and therefore total spending in the economy falls.

In terms of our 45° line diagram, then, a rise in the price level will lower the consumption function depicted in Figure 8-2 and, hence, will lower the total expenditure schedule as well. Conversely, a fall in the price level will raise both the C and $C + I$ schedules in the diagram. Figure 8-4 illustrates both these sorts of shifts.

What, then, do changes in the price level do to the equilibrium level of real GNP on the demand side? Common sense says that, with lower spending, equilibrium GNP should fall. And Figure 8-5 shows that this conclusion is correct. Part (a) shows that a rise in the price level, by shifting the expenditure schedule downward from $C_0 + I$ to $C_1 + I$, leads to a reduction in the equilibrium quantity of real GNP demanded from Y_0 to Y_1. Part (b) shows that a fall in the price level, by shifting the expenditure schedule upward from $C_0 + I$ to $C_2 + I$, leads to a rise in the equilibrium quantity of real GNP demanded from Y_0 to Y_2. In summary:

A rise in the price level leads to a lower equilibrium level of real aggregate quantity demanded. This relationship between the price level and the equilibrium quantity

An **income-expenditure diagram**, also called a **45° line diagram**, plots total real expenditure (on the vertical axis) against real income (on the horizontal axis). The 45° line marks off points where income and expenditure are equal.

[2]Two warnings issued in Chapter 7 (page 126) are worth repeating: First, the effect referred to here comes from changes in the *price level*, not from changes in the *inflation rate*. Second, a higher price level does not reduce spending by reducing real income. Quite to the contrary, real income is held constant when we compare consumer expenditures at different price levels.

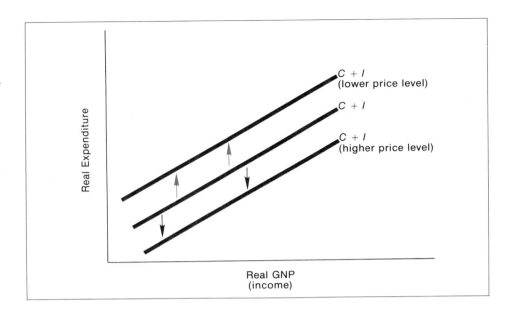

Figure 8-4

THE EFFECT OF THE PRICE LEVEL ON THE EXPENDITURE SCHEDULE

A higher price level will cause the $C + I$ schedule to shift downward, as shown by the black arrows. A lower price level will cause the $C + I$ schedule to shift upward, as shown by the blue arrows.

of real GNP demanded is depicted in Figure 8-6 and is precisely what we called the **aggregate-demand curve** in earlier chapters. It comes directly from the 45° line diagrams in Figure 8-5. Thus, points E_0, E_1, and E_2 in Figure 8-6 correspond to the points bearing the same labels in Figure 8-5.

Thus we have now learned the first reason why the aggregate-demand curve relating the price level to real GNP demanded slopes downward. (More reasons will come later in the book.) We have also been warned that:

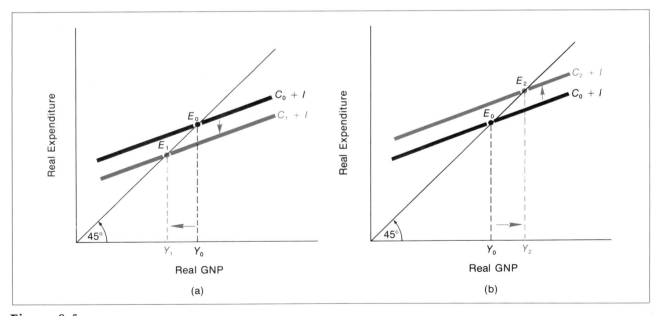

Figure 8-5

THE EFFECT OF THE PRICE LEVEL ON EQUILIBRIUM AGGREGATE QUANTITY DEMANDED

Because a change in the price level causes the expenditure schedule to shift, it changes the equilibrium quantity of real GNP demanded. Part (a) shows what happens when the price level rises, causing the expenditure schedule to shift downward from $C_0 + I$ to $C_1 + I$. Equilibrium quantity demanded falls from Y_0 to Y_1. Part (b) shows what happens when the price level falls, causing the expenditure schedule to shift upward from $C_0 + I$ to $C_2 + I$. Equilibrium quantity demanded rises from Y_0 to Y_2.

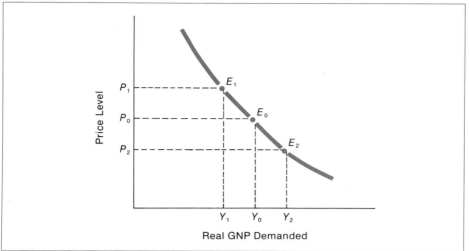

Figure 8-6
THE AGGREGATE-DEMAND
CURVE
The graphical analysis in Figure
8-5 showed that higher prices
lead to lower aggregate quantity
demanded. This relationship is
called the aggregate-demand
curve and is shown in this figure.

An income–expenditure diagram like Figure 8–3 can only be drawn up for a *specific* price level. At different price levels, the $C + I$ schedule will be different and, hence, the equilibrium quantity of GNP demanded will be different.

As we shall now see, this finding is critical to understanding the genesis of unemployment and inflation.

Demand-Side Equilibrium and Full Employment

We now turn to the second major question of this chapter: Will the economy achieve an equilibrium at full employment without inflation, or will there be unemployment, inflation, or both?

In the income–expenditure diagrams used so far, the equilibrium level of GNP demanded has been shown as the intersection of the expenditure schedule and the 45° line, regardless of whatever level of GNP might correspond to full employment of the nation's available resources. However, as we will see now, when equilibrium GNP exceeds the full-employment level of output, the result is inflation. And when equilibrium falls below full employment, there will be unemployment and recession.

This fact was one of the principal messages of Keynes's *General Theory of Employment, Interest, and Money*. Writing during the Great Depression, it was natural for him to stress the case in which equilibrium falls short of full employment so that there are unemployed resources. Figure 8–7 illustrates this possibility. A vertical line has been erected at the full-employment level of GNP (called "potential GNP"), which is assumed to be $500 billion in the example. We see that the $C + I$ curve cuts the 45° line at point E, which corresponds to a GNP ($Y = \$400$ billion) below potential GNP. In this case, the $C + I$ curve is too low to lead to full employment. Such a situation might arise because either consumers or investors are unwilling to spend at normal rates, or because the price level is "too high," thereby depressing the $C + I$ curve. Unemployment must occur because not enough output will be demanded to keep the entire labour force busy.

The distance between the equilibrium level of output demanded and the full-employment level of output (that is, potential GNP) is called the **recessionary gap**—and is shown by the horizontal distance from E to B.

The **recessionary gap** is the amount by which the equilibrium level of real GNP falls short of potential GNP.

Biographical Note: John Maynard Keynes (1883–1946)

It may be one of history's great ironies that the death of Karl Marx, the prophet of capitalism's doom, and the birth of John Maynard Keynes, who many consider capitalism's saviour, both occurred in the same year—1883. The son of a prominent upper-class British economist, Keynes was something of a child prodigy. After an outstanding scholastic career at Eton and Cambridge, Keynes took the civil service examination. His second-place score was not good enough to land him the position he wanted and should have had (in the Treasury), so in 1907 he found himself in the India Office. Some years later, reflecting on the fact that his lowest score on the exam was in the economics section, he suggested with characteristic immodesty that, "The examiners presumably knew less than I did."* He was probably right.

While Keynes disliked his work at the India Office, his time there was not wasted. It was during that period that he wrote his *Treatise on Probability* (1909), which drew the admiration of Bertrand Russell and won Keynes election as a lifetime Fellow of Cambridge's King's College.

During World War I, Keynes was called to the Treasury to assist in planning various financial aspects of the war. There his "unique combination of the guts of a burglar and the intellect of a first-class economist"‡ established him as a dominant figure. At the war's end, though only 36, Keynes represented the British Treasury at the peace conference in Versailles.

The conference was a turning point in Keynes's life, though it was one of his few failures. He sought unsuccessfully to persuade the Allies to take a less punitive attitude toward the vanquished Germans, and then left the conference in protest in June 1919, telling David Lloyd George, the English Prime Minister, "I am slipping away from this scene of nightmare."§ Keynes immediately went to work on his *Economic Consequences of the Peace*, which created a furor when it was published in 1919. In addition to stinging personal portraits of Lloyd George, Georges Clemenceau, and Woodrow Wilson ("the blind and deaf Don Quixote"), Keynes demonstrated with exquisite logic that the Germans could never meet the

Figure 8–7

A RECESSIONARY GAP
Sometimes equilibrium GNP may fall below potential GNP, so that some workers are unemployed. This diagram illustrates such a case. The horizontal distance *EB* between equilibrium GNP and potential GNP is called the recessionary gap.

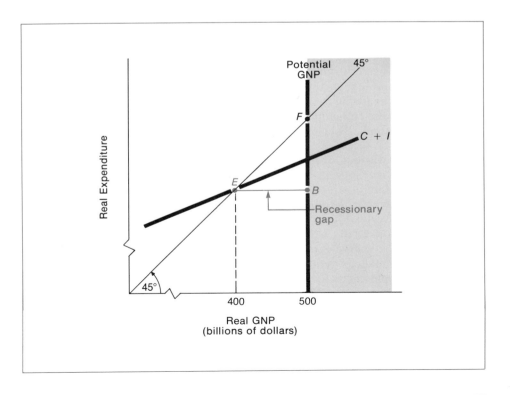

harsh economic terms of the treaty and that its very viciousness posed the threat of continued instability and perhaps another war in Europe. Sadly, his visions were remarkably accurate.

No longer welcome in government, Keynes returned to Cambridge and to his distinguished circle of literary and artistic friends in London's Bloomsbury district—a group that included Virginia Woolf, Lytton Strachey, and E. M. Forster. In 1925 he married the beautiful ballerina Lydia Lopokova, who gave up her stage career for him (though she later acted in a theatre that Keynes himself established).

Between the wars, Keynes devoted himself to making money (both for himself and for King's College), to economic theory, and to political economy. Spending about one-half hour each morning with newspapers and financial reports (apparently while still in bed!), Keynes managed to make himself a rich man and increase his college's unrestricted fund from £30,000 to £380,000 by speculating in international currencies and commodities. As a scholar, he wrote the *Tract on Monetary Reform* (1923), a stunning denunciation of the gold standard, which was published two years before Churchill once again tied the pound to gold and, in the view of modern observers, sealed Britain's economic doom. In 1936, he published his masterpiece, *The General Theory of Employment, Interest, and Money*, upon which modern macroeconomics is based. Finally, as a tireless political activist and polemicist, he used newspaper and magazine articles, and visits to Whitehall and Washington, to urge governments to lift their economies out of the Depression (which began for Britain in the 1920s) through policies that we would now call "Keynesian."

A heart attack in 1937 reduced Keynes's activities somewhat, though he maintained careers as both an academic economist and a businessman. He returned to the Treasury during World War II and conducted several delicate financial negotiations with the Americans. Then, as the capstone to a truly remarkable career, he represented the United Kingdom—and by all accounts dominated the proceedings—at the conference in Bretton Woods, New Hampshire, in 1944 that established an international financial system that served the Western world for 27 years. (See Chapter 16.)

He died of a heart attack at his home on Easter Sunday of 1946 as Lord Keynes, Baron of Tilton, a man who had achieved almost everything that he sought, and who had only one regret: He wished he had drunk more champagne.

*Quoted in E. A. G. Robinson, "John Maynard Keynes," in R. Lekachman, ed., *Keynes' General Theory: Reports of Three Decades* (New York: St. Martin's Press, Inc., 1964), page 25.

‡Robert Lekachman, *The Age of Keynes* (New York: Random House, 1966), page 27. This book contains a marvelous biography of Keynes, as does Robert Heilbroner's *The Worldly Philosophers*, 4th edition (New York: Simon and Schuster, 1972).

§Quoted in R. F. Harrod, *The Life of John Maynard Keynes* (New York: Macmillan, 1951), page 253.

It is clear from Figure 8–7 that full employment can be reached only by raising the total spending schedule to eliminate the recessionary gap. Specifically, the $C + I$ schedule must move upward until it cuts the 45° line at point F. Can this happen without government intervention? We shall return to this question after we have brought the supply side into the picture. But first let us consider the other case, in which equilibrium GNP exceeds full employment.

Figure 8–8 illustrates this possibility. The expenditure schedule intersects the 45° line at point E, where GNP is $600 billion. But this exceeds the full-employment level, $Y = $500 billion. A case like this can arise when consumer or investment spending is unusually buoyant or when a "low" price level pushes the $C + I$ curve upward.

To reach an equilibrium at full employment, the price level would have to rise enough to drive the $C + I$ schedule *down* until it passed through point F. The horizontal distance BE—which indicates the amount by which the quantity of GNP demanded exceeds potential GNP—is called the **inflationary gap**. If there is an inflationary gap, a higher price level or some other means of reducing total expenditure is necessary to reach an equilibrium at full employment.

The **inflationary gap** is the amount by which equilibrium real GNP exceeds the full-employment level of GNP.

In sum, only if the price level and the spending plans of consumers and investors are "just right" will the $C + I$ curve intersect the 45° line precisely at full employment, so that neither a recessionary gap nor an inflationary gap occurs. Are there reasons to expect this outcome? Does the economy have a self-correcting mechanism that automatically eliminates recessionary or inflationary gaps and propels it toward full employment? And how is it that inflation and unemployment sometimes occur together? These are questions we are not quite ready to address

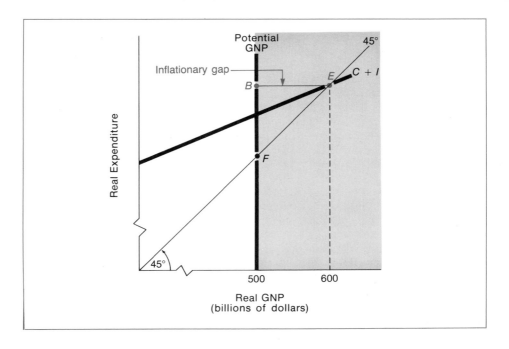

Figure 8-8

AN INFLATIONARY GAP
Sometimes equilibrium GNP may
lie above potential GNP, meaning
that there are more jobs than
required for full employment. This
diagram illustrates such a case.
The horizontal distance *BE*
between potential GNP and
equilibrium GNP is called the
inflationary gap. It is gradually
eliminated by rising prices, which
pull the *C + I* schedule down until
it passes through point *F*.

because we have yet to bring *aggregate supply* into the picture. And, as we learned in Chapter 4, the price level is determined by the interaction of *both* aggregate demand *and* aggregate supply. However, it is not too early to get an idea about why things can go wrong, why the economy can find itself far away from full employment.

The Co-ordination of Saving and Investment

To understand what goes wrong with the economy in a recession, it is useful to pose the following question: How can the full-employment level of GNP fail to be an equilibrium?

To find an answer look back at the simplified circular flow diagram (Figure 8-1 on page 144). Suppose that firms produce the full-employment level of GNP, and this becomes the national income that emerges at point 4 in the diagram. This full-employment level of income then flows to consumers at point 5, who save some of it and spend the rest. The saving, you will note, "leaks out" of the circular flow at point 1. So, once we pass this point, consumption is less than full-employment GNP. But then at point 2, an additional source of spending enters: investment. Recalling that the condition for equilibrium is that the sum *C + I* equals the GNP, we have the following conclusion:

The economy will reach an equilibrium at full employment only if the amount that consumers wish to save out of full-employment incomes is precisely equal to the amount that investors want to invest. If these two magnitudes happen to be unequal, then full employment will not be an equilibrium for the economy.

Specifically, we can see from the circular flow diagram that if saving exceeds investment at full employment, then the total demand arriving at the firms (point 3) will fall short of total output because the added investment spending is not enough to replace the leakage to saving. With demand inadequate to support production at full employment, we know that the GNP must fall below potential. There will be a recessionary gap. Conversely, if investment exceeds saving when the economy is at full employment, then total demand (*C + I*) will exceed potential

GNP and production will rise above the full-employment level. There will be an inflationary gap.

Now this discussion does nothing but restate what we already know in different words.[3] But these words hold the key to understanding why the economy can find itself stuck below full employment (or above it, for that matter), for *the people who do the investing are not the same people who do the saving.* In a modern capitalist economy, investing is done by one group of individuals (corporate executives and home buyers) while saving is done by another group.[4] It is easy to imagine that their plans may not be well co-ordinated. If they are not, we have just seen how either unemployment or inflation can arise.

Notice that these problems would never arise if the acts of saving and investing were not separated. Imagine a primitive economy of farmers, each of whom invests only in his own farm. There is no borrowing or lending, and no financial system. In this world, any farmer wanting to buy a new plough or tractor (that is, wanting to *invest*) would have to refrain from consuming part of his income (that is, would have to *save*). Therefore, the amount that all farmers together planned to save out of full-employment income would of necessity be equal to the amount of planned investment. Total spending and production would always have to be equal at full employment.

Almost the same sequence holds true in a centrally planned economy like that of the Soviet Union. There, the state decides how much will be invested and has a great deal of leverage over how much saving people do. If the planners do their calculations correctly, they can force saving to be equal to investment at full employment. Consequently, business fluctuations are not a major problem in the Soviet Union. (They have plenty of others!)

Keynes observed that modern market economies differ from either primitive societies or centrally planned societies in this fundamental way and that this separation of decisions within the market system is what leaves them vulnerable to recessions. However, one should not conclude that in order to avoid unemployment and recession the Canadian economy should revert either to a primitive form of capitalism or to rigid central planning. These "remedies" may be far worse than the disease. Fortunately, there are policies the government can follow in an advanced capitalist economy to ease the pain of unemployment and recession—policies that we shall be studying in the following chapters.

---

[3]In symbols, our previous equilibrium condition was $C + I = Y$. If we note that Y is also the sum of consumption plus saving, $Y = C + S$, it follows that $C + I = C + S$, or $I = S$, is a restatement of the equilibrium condition. The saving = investment approach is described in an appendix to this chapter.

[4]In a modern economy, it is not only households that save. Businesses save also, in the form of retained earnings. None the less, households are the ultimate source of the saving needed to finance investment.

Summary

1. Investment is the most volatile component of aggregate demand, largely because it is tied so closely to the state of business confidence and to expectations about the future performance of the economy.
2. Government policy cannot influence business confidence in any reliable way, so policies designed to alter investment spending are aimed at more objective, though possibly less important, determinants of investment. Among these are interest rates, the overall state of aggregate demand, and corporate tax incentives.
3. The equilibrium level of national income on the demand side is the level at which total spending just equals production (GNP). In this chapter we ignore government and foreign demand, so total spending is the sum of consumption plus investment. Thus, in symbols, the condition for equilibrium is $Y = C + I$.
4. Income levels below equilibrium are bound to rise because, when spending exceeds output, firms will see their inventory stocks being depleted and will react by stepping up production.
5. Income levels above equilibrium are bound to fall because, when total spending is insufficient to absorb total output, inventories will pile up and firms will react by curtailing production.
6. The determination of the equilibrium level of GNP on the demand side can be portrayed on a convenient "income–expenditure diagram" as the point at which the expenditure schedule—defined as the sum of the consumption and investment schedules—crosses the 45° line. The 45° line is significant because it marks off points at which spending and output are equal (that is, at which $C + I = Y$), and this is the basic condition for equilibrium.
7. An income–expenditure diagram can only be drawn up for a specific price level, however. Thus the equilibrium GNP so determined depends on the price level.
8. Because higher prices reduce the purchasing power of consumers' wealth, and hence reduce their spending, equilibrium real GNP demanded is lower when prices are higher. This downward-sloping relationship is known as the aggregate-demand curve.
9. Equilibrium GNP can be above or below potential GNP, which is defined as the GNP that would be produced if the labour force were fully employed.
10. If equilibrium GNP exceeds potential GNP, the difference is called an inflationary gap. If equilibrium GNP falls short of potential GNP, the resulting difference is called a recessionary gap.
11. Such gaps can occur in a decentralized economy because the saving that consumers want to do at full-employment income levels may differ from the investing that investors want to do. This problem is not likely to arise in a planned economy or in a primitive economy.

Concepts for Review

Depreciation allowances	Income–expenditure (or 45° line)	Recessionary gap
Equilibrium level of GNP	diagram	Inflationary gap
Expenditure schedule	Aggregate–demand curve	Co-ordination of saving and
Induced investment	Full-employment level of GNP (or	investment
$C + I = Y$	potential GNP)	

Questions for Discussion

1. Why would someone interested in stabilization policy want to study a model of an economy in which there is no government?
2. Analysts of the economy often argue that the rate of business investment in Canada is too low. Does this chapter give you any ideas about what is meant by the phrase "too low"? What factors do you think accounted for the low level of investment spending in the early 1980s? (You may want to discuss this last issue with your instructor.)
3. Why is not any arbitrary level of GNP an equilibrium for the economy? (Do not give a mechanical answer to this question but explain the economic mechanism involved.)
4. From the following data, construct an expenditure schedule on a piece of graph paper. Then use the income–expenditure (45° line) diagram to determine the equilibrium level of GNP.

INCOME	CONSUMPTION	INVESTMENT
1100	980	130
1150	1025	130
1200	1070	130
1250	1115	130
1300	1160	130

PRICE LEVEL	CONSUMER SPENDING
80	740
90	720
100	700
110	680
120	660

5. From the following data, construct an expenditure schedule on a piece of graph paper. Then use the income–expenditure (45° line) diagram to determine the equilibrium level of GNP.

INCOME	CONSUMPTION	INVESTMENT
1100	1010	100
1150	1040	115
1200	1070	130
1250	1100	145
1300	1130	160

Compare your answer with your answer to Question 4.

6. Suppose investment spending were always $200, and consumer spending depended on the price level in the following way:

On a piece of graph paper, use these data to construct an aggregate-demand curve. Why do you think this example supposes that consumption declines as the price level rises?

7. Does the economy this year seem to have an inflationary gap or a recessionary gap? (If you do not know the answer from reading the newspaper, ask your instructor.)

8. Why are there no recessions in the Soviet Union?

9. (More difficult.)* Consider an economy in which the consumption function takes the following simple algebraic form:

$$C = 100 + 0.8Y$$

and in which investment (I) is always 700. Find the equilibrium level of GNP from the requirement that $C + I = Y$. Compare your answer to Table 8-2 and Figure 8-3.

*The answer to this question is provided in Appendix B.

Appendix A
The Saving and Investment Approach

As we mentioned in the chapter, there is another way of looking at the determination of the equilibrium level of GNP on the demand side. Instead of studying the condition that total expenditure $(C + I)$ is equal to production (Y), we can study the condition that saving (S) is equal to investment (I). This is what we will do in this appendix.

It must be emphasized at the outset that this is not a *new* approach. It is merely another way of looking at precisely the same phenomenon. The reason is that income (Y) must be either spent on consumer goods (C) or saved (S). Since $Y = C + S$ *always*, and since $Y = C + I$ *when Y is at its equilibrium value*, we can describe equilibrium by the condition that $C + S = C + I$, or simply:

$$S = I.$$

Graphical Analysis

This way of looking at equilibrium has a different graphical representation: It does not use the 45° line

diagram, but it contains precisely the same information. Recall that in an appendix to Chapter 7 we constructed the saving schedule, which we repeat here as Figure 8-9. Since the equilibrium condition now under scrutiny is $S = I$, we can complete the story by providing an investment schedule. In the example used in the text, investment was taken to be a fixed number irrespective of income. We again do this here, so the investment schedule is as shown in Figure 8-10.

To find the point at which saving and investment are equal, we need only put both curves on the same diagram, which we have done in Figure 8-11. Point E shows the equilibrium level of GNP, which is at an income level of $400 billion. As must be the case, this is the same answer we obtained with the 45° line diagram.

You will notice that at income levels below $400 billion, investment exceeds saving, just as $C + I$ exceeded output in the 45° line diagram. Similarly, at income levels above $400 billion, S exceeds I. (In the

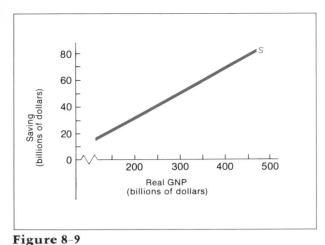

Figure 8-9
THE SAVING SCHEDULE
This diagram shows the relationship between saving and income in Macroland and duplicates Figure 7-10 (page 132).

45° line diagram, Y exceeded $C + I$ in this range.) This must be the case since the two graphs are alternative depictions of the same phenomena. The economic analyses behind them are precisely the same.

Induced Investment

In the chapter we mentioned the possibility of *induced investment*, that is, of an investment schedule that rises as GNP rises, but we did not examine this possibility in our graphs. (However, this case did arise in Discussion Question 5.) The reason is that what matters in the 45° line diagram is the slope of the *combined $C + I$* schedule, not the *individual* slopes of the C and I schedules. So an upward-sloping invest-

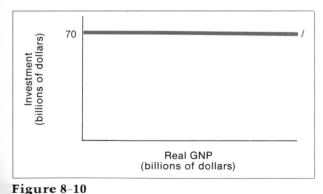

Figure 8-10
THE INVESTMENT SCHEDULE
In this simple example, investment spending is a fixed number—$70 billion—regardless of the level of GNP. Therefore, the investment schedule is a horizontal line at $70 billion.

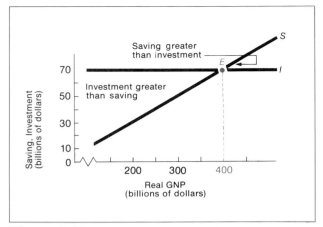

Figure 8-11
DETERMINATION OF EQUILIBRIUM GNP BY SAVING-INVESTMENT
This diagram, which combines Figures 8-9 and 8-10, depicts the equilibrium of the economy at point E, where the saving and investment schedules intersect. The equilibrium is at a real GNP of $400 billion, which, as must be the case, is the same conclusion that we reached with the aid of the 45° line diagram (Figure 8-3 on page 148).

ment schedule does not make much difference to the analysis.

When using the saving and investment approach, however, the slope of the investment schedule becomes more apparent, if not more important. So Figure 8-12 illustrates the case of induced investment. In

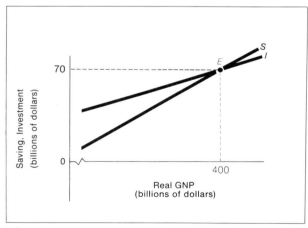

Figure 8-12
INCOME DETERMINATION WITH INDUCED INVESTMENT
When investment rises with GNP ("induced investment"), the investment schedule acquires a positive slope. Apart from this, the determination of equilibrium output is precisely as it was before. Point E, where the S and I schedules cross, is the equilibrium.

this diagram, the investment schedule is upward sloping. Equilibrium, however, is still at point E—where the S and I schedules cross. Thus, allowance for induced investment does not change our analysis in any significant way.[5]

[5]Some students may wonder what happens if the slope of the investment schedule exceeds that of the saving schedule. This is a difficult question and one that is best reserved for more advanced courses. Suffice it to say here that the simple model of income determination constructed in this chapter will not work in such a case.

Summary

1. The condition for equilibrium GNP—which we gave in the chapter as the equation of total spending with output $(C + I = Y)$—can be restated as the requirement that saving and investment be equal $(S = I)$. This does not change anything, but simply says the same thing in different words.
2. These different words lead to a different graphical presentation, in which we look for equilibrium at the point where the saving schedule crosses the investment schedule.
3. Induced investment—that is, investment that rises as the GNP rises—leads to an upward-sloping investment schedule, but requires no other change in the analysis.

Concepts for Review

$S = I$
Saving schedule

Investment schedule
Induced investment

Questions for Discussion

1. From the data in Discussion Question 4 at the end of the chapter, construct the saving schedule and the investment schedule on a piece of graph paper. (In doing so, remember that any income that is not consumed must have been saved.) Use these constructions to find the equilibrium level of GNP.

2. Do the same thing with the data in Discussion Question 5. (*Hint*: You will find *negative* saving at income level 100. There is nothing wrong with this. You do negative saving any time you draw down your bank account balance.)

Appendix B
The Simple Algebra of Income Determination

The model of demand-side equilibrium that the chapter presented graphically and in tabular form can also be handled with some simple algebra.

Written as an equation, the consumption function in our example is:

$$C = 10 + 0.8Y.$$

This is simply the equation of a straight line with intercept 10 and slope 0.8. Investment in the example was assumed to be 70, regardless of the level of income. So the sum $C + I$ is:

$$C + I = 10 + 0.8Y + 70 = 80 + 0.8Y.$$

This is the equation of the $C + I$ curve found in Figure 8–3.

Since the equilibrium quantity of GNP demanded is defined by:

$$Y = C + I,$$

we can solve for the equilibrium value of Y algebraically by substituting $80 + 0.8Y$ for $C + I$. Thus, we have:

$$Y = C + I = 80 + 0.8Y.$$

To solve this equation for Y, first subtract $0.8Y$ from both sides to get:

$$0.2Y = 80.$$

Then divide both sides by 0.2 to obtain the answer:

$$Y = 400.$$

This, of course, is precisely the solution we found by graphical and tabular methods in the chapter.

The method of solution is easily generalized to deal with any set of numbers in our equations. Suppose the consumption function is:

$$C = a + bY.$$

(In the example, $a = 10$ and $b = 0.8$.) Then the equilibrium condition that $Y = C + I$ implies:

$$Y = a + bY + I.$$

Subtracting bY from both sides leads to:

$$(1 - b)Y = a + I,$$

and dividing through by $1 - b$ gives:

$$Y = \frac{a + I}{1 - b}.$$

This formula, which is certainly not to be memorized, is valid for any numerical values of a, b, and I (so long as b is between zero and one).

Questions for Discussion

1. Find the equilibrium level of GNP demanded in an economy in which investment is always $200 and the consumption function is described by the following algebraic equation:

$$C = 120 + 0.8Y.$$

2. Do the same for an economy in which investment is fixed at $150 and the consumption function is:

$$C = 250 + 0.5Y.$$

3. In each of the above cases, how much saving is there in equilibrium? (*Hint*: Income not consumed must be saved.) Is saving equal to investment?

4. Imagine an economy in which consumer expenditure is represented by the following equation:

$$C = 100 + 0.75Y.$$

Imagine also that investors want to spend $500 at every level of income: $I = 500$.

a. What is the equilibrium level of income?
b. If the full employment level of income is $2000, is there a recessionary or inflationary gap? If so, how much?
c. What will happen to the equilibrium level of income if investors become pessimistic about the country's future and reduce their investment to $250?
d. Is there a recessionary or inflationary gap now? How much?

5. Ivyland has the following consumption function:

$$C = 200 + 0.75Y.$$

Firms in Ivyland always invest $200.
a. Find the equilibrium level of GNP.
b. How much is saved? Is saving equal to investment?
c. Suppose consumers are given an inducement to save, so that the consumption function falls to $C = 150 + 0.75Y$, but at the same time firms boost investment spending to $240. Answer questions (a) and (b) under these new circumstances.

Changes on the Demand Side: Multiplier Analysis

9

A definite ratio, to be called
the Multiplier, can be
established between income
and investment.
JOHN MAYNARD KEYNES

I n the last chapter we derived the economy's aggregate-demand curve, which
shows how the equilibrium quantity of real GNP demanded depends on the
price level—holding all other factors constant. But often these "other factors"
do not remain constant and, as a consequence, the entire aggregate-demand curve
shifts. This chapter is the first of several that are devoted to enumerating these
"other factors" and explaining how and why they make the aggregate-demand
curve shift.

The central concept of this short chapter is the *multiplier*—the idea that an
increase in spending will bring about an *even larger* increase in overall demand.
We approach this idea from three different perspectives, each of which provides
the reader with different and significant insights into the multiplier process. First,
the multiplier is illustrated graphically using the income–expenditure diagram
from Chapter 8. Next, we reach the same conclusion through the use of a numerical
example, and finally, we offer an algebraic statement.

At the end of the chapter, we use multiplier analysis to explain why a drive to
increase national saving might not succeed.

The Magic of the Multiplier

Because it is subject to such abrupt swings, investment spending is often the cause
of business fluctuations in Canada and elsewhere. Let us, therefore, ask what
would happen to equilibrium income in our fictitious country, Macroland, if firms
there suddenly decided to spend more on investment goods. As we shall see, such
a decision would have a *multiplied* effect on GNP in Macroland. The same would
be true in the Canadian economy.

For simplicity, we begin by assuming that the price level is fixed—an
assumption we maintain *only* for this short chapter. Refer first to Table 9–1, which
looks very much like Table 8–1 (page 146). The only difference is that we assume
here that, for some reason, firms in Macroland now want to invest $20 billion
more than they previously did—for a total of $90 billion. The multiplier principle
says that Macroland's GNP will rise by more than the $20 billion increase in
investment. Specifically, **the multiplier** is defined as the ratio of the change in
equilibrium GNP (Y) divided by the original change in spending that causes the

The multiplier is the
ratio of the change in
equilibrium GNP (Y) divided
by the original change in
spending that causes the
change in GNP.

Table 9-1

TOTAL EXPENDITURE AFTER THE RISE IN INVESTMENT SPENDING (billions of dollars)

(1) INCOME (Y)	(2) CONSUMPTION (C)	(3) INVESTMENT (I)	(4) TOTAL EXPENDITURE ($C + I$)
200	170	90	260
250	210	90	300
300	250	90	340
350	290	90	380
400	330	90	420
450	370	90	460
500	410	90	500
550	450	90	540
600	490	90	580

This table shows the construction of a total expenditure schedule for Macroland after investment has risen to $90 billion. As indicated by the numbers shaded in blue, only income level Y = $500 billion is equilibrium on the demand side of the economy because only at this level is total spending ($C + I$) equal to production (Y).

change in GNP. In shorthand, when we deal with the multiplier for investment (I), the formula is:

$$\text{Multiplier} = \frac{\text{Change in } Y}{\text{Change in } I}.$$

Let us verify that the multiplier is indeed greater than 1. Table 9-1 shows how to derive a new expenditure schedule by adding up C and I at each level of Y, just as we did in Chapter 8. If you compare the last column of Table 9-1 to that of Table 8-1, you will see that the new expenditure schedule lies uniformly above the old one by $20 billion. Figure 9-1 illustrates this diagrammatically. The schedule marked $C + I_0$ is derived from the last column of Table 8-1, while the higher schedule marked $C + I_1$ is derived from the last column of Table 9-1. The two $C + I$ lines are parallel and $20 billion apart.

So far no act of magic has occurred—things look just as you might expect. But one more step will bring the multiplier rabbit out of the hat. Let us see what the upward shift of the $C + I$ line does to equilibrium income. We see in Figure 9-1 that equilibrium moves outward from point E_0 to point E_1, that is, from $400 billion to $500 billion. The difference is an increase in national income of $100 billion. All this from a $20 billion stimulus to investment? That is the magic of the multiplier.

Because the change in I is $20 billion and the change in equilibrium Y is $100 billion, by applying our definition, the multiplier is:

$$\text{Multiplier} = \frac{\text{Change in } Y}{\text{Change in } I} = \frac{\$100 \text{ billion}}{\$20 \text{ billion}} = 5.$$

This tells us that, in our example, every additional dollar of investment demand will add $5 to the equilibrium GNP!

This does indeed seem mysterious. Can something be created from nothing? Let us, therefore, check to be sure that the graph has not deceived us. The first and last columns of Table 9-1 show in numbers what Figure 9-1 shows in a picture. Notice that, at any income level below $500, spending ($C + I$) exceeds output ($Y$). As we know, this cannot be an equilibrium situation because inventories would be disappearing. On the other hand, at any income level above $500, inventories would be piling up, since $C + I$ is less than Y.

Only at Y = $500 billion are spending and production in balance, as Table 9-1 shows. This is $100 billion higher than the $400 billion equilibrium GNP obtained

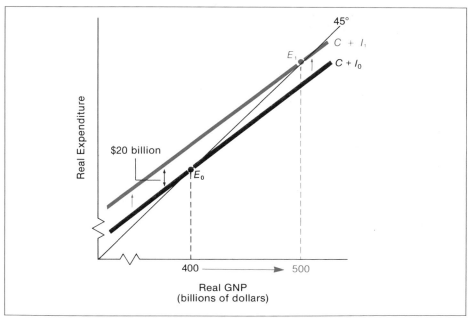

Figure 9-1
ILLUSTRATION OF THE
MULTIPLIER
This figure depicts the multiplier
effect of a rise in investment
spending of $20 billion. The
expenditure schedule shifts
upward from $C + I_0$ to $C + I_1$, thus
moving equilibrium from point E_0 to
point E_1. The rise in income is
$100 billion, so the multiplier is
$100/$20 = 5.

in the discussion of Table 8-1, where investment was only $70 billion. Thus a $20 billion rise in investment leads to a $100 billion rise in equilibrium GNP, which goes up from an initial value of $400 billion to $500 billion. The multiplier really is 5.

Demystifying the Multiplier: How It Works

The multiplier result seems peculiar at first, but it loses its mystery once we remember the circular flow of income and expenditure, and the simple fact that one person's spending is another person's income. To illustrate the logic of the multiplier, and see why it is exactly 5 in our model economy, let us look more closely at what actually happens if businesses decide to spend an additional $1 million on investment goods.

For the sake of concreteness, suppose that Generous Motors—a major corporation in Macroland—decides to spend $1 million to retool a factory to manufacture pollution-free electronically powered automobiles. Its $1 million expenditure goes to construction workers and owners of construction companies as wages and profits. That is, it becomes their *income*.

But the owners and workers of the construction firms will not simply keep their $1 million in the bank. They will spend some of it. If they are "typical" consumers, their spending will, by definition, be $1 million times the marginal propensity to consume (MPC). In our example, the MPC is 0.8. So let us assume that they spend $800,000 and save the rest. *This $800,000 expenditure is a net addition to the nation's demand for goods and services exactly as GM's original $1 million expenditure was.* So, at this stage, the $1 million investment has already pushed GNP up some $1.8 million.

But the process by no means stops here. Shopkeepers receive the $800,000 spent by construction workers, and these shopkeepers in turn also spend 80 percent of their new income. This accounts for $640,000 (80 percent of $800,000) in additional consumer spending in the "third round." Next follows a fourth round in which the recipients of the $640,000, in their turn, spend 80 percent of this amount, or $512,000, and so on. At each stage in the spending chain, people spend 80 percent of the additional income they receive, and the process continues.

Where does it all end? Does it all end? The answer is that it does, indeed, eventually end—with GNP a total of $5 million higher than it was before Generous Motors spent the original $1 million. The multiplier, as stated, is 5.

Table 9-2 displays the basis for this conclusion. In the table, "round 1" represents GM's initial investment, which creates $1 million in income for construction workers; "round 2" represents the construction workers' spending, which creates $800,000 in income for shopkeepers. The rest of the table proceeds accordingly. Each entry in column 2 is 80 percent of the previous entry, and column 3 tabulates the running sum of column 2.

We see that after 10 rounds of spending the initial $1 million investment has mushroomed to nearly $4.5 million, and the sum is still growing. After 20 rounds, the total increase in GNP is over $4.9 million—quite near its eventual value of $5 million. While it takes quite a few rounds of spending before the multiplier chain is near 5, we see from the table that it approaches 4 within seven periods.

Figure 9-2 provides a graphical presentation of the numbers in the last column of Table 9-2. Notice how the multiplier builds up rapidly at first, and then tapers off to approach its ultimate value (5 in this example) gradually.

Algebraic Statement of the Multiplier

Figure 9-2 and Table 9-2 probably make a persuasive case for the fact that the multiplier eventually reaches 5. But for the remaining skeptics we offer a simple algebraic proof.[1] Most of you learned about an "infinite geometric progression" in high school. This is simply an infinite series of numbers, each one of which is a fixed fraction of the previous one. This fraction is called the "common ratio." A geometric progression beginning with 1 and having a common ratio equal to 0.8 would look like this:

$$1 + 0.8 + (0.8)^2 + (0.8)^3 + \ldots.$$

More generally, a geometric progression beginning with 1 and having a common ratio R would be:

$$1 + R + R^2 + R^3 \ldots.$$

A simple formula enables us to sum such a progression as long as R is less than 1.[2]

The formula is:[3]

$$\text{Sum of infinite geometric progression} = \frac{1}{1 - R}.$$

Now we can recognize that the multiplier chain in Table 9-2 is just an infinite geometric progression with 0.8 as its common ratio. That is, each $1 spent by GM

---

[1]Students who blanch at the sight of algebra should not be put off. Anyone who can balance a chequebook (even many who cannot!) will be able to follow the argument.

[2]If R exceeds 1, nobody can possibly sum it—not even with the aid of a modern computer!

[3]The proof is simple. Let the symbol S stand for the (unknown) sum of the series:

$$S = 1 + R + R^2 + R^3 + \ldots.$$

Then, multiplying by R,

$$RS = R + R^2 + R^3 + \ldots.$$

By subtracting RS from S, we obtain:

$$S - RS = 1$$

or

$$S = \frac{1}{1 - R}.$$

---

leads to a $(0.8) \times \$1$ expenditure by construction workers, which in turn leads to a $(0.8) \times (0.8 \times \$1) = (0.8)^2 \times \$1$ expenditure by the shopkeepers, and so on. Thus, for each initial dollar of investment spending, the progression is:

$$1 + 0.8 + (0.8)^2 + (0.8)^3 + (0.8)^4 + \ldots.$$

Table 9-2
THE MULTIPLIER SPENDING CHAIN

(1) ROUND NUMBER	(2) SPENDING IN THIS ROUND	(3) CUMULATIVE TOTAL
1	$1,000,000	$1,000,000
2	800,000	1,800,000
3	640,000	2,440,000
4	512,000	2,952,000
5	409,600	3,361,600
6	327,680	3,689,280
7	262,144	3,951,424
8	209,715	4,161,139
9	167,772	4,328,911
10	134,218	4,463,129
. . .	. . .	. . .
20	14,412	4,942,354
. . .	. . .	. . .
50	18	4,999,929
. . .	. . .	. . .
"Infinity"	0	5,000,000

This table shows how the multiplier unfolds through time. Round 1 is GM's initial spending, which leads to $1 million in additional income to construction workers. Round 2 shows the construction workers spending 80 percent of this amount, since the marginal propensity to consume is 0.8. The other rounds proceed accordingly, with spending in each successive round equal to 80 percent of that in the previous round. Technically, the full multiplier of 5 is reached only after an "infinite" number of rounds. But, as can be seen, we are quite close to the full amount after 20 rounds.

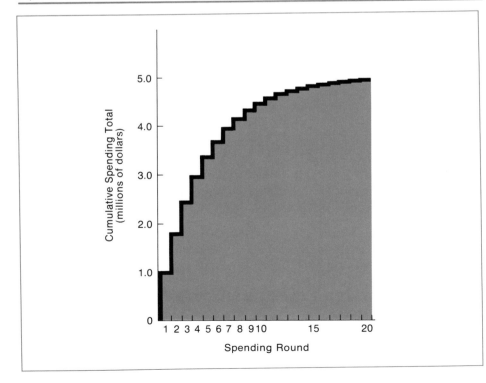

Figure 9-2
HOW THE MULTIPLIER BUILDS
This diagram portrays the numbers from Table 9-2 and shows how the multiplier builds through time. Notice how the effect grows quickly at first and how the full effect is almost reached after 15 rounds.

Applying the formula for the sum of such a series, we find that:

$$\text{Multiplier} = \frac{1}{1 - 0.8} = \frac{1}{0.2} = 5.$$

Notice how this result can be generalized. If we did not have a specific numerical value for the marginal propensity to consume, but simply called it "MPC," the geometric progression would have been:

$$1 + \text{MPC} + (\text{MPC})^2 + (\text{MPC})^3 + \ldots,$$

which has the MPC as its common ratio. Applying the same formula for summing a geometric progression to this more general case gives us the following general result:

Oversimplified Formula for the Multiplier

$$\text{Multiplier} = \frac{1}{1 - \text{MPC}}.$$

We call this formula "oversimplified" because it ignores many factors that are important in the real world. One of them is *inflation*, a complication to which we will turn in the next chapter. A second is *income taxation*, and a third is *imports*; both of these points will be elaborated on in Chapter 11. Two further factors, interest rates and exchange rates, arise from the financial system. We explain these complications in Chapters 14 and 15, after money and banking is explained. As it turns out, *all* of these factors *reduce* the size of the multiplier.

The *simplified multiplier formula* ignores the effects of inflation, taxation, imports, interest rates, and exchange rates. Later chapters show how all these factors lower the multiplier.

We can begin to appreciate just how unrealistic the "oversimplified" formula is by considering some real numbers for the Canadian economy. The marginal propensity to consume (MPC) has been estimated many times, and is about 0.9. From our oversimplified formula, then, it would seem that the multiplier should be:

$$\text{Multiplier} = \frac{1}{1 - 0.9} = \frac{1}{0.1} = 10.$$

In fact, the actual multiplier for the Canadian economy is believed to be no more than 2. This is quite a discrepancy! But it does not mean that anything we have said about the multiplier so far is incorrect. Our story is simply incomplete. As we progress through the following chapters, you will learn why the multiplier is close to 2 even though the MPC is close to 0.9. For now we simply point out that:

While the multiplier is larger than 1 in the real world, it cannot be calculated with any degree of accuracy from the oversimplified formula. The actual multiplier is *lower* than the formula suggests.

The Multiplier Effect of Consumer Spending

Business firms that invest are not the only ones that can work the magic of the multiplier; so can consumers. Let us see how the multiplier works when the process is initiated by an upsurge in consumer spending.

First, we need to distinguish between two types of change in consumer

Table 9-3

TOTAL EXPENDITURE AFTER CONSUMERS DECIDE TO SPEND $20 BILLION MORE (billions of dollars)

(1) INCOME (Y)	(2) CONSUMPTION (C)	(3) INVESTMENT (I)	(4) TOTAL EXPENDITURE (C + I)
200	190	70	260
250	230	70	300
300	270	70	340
350	310	70	380
400	350	70	420
450	390	70	460
500	430	70	500
550	470	70	540
600	510	70	580

This table shows the construction of the total expenditure schedule for Macroland following an autonomous increase of $20 billion in consumption rather than in investment. Notice that columns 2 and 3 differ from the corresponding columns in Table 9-1, but column 4 is the same in both tables. Thus the expenditure schedule in the 45° line diagram is the same as in the earlier example.

spending. When C rises because income rises—that is, when consumers move outward *along a fixed consumption function*—we call the increase in C an **induced increase in consumption**. However, if instead C rises because the entire consumption function *shifts* up, we call this an **autonomous increase in consumption**. The name indicates that consumption changes independently of income, and Chapter 7's discussion pointed out that a number of events, such as a change in the price level or in the value of the stock market, can initiate such a shift.

Let us suppose that, for some reason, consumer spending rises autonomously by $20 billion. In this case, our table of aggregate demand would have to be revised to look like Table 9-3. Comparing this to Table 9-1 on page 162, we note that each entry in column 2 is $20 billion *higher* than the corresponding entry in Table 9-1 (because consumption is higher) and each entry in column 3 is $20 billion *lower* (because investment is lower).

The equilibrium level of income is clearly Y = $500 billion once again. Indeed, the entire expenditure schedule is the same as it was in Table 9-1. The initial rise of $20 billion in spending leads to an ultimate rise of $100 billion in GNP, just as occurred in the case of higher investment spending. In fact, Figure 9-1 applies to this case without any changes. The multiplier for autonomous changes in consumer spending, then, is also 5 ($100/$20).

The reason is straightforward. It does not matter who injects an additional dollar of spending into the economy, whether it is business investors or consumers. Wherever it comes from, 80 percent of it will be respent if the MPC is 0.8, and the recipients of this second round will in turn spend 80 percent of their additional income, and so on and on. And that is what constitutes the multiplier process. In the next chapter we will learn, not surprisingly, that this same multiplier applies equally well to the third component of aggregate demand—government purchases of goods and services.

An **induced increase in consumption** is an increase in consumer spending that stems from an increase in consumer incomes. It appears on a graph as a movement along a fixed consumption function.

An **autonomous increase in consumption** is an increase in consumer spending without any increase in incomes. It appears on a graph as a shift of the entire consumption function.

The Multiplier in Reverse

A good way to check your understanding of the multiplier process is to run it in reverse: What happens if, for example, consumers autonomously decide to spend less? For example, suppose a wave of thriftiness comes over the people of Macroland so that, no matter what their total income, they now want to spend $20 billion *less* than they did previously.

A decision to spend $20 billion less out of any given level of income is, by definition, a *downward* shift of the total expenditure schedule by $20 billion. This is shown in Figure 9–3, where the $C + I$ schedule falls from $C_0 + I$ to $C_1 + I$. The horizontal distance between these two parallel lines is the $20 billion drop in spending.

There are two ways of calculating the multiplier. First, our oversimplified multiplier formula tells us that the multiplier is

$$\frac{1}{1 - \text{MPC}} = \frac{1}{1 - 0.8} = \frac{1}{0.2} = 5.$$

So a $20 billion drop in spending will lead to a multiplier effect of $100 billion. Alternatively, we can read this conclusion from Figure 9–3. Here the economy's equilibrium point moves down the 45° line from point E_0 to E_1; income drops from $400 billion to $300 billion—a decline of $100 billion.

Now compare the analysis of a decline in spending that is summarized in Figure 9–3 with our previous analysis of an increase in spending, as shown in Figure 9–1 on page 163. You will see that everything is simply turned in the opposite direction. The multiplier works in either direction.

The Paradox of Thrift

This last example of multiplier analysis teaches us an important lesson: It shows that an increase in the desire to save will lead to a cumulative fall in GNP. And, *because saving depends on income*, the resulting decline in national income will pull saving down.

Let us be a bit more specific about this. Before the upsurge in saving, consumers were spending $330 billion out of a total national income of $400 billion, as we can see in Table 8–1 on page 146. Hence $70 billion was being saved. In Figure 9–3, income falls to $300 billion. Since investment is still $70 billion, and $C + I$ must add up to Y, we know that consumption at point E must be $230 billion. So total saving is still $70 (= $300 – $230) billion. The effort to save more has been totally frustrated by the decline in GNP.[4]

[4]It is even possible for total saving to go down when people attempt to save more. This occurs in this model economy if there is induced investment (that is, if the investment line is positively sloped).

Figure 9–3

THE MULTIPLIER IN REVERSE

This diagram shows the multiplier effect of an autonomous decline in consumer spending of $20 billion. The decline appears as a downward shift of $20 billion in the expenditure schedule, which falls from $C_0 + I$ to $C_1 + I$. Equilibrium, which is always at the intersection of the expenditure schedule and the 45° line, moves from point E_0 to point E_1, and income falls from $400 billion to $300 billion.

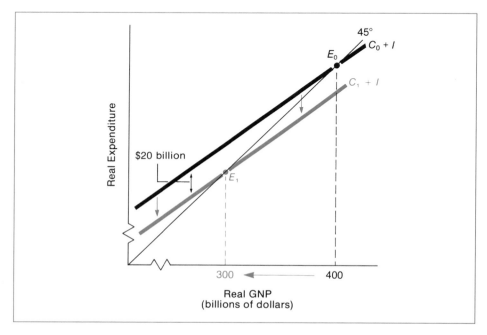

This remarkable result is called the **paradox of thrift**, because it shows that, while saving may pave the road to riches for an individual, if the nation as a whole decides to save more, the result may be a recession and lower incomes for all. The paradox of thrift is important because it is contrary to most people's thinking, and it means that greater saving may be a mixed blessing if it is not accompanied by equally greater investment. The paradox of thrift reminds us that it is not always accurate to think of the nation's economic problems as simply a big version of an individual family's economic problems.

The Multiplier and the Aggregate-Demand Curve

At this point we must recall something that was mentioned at the start of this chapter: Income–expenditure diagrams such as Figures 9–1 or 9–3 can be drawn up only for a given price level. A different price level leads to a different total-

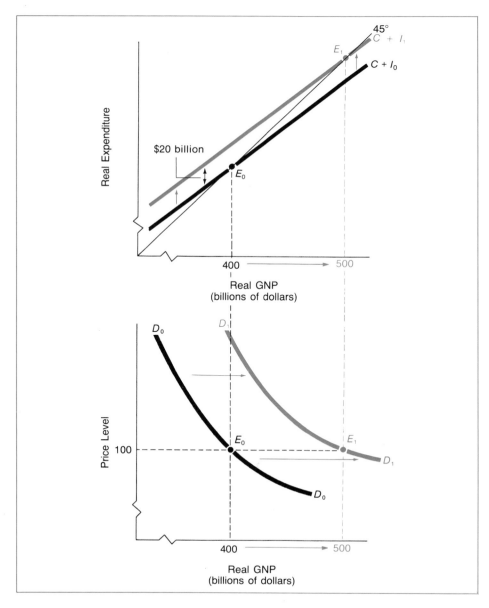

Figure 9–4
TWO VIEWS OF THE MULTIPLIER
The top panel repeats Figure 9–1. The bottom panel shows two aggregate-demand curves. Curve D_0D_0, which applies when investment is $70 billion, shows that equilibrium GNP on the demand side comes at $Y=\$400$ billion when $P=100$ (point E_0). Curve D_1D_1, which applies when investment is $90 billion, shows that equilibrium GNP on the demand side comes at $Y=\$500$ billion when $P=100$ (point E_1). The horizontal distance between points E_0 and E_1 in the bottom panel indicates the oversimplified multiplier effect.

expenditure curve. This means that our oversimplified multiplier formula measures *the increase in real GNP demanded, that is, the increase in the level of GNP that would occur if the price level were fixed*. In other words, it measures the horizontal shift of the economy's aggregate-demand curve.

Figure 9–4 illustrates this conclusion by supposing that the price level that underlies Figure 9–1 is $P=100$. The top panel simply repeats Figure 9–1 and shows how an increase in investment spending from $70 billion to $90 billion leads to an increase in GNP from $400 billion to $500 billion.

The bottom panel shows two downward-sloping aggregate-demand curves. The first, labelled D_0D_0, depicts the situation when investment is $70 billion. Point E_0 on this curve indicates that, at the given price level ($P=100$), the equilibrium quantity of GNP demanded is $400 billion. It corresponds exactly to point E_0 in the top panel. The second aggregate-demand curve, D_1D_1, depicts the situation after investment has risen to $90 billion. Point E_1 on this curve indicates that the equilibrium quantity of GNP demanded when $P=100$ has risen to $500 billion, which corresponds exactly to point E_1 in the top panel.

As Figure 9–4 shows, the horizontal distance between the two aggregate-demand curves is exactly equal to the increase in real GNP shown in the income–expenditure diagram—in this case, $100 billion. Thus:

An autonomous increase in spending leads to a horizontal shift of the aggregate-demand curve by an amount given by the oversimplified multiplier formula.

In the next chapter, after we bring the aggregate-supply curve into the picture, we will use this finding to explain one reason why GNP actually rises by *less* than the oversimplified multiplier formula suggests.

Summary

1. Any autonomous increase in expenditure has a multiplier effect on GNP, that is, it increases GNP by more than the original increase in spending.
2. The reason for this multiplier effect is that one person's additional expenditure constitutes a new source of income for another person, and this additional income leads to still more spending, and so on.
3. The multiplier also works in reverse: an autonomous decrease in any component of aggregate demand leads to a multiplied decrease in national income.
4. A simple formula for the multiplier says that its numerical value is $1/(1-MPC)$. This formula, which is

too simple to give accurate results, measures the horizontal shift of the aggregate-demand curve.
5. The simplified multiplier formula ignores the effects of inflation, taxation, imports, interest rates, and exchange rates. Later chapters show how all these factors lower the multiplier.
6. If the nation as a whole decides to save more, that is, to consume less, the resulting decline in national income may serve to make everyone poorer. This possibility that thriftiness, while helpful for the individual, may be disastrous for an entire nation, is called the paradox of thrift.

Concepts for Review

The multiplier
Induced increase in consumption

Autonomous increase in
consumption

Paradox of thrift

Questions for Discussion

1. Try to remember where you last spent a dollar. Explain how this dollar will lead to a multiplier chain of increased income and spending. (Who received the dollar? What will he or she do with it?)

2. Use both numerical and graphical methods to find the multiplier effect of the following shift in the consumption function in an economy in which investment is always $110.

INCOME	CONSUMPTION BEFORE SHIFT	CONSUMPTION AFTER SHIFT
$510	$440	$470
540	460	490
570	480	510
600	500	530
630	520	550
660	540	570
690	560	590
720	580	610

(*Hint*: What is the marginal propensity to consume?)

3. Turn back to Discussion Question 4 in Chapter 8 (page 156). Suppose investment spending rises to $140 and the price level is fixed. By how much will the equilibrium GNP increase? Derive the answer both numerically and graphically.

4. Explain the paradox of thrift. Why do you think it is called a paradox?

5. (More difficult.) Suppose the consumption function is as given in Discussion Question 9 of Chapter 8 (page 157)

$$C = 100 + 0.8Y$$

and investment (*I*) rises to $900. Use the equilibrium condition $Y = C + I$ to find the equilibrium level of GNP. (In working out the answer, assume the price level is fixed.) Compare your answer to Table 9-1 and Figure 9-1. Now compare your answer to the answer to Discussion Question 9 of Chapter 8. What do you learn about the multiplier?

Appendix
The Simple Algebra of the Multiplier

In Appendix B to Chapter 8, we worked out a general expression for the equilibrium level of GNP when the price level is fixed, investment is some fixed number, *I*, and the consumption function is:

$$C = a + bY.$$

The answer obtained there (which can be found on page 160) was:

$$Y = \frac{a + I}{1 - b}$$

From this formula it is easy to derive the over-simplified multiplier formula algebraically and to show that it applies equally well to a change in investment or to a change in autonomous consumer spending. To do this, suppose that *either I or a* increased by 1 unit. In either case, the sum $C + I$ would rise from:

$$C + I = a + bY + I,$$

to:

$$C + I = a + bY + I + 1.$$

Using the equilibrium condition that *Y* must be equal to $C + I$, we can solve for *Y* just as we did in Appendix B of Chapter 8:

$$Y = C + I$$

so that:

$$Y = a + bY + I + 1$$

and therefore:

$$(1 - b)Y = a + I + 1,$$

or:

$$Y = \frac{a + I + 1}{1 - b}.$$

By comparing this with our previous expression for *Y*, we see that a 1 unit change in *either a or I* changes equilibrium GNP by:

$$\text{change in } Y = \frac{a + I + 1}{1 - b} - \frac{a + I}{1 - b}$$

$$\text{change in } Y = \frac{a + I + 1 - (a + I)}{1 - b}$$

or:

$$\text{change in } Y = \frac{1}{1 - b}.$$

Recalling that *b* is the marginal propensity to consume, we see that this is precisely the over-simplified multiplier formula.

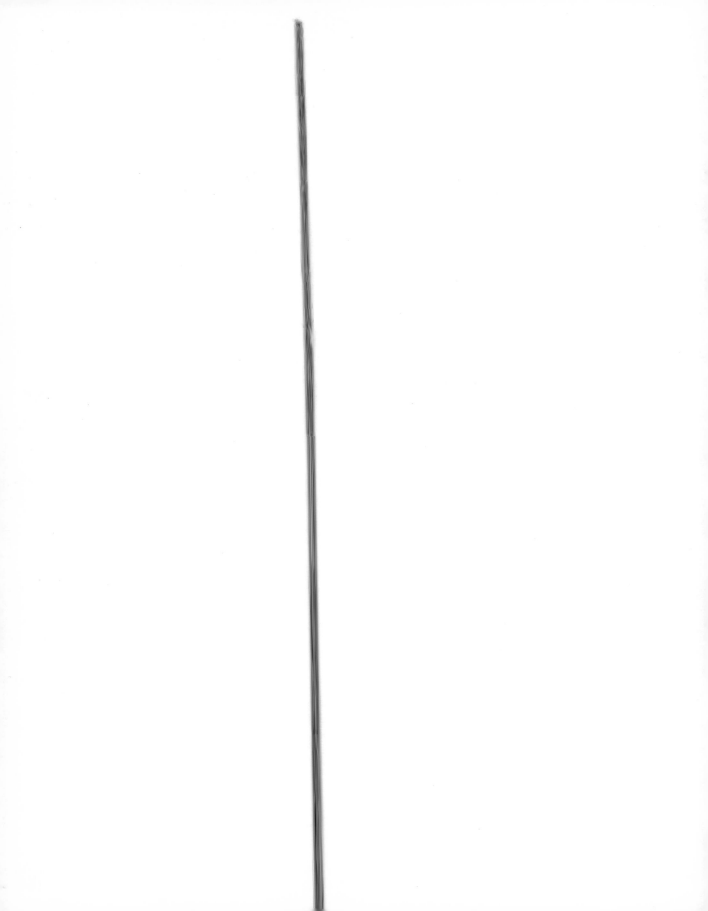

Supply-Side Equilibrium: Unemployment *and* Inflation?

We might as well reasonably
dispute whether it is the upper or
the under blade of a pair of
scissors that cuts a piece of paper,
as whether value is governed by
[demand] or [supply].

ALFRED MARSHALL

In Chapter 8 we learned that the level of prices, in conjunction with the economy's consumption and investment schedules, governs whether the economy will experience a recessionary or an inflationary gap. If the $C + I$ schedule is "too low," a *recessionary gap* will arise, while a $C + I$ schedule that is "too high" leads to an *inflationary gap*. Which sort of gap actually occurs is of some importance because, as we shall see in this chapter, a recessionary gap normally spells unemployment while an inflationary gap means inflation.

The tools provided in Chapter 8, however, are not sufficient to determine which sort of gap will arise, because the position of the $C + I$ schedule depends on the price level—and the price level is determined by *both* aggregate demand *and* aggregate supply. Thus, the task of the present chapter is to bring the supply side of the economy into the picture.

After reviewing some puzzling aspects of recent economic history, we explain how the *aggregate-supply curve* is derived from business costs. Next we consider the interaction of aggregate supply and aggregate demand, and the joint determination of output and the price level. With this apparatus in hand, we return to the phenomena of recessionary and inflationary gaps and study how the economy adjusts to each type. Doing this puts us in a position to deal with the crucial question raised in earlier chapters: Does the economy have an efficient self-correcting mechanism? As we shall learn, the economy is better at curing inflationary gaps than recessionary gaps. Finally, we use aggregate-supply–aggregate-demand analysis to explain the vexing problem of *stagflation*—the simultaneous occurrence of high unemployment *and* high inflation—which has plagued the economy so often since the mid-1970s. The chapter ends by explaining how inflation affects the multiplier.

The Mystery of Stagflation.

The analysis of demand-side equilibrium presented in Chapter 8 seems to suggest that while we can have *either* unemployment (from a recessionary gap) *or* inflation (from an inflationary gap), we should not have both at the same time. And, for many decades, this seemed to be the way things worked out. The Great Depression witnessed severe unemployment and falling prices; World War II led to an inflationary boom; there was very little inflation during the 1958–62 recession.

But things started to change in the 1970s, the decade of stagflation. The inflation rate fell only slightly during the 1971 recession, and it rose dramatically during the 1971–76 period, when unemployment also rose. Inflation also increased during the 1980 recession. Thus, recent events have made clear that inflation and unemployment can coexist in unhappy wedlock.

Throughout the 1970s, and right up to the present time, journalists, politicians, and even some economists have proclaimed frequently that the phenomenon of stagflation is a mystery to economists, that somehow it "defies the laws of economics." A *New York Times* article in 1970 was entitled "Impossible! Recession *and* Rising Prices?" Even today the coexistence of high unemployment and inflation leads many to view macroeconomics as a bankrupt discipline.

Despite the many times such claims have been made, the plain fact is that they are false. Standard economic theory *does* provide an explanation of stagflation; and by the end of this chapter, you will be able to explain it yourself. But, unfortunately, *understanding* why stagflation occurs and being able to *cure* it are two very different things. We might as well admit right now that, while some suggestions have been made, no economist has a costless cure for stagflation.

The Aggregate-Supply Curve

In earlier chapters we noted that *aggregate demand* is a schedule, not a fixed number. The quantity of real GNP that will be demanded depends on the price level, as summarized in the economy's *aggregate-demand curve*.

Analogously, the concept of *aggregate supply* does not refer to a fixed number but, rather, to a schedule (to a supply *curve*). The volume of goods and services that will be provided by profit-seeking enterprises depends on the prices they obtain for their outputs, wages and other production costs, the state of technology, and other things. The relationship between the price level and the quantity of real GNP supplied, *holding all other determinants of quantity supplied constant*, is called the economy's **aggregate-supply curve**.

The **aggregate-supply curve** shows, for each possible price level, the quantity of goods and services that all the nation's businesses are willing to produce, holding all other determinants of aggregate quantity supplied constant.

A typical aggregate-supply curve is drawn in Figure 10–1. It slopes upward, meaning that as prices rise more output is produced, *other things held constant*. It is not difficult to understand why this curve slopes upward. Producers in the Canadian economy are motivated mainly by profit. Since the profit made by producing a unit of output is simply the difference between the price at which it is sold and the unit cost of production,

$$\text{Profit per unit} = \text{Price} - \text{Cost per unit},$$

it is clear that the response of production to a rising price level (henceforth, P) depends on the response of costs.[1]

One critical fact affecting this response is that labour and other inputs used by firms normally are available at *relatively fixed prices* for some period of time—though certainly not forever. There are many reasons for this. Some workers and firms enter into long-term labour contracts that set money wages up to three years in advance. Even where there are no explicit contracts, employees typically have their wages increased only about once per year. During the interim period, money wages are fixed. Much the same is true of other factors of production. Many firms get deliveries of raw materials under long-term contracts according to which suppliers have agreed to provide the materials at prearranged prices. None of these contracts lasts forever, of course, but many of them last long enough to be of importance.

Why is it significant that firms often purchase inputs like labour and raw materials at prices that stay fixed for considerable periods? Because firms decide

[1]For a full discussion of business output decisions and how they respond to costs, see Chapter 23.

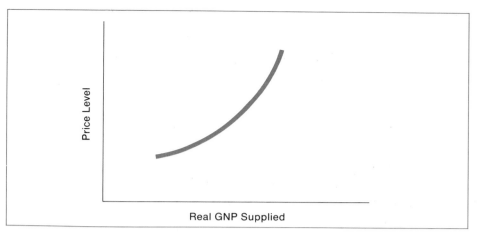

Figure 10–1
AN AGGREGATE-SUPPLY
CURVE
This graph shows a typical
aggregate-supply curve. It has a
positive slope (that is, it rises as
we move to the right), meaning
that the quantity of output supplied
rises as the price level rises.

Price Level

Real GNP Supplied

how much to produce by comparing selling prices with costs of production; and production costs obviously depend on input prices. If the selling prices of the firm's products rise while wages and other factor costs are relatively fixed, production becomes more profitable, and so firms are persuaded to increase output.

A simple example will illustrate the idea. Suppose a firm uses one hour of labour time to manufacture a gadget that sells for $9. If workers earn $8 per hour, and the firm has no other production costs, its profit per unit is:

$$\text{Profit per unit} = \text{Price} - \text{Cost per unit}$$
$$= \$9 \quad - \$8$$
$$= \$1 .$$

Let us assume that this level of profit is just enough to compensate firms for the risks involved, and so make the current production level worthwhile. Now what happens if the price of a gadget rises to $10, but wage rates remain constant? The firm's profit per unit becomes:

$$\text{Profit per unit} = \text{Price} - \text{Cost per unit}$$
$$= \$10 \quad - \$8$$
$$= \$2 .$$

With production more profitable, it is likely that the firm will supply more gadgets.

The same process operates in reverse. Suppose selling prices fall while input costs are relatively fixed. Since this squeezes their profit margins, firms may react by cutting back on production. For example, if the price of a gadget fell from $9 to $8.50, profit per unit would fall from $1 to 50¢, and firms would probably produce less.

The behaviour we have just described is summarized by the upward slope of the aggregate supply curve: Production rises when the price level (P) rises, and falls when P falls. In other words:

The aggregate-supply curve slopes upward because firms normally can purchase labour and other inputs at fixed costs for some period of time. Thus, higher selling prices make production more attractive.

The phrase "for some period of time" alerts us to the possibility that the aggregate-supply curve may not stand still for long. If wages or prices of other inputs change, as they surely will during inflationary times, then the aggregate-supply curve will shift.

Shifts of the Aggregate-Supply Curve

We have concluded so far that, for any given levels of wages and other input prices, there will be an upward-sloping aggregate-supply curve relating aggregate quantity supplied to the price level. But what factors determine the *position* of this curve? What things can make it shift?

The Wage Rate

Our previous discussion suggests that the most obvious determinant of the position of the aggregate-supply curve is the wage rate. Wages are the major element of cost for most firms, typically accounting for something like 70 percent of all expenses. Higher wages spell higher costs, thereby lowering profits at any given price.

Let us return to our example and consider what would happen to a gadget producer if the wage rate rose to $8.75 per hour while the price of a gadget remained $9. Profit per unit would decline from $9 – $8 = $1 to $9 – $8.75 = $0.25. With profits squeezed, the firm would probably cut back on production, since this lower level of profits would be less than that which had previously just made it worthwhile for the firm to bear the associated risks.

This is the typical reaction of firms in our economy to a rise in wages. Therefore, a wage increase leads to a decrease in aggregate quantity supplied at current prices. Graphically, the aggregate-supply curve shifts to the left (or inward), as shown in Figure 10-2. In this diagram, when wages are low, firms are willing to supply $400 billion in goods and services at a price level of 100 (point A). After wages increase, however, these same firms are willing to supply only $350 billion at this price level (point B). By similar reasoning, the aggregate-supply curve will shift to the right (or outward) if wages fall. Thus:

A rise in the money wage rate causes the aggregate-supply curve to shift inward, meaning that the quantity supplied at any price level declines. A fall in the money

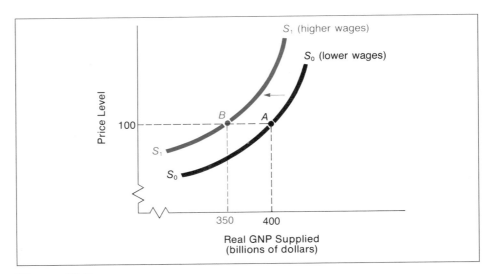

Figure 10-2

A SHIFT OF THE AGGREGATE-SUPPLY CURVE

This diagram shows what happens to the economy's aggregate-supply curve when money wages rise. Higher wages shift the supply curve inward from S_0S_0 to S_1S_1, leading, for example, to an output level of $350 billion (point B), rather than $400 billion (point A), when the price level is 100. The aggregate-supply curve will shift inward in the same manner if the price of any other input (such as energy) increases. Since some inputs are imported, a fall in the foreign value of the Canadian dollar also shifts the supply curve inward.

wage rate causes the aggregate-supply curve to shift outward, meaning that the quantity supplied at any price level increases.

Prices of Other Inputs

In this regard, there is nothing special about wages. An increase in the price of *any* input that firms buy will shift the aggregate-supply curve in the same way. That is:

The aggregate-supply curve is shifted inward by an increase in the price of any input to the production process, and is shifted outward by a decrease.

While there are many inputs other than labour, the one that has attracted the most attention in recent years is energy. We shall have much to say about energy in this book, including further discussion in this chapter and in an entire chapter on the energy problem (Chapter 35). But for present purposes the important thing to realize is that increases in the price of energy, such as those that took place in the 1970s, push the aggregate-supply curve inward more or less as shown in Figure 10–2.

The Exchange Rate

Since some production inputs are imported intermediate goods, a fall in the foreign value of the Canadian dollar raises business costs. Thus, the **exchange rate** is an important shift variable for the aggregate-supply curve as well.

The aggregate-supply curve is shifted inward by depreciation in the foreign value of the Canadian dollar and is shifted outward by an appreciation of the Canadian dollar.

The **exchange rate** states the price at which one currency can be bought in terms of another currency.

Technology and Productivity

Another factor that determines the position of the aggregate-supply curve is the state of technology. Suppose, for example, that a technological breakthrough increases the **productivity** of labour. Such an improvement in productivity will *decrease* business costs and thus improve profitability and encourage more production.

Once again, our gadget company will help us understand how this works. Suppose the price of a gadget stays at $9 and the hourly wage rate stays at $8, but gadget workers become much more productive. Specifically, suppose the labour input required to manufacture a gadget falls from one hour (which costs $8) to three-quarters of an hour (which costs $6). Then profit per unit rises from $9 – $8 = $1 to $9 – $6 = $3. The lure of higher profits should induce gadget manufacturers to increase production. In brief, we have concluded that:

Productivity is the amount of output produced by a unit of input.

Improvements in productivity shift the aggregate-supply curve outward.

Figure 10–2 can be viewed as applying to a *decline* in productivity. As we shall learn in later chapters, especially Chapter 39, slow growth of productivity is one factor that contributed to the stagflation of the 1970s, and it remains a source of great concern for the 1980s.

Available Supplies of Labour and Capital

The last determinant of the position of the aggregate-supply curve is quite obvious, but we list it anyway for the sake of completeness. The bigger the economy—as measured by its available supplies of labour and capital—the more it is capable of producing. So:

As the labour force grows, and as the capital stock is increased by investment, the aggregate-supply curve will shift outward (to the right), meaning that more output will be produced at any given price level.

These, then, are the "other things" that we hold constant when drawing up an aggregate-supply curve: wage rates, prices of other inputs (like energy), the exchange rate, technology, labour force, and capital stock. While a change in the price level moves the economy *along a given supply curve*, a change in any of these other determinants of aggregate quantity supplied *shifts the entire supply schedule*.

The Shape of the Aggregate-Supply Curve

One other feature of the aggregate-supply curve depicted in Figure 10–1 merits comment. We have drawn our supply curve with a characteristic curvature: It is relatively flat at low levels of output and gets steeper at high levels of output (as we move to the right). There is a reason for this.

When economic activity is weak, product demand slack, and capacity utilization low, firms are likely to respond to an upsurge in demand by bringing their unused capital and labour resources back into production. They will find it neither necessary nor advisable to raise prices very much. The aggregate-supply curve, in a word, will be relatively flat.

By contrast, if the economy is booming, demand is buoyant, and production is straining capacity, firms will be unable to increase output without incurring higher costs. Price increases will thus become necessary because of cost developments and, incidentally, they will not be resisted very forcefully on the demand side. In this case, the aggregate-supply curve will be rather steep. Thus:

The slope of the aggregate-supply curve, which tells us the price increase that is associated with a unit increase in quantity supplied, generally rises as the degree of resource utilization rises.

Equilibrium of Aggregate Demand and Supply

In Chapter 8 we learned that the level of prices is a crucial determinant of whether equilibrium GNP is below full employment (a recessionary gap), precisely at full employment, or above full employment (an inflationary gap). We are now in a position to analyse which type of gap, if any, will actually occur in any particular case by combining the analysis of aggregate supply just completed with the analysis of aggregate demand from the last two chapters to determine *simultaneously* the equilibrium level of real GNP (Y) and the equilibrium price level (P).

Figure 10–3 shows the mechanics graphically. The aggregate-demand curve *DD* and the aggregate-supply curve *SS* intersect at point *E*, where real GNP is $400 billion and the price level is 100. As can be seen in the graph, at any higher price level, such as 120, aggregate quantity supplied would exceed aggregate quantity demanded. There would be a glut on the market as firms found themselves unable to sell all their output. As inventories piled up, firms would compete more vigorously for the available customers, thereby forcing prices down. The price level would fall.

At any price level lower than 100, such as 80, quantity demanded would exceed quantity supplied. There would be a shortage of goods on the market. With inventories disappearing and customers knocking on their doors, firms would be encouraged to raise prices. The price level would rise.

Only when the price level is 100 are the quantities of real GNP demanded and supplied equal. Hence, only the combination $P = 100$, $Y = \$400$ billion is an equilibrium.

Table 10–1 illustrates this same conclusion in another way, using a tabular analysis similar to that of Chapter 8 (refer back to Table 8–2 on page 147). Columns 1 and 2 constitute an aggregate-demand schedule corresponding to the aggregate-demand curve *DD* in Figure 10–3. Columns 1 and 3 constitute an aggregate-supply

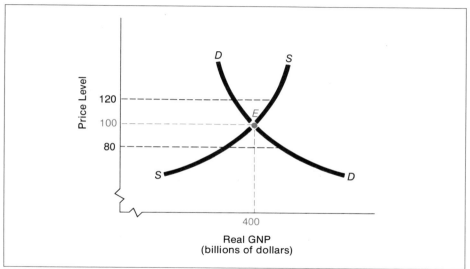

Figure 10-3
EQUILIBRIUM OF REAL GNP AND THE PRICE LEVEL
This diagram shows how the equilibrium levels of real GNP and the price level are simultaneously determined by the intersection of the aggregate-demand curve (*DD*) and the aggregate-supply curve (*SS*). In this example, equilibrium occurs at point *E*, with a real GNP of $400 billion and a price level of 100.

schedule with the general shape discussed in this chapter. It corresponds exactly to aggregate-supply curve *SS* in the figure.

It is clear from the table that equilibrium occurs only at *P* = 100 and *Y* = $400 billion. At any other price level, aggregate quantities supplied and demanded would be unequal, with consequent upward or downward pressure on prices. For example, at a price level of 80, customers demand $430 billion worth of goods and services, but firms wish to provide only $370 billion. The price level is too low and will be forced upward. Conversely, at a price level of, say, 120, quantity supplied ($420 billion) exceeds quantity demanded ($380 billion), implying that the price level must fall.

Recessionary and Inflationary Gaps Revisited

Let us now reconsider a question we posed, but could not answer, in Chapter 8: Will equilibrium occur at, below, or above full employment?

We could not give a complete answer to this question in Chapter 8 because we had no way to determine the equilibrium price level, and therefore no way to tell which type of gap, if any, would arise. The aggregate supply and demand analysis summarized in Figure 10-3 gives us the information we need to determine

Table 10-1
THE DETERMINATION OF THE EQUILIBRIUM PRICE LEVEL

(1) PRICE LEVEL (P)	(2) AGGREGATE QUANTITY DEMANDED (billions of dollars)	(3) AGGREGATE QUANTITY SUPPLIED (billions of dollars)	(4) BALANCE OF SUPPLY AND DEMAND	(5) PRICES WILL:
75	440	360	Quantity demanded exceeds quantity supplied	Rise
80	430	370	Quantity demanded exceeds quantity supplied	Rise
100	400	400	Quantity demanded equals quantity supplied	Remain the same
120	380	420	Quantity supplied exceeds quantity demanded	Fall
150	360	440	Quantity supplied exceeds quantity demanded	Fall

the price level. But we find that our answer is none the less the same as it was in Chapter 8: Anything can happen.

The reason is that nothing in Figure 10–3 tells us where full employment is; it could be above the $400 billion equilibrium level or below it. Depending on the locations of the aggregate-demand and aggregate-supply curves, then, we can reach equilibrium above full employment (an inflationary gap), at full employment, or below full employment (a recessionary gap).

All three possibilities are illustrated in Figure 10–4. The three upper panels are familiar from Chapter 8. As we move from left to right, the $C + I$ schedule rises from $C + I_0$ to $C + I_1$ to $C + I_2$, leading respectively to a recessionary gap, an equilibrium at full employment, and an inflationary gap. In fact, the upper left-hand diagram is a repeat of Figure 8–7 (page 152), and the upper right-hand diagram repeats Figure 8–8 (page 154). We stressed in Chapter 8 that any one of the three cases is possible, depending on the price level and on the consumption and investment schedules.

In the three lower panels, the equilibrium price level is determined at point E by the intersection of the aggregate-supply curve (SS) and the aggregate-demand curve (DD). But the same three possibilities emerge none the less.

In the lower left-hand panel, aggregate demand is too small to provide jobs for the entire labour force, so there is a recessionary gap equal to distance EB, or $100 billion. This corresponds precisely to the situation depicted on the income–expenditure diagram immediately above it.

In the lower right-hand panel, aggregate demand is so high that the economy reaches an equilibrium well beyond full employment. There is an inflationary gap equal to BE, or $100 billion, just as in the diagram immediately above it.

In the lower middle panel, the aggregate-demand curve D_1D_1 is at just the right level to produce an equilibrium at full employment. There is neither an inflationary nor a recessionary gap, as in the diagram just above it.

Thus, it may seem that we have done nothing but restate our previous conclusions. But, in fact, we have done much more, because now that we have studied the determination of the equilibrium price level, we are in a position to examine how the economy adjusts to either a recessionary gap or an inflationary gap.

Adjusting to an Inflationary Gap: Inflation

We have already suggested that an inflationary gap sets the stage for inflation. As we shall see now, this happens because the economy, if left to its own devices, produces an inflation that eventually eliminates an inflationary gap. In other words, the gap self-destructs, although the process may be slow and painful. Let us see how this works.

When equilibrium GNP is above potential, jobs are plentiful and labour is in great demand. Although some workers are unemployed, this minimal unemployment is less than the frictional (and structural) level—that is, less than the number we expect to be jobless because they are moving, changing occupations, and so on; or because the existing job vacancies do not match the skills and aspirations of the unemployed (labour force composition problems). Because of the low level of unemployment, many firms have trouble finding workers. They may even be having trouble hanging on to their current employees, as other firms try to lure them away with higher wages.

Such a situation is bound to lead to rising wages, and rising wages add to business costs, thus shifting the aggregate-supply curve inward. But as the aggregate-supply curve shifts inward—eventually moving from S_0S_0 to S_1S_1 in Figure 10–5, for example—the size of the inflationary gap steadily declines. Thus, inflation erodes the inflationary gap, eventually leading the economy to an equilibrium at full employment (point F in Figure 10–5).

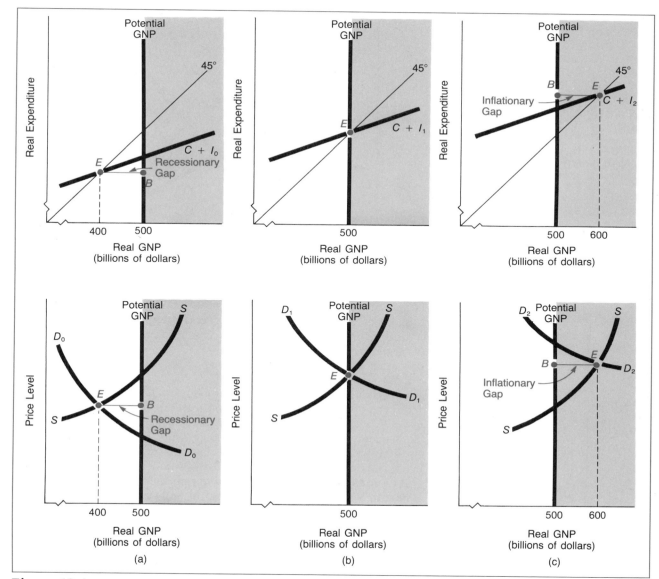

Figure 10-4

RECESSIONARY AND INFLATIONARY GAPS REVISITED

This figure shows three possible types of equilibrium on two different diagrams. In the top row, income–expenditure diagrams from Chapter 8 are used to depict a recessionary gap, an equilibrium at full employment, and an inflationary gap. In the bottom row, these same three situations are shown on aggregate supply and demand diagrams. In each case, the aggregate-supply curve is the same (SS), equilibrium occurs at point E, and full employment GNP is $500 billion. In part (a), the aggregate-demand curve D_0D_0 is relatively low, so that equilibrium falls below full employment. There is a recessionary gap measured by the distance EB, or $100 billion. In part (b), the aggregate demand-curve D_1D_1 is higher, and equilibrium occurs precisely at full employment. There is no gap of either kind. In part (c), the aggregate-demand curve D_2D_2 is so high that equilibrium occurs beyond full employment. There is an inflationary gap measured by the distance BE, or $100 billion.

There is a straightforward way of looking at how this self-correcting process works. The trouble arises in the first place because consumers and investors are demanding more output than the economy is capable of producing at normal operating rates. To paraphrase an old cliché, there is too much demand chasing too little supply. Naturally, prices will be rising in such an environment. And the rising prices will eat away at the purchasing power of consumers' wealth, forcing them to cut back on consumption, as explained in Chapter 7. Eventually,

Figure 10–5

THE ELIMINATION OF AN INFLATIONARY GAP

When the aggregate-supply curve is S_0S_0 and the aggregate-demand curve is DD, the economy will initially reach equilibrium (point E) with an inflationary gap. The resulting inflation of wages will push the supply curve inward until it has shifted to the position indicated by curve S_1S_1. Here, with equilibrium at point F, the economy is at normal full employment. But, during the adjustment period from E to F, there will have been inflation.

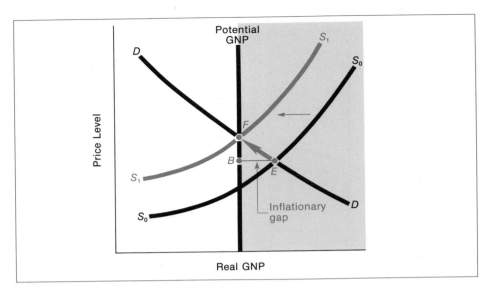

consumers' appetites for goods will be scaled down to the economy's capacity to provide those goods; and at this point, the self-correcting process stops. That, in essence, is the unhappy process by which the economy cures itself of the problem of excessive aggregate demand.

One caveat should be entered. The conclusion that an inflationary gap sows the seeds of its own destruction holds *only in the absence of further forces propelling the aggregate demand curve outward.* But in Chapter 9 we have already encountered several forces that might shift the aggregate-demand curve outward. As you can see by manipulating the aggregate-demand–aggregate-supply diagram, if aggregate demand is shifting out at the same time that aggregate supply is shifting in, there will certainly be inflation, but the inflationary gap may not shrink. (Try this as an exercise, to make sure you understand how to use the apparatus.) As a historical proposition, then, not all inflationary episodes have come to a smooth and gradual end. At times, the self-correcting mechanism is overridden by rapid expansion of aggregate demand—which is sometimes even due to government policy!

Demand Inflation and Stagflation

Simple as it is, this adjustment model teaches us a number of important lessons about inflation in the real world. First of all, Figure 10–5 reminds us that the real culprit in this particular inflation is the excessive level of aggregate demand. The aggregate-demand curve is initially so high that it intersects the aggregate-supply curve at an output level higher than full employment. The resulting intense demand for workers pushes wages higher; and higher wages spell higher prices. While excessive demand is not the only possible cause of inflation in the real world, it certainly is the cause in our example.

However, business managers and journalists are very likely to blame inflation on rising wages. In a superficial sense, of course, they are right, because higher wages do indeed lead firms to raise their prices. But in a deeper sense they are wrong. Both rising wages and rising prices are only symptoms of an underlying malady: too much aggregate demand. Blaming labour for inflation in such a case is a bit like blaming high doctor bills for making you ill.

Second, we see that output falls while prices rise as the economy adjusts from point E to point F in Figure 10–5. This process thus provides our first (but not our last!) explanation of the phenomenon of stagflation. We see that:

A period of stagflation is part of the normal aftermath of a period of excessive aggregate demand.

It is easy enough to understand why stagflation occurs. When aggregate demand is excessive, the economy will (temporarily) produce beyond its normal capacity. Labour markets become very tight and wages rise. Machinery and raw materials may also become scarce and so start rising in price. Faced by higher costs, the natural reaction of business firms is both to produce less and to charge a higher price. This is stagflation.

It may be useful to review what we have learned about inflationary gaps thus far.

If aggregate demand is exceptionally high, the economy may reach an equilibrium above full employment (an inflationary gap). When this occurs, the tight situation in the labour market soon forces wages to rise. Since wages are business costs, prices rise and there is inflation. With cuts in consumer purchasing power, the inflationary gap begins to close. As the inflationary gap is closing, output falls while prices continue to rise, so the economy experiences stagflation until the inflationary gap is eliminated. At this point, a long-run equilibrium is established with a higher price level and with GNP equal to potential GNP.

Examples from Canadian History

Because inflationary gaps have been rare birds in recent years, we have to go back to the late 1960s, and to the 1973–75 period, to find a "textbook" example of an inflationary gap that extinguished itself in this way. During the 1966–69 period, the Canadian economy was booming, unemployment got down to 4 percent, and jobs were plentiful. According to official estimates of potential GNP, there was an inflationary gap.

Our analysis suggests that wages should have been accelerating, and indeed they were. The bright blue bars in Figure 10–6 illustrate this acceleration. The dark blue bars show that the rate of price inflation followed the rate of increase of

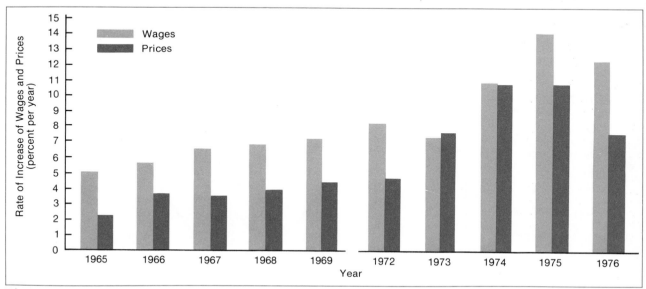

Figure 10-6
GROWTH RATES OF WAGES AND PRICES IN CANADA, 1965–1969 and 1972–1976
These data illustrate what happened when an inflationary gap arose in the late 1960s. Notice the acceleration of both wages and prices. By 1969, the gap was eliminated and wage increases levelled off. Price increases subsequently fell back to 2.9 percent in 1971. The second inflationary gap appeared in 1973-74. Again the wage increases first accelerated and then levelled off after the inflationary gap was eliminated.
SOURCE: Statistics Canada.

wages—rising from 2.4 percent a year to over 4.6 percent. This is, again, in line with what our model predicts.

The upsurge in inflation naturally ate away at the inflationary gap, which was gone by 1969. Price inflation subsequently fell back to 2.9 percent by 1971. Despite outcries of "excessive" wage demands that "caused" inflation, it is clear that the ultimate cause of the acceleration in both wages and prices was the excessive aggregate demand caused by large increases in government expenditure and exports (due to the boom in the United States that resulted from the Vietnam War).

The second example of an inflationary gap occurred in 1973-75, as the Canadian government over-stimulated aggregate demand in an attempt to avoid a recession following the OPEC oil price increases in 1973. Again, Figure 10-6 shows the acceleration in wages and prices that occurred. However, as the inflation eliminated the inflationary gap (as the higher wages shifted the aggregate-supply curve to the left), the unemployment rate rose (from 5.4 percent in 1974 to 7.1 percent in 1976). Once again, the economy behaved just as our simple model suggests.

Adjusting to a Recessionary Gap: Deflation or Unemployment?

Let us now consider what can happen when the economy finds itself in equilibrium *below* full employment—that is, when there is a recessionary gap. This might be caused, for example, by inadequate consumer spending or by anemic investment spending.

Figure 10-7 illustrates such a case and gives an impression of the economic situation of the early 1980s.

You might expect that we could just run our previous analysis in reverse: High unemployment leads to falling wages; falling wages reduce business costs and shift the aggregate-supply curve outward, so firms cut prices; falling wages and prices eliminate the recessionary gap by propping up consumer spending; and full employment is restored. The economy moves smoothly from point E to point F in Figure 10-7. Very simple. And very misleading in our modern economy!

Why is it misleading? While the economy may have operated like this long ago, it certainly does not work this way now. The history of Canada and other similar Western economies shows *many examples* of falling wages and prices before World War II but *none* since then. Not even the severe recession of 1981-84,

Figure 10-7

THE ELIMINATION OF A RECESSIONARY GAP?

At point E, there is a recessionary gap because the aggregate-demand curve DD crosses the aggregate-supply curve S_0S_0 below the level of potential GNP. If wages fall, the aggregate-supply curve gradually shifts outward until it reaches the position indicated by supply curve S_1S_1. Here the economy has attained a full-employment equilibrium at point F. But if wages refuse to fall, the economy gets stuck with a recessionary gap and a long period of unemployment.

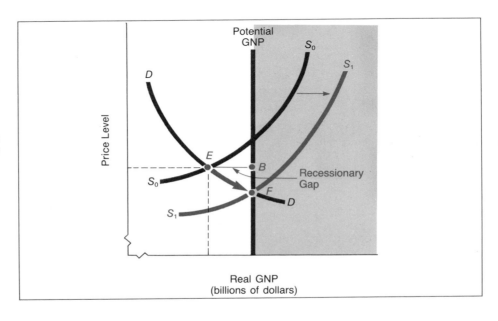

during which unemployment climbed above 12 percent, was able to force average prices and wages down.

Exactly *why* wages and prices are rigid in the downward direction in our modern economy has been a subject of intense controversy among economists for years. And the controversy continues.

Some economists emphasize institutional features like minimum-wage laws, union contracts, and a variety of government regulations that place legal floors under particular wages and prices. Because most of these institutions are of relatively recent vintage, this theory successfully explains why wages and prices are more rigid now than they were before World War II. However, most of the Canadian economy is not subject to legal restraints on cutting wages and prices. So it seems doubtful that legal restrictions can provide a complete explanation.

Other observers subscribe to the theory that holds that workers have a profound psychological resistance to accepting a wage reduction. This theory certainly has the ring of truth. Think how you would react if your boss announced that she was cutting your hourly wage rate. You might quit, or you might devote less care and attention to your job. Genuine wage "concessions" are rare enough to be news headlines. For example, Chrysler workers accepted paycuts in the early 1980s, but only when it appeared that the company was in grave danger of going bankrupt. And they demanded that their wages be restored as soon as the company was back on its feet.

While no one doubts that wage cuts are bad for morale, the psychological theory has one major drawback. It fails to explain why the psychological resistance to wage cuts apparently started only after World War II. Until a satisfactory answer to this question is provided, many economists will remain skeptical.

A third explanation is based on a fact we emphasized in Chapter 5—that business cycles have been far less severe in the postwar period than they were in the prewar period. Because of the government commitment to "full" employment, firms and workers know that recessions will not turn into depressions. Thus, workers and firms may decide to wait out the bad times rather than accept wage or price reductions that they will later regret. It is this explanation that was favoured by the Reagan and Thatcher administrations. They rejected the previous approaches, which involved an "inflationary bias." They observed that previous governments had always stimulated aggregate demand sufficiently to keep unemployment from rising too much. Taking employment for granted, labour leaders pushed for large wage increases. Either some wage- and price-control scheme seemed to be necessary to preclude labour's quite natural reaction to the inflationary gap, or they must not be allowed to take employment for granted. By essentially dropping any commitment to full employment, and by bluntly announcing that they would not permit an inflationary gap, these governments attempted to reduce the downward inflexibility of wages.

There are other theories as well, none of which commands anything like universal acceptance. But, regardless of the cause, we might as well accept the fact that, in the modern Canadian economy, prices and wages will rise when demand is strong but generally will not fall significantly when demand is weak.

The implications of this rigidity are quite serious, for a recessionary gap cannot cure itself without some deflation. And if wages and prices will not fall, *the economy gets stuck at a point like E in Figure 10–7, that is, at an equilibrium below full employment.* Keynes was the first economist to point out the possibility of a long-lasting equilibrium below full employment and to distinguish it from the full-employment equilibrium that we have just been considering.

When aggregate demand is low, the economy may get stuck in an *unemployment equilibrium.* There is a recessionary gap, but wages and prices refuse to fall; so the gap persists. The economy endures a prolonged period of production below potential GNP.

Does the Economy Have a Self-Correcting Mechanism?

Now a situation like this would, presumably, not last forever. As the recession lengthened, and perhaps deepened, more and more workers would be unable to obtain jobs at the prevailing high wages. Eventually their resistance to wage cuts, whatever its cause, would be worn down by their need to be employed.

Firms, too, would become increasingly willing to cut prices as the period of weak demand lasted longer and longer, and managers became convinced that the slump was not merely a temporary aberration. Prices and wages did, in fact, fall during the Great Depression of the 1930s. And they might fall again if a sufficiently drastic depression were allowed to occur.

Nowadays, political leaders of all three major parties believe it is folly to wait for falling wages and prices to eliminate a recessionary gap. But while they agree that *some* government action is both necessary and appropriate under recessionary conditions, there is still vocal—and highly partisan!—debate over how much and what kind of intervention is warranted.

One reason for this disagreement is that the **self-correcting mechanism** does operate—if only weakly—to cure recessionary gaps. Recent history provides a vivid illustration.

The Economy in the 1980s: A Case Study

As the current decade opened, the Canadian economy was operating not too far below full employment, but the inflation rate was very high. A policy-induced recession (to fight inflation) drove the unemployment rate up from only 7.5 percent in 1980 to 12.0 percent in 1983. Throughout this period, the recessionary gap was growing larger, not smaller. Does this mean that the self-correcting mechanism failed to work? Not quite. It just worked weakly, and with some delay.

Between 1980 and 1981, as the recessionary gap increased, wage and price inflation accelerated slightly, as Figure 10–8 shows. According to our model of the self-correcting mechanism, this is not supposed to happen. But then, with unemployment and the recessionary gap setting postwar records, things began to change. While wages and prices did not actually decline, their rates of increase did slow down markedly in 1982–83. By 1983, as you can see in Figure 10–8, the rate of inflation had fallen to just over half its 1980 level.

Figure 10–8
GROWTH RATES OF WAGES AND PRICES IN CANADA, 1980–1983
These data illustrate what happened when the Canadian economy developed a large recessionary gap in 1980–83. Notice that wage and price inflation did not slow down in 1980–81 but then did drop markedly in 1982 and 1983. SOURCE: Statistics Canada.

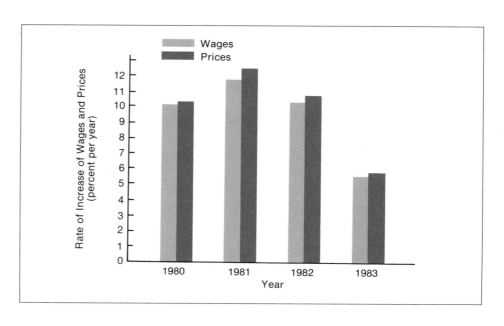

Inflation was significantly lowered, but at substantial cost. More than a million unemployed workers and hundreds of bankrupted businesses were the casualties of the war against inflation. The self-correcting mechanism is a rocky road to full employment.

Our overall conclusion about the economy's ability to right itself, then, seems to run something like this:

The economy does indeed have a self-correcting mechanism that tends to eliminate either unemployment or inflation. However, this mechanism is much more efficient at curing inflationary gaps through inflation than at curing recessionary gaps through deflation. In addition, its ability to curb inflation is sometimes overridden by increases in aggregate demand. Thus the self-correcting mechanism cannot always be relied upon.

Stagflation from Supply Shifts

We have so far encountered one type of stagflation in this chapter—the stagflation that often follows in the aftermath of an inflationary boom. As we saw, the "mystery" of the Canadian stagflations of the late 1960s and 1970s is solved in this way. However, the same model does not fit the facts of the more serious stagflationary episodes of 1973–75 and 1978–80 in the United States. What happened during these "mysteries"?

The economic boom of 1972–73 left the U.S. economy with an inflationary gap. In 1973, the U.S. unemployment rate stood at 4.9 percent—a rate considered to be below the full-employment level. By 1975, however, it had skyrocketed to 8.5 percent—well above even the most pessimistic estimates of the full-employment rate. This hardly looks like the workings of a smoothly functioning self-correcting mechanism. On the inflation front, the Consumer Price Index, which had risen only 3.4 percent during 1972, rose 8.8 percent in 1973 and 12.2 percent in 1974.

What was going on during 1973–75 that caused so much more unemployment and inflation than was expected? What were the causes of this more virulent type of stagflation? Several things, but the principal villain was the rising price of energy.

In 1973, the Organization of Petroleum Exporting Countries (OPEC) reached a collusive agreement to limit production that succeeded in quadrupling the price of crude oil in only a few months. American consumers found the prices of gasoline and home-heating fuels increasing sharply. American businesses found that one of the most important inputs into the production process—energy—rose drastically in price, thus increasing the cost of doing business. Other raw materials prices also skyrocketed in 1974.

Higher energy prices, we observed earlier, shift the economy's aggregate-supply curve inward in the manner shown in Figure 10–2 (page 176). If the aggregate-supply curve shifts inward, as it surely did for the United States in 1973–74, production will be reduced. And in order to reduce demand to the available supply, prices will have to rise. The result is the worst of both worlds: falling production and rising prices.

This conclusion is shown in Figure 10–9, which superimposes an aggregate-demand curve, *DD*, on the two aggregate-supply curves of Figure 10–2. The economy's equilibrium shifts upward to the left, from point *E* to point *A*. Thus, output falls while prices rise.

Stagflation is the typical result of adverse supply shifts.

The numbers used in Figure 10–9 are roughly indicative of what happened in the United States between 1973 (represented by supply curve S_0S_0 and point *E*) and 1975 (represented by supply curve S_1S_1 and point *A*). Real GNP, in 1972 prices, fell by about $22 billion, while the price level rose almost 20 percent.

Figure 10-9

STAGFLATION FROM A SHIFT IN AGGREGATE SUPPLY

This diagram illustrates how stagflation arises if the aggregate-supply curve shifts inward to the left (from S_0S_0 to S_1S_1). If the aggregate-demand curve does not change, equilibrium moves from point E to point A. Output falls as prices rise, which is what we mean by stagflation. The diagram indicates roughly what happened in the United States during 1973–75, when higher energy prices caused stagflation.

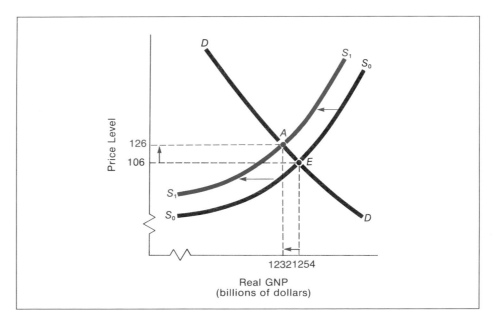

By 1978 the U.S. economy had just about recovered from the severe dislocations of 1973 and 1974, only to be clobbered by OPEC again. The ousting of the Shah of Iran in early 1979 led to a cutoff of Iranian oil supplies and virtual panic in the world oil market. Oil prices escalated as consumers scrambled to secure sources of supply and to build inventories. OPEC was only too happy to follow suit by raising prices.

The results of this second "energy shock" were much the same as those of the first. The inflation rate, which had been 9 percent in 1978, rose to 13.3 percent in 1979, and to 16 percent in the first half of 1980. Americans were almost panic-stricken over these unprecedented inflation rates, which dwarfed even the worst months of 1974.

As was the case in 1973–75, recession followed inflation. The economy, which had operated near the full-employment range (approximately 6 percent unemployment) throughout 1978, began to weaken slightly in 1979 and slipped into recession in early 1980. The unemployment rate rose to nearly 8 percent.

The general lesson to be learned from the experience of the United States during the 1970s is as important as it is clear:

The typical results of an adverse supply shock are a fall in output and an acceleration in inflation. This is one reason why the world economy was plagued by stagflation in the mid-1970s and early 1980s. And it can happen again if another series of supply-reducing events takes place.

Why didn't Canada suffer the adverse supply shocks to the same extent as the United States during the 1970s? The answer is that our government followed a rather different policy. Much to the chagrin of the oil-producing provinces, the federal government prevented domestic oil prices from rising as much as world prices did. For oil consumers in the eastern provinces who relied on imported oil, the government paid the difference between the high world price and the much lower domestic price. To a large extent, therefore, the Canadian policy precluded any big leftward shift of the aggregate-supply schedule from occurring.

Another aspect of Canadian policy was also important. The authorities correctly predicted the recession that followed OPEC in the United States and elsewhere, and they knew that this would decrease the demand for Canadian-produced goods. In an attempt to override this expected leftward shift of our aggregate-demand curve, the government stimulated aggregate demand rather dramatically. (The specific policies involved are discussed in the next few chapters.) As a result, Canada had an inflationary gap in 1973–74, not a deflationary gap as did the United States.

Was Canada's reaction to the world oil-price shocks a good policy? By comparing our experience with that of the United States, we see that Canadians suffered less unemployment. However, Canada's inflation performance has been somewhat worse. Also, citizens of the oil-producing provinces are very bitter about the big loss in their income caused by the ceiling imposed on domestic oil prices. Finally, to some extent the Canadian policy has only delayed, not eliminated, the adverse supply shifts. The Canadian oil price was gradually increased each year following 1974. Also, to cover part of the mushrooming budget deficit (partly caused by the government's oil-price subsidy to eastern consumers during the 1970s), the federal government raised the manufacturers' sales tax in 1984. This increased business costs and shifted the aggregate-supply curve inward, thereby worsening the recession of the 1980s instead of the one in the 1970s.

Inflation and the Multiplier

When we introduced the concept of the multiplier in Chapter 9, we said that there were several reasons why its actual value is smaller than that suggested by the oversimplified multiplier formula. We are now in a position to understand one of these reasons: *Inflation reduces the size of the multiplier.*

The basic idea is quite simple. In Chapter 9, we described a multiplier process in which one person's spending became another person's income, which led to further spending by the second person, and so on. But this story is confined to the demand side of the economy.

Let us therefore consider what is likely to happen on the supply side as the multiplier process unfolds. Will the additional demand be taken care of by firms without raising prices?

If the aggregate-supply curve is upward sloping, the answer is no; more goods will only be provided at higher prices. Thus, as the multiplier chain progresses, pulling income and employment up, prices will also rise. And this, as we know from Chapter 7, will dampen consumer spending because rising prices reduce the purchasing power of consumers' wealth. So the multiplier chain will not proceed as far as it would have in the absence of inflation. How much inflation results from the rise in demand? How much of the multiplier chain is cut off by inflation? The answers depend on the slope of the economy's aggregate-supply curve.

For a concrete example of the analysis, let us return to the $20 billion increase in investment spending used in Chapter 9. As we learned there (see especially page 169) $20 billion in additional investment spending eventually leads—through the multiplier process—to *a horizontal shift of $100 billion in the aggregate-demand curve.* But to know the actual quantity that will ultimately be produced, and the actual price level, we must bring the aggregate-supply curve into the picture.

Figure 10–10 does this. Here we show the $100 billion horizontal shift of the aggregate-demand curve, from D_0D_0 to D_1D_1, that is derived from the oversimplified multiplier formula (which ignored rising prices). The aggregate-supply curve, SS, then tells us how this expansion of demand is apportioned between higher output and higher prices. We see that as the economy's equilibrium moves from point E_0 to point E_1, real GNP does not rise by $100 billion. Instead, prices rise, which, as we know, tends to cancel out part of the rise in quantity demanded. So output increases only from $400 billion to $480 billion—an increase of $80 billion. Thus, in our example, inflation has reduced the multiplier from $100/$20 = 5 to $80/$20 = 4. In general:

As long as the aggregate-supply curve is upward sloping, any increase in aggregate

Figure 10-10

INFLATION AND THE MULTIPLIER

This figure illustrates the complete analysis of the multiplier, including the effect of inflation. The simple multiplier of Chapter 9, which ignored changes in the price level, appears here as a *horizontal* shift of $100 billion in the aggregate-demand curve, meaning that the multiplier would be $100/$20 = 5 if prices did not rise. However, when aggregate demand shifts from $D_0 D_0$ to $D_1 D_1$, prices rise. In the diagram, the price level increases from 100 to 120 or by 20 percent. Consequently, equilibrium real income increases from $400 billion to only $480 billion—for a rise of $80 billion, or a multiplier of $80/$20 = 4.

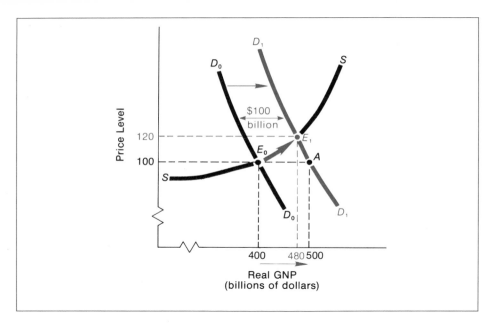

demand will push up the price level. This will, in turn, drain off some of the higher real demand by eroding the purchasing power of consumer wealth. Thus, inflation reduces the multiplier below that suggested by the oversimplified formula.

Notice also that the price level in this example has been pushed up (from 100 to 120, or 20 percent) by the rise in investment demand. This, too, is a general result:

As long as the aggregate-supply curve is upward sloping, any upward shift in the aggregate demand curve will cause some rise in prices in the economy.

The economic behaviour behind these results certainly cannot be considered surprising. Firms faced with a large increase in aggregate quantity demanded at their original prices respond to the changed circumstances in two natural ways: They raise production (so GNP rises) and they raise prices (so the price level rises). But this rise in the price level reduces the purchasing power of the bank accounts and bonds held by consumers, and they also react in the natural way: They cut down on their spending. Such a reaction amounts to a movement *along* aggregate-demand curve $D_1 D_1$ in Figure 10-10 from point A to point E_1.

Higher prices thus play their usual dual role in a market economy: They encourage suppliers to produce more and, at the same time, encourage demanders to consume less. In this way, equilibrium is re-established at higher levels of output and higher prices through the process of inflation.

Figure 10-10 also shows us exactly where the oversimplified multiplier formula goes wrong. By ignoring the effects of the higher price level, the oversimplified formula supposes the economy moves horizontally from point E_0 to point A. As the diagram clearly shows, output does not actually rise this much. Output *would* rise this much *only* if the aggregate-supply curve were horizontal. (Verify this for yourself by pencilling in an imaginary horizontal aggregate-supply curve through points E_0 and A in Figure 10-10.) That is, the oversimplified multiplier formula tacitly assumes that the aggregate-supply curve is horizontal. Normally, this is an unrealistic assumption, and that is one reason why the oversimplified formula exaggerates the size of the multiplier.

As a summary, it may be useful to put together what we have learned about multiplier analysis in Chapters 9 and 10.

STEPS IN CALCULATING THE MULTIPLIER

1. Shift the expenditure schedule in the 45° line diagram vertically by the amount of the autonomous shift in spending (as, for example, in Figure 9–1 on page 163).

2. Use the 45° line diagram, or the oversimplified multiplier formula, to calculate the multiplier effect on the GNP that *would* occur *if* the price level, wage rates, interest rate, exchange rate, and level of imports stayed constant (see again Figure 9–1).

3. Now move from the 45° line diagram to an aggregate supply and demand diagram like Figure 10–10 to see how the price level will react. Enter the multiplier effect calculated in Step 2 as a horizontal shift of the aggregate-demand curve in the supply–demand diagram.

4. The supply–demand diagram shows what *would* happen to real output and the price level *if* wages, the interest and exchange rates, and imports were constant.

We consider these remaining provisos in following chapters. It turns out that the exchange rate and interest rates will remain roughly constant in the face of a shift in autonomous expenditure, *if* the central bank follows a fixed exchange-rate policy (as explained in Chapter 15). However, the assumptions that imports and wages are constant are not plausible. The analysis in Chapter 14 indicates that making more plausible assumptions about the response of wages raises the effect of aggregate demand increases on the price level and lowers its effect on real output.

Summary

1. The economy's aggregate-supply curve relates the quantity of goods and services that will be supplied to the price level. It normally slopes upward to the right because the costs of labour and other inputs are relatively fixed in the short run, meaning that higher selling prices make input costs relatively "cheaper" and therefore encourage greater production.

2. The position of the aggregate-supply curve can be shifted by changes in wage rates, prices of other inputs, the exchange rate, technology, or the quantities of labour and capital available for employment.

3. The aggregate-supply curve normally gets steeper as output increases. This means that, as output and capacity utilization rise, any given increase in aggregate demand leads to more inflation and less growth of real output.

4. The equilibrium price level and the equilibrium level of real GNP are jointly determined by the intersection of the economy's aggregate-supply and aggregate-demand schedules. This intersection may come at full employment, below full employment (a recessionary gap), or above full employment (an inflationary gap).

5. If there is an inflationary gap, the economy has a self-correcting mechanism that erodes the gap through a process of inflation. Specifically, unusually strong job prospects push wages up, which shifts the aggregate-supply curve to the left and reduces the inflationary gap.

6. One consequence of this self-correcting mechanism is that, if a surge in aggregate demand opens up an inflationary gap, part of the economy's natural adjustment to this event will be a period of stagflation; that is, a period in which prices are rising while output is falling.

7. The economy also has a self-correcting mechanism that erodes a recessionary gap. However, this mechanism works much more slowly and less reliably than the inflationary-gap mechanism because it relies on falling wages to shift the aggregate-supply curve outward, and wages do not fall easily.

8. An inward shift of the aggregate-supply curve will cause output to fall while prices rise; that is, it will cause stagflation. Among the events that have caused such a shift are the abrupt increases in the price of foreign oil and the falling foreign currency value of the Canadian dollar.

9. Adverse supply shifts like this have occurred: foreign oil-price increases in the 1970s, and a falling value of the Canadian dollar in the 1980s. Thus the stagflation of the 1970s and 1980s is no mystery at all.

10. Among the reasons why the oversimplified multiplier formula is wrong is the fact that it ignores any inflation that may be caused by an increase in aggregate demand. Such inflation decreases the multiplier by reducing consumer spending, because consumers as a group suffer a loss of purchasing power when prices rise.

Concepts for Review

Aggregate-supply curve
Productivity
Equilibrium of real GNP and the
    price level

Inflationary gap
Self-correcting mechanism
Stagflation

Recessionary gap
Inflation and the multiplier

Questions for Discussion

1. In an economy with the following aggregate-demand and aggregate-supply schedules, find the equilibrium levels of real output and the price level. Graph your solution. If full employment comes at $1800 billion, is there an inflationary or a recessionary gap?

AGGREGATE QUANTITY DEMANDED (in billions)	PRICE LEVEL	AGGREGATE QUANTITY SUPPLIED (in billions)
2000	75	1400
1950	80	1450
1800	100	1600
1700	120	1700
1600	150	1800

2. Suppose a worker receives a wage of $9.50 per hour. Compute the *real* wage (money wage deflated by the price index) corresponding to each of the following possible price levels: 85, 95, 100, 110, 120. What do you notice about the relationship between the real wage and the price level? Relate this to the slope of the aggregate-supply curve.

3. In 1980, capacity utilization averaged 80 percent in Canada. In 1982 it averaged 70 percent. In which year do you think the economy found itself on a steeper portion of its aggregate-supply curve? Explain why.

4. Explain why an increase in the price of foreign oil shifts the aggregate-supply curve inward to the left. What are the consequences of such a shift?

5. Comment on the following statement: "Inflationary and recessionary gaps are nothing to worry about because the economy has a built-in mechanism that cures either type of gap automatically."

6. Give *two* different explanations of how the economy can suffer from stagflation.

7. Why do you think wages tend to be rigid in the downward direction?

8. Add the following aggregate-supply and aggregate-demand schedules to the data in Question 3 of Chapter 9 (page 171) to see how inflation affects the multiplier.

(1) PRICE LEVEL	(2) AGGREGATE DEMAND (when investment is $130)	(3) AGGREGATE DEMAND (when investment is $140)	(4) AGGREGATE SUPPLY
90	$1210	$1310	$1110
95	1205	1305	1155
100	1200	1300	1200
105	1195	1295	1245
110	1190	1290	1290
115	1185	1285	1335

Draw these schedules on a piece of graph paper. Then:

a. Notice that the difference between columns 2 and 3 (the aggregate-demand schedule at two different levels of investment) is always $100. Discuss how this relates to your answer in the previous chapter.

b. Find the equilibrium GNP and the equilibrium price level both before and after the increase in investment. What is the value of the multiplier?

9. Explain in words why rising prices reduce the multiplier effect of an autonomous increase in aggregate demand.

10. Use an aggregate supply and demand diagram to show that multiplier effects are smaller when the aggregate-supply curve is steeper. Which case gives rise to more inflation—the steep aggregate-supply curve or the flat one?

III

Fiscal, Monetary, and Exchange-Rate Policy

Fiscal Policy and Supply-Side Economics

11

Facts do not cease to exist because they are ignored.
ALDOUS HUXLEY

In the last several chapters, we have constructed and analysed a model of an economy in which there is no government spending, taxes, exports, or imports. We have seen how equilibrium is determined and how changes in the consumption and investment components of aggregate demand can change that equilibrium.

But in the Canadian economy, the government's budgetary decisions exercise a profound influence over aggregate demand, and we export and import more than one-quarter of our national product. Furthermore, net exports is almost as volatile a component of aggregate demand as is investment. Thus, to make our model fit the Canadian economy, our task in this chapter is to put the government and the foreign sector back into the picture. More than a desire for realism dictates that we bring the government into the model. Without including the government we cannot study what national economic policy can do about inflation and unemployment, and this is perhaps the main purpose of macroeconomic analysis.

Traditionally, the government has used its taxing and spending powers to manage aggregate demand. So this chapter begins there. Specifically, we expand the basic model to allow, first, for government purchases of goods and services as a component of aggregate demand, and second, for an income tax that makes disposable income less than national income. As we shall see, neither of these complications requires any fundamental change in the way we analyse the determination of GNP and the price level, although taxes do reduce the multiplier. But, while the *model* does not change much when the government is introduced, the *policy implications* of the analysis are drastically altered. In fact, the main topic of this chapter is how the government can use its spending and taxes to influence economic activity.

When Ronald Reagan became the U.S. president in 1981, he rejected the conventional emphasis on aggregate-demand management and argued that the government could and should use tax policy to influence aggregate supply. The terms "Reaganomics" and "supply-side economics" became the popular labels for this approach, which we analyse in the final part of this chapter.

Government Purchases and Equilibrium Income

The government's **fiscal policy** is its plan for spending and taxation. It is designed to steer aggregate demand in some desired direction.

The federal Minister of Finance normally presents a budget to Parliament each year. This economic report outlines the government's proposed **fiscal policy**, a highly volatile issue. In these statements, the finance minister outlines taxing and spending proposals, explains the effects that government economists expect these proposals to have on aggregate demand, and offers an explanation indicating why this is the right policy at that time.

This chapter is concerned with how these important budget decisions are, or should be, made. If you were a member of parliament, how would you evaluate the budget? How much spending is the right amount? How much taxation is appropriate? Perhaps more to the point, how can you as a voter decide whether your elected representatives have made sound decisions?

Before attempting to answer questions like these, we must integrate the government into our model of the determination of national income and the price level. We do this in stages, starting first with **government purchases of goods and services** (G), and then adding taxes. Thus, in considering once again the circular flow of income and expenditure (see Figure 11–1), we ignore for the moment the flows of tax revenues and transfer payments at point 5. How would the equilibrium level of GNP be determined in an economy in which the government bought goods but did not levy taxes or make transfers?

The circular flow diagram shows us the answer, just as it did in an economy with no government (Chapter 8). If the size of the circular flow of income and expenditure is to be maintained, then the total amount of new goods and services that firms produce at point 4 (Y) must be equal to the sum of the demands of consumers at point 1 (C), investors at point 2 (I), and government at point 3 (G). We

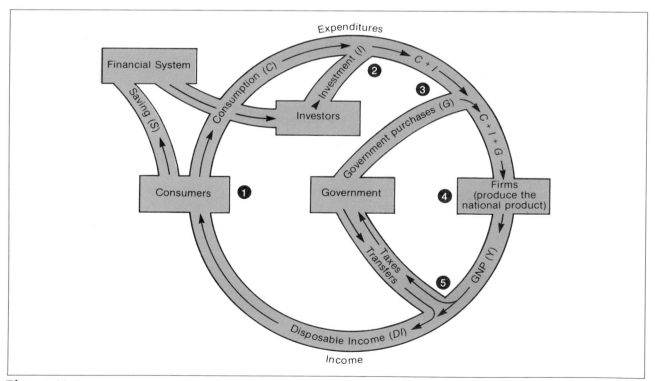

Figure 11–1
THE CIRCULAR FLOW OF EXPENDITURE AND INCOME

thus obtain the following restatement of the condition for equilibrium on the demand side of the economy:

For any given price level, equilibrium GNP on the demand side of the economy occurs when the sum of consumption demand, investment demand, and government demand for goods and services just equals the GNP. In symbols:

$$Y = C + I + G.$$

The reasoning behind this equilibrium condition is precisely the same as it was in Chapter 8. At income levels below equilibrium, the sum $C + I + G$ would exceed Y; and so inventories would be disappearing, signaling firms that they should raise their production. Conversely, at income levels above equilibrium, $C + I + G$ would be less than Y, so that unwanted inventories would be accumulating and firms would have incentives to cut back production.

Table 11–1, which may usefully be compared to Table 8–1 in Chapter 8 (page 146, illustrates this process. The first three columns give the same consumption and investment schedules that we worked with there. The fourth column reflects the assumption that government purchases will be $80 billion, irrespective of the level of GNP. Summing these three components gives us our new total expenditure schedule in columns 1 and 5.

What, then, is the equilibrium level of GNP? As the table indicates, only a GNP of $800 billion can be an equilibrium, for only at this level is total spending in balance with production.

Figure 11–2 shows the same conclusion graphically. The line labelled C is the same consumption function we used in previous chapters. The line labelled $C + I$ adds the fixed $70 billion in investment to this; again, this amount is taken from previous chapters. Finally, the line labelled $C + I + G$ adds an additional $80 billion in government spending to the $C + I$ line, which gives us our new total expenditure schedule.

Just as in previous chapters, the equilibrium of the economy is at point E, where the total expenditure schedule crosses the 45° line. This is because the 45° line includes all the points at which $C + I + G$ add up to Y. The diagram shows that equilibrium is at a GNP of $800 billion, which consists of $650 billion in consumption, $70 billion in investment, and $80 billion in government purchases. This agrees precisely with Table 11–1, as must be the case. If all this seems

Table 11–1
DERIVATION OF A TOTAL EXPENDITURE SCHEDULE WITH GOVERNMENT PURCHASES

(1) NATIONAL INCOME (Y) (billions of dollars)	(2) CONSUMPTION (C) (billions of dollars)	(3) INVESTMENT (I) (billions of dollars)	(4) GOVERNMENT PURCHASES (G) (billions of dollars)	(5) TOTAL EXPENDITURE (C + I + G) (billions of dollars)
400	330	70	80	480
450	370	70	80	520
500	410	70	80	560
550	450	70	80	600
600	490	70	80	640
650	530	70	80	680
700	570	70	80	720
750	610	70	80	760
800	650	70	80	800
850	690	70	80	840

This table adds government purchases of $80 billion to our model economy. Notice that the equilibrium level of GNP grows to $800 billion, for this is the level at which output is equal to total spending (the sum of $C + I + G$).

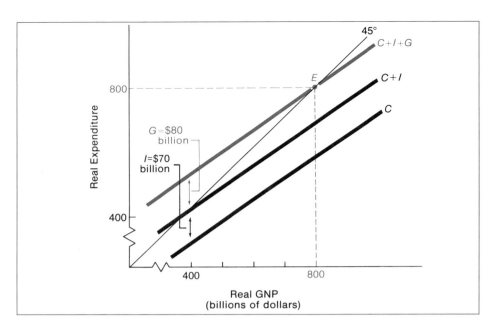

Figure 11-2

INCOME DETERMINATION WITH GOVERNMENT SPENDING

This diagram adds government purchases of goods and services (G) to the income–expenditure diagrams that we have been using. The C + I + G curve is the total expenditure schedule, and the point where it crosses the 45° line (point E) marks the equilibrium level of GNP. The C + I + G line is parallel to the C + I line because of the assumption that whatever the level of GNP, government spending remains at $80 billion.

familiar from previous chapters, it should; for the analysis is precisely the same.[1]

In Chapter 9 we stated that when government spending was introduced, the multiplier for G would be the same as the multiplier for autonomous changes in C and I. We can now demonstrate this conclusion.

If you flip back to page 147, you will see that the equilibrium reached there was at a level of output Y = $400 billion. Now, in an economy that is identical with the one in Chapter 8 except for the $80 billion in government spending, we see that the equilibrium is at Y = $800 billion. Thus an $80 billion increment in G (from zero to $80 billion) has pushed up GNP by $400 billion. In this example, then, the multiplier for government spending is $400/$80 = 5, which, you will recall, was also the value of the multiplier for autonomous increases in investment or consumption.

The two multipliers are identical because the logic behind them is identical. In Chapter 9 we studied an example of a multiplier spending chain set in motion when Generous Motors spent $1 million to build a factory. This process could equally well have been kicked off by the federal government buying $1 million worth of new cars from GM. Thereafter, each recipient of additional income would spend 80 percent of it (the assumed marginal propensity to consume), until $5 million in new income had eventually been created.

And the qualification that we placed on the oversimplified multiplier formula in Chapter 10 also applies here. Government spending normally leads to some inflation, which pulls down consumer spending and thus reduces the value of the multiplier below our illustrative figure of 5.

Income Taxes and the Consumption Schedule

You can see, then, that it takes little effort to bring government purchases into our model of income determination. Let us turn our attention next to taxes and, in particular to the personal income tax.

For present purposes, the most important aspect of taxes is that they create a discrepancy between gross national product (GNP) and disposable income (DI), as

[1] An algebraic version of this and other topics discussed here can be found in the appendix to this chapter.

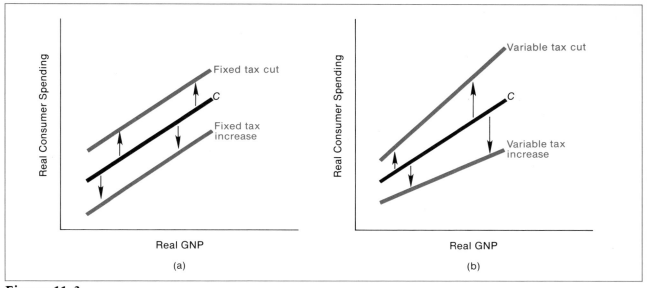

Figure 11-3

HOW TAX POLICY SHIFTS THE CONSUMPTION SCHEDULE

Because consumption depends on disposable income, not GNP, any change in taxes will shift the consumption schedule relating consumption to GNP. Part (a) shows how the curve shifts for changes in taxes of fixed amounts. Part (b) shows how the C curve shifts if the tax cut (or tax increase) is larger at high incomes than at low incomes.

can be seen in the circular flow diagram (Figure 11–1). Tax revenues flow out of the circular flow and into the hands of the government. (The effects of the transfer payments, which enter the circular flow at point 5, will be considered presently.)

We learned in Chapter 7 that there is a close and reliable relationship between consumer spending and *disposable* income. Therefore, if we want to construct a relationship between consumer spending and GNP, we first have to allow for the fact that taxes are deducted from GNP before *DI* is arrived at. The importance of this piece of accounting is that when taxes are increased, disposable income falls—and hence so does consumption—*even if GNP is unchanged.* As a result:

An increase in personal income taxes shifts the consumption schedule in our 45° line diagram downward. Similarly, a reduction in taxes shifts the consumption schedule upward.

The specific manner in which the consumption schedule shifts depends on the nature of the tax change. One way to reduce taxes is to introduce a flat, per person tax credit. The increase in disposable income from this legislation is the *same* regardless of the level of GNP; hence the increase in consumer spending is the same. In a word, the *C* schedule shifts upward in a parallel manner, as shown in Figure 11–3(a).

But often tax policy is designed to make the change in disposable income depend on the level of income, normally being larger at high income levels than at low ones. This is true, for example, when the government changes tax *rates*. Since this sort of tax policy changes disposable income more when GNP is higher, the upward or downward shift in the *C* schedule is sharper at high income levels than at low ones. Figure 11–3(b) illustrates how this type of tax policy shifts the consumption schedule.

Tax Policy and Equilibrium Income

We are now in a position to put taxes into our model of income determination. To do this, we must first adjust the consumption schedule we have been using to allow for an income tax.

Table 11-2

DERIVATION OF A CONSUMPTION SCHEDULE WITH INCOME TAXATION

(1) GROSS NATIONAL PRODUCT (billions of dollars)	(2) TAXES (billions of dollars)	(3) DISPOSABLE INCOME (GNP minus taxes) (billions of dollars)	(4) CONSUMPTION (billions of dollars)
250	62.5	187.5	160
300	75.0	225.0	190
350	87.5	262.5	220
400	100.0	300.0	250
450	112.5	337.5	280
500	125.0	375.0	310
550	137.5	412.5	340

Because taxes (column 2) must be subtracted from gross national product (column 1) to get disposable income (column 3), this table shows how an income tax lowers the consumption schedule (column 4) in a concrete example. (Compare column 4 with the consumption schedule in Table 11-1 to see that the C schedule has indeed fallen.)

Table 11-2 does this on the assumption that taxes are 25 percent of GNP. Column 1 shows alternative values of GNP ranging from $250 billion to $550 billion, and column 2 indicates that taxes are always one-quarter of this amount. Column 3 subtracts column 2 from column 1 to arrive at disposable income (DI). Column 4 then shows the amount of consumer spending corresponding to each level of DI. Note that columns 3 and 4 just repeat the consumption function that we studied in Chapter 7. But the consumption schedule that we need for our 45° line diagram relates C to Y, not to DI—that is, it relates spending to total consumer income, not to income net of taxes—and the schedule is therefore found in columns 1 and 4.

To derive the new expenditure schedule for an economy with taxes, we need only replace the old consumption schedule with this new one—that is, we must replace column 2 of Table 11-1 with column 4 of Table 11-2. This is done numerically in Table 11-3, and the results are shown diagrammatically in Figure 11-4. In particular, the expenditure schedule contained in columns 1 and 5 of Table 11-3 is shown as the $C + I + G$ line in Figure 11-4. Naturally, the inclusion of taxes has lowered the expenditure schedule.

Since the 45° line is given in the diagram, we can immediately locate the equilibrium level of GNP at point E. Here, gross national product is $400 billion, consumption is $250 billion, investment is $70 billion, and government purchases

Table 11-3

THE TOTAL EXPENDITURE SCHEDULE WITH TAXES AND GOVERNMENT PURCHASES

(1) GROSS NATIONAL PRODUCT (Y) (billions of dollars)	(2) CONSUMPTION (C) (billions of dollars)	(3) INVESTMENT (I) (billions of dollars)	(4) GOVERNMENT PURCHASES (G) (billions of dollars)	(5) TOTAL EXPENDITURE (C + I + G) (billions of dollars)
250	160	70	80	310
300	190	70	80	340
350	220	70	80	370
400	250	70	80	400
450	280	70	80	430
500	310	70	80	460
550	340	70	80	490

This table replaces the previous consumption schedule with a new one that adjusts for the income tax (as shown in Table 11-2) and shows that the equilibrium level of income is $400 billion.

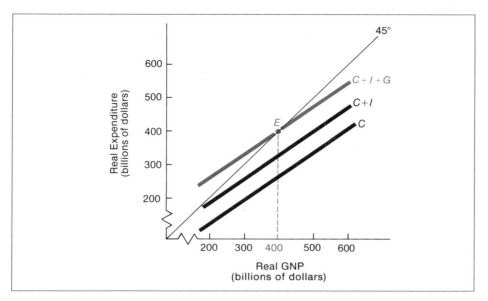

Figure 11-4
INCOME DETERMINATION WITH GOVERNMENT SPENDING AND TAXATION
This diagram adds a 25 percent income tax to the model economy portrayed in Figure 11-2. Because of this, the *C* schedule is shifted down (and hence the *C* + *I* and *C* + *I* + *G* schedules are also shifted down). Equilibrium is at point *E*, where the *C* + *I* + *G* schedule crosses the 45° line. Thus equilibrium GNP is $400 billion, the same as it was in the economy with no government. This, however, is certainly not a general result; government actions can either raise or lower GNP.

are $80 billion. As we know, full employment may occur above or below *Y* = $400 billion. If below, there is an inflationary gap. Prices probably will start to rise, pulling the expenditure schedule down and reducing equilibrium GNP. If above, there is a recessionary gap, and history suggests that prices will fall only slowly. In the interim, there will be a period of high unemployment.

In a word, once we adjust the expenditure schedule to include the effects of taxes, the determination of national income proceeds exactly as before. The effects of government spending and taxation, therefore, are fairly straightforward, and can be summarized as follows:

Government purchases of goods and services add to total spending directly through the *G* component of *C* + *I* + *G*. Taxes indirectly *reduce* total spending by lowering disposable income, and thus reduce the *C* component of *C* + *I* + *G*. On balance, then, the government's actions may raise or lower the equilibrium level of GNP, depending on how much spending and taxing it does.

Multipliers for Tax Policy

We saw earlier that government purchases (*G*) have a multiplier effect on GNP. So do changes in tax policy. But because they work indirectly via consumption, the multipliers for tax changes must be worked out in two steps.

Step 1. Before turning to the 45° line diagram, we must figure out what any proposed change in the tax law is likely to do to the consumption schedule.

Step 2. We can then enter this effect as a shift of the *C* + *I* + *G* schedule in the 45° line diagram, and work out the multiplier.

A reduction in income taxes provides a convenient example of this two-step analysis, because we have already done Step 1 in an earlier chapter. Specifically, in Chapter 7 we studied how consumer spending would respond to a cut in income taxes. We concluded that if the tax reduction were viewed as permanent, consumers would increase their spending by an amount equal to the tax cut times the marginal propensity to consume. (If you need review, turn back to pages 119-124.)

Figure 11-5

THE MULTIPLIER FOR A
REDUCTION IN INCOME
TAXES

In this example, the $C + I + G$
schedule is shifted upward, from
$C_0 + I + G$ to $C_1 + I + G$, by a tax
cut. Equilibrium GNP therefore
increases from Y_0 to Y_1.

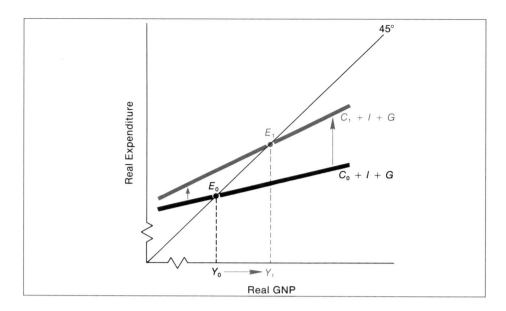

This is the shift that must be entered in the 45° line diagram to complete Step 2, and Figure 11-5 displays such a shift. The tax cut raises the expenditure schedule from $C_0 + I + G$ to $C_1 + I + G$ by raising its C component. The diagram then shows the multiplier effect on GNP, which rises from Y_0 to Y_1.

Government Transfer Payments

Finally, we should mention the last major tool of fiscal policy: **government transfer payments**. How are transfers treated in our models of income determination—like purchases of goods and services (G) or like taxes?

The answer follows readily from the circular flow diagram on page 196 or the accounting identity back on page 116. The important thing to understand about transfer payments is that they intervene between gross national product (Y) and disposable income (DI) in precisely the *opposite* way from income taxes. Specifically, starting with the wages, interest, rents, and profits that constitute the national income, we *subtract* income taxes to calculate disposable income. We do so because these taxes represent the portion of incomes that are *earned* but never *received* by consumers. But then we must *add* transfer payments because they represent sources of income that are *received* though they were not *earned* in the process of production. Thus, transfer payments are basically *negative taxes*, and giving a consumer $1 in the form of a transfer payment is equivalent to reducing her taxes by $1.

So to answer our question, in terms of the 45° line diagram, *increases in transfer payments can be treated simply as decreases in taxes.* And we see that Figure 11-5, which we devised to illustrate a tax cut, can also be used to illustrate a rise in unemployment benefits, or in social security benefits, or in any other such transfer payment. Similarly, the analysis of a decrease in transfer payments would proceed exactly like the analysis of an increase in taxes.

The Multiplier Revisited

We now have acquired most of the tools we need to understand how fiscal policy decisions are made. But, before members of parliament vote on the budget, they should have an idea of the magnitude of the multiplier. Our figure of 5 is too high, and we can now understand how the income tax works to lower its value. But before getting involved in the mechanics, let us understand the basic reason.

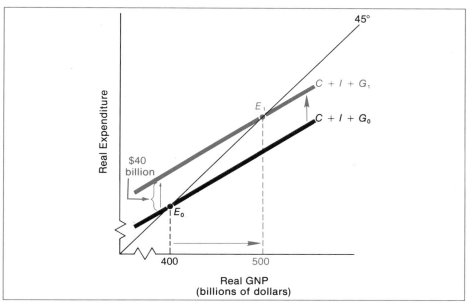

Figure 11-6
THE MULTIPLIER IN THE
PRESENCE OF AN INCOME
TAX
This diagram illustrates that an
economy with an income tax (in
this case a 25 percent income tax)
has a lower multiplier than an
economy without one. Specifically,
the $C + I + G$ curve is shifted
upward by a $40 billion increase in
G, and the diagram shows that
equilibrium GNP rises by $100
billion—from $400 billion to $500
billion. The multiplier is, therefore,
$100/$40 = 2½, whereas without
an income tax it was 5.

As we learned in Chapter 9, the multiplier works through a chain of spending and respending, as one person's expenditure becomes another's income. But through taxation some of the additional income leaks out of the circular flow at each stage. Specifically, if the income tax rate is 25 percent, when Generous Motors spends $1 million on salaries, workers actually receive only $750,000 in *after-tax* (or disposable) income. If workers spend 80 percent of this amount (based on a marginal propensity to consume of 0.8), spending in the next round will be only $600,000. Notice that this is only *60 percent* of the original expenditure, not *80 percent* as in our earlier example. Thus the multiplier chain for each original dollar of spending shrinks from:

$$1 + 0.8 + (0.8)^2 + (0.8)^3 + \ldots = \frac{1}{1 - 0.8} = \frac{1}{0.2} = 5$$

to:

$$1 + 0.6 + (0.6)^2 + (0.6)^3 + \ldots = \frac{1}{1 - 0.6} = \frac{1}{0.4} = 2\frac{1}{2}\,.$$

This is clearly a very large reduction in the multiplier. We thus have a second reason why our oversimplified multiplier formula of Chapter 9 gives an exaggerated impression of the size of the multiplier:

REASONS WHY THE OVERSIMPLIFIED MULTIPLIER FORMULA IS WRONG

1. It ignores price-level changes, which serve to reduce the size of the multiplier.

2. It ignores income taxes, which serve to reduce the size of the multiplier.

Later in this chapter, and in later chapters, we shall encounter still more reasons.

This conclusion about the multiplier is shown graphically in Figure 11-6, where we have drawn our $C + I + G$ schedules with a slope of 0.6 to reflect an MPC of 0.8, and a tax rate of 25 percent rather than the 0.8 slope that we used previously. The figure depicts the effect of an increase in government purchases of goods and services of $40 billion, which shifts the $C + I + G$ schedule from $C + I + G_0$ to $C + I + G_1$. Equilibrium moves from point E_0 to point E_1—a growth in GNP from $Y = \$400$ billion to $Y = \$500$ billion. Thus, if we ignore for the moment any increases in the price level (which would reduce the multiplier shown in Figure 11-6), a $40 billion increment in government spending leads to a $100 billion increment in GNP. So when taxes are included in our model, the multiplier is only $100/$40 = 2½, just as we concluded before.

To test your understanding of the multiplier, consider how the multiplier would work if the government decided to cut taxes by a fixed amount, such as $50 billion. According to our previous analysis, we should multiply $50 billion by the MPC to arrive at the implied shift in the C schedule (Step 1). Since the MPC in our example is 0.8, we obtain a figure of $40 billion. Next, we should enter this shift on a 45° line diagram to see how GNP changes (Step 2). But Figure 11–6 has already done this for us. In showing the effect of an *increase* in government spending of $40 billion, it also shows the effect of a *decrease* in fixed taxes of $50 billion because both policies shift the $C + I + G$ schedule upward by $40 billion. This example illustrates a very general point:

The multiplier for changes in fixed taxes is smaller than the multiplier for changes in government purchases.

The reason is quite straightforward. While G is a direct component of $C + I + G$, taxes are not. Taxes work indirectly, first by changing disposable income and then by changing C. But some of the higher disposable income caused by a tax cut will be saved, not spent, and hence a dollar of tax cut does not have as much effect on spending as does a dollar of G.

Equilibrium Income with Exports and Imports

The complete circular flow diagram that we studied in Chapter 7 (Figure 7–1, page 115) involved one additional injection and leakage of funds which we have so far ignored. The additional sector is the rest of the world. *Exports* (X) represent foreign purchases of our goods and thus constitute the final injection. *Imports* (IM) represent purchases by Canadians that do *not* involve sales by firms producing in Canada, and so they represent an important leakage of funds. Using the same reasoning as before, we now obtain the final restatement of the condition for equilibrium on the demand side of the economy:

For any given price level, equilibrium GNP on the demand side occurs when the sum of consumption, investment, government, and net exports just equals GNP. In symbols:

$$Y = C + I + G + X - IM.$$

Let us now see how exports and imports can be brought into our model of income determination and the multiplier.

While both exports and imports depend on many factors, the predominant one is national income. Some of the additional consumption and investment goods that Canadian consumers and firms buy as income rises are foreign goods. So to construct a simple model of an economy with international trade:

We assume that our imports rise as our GNP rises and fall as our GNP falls.

Similarly, our exports are the imports of other countries, so it is natural to assume that our exports depend on *their* GNPs, not on *ours*. Thus:

We assume that our exports are insensitive to our own GNP.

These two assumptions enable us to bring international trade into our income determination model.

Table 11-4

INCOME DETERMINATION WITH INTERNATIONAL TRADE

(1) GROSS NATIONAL PRODUCT (Y) (billions of dollars)	(2) DOMESTIC EXPENDITURE (C + I + G) (billions of dollars)	(3) EXPORTS (X) (billions of dollars)	(4) IMPORTS (IM) (billions of dollars)	(5) NET EXPORTS (X − IM) (billions of dollars)	(6) TOTAL EXPENDITURE (C + I + G + X − IM) (billions of dollars)
250	310	40	25	15	325
300	340	40	30	10	350
350	370	40	35	5	375
400	400	40	40	0	400
450	430	40	45	−5	425
500	460	40	50	−10	450
550	490	40	55	−15	475

Table 11-4 displays the mechanics in a concrete example. The first two columns are an abbreviated version of Table 11-3 on page 200; they show the sum of C + I + G—now labelled "Domestic Expenditure"—at alternative levels of GNP.

Columns 3 and 4 provide specific numerical versions of the assumptions we have just listed: Exports are assumed to be $40 billion regardless of (our) GNP, and imports are assumed to rise by $5 billion for every $50 billion rise in GNP. Column 5 simply subtracts imports from exports to get net exports, X – IM, and column 6 adds net exports to domestic expenditure to get total expenditures, C + I + G + X – IM.

The equilibrium, you can see, comes at Y = $400 billion. At any lower level of GNP, Y is less than C + I + G + X – IM, so output will rise. At any higher level of GNP, Y is greater than C + I + G + X – IM, so output will fall.

Figure 11-7 shows the same conclusion graphically. The line labelled C + I + G shows how domestic expenditures vary with GNP, and duplicates the C + I + G line in Figure 11-4 (page 201). The line labelled C + I + G + X – IM adds net exports to get total expenditures. (Net exports are therefore shown on the diagram by the vertical distance between the C + I + G + X – IM line and the C + I + G line.) Equilibrium occurs where Y = C + I + G + X – IM, that is, where the C + I + G + X – IM line crosses the 45° line—at point E in the diagram.

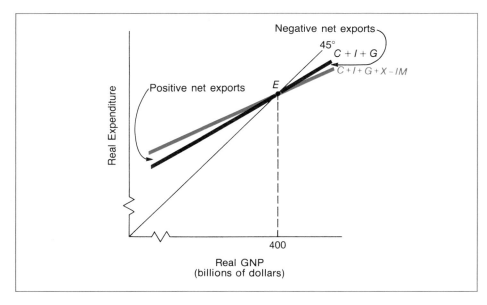

Figure 11-7

EQUILIBRIUM GNP WITH FOREIGN TRADE

In the presence of foreign trade, equilibrium GNP occurs where the C + I + G + X – IM line crosses the 45° line, for here Y = C + I + G + X – IM. In the graph, equilibrium is at point E, where GNP is $400 billion. This matches the equilibrium we found in Figure 11-4 (on page 201) without international trade because our example assumes that net exports are zero when Y = $400 billion. In the diagram, net exports are shown by the vertical distance—positive or negative—between the C + I + G + X – IM line and the C + I + G line. The C + I + G + X – IM line is *flatter* than the C + I + G line because net exports decline as GNP rises.

If you turn back to Figure 11-4 on page 201, you will see that Y = \$400 billion is the same equilibrium we found in an economy with no international trade. (Figure 11-7 shows this quite clearly, since the $C + I + G$ and $C + I + G + X - IM$ lines both cross the 45° line at Y = \$400 billion.) Does international trade therefore not affect domestic income?

Hardly. Notice in the table or the figure that we have constructed our example so that exports exactly balance imports (net exports are zero) when GNP is \$400 billion. This is just a coincidence. And because of this coincidence, net exports have no effect on equilibrium GNP.

The Foreign Trade Multiplier

But this is not the normal state of affairs. Let us consider what happens if exports rise to \$65 billion while imports remain as in Table 11-4. Table 11-5 shows us that equilibrium now occurs at a GNP of Y = \$450 billion. So world trade has raised domestic GNP. In general:

When net exports are positive, world trade raises equilibrium GNP. When net exports are negative, world trade lowers equilibrium GNP.

More specifically, in this example a rise of \$25 billion in exports (from \$40 billion to \$65 billion) leads to a rise of \$50 billion in GNP (from \$400 billion to \$450 billion). So the **foreign trade multiplier** is 2 (= \$50/\$25).[2] This same conclusion is shown graphically in Figure 11-8, where the line $C + I + G + X_0 - IM$ represents the original expenditure schedule and the line $C + I + G + X_1 - IM$ represents the expenditure schedule after the rise in exports. Equilibrium shifts from point E to point A, and GNP rises by \$50 billion.

Notice that the multiplier in this example is 2, whereas in the absence of international trade it was 2½. There is nothing special that makes the multiplier for exports different from any other multiplier. The same multiplier of 2 would apply to an autonomous change in any component of total expenditure.[3] What we have discovered is that:

International trade lowers the value of the multiplier.

[2]EXERCISE: Construct a version of Table 11-4 to show what would happen if imports rose by \$25 billion at every level of GNP. You should be able to show that the new equilibrium would be Y = \$350 billion.

[3]EXERCISE: Construct a version of Table 11-4 that shows the effects of a rise in domestic expenditure by \$25 billion at every level of GNP. Show that the new equilibrium occurs at Y = \$450.

Table 11-5
EQUILIBRIUM GNP AFTER A RISE IN EXPORTS

(1) GROSS NATIONAL PRODUCT (Y) (billions of dollars)	(2) DOMESTIC EXPENDITURE ($C + I + G$) (billions of dollars)	(3) EXPORTS (X) (billions of dollars)	(4) IMPORTS (IM) (billions of dollars)	(5) NET EXPORTS ($X - IM$) (billions of dollars)	(6) TOTAL EXPENDITURE ($C + I + G + X - IM$) (billions of dollars)
250	310	65	25	40	350
300	340	65	30	35	375
350	370	65	35	30	400
400	400	65	40	25	425
450	430	65	45	20	450
500	460	65	50	15	475
550	490	65	55	10	500

Figure 11-7 shows us graphically why this is true. Because net exports decline as GNP rises, the total expenditure line is *flatter* in the presence of international trade $(C + I + G + X - IM)$ than in its absence $(C + I + G)$. As we know already, the size of the multiplier depends on the *slope* of the expenditure schedule—steeper expenditure schedules lead to larger multipliers. Since international trade flattens the expenditure schedule, it lowers the multiplier.

Thus international trade gives us yet another reason why the oversimplified multiplier formula first given in Chapter 9 (page 166) overstates the true value of the multiplier.

The Canadian and World Economies

In Canada we export more than one-quarter of our national product, and as a result we are tremendously exposed to business conditions in the rest of the world. Since the lion's share of our exports is to the United States, whenever they have a recession, our spending schedule shifts down by a significant amount (exports decrease), and we have a recession too.

But our heavy reliance on foreign trade is not all bad. Our high tendency to import means that Canada's total expenditure line is quite flat so that our multiplier is quite small. Thus, the openness of our economy is a mixed blessing. It exposes us to additional shocks to aggregate demand, especially from the United States. But it also means that domestically generated shocks have a smaller multiplier effect than they would in an economy less involved in foreign trade.

One final point concerning exports and imports should be stressed. Since both are affected by the exchange rate and tariffs, these variables become important influences on aggregate demand. If foreigners put a tax on their imports (that is, a **tariff**), our exports fall. This shifts our $C + I + G + X - IM$ line down, moving our aggregate-demand curve to the left. Similarly, if we put a tariff on our imports, less domestic spending leaks out of the circular flow, so aggregate demand is increased.

A **tariff** is a tax on imports

When recessions occur, countries are often tempted to raise tariffs to "export" their unemployment problem. However, all countries cannot do this, and an attempt to do this can involve a series of retaliations, which very much restricts world trade. As a result, most Western countries have agreed to avoid using tariffs to stimulate domestic demand.

The exchange rate is also an important influence on exports and imports. The lower the foreign value of the Canadian dollar, the less it costs foreigners to buy

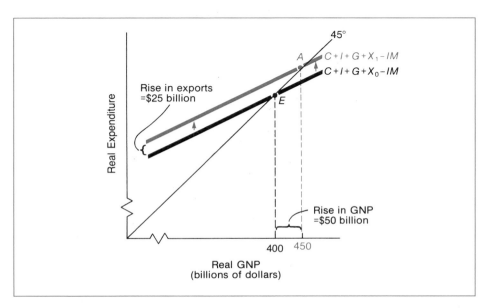

Figure 11-8

THE FOREIGN TRADE MULTIPLIER

This diagram shows a $25 billion increase in exports as a vertical shift of the total expenditure schedule from $C + I + G + X_0 - IM$, to $C + I + G + X_1 - IM$. As a result, equilibrium shifts from point E to point A, and GNP rises from $400 billion to $450 billion. The multiplier is therefore 2 (= $50/$25).

our exports and the more it costs Canadians to buy foreign imports. Thus:

A depreciation of the Canadian dollar raises net exports $(X - IM)$, shifts the $C + I + G + X - IM$ line up, and so moves the aggregate-demand curve to the right. For the same reason, an appreciation of the Canadian dollar lowers net exports and shifts the aggregate-demand curve to the left. Our general summary is:

Government expenditures, tax rates, transfer payments, exports, tariffs, and the exchange rate are all important variables that shift the aggregate-demand curve.

Planning Expansive Fiscal Policy

Now, at last, you are ready to pretend that you are a member of parliament deciding how to respond to the finance minister's proposed budget. Suppose that the economy would have a GNP of $400 billion if last year's budget were simply repeated. Suppose further that your goal is to achieve a fully employed labour force and that staff economists tell you that your goal can be achieved with a GNP of approximately $500 billion. Further, just to keep the calculations manageable, suppose that the price level is fixed. (We will drop this unrealistic assumption in just a few pages.) What budget should you support?

First we must consider what options are available if we want to raise GNP by $100 billion. This chapter has taught us that the government can raise government purchases, reduce taxes, or increase transfer payments by enough to close the recessionary gap between actual and potential GNP.

Figure 11–9 illustrates the problem, and its cure through higher government spending, on our 45° line diagram. Figure 11–9 (a) shows the equilibrium of the economy if no changes are made in the budget. Except for the full-employment line at $Y = $500 billion, the corresponding recessionary gap, and the extended label for the total spending line, it looks like Figure 11–4. With an expenditure multiplier of 2, you can figure out that an additional $50 billion of government spending will be needed to push the GNP up $100 billion and eliminate this gap ($100 billion/2 = $50 billion).

So you might vote to raise G from $G_0 = $80 billion to $G_1 = $130 billion, hoping to move the $C + I + G + X - IM$ line in Figure 11–9 (a) out to the position indicated in Figure 11–9 (b), thereby achieving full employment. Of course you might prefer to achieve this fiscal stimulus by lowering income taxes rather than increasing expenditures. Or you might prefer to rely on more generous transfer payments. The point is that there are a variety of budgets capable of pushing the economy up to full employment by increasing GNP by $100 billion. Figure 11–9 applies equally well to any of them.

Planning Restrictive Fiscal Policy

The preceding example assumed that the basic problem of fiscal policy is to overcome a deficiency of aggregate demand, as is often the case. But at other times the problem is that demand is excessive relative to the economy's capacity to produce. In this case, fiscal policy should assume a restrictive stance in order to reduce inflation.

It does not take much imagination to run our previous analysis in reverse. If, under a continuation of current budget policies, there would be an inflationary gap, there are fiscal policy tools that can eliminate it. Either by cutting spending programs out of the budget, or by raising taxes, or by some combination of these policies, the government can pull the $C + I + G + X - IM$ schedule down to a noninflationary position and achieve an equilibrium at full employment.

Notice the difference between this way of eliminating an inflationary gap and the natural self-correcting mechanism of the economy that we discussed in Chapter

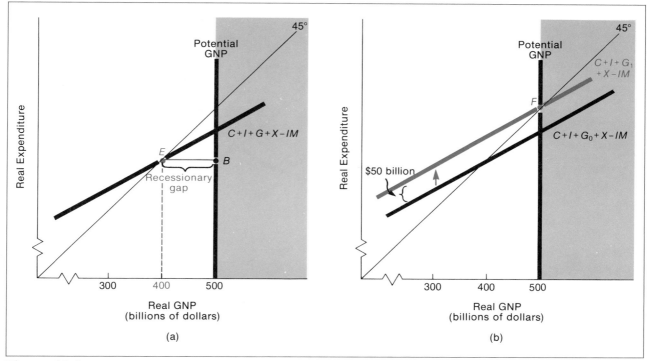

Figure 11-9

FISCAL POLICY TO ELIMINATE A RECESSIONARY GAP

This diagram shows, with more precision than can actually be achieved in practice, how fiscal policy can eliminate a recessionary gap. Part (a) shows the gap: Equilibrium GNP ($400 billion) falls short of potential GNP ($500 billion). Part (b) shows how fiscal policy—by moving the $C + I + G + X - IM$ line up just enough—can wipe out this gap and restore full employment. With a multiplier of 2, a rise in G of $50 billion or a cut in taxes large enough to shift C up by $50 billion would do the trick.

10. There we observed that if the economy were left to its own devices, a cumulative but self-limiting process of inflation eventually would eliminate the inflationary gap and return the economy to full employment. Here we see that it is not necessary to put the economy through the inflationary wringer. Instead, a restrictive fiscal policy can limit aggregate demand to the level that the economy can produce at full employment.

The Choice Between Spending Policy and Tax Policy

In principle, fiscal policy can nudge the economy in the desired direction equally well by changing government spending or by changing taxes. For example, if the government wants to expand the economy, it can raise G or lower taxes. Either policy shifts the total expenditure schedule upward, as depicted in Figure 11-9, thereby raising the equilibrium GNP on the demand side.

In terms of our aggregate demand and supply diagram, either policy shifts the aggregate-demand curve outward from D_0D_0 to D_1D_1 in Figure 11-10. As a result, the economy's equilibrium moves from point E to point A. Both real GNP and the price level rise. As this diagram points out, any combination of higher spending and lower taxes that produces the same aggregate-demand curve leads to the same increases in real GNP and prices.

How, then, do we decide whether it is better to raise spending or to cut taxes? The answer depends mainly on how large a public sector we want, and this is a contentious issue.

One point of view, expressed most eloquently in the writings of Canadian-born

Figure 11-10
EXPANSIONARY FISCAL POLICY

Any of a variety of expansionary fiscal policies will push the aggregate-demand curve outward to the right, as depicted by the shift from D_0D_0 to D_1D_1, in this aggregate-supply and demand diagram. The economy's equilibrium moves upward to the right along aggregate-supply curve SS, from point E to point A. Comparing A with E, we note that output is higher but prices are also higher. The expansionary policy has caused some inflation.

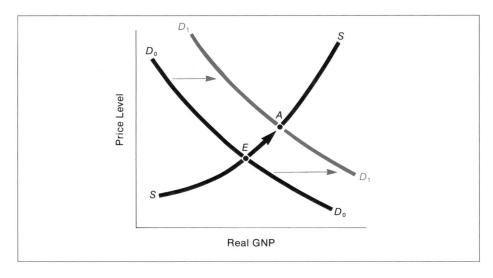

economist John Kenneth Galbraith, is that there is something amiss when a country as wealthy as the United States has such an impoverished public sector. In Galbraith's view, America's most pressing needs are not for more designer jeans, sports cars, and video games, but rather for better schools, more efficient public-transportation systems, and cleaner city streets and lakes. Those who agree with him believe that we should *increase G* when the economy needs stimulus and pay for these improved public services by *increasing taxes* when the economy needs to be reined in.

An opposing opinion, advocated by conservative politicians in all the Western countries, is that the government sector is already too large; that we are foolish to rely on government to do things that private individuals and businesses could do better on their own; and that the growth of government interferes too much in our everyday lives and in so doing circumscribes our freedom. Those who hold this view argue for *tax cuts* when macroeconomic considerations call for expansionary fiscal policy, and for *reductions in public spending* when restrictive policy is required.

This is an important point, and one on which so many people are confused. Too often the use of fiscal policy for economic stabilization is erroneously associated with a large and growing public sector—that is, with "big government." This need not be the case. Individuals favouring a smaller public sector can advocate an active fiscal policy just as well as those who favour a larger public sector. Advocates of big government budgets should seek to expand demand (when appropriate) through higher government spending and contract demand (when appropriate) through tax increases. By contrast, advocates of small public budgets should seek to expand demand by cutting taxes and reduce demand by cutting expenditures.

There are potentially legitimate arguments against an active stabilization policy, as we noted in Chapter 10. For example, the downward rigidity of wages may be strengthened if workers can count on the government's active commitment to full employment. But this issue is entirely separate from questions concerning the relative worth of big or small government.

Some Harsh Realities

The mechanics outlined so far in this chapter make the fiscal policy planner's job look rather simple. The elementary diagrams suggest, rather misleadingly, that the authorities can drive GNP to any level they please simply by manipulating their spending and tax programs. It seems as though they should be able to hit the full-employment bull's-eye every time.

But, in fact, a better analogy is shooting through dense fog at an erratically moving target with a gun of uncertain accuracy. The target is moving because, in the real world, the investment schedule (and, to a lesser extent, the consumption schedule) is constantly shifting on account of changes in expectations, new technological breakthroughs, changes in consumers' tastes, and the like. Furthermore, the export and import schedules often shift due to unforeseen events in other countries. This means that the policies decided upon today, which are to take effect at some future date, may no longer be appropriate by the time that future date rolls around. Policy must be based, to some extent, on *forecasting*, and no one has yet discovered a foolproof method of economic forecasting. Since our forecasting ability is so modest, and because fiscal policy decisions sometimes take a long time to be carried out, the government may occasionally find itself fighting the last inflation just when the new recession gets under way.

A second misleading feature of our diagrams is that multipliers are not known with as much precision as our examples may suggest. Thus, while the "best guess" may be that a $10 billion cut in government purchases will reduce GNP by $20 billion, the actual outcome may be as little as $12 billion or as much as $28 billion. It is therefore impossible to "fine tune" every wobble out of the economy's growth path through fiscal policy; economics is simply not that precise a science. The point is even more cogent with respect to tax policy. For example, we get involved in trying to guess whether consumers will view tax changes as permanent or temporary.

A third complication is that our target—full-employment GNP—may be only dimly visible, as if through a fog. Especially when the economy's last experience with full employment is very far in the past, economists may have difficulty estimating the GNP level that represents full employment. In fact, as was mentioned in Chapter 6, there is a great deal of controversy over how much unemployment constitutes "full employment" right now.

Finally, in trying to decide whether to push the economy out of a position of unemployment, legislators would like to know what the inflationary costs will be. As Figure 11–10 reminds us, any expansionary fiscal policy that closes a recessionary gap by increasing aggregate demand also pushes prices higher, that is, causes more inflation. This undesired side-effect may make the government hesitant to use fiscal policy to end a recession.

Is there a way out of this dilemma? Can we stimulate the economy by fiscal policy without worsening inflation? During the late 1970s and early 1980s, a small but influential minority of economists and politicians argued that we could. They called their approach "supply-side economics."

The Idea Behind Supply-Side Tax Cuts

The central idea of supply-side economics is that certain types of tax cuts increase aggregate supply at the same time as they increase aggregate demand. What kinds of measures are these? The basic principle is simple to state but not quite so simple to carry out.

If taxes can be cut in such a way that people's incentives to work are increased, *and if people actually respond to these incentives*, then the tax system can be used to increase the total amount of labour that is available for employment. Similarly, if the tax system is changed in ways that encourage households to save more and businesses to invest more, *and if people respond to these changes in the way that policy-makers hope*, then the total amount of capital that is available for use will begin to rise. Both sorts of tax policies, if successful, increase aggregate supply.

Figure 11–11 illustrates this conclusion on an aggregate supply and demand

Figure 11–11

THE IDEA BEHIND SUPPLY-SIDE TAX CUTS

The basic idea of supply-side cuts is that if they achieve their desired objective, they will cause the economy's aggregate-supply curve to shift outward to the right. For example, the aggregate-supply curve might be S_1S_1 under a program of supply-side tax cuts, whereas it would only be S_0S_0 without such tax cuts. In this case, if aggregate demand is the same in either case, the tax cuts would lead to the equilibrium point B instead of the equilibrium point A. Comparing B with A, we see that the program leads to lower prices and higher output.

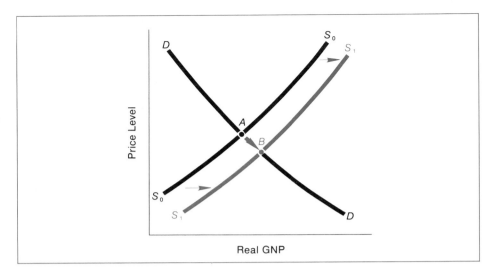

diagram. If policy measures can shift the economy's aggregate supply to position S_1S_1, then prices will be lower and output higher than if the aggregate-supply curve were S_0S_0. Policy-makers will have succeeded in reducing inflation and raising real output (lowering unemployment) at the same time. The trade-off between inflation and unemployment will have been defeated. This is the goal of supply-side economics.

What sorts of policies do supply-siders advocate? There is a long list, but most supply-side tax cuts are aimed at stimulating capital formation. For example:

1. **Accelerated Depreciation.** As mentioned in Chapter 8, a company investing in a machine or factory is not permitted to take the entire cost of that asset as a tax write-off in the year it is purchased. Instead, it must spread the cost over the lifetime of the asset in a series of **depreciation allowances**, which are annual tax deductions that in total add up to the value of the asset. Naturally, firms prefer to take their depreciation allowances sooner rather than later, because higher depreciation allowances in the early years of an investment mean lower immediate tax burdens.

   Many supply-siders argue that an effective way to provide greater incentives for investment is to speed up ("accelerate") depreciation allowances. There are many ways to do this, and the details are best left to courses on accounting. However, one very straightforward way is simple enough to explain right here. If the government reduces the "lifetime" of a machine for tax purposes from, say, seven years to five, then obviously firms will get the tax savings from depreciation faster. This is precisely the course of action taken in Canada. Since 1972, the official lifetime (for tax purposes) of a machine in the manufacturing and processing sector has been two years.

2. **Reducing the Corporation Income Tax.** Another type of tax cut that supply-siders often favour is reducing the statutory rates of taxation on corporate income. By letting companies retain more of their pre-tax income, it is argued, government will provide both greater investment incentives (by raising the profitability of investments) and more investable funds (by letting companies keep more of their earnings). This policy has also been implemented in Canada. In 1972 the main corporate tax rate in the manufacturing and processing sectors was cut from 50 percent to 40 percent.

A **capital gain** is an increase in the market value of a piece of property, such as a common stock or a parcel of land, that occurs during the period between when it is bought and when it is sold. A **capital loss** is a decrease in that property's value.

3. **Reducing Taxes on Capital Gains.** Many investments, particularly financial investments such as stocks and bonds, often lead to **capital gains and losses.** For example, if Mr. Cabot purchases Canadian Pacific shares in 1960

for $10,000 and sells them in 1985 for $100,000, the law says he has reaped a $90,000 *capital gain*, and must pay tax. Supply-siders argue that lower taxes on capital gains would provide greater incentives for individuals and firms to invest more. Partly for these reasons, the Canadian government taxes capital gains at only half the normal rates.[4]

Not all supply-side tax cuts are aimed at spurring investment. If there is to be more investment, someone must be providing the saving to finance it. Thus, supply-siders typically favour:

4. Reducing Taxes on Income from Savings. One extreme form of this proposal would simply exempt from taxation all income from interest and dividends. Since income must be either consumed or saved, this would, in effect, change our present personal income tax into a tax on consumer spending. While this has not been adopted explicitly in Canada, our income-tax system allows a substantial part of interest income to be exempt. Registered Retirement Savings Plans (RRSPs), Registered Home Ownership Savings Plans (RHOSPs), and the $1,000 exemption for interest earnings are the three most common provisions used to shield the earnings on savings from tax.

Supply-siders recognize that capital is not the only factor of production. Aggregate supply can be expanded by increasing the supply of labour services as well. For this reason, they generally advocate:

5. Lowering Personal Income-Tax Rates. Such cuts, they argue, encourage people to work harder and for longer hours, and induce them to spend more time at productive activities and less time worrying about how to avoid taxes. In fact, sharp cuts in personal taxes have been the cornerstone of the economic strategies of both Thatcher in England and Reagan in the United States.

Aggregate supply depends on the state of technology and the availability of raw materials. So supply-siders are interested in using the tax system to encourage technological progress and resource exploration by offering:

6. Tax Credits for Research and Exploration. Canadian corporate tax law has consistently allowed companies that spend money on research and development (R & D) and resource exploration to have dramatic reductions in their tax bills. The hope is obvious: Tax incentives should increase spending on R & D, and more R & D should lead to improvements in technology. Similarly, tax incentives should increase spending on drilling for oil (etc.), and more energy resources and other raw materials should lead to lower business costs.

Finally, business costs can be decreased by:

7. Reducing Sales and Payroll Taxes. If firms are allowed to pay less to the government in the form of sales taxes or Canada pension and unemployment insurance contributions, they can afford to lower their selling prices (so the aggregate-supply curve should shift down). Given the government's goals at the time, it is unfortunate that the large government budget deficit forced increases in all these levies in 1983 and 1984. Since these tax increases shift the aggregate supply curve to the left, they result in stagflation.

Let us suppose, for the moment, that a successful supply-side tax cut is enacted to help close a recessionary gap. Since *both* aggregate demand *and* aggregate supply increase simultaneously, the economy may be able to avoid the painful inflationary consequences of an expansionary fiscal policy that were shown in Figure 11–10.

Figure 11–12 illustrates this conclusion. The two aggregate-demand curves and the initial aggregate-supply curve S_0S_0 are carried over directly from Figure 11–10. But we have introduced an additional supply curve, S_1S_1, to reflect the

[4]More will be said about capital gains taxation, which is viewed by many as a major tax shelter, in Chapter 33.

Figure 11-12

A SUCCESSFUL SUPPLY-SIDE TAX REDUCTION

A tax cut specifically aimed at the supply side, if successful, will shift *both* aggregate demand and aggregate supply to the right. In this diagram, equilibrium is initially at point E, where demand curve $D_0 D_0$ intersects supply curve $S_0 S_0$. After the supply-side tax cut, the aggregate-demand curve is $D_1 D_1$ and the aggregate-supply curve is $S_1 S_1$, so equilibrium is at point C. As compared with the results of a tax cut that works only on the demand side (point A), the supply-side tax cut raises output more and prices less.

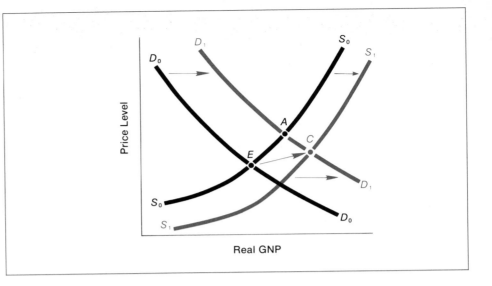

successful supply-side tax cut depicted in Figure 11–11. The equilibrium of the economy moves from E to C, whereas with a conventional demand-side tax cut it would have moved from E to A. As compared with point A, output is higher and prices are lower at point C.

A good deal, you say! Indeed it is. The supply-side argument is extremely attractive. It certainly was appealing to Ronald Reagan in 1980 and, as a consequence, it has had a profound influence on U.S. economic policy. Also, as just noted, the Canadian government has applied supply-side reasoning for years. But does the supply-side approach work in practice? Can we actually do what is depicted in Figure 11–12? Let us consider some difficulties.

Some Flies in the Ointment

Supply-side economics has been controversial. Supporters have touted it as a painless remedy for all our economic ills. Detractors have derided it as wishful thinking. But the critics of supply-side economics rarely question the goals of the program. Nor do they question the basic idea that the tax system can be used to improve incentives. They argue, instead, that supply-siders exaggerate the beneficial effects of supply-side tax cuts and ignore some undesirable side effects. Here is a list of the main objections to supply-side tax cuts that have fuelled the debate.

1. **The Uncertainty of Supply-Side Effects**. The first objection is that supply-siders are simply too optimistic: We really do not know how to do what Figure 11–9 shows. It is easy to design tax cuts that, for example, make working more *attractive* financially; that is, which raise take-home pay. All you have to do is cut tax rates. Doing this, however, does not guarantee that people will actually work more. Instead, they may find themselves able to afford the goods and services they want with fewer hours of labour and react by working less. Similarly, if tax cuts raise the return on savings, people may find their savings goals easier to achieve and react by saving less.

   Most of the statistical evidence suggests that it is unrealistic to expect tax reductions to lead to very substantial increases in either labour supply or household savings.

2. **Demand-Side Effects**. The second objection is that supply-siders underestimate the effects of tax cuts on aggregate demand. If you cut personal taxes, individuals *may possibly* work more, but they *will certainly* spend more. If you reduce business taxes and successfully encourage expansion of industrial

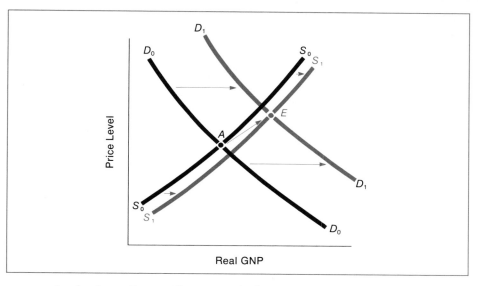

Figure 11-13

A MORE PESSIMISTIC VIEW
OF SUPPLY-SIDE TAX CUTS
If the effect of supply-side tax
initiatives on the aggregate-supply
curve is actually much smaller
than suggested by Figure 11-11,
the anti-inflationary impact will be
correspondingly smaller. As you
can see in this diagram, it is
possible that a large shift in the
aggregate-demand curve could
overwhelm the favourable effects
of the tax cuts on the price level.

capacity, business firms will necessarily demand more investment goods.

Reagan's response to this criticism was to link the tax cuts to reductions in government spending that would cancel out the demand-side effects. Let us review the reasoning briefly. We learned in earlier chapters that tax cuts raise aggregate demand while reductions in government spending reduce it. Thus, whatever demand stimulus is caused by the tax cuts, there is some expenditure reduction big enough to cancel its demand-side effects. By combining these two programs into a fiscal package, it may be possible to obtain the situation depicted in Figure 11-11: a rise in aggregate supply with no accompanying rise in aggregate demand.

The problem with this strategy is that if *large* tax cuts are made, then *large* spending cuts must accompany them. Many observers in 1981 worried that the expenditure cuts proposed by President Reagan, while substantial, were not nearly as large as the tax cuts. They turned out to be right.

If we put these two objections together, we are led to Figure 11-13. Here we depict a small outward shift in the aggregate-supply curve (which reflects the first objection) and a large outward shift of the aggregate-demand curve (which reflects the second). The result is that the economy's equilibrium moves from point A (the intersection of $S_0 S_0$ and $D_0 D_0$) to point E (the intersection of $S_1 S_1$ and $D_1 D_1$). Prices rise as output expands. The outcome differs only a little from the straight "demand side" fiscal stimulus depicted in Figure 11-10 (page 210).

3. **Problems in Timing**. The most popular types of supply-side tax cuts in Canada seek to encourage greater business investment by, for example, making depreciation allowances more generous. But investment does not create new industrial capacity overnight. It takes time to plan new investment projects, arrange the financing, get delivery on machinery, build factories, and then actually put these things into operation. The crucial point is that the *expenditures* on investment goods come before the *expansion of capacity*. Thus, even if supply-side policies are successful, aggregate *demand* expands first and aggregate *supply* follows later.

4. **Limited Effect on Inflation**. Supply-side policies were offered as a cure for inflation. Unfortunately, even a very successful supply-side program can be expected to make only a small dent in the inflation rate.

Inflation depends on the *difference* between the rates at which the *aggregate-demand* and *aggregate-supply* curves are shifting outward over time. Aggregate supply is, as a matter of definition, the product of the amount of labour available times the amount of output produced by each hour of labour—

The **productivity of labour** is the amount of output produced per hour of labour input.

the **productivity of labour**. There is little that can be done to affect the long-run growth rate of labour supply, which depends fundamentally on population growth. Thus, if supply-side policies are to increase the growth rate of aggregate supply, they must focus on productivity.

But the historical growth rate of productivity in Canada is only about 2 percent per year.[5] A 50 percent improvement in productivity growth (from 2 percent to 3 percent) would constitute a truly remarkable achievement. No serious economist thinks we really known how to achieve such a feat. But even a supply-side miracle of this magnitude would add only one percentage point to the growth rate of aggregate supply, and therefore would lower the inflation rate by only about one percentage point, a very small effect.

5. *Effect on the Distribution of Income*. The preceding objections all pertained to the likely effects of supply-side policies on aggregate supply and demand. But there is a very different problem that bears mention: Most supply-side initiatives would increase income inequality. Why? Because, while raising the incomes of the wealthiest members of our society may not be their primary aim, most supply-side cuts cannot help but concentrate benefits on the rich simply because it is the rich who earn most of the capital gains, interest, and dividends, and who own most of the corporations.

Indeed, this tilt toward the rich is almost an inescapable corollary of supply-side logic. The basic aim of supply-side economics is to increase the incentive for working and investing; that is, to increase the gap between the rewards of those who succeed in the economic game (by working hard, investing well, and so on) and those who fail. It can hardly be surprising therefore, that supply-side policies tend to increase economic inequality.

6. *Losses of Tax Revenue*. You can hardly help noticing that most of the policies suggested by supply-siders involve reductions in one tax or another. Thus, unless some other tax is raised or spending is cut, supply-side tax cuts are bound to raise the government budget deficit. Critics of President Reagan's program, for example, argued that such large tax cuts would leave monstrous budget deficits for years to come.

Once again, extreme supply-siders answered this objection by denying the obvious. Lower tax rates, they argued, need not lead to lower tax revenues if the tax base grows quickly enough. For example, suppose the GNP starts at $400 billion when the tax rate is 25 percent; so the government collects $100 billion in tax revenues. Then, if the tax rate is cut to 20 percent, but GNP grows to $500 billion as a result, tax receipts will remain at $100 billion. Reasoning like this led extreme supply-siders like Professor Arthur Laffer of the University of California at Los Angeles to predict that the Reagan tax cuts would actually lead to more tax revenue and smaller budget deficits![6]

To the vast majority of economists, this claim was implausible. In the preceding example, if the GNP starts at $400 billion, a cut in the tax rate from 25 percent to 20 percent lowers tax revenues initially by $20 billion (from $100 billion to $80 billion). For this to cause a $100 billion increase in the GNP (from $400 billion to $500 billion), the tax multiplier would have to be $100/$20 = 5. This is about three times as large as the actual multiplier. Turning from hypothetical examples to reality, U.S. federal tax revenues did not rise, but rather fell sharply after the 1981–83 tax cuts—just as the critics had predicted. And the large budget deficits that ensued have been a major economic issue ever since.[7]

[5]See Chapter 39 for a full discussion of productivity growth in Canada and why it has slowed in recent years.

[6]The famous, or infamous, Laffer Curve is a graph showing how tax revenues first rise, but then fall, as the tax rate rises from zero, to 10 percent, then 20 percent, and so on, up to 100 percent. Therefore, if tax rates are high enough, we can actually raise more revenue by cutting rates.

[7]Chapter 17 is devoted to the causes and consequences of budget deficits.

Corporate Tax Concessions in Canada

Canadians have been actively involved with supply-side economics, both at the academic and policy levels. The acknowledged intellectual leader of this school of thought is Robert Mundell, a Canadian economist who currently teaches at Columbia University. (Mundell has also taught at the universities of British Columbia, Waterloo, McGill, Stanford, Chicago, and Bologna.) Mundell had worked out the principles underlying the supply-side approach a full decade before the terms "supply-side" and "Reaganomics" were invented.

At the policy level, the Canadian federal government has been using corporate tax concessions as its favourite instrument of fiscal policy for more than 30 years. Its intention has been to stimulate investment spending. While this policy is an attempt to raise aggregate demand, and therefore create jobs while the new equipment is constructed and installed, the government has consistently stressed the supply-side motivation of their policies. The idea is to get new and better equipment in place so that Canadian labour is more productive and our level of potential GNP is increased.

One indication of the extent to which these policies were used is the fact that in 1969 Statistics Canada began publishing two separate volumes entitled *Corporation Taxation Statistics* and *Corporation Financial Statistics*. Mr. Duffett, the Chief Statistician at the time, gave the following explanation for the two volumes:

During the early part of the twenty-year period that the Department of National Revenue compiled financial statistics on corporations, corporation profit was essentially the same as taxable income and therefore it was possible to satisfy both needs with one set of statistics. However, during this period (1944–64) and particularly during the last decade, taxation legislation, through special provisions, has been used to an increasing extent as an instrument of government policy.... As a result, it was becoming increasingly difficult to use the same information to satisfy the needs for data of both corporation finance generally and corporation income taxation.*

Perhaps the most dramatic use of corporate tax concessions came in the 1972 Budget, when the corporate profits tax rate was cut from 50 percent to 40 percent, and firms in the manufacturing and processing sector were allowed to claim for tax purposes that machines and equipment were fully worn out within two years of purchase. An election occurred before the budget was passed, and the Liberals just stayed in office with a minority government. Most analysts credit the NDP's criticism of the tax concessions as an important reason for the decline in the government's support (although others criticized, too, as the cartoon from the *Toronto Star* indicates). The political problem facing the Con-

Tit for tat

servatives was that they wanted to support the tax concessions, but they had to express concern about their unpopularity. They decided to support the government, provided the government conducted a study of the effectiveness of the tax cuts.

In the study, the Department of Finance surveyed companies and simply asked them whether the tax cuts had *any* effect on their investment spending. When the answers were published in 1975, we learned that only 47 percent of the firms said "yes"! This is a surprising answer, since the tax concessions definitely increase a firm's profits. However, the fact that many firms in Canada are foreign-owned may explain this surprise. When foreign-owned firms file for corporation profits taxes in their home country (say, the United States) they are allowed a tax credit equal to the amount of taxes already paid in other countries (like Canada). Thus, if the Canadian government collects less revenue as a result of our tax concessions, the foreign-owned firm qualifies for precisely that much less of a tax credit when filing in the United States. The end result is that the Canadian government has given revenue to the American government, and the firm (and its investment decision) is unaffected.

Despite these and other problems, corporate tax concessions formed a major part of the 1977 and 1983 federal government Budgets. In 1983, the motivation was simply to avoid bankruptcies that were threatening Canadian-owned firms because of the severity of the recession.

**Corporation Taxation Statistics* (Ottawa: Revenue Canada, 1965), Introduction.

Toward Assessment of Supply-Side Economics

On balance, most economists have reached the following conclusions about supply-side tax initiatives:

1. The likely effectiveness of supply-side tax cuts depends very much on what kinds of taxes are cut. Tax reductions aimed at stimulating business investment can pack more punch than tax reductions aimed at getting people to work longer hours or to save more.

2. Such tax cuts probably *will* increase aggregate supply, but the increase in aggregate supply will come much more slowly than the increase in aggregate demand.

3. The demand-side effects are very likely to be larger than the supply-side effects.

4. Supply-side policies can be expected to make, at most, only a small dent in the inflation rate.

5. Supply-side income-tax cuts are likely to benefit the rich more than the poor. However, this defect does not hold for sales-tax cuts.

6. Supply-side tax cuts are almost certain to lead to bigger, not smaller, budget deficits.

But this list does not close the books on the issue. It does not even tell us whether supply-side tax cuts are a good idea or a bad one. Some people will look over this list and decide that they favour supply-side tax cuts; indeed, the Canadian government budgets have included an almost endless series of corporate tax concessions over the last 20 years. Also, many economists and most of the U.S. Congress supported President Reagan's program in 1981. Others, perusing the same facts, will reach the opposite conclusion. We cannot say that either group is "wrong" because, like almost every economic policy, supply-side economics has its pros and cons. While the claims made by the most ardent supply-siders in the United States were clearly excessive, there is definitely some truth in supply-side economics. Reductions in marginal tax rates do improve economic incentives. Sales-tax reductions definitely lower prices. Hence, any specific supply-side tax cut must be judged on its individual merits.

How did things work out in the United States after the Reagan tax cuts of 1981? Although supply-siders had predicted an exuberant boom, the U.S. economy in 1981–82 suffered through its worst recession since the Great Depression. But, when recovery finally came, the economy grew rapidly in 1983—confounding many pessimistic forecasters. There has been very little evidence to date that supply-side incentives have increased saving, investment, or labour supply to any noticeable degree. But inflation did fall rapidly in the early 1980s. Finally, income inequality did grow larger and, as already mentioned, the budget deficit grew ominously.

In a nutshell, then, the specific supply-side tax cuts enacted in the United States in 1981 appear to have had some beneficial effects and some harmful ones—as was to be expected.

Summary

1. The government's fiscal policy is its plan for managing aggregate demand through its spending and taxing programs. It is announced and described in the federal budget.

2. Government purchases of goods and services (G) and net exports ($X - IM$) are direct components of the total spending. Therefore, they have the same multiplier as do autonomous changes in consumption or investment.

3. When income taxes are introduced, there is a dif-

ference between GNP and disposable income. Since consumer spending (C) depends on disposable income, any change in taxes will shift the consumption schedule on a 45° line diagram.

4. Shifts in the consumption function caused by tax policy are subject to the same multiplier as autonomous shifts in the consumption schedule. However, the income tax reduces the size of this common multiplier just as it reduces the size of the multiplier for G, I, or X. High tendencies to import also reduce the size of the multiplier.

5. Government transfer payments are treated like negative taxes, not like government purchases of goods and services, because they influence total spending only indirectly through their effect on consumption.

6. The net effect of the government on aggregate demand—and hence on equilibrium output and prices—depends on whether the expansionary effects of its spending are greater or smaller than the contractionary effects of its taxes.

7. If the multipliers were known precisely, it would be possible to plan fiscal policies to eliminate either a recessionary or an inflationary gap. Recessionary gaps can be cured by raising G, cutting taxes, or increasing transfers. Inflationary gaps can be cured by cutting G, raising taxes, or reducing transfers.

8. Active stabilization policy can be carried out either by means that tend to expand the size of government (by raising either G or taxes when appropriate) or by means that hold back the size of government (by reducing either G or taxes when appropriate).

9. Expansionary fiscal policy can lessen recessions, but it normally exacts a cost in terms of higher inflation. This dilemma has led to interest in "supply-side" tax cuts designed to stimulate aggregate supply.

10. Supply-side tax cuts aim to push the economy's aggregate-supply curve outward to the right. If successful, they can expand the economy and reduce inflation at the same time—a desirable outcome.

11. But critics point out five problems of supply-side tax cuts: They also stimulate aggregate demand; the beneficial effects on aggregate supply may be quite small; the demand-side effects occur before the supply-side effects; they make the income distribution more unequal; and large tax cuts lead to large budget deficits.

12. Supply-side policies can be expected to make only a small contribution to the long-term battle against inflation.

Concepts for Review

Fiscal policy	Tariffs	Supply-side tax cuts
Government purchases of goods and services (G)	Government transfer payments	Depreciation allowances
Net exports (X – IM)	Effect of income taxes and imports on the multiplier	Capital gains and losses
		Productivity of labour

Questions for Discussion

1. Consider an economy involved in no foreign trade, in which tax collections are always $200 and in which the three components of aggregate demand are as follows:

GNP	TAXES	DI	C	I	G
$480	$200	$280	$210	$100	$215
540	200	340	255	100	215
600	200	400	300	100	215
660	200	460	345	100	215
720	200	520	390	100	215

Find the equilibrium of this economy graphically. What is the marginal propensity to consume? What is the multiplier? What would happen to equilibrium GNP if government purchases were raised by $15 and the price level were unchanged?

2. Now consider a related economy in which investment is also $100, government purchases are also $215, and the price level is also fixed. But taxes now vary with income, and as a result the consumption

schedule looks like the following:

GNP	TAXES	DI	C
$480	$160	$320	$255
540	180	360	285
600	200	400	315
660	220	440	345
720	240	480	375

Find the equilibrium graphically. What is the marginal propensity to consume? What is the tax rate? Use your diagram to show the effect of an increase of $15 in government purchases. What is the multiplier? Compare this answer with your answer to Question 1 above. What do you conclude?

3. Explain why G has the same multiplier as autonomous shifts in C or I, while taxes have a different multiplier.

4. Return to the hypothetical economy in Question 1 and suppose that both taxes and government purchases are increased by $60. Find the new equilib-

rium under the assumption that consumer spending continues to be exactly three-quarters of disposable income (as it is in Question 1).

5. If the government today decides that aggregate demand is excessive and is causing inflation, what options are open to it? What if it decides that aggregate demand is too weak instead?

6. Discuss the difference between a government purchase of a good or service and a government transfer payment.

7. Suppose that you are in charge of the fiscal policy of the economy in Question 1. There is an inflationary gap with income at $660, and you want to reduce income to $600. What specific actions can you take to achieve this goal?

8. Now put yourself in charge of the economy in Question 2, and suppose that full employment comes at a GNP of $720. How can you push income up to that level?

9. Which of the proposed supply-side tax cuts appeals to you most? Draw up a list of arguments for and against enacting such a cut right now.

10. (More difficult.) Consider an economy with a horizontal aggregate-supply curve. Investment is fixed at

$700, government purchases are $800, the consumption function is:

$$C = 100 + 0.8DI,$$

and taxes are one-quarter of GNP—making disposable income (DI) equal to three-quarters of GNP. Find the equilibrium level of GNP. How would this equilibrium change if taxes were abolished? Compare your answer with the examples in this chapter.

11. Consider the following fictitious economy.

GNP	SAVINGS	IMPORTS
$500	$50	$10
600	70	20
700	90	30
800	110	40
900	130	50
1000	150	60
1100	170	70
1200	190	80

Investment and exports are $100 and $110, respectively. What is the equilibrium value of GNP? What is the multiplier? What is equilibrium GNP if exports drop to $80?

Appendix
Algebraic Treatment of Fiscal Policy and Aggregate Demand

In this appendix we explain the simple algebra behind the fiscal policy multipliers discussed in the chapter. In so doing, we deal only with a simplified case in which prices do not change. While it is possible to work out the corresponding algebra for the more realistic aggregate demand–aggregate supply analysis with variable prices, the analysis is rather complicated and is best left to more advanced courses.

We start with the example used in the chapter (especially on pages 199–202 and 204–206). The government spends $80 billion on goods and services (G = 80), and levies an income tax equal to 25 percent of GNP. So, if the symbol T denotes tax receipts:

$$T = 0.25 \ Y.$$

Since the consumption function we have been working with is

$$C = 10 + 0.8 \ DI,$$

where DI is disposable income, and since disposable income and GNP are related by the accounting identity

$$DI = Y - T,$$

it follows that the C schedule used in the 45° line diagram is described by the algebraic equation:

$$
\begin{aligned}
C &= 10 + 0.8 \ (Y - T) \\
&= 10 + 0.8 \ (Y - 0.25 \ Y) \\
&= 10 + 0.8 \ (0.75 \ Y) \\
&= 10 + 0.6 \ Y.
\end{aligned}
$$

We can now apply the equilibrium condition for an economy with a government, which is:

$$Y = C + I + G.$$

Since investment in this example is $I = 70$, substituting for C, I, and G into this equation gives:

$$
\begin{aligned}
Y &= 10 + 0.6 \ Y + 70 + 80 \\
0.4 \ Y &= 160 \\
Y &= 400.
\end{aligned}
$$

This is all there is to finding equilibrium GNP in an economy with a government, but no foreign sector.

To find the multiplier for government spending, increase G by 1 and resolve the problem:

$$Y = C + I + G$$
$$Y = 10 + 0.6\ Y + 70 + 81$$
$$0.4\ Y = 161$$
$$Y = 402.5.$$

So the multiplier is $402.5 - 400 = 2.5$, as stated in the text.

To find the multiplier for an increase in fixed taxes, change the tax schedule to:

$$T = 0.25\ Y + 1.$$

Disposable income is then

$$DI = Y - T = Y - (0.25\ Y + 1) = 0.75\ Y - 1,$$

so the consumption function is

$$C = 10 + 0.8\ DI$$
$$= 10 + 0.8\ (0.75\ Y - 1)$$
$$= 9.2 + 0.6\ Y.$$

Solving for equilibrium GNP as usual gives

$$Y = C + I + G$$
$$Y = 9.2 + 0.6\ Y + 70 + 80$$
$$0.4\ Y = 159.2$$
$$Y = 398.$$

So a $1 increase in fixed taxes lowers Y by $2. The tax multiplier is –2.

Now let us proceed to a more general solution, using symbols rather than specific numbers. The equations of the model that involves no foreign sector are as follows:

$$(1) \quad Y = C + I + G$$

is the equilibrium condition, as usual;

$$(2) \quad C = a + b\ DI$$

is the same consumption function we have used in the appendixes of Chapters 8 and 9;

$$(3) \quad DI = Y - T$$

is the accounting identity relating disposable income to GNP;

$$(4) \quad T = T_0 + tY$$

is the tax function, where T_0 represents fixed taxes

(which were zero in our numerical example) and t represents the tax rate (which was 0.25 in the example). Finally, I and G are just fixed numbers.

We begin the solution by substituting (3) and (4) into (2) to derive the consumption schedule relating C to Y:

$$C = a + b\ DI$$
$$C = a + b(Y - T)$$
$$C = a + b(Y - T_0 - tY)$$
$$(5) \quad C = a - bT_0 + b(1 - t)Y.$$

You will notice that a change in fixed taxes (T_0) shifts the intercept of the C schedule while a change in the tax rate (t) changes its slope, as explained in the text (pages 198–99).

Next substitute (5) into (1) to find equilibrium GNP:

$$Y = C + I + G$$
$$Y = a - bT_0 + b(1 - t)Y + I + G$$
$$[1 - b(1 - t)]\ Y = a - bT_0 + I + G$$

or

$$(6) \quad Y = \frac{a - bT_0 + I + G}{1 - b(1 - t)}.$$

Equation (6) shows us that G has the same multiplier as I or a, and that this multiplier is:

$$\text{Multiplier} = \frac{1}{1 - b(1 - t)}.$$

To see that this is in fact the multiplier, raise G or I or a by 1 unit. In each case, equation (6) would be changed to read:

$$Y = \frac{a - bT_0 + I + G + 1}{1 - b(1 - t)}.$$

Subtracting equation (6) from this expression gives the change in Y stemming from a one-unit change in G or I or a:

$$\text{Change in } Y = \frac{1}{1 - b(1 - t)}.$$

We noted in Chapter 9 (page 166) that if there were no income tax $(t = 0)$, a realistic value for b (the marginal propensity to consume) would yield a multiplier of 10, which is much bigger than the true multiplier. Now that we have added taxes to the model, our multiplier formula produces much more realistic numbers, but only for an economy with a relatively insignificant foreign sector like the United

States. Reasonable values for the parameters for the U.S. economy are $b = \frac{9}{10}$ and $t = \frac{1}{3}$. The multiplier formula then gives:

$$\text{Multiplier} = \cfrac{1}{1 - \dfrac{9}{10}\left(1 - \dfrac{1}{3}\right)} = \cfrac{1}{1 - \dfrac{9}{10} \times \dfrac{2}{3}}$$

$$= \cfrac{1}{1 - \dfrac{6}{10}} = \cfrac{1}{\dfrac{4}{10}} = 2.5,$$

which is not far from its true value, approximately 2.

Finally, we can see from equation (6) that the multiplier for a change in fixed taxes (T_0) is:

$$\text{Tax multiplier} = \frac{-b}{1 - b(1 - t)}.$$

For the example considered in the text and earlier in this appendix, $b = 0.8$ and $t = 0.25$, so the formula gives:

$$\frac{-0.8}{1 - 0.8(1 - 0.25)} = \frac{-0.8}{1 - 0.8(0.75)}$$

$$= \frac{-0.8}{1 - 0.6} = \frac{-0.8}{0.4} = -2.$$

According to these figures, each $1 *increase* in T_0 *reduces* Y by $2.

For an economy *with* foreign trade, the equilibrium condition is:

$$\text{(1a)} \quad Y = C + I + G + X - IM,$$

and we add an import function:

$$\text{(7)} \quad IM = i_0 + iY,$$

where i is the marginal propensity to import. Similar substitution of (5) and (7) into (1a) yields the revised expression for equilibrium output:

$$\text{(6a)} \quad Y = \frac{a - bT_0 + I + G + X - i_0}{1 - b(1 - t) + i}.$$

The expenditure multiplier for the open economy is therefore:

$$\frac{1}{1 - b(1 - t) + i}$$

For the plausible parameter values $(b = 0.9, t = 0.33,$ and $i = 0.2)$ the multiplier formula gives a most realistic answer for Canada, 1.67.

Questions for Discussion

1. In an economy described by the following set of equations:

$$C = 10 + 0.9\, DI$$
$$I = 180$$
$$G = 255$$
$$T = 50 + (\tfrac{1}{3})\, Y,$$

find the equilibrium level of GNP. Then find the multipliers for government purchases and for fixed taxes. If it is desired to lower GNP by $100, what are some policies that would do the trick?

2. This is a variant of the previous problem that approaches things the way a fiscal policy planner might. In an economy whose consumption function and tax function are as given in Question 1, and with investment fixed at $180, find the value of G that would make GNP equal to $1200.

3. You are given the following information about an economy.

$$C = 50 + 0.8\, (Y - T)$$
$$I = 120$$
$$G = 550$$
$$T = 0.25\, Y$$

a. Find equilibrium GNP and the budget deficit.
b. Suppose the government, unhappy with the budget deficit, decides to cut government spending by precisely the amount of the deficit in (a). What actually happens to the budget deficit and why?

4. (More difficult.) In the economy considered in Question 3, suppose the government, seeing that it has not wiped out the deficit, keeps cutting G until it succeeds in balancing the budget. What level of GNP will then prevail?

5. You are given the following information about an economy.

$$C = 40 + 0.75\, (Y - T)$$
$$I = 100$$
$$G = 80$$
$$X = 80$$
$$T = 0.2\, Y$$
$$IM = 0.2\, Y$$

Find the equilibrium values for GNP, budget surplus, and trade surplus.

Banking and the Creation of Money

12

[Money] is a machine for
doing quickly and
commodiously what would
be done, though less quickly
and commodiously,
without it.

JOHN STUART MILL

T he circular flow diagrams that were used in earlier chapters to explain equilibrium GNP (see, for example, Figure 11–1 on page 196) had a "financial system" in their upper left-hand corners. Savings flowed into this system and investment flowed out. Something obviously goes on inside the financial system to channel the saving into investment, and it is time we learned just what this something is.

There is another, equally important, reason for studying the financial system. *Fiscal policy* is not the only lever the government has on the economy's aggregate-demand curve: It also exercises significant control over aggregate demand by manipulating *monetary and exchange-rate policy*. If we are to understand monetary and exchange-rate policy (the subjects of Chapters 13–15), we must first acquire some understanding of the financial system.

The present chapter has three major objectives. It first seeks to explain the nature of money: What it is, what purposes it serves, and how it is measured. Once this is done, we turn our attention to the banking system, explaining its historical origins, the nature of banking as a business, and why this industry is so heavily regulated. Finally, we learn how banks create money—a subject that is of great importance because it is simply impossible to understand monetary policy without knowing how money is created.

At the end of the chapter, we will see why government authorities must exercise control over the supply of money in a modern economy, and this leads naturally into the discussion in Chapter 13 of *central banking*, that is, the techniques used to implement monetary and exchange-rate policy. In Chapters 14 and 15, we integrate what we will by then have learned about money and monetary policy into our model of income determination, as the culmination of our study of macroeconomic theory.

Policy Issue: Competition Among Banks

Excluding a class of special banks that deal mostly with the financial markets, there are only thirteen regular chartered banks in Canada, and the "big five" account for over 90 percent of all bank deposits across the country. Each of these five companies has more than 1000 branches. This situation is in stark contrast to the

U.S. banking system, where branching across state lines is not permitted. As a result, there are 15,000 separate banks in the United States. In 1980 significant legal changes were made in the United States to deregulate the operations of their many banks. One of the purposes of deregulation is to provide benefits to households through increased industry competition.

With Canada's highly concentrated banking industry, it would seem that increased competition would be desirable here too. This was the opinion of a Royal Commission in the 1960s and a study by the Economic Council of Canada in the 1970s. Some small steps in this direction were taken in 1980. But to form a judgment on deregulation, we must first address an even more basic question: Why were banks so heavily regulated in the first place?

One reason is that governments often feel compelled to regulate any monopolized industry. The intention is that government regulation can insure that "the public interest" gets some weight in the decision-making process of these private firms. The Canadian banking industry has certainly become more concentrated through time. The largest number of banks in Canada was 51, in 1874. By 1914, that number was down to 22. During that period, there were 17 new banks established; however, there were also 25 failures and 21 mergers. But industry concentration cannot be the only reason for regulation, since the U.S. banks have historically been subject to even more regulation than banks in Canada.

A major reason for regulation is simply that the major "output" of the banking industry—the nation's supply of money—is of vital importance to the health of the economy. Bank managers presumably do what is best for their shareholders. That, at any rate, is their job. But, as we shall see, what is best for bank shareholders may not be best for the whole economy. For this reason, the government does not allow bankers to determine the level of the nation's money supply by profit considerations alone.

Another reason for the extensive regulation of banks is concern for the safety of depositors. In a free-enterprise system, new businesses are born and die every day; and no one save those people immediately involved takes much notice of these goings-on. When a firm goes bankrupt, shareholders lose money and employees may lose their jobs. (The latter may not even happen if new management takes over the assets of the bankrupt firm.) But, except for the case of very large firms, that is about it.

A **run on a bank** occurs when many depositors withdraw cash from their accounts simultaneously.

But banking is different. If banks were treated like other firms, depositors would lose money whenever one went bankrupt. That is bad enough by itself, but the real danger comes in the case of a **run on a bank**. When depositors get jittery about the security of their money, they may all rush in at once to cash in their accounts. For reasons we will learn in this chapter, most banks could not survive a "run" like this and would be forced into insolvency. Worse yet, this disease is highly contagious. If Mrs. Smith hears that her neighbour has just lost her life savings because the Victoria Street National Bank went broke, she is quite likely to rush to her own bank to make a hefty withdrawal.

Without modern forms of bank regulation, therefore, one bank failure might lead to another; and indeed, as noted above, bank failures certainly did occur in the past. They were much more common in the United States. For instance, failures were not an important feature of the Great Depression in Canada, while 2200 banks failed in 1932 alone in the United States. Failures of banks in the United States are relatively rare nowadays, although there were 42 of them in 1982. Failures are very infrequent in Canada, because "head office" can always bail out any local branch that may get into difficulties. Nevertheless, the governments in both Canada and the United States have taken steps to ensure that the infectious disease of bank failure, if it occurs, will not spread. It has done this in several ways that will be mentioned later in this chapter.

Barter Versus Monetary Exchange

Money is so much a part of our day-to-day existence that we are likely to take it for granted, failing to appreciate all that it accomplishes. But it is important to realize that money is very much a social contrivance. Like the wheel, it had to be invented. The most obvious way to trade commodities is not by using money, but by **barter**—a system in which people exchange one good directly for another. And the best way to appreciate what monetary exchange accomplishes is to imagine a world without it.

Under a system of direct barter, if Farmer Jones grows corn and has a craving for spinach, he has to find a spinach farmer with a taste for corn. If he finds such a person (this was called the *double coincidence of wants* by the classical economists), they make the trade. If this sounds easy, try to imagine how busy Farmer Jones would be if he had to repeat the sequence for every commodity he consumed in a week. For the most part, the desired double coincidences of wants are more likely to turn out to be double wants of coincidence, where Jones gets no spinach and the spinach farmer gets no corn. Worse yet, with so much time spent looking for trading partners, Jones would have far less time to grow corn.

Money greases the wheels of exchange, and thus makes the whole economy more productive.

Under a monetary system, the corn farmer gives up his corn for money. He does so not because he wants the money per se, but because of what that money can buy. Money makes Farmer Jones's shopping tasks much easier, for it allows him simply to locate a spinach farmer who wants money. And what spinach farmer does not?

For these reasons, monetary exchange replaced barter at a very early stage of human civilization, and only extreme circumstances, like massive wars and runaway inflations, have been able to bring barter (temporarily) back.

Barter is a system of exchange in which people directly trade one good for another, without using money as an intermediate step.

The Conceptual Definition of Money

Monetary exchange is the alternative to direct barter. In a system of monetary exchange, people trade **money** for goods when they purchase something and trade goods for money when they sell something, but they do not trade goods directly for other goods. This defines money's principal role as the **medium of exchange**. But once it has come into use as the medium of exchange, whatever object is serving as money is bound to take on other functions as well. For one, it

Money is the standard object used in exchanging goods and services. In short, money is the **medium of exchange**.

The unit of account is the standard unit for quoting prices.

A store of value is an item used to store wealth from one point in time to another.

will inevitably become the **unit of account**, that is, the standard unit for quoting prices. Thus, if inhabitants of an idyllic tropical island used coconuts as money, they would be foolish to quote prices in terms of sea shells.

Money may also come to be used as a **store of value**. If Farmer Jones temporarily produces and sells corn of more value than he wants to consume right away, he may find it convenient to store the difference in the form of money until he wants to use it. This is because he knows that money can be "sold" easily for goods and services at a later date, whereas land, gold, and other stores of value might not be. Of course, if money pays no interest and inflation is substantial, he may decide to forgo the convenience of money and store his wealth in some other form rather than see its purchasing power rapidly eroded. So this role of money is far from inevitable.

Since money may not always serve as a store of value, and since there are many stores of value other than money, it is best not to include the store-of-value function as part of our conceptual definition of money. Instead, we simply label as "money" whatever serves as the medium of exchange.

What Serves as Money?

Anthropologists and historians will testify that a bewildering variety of things have served as money in different times and places. Cattle, stones, candy bars, cigarettes, woodpecker scalps, porpoise teeth, and giraffe tails are a few of the more colourful examples. In the early settlements in Quebec, playing cards were used as money.

A commodity money is an object in use as a medium of exchange that also has a substantial value in alternative (non-monetary) uses.

In primitive or less organized societies, the commodities that served as money generally had value in themselves. If not used as money, cattle could be slaughtered for food, cigarettes could be smoked, and so on. But such **commodity money** generally runs into several severe difficulties. To be useful as a medium of exchange the commodity must be divisible. This makes cattle a very poor choice. It must also be of uniform, or at least readily identifiable, quality so that inferior substitutes are easy to recognize. This may be why woodpecker scalps never achieved great popularity. The medium of exchange must also be storable and durable, which presents a serious problem for candy-bar money. Finally, because commodity moneys need to be carried and stored, it is helpful if the item is compact, that is, has high value per unit of volume and weight. (See the boxed insert on page 227.)

All of these traits make it sensible that gold and silver have circulated as money since the first coins were struck about 2500 years ago. Since they have high value in non-monetary uses, a lot of purchasing power can be carried without too much weight. Pieces of gold are also storable, divisible (with a little trouble), and of identifiable quality (with a little more trouble).

The same characteristics suggest that paper would make an ideal money. Since we can print any number on it that we want, we can make paper money as divisible as we please and also make it possible to carry a large value in a lightweight and compact form. Paper is easy to store and, with a little cleverness, we can make counterfeiting very hard (though never impossible). The Chinese apparently originated paper money in the 12th century.

Fiat money is money that is decreed as such by the government. It is of little value as a commodity, but it maintains its value as a medium of exchange because people have faith that the issuer will stand behind the pieces of printed paper and limit their production.

Paper cannot, however, serve as a commodity money because its value per square inch in alternative uses is so small. A paper currency that is repudiated by its issuer can, perhaps, be used as wallpaper or to wrap fish, but these uses will surely represent only a small fraction of the paper's value as money. Contrary to the popular expression, such a currency literally *is* worth the paper it is printed on, which is to say that it is not worth very much. Thus paper money is always **fiat money**.

Contemporary Canadian money is fiat money. Look at a dollar bill. Between the Coat of Arms and the Queen's picture it states: "This note is legal tender."

Dealing by Wheeling on Yap

As this extract from a recent newspaper article shows, primitive forms of money still exist in some remote places.

YAP, Micronesia—On this tiny South Pacific Island... the currency is as solid as a rock. In fact, it is rock. Limestone to be precise.

For nearly 2,000 years the Yapese have used large stone wheels to pay for major purchases, such as land, canoes and permission to marry. Yap is a U.S. trust territory, and the dollar is used in grocery stores and gas stations. But reliance on stone money... continues.

Buying property with stones is "much easier than buying it with U.S. dollars," says John Chodad, who recently purchased a building lot with a 30-inch stone wheel. "We don't know the value of the U.S. dollar."

Stone wheels don't make good pocket money, so for small transactions, Yapese use other forms of currency, such as beer....

Besides stone wheels and beer, the Yapese sometimes spend *gaw*, consisting of necklaces of stone beads strung together around a whale's tooth. They also can buy things with *yar*, a currency made from large sea shells. But these are small change.

The people of Yap have been using stone money ever since a Yapese warrior named Anagumang first brought the huge stones over from limestone caverns on neighboring Palau, some 1,500 to 2,000 years ago. Inspired by the moon, he fashioned the stone into large circles. The rest is history....

By custom, the stones are worthless when broken. You never hear people on Yap musing about wanting a piece of the rock....

SOURCE: Adapted from Art Pine, "Hard Assets, or Why a Loan in Yap is Hard to Roll Over," *The Wall Street Journal*, March 29, 1984, page 1.

Nowhere on the certificate is there a promise, stated or implied, that the Canadian government will exchange it for anything else. A dollar bill is convertible into 4 quarters, or 10 dimes, or 20 nickels, or any other similar combination, but not into gold, chocolate, or any other commodity.

Why do people hold these pieces of paper? Only because they know that others are willing to accept them for things of intrinsic value—food, rent, shoes, and so on. If this confidence ever evaporated, these dollar bills would cease serving as a medium of exchange and, given that they make ugly wallpaper, would become virtually worthless.

But don't panic. This is not likely to occur. Our current monetary system has evolved over hundreds of years during which *commodity money* was first replaced by *"full-bodied" paper money*—paper certificates that were backed by gold or silver of equal value held in the issuer's vaults. Then the full-bodied paper money was replaced by certificates that were only partially backed by gold and silver. Finally, we arrived at our present system, in which paper money has no "backing" whatsoever. Like a hesitant swimmer who first dips her toes, then her legs, then her whole body into a cold swimming pool, we have "tested the water" at each step of the way—and found it to our liking. It is unlikely that we will ever take a step back in the other direction.

How the Quantity of Money Is Measured

As we will learn in coming chapters, the amount of money circulating in the economy is of profound importance for the determination of national income and the price level. Thus it becomes important for the government to know how much money there is at any given time.

Our conceptual definition of money describes it as the medium of exchange.

But this raises questions about just what items should be included and what items excluded when we count up the money supply. Some items are easy. All of our coins, the small change of our economic system, clearly should count as money. So should paper money, which accounts for a far greater volume of transactions. But we cannot stop here if we want to include the main vehicle for making payments in our society, because the lion's share of our nation's payments are made neither in metal nor in paper money, but by cheque.

Chequing deposits are actually no more than bookkeeping entries in bank ledgers. Many people think of cheques simply as a convenient way to give coins or dollar bills to someone else. But, in fact, cheques are something quite different, which is why the country can have more money in the form of chequing deposits than it has in the form of currency. For example, if you pay the grocer $50 by cheque, no dollar bills or coins normally will change hands. Instead, that cheque will travel back to your bank, where $50 will be deducted from the bookkeeping entry that records your account and added to the bookkeeping entry for your grocer's account. (If you and the grocer hold accounts at different banks, more books get involved; but still no coins or bills are likely to be moved.) Since so many transactions are made by cheque, it seems imperative that chequing deposits be included in any specific definition of the money supply.

One popular definition of the money supply stops here and includes only currency held outside chartered bank vaults, plus chequing deposits at chartered banks. In the official statistics, this narrowly defined concept of money is called **M1**. The left-hand side of Figure 12–1 shows the composition of M1 as of January 1984.

But there are other types of accounts that allow withdrawals by cheque, and which therefore are candidates for inclusion in the money supply. Strictly speaking, withdrawals from the savings account at your bank can require up to seven days prior notice. However, in practice this procedure is not followed, and everyone

The narrowly defined money supply, usually abbreviated **M1**, is the sum of all coins and paper money in circulation, plus pure chequing deposits at chartered banks.

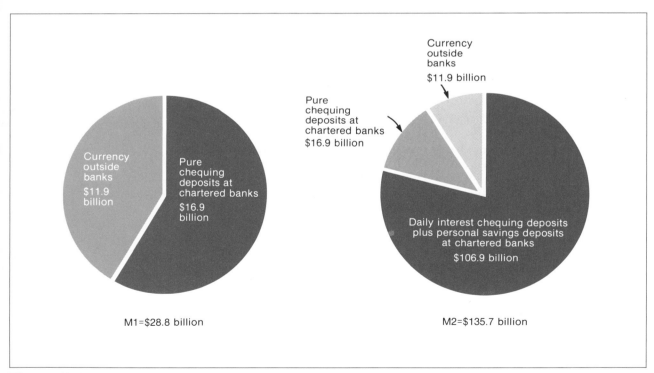

Figure 12–1
DEFINITIONS OF THE MONEY SUPPLY (JANUARY 1984)
SOURCE: Bank of Canada *Review*.

regards their savings-account holdings as equivalent to money. Furthermore, since many banks offer convenient electronic transfers of funds from one account to another, either by telephone or by pushing a button on an automated teller, savings balances can serve the same purposes as chequing balances. For this reason, savings accounts are included in the broader statistical definition of the money supply known as **M2**.

The composition of M2 as of January 1984 is shown on the right-hand side of Figure 12–1. You can see that the savings accounts predominate, dwarfing everything that is included in M1.

Some economists do not want to stop counting at M2; they prefer still broader definitions of money that include other closely related assets. For example, many people do their "banking" at trust companies or credit unions; this is especially true in Quebec, with the Caisses Populaires. The problem with extending the definition of the money supply by including the deposits at these institutions is that there is no clear-cut place to stop. There is no obvious line of demarcation between those assets that *are* money and those that are merely *close substitutes* for money—so-called **near moneys**.

If we define an asset's **liquidity** as the ease with which it can be converted into cash, then there is a range of assets of varying degrees of liquidity. Everything in M1 is completely "liquid"; savings accounts included in M2 are a bit less so; and so on, until we encounter such things as short-term government bonds, which, while still quite liquid, would not normally be included in the money supply. Any number of different "M's" can be defined—and have been—by drawing the line in different places.

And there are still more complexities. For example, credit cards clearly serve as a medium of exchange. So should they be included in the money supply? Yes, you say. But how would we do this? How much money does your credit card represent? If you think about questions like this for a while, you will realize that there are no good answers—which is one reason why research on the definition of money continues. But, in a first course in economics, we do not want to get bogged down in complex definitional issues. So we will simply adhere to the convention that *"money" consists only of coins, paper money, and chequing deposits at chartered banks.*

Now that we have defined money and seen how it can be measured, we turn our attention to the principal creators of money—the banks.

How Banking Began

When Adam and Eve left the Garden of Eden, they did not encounter a bank. Banking had to be invented, and some time passed before it came to be practised as it is today. With a little imagination, we can see how the first banks must have begun.

When money was made of gold it was most inconvenient for consumers and merchants to carry it around and to have to weigh and assay it for purity every time a transaction was made. So it is not surprising that the practice developed of leaving one's gold in the care of a goldsmith, who had safe storage facilities, and carrying in its place a receipt from the goldsmith stating that John Doe did indeed own five ounces of gold of a certain purity. The goldsmiths, of course, charged a fee for this service. When people began trading goods and services for the goldsmiths' receipts, rather than for the gold itself, the receipts became an early form of paper money.

At this stage, paper money was fully backed by gold. But gradually the goldsmiths began to notice that the amount of gold they were actually required to pay out in a day was but a small fraction of the total gold they had stored in their warehouses. Then one day some enterprising goldsmith hit upon a momentous idea that must have made him fabulously wealthy.

The broadly defined money supply, usually abbreviated **M2,** is the sum of currency in public hands, plus chequing and all savings deposits at chartered banks.

Near moneys are liquid assets that are close substitutes for money.

An asset's **liquidity** refers to the ease with which it can be converted into cash.

His thinking probably ran something like this. "I have 2000 ounces of gold stored away in my vault, for which I collect storage fees from my customers. If I get much more, I'll need an expensive new vault. But in the last year, I was never called upon to pay out more than 100 ounces on a single day. What harm could it do if I lent out, say, half the gold I now have? I'll still have more than enough to pay off any depositors that come in for a withdrawal, so no one will ever know the difference. And I could earn 30 additional ounces of gold each year in interest on the loans I make (at 3 percent interest on 1000 ounces). With this profit, I could lower my service charges to depositors and so attract still more deposits. I think I'll do it."

With this resolution, the modern system of **fractional reserve banking** was born. This system has three important features—features that are crucially important to this chapter.

Fractional reserve banking is a system under which bankers keep in their vaults as reserves only a fraction of the funds they hold on deposit.

1. ***Bank profitability***. By getting deposits at zero interest and lending some of them out at positive interest rates, goldsmiths made a profit. The history of banking as a profit-making industry was begun and has continued to this date. *Banks, like other enterprises, are in business to earn profits.*

2. ***Bank discretion over the money supply***. When goldsmiths decided that they could get along by keeping only a fraction of their total deposits on reserve in their vaults and lending out the balance, they acquired the ability to *create money*. As long as they kept 100 percent reserves, each gold certificate represented exactly one ounce of gold. So whether people decided to carry their gold or leave it with their goldsmith did not affect the money supply, which was set by the volume of gold.

   With the advent of fractional reserve banking, however, new paper certificates were added whenever goldsmiths lent out some of the gold they held on deposit. The loans, in effect, created new money. In this way, the total amount of money came to depend on the amount of gold that each goldsmith felt compelled to maintain as reserves in his vault. For any given volume of gold on deposit, the lower the reserves the goldsmiths kept, the more loans would be made, and therefore the more money there would be. While we no longer use gold to back our money, this principle remains true today. *Bankers' business decisions influence the supply of money.*

3. ***Exposure to runs***. A goldsmith who kept 100 percent reserves never had to worry about a run on his vault. Even if all his depositors showed up at the door at once, he always had enough gold to return their deposits. But as soon as the first goldsmith decided to get by with only fractional reserves, the possibility of a run on the vault became a real concern. If that first goldsmith who lent out half his gold had found 51 percent of his customers at his door one unlucky day, he would have had a lot of explaining to do. Similar problems have worried bankers for centuries. *The danger of a run on the bank has induced bankers to keep prudent reserves and to lend out money carefully.*

Principles of Bank Management: Profits Versus Safety

Bankers have a reputation, probably deserved, for conservatism in politics, dress, and business affairs. From what has been said so far, the economic rationale for this conservatism should be clear. Today's chequing deposits are pure fiat money. For years now these deposits have been "backed" by nothing more than the bank's promise to convert them into currency on demand. Thus, banks depend entirely on people's trust, and so must acquire a reputation for prudence. This they did (and continue to do) in two principal ways. First, they had to maintain a sufficiently generous level of reserves to minimize their vulnerability to runs. Second, they had to be somewhat cautious in making loans and investments, since any large losses on their loans could undermine the confidence of depositors.

It is important to realize that banking under a system of fractional reserves is an inherently risky business that is rendered relatively safe only by cautious and prudent management. The history of bank failures in the United States before World War II bears sober testimony to the fact that many bankers were neither cautious nor prudent. Why? Because this is not a recipe for high profits. Bank profits are maximized by keeping reserves as low as possible, by making at least some risky investments, and by giving loans to borrowers of questionable credit standing (because these borrowers will pay the highest interest rates). The art of bank management is to strike the appropriate balance between the lure of profits and the need for safety. When a banker errs by being too stodgy, his bank will earn inadequate profits. When he errs by taking unwarranted risks, his bank may not survive at all.

Bank Regulation

The public authorities apparently have decided that the balance struck by profit-minded bankers often would not be at the place where society would like it struck. So government has thrown up a web of regulations designed to insure the safety of depositors and to control the supply of money.

The principal innovation guaranteeing the safety of bank deposits is **deposit insurance**. Today most bank deposits are insured against loss by the federal government, up to an amount of $60,000 per account regardless of what happens to the bank. Thus, while bank failures may spell disaster for the bank's shareholders, they do not give many depositors cause for concern. Deposit insurance eliminates the motive for customers to rush to their bank just because they hear some bad news about the bank's finances. Many observers give this innovation much of the credit for the pronounced decline in bank failures in the United States since 1933 (the year in which deposit insurance was started there). They had 2200 bank failures in 1932, and 60 in 1934.

Deposit insurance is a system that guarantees that depositors will not lose money even if their bank goes bankrupt.

In addition to insuring depositors against loss, the government takes steps to see that banks do not get into financial trouble. For one thing, various regulatory authorities conduct periodic *bank examinations and audits* in order to keep tabs on the financial condition and business practices of the banks under their purview. For another, laws and regulations *limit the kinds and quantities of assets in which banks may invest*. For example, banks are limited in the amount of common stock they may purchase, and it wasn't until 1954 that banks were allowed to make household mortgages. Both these forms of regulation are clearly aimed at maintaining bank safety.

A final type of regulation also has some bearing on safety but it is motivated primarily by the government's desire to control the money supply. We have seen that the amount of money any bank will issue depends on the amount of reserves it elects to keep. For this reason, most banks are subject by law to minimum **required reserves**. While banks may (and sometimes do) keep reserves in excess of these legal minimums, they may not keep less. It is this regulation that places an upper limit on the money supply. The rest of this chapter is concerned with the details of this mechanism.

Required reserves are the minimum amount of reserves (in cash or the equivalent) that is mandated by law. Normally, required reserves are proportional to the volume of deposits.

How Bankers Keep Books

Before we can fully understand the mechanics of modern banking and the process by which money is "created," we must acquire at least a nodding acquaintance with the way in which bankers keep their books. The first thing to know is how to distinguish assets from liabilities.

An **asset** of an individual or business firm is an item that the individual or firm owns.

A **liability** of an individual or business firm is an item that the individual or firm owes. Many liabilities are known as "debts."

A **balance sheet** is an accounting statement listing the values of all the assets on the left-hand side and the values of all the liabilities and **net worth** on the right-hand side.

Net worth is the value of all assets minus the value of all liabilities.

An **asset** of a bank is something that the bank *owns*. This "thing" may be a physical object, such as the bank building, a typewriter, or a vault, or it may be just a piece of paper, such as an IOU of a customer to whom the bank has made a loan. A **liability** of a bank is something that the bank *owes*. Most bank liabilities take the form of bookkeeping entries. For example, if you have a chequing account in the Victoria Street Bank, your bank balance there is a liability of the bank. (It is, of course, an asset for you.)

There is an easy test to see whether some piece of paper or bookkeeping entry is a bank's asset or a liability. Ask yourself whether, if this paper were converted into cash, the bank would receive the cash (if so, it is an asset) or pay it out (if so, it is a liability). This test makes it clear that loans to customers are bank assets (when the loans are repaid, the bank collects), while customers' deposits are bank liabilities (when deposits are cashed in, the bank must pay up).

When accountants draw up a complete list of all the bank's assets and liabilities, the resulting document is called the bank's **balance sheet**. Typically, the value of all the bank's assets exceeds the value of all its liabilities. (On the rare occasions when this is not the case, the bank is in serious trouble.) In what sense, then, do balance sheets "balance"?

They balance because accountants have invented the concept of **net worth** to balance the books. Specifically, they have defined the net worth of a bank to be the difference between the value of all its assets and the value of all its liabilities. Thus, by definition, when accountants add net worth to liabilities, the sum they get must be the same as the value of the bank's assets. In short:

$$\text{Assets} = \text{Liabilities} + \text{Net worth.}$$

Table 12–1 illustrates this with the balance sheet of a fictitious bank, Bank-a-mythica, whose finances are extremely simple. On December 31, 1984, it had only two kinds of assets (listed on the left-hand side of the balance sheet)—$1 million in cash, which it held as reserves in its vault, and $4.5 million in outstanding loans to its customers, that is, in customers' IOUs. And it had only one type of liability (listed on the right-hand side)—$5 million in chequing deposits. The difference between total assets ($5.5 million) and total liabilities ($5 million) was the bank's net worth ($500,000), shown on the right-hand side of the balance sheet.

The Limits to Money Creation by a Single Bank

Let us now turn to the process of deposit creation. Many bankers will deny that they have any ability to "create" money. (The very phrase has a suspiciously

Table 12–1
BALANCE SHEET OF BANK-A-MYTHICA, DECEMBER 31, 1984

ASSETS		LIABILITIES AND NET WORTH	
Assets		**Liabilities**	
Cash in vault	$1,000,000	Chequing deposits	$5,000,000
Loans oustanding	4,500,000		
Total	$5,500,000		
Addendum: Bank Reserves		**Net Worth**	
Actual reserves	$1,000,000	Shareholders' equity	500,000
Required reserves	1,000,000		
Excess reserves	0	Total	$5,500,000

hocus-pocus sound to it.) But they are not quite right. For although any individual bank's ability to create money is severely limited in a system with many banks, the banking system as a whole can achieve much more than the sum of its parts. Through the modern alchemy of **deposit creation**, it can turn one dollar into many dollars. But to understand this important process, we had better proceed in steps, beginning with the case of a single bank, our hypothetical Bank-a-mythica.

According to the balance sheet in Table 12–1, Bank-a-mythica is holding cash reserves in its vault that are equal to 20 percent of its deposits ($1 million in cash is equal to 20 percent of the $5 million in deposits). Let us assume that this is the minimum reserve ratio prescribed by law and that the bank strives to keep its reserves down to the legal minimum; that is, it strives to keep its **excess reserves** down to zero.

Now let us suppose that on January 2, 1985, an eccentric widower comes into Bank-a-mythica and deposits $100,000 in cash in his chequing account. The bank now has acquired $100,000 more in cash reserves, and $100,000 more in chequing deposits. But since deposits are up by $100,000, *required* reserves are up by only 20 percent of this amount, or $20,000, leaving $80,000 in *excess* reserves. Table 12–2 illustrates the effects of this transaction on Bank-a-mythica's balance sheet. It is tables such as this, which show *changes* in balance sheets rather than the balance sheets themselves, that will help us follow the money-creation process.

If Bank-a-mythica does not want to hold excess reserves, it will be unhappy with the situation illustrated in Table 12–2, for it is holding $80,000 in excess reserves on which it earns no interest. So as soon as possible it will lend out the extra $80,000—let us say to Hard-Pressed Construction Company. This loan leads to the balance sheet changes shown in Table 12–3: Bank-a-mythica's loans rise by $80,000 while its holdings of cash reserves fall by $80,000.

Excess reserves are any reserves held in excess of the legal minimum.

Table 12–2
CHANGES IN BANK-A-MYTHICA'S BALANCE SHEET, JANUARY 2, 1985

ASSETS		LIABILITIES	
Cash in vault	+ $100,000	Chequing deposits	+ $100,000
Addendum: Bank Reserves			
Actual reserves	+ $100,000		
Required reserves	+ 20,000		
Excess reserves	+ $ 80,000		

Bank-a-mythica receives a $100,000 cash deposit. It now holds excess reserves of $80,000, since required reserves rise by only $20,000 (20 percent of $100,000).

Table 12–3
CHANGES IN BANK-A-MYTHICA'S BALANCE SHEET, JANUARY 3–6, 1985

ASSETS		LIABILITIES	
Loans outstanding	+ $80,000	No change	
Cash in vault	– $80,000		
Addendum: Changes in Reserves			
Actual reserves	– $80,000		
Required reserves	No change		
Excess reserves	– $80,000		

Bank-a-mythica gets rid of its excess reserves by making a loan of $80,000 to Hard-Pressed Construction Company.

Table 12-4

CHANGES IN BANK-A-MYTHICA'S BALANCE SHEET, JANUARY 2-6, 1985

ASSETS		LIABILITIES	
Cash in vault	+ $20,000	Chequing deposits	+ $100,000
Loans outstanding	+ 80,000		
Addendum: Changes in Reserves			
Actual reserves	+ $20,000		
Required reserves	+ 20,000		
Excess reserves	No change		

When it receives $100,000 in cash deposits, Bank-a-mythica keeps only the required $20,000 in reserves and lends out the remaining $80,000 to Hard-Pressed Construction Company. Its excess reserves return to zero.

By combining Tables 12-2 and 12-3, we arrive at Table 12-4, which summarizes all the bank's transactions for the week. Cash reserves are up $20,000, loans are up $80,000, and now that the bank has had a chance to adjust to the inflow of deposits, it no longer holds excess reserves.

Looking at Table 12-4 and keeping in mind our specific definition of money, it appears at first that the chairman of Bank-a-mythica is right when he claims not to have engaged in the nefarious practice of "money creation." All that happened was that, in exchange for the $100,000 in cash it received, the bank issued the widower a chequing balance of $100,000. This does not change M1, it merely converts one form of money into another.

But wait. What happened to the $100,000 in cash that the eccentric man brought to the bank? The table shows that $20,000 was retained by Bank-a-mythica in its vault. Since this currency is no longer in circulation, it no longer counts in the official money supply. (Notice that Figure 12-1 included only "currency outside banks.") But the other $80,000, which the bank lent out, is still in circulation. It is held by Hard-Pressed Construction, which probably will redeposit it in some other bank. But even before this happens, the original $100,000 in cash has supported a rise in the money supply: There is now $100,000 in chequing deposits of the widower and $80,000 of cash in circulation, making a total of $180,000. The money-creation process has begun.

Multiple Money Creation by a Series of Banks

Let us now trace the $80,000 in cash and see how the process of money creation gathers momentum. Suppose that Hard-Pressed Construction Company, which banks across town at the First National Bank, deposits the $80,000 into its bank account. First National's reserves increase by $80,000. But because deposits are up by $80,000, *required* reserves rise by only 20 percent of this amount or $16,000. If the management of First National Bank behaves like that of Bank-a-mythica, the $64,000 of excess reserves will be lent out.

Table 12-5 shows the effects of these events on First National Bank's balance sheet. (The preliminary steps corresponding to Tables 12-2 and 12-3 are not shown separately.) At this stage in the chain, the original $100,000 in cash has led to $180,000 in deposits—$100,000 at Bank-a-mythica and $80,000 at First National Bank—and $64,000 in cash, which is still in circulation (in the hands of the recipient of First National's loan—Al's Auto Shop). Thus, from the original $100,000, a total of $244,000 has been added to the money supply ($180,000 in chequing deposits plus $64,000 in cash).

Table 12-5

CHANGES IN FIRST NATIONAL BANK'S BALANCE SHEET

ASSETS		LIABILITIES	
Cash in vault	+ $16,000	Chequing deposits	+ $80,000
Loans outstanding	+ 64,000		
Addendum: Changes in Reserves			
Actual reserves	+ $16,000		
Required reserves	+ 16,000		
Excess reserves	No change		

Hard-Pressed deposits its $80,000 in First National Bank, which sets aside the required $16,000 in reserves (20 percent of $80,000) and lends $64,000 to Al's Auto Shop.

Table 12-6

CHANGES IN SECOND NATIONAL BANK'S BALANCE SHEET

ASSETS		LIABILITIES	
Cash in vault	+ $12,800	Chequing deposits	+ $64,000
Loans outstanding	+ 51,200		
Addendum: Changes in Reserves			
Actual reserves	+ $12,800		
Required reserves	+ 12,800		
Excess reserves	No change		

When Al deposits his $64,000 in Second National Bank, that bank retains $12,800 as required reserves (20 percent of $64,000) and lends out the remaining $51,200.

But, to coin a phrase, the bucks do not stop here. Al's Auto Shop will presumably deposit the proceeds from its loan into its own account at Second National Bank, leading eventually to the balance sheet adjustments shown in Table 12–6 when Second National makes an additional loan rather than hold on to excess reserves. You can see how the money-creation process continues.

Table 12–7 adds up the balance-sheet changes of the first five banks in the chain (from Bank-a-mythica through the Fourth National Bank) on the assumptions that each bank holds exactly the 20 percent required reserves (no excess reserves), and that each loan recipient redeposits the proceeds in his own bank. At this stage, $336,160 in bank deposits have been created, and there is still $32,768 in cash circulating (the original $100,000 less $67,232 in bank vaults), for a total increase in the money supply of $268,928 ($368,928 less the original $100,000).

But the chain does not end there. For the Main Street Movie Theatre, which received the $32,768 loan from the Fourth National Bank, then deposits these funds into the Fifth National Bank. Fifth National has to keep only 20 percent of this deposit, or $6,553.60, on reserve and will lend out the balance. And so the chain continues.

What are the final effects on the money supply? If you look carefully at the three sections of Table 12–7, you will see that each column of numbers forms a *geometric progression*; specifically, each entry is equal to exactly 80 percent of the entry that preceded it. Recall that in the discussion of the multiplier in Chapter 9 we learned how to sum an infinite geometric progression, which is just what each

Table 12-7

CHANGES IN THE COMBINED BALANCE SHEETS OF THE FIRST FIVE BANKS

ASSETS		LIABILITIES	
Cash in Vault		**Chequing Deposits**	
Bank-a-mythica	+ $20,000	Bank-a-mythica	+ $100,000
First National Bank	+ 16,000	First National Bank	+ 80,000
Second National Bank	+ 12,800	Second National Bank	+ 64,000
Third National Bank	+ 10,240	Third National Bank	+ 51,200
Fourth National Bank	+ 8,192	Fourth National Bank	+ 40,960
Total	+ $67,232	Total	+ $336,160
Loans Outstanding			
Bank-a-mythica	+ $80,000		
First National Bank	+ 64,000		
Second National Bank	+ 51,200		
Third National Bank	+ 40,960		
Fourth National Bank	+ 32,768		
Total	+ $268,928		
Total change in assets	+ $336,160		

After five banks have participated, the chain of deposit creation looks like this. But there are still excess reserves in the system (held by Fifth National Bank), so the chain continues.

of these chains eventually will be. In particular, if the common ratio is R, the sum of an infinite geometric progression is

$$1 + R + R^2 + R^3 + \ldots = \frac{1}{1 - R} .$$

By applying this formula to the chain of chequing deposits on the right-hand side of Table 12–7, we get:

$$
\begin{aligned}
&\$100,000 + \$80,000 + \$64,000 + \$51,200 + \ldots \\
&= \$100,000 \times (1 + 0.8 + 0.64 + 0.512 + \ldots) \\
&= \$100,000 \times (1 + 0.8 + 0.8^2 + 0.8^3 + \ldots) \\
&= \$100,000 \times \frac{1}{1 - 0.8} = \frac{\$100,000}{0.2} = \$500,000.
\end{aligned}
$$

So eventually the original $100,000 in cash will support $500,000 in new chequing deposits—a multiple expansion of $5 for every one original dollar. Table 12–8 shows the ultimate effect of the entire chain of deposit creation on the balance sheet of the banking system as a whole. The banks have converted $100,000 in cash into $500,000 in chequing deposits.

Notice that 5 is the reciprocal of 20 percent (that is, 5 = 1/0.2). This suggests the general formula for multiple deposit creation when the required reserve ratio is some number other than 20 percent:

OVERSIMPLIFIED MONEY-MULTIPLIER FORMULA
If the required reserve ratio is some fraction, m, an injection of $1 of reserves into the banking system can lead to the creation of $1/m$ in new deposits. That is, the so-called "money multiplier" is given by:

Change in deposits = $(1/m)$ × Change in reserves.

Table 12–8

CHANGES IN COMBINED BALANCE SHEET OF THE ENTIRE BANKING SYSTEM

ASSETS		LIABILITIES	
Cash in vault	+ $100,000	Chequing deposits	+ $500,000
Loans outstanding	+ 400,000		
Addendum: Changes in Reserves		**Addendum: Changes in Money Supply**	
Actual reserves	+ $100,000	Demand deposits	+ $500,000
Required reserves	+ 100,000	Currency outside banks	− 100,000
Excess reserves	No change	Net change	+ $400,000

By the end of the chain of deposit creation, the entire $100,000 of cash has found its way into bank vaults, where it can support $500,000 in deposits. No excess reserves remain; and the money supply has expanded by $400,000.

While we have derived this formula in a rather mechanical fashion, there is a simple piece of logic behind it. If banks want to hold only the legal minimum in cash reserves, then an injection of $1 in new reserves into the banking system must induce them to expand their loans until *required* reserves have risen by $1. For only then will all *excess* reserves have been eliminated.

But if each dollar of deposits requires only a fraction m (one-fifth in our example) of a dollar in reserves, then deposits must expand by $1/m$ for each dollar of new reserves. This is the common sense behind the money-multiplier formula.

Since later chapters will be concerned with changes in the *money supply*, not just with changes in *bank deposits*, it is worth pointing out that the money supply grew by only $400,000, not $500,000, in Table 12–8. The reason is that the original $100,000 cash deposit was part of the money supply before it was deposited in Bank-a-mythica. While the *chequing-deposit* component of the money supply rose by $500,000 (as our formula suggests), the *cash* component of the money supply fell by $100,000, leaving a net increase of $400,000. You will avoid confusion if you keep in mind the fact that the money supply has *two* components: cash (outside banks) and deposits.

The Process in Reverse: Multiple Contractions of the Money Supply

Let us now briefly consider how this deposit-creation mechanism operates in reverse—as a system of deposit *destruction*. In particular, suppose that our eccentric widower came back to Bank-a-mythica to withdraw $100,000 from his checking account and return it to his mattress, where it rightfully belongs. Bank-a-mythica's *required* reserves would fall by $20,000 as a result of this transaction (20 percent of $100,000), but its *actual* reserves would fall by $100,000. The bank would be $80,000 short, as indicated in Table 12–9(a).

How does it react to this discrepancy? As some of its outstanding loans are routinely paid off, the bank will cease granting new ones until it has accumulated the necessary $80,000 in required reserves. The data for Bank-a-mythica's contraction are shown in Table 12–9(b), assuming that borrowers pay off their loans in cash.[1]

But where did the borrowers get this money? Probably by making withdrawals from other banks. In this case, let us assume it all came from First National Bank, which loses an $80,000 deposit and $80,000 in reserves. It finds itself short some

[1]In reality, they would probably pay with cheques drawn on other banks. Bank-a-mythica would then cash these cheques to acquire the reserves.

Table 12–9

CHANGES IN THE BALANCE SHEET OF BANK-A-MYTHICA

(a)			(b)	
ASSETS	LIABILITIES		ASSETS	LIABILITIES
Cash in vault − $100,000	Chequing deposits − $100,000		Cash in vault + $80,000	
			Loans outstanding − 80,000	
Addendum: Changes in Reserves			**Addendum: Changes in Reserves**	
Actual reserves − $100,000			Actual reserves + $80,000	
Required reserves − 20,000			Required reserves No change	
Excess reserves − $ 80,000			Excess reserves + $80,000	

When Bank-a-mythica loses a $100,000 deposit, it must reduce its loans by $80,000 to replenish its reserves.

$64,000 in reserves [see Table 12–10(a)] and therefore must reduce its loan commitments by $64,000 [see Table 12–10(b)]. This, of course, causes some other bank to suffer a loss of reserves and deposits of $64,000, and the whole process repeats just as it did in the case of deposit expansion.

After five banks had become involved, the picture would be just as shown in Table 12–7, except that all the *plus* signs would be *minus* signs. And the final results are just the mirror image of Table 12–8. Deposits shrink by $500,000, loans fall by $400,000, bank reserves are reduced by $100,000, and the money supply falls by $400,000. As suggested by our money-multiplier formula with $m = 0.2$, the decline in deposits is $1/0.2 = 5$ times as large as the decline in reserves.

During the height of the radical student movements of the late 1960s, a circular appeared in Cambridge, Massachusetts, urging citizens to withdraw all funds from their chequing accounts on a prescribed date, hold them in cash for one week, and then redeposit them. This act, the circular argued, would surely wreak havoc upon the capitalist system. Obviously, some of these radicals were well-schooled in modern money mechanics, for the argument was basically correct. The tremendous multiple contraction of the banking system and consequent multiple expansion that a successful campaign of this sort could have caused might have disrupted the local financial system quite seriously. But history records that the appeal met with little success.

Table 12–10

CHANGES IN THE BALANCE SHEET OF FIRST NATIONAL BANK

(a)			(b)	
ASSETS	LIABILITIES		ASSETS	LIABILITIES
Cash in vault − $80,000	Chequing deposits − $80,000		Cash in vault + $64,000	
			Loans outstanding − 64,000	
Addendum: Changes in Reserves			**Addendum: Changes in Reserves**	
Actual reserves − $80,000			Actual reserves + $64,000	
Required reserves − 16,000			Required reserves No change	
Excess reserves − $64,000			Excess reserves + $64,000	

First National Bank's loss of an $80,000 deposit forces it to cut back its loans by $64,000.

Why the Money-Creation Formula Is Oversimplified

So far, our discussion of the process of money creation has made it all seem rather mechanical. If all proceeds according to formula, each $1 in new reserves will lead to a $1/m increase in deposits. But in reality things are not this simple. Just as we did in the case of the expenditure multiplier, we must stress that the oversimplified formula for money creation is accurate only under very particular circumstances. These circumstances require that:

1. Every recipient of a bank loan must redeposit the proceeds of that loan into another bank rather than hold it in cash.
2. Every bank must hold reserves no larger than the legal minimum.

Let us see what happens to the chain of deposit creation when either of these assumptions is violated.

Suppose first that the business firms and individuals who receive bank loans decide not to redeposit all of the proceeds into their bank accounts. For example, Hard-Pressed Construction Company and all the other borrowers might decide to hold half of their loan proceeds in cash and deposit only the remaining half. Then First National Bank would receive only a $40,000 deposit, and could, therefore, make only a $32,000 loan. Second National Bank would then receive only $16,000 (half of $32,000), and so on. The whole chain of deposit creation would be reduced drastically. Thus:

If individuals and business firms decide to hold more cash, the multiple expansion of the money supply will be curtailed because fewer dollars of cash will be available in bank vaults to be used as reserves to support new chequing deposits. Consequently, the money supply will be smaller.

The basic idea here is simple. Each $1 of cash held by a bank can support several dollars (specifically, $1/m) of money. But each $1 held by an individual is exactly one dollar of money. Hence, any time cash leaves the banking system, the money supply will decline. And any time cash enters the banking system, the money supply will rise.

Next, suppose that Bank-a-mythica's management becomes very conservative, or that the outlook for loan repayments worsens because of a recession. The bank might then decide to keep more reserves than the legal requirement (say, 30 percent) and lend out less than the $80,000 assumed in Table 12-4 (say, $70,000). If this happens, then First National Bank will receive a smaller injection of cash reserves than that shown in Table 12-5. And if First National's management is as jittery as Bank-a-mythica's, it too will hold more in reserves and lend out less. Thus:

If banks wish to keep excess reserves, the multiple expansion of the money supply will be restricted. A given amount of cash will support a smaller supply of money than would be the case if banks held no excess reserves.

The Need for Monetary Control

If we pursue this point a bit further, we will see why government regulation of the money supply is so important for economic stability. We have just suggested that banks will wish to keep excess reserves when they do not foresee profitable and secure opportunities to make loans. This is likely to happen during the downswing and around the bottom of a business contraction. If it occurs, the propensity of banks to hold excess reserves will turn the money-creation process into one of money destruction.

During a recession, profit-oriented banks would be prone to reduce the money supply by increasing their excess reserves—if the monetary authorities did not intervene. As we will learn in subsequent chapters, the money supply is an important influence on aggregate demand, so such a contraction of the money supply would exacerbate the severity of the recession.

On the other hand, banks will want to squeeze the maximum possible money supply out of any given amount of cash reserves by keeping their reserves at the bare minimum when the demand for bank loans is buoyant, profits are high, and many investments suddenly start to look profitable. This reduced incentive to hold excess reserves in prosperous times means that:

During an economic boom, the behaviour of profit-oriented banks is likely to make the money supply expand, adding undesirable momentum to the booming economy and paving the way for a burst of inflation. The authorities must intervene to prevent this.

Regulation of the money supply, then, is necessary because bankers, in the pursuit of profit, might otherwise provide the economy with a widely fluctuating money supply that dances to the tune of the business cycle. Precisely how the authorities can keep the money supply under control is the subject of the next chapter.

Summary

1. It is much more efficient to exchange goods and services by using money as a medium of exchange than by bartering them directly.
2. In addition to being the medium of exchange, whatever serves as money is likely to become the standard unit of account and a popular store of value.
3. Throughout history, all sorts of things have served as money. Commodity moneys gave way to full-bodied paper money (certificates backed 100 percent by some commodity, like gold), which in turn gave way to partially backed paper money. Nowadays our paper money has no commodity backing whatsoever: that is, it is pure fiat money.
4. The most widely used definition of the Canadian money supply is M1, which includes coins and paper money held outside banks, and chequing deposits. However, many economists prefer the M2 definition, which adds to M1 savings and most notice deposits held at chartered banks.
5. Under our modern system of fractional reserve banking, banks keep cash reserves equal to only a fraction of their total deposit liabilities. This is the key to their profitability, since their remaining funds can be loaned out at interest. But it also leaves them potentially vulnerable to runs.
6. Because of this vulnerability, bank managers are

generally very conservative in their investment strategy, and they also like to keep a prudent level of reserves. Even so, the government keeps a watchful eye over banking practices.

7. Before bank mergers and deposit insurance, bank failures were fairly common. Some still occur in the United States, where branching across state lines is not permitted.
8. Because it holds only fractional reserves, even a single bank can create money. But its ability to do so is severely limited because the funds it lends out probably will be deposited in another bank.
9. As a whole, the banking system can create several dollars of deposits for each dollar of cash reserves it receives. Under certain assumptions, the ratio of new deposits to new reserves will be $1/m$, where m is the required reserve ratio.
10. The same process works in reverse, as a system of money destruction, when cash is withdrawn from the banking system.
11. Because banks and individuals may want to hold more cash when the economy is shaky, the money supply would probably contract under such circumstances if the monetary authorities did not intervene. Similarly, the money supply would probably expand rapidly in boom times if it were unregulated.

Concepts for Review

Run on a bank	Fiat money	Asset
Barter	M1 versus M2	Liability
Unit of account	Near moneys	Balance sheet
Money	Liquidity	Net worth
Medium of exchange	Fractional reserve banking	Deposit creation
Store of value	Deposit insurance	Excess reserves
Commodity money	Required reserves	

Questions for Discussion

1. If ours were a barter economy, how would you pay your tuition bill? What if your university did not want the goods or services you offered in payment?

2. How is "money" defined, both conceptually and in practice? Does the Canadian money supply consist of commodity money, full-bodied paper money, or fiat money?

3. What is fractional reserve banking, and why is it the key to bank profits? (*Hint:* What opportunities to make profits would banks have if reserve requirements were 100 percent?) Why does fractional reserve banking give bankers discretion over how large the money supply will be? Why does it make banks potentially vulnerable to runs?

4. Do you hold an account in a bank? If so, what will happen to your account if the bank goes bankrupt?

5. Suppose that no banks keep excess reserves and no individuals or firms hold on to cash. If someone suddenly discovers $1 million in buried treasure, explain what will happen to the money supply if the required reserve ratio is one-sixth (16.67 percent).

6. How would your answer to Question 5 differ if the reserve ratio were 25 percent? If the reserve ratio were 100 percent?

7. Each year during the Christmas shopping season, consumers and stores wish to increase their holdings of cash. Explain how this could lead to a multiple contraction of the money supply. (As a matter of fact, the authorities prevent this contraction from occurring by methods explained in the next chapter.)

8. Excess reserves make a bank less vulnerable to runs. Why, then, don't bankers like to hold excess reserves? What circumstances might persuade them that it would be advisable to hold excess reserves?

9. Use tables such as Tables 12–2 and 12–3 to illustrate what happens to bank balance sheets when each of the following transactions occurs:
   a. You withdraw $200 from your chequing account to purchase textbooks at the university book store.
   b. Paul steals $100 in cash from Peter and deposits it into his chequing account.
   c. Mary Q. Contrary withdraws $500 in cash from her account at Hometown Bank, carries it to the city, and deposits it into her account at Big City Bank.

10. For each of the transactions listed in Question 9, what will be the ultimate effect on the money supply if the required reserve ratio is 10 percent? (Assume that the oversimplified money-multiplier formula applies.)

Central Banking and Monetary Policy

13

Victorians heard with grave attention that the Bank Rate had been raised. They did not know what it meant. But they knew that it was an act of extreme wisdom.

J.K. GALBRAITH

From what we learned in Chapter 12 about the normal practices of profit-oriented banks we might expect the money supply to expand rapidly during prosperous times and to grow sluggishly, or even to shrink, during recessions. Fortunately, the historical record for *postwar* Canada does not exhibit this pattern. Why not? One reason is that Canada's *central bank*, the Bank of Canada, has prevented it from happening.

The Bank of Canada is a very special kind of bank. Its customers are banks rather than individuals, and it performs some of the same services for them that your bank performs for you. Though it turns out to be quite an effective profit-maker, its actions are not guided by the profit motive. Instead, the Bank of Canada acts in what it perceives to be the national interest. While its actions are certainly not free from error, and while many people do not share its view of what constitutes the national interest, the Bank of Canada's actions have by and large caused the money supply to be a stabilizing influence on the Canadian economy. Just how the Bank of Canada regulates the money supply and the international value of the Canadian dollar, and why its performance has fallen short of perfection, are the main subjects of this chapter.

The Bank of Canada

The Bank of Canada was officially created by the Bank of Canada Act of 1935. It was originally a privately owned bank with approximately 12,000 individual shareholders. In 1938, complete nationalization took place when the federal government bought all the shares. The Bank of Canada is now a crown corporation, and all its profits accrue to the government.

Before the creation of the Bank of Canada, much of our currency was dollar bills, or notes, issued by the various chartered banks. In 1934, 53 percent of the currency was Dominion of Canada notes, while 47 percent was private bank liabilities. In 1950, all chartered bank notes were withdrawn from circulation.

One of the reasons for the creation of the Bank of Canada was to provide more stability for the economy. During the first four years of the Great Depression, the Canadian money supply fell by 12.5 percent. While no chartered banks failed, this contraction in the money supply accentuated the fall in aggregate demand that took place. Now the Bank of Canada tries to control Canada's money supply in an attempt to have the "appropriate" level of aggregate demand.

The Independence of the Bank of Canada

Canadians have had four governors of its central bank. According to the original act, the governor was appointed for seven years, and once appointed, he could not be removed by the government. This institutional independence of the governor was looked upon as a source of pride by some and as an anti-democratic embarrassment by others. The proponents of central bank independence argue that it enables monetary-policy decisions to be made on objective, technical criteria and keeps monetary control out of the "political thicket." Without this independence, it is argued, there would be a tendency for politicians to force the Bank of Canada to expand the money supply too rapidly, thereby contributing to chronic inflation and undermining faith in the financial system.

Opponents of this view counter that there is something profoundly undemocratic about having an unelected banker and his advisors make decisions that affect the well-being of all Canadians. Monetary policy, they argue, ought to be formulated by the elected representatives of the people, just like fiscal policy. Those who argue for government control over the Bank can point to historical instances in which monetary and fiscal policy have been at loggerheads—with the Bank of Canada undoing or even overwhelming the effects of fiscal-policy decisions.

This conflict did not occur under our first governor, Graham Towers, who headed the central bank from 1935 to 1954. However, the second governor, James Coyne (1955–61), was the centre of a dramatic conflict with the Diefenbaker government. During the severe recession of the late 1950s, Diefenbaker's government used expansionary fiscal policy in an attempt to create jobs. Coyne was more concerned with avoiding inflation and a possible depreciation of the Canadian dollar. Thus, he put a tight limit on the growth of the money supply and operated a contractionary monetary policy. This counteracted the government's fiscal policy. After much wrangling, the government's constitutional advisors suggested that an act be passed declaring the governor's seat to be vacant. The government could not fire Mr. Coyne, but they could define his position out of existence. Although the Senate refused to pass this bill, Mr. Coyne felt that he had had his chance to have his reasoning officially recorded during the Senate hearings, and he resigned.

When our third governor, Louis Rasminsky (1961–73), took office, he formally acknowledged that the government had the final power "to direct the Bank as to the policy which the Bank is to carry out." This principle was officially included in the 1967 revision of the Bank of Canada Act. As a result, our fourth and current governor, Gerald Bouey, must take his basic instructions from the government. However, should he consider the government's dictates to be irresponsible monetary policy, he can resign and explain his reasons. Since this would be extremely embarrassing for the government, from a political point of view, the governor still has a significant degree of power. For example, since 1975, the governor has consistently warned the government that the Bank of Canada is not printing up new money to buy up very many of the government bonds being issued to cover the record budget deficits. Several recent annual reports of the Bank stress that the government must get better control of its deficit. Hence, the governor of the Bank is not a pawn of the government.

Controlling the Money Supply: Reserve Requirements

Chapter 12 taught us one important way in which the monetary authorities can control the money supply: by varying the minimum required reserve ratio. The lower is the reserve ratio, the more the chartered banks can loan out, and therefore the more deposit money they can create. However, since the 1967 revision of the Bank Act, the main reserve ratio has been fixed by law, and so the reserve requirement is no longer an instrument of monetary control.

The reserve requirements that rule today are those that were set in the 1980 revision of the Bank Act. Chartered banks must hold at least the following amounts in their vaults, or in their deposits at the Bank of Canada: 10 percent of their chequing deposit obligations; 2 percent of the first $500 million of savings and notice deposit obligations; 3 percent of the remaining savings and notice deposits; 3 percent of their foreign currency deposit obligations.

The fact that there are several different reserve requirements means that the actual money-creation formula is more complicated than the one we derived in Chapter 12. The fact that the reserve requirement is less stringent on deposit accounts that formally require prior notice of withdrawals is an anachronism. The reserves are not required for public confidence, given the existing deposit insurance. Unfortunately, this anachronism has a cost, since it makes monetary control more difficult. Chartered banks can vary deposit interest rates and service charges for cheques to induce the public to change the proportion of the deposits it holds in chequing accounts. By doing so, the chartered banks (not the central bank) can control the overall reserve requirement ratio.

Controlling the Money Supply: Open-Market Operations

The Bank of Canada buys and sells in the nation's bond markets, and this is its main method of affecting chartered bank reserves. Since these operations involve the Bank of Canada as simply one (sometimes large) participant in the bond markets that are open to anyone, they are called **open-market operations**. To appreciate the mechanics of this policy, we must consider the balance sheet of the central bank; this is presented in Table 13–1.

We see from Table 13–1 that the Bank of Canada limits most of its purchases to one class of assets: Government of Canada bonds. Either the Bank purchases newly printed bonds that have been issued by the government to cover some of its current budget deficit, or it purchases existing government bonds previously held by members of the private sector. The latter operation, which is called an open-market purchase, allows the Bank to increase the money supply even if there is no current budget deficit, as we shall presently see. Unlike the chartered banks, the Bank of Canada returns all bond-interest earnings to the government.

The other major asset purchased by the Bank is foreign exchange. Some of these holdings are gold (since gold was the original international medium of

Open-market operations refer to the Bank of Canada's purchase or sale of government securities through transactions in the open bond market.

Table 13–1

THE CONSOLIDATED BALANCE SHEET OF THE BANK OF CANADA AND THE EXCHANGE FUND ACCOUNT, 1983

ASSETS (billions of dollars)		LIABILITIES (billions of dollars)	
Government of Canada bonds	17.03	Notes in circulation (currency)	14.16
		Deposits:	
Gold and foreign currency reserves	5.45	of chartered banks	3.45
		of federal government	0.09
Advances	0.03	Miscellaneous accounts and net worth	4.81

SOURCE: Bank of Canada *Review.*

exchange) and the rest are stocks of various major foreign currencies. Our discussion of the reasons for, and the implications of, the Bank's purchasing or selling foreign exchange is postponed until later in this chapter. What we emphasize now is simply the fact that exchange-rate policy is carried out by the Bank of Canada.[1]

Table 13-1 also shows that the bulk of the Bank of Canada "liabilities" is the stock of currency that is used by chartered banks and the general public. We also see that the Bank of Canada serves as a bank for the chartered banks. A large part of the reserves held by the chartered banks to satisfy the reserve requirement laws are held in the form of chequing deposits at the Bank of Canada. The cheque-clearing process between chartered banks is accomplished by the banks writing cheques (to each other) drawn against their own accounts at the Bank of Canada. The federal government also holds an account with the Bank of Canada; and, of course, the government has deposit accounts at the various chartered banks as well. The government uses all of these accounts to store tax revenue as it comes in and to write cheques to make payments.

An open-market purchase of federal government bonds (previously held by the general public) by the Bank of Canada on January 2, 1985, is illustrated in Table 13-2.

The +$100,000 entry on the asset side of the Bank of Canada's balance sheet indicates its purchase of bonds from some member of the general public on the open market. The Bank of Canada pays for the bond by cheque, and the bond dealer gives the cheque to the member of the public for whom he sold the bond. The member of the public then deposits the cheque for $100,000 in his chartered bank, and this is recorded as the +$100,000 entry on the liability side of the

[1]The third asset, advances, is explained on pages 247–48.

Table 13-2
CHANGES IN THE BALANCE SHEETS OF THE BANK OF CANADA AND THE CHARTERED BANKS FOLLOWING AN OPEN MARKET PURCHASE OF BONDS

CHANGES IN BALANCE SHEET OF BANK OF CANADA, JANUARY 2, 1985

ASSETS		LIABILITIES	
Government bonds	+$100,000	Currency outstanding	
Foreign exchange		Deposits:	
		of federal government	
Advances to chartered banks		of chartered banks	+$100,000

CHANGES IN BALANCE SHEET OF CHARTERED BANKS, JANUARY 2, 1985

Reserves:		Deposits:	
vault cash		of general public	+$100,000
deposits at the Bank of Canada	+$100,000	of federal government	
Loans		Advances from Bank of Canada	

Addendum: Changes in Reserves	
Actual reserves	+$100,000
Required reserves	+ $20,000
Excess reserves	+ $80,000

A multiple expansion of loans and deposits begins as the chartered banks get rid of their excess reserves by making new loans totalling $80,000.

chartered bank's balance sheet. The other entries on the balance sheets indicate the cheque-clearing process. The chartered bank sends the cheque back to the Bank of Canada, and the central bank pays the chartered bank by simply granting it an increase of $100,000 in its deposits at the Bank of Canada. This cheque-clearing operation requires two entries on the balance sheet, since the chartered bank's deposit is both its own asset *and* the Bank of Canada's liability.

The net result of this transaction is that the chartered bank has its reserves increase by the same amount as its deposits. Given the low reserve requirements, most of this increase is excess reserves; so the chartered banking system is now in a position to commence the process of multiple expansion in loans and deposits that we described in Chapter 12. For example, if we continue to assume a reserve requirement ratio of 0.2 for our illustration, the open-market purchase of bonds by the Bank of Canada eventually results in an increase of the public's deposits in chartered banks equal to $500,000. We need not repeat the details of that multiple expansion process. Our purpose here is only to explain how the Bank of Canada actually creates the initial increase in reserves that starts the expansion of the money supply. By a similar process, an open-market sale of government bonds by the Bank of Canada involves minus signs on the four entries in Table 13–2, and so leads to a multiple contraction of chartered bank loans and deposits.

Open-market operations constitute the major tool of monetary policy by which the Bank of Canada varies the rate of growth of the money supply.

The Bank of Canada buys bonds whenever it wants to increase the money supply; and it sells bonds whenever it wants to decrease the money supply.

To anticipate our discussion on exchange-rate policy in the next section of this chapter, we emphasize one important point now. *It does not matter what the Bank of Canada buys or sells; the effect on the money supply is the same.* Thus, as we shall see, Bank of Canada purchases of foreign exchange constitute an expansionary monetary policy, and Bank of Canada sales of foreign-exchange reserves constitute a contractionary monetary policy.

Controlling the Money Supply: Changes in Bank Rate

If the chartered banks ever get over-extended in loan operations and do not have the reserves required by the Bank Act, they can borrow the reserves from the Bank of Canada. The rate of interest charged by the Bank of Canada for these advances is called the **bank rate**. Since the chartered banks virtually never require an advance from the central bank, the bank rate is usually just employed as a summary signal, so that the private sector is aware of the behind-the-scenes operations of the Bank. For example, if the Bank has been selling government bonds, and intends to continue this action, it raises the bank rate. This represents an easily understood signal that the Bank is trying to reduce the money supply and tighten credit. Thus, changes in the bank rate merely reflect the stance of monetary policy as defined by the more basic tool of open-market operations.

Many people misunderstand the role of bank-rate announcements, since these changes are often *followed by* adjustments in the prime lending rates charged by chartered banks. Given this observed sequence of events, it appears that the bank rate is the fundamental causal influence. In fact, the Bank of Canada's contraction of reserves (due to open-market bond sales) is the real cause of loans becoming scarce and chartered bank loan rates increasing. However, the chartered banks can achieve a gain in public relations by waiting for the central bank to raise the bank rate before increasing their loan rates. Then they can talk about necessarily having to "pass on cost increases."

Before 1979, the bank rate was changed by the Bank of Canada on a relatively

The **bank rate** is the rate of interest charged by the Bank of Canada when reserves are loaned to the chartered banks (advances from the central bank). It is used as a signal of the direction of monetary policy.

infrequent basis. In the autumn of 1979, the true role of the bank rate became more transparent as the Bank of Canada adopted a policy of weekly adjustments in the bank rate. Every week the federal government auctions its new issue of treasury bills, a type of bond that it uses to obtain operating funds. The yield on the treasury bills is determined in a free market by supply and demand. The bank rate is now set every week at one-quarter of one percentage point above that week's treasury bill yield. This arrangement makes explicit what has been true for years: The bank rate is set to be *consistent with* going market interest rates; it *does not determine* market interest rates. Monetary policy has its fundamental effects on market interest rates by affecting the quantity of bonds and reserves that are available to the private sector through open-market operations.

Flexible Exchange Rates: A Prerequisite for Independent Control of the Money Supply

The Bank of Canada intervenes in the foreign-exchange market on a daily basis, in order to control the value of the Canadian dollar. Since this intervention involves either buying or selling foreign exchange, the quantity of central-bank liabilities outstanding becomes residually determined. This means that the more the Bank tries to fix a particular price for the Canadian dollar (the exchange rate), the more it loses the ability to fix the nation's money supply at any particular value. Thus, exchange-rate policy and monetary policy are one and the same. Because of this connection, we now give a detailed explanation of exchange rates, and how they can be fixed by the central bank.

What Are Exchange Rates?

While we have mentioned exchange rates at numerous points in earlier chapters, it is now time for a more thorough discussion. In the next several pages we will explain the distinction between a policy of fixed exchange rates and one of floating exchange rates. Then we will discuss how the choice of policy affects the ability of the Bank of Canada to control the nation's money supply.

International trade is more complicated than domestic trade. There are no national borders to be crossed when, say, apples from British Columbia are shipped to Ontario. The consumer in Ottawa pays with *dollars*, just the currency that the farmer in the Okanogan wants. But if that same farmer ships his apples to Japan, consumers there will have only Japanese *yen* with which to pay, rather than the dollars the farmer in B.C. wants. Thus, if international trade is to take place, there must be a way to transform one currency (yen) into another (dollars). The rates at which such transformations are made are called **exchange rates**.

The **exchange rate** states the price, in terms of one currency, at which another currency can be bought.

There is an exchange rate between every pair of currencies. For example, $1 Canadian is currently the equivalent of about 6 French francs. The exchange rate between the franc and the dollar, then, may be expressed as "6 francs to the dollar" (meaning that it costs 6 francs to buy a dollar) or about "16 cents to the franc" (meaning that it costs 16 cents to buy a franc). Although exchange rates change all the time, Table 13–3 gives an indication of exchange rates prevailing in June 1984, showing how many Canadian dollars it cost at that time to buy each unit of foreign currency.

Under our present system, currency rates change frequently. When other currencies get more expensive in terms of dollars, we say that they have **appreciated** relative to the dollar. Alternatively, we can look at this same event in terms of the dollar buying less foreign currency, meaning that the dollar has **depreciated** relative to another currency.

A nation's currency is said to **appreciate** when exchange rates change so that a unit of its own currency can buy more units of foreign currency. The currency is said to **depreciate** when exchange rates change so that a unit of its currency can buy fewer units of foreign currency.

What is a depreciation to one country must be an appreciation to the other.

For example, if the dollar cost of a German mark rises from 48 cents to 60 cents,

Table 13-3

EXCHANGE RATES WITH THE CANADIAN DOLLAR, JUNE 1984
(dollars per unit of foreign currency)

COUNTRY	CURRENCY UNIT	SYMBOL	COST IN CANADIAN DOLLARS
Australia	dollar	$	1.17
France	franc	FF	0.16
Germany	mark	DM	0.48
Italy	lira	L	0.00079
Japan	yen	¥	0.0056
Mexico	peso	$	0.0068
Sweden	krona	Kr	0.16
Switzerland	franc	S. Fr.	0.58
United Kingdom	pound	£	1.82
United States	dollar	$	1.30

SOURCE: *The Financial Post*

the cost of a Canadian dollar in terms of marks simultaneously falls from just over 2 marks to 1.67 marks. The Germans have had a currency *appreciation* while we have had a currency *depreciation.*

Notice also that, when many currencies are changing in value, the dollar may be appreciating with respect to one currency but depreciating with respect to another. Consider, for example, this set of actual recent exchange rates:

	ACTUAL EXCHANGE RATES	
	January 1982	**June 1984**
British pound	1 pound = $2.23	1 pound = $1.82
U.S. dollar	1 U.S. dollar = $1.19	1 U.S. dollar = $1.30

Between January 1982 and June 1984, the Canadian dollar *depreciated* relative to the U.S. dollar but *appreciated* relative to the pound.

While this is the terminology used to describe movements of exchange rates in free markets, another set of terms is used to describe decreases and increases in currency values when these values are set by government decree. When an officially set exchange rate is altered so that a unit of a nation's currency can buy *fewer* units of foreign currency, we say there has been a **devaluation** of that currency. When the exchange rate is altered so that the currency can buy *more* units of foreign currency, we say there has been a **revaluation**.

Exchange-Rate Determination in a Free Market

Why is it that a German mark costs 48 cents and not 40 cents or 55 cents? In a world of **floating exchange rates** (also called **flexible exchange rates**), with no government interferences, the answer would be fairly straightforward. Exchange rates would be determined by the forces of supply and demand, just like the prices of apples, or typewriters, or haircuts.

In a leap of abstraction, imagine that Canada and West Germany were the only countries on earth, so there was only one exchange rate to be determined. Figure 13-1 depicts the determination of this exchange rate at the point (denoted *E* in the figure) where demand curve *DD* crosses supply curve *SS*. At this price (48 cents per mark), we know that the number of marks demanded is equal to the number of marks supplied.

In a free market, exchange rates are determined by the law of supply and demand. If the rate were below the equilibrium level, the quantity of marks

A **devaluation** is a reduction in the official value of a currency.

A **revaluation** is an increase in the official value of a currency.

Floating exchange rates (also known as **flexible exchange rates**) are rates determined in free markets by the law of supply and demand.

Figure 13-1

DETERMINATION OF
EXCHANGE RATES IN A
FREE MARKET

Like any price, an exchange rate
will be determined by the
intersection of the demand and
supply curves in a free market.
Point *E* depicts this point for the
exchange rate between the
Canadian dollar and the German
mark, which settles at 48 cents
per mark in this example.

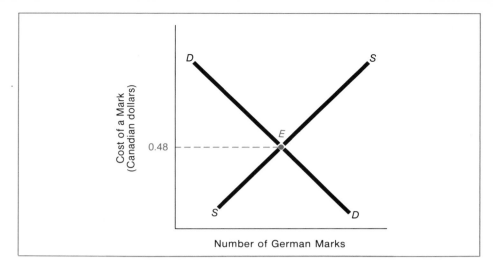

demanded would exceed the quantity of marks supplied, and the price of a mark would be bid up. If the rate were above the equilibrium level, quantity supplied would exceed quantity demanded, and the price of a mark would fall. Only at the equilibrium exchange rate is there no tendency for the exchange rate to change.

As usual, supply and demand determine price. What we must ask in this case is: Where do the supply and demand come from? Why does anyone demand a German mark?

1. **International trade in goods and services.** If, for example, Jane Doe, a Canadian, wants to buy a German automobile, she will first have to buy marks with which to pay the dealer in Munich.[2] So Jane's demand for a German *car* leads to a demand for German *marks*. In general, *demand for a country's export goods and services leads to a demand for its currency.*

2. **International trade in financial instruments like stocks and bonds.** For example, if Canadian investors want to purchase German stocks, they will first have to acquire the marks that the sellers will insist on. In this way, demand for German financial assets leads to demand for German marks. Thus, *demand for a country's financial assets leads to a demand for its currency.*

3. **Purchases of physical assets like factories and machinery overseas.** If a company in Canada wants to buy out a small German manufacturer, the owners will no doubt want to receive marks. So the Canadian company will first have to acquire German currency. In general, *direct foreign investment leads to a demand for a country's currency.*

Now, where does the supply come from? To answer this, we need only turn all of these transactions around. Germans wanting to buy Canadian goods and services, or to invest in Canadian financial markets, or to make direct investments in Canada will have to offer their marks for sale in the foreign-exchange market (which is similar to the stock market) to acquire the needed dollars. To summarize:

The *demand* for a country's currency is derived from the demands of foreigners for its export goods and services and for its assets, including financial assets, factories,

---

[2]Actually she will not do this because banks generally handle foreign-exchange transactions for consumers. A Canadian bank probably will buy the marks for her. But the effect is exactly the same as if Jane had done it herself.

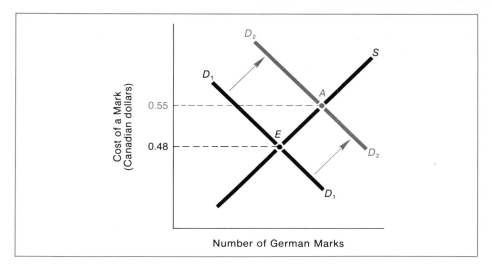

Figure 13-2
THE EFFECT OF AN
ECONOMIC BOOM ON THE
EXCHANGE RATE
If the Canadian economy
suddenly booms, Canadians will
spend more on imports from
Germany. Thus, the demand
curve for German marks will rise
from D_1D_1 to D_2D_2 as Canadians
seek to acquire the marks they
need. The diagram shows that
this will cause the mark to
appreciate, from 48 cents to 55
cents, as equilibrium shifts from
point E to point A. Looked at from
the Canadian perspective, the
dollar will depreciate.

and machinery. The *supply* of a country's foreign currency to individuals and firms in the rest of the world arises from its imports, and from foreign investment by its own citizens.

To appreciate the usefulness of even this simple supply and demand analysis, let us consider how the exchange rate between the Canadian dollar and the mark would change if there were an economic boom in Canada. One important effect of such a boom would be to stimulate Canadian demand for German products, such as automobiles, cameras, and wines. In terms of the supply–demand diagram shown in Figure 13-2, the increased desires of Canadians for German products would shift the demand curve for German marks out from D_1D_1 (the black line in the figure) to D_2D_2 (the blue line). Equilibrium would shift from point E to point A, and the exchange rate would rise from 48 cents per mark to 55 cents per mark. In a word, the increased demand for marks by Canadian citizens causes the mark to appreciate relative to the dollar.

EXERCISE
Test your understanding of the supply and demand analysis of exchange rates by showing why each of the following events would lead to a depreciation of the mark (appreciation of the dollar) in a free market:

1. A recession in Canada cuts Canadian purchases of German goods.

2. German investors are attracted by prospects for profit in the Canadian stock market.

3. Interest rates on government bonds rise in Canada but are stable in Germany. (*Hint*: Which country's citizens will be attracted by high interest rates to the other country?)

We will discuss the other important factors that shift the supply and demand curves for foreign exchange in Chapter 16. Here our focus is on the way central banks limit the flexibility of exchange rates (no matter what shifts the supply and demand curves for foreign exchange).

Fixed Exchange Rates
History records rather few instances of truly free exchange rates, determined by

supply and demand without government interference. Much more typical are cases where governments have resisted market forces and kept their exchange rates either above or below the equilibrium price for long periods of time. For this reason, we turn our attention next to the opposite of floating exchange rates, a system of **fixed exchange rates**, or rates that are set by governments. Naturally, under such a system the exchange rate, being fixed, is not closely watched. Instead, international financial specialists focus on a country's **balance of payments**—a term we are now ready to define.

To understand what the balance of payments is, look at Figure 13–3, which depicts a situation that might represent, say, Great Britain before its major devaluation in 1967—an *overvalued* currency. While the supply and demand curves for British pounds indicate an equilibrium exchange rate of $2.60 to the pound (point *E*) the British government is keeping the rate at $3.00. Notice that at $3.00 more people are supplying pounds than are demanding them. In the example, suppliers are selling £22 billion per year, but demanders are purchasing only £20 billion.

This gap between the £22 billion that some people sell and the £20 billion that other people buy is what we mean by Britain's **balance of payments deficit**—£2 billion per year in this case. It is shown by the horizontal distance between points *A* and *B* in Figure 13–3.

How can market forces be flouted in this way? Since sales and purchases on any market must be equal, as a simple piece of arithmetic, the excess of quantity supplied over quantity demanded of British currency (£2 billion per year in this example) must be bought by the Bank of England, Britain's central bank. In buying these pounds, it must give up some of the gold and foreign currencies that it keeps as *foreign-exchange reserves*. Thus, the Bank of England would be losing £2 billion in reserves per year as the cost of keeping the pound at $3.00.

Naturally, this cannot go on forever; the reserves eventually will run out. And this is the fatal flaw in the system of fixed exchange rates. Once speculators become convinced that the exchange rate can be held only a short while longer, they will sell pounds in massive amounts rather than hold on to a currency whose value they soon expect to fall sharply. The supply curve of pounds will shift outward drastically, as shown in Figure 13–4, causing an astronomical rise in the balance of payments deficit (from £2 billion to £4 billion in the example). This is called a "run" on the currency. Lacking sufficient reserves, the Bank of England will have to permit the exchange rate to fall to its equilibrium level, and this

Fixed exchange rates are rates that are set by government decisions and maintained by central bank actions.

The **balance of payments deficit** is the amount by which the quantity supplied of a country's currency (per year) exceeds the quantity demanded. Balance of payments deficits arise whenever the exchange rate is pegged at an artificially high level.

Figure 13–3

A BALANCE OF PAYMENTS DEFICIT

At a fixed exchange rate of $3.00 per pound, which is well above the equilibrium level of $2.60 per pound, England's currency is overvalued in this example. As a consequence, more pounds will be supplied (point *B*) than are demanded (point *A*). The difference—distance *AB*, or £2 billion per year—represents Britain's balance of payments deficit.

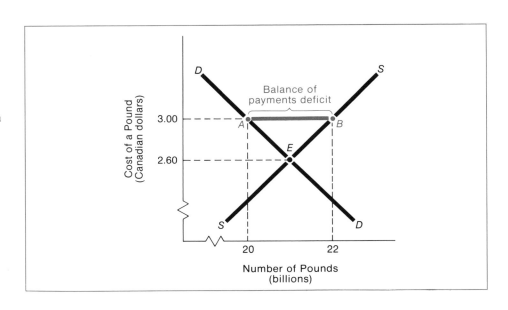

might amount to an even larger devaluation than would have been required before the speculative run on the pound began.

For an example of the reverse case, a severely *undervalued* currency, let us consider Germany in 1973. Figure 13–5 depicts demand and supply curves for marks that intersect at an equilibrium price of 40 cents per mark (point *E* in the diagram). Yet, in the example, we suppose that the German authorities are holding the rate at 35 cents. At this rate, the quantity of marks demanded (50 billion) greatly exceeds the quantity supplied (40 billion). The difference is Germany's **balance of payments surplus**, and is shown by the horizontal distance *AB*.

Germany can keep the rate at 35 cents only by providing the marks that foreigners want to buy: 10 billion marks per year in this example. In return, it receives U.S. dollars, British pounds, French francs, gold, and so on. All of this serves to increase Germany's reserves of foreign currencies. But notice the important difference between this case and Britain's overvalued pound.

The **balance of payments surplus** is the amount by which the quantity demanded of a country's currency (per year) exceeds the quantity supplied. Balance of payments surpluses arise whenever the exchange rate is pegged at an artificially low level.

The accumulation of foreign-exchange reserves rarely will *force* a central bank to revalue in the way that depletion of reserves can force a devaluation.

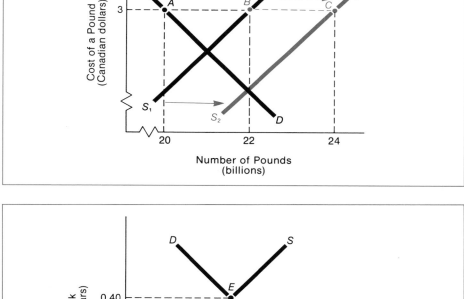

Figure 13-4

A SPECULATIVE RUN ON THE POUND

When speculators become convinced that a devaluation of the pound is in the offing, they will rush to sell all their pounds. Their actions shift the supply curve outward from S_1S_1 to S_2S_2 and, in the process, widen England's balance of payments deficit from *AB* to *AC*.

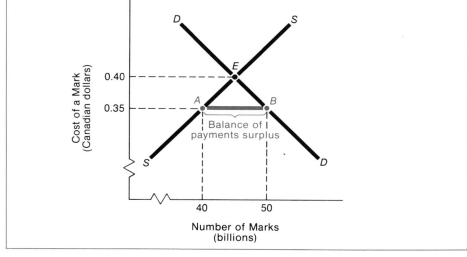

Figure 13-5

A BALANCE OF PAYMENTS SURPLUS

In this example, Germany's currency is undervalued at 35 cents per mark, since the equilibrium exchange rate is 40 cents per mark. Consequently, more marks are being demanded (point *B*) than are being supplied (point *A*). The gap between quantity demanded and quantity supplied—distance *AB*, or 10 billion marks per year—measures Germany's balance of payments surplus.

This was another weakness of the system of fixed exchange rates. In principle, imbalances in exchange rates could be cured either by a devaluation by the country with a balance of payments deficit or by an upward revaluation by the country with a balance of payments surplus. In practice, though, it was almost always the deficit countries that were forced to act.

Why did the surplus countries refuse to revalue? One reason was a simple misunderstanding of basic economics. They viewed the disequilibrium as the problem of the deficit countries and believed that the deficit countries, therefore, should take the corrective steps. This, of course, is nonsense. Some currencies are overvalued *because* some other currencies are undervalued. In fact, the two statements mean exactly the same thing.

The other reason is that exporters in Germany, Japan, and other surplus countries resisted upward revaluations because they knew that such actions would make their products more expensive to foreigners and thus cut into their export sales. And these exporters had the political clout to make that view stick. Meanwhile, since the values of the mark and the yen on world markets were artificially held down, German and Japanese consumers were put in the unenviable position of having to pay more for imported goods than they need have paid. Rather than buy these excessively expensive foreign goods, they watched domestically produced goods go overseas in return for pieces of paper (dollars, francs, pounds, and so on).

A more thorough investigation of the reasons why countries have tried to fix their exchange rates takes place in Chapter 16. Here we simply stress that fixing the exchange rate necessarily involves the country's central bank either buying up, or selling off, foreign exchange. Thus, pegging the exchange rate would involve the Bank of Canada performing an open-market operation in the foreign-exchange market, instead of the domestic bond market. The implications for the money supply are the same. This can be appreciated by simply moving the +$100,000 entry on the asset side of the Bank of Canada balance sheet in Table 13–2. The effect on chartered bank reserves is the same whether this entry is on the government-bond line or on the foreign-exchange line. Thus pegging the exchange rate involves allowing the growth in the Canadian money supply to be determined by the gap between the private demand and supply for foreign exchange.

The Bank of Canada can control our exchange rate or our money supply but not both.

The Money-Supply Mechanism: A Summary

This completes our discussion of the Bank of Canada's methods of controlling the money supply. We can now begin to integrate what we have just learned about the financial system into the macroeconomic model presented in Chapters 8 through 11, and to study how money affects the national economy. For this purpose, the analyses of the last chapter and the present one can be summed up in the following statement:

As interest rates rise, banks normally find it more profitable to expand their volume of loans and deposits, thus increasing the supply of money. This poses the danger that the money supply might expand rapidly during a period of inflation and economic boom and advance slowly, or even contract, during a period of recession—just the opposite from what stabilization policy requires.

However, the Bank of Canada can shift the relationship between the money supply and interest rates by employing its principal weapon of monetary control: open-market operations.

These ideas are depicted graphically in Figure 13–6. Part (a) shows a typical

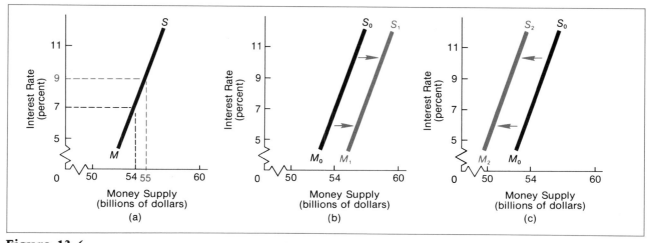

Figure 13-6

THE SUPPLY SCHEDULE FOR MONEY

Part (a) shows a typical supply schedule for money. It is rising as we move toward the right, meaning that banks will supply more money when interest rates are higher. Part (b) illustrates what happens to the money-supply schedule when the Bank of Canada purchases securities in the open market: The supply schedule shifts outward. Part (c) depicts the effect of a sale of bonds by the Bank of Canada. With this contractionary policy, the supply schedule shifts inward.

money-supply schedule labelled *MS*, illustrating that bank behaviour makes the money stock rise as interest rates rise. Notice that the sensitivity of the money supply to interest rates is rather weak in the diagram—a large rise in the rate of interest (from 7 percent to 9 percent) induces only a small increase in the supply of money (from \$54 billion to \$55 billion). The drawing is deliberately constructed that way because that is what the statistical evidence shows.

The curve in Figure 13–6(a) shows the money-supply schedule corresponding to some specific monetary policy. Figure 13–6(b) portrays how the money-supply schedule responds to an *expansionary change in monetary policy*, such as an open-market purchase of government bonds. The money-supply schedule shifts outward from M_0S_0 to M_1S_1, as indicated by the arrows. After banks have adjusted to the change, there is more money at any given interest rate. Figure 13–6(c) shows what happens in the reverse case—*contractionary monetary policy*, such as an open-market sale of securities. The money-supply schedule shifts inward from M_0S_0 to M_2S_2.

The diagrams make things look rather more precise than they actually are. Since the Bank of Canada's control over the money-supply schedule is imperfect in the short run, the actual *MS* schedule is obscured by a bit of fog. In what follows, we portray all the graphs as clean straight lines only for pedagogical simplicity. The Bank of Canada wishes things were so simple in the real world!

The Demand for Money

Just as we must know something about both the supply of and the demand for wheat before we can predict how much will be sold and at what price, it is necessary to know something about the **demand for money** if we are to understand the amount of money actually in existence and the prevailing interest rate.

The definition of money given in Chapter 12 suggests the most important reason why people hold money balances: The medium of exchange is needed to carry out purchases and sales of goods and services. Since the nominal gross national product (GNP) is considered to be the best measure of the total money value of all goods and services traded in the economy, it seems safe to assume that the higher the nominal GNP, the higher will be the demand for money. And, indeed, an impressive amount of statistical evidence supports this supposition. Notice that nominal GNP, and hence the demand for money, rises if *either* real output or the price level rises—a fact that will assume some importance in the next chapter.

But income is not the only factor affecting the demand for money; interest rates matter, too. At first, that may seem surprising because many forms of money, such as currency and some chequing deposits, pay no interest. Why, then, are interest rates relevant? They are relevant because money is only one of a variety of forms in which individuals can hold their wealth. Holders of money *give up* the opportunity to hold one of these other assets, such as government bonds, in order to gain the convenience of money. In so doing, they *give up* the interest that they could have earned on one of these alternative assets.

This is another example of the concept of *opportunity cost.*[3] On the surface, it seems virtually costless to hold money. But, *compared with the next best alternative*, this action is not costless at all. For example, if the next best alternative to holding $200 in cash is to put those funds into a government bond that pays 10 percent interest, then the opportunity cost of holding that money is $20 per year (10 percent of $200).

How, then, should the rate of interest influence the quantity of money that people demand? It is natural to assume that when interest rates are high people will make strenuous efforts to economize on their holdings of money balances, efforts that would not be worthwhile at lower interest rates. In a word, rational behaviour of consumers and business firms should make the demand to hold money *decline* as the interest rate *rises*. And once again, careful analysis of the data shows this to be true. To summarize:

People and business firms hold money primarily to finance their transactions. Therefore, the quantity of money demanded increases as real output rises or as prices rise. However, the quantity of money demanded decreases as the rate of interest rises because the rate of interest is the opportunity cost of holding money balances.

It is possible to portray the demand for money by a graphical device, as shown in Figure 13–7. There we show a downward-sloping demand schedule for money

[3]If you need to review this concept, see Chapter 3.

Figure 13-7
THE DEMAND SCHEDULE FOR MONEY
The downward-sloping curve *MD* is a typical demand schedule for money. It slopes down because money is a less-attractive asset when interest rates on alternative assets are higher. The entire curve is shifted if either the number of transactions (which is often measured by real GNP) or the average price of a transaction (which is measured by the price level) changes.

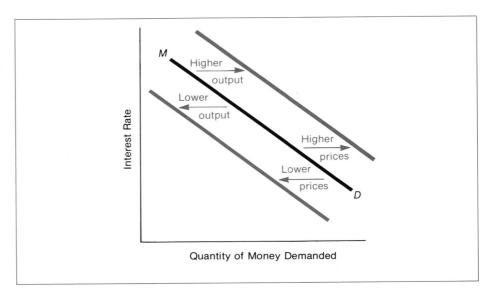

(the curve labelled *MD*)—the quantity of money demanded decreases as the rate of interest rises. But since the quantity of money demanded also depends on real output and the price level, we must hold both real output and the price level constant in drawing up such a curve. Changes in either of these variables will shift the *MD* curve in the manner indicated in the diagram because at higher levels of nominal GNP, demand for money is higher; and at lower levels of nominal GNP, it is lower.

Equilibrium in the Money Market When Foreign and Domestic Financial Markets Are Independent

As is usual in supply and demand analysis, it is useful to put both sides of the market together on a single graph. Figure 13–8 combines the money-supply schedule of Figure 13–6(a) (labelled *MS*) with the money-demand schedule of Figure 13–7 (labelled *MD*).

There is no curve representing foreigners' actions in this market, since, for the moment, we are assuming that funds cannot flow across international borders, so that interest rates in Canada can diverge from the level of U.S. interest rates. Point *E* is the equilibrium of the money market. The diagram thus shows that *given* real output and the price level (which locates the *MD* curve) and *given* the monetary policy (which locates the *MS* curve), the money market is in equilibrium at an interest rate (*r*) of 9 percent and a money stock (*M*) of $55 billion.

Since the central bank can shift the *MS* curve, it can alter this equilibrium through its **monetary policy**. Expansionary monetary-policy actions involve purchasing government securities in the open market. This action provides additional excess reserves to the banking system, thus encouraging banks to increase their loans and deposits. As money becomes more plentiful, interest rates drop.

Our supply–demand analysis of the money market shows this in Figure 13–9(a). By shifting the money-supply schedule outward from M_0S_0 to M_1S_1, the central bank moves the market equilibrium from point *E* to point *A*—thus forcing the interest rate down.

Contractionary monetary-policy actions, such as selling securities in the open

Monetary policy refers to actions that the Bank of Canada takes in order to change the equilibrium of the money market, that is, to alter the money supply, move the exchange rate, or both.

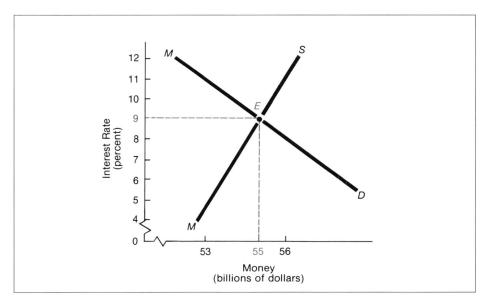

Figure 13–8
EQUILIBRIUM IN THE MONEY MARKET WITH FOREIGN TRANSACTIONS OMITTED
Equilibrium in the market for money is determined by the intersection of demand curve *MD* and supply curve *MS*. At point *E*, the interest rate is 9 percent, and the money supply is $55 billion. At no other interest rate would the demand for and the supply of money be in balance.

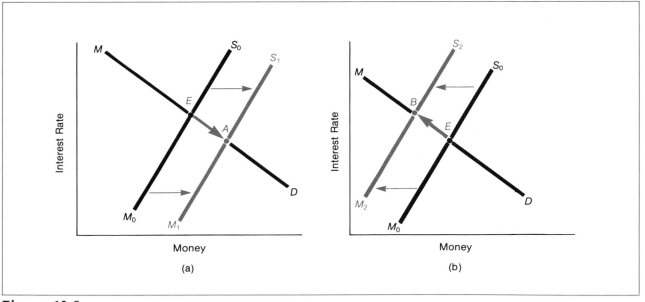

Figure 13-9
THE EFFECTS OF MONETARY POLICY ON THE MONEY MARKET
The two parts of this figure show the effects of monetary policy on the money supply (M) and the rate of interest (r). In part (a), expansionary monetary policies shift the supply schedule from M_0S_0 to M_1S_1 and push the equilibrium from point E to point A; M rises while r falls. In part (b), contractionary policies pull the supply schedule in from M_0S_0 to M_2S_2, causing equilibrium to move up from point E to point B; M falls as r rises.

market, have the opposite effect. They push interest rates up, as Figure 13–9(b) shows. Thus:

Monetary policies that expand the money supply normally lower interest rates. Monetary policies that reduce the money supply normally raise interest rates.

During the early 1980s the U.S. central bank rigidly restricted the growth of the U.S. money supply to fight inflation. The theory was that the resulting high interest rates would discourage investment spending and so decrease aggregate demand. Those high interest rates have caused much concern in Canada and other Western countries.

Equilibrium in the Money Market When Foreign and Domestic Financial Markets Are Integrated

In the previous section, we discussed the determination of the level of interest rates, without any reference to the level of foreign interest rates. While this analysis is useful for a country like the United States, it is unrealistic for Canada. Since it is so easy for Americans to buy Canadian bonds, and vice versa, and since Canadian bonds constitute such a small proportion of the North American financial market, the North American interest rate is essentially determined by U.S. monetary policy in the manner we have just described. Competition among sellers of bonds precludes a different rate of interest from being "made in Canada."

Figure 13–10, which reproduces the demand and supply curves from Figure 13–8, shows how this works. Assume that the value of the U.S. interest rate has just risen from 9 to 11 percent. Equilibrium in the Canadian market can no longer be at point E, since that outcome involves Canadians earning only 9 percent on their bonds, while 11 percent is available through buying U.S. bonds. Thus, households and firms will choose to be at point A on their demand-for-money curve.

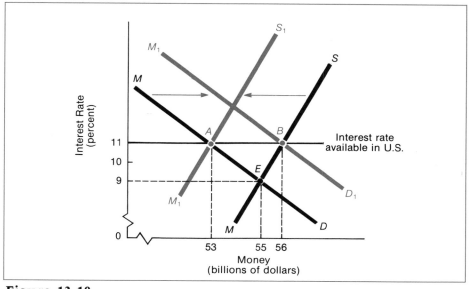

Figure 13-10

EQUILIBRIUM IN THE MONEY MARKET WHEN THE AVAILABILITY OF FOREIGN
BONDS PEGS THE RATE OF INTEREST

Under fixed exchange rates, the Bank of Canada must accept the otherwise unwanted Canadian
currency (given by distance AB). This decreases the amount of money in circulation so the money-
supply curve shifts left (to M_1S_1), and equilibrium obtains at point A. Under flexible exchange rates,
the Canadian dollar depreciates (because of the excess supply, AB). This raises import costs and
stimulates exports. The resulting increase in nominal GNP shifts the money-demand curve to the
right (to M_1D_1), and equilibrium obtains at point B.

Given this choice by demanders, and given the interest rate of 11 percent, there is
an excess supply of domestic money equal to the distance AB in Figure 13–10 ($3
billion in our example).

How is this disequilibrium resolved? There are two possible methods of
resolution, depending on whether the country has adopted a fixed or flexible
exchange-rate policy.

Fixed Exchange Rates

Under a fixed-exchange-rate regime, the Bank of Canada must intervene in the
money market to support the exchange rate. In this case, there is excess supply of
Canadian dollars, equal to $3 billion and shown by distance AB in the diagram.
The mirror image of this excess supply of Canadian dollars is the equivalent
excess demand for U.S. dollars, which savers need to buy the desired U.S. bonds.
Since the U.S. dollar is in demand, while the Canadian dollar is not, a fall in the
value of the Canadian dollar will occur unless the Bank intervenes. To avoid the
fall in the value of the Canadian dollar, the Bank of Canada must buy up the
otherwise unwanted $3 billion of Canadian dollars, by selling the corresponding
amount of U.S. dollars from the country's foreign-exchange reserves. As a result of
this foreign-exchange operation, there will be less Canadian money circulating
than before (by amount AB). So the money-supply curve will be shifted to the left
by this distance (to position M_1S_1), and all three curves intersect at point A. Thus,
a complete equilibrium can be obtained under fixed exchange rates but with an
adjustment that amounts to a contractionary monetary policy—an open-market
sale of foreign exchange.

A policy of fixed exchange rates involves giving up the ability to conduct an
independent monetary policy. Under fixed exchange rates, the private agents
involved in the foreign-exchange market dictate what open-market operation the
Bank of Canada must do to peg the exchange rate. Both the magnitude and
direction of this open-market operation is determined for the central bank.

Flexible Exchange Rates

How is full equilibrium achieved under a flexible-rate policy? Without intervention by the Bank of Canada, the attempt by private agents to trade away Canadian for U.S. dollars means that the Canadian dollar will depreciate in value. This makes our imports more expensive and so raises our price level. It also makes our exports cheaper for foreigners to buy, and so raises aggregate demand. Both of these influences raise nominal GNP in Canada, and so shift the money-demand curve to the right. The depreciation of the Canadian dollar continues until the excess supply of Canadian dollars is eliminated by the demand-for-money curve shifting to position M_1D_1 in Figure 13–10. Thus, a complete equilibrium is obtained under flexible exchange rates at point B, and the adjustment involves inflation and an increase in aggregate demand.

When foreign interest rates increase, competition forces Canadian interest rates to increase. Our only policy choice is whether we want aggregate demand to expand or contract along with this rise in interest rates. Contraction follows if the Bank of Canada fixes the exchange rate, since the bank must absorb the excess supply of Canadian dollars that results from bond-holders switching to foreign bonds. The bank can refuse to supply foreign currency in exchange for the Canadian dollars that bond-holders want to sell, but then the Canadian dollar depreciates. This raises the price of imports and stimulates aggregate demand, and so leads to inflation.

The applicability of this analysis can be demonstrated in two ways. First, we can illustrate the direct connection between Canadian and U.S. interest rates that exists in the data; and second, we can consider the annual report of the Bank of

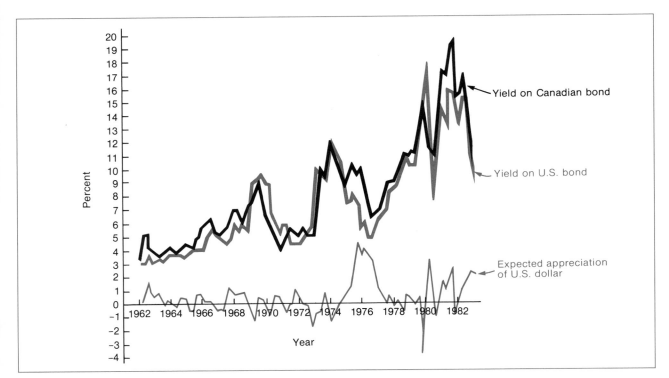

Figure 13–11
CANADIAN AND U.S. INTEREST RATES AND THE EXPECTED APPRECIATION OF THE U.S. DOLLAR, 1962–1982
This graph shows that a significant interest-rate differential has only emerged when a significant change in the exchange rate was expected by market participants. SOURCE: Cansim

Bank of Canada Policy

The following article from *The Globe and Mail* illustrates how directly the Bank of Canada relies on the economic analysis that we have covered in this chapter.

OTTAWA—Bank of Canada Governor Gerald Bouey says he cannot ease up on high interest rates at the expense of the Canadian dollar because this would risk further inflation....

In the Bank of Canada's annual report ... Mr. Bouey said that he will do everything within reason to fight rising prices—including resisting "sharp downward movements" in the value of the Canadian dollar.

The Bank of Canada allowed interest rates to rise on Thursday, in order to attract liquid capital into Canada and thus keep the value of the dollar up....

... at a press conference in which he released the annual report, Mr. Bouey told reporters that the central bank had little choice except to let interest rates go up.

He said the Bank of Canada would have had to print $2-billion worth of money on Thursday and buy up all government treasury bills to keep interest rates down. (The central bank lending rate is set at a weekly auction of these government treasury bills.)...

"I don't want a serious devaluation of the Canadian dollar. That is a sure way to inflation."

In his report, the central bank chief warned that it would be folly for the Government to deliberately try to devalue the currency in order to lower interest rates and create jobs. Such a move could only weaken private sector confidence in the Government's determination to bring down inflation.

If that were to happen, he said, interest rates might dip for a short period but then they would rise again....

Mr. Bouey said interest rates in Canada can come down significantly only if the United States lowers its federal deficit. This, by alleviating fears of inflation among Wall Street financiers, would let U.S. interest rates, and thus Canadian rates, come down.

He said that while he supports the idea of reducing the Canadian deficit, such a reduction would lower interest rates only minimally. Canadian interest rates, he said, are in large measure set in the U.S.

SOURCE: *The Globe and Mail*, Toronto, March 17, 1984, page 1.

Canada. Figure 13–11 certainly verifies that Canada has had to accept the high and volatile interest rates that have followed from U.S. monetary policy in the 1980s. The graph demonstrates that a significant interest-rate differential has only emerged when a significant change in the exchange rate was expected by market participants.

The only policy decision that exists for the Bank of Canada is whether we follow a fixed or a flexible exchange-rate policy. As the accompanying box explains, the Bank of Canada relies on this analysis and has chosen to fight inflation rather than unemployment, and therefore to resist depreciation of the Canadian dollar. It is possible to criticize the Bank for caring too much about inflation, but it cannot be blamed for the high interest rates.

Conclusion and Preview

We now understand how the Bank of Canada is organized, what tools it has available for regulating the money supply, how monetary policy is connected with exchange-rate policy, and how interest rates and exchange rates are determined. We can now investigate how these monetary-policy decisions affect unemployment, inflation, and the overall state of the economy, a task to which we turn in the next chapter.

Summary

1. The Bank of Canada is our central bank, which serves as a bank for the chartered banks. It is the institution that conducts Canada's monetary and exchange-rate policy.

2. The Bank of Canada uses open-market operations to change the reserves available to the chartered banks.

3. Open-market purchases of government bonds or foreign exchange by the Bank of Canada increase the money supply. Open-market sales of government bonds or foreign exchange by the Bank decrease Canada's money supply.

4. Bank rate is the rate the chartered banks must pay the Bank of Canada if they need to borrow reserves. Since very little borrowing of reserves occurs, the weekly adjustment in the bank rate serves only as a signal of the direction of monetary policy. A decrease in the bank rate indicates that the Bank of Canada has been conducting policies that increase the money supply.

5. The Bank of Canada does not have perfect control over the money supply in the short run, because it cannot predict perfectly how far the process of deposit creation or destruction will go.

6. Exchange rates state the value of one currency in terms of another, and thus influence the patterns of world trade in important ways.

7. If governments do not interfere, exchange rates will be determined in free markets by the usual laws of supply and demand. Such a system is called floating or flexible exchange rates.

8. Demand for a nation's currency is derived from foreigners' desires to purchase that country's goods and services or to invest in its assets. Any change that increases the demand for a nation's currency will cause its exchange rate to appreciate under floating rates.

9. Supply of a nation's currency is derived from the desire of that country's citizens to purchase foreign goods and services or to invest in foreign assets. Any change that increases the supply of a nation's currency will cause its exchange rate to depreciate under floating rates.

10. Exchange rates can be fixed at non-equilibrium levels by governments that are willing and able to mop up any excess of quantity supplied over quantity demanded, or provide any excess of quantity demanded over quantity supplied. In the first case, the country is suffering from a balance of payments deficit because of its overvalued currency. In the second, an undervalued currency has given it a balance of payments surplus.

11. When the Bank of Canada fixes the exchange rate, it performs an open-market operation in the foreign-exchange market instead of the domestic bond market. As a result, the central bank cannot set both the money supply and the exchange rate.

12. The money-supply schedule shows that more money is supplied at higher interest rates because, as interest rates rise, banks find it more profitable to expand their loans and deposits. This schedule can be shifted by Bank of Canada policy.

13. The money-demand schedule shows that less money is demanded at higher interest rates because interest is the opportunity cost of holding money. This schedule shifts when output or the price level changes.

14. The equilibrium money stock (M) and the equilibrium rate of interest (r) are determined by the intersection of the money-supply and money-demand schedules, as long as foreign and domestic financial markets are independent.

15. Central bank policy can shift this equilibrium. Expansionary policies cause M to rise and r to fall. Contractionary policies reduce M and increase r.

16. Canadian interest rates are determined in the United States. Increased foreign interest rates are accompanied by inflation if we let the Canadian dollar depreciate, and by a contraction in the money supply and aggregate demand if the Bank of Canada pegs the exchange rate.

Concepts for Review

Bank of Canada
Reserve requirements
Exchange rate
Appreciation
Depreciation
Devaluation
Revaluation
Supply of and demand for foreign exchange

Floating, or flexible, exchange rates
Open-market operations
Contraction and expansion of the money supply
Bank rate
Fixed exchange rates
Balance of payments deficit and surplus
Interest-rate differential

Supply of money
Demand for money
Equilibrium in the money market
Controlling M versus controlling exchange rate

Questions for Discussion

1. Why does a modern industrial economy need a central bank?

2. Do you think it is a good idea to have an independent central bank? Explain your reasons.

3. Suppose there is $80 billion of cash in existence, and that all of it is held in bank vaults as *required* reserves (that is, banks hold no *excess* reserves). How large will the money supply be if the required reserve ratio is 16⅔ percent? 20 percent? 25 percent?

4. Show the balance-sheet changes that would take place if the Bank of Canada purchased an office building from the Bank of Commerce for a price of $100 million. Compare this to the effect of an open-market purchase of securities shown in Table 13–2. What do you conclude?

5. Suppose that the Bank of Canada purchases $5 million worth of government bonds from E.P. Taylor who banks at the Bank of Montreal. Show the effects on the balance sheets of the central bank, the Bank of Montreal, and E.P. Taylor. (*Hint*: What will Taylor do with the $5 million cheque he receives from the Bank of Canada?) Does it make any difference if the Bank of Canada buys bonds from a bank or from an individual?

6. Why would the Bank of Canada's control over the money supply be tighter if all chartered bank deposits were subject to the same reserve requirements?

7. Explain why Governor Bouey has stated that he would resign rather than carry out written instructions from the government to try to lower interest rates by allowing the Canadian dollar to depreciate.

Stabilization Policy: Without International Capital Flows

In this chapter and the next, we bring together our analysis of income determination and the price level from Chapters 7 through 11 and our analysis of money and monetary policy from Chapters 12 and 13. In doing so, we complete the construction of our model of the entire macroeconomy. We will then use this model to see how and to what extent the Bank of Canada's ability to manage the money supply also enables it to manage the level of aggregate demand—and hence to influence unemployment and inflation.

We begin the chapter by integrating the financial system into the Keynesian $C + I + G + X - IM$ model described in Chapters 7 through 11. The mechanisms by which monetary policy affects aggregate demand are spelled out and analysed, and we learn an additional reason why the aggregate-demand curve slopes downward.

Then we turn to a very old and very simple macroeconomic model—the *quantity theory of money*, and its modern reincarnation, *monetarism*—for an alternative view of the effects of money on the economy. Although the monetarist and Keynesian theories seem to be two contradictory views of how monetary and fiscal policy work, we will see that the conflict is more apparent than real. In fact, the disagreement is akin to hearing a Briton say, "Yes," and a Frenchman say, "Oui." The uninitiated hear two different languages, but knowledgeable listeners understand that they mean the same thing.

However, while a major objective of this chapter is to show that the differences between the two theories are greatly exaggerated, there *are* significant differences between the two schools of thought—not outright contradictions but differences in emphasis. These differences occupy the rest of this chapter.

The analysis in this chapter rests on the unrealistic but simplifying assumption that Canada's financial markets operate independently of foreign financial markets. That is, we assume that Canadian interest rates can diverge from the level of U.S. interest rates. This is *not* realistic, but for the sake of clearer exposition we discuss the Keynesian–monetarist controversy and the foreign-exchange market complications in two separate steps. We will consider the more realistic case of integrated financial markets in Chapter 15.

A Study Hint

Because it integrates so many aspects of the macroeconomic theory we have already constructed, this chapter requires you to keep many things in mind at the same time. In this respect, it requires careful study. Fortunately, however, it does not introduce any new technical apparatus. Literally everything we need can be borrowed from earlier chapters. The following is a list of the things we will be referring to in the pages to come, indicating where you should look if you need to review any of them:

- How aggregate supply and aggregate demand interact to determine the price level (Chapters 5 and 10).
- How the circular flow of income and expenditure determines equilibrium output (Chapter 8).
- The analysis of the multiplier (Chapters 9 and 11).
- The workings of fiscal policy (Chapter 11).
- How the supply of and the demand for money interact to determine the quantity of money and the interest rate, and how the central bank can influence this equilibrium (Chapter 13).

Money and Income: The Important Difference

First, a review of some important vocabulary. As pointed out in Chapter 1, the words "money" and "income" are used almost interchangeably in common parlance. This is a pitfall we must learn to avoid.

Money is a snapshot concept. It is the answer to questions like: "How much money do you have right now?" or "How much money did you have at 3:32 P.M. on Friday, November 5th?" To answer questions like these, you would add up the cash you are (or were) carrying and whatever bank balances you have (or had), and answer something like: "I have $126.33," or "On Friday, November 5th, at 3:32 P.M., I had $31.43."

Income, by contrast, is more like a motion picture; it comes to you only over a period of time. If you are asked "What is your income?" you must respond by saying "$300 *per week*," or "$1200 *per month*," or "$14,400 *per year*," or something like that. Notice that there is a unit of time attached to each of these responses. If you just say "My income is $452.19," without indicating whether it is per week or per month or per year, no one will understand what you mean.

That the two concepts are very different is easy to see. A typical Canadian family has an income of about $32,000 per year, but its holdings of *money* at any point in time (using the M1 definition) are $4500. Similarly, at the national level, nominal GNP in 1983 was about $389 billion, while the money stock (M1) was only about $30 billion.

While money and income are very different, they are certainly related. This chapter is precisely about that relationship. Specifically, we will look at how the stock of *money* in existence at any moment of time influences the rate at which people will be earning *income*, that is, how money affects the GNP.

Money and Total Expenditure in the Keynesian Model

To begin, we go back to the analysis of Chapters 7–11, where we learned that aggregate demand is the sum of consumption spending (C), investment spending (I), government purchases of goods and services (G) and net exports ($X - IM$). We know that *fiscal policy* controls G directly and exerts influence over both C and I through the tax laws. We now want to find out how *monetary policy* influences $C + I + G + X - IM$.

Most economists agree that, of the four components of aggregate demand, investment (I) is the most sensitive to monetary policy. *Business investment in* new factories and machinery is sensitive to interest rates for reasons that have been explained in earlier chapters.[1] Since the rate of interest that must be paid on borrowings is one element of the cost of making an investment, business executives will find investment prospects less attractive as interest rates rise. Therefore, they will spend less. For similar reasons, *investment in housing* by individuals may also be deterred by high interest rates. Since the interest cost of a home mortgage is the major component of the total cost of owning a home, fewer families will want to buy a new home when interest rates are high than when interest rates are low. We conclude that:

Higher interest rates lead to lower investment spending. But investment (I) is a component of total spending ($C + I + G + X - IM$). Therefore, when interest rates rise, total spending falls. In terms of the 45° line diagram of previous chapters, a higher interest rate leads to a lower $C + I + G + X - IM$ schedule. Conversely, a lower interest rate leads to a higher $C + I + G + X - IM$ schedule (see Figure 14-1).

Monetary Policy in the Keynesian Model

The effect of interest rates on spending provides the mechanism by which monetary policy affects aggregate demand in the Keynesian model. We know from our analysis of the money market in Chapter 13 that monetary policy can have a profound effect on the rate of interest. Let us, therefore, outline the effects of monetary policy in the Keynesian model, starting first on the demand side of the economy.

Suppose the Bank of Canada, seeing the economy stuck with unemployment and a recessionary gap, raises the money supply. We learned in Chapter 13 that it normally would do this by purchasing government securities in the open market. With the demand schedule for money (temporarily) fixed, such an increase in the supply of money has the effect that an increase in supply always has in a free market—it lowers the price. In this case, the price of renting money is the rate of interest, r; so r falls.

Next, for reasons we have just outlined, investment spending (I) rises in response to the lower interest rates. But, as we learned in Chapter 9, such a rise in

[1]See, for example, Chapter 8, page 142.

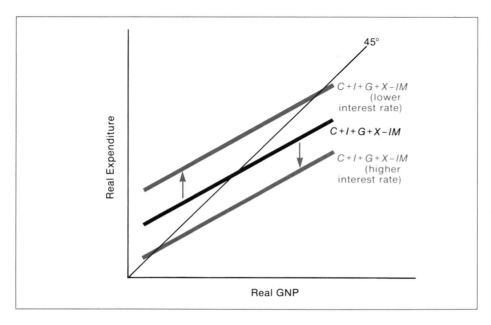

Figure 14-1
THE EFFECT OF INTEREST RATES ON AGGREGATE DEMAND
Because interest rates are an important determinant of investment spending, I, the $C + I + G + X - IM$ schedule shifts whenever the rate of interest changes. Specifically, as shown here, lower interest rates shift the curve upward and higher interest rates shift it downward.

investment kicks off a multiplier chain of increases in output and employment. Thus, finally, we have completed the links from the money supply to the level of aggregate demand. In brief, monetary policy works as follows:

A higher money supply leads to lower interest rates, and these lower interest rates encourage investment, which has multiplier effects on aggregate demand.

The process operates equally well in reverse. By contracting the money supply, the Bank of Canada can force interest rates up, causing investment spending to fall and pulling down aggregate demand via the multiplier mechanism.

This, in outline form, is how monetary policy operates in the Keynesian model. Since the chain of causation is fairly long, the following schematic diagram may help clarify it.

In this causal chain, link 1 indicates that the actions of the Bank of Canada affect money and interest rates. Link 2 stands for the effect of interest rates on investment. Link 3 simply notes that investment is one component of total spending. And link 4 is the multiplier, relating an autonomous change in investment to the ultimate change in aggregate demand.

Let us next review what we have learned about each of these links in previous chapters. In the process, we will see what Keynesians must study if they are to estimate the effect of monetary policy.

Link 1 was the subject of the last chapter, and Figure 14–2 reviews the analysis. Given the initial level of real GNP and prices, the demand schedule for money is shown by curve MD. The Bank of Canada's expansionary action shifts the supply schedule out from $M_0 S_0$ to $M_1 S_1$, resulting in an increase in the money stock from $55 billion to $59 billion in this example, and a decline in the interest rate from 9 percent to 7 percent. Thus the first thing a Keynesian economist must know is how sensitive interest rates are to changes in the supply of money.

Figure 14-2
THE EFFECT OF EXPANSIONARY MONETARY POLICY ON THE MONEY SUPPLY AND RATE OF INTEREST
An expansionary monetary policy pushes the money-supply schedule outward from $M_0 S_0$ to $M_1 S_1$, causing equilibrium in the money market to shift from point E_0 to point E_1. The money supply rises from $55 billion to $59 billion, while the interest rate falls from 9 percent to 7 percent.

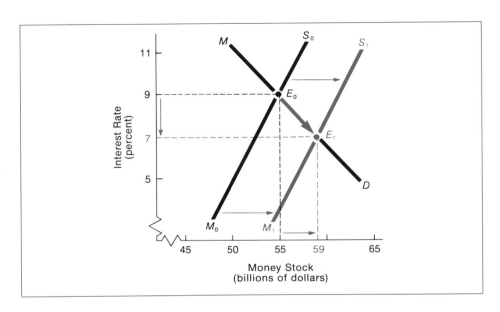

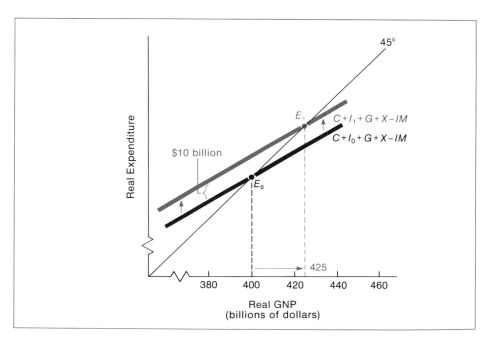

Expansionary monetary policies, which lower the rate of interest, will cause the $C + I + G + X - IM$ schedule to shift upward from $C + I_0 + G + X - IM$ to $C + I_1 + G + X - IM$ as shown here. In this example, since the multiplier is 2.5, a $10 billion rise in investment leads, via the multiplier process, to a $25 billion rise in GNP.

Link 2 translates the drop in the interest rate into an increase in investment spending (I), which we take to be $10 billion in this example. To estimate this effect in practice, a Keynesian economist must study the sensitivity of investment to interest rates.

Link 3 instructs us to enter this $10 billion rise in I as an autonomous shift in the $C + I + G + X - IM$ schedule of a 45° line diagram. Figure 14–3 carries out this step. The expenditure schedule rises from $C + I_0 + G + X - IM$ to $C + I_1 + G + X - IM$.

Finally, link 4 applies multiplier analysis to this vertical shift in the expenditure schedule in order to predict the eventual increase in real GNP demanded. In this example, we assume a multiplier of 2.5, so multiplying $10 billion by 2.5 gives the final effect on aggregate demand—a rise of $25 billion. This is shown in Figure 14–3 as a shift in equilibrium from E_0 (where GNP is $400 billion) to E_1 (where GNP is $425 billion). Of course, the size of this multiplier itself must also be estimated. To summarize:

The effect of monetary policy on aggregate demand depends on the sensitivity of interest rates to the money supply, on the responsiveness of investment spending to the rate of interest, and on the size of the multiplier.

Money and the Price Level: The Complete Keynesian Model

One need only recall the inflation of past decades to realize that we have forgotten something. What happens to the price level? To answer this, we must simply remember once again that prices and output are determined jointly by aggregate supply *and* aggregate demand. The analysis of monetary policy that we have completed so far has shown us how an increase in the money supply shifts the aggregate-demand curve; that is, increases the *aggregate quantity demanded at any given price level*. But to learn what happens to the price level and to real output, we must bring *aggregate supply* into the picture as well.

Specifically, in considering shifts in aggregate demand caused by *fiscal* policy in Chapter 11, we noted that an upsurge in total spending normally induces firms to increase output somewhat *and* to raise prices somewhat. This is just what an aggregate-supply curve shows. Whether prices or real output exhibit the greater response depends mainly on the degree of capacity utilization. An economy operating near full employment has only a limited ability to increase production; it therefore responds to greater demand mainly by raising prices. On the other hand, an economy with a substantial amount of unemployed labour and unused capital is able to increase output a great deal without raising prices.

Now this analysis of output and price responses applies equally well to monetary policy or, for that matter, to anything else that raises aggregate demand. We conclude, then, that:

Expansionary monetary policy causes some inflation under normal circumstances. But how much inflation it causes depends on the state of the economy. If the money supply is expanded when unemployment is high and there is much unused industrial capacity, then the result may be little inflation. If, however, increases in the money supply occur when the economy is fully employed, then the main result is inflation.

The effect of a rise in the money supply on the price level is depicted graphically on an aggregate-supply-and-demand diagram in Figure 14–4. The curved shape of aggregate-supply curve SS reflects the assumptions that output rises with little inflation when the economy is depressed, while prices rise with little gain in output when the economy is near full employment.

In the example we have been using, the Bank of Canada's actions raise the money supply by $4 billion, and this increases aggregate demand (through the multiplier) by $25 billion. We enter this in Figure 14–4 as a horizontal shift of $25 billion in the aggregate-demand curve, from D_0D_0 to D_1D_1. The diagram shows that this expansionary monetary policy raises the economy's equilibrium from point E to point B—the price level therefore rises from 100 to 103, or 3 percent. The diagram also shows that real GNP rises by only $20 billion, which is less than the $25 billion stimulus to aggregate demand. The reason, as we know from earlier chapters, is that rising prices stifle demand.

By taking account of the effect of an increase in the money supply on the price level, we have completed our story about the role of monetary policy in the Keynesian model. We can thus expand our schematic diagram of monetary policy as follows:

Figure 14–4

THE INFLATIONARY
EFFECTS OF EXPANSIONARY
MONETARY POLICY

Raising the money supply normally causes inflation. When expansionary monetary policy causes the aggregate-demand curve to shift outward from D_0D_0 to D_1D_1, the economy's equilibrium shifts from point E to point B. Real output expands (in this case by $20 billion), but prices also rise (in this case by 3 percent).

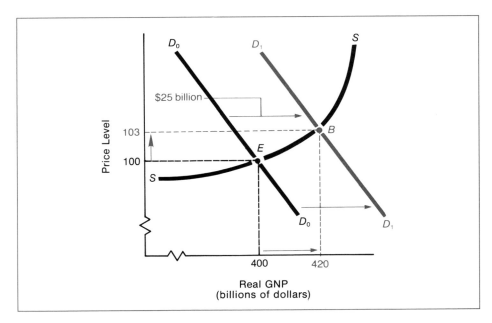

The last link now recognizes that *both* output *and* prices normally are affected by changes in the money supply.

Why the Aggregate-Demand Curve Slopes Downward

This analysis of the effect of money on the price level puts us in a better position to understand why higher prices reduce aggregate quantity demanded; that is, why the aggregate-demand curve slopes downward. In earlier chapters, we explained this phenomenon by observing that rising prices reduce the purchasing power of certain assets held by consumers, especially money and government bonds, and that this in turn retards consumption spending. There is nothing wrong with this analysis. But higher prices have much more important effects on aggregate demand through channels that we are now in a position to understand.

Money is demanded primarily to conduct transactions, and we saw in Chapter 13 that a rise in the *average money cost* of each transaction—as a result of a rise in the price level—will increase the quantity of money demanded. It simply takes more cash to buy a given amount of goods at higher prices. This means that when expansionary policy of any kind pushes the price level up, more money will be demanded at any given interest rate.

But, if the supply of money is *not* increased, an increase in the quantity of money demanded at any given interest rate must force the cost of borrowing money—the rate of interest—to rise. As we know, increases in interest rates reduce investment and, hence, reduce aggregate demand. This, then, is the main reason why the economy's aggregate-demand curve has a negative slope, meaning that aggregate quantity demanded is lower when prices are higher.

At higher price levels, the quantity of money demanded is greater. Given a fixed supply schedule, a higher price level must lead to a higher interest rate. Since high interest rates discourage investment, aggregate quantity demanded is lower when the price level is higher. That is, the aggregate-demand curve slopes downward to the right.

There exists yet another reason for the downward slope of the aggregate-demand curve. The higher the domestic price level, the more expensive are our goods relative to foreign products. As a result, both domestic residents and foreigners buy fewer Canadian-produced goods. This means that net exports $(X - IM)$ fall, leading to an overall drop in aggregate-demand when our price level rises.

Velocity and the Quantity Theory of Money

We have now seen how money influences real output and the price level in the Keynesian model. But there is another way to look at these matters using a model that is much older than the Keynesian model, and yet is at the heart of some very modern critiques of Keynesian economics. This model is known as the **quantity theory of money**, and it is easy to understand once we have introduced one new concept—*velocity*.

We learned in Chapter 12 that because barter is so cumbersome, virtually all economic transactions in advanced economies are conducted by the use of money. This means that if there are, say, $350 billion worth of transactions in the economy during a particular year, and there is an average money stock of $70 billion during that year, then each dollar of money must get used an average of five times during the year (since 5 × $70 billion = $350 billion).

The number 5 in this example is called the **velocity of circulation**, or just **velocity** for short, because it indicates the speed at which money circulates.

Velocity indicates the number of times per year that an "average dollar" is spent on goods and services. It is the ratio of nominal GNP to the number of dollars in the money stock. That is:

$$\text{Velocity} = \frac{\text{Nominal GNP}}{\text{Money stock}}.$$

For example, a particular dollar bill might be used to pay for a haircut in January; the barber might use it to buy a sweater in March; the storekeeper might then use it to buy gasoline in May; the gas station owner could pay it out to a painter who paints his house in October; and the painter might spend it on a Christmas present in December. This would mean that the dollar was used five times during the year. If it were used only four times during the year, its velocity would be only 4, and so on. Similarly, a $20 bill circulating with a velocity of 4 would be the monetary instrument used to finance $80 worth of transactions in that year.

As we noted in Chapter 13, the gross national product in current prices (nominal GNP) is the most widely used measure of the value of the economy's total transactions (the number of dollars changing hands in a year). This measure leads to a concrete definition of velocity as the ratio of nominal GNP to the number of dollars in the money stock. Since nominal GNP is the product of real GNP times the price level, we can write this definition in symbols as:

$$V = \frac{\text{Value of transactions}}{\text{Money stock}} = \frac{\text{Nominal GNP}}{M} = \frac{P \times Y}{M}.$$

The **equation of exchange** states that the money value of GNP transactions must be equal to the product of the average stock of money times velocity. That is: $M \times V = P \times Y$.

By multiplying both sides of the equation by M, we arrive at an identity called the **equation of exchange** that relates the money supply and nominal GNP:

Money supply × Velocity = Nominal GNP.

Alternatively, stated in symbols, we have:

$$M \times V = P \times Y.$$

Here we have quite an obvious link between the stock of money, M, and the nominal value of the nation's output. But it is only a matter of arithmetic, not of economics. For example, it does not imply that the Bank of Canada can raise nominal GNP by increasing M. Why not? Because V might simultaneously fall by enough to prevent $M \times V$ from rising. That is, if there were more dollar bills in circulation than before, but each bill changed hands more slowly, total spending would not necessarily rise.

The *quantity theory of money* transforms the equation of exchange from an accounting identity into an economic model *by assuming* that changes in velocity are so minor that, for practial purposes, velocity can be taken to be a constant.

You can see that if V never changed, the equation of exchange would be a marvellously simple model of the determination of nominal GNP—one that is far simpler than the Keynesian model. To see this, we need only to turn the equation of exchange around to read,

$$P \times Y = V \times M.$$

This equation says, for example, that if the Bank of Canada wants to increase nominal GNP by 12.7 percent, it need only raise the money supply by 12.7 percent. In such a simple world, economists could use the equation of exchange to *predict* nominal GNP simply by predicting the quantity of money. And policy-makers could *control* nominal GNP simply by controlling the money supply.

In the real world things are not so simple, because velocity is not a fixed number. But this does not necessarily destroy the usefulness of the quantity theory. We explained in Chapter 1 why all economic models make assumptions that are at least mildly unrealistic—without such assumptions they would not be models at all, just tedious descriptions of reality. The question is really whether

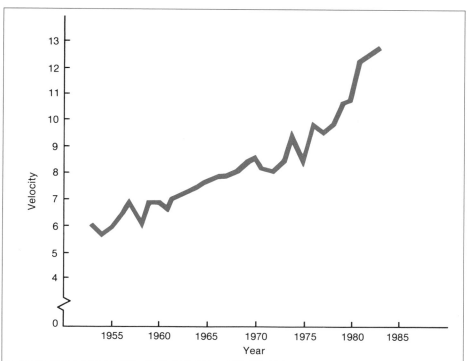

Figure 14-5
VELOCITY OF CIRCULATION,
1953–1983
Velocity displays both a trend and
short-run fluctuations.
SOURCE: Historical Statistics of Canada
(series J22), and Bank of Canada
Review, selected issues.

the assumption of constant velocity is a useful abstraction from annoying detail or a gross distortion of facts.

Figure 14–5 sheds some light on this question by showing the behaviour of velocity since 1953. You will undoubtedly notice an upward trend throughout this period. Quite clearly, *velocity is not constant over long periods of time.* Also we see some rather substantial fluctuations of velocity about its trend. Such fluctuations have led most economists to the conclusion that *velocity is not constant in the short run either.* Nor have predictions of nominal GNP based on the product of V times M fared very well. It seems, then, that the strict quantity theory of money is not an adequate model of aggregate demand.

The Determinants of Velocity

Since it is abundantly clear that velocity is a variable, not a constant, we can use the equation of exchange as a model of GNP determination only by examining the determinants of velocity. What factors decide whether V will be 6 or 8 or 10; that is, whether a dollar will be used to buy goods and services six or eight or ten times a year?

Perhaps the principal factor is the *frequency with which paycheques are received.* This can best be explained through a numerical example. Consider a worker who earns $12,000 a year, paid to her in 12 monthly *paycheques* of $1000 each. Suppose that she spends the whole $1000 over the course of each month and maintains a minimum balance in her chequing account of $500. Each payday her bank balance will shoot up to $1500 and then be gradually whittled down as she makes withdrawals to purchase goods and services. Finally, on the day before her next paycheque arrives, her chequing balance will be just $500. Over the course of a typical month, then, her average chequing account balance will be $1000 (halfway between $1500 and $500).

Now suppose her employer switches to a twice-a-month payroll. Her paycheques come twice as often but are reduced to $500 each. There is no reason for her rate of spending to change, but her *cash balances* will change. For now her chequing balance will rise only to $1000 on payday (the $500 minimum balance plus the $500 paycheque), and it will still be drawn down gradually to $500. Her average cash balance will therefore decline to $750 (halfway between $1000 and $500). Why is this so? Because, with the next paycheque coming sooner than before, it is not necessary to keep as much cash in the bank in order to carry out a given quantity of transactions.

But what does this have to do with velocity? Notice that when she was on a monthly payroll, this worker's personal velocity was:

$$V = \frac{\text{Annual income}}{\text{Average cash balance}} = \frac{\$12,000}{\$1000} = 12.$$

When she switched to a semimonthly payroll, velocity rose to:

$$V = \frac{\text{Annual income}}{\text{Average cash balance}} = \frac{\$12,000}{\$750} = 16.$$

The general lesson to be learned is that:

More frequent wage payments mean that people can conduct their transactions with lower average cash balances. Since they will want to hold less cash, money will circulate faster. In other words, velocity will rise.

A second factor influencing velocity is the *efficiency of the payments mechanism*, including how quickly cheques clear through banks, the use of credit cards, and other methods of transferring funds. It is easy to see how this works.

The example in the previous paragraph assumed that our worker holds her entire paycheque in the form of money until she uses it to make a purchase. But, given that many forms of money pay little or no interest, this method may not be the most rational behaviour. If it is possible to convert interest-bearing assets into money on short notice and at low cost, a rational individual might use her paycheque to purchase such assets and then use credit cards for most purchases, making periodic transfers to her chequing account as necessary. For the same amount of total transactions, then, she would require lower money balances. This means that money would circulate faster: Velocity would rise.

The incentive to limit cash holdings depends on the ease and speed with which it is possible to exchange money for other assets. This is what we mean by the "efficiency of the payments mechanism." As computerization has speeded up the bookkeeping procedures of banks, as financial innovations have made it possible to transfer funds rapidly between chequing accounts and other assets, and as credit cards have come to be used instead of cash, the need to hold money balances has declined. By definition, then, velocity has risen.

Fortunately such basic changes in the payments mechanism usually take place only gradually, and thus often are easy to predict. But this is not always so. For example, a host of financial innovations in the 1980s—some of which were mentioned in Chapter 12's discussion of the definitions of money—gave analysts fits in predicting velocity.

A third determinant of velocity is the *rate of interest*. The basic motive for economizing on money holdings is that most money (at least M1) pays little or no interest, while many alternative stores of value pay higher rates. The higher these alternative rates of interest, the greater the incentive to economize on holding money. Therefore, as interest rates rise, people want to hold less money. So the existing stock of money circulates faster, and velocity rises.

It is this factor that most directly undercuts the usefulness of the quantity theory of money as a guide for monetary policy. For in the last chapter we learned that expansionary monetary policy, which increases M, normally also decreases the interest rate. But if interest rates fall, other things equal, velocity (V) will also fall. Thus, *when the central bank raises the money supply (M), the product M × V may go up by a smaller percentage than does M itself.*

One component of the interest rate is worth singling out for special attention: *the expected rate of inflation.* We explained in Chapter 6 why an "inflation premium" equal to the expected inflation rate often gets built in to market interest rates.[2] Thus, in many instances, high inflation is the principal cause of high nominal interest rates. High rates of inflation, which erode the purchasing power of money, therefore lead both individuals and businesses to hold as little money as they can get by on—actions that increase velocity. To summarize this discussion of the determinants of velocity:

Velocity is not a strict constant but depends on such things as the frequency of payments, the efficiency of the financial system, the rate of interest, and the rate of inflation. Only by studying these determinants of velocity can we hope to predict the level of nominal GNP from knowledge of the money supply.

Monetarism: The Quantity Theory Modernized

The foregoing does not mean, however, that the equation of exchange cannot be a useful framework within which to organize macroeconomic analysis. It can be. And during the past 30 years a group of economists called *monetarists* have convincingly demonstrated that this is so.

Monetarists recognize that velocity is not a constant. But they stress that it is fairly *predictable*—certainly in the long run and probably also in the short run. This leads them to the conclusion that the best way to study economic activity is to start with the *equation of exchange: M × V = P × Y.* From here, careful study of the determinants of M (which we provided in the previous two chapters) and of V (which we just completed) can be used to *predict* the behaviour of nominal GNP. Similarly, given an understanding of movements in V, control over the money supply gives the central bank *control* over nominal GNP.

These are the central tenets of **monetarism**. When something happens in the economy, monetarists ask two questions:

Monetarism is a mode of analysis that uses the equation of exchange to organize macroeconomic data.

1. What does this event do to the stock of money?

2. What does this event do to velocity?

From the answers, they assert that they can predict the path of nominal GNP.

By comparing the monetarist approach with the Keynesian approach that we described earlier in this chapter, we can put both doctrines into perspective and understand the limitations of each. As we mentioned earlier, they differ more in style than in substance. Keynesians, as we learned in earlier chapters, divide economic knowledge into four neat compartments—marked "C," "I," "G," and "$X – IM$"—and unite them all with the equilibrium condition that $C + I + G + X – IM = Y$. In Keynesian analysis, money affects the economy by first affecting interest rates.

[2]If you need review, turn back to pages 100–101.

Monetarists on the other hand, organize their knowledge into two alternative boxes—labelled "M" and "V"—and then use a simple identity that says $M \times V = P \times Y$ to bring this knowledge to bear in predicting aggregate demand. The role of money in the national economy is not necessarily limited to working through interest rates in the monetarist model.

The bit of arithmetic that multiplies M by V to get P multiplied by Y is neither more nor less profound than the one that adds C, I, G, and $X - IM$ to get Y. And certainly both approaches are correct. The only substantive difference is that the monetarist equation leads to a prediction of *nominal* GNP, that is, the demand for goods and services measured in money terms, whereas the Keynesian equation leads to a prediction of *real* GNP, that is, the demand for goods and services measured in dollars of constant purchasing power.

Why, then, do we not simply mesh the two theories—using the monetarist approach to study nominal GNP and the Keynesian approach to study real GNP? It seems that by doing so we could use the separate analyses of real and nominal GNP to obtain a prediction of the future behaviour of the price level, which, of course, is the source of any difference in behaviour between real and nominal GNP.

The reason that this appealing procedure will not work helps point out the major limitation of each theory. *Taken by itself, either theory is incomplete.* Each gives us a picture of the *demand* side of the economy without saying anything about the *supply* side. To try to predict both the price level and real output solely from these demand-oriented models would be like trying to predict the price of spinach by studying only the behaviour of consumers and ignoring that of farmers. It just will not work. In terms of our earlier aggregate-supply-and-demand analysis:

Both the monetarist and Keynesian analyses are ways of studying the *aggregate-demand curve*. In neither case is it possible to learn anything about both output and the price level without also studying the *aggregate-supply curve*.

Economists thus are forced to choose between two alternative ways of predicting aggregate demand. If the monetarist route is chosen, the economist will use velocity and the money supply to study the demand for *nominal* GNP, and then turn to the supply side to estimate how any predicted change in nominal income gets apportioned between changes in production and changes in prices. The schematic diagram on page 271, with its emphasis on interest rates, plays little role in the monetarist analysis of the transmission mechanism for monetary policy.

On the other hand, an economist working with the Keynesian $C + I + G + X - IM$ approach will start by using the schematic diagram on page 271, to predict how monetary policy affects the demand for *real* GNP. Then he will turn to the aggregate-supply curve to estimate the inflationary consequences of this real demand.

Which approach works better? There is no generally correct answer for all economies in all periods of time. Therefore, it is not surprising that some economists prefer one approach while others favour the alternative.

Reconciling the Keynesian and Monetarist Views

We have already come quite a long way toward reconciling the Keynesian and monetarist views of how the economy operates. Keynesian analysis lends itself naturally to the study of fiscal policy, since G is a part of $C + I + G + X - IM$. But we have learned in this chapter that Keynesian economics also provides a powerful and important role for monetary policy: An increase in the money supply reduces interest rates, which, in turn, stimulates the demand for investment.

Monetarist analysis provides an obvious and direct route by which monetary policy influences both output and prices. But can the monetarist approach also handle fiscal policy? It can, because fiscal policy has an important effect on the rate of interest. And it is not hard to understand how this effect operates.

Let's see what happens to real output and the price level following, say, a rise in government purchases of goods and services. We learned in Chapter 11 that both real GNP (Y) and the price level (P) rise. But Chapter 13's analysis of the demand for money taught us that rising Y and P push the demand curve for money outward to the right. With no change in the supply curve for money, the rate of interest must rise. So expansionary fiscal policy raises interest rates.

If the government uses its spending and taxing weapons in the opposite direction, the same process works in reverse. Falling output and (possibly) falling prices shift the demand curve for money inward to the left. With a fixed supply curve for money, equilibrium in the money market leads to a lower interest rate. Thus:

Monetary policy is not the only type of policy that affects interest rates. Fiscal policy also affects interest rates. Specifically, increases in government spending or tax cuts normally push interest rates higher, whereas restrictive fiscal policies normally pull interest rates down.

The fact that fiscal policy affects interest rates gives it a role in the monetarist model despite the fact that the equation of exchange, $M \times V = P \times Y$, does not include either government spending or taxation among its variables. The way it works is that a rise in government spending, for example, pushes up the rate of interest. And rising interest rates push up velocity because people want to hold less money when the interest they can earn on alternative assets increases. So it is through the V term in $M \times V$ that fiscal policy does its work in the monetarist framework.

Any of the government policies that a Keynesian would call expansionary—higher spending, lower taxes, and so on—forces interest rates higher, thus increasing V. The equation of exchange, $M \times V = P \times Y$, then implies that nominal GNP must rise when government spending increases, even if M is fixed. The given supply of money can finance more transactions when velocity is higher.

Conversely, restrictive fiscal policies, like tax increases and expenditure cuts, reduce the quantity of money demanded and lower interest rates. The consequent drop in velocity lowers income through the equation of exchange, because the money supply circulates more slowly.

The translation, then, seems to be complete. The Keynesian story about how fiscal policy works can be phrased in the monetarist dialect. And the monetarist tale about monetary policy can be told with a Keynesian accent. Furthermore, both modes of analysis help only to explain the mysteries of aggregate *demand*, and must be supplemented by an analysis of aggregate *supply* to be complete. We must conclude then, that:

The differences between Keynesians and monetarists have been grossly exaggerated by the news media. Indeed, when it comes to matters of basic economic theory, there are hardly any differences at all.

But this does not mean that Keynesians and monetarists must agree on everything any more than the fact that English prose can be translated into French implies that the English and the French always see eye to eye. There are important differences of emphasis and policy that we will take up in the remainder of this chapter.

The Multiplier Formula Once Again

But first, the fact that expansionary fiscal policy pushes up interest rates has another important consequence that we should mention. Recall that higher interest rates deter private investment spending. This means that when the government raises the G component of $C + I + G + X - IM$ one of the side effects of its action will be to reduce the I component (by raising interest rates). Consequently, the sum $C + I + G + X - IM$ will not rise as much as simple multiplier analysis might suggest. In a word, the surge in government demand (G) discourages some private demand (I). This phenomenon provides another reason why the oversimplified multiplier formula, $1/(1 - MPC)$, exaggerates the size of the multiplier:

Because any rise in G (or, for that matter, any autonomous rise in C or I or $X - IM$ pushes interest rates higher, and hence deters some investment spending, the increase in the sum $C + I + G + X - IM$ is smaller than what the oversimplified multiplier formula predicts.

Combining this observation with our previous analysis of the multiplier, we now have a more complete list of:

REASONS WHY THE OVERSIMPLIFIED MULTIPLIER FORMULA IS WRONG

1. It ignores price-level changes, which reduce the size of the multiplier.

2. It ignores the income tax, which reduces the size of the multiplier.

3. It ignores imports, which reduce the size of the multiplier.

4. It ignores the rising interest rates that accompany any autonomous increase in spending, which also reduce the size of the multiplier.

Keynesians Versus Monetarists: Fiscal Versus Monetary Policy

Although the Keynesian and monetarist approaches can be thought of as two languages, it is well known that language can influence attitudes in many subtle ways. And it must be admitted that Keynesians and monetarists have not lacked things to argue about.

For years they conducted a spirited, and well-publicized, debate over whether the government should rely mainly on fiscal policy or monetary policy to manage aggregate demand. While one would guess from reading the newspapers that this is the most important issue in the Keynesian–monetarist debate today, it is in fact the *least* important. It is unimportant because, as we have seen, each approach allows a role for each type of policy.

None the less, the Keynesian language biases things subtly toward thinking that fiscal policy is very important simply because fiscal actions influence aggregate demand so directly. G is, after all, a part of $C + I + G + X - IM$. Monetarists, on the other hand, see a more indirect channel that works through interest rates and velocity, and they wonder if something might not go wrong along the way.

The roles are reversed in the analysis of monetary policy. To monetarists, the effect of the money supply on aggregate demand is simple—it follows directly from velocity through the equation of exchange: $M \times V = P \times Y$. While monetary policy also affects aggregate demand in the Keynesian model, the mechanisms are rather complex, and there is obviously room for a slip-up. Monetary expansion might not affect the interest rate very much, or a fall in the interest rate might not induce much additional investment. Thus some Keynesians have their doubts when monetarists attribute great stabilizing powers to monetary policy.

During the 1960s and early 1970s the choice between fiscal and monetary policy dominated the debate between the more partisan Keynesians and monetarists. Extreme monetarists claimed that fiscal policy was futile, while extreme Keynesians countered that monetary policy was useless. We shall see in the next chapter that these conclusions can be perfectly correct, *if* the country's financial markets are integrated with those of the rest of the world (as Canada's are). It turns out that monetary policy cannot have a significant effect on aggregate demand if a country follows a fixed exchange-rate policy, while fiscal policy has no significant effect on aggregate demand if a flexible exchange-rate policy is followed. However, a country such as the United States is much more capable of setting its own level of interest rates, and for it, the analysis of this chapter is directly relevant. U.S. evidence has rejected the extreme claims of both Keynesians and monetarists, so that now both groups agree that both fiscal and monetary policy have significant effects on aggregate demand. However, Keynesians still tend to look more toward fiscal policy while monetarists tend to rely more on monetary policy.

Keynesians Versus Monetarists: Lags in Fiscal and Monetary Policy

More important than the issue of which type of policy is more *powerful* is the related question: Which type of medicine—fiscal or monetary—cures the patient more *quickly*? In our discussions of fiscal and monetary policy so far, we have ignored such subtle questions of timing and proceeded as if the authorities instantly noticed the need for stabilization policy, decided upon a course of action, and administered the appropriate medicine. In reality, each of these steps is time consuming.

First, delays in data collection and processing mean that the latest macroeconomic data pertain to the economy as it was a few months ago. Second, one of the prices of democracy is that the government often takes a good deal of time to decide what should be done, to muster the necessary political support, and to put its decisions into effect. Finally, our economy is a bit like a sleeping elephant—it reacts rather sluggishly to moderate fiscal and monetary prods. As it turns out, these **lags in stabilization policy**, as they are called, play a pivotal role in the choice between fiscal and monetary policy. It is not hard to see why.

The main policy tool for manipulating consumer spending (C) is the personal income tax, and Chapter 7 documented why the fiscal-policy planner can feel fairly secure that each $1 of tax reduction will lead to about 90¢ of additional spending *eventually*. But not all of this will happen at once.

First, consumers must learn about the tax change. Then, more time may elapse before many consumers are convinced that the change is permanent. Finally, there is the simple force of habit: Households need time to adjust their spending habits when circumstances change. For all these reasons, consumers may increase their spending by only 30¢ to 50¢ for each $1 of additional income within the first few months after a tax cut. Only gradually, over a period of perhaps several years, will they raise their spending until they are finally consuming 90¢ of each additional dollar of income.

Lags are much longer for investment (I), which, while it also can be influenced by fiscal policy (tax incentives), provides the main vehicle by which monetary policy affects aggregate demand. Planning for capacity expansion in a large corporation is a long, drawn-out process. Ideas must be submitted and approved. Plans must be drawn up, funding acquired, orders for machinery or contracts for new construction placed. And most of this occurs *before* any appreciable amount of money is spent. Economists have found that most of the response of investment to changes in interest rates or tax provisions is delayed for several years.

The fact that C responds more quickly than I has important implications for the choice among alternative stabilization policies. The reason is that the most common varieties of fiscal policy affect aggregate demand either directly (G is a component of $C + I + G + X - IM$) or work through consumption with a relatively short lag, while monetary policy has its major effects on investment. Therefore:

Conventional types of fiscal-policy actions, such as changes in G or in personal taxes, probably affect aggregate demand much more promptly than do monetary-policy actions.

Notice that the statement says nothing about which instrument is more *powerful*. It simply asserts that the fiscal weapon, whether it is stronger or weaker, acts more *quickly*. This important fact has been used to build a case that fiscal policy should bear the major burden of economic stabilization. But before you jump to such a conclusion, you should realize that the sorts of lags we have been discussing are not the only ones affecting the timing of stabilization policy.

Apart from these lags in expenditure, which are beyond the control of policy-makers, there are further lags that are due to the behaviour of the policy-makers themselves! We are referring here to the delays that occur while the policy-makers are studying the state of the economy, contemplating what steps they should take, and putting their decisions into effect. And here most observers believe that monetary policy has an important edge; that is:

Policy lags are normally shorter for monetary policy than for fiscal policy.

The reasons are apparent. The Governor of the Bank of Canada meets frequently with his advisors, so monetary-policy decisions are made almost every month. And once the Bank of Canada decides on a course of action, it normally can be executed almost instantly by buying or selling bonds on the open market.

Contrast this with fiscal policy. Federal budgeting procedures operate on an annual budget cycle. Except in rare circumstances, then, *major* fiscal-policy initiatives that affect spending can occur only at the time of the budget. Tax laws can be changed at any time, but the wheels of Parliament grind slowly and it may take many months before Parliament acts on a bill to change taxes. In sum, one has to be very optimistic to suppose that important fiscal-policy actions can be taken on short notice.

Where does the combined effect of expenditure lags and policy lags leave us? With nothing conclusive, we are afraid. As the late Arthur Okun put it, the debate over whether the nation should rely only on monetary policy or only on fiscal policy is a bit like arguing whether a safe car is one with good headlights or one with good brakes. It is not very wise to drive at night unless you have both.

Keynesians Versus Monetarists: The Aggregate-Supply Curve

But the Keynesian–monetarist battles did not end there. As the debate over fiscal versus monetary policy fizzled, the two schools of thought regrouped along new, and more productive, battle lines.

One major controversy that is very much alive today is over whether the government should conduct *any* stabilization policy at all, be it monetary or fiscal. This argument is not surprising given the political differences between the two groups. As it happens, monetarists tend to be conservative politically and Keynesians tend to be liberal, which helps explain why the two schools differ markedly in the degree to which they think the government should try to manage the economy. Since this important and controversial issue transcends the Keynesian–monetarist debate, we defer discussion of it until Chapter 19.

Another major battleground in the Keynesian–monetarist debate today is over the shape of the economy's aggregate-supply curve. As we have noted, either the Keynesian or the monetarist model must be supplemented by an aggregate-

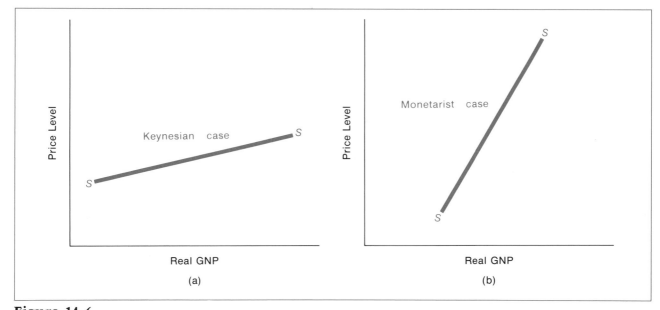

Figure 14-6
ALTERNATIVE VIEWS OF THE AGGREGATE-SUPPLY CURVE
Keynesians tend to think of the economy's aggregate-supply schedule as very flat, as in part (a), whereas monetarists tend to think of it as quite steep, as in part (b).

supply curve if it is to tell us anything about output and prices. Most Keynesians tend to think of the aggregate-supply curve as fairly flat in the short run, as in Figure 14-6(a), so that large increases in output can be achieved with rather little inflation. Monetarists, by contrast, picture the supply curve as quite steep, as in Figure 14-6(b), so that prices are very responsive to changes in output. The differences for public policy are substantial.

In the Keynesian view, expansionary fiscal or monetary policy that raises the aggregate-demand schedule can buy large gains in real GNP at little cost in terms of inflation. This is shown in Figure 14-7(a). Here, stimulation of demand raises the aggregate-demand curve from D_0D_0 to D_1D_1 and moves the economy's equilibrium from point E to point A. There is a substantial rise in output ($40 billion) with only a pinch of inflation (1 percent).

Conversely, when the supply curve is so flat, a restrictive stabilization policy is not a very effective way to cure inflation; instead, it serves mainly to reduce real output, as Figure 14-7(b) shows. Here, a leftward shift of the aggregate-demand curve moves equilibrium from point E to point B, lowering real GNP by $40 billion, but cutting the price level merely 1 percent.

The monetarists see things differently. To them, the aggregate-supply curve is so steep that expansionary fiscal or monetary policies are likely to cause a good deal of inflation without adding much to real GNP. [See Figure 14-8(a), where expansionary policies shift equilibrium from E to A.] Similarly, contractionary policies are effective ways of bringing down the price level without much sacrifice of real output, as shown by the shift from E to B in Figure 14-8(b).

The resolution of this debate is of fundamental importance for the proper conduct of stabilization policy. If the Keynesian view is right, stabilization policy is much more effective at combating recession than inflation. If the monetarist view is correct, the reverse is true.

Why, then, does the argument persist? Why cannot economists determine whether the aggregate-supply curve is flat or steep, and stop arguing? The answer is that supply conditions in the real world are far more complicated than our simple diagrams suggest. Some industries may have flat supply curves while others have

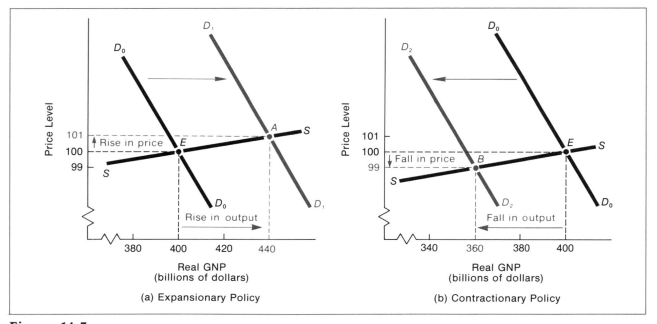

Figure 14-7
STABILIZATION POLICY WITH A FLAT AGGREGATE-SUPPLY CURVE: THE KEYNESIAN CASE
These two diagrams show that stabilization policy is much more effective as an anti-recession policy than as an anti-inflation policy when the aggregate-supply curve is very flat. In part (a), monetary or fiscal policies push the aggregate-demand curve outward from D_0D_0 to D_1D_1, causing equilibrium to shift from point E to point A. It can be seen that output rises substantially (from $400 billion to $440 billion), while prices rise only slightly (from 100 to 101, or 1 percent). So the policy is quite successful. In part (b), contractionary policies are used to combat inflation by pushing the aggregate-demand curve inward from D_0D_0 to D_2D_2. Prices do fall slightly (from 100 to 99) as equilibrium shifts from point E to point B, but real output falls much more dramatically (from $400 billion to $360 billion); so the policy has had little success. Keynesians tend to believe in this case.

steep ones. For reasons explained in Chapter 10, supply curves change over time. And, unlike many laboratory scientists, economists cannot perform the controlled experiments that would reveal the shape of the aggregate-supply curve directly. Instead, they must use statistical inference to make educated guesses.

Although empirical research on aggregate supply is proceeding, our understanding of aggregate supply remains much less settled than our understanding of aggregate demand. Nevertheless, many economists believe that the dim outline of a consensus view is emerging. This view stresses that the steepness of the aggregate-supply schedule depends on the degree of slack in the economy.

If industry has a great deal of spare capacity, then increases in demand will not call forth large price increases. Similarly, when many workers are unemployed, employment can rise without causing much acceleration in the rate at which wages are growing. In a word, the aggregate-supply curve is quite flat. On the other hand, when businesses are producing near capacity and unemployment is near the frictional level, greater demand for goods will induce firms to raise prices; and greater demand for labour will push wages up faster. In brief, the aggregate-supply schedule will be steep.

Figure 14–9 shows a version of the aggregate-supply curve that embodies these ideas. It has the same general shape as most of the supply curves that we have used in this book. At low levels of GNP, like Y_1, it is nearly horizontal; then its slope starts to rise gradually until at very high levels of GNP, like Y_2, it becomes almost vertical. The implication is that any change in aggregate demand will have most of its effect on *output* when economic activity is slack (the Keynesian case) but on *prices* when the economy is operating near full employment (the monetarist case). In summary:

1. Keynesians believe that the aggregate-supply curve is rather flat in many

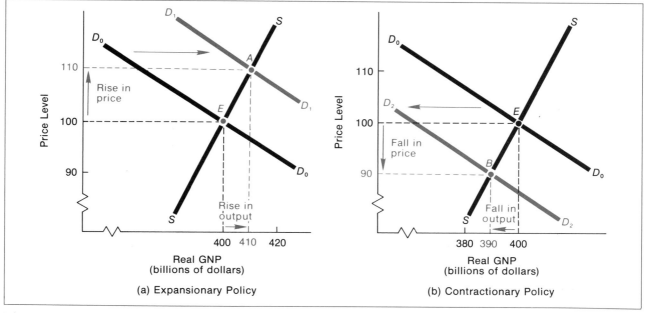

Figure 14-8

STABILIZATION POLICY WITH A STEEP AGGREGATE-SUPPLY CURVE: THE MONETARIST CASE

These two diagrams show that stabilization policy is much more effective at fighting inflation than at fighting recession when the aggregate-supply curve is very steep. In part (a), expansionary policies that push aggregate demand outward from D_0D_0 to D_1D_1 raise output by only $10 billion but push up prices by 10 percent, as equilibrium moves from point E to point A. So demand management is not a good way to end a recession. In part (b), contractionary policies that pull aggregate demand inward to D_2D_2 are successful in that they lower prices quite markedly (from 100 to 90, or about 10 percent) but reduce output only slightly (from $400 billion to $390 billion). Monetarists tend to believe in this case.

circumstances, especially when the economy is operating at low levels of resource utilization. They therefore stress the effects of demand management on output, and belittle the effects on prices.

2. Monetarists believe that the aggregate-supply curve is rather *steep* in many circumstances, especially when the economy has little slack. They therefore

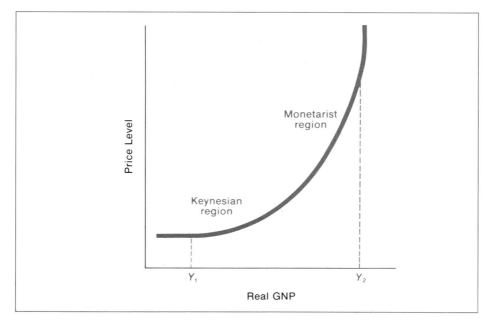

Figure 14-9

AN AGGREGATE-SUPPLY CURVE WITH BOTH STEEP AND FLAT REGIONS

As this diagram suggests, either the Keynesians or the monetarists may be right under the appropriate circumstances. The Keynesian view of a flat supply curve is likely to be most accurate when there is much unemployment and unused capacity. The monetarist view of a steep supply curve is likely to be more accurate when there is full employment and high capacity utilization.

emphasize the effects of demand management on prices, and belittle the effects on real output.

3. A middle-of-the-road view would hold that the Keynesian case is quite strong when there is a great deal of unemployment, while the monetarist case is stronger when the economy is near full employment. Not all economists accept this middle-of-the-road view, but many do.

Since the nature of the trade-off between output gains (which reduce unemployment) and inflation, as embodied in the slope of the aggregate-supply schedule, plays such a fundamental role in the design of an appropriate stabilization policy, we shall devote all of Chapter 18 to an exploration of this trade-off.

Summary

1. Monetarist and Keynesian analyses are two different ways of studying the determination of aggregate demand. Neither is a complete theory of the behaviour of the economy until aggregate supply is brought into the picture.

2. Investment spending (I), including business investment and investment in new homes, is sensitive to interest rates (r). Specifically, I is lower when r is higher.

3. This fact explains how monetary policy works in the Keynesian model. Raising the money supply (M) leads to lower r; the lower interest rates stimulate more investment spending; and this investment stimulus, via the multiplier, then raises aggregate demand.

4. However, prices are likely to rise as output rises. The amount of inflation caused by increasing the money supply depends on the levels of unemployment and of capacity utilization. There will be much inflation when the economy is near full employment, but little inflation when there is a great deal of slack.

5. An important reason why the aggregate-demand curve slopes downward is that higher prices increase the demand to hold money in order to finance transactions. Given the money supply, this pushes interest rates up; and this, in turn, discourages investment.

6. A second reason why the aggregate-demand curve slopes downward is that higher domestic prices make our exports less competitive internationally so net export demand falls.

7. Velocity (V) is the ratio of nominal GNP to the stock of money. It indicates how quickly money circulates, that is, how many times money changes hands in a year.

8. Among the determinants of velocity is the rate of interest (r). At higher interest rates, people find it less attractive to hold money because most money pays no interest. Thus, when r rises, money circulates faster, and V rises.

9. Monetarism is a type of analysis that focuses attention on velocity and the money supply (M). Though monetarists realize that V is not constant, they believe that it is predictable enough to make it a useful tool for policy analysis and forecasting.

10. Because it raises output and prices, and hence increases the demand for money, expansionary fiscal policy pushes interest rates higher. This is how a monetarist explains the effect of fiscal policy. Because higher r leads to higher velocity, it leads to a higher product $M \times V$ even if M is unchanged.

11. While Keynesian and monetarist theories both lead us to expect that fiscal *and* monetary policies can each affect aggregate demand, Keynesians tend to believe more in the effectiveness of fiscal policy while monetarists tend to believe more in the effectiveness of monetary policy.

12. Because fiscal-policy actions affect aggregate demand either directly through G or indirectly through C, the expenditure lags between fiscal actions and their effects on aggregate demand are probably fairly short. By contrast, monetary policy operates mainly on investment, I, which responds very slowly to changes in interest rates.

13. However, the policy-making lag normally is much longer for fiscal policy than for monetary policy. Hence, when the two lags are combined, it is not clear which type of policy acts more quickly.

14. Keynesians believe that the aggregate-supply curve is rather flat in the short run. This means that increases in aggregate demand will add much to the nation's real output and add little to the price level. Stabilization policy thus has much to recommend it as an anti-recession device, but it has little power to combat inflation.

15. Monetarists believe that the aggregate-supply curve is very steep. This means that increases in aggregate demand increase real output rather little and succeed mostly in pushing up prices. Consequently, while stabilization policy can do much to fight inflation, it is not a very effective way to cure unemployment.

16. The Keynesian view probably is most applicable to an economy with much unemployment, while the monetarist view applies best to an economy producing near capacity levels.

Concepts for Review

Why the aggregate-demand curve slopes downward	Effect of interest rate on velocity	Lags in stabilization policy
Quantity theory of money	Monetarism	Shape of the aggregate-supply curve
Velocity	Effect of monetary policy on inflation	
Equation of exchange	Effect of fiscal policy on interest rates	

Questions for Discussion

1. How much money (including cash and chequing account balances) do you typically have at any particular moment? Divide this into your total income over the past 12 months to obtain your own personal velocity. Are you typical of the nation as a whole?

2. Just below you will find data on nominal gross national product and the money supply (M1 definition) for selected years. Compute velocity in each year. Can you see any trend?

YEAR	NOMINAL GNP (billions of dollars)	MONEY SUPPLY (M1) (billions of dollars) (end of year)
1963	46.0	6.3
1973	123.6	14.5
1983	388.7	30.2

3. Use the concept of opportunity cost to explain why velocity is higher at higher interest rates.

4. How does monetarism differ from the quantity theory of money? How does it differ from Keynesian analysis?

5. Explain why both business investments and purchases of new homes are expected to decline when interest rates rise.

6. Explain what a $60 billion increase in the money supply will do to real GNP under the following assumptions:

a. Each $20 billion increase in the money supply reduces the rate of interest by 1 percentage point.

b. Each 1 percentage point decline in interest rates stimulates $40 billion of new investment spending.

c. The expenditure multiplier is 2.

d. There is so much unemployment that prices do not rise noticeably when demand increases.

7. Explain how your answer to Question 6 would differ if each of the assumptions were changed. Specifically, what sorts of changes in the assumptions would make monetary policy very weak?

8. Explain why the aggregate-demand curve has a negative slope.

9. Distinguish between the expenditure lag and the policy lag in stabilization policy. Does monetary policy or fiscal policy have the shorter expenditure lag? What about the policy lag?

10. Explain why their contrasting view on the shape of the aggregate-supply curve lead Keynesians to argue much more strongly for stabilization policies to fight unemployment while monetarists argue much more strongly for stabilization policies to fight inflation.

11. (More difficult.) Consider an economy in which government purchases, taxes, and net exports are zero; the consumption function is:

$$C = 100 + 0.8\ Y,$$

and investment spending (I) depends on the rate of interest (r) in the following way:

$$I = 500 - 800\ r.$$

Find the equilibrium GNP if the central bank makes the rate of interest (a) 5 percent ($r = 0.05$), (b) 10 percent, (c) zero.

Stabilization Policy: With International Capital Flows

The truth is never pure
and rarely simple.
OSCAR WILDE

I n Chapter 14 we explained how fiscal and monetary policy affect GNP, the price level, and the level of interest rates. We now must admit, however, that we cut the story short by assuming that Canadian interest rates can move independently of foreign interest rates. On the contrary, as we stressed in Chapter 13, interest-rate differentials cause large flows of funds across the border as asset holders strive to acquire bonds giving a higher yield. These flows of funds represent shifts in the demand and supply curves for foreign exchange. Such shifts must result in one of two things: either a movement of the exchange rate (if we are on a flexible-rate policy) so that net exports will change; or a change in the domestic money supply (if we are on a fixed exchange-rate policy). In either case, there are further effects on aggregate demand. We now complete the analysis by examining four separate cases:

1. Fiscal policy under fixed exchange rates.

2. Fiscal policy under flexible exchange rates.

3. Monetary policy under fixed exchange rates.

4. Monetary policy under flexible exchange rates.

Our conclusion is that the usefulness of monetary and fiscal policies as demand-management tools depends critically on the government's exchange-rate policy. Thus, although this is one of the shorter chapters in the book, it is indispensible to a proper understanding of macroeconomic policy.

Fiscal Policy Under a Fixed Exchange-Rate Regime

Consider an increase in government spending. Our earlier analysis suggested that this policy leads to an increase in GNP and the price level, and that the higher nominal value of transactions induces households and firms to try to acquire more money. As a result, the money-demand curve shifts to the right, and there is an increase in the Canadian interest rate. This review of our earlier analysis is summarized by the shift from point A to point B in both panels of Figure 15–1.

Both real GNP and the price level increase, from $400 billion to $420 billion and from 100 to 105 in this example; and there is what we now recognize as a *temporary* increase in the Canadian interest rate to 11 percent. Canadian interest rates now exceed foreign interest rates by two percentage points in this example.

Now let us trace through the international effects of the higher Canadian interest rate depicted in Figure 15-1(b). It causes foreign investors to send more funds into Canada as they shift their portfolios of assets to acquire more of the now-appealing high-yield Canadian bonds. To acquire our bonds, they need our currency; therefore, they sell foreign exchange to obtain our currency. Similarly, Canadians reduce their demand for foreign exchange as they have increased incentive to hold their own bonds.

The net effect on the foreign-exchange market is that the Canadian dollar is more in demand so Canada's balance of payments must move in the direction of a surplus. Under a fixed exchange-rate regime, the Bank of Canada avoids any appreciation of the Canadian dollar by buying up the otherwise unwanted quantity of foreign exchange, thereby issuing more Canadian money.

The higher quantity of domestic money is shown by a shift to the right of the money-supply line in Figure 15-1(b) from M_0S_0 to M_1S_1. This easing of domestic credit conditions, which necessarily follows from the Bank of Canada's intervention in the foreign-exchange market, eliminates the interest-rate differential. The final outcome in the domestic-money market is given by point C in Figure 15-1(b). The return of the Canadian interest rate to its original level reverses any cut-back of investment spending that originally occurred, so aggregate demand is stimulated further, as shown by the aggregate-demand curve shifting further to position D_2D_2 in Figure 15-1(a).

We conclude that the initial direct expansionary effect of the fiscal policy (the movement from point A to point B in Figure 15-1) is *reinforced* by the subsequent effects of the policy that are induced by the Bank of Canada's intervention to keep the exchange rate fixed (the movement from point B to point

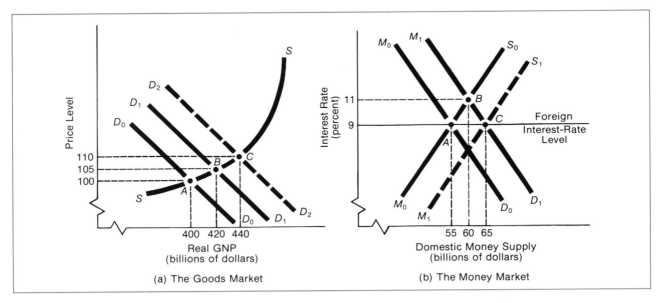

Figure 15-1

FISCAL POLICY WITH INTERNATIONAL CAPITAL FLOWS

An increase in government spending shifts the aggregate-demand curve from D_0D_0 to D_1D_1. The resulting higher nominal GNP shifts the money-demand curve from M_0D_0 to M_1D_1. The higher rate of interest attracts foreign funds into Canada so that: either the Canadian dollar appreciates (and net exports fall, returning the demand curves to D_0D_0 and M_0D_0) under flexible exchange rates, or the Bank of Canada buys the incoming foreign funds (so that the domestic money supply increases to M_1S_1, and aggregate demand is further stimulated to D_2D_2) under fixed exchange rates.

C in Figure 15–1). In our example then, the expansionary fiscal policy raises real GNP from \$400 billion to \$440 billion and raises the price level from 100 to 110. The reason for these large effects is that the Bank of Canada was forced, by its commitment to fix the exchange rate, to perform a complementary monetary policy. The open-market purchase of foreign exchange increases the Canadian money supply (to \$65 billion in our example). The interest rate only rises from 9 percent to 11 percent *temporarily*; in the end, the Canadian interest rate has returned to the level of foreign interest rates.

Fiscal Policy Under a Flexible Exchange-Rate Regime

Now consider the same increase in government spending when exchange rates are floating freely. The initial effects are the same as in Figure 15–1 (to which we continue to refer): higher GNP (shown by the move from *A* to *B*), Canadian interest rates rising above foreign rates, and an increased demand for Canadian dollars on the foreign-exchange market. Under flexible exchange rates, the Bank of Canada makes no attempt to buy up the otherwise unwanted quantity of foreign exchange, so the Canadian dollar appreciates in value. With no transactions by the Bank of Canada, the money supply is constant so the money-supply schedule remains at position M_0S_0 in Figure 15–1(b). But the appreciating Canadian dollar makes our imports cheaper, and foreigners find our exports more expensive. As a result, *net exports fall*, and so the aggregate-demand curve shifts back to the left from D_1D_1 toward D_0D_0 in Figure 15–1(a).

How far will this process go? The induced appreciation of the Canadian dollar must continue as long as the Canadian interest rate remains above foreign rates. Hence, the process can come to an end only when the aggregate-demand curve has shifted leftward enough to re-establish the original equilibrium point *A*. With prices and real output back at their original levels, the demand-for-money curve will be back at its original position, so Canadian interest rates will be back down to the level of foreign interest rates. At this point, the shift of funds across the border by savers stops. In the end, then, the initial direct expansionary effect of fiscal policy is eventually completely eliminated by the induced exchange-rate effects.

The effort to raise GNP by government spending fails under flexible exchange rates; aggregate demand is only affected temporarily, since all that the higher government spending does is *replace* pre-existing export demand for Canadian products.

This scenario is a perfect description of the Canadian situation during the late 1950s and early 1960s. We were in a recession, with unemployment in excess of 7 percent and very little inflation. James Coyne, the governor of the Bank of Canada, felt that unemployment was not a concern of the central bank. Technically he was right; the Bank Act states that the Bank of Canada's job is to preserve the value of our currency, and that means keeping the purchasing power of our dollar from being eroded by inflation. Coyne tried to ensure that this would not occur by restricting the quantity of money in the system. This policy put upward pressure on interest rates, and the resulting increase in the foreign demand for our bonds pushed up the value of the Canadian dollar. The problem was that both the temporarily higher interest rates and the more expensive Canadian dollar made the unemployment problem worse. The Department of Finance ran large deficits in an attempt to lessen unemployment, but as we have just learned, there is no lasting effect on aggregate demand from fiscal policy under flexible exchange rates. It is no wonder that the Diefenbaker government wanted Coyne to resign; they were left with fiscal policy as the only tool for "curing" the recession, and it is essentially a useless tool in a flexible exchange-rate setting. It is not surprising that major Canadian economists ran a full-page item in leading newspapers at the time, urging the Bank of Canada to relieve the constraint it had placed on stabilization policy.

Monetary Policy Under a Fixed Exchange-Rate Regime

We now consider monetary policy in each of the polar case exchange-rate regimes. Suppose the Bank of Canada wants to fight inflation and so decreases the domestic money supply. The analysis in Chapter 14 suggested that this policy leads to a decrease in GNP and the price level, and a higher interest rate due to tighter credit conditions. This is illustrated in Figure 15–2. The decrease in the domestic money supply is shown by the leftward shift of the money-supply line (from M_0S_0 to M_1S_1) in Figure 15–2(b). The resulting tighter credit conditions are indicated by the fact that Canadian interest rates have risen from 9 percent to 11 percent, at point B in panel (b). The higher borrowing costs mean lower investment spending by firms, so the aggregate-demand curve shifts left from D_0D_0 to D_1D_1 in panel (a). Thus, the economy moves from point A to point B in both panels of Figure 15–2. The initial effects of the contractionary monetary policy in this example are to reduce real GNP from $400 billion to $380 billion, to reduce the price index from 100 to 95, and to raise borrowing costs from 9 percent to 11 percent. As we have seen before, however, the resulting gap between foreign and domestic interest rates cannot last.

The interest-rate differential causes portfolio shifts on the part of bond-holders toward Canadian bonds. Foreigners will supply more foreign exchange to the trading market, to get the Canadian dollars that are required to pay for the high-yield Canadian bonds. Canadians will demand less foreign exchange, since they now have a decreased demand for foreign financial assets. These reactions to the temporary interest-rate differential mean upward pressure on the value of the

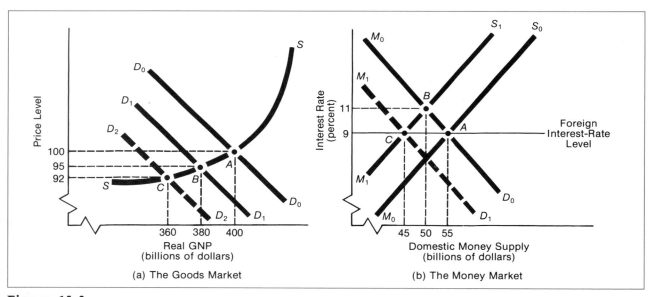

Figure 15–2
MONETARY POLICY WITH INTERNATIONAL CAPITAL FLOWS
A decrease in the money supply shifts the money-supply curve from M_0S_0 to M_1S_1. The resulting higher borrowing costs reduce aggregate demand from D_0D_0 to D_1D_1. The higher rate of interest also attracts foreign funds into Canada so that: either the Canadian dollar appreciates (and net exports fall, pushing aggregate demand down to D_2D_2) under flexible exchange rates, or the Bank of Canada buys the incoming foreign funds (so that the domestic money supply increases back to supply-curve position M_0S_0) under fixed exchange rates.

Canadian dollar. Under a fixed exchange-rate regime, the Bank of Canada precludes this appreciation of the dollar by buying the otherwise unwanted quantity of foreign exchange. That is, Canada sustains an increase in the balance-of-payments surplus, and the Bank of Canada issues more domestic currency to pay for this accumulation of foreign-exchange reserves. Since the money supply increases automatically as a result of this open-market purchase of foreign exchange, the money-supply curve in Figure 15–2(b) shifts back to the right. This easing of credit conditions causes Canadian interest rates to start falling back down from 11 percent, and as a result, the aggregate-demand curve starts to shift back to the right, from position D_1D_1 in Figure 15–2(a). Thus, the original decreases in real GNP and the price level are reversed.

How far will this process go? The increase in the money supply that is induced by the flow of foreign funds into Canada must continue as long as the Canadian interest rate is significantly above foreign rates. Hence, the process comes to an end when the money-supply line shifts far enough to the right that it returns to position M_0S_0, and the interest rate is 9 percent, at point A in Figure 15–2(b). But if borrowing costs return to their original level, investment spending by firms will be restored to its initial level. Thus, the aggregate-demand curve will return to its starting position, D_0D_0, in Figure 15–2(a). In the end, then, we return to point A in both panels of Figure 15–2, and there is no lasting effect of monetary policy.

By committing themselves to issue or withdraw money according to the outcome in the foreign-exchange market, the authorities have relinquished the ability to set the domestic money supply at any independently specified value.

In spite of the fact that the flexible exchange-rate version of this model explained the "Coyne Affair" so well, the Bank of Canada ignored it again by trying a rather dramatic contractionary monetary policy in 1969, while we were then still in a fixed exchange-rate regime. This move was part of the Trudeau government's fight against inflation. The money supply was cut in mid-1969, and Canadian interest rates rose. The effect on the balance of payments was dramatic. We had a surplus of $65 million in 1969; then, with the foreign currency attracted by high Canadian interest rates, the balance-of-payments surplus rose to $1663 million in 1970, and the Bank had only maintained the fixed exchange-rate policy until May of that year! The Bank tried to insulate the domestic money supply from the balance-of-payments surplus by using open-market operations in the bond market. That is, as rapidly as it was issuing new Canadian money to buy the incoming foreign exchange, it tried to balance this by selling government bonds to decrease chartered bank reserves. However, the Bank soon realized that selling bonds to the general public (to get the new money back out of the system) produced a vicious circle. Big bond issues are only purchased if the interest rate involved is favourable. Thus, the big bond sales further raised interest rates, caused a larger inflow of foreign exchange (resulting in an even larger balance-of-payments surplus), and forced the government to sell even more bonds, etc., etc., if the money supply was to remain contracted.

The government finally realized it was trapped in this vicious circle, and it broke the chain in May 1970 by removing the promise to fix the exchange rate. As the model predicts, the value of the Canadian dollar increased noticeably immediately following this decision. It is ironic that after moving to a floating-rate policy (which we have just shown to be a necessary condition for conducting a successful monetary policy), the Bank gave up its fight against inflation and embarked on an expansionary monetary policy. This was "effective" (given the new floating exchange-rate environment), and the acceleration of inflation was the result.

Monetary Policy Under a Flexible Exchange-Rate Regime

To discuss monetary policy under flexible exchange rates we consider the same decrease in money supply and continue to refer to Figure 15-2. The initial effects are the same: lower GNP, lower price level, the Canadian interest rate going higher than foreign rates, and the interest-rate differential causing foreign funds to flow into Canada. The difference is that without the Bank of Canada's involvement in the foreign-exchange market there is no further move in the position of the money-supply curve from M_1S_1. Instead, the Canadian dollar appreciates as the foreign funds enter the country, and this makes our imports cheaper to buy, and our exports more expensive for foreigners to buy. As our net exports fall, the aggregate-demand curve shifts leftward in the direction of D_2D_2, so the price level and real GNP are further reduced.

How far will this process go? The appreciation of the Canadian dollar must continue as long as the Canadian interest rate is significantly above foreign interest rates. The process ends when the aggregate-demand curve has shifted down enough to lower nominal GNP enough to shift the demand-for-money curve to position M_1D_1 in panel (b). At this stage, the economy is at point C in both panels of Figure 15-2. In our example, the price index has fallen from 100 to 92, and real GNP has fallen to $360 billion. The money supply has fallen to the $45 billion level, and the interest rate has returned to its original value of 9 percent, which is the level of foreign interest rates. Since the interest rate differential is eliminated, we see that:

Monetary policy works through the sensitivity of net exports to the exchange rate, not the sensitivity of investment spending to the interest rate.

We have analysed a *contractionary* monetary policy in the flexible exchange-rate case, so you can directly compare the effects to the earlier discussion of actual policy taken in 1969–70 under fixed exchange rates. As a matter of fact, however, the 1971–74 period was characterized by *expansionary* monetary policy. The same reasoning can be used in reverse to explain how this does have a lasting expansionary effect on aggregate demand, but only under floating rates.

Monetary policy certainly was expansionary in the early 1970s. The rate of growth of Canada's money supply rose from 4.7 percent in 1969 to 19.9 percent in 1974. Given that the average annual growth in Canada's real GNP since 1953 has been less than 4.7 percent, this policy clearly involved an excessive stimulation of spending.

The Bank of Canada accepted this interpretation and, in September 1975, reversed its policy position. During the 1975–82 period, the Bank emphasized repeatedly that it was attempting to ensure that Canada's money supply did not increase at more than a specified rate (to be lowered systematically so that inflation could be gradually reduced). The news media referred to this period as "Canada's experiment with monetarism." One interesting question is why the Bank permitted the overstimulation of aggregate demand in the 1971–74 period. The answer to this question will make clear the underlying cause of inflation.

The key to the answer is found in the 1971 *Annual Report* of the Bank of Canada. The report notes that the expansion in Canada's money supply was needed to "avoid contributing to undue appreciation of our currency," which would have "exacerbated the difficulties of important export and import competing industries and impeded the expansion of economic activity." Essentially, the Bank was concerned about unemployment, not inflation, and felt that rising interest rates and the resulting increase in the foreign value of the Canadian dollar would aggravate unemployment.

It is true that *if* foreign countries were not inflating, the higher value of the Canadian dollar would have hurt our exports, since a given amount of foreign currency earned as sales receipts would translate into fewer Canadian dollars to be used for financing domestic production costs. This is what the Bank of Canada was trying to avoid, and they probably regarded this possibility with particular concern since this is exactly what happened in the 1958–61 period of tight monetary policy, that is, during the "Coyne Affair." However, there was an important difference in the 1970s: foreign countries *were* inflating. Thus, as long as the rate at which the Canadian dollar appreciated was no larger than the rate of foreign inflation, Canadian exporters would *not* be subject to a cost squeeze *at all*. Given the foreign environment, then, the Bank's inappropriate resistance to currency appreciation led to the overly expansive aggregate-demand policy in the 1971–74 period.

Review of Aggregate-Demand Policy Options

1. Fiscal policy has a lasting effect on aggregate demand under fixed exchange rates. The temporary rise in interest rates following the expansion attracts foreign funds, which the Bank of Canada must absorb to peg the exchange rate. The increase in the domestic money supply that the Bank must allow to buy the incoming foreign exchange reinforces the initial fiscal expansion.

2. Fiscal policy has no lasting effect on aggregate demand under a floating exchange rate. Any initial expansion of demand just causes temporarily higher interest rates, which attract foreign funds. The Canadian dollar appreciates, forcing a contraction in net export demands.

3. Monetary policy has no lasting effect on aggregate demand under fixed exchange rates. Any initial expansion of demand involves temporarily lower domestic interest rates, which cause foreign funds to leave the country. The Bank of Canada must accept the domestic currency that is relinquished as foreign exchange is purchased to buy foreign bonds. The resulting decrease in domestic money circulating counteracts the original policy.

4. Monetary policy has a lasting effect on aggregate demand under a floating exchange rate. An expansion of demand by the central bank initially involves lower domestic interest rates. As foreign funds leave the country, the Canadian dollar depreciates. The resulting stimulation of net exports reinforces the initial expansionary monetary policy.

These strong conclusions depend on the assumption that Canada has absolutely no ability to maintain interest rates at values that differ significantly from those in the United States. This assumption is not literally true, but as we noted in Chapter 13 (pages 258–59) it is very close to being completely true. Thus, while the aggregate-demand effects summarized above are *far* more relevant than those discussed in Chapter 14, we should probably temper them a little bit. Capital flows across the U.S.–Canadian border are not instantaneous. The following summary table gives the conclusions in this slightly weaker form.

To utilize this summary table, we must know what Canada's exchange-rate policy is. However, there is no simple answer to this question. We had a flexible

EFFECTS ON AGGREGATE DEMAND OF:		
	FISCAL POLICY	MONETARY POLICY
Under a fixed exchange-rate regime	Strong	Weak
Under a flexible exchange-rate regime	Weak	Strong

exchange-rate regime in the 1950s, a fixed exchange-rate regime in the 1960s, and a mixture of the two since 1970.[1]

Canada is currently following a policy of heavily managing the exchange rate. While the exchange rate is not absolutely fixed, intervention by the Bank of Canada is dramatic at times. Only limited variation in the exchange rate around its ongoing trend of depreciation (a trend that has occurred since 1976) is permitted. Thus, it is probably best to take the conclusions contained in the fixed exchange-rate row of the summary table as being roughly appropriate.

As an example of the use of the summary table, let us consider the Foreign Investment Review Agency (FIRA) and the National Energy Policy (NEP), which were introduced by the Trudeau government at the start of the 1980s. Most analysts have concluded that these policies discouraged investment spending by foreign-owned firms in Canada. As a result, these policies shifted the total-expenditure $(C + I + G + X - IM)$ line down, in the same manner as would a decrease in government expenditure. To use the summary table, then, we consult the entry for fiscal policy under a fixed exchange-rate regime. The "strong" entry means that our model supports those who claimed that FIRA and the NEP had contractionary effects on the Canadian economy.

Defenders of these policies can react in two ways. First, they can claim that significant depreciation of the Canadian dollar has occurred during the 1980s, so perhaps the flexible exchange-rate row of the summary table is more appropriate. As we see, this entry says the contractionary effects of FIRA and NEP are weak, but this is because they would have contributed to the weaker dollar. Second, the defenders can claim that certain microeconomic benefits of these policies are worth the macroeconomic costs.

Exchange Rates and Aggregate Supply

We emphasized in Chapter 11 that the exchange rate is a shift variable for the aggregate-supply curve. Since some imports are intermediate products, an appreciating Canadian dollar lowers one component of domestic costs and shifts the aggregate-supply curve down. Similarly, a depreciating Canadian dollar raises this component of domestic costs and shifts the aggregate-supply curve up. With this reminder, we are in a position to extend our discussion beyond aggregate demand and to derive the complete real GNP and price-level effects of monetary and fiscal policies under each exchange-rate regime.

An increase in government spending under fixed exchange rates is shown in Figure 15–3(a). We have already shown that there is a lasting effect on aggregate demand in this case, and this is indicated by the rightward shift of the aggregate-demand curve from D_0D_0 to D_1D_1. Since the exchange rate is fixed, the aggregate-supply curve does not move. We conclude that expansionary fiscal policy under fixed exchange rates raises both prices and real output.

The same increase in government spending under flexible exchange rates is shown in Figure 15–3(b). We discovered earlier that there is no lasting effect on aggregate demand in this case, so there is no rightward shift of the aggregate-demand curve. The reason for this is that the appreciation of the Canadian dollar reduces net exports and lowers aggregate demand by as much as the higher government spending raises demand. There is nothing to counteract the cost-saving effect of the currency appreciation, however, so the aggregate-supply curve shifts down from S_0S_0 to S_1S_1. We conclude that expansionary fiscal policy under flexible exchange rates raises real GNP and lowers the price level.

An increase in the domestic money supply is considered in the remaining two panels of Figure 15–3. Since there is no lasting effect on aggregate demand under

---

[1]The historical development of the international monetary system is discussed in the next chapter.

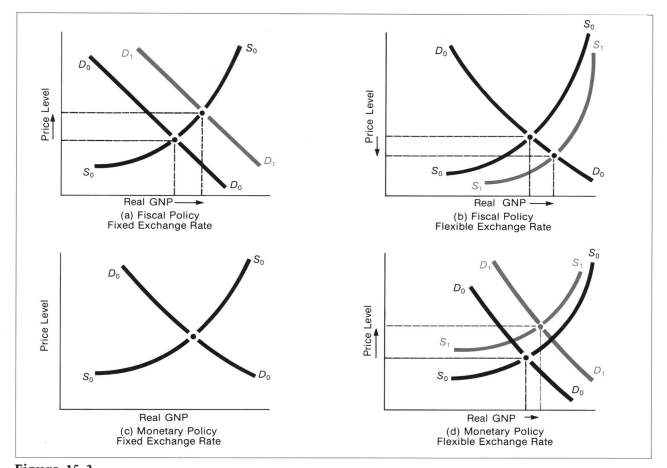

Figure 15-3

FISCAL AND MONETARY EFFECTS ON AGGREGATE DEMAND AND SUPPLY

Both monetary and fiscal policies have direct aggregate-supply effects under a floating exchange-rate regime, since the exchange rate affects the costs of imported intermediate products.

fixed exchange rates, nor any shift in the supply curve without an exchange-rate change, neither curve is shifted in Figure 15-3(c). We conclude that monetary policy has no effect on real GNP or the price level under fixed exchange rates. A more accurate description of this outcome is that an independent monetary policy cannot be set if the central bank has already committed the money supply to be whatever is required to peg the exchange rate.

An increase in the money supply is possible if the central bank does not intervene in the foreign-exchange market. This policy is considered in Figure 15-3(d). Since there is a lasting effect of the monetary expansion on aggregate demand, the demand curve shifts to the right from D_0D_0 to D_1D_1. However, the reason for this is that the depreciation in the Canadian dollar raises net exports. This depreciation also raises business costs, so the aggregate-supply curve shifts up from S_0S_0 to S_1S_1. We conclude that expansionary monetary policy under flexible exchange rates results in higher prices, and (at best) in only a small increase in real GNP.

Review

Before an informed opinion concerning the effects of government policy on unemployment and inflation can be had, we must know what the government's exchange-rate policy is. Although a noticeable depreciation of the Canadian dollar has taken place during the early 1980s, the government's policy has been one of significant management of the exchange rate. Thus we can take the fixed exchange-rate predictions of our analysis as roughly appropriate. As a result, we cannot expect Canada to have a monetary policy that is much different from that in the United States. Fiscal policy can be used as an independent instrument, but it involves the standard trade-off between the real GNP and price-level goals.

Foreign Interest-Rate Increases and Aggregate Supply

We considered the aggregate-demand effects of an increase in foreign interest rates in Chapter 13 (pages 258–60). Here we bring in the aggregate-supply effects that are involved if the exchange rate is allowed to float.

Until Canadian interest rates are pulled up to the level of foreign interest rates through competition, investors will sell Canadian bonds, to buy the higher-yield foreign bonds. To accomplish this shift, investors must buy foreign currency by selling Canadian dollars. If the exchange rate is flexible, this shift causes a fall in the value of the Canadian dollar. The depreciation of the Canadian dollar stimulates foreign demand for our exports, so that the aggregate-demand curve shifts out from D_0D_0 to D_1D_1 in Figure 15–4(a). The depreciated Canadian dollar also increases business costs, so the aggregate-supply curve moves from S_0S_0 to S_1S_1. The net result is significant upward pressure on the price level, and perhaps even a decrease in production.

A lower level of production is particularly likely in the short run, since the increase in business costs occurs without a lag. In contrast to this, there is often a

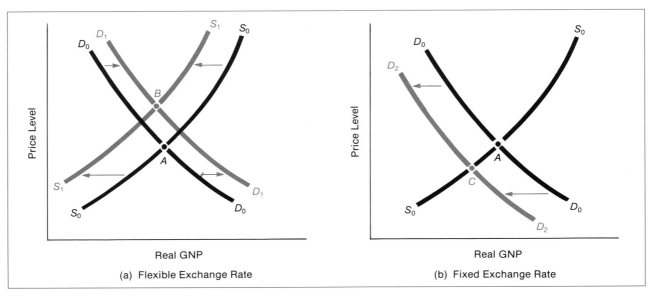

Figure 15–4

AGGREGATE-DEMAND AND AGGREGATE-SUPPLY EFFECTS OF FOREIGN INTEREST-RATE INCREASES

Foreign interest-rate increases lead investors to trade Canadian bonds for foreign bonds, and this requires exchanging Canadian dollars for foreign currencies. If there is a floating exchange rate, the depreciation of the Canadian dollar stimulates export demand (so demand shifts from D_0D_0 to D_1D_1) and increases business costs (so supply shifts from S_0S_0 to S_1S_1). We move from point A to point B in panel (a). If the exchange rate is fixed, the Bank of Canada buys the previously circulating Canadian currency to avoid depreciation, so the domestic money supply shrinks and aggregate demand shifts from D_0D_0 to D_2D_2. Without a change in the exchange rate, there is no direct effect on business costs, so no shift in the aggregate-supply curve. We move from point A to point C in panel (b). Output can fall under either exchange-rate regime, but more inflation occurs under a floating rate.

significant lag following an exchange-rate change, before foreign buyers decide that a change is permanent enough to warrant switching orders from one country to another.

To maintain a fixed exchange rate after an increase in foreign interest rates, the Bank of Canada must sell foreign exchange. Investors who desire high-yield bonds will be trading in Canadian dollars to get the necessary foreign exchange. As the previously circulating Canadian dollars are absorbed by the Bank of Canada (in payment for its sales of foreign exchange), the domestic money supply shrinks. As a result, the aggregate-demand curve shifts in from D_0D_0 to D_2D_2 in Figure 15–4(b). With no change in the exchange rate under a fixed exchange-rate policy, there is no direct effect on business costs, so there is no shift in the aggregate-supply curve.

To summarize, an increase in foreign interest rates leaves Canada with the following alternatives:

1. Peg the exchange rate, so the higher interest rate is accompanied by lower output and downward pressure on prices (a move from point A to point C in Figure 15–4(b)); or

2. Float the exchange rate, so the higher interest rate is accompanied by higher prices, and probably a mild slump in output (a move from point A to point B in Figure 15–4(a)).

One's choice between these alternatives depends (among other things) on one's beliefs concerning the relative sizes of the costs of unemployment and inflation.

As we learned in Chapter 13, the Bank of Canada has permitted some depreciation of the Canadian dollar in the face of U.S. interest-rate increases in the early 1980s, but the exchange rate has been heavily managed. The Bank has followed this policy since it regards the costs of inflation to be very high.

Summary

1. The usefulness of monetary and fiscal policies as tools of demand management depends critically on the government's exchange-rate policy.

2. Fiscal policy has no lasting effect on aggregate demand under a floating exchange rate. Any initial expansion of demand just causes temporarily higher interest rates, which attract foreign funds. The Canadian dollar appreciates, forcing a contraction in net export demands. The truth of this proposition was dramatically illustrated by the conflict between the Bank of Canada and the Diefenbaker government, known as the "Coyne Affair."

3. Fiscal policy has a lasting effect on aggregate demand under fixed exchange rates. The temporary rise in interest rates following the expansion attracts foreign funds, which the Bank of Canada must absorb to peg the exchange rate. The increase in the domestic money supply which the Bank must allow to buy the incoming foreign exchange reinforces the initial fiscal expansion.

4. Monetary policy cannot be used as an independent instrument in a fixed exchange-rate regime. Any initial expansion of demand involves temporarily lower domestic interest rates, which cause foreign funds to leave the country. The Bank of Canada must accept the domestic currency that is relinquished as foreign exchange is purchased to buy foreign bonds. The resulting decrease in domestic money circulating counteracts the original policy. The truth of this proposition was dramatically illustrated in the 1969–70 period. Canada tried a contractionary monetary policy with a pegged exchange rate, while the U.S. policy was expansionary due to the Vietnam war.

5. Monetary policy has a lasting effect on aggregate demand under a floating exchange rate. An expansion of demand by the Bank of Canada initially involves lower domestic interest rates. As foreign funds leave the country, the Canadian dollar depreciates. The resulting stimulation of net exports reinforces the initial expansionary monetary policy.

6. Both monetary and fiscal policies can have direct aggregate-supply effects under a floating exchange-rate regime. Since the exchange rate affects the costs of imported intermediate products, it affects business costs and shifts the position of the aggregate-supply curve.

7. The Bank of Canada has followed a policy of heavily managing the exchange rate during the 1980s. As a result, our monetary policy is largely determined in the United States. Fiscal policy remains an independent instrument that can be used for demand management, but it involves the standard short-run trade-off: Higher levels of real GNP can be had only with increases in the price level.

Concepts for Review

Interest-rate differential
Foreign exchange market
    intervention
Floating, or flexible, exchange rates

Questions for Discussion

1. Why did the Bank of Canada resist appreciation of the Canadian dollar in the early 1970s?
2. Why did the Bank of Canada resist depreciation of the Canadian dollar in the early 1980s?
3. In the text we examined an expansionary fiscal policy and a contractionary monetary policy, under both exchange-rate regimes. Show that the conclusions in the table on page 293 are equally valid for a contractionary fiscal policy and an expansionary monetary policy.
4. Does exchange-rate policy make a difference for the effects of a foreign tariff on the Canadian economy?

The International Monetary System

16

All decent people live beyond
their incomes nowadays, and
those who aren't respectable live
beyond other people's. A few gifted
individuals manage to do both.

SAKI

This chapter takes a look at the system that has been set up to handle the international movement of money—the **international monetary system**. We have already discussed the two polar forms of international monetary arrangements—the fixed and flexible exchange-rate regimes, at least from one country's point of view. In the first part of this chapter, we continue our investigation of these two exchange-rate regimes. First, we examine why some countries' currencies appreciate while others depreciate. Second, in discussing fixed exchange rates, we consider how the *balance of payments* is measured.

But the two polar exchange-rate systems are studied to illustrate some important principles, *not* to describe the actual international monetary system as it is now. Therefore, in the remainder of the chapter we turn to more realistic intermediate systems that have elements of both pure forms, including the old *gold standard*, the so-called *gold-exchange system* that prevailed from 1944 until 1971, and the current *mixed* system—a system that defies any short description because each country, it seems, handles its international monetary relations somewhat differently.

What Determines Exchange Rates?

When exchange rates are flexible, they are determined by the forces of supply and demand. But what factors move the supply and demand curves? Economists believe that the principal determinants of exchange-rate movements are rather different in the long, medium, and short runs. So we turn in the next three sections to the analysis of exchange-rate movements over these three "runs." We begin with the long run.

The Purchasing-Power Parity Theory: The Long Run

As long as there is free trade across national borders, exchange rates should eventually adjust so that the same product costs the same number of dollars (or the same amount of any other currency) in every country, except for differences attributable to transportation costs and the like. This simple statement forms the basis of the major theory of exchange-rate determination in the long run.

The **purchasing-power parity theory of exchange-rate determination** holds that the exchange rate between any two national currencies adjusts to reflect differences in the price levels in the two countries.

An example will bring out the basic truth in this theory and also suggest some of its limitations. Suppose that Swedish and Canadian steel are identical and that these two nations are the only producers of steel for the world market. Suppose further that steel is the only tradable good that either country produces.

Question: If Canadian steel costs $120 per ton and Swedish steel costs 1000 kronor per ton, what must be the exchange rate between the dollar and the krona?

Answer: Since 1000 kronor must be the equivalent of $120, each krona must be worth 12 cents. Why? Because if a krona cost 15 cents, then Swedish steel would cost $150 per ton (1000 kronor at 15 cents each) while Canadian steel would cost $120 per ton, and all foreign customers would shop for their steel in Canada. The exchange rate of 15 cents per krona would be too high.

EXERCISE
Show why an exchange rate of 10 cents per krona is too low.

The purchasing-power parity theory is used to make long-run predictions about the effects of inflation on exchange rates. To continue our example, suppose that over a five-year period, prices in Canada rise by one-third while prices in Sweden rise by 60 percent. The purchasing-power parity theory predicts that the krona would depreciate relative to the dollar. It also predicts the amount of the currency depreciation. Say that after the inflation, Canadian steel costs $160 per ton (one-third more than $120), while Swedish steel costs 1600 kronor per ton (60 percent more than 1000 kronor). For these two prices to be equivalent, 1600 kronor must be worth $160, or one krona must be worth 10 cents. The value of the krona, therefore, must have fallen from 12 cents to 10 cents.

According to the purchasing-power parity theory, differences in domestic inflation rates are a major cause of adjustments in exchange rates. For instance, if one country has a faster rate of inflation than another, then its exchange rate must be depreciating.

For many years, the theory seemed to work tolerably well. While precise numerical predictions based on purchasing-power parity calculations were not very accurate (see the accompanying box), nations with higher inflation did at least experience depreciating currencies. But in the early 1980s even this theory broke down. For example, while the U.S. inflation rate was slightly higher than West Germany's and much higher than Japan's between 1980 and 1983, the U.S. dollar none the less rose relative to both the mark and the yen during this period. Clearly, the theory is missing something. There are a number of complications that the purchasing-power theory ignores.

First, changes in any of the interferences with free trade, such as tariffs and quotas, can upset simple calculations based on purchasing-power parity. For example, if Swedish prices rise faster than Canadian prices but, at the same time, foreign countries erect tariff barriers to keep Canadian (but not Swedish) steel out, then the krona might not have to depreciate.

Second, some goods and services cannot be traded across national frontiers. Land and buildings are only the most obvious examples; most services can be traded only to a limited extent (as when tourists from one country have their hair cut in another). Inflation rates for goods and services that are *not tradable* have little bearing on exchange rates.

Third, few of the goods that different nations produce and trade are as uniform

Purchasing-Power Parity and the Big Mac

In July 1983, *The New York Times* used a well-known international commodity to assess the purchasing-power parity theory. As this article shows, the theory did not work very well.

The French have been most vociferous in complaining that the U.S. dollar's value has been too high. But if the cost of lunch at McDonald's is any guide, it is the franc, more than the dollar, that should be devalued.

Theoretically, at least, if all exchange rates were where they should be, prices of the same goods should be identical in every country. Using McDonald's as an example, exchange rates, indeed, are out of line and the dollar is overvalued against all the major currencies, except the franc.

Last Wednesday, in New York, it cost $3.39 to buy a Big Mac, a small order of fries, and a small Coke. This was substantially higher than the cost of a comparable McDonald's lunch in five major foreign cities.

In Paris, however, the dollar-equivalent price was $3.82, based on the franc's June 28 value of 13.08 cents. The biggest bargain was in Amsterdam, where the price of a McDonald's lunch was only $2.40. In Switzerland, the cost of a comparable meal was $3.23; in Tokyo, $2.62; in Germany, $2.57, and in London, $2.40.

If the seven currencies were to be made equal on the "MacIndex," using the New York price as the yardstick, the Swiss franc would have to be revalued upward by 4.7

percent against the dollar; the Japanese yen 22.7 percent; the German mark 24 percent; the British pound 25.7 percent; and the Dutch guilder 29.2 percent. The French franc would have to be devalued 11.3 percent.

SOURCE: *The New York Times*, July 3, 1983.

AUTHORS' NOTE: Actually, the theory did not do all that badly. Over the next several months, the French franc depreciated 10.9 percent relative to the U.S. dollar.

---

as the Swedish and Canadian steel in our example. A Volvo and a Buick, for example, are not identical products. So the price of a Volvo *in Canadian dollars* can rise faster than the price of a Buick without driving Volvos out of the market entirely. On balance:

Most economists believe that other factors are much more important than relative price levels for exchange-rate determination in the short run. But in the long run, purchasing-power parity plays an important role.

Economic Activity and Exchange Rates: The Medium Run

Consumer spending increases quite regularly when income expands, and decreases when income contracts, and the same is true for imported goods. Thus, as we stressed in Chapter 11:

A country's imports will rise quickly when its economy is booming and slowly when its economy is stagnating.

A boom in Canada would shift the demand curve for marks outward and therefore lead to an appreciation of the mark (depreciation of the dollar) and Canadian imports from Germany would surge. However, if Germany were booming at the same time, German citizens would be buying more Canadian exports, which would shift the supply curve of marks outward. On balance, the value of the dollar might or might not fall. What matters is whether exports are growing faster than imports. The general lesson is that:

Holding other things equal, a country that grows faster than the rest of the world normally finds its currency depreciating because its imports grow faster than its exports, so that its demand curve for foreign currency shifts outward more rapidly than its supply curve.

The exchange rate between the U.S. dollar and the mark in the 1970s (but not in the 1980s!) is a case in point. During the recovery from the worldwide recession of 1974–76, the U.S. economy expanded quite a bit more rapidly than the German economy. This is one reason why the dollar depreciated and the mark rose in value from late 1976 to late 1978.

Interest Rates and Exchange Rates: The Short Run

While economic activity is very important for exchange-rate determination in the medium run, "other things" often are not equal in the very short run. Specifically, one factor that often seems to call the tune in determining exchange rates in the short run is *interest-rate differentials*. There is an enormous fund of so-called "hot money"—owned by banks, multinational corporations, and wealthy individuals of all nations, and amounting to perhaps $500 billion to $700 billion—that travels around the globe in search of the highest interest rates.

Thus, suppose that British government bonds are paying a 10 percent rate of interest when yields on equally safe Canadian government securities rise to 15 percent. British investors will be attracted by the high interest rates in Canada and will offer pounds for sale in order to buy dollars, planning to use those dollars to buy Canadian securities. At the same time Canadian investors will find investing in Canada more attractive than ever, so fewer pounds will be demanded by Canadians.

When the demand schedule falls and the supply curve rises, the effect on price is quite predictable: the pound will depreciate, as Figure 16–1 shows. In the figure, the supply curve of pounds shifts outward from S_1S_1 to S_2S_2 when British investors seek to sell pounds in order to purchase Canadian securities. At the same time, Canadian investors wish to buy fewer pounds because they no longer

Figure 16-1
THE EFFECT OF A RISE IN CANADIAN INTEREST RATES
When Canada raises its interest rates, more English investors will want to buy Canadian bonds, and so the supply curve of pounds will shift outward from S_1S_1 to S_2S_2. At the same time, fewer Canadians will seek to buy British bonds, so the demand curve for pounds will shift inward from D_1D_1 to D_2D_2. The combined effect of these two shifts is to move the market equilibrium from point E_1 to point E_2. The British pound depreciates, and the dollar appreciates.

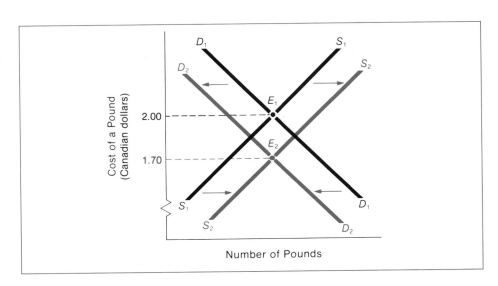

wish to invest in British securities. Thus, the demand curve shifts inward from D_1D_1 to D_2D_2. The result, in our example, is a depreciation of the pound from \$2.00 to \$1.70. In general:

Holding other things equal, countries with high interest rates are able to attract more capital than are countries with low interest rates. Thus a rise in interest rates often will lead to an appreciation of the currency, and a drop in interest rates will lead to a depreciation.

The Canadian dollar in 1981–83 provided a vivid example of the power of this phenomenon when high U.S. interest rates caused a sharp appreciation of the U.S. dollar and a depreciation of the Canadian dollar. Most experts in international finance agree that international money is so volatile that interest-rate movements are the chief determinant of exchange-rate fluctuations in the short run.

Market Determination of Exchange Rates: Summary

We can summarize this discussion of exchange-rate determination in free markets as follows:

1. Currencies generally will be *appreciating* in countries whose inflation rates are lower than the rest of the world, for otherwise it would be increasingly difficult for the other countries to market their goods.

2. Exchange rates would also be expected to rise in countries whose levels of economic activity are lower than average, because these countries will be importing rather little.

3. We expect to find appreciating currencies in countries whose interest rates are high because these countries will attract capital from all over the world.

Reversing each of these, we expect that currencies will be *depreciating* in countries with relatively high inflation rates, or high levels of economic activity, or low interest rates.

Fixed Exchange Rates and the Definition of the Balance of Payments

From our discussion of fixed exchange rates in Chapter 13 (pages 248–54) it may seem that measuring a nation's balance-of-payments position is a simple task: We simply count up the private demand for and supply of its currency and subtract quantity supplied from quantity demanded. Conceptually, this is all there is to it. But, in practice, the difficulties are great because we never have statistics on the number of dollars demanded and supplied. There is no way to observe these directly.

If we look at actual market transactions, we will see that the number of Canadian dollars actually *purchased* and the number of Canadian dollars actually *sold* on the foreign-exchange market are identical. Unless someone has made a bookkeeping error, this must always be so. How, then, can we recognize a balance-of-payments surplus or deficit? Easy, you say. Just look at the transactions of the central bank, whose purchases or sales must make up the difference between private demand and private supply. If the Bank of Canada is buying Canadian dollars, its purchases measure our balance-of-payments deficit. If it is selling, its sales represent our balance-of-payments surplus. Thus, we measure the balance of payments by *excluding official transactions among governments.*

The Canadian Balance-of-Payments Accounts

Using 1983 as an example, Table 16-1 shows the official Canadian balance-of-payments accounts. The top section of the table summarizes Canada's trade in currently produced goods and services—the so-called *current account*. The positive or negative sign attached to each entry indicates whether the transaction represented a *gain* (+) or a *loss* (−) of foreign currency.

Looking first at the top of the table, we see that in merchandise transactions Canadians exported about $18 billion more than they imported, leading to a surplus in merchandise trade (lines 1–3). Almost as big an amount, but in this case a deficit, took place in the trade of services. Lines 4 and 5 indicate that Canadians spent more on foreign travel and on making interest payments to foreigners to service our international debt than we received from foreign tourists and from our investments abroad. The transfer payments in line 6 include items such as gifts and foreign aid. Line 7 gives the net result of all trading in goods and services—the balance on current account. The entry means that Canada received $1.6 billion more than it spent during 1983.

Lines 8–11 record trades of financial assets, and this section is called the *capital account* of the balance of payments. Line 8 indicates that Canadians purchased more shares in foreign companies than foreigners purchased in Canadian companies in 1983. Much of this is due to our banks and real estate companies, and the Canadianization that has taken place in the energy industry. Lines 9 and 10 indicate that Canadians sold $7.1 billion of long- and short-term bonds to foreigners, more than foreigners sold to Canadians. The balance on the capital account is given in line 11. It indicates that $5.5 billion entered Canada during 1983, as a result of all the recorded trades of stocks and bonds that took place across the border that year.

One would think that with a surplus on both the current and capital accounts,

---

Table 16-1

CANADIAN BALANCE-OF-PAYMENTS ACCOUNTS, 1983 (billions of dollars)

Current Account			
1) Merchandise exports	+91.3		
2) Merchandise imports	−73.3		
3) Balance of merchandise trade		+18.0	
4) Service exports			
(Foreign travel in Canada, Canadian interest and dividend receipts from abroad)		+16.9	
5) Service imports			
(Canadian travel abroad, foreign interest and dividend receipts from Canada)		−34.2	
6) Net transfer payments		+0.9	
7) Balance on current account			+1.6
Capital Account			
8) Net direct foreign investment in Canada		−1.6	
9) Net long-term portfolio investment in Canada		+4.4	
10) Net short-term investment in Canada		+2.7	
11) Balance on capital account			+5.5
Summary			
12) Errors and omissions			−6.6
13) Balance of payments			
(Change in official foreign-exchange reserves)			−0.5

SOURCE: Bank of Canada *Review*

Where Has All the Money Gone?

Canada is not the only country that cannot balance its international books. As the following news report indicates, "statistical discrepancies" are causing problems all over the world—and the problem is getting worse.

WASHINGTON, July 29—Somewhere, in ships on the high seas, in the mails, in secret bank deposits, in some countries' ill-kept accounts and in a multitude of other places, about $100 billion a year is disappearing from the books of the world economy.

The figure represents the disparity in the sums of all countries' payments to each other for all the business they conduct across their borders—everything from sales of automobiles and airline tickets to the dividends a company in one country pays to stockholders in another.

A payment made in one country should show up as a receipt for an equal amount on the other country's books. And at the end of the year, the final accounting of all countries' payments on one side, and receipts on the other, should be equal, even though some individual countries have deficits and some have surpluses.

But lately, the figures have not come close.

"The world balance of payments doesn't add up," said Henry C. Wallich, a governor of the Federal Reserve Board and an expert on international commerce. "This question irritates a lot of people who can't answer it."

The country showing the largest shortfall is the United States.

According to economists for the international lending agency, the discrepancy is growing fastest in the category called "other services." These include construction and other contractual work that rapidly developing nations—recently, members of the Organization of Petroleum Exporting Countries—purchase from foreign companies and individuals. Payments go to some individuals "who have fiscal incentives for under-reporting or routing payments via tax havens," the I.M.F. reported in a seven-page appendix on the subject in last month's 1983 outlook.

Many other transactions bypass the world's bookkeepers entirely. When a ship that flies a flag of convenience picks up a cargo, one country makes note of payment of the shipping fees, but none records receipt of the payment.

C. Fred Bergsten, head of the Institute for International Economics, a research centre here, suspects that many travel transactions are inadequately reported as spendthrift American tourists, for example, travel across Europe.

"It's very important, because if everybody thinks he has a deficit and nobody thinks he has a surplus, then somebody thinks his problem is worse than it is," Mr. Bergsten said. "Right now, there's no one on the surplus side except Japan to take balancing action."

SOURCE: Peter T. Kilborn, "Global Trade Mystery: A Vanishing $100 Billion," *The New York Times*, July 30, 1983.

Canada would have had an overall balance-of-payments surplus in 1983. That is, official exchange reserves would increase as foreign exchange flowed into Canada. However, there is one other line in the table—line 12, errors and omissions. This entry shows that during 1983, $6.6 billion flowed out of Canada in unidentified forms.

While part of this huge discrepancy simply comes from errors in data collection and computation, the lion's share reflects the Canadian government's inability to monitor all the flows of money, goods, and services across its borders. (See the accompanying boxed insert.)

As a result, the official balance of payments shows a small deficit of $0.5 billion, so our foreign-exchange reserves decreased by this amount in 1983.

A Bit of History: The Gold Standard

About the only time exchange rates were truly fixed was under the old **gold standard**, at least when it was practised in its ideal form.[1]

Under the gold standard, fixed exchange rates were maintained by an automatic equilibrating mechanism that went something like this: All currencies were defined in terms of gold; indeed, some were actually made of gold. When a nation had a deficit in its balance of payments, this meant, essentially, that more gold was flowing *out* than was flowing *in*. Since the domestic money supply was based on gold, losing gold to foreigners meant that the quantity of money automatically fell. Thus, "monetary policy" *automatically* turned restrictive, and interest rates rose, attracting foreign capital. At the same time, the restrictive monetary policy pulled down national output and prices, thus discouraging imports and encouraging exports. The balance-of-payments problem quickly rectified itself. This means, however, that:

Under the gold standard, no nation had control of its domestic monetary policy, and therefore no country could control its domestic economy very well.

At least in principle, the effects on surplus countries were perfectly symmetrical under the gold standard. A balance-of-payments surplus led, via gold inflows, to an increase in the domestic money supply whether the surplus country liked the idea or not. This raised prices (which decreased exports) and raised real GNP (which increased imports). And it also lowered interest rates, thereby encouraging outflows of capital. Because of these automatic adjustments, nations rarely reached the point at which devaluations or revaluations were necessary. Exchange rates were fixed as long as countries abided by the rules of the gold-standard game.

In addition to the complete loss of control over domestic monetary conditions, the gold standard posed one other serious difficulty.

A fundamental problem with the gold standard was that the world's commerce was at the mercy of gold discoveries.

Discoveries of gold meant higher prices in the long run and higher real economic activity in the short run, through the standard monetary-policy mechanisms that we studied in Chapters 12–14. And when the supply of gold did not keep pace with growth of the world economy, prices had to fall in the long run and employment had to fall in the short run.

An examination of the periods containing the world's great gold discoveries during the last several centuries provides a direct test of our understanding of these arrangements. These periods are precisely the times when there were major world inflations, just as our analysis suggests.

The Bretton Woods System and the International Monetary Fund

The gold standard, which had faltered many times before, finally collapsed amid the financial chaos of the Great Depression of the 1930s. Without it, the world struggled through nearly 15 years of almost complete breakdown in international trade.

Then, as World War II drew to a close, with much of Europe in ruins and with the United States holding the lion's share of the free world's reserves, officials of

---

[1] As a matter of fact, while the gold standard lasted (on and off) for hundreds of years, it was rarely practised in its ideal form. Except for a brief period of fixed exchange rates in the late nineteenth and early twentieth centuries, there were periodic adjustments of exchange rates even under the gold standard.

the industrial nations met at Bretton Woods, New Hampshire, in 1944 to try to establish a stable monetary environment that would facilitate world trade. And since the U.S. dollar was the only "strong" currency at that time, it was natural for them to turn to the dollar as the basis of the new international economic order.

That is just what they did. The Bretton Woods agreements re-established a system of fixed exchange rates based not on the old gold standard but on the free convertibility of the U.S. dollar into gold. The United States agreed to buy or sell gold to maintain the $35 per ounce price that had been established by President Franklin Roosevelt in 1933. And the other signatory nations, which had almost no gold in any case, agreed to buy and sell U.S. dollars to maintain their exchange rates at agreed-upon levels. Thus all currencies were indirectly on a modified "gold standard." A holder of French francs, for example, could exchange these for U.S. dollars at (roughly) 5 francs per dollar and then exchange these into gold at $35 per ounce. In this way, the value of the franc was fixed at 175 francs per ounce of gold (5 francs per dollar times 35 dollars per ounce). The new system was dubbed the **gold-exchange system**, and often referred to as the **Bretton Woods system**.

The **International Monetary Fund (IMF)** was set up to police and manage this new system. Using funds that had been contributed by member countries, the IMF was empowered to make loans to countries that were running low on reserves. Only in the case of a "fundamental disequilibrium" in a nation's balance of payments was a change in exchange rates to be permitted. For it was believed that only relatively fixed exchange rates could provide the stable climate needed to restore world trade.

Of course, the Bretton Woods conferees did not define clearly what a "fundamental disequilibrium" was, nor could they have. As the system evolved, it came to mean a chronic deficit in the balance of payments of sizable proportions. Such nations would then *devalue* relative to the U.S. dollar; that is, they would reduce the value of their currencies in terms of U.S. dollars. So the system was not really one of fixed exchange rates but rather one where rates were "fixed until further notice."

Several flaws in the Bretton Woods system were evident in our discussion of the pure system of fixed exchange rates in Chapter 13 (pages 251–54). First, since devaluations were permitted only after a long run of balance-of-payments deficits, these devaluations (a) could be clearly foreseen, and (b) normally had to be quite large. Speculators then saw opportunities for profit and would "attack" weak currencies with a wave of selling.

This problem led many economists to question whether the system of fixed exchange rates was really providing the stable climate for world trade that had been intended. Was a system where rates were constant for long periods and then altered by very large amounts really more conducive to international trade than one where overvalued currencies would gradually depreciate, as they would under a system of floating rates?

The second problem arose from the custom that deficit nations were expected to devalue when forced to, while surplus nations (mainly Germany and Japan) could resist upward revaluations. Since the U.S. dollar defined the monetary value of gold (at $35 per ounce), the United States was the one nation in the world that had no way to devalue its currency relative to gold, no matter how "fundamental" the disequilibrium became. The only way exchange rates between the U.S. dollar and foreign currencies could change was if the surplus nations revalued their currencies upward relative to the U.S. dollar. They did not do this frequently enough, so the United States, with its chronically overvalued currency, ran persistent balance-of-payments deficits.

This represented an adjustment problem for the system as a whole, but it was a benefit for the United States. Whenever other countries had large balance-of-payments deficits, they had to do something about it before they ran out of foreign-exchange reserves. But the United States could not run out of "foreign exchange," since they could simply print more. It certainly was convenient for the United States. They could import more than they exported and could buy up ownership in companies operating in other countries, and all they had to give in return were U.S. dollars, which they could print at essentially no cost.

Adjustment Mechanisms Under the Bretton Woods System

Under the Bretton Woods system, devaluation was viewed as a last resort, to be used only after other methods of adjusting to payments imbalances had failed. What were these other methods?

We have already encountered most of them in our discussion of exchange-rate determination in free markets (see Chapter 13, pages 260–61). Any factor that increases the demand for, say, British pounds or that reduces the supply will push the exchange rate upward if it is free to adjust. If, however, the exchange rate is pegged, it is the balance-of-payments deficit rather than the exchange rate that will adjust when supply of or demand for a nation's money changes. Specifically, the British balance-of-payments deficit will shrink if either the demand for pounds increases or the supply decreases.

The two panels of Figure 16–2 illustrate this adjustment. In each case, the United Kingdom has a payments deficit, since the official exchange rate ($3.00) exceeds the equilibrium rate ($2.60). The deficit starts at AB in each diagram. Then either the demand curve moves outward as in part (a), or the supply curve moves inward as in part (b). With the exchange rate held at $3.00, the balance-of-payments deficit shrinks—to CB in part (a) or AC in part (b).

Referring back to our earlier discussions of the factors that underlie the demand and supply curves, then, we see that one way a deficit nation can improve its balance of payments is to *reduce its aggregate demand*, thus discouraging imports and cutting down its demand for foreign currency. Another is to *slow its*

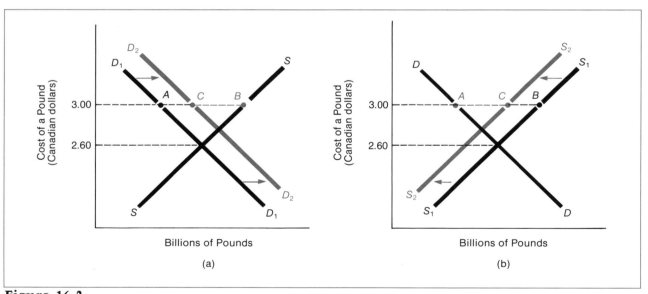

Figure 16-2
ADJUSTING TO BALANCE-OF-PAYMENTS DEFICITS

The two parts of this diagram illustrate alternative ways to cut Britain's balance-of-payments deficit while maintaining the exchange rate at $3.00 per pound. Part (a) might represent a reduction in British inflation, which would increase world demand for her export products. Or it could represent a rise in British interest rates, which would attract foreign capital. Part (b) might represent a reduction in British incomes, which would diminish English appetites for foreign goods. In either case, whether demand rises or supply falls, the balance-of-payments deficit is reduced: from AB to CB in part (a) and from AB to AC in part (b).

rate of inflation, thus encouraging exports and discouraging imports. Finally, it can *raise its interest rates* in order to attract more foreign capital.

In a word, deficit nations were expected to follow restrictive monetary and fiscal policies *voluntarily* just as they would *automatically* have done under the old gold standard. However, just as under the gold standard, this medicine was often unpalatable, so deficit nations frequently resorted to a bewildering variety of **exchange controls**—laws and regulations that made it very difficult for its nationals to sell their own currency to get foreign exchange. Many countries still have such controls.

Surplus nations could, of course, have taken the opposite measures: pursuing expansive monetary and fiscal policies to increase economic growth and lower interest rates. But they often did not relish the inflation that would come with such actions, and, once again, left the burden of adjustment to the deficit nations. The general point about fixed exchange rates is that:

Under a system of fixed exchange rates, the government of a country loses some control over its domestic economy. There may be times when balance-of-payments considerations force it to contract its economy in order to cut down its demand for foreign currency, even though domestic needs are calling for expansion. Conversely, there may be times when the domestic economy needs to be reined in, but balance-of-payments considerations suggest expansion.

The system worked fairly well for a number of years, but it finally broke down over its inability to "devalue" the U.S. dollar with respect to the other world currencies. During the mid-1960s, the size of the U.S. balance-of-payments deficit grew tremendously. This was primarily due to their large expenditures on the Vietnam war and on domestic social programs, and on the fact that the stock of U.S. dollars in foreign hands had reached a level that was many times larger than the U.S. government's holdings of gold. The demand for U.S. dollars fell, and the demand for gold rose, as many speculators anticipated that the United States would effectively increase their reserves of gold by raising the official price above $35 per ounce. But the larger U.S. balance-of-payments deficits meant that the *world money supply was growing very rapidly*. So the late 1960s was just like one of the earlier periods of large gold discoveries, and just like in those periods, a world inflation ensued. Since the other nations had no way of stopping the overly expansive U.S. monetary policy, the only way they could control their own inflation rate was to cut the link with the U.S. dollar. Many countries floated their exchange rate, as Canada did in 1970. The Bretton Woods system ended when the monetary policy of the base-currency country, the United States, became irresponsible in the eyes of the other countries.

In August 1971, President Nixon formally abolished the Bretton Woods system by announcing that the United States would no longer peg the value of the dollar by buying and selling gold. Actually, the system had already ended.

Most observers today agree that the gold-exchange system could not have survived the incredible events of the 1970s in any case. The worldwide inflationary boom of 1972, the poor food harvests in 1972–74, the huge increases in the price of oil in 1973–74 and again in 1979–80, and the great worldwide recession of 1974–76 all helped create a world in which the major countries were experiencing dramatically different inflation rates.

For example, between 1972 and 1982 inflation averaged 5 percent per year in Germany, 9 percent in the United States, and 16 percent in Italy. As the purchasing-power theory reminds us, large differences in inflation rates call for *major* changes in currency values. And the Bretton Woods system was ill-suited to handle such major changes.

Exchange controls are laws restricting the exchange of one nation's currency for another's.

Why Try to Fix Exchange Rates?

"Then it's agreed. Until the dollar firms up, we let the clamshell float."
Drawing by Ed Fisher
© 1971, The New Yorker Magazine, Inc.

In view of these and other severe problems with the Bretton Woods system, why did the international financial community work so hard to maintain fixed rates for so many years? The answer is that floating exchange rates, determined in free markets by supply and demand, also pose problems.

Chief among these is the possibility that freely floating rates might be highly variable rates, which add an unwanted element of riskiness to foreign trade. For example, if the exchange rate is 16 cents to the French franc, then a 2000-franc Parisian dress will cost $320. But should the franc appreciate to 20 cents, this same dress would cost $400. A Canadian department store thinking of buying this dress may need to place its order far in advance and will want to know the cost *in dollars*. It may be worried about the possibility that the value of the franc will rise, so that the dress will cost more than $320. And such worries might inhibit trade.

There are two answers to this worry. First, we could hope that freely floating rates would prove not to be very volatile. Prices of many domestic consumer goods, for example, are determined by supply and demand in free markets and yet do not fluctuate unduly. Second, speculators might relieve business firms of exchange-rate risks—for a fee, of course. Consider the department store example. If French francs cost 16 cents today, the department store manager can assure herself of paying exactly $320 for the dress several months from now by arranging for a speculator to deliver francs to her at 16 cents on the day she needs them. If the franc appreciates in the interim, it is the speculator, not the department store, that will take the financial beating. (And, of course, if the franc depreciates, the speculator will pocket the profits.)

This role of speculation is described more fully in our discussion of the stock market in Chapter 24. The widespread fears that speculative activity in free markets will lead to wild gyrations in prices, while occasionally valid, are more often unfounded. The reason is quite simple. International currency speculators, if they are to make profits, must buy a currency when its value is low (thus helping to support the currency by pushing up its demand curve) and sell it when its value is high (thus holding down the price by adding to the supply curve).

This means that, if they are successful, speculators will be coming into the market as *buyers* just when demand is weak (or when supply is strong), and coming in as *sellers* just when demand is strong (or supply is scant). In doing so, they will help limit price fluctuations. Looked at the other way around, speculators can destabilize prices only if they are systematically willing to lose money.

Notice the stark contrast to the system of fixed exchange rates in which speculation often led to wild "runs" on currencies that were on the verge of devaluation. Speculative activity, which may very well be destabilizing under fixed rates, is likely to be stabilizing under floating rates.

We do not mean to imply here that there are no difficulties at all under floating exchange rates. Indeed, it may prove impossible to eliminate all exchange-rate risks through speculation. And at the very least, speculators will demand a fee for their services—a fee that adds to the costs of trading across national borders. We only suggest that life is liable to be more placid than is commonly supposed.

The experience under floating rates since 1973 has delivered clear verdicts on these two issues. First, exchange rates have in fact proven to be quite volatile—more volatile than many of the advocates of floating rates anticipated. Second, however, international trade has flourished despite this volatility. Speculators, we may surmise, are doing their job.

The Current Mixed System

Our current international financial system—where some currencies are still pegged in the old Bretton Woods manner, others are floating freely, and many more are floating subject to government interferences—has evolved gradually since 1971. Though it continues to change and adapt, at least three features are quite evident.

The first is the decline in the notion that exchange rates should be fixed for relatively long periods of time. The demand by many countries in the early 1970s that the world quickly return to fixed exchange rates had largely subsided by the mid-1970s. Even where rates are still pegged to the U.S. dollar, devaluations and revaluations are now much more frequent—and smaller—than they were in the 1944–71 period. Most free-world currency rates change very slightly on a day-to-day basis, and market forces generally determine the basic trends, up or down.

Second, however, some central banks do not hesitate to intervene to moderate exchange movements whenever they feel that such actions are appropriate. Typically, these interventions are aimed at ironing out transitory fluctuations. But there have been instances in which central banks have, for a time, opposed basic trends in exchange rates. Deficit nations have bought their own currencies to prevent them from depreciating. Surplus nations have sold their own currencies to prevent them from appreciating. While we certainly no longer have many fixed exchange rates, many of the major currencies are floating less than freely. The terms "dirty float" or "managed float" have been coined to describe this mongrel system.

Figure 16–3 illustrates these tendencies in Canada. The decade of the 1960s was rather tranquil. Despite Canada's maintaining a fixed exchange rate from 1962 to 1969, our balance-of-payments surpluses and deficits were small. In the 1970s and 1980s, there were quite dramatic changes in the exchange rate *and* much larger balance-of-payments surpluses and deficits. The balance-of-payments data show that the Bank of Canada limited the fluctuations in the exchange rate. The

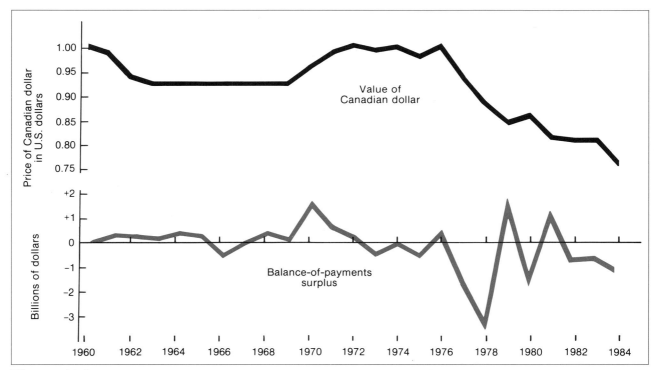

Figure 16–3
CANADA'S BALANCE OF PAYMENTS AND THE VALUE OF THE CANADIAN DOLLAR
This graph shows that the Bank of Canada has resisted movements in the exchange rate. The balance-of-payments surpluses in the early 1970s indicate that the Bank was accumulating foreign-exchange reserves (that is, selling Canadian dollars) to limit the rise in the Canadian dollar that took place. Also, balance-of-payments deficits occurred in 1976–78 and 1982–84, since the Bank was buying up Canadian dollars to limit the fall in our currency's value that was taking place.

surpluses in the early 1970s prove that the Bank of Canada was accumulating foreign-exchange reserves (that is, selling Canadian dollars) to limit the rise in the value of the Canadian dollar that did take place. Similarly, the deficits during 1976–78 and 1982–84 prove that the Bank of Canada was selling off foreign-exchange reserves (that is, buying Canadian dollars) to limit the fall in the value of the Canadian dollar.

Incidentally, most analysts attribute the rise in the Canadian dollar in the 1969–70 period to the temporarily higher interest rates, and the lower inflation rate in Canada (compared to the United States). Similarly, the fall in the Canadian dollar in the later 1970s and the 1980s is due to the higher inflation rate in Canada, and our attempt to maintain interest rates lower than the United States.

The third unmistakable feature of the present international monetary system is the virtual elimination of any role for gold. The trend away from gold actually began before President Nixon's dramatic announcement in 1971, and by now it is only a minor exaggeration that gold plays no role in the world's financial system.

Nowadays there is a *free market* in gold, which enables those who wish to invest in gold—dentists, jewelers, industrial users, speculators, and ordinary citizens who think of gold as a good store of value—to buy or sell as they wish. The price of gold, determined each day by the law of supply and demand, has proved to be quite volatile. Fortunes have been made and lost by investors in gold.

Developments in International Financial Markets Since 1973

Oil Prices and "Petrodollars"

The system of "dirty floating" is generally dated from early 1973. It received its first test in late 1973 and early 1974, when the Organization of Petroleum Exporting Countries (OPEC) quadrupled the price of oil. This naturally led to huge surpluses in the current accounts of the OPEC nations: Their combined surplus in 1974, for example, was a colossal $70 billion (U.S.). Because the sum of the current-account balances of all nations must necessarily be zero (since the country's exports are another's imports), this meant that the rest of the world had a combined deficit of $70 billion. And since this $70 billion (U.S.) total deficit was distributed quite unevenly across the nations of the world, it is hard to imagine how fixed exchange could have been maintained.

In particular, with OPEC earning so much more foreign currency than it was spending, it had to find places to invest its unspent revenues. Since OPEC invested mainly in New York, Zurich, and other financial centres, a problem arose that journalists dubbed "recycling petrodollars." Specifically, while the advanced industrial nations were paying more for oil, they were also receiving capital inflows from OPEC. So they found their balance-of-payments problems manageable. But the less developed countries (LDCs) had no such luck. They needed more foreign exchange to pay OPEC for oil but did not receive any through capital inflows.

The problem, then, was clear: How could OPEC's savings be channelled to the LDCs that needed the funds? At first, the IMF took the lead in this "recycling" effort. But soon the job was taken over by the big international banks, especially American banks, which received funds from OPEC and made loans to less developed countries. The short-term problem was solved, but a long-term problem was created: How were the less developed countries ever going to repay the loans?

The LDC Debt Problem*

Before anyone had an answer, OPEC struck again. The price of oil more than doubled during 1979, and the combined current-account surplus of the OPEC

---

*For more on this problem, see Chapter 40, especially page 804.

nations (the rest of the world's deficit) skyrocketted to $111 billion (U.S.) in 1980. As in 1974, the currencies of the developed countries withstood the shock fairly well; they once again financed their oil deficits through capital inflows. And the non-oil-developing nations again turned to borrowing on the private market; but the debts were getting unmanageably large.

Then two further problems beset the LDCs. First, the worldwide recession of 1981–83 made it harder for them to earn foreign currency by exporting goods to the industrial countries. Second, real interest rates rose dramatically, making the burden of paying interest on the debt much harder to bear. As a result, the 1980s so far have been marked by a series of near-crises in the international financial system as Mexico, Argentina, Brazil, and other nations have encountered difficulty in meeting their debt obligations.

To date, a series of special arrangements negotiated by governments and banks have kept the system afloat and avoided a panic. But no one is declaring the problem solved. And there is continued concern that major defaults on loans by LDCs could threaten the solvency of some banks in the developed countries.

The European Monetary System

As noted earlier, floating exchange rates are no magical cure-all. One particular problem beset the members of the European Economic Community (EEC). These Common Market countries seek a unified large market like the United States and have a long-range goal of establishing a single currency for all member countries. Floating rates would make this goal impossible. So in 1973 some of the member countries entered into an agreement whereby exchange rates among their currencies could remain relatively *fixed* while Common Market currencies as a group would rise or fall *relative to the rest of the world*.

Within a short time, however, both Britain and Italy found themselves unable to maintain parity with the strong currencies of Germany and the Netherlands. Britain was the first to let the pound float, but soon Italy and France also had to devalue relative to the mark. In 1979 the arrangement was strengthened and formalized in the **European Monetary System (EMS)**, which currently has eight member nations. The EMS includes detailed provisions for coping with exchange rates that threaten to get out of line with the others, and it is widely regarded as the first step, albeit a small one, toward a unified European currency.

Concluding Remark: Summits and Precipices

The past 15 years have been tumultuous ones for the international monetary system. Several crises have been faced and several changes have been made. No doubt, we will have more of both in the coming years.

Since 1975, the leaders of the major industrial nations have held annual summit meetings to discuss international economic problems. Sometimes these discussions are frank and fruitful. Sometimes they are public-relations exercises that paper over disagreements rather than resolve them. But most observers find the summits a useful and productive enterprise in any case. In today's small world, the major economies are too interrelated to ignore the need for international co-operation.

No one can predict with confidence the agendas for summit meetings to come. But it would be surprising indeed if the issues dealt with in this chapter did not arise again and again.

Summary

1. Several factors are important in the determination of exchange rates. In the long run, purchasing-power parity plays a major role in exchange-rate movements. The purchasing-power parity theory states that relative price levels in any two countries determine the exchange rate between their currencies. Therefore, countries with relatively low inflation rates normally will have appreciating currencies.

2. Over shorter periods, the pace of economic activity and the level of interest rates exert a greater influence on the exchange rate.

3. The balance of payments is difficult to measure, since many transactions across borders are difficult to monitor. However, the estimated accounts show that Canada typically has a surplus on merchandise trade, a deficit on the services account (which is due mostly to the interest payments on our foreign debt), and a surplus on the capital account (which is due to the fact that our foreign debt is increasing).

4. In the early part of this century, the world was on a particular system of fixed exchange rates called the gold standard, in which the value of every nation's currency was fixed in terms of gold. But this created problems because nations could not control their own money supplies and because the world could not control its total supply of gold.

5. After World War II, the gold standard was replaced by the gold-exchange (or Bretton Woods) system where rates were again fixed, or rather, fixed until further notice. In this system, the U.S. dollar was the basis of international currency values.

6. The gold-exchange system served the world well and helped restore world trade, but it got into trouble when U.S. monetary policy became overly expansionary, making the U.S. dollar overvalued. The system provided no way to remedy this situation.

7. Since 1971, the world has gradually been moving toward a system of relatively free exchange rates, though there are plenty of exceptions. We now have a thoroughly mixed system of "dirty" or "managed" floating, which continues to evolve and adapt.

8. Canada's managed exchange rate has fallen since 1976, mostly because of our relatively inferior inflation performance, and because we have tried to maintain slightly lower interest rates than those in the United States.

9. Floating rates are not without their problems; importers and exporters justifiably worry about fluctuations in exchange rates. But these problems seem manageable, if not completely solvable, and few people think that a return to fixed exchange rates is likely.

10. Under floating exchange rates, investors who speculate on international currency values provide a valuable service by assuming the risks of those who do not wish to speculate. Normally, speculators stabilize rather than destabilize exchange rates, because that is how they make profits.

Concepts for Review

Purchasing-power parity
Current account
Capital account
Balance of payments
Gold standard

Gold-exchange system (Bretton Woods system)
International Monetary Fund (IMF)
Exchange controls
"Dirty" or "managed" floating

The LDC debt problem
The European Monetary System (EMS)

Questions for Discussion

1. What items do you own, or routinely consume, that are produced abroad? What countries do these come from? How have your purchases affected the exchange rates between the dollar and these currencies?

2. If the Canadian dollar appreciates relative to the Japanese yen, will the Sony stereo you have longed for become more or less expensive? What effect do you imagine this will have on Canadian demands for Sonys? Does the demand curve for yen, therefore, slope upward or downward? Explain.

3. Inflation in West Germany has generally been below that in Canada. What, then, does the purchasing-power parity theory predict should have happened to the exchange rate between the mark and the dollar?

Ask your instructor what actually has happened.

4. Use supply and demand diagrams to analyse the effect on the exchange rate between the Canadian dollar and the British pound if:
   a. Britain's flow of North Sea oil ceases.
   b. British dockworkers refuse to unload ships that arrive with cargo from Canada but continue to load ships that sail from Britain.
   c. Both Britain and Canada slip into recession, but the Canadian recession is far more severe.
   d. Polls suggest that Mrs. Thatcher's government will be replaced by radicals who vow to nationalize all foreign-owned assets.

5. How are the problems of a country faced with a

balance-of-payments deficit similar to those posed by a government regulation that holds the price of milk above the equilibrium level? (*Hint:* Think of each in terms of a supply–demand diagram.)

6. Look at the Canadian balance-of-payments accounts table in the text (Table 16–1 on page 304). Figure out where each of the following actions you could have taken in 1983 would have been recorded in these accounts:
   a. You spent the summer travelling in Europe.
   b. Your uncle in France sent you $50 as a birthday present.
   c. You bought a new Toyota.
   d. You bought stock on the Japanese stock market.
   e. You drove over the American border carrying Canadian records in your truck and sold them to a friend in the United States. (*Hint:* Would your sale have been recorded anywhere?)

7. For each of the transactions listed in Question 6, indicate how it would affect:
   a. The Canadian balance of payments, if exchange rates were fixed.
   b. The international value of the Canadian dollar, if exchange rates were floating.

8. Explain why the members of the Bretton Woods conference in 1944 wanted to establish a system of fixed exchange rates. What was the flaw that led to the ultimate breakdown of the system in 1971?

9. Suppose you want to reserve hotel rooms in Rome for the coming summer but are worried that the value of the lira may rise between now and then, making the rooms too expensive for your budget. Explain how a speculator could relieve you of this worry. (Don't actually try it. Speculators deal only in very large sums!)

10. On page 310, it is pointed out that successful speculators buy a currency when demand is weak and sell it when demand is strong. Use supply and demand diagrams for two different periods (one with weak demand, the other with strong demand) to show why this will limit price fluctuations.

Budget Deficits and the National Debt: Fact and Fiction

17

Blessed are the young, for they shall inherit the national debt.

HERBERT HOOVER

There is a widespread belief that there is something inherently wrong with government budget deficits. Public-opinion polls consistently show that the public wants the budget balanced, and politicians of all parties constantly rail against deficits. Yet the federal budget has shown a deficit in 18 of the last 26 years.

Why is the federal budget so frequently in the red? What kinds of problems do large deficits pose for the economy, both now and in the future? Should we strive to balance the budget? And, if so, by what means? These are the questions to be addressed in this chapter.

We begin by explaining why the principles of stabilization policy that we learned in Part Three do not lead to the conclusion that the budget should always be balanced. (Neither, however, do they lead to the conclusion that it should always be in deficit!) Then we try to get the facts straight. We discuss the size of the national debt, and how it grew so large. Then we turn to the federal budget deficit and why some economists claim that it is badly mismeasured.

With the facts established, we examine the alleged ill effects of deficits. We shall see that many popular arguments against deficits are based on faulty reasoning. But not all are. In particular, we devote special attention to two potentially severe costs of deficit spending: It can be inflationary, and it can "crowd out" private investment spending or export sales.

Should the Budget Be Balanced?

The basic principles of fiscal policy that we discussed in Chapter 11 certainly do not lead to the conclusion that the government should always balance its budget. Instead, they point to the desirability of budget *deficits* when private demand ($C + I + X - IM$) is too weak and budget *surpluses* when private demand is too strong. The budget should be balanced, according to these principles, only when $C + I + G + X - IM$ approximately equals the full employment level of output. This may sometimes occur, but it will not necessarily be the norm.

In brief, according to this approach, the focus of fiscal policy should be on *balancing aggregate supply and aggregate demand*, not on balancing the budget. The reason why a balanced budget may not achieve a balanced economy is clear from our earlier discussion of stabilization policy.

Consider the fiscal policy that would be followed by a government that believed in balanced budgets. If private spending sagged for some reason, the multiplier would pull GNP down. Since personal and corporate tax receipts fall sharply when GNP declines, the budget would inevitably swing into the red. To a true budget-balancer, this would be a signal either to reduce spending or to raise taxes—exactly the opposite of the appropriate policy response.

Thus, budget balancing—as was practised during the early part of the Great Depression—will prolong and deepen recessions.

Budget balancing can also lead to inappropriate fiscal policy when an economic boom begins. If rising tax receipts induce a budget-balancing government to spend more or cut taxes, fiscal policy will accentuate the boom—with inflationary consequences. Fortunately, believers in budget balancing usually are not alarmed by surpluses.

This analysis explains why a balanced budget should not be expected to be the norm. But it does not explain why all of the last nine budgets have shown deficits. Why not, for example, five deficits and four surpluses? That is a good question, but a complicated one. So, before attempting an answer, we should get the facts straight.

Deficits and Debt: Some Terminology

First some critical terminology. The title of this chapter contains two terms that seem similar but mean different things: *budget deficits* and the *national debt*. We must learn to distinguish between the two.

The **budget deficit** is the amount by which the government's expenditures exceed its receipts during some specified period of time, usually one year. For example, during fiscal year 1983–84, the federal government raised about $58.6 billion in taxes but spent almost $90.1 billion, leaving a deficit of almost $31.5 billion.[1]

The **national debt**, also called the public debt, is the total value of the government's indebtedness at a moment in time. Thus, for example, the national debt at the end of fiscal year 1983–84 was $151 billion.

The two concepts—debt and deficit—are closely related because the government accumulates *debt* by running *deficits* or reduces its debt by running surpluses. The relationship between the debt and the deficit can be explained by a simple analogy. As you run water into a bathtub ("run a deficit"), the level of water in the tub ("the debt") rises. Alternatively, if you let water out of the tub ("run a surplus"), the level of the water ("the debt") falls. Analogously, budget deficits raise the national debt while budget surpluses lower it.

Having made this distinction, let us look first at the size and nature of the accumulated public debt, and then at the annual budget deficit.

Some Facts About the National Debt

How large a public debt do we have? How did we get it? Who owns it? Is it really growing rapidly?

To begin with the simplest question, the public debt is enormous. At the end of fiscal 1983–84 it amounted to more than $151 billion, over $6,000 for every man, woman, and child in Canada. When we compare the debt with the gross national product—the volume of goods and services our economy produces in a year—it does not seem so large after all. With a nominal GNP of $390 billion in

The **budget deficit** is the amount by which the government's expenditures exceed its receipts during a specified period of time, usually one year.

The **national debt** is the federal government's total indebtedness, which has resulted from previous deficits.

[1]*Reminder*: The fiscal year of the Canadian government ends on March 31. Thus, fiscal year 1983–84 ran from April 1, 1983, to March 31, 1984.

Table 17-2

INFLATION ACCOUNTING AND THE DEFICIT

YEAR	ACTUAL DEFICIT* (billions of dollars)	INFLATION ADJUSTMENT (billions of dollars)	INFLATION-ADJUSTED DEFICIT (-) OR SURPLUS (+) (billions of dollars)
1980	-9.9	+4.7	-5.2
1981	-7.0	+6.2	-0.8
1982	-20.5	+5.6	-14.9
1983	-24.3	+4.2	-20.1
1984	-26.6	+6.7	-19.9

*Measured on a national-accounts basis. The deficit data reported in Figure 17-3 are on a public-accounts basis, as reported to Parliament on a fiscal-year basis. The deficits reported in this table are defined on a national-accounts basis since the government has calculated its inflation adjustments with deficits measured on a national-accounts basis. The main differences in the two methods are that the national-accounts procedure involves the calendar year, and its revenue items are recorded on the basis of when revenues were earned (not when they were actually paid).

SOURCE: Department of Finance, *The Fiscal Plan* (1984), page 58.

$1100 is treated as repayment of principal, leaving only $22 ($1122 – $1100) to be treated as interest. The correct inflation accounting treatment of the loan is shown in column 3 of Table 17-1.

To recapitulate, the proper economic treatment of a loan in an inflationary environment must recognize that more dollars (in our example, $1100) must be returned to the lender in order to give back the purchasing power of the original loan ($1000). Only the excess of the nominal interest payment ($122) over the compensation for inflation ($100) should be counted as interest.

This example holds the following lesson for interpreting budget-deficit figures:

Inflation distorts the government budget under conventional accounting procedures by exaggerating interest expenses.

The example also suggests how this error can be corrected:

To correct the deficit for inflation, we must subtract the inflation premium from the interest paid on the national debt, thereby counting only *real* interest payments.

This treatment, by the way, corresponds exactly to the way inflation accounting is done by major corporations.

As Table 17-2 shows, making the inflation adjustment to interest payments would have reduced reported deficits by an average of about $5 billion in recent years. Starting in 1982, the federal government began running large deficits even after correction for inflation accounting.

The High-Employment Budget

The second major issue in making sense of the budget deficit is not a problem of measurement, but rather one of interpretation.

As we learned in Chapter 11, the government's taxing and spending decisions affect the level of economic activity. For example, higher spending or lower taxes lead—via the multiplier process—to higher aggregate demand and therefore to a higher GNP. This makes it natural to think that big deficits signify expansionary fiscal policy.

But that view may be incorrect because the state of the economy also affects the budget. In particular, recessions tend to enlarge the budget deficit. The reason is simple. Remember that the deficit is the difference between government expenditures and tax receipts, that is:

$$\text{Deficit} = G + \text{Transfers} - \text{Taxes}.$$

The government's most important sources of tax revenue—income taxes, corporate profit taxes, sales taxes, and payroll taxes—all shrink when GNP falls because firms and people pay less tax when they earn less. Similarly, some government spending, notably transfer payments like unemployment benefits, rise when GNP falls because more people are out of work. Since spending goes up and tax receipts go down as GNP falls:

The deficit rises in a recession (and falls in a boom), even when there is no change in fiscal policy.

The **high-employment budget** is the hypothetical budget we *would have* if the economy were operating near full employment.

Because the deficit changes even when policy does not, the deficit is a poor measure of the government's fiscal policy. For this reason, many economists feel that we should pay less attention to the actual deficit or surplus and more attention to the deficit or surplus in what is called the **high-employment budget**. This is a hypothetical construct that replaces both the spending and taxes in the *actual* budget by estimates of how much the government *would be* spending and receiving, given current tax rates and expenditure rules, if the economy were operating near full employment.

Since it is based on the spending and taxing the government would be doing at full employment, rather than on actual expenditures and receipts, the high-employment budget is not sensitive to the state of the economy. It will change only when policy changes. For this reason, most economists believe it is a better measure of the thrust of fiscal policy than the actual deficit. Using this new concept, we can provide a useful restatement of our previous conclusion about the effect of a recession on the budget deficit:

When unemployment rises, the actual budget deficit grows larger even if the high-employment budget is unchanged.

This simple observation helps us understand the genesis of the large budget deficits of the early 1980s: They were partly attributable to the consistently high unemployment rates that marked this period. Table 17–3 shows just how important

Table 17-3
UNEMPLOYMENT AND THE FEDERAL DEFICIT

YEAR	DEFICIT* (billions of dollars)	ADJUSTMENT TO HIGH EMPLOYMENT† (billions of dollars)	HIGH-EMPLOYMENT DEFICIT (billions of dollars
1980	-9.9	+2.4	-7.5
1981	-7.0	+1.9	-5.1
1982	-20.5	+9.2	-11.3
1983	-24.3	+11.6	-12.7
1984	-26.6	+10.2	-16.4

*Measured on a national-accounts basis.
†Based on a 7 percent unemployment rate.

SOURCE: Department of Finance, *The Fiscal Plan* (1984), pages 54, 56, 58, 63.

the distinction between the actual deficit and the high-employment deficit has been in recent years. For 1982 through 1984, the deficits in the high-employment budget were rather small even though the deficits in the actual budget were quite large. Nevertheless, even the high-employment budget has been deeply in the red.

Other Measurement Issues

There are many other complicated issues in measuring and interpreting the federal budget deficit. We conclude this section by mentioning just three of them.

1. *Junior-level government budget surpluses.* Some analysts argue that it is the combined deficit of all levels of government that matters, not just the federal deficit. In this regard, it is useful to realize that the junior-level governments together have been running surpluses in recent years—averaging $3 billion per year throughout the 1980–84 period. Part of the reason for these surpluses—and for the federal deficit—is that the federal government gives a good deal of money to the provincial governments in the form of grants each year.

2. *Capital expenditures.* A further point is that some federal spending goes to purchase capital of various sorts—government buildings, military equipment, and so on. There is nothing unusual about borrowing to purchase assets. Private businesses and individuals do it all the time. For this reason, many people have suggested that the federal government compile a separate capital budget—which is precisely what municipal governments do.

3. *Off-budget activities.* Another source of ambiguity stems from the lending activities of the so-called "off-budget" agencies. (A familiar example is loans for low-income housing.) In recent years, these agencies have run deficits that are not included in the official budget deficit.

Conclusion: What's New About the Recent Deficits?

Table 17-4 puts our two major adjustments—for inflation accounting and for unemployment—together and compares recent deficits (column 1) with corresponding figures on the high-employment, inflation-corrected deficit (column 4). The difference between the two columns is startling. Only since 1982 has the high-employment, inflation-corrected budget been in substantial deficit. But this does represent a major swing in the federal budget position. Much of the actual deficit is understandable, given the high levels of inflation and recession prevailing in the early 1980s. But these considerations account for only about 66 percent of the 1984 federal deficit. It is because the *corrected* deficit has never been near these levels in peace time that there has been such concern.

Table 17-4
ACTUAL AND ADJUSTED BUDGET DEFICITS

YEAR	(1) ACTUAL DEFICIT* (billions of dollars)	(2) ADJUSTMENT FOR INFLATION (billions of dollars)	(3) ADJUSTMENT TO HIGH EMPLOYMENT (billions of dollars)	(4) ADJUSTED DEFICIT (–) OR SURPLUS (+) (billions of dollars)
1980	-9.9	+4.7	+2.4	-2.8
1981	-7.0	+6.2	+1.9	+1.1
1982	-20.5	+5.6	+9.2	-5.7
1983	-24.3	+4.2	+11.6	-8.5
1984	-26.6	+6.7	+10.2	-9.7

*Measured on a national-accounts basis.

SOURCE: Tables 17-2 and 17-3.

Bogus Arguments About the Burden of the Debt

Having gained some perspective on the facts, let us now turn to some of the arguments advanced by those who claim that by running budget deficits we are placing an intolerable burden on future generations.

Argument 1: Our children and grandchildren will be burdened by heavy interest payments. To meet these payments there will have to be higher taxes.

Answer: It is certainly true that a higher debt will necessitate higher interest payments and, other things being equal, this will lead to higher taxes paid by our children and grandchildren. But think who will receive the higher interest payments as income: our children and grandchildren! Thus one group of future Canadians will, essentially, be making interest payments to another group of future Canadians. While some people will gain and others will lose, the future generation as a whole will come out even. We conclude that:

As long as the national debt is owned by domestic citizens, the future interest payments merely shuffle money from one group of Canadians to another. These transfers may or may not be desirable, but they hardly constitute a burden to the nation as a whole.

However, this argument *is* valid for that portion of our debt that is held by foreigners. To pay the interest on this portion of the debt *will* be a burden on future generations of Canadians.

Argument 2: It will ruin the nation when we have to repay the enormous debt.

Answer: A first answer to this merely rephrases the answer to the previous argument: Only the part owned by foreigners involves any burden; the rest is paid by one group of Canadians to another. But there is a much more fundamental point. *Unlike a private family, the nation need never pay off its debt.* Instead, each time the principal is due, the government can simply "roll it over" by floating more debt. Indeed, this is precisely what the government does.

Is this a bit of chicanery? How can the government get away with making loans that it never intends to pay back? The answer is found by recognizing the fallacy of comparing the government to a family or individual. People cannot be extended credit in perpetuity because they will not live that long. Sensible lenders will not extend long-term credit to very old people because their heirs cannot be forced to pay up. But the Canadian government will never "die"; at least, we hope not! So this factor does not arise. In this respect, the government is in much the same position as a large corporation. General Motors never worries about paying off its debt. It too rolls it over by floating new debt all the time.

Argument 3: It will bankrupt the nation. Like any family or any business firm, a nation has a limited capacity to borrow. If it exceeds this limit, it is in danger of being unable to pay its creditors. It may go bankrupt with calamitous consequences for everyone.

Answer: This is another example of a false analogy. What is claimed about private debtors is certainly true. But the Canadian government need never fear defaulting on its debt. Why? First, because it has enormous power to raise revenues by taxation. If you had such power, you would never have to fear bankruptcy either.

Furthermore, a good part of the Canadian national debt is an obligation to pay *Canadian* dollars: Each debt certificate obligates the government to pay the holder so many Canadian dollars on a prescribed date. But the Canadian government is the source of these dollars; it prints them! *No nation need ever fear defaulting on debts that call for repayment in its own currency.* At the very worst, it can always print whatever money it needs to pay off its creditors.

It does not follow, however, that acquiring debt through budget deficits is therefore always a good idea. Sometimes it is clearly a very bad idea. Printing money to pay the debt will expand aggregate demand and cause inflation, and this often will be undesirable. The point is not that budget deficits are either good or bad—we already know that they can be either under the appropriate circumstances. Rather, the point is that worrying about a possible default on the national debt is quite unnecessary, unless a very significant portion of that debt, or the debts of the nation's households and firms, are obligations to pay *foreign* currencies. A large foreign debt cannot be paid by simply printing more domestic currency. This is a problem for a number of less-developed countries, but Canada's foreign debt is not at such levels.

Having cleared the air of these fallacious arguments, we are now in a position to explore some real problems that may arise when the government spends more than it takes in through taxation.

Budget Deficits and Inflation

One indictment of deficit spending that certainly *does* have validity under most circumstances is the charge that it is inflationary. Why? Because when government policy pushes up aggregate demand, firms may find themselves unwilling or unable to produce the higher quantities that are being demanded at the going prices. Prices will therefore have to rise.

Figure 17-4 is an aggregate-supply-and-demand diagram that shows this analysis graphically. Initially, equilibrium is at point E_0—where demand curve D_0D_0 and supply curve SS intersect. Output is \$400 billion, and the price index is at 100. The diagram indicates that the economy is operating below full employment; there is a recessionary gap. If the government does nothing to reduce the resulting unemployment, we know from Chapter 10 that this recessionary gap will linger for a long time. The economy will suffer through a prolonged period of unemployment.

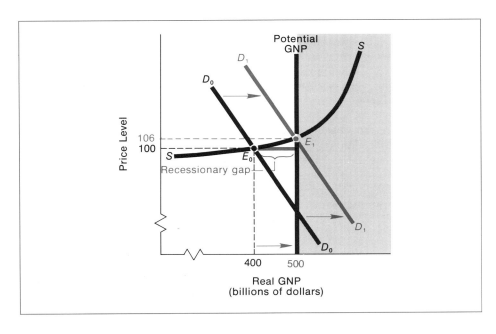

Figure 17-4
THE INFLATIONARY EFFECTS OF DEFICIT SPENDING
In this diagram, expansionary fiscal policy pushes the aggregate-demand curve out from D_0D_0 to D_1D_1, causing equilibrium to move from E_0 (where there is unemployment) to E_1 (where there is full employment). But because aggregate-supply curve SS slopes upward, the price level is pushed up from 100 to 106; that is, there is a 6 percent inflation.

Figure 17-5

FISCAL EXPANSION AND
INTEREST RATES

If expansionary fiscal policy
pushes real GNP and the price
level higher, the demand curve for
money will shift outward from
M_0D_0 to M_1D_1. Equilibrium in the
money market shifts from point A
to point B, so interest rates rise.

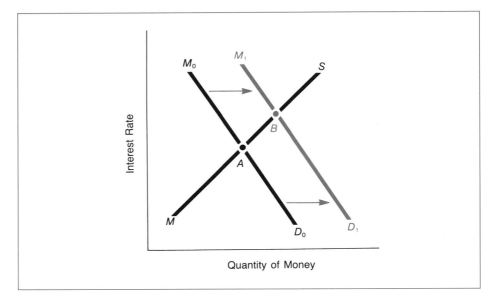

Rather than permit such a long recession, we know that the government can raise its spending or cut its taxes enough to shift the aggregate-demand schedule upward from D_0D_0 to D_1D_1. Such a policy can wipe out the recessionary gap and the associated unemployment—but not without an inflationary cost. The diagram shows that the new equilibrium price level is at 106—6 percent higher than before the government acted.

Thus the cries that budget deficits are "inflationary" have the ring of truth. How much truth, of course, depends on the slope of the aggregate-supply curve. Deficit spending will not cause much inflation if the economy has lots of slack and the aggregate-supply curve consequently is flat. But deficit spending will be highly inflationary in a fully employed economy with a steep aggregate-supply curve.

The Monetization Issue

Some people worry about the inflationary consequences of deficits for a rather different reason. They fear that the Bank of Canada may have to "monetize" part of the deficit, by which they mean that the Bank may feel compelled to purchase some of the newly issued government debt. Let us explain, first, why the Bank might make such purchases, and second, why these purchases are called **monetizing the deficit**.

The central bank is said to **monetize the deficit** when it purchases the bonds that the government issues.

Deficit spending, we have just noted, normally drives up both real GNP and the price level. As we have emphasized before, such an economic expansion shifts the demand curve for money outward to the right—as depicted in Figure 17-5. The figure shows that, if the Bank of Canada takes no actions to shift the money supply curve, interest rates will rise.

Suppose now that the Bank does not want interest rates to rise. What can it do? To prevent the incipient rise in r, it must engage in expansionary monetary policies that shift the supply curve for money outward to the right—as indicated in Figure 17-6. And, as noted in Chapter 13, expansionary monetary policies normally take the form of open-market purchases of government bonds. For this reason, deficit spending sometimes induces the Bank of Canada to increase its purchases of government bonds, that is, to buy up some of the newly issued debt.

Even if the Bank of Canada makes no explicit response to the pressure for higher interest rates, the reaction of foreign bond-holders forces the same result.

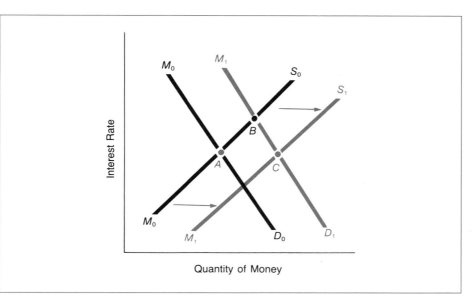

Figure 17-6

MONETIZATION AND
INTEREST RATES

If the Bank of Canada does not
want a fiscal expansion to raise
interest rates, it must increase the
money supply. In this diagram, the
fiscal expansion shifts the demand
curve for money from M_0D_0 to
M_1D_1, precisely as it did in Figure
17-5. To keep the rate of interest
constant, the Bank of Canada will
have to shift the money-supply
curve outward from M_0S_0 to M_1S_1.
Points A and C correspond to the
same rate of interest.

As foreigners move to acquire the relatively high-yield Canadian bonds, they must enter the foreign-exchange market to get the required amount of Canadian dollars to buy the bonds. This puts upward pressure on the value of the Canadian dollar. The Bank of Canada frequently resists any significant appreciation of the Canadian dollar, to avoid a potential squeeze on the profits of Canadian exporters. This requires intervention in the foreign-exchange market, to make available the additional Canadian dollars demanded by the foreign investors. Thus, the pursuit of maximum interest yields by foreign bond-holders keeps Canadian interest rates from rising significantly, and a fixed exchange-rate policy by the Bank of Canada means that the domestic money supply must increase following newly issued government debt.

Why is this process called *monetizing* the deficit? The reason is simple. As we learned in Chapter 13, open-market purchases of bonds by the central bank give the chartered banks more reserves, which leads, eventually, to an increase in the money supply. This is also shown in Figure 17-6: The outward shift of the money-supply schedule from M_0S_0 to M_1S_1 leads to an increase in the money supply. By this indirect route, then, larger budget deficits may lead to an expansion of the money supply. To summarize:

If the Bank of Canada takes no countervailing actions, an expansionary fiscal policy that raises the budget deficit will raise real GNP and prices, thereby shifting the demand curve for money outward and putting upward pressure on interest rates. If the Bank does not want either interest rates or the exchange rate to rise, it can engage in expansionary open-market operations, that is, purchase more government debt. If the Bank of Canada does this, the money supply will increase. In this case, we say that part of the deficit is *monetized*.

Monetized deficits are more inflationary than non-monetized deficits for the simple reason that expansionary monetary and fiscal policies together are more inflationary than expansionary fiscal policy alone. Figure 17-7 illustrates this conclusion. The aggregate-supply curve and aggregate-demand curves D_0D_0 and D_1D_1 are carried over without change from Figure 17-4. The shift from D_0D_0 to D_1D_1 represents the effect of expansionary fiscal policy (raising the budget deficit). If, in addition, the central bank monetizes part of the deficit, the aggregate-demand

Figure 17-7

MONETIZED DEFICIT
SPENDING

Expansionary fiscal policies that
raise the budget deficit push the
aggregate-demand curve outward
from D_0D_0 to D_1D_1. If the Bank of
Canada monetizes some of the
deficit, then expansionary
monetary policy pushes the
aggregate-demand curve out even
further—to D_2D_2. Monetized
deficits (point C) are therefore
more inflationary than deficits that
are not monetized (point B).

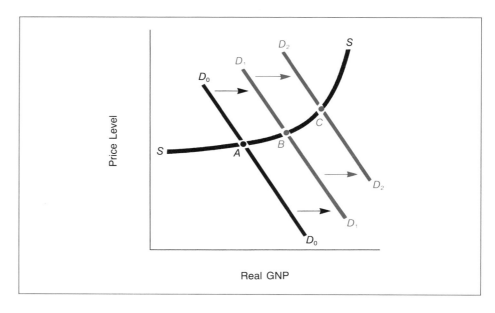

curve will shift out still further—perhaps to the position indicated by D_2D_2. Thus, the price level will rise even more (compare points B and C).

Many economists and business leaders have been concerned about monetization in the 1980s. The reason is simple arithmetic. When budget deficits are extremely large, even a small percentage of monetization can lead to a substantial increase in bank reserves and the money supply.

Deficits, Interest Rates, and Crowding Out

So far we have been looking for possible burdens of the national debt on the *demand* side of the economy. But a serious burden also comes on the *supply* side because large budget deficits discourage investment and therefore retard the growth of our nation's capital stock. The mechanism is easy to understand.

We have just seen that budget deficits create pressure for higher interest rates unless the Bank of Canada engages in substantial monetization. But the rate of interest (r) is a major determinant of investment spending (I). In particular, higher r leads to lower I. And if we do less spending on I today, we will have a smaller capital stock tomorrow. This, according to most economists, is the true sense in which a large national debt may put a burden on future generations:

Because of the large national debt, we may bequeath less physical capital to future generations. If they inherit less plant and equipment, these generations will be burdened by a lower productive capacity—a lower potential GNP.

There is another way of looking at this problem—a way that explains why it is often called the **crowding-out effect**. Consider what happens in financial markets when the government engages in deficit spending. When it spends more than it takes in through tax revenues, the government must borrow the balance from private citizens. It does this by issuing bonds, and these bonds compete with corporate bonds and other financial instruments for the available supply of funds. When some private savers are persuaded to buy government bonds, there must be a decline in the funds remaining to invest in private bonds. Thus some private borrowers will get "crowded out" of the financial markets as the government claims an increasing share of the economy's total pool of saving.

Crowding out occurs
when deficit spending by the
government forces private
investment spending or
exports to contract.

Some critics of deficits who have taken this lesson to its illogical extreme argue that each $1 of deficit spending by government crowds out exactly $1 of private spending, so that expansionary fiscal policy has no net effect on total demand. In their view, when G rises, I falls by the same amount, so that $C + I + G + X - IM$ is unchanged.

Other analysts feel that as long as a severe recession exists, firms will not be borrowing to expand anyway. According to this view, crowding out becomes a real issue only if the deficit remains large after the economy improves.

Some analysts challenge the relevance of the crowding-out problem even when the economy is recovering. They argue that the notion of "room in the bond market" for both government and private borrowing makes limited sense for Canada. We always have the option of foreign borrowing, so the relevant bond market is very big relative to all Canadian participants. With the option of foreign borrowing, there should be little increase in interest rates following deficit finance, so there should be little crowding out of investment.

We must remember, however, that foreign borrowing involves foreign exchange entering the country. This foreign exchange must be converted to domestic currency to finance the increased domestic expenditures. If the exchange rate is flexible, it is the international value of the Canadian dollar that gets bid up, not the domestic rate of interest. But an appreciating Canadian dollar makes our exports more expensive to foreigners, so there is still a crowding out effect— exports are crowded out by the increase in government spending. Investment spending by these exporting firms also diminishes, without an increase in interest rates.

Exchange-rate crowding out can be avoided if the Bank of Canada fixes the exchange rate. Thus, we can summarize as follows:

Both interest-rate and exchange-rate reasons for crowding out can be avoided, but only by monetizing the deficit and/or by allowing the foreign-owned portion of the national debt to rise. Either option yields a burden: either inflation or large interest payment obligations to foreigners in the future.

The True Burden of the National Debt

With this analysis of crowding out, we are in a position to understand why budget deficits might, or might not, impose a burden on future generations: When government budget deficits take place in a high-employment economy, the crowding-out effect becomes important, so the deficits will exact a burden by leaving a smaller capital stock to future generations. However, deficits in a slack economy may well lead to more investment rather than less since economic activity is stimulated. In this case, the debt may be a blessing rather than a burden.

Which case applies to the Canadian national debt? To answer this, let us go back to the historical facts and recall how we have accumulated such a large debt. The first cause was the financing of World War II. This debt was contracted in a fully employed economy, and thus undoubtedly constituted a burden in the formal sense. It left future generations with less capital because some of our nation's resources were diverted from private investment into government production. The bombs, ships, and planes that it financed were used up in the war, not bequeathed as capital to future generations.

Yet what were the alternatives? We could have tried to finance the entire war by taxation, and thus placed the burden on consumption rather than on investment. But that would truly have been ruinous, and probably even impossible, given the colossal wartime expenditures. Or we could have printed money, but that would have unleashed an inflation that nobody wanted. Or we could have just done much less government spending and would therefore have contributed less toward winning the war. So, in retrospect, the generations alive today and in the future may not feel unduly burdened by the decisions of the people in power in the 1940s.

The second major contributor to the national debt has been a series of recessions. But these are precisely the circumstances under which increasing the debt might prove to be a blessing rather than a burden. So, if we look for the classic type of deficits to which the valid burden-of-the-debt argument applies—deficits acquired in a fully employed peacetime economy—we do not find many in the Canadian record *until after 1973*.

It is in this context that current budget deficits are a sharp departure from the past. Our examination of the inflation and high-employment adjustments showed that large deficits would exist today even if the Canadian economy had "full" employment and no inflation. This is not something that has happened before, at least on an on-going basis, and it poses a real threat of severe crowding out and a serious potential burden on future generations.

The Burden of the National Debt

Let us now summarize our evaluation of the burden of the national debt and thereby clarify one of the **12 Ideas for Beyond the Final Exam** introduced in Chapter 1. First, the arguments that a large national debt may lead the nation into bankruptcy, or unduly burden future generations who have to make onerous payments of interest and principal, are mostly bogus. They are important arguments only if the country is significantly in debt to foreigners. Second, the national debt *will* be a burden if it is contracted in a fully employed peacetime economy, because in that case it will reduce the nation's capital stock. Third, there are circumstances in which budget deficits are quite appropriate for stabilization reasons. Fourth, and finally, before 1973 the actual public debt of the Canadian federal government was mostly contracted as a result of the war and recessions—precisely the circumstances under which the valid burden-of-the-debt argument does not apply. However, the large deficits since 1973 are worrisome from this point of view.

Conclusion: What Should Be Done About the Deficit?

It is a matter of simple arithmetic that you close a budget deficit by raising taxes and/or reducing spending. Either of these routes is a contractionary fiscal policy, and will retard the growth of the real GNP. Given this fact of life, should we try to close the deficit? The correct answer would be "No," if the inflation-adjusted, high-employment deficit were zero. But even after these adjustments, the federal government deficit exists and is large, so some closing of the deficit is called for. Thus, one of the very real costs of the deficit is that it constrains the government's ability to undertake any job-creation policies.

Is there any way around the problem that moves to close the deficit are contractionary? The government has tried to lessen this problem by waiting until significant economic recovery before attempting to close the deficit. Another answer to this problem is that fiscal and monetary policies could be better co-ordinated. If fiscal policy must turn contractionary to reduce the deficit, monetary policy can turn expansionary to counteract the effects on aggregate demand. In this way, we can hope to shrink the deficit without shrinking the economy in the process. Such a change in the policy "mix" would put downward pressure on interest rates, since both tighter budgets and easier money tend to push interest rates down.

The problem with this policy mix is that it would lead to a depreciation in the foreign value of the Canadian dollar. Pressure for lower interest rates in Canada leads to foreign investors' selling off Canadian bonds in favour of higher yields elsewhere. A depreciated Canadian dollar *stimulates* aggregate *demand* (through higher net export sales), but it *contracts* aggregate *supply* (by raising business costs). Despite this unfavourable supply-side effect, quite a few economists, including those at the Economic Council of Canada, have advocated a shift in the policy mix toward tighter budgets and easier monetary policy. However, the history of the 1980s so far has given us precisely the opposite combination: loose fiscal policy and tight money. If this continues, deficits will persist and will become increasingly burdensome.

Summary

1. Rigid adherence to budget balancing would make the economy less stable by reducing aggregate demand (via tax increases and reductions in *G*) when private spending is low, and raising aggregate demand when private spending is high.

2. The national debt has grown dramatically since the early 1970s. Before then it grew only because of recessions and World War II.

3. Inflation makes the deficit look bigger than it really is because all nominal interest payments are counted as expenditures. Under inflation accounting, only real interest payments would count as expenditures, and the corrected deficit is seen to be much smaller than it appears.

4. Part of the reason for large budget deficits in recent years is the fact that the economy has operated well below full employment. The high-employment deficit, which uses estimates of what the government's receipts and outlays would be at full employment, has been much smaller than the official deficit.

5. If we correct the official deficit for inflation and adjust it to high levels of employment, we find that large deficits in the high-employment, inflation-corrected budget began only in 1982.

6. Arguments that the public debt will burden future generations, who will have to make huge payments of interest and principal, are based on false analogies. In fact, most of these payments are simply transfers from some Canadians to other Canadians. However, some of the debt is foreign-owned, and the associated interest obligations *do* represent a burden in the future.

7. Under normal circumstances, budget deficits are somewhat inflationary. They are even more inflationary if they are "monetized," that is, if the Bank of Canada buys some of the newly issued government debt in the open market to keep interest rates from rising or to fix the exchange rate.

8. Unless the deficit is substantially monetized, deficit spending forces interest rates higher and discourages private investment spending. This is called the crowding-out effect. If there is a great deal of crowding out, then deficits really do impose a burden on future generations by leaving them a smaller capital stock to work with.

9. Even if foreigners purchase most of the newly issued Canadian debt, so that interest rates do not rise, the increased foreign demand for Canadian dollars results in an appreciation of the Canadian dollar so that export demand is crowded out.

10. Crowding out may not be very important when unemployment is high. Indeed, higher output levels may induce firms to raise investment spending. But when the economy is near full employment, the proponents of the crowding-out hypothesis are probably right: High government spending just displaces private investment and exports.

11. Whether or not deficits are a burden depends on how and why the government ran these deficits in the first place. If deficits are contracted to fight recessions, it is possible that more investment is actually stimulated. Deficits contracted to carry on wars certainly impair the future capital stock, though they may not be considered a burden for non-economic reasons. Since these two cases account for most of Canada's national debt that was incurred before 1973, this debt cannot reasonably be considered a serious burden. However, a noticeable part of the debt incurred since 1973 does represent an overly expansionary fiscal policy.

12. Since the size of the deficit depends on the state of the economy, and since the state of the economy is affected by the deficit, simple correlations between the deficit and other economic variables cannot be used to deduce causation.

Concepts for Review

Budget deficit	Inflation accounting	Interest-rate crowding out
National debt	High-employment budget	Exchange-rate crowding out
Real versus nominal interest rates	Monetization of deficits	Burden of the national debt

Questions for Discussion

1. Explain the difference between the budget deficit and the national debt. If we reduce the deficit, will the debt stop growing?
2. Explain how the Canadian government has managed to accumulate a debt of more than $150 billion. To whom does it owe this debt? Can this debt be considered a burden on future generations?
3. Comment on the following: "Deficit spending paves the road to ruination. If we keep it up, the whole nation will go bankrupt. Even if things do not go this far, what right have we to burden our children and grandchildren with these debts while we live high on the hog?"
4. Calculate the budget deficit and the inflation-corrected deficit for an economy with the following data:
   Government expenditures other than interest = $80
   Tax receipts = $85
   Interest payments = $60
   Interest rate = 12 percent
   Inflation rate = 10 percent
   National debt at start of year = $500.
   (*Note*: 12 percent interest on a $500 debt is $60.)
5. Explain why the high-employment budget might show a surplus while the actual budget is in deficit.
6. If the Bank of Canada begins to increase the money supply more rapidly than before, what will happen to the government budget deficit? (*Hint*: What will happen to tax receipts and interest expenses?) If the government wants to offset the effects of the Bank's actions on aggregate demand, what might it do? How will this affect the deficit?
7. Given the current state of the economy, do you think the Bank of Canada should monetize a sizeable proportion of the deficit? (*Note*: There is no one correct answer to this question. It is a good question to discuss in class.)
8. Explain both interest-rate and exchange-rate mechanisms for crowding out. Given the current state of the economy, do you think crowding out is an issue?
9. Evaluate each of the following statements. (*Note*: The facts in each case are correct; concentrate on the conclusion that is reached.)
   a. "In 1978, we had a small deficit and strong GNP growth. In 1982, we had a huge deficit and a recession. Therefore, deficit spending does not stimulate the economy."
   b. "If we compare 1981 with 1983, we find a much larger deficit but much lower inflation in 1983. Therefore, it is clear that deficit spending is not inflationary."

The Trade-Off Between Inflation and Unemployment

All progress is precarious, and the solution of one problem brings us face to face with another problem.

MARTIN LUTHER KING

Between 1980 and 1983 the rate of inflation, as measured by the deflator for GNP, declined from just over 11 percent to just under 6 percent, reversing a worrisome trend toward higher inflation rates. At the same time, the economy suffered a severe recession and the unemployment rate climbed ominously, from 7.5 percent in 1980 to 11.9 percent in 1983.

Most economists believe that this conjunction of events was no coincidence. Rather, they insist, the period of high unemployment was the price we paid to reduce the rate of inflation. Although some optimists claim that it is possible to reduce inflation without suffering from unemployment, the Canadian economy clearly paid a heavy price for the disinflation of the early 1980s. Was this price inevitable, or could we have avoided it? That is the question for this chapter.

You may recall from Chapter 1 that the existence of an agonizing trade-off between inflation and unemployment is one of the **12 Ideas for Beyond the Final Exam**. The importance of this trade-off can hardly be overestimated. It is probably the one area of macroeconomics where confusion is most widespread. And because this confusion can have disastrous consequences for the conduct of stabilization policy, the trade-off merits the comprehensive examination that we give it in this chapter. Without a thorough understanding of the dimensions of this trade-off, it is impossible for a citizen to make an informed judgment about macroeconomic policy.

Demand-Side Inflation Versus Supply-Side Inflation: A Review

Let us begin our investigation of the trade-off by reviewing some of what we have learned about inflation in earlier chapters.

One major cause of inflation, though not the only one, is *excessive growth of aggregate demand*. What happens if, for some reason, consumers, investors, the government, or foreigners decide to increase spending? We know, first of all, that such an autonomous increase in spending will have a multiplier effect on aggregate

Figure 18-1

INFLATION FROM THE
DEMAND SIDE

An increase in aggregate demand,
whether it comes from consumers,
investors, the government, or
foreigners, shifts the aggregate-
demand curve outward from D_0D_0
to D_1D_1. The economy's
equilibrium moves from point A to
point B. Since point B corresponds
to a higher price level than does
point A, there is *inflation* (that is, a
rising price level) as the economy
moves from A to B.

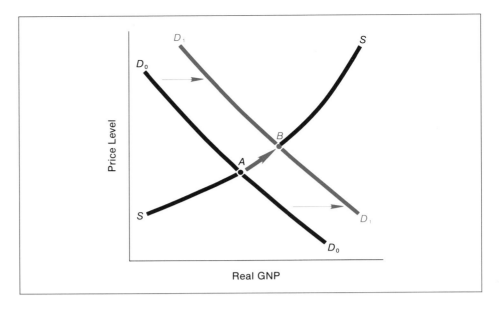

demand; that is, each additional $1 of C, I, G, or $X - IM$ will lead to perhaps $2 of
additional demand, assuming we are on a fixed exchange rate. Second, we know
that such a stimulus to aggregate demand will normally pull up *both* real output
and prices. The reason, to review our earlier findings, is that firms normally will
find it profitable to supply the additional output only at higher prices.

Figure 18-1, which is familiar from earlier chapters, displays this conclusion.
Initially, the economy is at point A, where aggregate-demand curve D_0D_0 intersects
aggregate-supply curve SS. Then something happens to increase demand, and the
aggregate-demand curve shifts horizontally to D_1D_1. The new equilibrium is at
point B, where both prices and output are higher than they were at A.

The slope of the aggregate-supply curve measures the amount of inflation that
accompanies any specified rise in output and therefore embodies the most
important aspects of the trade-off between unemployment and inflation. We
concluded in Chapter 14 that this trade-off will be favourable when the economy
is operating at low levels of capacity utilization and high levels of unemployment.
Under such circumstances, firms can expand their operations substantially
without running into higher costs. On the other hand, if demand stimulus occurs
in a fully employed economy, firms will find it quite difficult to raise output and
so will respond mostly by raising prices. Thus, the trade-off is very unfavourable
when unemployment is low.

But we have learned in this book (especially in Chapter 10) that inflation need
not always emanate from the demand side. Restrictions in the growth of aggregate
supply—caused, for example, by an increase in the price of foreign oil—can shift
the economy's aggregate-supply curve inward (or upward). This is illustrated in
Figure 18-2, where the aggregate-supply curve shifts from S_0S_0 to S_1S_1, and the
economy's equilibrium consequently moves from point A to point B. Prices rise as
output falls; we have *stagflation*. Thus, while inflation can be initiated from either
the demand side or the supply side of the economy, there is a crucial difference.
Demand-side inflation is normally accompanied by rising real GNP (see Figure
18-1), while supply-side inflation may well be accompanied by falling GNP (see
Figure 18-2). This is an important distinction, as we shall see in this chapter.

Applying the Model to a Growing Economy

You may have noticed that our simple model of aggregate supply and aggregate
demand determines an equilibrium *price level* and an equilibrium *level of real*

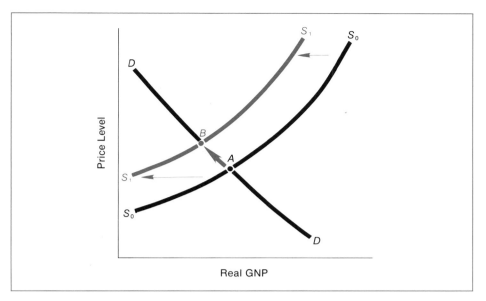

Figure 18-2
INFLATION FROM THE SUPPLY SIDE
A decrease in aggregate supply—which can·be caused by such factors as an autonomous increase in wages, or by an increase in the price of foreign oil—can cause inflation. When the aggregate-supply curve shifts to the left, from S_0S_0 to S_1S_1, the equilibrium point moves from A to B. Comparing B with A, we see that the price level is higher, which means there must have been *inflation* (rising prices) in the interim. Notice also that adverse supply shifts make real output decline while prices are rising; that is, they produce *stagflation*.

GNP. But in the real economy, we do not see an unchanged price level and an unchanged level of real GNP for long periods of time. Instead, the price level and the level of real GNP change every year.

This is illustrated in Figure 18-3, which is a scatter diagram of the Canadian price level and the level of GNP for every year from 1960 to 1983. The points are labelled for your convenience, and it is quite clear that the general march of the economy through time is upward and to the right—toward higher prices and higher levels of output.

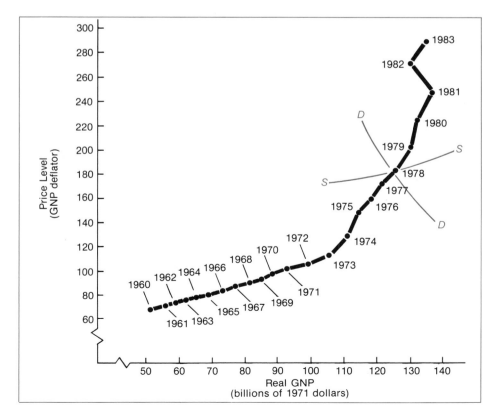

Figure 18-3
THE PRICE LEVEL AND REAL OUTPUT IN CANADA, 1960-1983
This scatter diagram shows, for each year from 1960 to 1983, the price level (GNP deflator) and real GNP for Canada. Clearly the normal state of affairs is for both variables to rise from one year to the next.
SOURCE: Statistics Canada

Figure 18-4

AGGREGATE SUPPLY AND
DEMAND ANALYSIS OF A
GROWING ECONOMY
This diagram illustrates how the
aggregate supply and demand
analysis of earlier chapters can be
applied to a real-world economy,
in which both the supply curve and
the demand curve normally shift
outward from one year to the next.
In this example, demand curve
D_0D_0 and supply curve S_0S_0
represent the Canadian economy
in late 1982. Equilibrium was at
point A, with a price level of 274
and real GNP of $130 billion.
Demand curve D_1D_1 and supply
curve S_1S_1 represent the end of
1983. During the year, the price
index rose by 16 points (about 6
percent) and output increased by
$4 billion (about 3 percent).

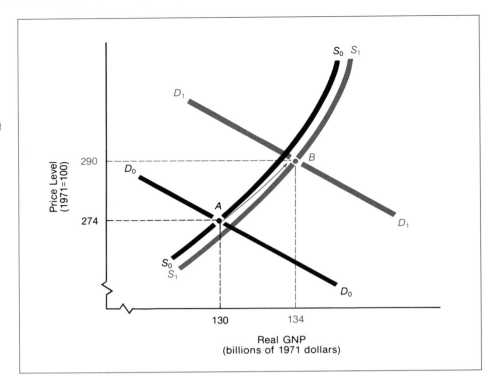

It is certainly no mystery why this occurs. The economy's aggregate-supply and aggregate-demand curves change each year. Aggregate supply normally grows because there are more workers, more machinery, and more factories each year, and because technology is improving. Aggregate demand normally grows because, with a growing population, there is more demand for both consumer and investment goods by both domestic and foreign residents, and because the government increases its spending and the Bank of Canada increases the money supply. We can think of each point in Figure 18–3 as the intersection of an aggregate-supply curve and an aggregate-demand curve for that particular year. To help you visualize this, the curves for 1978 are sketched in the diagram.

One thing is clear from this diagram: If we want to apply our theoretical model to the real world, we must recognize that the normal state of affairs is for *both* the aggregate-demand curve *and* the aggregate-supply curve to shift to the right each year. As a consequence, we expect to find both the price level and real GNP rising from year to year.

Figure 18–4 illustrates this idea. The numbers are chosen so that curves D_0D_0 and S_0S_0 approximately represent the end of 1982, and the curves D_1D_1 and S_1S_1 approximately represent the end of 1983. Thus the equilibrium late in 1982 was at point A, with real GNP of $130 billion (in 1971 dollars) and a price level of 274, while the equilibrium one year later was at point B, with real GNP at $134 billion and the price level at 290. The blue arrow in the diagram shows how equilibrium moved during 1983. It points upward and to the right, meaning that both prices and output increased.

Demand-Side Inflation and the Phillips Curve

Let us now use our theoretical model to rerun history. Suppose that during 1983 the aggregate-demand curve grew either faster or slower than it actually did. What difference would this have made for the performance of the national economy?

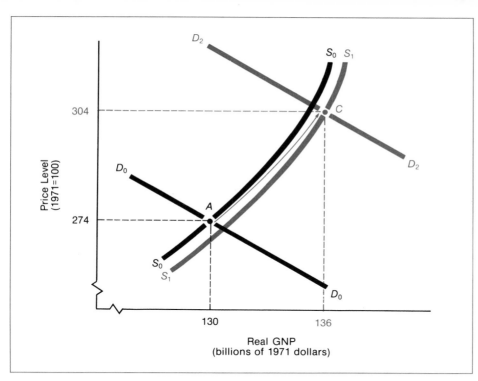

Figure 18-5
THE EFFECTS OF FASTER
GROWTH OF AGGREGATE
DEMAND
In this hypothetical example, we
imagine that, because either
private citizens spent more or the
government pursued more
expansionary policies, aggregate
demand grew faster between late
1982 and late 1983 than it did in
Figure 18-4. The consequence is
that in this diagram the price level
rises 30 points (about 11 percent)
during 1983, compared with the 16
points (6 percent) in Figure 18-4.
Growth of real output is also
greater. $6 billion here and only $4
billion in the previous figure.

The next two figures are intended to provide the answers.

In Figure 18-5 we imagine that aggregate demand grew even *faster* during 1983 than it actually did. Thus, the demand curve D_0D_0 and both supply curves are exactly as they were in the previous diagram, but the demand curve D_2D_2 in Figure 18-5 is farther to the right than the demand curve D_1D_1 in Figure 18-4. Equilibrium is at point A late in 1982 and point C late in 1983. Comparing point C in Figure 18-5 with point B in Figure 18-4, we see that output would have increased more during 1983 ($6 billion versus $4 billion) and prices would also have increased more (to 304 instead of 290); that is, there would have been more inflation. This is generally what happens when the growth rate of aggregate demand speeds up.

For any given rate of growth of the aggregate-supply curve, a faster rate of growth of the aggregate-demand curve will lead to more inflation and faster growth of real output.

Figure 18-6 illustrates the opposite case. Here we imagine that the aggregate-demand curve shifted outward *less* than in Figure 18-4. That is, demand curve D_3D_3 in Figure 18-6 is to the left of demand curve D_1D_1 in Figure 18-4. The consequence, we see, is that the shift of the economy's equilibrium during 1983 (from point A to point E) would have entailed *less inflation* and *slower growth of real output* than actually took place. This again is generally the case.

For any given rate of growth of the aggregate-supply curve, a slower rate of growth of the aggregate-demand curve will lead to less inflation and slower growth of real output.

If we put these two findings together, we have a very clear prediction from our theory:

If fluctuations in the economy's real growth rate from year to year are caused

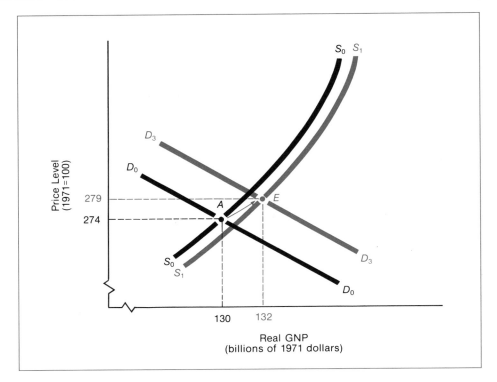

Figure 18-6

THE EFFECTS OF SLOWER GROWTH OF AGGREGATE DEMAND

Here, the aggregate-demand curve is assumed to shift outward less than it did in Figure 18-4. Consequently, the movement from equilibrium point A to equilibrium point E during 1983 entails a smaller rise in the price level and a smaller increase in real output than actually occurred.

primarily by variations in the rate at which the aggregate-demand curve shifts outward, then the data should show that the most rapid inflation occurs during years when output expands most rapidly, and the slowest inflation occurs when output expands more slowly.

Does the theory fit the facts? We will put it to the test in a moment, but first let us translate it into a prediction about the relationship between inflation and unemployment. Faster growth of real output naturally means faster growth in the number of jobs and, hence, *lower unemployment*. Conversely, slower growth of real output means slower growth in the number of jobs and, hence, *higher unemployment*. Thus, the unemployment rate and the growth rate of output should be inversely related—the faster the economy grows the lower the unemployment rate, and the slower the economy grows the higher the unemployment rate.

Figure 18-7 illustrates this idea. The actual unemployment rate in Canada in 1983 was about 12 percent, and the inflation rate during the year was about 6 percent. This is point *b* in Figure 18-7, which corresponds to equilibrium point *B* in Figure 18-4. The faster growth rate of demand depicted by point *C* in Figure 18-5 would have led to higher inflation and lower unemployment. For the sake of a concrete example, we suppose that unemployment would have been 10 percent and inflation would have been 11 percent; this is point *c* in Figure 18-7. Point *E* in Figure 18-6 summarized the results of slower growth of aggregate demand: Unemployment would have been higher and inflation lower. In Figure 18-7, this is represented by point *e*, with an unemployment rate of 15 percent and an inflation rate of 2 percent. This figure shows quite graphically the principal empirical implication of our theoretical model:

If fluctuations in economic activity are primarily caused by variations in the rate at which the aggregate-demand curve shifts outward from year to year, then the data should show that low unemployment rates are associated with high inflation rates and high unemployment rates are associated with low inflation rates.

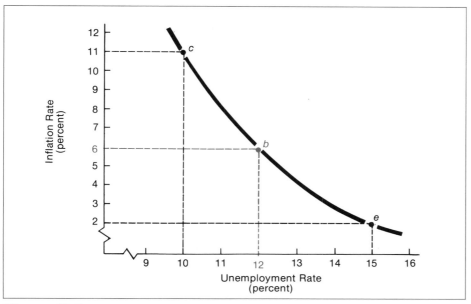

Figure 18-7

ORIGINS OF THE PHILLIPS CURVE

The three previous diagrams indicated three different rates of growth of real GNP between late 1982 and late 1983 and three different inflation rates. Since each different real growth rate corresponds to a different rate of unemployment, we can put the information contained in the three preceding diagrams together in a scatter diagram to show the relationship between inflation and unemployment. Points *b*, *c*, and *e* in this figure correspond to points *B*, *C*, and *E* in Figures 18-4, 18-5, and 18-6, respectively. The inflation numbers are read directly from the previous three graphs. The unemployment numbers are fabricated to represent the fact that faster growth (Figure 18-5) is associated with lower unemployment (point *c*) while slower growth (Figure 18-6) is associated with higher unemployment (point *e*). Scatter diagrams like this one are called "Phillips curves," after their inventor, A. W. Phillips.

Now we are ready to look at real data. Do we actually observe such an inverse relationship between inflation and unemployment? About 27 years ago, economist A. W. Phillips plotted data on unemployment and the rate of change of *wages* (not prices) for several extended periods of British history on a series of scatter diagrams, one of which is reproduced as Figure 18-8. He then sketched in a curve that seemed to "fit" the data. This type of curve, which is now called a **Phillips curve**, shows that wage inflation normally is high when unemployment is low and is low when unemployment is high. So far, so good.

Phillips curves have also been constructed for *price* inflation, and one of these for Canada in the 1950s and 1960s is shown in Figure 18-9. The curve appears to fit the data fairly well, although there are two exceptions, 1953 and 1955. As viewed through the eyes of our theory, these facts suggest that economic fluctuations in England between 1861 and 1913 and in Canada between 1952 and 1969 probably were accounted for primarily by changes in the growth of aggregate demand; that is, by changes in the spending habits of consumers, investors, foreigners, and the government. The simple model of demand-side inflation really does seem to describe what happened.

During the 1960s and early 1970s, economists often thought of the Phillips curve as a "menu" of the choices available to policy-makers. In this view, policy-makers could opt for low unemployment and high inflation—as was done in 1967. Or they might prefer higher unemployment coupled with lower inflation—as, for example, in 1961. The Phillips curve, it was thought, described the *quantitative* trade-off between inflation and unemployment. And, for a number of years, it worked rather well.

Then something happened. The economy in the 1970s behaved far worse than

A **Phillips curve** is a graph depicting the rate of unemployment on the horizontal axis and either the rate of inflation or the rate of change of money wages on the vertical axis. Phillips curves are normally downward sloping, indicating that higher inflation rates are associated with lower unemployment rates.

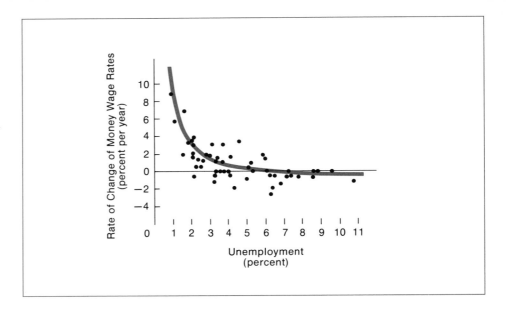

Figure 18-8

THE ORIGINAL PHILLIPS CURVE

This scatter diagram, reproduced from the original article by A. W. Phillips, shows the rate of change of money wages and the rate of unemployment in the United Kingdom between 1861 and 1913. Each year is represented by a point in the diagram.

SOURCE: A. W. Phillips, "The Relationship Between Unemployment and the Rate of Change of Money Wages in the United Kingdom, 1861-1957." *Economica*, New Series, vol. 25, November 1958.

expected in terms of the Phillips curve shown in Figure 18-9. In particular, given the unemployment rates in each of those years, inflation was astonishingly high by historical standards. This is shown in Figure 18-10, which simply adds to Figure 18-9 the points for 1970-83. Clearly something had gone wrong with the old view of the Phillips curve as a menu for policy choices. As a result, a new view of the Phillips curve has emerged. We will discuss this "new view" next, and then return to the implications of the Phillips curve for the conduct of economic policy.

What the Phillips Curve Is Not

One view of what went wrong in the 1970s holds that policy-makers misinterpreted the Phillips curve and tried to pick combinations of inflation and unemployment that were not in fact on the menu. Specifically, the Phillips curve is a *statistical relationship* between inflation and unemployment that we expect to emerge *if*

Figure 18-9

A PHILLIPS CURVE FOR CANADA

This Phillips curve relates price inflation (using the GNP price deflator rather than wage inflation) to the unemployment rate in Canada for the years 1952-69. Though it misses badly in two instances (1953 and 1955), it generally "fits" the data fairly well.

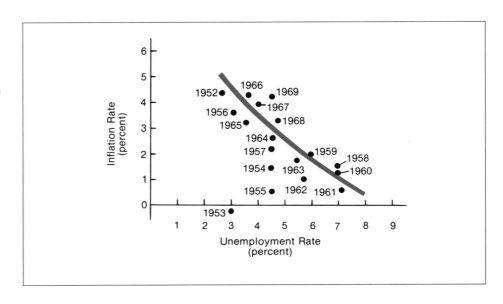

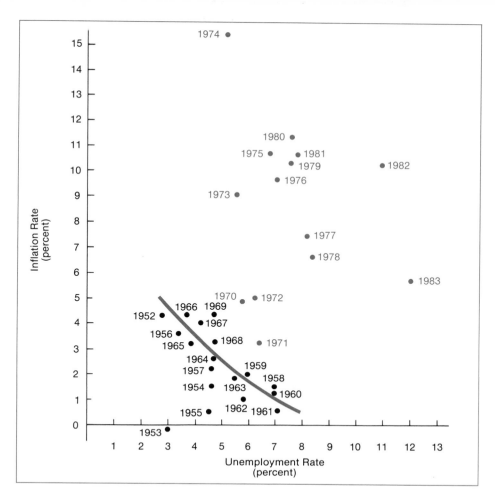

Figure 18-10
A PHILLIPS CURVE FOR
CANADA?
This scatter diagram adds the
points for 1970–83 to the scatter
diagram shown in Figure 18–9. It is
clear that inflation in each of those
years was much higher than the
Phillips curve would have led us to
predict.

*changes in the growth of aggregate demand are the predominant factor accounting
for economic fluctuations.* But the curve was widely misinterpreted as depicting a
number of *alternative equilibrium points* that the economy could achieve and
from which policy-makers could choose.

We can understand the flaw in this reasoning by quickly reviewing an earlier
lesson. We know from Chapter 10 that the economy has a **self-correcting
mechanism** that will cure both inflations and recessions *eventually* even if the
government does nothing. Why is this relevant here? Because it tells us that many
combinations of output and prices cannot be maintained indefinitely. Some will
"self-destruct." Specifically, if the economy finds itself far away from the normal
"full-employment" level of unemployment, forces will be set in motion that tend
to erode the inflationary or recessionary gap.

For example, consider the case of a recessionary gap where aggregate-supply
curve S_0S_0 intersects aggregate-demand curve DD as in Figure 18–11. With
equilibrium output well below potential GNP at point A, there is unused industrial
capacity and unsold output. So firms will not raise prices very much. At the same
time, the availability of unemployed workers eager for jobs limits the rate at
which labour can push up wage rates. But wages are the main component of
business costs, so when wages decline (relative to what they would have been
without a recession) so do costs. And lower costs stimulate greater production.
This idea is depicted in Figure 18–11 as an outward shift of the aggregate-supply
curve—from S_0S_0 to S_1S_1.

Figure 18-11

THE ELIMINATION OF A
RECESSIONARY GAP
When the aggregate-supply curve
is S_0S_0 and the aggregate-demand
curve is DD, the economy will
reach an equilibrium with a
recessionary gap (point A). The
resulting deflation of wages will
cause the aggregate-supply curve
to shift outward (downward) from
S_0S_0 to S_1S_1 and eventually to
S_2S_2. Here, with equilibrium at
point C, the recessionary gap is
gone and the economy is back at
"full employment."

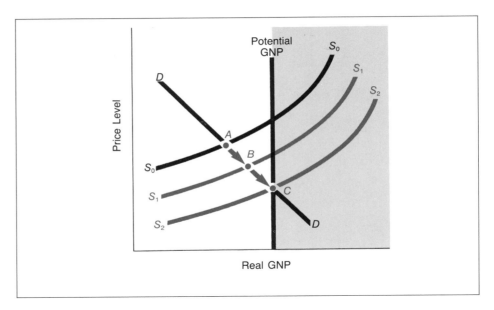

As can be seen in the figure, the outward shift of the aggregate-supply curve
brought on by the recession causes equilibrium output to rise as the economy
moves from point A to point B. Thus the recessionary gap begins to shrink. This
process continues until the aggregate-supply curve reaches the position indicated
by S_2S_2 in Figure 18-11. Here wages have fallen enough to eliminate the
recessionary gap, and the economy has reached a full-employment equilibrium at
point C.[1]

So far this is all review. Now let us relate it to our discussion of the origins of
the Phillips curve. Figure 18-12, which is a hypothetical Phillips curve, will help
us do this.

Point a in Figure 18-12 corresponds to point A in Figure 18-11: It shows the
initial recessionary gap with unemployment (at 9 percent) above full employment,
which we assume to occur at 7 percent. But we have just seen that point A in
Figure 18-11—and therefore also point a in Figure 18-12—is not sustainable. The
economy tends to rid itself of the recessionary gap through the process of
disinflation that we have just described. The adjustment path from A to C that we
analysed in Figure 18-11 would appear on our Phillips curve diagram as a
movement toward less inflation and less unemployment—something like the blue
arrow from point a to point c in Figure 18-12.

Similarly, points representing inflationary gaps—such as point d in Figure
18-12—are not sustainable. They are also gradually eliminated by the self-
correcting mechanism that we studied in Chapter 10. To review briefly, wages are
forced up by the abnormally low unemployment, and this in turn pushes prices
higher. Higher prices deter export spending by foreigners, and they reduce
investment spending by forcing up interest rates. And they also deter consumer
spending by lowering the purchasing power of consumer wealth. The inflationary
process continues until the amount people want to spend is brought into balance
with the amount firms want to supply at normal full employment. During such an
adjustment period, unemployment and inflation are both rising—as indicated by
the blue path from point d to point f in Figure 18-12.

[1]This simple analysis assumes that the aggregate-demand curve does not move during the
adjustment period. If it is shifting to the right, the recessionary gap will disappear even faster, but
inflation will not slow down as much. *Exercise*: Construct the diagram for this case by adding a
shift in the aggregate-demand curve to Figure 18-11.

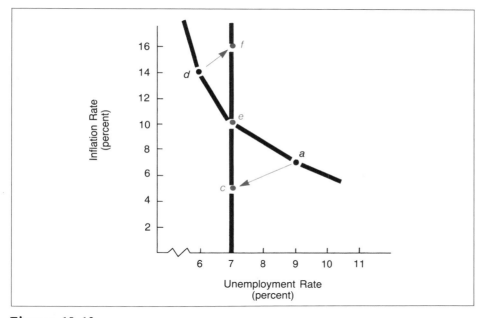

Figure 18-12

THE VERTICAL LONG-RUN PHILLIPS CURVE

In the long run, points like *a*, where unemployment is above the normal "full-employment" unemployment rate, are unsustainable. The economy's natural self-correcting mechanism (which was described in Figure 18-11) will erode the recessionary gap by reducing both inflation and unemployment. In the diagram, this will force the economy toward a point like *c*. The long-run choices, therefore, are among points like *c* and *f*, which constitute what is called the *vertical (long-run) Phillips curve*, not among points like *d* and *a* on the downward-sloping (short-run) Phillips curve.

Putting these two conclusions together, we see that:

On a Phillips curve diagram, neither points corresponding to an inflationary gap (like *d* in Figure 18–12) nor points corresponding to a recessionary gap (like *a* in Figure 18–12) can be maintained indefinitely. Inflationary gaps lead to rising unemployment and rising inflation. Recessionary gaps lead to falling inflation and falling unemployment. All the points that are sustainable in the long run (such as *c, e,* and *f* in Figure 18–12) correspond to the same rate of unemployment, which is therefore called the **natural rate of unemployment**. The natural rate corresponds to what we have so far been calling the "full-employment" unemployment rate.

> The economy's self-correcting mechanism always tends to push the unemployment rate back toward a specific rate of unemployment that we call the **natural rate of unemployment**.

Now we can see why the Phillips curve connecting points *d, e,* and *a* does not represent a menu of policy choices. While we can move from a point like *e* to a point like *d* by stimulating aggregate demand sufficiently, there is no way that we can *stay* at point *d*. Unemployment cannot be kept this low indefinitely. Instead, policy-makers must choose from among points like *e, f,* and *c*, all of which are vertically above one another at the natural rate of unemployment. For rather obvious reasons, the line connecting these points has been dubbed the **vertical (long-run) Phillips curve**. It is this vertical Phillips curve (connecting points like *e, f,* and *c*) that represents the true long-run "menu" of policy choices.

> The **vertical (long-run) Phillips curve** shows the menu of inflation/ unemployment choices available to society in the long run. It is a vertical straight line at the natural rate of unemployment.

Our conclusions about the Phillips curve can be summarized in three statements:

SUMMARY

1. To the extent that economic fluctuations emanate from the demand side, we expect to find an inverse relationship between unemployment and inflation—a downward-sloping Phillips curve.

2. In the short run, it is possible to "ride up the Phillips curve" toward lower levels of unemployment by stimulating aggregate demand. Conversely, by restricting the growth of demand, it is possible to "ride down the Phillips curve" toward lower rates of inflation (see, for example, point *a* in Figure 18–12). There is, thus, a *trade-off between unemployment and inflation.* Stimulating demand will improve the unemployment picture but worsen inflation; restricting demand will lower inflation but aggravate the unemployment problem.

3. However, there is no such trade-off in the long run. The economy's self-correcting mechanism ensures that unemployment eventually will return to the "natural rate," no matter what happens to aggregate demand. In the long run, faster growth of demand leads only to higher inflation, not to lower unemployment; and slower growth of demand leads only to lower inflation, not to higher unemployment.

Fighting Inflation with Fiscal and Monetary Policy

Let us now apply this analysis to a concrete policy problem, one that has vexed our ministers of finance for years. How should the government's ability to manage aggregate demand through fiscal and monetary policy be used to fight inflation?

We have already spent many chapters discussing how the government's monetary and fiscal policy tools—tax rates, government spending, open-market operations, and so on—can be used to increase or decrease aggregate demand. We have also discussed some of the practical problems that arise in using each of these weapons and some of the issues involved in choosing among them. Rather than repeat all this, let us just suppose that the government somehow controls aggregate demand and wishes to use this ability to fight inflation. What has our discussion of the trade-off between inflation and unemployment taught us about this problem?

To create a somewhat realistic example, let us imagine that a new government takes office when the inflation rate is 10 percent and the unemployment rate is 7 percent—point *e* in Figure 18–12. Suppose the new government adopts a policy of restricting the growth of aggregate demand by contractionary fiscal and monetary policies, thereby opening up a recessionary gap. In a word—though no politician would ever use such blunt language—he decides to fight inflation by causing a recession.

At first, the economy "rides down" the short-run Phillips curve from point *e* to point *a* in Figure 18–12. The recession pushes unemployment up from 7 percent to 9 percent but reduces inflation from 10 percent to 7 percent. Lower inflation has been "bought" by causing higher unemployment. This scenario roughly describes what happened in Canada between 1980 and 1982, except that the recession was much more severe in reality than in the example.

But the anti-inflation dividends of recession do not end there. The economy's self-correcting mechanism begins to work and gradually erodes the recessionary gap. Inflation continues to decline as the economy recovers and unemployment falls. In the example, inflation falls from 7 percent to 5 percent as the economy recovers along the path from *a* to *c* in Figure 18–12. In the actual Canadian case, inflation continued to decline as recovery progressed in 1983, but the economy had still not returned to full employment when this book went to press.

When all the dust has settled, the economy in our hypothetical example has moved from point *e* to point *c* in Figure 18–12. Comparing these two points shows that, in the end, there is less inflation and no more unemployment. In what sense, then, do policy-makers have to face up to a trade-off between inflation and unemployment? The answer is that:

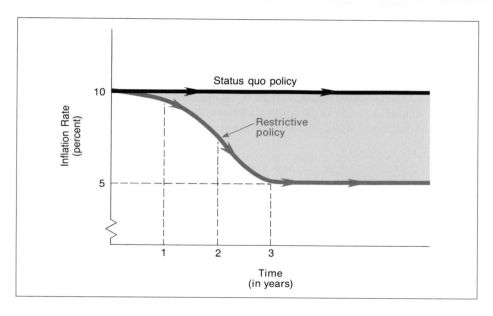

Figure 18-13

THE PAYOFF TO ANTI-INFLATION POLICY
If a recession is caused by restrictive fiscal and monetary policy, the inflation rate will not respond very much at first. Gradually, however, inflation will yield to the slack caused by the restrictive policy. In this example the inflation rate begins at 10 percent, falls only to 9 percent after one year, but is down to 7½ percent after two years, and 5 percent after three years. The shaded area indicates the gains that the policy has reaped on the inflation front.

The cost of reducing inflation by restrictive fiscal and monetary policies is a *temporary* rise in unemployment.

Figures 18-13 and 18-14 are intended to give the flavour of what the real menu of choices looks like to a policy-maker who is considering embarking on such a program. Figure 18-13 contrasts the behaviour of the inflation rate over time under a "status quo policy" (which makes the unemployment rate unchanged at 7 percent) with the behaviour under a restrictive anti-inflationary policy (which deliberately slows the growth rate of aggregate demand and makes unemployment rise).

Inflation will continue at 10 percent per year if the government does not restrain the growth of demand and unemployment remains at 7 percent. This is the status quo policy path shown in black in Figure 18-13. It corresponds to the case where the economy remains indefinitely at point *e* in Figure 18-12.

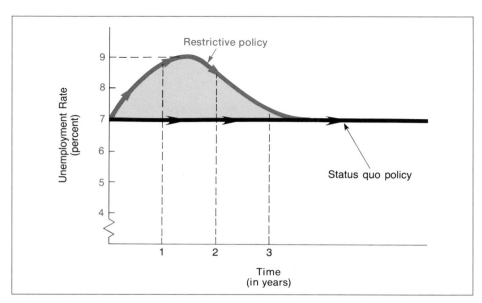

Figure 18-14

THE COST OF ANTI-INFLATION POLICY
The inflation gains depicted in the preceding figure do not come to us without cost. The restrictive policy increases unemployment for a period; that is, it induces a recession. In this example, the unemployment rate takes about a year to rise from 7 percent to 9 percent (the recession period), and then takes over two years to return to 7 percent (the recovery period). The shaded area indicates the extra unemployment that must be endured in order to get the inflation rate down from 10 percent to 5 percent.

On the other hand, if a restrictive policy is followed and the growth of aggregate demand is restrained, inflation will begin to fall, slowly at first but then with increasing speed. In the example, we suppose that the inflation rate falls little in the first year, more in the second year, and is essentially down to 5 percent after three years. This is the restrictive-policy path shown in blue in Figure 18-13. It corresponds to the path from *e* to *a* to *c* in Figure 18-12.

The shaded area in the figure summarizes the difference between these two paths, and therefore depicts the payoff to anti-inflation policy. But there are also costs.

Figure 18-14 gives a rough impression of how the unemployment rate might behave under the two alternative policies. The status quo policy keeps the unemployment rate at 7 percent, which is the natural rate. The restrictive policy results in a recession: Unemployment rises gradually from 7 percent to 9 percent and then gradually falls back to the natural rate of 7 percent. The shaded area in Figure 18-14 shows what it costs to get the inflation rate down: For over three years unemployment is above the natural rate.

Notice the differences in timing between Figure 18-13 and Figure 18-14. In the early stages of the disinflation program (say, the first year), progress against inflation is meagre even though the losses on the unemployment front are substantial. This reflects an underlying reality that we have mentioned before: Inflation gives way only grudgingly to economic slack. Because of this, policy-makers who embark on a disinflationary course must be patient. The costs in terms of unemployment, although temporary, come sooner. The gains on the inflation front, though more durable, appear later.

What Should Be Done?

Should the government pay the recessionary cost of fighting inflation? When the benefits depicted in Figure 18-13 are balanced against the costs shown in Figure 18-14, have we made a good bargain? While each of you will have to answer this question for yourself, our analysis has highlighted three critical issues on which your answer should rest.

The Costs of Inflation and Unemployment
We spent an entire chapter early in the book (Chapter 6) examining the social costs of inflation and unemployment. Most of the costs of the extra unemployment depicted in Figure 18-14, we concluded, are easy to translate into dollars and cents. Basically, we only need to estimate the real GNP that is lost each year. However, the costs of inflation are harder to put a price tag on, and hence the benefits from reducing inflation are harder to measure. Thus, there is considerable controversy over the costs and benefits of using recession to fight inflation.

Some economists and public figures believe that inflation is extremely costly, and so they look with favour on the trade-off that is embodied in Figures 18-13 and 18-14. Others have a lower estimate of the costs of inflation and find recession a terribly high price to pay. Thus, in particular, some observers believe that we paid an excessively high price to reduce inflation from 11 percent to 6 percent in 1980-83, while others applaud the policy and maintain that the price was worth paying.

The Position of the Economy
We have stated several times in this book that the shape of the economy's aggregate-supply curve, and hence the shape of the short-run Phillips curve, depends very much on the degree of resource utilization. If resources are virtually fully employed, the aggregate-supply curve (and thus the Phillips curve) will be rather steep, which means that the inflation gains will be substantial and the unemployment costs will be minimal. On the other hand, if there is a great deal of

unemployed labour and unutilized industrial capacity, the aggregate-supply curve (and hence the short-run Phillips curve) may be nearly horizontal. In that case, a great deal of unemployment will be needed to achieve even a slight reduction in inflation. The Phillips curves we have drawn in this chapter have this characteristic shape.

Because the Phillips curve is shaped this way the trade-off depicted in our last two diagrams will look more favourable when the economy is in a boom and less favourable when there is already a good deal of unemployment.

The Efficiency of the Economy's Self-Correcting Mechanism

We have stressed that once government policy causes a recession, it is the economy's natural self-correcting mechanism that cures the recessionary gap. The obvious question here is: How long do we have to wait? If the self-correcting mechanism—which works through reductions in the rate of wage inflation—is slow and halting, the costs of fighting inflation will be enormous. On the other hand, if wage inflation responds promptly, the recession necessary to bring down inflation may not be very severe.

This is another issue that is surrounded by controversy. Most economists believe that the weight of the evidence points to very sluggish wage behaviour. The rate of wage inflation appears to respond only slowly to economic slack. In terms of our Figure 18–12 (page 345), this means that the economy will traverse the path from *a* to *c* at an agonizingly slow pace, so that a very long recession will be necessary if there is to be any appreciable effect on inflation.

But a significant minority opinion finds this assessment far too pessimistic. Economists in this group argue that the costs of reducing inflation are not nearly so severe and that the key to a successful anti-inflation policy is its effect on people's *expectations*. But, to understand this argument, we must first examine why expectations are relevant to the Phillips curve trade-off.

Inflationary Expectations and the Phillips Curve

The explanation starts with some more review. Recall from Chapter 10 that the main reason why the economy's aggregate-supply curve slopes upward—that is, why output increases as the price level rises—is that businesses typically purchase labour and other inputs under long-term contracts that stipulate the cost of the input in *money* terms (for example, the nominal wage rate). If such contracts are in force when prices go up, then *real* wages fall as prices rise. From businesses' point of view, labour becomes cheaper in real terms, and firms are induced to expand employment and output. Buying cheaply and selling dearly is, after all, the route to higher profits. Long-term contracts that set the nominal wage rate, then, explain why higher prices lead to more output; that is, why the aggregate-supply curve slopes upward.

Table 18–1 illustrates how this works in a concrete example. We suppose that workers and firms agree today that the money wage to be paid a year from now will be $10 per hour. The table then shows the real wage that corresponds to each alternative rate of inflation.[2] Clearly, the higher the inflation rate, the higher the price level at the end of the year and the lower the real wage.

Lower real wages provide an incentive for the firm to increase output, as we have just noted. But lower real wages also impose losses of purchasing power on workers. Thus, there is a sense in which workers are being "cheated" by inflation if

---

[2]Each real-wage figure is obtained by dividing the $10 nominal wage by the corresponding price level a year later and multiplying by 100. Thus, for example, when the inflation rate is 4 percent, the real wage at the end of the year is ($10/104) × 100 = $9.62.

Table 18-1

MONEY AND REAL WAGES UNDER INFLATION

INFLATION RATE (percent)	PRICE LEVEL ONE YEAR FROM NOW	MONEY WAGE ONE YEAR FROM NOW (dollars per hour)	REAL WAGE ONE YEAR FROM NOW (dollars per hour)
0	100	10.00	10.00
4	104	10.00	9.62
8	108	10.00	9.26
12	112	10.00	8.93

they sign a contract specifying a fixed money wage in an inflationary environment.

Many economists wonder why workers would sign such a contract if they can see inflation coming. Would it not be more reasonable, these economists ask, to insist on being compensated for inflation in advance? After all, firms should be willing to provide compensation for expected inflation because they realize that it does not raise real wages.

Table 18-2 illustrates how the money wage specified in a contract can be adjusted for expected inflation. For example, if 4 percent inflation is expected, the contract could stipulate that the wage rate be increased to $10.40 (which is 4 percent more than $10) at the end of the year. That would keep the real wage at $10, the same as it would be under zero inflation. The remaining money wage figures in Table 18-2 are derived similarly.

If workers and firms actually adjust money wages in the way suggested in Table 18-2, then the expected real wage will not decline as the expected price level rises. (In the example, the expected future real wage is always $10 per hour.) Then, if expectations prove correct, prices and wages will go up together, leaving the real wage unchanged. Workers will not lose from inflation and firms will not gain. But, of course, that means that there will be no special incentive for firms to produce more as prices rise. In a word, the aggregate-supply curve would become *vertical*. In general:

If workers can see inflation coming, and if they receive compensation for it in advance so that inflation does not erode *real* wages, then the economy's aggregate-supply curve will not slope upward. It will be a vertical line at the level of output corresponding to potential GNP.

Such a curve is shown in part (a) of Figure 18-15. Since we derived the Phillips curve from the aggregate-supply curve earlier in the chapter, it follows that even the *short-run* Phillips curve will become vertical under these circumstances [see part (b) of Figure 18-15].[3]

[3]See Discussion Question 10 at the end of the chapter.

Table 18-2

MONEY AND REAL WAGES UNDER EXPECTED INFLATION

EXPECTED INFLATION RATE (percent)	EXPECTED PRICE LEVEL ONE YEAR FROM NOW	MONEY WAGE ONE YEAR FROM NOW (dollars per hour)	EXPECTED REAL WAGE ONE YEAR FROM NOW (dollars per hour)
0	100	10.00	10.00
4	104	10.40	10.00
8	108	10.80	10.00
12	112	11.20	10.00

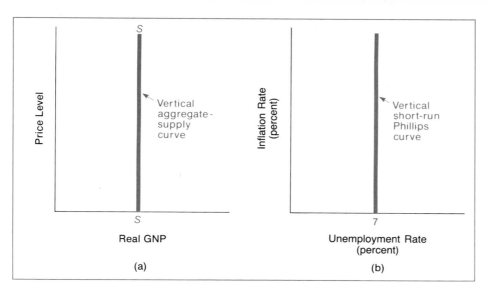

Figure 18-15

A VERTICAL AGGREGATE-SUPPLY CURVE AND THE CORRESPONDING VERTICAL PHILLIPS CURVE

If workers foresee inflation, and if they also receive full compensation for it in advance, then inflation will no longer erode real wages. In that case, firms will have no incentive to raise production as prices rise, and the aggregate-supply curve will be vertical as in part (a). Since we derived the short-run Phillips curve from the aggregate-supply curve, the short-run Phillips curve will also become vertical [part (b)].

If this analysis is correct, it has profound implications for the trade-off and for the costs and benefits of inflation-fighting. This can be seen by referring back to Figure 18–12 on page 345, where we depicted the strategy of fighting inflation by causing a recession. We concluded there that in order to move from point *e* (representing 10 percent inflation) to point *c* (representing 5 percent inflation), the economy would have to take a detour through point *a*; that is, it would have to endure a recession. If, however, even the *short-run* Phillips curve were *vertical* rather than downward sloping, this detour would not be necessary. It would be possible for inflation to fall without unemployment rising. The economy could jump directly from point *e* to point *c*.

Is this analysis correct? Can we really slay the inflationary dragon so painlessly? As a piece of pure logic, the argument is impeccable. Yet things do not seem to have worked out this way. In practice, inflation fighting has been very costly. We must, therefore, ask ourselves whether the premises on which the analysis rests are realistic. There are several reasons why many economists think the expectations argument should not be applied uncritically to the modern economy.

Point 1. The argument is predicated on the notion that inflation can be accurately foreseen. But many contracts for labour and other raw materials cover such long periods of time that the expectations that were held when the contracts were written may be very different from the current reality. If a restrictive policy reduces inflation below the rate firms and workers were expecting when they made their wage agreement, real wages will wind up higher than was intended, and hence firms will want to reduce employment and produce less.

Point 2. Many people believe that inflationary expectations are quite sluggish, that they do not adapt quickly to changes in the economic environment. If, for example, the government embarks on an anti-inflation policy, workers will continue to expect high inflation for quite a while. Thus they will continue to insist on high rates of increase in money wages. Then, if inflation actually slows down, real wages will wind up rising faster than anyone expected. Firms will therefore find labour "too expensive" relative to current selling prices, and unemployment will result. With lags in the reaction of expectations, then, the short-run Phillips curve retains its downward slope and inflation-fighting is costly.

The Theory of Rational Expectations

These two points, and others we have not mentioned, have persuaded most economists that the expectations argument, while valid in part, should not be taken to extremes. Most economists nowadays accept the notion that the Phillips curve is downward sloping in the short run, and hence that a short-run trade-off does exist.

But a vocal minority of economists disagrees. This group, believers in the doctrine of **rational expectations**, insists that the only type of inflation that leads to *increases* in output is *unexpected* inflation, because only unexpected inflation will reduce real wages. (To see this, compare Tables 18–1 and 18–2.) Similarly, they argue, the only type of reduction in inflation that leads to recession is an *unexpected* reduction.

To explain this point of view, we must first explain what rational expectations are. Then, we will be in a position to understand why the hypothesis of rational expectations has such radical implications for the Phillips curve.

Rational expectations are forecasts that, while not necessarily correct, are the best that can be made given the available data. Rational expectations, therefore, cannot err systematically. If expectations are rational, forecasting errors are pure random numbers.

What Are Rational Expectations?

In many economic problems, people must formulate expectations about what the future will bring. For example, those who invest in the stock market need to forecast the future prices of the stocks they buy and sell. And we have just discussed why workers and businesses may want to forecast the future price level before they agree on a money wage. *Rational expectations* is a controversial hypothesis about how such forecasts are made.

As used by economists, a forecast (an "expectation") of a future variable is considered rational if the forecaster makes *optimal* use of all information that is both *available* and *relevant*. Let us elaborate on the italicized words in this definition, using as an example a hypothetical stock-market investor who has rational expectations.

First, believers in the doctrine of rational expectations recognize that *information is limited*. An investor who is interested in buying Canadian Pacific stock would like to know how much profit the company will make in the coming years. Armed with such information, she could predict the future price of CP stock more accurately. But that information is not available; no one knows it. Her forecast of the future price of CP stock is not "irrational" just because she does not know CP's future profits. On the other hand, if CP stock normally goes down on Fridays and up on Mondays, she should be aware of this fact.

Second, *not all information is important*. Some publicly available facts may be irrelevant to predicting the variables of interest. If so, a rational forecaster can afford to be ignorant of them. For example, anyone who cares to can find out how many babies were born last year in Fredericton. But this fact may not tell you much about the future performance of Canadian Pacific. So our investor need not have this information to be rational. However, if there is a clear Friday/Monday pattern in CP stock prices, she had better know what day of the week it is!

Finally, we have the word *optimal*. As used by economists, this means using proper statistical inference to process all the relevant information that is available before making a forecast. Thus, to have rational expectations, your forecasts do not have to be correct, but they cannot have systematic errors that could have been avoided by applying better statistical methods. This requirement, while exacting, is not quite as outlandish as it may seem. A good billiards player makes expert use of the laws of physics, even though he may have no understanding of the theory. Similarly, an experienced stock-market investor may make good use of information even without formal training in statistics.

Rational Expectations and the Trade-Off

Let us now see how the doctrine of rational expectations has been applied to deny that there exists any trade-off between inflation and unemployment—even in the short run.

Even though they recognize that inflation cannot always be predicted accurately, rational expectationists claim that workers will not make *systematic* errors in forecasting inflation. Note that Point 2 above suggests that inflationary expectations are typically *too low* when inflation is rising and *too high* when inflation is falling. Rational expectationists deny that this is possible. Workers, they argue, will always make the best possible forecast of inflation, using all the latest data and the best available economic models. Such forecasts will not err systematically in one direction or the other regardless of whether inflation is rising or falling. Consequently:

If expectations are rational, the difference between the *actual* rate of inflation and the *expected* rate of inflation (the forecasting error) will be a pure random number.

Now recall that the basic expectationist argument summarized in the previous section claims that employment is affected by inflation only to the extent that inflation differs from what was expected. It follows, therefore, that:

If expectations are rational, and there are no long-term contracts, the inflation rate can be reduced without the need for a period of high unemployment.

Except for some random—and totally unpredictable—gyrations due to forecasting errors, unemployment will always remain at the natural rate.

The implications of rational expectations for the conduct of economic policy are really quite revolutionary, at least when long-term contracts are not important. According to this view, the government's ability to manipulate aggregate demand does not give it any control over real output and unemployment because the aggregate-supply curve is vertical—even in the short run. [To see why, experiment by moving an aggregate-demand curve when the aggregate-supply curve is vertical as in Figure 18–15(a).] Any *predictable* change in aggregate demand will lead to a change in the expected rate of inflation, and hence will leave real wages unaffected.

The government can influence output only by making *unexpected* changes in aggregate demand. But this is not easy to do when expectations are rational because people are well informed about what policy-makers are up to. According to the rational expectationists, if the monetary and fiscal authorities typically react to high inflation by reducing aggregate demand, people will soon come to anticipate this reaction. And, as just mentioned, anticipated reductions in aggregate demand will not affect unemployment because they will not cause *unexpected* changes in inflation.

An Evaluation

The hypothesis of rational expectations is now embraced by many economists, but the proposition that inflation can be reduced without significant output losses is not. There are many reasons for this.

For one, Point 1 above remains valid even if expectations are rational. When long-term contracts are made, people get locked into provisions that, while rational when they were made, may seem irrational from today's point of view. For example, consider a labour contract drawn up in 1980 that specified a money wage rate to be paid in 1983. Given what people knew in 1980, it may have been rational to expect the 1983 price level to be 30 percent higher than the 1980 price level. So the money wage may have been set to rise 33 percent over the three years. Then inflation slowed dramatically. If the money wage specified in the contract was actually paid, the real wage was higher than had been intended. But no one behaved irrationally. Thus, the hypothesis of rational expectations is a *necessary* assumption for defending the proposition that inflation can be reduced without a recession, but it is *not sufficient*. There must also be no long-term contracts.

Since long-term contracts do exist, it is perhaps not surprising that the facts have not been kind to the costless disinflation proposition. The theory suggests that unemployment should hover around the natural rate most of the time. Yet this does not seem to be the case. The theory also denies that predictable monetary- and fiscal-policy actions will have effects on real output. Yet most observers think they can identify episodes in the past, such as the policy-induced recession of the early 1980s, where such actions had significant effects on real GNP and unemployment. Finally, some direct tests of the rationality of expectations have cast some doubt on the hypothesis.

At this writing, there is a great deal of controversy over how best to apply the idea of rational expectations to macroeconomic issues. The issues are far from resolved. But the evidence to date has led most economists to reject the extreme costless disinflation proposition and to affirm the existence of a short-run trade-off between inflation and unemployment.

Fighting Recessions with Fiscal and Monetary Policy

We have covered a lot of ground in this chapter already, and we have introduced a number of new concepts. At this point it may be useful to pause and take stock of what we have learned. A good way to test your understanding is to run the analysis in reverse. Up to now we have been considering the use of monetary and fiscal policies to combat *inflation*. Let us now suppose instead that the crucial macroeconomic problem is *unemployment*.

We again turn to the Phillips curve diagram, Figure 18–12 on page 345, for a concrete example. Suppose that the economy somehow finds itself at a point like *a*, in a recession. And suppose that the government wants to get the economy back to full employment. What should it do?

We already know from our previous analysis what will happen if the current rate of growth of aggregate demand is simply maintained. Point *a* on the short-run Phillips curve represents a recessionary gap, so the economy's self-correcting mechanism starts to work. High unemployment slows the rate of increase of money wages, which tends to push the aggregate-supply curve downward (compared with where it would have been if full employment were maintained). This both puts a brake on inflation and encourages employment. The economy slowly travels down the path indicated by the blue arrow in Figure 18–12, from point *a* to point *c*. But, as we have noted before, the road from *a* to *c* may be slow and bumpy.

Is there a better way out of our economic problems? Perhaps. As we have learned, expansionary measures such as tax cuts, increases in government spending, or open-market purchases of government securities can speed up the rate at which the aggregate-demand curve moves to the right. (Compare Figure 18–5 and Figure 18–4.) Such a policy would enable the economy to "ride up" the short-run Phillips curve toward point *e*.

Let us compare this active anti-recession policy with the more passive "status quo policy." Figures 18–16 and 18–17 will assist in the comparison. Under the status quo policy of relying on the economy's self-correcting mechanism, the unemployment rate gradually falls from the 9 percent that corresponds to point *a* on the Phillips curve to the 7 percent that corresponds to point *c*. But progress is agonizingly slow. The status quo policy path shown in black in Figure 18–16 indicates that it takes three uncomfortable years to return to full employment.

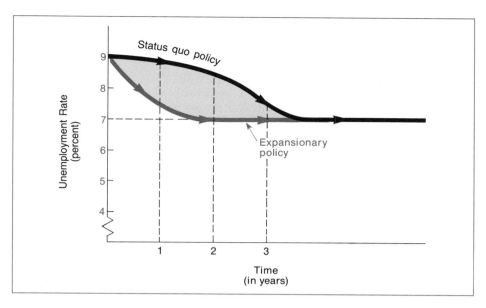

Figure 18-16
THE PAYOFF TO ANTI-
RECESSION POLICY
By stimulating aggregate demand
through monetary and fiscal policy,
the government can reduce
unemployment more rapidly. If it
relies exclusively on the
economy's ability to right itself,
unemployment will follow the black
"status quo policy" path. If,
instead, the government takes an
active hand in fighting the
recession, unemployment will
follow the blue "expansionary-
policy" path. The shaded area
measures the reduction in
unemployment that the
expansionary policy achieves.

By contrast, if expansionary monetary- and fiscal-policy actions are taken, the return to full employment is much quicker. According to the blue "expansionary-policy" path in Figure 18–16, we get there in about one and one-half years. The shaded area in the figure measures the payoff to anti-recession policy; it shows how much unemployment we save during the three-year period.

But, as we have by now come to expect, these gains are made at some cost. The black status quo policy path in Figure 18–17 shows the likely behaviour of the inflation rate under the policy of waiting for the economy's self-corrective forces to work. Inflation falls gradually from the 7 percent rate that corresponds to point *a* on the Phillips curve to the 5 percent rate that corresponds to point *c*. But if the expansionary policy is pursued, inflation will not creep downward; instead it will creep upward, as indicated by the blue expansionary-policy path in Figure 18–17. The shaded area in this figure shows the cost of fighting recession with monetary and fiscal policy: We wind up with more inflation.

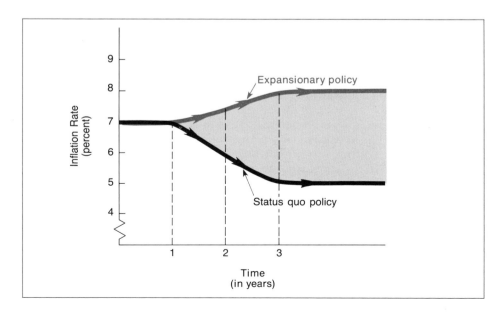

Figure 18-17
THE COST OF ANTI-
RECESSION POLICY
The unemployment gains depicted
in the previous figure are not
obtained without cost. By
stimulating the economy, the
government policies cause a rise
in the inflation rate—as shown by
the blue "expansionary-policy"
path. If, instead, the government
had simply waited for the
economy's natural self-correcting
mechanism to work, inflation would
have fallen—see the black "status
quo policy" path. The difference
between these two paths (the
shaded area) represents the
inflationary cost of fighting the
recession.

In considering whether or not to fight a recession, policy-makers face a trade-off between unemployment and inflation. If they take expansionary actions to reduce unemployment, they may end up with a higher inflation rate.

Are the inflationary costs depicted in Figure 18–17 worth the benefits of the lower unemployment shown in Figure 18–16? This is not a question that can be answered with any assurance. The answer hinges on the same three issues we isolated before when considering anti-inflation policy:

1. *The social costs of inflation and unemployment*. Those who regard inflation as very costly will not want to pay the price of shortening the recession. Those who are more concerned with unemployment will find recession-fighting a good idea.

2. *The position of the economy*. As we have noted, the Phillips curve is likely to be flatter at higher rates of unemployment. As you can see by studying Figure 18–12, if the Phillips curve is rather flat, the extra inflation caused by fighting a recession will be minimal. On the other hand, if the short-run Phillips curve is steep, the inflationary price tag will be high. Thus the case for fighting deep recessions is stronger than the case for fighting shallow ones.

3. *The efficiency of the economy's self-correcting mechanism*. Naturally, if the economy's self-corrective forces worked rapidly, there would be little reason for the government to try to speed things up. On the other hand, if the mechanism is slow and unreliable or, worse yet, if it breaks down entirely, the case for government intervention is much stronger.

Why Economists (and Politicians) Disagree

These three factors help explain why economists sometimes differ so radically from one another in their recommendations as to the proper conduct of national economic policy. And they also help account for disagreements among politicians.

The question is: When a recession occurs, should the government take actions to bring it to a rapid end? You will say *yes* if you believe that (1) unemployment is more costly than inflation, (2) the short-run Phillips curve is rather flat, and (3) the economy's self-correcting mechanism—which works as unemployment slows the rate of growth of wages—is slow and unreliable. These views on the economy tend to be associated with economists of the Keynesian school and with the (generally liberal) politicians who listen to them.

But you will say *no* if you believe that (1) inflation is more costly than unemployment, (2) the short-run Phillips curve is quite steep, and (3) the self-correcting mechanism works smoothly and quickly. These views are held by most monetarists and rational expectationists, so it is not surprising that the (generally conservative) politicians who follow their advice typically oppose strong measures to fight recessions.

The tables turn, however, when the question is whether or not to use policy to fight inflation. The Keynesian view of the world—that unemployment is costly, that the short-run Phillips curve is flat, and that the self-correcting mechanism is unreliable—leads to the conclusion that the costs of fighting inflation are high while the benefits are low. The monetarist and rational-expectationist positions on these three issues are just the reverse, and so are the policy conclusions.

Supply-Side Inflation and the Phillips Curve

Let us now return to the question posed early in the chapter: Why did the Phillips curve, which worked reasonably well in the 1950s and 1960s, seem to fall apart in the 1970s? (It may be useful to refer back to Figure 18–10 on page 343 to see the

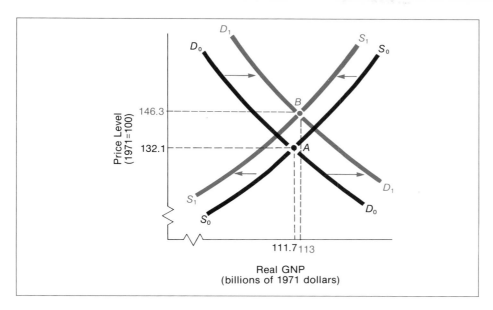

Figure 18-18
STAGFLATION FROM A
SUPPLY SHOCK
Instead of shifting outward as it
normally does, the aggregate-
supply curve shifted inward—from
S_0S_0 to S_1S_1—between 1974 and
1975. Coupled with some growth
of the aggregate-demand curve—
from D_0D_0 in 1974 to D_1D_1 in
1975—equilibrium moved from
point A to point B. There was only
a very slight increase in real
output, and prices rose rapidly.

evidence.) The analysis that we have provided in this chapter so far gives one answer: Economists and policy-makers at that time mistakenly viewed the Phillips curve as a menu of *long-run* policy choices. Wanting to lower unemployment, the government adopted policies that pushed the economy up the Phillips curve. But, as we know, unemployment rates below the natural rate are not sustainable, and these policy-makers got much more inflation than they had bargained for.

There is another answer that operates along with the first effect. This answer is that some of the inflation of the 1970s did not emanate from the demand side. Instead, the 1970s contained adverse "supply shocks," events that pushed the economy's aggregate-supply curve inward, to the left. What kind of Phillips curve will be generated when economic fluctuations come from the supply side?

Figure 18-2 already gives us the answer: The price level increases, and real output falls. Falling output means fewer jobs available, so unemployment increases. Thus:

If fluctuations in economic activity emanate mainly from the supply side, higher rates of inflation will be associated with higher rates of unemployment, and lower rates of inflation will be associated with lower rates of unemployment.

There were numerous supply shocks during the 1970s. Food prices boomed between 1972 and 1974 and again in 1978. World energy prices soared in 1973–74 and again in 1979–80. The Canadian government shielded our economy from some of these shocks (as we discussed in Chapter 10), but we were not completely insulated. The government also increased aggregate demand in reaction to these shocks, in an attempt to keep unemployment from rising. The combined effect of the supply-side shock and the expansion in aggregate demand can be clarified by considering a specific example. In Figure 18-18, aggregate-demand curve D_0D_0 and aggregate-supply curve S_0S_0 represent the economic situation in 1974. Equilibrium was at point A, with a price level of 132.1 and real output of $111.7 billion. In 1974, OPEC raised the world price of oil by a factor of four. The Canadian price of oil increased but not to this extent. As a result, instead of shifting to the *right* as it normally does from one year to the next, the aggregate-supply curve shifted to the *left* during 1974, to S_1S_1.

By 1975, the aggregate-demand curve had shifted out to the position indicated by D_1D_1. The equilibrium for 1975 (point B in the figure), therefore wound up almost vertically above the equilibrium point for 1974. Real output only increased slightly. Prices rose rapidly (10.7 percent).

Now, in a growing population with more people looking for jobs each year, a stagnant economy that is not generating new jobs will suffer a rise in the unemployment rate. This is precisely what happened in Canada; the unemployment rate averaged 5.4 percent in 1974 and 6.9 percent in 1975. Thus the inflation rate and the unemployment rate increased at the same time. The Phillips curve was upward sloping! We conclude that a model involving both demand-side *and* supply-side inflation shocks can easily explain our unemployment and inflation experience since 1970.

The Dilemma of Demand Management

We have just learned that when inflation comes from the supply side, inflation and unemployment will be *positively* associated: We will suffer from more of both or enjoy less of each. Does this mean that monetary and fiscal policy-makers can escape the trade-off between inflation and unemployment? Certainly not.

Adverse shifts in the aggregate-supply curve can cause both inflation and unemployment to rise together and thus can destroy the Phillips curve relationship. Nevertheless, anything that monetary and fiscal policy can do will make unemployment and inflation move in opposite directions. The reason is that monetary and fiscal policy only gives the government control over the *aggregate-demand* curve, not the *aggregate-supply* curve. If the government stimulates demand to cut down on unemployment, it will make inflation worse; if it restricts demand to fight inflation, it will increase unemployment.

Thus, no matter what the source of inflation, and no matter what happens to the Phillips curve, the makers of monetary and fiscal policy must still face up to the disagreeable trade-off between inflation and unemployment. This is a principle that many policy-makers have failed to recognize and one of the **12 Ideas** that we hope you will remember well **Beyond the Final Exam**.

Naturally, the unpleasant nature of this trade-off has led to a vigorous search for a way out of the dilemma. Both economists and public officials have sought a policy that might offer improvements on both fronts simultaneously, or that might ease the pain of either unemployment or inflation. The next chapter will consider some of these ideas.

Summary

1. Inflation can be caused either by rapid growth of aggregate demand or by sluggish growth of aggregate supply.

2. When fluctuations in economic activity emanate from the demand side, prices will rise rapidly when real output grows rapidly. Since rapid growth means more jobs, unemployment and inflation will be inversely related.

3. This inverse relationship between unemployment and inflation is called the Phillips curve. It explains Canadian data for the 1950s and 1960s rather well but fails miserably to account for the 1970s.

4. One reason for this failure is that the Phillips curve was misinterpreted as a menu of *long-run* policy choices for the economy. This view is incorrect because the economy's self-correcting mechanism guarantees that neither an inflationary gap nor a recessionary gap can last indefinitely.

5. Because of the self-correcting mechanism, the economy's true long-run choices lie along a *vertical* Phillips curve, which shows that the so-called *natural rate of unemployment* is the only unemployment rate that can persist indefinitely.

6. In the short run, the economy can move up or down its short-run Phillips curve. *Temporary* reductions in unemployment can be achieved at the cost of higher inflation. Similarly, *temporary* increases in unemployment can be used to fight inflation.

7. Whether it is advisable to use unemployment to fight inflation depends on three principal factors: The relative social costs of inflation versus unemployment; the efficiency of the economy's self-correcting mechanism; and the current position of the economy (which influences the shape of the short-run trade-off between inflation and unemployment).

8. Since controversy surrounds each of these three factors, both economists and politicians often disagree on the proper conduct of stabilization policy.

9. If workers expect inflation to occur, and if they demand (and receive) compensation for inflation, output will be independent of the price level. Both the aggregate-supply curve and the short-run Phillips curve are vertical in this case.

10. However, errors in predicting inflation will still change real wages and hence will still change the quantity of output that firms wish to supply. Thus, *unpredicted* movements in the price level will lead to the normal sort of upward-sloping aggregate-supply curve.

11. According to the doctrine of rational expectations, errors in predicting inflation will be purely random. This, means that, except for some random (and uncontrollable) gyrations, the aggregate-supply curve is vertical even in the short run.

12. Many economists reject the rational expectations view of the world. Some deny that expectations are "rational," and believe instead that people tend, for example, to underpredict inflation when it is rising. Others point out that contracts signed years ago cannot possibly embody expectations that are "rational" in terms of what we know today.

13. When fluctuations in economic activity are caused by shifts of the aggregate-supply curve, output will grow slowly (causing unemployment to rise) when inflation speeds up. Hence, the rates of unemployment and inflation will be positively related.

14. Many observers feel that the adverse supply shifts during the 1970s help explain why the Phillips curve collapsed.

15. Even if inflation is initiated by supply-side problems, so that inflation and unemployment occur together, the monetary and fiscal authorities still face this trade-off: Anything they do to improve unemployment is likely to worsen inflation, and anything they do to reduce inflation is likely to aggravate unemployment. The reason is that monetary and fiscal policy mainly influences the aggregate-demand curve, not the aggregate-supply curve. This is one of our **12 Ideas for Beyond the Final Exam**.

Concepts for Review

Demand-side inflation
Supply-side inflation
Phillips curve
Self-correcting mechanism
Natural rate of unemployment

Vertical (long-run) Phillips curve
Trade-offs between unemployment
    and inflation in the short run
    and in the long run
Inflationary expectations

Rational expectations
Stagflation caused by supply
    shocks

Questions for Discussion

1. Some observers during the 1970s claimed that policy-makers no longer faced a trade-off between inflation and unemployment. Why did they think this? Were they correct?

2. "There is no sense in trying to shorten recessions through fiscal and monetary policies because the effects of these policies on the unemployment rate are sure to be temporary." Comment on both the truth of this statement and its relevance for policy formulation.

3. Why is the economy's self-correcting mechanism more efficient at eliminating inflationary gaps than it is at eliminating recessionary gaps?

4. Why is it said that decisions on fiscal and monetary policy are, at least in part, political decisions that cannot be made on "objective" economic criteria?

5. Does the economy have a recessionary gap or an inflationary gap today? What should be done about this? What facts would you want to know in preparing an answer to this question?

6. What is a "Phillips curve"? Why did it seem to work so much better in the 1950s and 1960s than it did in the 1970s?

7. Explain the dilemma that policy-makers face when there is an episode of supply inflation. What would you recommend if there were a severe bout of supply inflation today?

8. Why do expectations about inflation affect the wages resulting from labour–management bargaining?

9. What is meant by "rational" expectations? Why does the doctrine of rational expectations have such stunning implications for economic policy? Would believers in rational expectations want to shorten a recession by expanding aggregate demand? Would they want to fight inflation by reducing aggregate demand?

10. Show that, if the economy's aggregate-supply curve is vertical, fluctuations in the growth of aggregate demand produce only fluctuations in inflation with no effect on output. Relate this to your answer to the previous question.

Further Controversies Over Stabilization Policy

19

Where there is much desire
to learn, there of necessity
will be much arguing.
JOHN MILTON

W
e have pointed out that stabilization-policy decisions are inherently political and, as a consequence, are usually immersed in controversy. Several of these controversies were examined in the preceding chapters, and we now turn our attention to two others.

In the first part of the chapter, we investigate a number of suggestions that have been offered to improve the trade-off between inflation and unemployment or, better yet, to eliminate it entirely. Some of these plans have actually been tried; others are still untested ideas. They range from governmental exhortations to hold down inflation to outright prohibition of wage or price increases. They include efforts to improve the functioning of labour markets, plans to enlist the tax system in the battle against inflation, and institutional changes designed to rob inflation of its social costs. Although each of these ideas is worthy of consideration, we must emphasize in advance that all are controversial and none is a panacea.

The second part of the chapter turns to an even more fundamental question: Should the government conduct any stabilization policy at all? Much that we have said in earlier chapters seems to indicate that it should. But, as we shall see, there are several important factors that point in the opposite direction—factors that we have not yet considered. These factors lead a number of economists, many of them monetarists, to conclude that it is unwise to try to stabilize the economy through monetary and fiscal policy.

Can We Improve the Trade-Off Between Inflation and Unemployment?

In the last chapter, we learned that one way to fight inflation is to create economic slack by slowing the growth of aggregate demand; that is, to use recession to fight inflation. Though it is a genuine alternative, politicians react to it somewhat like children react to spinach. For, in addition to its obvious economic costs, fighting inflation by causing unemployment is politically unpopular.

Because of the agonizing nature of the Phillips curve trade-off, economists and politicians have been searching for years for policies that promise to improve the terms of the trade-off a bit. Since the long-run Phillips curve is believed to be approximately vertical, such policy initiatives in effect seek to *reduce the natural rate of unemployment.*

Attempts to Reduce the Natural Rate of Unemployment

One class of policies that attempts to reduce the natural rate of unemployment is vocational training and retraining programs. When successful, they help unemployed workers with obsolete skills acquire abilities that are currently in demand. In doing so, they help alleviate upward pressures on wage rates in jobs where qualified workers are in short supply. For example, if an unemployed steelworker is taught to assemble computers, then progress is made against both inflation and unemployment, since one former steelworker leaves the ranks of the unemployed while one new worker helps alleviate the shortage of skilled labour in the computer industry.

Although the idea sounds appealing and has attracted many adherents, successes achieved through training programs have, in practice, been rather limited. Too often, people are trained for jobs that do not exist by the time they finish their training—if indeed they ever existed. Even when successful, these programs are quite expensive, which restricts the number of workers that can be accommodated. Despite these difficulties, revised versions of these retraining schemes continue to be developed. A recent scheme is the National Training Program, introduced in August 1982.

The Canada Employment Centres also try to improve the match of workers to jobs but not by retraining workers. Instead, they seek to funnel information from prospective employers to prospective employees. Firms are encouraged to list their job vacancies with the centres and to inspect the centres' lists of people looking for work. Unemployed workers, or people wanting to change jobs, are encouraged to register with the Canada Employment Centres and to study its lists of openings. In this way, it is hoped, the simultaneous occurrence of unemployed workers and unfilled jobs will be reduced.

The centres also co-ordinate recent initiatives such as the New Employment Expansion Development (NEED) program, and other direct job-creation schemes, which are intended to provide jobs for persons whose unemployment insurance has run out. The federal government also operates the Industry and Labour Adjustment Program (ILAP), which pays two-thirds of workers' former wages (after their unemployment insurance has expired—until retirement if necessary) if the workers are over 45 years of age and have been released by declining, low-productivity industries. This experimental program may be a useful way to raise aggregate productivity, since it is a substitute for continually propping up industries in which Canada is not competitive.

Another federal government program aimed at reducing frictional unemployment is one involving relocation grants. If the unemployed live in one province and job vacancies occur in others, the government moving allowance permits the family to move and therefore to take the job. Some analysts argue that other grants to high-unemployment regions tend to cancel out the effectiveness of the moving allowances. While it may not be due to any government programs, it is noteworthy that Newfoundland, Prince Edward Island, and Nova Scotia all experienced net immigration during the 1970s.

Despite the many government programs that are aimed at improving the functioning of the labour market, unemployment insurance still represents the major commitment of funds. During the 1982–83 fiscal year, the government spent $9.7 billion on unemployment insurance and $1.6 billion on all other job creation, training, and related employment services.

While these government programs are intended to improve the Phillips curve, many other schemes—such as government regulations ranging from agricultural price supports, to control of airline-passenger fares, to requirements that trucks return empty after delivering their loads—have been criticized on the grounds that they make prices higher at any given level of unemployment. Over recent years many of these government interferences with free-market processes have come under vigorous verbal assault, with the result that some deregulation has now occurred in the airline, trucking, and telecommunications industries.

An added impetus for deregulation in Canada has been provided by the Reagan administration in the United States, which made deregulation one of its top priorities. It has deregulated the airline and telecommunications industries, expedited the demise of price controls on energy products, halted the rise of the minimum wage, and generally reduced the amount of red tape imposed on businesses.[1] It has also sparked several acrimonious debates by slackening federal enforcement efforts in the areas of environmental protection and occupational health and safety.

Incomes Policy

Yet another way to improve the trade-off, an approach that has been tried intermittently in Canada, is **incomes policy**. As practised in this country during the last 20 years, incomes policy has run the gamut from verbal admonitions all the way to outright prohibition of wage and price increases beyond a certain guideline (in the 1975–78 period). In some foreign countries that rely upon incomes policy more heavily than we do, a still more bewildering variety of alternative measures has emerged. Indeed, there may be only one common thread linking these disparate policies: No hard evidence exists that any of them has succeeded *permanently* in improving the trade-off between unemployment and inflation. Note that the emphasis here is on the word "permanently," for many attempts at incomes policy—including some in this country—have had temporary success.

The Canadian 1975–78 episode stands out as perhaps the most successful use of incomes policy ever tried in a Western economy since World War II. All studies show that our controls program lessened the magnitude of the temporary increases in unemployment that accompanied the contractionary aggregate-demand policy at the time. The reason for the relative success of the Canadian experience is given later in this chapter.

> **Incomes policy** is a generic term used to describe a wide variety of measures aimed at curbing inflation *without* reducing aggregate demand.

Jawboning

The mildest form of incomes policy is commonly referred to as **jawboning**. The term is descriptive. It is meant to conjure up in your mind an image of the Prime Minister's Office communicating directly with corporate executives, applying pressure to limit price increases deemed to be contrary to the national interest. Since corporate executives may feel somewhat threatened under these circumstances, jawboning has occasionally enjoyed some success.

The main argument in favour of jawboning is that it is a relatively painless way to try to improve the trade-off between inflation and unemployment. Large corporations, it is argued, have the market power to raise prices even when price rises are not justified by cost increases. But, since these corporate giants are also very conscious of their public-relations images, proponents of jawboning argue, why not use the prestige of the federal government to dissuade them from exercising their market power?

Opponents of jawboning respond that market power, which undoubtedly exists, can explain *high* prices. But why, they ask, would a firm with market power wait until this month to raise prices when it could have done so last month, or the month before? They answer that large corporations raise prices only when changes

> **Jawboning** refers to informal pressures on firms and unions to slow down the rates at which prices and wages are rising.

[1]For a full discussion of regulation and deregulation, see Chapter 30.

in demand or cost considerations make it profitable to do so, not because they have a residue of unused market power. Furthermore, there is an inevitable element of inequity in jawboning. By its very nature it must be discriminatory, picking on some firms while letting others go scot-free.

On balance, a fair assessment of jawboning would probably conclude that it does little good and little harm.

Wage-Price Guidelines

Wage-price guidelines are numerical standards for permissible wage and price increases.

The next step up from jawboning is the establishment of an official standard for "permissible" rates of increase in wages and prices. This was the Canadian approach in the late 1960s, when the Prices and Incomes Commission was set up. However, lacking any enforcement mechanism, there was no chance that the **wage-price guidelines** could be effective in the face of the excessive aggregate demand that characterized this period.[2]

The logic behind guidelines is both simple and compelling. In an ideally functioning economy, if worker productivity rises by 2 percent a year, then wages can rise by 2 percent a year with no increase in costs or prices. Alternatively, wages can increase at a 4 percent annual rate while prices rise at 2 percent a year, and so on. In general, price inflation proceeds at a rate roughly 2 percentage points below wage inflation. A set of wage-price guidelines is obtained by picking a target rate of inflation, say 4 percent a year, and adding 2 percent to get a consistent target for wage increases—6 percent in this example. The government then announces that (a) wage increases that exceed this standard will be deemed "inflationary," (b) firms enjoying productivity increases faster than the national average are expected to raise their prices more slowly than 4 percent a year while, (c) firms obtaining sub-par productivity improvements are allowed to have higher-than-average price increases so that, (d) the overall price level can increase at a rate of 4 percent a year.

As noted, guidelines are quite logical. The problem comes in deciding what to do if some union or corporation violates them. Experience shows that voluntarism goes only so far when economic self-interest is threatened. If the government responds by jawboning we are back to the first type of incomes policy, but with one important difference. The uniformity of the guidelines means that the firms or unions singled out for public scrutiny earned that status. Official guidelines remove much of the element of capriciousness from an *ad hoc* jawboning policy. An alternative approach is to give the guidelines the force of law, which brings us to the next variety of incomes policy.

Wage-Price Controls

Wage-price controls are legal restrictions on the ability of industry and labour to raise wages and prices.

Once the government is given the legal authority to *force* labour and industry to adhere to a set of guidelines, we have moved to a system of mandatory **wage-price controls**. Canada used such a policy during World War II and during the 1975–78 period, when the Anti-Inflation Board (AIB) was in existence.

A major justification for controls is that inflation gathers substantial momentum once workers, consumers, and business managers begin to expect that it will continue. **Inflationary expectations** encourage workers to demand higher wage increases. Firms, in turn, are willing to grant the workers' demands because they believe they will be able to pass the cost increases on to consumers in a general inflationary environment. Consumers contribute their part to the shell game by purchasing durable goods ahead of their needs in anticipation of higher prices in the future, an action that increases demand and helps fuel the inflation engine. Thus, to a great extent, *inflation occurs because people expect it to occur.*

[2]By mid-1969, Prime Minister Trudeau gave up on the Commission and tried a contractionary monetary policy to solve inflation. However, this was attempted during a fixed exchange-rate period—a policy error that we described in Chapter 15.

In terms of our aggregate supply and demand analysis, inflationary expectations shift the aggregate-supply curve upward because workers insist on—and get—higher money wages to compensate them for the coming inflation.[3] Phrased in terms of the Phillips curve, this means that *inflationary expectations shift the Phillips curve upward*, so that any given rate of unemployment corresponds to a higher rate of inflation.

This analysis provides the best intellectual case for controls. A tough and thorough program of wage and price controls, it is argued, can break the vicious cycle of inflationary expectations. By announcing a controls program, the government serves notice on workers that they do not need anticipatory wage increases to preserve their purchasing power. Firms are warned that they may not be able to pass on higher costs to consumers. And consumers may conclude that buying now to beat future price increases is a poor strategy. By breaking inflationary expectations, supporters argue, a controls program can shift the Phillips curve down and reduce the rate of inflation. Under the right conditions, this argument may be correct. However, many economists question whether this line of reasoning is generally valid. For example, it may be that astute workers, business executives, and consumers realize that no controls program can remain in force forever—at least not in a free-market economy like ours. They may then view the temporary dip in the inflation rate caused by controls as an aberration soon to be corrected and therefore not as a major event that warrants changing their long-term expectations.

Why cannot wage–price controls be a permanent feature of the Canadian economy? We learned the answer to this back in Chapter 4. When price ceilings are effective, they force the price below the equilibrium price, so that quantity demanded exceeds quantity supplied. This is shown in Figure 19-1, where the equilibrium price of hamburgers is assumed to be $1. If controls do not allow the price of hamburgers to rise above 75¢, quantity demanded will exceed quantity supplied by one million hamburgers.

With price no longer serving as the rationing device, some other method of rationing is necessary. One possibility is long lines of eager eaters waiting their turn for hamburgers. Scenes like this are quite typical in the Soviet Union and were witnessed in the United States at gas stations during 1979, when gasoline

[3]To review this idea, refer back to pages 349–51 in Chapter 18.

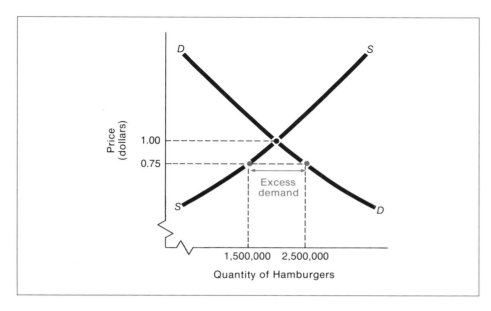

Figure 19-1

THE EFFECTS OF PRICE CONTROLS

This diagram portrays the market for hamburgers under an effective price-control system. Since the equilibrium price is $1 per hamburger, a regulation that holds the price at 75¢ makes the quantity of hamburgers demanded (2,500,000 per year) exceed the quantity supplied (1,500,000 per year). There is a shortage of one million hamburgers per year, and some sort of rationing scheme probably will be necessary.

was in short supply. Another is government ration coupons, giving the owner the right to buy a hamburger—a device used successfully for many goods during World War II. Neither of these measures is likely to be popular with the electorate in peacetime. And both are likely to spawn a black market, which erodes respect for law and order at the same time that it abrogates the effects of controls. As critics of controls are fond of pointing out, controls give law-abiding citizens an incentive to become criminals by participating in illicit black-market activities.

And the problems spawned by price controls go deeper than this. Among the principal factors determining the equilibrium price of hamburgers are the prices of various raw agricultural commodities such as beef. But prices of raw agricultural commodities cannot be controlled by the government because they are so dependent on the weather and other acts of nature. If price controls hold the price of hamburgers at 75¢ while the price of beef skyrockets, it may become unprofitable to sell hamburgers. If so, firms will start leaving the hamburger industry.

With hamburgers unavailable, consumers will increase their purchases of others goods, thereby putting upward pressure on the prices of goods such as fish and soybeans. Thus, price controls on hamburgers will cause the hamburger industry to contract and necessitate additional price controls on fish and soybeans. And so it goes. Each extension of price controls to a new commodity requires additional controls to support it, in a never-ending chain. Thus, for price controls to be effective, they must be nearly universal—which is, of course, next to impossible.

This analysis also explains why wage and price controls have almost always failed to work. Most governments who used controls (for example, the British during the 1960s and 1970s) saw them as "solving" the inflation problem and thereby freeing monetary and fiscal policy to be used without restraint for achieving employment objectives. As a result, aggregate-demand policy and incomes policy were often inconsistent. Monetary and fiscal policy pushed demand curves to the right, while the incomes policy made it unlawful for the prices to adjust to equilibrium. Most analysts have likened these policy episodes to putting a pot of water on the stove and trying to wire on the lid while the burner is turned on high. Little steam emerges for a while but eventually it all blasts out. This is exactly what happened with the many European experiments with controls, and with the Nixon controls in the United States. Lower inflation rates prevailed while the controls were in effect, but these were counterbalanced by higher inflation rates during the year or so after controls were lifted. Instead of improving the trade-off, the controls just managed to increase the *variability* of inflation. In Chapter 6 we pointed out that the *variability* of inflation often exacts more serious social costs than the *average level*. In this sense, then, these control programs were counter productive, and this is why most economists say that they "failed."

The Canadian AIB experiment avoided this problem to some degree, since it was imposed as a *complement* to, not a *substitute for*, contractionary aggregate-demand policy. During this period, the government used monetary and fiscal policy to limit the rightward shifts of demand curves, and the controls were only intended to shorten the lags in the downward revision of inflationary expectations.

Wage–Price Freezes

A **wage–price freeze** is an outright ban on wage or price increases.

An extreme case of mandatory controls is a **wage–price freeze**—a statute making it illegal to increase wages or prices above their levels on some specified date. Nixon ushered in his U.S. controls program with a three-month freeze beginning in mid-August 1971. Such an action cannot be considered a constructive incomes policy; it is meant to be a shock treatment—a dramatic action intended to break inflationary expectations. A wage–price freeze also gives an administration contemplating controls some breathing space to plan a rational program. Nothing could be worse than letting people know today that a controls program is on the way. News reports that a controls program *may* begin can cause price increases just in case. According to the U.S. Secretary of the Treasury an epidemic of rumours of impending controls forced President Nixon's hand in 1971.

Incomes Policies in the Future

There are many problems with incomes policies. They limit relative price adjustments and so diminish the effectiveness of the market mechanism for allocating scarce resources. It is difficult to command lasting commitment for an incomes policy when the freedoms of individuals and firms are curtailed and when import prices cannot be controlled. Furthermore, since wage rates are easier to control than managerial salaries or prices, many feel that controls hurt the real income position of the lower-income groups. Also, the administrative costs become horrendous the longer the controls are left in place.

One implementation issue in Canada is a constitutional one. Before the AIB, most economists and lawyers regarded a wage-and-price-control scheme imposed by the federal government as illegal. The BNA Act stipulates that provincial governments have the power to oversee the setting of domestic wages. Because of this, and because the AIB was expected to control wages more effectively than prices, organized labour tested the legality of the AIB in the Supreme Court. The only possible argument the federal government could give for the legality of the AIB was that Canada faced a "national emergency" without it. (The constitution provides a justification for virtually any federal government action, if this claim can be sustained.)

The analysis submitted to the Supreme Court showed that no emergency existed, in the sense that Canada's inflation was not extraordinary by historical standards, nor when compared to that of other countries. Nor was there a crisis in the sense that alternative anti-inflation policies did not exist. Nevertheless, the Supreme Court ruled that while an emergency may not have existed in 1975, one would exist if the controls were lifted before their intended expiry date. It would seem that legal precedent now exists for the future wage–price control programs.

While the economics profession maintains a healthy skepticism about inordinate reliance on incomes policies, the general public seems more optimistic. When a Gallup poll released in April 1982 indicated that a majority of Canadians favoured wage and price controls, the federal government responded with the "6 and 5" program in the June 1982 budget. This program limited wage increases in the public sector to 6 percent for the first year and 5 percent in the second year. Also, the program involved a form of jawboning, as government contracts only went to firms who respected the 6 and 5 guidelines in their wage settlements. It is difficult to know whether the 6 and 5 program made any significant addition to the effect of the severe recession on lowering inflation during the early 1980s. Nevertheless, incomes policies seem to command much general acceptance, despite administrative and other costs.

Primarily because of the resource-misallocation problems, many economists oppose incomes policies. They agree with the summary of incomes policies given by the famous Canadian economist Harry Johnson, who likened incomes policies to a farmer's attempts to make his donkey behave. The policy always begins as gentle ear-stroking but seems eventually to turn into ear-twisting and then attempts to grope for more sensitive parts of the animal.

A more constructive incomes policy is one that does not try to force the donkey to ignore its private interest but to change the signals facing the donkey so that its private interest and the public interest coincide. This is the idea behind tax-based incomes policies.

Tax-Based Incomes Policy

Tax-based incomes policy uses the tax system to provide incentives favouring non-inflationary behaviour.

Advocated originally by Governor Henry Wallich of the U.S. Federal Reserve System, Professor Sidney Weintraub of the University of Pennsylvania, and the late Arthur Okun of the Brookings Institution in Washington, **tax-based incomes policy (TIP)** seeks to use the tax system to fight inflation. The idea behind TIP is simple, though its implementation might be quite complex in practice. TIP would give employers and employees a financial stake in fighting inflation by lowering taxes for firms or workers who abided by national guidelines for wage–price behaviour, or by raising taxes for those who violated them.

While there are many TIP plans, one particular example will bring out the flavour of all of them. Suppose the government wants to limit wage increases to 5 percent a year. It could pass legislation granting a 2 percent *decrease* in payroll taxes to all employees of firms in which average wages increased by no more than 5 percent. Then, for example, workers who settled for a (non-inflationary) 4½ percent raise would actually wind up with *more* after-tax income than those who settled for an (inflationary) 6 percent raise. They would get 4½ percent more from their employers, plus 2 percent more from the government in the form of lower taxes, for a total gain of 6½ percent. This incentive, it is hoped, would lead labour and management to settle for slower growth in wages; and these slower wage increases, in turn, would lead to slower price increases.

Other TIP plans focus on corporation taxes rather than on payroll taxes, or utilize the "stick" rather than the "carrot" by penalizing the violators of the wage–price guidelines rather than rewarding those who obey. But the basic goal is always the same: to make non-inflationary behaviour profitable for either firms or workers, or both.

Is TIP workable? We really have no way of knowing because it has never been tried. In 1978, President Carter asked the U.S. Congress to enact a modified version of TIP, but Congress never gave the idea serious consideration. The Economic Council of Canada has suggested that TIPs warrant further study.

Making Wages More Flexible

Other countries seem to have had success in eliminating some of the downward inflexibility in wage rates. This makes the economy's self-correcting mechanism work faster, so that anti-inflation policy involves a smaller and less prolonged recession. For example, the West Germans have a "concerted-effort program," which involves regular discussions between unions, firms, and the government. The intention is to reach a consensus on how income can be divided up without inflation. For example, if all participants agree that a recession is coming, slower wage-and-price growth can be agreed upon *in advance*, thereby lessening the recession.

Indexing refers to provisions in a law or a contract whereby monetary payments are automatically adjusted whenever a specified price index changes. Wage rates, pensions, interest payments on bonds, income taxes, and many other things can be indexed in this way, and have been. Sometimes such contractual provisions are called *escalator clauses*.

Japan provides another example, which the Canadian government considered within the "gain-sharing" proposals of the 1984 Federal Budget. Workers in Japan receive a regular wage plus a bonus every six months that is geared to the employer's profits. Since profits are high in the good years, but very low during recessions, this system makes total wages go up and down dramatically over the cycle, too. The much lower wages during the recession result in fewer job losses.

Indexing

A very different approach to the inflation–unemployment dilemma is **indexing**. Indexing refers to provisions in a law or a contract whereby monetary payments are automatically adjusted whenever a specified price index changes. The idea behind indexing is to lessen the magnitude of the temporary recession that results from standard contractionary aggregate-demand policies, and to reduce the social costs of inflation at the same time.

The mechanics of indexing can be explained best through an example. In Canada the most common form of indexed contract is an *escalator clause* in a wage agreement. An escalator clause provides for an automatic increase in money wages—without the need for new contract negotiations—any time the price level rises by more than a specified amount. Suppose that with the Consumer Price Index (CPI) sitting at 300, a union and a firm agree on a three-year contract setting wages at $7 per hour this year, $8 next year, and $9 in the third year. They might then add an escalator clause stating that wages will be increased above these stipulated amounts by 5 cents per hour for each point by which the CPI exceeds 330 in any future year of the contract. Then, if the CPI in year three of the contract reaches 340, workers will receive an additional 50 cents per hour (5 cents for each of the 10 points by which 340 exceeds 330), for a total wage of $9.50 per hour. In this way, workers are partly protected from inflation. Nowadays, more than half of all workers employed by large unionized firms in Canada are covered by some sort of escalator or cost-of-living clause.

Interest payments on bonds or savings accounts can also be indexed, although this is not currently done in Canada.[4] The mechanics here are quite simple. If you had an indexed savings account, your bank might guarantee you a 1 percent *real interest rate* on your savings by automatically increasing your balance by the amount of inflation. For example, suppose you deposited $1000 on January 1 and withdrew it on December 31. An ordinary savings account, paying 6 percent interest, would pay you $1060 at the end of the year—your original $1000 plus 6 percent interest. But if this were an indexed bank account paying 1 percent, and prices rose by 10 percent during the year, your balance at year-end would be $1110—your original $1000 plus 1 percent real interest ($10) plus 10 percent ($100) to compensate you for your loss of purchasing power. The *nominal interest rate* would thus be 11 percent.[5] In general, the nominal rate would be 1 percent *plus* the rate of inflation. Thus, if inflation turned out to be less than 5 percent that year, you would receive less than $1060.

Indexing is not designed to keep interest rates *high*, but to make real interest payments independent of inflation—to cut down the chances that the purchasing power of savings will be eroded by inflation.

With a conventional 6 percent savings account you get a real interest rate of 6 percent if there is zero inflation, 2 percent if there is 4 percent inflation, –2 percent if there is 8 percent inflation, and so on. With an imaginary 1 percent indexed account, you would receive 1 percent real interest no matter what the inflation rate. Indexing thus enables the saver to avoid gambling on inflation. For this reason, some economists have advocated that the Canadian government issue an indexed savings bond that small savers could use to protect themselves against inflation. This idea was proposed by Conservative leader Robert Stanfield in the early 1970s, but the government opted for the arbitrary $1000 interest-income exemption instead. While the personal deduction and tax bracket cut-offs in the personal income-tax system have been indexed since 1973, the interest-income exemption is not indexed. Thus its real value has shrunk dramatically over the last decade.

Indexing and the Social Costs of Inflation

The most extensive government use of indexing to be found in Canada today is in transfer payments and the personal income-tax system. Canada Pension Plan

---

[4]Some other countries, with much higher inflation than ours, do extensive indexing of interest rates. Brazil and Israel are notable examples.

[5]The distinction between real and nominal interest rates, one of our 12 Ideas for Beyond the Final Exam, was discussed in detail in Chapter 6.

benefits are fully indexed so that retirees are not victimized by inflation. A variety of government income-maintenance and social-insurance programs also pay benefits that are tied directly to prices. Some economists believe that Canada should adopt a much more widespread system of indexing. Why? Because, they argue, it would take most of the sting out of inflation. To see how indexing would accomplish this, let us review some of the social costs of inflation that we enumerated in Chapter 6.

One important cost is the capricious redistribution of income caused by unexpected inflation or deflation. We saw that borrowers and lenders normally incorporate an *inflation premium* equal to the *expected rate of inflation* into the nominal interest rate. Then, if inflation turns out to be higher than expected, the borrower has to pay to the lender only the agreed-upon nominal interest rate, including the premium for expected inflation; he does not have to compensate the lender for the (higher) actual inflation. Thus the borrower enjoys a windfall gain and the lender loses out. The opposite happens if inflation turns out to be lower than was expected. Again the borrower pays the lender the agreed-upon nominal interest rate, but now his rate includes an inflation premium that overcompensates the lender for the actual inflation. But if interest rates on loans were indexed, none of this would occur. Borrowers and lenders would agree on a fixed *real* rate of interest, and then the borrower would compensate the lender for whatever *actual inflation* occurred. No one would have to guess what the inflation rate would be.

A second social cost we mentioned in Chapter 6 stems from the fact that our tax system levies taxes on nominal interest and nominal capital gains. As we learned, this flaw in the tax system leads to extremely high effective tax rates in an inflationary environment. But indexing could fix this problem easily. We need only rewrite the tax code so that only real interest payments and real capital gains are taxed.

A final problem noted in Chapter 6 is that uncertainty over future price levels makes it difficult to enter into long-term contracts—rental agreements, construction agreements, and so on. One way out of this problem is to write indexed contracts, which specify all future payments in real terms.

In the face of all these benefits, and others we have not mentioned here, why do many economists oppose a move toward more complete indexing? One reason is the fear that indexing will lead to an acceleration of inflation. With the costs of inflation reduced so markedly, they argue, what will persuade governments to pay the price of fighting inflation? What will stop them from inflating more and more? They fear that the answer to these questions is, Nothing. Voters who stand to lose nothing from inflation are unlikely to pressure their legislators to stop it. Opponents of indexing worry that a mild inflationary disease could turn into a ravaging epidemic in a highly indexed economy. Hyperinflation often involves dramatic political changes.

Can We Conduct a Successful Stabilization Policy?

It seems fitting to conclude Part Three by considering what may be the most fundamental and controversial issue of all: Is it likely that the government can conduct a successful stabilization policy? Or are its well-intentioned efforts likely to be harmful, so that it would be better to adhere to *fixed rules*?

This controversy has raged for several decades now, with no clear resolution of the issue. Often the protagonists in the debate have been monetarists arguing for fixed rules, against Keynesians arguing for discretionary adjustments of policy.

Monetarists point to the lags and uncertainties that surround the operation of both fiscal and monetary policies—lags and uncertainties that we have stressed repeatedly in earlier chapters. Will the Bank of Canada's actions have the desired effects on the money supply? How long will these actions have significant effects on interest rates? How will they affect spending, and how long will it take before the effects appear? Can fiscal-policy actions be taken promptly? Will consumers view tax changes as temporary or permanent? How large is the expenditure multiplier? The list could go on and on.

Monetarists look at this formidable catalogue of difficulties, add a dash of skepticism about our ability to forecast the economy's future, and conclude that stabilization policy is likely to do more harm than good. They advise both the fiscal and monetary authorities to pursue a passive policy rather than an active one—adhering to fixed rules that, while they will not iron out all the bumps in the economy's growth path, will at least keep it roughly on track in the long run.

Keynesians, though they admit that perfection is unattainable, are much *more optimistic* about the possibility of achieving a successful stabilization policy. And they are much *less optimistic* than the monetarists about how smoothly the economy would function in the absence of demand management. They therefore advocate discretionary increases in government spending (or decreases in taxes) and more rapid growth of the money supply when the economy has a recessionary gap. By this policy mix, they believe, government can keep the economy closer to its full-employment growth path.

Naturally, each side can point to evidence that buttresses its own view. Keynesians like to remind us of the U.S. government's tax cut of 1964 and the sustained period of economic growth that it helped usher in. Monetarists remind us of the government's refusal to curb what was obviously a situation of runaway demand during the late 1960s.

The historical record of fiscal and monetary policy is far from glorious. It shows that while there were many instances in which appropriate stabilization policy could have been helpful, the authorities instead either took inappropriate steps or did nothing at all. We examined some of these mistakes in Chapter 15. It seems, therefore, that the question of whether the government should adopt passive rules or attempt an activist stabilization policy merits a closer look. As we shall see, the lags in the effects of policy play a pivotal role in the debate.

Lags and the Rules-Versus-Discretion Debate

The reason that lags lead to a fundamental difficulty for stabilization policy—a difficulty so formidable that it has led many economists to conclude that attempts to stabilize economic activity are likely to do more harm than good—can be explained best by reference to Figure 19–2. Here we chart the behaviour of both actual and potential GNP over the course of a business cycle in a hypothetical economy in which no stabilization policy is attempted. At point *A*, the economy begins to slip into a recession and does not recover to full employment until point *D*. Then, between points *D* and *E*, it overshoots and is in an inflationary boom.

The case for stabilization policy runs like this. The recession is recognized to be a serious problem at point *B*, and appropriate actions are taken. These have their major effects around point *C* and thus curb both the depth and length of the recession.

But suppose the lags are really much longer than this. Suppose, for example, that delays in taking action postpone policy initiatives until point *C* and that stimulative policies do not have their major effects until after point *D*. Then policy will be of little help during the recession, and will actually do harm by overstimulating the economy during the ensuing boom. Thus:

In the presence of long lags, attempts at stabilizing the economy can actually succeed in destabilizing it.

Figure 19-2

A TYPICAL BUSINESS CYCLE
This is a stylized representation of the relationship between actual and potential GNP during a typical business cycle. The imaginary economy slips into a recession at point A, bottoms out around point B, and is in a recovery period until point D. After point D, it enters an inflationary boom that lasts until point E.

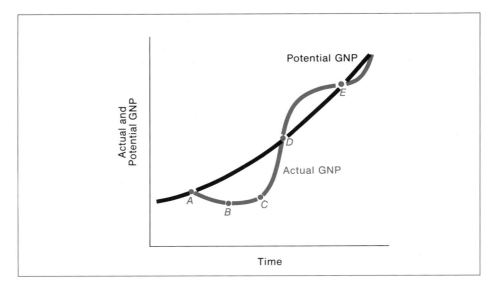

Because of this, some economists, like Milton Friedman, have argued that we are better off letting the economy alone and relying on its natural self-corrective forces to cure recessions and inflations. Instead of embarking on periodic programs of monetary and fiscal stimulus or restraint, they advise policy-makers to stick to fixed rules; that is, to rigid formulas that ignore current economic events.

The rule most emphasized by monetarists is that the Bank of Canada simply keep the money supply growing at a constant rate. The corresponding rule for fiscal policy is to *keep the high-employment budget in balance.*

The concept of the high-employment budget was introduced and explained in Chapter 17 (pages 323–25). Under this rule for fiscal policy, the actual budget would swing from surplus to deficit during a recession and from deficit to surplus during an inflationary boom. The main reason is that tax receipts automatically rise when GNP rises and fall when GNP falls. In addition, some items of government expenditure, such as transfer payments, automatically increase when unemployment rises and decrease when unemployment falls. So fiscal policy automatically swings toward expansion when the economy sags and toward contraction when the economy booms.

Automatic Stabilizers

An **automatic stabilizer** is any arrangement that automatically serves to support aggregate demand when it would otherwise sag and to hold down aggregate demand when it would otherwise surge ahead. In this way, an automatic stabilizer reduces the sensitivity of the economy to shifts in demand.

This discussion actually illustrates a general class of mechanisms called **automatic stabilizers**—features of the economy that reduce its sensitivity to shocks. Examples of automatic stabilizers are not hard to find in the federal budget. The personal income tax is the most obvious example.

The ability of the income tax to act as a shock absorber derives from the fact that it makes disposable income, and thus consumer spending, less sensitive to fluctuations in GNP. When GNP rises, disposable income (*DI*) rises also, but by less than the rise in GNP because part of the income is siphoned off by the government. This helps limit the upward fluctuation in consumption spending. And when GNP falls, *DI* falls less sharply because part of the loss is absorbed by the government rather than by consumers. So consumption does not drop as much as it otherwise might. Thus, although everybody likes to grumble about it, the personal income tax—which affected very few families in 1929, but affects almost everyone now—is one of the many modern institutions that helps ensure us against a repeat performance of the Great Depression.

There are many other automatic stabilizers in our economy. For example, in Chapter 6 we studied the Canadian system of unemployment insurance. This serves as an automatic stabilizer in a similar way. When GNP begins to fall and people lose their jobs, unemployment benefits prevent the disposable incomes of the jobless from falling as much as their earnings. As a result, unemployed workers can maintain their spending, and consumption need not fluctuate as dramatically as employment.

And the list could continue. The basic principle is the same: Each of these automatic stabilizers, in one way or another, serves as a shock absorber, and each does so without the need for any decision-maker to take action. In a word, they work *automatically*.

Stabilization Policy: Discretionary Measures or Fixed Rules?

Believers in fixed rules assert that we should forget about discretionary policy and rely solely on automatic stabilizers and the economy's natural self-correcting mechanisms. Are they right? As usual, the answer depends on many factors.

How Fast Does the Economy's Self-Correcting Mechanism Work?

We stressed in Chapter 10 that the economy does have a self-correcting mechanism. If the economy can cure recessions and inflations very quickly by itself, then the case for intervention is weak. For if such problems typically last only a short time, then lags in discretionary stabilization policy mean that the medicine will often have its major effects only after the disease is over. (In terms of Figure 19–2, this would be a case where point D comes very close to point A.)

While the more extreme advocates of rules argue that this is what indeed happens, most economists agree that the economy's self-correcting mechanism is slow and not terribly reliable, even when supplemented by the automatic stabilizers. On this count, then, a point is scored for discretionary policy.

How Long Are the Lags in Stabilization Policy?

As we explained, long lags before stabilization measures are adopted or can take effect make it unlikely that policy can do much good, while short lags point in the other direction. Thus, advocates of fixed rules emphasize the length of lags while proponents of discretion discount them.

Who is really right depends on the circumstances. In the most optimistic scenario, fiscal-policy actions are taken promptly, and the economy feels much of the stimulus from expansionary policy in less than a year after slipping into a recession. While far from an instant curve, these actions certainly are felt soon enough to do a lot of good. But, as we have seen, more pessimistic scenarios raise the possibility that policy may actually be destabilizing. History offers examples of both types of scenarios. No general conclusion can be drawn.

How Accurate Are Economic Forecasts?

One way to cut down the policy-making lag is to have good economic forecasts. If we could see a recession coming a full year ahead of time (which we certainly *cannot* do), even a rather slow-acting policy response would still be timely. (In terms of Figure 19–2, this would be a case where the coming recession is predicted well before point A arrives.) Unfortunately, however, to forecast Canadian economic performance, we must be able to predict U.S. interest rates, foreign-government policies that affect our export performance, and such intangibles as inflationary expectations. The evidence is that forecasting is certainly not good enough to support so-called "fine tuning," that is, attempts to keep the economy always within a hair's breadth of full employment. But it probably is good enough if our interest in using discretionary stabilization policy is simply to avoid sizable gaps between actual and potential GNP.

Other Dimensions of the Rules-Versus-Discretion Debate

While lags and forecasting play major roles in the debate between advocates of rules and advocates of discretionary policy, these are not the only battlegrounds.

The Size of Government

One bogus argument that is none the less quite often heard is that an activist fiscal policy must inevitably lead to a growing public sector. Since proponents of fixed rules tend also to be opponents of big government, they view this as undesirable. Of course, others think that a large public sector is just what society needs. This argument is, however, completely beside the point, as we pointed out in Chapter 11 (pages 209–210).

One's opinion about the proper size of government should have nothing to do with one's view on stabilization policy. When recessions occur, advocates of big government can call for greater spending while advocates of small government can insist on tax cuts. Similarly, if there is a need to contract aggregate demand to fight inflation, we can make the public sector smaller by cutting expenditures or bigger by raising taxes. While such choices may be quite momentous from other points of view, they simply do not bear on the question of whether we should fight the recession or the inflation.

A particularly clear example of this point came in the early days of the Reagan administration. Reagan embarked on an extremely *activist* stabilization policy based on *shrinking* the size of the public sector through reductions in both taxes and government spending.

Uncertainties Caused by Government Policy

Advocates of rules are on stronger ground when they argue that frequent changes in tax laws, government spending programs, or monetary conditions will make it difficult for firms and consumers to formulate and carry out rational plans. They argue that by adhering to fixed rules, which are known to businesses and consumers, the authorities can provide a more stable environment for the private sector. One of the points stressed by advocates of rules is that the downward flexibility of wages and prices has been undermined by the government's commitment to activist stabilization policy. Why lower your wage or price during a recession, if you expect that the government is about to stimulate demand?

Supporters of discretionary policy tend to ignore this issue and instead stress the difference between stability in the government budget (or in Bank of Canada operations) and stability in the economy. The goal of stabilization policy is to help *prevent* gyrations in the pace of economic activity by *causing* timely gyrations in the government budget (or in monetary policy). Which atmosphere is better for business, they ask, one in which fiscal and monetary rules keep things peaceful on Parliament Hill and at the Bank of Canada while recessions and inflation hit the economy, or one in which policy instruments are changed abruptly on occasion but the economy grows more steadily? They think that the answer is self-evident.

A Political Business Cycle

A final argument used by advocates of rules is political rather than economic in nature. Fiscal policy, they note, is decided upon by elected politicians. At least when elections are on the horizon, these men and women are likely to be at least as concerned with keeping their offices as with doing what is right for the economy. This leaves fiscal policy subject to all sorts of political manipulations, meaning that inappropriate actions may be taken to attain short-run political goals. In a system of purely automatic stabilization, its proponents argue, a rule of law would replace the rule of men, and this peril would be eliminated.

There is certainly a *possibility* that politicians could deliberately *cause*

Political Business Cycles

Since the Phillips curve trade-off is reasonably favourable in the short run (so that lower unemployment can be bought rather cheaply in terms of inflation), and since elected officials tend to have a hard time seeing past the next election, there is the possibility that politicians might deliberately cause business cycles in order to promote their own political ends.

Let us see how this might work with a hypothetical scenario. In January 1993, Les Scruples, a clever politician, takes office. The inflation rate is 8 percent and the unemployment rate is 7 percent (see the accompanying figure). Scruples remembers from his university political science course that (a) voters tend to blame the government when economic conditions are bad and reward them when economic conditions are good, and (b) voters have very short memories when they go to the polls. In fact, Scruples has seen studies that suggest that voters care only about the economy's real growth rate in the *one year prior to election day.* (This, in fact, is what the studies do suggest.)

This gives Scruples an idea. "By wringing inflation out of the system with a recession early in my term, and then stimulating demand near the end of my term, I should be able to stand for re-election with the inflation rate well below 8 percent and the unemployment rate well below 7 percent. Sounds great. I wonder if I can do it?" Scruples consults his economic advisers who explain to him that while the long-run Phillips curve is vertical, the short-run Phillips curve is probably quite flat, so his plan should work.

During his first year in office Scruples raises taxes and cuts government spending. A serious recession ensues: unemployment rises to 10 percent (again, see the accompanying figure). During the second, third, and fourth years of his term, the economy's natural self-

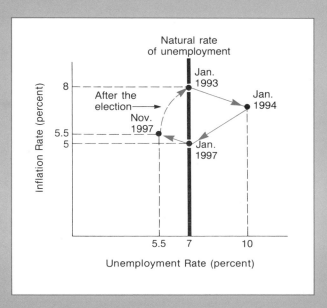

correcting mechanism slowly and painfully erodes the recessionary gap, so that by January 1997—an election year—inflation is down to 5 percent and unemployment is back to 7 percent (see the figure).

Now Les Scruples opens the sluice gates of federal spending and enacts a huge tax cut. The economy travels leftward along its short-run Phillips curve until, on election day 1997, the unemployment rate is down to 5½ percent and inflation is only 5½ percent. Scruples runs "on his record" as the prime minister who brought down both inflation and unemployment. His party is re-elected in a landslide. After the election, inflation accelerates and unemployment rises.

economic instability to help their own re-election. (See the boxed insert above.) And some observers of these "political business cycles" have claimed that several leaders have taken full advantage of the opportunity. Furthermore, even if there is no insidious intent, politicians may take the wrong actions for perfectly honourable reasons. Decisions in the political arena are never clear-cut, and it certainly is easy to find examples of large errors in the history of Canadian stabilization policy. Again, we refer the reader to Chapter 15, which described the government's attempts to use fiscal policy in a floating exchange-rate regime, and its attempts to use monetary policy in a fixed exchange-rate regime.

So, taken as a whole, the political argument against discretionary policy seems to have a great deal of merit. But what are we to do about it? It is foolhardy to believe that fiscal and monetary decisions could or should be made by a group of objective and non-partisan technicians. Steering the economy is not like steering a rocket to the moon. Because policy actions that help on the employment front normally do harm on the inflation front, and vice versa, the "correct" policy action is almost always an inherently political matter. In a political democracy, if we take such decisions out of the hands of elected officials, in whose hands shall we put them?

Ethical Reflections on the Economic Crisis

Many Canadians have been shocked by the depth of the recession of the 1980s. The Canadian Conference of Catholic Bishops made public its *Ethical Reflections on the Economic Crisis* in January 1983 and much public discussion followed. The following three statements capture the general thrust of the Bishops' views:

1. Unemployment rather than inflation should be recognized as the number-one problem, and expansion in aggregate demand is warranted.
2. Wage and price controls represent a more balanced and equitable means of controlling inflation than does contractionary demand policy.
3. Investment should take place in labour-intensive, not capital-intensive, industries.

All of these comments stem from the Bishops' deep concern for the poor. But each statement involves both a positive and a normative element; that is, each involves an economic issue (that may be true or false) and a moral issue (upon which the Bishops can comment). Economists, in their role as technical advisers, must limit their evaluation of these policy suggestions to the positive, or factual, aspects. We consider each statement in turn.

1. Statement One involves the proposition that unemployment can be traded-off with inflation (a factual issue) and the view that the costs of unemployment are more important than the costs of inflation. We have learned that it is very unlikely that unemployment and inflation can be traded off in the long run, so that *in the long run* (but not the short run!), moral disagreements concerning the relative burdens of unemployment and inflation are not critical for the conduct of policy.

2. Statement Two involves the assumption that wage and price controls work, even when aggregate-demand policy is expansionary (the factual question), and the view that unemployment is more important than the misallocation of resources that follows from controls (the moral question). Unfortunately, history has given a very clear answer regarding the factual question: While controls can work for a year or two, they have *never* provided *any lasting* help in fighting inflation when used as a substitute for (rather than a complement to) contractionary demand policy. If controls do not work, moral debates concerning their costs are beside the point.

3. Statement Three involves the assumption that jobs created by new industries involve less total employment than jobs that are lost during the adjustment period that follows automation. This is the factual issue. The moral proposition is that jobs are more important than cost-saving techniques. Regarding the economic issue, history has shown that the industrial revolution led to more jobs *and* higher income standards. Again, it seems that in the *long run*, the moral issue may not arise.

The point of this discussion is to emphasize that while economists *cannot* referee moral disputes, they can contribute toward minimizing them by drawing attention to, and commenting on, the positive aspects of policy disagreements. As we have seen in these examples, the factual issue *can* be logically prior to the moral question. Nevertheless, the current state of economic analysis *only* permits this strong conclusion if one is prepared to stress the *longer run*. In the short run, there *is* an unemployment–inflation trade-off, controls do slow inflation temporarily, and automation does cause significant dislocation. Regarding short-run policy options then, heated debate will continue even if all participants are careful to separate positive and normative issues.

This harsh fact may seem worrisome in view of the possibilities for political chicanery, but it should not bother us any more (or any less!) than similar manoeuvring in other areas of policy-making. After all, the same thing applies to international relations, formulation of the law, and so on. Politicians make all these decisions for us, subject only to sporadic accountability at election times. Is there really any reason why economic decisions should be different?

Conclusion: What Should Be Done?

Where do all these considerations leave us? On balance, is it better to conduct discretionary policy as best we can, knowing full well that we will never do it perfectly? Or is it wiser to rely on fixed rules and automatic stabilizers?

In weighing the pros and cons that we have discussed in this chapter, one's basic view of the economy is very important. Some economists believe that the economy, if left unmanaged, would generate a series of ups and downs that are hard to predict, but that it would correct each of them by itself in a relatively short period of time. They conclude that, because of long lags and poor forecasts our ability to anticipate whether the economy will be heading up or down by the time policy actions have their effects is quite limited. And so they are led to advocate fixed rules.

Other economists liken the economy to a giant glacier with a great deal of inertia. This means that if we observe an inflationary or recessionary gap today, it is likely still to be there a year or two from now because the self-correcting mechanism is so slow. In such a world, accurate forecasting is not imperative, even if policy lags are long. If we base policy on a forecast of a $10 billion gap between actual and potential GNP a year from now, and the gap turns out to be only $5 billion, then we still will have done the right thing despite the horrible forecast. Holders of this view of the economy, then, are likely to advocate the use of discretionary policy.

While there is no consensus on this issue either among economists or among politicians, a prudent view might be that:

The case for active discretionary policy is strong when the economy has a serious deficiency or excess of aggregate demand. However, advocates of fixed rules are right that it is unwise to try to iron out every little wiggle in the growth path of GNP.

But the decision cannot be made solely on economic grounds. Political judgments enter as well. In the end:

The question of whether the government should take an active hand in managing the economy, which is one of the main bones of contention between Keynesians and monetarists today, is as much a matter of ideology as of economics. Liberals have always looked to government activism to solve social problems, while conservatives have consistently pointed out that many efforts of government fail despite the best of intentions.

Since no one can decide whether liberal or conservative political attitudes are the "correct" ones on purely objective criteria, the rules-versus-discretion debate is likely to go on for quite some time.

Summary

1. Policies that improve the functioning of the labour market—including retraining programs and various types of employment services—can improve the trade-off between inflation and unemployment by lowering the natural rate of unemployment. To date, however, Western governments have had only modest success with these measures.

2. Some small amount of progress against inflation may also be made by eliminating some of the government regulations that keep prices high.

3. Many varieties of incomes policies have been used in this and other countries in an effort to improve the trade-off between inflation and unemployment. While some have led to notable temporary improvements, a surge of inflation often follows the controls period.

4. The weakest varieties of incomes policies simply set up standards for permissible wage and price increases (wage–price guidelines) and apply verbal admonitions against violators (jawboning). Stronger variants may actually set legal limits on wage and price increases or even ban them outright (a wage–price freeze). But such policies seriously interfere with the workings of our market economy.

5. One argument in favour of short-term wage–price controls is that they can reduce inflationary expectations and thereby rob inflation of some of its momentum and reduce the magnitude of the temporary recession that must accompany contractionary aggregate-demand policy. The Canadian AIB made a significant contribution in this regard.

6. A new and different approach to incomes policy would use tax incentives to encourage more moderate wage and price increases. This so-called "tax-based incomes policy" has yet to be tried.

7. Indexing is another way to approach the trade-off problem. Instead of trying to improve the trade-off, it concentrates on reducing the social costs of inflation.

Opponents of indexing worry, however, that the economy's resistance to inflation may be lowered by indexing.

8. When there are long lags in the operation of fiscal and monetary policy, it becomes possible that attempts to stabilize economic activity may actually succeed in destabilizing it.

9. The Canadian economy has a number of automatic stabilizers that make it less vulnerable to shocks than it would otherwise be. Among these are the personal income tax and unemployment benefits.

10. Many monetarists believe that our imperfect knowledge of the channels through which stabilization policy works, and the long lags involved, make it unlikely that discretionary stabilization policy can succeed.

11. Keynesians recognize these difficulties but do not believe they are as serious as monetarists think. On the other hand, Keynesians place much less faith in the economy's ability to cure recessions and inflations on its own. They therefore think that discretionary policy is not only advisable, but essential.

Concepts for Review

Incomes policy	Anti-Inflation Board (AIB)	Indexing (escalator clauses)
Jawboning	Inflationary expectations	Real versus nominal interest rates
Wage–price guidelines	Wage–price freezes	Rules versus discretionary policy
Wage–price controls	Tax-based incomes policy (TIP)	Automatic stabilizers

Questions for Discussion

1. Do you think it is proper for the Prime Minister's Office to "jawbone" some corporations into reducing their price increases?

2. Explain some of the differences between wage–price guidelines and wage–price controls.

3. Suppose that a program of wage–price controls is under consideration by the government. What are the possible benefits to the nation from such a program? What are the possible costs? How would you go about balancing the benefits against the costs?

4. Explain the basic idea behind "TIP" (tax-based incomes policy). Try to devise a TIP plan of your own. Can you foresee some practical difficulties with your plan?

5. At the time of writing (late 1984), ordinary savings accounts paid approximately 8 percent *nominal* interest. Would you prefer to trade yours in for an indexed bank account that paid a zero *real* rate of interest? What if the real interest rate offered were 2 percent? What if it were –2 percent? What do your answers to these questions reveal about your personal attitudes toward inflation?

6. Explain why lags make it possible for policy actions intended to stabilize the economy to actually destabilize it instead.

7. Name some automatic stabilizers and explain how and what they "stabilize."

8. Which of the following events would strengthen the argument for the use of discretionary policy, and which would strengthen the argument for rules?
   a. Structural changes make the economy's self-correcting mechanism faster and more reliable than before.
   b. New statistical methods are found that improve the accuracy of economic forecasts.

IV

Essentials of Microeconomics: Consumers and Firms

The Common Sense of Consumer Choice

20

Everything is worth what its
purchaser will pay for it.
PUBLILIUS SYRUS (1st century B.C.)

It is clear from our initial look at supply and demand in Chapter 4 that if we are to understand how markets function and how they react to changes in the economic environment, we will have to delve more deeply into the nature of both demand and supply. What influences determine the shapes and positions of the demand and supply curves? How do the curves shift in response to various events? The purpose of Part Four is to answer questions like these and thereby to provide the analytical tools we will need to pursue the central theme of this book: the virtues and shortcomings of the market mechanism.

We begin on the demand side of the market. In this chapter we emphasize that the demand curves of Chapter 4 depend on choices made by consumers, and we explore the logic underlying these choices. Since a demand curve tells us how much of a good consumers want to purchase at each possible price, its origins must in some sense rest in consumer psychology. But since economists claim no qualifications for making deep pronouncements about consumer psychology, our exploration will not go very far below the surface. It will, however, describe some powerful tools used in the analysis of consumer choice and cast some light on a number of important issues, including the negative slope of the demand curve.

In Chapter 21 we take up some further aspects of demand curves that are essential for understanding the workings of the market mechanism and expand our analysis from demand curves for single consumers to demand curves for a total market. Then, in Chapters 22 and 23, we turn our attention to the supply side of the market.

A Puzzle:
Should Water Be Worth More than Diamonds?

When Adam Smith was lecturing at the University of Glasgow in the 1760s, he introduced the study of demand by posing a puzzle. Common sense, he said, suggests that the price of a commodity must somehow depend on what that good is worth to consumers—on the amount of *utility* that commodity offers. Yet, Smith pointed out, there are cases in which a good's utility apparently has little influence on its price.

Two examples he gave were diamonds and water. He noted that water, which is essential to life and therefore undoubtedly of enormous value to most consumers, generally sells at a very low price, while diamonds, on the other hand, cost thousands of dollars even though their uses are quite limited. A century later, this puzzle, called the **diamond–water paradox**, helped stimulate the invention of what is perhaps the most powerful set of tools in the economist's toolkit—*marginal analysis*. Fortunately, we need only wait a few pages, not a century, to learn how marginal analysis—a general method for making optimal decisions—helps to resolve the paradox.

Total and Marginal Utility

In the Canadian economy, millions of consumers make millions of decisions every day. You decide to buy a movie ticket instead of a paperback novel. Your roommate decides to buy two kilograms of cheese rather than one or three. How are these decisions made?

Economists have constructed a simple theory of consumer choice based on the hypothesis that each consumer spends his or her income in the way that yields the greatest amount of satisfaction, or *utility*. This seems a reasonable starting point, since it says little more than that people do what they prefer. But, to make the theory operational, we need a way to measure utility.

A century ago, economists thought that utility could be measured directly in some kind of psychological units (sometimes called "utils"), after somehow reading the consumer's mind. But gradually it came to be realized that this was an unnecessary and, perhaps, impossible task. How many utils did you get from the last movie you saw? You probably cannot answer that question because you have no idea what a util is.

But you may be able to answer a different question like, How many hamburgers would you give up to get that movie ticket? If you answer "three," we still do not know how many utils you get from a movie. But we do know that you get more than you get from a hamburger. Hamburgers, rather than utils, become the unit of measurement, and we can say that the utility of a movie (to you) is three hamburgers.

Early in the twentieth century, economists concluded that this more indirect way of measuring utility was all they needed to build a theory of consumer choice. We can measure the utility of a movie ticket by asking how much of some other commodity (like hamburgers) you are willing to give up for it. Any commodity will do for this purpose. But the simplest choice, and the one we will use in this book, is money.[1]

The **total utility** of a quantity of goods to a consumer (measured in money terms) is the maximum amount of money he or she is willing to give in exchange for it.

Thus, we are led to define the **total utility** of some bundle of goods to some consumer as *the largest sum of money she will voluntarily give up in exchange for it*. For example, suppose Jennifer is considering purchasing six kilograms of bananas. She has determined that she will not buy them if they cost more than $4.44, but she will buy them if they cost $4.44 or less. Then the *total utility* of six kilograms of bananas to her is $4.44—the maximum amount she is willing to spend to have them.

Total utility measures the benefit Jennifer derives from her purchases. It is total utility that really matters. But to understand which decisions most effectively promote *total* utility we must consider the related concept of **marginal utility**. This term refers to the *additional utility that an individual derives by consuming one more unit of any good*.

The **marginal utility** of a commodity to a consumer (measured in money terms) is the maximum amount of money he or she is willing to pay *for one more unit* of it.

Table 20–1 helps clarify the distinction between marginal utility and total utility, and shows how the two are related. The first two columns show how much *total* utility (measured in money terms) Jennifer derives from various quantities of

---

[1]*NOTE TO INSTRUCTORS:* You will recognize that while not using the terms, we are distinguishing between neoclassical *cardinal utility* and *ordinal utility*. Moreover, throughout the book marginal utility in money terms or money marginal utility is simply a synonym for the marginal rate of substitution between money and the commodity in question.

Table 20-1

TOTAL AND MARGINAL UTILITY OF BANANAS (MEASURED IN MONEY TERMS)

NUMBER OF KILOGRAMS	TOTAL UTILITY (in dollars)	MARGINAL UTILITY (in dollars)
0	0	
1	1.20	1.20
2	2.32	1.12
3	3.20	0.88
4	3.92	0.72
5	4.28	0.36
6	4.44	0.16
7	4.52	0.08
8	4.52	0

bananas ranging from zero to eight. For example, a single kilogram is worth (no more than) $1.20 to her, two kilograms are worth $2.32, and so on. The *marginal* utility is the *difference* between any two successive total-utility figures. For example, if the consumer already has three kilograms (worth $3.20 to her), an *additional* kilogram brings her total utility up to $3.92. Her marginal utility is thus the difference between the two, or 72¢.

Remember: Whenever we use the terms *total utility* and *marginal utility*, we are defining these in terms of the consumer's willingness to part with money for the commodity—not in some unobservable (and imaginary) psychological units.

The "Law" of Diminishing Marginal Utility

With these definitions we can now propose a simple hypothesis about consumer tastes: The more of a good a consumer has, the less will be the *marginal* utility of an additional unit.

In general, this is a plausible proposition. The idea is based on the assertion that every person has a hierarchy of uses to which he or she will put a particular commodity. All of these uses are valuable, but some are more valuable than others. Let's consider bananas again. Jennifer may use them to give to her family to eat, to feed a pet monkey, to make banana cream pie (which is a bit rich for her tastes), or to give to a brother-in-law for whom she has no deep affection. If she has only one kilogram, it will be used solely for the family to eat. The second, third, and fourth kilograms may be used to feed the monkey; and the fifth may go into the banana cream pie. But the only use she has for the sixth kilogram, alas, is to give it to her brother-in-law.

The point is obvious. Each kilogram of bananas contributes something to the satisfaction of Jennifer's needs for the product. But each additional kilogram contributes less (relative to money) than its predecessor because the use to which it can be put has a lower priority. This, in essence, is the logic behind the **"law" of diminishing marginal utility**.

The last column of Table 20-1 illustrates this concept. The marginal utility (abbreviated MU) of the first kilogram of bananas is $1.20; that is, Jennifer is willing to pay up to $1.20 for the first kilogram. The second kilogram is worth no more than $1.12, the third kilogram only 88¢, and so on until, after the fifth kilogram, the consumer is willing to pay only 16¢ for an additional kilogram (the MU of the sixth kilogram is 16¢).

The assumption upon which this "law" is based is plausible for most consumers and for most commodities. But, like most laws, there are exceptions. For some people, the more they have of a particular good, the more they want. Consider the needs of addicts and collectors, for example. The stamp collector who has a few stamps may consider the acquisition of one more to be mildly amusing. The person who has a large and valuable collection may be prepared to

The **"law" of diminishing marginal utility** asserts that additional units of a commodity are worth less and less to a consumer in money terms. As the individual's consumption increases, the marginal utility of each additional unit declines.

go to the ends of the earth for another stamp. Similarly, the alcoholic who finds a dry martini quite pleasant when he first starts drinking may find one more to be absolutely irresistible once he has already consumed four or five. Economists, however, generally treat such cases of *increasing marginal utility* as anomalies. For most goods and most people, marginal utility probably declines as consumption increases.

The Optimal Purchase Rule

Now let us put the concept of marginal utility to work in analysing consumer choice. Every consumer has a limited amount of money to spend. Which items will he or she buy, and in what quantities? The theory of consumer choice is based on the hypothesis that consumers will spend their money in the way that *maximizes their total utility*. This hypothesis leads to the following **optimal purchase rule**:

It always pays the consumer to buy more of any commodity whose marginal utility (measured in money) exceeds its price, and less of any commodity whose marginal utility is less than its price. When possible, the consumer should buy the quantity of each good at which price (*P*) and marginal utility (MU) are exactly equal; that is, at which

$$P = MU,$$

because only these quantities will maximize the *total utility* he or she gains from the purchases given the fact that the money available must be divided up among all the goods bought.[2]

Notice that while our concern is with *total* utility, the rule is framed in terms of *marginal* utility. Marginal utility is not important for its own sake, but rather as an instrument used to calculate the level of purchases that maximizes total utility.

To see why this rule works, refer back to the table of marginal utilities of bananas (Table 20-1). Suppose the supermarket is selling bananas for 46¢ a kilogram and Jennifer considers buying only two kilograms. We see that this is not a wise decision, because the marginal utility of the third kilogram of bananas (88¢) is greater than its 46¢ price. If Jennifer were to increase her purchase to three kilograms, the additional kilogram would cost 46¢ but yield 88¢ in marginal utility; thus the additional purchase would bring her a clear net gain of 42¢. Obviously, at the 46¢ price she is better off with three kilograms of bananas than with two.

Similarly, at this price, five kilograms is *not* an optimal purchase because the 36¢ marginal utility of the fifth kilogram is less than its 46¢ price. Jennifer would be better off with only four kilograms, since that would save her 46¢ with only a 36¢ loss in utility—a net gain of 10¢ from the decision to buy one kilogram less. Our rule for optimal purchases tells us that Jennifer should buy four kilograms, since any purchase above this amount yields a marginal utility that is less than price, and any purchase below this amount leaves MU greater than *P*.

It should be noted that price is an objective, observable figure determined by the market, while marginal utility is subjective and reflects the tastes of the consumer. Since consumers lack the power to influence the price, they must adjust their purchases to make the marginal utility of each good equal to the price given by the market.

[2]We can equate a dollar price with marginal utility only because we measure marginal utility in money terms (or, as the matter is usually put by economists, because we deal with the marginal rate of substitution of money for the commodity in question). If marginal utility were measured in some psychological units not directly translatable into money terms, a comparison of *P* and MU would have no meaning. However, MU could also be measured in terms of any commodity other than money. (*Example:* How much root beer is Jennifer willing to trade for an additional banana?)

Table 20-2

LIST OF OPTIMAL QUANTITY TO PURCHASE AT ALTERNATIVE PRICES

PRICE (in dollars)	QUANTITY TO PURCHASE
0.04	7
0.12	6
0.28	5
0.44	4
0.80	3
1.00	2
1.16	1

From Marginal Utility to the Demand Curve

We can use the optimal purchase rule to show that the "law" of diminishing marginal utility implies that demand curves typically slope downward to the right; that is, they have negative slopes.[3] For example, it is possible to use the list of marginal utilities in Table 20-1 to determine precisely how many bananas Jennifer would buy at any price. Table 20-2 gives several alternative prices, and the optimal purchase quantity corresponding to each. (To make sure you understand the logic behind the optimal purchase rule, verify that the entries in the right-hand column of Table 20-2 are in fact correct.) This *demand schedule*, which relates quantity demanded to price, may be translated into Jennifer's *demand curve* shown in Figure 20-1. You can see that it has the characteristic negative slope commonly associated with demand curves.

Let us examine the logic underlying the negatively sloped demand curve a bit more carefully. If Jennifer is purchasing the optimal number of bananas, and then the price falls, she will find that her marginal utility of bananas is now above the suddenly reduced price. For example, Table 20-1 tells us that at a price of 80¢ per kilogram it is optimal to buy three kilograms, because the marginal utility (MU) of the fourth kilogram is 72¢. But, if price is reduced to 60¢, it then pays to purchase the fourth kilogram because its MU exceeds its price. This additional kilogram of bananas will lower the marginal utility of the next kilogram of bananas (to 36¢ in the example) and thereby bring it back into balance with price, as prescribed in the optimal purchase rule.

[3]If you need review, turn back to pages 21–23 in Chapter 2.

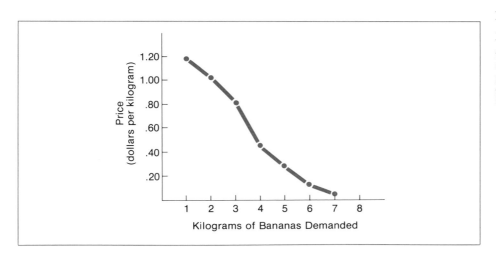

Figure 20-1

A TYPICAL DEMAND CURVE
This demand curve is derived from the consumer's table of marginal utilities by following the optimal purchase rule. The points in the graph correspond to the numbers in Table 20-2.

Note the critical role of the "law" of diminishing marginal utility. If P falls, a consumer who wishes to maximize total utility will see to it that MU falls. According to the "law" of diminishing marginal utility, the only way to do this is to increase the quantity purchased.

While this explanation is a bit abstract and mechanical, it can easily be rephrased in practical terms. We have seen that the various uses to which an individual puts a commodity have different priorities. For Jennifer, giving bananas to her family has a higher priority than using them to make pie, which in turn is of higher priority than giving them to her brother-in-law. If the price of bananas is high, Jennifer will buy only enough for the high-priority uses—those that offer a high marginal utility. When price declines, however, it pays to purchase more of the good—enough for some lower-priority uses. This is the essence of the analysis. It tells us that the same assumption about consumer psychology underlies both the law of diminishing marginal utility and the negative slope of the demand curve. They are really two different ways of describing the assumed attitudes of consumers.

The Diamond–Water Paradox: The Puzzle Resolved

We can use marginal utility analysis to solve the mystery of Adam Smith's diamond–water paradox—his observation that the price of diamonds is much higher than the price of water even though water seems to offer far more utility. The resolution of the diamond–water paradox is based on the distinction between marginal and total utility.

The *total* utility of water—its life-giving benefit—is indeed much higher than that of diamonds, just as Smith observed. But price, as we have seen, is not related directly to total utility. Rather, the optimal purchase rule tells us that price will tend to be equal to *marginal* utility. And there is every reason to expect the marginal utility of water to be very low while the marginal utility of diamonds is very high. Water is extremely plentiful in many parts of the world, and so its price is generally quite low. Consumers use correspondingly large quantities of water. By the principle of diminishing marginal utility, therefore, the marginal utility of water to a typical household will be pushed down to a very low level.

On the other hand, diamonds are very scarce. As a result, the quantity of diamonds consumed is not large enough to drive the MU of diamonds down very far and so buyers are willing to pay high prices for them. The scarcer the commodity, the higher its *marginal utility* and its market price will be, regardless of the size of its *total* utility.

Thus, like many paradoxes, the diamond–water puzzle has a straightforward explanation. In this case, all one has to remember is that:

Scarcity raises price and *marginal* utility but not necessarily *total* utility.

Prices, Income, and Quantity Demanded

Our study of marginal analysis has enabled us to examine the relation between the price of a commodity and the quantity that will be purchased. But the quantity of the good demanded by a consumer also depends on the consumer's income. Let us first consider briefly how a change in income affects quantity purchased. Then we will use this information to learn more about the effects of a price change.

The Effect of a Change in Income
The consumer's purchase of commodity X depends on both his income and the price of X. Let us consider what happens to the amount of X a consumer will buy

when his real income rises. It may seem almost certain that he will buy more X than before, but that is not necessarily so. A rise in real income can either increase or decrease the quantity of X purchased.

Why might it do the latter? There are some goods and services that people buy only because they cannot afford any better. They eat bologna three days a week and filet mignon twice a year, but would rather have it the other way around. They use margarine instead of butter, or purchase most of their clothing secondhand. If their real income rises, they may then buy more filet mignon and less bologna, more butter and less margarine, more new shirts and fewer second-hand shirts. Thus, a rise in real income will reduce the quantities of bologna, margarine, and secondhand shirts demanded. Economists have given the rather descriptive name **inferior goods** to the class of commodities for which quantity demanded falls when income rises.

The upshot of this discussion is that we cannot draw definite conclusions about the effects of a rise in consumer incomes on quantity demanded. For most commodities, if incomes rise and prices do not change, there will be an increase in quantity demanded. (Such items are often called *normal goods*.) But for the inferior goods there will be a decrease in quantity demanded.

The Effects of a Change in Price*

When the price of some good, say heating oil, falls, it has two consequences. First, it makes fuel oil cheaper relative to electricity, gas, or coal. We say, then, that the *relative price* of fuel oil has fallen. Second, this price decrease leaves homeowners with more money to spend on movie admissions, soft drinks, or clothing. In other words, the decrease in the price of fuel oil *increases the consumer's real income—* her power to purchase other goods.

While a fall in the price of a commodity always produces these two effects simultaneously, our analysis will be easier if we separate the effects from one another and study them one at a time.

1. ***The income effect.*** As we have just noted, a fall in the price of a commodity leads to a rise in the consumer's *real* income—the amount that her wages will purchase. The consequent effect on quantity demanded is called the **income effect** of the price fall.

    The income effect caused by a fall in a commodity's price is much the same as if the consumer's wages had risen: She will buy more of any commodity that is not an inferior good. The process producing the income effect has three stages: (1) the price of the good falls causing (2) an increase in the consumer's real income, which leads to (3) a change in quantity demanded. Of course, if the price of a good rises, it will produce the same effect in reverse. The consumer's real income will decline, leading to the opposite change in quantity demanded.

2. ***The substitution effect***. A change in the price of a commodity produces another effect on quantity demanded that is rather different from the income effect. This is the **substitution effect**, which is the effect on quantity demanded attributable to the fact that the new price is now higher or lower than before *relative to the prices of other goods*. The substitution effect of a price change is the portion of the change in quantity demanded that can be attributed *exclusively* to the resulting change in relative prices rather than to the associated change in real income.

    There is nothing mysterious or surprising about the effect of a change in relative prices when the consumer's real income remains unchanged. Whenever it is possible for the consumer to switch between two commodities, she can be expected to buy more of the good whose relative price has fallen and less of the

An **inferior good** is a commodity whose quantity demanded falls when the purchaser's real income rises, all other things remaining equal.

The **income effect** is a *portion* of the change in quantity of a good demanded when its price changes. A rise in price cuts the consumer's purchasing power (real income), which leads to a change in the quantity demanded of that commodity. That change is the income effect.

The **substitution effect** is the change in quantity demanded of a good resulting from a change in its relative price, exclusive of whatever change in quantity demanded may be attributable to the associated change in real income.

*This section contains rather more difficult material, which, in shorter courses, may be omitted without loss of continuity.

The Theory of Consumer Choice and White Rats

A few years ago, a team of economists and psychologists studied whether the theory of consumer choice that we have just outlined—including the different income and substitution effects of a price change—applies to animal species other than *homo sapiens*. According to their research, it does.*

In one experiment, standard laboratory rats were placed in experimental chambers equipped with two levers; pressing one lever rewarded them with a prescribed amount of commodity A (say, water) while pressing the other rewarded them with a prescribed amount of commodity B (say, food). The rats were given a limited "budget" because they could only press the levers a fixed number of times per day. Once they had exhausted their "income" by pressing the levers, say, 250 times, the lights above the levers would go out, signalling the rats that their presses would no longer result in rewards. Apparently, the little creatures learned the meaning of the lights quite quickly.

In this controlled environment, *income effects* could be observed by varying the permitted number of lever presses per day. The results showed clearly that when more lever presses were allowed, rats chose to consume more of both goods. Apparently, none of the goods, such as food, water, root beer, and Tom Collins mix, are inferior goods from the point of view of rats.

Measuring *substitution effects* was a bit trickier since, as we have stressed, a price change sets in motion *both* an income effect *and* a substitution effect. In the experiment, the "price" of each commodity was controlled by the amount of food or liquid produced by each lever press. Substitution effects were measured, for example, by raising the "price" of food (i.e., reducing the amount of food yielded by each press), while at the same time allowing the rat enough additional lever presses to compensate him for his loss of purchasing power. As the analysis of this chapter has suggested, the rats responded to this change in their environment by "buying" less food.

Putting the two effects together, then, a higher price of food led to less consumption of food via the income effect and also to less consumption of food via the substitution effect. The demand curves of these rats were indeed negatively sloped.

*John H. Kagel, Raymond C. Battalio, Howard Rachlin, and Leonard Green, "Demand Curves for Animal Consumers," *Quarterly Journal of Economics*, vol. XCVI, February 1981, pages 1–16.

---

good whose relative price has risen. For example, a few years ago the telephone company instituted sharp reductions in the prices of evening long-distance telephone calls relative to daytime calls. The big decrease in the relative price of evening calls brought about a large increase in calling during the evening hours and a decrease in daytime calling, just as the telephone company had hoped. Similarly, a fall in the relative price of fuel oil will induce more of the people who are building new homes to install oil heat instead of electric heat.

When the price of any commodity X rises relative to the price of some other commodity Y, a consumer whose real income has remained unchanged can be expected to buy less X and more Y than before. Thus, *if we consider the substitution effect alone*, a decline in price always increases quantity demanded and a rise in price always reduces quantity demanded.

These two concepts, the income effect and the substitution effect, which many beginning economics students think were invented to torture them, are really quite useful. Let us consider an example of how economists use them. Suppose the price of hamburgers declines while the price of cheese remains unchanged. The *substitution effect* clearly induces the consumer to buy more hamburgers in place of grilled cheese sandwiches, because hamburgers are now comparatively cheaper. What of the *income effect*? Unless hamburger is an inferior good, it leads to the same decision. The fall in price makes consumers richer,

---

which induces them to increase their purchases of all but inferior goods. This example alerts us to two general points:

If a good is not inferior, it must have a downward-sloping demand curve, since income and substitution effects reinforce each other. However, an inferior good may violate this pattern of demand behaviour because the income effect of a decline in price leads consumers to buy less.

Do *all* inferior goods, then, have upward-sloping demand curves? Certainly not, for we have the substitution effect to reckon with; and the substitution effect always favours a downward-sloping demand curve. Thus, we have a kind of tug-of-war in the case of an inferior good. If the *income effect* predominates, the demand curve will slope upward; if the *substitution effect* prevails, the demand curve will slope downward.

Economists have concluded that the substitution effect generally wins out; so while there are many examples of inferior goods, there are few examples of upward-sloping demand curves. When might the income effect prevail over the substitution effect? Certainly not when the good in question (say, margarine) is a very small fraction of the consumer's budget, for then a fall in price makes the consumer only slightly "richer," and therefore creates a very small income effect. But the demand curve could slope upward if an inferior good constitutes a substantial portion of the consumer's budget.

We conclude this discussion of income and substitution effects with a warning against an error that is frequently made. Many students mistakenly close their books thinking that price changes cause substitution effects while income changes cause income effects. This is incorrect. As the foregoing example of hamburgers made clear:

Any change in price sets in motion both a substitution effect and an income effect, both of which affect quantity demanded.

This completes our discussion of the logic behind consumer choice. In the next chapter we will use this analysis as a base upon which to build a theory of demand, thereby taking our first major step toward understanding how the market system operates.

Summary

1. Economists distinguish between total utility and marginal utility. Total utility, or the benefit a consumer derives from a purchase, is measured by the maximum amount of money he or she would give up in order to have the good in question. Rational consumers seek to maximize total utility.

2. Marginal utility is the maximum amount of money a consumer is willing to pay for an additional unit of a particular commodity. Marginal utility is useful in calculating what set of purchases maximizes total utility.

3. The "law" of diminishing marginal utility is a psychological hypothesis stating that as a consumer acquires more and more of a commodity, the marginal utility of additional units to the commodity will decrease.

4. To maximize the total utility obtained by spending money on some commodity X, given the fact that the other goods can be purchased only with the money that remains after buying X, the consumer must purchase a quantity of X such that the price is equal to the commodity's marginal utility (in money terms).

5. If the consumer acts to maximize utility, and if his marginal utility of some good declines when larger quantities are purchased, then his demand curve for the good will have a negative slope. A reduction in price will induce the purchase of more units, leading to a lower marginal utility.

6. Abundant goods tend to have a low price and low marginal utility regardless of whether their total utility is high or low. That is why water can have a low price despite its high total utility.

7. An inferior good, such as secondhand clothing, is a commodity consumers buy less of when they get richer, all other things held equal.

8. A rise in the price of a commodity has two effects on quantity demanded: (a) a substitution effect, which makes the good less attractive because it has become more expensive than it was previously, and (b) an income effect, which decreases the consumer's total utility because higher prices cut his purchasing power.

9. Any increase in the price of a good always has a *negative* substitution effect; that is, considering only the substitution effect, a rise in price must reduce the quantity demanded.

10. The income effect of a rise in price may, however, push quantity demanded up or down. For normal goods, the income effect of a higher price (which makes consumers poorer) reduces quantity demanded; for inferior goods, the income effect of higher prices actually increases quantity demanded.

Concepts for Review

Diamond–water paradox	The "law" of diminishing marginal	Inferior goods
Marginal analysis	utility	Income effect
Total utility	Optimal purchase rule (P = MU)	Substitution effect
Marginal utility	Scarcity and marginal utility	

Questions for Discussion

1. Describe some of the different things you do with water. Which would you give up if the price of water rose a little? If it rose by a fairly large amount? If it rose by a very large amount?

2. Which is greater: your *total* utility from 10 litres of water per day or from 20 litres per day? Why?

3. Which is greater: your *marginal* utility at 10 litres per day or your marginal utility at 20 litres per day? Why?

4. Some people who do not understand the optimal purchase rule argue that if a consumer buys so much of a good that its price equals its marginal utility, he could not possibly be behaving optimally. Rather, they say, he would be better off quitting when ahead, that is, buying a quantity such that marginal utility is much greater than price. What is wrong with this argument? (*Hint*: What opportunity does the consumer then miss? Is it maximization of marginal or total utility that serves the consumer's interests?)

5. What inferior goods do you purchase? Why do you buy them? Do you think you will continue to buy them when your income is higher?

6. Which of the following items are likely to be normal goods to a typical consumer? Which are likely to be inferior goods?
   a. Vintage champagne
   b. Paper napkins
   c. Secondhand clothing
   d. Overseas trips

7. Suppose that gasoline and safety pins each rise in price by 10 percent. Which will have the larger income effect on the purchases of a typical consumer? Why?

8. Around 1850, Sir Robert Giffen observed that Irish peasants actually consumed more potatoes as the price of potatoes increased. Use the concepts of income and substitution effects to explain this phenomenon.

Appendix
Indifference Curve Analysis

The analysis of consumer demand presented in this chapter, while correct as far as it goes, has one shortcoming: By treating the consumer's decision about the purchase of each commodity as an isolated event, it conceals the necessity of choice imposed on the consumer by his limited budget. It does not indicate explicitly the hard choice behind every purchase decision—the sacrifice of some goods to obtain others. The idea, of course, is implicit because the purchase of a commodity involves a trade-off between that good and money. If you spend more money on rent, you have less to spend on entertainment. If you buy more clothing, you have less money for food. But to represent the consumer's choice problem explicitly, economists have invented two geometric devices, the *budget line* and the *indifference curve*, which this appendix describes.

Geometry of the Available Choices: The Budget Line

Suppose, for simplicity, that there were only two commodities produced in the world, cheese and records. The decision problem of any household then would be to determine the allocation of its income between these two goods. Clearly, the more it spends on one the less it can have of the other. But just what is the trade-off? A numerical example will answer this question and also introduce the graphical device that economists use to portray the trade-off.

Suppose that cheese costs $2 per kilogram, records sell at $3 each, and our consumer has $12 at his disposal. He obviously has a variety of choices—as displayed in Table 20–3. For example, if he buys no records, he can go home with six kilograms of cheese, and so on. Each of the combinations of cheese and records that the consumer can afford can be shown in a diagram in which the axes measure the quantities of each commodity that are purchased. In Figure 20–2, kilograms of cheese are measured along the vertical axis, number of records is measured along the horizontal axis, and each of the combinations enumerated in Table 20–3 is represented by a labelled point. For example, point A corresponds to spending everything on cheese, point E corresponds to spending everything on records, and point C corresponds to buying two records and three kilograms of cheese.

If we connect points A through E by a straight line, the blue line in the diagram, we can trace all the possible ways to divide the $12 between the two goods. For example, point D tells us that if the consumer buys three records, there will be only enough money left to purchase one and one-half kilograms of cheese. This is readily seen to be correct from Table 20–3. Line AE is therefore called the **budget line**.

The **budget line** for a household represents graphically all the possible combinations of two commodities that it can purchase, given the prices of the commodities and some fixed amount of money at its disposal.

Properties of the Budget Line

Let us now use r to represent the number of records purchased by our consumer and c to indicate the

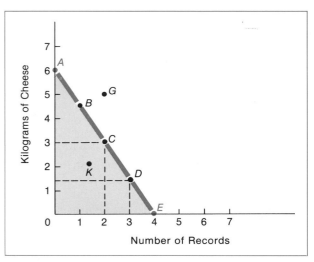

Figure 20–2
A BUDGET LINE
This budget line shows the different combinations of cheese and records the consumer can buy with $12 if cheese costs $2 per kilogram and records cost $3 each. At point A the consumer buys six kilograms of cheese and has nothing left over for records. At point E he spends the entire budget on records. At intermediate points (such as C) on the budget line, the consumer buys some of both goods (two records and three kilograms of cheese).

amount of cheese he acquires. Thus, at $2 per kilogram, he spends on cheese a total of $2 \times$ (number of kilograms of cheese bought) = $2c$ dollars. Similarly, he spends $3r$ dollars on records, making a total of $2c + 3r$ = $12, if the entire $12 is spent on the two commodities. This is the equation of the budget line. It is also the equation of the straight line drawn in the diagram.[4]

[4]The reader may have noticed one problem that arises in this formulation. If every point on the budget line AE is a possible way for the consumer to spend his money, there must be some manner in which he can buy fractional records. Perhaps the purchase of one and one-half records can be interpreted to include a down payment of $1.50 on a record on his next shopping trip! Throughout this book it is convenient to assume that commodities are available in fractional quantities when drawing diagrams. This makes the graphs clearer and does not really affect the analysis.

Table 20–3
ALTERNATIVE PURCHASE COMBINATIONS FOR A $12 BUDGET

NUMBER OF RECORDS (at $3 each)	EXPENDITURE ON RECORDS (in dollars)	REMAINING FUNDS (in dollars)	NUMBER OF KILOGRAMS OF CHEESE (at $2 per kilogram)	LABEL IN FIGURE 20–2
0	0	12	6	A
1	3	9	4½	B
2	6	6	3	C
3	9	3	1½	D
4	12	0	0	E

We note also that the budget line represents the *maximal* amounts of the commodities that the consumer can afford. Thus, for any given purchase of records, it tells us the greatest amount of cheese his money can buy. If our consumer wants to be thrifty, he can choose to end up at a point below the budget line, such as K. Clearly, then, the choices he has available include not only those points on the budget line AE, but also any point in the shaded triangle formed by the budget line AE and the two axes. By contrast, points above the budget line, such as G, are not available to the consumer given his limited budget. A bundle consisting of five kilograms of cheese and two records would cost $16, which is more than he has to spend.

The position of the budget line is determined by two types of data: the prices of the commodities purchased and the income at the buyer's disposal. We can complete our discussion of the graphics of the budget line by examining briefly how a change in either of these magnitudes affects its location.

Obviously, any increase in the income of the household increases the range of options available to it. Specifically, *increases in income produce parallel shifts in the budget line*, as shown in Figure 20–3. The reason is simply that a, say, 50 percent increase in available income, if entirely spent on the two goods in question, would permit the family to purchase exactly

50 percent more of *either* commodity. Point A in Figure 20–2 would shift upward by 50 percent of its distance from the origin, while point E would move to the right by 50 percent.[5] Figure 20–3 shows three such budget lines corresponding to incomes of $9, $12, and $18, respectively.

Finally, we can ask what happens to the budget line when there is a change in the price of some commodity. In Figure 20–4, we see that when the price of records *decreases*, the budget line moves outward, but the move is no longer parallel because the point on the cheese axis remains fixed. Once again, the reason is fairly straightforward. A 50 percent reduction in the price of records permits the family's $12 to buy twice as many records as before: Point E is moved rightward to point H, at which eight records are shown as obtainable. However, since the price of cheese has not changed, point A, the amount of cheese that can be bought for $12, is unaffected. Thus we have the general result that *a reduction in the price of one of*

[5]An algebraic proof is simple. Let M (which is initially $12) be the amount of money available to our household. The equation of the budget line can be solved for c, obtaining

$$c = -(3/2)r + M/2.$$

This is the equation of a straight line with a slope of -3/2 and with a vertical intercept of M/2. A change in M, the quantity of money available, will not change the *slope* of the budget line; it will lead only to parallel shifts in that line.

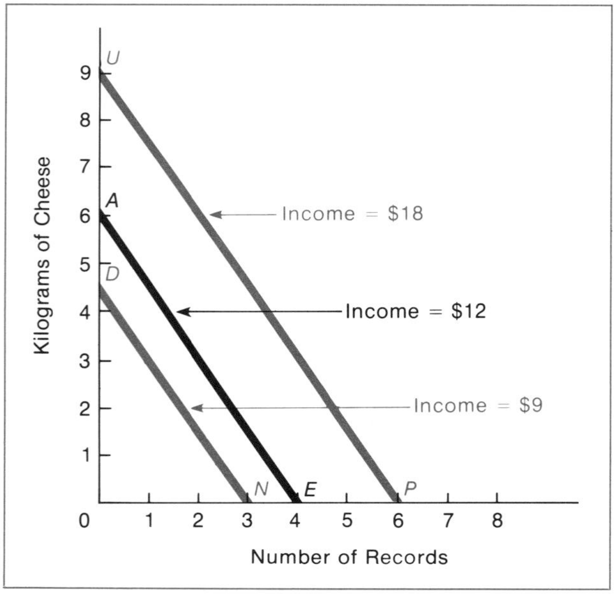

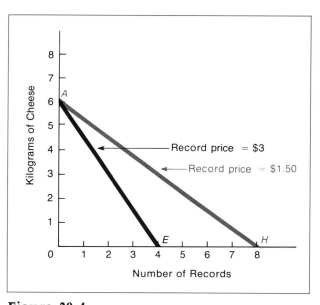

Figure 20-3
THE EFFECT OF INCOME CHANGES ON THE BUDGET LINE
A change in the amount of money in the consumer's budget causes a parallel shift in the budget line. A rise in the budget from $12 to $18 raises the budget line from AE to UP. A fall from $12 to $9 lowers the budget line from AE to DN.

Figure 20-4
THE EFFECT OF PRICE CHANGES ON THE BUDGET LINE
A fall in the price of records causes the end of the budget line on the records axis to swing away from the origin. A fall in record price from $3 to $1.50 swings the price line from AE to coloured line AH. This happens because at the higher price, $12 buys only four records, but at the lower price, it can buy eight records.

the two commodities swings the budget line outward along the axis representing the quantity of that item while leaving the location of the other end of the line unchanged.

What the Consumer Prefers: The Indifference Curve

The budget line tells us what choices are *available* to the consumer. We next must examine the consumer's *preferences* in order to determine which of these possibilities he will want to choose.

After much investigation, economists have determined what they believe to be the minimum amount of information they need about a purchaser in order to analyse his or her choices. This information consists of the consumer's *ranking* of the alternative bundles of commodities that are available. Suppose, for instance, the consumer is offered a choice between two bundles of goods, bundle *W*, which contains three records and one kilogram of cheese, and bundle *T*, which contains two records and three kilograms of cheese. The economist wants to know for this purpose only whether the consumer prefers *W* to *T*, *T* to *W*, or whether he is *indifferent* about which one he gets. Note that the analysis requires no information about *degree* of preference—whether the consumer is wildly more enthusiastic about one of the bundles or just prefers it slightly.

Graphically, the preference information is provided by a group of curves called **indifference curves** (Figure 20-5).

An **indifference curve** is a line connecting all combinations or the commodities in question that are equally desirable to the consumer.

But before we examine these curves, let us see how such a curve is interpreted. A single point on an indifference curve tells us nothing about preferences. For example, point *R* on curve I_a simply represents the bundle of goods composed of four records and one-half kilogram of cheese. It does *not* suggest that the consumer is indifferent between one-half kilogram of cheese and four records. For the curve to tell us anything, we must consider at least two of its points, for example, points *S* and *W*. Since they represent two different combinations that are on the same indifference curve, they are equally desirable to our consumer.

Properties of the Indifference Curves

We do not know yet which bundle our consumer prefers; we know only that a choice between certain

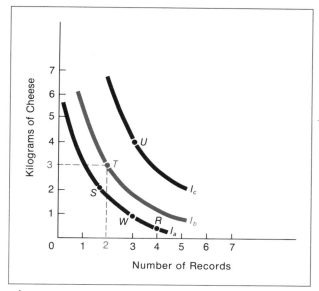

Figure 20-5

THREE INDIFFERENCE CURVES FOR CHEESE AND RECORDS

Any point in the diagram represents a combination of cheese and records (for example, *T* represents two records and three kilograms of cheese). Any two points on the same indifference curve (for example, *S* and *W*) represent two combinations of the goods that the consumer likes equally well. If two points, such as *T* and *W*, lie on different indifference curves, the one on the higher indifference curve is preferred by the consumer.

bundles will lead to indifference. So before we can use an indifference curve to analyse the consumer's choice, we must examine a few of its properties. Most important for us is the fact that:

As long as the consumer desires *more* of each of the goods in question, *every* point on a higher indifference curve (that is, a curve farther from the origin in the graph) will be preferred to *any* point on a lower indifference curve.

In other words, among indifference curves, higher is better. The reason is obvious. Given two indifference curves, say I_b and I_c in Figure 20-5, the higher curve will contain points lying above and to the right of some points on the lower curve. Thus, point *U* on curve I_c lies above and to the right of point *T* on curve I_b. This means that at *U* the consumer gets more records *and* more cheese than at *T*. Assuming that he desires both commodities, our consumer must prefer *U* to *T*. Since every point on curve I_c is, by definition, equal in preference to point *U*, and the same relation holds for point *T* and all other points along curve I_b, *every* point on curve I_c will be preferred to *any* point on curve I_b.

Another property that characterizes the indifference curve is its *negative slope*. Again, this holds only if the consumer wants more of both commodities. Consider two points, such as S and R, on the same indifference curve. If the consumer is indifferent between them, one cannot contain more of *both* commodities than the other. Since point S contains more cheese than R, R must offer more records than S, or the consumer would not be indifferent about which he gets. This means that if, say, we move toward the one with the larger number of records, the quantity of cheese must decrease. The curve will always slope downhill toward the right, a negative slope.

A final property of indifference curves is the nature of their curvature—the way they round toward the axes. As drawn, they are "bowed in"—they flatten out (their slopes decrease in absolute value) as they extend from left to right. To understand why this is so we must first examine the economic interpretation of the slope of an indifference curve.

The Slopes of an Indifference Curve and of a Budget Line

In Figure 20-6 the average slope of the indifference curve between points M and N is represented by

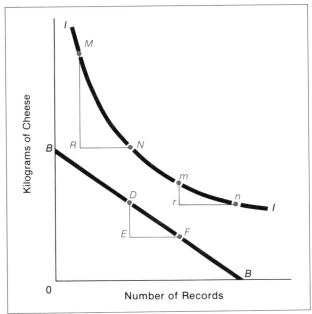

Figure 20-6
SLOPES OF A BUDGET LINE AND AN INDIFFERENCE CURVE
The slope of the budget line shows how many kilograms of cheese, *ED*, can be exchanged for *EF* records. The slope of the indifference curve shows how many kilograms of cheese, *RM*, the consumer is just willing to exchange for *RN* records. When the consumer has more records and less cheese (point *m* as compared with *M*), the slope of the indifference curve decreases, meaning that the consumer is only willing to give up *rm* kilograms of cheese for *rn* records.

RM/RN. RM is the quantity of cheese the consumer gives up in moving from M to N. Similarly, RN is the increased number of records acquired in this move. Since the consumer is indifferent between bundles M and N, the gain of RN records must just suffice to compensate him for the loss of RM kilograms of cheese. Thus, the ratio RM/RN represents the terms of which the consumer is just willing—*according to his own preferences*—to trade one good for the other. If RM/RN equals two, the consumer is willing to give up (no more than) two kilograms of cheese for one additional record.

The **slope of an indifference curve**, referred to as the **marginal rate of substitution** between the commodities involved, represents the maximum amount of one commodity the consumer is willing to give up in exchange for one more unit of another commodity.

The slope of the budget line BB in Figure 20-6 is also a rate of exchange between cheese and records. But it no longer reflects the consumer's subjective willingness to trade. Rather, the slope represents the rate of exchange the *market* offers to the consumer when he gives up money in exchange for cheese and records. Recall that the budget line represents all commodity combinations a consumer can get by spending a fixed amount of money. The budget line is thus a curve of constant expenditure. At current prices, if the consumer reduces his purchase of cheese by amount *DE* in Figure 20-6, he will save just enough money to buy an additional amount, *EF*, of records, since at points D and F he is spending the same total number of dollars.

The **slope of a budget line** is the amount of one commodity the market requires an individual to give up in order to obtain one additional unit of another commodity without any change in the amount of money spent.

The slopes of the two types of curves, then, are perfectly analogous in their meaning. The slope of the indifference curve tells us the terms on which the *consumer* is willing to trade one commodity for another, while the slope of the budget line reports the *market* terms on which the consumer can trade one good for another.

It is useful to carry our interpretation of the slope of the budget line one step further. Common sense tells us that the market's rate of exchange between cheese and records would be related to their prices, p_c and p_r, and it is easy to show that this is so. Specifically, the slope of the budget line is equal to the ratio of the prices of the two commodities. The reason is straightforward. If the consumer gives up one record, he has p_r more dollars to spend on cheese. Since the price of cheese is p_c per kilogram, these additional funds permit him to buy p_r/p_c more kilograms of cheese. Thus the slope of the budget line is p_r/p_c.

Before returning to our main subject, the study of consumer choice, we pause briefly and use our interpretation of the slope of the indifference curve to discuss the third of the properties of the indifference curve—its characteristic curvature—which we left unexplained earlier. With indifference curves being the shape shown, the slope decreases as we move from left to right. We can see in Figure 20–6 that at point *m*, toward the right of the diagram, the consumer is willing to give up far less cheese for one more record (quantity *rm*) than he is willing to trade at point *M*, toward the left. This is because at *M* he initially has a large quantity of cheese and few records, while at *m* his initial stock of cheese is low and he has many records. In general terms, the curvature premise on which indifference curves are usually drawn asserts that consumers are relatively eager to trade away a commodity of which they have a large amount but are more reluctant to trade goods of which they hold small quantities. This psychological premise is what is implied in the curvature of the indifference curve.

The Consumer's Choice

We can now use our indifference curve apparatus to analyse how the consumer chooses among the combinations he can afford to buy; that is, the combinations of records and cheese shown by the budget line. Figure 20–7 brings together in the same diagram the budget line from Figure 20–2 and the indifference curves from Figure 20–5.

Since according to the first of the properties of indifference curves the consumer prefers higher to lower curves, he will go to the point on the budget line that lies on the highest indifference curve attainable. This will be point *T* on indifference curve I_b. He can afford no other point that he likes as well. For example, neither point *K* below the budget line nor point *Z* on the budget line gets him on as high an indifference curve, and any point on an indifference curve above I_b, such as point *U*, is out of the question because it lies beyond his financial means. We end up with a simple rule of consumer choice:

Consumers will select the most desired combination of goods obtainable for their money. The choice will be that point on the budget line at which the budget line is tangent to an indifference curve.

We can see why no point except the point of tangency, *T* (two records and three kilograms of

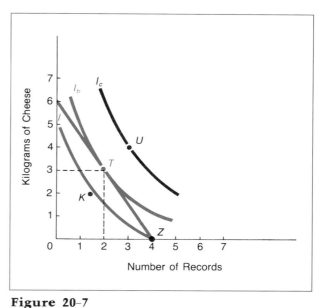

Figure 20-7

OPTIMAL CONSUMER CHOICE

Point *T* is the combination of records and cheese that gives the consumer the greatest benefit for his money. I_b is the highest indifference curve that can be reached from the budget line. *T* is the point of tangency between the budget line and I_b.

cheese), will give the consumer the largest utility that his money can buy. Suppose the consumer were instead to consider buying four records and no cheese. This would put him at point *Z* on the budget line and on indifference curve *I*. But then, by buying fewer records and more cheese (a move to the left on the budget line), he could get to an indifference curve that was higher and hence more desirable. It clearly does not pay to end up at *Z*. Only at the point of tangency, *T*, is there no room for improvement.

At a point of tangency where the consumer's benefits from purchasing cheese and records are maximized, the slope of the budget line equals the slope of the indifference curve. This is true by the definition of a point of tangency. We have just seen that the slope of the budget line is the ratio of the prices of records and cheese. We can therefore restate the requirement for the optimal division of the consumer's money between the two commodities in slightly more technical language:

Consumers will get the most benefit from their money by choosing a combination of commodities whose marginal rate of substitution is equal to the ratio of their prices.

It is worth reviewing the logic behind this conclusion. Why is it not advisable for the consumer to stop at a point like *Z*, where the marginal rate of substitution (slope of the indifference curve) is less than the price ratio (slope of the budget line)? Because by moving upward and to the left along his budget line, he can take advantage of market opportunities to obtain a commodity bundle that he likes better. And this will always be the case if the rate at which the consumer is *personally* willing to exchange cheese for records (his marginal rate of substitution) differs from the rate of exchange offered *on the market* (the slope of the budget line).

Consequences of Income Changes: Inferior Goods

Next, consider what happens to the consumer's purchases when there is a rise in income. We know that a rise in income produces a parallel outward shift in the budget line, such as the shift from *BB* to *CC* in Figure 20–8. This moves the consumer's equilibrium from tangency point *P* to tangency point *F* on a higher indifference curve.

A rise in income may or may not increase the demand for a commodity. In the case shown in Figure 20–8, the rise in income does lead the consumer to buy more cheese *and* more records. But his indifference curves need not always be positioned in a way that yields this sort of result. In Figure 20–9 we see that as the consumer's budget line rises from *BB* to *CC*, the tangency point moves leftward from *H* to *G*, so that when his income rises he actually buys *fewer* records. In this case we infer that records are an *inferior* good.

Consequences of Price Changes: Deriving the Demand Curve

Finally, we come to the main question underlying demand curves; How does our consumer's choice change if the price of one good changes? We learned earlier that a reduction in the price of a record causes the budget line to swing outward along the horizontal axis while leaving its vertical intercept unchanged. In Figure 20–10, we depict the effect a decline in the price of records has on the quantity of records demanded. As the price of records falls, the budget line swings from *BC* to *BD*. The tangency points, *T* and *E*, also move in a corresponding direction, causing the quantity demanded to rise from two to three. The price of records has fallen, and the quantity demanded has risen: The demand curve for records is negatively sloped.

The demand curve for records can be constructed directly from Figure 20–10. Point *T* tells us that two records will be bought when the price of a record is

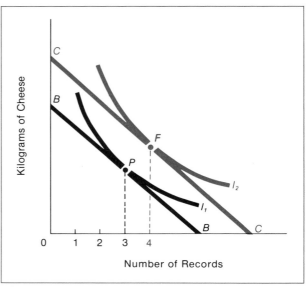

Figure 20–8
EFFECTS OF A RISE IN INCOME WHEN NEITHER GOOD IS INFERIOR
The rise in income causes a parallel shift in the budget line from *BB* to *CC*. The quantity of records demanded rises from three to four, and the quantity demanded of cheese also increases.

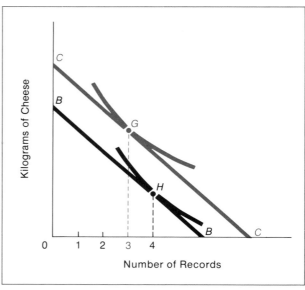

Figure 20–9
EFFECTS OF A RISE IN INCOME WHEN RECORDS ARE AN INFERIOR GOOD
The upward shift in the budget line from *BB* to *CC* causes the quantity of records demanded to fall from four (point *H*) to three (point *G*).

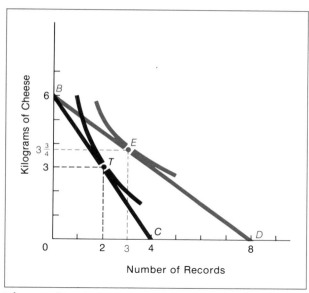

Figure 20-10

CONSEQUENCES OF PRICE CHANGES

A fall in record price swings the budget line outward from line *BC* to *BD*. The consumer's equilibrium point (the point of tangency between the budget line and an indifference curve) moves from *T* to *E*. The desired purchase of records increases from two to three, and the desired purchase of cheese increases from three kilograms to three and three-quarters kilograms.

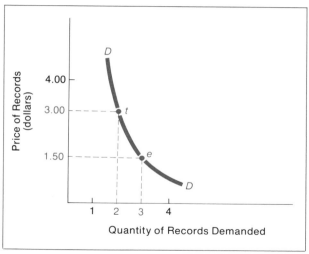

Figure 20-11

DERIVING THE DEMAND CURVE FOR RECORDS

The demand curve is derived from the indifference curve diagram by varying the price of the commodity in question. Specifically, when the price is $3 per record, we know from Figure 20-10 that the optimal purchase is two records (point *T*). This information is recorded here as point *t*. Similarly, the optimal purchase is three records when the price of records is $1.50 (point *E* in Figure 20-10). This is shown here as point *e*.

$3. Point *E* tells us that when the price of a record falls to $1.50, quantity demanded rises to three records.[6] These two pieces of information are shown in Figure 20-11 as points *t* and *e* on the demand curve for records. By examining the effects of other possible prices for records (other budget lines emanating from

[6]How do we know that the price of records corresponding to budget line *BD* is $1.50? Since the $12 total budget will purchase at most eight records (point *D*), the price per record must be $12 ÷ 8 = $1.50.

point *B* in Figure 20-10), we can find all the other points on the demand curve in exactly the same way.

The indifference curve diagram also brings out an important point that the demand curve does not show. A change in the *price of records* also has consequences for the *quantity of cheese demanded* because it affects the amount of money left for cheese purchases. In the example illustrated in Figure 20-10, the decrease in the price of records increases the demand for cheese from three to three and three-quarters kilograms.

Summary

1. Indifference-curve analysis permits us to study the interrelationships of the demands for two (or more) commodities.

2. The basic tools of indifference-curve analysis are the consumer's budget line and indifference curves.

3. A budget line shows all combinations of two commodities that the consumer can afford, given the prices of the commodities and the amount of money the consumer has available to spend.

4. The budget line is a straight line whose slope equals the ratio of the prices of the commodities. A change in price changes the slope of the budget line. A change in the consumer's income causes a parallel shift in the budget line.

5. Two points on an indifference curve represent two combinations of commodities such that the consumer

does not prefer one of the combinations over the other.

6. Indifference curves normally have negative slopes and are "bowed in" toward the origin. The slope of an indifference curve indicates how much of one commodity the consumer is willing to give up in order to get an additional unit of the other commodity.

7. The consumer will choose the point on his budget line that gets him to the highest attainable indifference curve. Normally this will occur at the point of tangency between the two curves. This choice indicates the combination of commodities that gives him the greatest benefits for the amount of money he has available to spend.

8. The consumer's demand curve can be derived from his indifference curve.

Concepts for Review

Budget line
Indifference curves
Marginal rate of substitution

Slope of an indifference curve
Slope of a budget line

Questions for Discussion

1. John Q. Public spends all his income on cheap wine and hot dogs. Draw his budget line when:
   a. His income is $70 and the cost of one bottle of wine and one hot dog is $1.40 each.
   b. His income is $105 and the two prices are as in part (a).
   c. His income is $70 and hot dogs cost $1.40 each and wine costs $2 per bottle.
2. Draw some hypothetical indifference curves for John Q. Public on a diagram identical to the one you constructed for part (a) of Question 1.

   a. Approximately how much wine and how many hot dogs will Public buy?
   b. How will these choices change if his income increases to $105, as in part (b) of Question 1? Is either good an inferior good?
   c. How will these choices change if wine prices rise to $2 per bottle, as in part (c) of Question 1?
3. Explain what information the *slope* of an indifference curve conveys about a consumer's preferences. Use this to explain the typical U-shaped curvature of indifference curves.

Consumer Demand and Elasticity

21

There was a time when a fool
and his money were soon parted,
but now it happens to everybody.
ADLAI STEVENSON

Economists who work for business firms are frequently assigned the task of studying consumer demand for the products their companies produce. Business managers count the results of such studies among the most important information they get. But they also know it is among the most difficult to obtain. Government agencies are also interested in information on demand, which they use for estimating such widely diverse variables as general business conditions and receipts from sales taxes.

The quantity demanded in any market depends on many things: the incomes of consumers, the price of the good, the prices of other goods, the volume and effectiveness of advertising, and so on. Demand analysis deals with all these influences, but it has traditionally focused on the price of the good in question. The reason is that the market price of a commodity plays a crucial role in influencing both quantity supplied and quantity demanded, and, in equilibrium, price is set so that these two quantities are equal. This role of price was studied in Chapter 4, and we will return to it time and again throughout the book.

We begin this chapter by showing how the market-demand curve for a product is derived from the individual-demand curves of each consumer. Next we turn to the "law" of demand, which tells us that quantity demanded decreases as price increases. Third, we pose a question: Who pays for the sales taxes levied on a product—consumers or producers? The important concept of elasticity is introduced as a way to measure the responsiveness of quantity demanded to price, and it is then used to answer this question. Fourth, we turn to the variables other than price that influence quantity demanded. And, finally, we explain the importance of the time period to which a demand curve applies and how this can create problems in obtaining demand information from statistical data.

From Individual-Demand Curves to Market-Demand Curves

In the last chapter we studied how *individual-demand curves* are derived from the logic of consumer choice. Each consumer seeks to attain the highest total utility permitted by his limited budget and, in the process, will typically react to a higher price by reducing his quantity demanded. But to understand how the market

A market-demand curve shows how the total quantity demanded of some product during a specified period of time changes as the price of that product changes, holding other things constant.

system works we must derive the relationship between price and quantity demanded in *the market as a whole*—the **market-demand curve**.

If each individual pays no attention to other people's purchase decisions when making his own, it is straightforward to derive the market-demand curve from the customers' individual-demand curves. We simply *add* the negatively sloping individual-demand curves *horizontally* as shown in Figure 21–1. There we see the individual-demand curves *DD* and *BB* for two people, David and Brian, and the total (market) demand curve *MM*.

Specifically, this market-demand curve is constructed as follows: *Step 1:* Pick any relevant price, say $10. *Step 2:* At that price, determine David's quantity demanded (9 units) from David's demand curve in part (a) and Brian's quantity demanded (6 units) from Brian's demand curve in part (b). Note that these quantities are indicated by line segment *AA* for David and line segment *RR* for Brian. *Step 3:* Add Brian's and David's quantities demanded at the $10 price (segment *AA* + segment *RR* = 9 + 6 = 15) to yield the total quantity demanded by the market at that price [line segment *CC*, with total quantity demanded equal to 15 units, in part (c)]. Now repeat the process for all alternative prices to obtain other points on the market-demand curve until the shape of the entire curve *MM* is indicated. That is all there is to the adding-up process.

The "Law" of Demand

The **"law" of demand** states that a lower price generally increases the amount of a commodity that people in a market are willing to buy. So, for most goods, demand curves have a negative slope.

A formal definition of the demand curve for an entire market was given in Chapter 4 and again at the top of this page. We shall pay much attention in this chapter to the "other things" referred to in this definition. But for now, let us focus on price, and note that the total quantity demanded by the market normally moves in the opposite direction from price. Economists call this relationship the **"law" of demand**.

Notice that we have put the word *law* in quotation marks. By now you will have observed that economic laws are not always obeyed, and we shall see in a moment that the "law" of demand is not without its exceptions. But first let us see why the "law" usually holds.

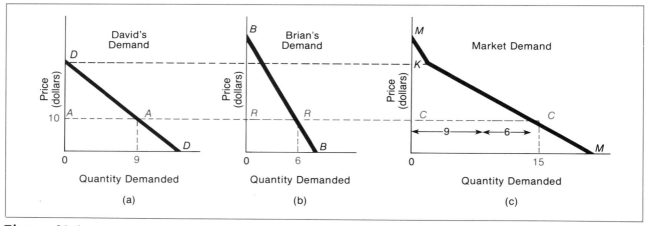

Figure 21-1

THE RELATIONSHIP BETWEEN TOTAL MARKET DEMAND AND THE DEMANDS OF INDIVIDUAL CONSUMERS WITHIN THAT MARKET

If David and Brian are the customers for a product, and at a price of $10 David demands 9 units [line *AA* in part (a)] and Brian demands 6 units [line *RR* in part (b)], then total quantity demanded by the market at that price is 9 + 6 = 15 [line *CC* in part (c)]. In other words, we obtain the market-demand curve by adding horizontally all points on each consumer's demand curve at each given price. Thus, at a $10 price we have length *CC* on the market-demand curve, which is equal to *AA* + *RR* on the individual-demand curves. (The sharp angle at point *K* on the market curve occurs because it corresponds to the price at which David, whose demand pattern is different from Brian's, first enters the market. At any higher price, only Brian is willing to buy anything.)

In Chapter 20 we learned that individual-demand curves are usually downward sloping because of the "law" of diminishing marginal utility. If individual-demand curves slope downward, then we see from the preceding discussion of the adding-up process that the market-demand curve must also slope downward. This is just common sense: If every consumer in the market buys fewer bananas when the price of bananas rises, then the total quantity demanded in the market must surely fall.

But market-demand curves may slope downward even when individual-demand curves do not, because not all consumers are alike. For example, if a bookstore reduces the price of a popular novel, it may draw many new customers, but few customers will be induced to buy two copies. Similarly, people differ in their fondness for bananas. True devotees may maintain their purchases of bananas even at exorbitant prices, while others will not eat a banana even if it is offered free of charge. As the price of bananas rises, the less enthusiastic banana-eaters drop out of the market entirely, leaving the expensive fruit to the more devoted consumers. Thus, the quantity demanded declines as price rises simply because higher prices induce more people to kick the banana habit. Indeed, for many commodities, it is the appearance of new customers in the *market* when prices are lower, rather than the negative slope of *individual* demand curves, that accounts for the law of demand.

We conclude, therefore, that the law of demand stands on fairly solid ground. If individual-demand curves are downward sloping, then the market-demand curve surely will be, too. And the market-demand curve may slope downward even when individual-demand curves do not.

Nevertheless, exceptions to the law of demand have been noted. One common exception occurs when quality is judged on the basis of price—the more expensive the better. For example, some people buy vegetables labelled "organic" even though they are more expensive than other vegetables. Even if the two kinds of vegetables are identical to a biologist, some consumers may assume that the organic vegetables are superior simply because they are more expensive. If organic vegetables then become cheaper, consumers might assume that they are no longer superior and actually reduce their purchases.

Another possible cause of an upward-sloping demand curve is snob appeal. If part of the reason for purchasing a Rolls Royce is to advertise one's wealth, a decrease in the car's price may actually reduce sales, even if the quality of the car is unchanged. Other types of exceptions have also been noted by economists; but, for most commodities, it seems quite reasonable to assume that demand curves have a negative slope, an assumption that is supported by the data.

Application: Who Pays an Excise Tax?

The law of demand has many applications. Suppose, for example, that 18 million records are sold per year, and the government considers placing a $4 tax on each record sold (called an **excise tax**), hoping to collect $72 million in revenue per year ($4 per record times 18 million records). The law of demand tells us that the government will collect less than $72 million. Why? Because the excise tax will push up the price and that will reduce quantity demanded below 18 million.

Knowing that revenues will rise by less than $72 million is useful; but it is not enough. To determine its tax receipts, the government needs to estimate *how much* the price will rise and *how much* quantity demanded will fall. For this purpose, the government needs a *quantitative measure* of the responsiveness of quantity demanded to price. Such a measure is the main subject of this chapter. But, to see how tax revenues can be estimated, we must detour briefly. In the process, we will also learn who really pays the excise tax.

Table 21–1 presents hypothetical supply and demand schedules for records in a format that is familiar from Chapter 4. You can see that the equilibrium price is

An **excise tax** is a tax levied on a particular commodity or service, as a fixed amount of money per unit of product sold or as a fixed percentage of the purchase price.

Table 21-1

DEMAND AND SUPPLY SCHEDULES FOR RECORDS

PRICE (dollars)	QUANTITY SUPPLIED	QUANTITY DEMANDED
	(millions of records per year)	
10	30	0
9	27	1
8	24	3
7	21	9
6	18	18
5	15	27
4	12	36
3	9	45

$6 per record and the equilibrium quantity is 18 million records per year [point A in Figure 21-2(a)]. Now, what happens if the government imposes a $4 per record excise tax? To find the answer we must first determine what a $4 excise tax does to the supply curve.

The Effect of the Tax on the Supply Curve

We do this by answering a series of hypothetical questions about how sellers would react to the tax at different levels of market price.

First, if records sell for $12, including the tax, how many will be supplied? The key point here is that suppliers will receive only $8 per record—$12 minus the $4 tax. Therefore, the tax-free supply schedule in Table 21-1 tells us (third line) that quantity supplied will be 24 million records per year. Thus, at a price to customers of $12 each, quantity supplied is 24 million records. This information is recorded in the top row of Table 21-2.

The rest of the supply schedule in Table 21-2 is constructed similarly. For example, a $10 price nets the seller $6, which, according to Table 21-1, leads to a quantity supplied of 18 million records. And so on.

A pattern is apparent in Table 21-2. At any given price, suppliers will provide the same quantity after the tax as they previously provided at a price $4 lower. Thus, we conclude that:

An excise tax shifts the supply curve upward by the amount of the tax.

This conclusion is just common sense. After all, suppliers care about the price they receive, not about the price buyers pay. Graphically, our conclusion is depicted in part (a) of Figure 21-2, which shows the demand curve D_0D_0 and the

Table 21-2

EFFECT OF A $4 EXCISE TAX ON THE RECORD MARKET

PRICE INCLUDING TAX (dollars)	PRICE RECEIVED BY SUPPLIERS (dollars)	QUANTITY SUPPLIED	QUANTITY DEMANDED
		(millions of records per year)	
12	8	24	0
11	7	21	0
10	6	18	0
9	5	15	1
8	4	12	3
7	3	9	9
6	2	6	18
5	1	3	27

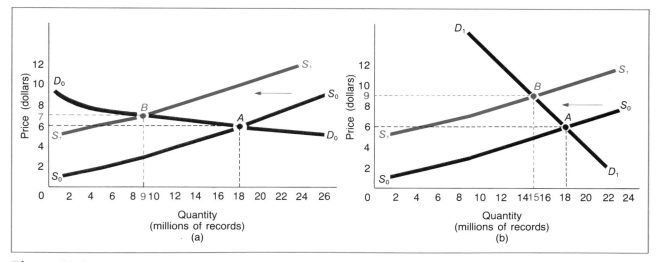

Figure 21-2

WHO PAYS AN EXCISE TAX?

A $4 excise tax shifts the supply curve vertically upward by $4—from S_0S_0 to S_1S_1. The market equilibrium therefore shifts from point A to point B. In part (a), the demand curve D_0D_0 is rather flat, so the price rises only $1 (from $6 to $7) while the quantity falls dramatically (from 18 million to 9 million). Producers pay most of the tax. In part (b), the demand curve D_1D_1 is much steeper, so the price rises by $3 and quantity falls by much less (only 3 million records). Consumers pay most of the tax.

two supply curves—S_0S_0 before tax and S_1S_1 after tax. The two supply curves are parallel and $4 apart.

The Role of the Shape of the Demand Curve

Now we can answer the questions of interest: How much will the market price rise as a result of the tax? How much will the quantity fall? And how much revenue will the government collect?

The answers depend on the responsiveness of quantity demanded to price changes, that is, on the shape of the demand curve. We start with a case in which demand is relatively responsive [part (a) of Figure 21–2]; that is, a small (vertical) change in price leads to a large (horizontal) change in quantity, making the demand curve rather flat.

Figure 21–2(a) shows that in this case the $4 excise tax raises the equilibrium price from $6 per record (point A) to $7 (point B). Because this lowers the quantity sold from 18 million to 9 million records per year, the government will collect only $36 million ($4 times 9 million) rather than $72 million.

In this example, the price rises by only one-fourth as much as the tax (from $6 to $7), so consumers wind up paying only one-fourth of the tax. The other $3 of tax is paid by businesses, which now collect only $3 per record ($7 less $4 tax) instead of $6. But consumers do not always pay such a small fraction of an excise tax. The way the tax burden is shared depends on how responsive quantity demanded is to price. In this example, quantity demanded responds very strongly.[1]

Part (b) of Figure 21–2 shows that things work out quite differently if quantity demanded is much less responsive to price. Demand curve D_1D_1 is much steeper than demand curve D_0D_0, meaning that a given change in price elicits a much smaller quantity response.[2] As a result, the equilibrium price rises by much more ($3 instead of $1), and the quantity demanded falls by much less (only 3 million instead of 9 million).

[1] The distribution of the tax burden also depends on the responsiveness of quantity *supplied* to price. But we are concentrating on demand here.

[2] The reader should verify that a fall in price from $7 to $6 per record raises quantity demanded by 9 million records in part (a) but only by about 1 million in part (b).

With the (steep) demand curve D_1D_1, consumers pay three-quarters of the tax and firms pay only one-quarter. And, since the decline in quantity is much smaller in part (b) than in part (a), the government collects more revenue—$60 million per year ($4 times 15 million) in part (b) rather than the $36 million in part (a). Thus we conclude:

The steeper the demand curve is, the larger the share of any excise tax that is paid by consumers, other things being equal, and the more total tax revenue the government collects.

Elasticity: The Measure of Responsiveness

The excise-tax example makes it clear that governments need a way to measure the responsiveness of quantity demanded to price. So do other users of demand information, such as business firms, which need it for decisions on pricing of products, on whether to develop new models of their products, and so on. Let us therefore see how economists measure this responsiveness. To understand the formula that economists use, we first consider a more common-sense approach which, unfortunately, does not work but which indicates the logic of the economist's approach.

At first, it may seem that the slope of the demand curve conveys the information we need: Curve D_1D_1 is much steeper than curve D_0D_0. But slope will not do because the slope of any curve depends on the units of measurement, and in economics there are no standardized units of measurement. Cloth output may be measured in yards or metres; milk in quarts or litres; and coal in tons or kilograms. An example will illustrate the problem.

Figure 21–3(a) repeats the demand curve D_0D_0 from Figure 21–2(a). It looks flat. Specifically, its slope between points A and B is:

$$\text{Slope} = \frac{\text{Change in price}}{\text{Change in quantity demanded}} = \frac{\$1.00}{9} = 0.11.$$

But suppose we measure quantity in millions of two-record albums, instead of in millions of records. This is done in Figure 21–3(b), and here the demand curve looks very steep. Between points A and B price changes by $2 per album (that is, $1 per record) and quantity demanded changes by 4.5 million albums (9 million records); so the slope is now

$$\text{Slope} = \frac{\text{Change in price}}{\text{Change in quantity demanded}} = \frac{\$2.00}{4.5} = 0.44.$$

This is quite a change in slope. But nothing has really changed. Points A and B represent exactly the same quantities and prices in both figures. Only the units of measurement have changed.

A parallel problem arises if we measure prices in dimes or millions of dollars, instead of in dollars. Here you may object that the dollar is the standard unit for measuring prices. But the economic significance of a dollar varies. A $1 increase in the price of a car is insignificant. But a $1 increase in the price of a ball-point pen may be quite substantial.

Because of this problem, economists use an alternate measure of responsiveness, one that is based on *percentage* changes in price and quantity rather than *absolute* changes. This measure is called the **price elasticity of demand**, or sometimes simply the **elasticity of demand**, and it is defined as the ratio of

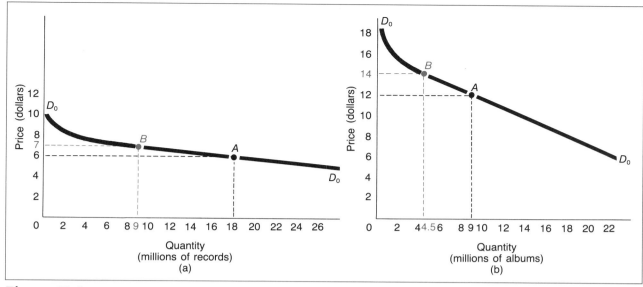

Figure 21-3

THE SENSITIVITY OF SLOPE TO UNITS OF MEASUREMENT

The slope of a curve changes whenever we change units of measurement. Part (a) repeats Figure 21-2(a); the demand curve looks very flat. In part (b), we measure quantity in two-record albums, so all the quantities are cut in half and all the prices are doubled. As a result, the demand curve looks rather steep. But the two demand curves present exactly the same information.

the *percentage* change in quantity demanded to the associated *percentage* change in price. Specifically:

$$\text{Elasticity of demand} = \frac{\text{\% change in quantity demanded}}{\text{\% change in price}}$$

Application of this formula to our example illustrates that it really does solve the units problem. In moving from point *A* to point *B* in either version of Figure 21-3, quantity demanded declines by 50 percent—from 18 million to 9 million in part (a), or from 9 million to 4.5 million in part (b). Similarly the percentage rise in price from $6 to $7 in part (a) or from $12 to $14 in part (b) is 16.67 percent whether we use dollars, dimes, or pennies.

The elasticity formula solves the units problem because percentages are unaffected by units of measurement. If nominal GNP doubles, it goes up by 100 percent, whether measured in millions or billions of dollars. If a person's height doubles between the ages of 5 and 15, it goes up 100 percent, whether measured in inches or in centimetres.[3]

Let us now summarize the features of the formula that is actually used by businesses and government to measure price elasticity of demand. It has three features:

1. Both the change in quantity demanded and the change in price are expressed as *percentages*.

2. The change in quantity is not calculated either as a percentage of the "initial" quantity or as a percentage of the "subsequent" quantity, but *as a percentage of*

The **(price) elasticity of demand** is the ratio of the *percentage* change in quantity demanded to the *percentage* change in price that brings about the change in quantity demanded; that is,

Price elasticity of demand

$$= \frac{\begin{array}{c}\text{\% change} \\ \text{in quantity demanded}\end{array}}{\text{\% change in price}}$$

[3]Mathematically, the reason is straightforward. If H_a and H_b represent height at age 5 and age 15, respectively, the formula for the percentage rise in height is $(H_b - H_a)/H_a$. Since an inch is about 2.5 centimetres, if we switch from inches to centimetres, in this formula both the numerator and the denominator are multiplied by 2.5. These 2.5's then cancel out, leaving the percentage figure unaffected by the switch from inches to centimetres.

the average of the two quantities. Similarly, the change in price is expressed as a percentage of the average of the two prices in question.

3. Minus signs are eliminated.

We already understand the purpose of the first of these features. Let us next consider what the other two attributes of the elasticity formula mean and the reasons for their adoption.

The Use of an Average for the Base of the Percentage

Consider the demand information presented in Table 21-1 (page 402): At a price of $6, quantity demanded is 18 million records; at a price of $7, quantity demanded is 9 million records. Suppose that a record company is deciding whether to price its product at $6 or $7. The difference in sales volume is 18 million – 9 million = 9 million. But this 9 million difference in sales is 50 percent of 18 million and 100 percent of 9 million. Which is the correct figure to use as the percentage change in quantity?

This problem is always with us because any given change in quantity must involve some larger quantity Q_L (18 million in our example) and some smaller quantity Q_S (9 million), so that a given change in quantity must be a relatively small percentage of Q_L and a relatively large percentage of Q_S. Obviously, neither of these can claim to be *the* right percentage change in quantity. We therefore use what appears to be a compromise—the *average* of the two quantities. In terms of our example, we use the average of 18 million and 9 million, that is, 13.5 million in our calculation of the percentage change in quantity. Thus:

Percentage change in quantity = 9 million as a percentage of 13.5 million
= 66 ⅔ percent

Similarly, in calculating the percentage change in price, we take the $1 change in price as a percentage of the average of $7 and $6, giving us $1/$6.50, or 15.4 percent, approximately.

Elimination of Minus Signs

We come now to the last feature of the elasticity formula—the removal of all minus signs. Recall that, by the law of demand, when price increases, quantity demanded will normally decrease, and vice versa. That is, when the percentage change in price is positive, the percentage change in quantity demanded will be negative, and vice versa. So our elasticity formula would normally produce a negative number. In calculating elasticity it is customary to disregard the minus sign to make the elasticity a positive number. That way, a *larger* elasticity number means that demand is *more* responsive to price.

We can now state the formula for price elasticity of demand. Keeping in mind all three features of the formula, we have:

Price elasticity of demand =

$$\frac{\text{Change in quantity as \% of average of the two quantities}}{\text{Change in price as \% of average of the two prices}},$$

so that in our example,

$$\text{Elasticity} = \frac{\text{9 million as \% of (18 million + 9 million)/2}}{\text{\$1 as \% of (\$7 + \$6)/2}}$$

$$= \frac{66.67\%}{15.38\%} = 4.33.$$

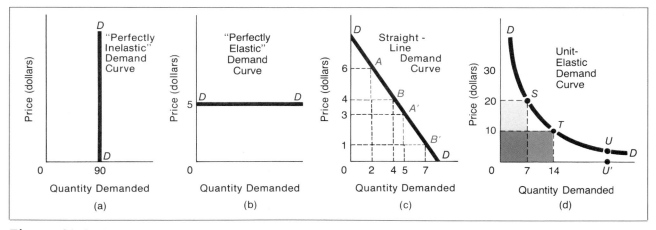

Figure 21-4

DEMAND CURVES WITH DIFFERENT ELASTICITIES

The vertical demand curve in part (a) is *perfectly inelastic* (elasticity = 0)—quantity demanded remains the same regardless of price. The horizontal demand curve in part (b) is *perfectly elastic*—at any price above $5, quantity demanded falls to zero. Part (c) shows a *straight-line demand curve*. Its *slope* is constant, but its *elasticity* is not. Part (d) depicts a *unit-elastic* demand curve whose constant elasticity is 1.0 throughout. A change in price pushes quantity demanded in the opposite direction but does not affect total expenditure. When price equals $20, total expenditure is price times quantity, or $20 × 7 = $140; and when price equals $10, expenditure equals $10 × 14 = $140.

Elasticity and the Shape of Demand Curves

Figure 21-4 indicates how elasticity of demand is related to the shape of the demand curve. We begin with two extreme but important cases. Part (a) depicts a demand curve that is simply a vertical line. This curve is called *perfectly inelastic* throughout because its elasticity is zero. That is, since quantity demanded remains at 90 units no matter what the price, the percentage change in quantity is always zero and hence the elasticity is zero. Such a demand curve is quite unusual. It may perhaps be expected when the price range being considered already involves very low prices from the consumer's point of view. (Will anyone use more salt if its price is lowered?) It may also occur when the item (such as medicine) is considered absolutely essential by the consumer, but even here the demand curve will remain vertical only so long as price does not exceed what the consumer can afford.

Part (b) of Figure 21-4 shows the opposite extreme: a horizontal demand curve. It is said to be *perfectly elastic* (or "infinitely elastic"). If there is the slightest rise in price, quantity demanded will drop to zero; that is, the percentage change in quantity demanded would be infinitely large. This may be expected to occur where a rival product that is just as good in the consumer's view is available at the going price ($5 in our diagram). In cases where no one will pay more than the going price, the seller will lose all his customers if he raises his price even one penny.

Part (c) depicts a case between these two extremes: a *straight-line* demand curve, which is neither vertical nor horizontal. Though the *slope* of a straight-line demand curve is constant throughout its length, its *elasticity* is not.

The reason is that the elasticity formula deals in *percentage* changes in quantity and in price, which behave in a curious way on a straight-line demand curve. At a point near the top of the curve [such as point *A* in part (c) of the figure], price is relatively high ($6) while at a point that is nearer the bottom of the curve (such as *A'*), price is lower ($3). Thus a $2 reduction in price from the $6 price at point *A* will represent a smaller *percentage* price decrease ($2 = 33⅓% of $6)[4] than the same $2 reduction from the $3 price at point *A'* ($2 = 66⅔% of $3). In

[4] To simplify the discussion in these paragraphs, we ignore the complication that the elasticity calculation is usually based on the *average* of the "initial" and "subsequent" prices and on the average of the two corresponding quantities.

other words, as we move down a demand curve to successively lower initial prices, a given reduction in price (a $2 price decrease) becomes a larger and larger *percentage* price reduction.

The opposite is true of percentage change in quantity. Toward the top of a straight-line demand curve, quantity is relatively small (2 units at point *A*); at a lower point, quantity demanded is relatively large (5 units at point *A'*). Thus, as we move downward and to the right along a demand curve, a given change in quantity becomes a smaller *percentage* change. The two-unit increase in quantity from *A* to *B* is a 100 percent increase from the two-unit quantity at point *A*, while an equal increase in quantity from *A'* to *B'* is only a 40 percent increase from the five-unit quantity at point *A'*.

To summarize, as we move down a straight-line demand curve, a given numerical change in quantity constitutes an ever smaller percentage change in quantity, while a given numerical change in price constitutes an ever larger percentage change in price. Since elasticity is defined as the percentage change in quantity divided by the percentage change in price, the numerator of the elasticity fraction gets smaller and the denominator gets larger as we move down a straight-line demand curve. Consequently:

Along a straight-line demand curve, the price elasticity of demand grows steadily smaller as we move from left to right. That is so because the quantity keeps getting larger, so that a given numerical change in quantity becomes an ever smaller percentage change, while the price keeps going lower so that a given numerical change in price becomes an ever larger percentage change.

Example: The elasticity of demand between points *A* and *B* in Figure 21–4(c) is:

$$\frac{\text{Change in } Q \text{ as \% of average } Q}{\text{Change in } P \text{ as \% of average } P} = \frac{2 \text{ as \% of } (2+4)/2}{2 \text{ as \% of } (4+6)/2}$$

$$= \frac{2/3}{2/5} = \frac{66\,^2/_3\,\%}{40\,\%} = 1.67 \text{ (approx.)}.$$

But the elasticity of demand between points *A'* and *B'* is:

$$\frac{2 \text{ as \% of } (5+7)/2}{2 \text{ as \% of } (3+1)/2} = \frac{2/6}{2/2} = \frac{33^1/_3\,\%}{100\,\%} = 0.33 \text{ (approx.)}.$$

If the elasticity of a straight-line demand curve varies from one part of the curve to another, what is the appearance of a demand curve with the same elasticity throughout its length? For reasons given in the next section, it looks like the curve in Figure 21–4(d), which is a curve with elasticity equal to one throughout (a *unit-elastic* demand curve). That is, a unit-elastic demand curve bends in the middle toward the origin of the graph, and at either end moves closer and closer to the axes but never touches or crosses the axes.

It is conventional to speak of a curve whose elasticity is greater than one as an *elastic* demand curve and of one whose elasticity is less than one as an *inelastic* curve. When elasticity is exactly one, we say the curve is unit elastic. This terminology is convenient for discussing the last important property of the elasticity measure.

Elasticity and Total Expenditure

The elasticity of demand conveys useful information about the effect of a price change on the buyer's *total expenditure*. In particular, it can be shown that:

If demand is elastic, a rise in price will decrease total expenditure. If demand is unit elastic, a change in price will leave total expenditure unaffected. If demand is inelastic, a rise in price will raise total expenditure.

These relationships hold because total expenditure equals price times quantity demanded, $P \times Q$, and a rise in price has two opposing effects on $P \times Q$. It increases P and, if the demand curve is negatively sloped, it decreases Q.

The two effects of a price rise on expenditure can be explained more fully as follows. First, there is *the price effect*, which increases expenditure by raising the amount of money a consumer spends on each unit of the good. Second, there is *the quantity effect*, which reduces the consumer's total expenditure on the good by cutting the number of units of the good that he buys. The net consequence for expenditure depends on the elasticity. If price goes up 10 percent and quantity demanded declines 10 percent (a case of *unit elasticity*), the two effects will cancel out: $P \times Q$ will remain constant. On the other hand, if price goes up 10 percent and quantity demanded declines 15 percent (a case of *elastic* demand), $P \times Q$ will decrease. Finally, if a 10 percent price rise leads to a 5 percent decline in quantity demanded (an *inelastic* case), $P \times Q$ will rise.

The connection between elasticity and total expenditure is easily seen in a graph. First we note that:

The total expenditure represented by any point on a demand curve (any price–quantity combination), such as point S in Figure 21–5, is equal to the area of the rectangle under that point (the area of rectangle $ORST$ in the figure). This is so because the area of a rectangle equals height times width = OR times OT = price times quantity, and, by definition, price times quantity equals total expenditure.

To illustrate the connection between elasticity and consumer expenditure, Figure 21–5 shows an elastic portion of a demand curve, DD. At a price of $6 per unit, the quantity sold is four units, so total expenditure is $4 \times \$6 = \$24$. This is represented by the shaded grey rectangle, because the formula for the area of a rectangle is area = height × width, which in this case is equal to $4 \times \$6 = \$24$. When price falls to $5 per unit, 12 units are bought. Consequently, the new expenditure ($\$60 = \$5 \times 12$), now measured by the coloured rectangle, will be larger than the old. In contrast, Figure 21–4(d), the unit-elastic demand curve, shows a case in which expenditure remains constant even though selling price changes. Total spending is $140 whether the price is $20 and 7 units are sold (point S) or the price is $10 and 14 units are sold (point T).

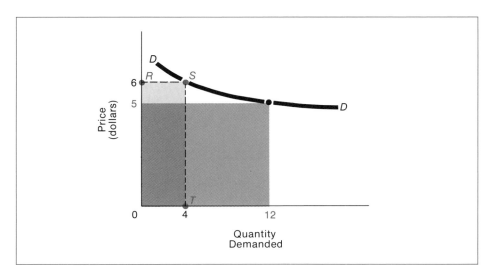

Figure 21-5
AN ELASTIC DEMAND CURVE
When price falls, quantity demanded rises by a greater percentage, increasing the total expenditure. Thus, when price falls from $6 to $5, quantity demanded rises from 4 to 12, and total expenditure rises from $6 × 4 = $24 to $5 × 12 = $60.

This discussion also indicates why a unit-elastic demand curve must have the shape depicted in Figure 21–4(d), hugging the axes closer and closer but never touching or crossing them. We have seen that when demand is unit-elastic, total expenditure must be the same at every point on the curve. It must be the same ($140) at point S and point T and point U. Suppose that at point U' (or some other point) the demand curve were to touch the horizontal axis. We will see now that this is impossible if expenditure at this point is to remain $140. It is impossible because if U' lies on the axis, the price at that point must be zero. Therefore, at that point we must have total expenditure = $P \times Q = 0 \times Q$ = zero. We conclude that if the demand curve is unit-elastic throughout, it can never cross the horizontal axis (where $P = 0$) or the vertical axis (where $Q = 0$). Since the slope of the demand curve is negative, the curve simply must get closer and closer to the axes as one moves away from its middle points. That is why a unit-elastic demand curve must always have the shape illustrated in Figure 21–4(d).

What Determines Elasticity of Demand?

What kinds of goods have elastic demand curves, meaning that quantity demanded responds strongly to price? And what kinds of goods have inelastic demand curves? Several considerations are relevant:

Nature of the Goods
Necessities, such as basic foodstuffs, have very inelastic demand curves. The quantity of bread demanded does not decline very much when the price of bread rises. In contrast, many *luxury goods*, such as restaurant meals, have rather elastic demand curves.

Availability of Close Substitutes
This factor is a critical determinant of elasticity. The demand for gasoline is inelastic because it is not easy to run a car without it. But the demand for *any particular brand* of gasoline is quite elastic, because another company's product will work just as well. This example suggests a general principle: The demand for narrowly defined commodities (like iceberg lettuce) is more elastic than the demand for more broadly defined commodities (like vegetables).

Fraction of Income Absorbed
The fraction of income absorbed by a particular item is also important. Who will buy less salt if the price of salt rises? But many families will buy fewer cars if auto prices go up.

Passage of Time
This factor is relevant because the demand for many products is more elastic in the long run than in the short run. For example, when the price of home heating oil rose in the 1970s, some homeowners switched from oil heat to gas heat. But, at first, very few homeowners switched; so the demand for oil was quite inelastic. It gradually became more elastic as time passed and more homeowners switched.

Elasticity Is a General Concept

We have spent much time studying the price elasticity of demand. But elasticity is a very general measure of the responsiveness of one economic variable to another. Here are two very common and similar elasticity measures.

1. ***Income elasticity of demand.*** As we know from earlier chapters, consumer income is an important determinant of quantity demanded. The ratio of the

percentage change in quantity demanded to the percentage change in income is called the *income elasticity of demand.*

2. ***Price elasticity of supply.*** Quantity supplied also changes when price changes. The ratio of the percentage change in quantity supplied to the percentage change in price is called the *price elasticity of supply*, or just the *elasticity of supply.*

Many other examples arise in all branches of economics, and some everyday uses of these elasticity measures are noted in this chapter's box (page 413).

Quantity Demanded Depends on Many Variables

It is clear from what we have said that a firm will be very interested in the price elasticity of its demand curve. But this is not where its interest in demand ends, for, as we have noted, quantity demanded depends on other things besides price. While it is impossible to list all the determinants of quantity demanded, it is worth mentioning some of the more important ones.

Consumer Incomes
An increase in consumer incomes clearly raises the quantity demanded of most goods. So a firm will also care about the income elasticity of demand.

Consumer Tastes
In Chapter 20 we learned how individual-demand curves, and hence the market-demand curve, depend on consumer preferences (tastes). While changes in tastes are difficult to predict and even to explain, it is clear that if fashions shift from French to Chinese restaurants, or from yo-yos to frisbees, this can have a substantial effect on the quantities of these products that are demanded.

Advertising Expenditures
Cognizant of this, many large firms try to influence consumer tastes by advertising. Although there is much disagreement over the degree to which this is successful, it is clear that if a firm is to decide rationally on the size of its advertising budget, it must have an estimate of the effect of advertising on quantity demanded. As we shall see at the end of the chapter, such information may be difficult to obtain.

Prices of Related Goods: Substitutes and Complements
There are many products whose quantities demanded depend on the quantities and prices of other products. Certain goods make one another *more* desirable. For example, cream and sugar can increase the desirability of coffee, and vice versa. The same is true of mustard or catsup and hamburgers. In some extreme cases, neither of two products ordinarily has any use without the other—an automobile and tires, a pair of shoes and shoelaces, and so on. Such goods, each of which makes the other more valuable, are called **complements**.

The demand curves of complements are interrelated, meaning that a rise in the price of coffee is likely to affect the quantity of sugar demanded. Why? When coffee prices rise, less coffee will be drunk and therefore less sugar will be demanded. The opposite will be true of a fall in coffee prices. A similar relationship holds for other complementary goods.

At the other extreme, there are goods that make one another *less* valuable. These are called **substitutes**. Ownership of a motorcycle, for example, may decrease the desire for a bicycle. If your pantry is stocked with cans of tuna, you are less likely to rush out and buy cans of salmon. As you might expect, demand curves for substitutes are also interrelated, but in the opposite direction.

Two goods are called **complements** if an increase in the price of one reduces the quantity demanded of the other, all other things remaining constant.

Two goods are called **substitutes** if an increase in the price of one raises the quantity demanded of the other, all other things remaining constant.

When the price of a new house rises, people demand fewer new houses, so the quantity of old houses demanded goes up. When the price of coffee goes up, people drink less coffee; instead, they consume more tea or tomato juice.

Yet another elasticity measure is useful for determining whether two products are substitutes or complements: their **cross elasticity of demand**. This measure is defined much like the ordinary price elasticity of demand, only instead of measuring the responsiveness of the quantity demanded of, say, coffee to a change in the price of coffee, cross elasticity of demand measures the responsiveness of the quantity demanded of coffee to a change in the price of, say, sugar. For example, if a 20 percent rise in the price of sugar reduces the quantity of coffee demanded by 5 percent (a change of *minus* 5 percent in quantity demanded), then the cross elasticity of demand will be

The **cross elasticity of demand** for product X to a change in the price of another product, Y, is the ratio of the percentage change in quantity demanded of product X to the percentage change in the price of product Y that brings about the change in quantity demanded.

$$\frac{\text{\% change in quantity of coffee demanded}}{\text{\% change in sugar price}} = \frac{-5\%}{20\%} = -0.25.$$

Using the cross elasticity of demand measure, we come to the following rule about complements and substitutes:

If two goods are substitutes, a rise in the price of one of them raises the quantity demanded of the other; so their cross elasticities of demand will normally be positive. If two goods are complements, a rise in the price of one of them tends to decrease the quantity demanded of the other item, so their cross elasticities will normally be negative.[5]

This result is really a matter of common sense. If the price of a good goes up and there is a substitute available, people will tend to switch to the substitute. If the price of Coke goes up (and the price of Pepsi does not), at least some people will switch to Pepsi. Thus, a *rise* in the price of Coke causes a *rise* in the quantity of Pepsi demanded. Both percentage changes are positive numbers and so their ratio, the cross elasticity of demand, is also positive.

On the other hand, if two goods are complements, a rise in the price of one will discourage its own use and will also discourage use of the complementary good. Automobiles and car radios are obviously complements. A large increase in the price of cars will depress the sale of cars, and this will in turn reduce the sale of car radios. Thus, a positive percentage change in the price of cars leads to a negative percentage change in the quantity of car radios demanded. The ratio of these numbers, the cross elasticity of demand for cars and radios, is therefore negative.

In addition to these rather general determinants of the quantity demanded of almost every good, there are always other variables that are pertinent to specific goods. For example, rainfall affects the quantity of umbrellas demanded; temperature affects the demand curves for air conditioners and for fuel; the amount of soot in the atmosphere affects the quantity of soap demanded; and so forth. You can easily think of more examples.

Shifts in Demand Curves

Demand is obviously a complex phenomenon. We have studied in detail the dependence of quantity demanded on price, and we have just seen that quantity demanded depends on other variables such as incomes, advertising, and tastes. Because of these "other variables," demand curves often do not retain the same

---

[5]Because cross elasticities can be positive or negative, it is *not* customary to drop minus signs as we do when calculating ordinary price elasticity of demand.

Elasticity in Practice

There are numerous examples which illustrate how business people and governments use the concept of elasticity. We have already seen that the revenue raised from a sales tax is higher, and the output/employment losses smaller, if the sales tax is levied on products that have inelastic demands. Is it any wonder, then, that the highest sales taxes in Canada are on gasoline, alcohol, and tobacco? For example, 75 percent of the price of a bottle of spirits is tax (one-third of this levied at the federal level, two-thirds at the provincial level).

Since these items are regarded as necessities by so many, they have very low price elasticities of demand. Many foods are necessities, too, and the resulting inelastic demand curves explain why governments set up policies to restrict farm outputs. When weather conditions are "good," making the supply curve for foods shift to the right, farmers' total receipts fall. With the inelastic demand curve, the bumper crop pushes the selling price down proportionately more than quantities sold increase. Thus, while consumers are worse off because of production quotas and adverse weather conditions that restrict supply, most food producers are better off.

Cross elasticity also has many important applications. For example, if a cross elasticity is high and negative, it indicates that the products in question are substitutes for one another. Establishing whether substitutes exist is important in a court of law if the government wishes to show that an industry is monopolized. When the Supreme Court in the United States ruled as to whether Dupont had monopolized trade in cellophane, they accepted the measured cross elasticity of demand as an important piece of evidence. Even though Dupont sold about 75 percent of the cellophane used in the United States, no monopoly was deemed to exist. The Supreme Court concluded that significant competition existed since a slight decrease in the price of cellophane was observed to cause a large switch in sales from the flexible wrappings to cellophane.

In Canada, provincial liquor boards have recognized cross elasticity. Whenever imported French wine prices are scheduled to increase, the liquor boards correctly predict that this will increase the demand for other (perhaps lesser known) imported wines from Spain, Portugal, and elsewhere.

Cross elasticity is also important in the urban-transportation field. Analysts have concluded that public-transit use is limited largely because of the low operating cost of the substitute good—private automobiles. Since car-users are not charged for the expressways or the pollution and congestion costs, the *relative* price of public transit (that consumers currently face) is high.

---

shape and position as time passes. Instead, they shift about. And, as we learned in Chapter 4, shifts in demand curves have predictable consequences for both quantity and price. But in public or business discussions, one often hears vague references to a "change in demand." By itself, this expression does not really mean anything. Remember from our discussion in Chapter 4 that it is vital to distinguish between a response to a price change (*which is a movement along the demand curve*) and a change in the relationship between price and quantity demanded (*which is a shift in the demand curve*).

When price falls, quantity demanded generally responds by rising. This is a movement *along* the demand curve. On the other hand, an effective advertising campaign may mean that more goods will be bought at *any given price*. This would be a rightward *shift* in the demand curve. In fact, such a shift can be caused by a change in the value of any of the variables affecting quantity demanded other than price. While the distinction between a shift in a demand curve and a movement along it may at first seem trivial, it is a significant difference in practice and can cause confusion if it is ignored. So let us pause for a moment to consider how changes in some of these other variables shift the demand curve.

As an example, consider the effect of a change in consumer income on the demand curve for jeans. In Figure 21-6(a), the black curve D_0D_0 is the original demand curve for jeans. Now suppose that parents start sending more money to their needy sons and daughters in university. If the price of jeans were to stay the same, we would expect students to use some of their increased income to buy more jeans. For example, if the price were to remain at $15, quantity demanded might rise from 40,000 (point R) to 60,000 (point S). Similarly, if price had instead been $10, and had remained at that level, there might be a corresponding change from T to U. In other words, the rise in income would be expected to *shift* the entire demand curve to the right from D_0D_0 to D_1D_1. In exactly the same way, a fall in consumer income can be expected to lead to a leftward shift in the demand curve for jeans, as shown in Figure 21-6(b).

Other variables that affect quantity demanded can be analysed in the same way. For example, a rise in TV advertising for jeans might lead to a rightward (outward) shift in the demand curve for jeans, as depicted in Figure 21-6(a). The same thing might occur if there were an increase in the price of a substitute product, such as skirts or corduroy trousers, because that would put jeans at a competitive advantage. That is, if two goods are substitutes, a rise in the price of one of them will tend to cause the demand curve for the other one to shift outward (to the right). Conversely, if a product that is complementary to jeans (perhaps a certain type of belt) becomes more expensive, we would expect the demand curve for jeans to shift to the left, as in Figure 21-6(b). In summary:

A demand curve is expected to shift to the right (outward) if consumer incomes rise, if tastes change in favour of the product, if substitute goods become more expensive, or if complementary goods become cheaper. A demand curve is expected to shift to the left (inward) if any of these factors goes in the opposite direction.

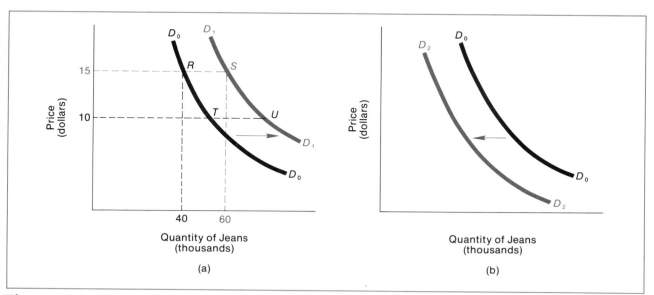

Figure 21-6
SHIFTS IN A DEMAND CURVE
A rise in consumer income or an increase in advertising or a rise in the price of a substitute product can all produce a rightward (outward) shift of the demand curve for a product, as depicted by the shift from the black curve D_0D_0 to the blue curve D_1D_1 in part (a). This means that at any fixed price (say $15), the quantity of the product demanded will rise. (In the figure, it rises from 40,000 units to 60,000 units.) Similarly, a fall in any of the variables, such as consumer income, will produce a leftward (inward) shift in the demand curve, as in part (b) of the figure.

The Time Dimension of the Demand Curve and Decision-Making

There is one more feature of a demand curve that does not show up on a graph but that is very important nevertheless. A demand curve indicates, at each possible price, the quantity of the good that is demanded *during a particular period of time*. That is, all the alternative prices considered in a demand curve must refer to the *same* time period. We do not compare a price of $10 for January with a price of $8 for September. This feature imparts a peculiar character to the demand curve and makes statistical estimates more difficult than might be supposed. Why, then, do economists adopt this apparently peculiar approach? The answer is that the time dimension of the demand curve is dictated inescapably by the logic of decision-making.

When a business undertakes to find the best price for one of its products for, say, the next six months, it must consider the range of alternative prices available to it for that six-month period and the consequences of each possible choice. For example, if management is reasonably certain that the best price lies somewhere between $3.50 and $5.00, it should perhaps consider each of the four possibilities, $3.50, $4.00, $4.50, and $5.00, and estimate how much it can expect to sell at each of these potential prices during the six-month period in question. The result of these estimates may appear in a format similar to that shown in the table below.

Potential price	$3.50	$4.00	$4.50	$5.00
Expected quantity demanded	75,000	73,000	70,000	60,000

This table, which supplies management with what it needs to know to make a pricing decision, also contains precisely the information an economist uses to draw a demand curve.

The demand curve describes a set of hypothetical responses to a set of potential prices, only one of which can actually be charged. All of the points on the demand curve refer to alternative possibilities for the *same* period of time—the period for which the decision is to be made.

Thus, the demand curve as just described is no abstract notion that is useful primarily in academic discussion. Rather it offers precisely the information that businesses need for rational decision-making.

Statistical Analysis of Demand Relationships*

The peculiar time dimension of the demand curve, in conjunction with the fact that many variables other than price can influence quantity demanded, makes it surprisingly hard to discover the shape of the demand curve from statistical data. It can be done, but the task is full of booby traps and can usually be carried out successfully only by using advanced statistical methods. Let us see why these two characteristics of demand curves cause problems.

The most obvious way to go about estimating a demand curve statistically is to collect a set of figures on prices and quantities sold in different periods, like those given in Table 21-3. These points can then be plotted on a diagram with price and quantity on the axes, as shown in Figure 21-7. One can then proceed to draw in a line (the dotted line *TT*) that connects these points reasonably well and

*This section contains more difficult material and, in shorter courses, may be omitted without loss of continuity.

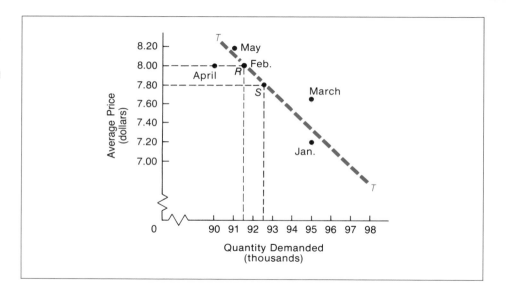

Figure 21-7

PLOT OF HISTORICAL DATA ON PRICE AND QUANTITY

The dots labelled Jan., Feb., and so on, represent actual prices and quantities sold in the months indicated. The blue line *TT* is drawn to approximate the dots as closely as possible.

Table 21-3

HISTORICAL DATA ON PRICE AND QUANTITY

	JANUARY	FEBRUARY	MARCH	APRIL	MAY
Price	$7.20	$8.00	$7.70	$8.00	$8.20
Quantity sold	95,000	91,500	95,000	90,000	91,000

that appears to be the demand curve. Unfortunately, line *TT*, which summarizes the historical data, may bear no relationship to the demand curve we are after.

You may notice at once that the prices and quantities represented by the historical points in Figure 21–7 refer to different periods of time, and that they all have been *actual*, not *hypothetical*, prices and quantities at some time. This distinction is significant. Over the period covered by the historical data the true demand curve, which is what we really want, may well have shifted because some of the other variables affecting quantity demanded changed.

What actually happened may be as shown in Figure 21–8. Here we see that in January the demand curve was given by *JJ*, but by February the curve had shifted to *FF*, by March to *MM*, and so on. That is, there was a separate and distinct demand curve for each of the relevant months, and none of them need have any resemblance to the plot of historical data, *TT*.

In fact, the slope of the historical plot curve, *TT*, can be very different from the slopes of the true underlying demand curves, as is the case in Figure 21–8. This means that the decision-maker can be seriously misled if he selects his price on the basis of the historical data. He may, for example, think that demand is quite insensitive to changes in price (as line *TT* in the diagram seems to indicate), and so he may reject the possibility of a price reduction when in fact the true demand curves show that a price reduction will increase quantity demanded substantially. For example, if in February he were to charge a price of $7.80 rather than $8, the historical plot would suggest to him a rise in quantity demanded of only 1000 units. (Compare point *R*, with sales of 91,500 units, and point *S*, with sales of 92,500 units, in Figure 21–7.) However, as can be seen in Figure 21–8, the true demand curve for February (line *FF* in Figure 21–8) promises him an increment in sales of 2500 units (from point *R*, with sales of 91,500, to point *W*, with sales of 94,000) if he reduces February's price from $8 to $7.80. A manager who based his decision on the historical plot, rather than on the true demand curve, might be led into serious error.

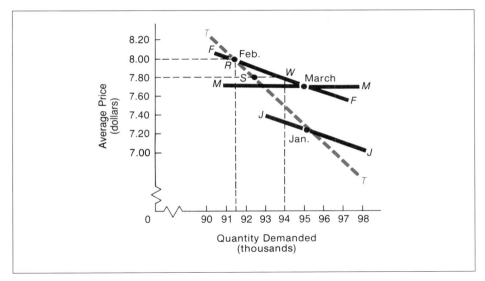

Figure 21-8
PLOT OF HISTORICAL DATA
AND TRUE DEMAND CURVES
FOR JANUARY, FEBRUARY,
AND MARCH
An analytical demand curve
shows how quantity demanded in
a particular month is affected by
the different prices considered
during that month. In the case
shown, the true demand curves
are much flatter (more elastic)
than is the line plotting historical
data. This means that a cut in
price will induce a far greater
increase in quantity demanded
than the historical data suggest.

In light of this discussion, it is astonishing how often in practice one encounters demand studies that use apparently sophisticated techniques to arrive at no more than a graph of historical data. One must not allow oneself to be misled by the apparent complexity of the procedures employed to fit a curve to historical data. If these merely plot historical quantities against historical prices, the true underlying demand curve is not likely to be found.

An Illustration: Did the Advertising Program Work?

A few years ago one of the world's largest producers of packaged foods conducted a statistical study to determine the effectiveness of its advertising expenditures, which amounted to nearly $100 million a year. A company statistician collected year-by-year figures on company sales and advertising outlays and discovered, to his delight, that they showed a remarkably close relationship to one another: Quantity demanded rose as advertising rose. The trouble was that the relationship seemed just too perfect. In economics, data about demand and any one of the elements that influence it almost never make such a neat pattern. Human tastes and other pertinent influences are just too variable to permit such regularity.

Suspicious company executives asked one of the authors of this book to examine the analysis. A little thought showed that the suspiciously close statistical relationship between sales and advertising expenditure resulted from a disregard for the principles just presented. The investigator had in fact constructed a graph of *historical* data on sales and advertising expenditure, analogous to *TT* in Figures 21–7 and 21–8 and therefore not necessarily similar to the truly relevant relationship.

The stability of the relationship actually arose from the fact that, in the past, the company had based its advertising outlays on its sales, automatically allocating a fixed percentage of its sales revenues to advertising. The *historical* advertising–demand relationship therefore described only the company's budgeting practices, not the effectiveness of its advertising program. If management had used this curve in planning its advertising campaigns, it might have made some regrettable decisions. *Moral:* Avoid the use of historical curves like *TT* in making economic decisions.

Summary

1. A market-demand curve for a product can be obtained by summing horizontally the demand curves of each individual in the market; that is, by adding up at each price the quantities demanded by each consumer.
2. The "law" of demand says that demand curves normally have a negative slope, meaning that a rise in price reduces quantity demanded.
3. To measure the responsiveness of quantity demanded to price we use the elasticity of demand, which is defined as the percentage change in quantity demanded divided by the percentage change in price.
4. If demand is elastic (elasticity greater than one), a rise in price will reduce total expenditure. If demand is unit elastic (elasticity equal to one), a rise in price will not change total expenditure. If demand is inelastic (elasticity less than one), a rise in price will increase total expenditure.
5. The more inelastic is the demand for a commodity, other things being equal, the higher is the share of any excise tax that is paid by consumers, and the higher is the tax revenue collected by the government.
6. Demand is not a fixed number. Rather, it is a relationship showing how quantity demanded is affected by price and other pertinent influences. if one or more of these other variables change, the demand curve will shift.
7. Goods that make each other more desirable (hot dogs and mustard, wrist watches and watch straps) are called *complements*. Goods such that if we have more of one we usually want less of another (steaks and hamburgers, Coke and Pepsi) are called *substitutes*.
8. Cross elasticity of demand is defined as the percentage change in the quantity demanded of one good divided by the percentage change in the price of the other good. Two substitute products normally have a positive cross elasticity of demand. Two complementary products normally have a negative cross elasticity of demand.
9. A rise in the price of one of two substitute commodities can be expected to shift the other's demand curve to the right. A rise in the price of one of two complementary goods is apt to shift the other's demand curve to the left.
10. All points on a demand curve refer to the *same* time period—the time during which the price will be in effect.
11. Simply comparing statistics of sales with prices over a period of time does not give us the demand curve, since demand curves are likely to shift from period to period.

Concepts for Review

Market-demand curve	Elastic, inelastic, and unit-elastic	Cross elasticity of demand
Excise tax	demand curves	Shift in a demand curve
"Law" of demand	Complements	
(Price) elasticity of demand	Substitutes	

Questions for Discussion

1. What variables besides price and advertising are likely to affect the quantity of a product that is demanded?
2. Describe the probable shifts in the demand curves for:
   a. railway trips when there is an improvement in the trains' on-time performance.
   b. automobiles when railway fares rise.
   c. automobiles when gasoline prices rise.
   d. electricity when average temperature in Canada rises during a particular year. (Note: The demand curve for electricity in Ontario and the demand curve for electricity in the Yukon should respond in different ways. Why?)
3. Which of the following goods may conceivably have positively sloping demand curves? Why?
   a. Diamonds.   b. Steel.   c. Aspirin.   d. Glue.
4. Explain why elasticity of demand is measured in *percentages*.
5. Explain why the elasticity-of-demand formula normally eliminates minus signs.
6. Give examples of commodities whose demand you expect to be elastic and some you expect to be inelastic.
7. Explain why the elasticity of a straight-line demand curve varies from one part of the curve to another.
8. A rise in the price of a certain commodity from $10 to $20 reduces quantity demanded from 60,000 units to 40,000 units. Calculate the price elasticity of demand.
9. Calculate the price elasticity of demand when price falls from $6 to $5 in Table 21–1.
10. If the price elasticity of demand for gasoline is 0.15, and the current price is 50 cents per litre, what rise

in the price of gasoline will reduce its consumption by 10 percent?

11. A rise in the price of a product whose demand is elastic will reduce the total revenue of the firm. Explain.

12. Which of the following product pairs would you expect to be substitutes and which would you expect to be complements?
   a. Trousers and belts.
   b. Gasoline and big cars.
   c. Bread and crackers.
   d. Butter and margarine.

13. For each of the previous product pairs, what would you guess about their cross elasticity of demand?
   a. Do you expect it to be positive or negative?
   b. Do you expect it to be a large or small number? Why?

14. (More difficult.) Explain why the following statement is true. "A firm with a demand curve which is inelastic at its current output level can always increase its profits by raising its price and selling less." (*Hint*: Refer back to the discussion of elasticity and total expenditure on pages 408–410.)

The Common Sense of Business Decisions: Inputs and Costs

22

"You realize this cost figure
is only an estimate. Of
course, the actual cost will
be higher."
ARCHITECT TO HIS CLIENT IN
AN OLD *NEW YORKER*
CARTOON

Having discussed the consumers' side of the market, we now turn to that of the producers. Just as the consumer must decide what combination of products to buy and how much of each to purchase, the producer must decide how much to produce and what combination of inputs to buy. And just as there is a key concept—the consumer's utility or preferences—that is crucial for the analysis of the buyer's behaviour, there is a fundamental phenomenon—production cost—that underlies the analysis of the seller's decisions.

Costs depend on the quantities of inputs needed to produce outputs. If output can be increased with only very small increases in input usage, then cost *per unit* will fall when output rises. On the other hand, if, say, a 10 percent increase in output requires a 20 percent increase in input use, then cost per unit will increase.

Because output decisions depend on costs, to understand the choice of output level, one must first analyse relation of output to cost. This chapter will therefore consider the logic of a firm's input decisions, while the next chapter will analyse its output choices.

For pedagogical purposes, this chapter is divided into two parts. In the first part we begin with the simple case in which the firm only varies the quantity of a single input. This will vastly simplify the analysis and enable us to see how the production relation between inputs and outputs gives the producer the cost information needed to determine output and price.

The second part of the chapter goes over the same territory but deals with the more realistic case in which several input quantities can be changed. Many new insights emerge from the multi-input analysis.[1]

Throughout the chapter we also assume that the price of each input is fixed by the market and is beyond the control of the firm that buys it.

Illustrative Issue: Do Large Firms Produce at Lower Cost?

Economies of large-scale production are thought to be a pervasive feature of modern industrial society. Automation, assembly lines, and sophisticated machinery are widely believed to reduce production costs dramatically. But if this equipment has enormous capacity and requires a very large investment, small companies will not be able to benefit much from these products of modern technology. In this case,

---

[1]*Note:* Some instructors may prefer to postpone this part until later in the course.

HISTORICAL COSTS FOR LONG-DISTANCE TELEPHONE TRANSMISSION
By 1983, the dollar cost per circuit mile had fallen to about 10 percent of what it was in 1942. Because prices had more than tripled in that period, the decline in *real* cost was even more sensational. In constant dollars, in 1983 the investment cost per circuit mile was about 2 percent of its 1942 level. Yet this diagram of historical costs is not legitimate evidence *one way or the other* about economies of scale in telecommunications.
SOURCE: AT&T.

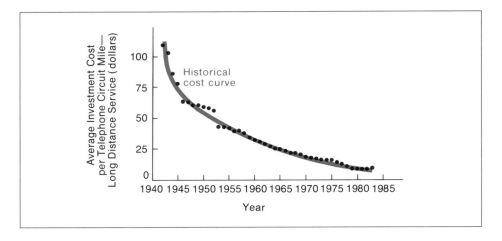

only large-scale production can offer the associated savings in costs. Where such *economies of scale*, as economists call them, exist, production costs per unit will decline as output expands.

But this favourable relationship between low costs and large size does not characterize every industry. When a court is called upon to decide whether a giant firm is operating against consumers' interests, officials need to know whether the industry has significant economies of scale. Those who want to break up large firms argue that industrial giants concentrate economic power, which is something these individuals wish to avoid. Those who oppose such breakups point out that if significant economies of scale are present, large firms will be much more efficient producers than will a number of small firms. It is crucial, therefore, to be able to decide whether economies of scale are present. What kind of evidence will speak to this issue?

Court cases of this sort have occurred in the United States, and sometimes data like those shown in Figure 22–1 are offered to the courts. These figures, provided by AT&T in the United States, indicate that since 1942, as the volume of messages rose, the capital cost of long-distance communication by telephone dropped enormously. Yet economists maintain that while this graph may be valid evidence of efficiency, innovation, and perhaps other virtues of the telecommunications industry, it does *not* constitute legitimate evidence, one way or another, about the presence of economies of scale. Specifically, though this information shows that costs fell as the telephone company's volume of business grew, it does *not* show that a large firm is more efficient than a small one. At the end of this chapter we will see precisely what is wrong with such evidence and what sort of evidence really is required.

The One-Variable Input Case

We begin our discussion with the unrealistic single-variable input case. That is, while any business firm uses many different inputs, we will assume for simplicity that it can only change the quantity of one.

Total, Average, and Marginal Physical Products

Consider, as an example of a firm, farmer Phil Pfister, who grows corn by himself on a 40-hectare plot of land. Ultimately, he can vary all his input quantities: He

Table 22-1

FARMER PFISTER'S TOTAL PHYSICAL PRODUCT SCHEDULE*

CORRESPONDING LABEL IN FIGURE 22-2	FERTILIZER INPUT (tonnes)	CORN OUTPUT (bushels)
A	0	1000
B	1	1250
C	2	1550
D	3	1900
E	4	2200
F	5	2450
G	6	2600
H	7	2650
I	8	2650
J	9	2600

*Data of the sort provided in this table do not represent the farmer's subjective opinion. They are *objective* information of the sort a soil scientist could supply from experimental evidence.

can hire many or few farmhands, buy more land, or sell some of the land he owns. But suppose for the moment that his only choice is how much fertilizer to apply to his land.

Farmer Pfister has studied the relationship between his input of fertilizer and his output of corn, and he has concluded that, at least up to a point, more fertilizer leads to more output. The relevant data are displayed in Table 22-1. We can see that 1000 bushels of corn will grow on the 40 hectares even with no fertilizer at all but that use of some fertilizer yields additional output; for instance, with four tonnes of fertilizer, output is 2200 bushels. Eventually, however, a saturation point is reached beyond which additional fertilizer actually reduces the corn crop (any amount beyond eight tonnes). These data are portrayed graphically in what we call a **total physical product (TPP) curve** in Figure 22-2.

Two other physical product concepts are added in Table 22-2. **Average physical product (APP)** is simply the total physical product divided by

The **average physical product (APP)** is the total physical product (TPP) divided by the quantity of input utilized.

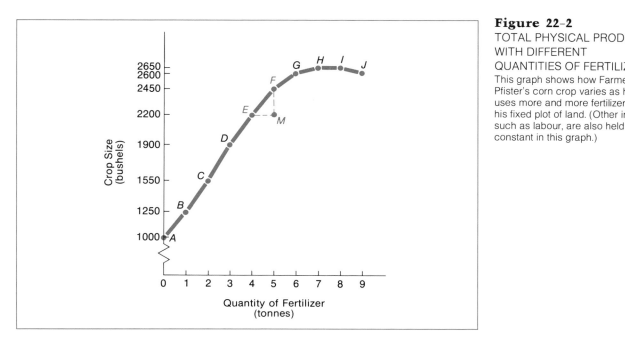

Figure 22-2

TOTAL PHYSICAL PRODUCT WITH DIFFERENT QUANTITIES OF FERTILIZER
This graph shows how Farmer Pfister's corn crop varies as he uses more and more fertilizer on his fixed plot of land. (Other inputs, such as labour, are also held constant in this graph.)

Table 22-2

FARMER PFISTER'S TOTAL, AVERAGE, AND MARGINAL PHYSICAL PRODUCT SCHEDULES

FERTILIZER INPUT (tonnes)	TOTAL PHYSICAL PRODUCT (corn output in bushels)	MARGINAL PHYSICAL PRODUCT (bushels)	AVERAGE PHYSICAL PRODUCT (bushels)
0	1000	—	—
1	1250	250	1250
2	1550	300	775
3	1900	350	633.3
4	2200	300	550
5	2450	250	490
6	2600	150	433.3
7	2650	50	378.6
8	2650	0	331.3
9	2600	–50	288.9

the quantity of input utilized. In our example, it is total corn output divided by number of tonnes of fertilizer used. APP is shown in the last column of Table 22–2, in which the TPP schedule is reproduced for convenience. For example, since 4 tonnes of fertilizer yield 2200 bushels of corn, the APP of 4 tonnes of fertilizer is 2200/4 = 550 bushels. (For a real example, see the box on page 425.)

If Farmer Pfister is to decide how much fertilizer to use, he must know how much *additional* corn output he can expect from each *additional* tonne of fertilizer. This concept is known as **marginal physical product (MPP)**. Thus, the marginal physical product of, for example, the fourth tonne of fertilizer is the total output of corn when four tonnes of fertilizer are used *minus* the total output when three tonnes are used.

The **marginal physical product (MPP)** of an input is the increase in total output that results from a one-unit increase in the input, holding the amounts of all other inputs constant.

The marginal physical product schedule of fertilizer on Farmer Pfister's land is given in the third column of Table 22–2. For example, since 3 tonnes of fertilizer yield 1900 bushels of corn and 4 tonnes yield 2200 bushels, the MPP of the fourth tonne is 2200 – 1900 = 300 bushels. The other MPP entries in Table 22–2 are calculated from the total product data in the same way. Figure 22–3 displays these numbers graphically in a **marginal physical product curve**.

The "Law" of Diminishing Marginal Returns

The marginal-physical-product curve in Figure 22–3 shows a pattern that will prove significant for our analysis. Up until three tonnes of fertilizer are used, the marginal physical product of fertilizer is *increasing*; between three tonnes and eight tonnes it is *decreasing*, but still *positive*; and beyond eight tonnes the MPP of fertilizer actually becomes *negative*. The graph has been divided into three zones to illustrate these three cases. The left zone is called the region of **increasing marginal returns**, the middle zone the region of **diminishing marginal returns**, and the right zone is the region of **negative marginal returns**. In this graph, the marginal returns to fertilizer increase at first and then diminish. This is a typical pattern.

The **"law" of diminishing marginal returns**, which has played a key role in economics for two centuries,[2] asserts that when we increase the amount of any one input, *holding the amounts of all others constant*, the marginal returns to the

---

[2]The "law" is generally credited to Anne Robert Jacques Turgot (1727–81), one of the great Comptrollers-General of France before the Revolution, whose liberal policies, it is said, represented the old regime's last chance to save itself. But, with characteristic foresight, the king fired him.

The Canadian Productivity Problem and Average Physical Product

In recent years there has been increasing concern in North America that the productivity of Japanese and other Asian workers is outstripping the productivity of Canadian and American workers. (See Chapter 39 on productivity for further discussion of these issues.) For example, statistics for two auto plants suggest that a Japanese auto worker, on the average, turns out nine engines per day, while his North American counterpart turns out only two. Thus, the productivity of labour in the auto industry is widely measured as the number of units of output produced per hour of labour.

But you will now recognize that the number of engines produced divided by the number of labour hours expended is exactly the same as the average physical product of an hour of labour in auto engine production. In other words, when you read in the newspapers about trends in the productivity of Canadian labour, or comparisons between that productivity and productivity in other countries, you will know that the report refers to the average physical product, which we discuss in this chapter.

---

expanding input ultimately begin to diminish. The so-called law is no more than an empirical regularity based on some observation of the facts; it is not a theorem deduced analytically.

The reason why returns to a single input are usually diminishing is straightforward. As we increase the quantity of one input while holding all others constant, the input whose quantity we are increasing gradually becomes more and more

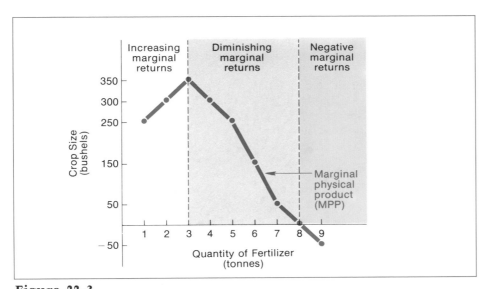

Figure 22-3
FARMER PFISTER'S MARGINAL PHYSICAL PRODUCT (MPP) CURVE
This graph of marginal physical product (MPP) shows how much *additional* corn Farmer Pfister gets from each application of an additional tonne of fertilizer. The relation between the MPP curve and the total product curve in Figure 22-2 is simple and direct: The MPP curve at each level of input shows the *slope* of the corresponding total product curve. To see why, suppose we want to know what happens when Farmer Pfister increases fertilizer usage from four tonnes to five tonnes; that is, we want to determine the MPP of the fifth tonne. In Figure 22-2 this takes us from point *E* to point *F* on the total product curve, so that output increases from 2200 bushels to 2450 bushels. The difference, 250 bushels, is the marginal physical product of the fifth tonne of fertilizer. It is measured by the slope of the total product curve between points *E* and *F* because it corresponds to the rise in the curve (distance *MF*) resulting from a move to the right by one unit (distance *EM*)—which is precisely the definition of slope.

Table 22-3

A PORTION OF FARMER PFISTER'S TOTAL COST SCHEDULE
(Obtained from the production data in Table 22-1, assuming fertilizer is the only variable input)

OUTPUT OF CORN (bushels)	TOTAL COST (dollars)
1000	$2200
1250	$2200 + $350 = $2550
1550	$2200 + 2 x $350 = $2900
1900	$2200 + 3 x $350 = $3250
2200	$2200 + 4 x $350 = $3600
2450	$2200 + 5 x $350 = $3950
2600	$2200 + 6 x $350 = $4300
2650	$2200 + 7 x $350 = $4650

abundant compared with the others. As the farmer uses more and more fertilizer with his fixed plot of land, the soil gradually becomes so well fertilized that adding yet more fertilizer does little good. Eventually the plants are absorbing so much fertilizer that any further increase in fertilizer will actually harm them. At this point the marginal physical product of fertilizer becomes *negative*.

Production, Input Quantities, and Cost

We can now use our two basic assumptions—that the price of fertilizer is beyond the control of the firm and that the quantities of all inputs other than fertilizer are somehow given—to deduce the firm's costs from the physical product schedules in Table 22-1 and Figure 22-2. We need simply record, for each quantity of output, the amount of fertilizer required to produce it, multiply that quantity of fertilizer by its price, and add this to the cost of the other inputs whose quantities we are holding constant.

Suppose that fertilizer costs $350 per tonne and that the cost of the fixed inputs (capital, labour, and land) is $2200. Then, from Table 22-1, we have the table of total costs shown in Table 22-3.

The point of this exercise is that:

The total-product curve tells us the input quantities needed to produce any given output. And from those input quantities and the price of the inputs, we can determine the *total cost* of producing any level of output. This is the amount the firm spends on the inputs needed to produce the output, plus any opportunity costs that arise in that production activity. Thus, the relation of total cost to output is determined by the technological production relations between inputs and outputs, and by input prices.

The Three Cost Curves

The behaviour of the firm's costs as output changes is obviously critical for output decisions. There are three interrelated cost curves that contain the pertinent information: the **total-cost curve**, the **average-cost curve**, and the **marginal-cost curve**, where marginal cost is a concept analogous to marginal physical product. As we shall see shortly, average and marginal costs are obtained directly from total costs (which we have just determined).

Total cost (TC) was just explained. But it is worth stressing that TC is not quite the same as the total expenditure of the firm. Expenditure and cost are not equal because, to an economist, "cost" must include the *opportunity costs* of

A firm's **total-cost curve** shows, for each possible quantity of output, the total amount that the firm must spend for its inputs to produce that amount of output plus any opportunity cost incurred in the process.

A firm's **average-cost curve** shows, for each output, the cost per unit; that is, total cost divided by output.

A firm's **marginal-cost curve** shows, for each output, the increase in the firm's total cost required if it increases its output by an additional unit.

Table 22-4

HYPOTHETICAL TOTAL, AVERAGE, AND MARGINAL COSTS OF A HOME-CONSTRUCTION FIRM

HOUSES BUILT PER PERIOD	TOTAL COST (thousands of dollars)	MARGINAL COST (thousands of dollars)	AVERAGE COST (thousands of dollars)
0	0		—
1	210	210	210
2	270	60	135
3	306	36	102
4	360	54	90
5	425	65	85
6	516	91	86
7	700	184	100

inputs provided by owners of the firm—even though the owners do not explicitly "charge" for those inputs. Thus, if to produce 2600 bushels of corn, Farmer Pfister must purchase $2600 in fertilizer, labour time, and other inputs, and in addition he himself provides labour time, capital, and land whose opportunity cost is $1700 (that is, it could have earned $1700 elsewhere), then the total cost of the 2600 bushels equals $2600 in input expenditures plus $1700 in opportunity cost, or $4300.

Average cost (AC), also called *unit cost*, is simply total cost divided by output; that is:

$$\text{Average cost} = \frac{\text{Total cost}}{\text{Quantity of output}},$$

or in symbols:

$$AC = \frac{TC}{Q}.$$

To determine the *marginal cost* (MC), we must know what would happen to TC if output were to increase by one unit. Table 22-4 presents the calculation systematically. For variety, we deal this time with the number of houses built per month by a construction firm that turns out standardized homes. We assume that the firm's total costs have already been determined from the relation between its inputs and its outputs, just as we did in the case of Farmer Pfister. For example, the coloured entries show that the total cost of four houses is $360,000, and of five houses, $425,000.

From the TC data we can next obtain the AC figure for each output. For example, we see that the AC of four houses is $360,000/4 = $90,000. We can also obtain the MC figures from the TC numbers. For example, by subtracting the TC of five houses from the TC of four houses, we see that the MC of producing the fifth house is $425,000 − $360,000 = $65,000. In general:

Once we know a firm's total costs for its various outputs, we can calculate its average costs and its marginal costs from the same information.[3]

Figure 22-4 plots the numbers in this table and thus shows the total-, average-, and marginal-cost curves for the construction firm. The shapes of the curves depicted here are considered typical. The TC curve is generally assumed to rise fairly steadily as the firm's output increases. After all, one cannot expect to produce

[3]The process also works the other way. If we know AC we can work backwards to find TC from the formula TC = AC × Q. Similarly, if we know all of the firm's marginal costs, we can work backwards and find its total costs.

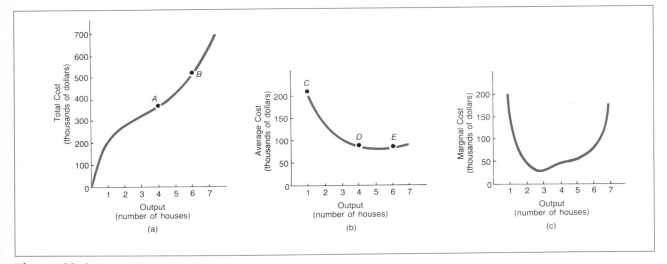

Figure 22-4

TOTAL, AVERAGE, AND MARGINAL COSTS

These cost curves of a hypothetical home-construction firm are based on figures presented in Table 22-4. These curves show how the firm's total, average, and marginal costs behave when the firm changes its decision on how many houses to produce.

three houses at a lower total cost than two houses. The AC curve and the MC curve are both shown to be shaped roughly like the letter U—first going downhill then gradually turning uphill again.

To explain these characteristic shapes, we must first distinguish between two important types of costs.

Fixed Costs and Variable Costs

A **fixed cost** is the cost of the indivisible inputs which the firm needs to produce any output at all. The total cost of these inputs does not change when the level of output changes. Any other cost of the firm's operation is called **variable cost**.

Total, average, and marginal costs are often divided into two components: **fixed costs** and **variable costs**. A *fixed cost* is the cost of the indivisible inputs that the firm needs to produce any output at all. The total cost of such inputs does not change when the firm changes its outputs by an amount that does not exceed the inputs' production capacity. Any other cost of the firm's operation is called *variable* because the total amount of that cost will increase when the firm's output rises.

The difference between fixed costs and variable costs can be illustrated by comparing the cost of a railway's fuel with that of its track construction. To operate between Winnipeg and Regina a railway must lay a set of tracks. It cannot lay half a set of tracks or a quarter set of tracks. We, therefore, call such an input "indivisible." The construction cost of the railway's tracks will be the same whether one train per month or five trains per day travel the route.[4] Thus up to a point, track-construction cost is not affected by output size, that is, by volume of traffic. On the other hand, the more trains that pass over those tracks, the higher the railway's total fuel bill will be. We therefore say that fuel costs are variable.

Although variable costs are only part of overall costs (fixed plus variable costs), the variable costs of a firm exhibit patterns of behaviour like those already shown in Table 22-4 and Figure 22-4. However, curves of *total fixed costs* (TFC), *average fixed costs* (AFC), and *marginal fixed costs* (MFC) have very special patterns, which are illustrated in Table 22-5 and Figure 22-5. We see that TFC remains the same, whether the firm produces a lot or a little, so long as it produces anything at all. As a result, any TFC curve, like the one in Figure 22-5(a), is

---

[4]Note, however, that an increase in traffic will increase annual maintenance and replacement costs, so that replacement and maintenance are variable costs.

Table 22-5

HYPOTHETICAL FIXED COSTS OF A HOME-CONSTRUCTION FIRM

HOUSES BUILT PER PERIOD	TOTAL FIXED COST (thousands of dollars)	MARGINAL FIXED COST (thousands of dollars)	AVERAGE FIXED COST (thousands of dollars)
0	0		—
1	120	120	120
2	120	0	60
3	120	0	40
4	120	0	30
5	120	0	24
6	120	0	20

horizontal—it has the same height at every output.

Average fixed cost, however, gets smaller and smaller as output increases because with TFC constant, AFC = TFC/Q gets smaller and smaller as output (the denominator) increases. Put another way, any increase in output permits the fixed cost to be spread among more units, leaving less and less of it to be carried by any one unit. For example, when only one house is built, the entire $120,000 of the firm's fixed cost must be borne by that one house. But if the firm constructs two homes, each of them need only cover half the total—$60,000.

However, AFC can never reach zero because even if the firm were to produce, say, a million houses, each would have to bear, on the average, one millionth of the TFC, which is still a positive number, even if it is a very small one. It follows that the AFC curve goes lower and lower as output increases, moving closer and closer to the horizontal axis but never crossing it. This is the pattern shown in Figure 22–5(b).

Finally, marginal fixed cost, as is shown by the table and the graph, is always zero after the first unit because total fixed cost does not grow with output. For example, MFC of the fifth house is the TFC of that house minus the TFC of the fourth house, that is, $120,000 – $120,000 = 0. This means that when output exceeds one unit, the MFC curve will always coincide with the horizontal axis, as shown in Figure 22–5(c).

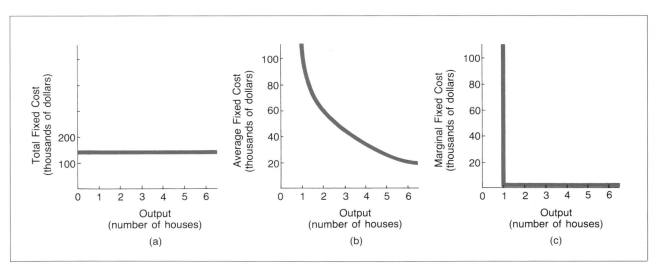

Figure 22-5

FIXED-COST CURVES: TOTAL, AVERAGE, AND MARGINAL

The total-fixed-cost curve [part (a)] is horizontal because, by definition, TFC does not change when output changes. AFC in part (b) decreases steadily as the TFC is spread among more and more units of output, but because AFC never reaches zero, the AFC curve never crosses the horizontal axis. Marginal fixed cost [part (c)] is always zero after the first unit of output because TFC does not change.

Since we have simply divided costs into two parts, fixed costs (FC) and variable costs (VC), we also have the rules:

$$TC = TFC + TVC \qquad AC = AFC + AVC \qquad MC = MFC + MVC.$$

The total-fixed-cost curve is always horizontal because, by definition, total fixed cost does not change when output changes. The average-fixed-cost curve declines when output increases, getting closer and closer to the horizontal axis but never crossing it. Marginal fixed cost is always zero when output is greater than one unit.

Shapes of the Average-Cost and Total-Cost Curves

Since the cost curves depend on the physical-product curves, these technological relationships should serve to explain the shapes of the cost curves. We will next discuss what they imply about the shapes of the AC and TC curves.

We have drawn the AC curve to be U-shaped in Figure 22–4(b): The leftward portion of the curve is downward sloping, and the rightward portion is upward sloping. Why should we expect AC to decline when output increases in the leftward portion of the AC curve? Fixed costs are a major element in the answer. As we have seen in Figure 22–5(b), the average-*fixed*-cost curve always falls as output increases, and it falls very sharply at the leftward end of the AFC curve. But AC = AFC + AVC, so that the AC curve of virtually any product contains a fixed-cost portion, AFC, which falls when output increases. That is the main reason we can expect the AC curve for any product to have a downward sloping portion such as *CD* in Figure 22–4(b)—a portion that is said to be characterized by economies of scale.

By *economies of scale* we mean that when quantity goes up by, say, 10 percent, total cost goes up by less than 10 percent, so that average cost, which is the ratio TC/Q, will fall. For example, if when Q = 100, TC = $1000, then AC = $1000/100 = $10. Now, suppose Q rises by 20 percent to 120 units; if TC rises by only 8 percent to $1080, then AC must fall to $1080/120 = $9. Since average cost is declining between points *C* and *D* in Figure 22–4(b), this suggests that our producer obtains economies of scale in that range.

Similarly, in the range to the right of point *E* in the same figure, AC is rising. This suggests that for those outputs there are *diseconomies of scale*—a given percentage rise in output requires a greater percentage rise in TC, so that AC = TC/Q must rise.

But why does the portion of the AC curve with economies of scale come to an end? There are two reasons: (1) the law of diminishing returns, and (2) the administrative (bureaucratic) problems of large organizations.

The first of these phenomena occurs because a firm may not be able to expand all of its inputs in proportion as its output increases. For example, it may not be able to expand the time the very top management of the company devotes to its operation because there are limits to the number of hours the president can put in. Even if all other inputs double, the president may not be able to double the amount of time she puts in. With some inputs not expanding while others are, diminishing returns to the expanding inputs can be expected because the proportions between the various inputs will grow less and less efficient and that will tend to raise average costs.

The second, and probably more important, source of diseconomies of scale stems from sheer size. Large firms tend to be relatively bureaucratic, impersonal, and costly to manage. As the personal touch of top management is lost and the firm becomes very large, costs will ultimately rise disproportionately, and average cost will ultimately be driven upward.

The point at which diseconomies of scale set in varies from industry to industry. It occurs at a much larger volume of output in automobile production than in farming—which is why no farms are as big as even the smallest of automobile producers. A large part of the reason is that the fixed costs of automobile production are far greater than those in farming, so the resulting economies of scale keep AC falling in auto production for a far larger range of output than they do in farming. Thus, although firms in both industries may have U-shaped AC curves, in auto production the bottom of the U occurs at a far larger output in auto production than in farming.

The typical AC curve of a firm is U-shaped. Its downward sloping segment is attributable to the economies of scale that occur as the firm's fixed costs are spread over larger and larger outputs. The upward-sloping segment is largely attributable to the disproportionate rise in administrative cost that occurs as the firm grows larger. The output at which economies of scale end, or at which diseconomies of scale begin, varies from industry to industry. The greater the relative size of fixed costs, the higher will tend to be the output at which the switchover occurs.

This, then, indicates the basis for economists' conclusion that AC curves tend to be U-shaped.[5] Since the shape of the TC curve does not play a major role in introductory discussions in microeconomics, only a few words will be said on this subject.

Going back to Figure 22-4(a), we see that between points 0 and *A* the TC curve is rising, but at a declining rate (its slope keeps falling). Roughly speaking, this means that in this region TC goes up less rapidly than Q. Farther to the right, however, TC rises at an increasing rate, so that TC goes up more rapidly than Q. Looked at in another way, what has just been said amounts to the assertion that portion 0*A* of the TC curve is the region of scale economies corresponding to the falling portion of the AC curve. On the other hand, region *AB* of the TC curve is the scale diseconomies portion of the TC curve corresponding to the rising portion of the AC curve. Thus, the shape of the 0*A* region of the TC curve corresponds to that of the region *CD* of the AC curve—both reflect the spreading of fixed costs over an increasing output. And, similarly, disproportionate increases in administrative costs can account for segment *AB* of the TC curve, just as it helps explain the rising portion of the AC curve.

Long-Run Versus Short-Run Costs

The cost to the firm of a change in its output depends very much on the period of time under consideration. The reason is that, at any point in time, many input choices are *precommitted* by past decisions. If, for example, the firm purchased machinery a year ago, it is committed to that decision for the remainder of the machine's economic life, unless the company is willing to take the loss involved in getting rid of it sooner.

An input to which the firm is committed for a short period of time, however, is not a fixed commitment when a longer planning horizon is considered. For example, a two-year-old machine with a nine-year economic life is a fixed commitment for the next seven years; but it is not a fixed commitment in plans that extend beyond the seven years. Economists summarize this notion by speaking of two different "runs" for decision-making—the **short run** and the **long run**.

These terms will recur time and again in this book. They interest us now

The **long run** is a period of time long enough for all the firm's commitments to come to an end.

The **short run** is a period of time briefer than the long run, so that some, but not all, of the firm's commitments will have ended. Obviously, there are many "intermediate runs."

[5]Empirical evidence confirms this view, though it suggests that the bottom of the U is often long and flat. That is to say, there is often a considerable range of outputs between the regions of scale economies and scale diseconomies. In this intermediate region the AC curve is approximately horizontal, meaning that there AC does not change when output increases.

because of their relationship to the shape of the cost curve. In the short run, there is relatively little opportunity for the firm to adapt its production processes to the size of its current output because the size of its plant has largely been predetermined by its past decisions. Over the long run, however, all inputs, including the size of the plant, become adjustable.

Consider the example of Farmer Pfister. Once the crop is planted, he has little discretion over how much of the various inputs to use. Over a somewhat longer planning horizon, he can decide how much labour to employ and how much seed to use. Over a still longer period, he can acquire new equipment and increase or decrease the size of his farm. Much the same is true of big industrial firms. In the short run, management has little control over the production technique. But with some advance planning, different types of machines using different amounts of labour and energy can be acquired, factories can be redesigned, and other choices can be made. Indeed, over the longest run, no inputs remain committed; all of them can be varied in both quantity and design.

It should be noted that the short and long runs do not refer to the same period of time for all firms; rather, they vary in length depending on the nature of the firm's commitments. If, for example, the firm can change its work force every week, its machines every two years, and its factory every twenty years, then twenty years will be the long run, and any period less than twenty years will constitute the short run.

The Average-Cost Curve in the Short and Long Runs

As we just observed, which inputs can be varied and which are precommitted depends on the time horizon under consideration. It follows that:

The average (and total) cost curve depends on the firm's planning horizon. The average (and total) cost curve pertinent to the long run differs from that for the short run because more inputs become variable.

We can, in fact, be much more specific about the relationships between short-run and long-run average-cost (AC) curves. Consider, as an example, the publisher of a small newspaper. In the short run, the firm can choose only the number of typesetters, printers, paper, and ink it uses; but in the long run, it can also choose between two different sizes of printing press. If the firm purchases the smaller press, the AC curve looks like curve SL in Figure 22–6. That means that if the paper is pleasantly surprised and its circulation grows to 50,000 copies per day, its cost will be 12 cents per copy (point V). It may then wish it had purchased the bigger press (whose AC curve is shown as BG), which would have enabled the firm

Figure 22-6

SHORT- AND LONG-RUN AVERAGE-COST CURVES FOR A NEWSPAPER

The publisher has a choice of two printing presses, a small one with AC curve SL, and a big one with AC curve BG. These are the short-run curves that apply as long as the newspaper is stuck with its chosen press. But in the long run, when it has its choice of press size, it can pick any point on the coloured lower boundary of these curves. This lower boundary, STG, is the long-run average-cost curve.

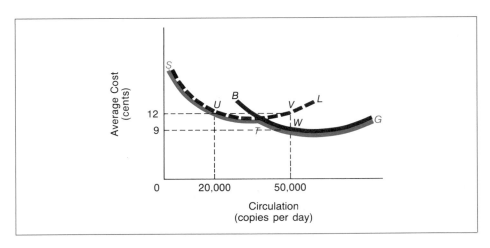

to cut unit cost to 9 cents per copy (point *W*). However, in the short run nothing can be done about this decision; the AC curve remains *SL*. Similarly, had it bought the larger press, its short-run AC curve would have been *BG* and it would have been committed to this cost curve even if business were to decline sharply.

In the long run, however, the machine must be replaced, and management has its choice once again. If it expects a circulation of 50,000 copies, it will purchase the larger press and its cost will be 9 cents per copy. Similarly, if it expects sales of only 20,000 copies, it will arrange for the smaller press and for average costs of 12 cents per copy (point *U*). In sum, in the long run, the firm will select the press size (that is, the short-run AC curve) that is most economical for the output level it expects to produce. The long-run average-cost curve then consists of all the *lower* segments of the short-run AC curves. In Figure 22–6, this composite curve is the coloured curve *STG*. Economies of scale are said to exist for output levels up to that which corresponds to the minimum point of this long-run average-cost curve.

The Multi-Input Case*

We come next to the more realistic case in which the firm decides on the quantities of several inputs—labour, land, fuel, as well as fertilizer.

So far, since only one input, fertilizer, was assumed to be controlled by the farmer, the quantity of the input used by the firm has appeared to follow mechanically from the magnitude of output. With the quantities of all other inputs fixed by assumption, the only way the farmer could increase his output was to buy more fertilizer. But that is not how things work in reality. Even given their output quantities, firms have some choices they can make about inputs. Next we will analyse how those choices can be made.

Substitutability: The Choice of Input Combinations

Casual observation of industrial processes deludes many people into thinking that management really has very little discretion in choosing its inputs. Technological considerations alone, it would appear, dictate such choices. A particular type of furniture-cutting machine may require two operators working for an hour on a certain amount of wood to make five desks, no more and no less. But this is an overly narrow view of the matter; whoever first declared that there are many ways to skin a cat saw things more clearly.

The furniture manufacturer may have several alternative production processes for making desks. For example, there may be simpler and cheaper machines that can change the same pile of wood into five desks using more than two hours of labour. Or still more workers could eventually do the job with simple hand tools, using no machinery at all. The firm will seek the *least costly* method of production. In advanced industrial societies, where labour is expensive and machinery is cheap, it may pay to use the most automated process; in more primitive societies, where machinery is scarce and labour abundant, making desks by hand may be the most economical solution.

In other words, one input can generally be *substituted* for another. A firm can produce the same number of desks with less labour, *if* it is prepared to sink more money into machinery. But whether it *pays* to make such a substitution depends on the relative costs of labour and machinery. Several general conclusions follow from this discussion.

---

*Instructors may want to teach this part of the chapter (up to page 442) now or they may prefer to wait until they come to Chapters 36 and 37 on the determination of wages, interest rates, profit, and rent.

1. Normally, there are different options available to a firm wanting to produce a particular volume of output. Input proportions are rarely fixed immutably by technological considerations.

2. Given a target level of production, if a firm cuts down on the use of one input (say, labour), it will normally have to increase its use of another input (say, machinery). This is what we mean when we speak of *substituting* one input for another.

3. Which combination of inputs represents the least costly way to produce the desired level of output depends on the relative prices of the various inputs.

A method of analysis that a business firm can use to select the least costly production process is described next. But you should know at the outset that the analysis is applicable well beyond the confines of business enterprises. Non-profit organizations, like your own university, are interested in finding the least costly ways to accomplish a variety of tasks (for example, maintaining the grounds and buildings); government agencies are concerned with meeting their objectives at minimum costs. Even in the household, there are many "cats" that can be "skinned" in different ways. Thus our present analysis of **cost minimization** is of very wide applicability.

We begin by dealing with one input at a time. Then we will deal with several at once.

Diminishing Returns and the Optimal Quantity of an Input

The **marginal revenue product (MRP)** of an input is the additional revenue the producer is able to earn as a result of increased sales when he uses an additional unit of the input.

The first two columns of Table 22–6 repeat Farmer Pfister's marginal physical product schedule from Table 22–2. (The third column will be explained presently.) Suppose fertilizer costs $350 per tonne, the farmer's product is worth $2 per bushel, and he is using three tonnes of fertilizer. Is this optimal for him? The answer is no, because the marginal physical product of the fourth tonne is 300 bushels (fourth entry in the marginal physical product column of Table 22–6). This means that although a fourth tonne of fertilizer would cost $350, it would yield an additional 300 bushels, which at the price of $2 would add $600 to his revenue. Thus he comes out $600 – $350 = $250 ahead if he adds a fourth tonne.

It is convenient to have a specific name for the additional revenue that accrues to a firm when it increases the quantity of some input by one unit; we call it **marginal revenue product**. So if Farmer Pfister's crop sells at a fixed price

Table 22-6
MARGINAL PHYSICAL PRODUCTS AND MARGINAL REVENUE PRODUCTS OF FARMER PFISTER'S FERTILIZER

FERTILIZER (tonnes)	MARGINAL PHYSICAL PRODUCT (bushels)	MARGINAL REVENUE PRODUCT (dollars)
1	250	500
2	300	600
3	350	700
4	300	600
5	250	500
6	150	300
7	50	100
8	0	0
9	−50	−100

(say, $2 per bushel), the marginal revenue product (MRP) of the input equals its marginal physical product (MPP) multiplied by the price of the product:

$$MRP = MPP \times \text{Price of output.}$$

For example, we have just seen that the marginal revenue product of the fourth tonne of fertilizer to Farmer Pfister is $600, which we obtained by multiplying the MPP of 300 bushels by the price of $2 per bushel. The other entries in Table 22–6 are obtained in precisely the same way. The concept of MRP enables us to formulate a simple **rule for the optimal use of any input**. Specifically:

When the marginal revenue product of an input exceeds its price, it pays the producer to expand his use of that input. Similarly, when the marginal revenue product of the input is less than its price, it pays the producer to use less of that input.

Let us test this rule in the case of Farmer Pfister. We have observed that three tonnes of fertilizer cannot be enough because the MRP of the fourth tonne ($600) exceeds its price ($350). What about the fifth tonne? Table 22–6 tells us that the MRP of the fifth tonne ($500) also exceeds its price; thus, stopping at four tonnes cannot be optimal. The same cannot be said of the sixth tonne, however. A sixth tonne is not a good idea, since its MRP is only $300, which is less than its $350 cost.

Notice the crucial role of diminishing returns in this analysis. Because the "law" of diminishing marginal returns holds true for Pfister's farm, the marginal *physical* product of fertilizer eventually begins to decline. Therefore, the marginal *revenue* product also begins to decline. At the point where MRP falls below the price of fertilizer, it is appropriate for Pfister to stop increasing his purchases. In sum, it always pays the producer to expand his input use until diminishing returns set in and reduce the MRP to the price of the input.

A common expression suggests that it does not pay to continue doing something "beyond the point of diminishing returns." As we see from this analysis, quite to the contrary, it normally pays to do so! Only when the marginal revenue product of an input has been reduced (by diminishing returns) to the level of the input's price has the proper amount of the input been employed. Thus, the optimal quantity of an input is that at which the MRP is equal to its price (P). In symbols:

$$MRP = P \text{ of input.}$$

Choice of Input Proportions: The Production Function

So far we have dealt with the choice of each input quantity as if it could be decided separately from the others by setting the MRP of each input equal to its price. This is somewhat misleading, for the choices of how much fertilizer, labour, and land to employ depend on one another. For example, the amount of fertilizer it pays Farmer Pfister to use clearly depends on the number of hectares he farms, because the marginal physical product of fertilizer depends on the amount of land that is used, and vice versa. Decisions about how much of each different input to employ are therefore interdependent.

To help select the combination of inputs that can produce the desired output most cheaply, economists have invented a concept they call the **production function**. The production function summarizes the technical and engineering information about the relationship between inputs and output in a given firm,

The **production function** indicates the *maximum* amount of product that can be obtained from any specified *combination* of inputs, given the current state of knowledge. That is, it shows the *largest* quantity of goods that any particular collection of inputs is capable of producing.

Table 22-7

A PRODUCTION FUNCTION

		QUANTITY OF LABOUR (months)					
		0	1	2	3	4	5
QUANTITY OF FERTILIZER (tonnes)	0	0	1000	—	—	—	2600
	1	0	1250	1900	2400	2600	—
	2	0	1550	2250	2600	2800	—
	3	0	1900	2450	2750	—	—
	4	0	2200	2600	—	—	—
	5	0	2450	3000	—	—	—
	6	0	2600	—	—	4900	—
	7	0	2650	—	—	—	—
	8	0	2650	3700	4600	5400	6000
	9	0	2600	—	—	—	—

taking *all* the firm's inputs into account. It indicates, for example, just how much output Farmer Pfister can produce if he has a given amount of land, labour, fertilizer, and so on.

When there are only two inputs—which are enough to indicate the basic principles involved—a production function can be represented graphically (which we do in the appendix to this chapter) or by a simple table. Table 22–7 indicates Farmer Pfister's production function for the use of labour and fertilizer to produce corn on his farm. To make the table easier to read, most of the numbers that normally would be entered (but that are irrelevant for our purposes) have been omitted and replaced by dashes.

The table is read like a mileage chart. So, to see how much can be produced with two tonnes of fertilizer, and three months of labour, we locate the 2 in the column of numbers on the left, which indicates the quantity of fertilizer, and the 3 in the row of numbers across the top, which represents the months of labour. Then, in the spot horizontally to the right of the 2 and vertically below the 3 we find the number 2600, meaning that this input combination can produce 2600 bushels of output per month. Similarly, you should be able to verify that with eight tonnes of fertilizer and three months of labour, 4600 bushels per month can be produced.

The zero entries in the first column of Table 22–7 tell us that Farmer Pfister can produce nothing with no labour. The second column, which corresponds to alternative amounts of fertilizer used in combination with *one* month of labour, is familiar to us already—it is just the total physical product schedule that we have been using for Farmer Pfister working alone with various amounts of fertilizer. The other columns represent alternative production arrangements in which Pfister hires one or more farmhands to help him.

How much labour and fertilizer should Farmer Pfister use if he wants to grow 2600 bushels of corn? The production-function table shows us that there are a variety of alternatives available to him. He can, for example, work alone and use six tonnes of fertilizer. Or he can hire a second worker and use only four tonnes. Or, at the other extreme, he can grow 2600 bushels without fertilizer by using five workers. The coloured entries in Table 22–7 indicate all the different ways in which Farmer Pfister can conceivably meet his 2600-bushel production target.

Which will he choose? Naturally, the one that costs him the least. Table 22–8 shows Farmer Pfister's cost calculations. It is assumed here that fertilizer costs $350 per tonne, that farm labour costs $500 per month, and that Pfister's fixed costs for such items as land and machinery amount to $1700 per month. Thus, for example, the first line tells us that Pfister can produce 2600 bushels using only his

Table 22-8

PRODUCTION COSTS UNDER ALTERNATIVE INPUT COMBINATIONS CAPABLE OF PRODUCING 2600 BUSHELS

QUANTITY OF LABOUR (months)	COST OF LABOUR (at $500 per month)	QUANTITY OF FERTILIZER (tonnes)	COST OF FERTILIZER (at $350 per tonne)	FIXED COSTS (for land, machinery, etc.)	TOTAL COST
1	$ 500	6	$2100	$1700	$4300
2	1000	4	1400	1700	4100
3	1500	2	700	1700	3900
4	2000	1	350	1700	4050
5	2500	0	0	1700	4200

own labour (which costs $500), six tonnes of fertilizer (which cost $2100), and land and machinery that cost $1700 per month, for a total cost of $500 + $2100 + $1700 = $4300. The other lines in Table 22-8 can be read the same way. We see that the cheapest way to produce 2600 bushels of corn is by using three workers and two tonnes of fertilizer, for a total cost of $3900, which is less than any other alternative.

Notice that two types of information are relevant to Farmer Pfister's decision. The *technological information* embodied in the production function tells Pfister all the possible ways that 2600 bushels can be produced; that is, it tells him about the possibilities for factor substitution. Then *financial information*—the prices of the two inputs—is needed to tell him which alternative is the least costly. If either set of data changes, Farmer Pfister's decision on input combinations is likely to change as well. For example, if fertilizer gets much more expensive, he might switch to an alternative that uses more labour and less fertilizer.

Does the "marginal revenue product equals price" rule continue to hold when there are two or more inputs? Let us see by testing whether the rule is satisfied when Pfister uses three months of labour and two tonnes of fertilizer. (Table 22-8 has just shown us that this input combination is the least costly way to produce 2600 bushels.) We know from Table 22-7 that when three months of labour are used, the marginal *physical* product (MPP) of the second tonne of fertilizer is 200 bushels (2600 bushels minus 2400 bushels). Since the price of a bushel of corn is $2, the marginal *revenue* product (MRP) of the second tonne of fertilizer is $400, which exceeds its price ($350). Therefore, Farmer Pfister should purchase the second tonne. But should he purchase the third? Its MPP is 150 bushels (2750 minus 2600), so its MRP is $2 × 150 = $300. This is less than what the third tonne would cost, so Pfister should stop at two tonnes.

What about months of labour? Reading across the row corresponding to two tonnes of fertilizer, we see that the MPP of the third month of labour is 350 bushels (2600 – 2250) while the MPP of the fourth month of labour is only 200 bushels. At a $2 price for corn, the corresponding MRPs are $700 for the third month of labour and only $400 for the fourth month. Since labour costs $500 per month, it is optimal to stop at three months.

Because we have not considered fractional amounts in our production-function table, we have not been able to satisfy the MRP = P rule exactly. But we can see that Farmer Pfister has indeed followed the basic logic of the rule and has come as close as possible to setting:

$$\text{MRP of fertilizer} = P \text{ of fertilizer}$$
$$\text{MRP of labour} = P \text{ of labour}.$$

If we remember that the MRP of each input is its marginal *physical* product times the price of corn, we can see that these rules are just a formalization of common sense. They say, for example, that if one input costs twice as much as another, then optimal input use requires that the first input be twice as productive (on the margin) as the second.[6]

This common-sense reasoning leads to an important conclusion. Suppose the price of fertilizer rises while the price of labour remains the same. The rule

$$P \text{ of fertilizer} = \text{MRP of fertilizer} = \text{MPP of fertilizer} \times \text{Price of corn}$$

tells us the optimal use of fertilizer now requires that the MPP of fertilizer must be higher than before. (The price of corn has not changed.) By the "law" of diminishing returns, the MPP of fertilizer is *higher* only when *less* fertilizer is used. Thus, a rise in the price of fertilizer leads the farmer to use *less* fertilizer and, if he still wants to produce 2600 bushels of output, *more* labour. In general:

As any one input becomes more costly relative to other competing units, the firm is likely to substitute one input for another; that is, to reduce its use of the input that has become more expensive and to increase its use of competing inputs.[7]

This general principle of input substitution applies in industry just as it does on the Pfister farm. For some applications of the analysis, see the box on page 439.

The Firm's Cost Curves

Earlier we calculated the firm's cost curves in the special case where the quantity of only one input—fertilizer—was selected by the firm. Now we can see how the cost curves can be determined in the more realistic case of choices about the quantities of several inputs.

In deciding on the quantity of output that serves its objectives best, the firm must consider alternative production levels and compare their costs. In the present example, an output of 2600 bushels is not likely to be the only possible production level that Farmer Pfister is considering. He might wonder, for example, about the least costly way to produce 2100 bushels or 3100 bushels.

By the same procedures outlined in Table 22–8 (page 437), Farmer Pfister can compute the minimum cost of producing *any* quantity of output, using the logic of the requirement that in such a cost-minimizing decision the relative marginal revenue products of any two inputs must equal their relative prices.

---

[6]A little algebra is helpful in restating this rule. Letting P_F, P_L, and P_C represent the prices of fertilizer, labour, and corn, respectively, and letting MRP_F and MPP_F represent the marginal revenue product and the marginal physical product of fertilizer, respectively, with similar notation for labour, our two rules for optimal input use become:

$$P_F = \text{MRP}_F = P_C \times \text{MPP}_F \quad \text{and} \quad P_L = \text{MRP}_L = P_C \times \text{MPP}_L.$$

Then if we divide the first optimality rule by the second, we obtain:

$$\frac{P_F}{P_L} = \frac{\text{MRP}_F}{\text{MRP}_L} = \frac{\text{MPP}_F \times P_C}{\text{MPP}_L \times P_C} \; .$$

Since P_C can be divided out of both numerator and denominator, the general rule for optimal input combinations is:

$$\frac{P_F}{P_L} = \frac{\text{MPP}_F}{\text{MPP}_L} \; .$$

In words, variable inputs should always be combined in such a way that their prices are proportional to their marginal physical products.

[7]*EXERCISE:* Suppose that fertilizer rises in price to $600 per tonne. Construct a new version of Table 22–8 (page 437) and use it to show that it will be optimal to reduce fertilizer use from two tonnes to zero and to increase the use of labour from three months to five months.

Input Substitution on the Range

When at the end of the 1970s the second fuel crisis hit North America, the newspapers carried a story about ranchers in the Southwest United States reportedly hiring additional cowhands to drive cattle on foot instead of carrying them on trucks. In other words, the rising price of oil had led ranchers to substitute the work of cowboys for the gasoline formerly used in driving cattle-carrying trucks. This is no scenario from a Wild West movie but an illustration of the way in which life follows the analytical principles described in the text, substituting inputs whose relative price has not risen for inputs whose relative price has risen.

There are many other illustrations of this phenomenon. It helps to explain the disappearance, in half a century, of personal servants who were once commonplace in the homes of middle-class families (in the 1920s "every" such home had at least a full-time maid) and the substitution of washing machines, clothes dryers, and dishwashers as real wages rose. It also helps to account

for the disappearance of wooden houses in England as forests disappeared and wood became increasingly expensive compared with other building materials. You can undoubtedly come up with other examples without difficulty.

Let us suppose that Farmer Pfister has calculated the minimum total costs for alternative production levels displayed in Table 22–9. Here we have the numbers Pfister needs to plot five different points on his *total-cost curve*, which is the curve shown in Figure 22–7. Point *A* shows the $2880 total cost of 1600 bushels of output, point *B* shows the $3360 total cost of 2100 bushels, and so on. As before, by dividing the total cost for each output by the quantity of the output, we obtain the corresponding *average cost*; that is, the cost per unit of output. For example, when output is 2600 bushels, total cost is $3900; so average cost is $3900/2600, or $1.50. Similarly, we can deduce the marginal-cost curve from the total cost figures, just as we did before.[8]

[8]*EXERCISE*: Provide the average- and marginal-cost columns for Table 22–9 and draw the AC and MC curves.

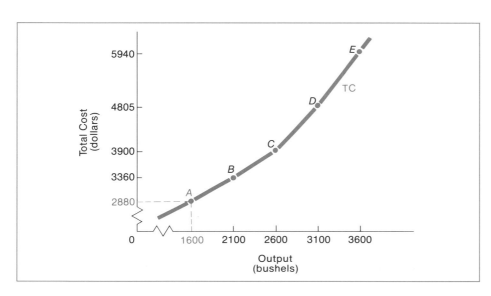

Table 22–9

DATA FOR PFISTER'S TOTAL-COST CURVE

OUTPUT LEVEL (bushels)	TOTAL COST (TC) (dollars)
1600	2880
2100	3360
2600	3900
3100	4805
3600	5940

Figure 22–7

TOTAL-COST CURVE

Point *A* shows that to produce 1600 bushels per month, a total of $2880 in cost must be incurred, just as Table 22–9 indicates.

Economies of Scale

We are now beginning to put together the apparatus we need to address the question posed at the start of this chapter: How can we tell if a firm has substantial **economies of scale**? We are now in a position to give a more careful definition than before.

The scale of operation of a business enterprise is defined by the quantities of the various inputs it uses. To see what happens when the firm doubles its scale of operations, we inquire about the effect on output of a doubling of each and every one of the firm's input quantities. As an example of economies of scale, turn back to the production function for Farmer Pfister in Table 22–7 on page 436 and assume that labour and fertilizer are the only two inputs.[9] Notice that with two months of labour and four tonnes of fertilizer, output is 2600 bushels. What happens if we double both inputs—to four months of labour and eight tonnes of fertilizer? The table shows us that output rises to 5400—that is, it more than doubles. So Farmer Pfister's production function, at least in this range, is said to display **increasing returns to scale** (economies of scale).

We can relate this definition of economies of scale to our earlier discussion where we interpreted economies of scale in terms of the *long-run* average-cost curve instead of the production function. Notice that the definition requires a doubling of *every* input to bring about more than a doubling of output. If all input quantities are doubled, then total cost must double. But if output *more* than doubles as a result, then cost per unit (average cost) must decline. In other words:

Production functions with economies of scale lead to long-run average-cost curves that decline as output expands.

An example will clarify the arithmetic behind this rule. We saw earlier (Table 22–8) that it costs $4100 to produce 2600 bushels with two months of labour and four tonnes of fertilizer. The average cost is thus $4100/2600, or approximately $1.58 per bushel. If, as the production function states, doubling all inputs (and thus doubling costs to $8200) leads to production of 5400 bushels, then cost per unit will become $8200/5400, or approximately $1.52. Economies of scale in the production function thus lead to *decreasing* average cost as output expands; in this case, average cost decreases by 6 cents—from $1.58 to $1.52.

A decreasing average-cost curve is depicted in Figure 22–8(a). But this is only one of three possible shapes the long-run average-cost curve can take. A second possibility is shown in part (b) of the figure. In this case we have an example of **constant returns to scale**, where both total cost (TC) and quantity of output (Q) double, so average cost (AC = TC/Q) remains constant. Finally, it is possible that output less than doubles when all inputs double. This would be a case of **decreasing returns to scale**, which leads to a rising long-run average-cost curve like the one depicted in part (c) of Figure 22–8.

It should be pointed out that the same production function can display increasing returns to scale in some ranges, constant returns to scale in others, and decreasing returns to scale in yet others. Farmer Pfister's production function in Table 22–7 provides an illustration of this. We have already seen that it displays increasing returns to scale when inputs are doubled from two months of labour and four tonnes of fertilizer to four months of labour and eight tonnes of fertilizer. But, looking back at Table 22–7 (page 436), we can see that there are constant returns to scale when inputs double from two months of labour and three tonnes of fertilizer (2450 bushels of output) to four months of labour and six tonnes of

Production is said to involve **economies of scale**, also referred to as **increasing returns to scale**, if, when all input quantities are doubled, the quantity of output is more than doubled.

---

[9]This is necessary because the table deals with only two inputs and the definition requires that *all* inputs be doubled simultaneously. So, to be true to the definition, because labour, fertilizer, *land, and machinery* were all used by the farmer, their quantities would all have to be doubled.

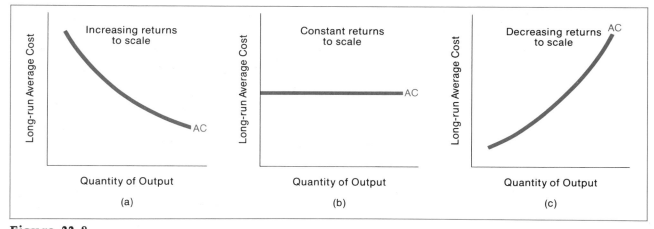

Figure 22-8

THREE POSSIBLE SHAPES FOR THE LONG-RUN AVERAGE-COST CURVE

In part (a), long-run average costs are decreasing as output expands because the firm has significant economies of scale (increasing returns to scale). In part (b), constant returns to scale lead to a long-run AC curve that is flat; costs per unit are the same for any level of output. In part (c), which pertains to a firm with decreasing returns to scale, long-run average costs rise as output expands.

fertilizer (4900 bushels). We can also find a region of decreasing returns to scale. Notice that with two months of labour and one tonne of fertilizer the yield is 1900 bushels, while with double those inputs—four months of labour and two tonnes of fertilizer—the yield is only 2800 bushels.

Diminishing Returns and Returns to Scale

Earlier in this chapter we discussed the "law" of diminishing marginal returns. Is there any relationship between economies of scale and the phenomenon of diminishing returns? It may seem at first that the two are contradictory. After all, if a producer gets diminishing returns from his inputs as he uses more of each of them, doesn't it follow that by using more of *every* input, he cannot obtain economies of scale? The answer is that there is no contradiction, for the two principles deal with fundamentally different issues.

1. **Returns to a single input**. Here we must ask the question, how much can output expand if we increase the quantity of just *one* input, *holding all other input quantities unchanged*?

2. **Returns to scale**. Here the question is: How much can output expand if *all* inputs are increased *simultaneously* by the same percentage?

The "law" of diminishing returns provides an answer to the first question while economies of scale pertain to the second.

Table 22-7 shows us that Farmer Pfister's production function satisfies the "law" of diminishing returns to a single input. To see this, we must hold the quantity of one input constant while letting the other vary. The row corresponding to eight tonnes of fertilizer will serve as an example, since an entry is provided for every quantity of labour. Reading across the row, we see from the second entry that the use of one month of labour and eight tonnes of fertilizer yields 2650 bushels of corn. The next entry shows that the same eight tonnes of fertilizer plus one additional month of labour produces a marginal product of 1050 bushels (that is, the total of 3700 bushels produced by the two months of labour minus the 2650 bushels obtained from the first month's labour). In the third column we find that another month of labour (still holding fertilizer use at eight tonnes) brings in a smaller marginal product of 900 (4600 total bushels minus 3700 bushels from the first two months). The "law" of diminishing returns is clearly satisfied.

Returns to scale, on the other hand, describe the production response to a proportionate increase in *all* inputs. We have already seen that this production function displays increasing returns to scale in some ranges, constant returns to scale in others, and decreasing returns to scale in yet others. Thus, the "law" of diminishing returns (to a single input) is compatible with *any* sort of returns to scale. In summary:

Returns to scale and returns to a single input (holding all other input quantities constant) refer to two distinct aspects of a firm's technology. A production function that displays diminishing returns to *a single input* may show diminishing, constant, or increasing returns when *all input quantities are increased proportionately*.

Historical Costs Versus Analytical Cost Curves

In the previous chapter, we made much of the fact that all points on a demand curve pertain to the *same* period of time, and that a plot of historical data on prices and quantities is normally not the demand curve that the decision-maker needs. A similar point relating to cost curves will resolve the problem posed at the beginning of the chapter as to whether declining historical costs are evidence of economies of scale.

All points on any of the cost curves used in economic analysis refer to the same period of time.

One point on the cost curve of an auto manufacturer tells us, for example, how much it would cost it to produce 2.5 million cars during 1985. Another point on the curve tells us what happens to the firm's costs if, *instead*, it produces, say, 3 million cars in 1985. Such a curve is called an **analytical cost curve** or, when there is no possibility of confusion, simply a cost curve. This curve must be distinguished from a diagram of **historical costs**, which shows how costs have changed from year to year.

The different points on an analytical cost curve represent *alternative possibilities*, all for the same time period. In 1985, the car manufacturer will produce either 2.5 or 3 million cars (or some other amount), but certainly not both. Thus, at most, only one point on this cost curve will ever be observed. The company may, indeed, produce 2.5 million in 1985 and 3 million in 1986; but the latter is not relevant to the 1985 cost curve. By the time 1986 comes around, the cost curve may well have shifted, so the 1985 cost figure will not apply to the 1986 cost curve. We can, of course, draw a different sort of graph that indicates, year by year, how costs and outputs have varied. Such a graph, which gathers together the statistics for a number of different periods, is not, however, a *cost curve* as that term is used by economists. An example of such a diagram of historical costs was given at the beginning of the chapter in Figure 22–1.

But why do economists rarely use historical cost diagrams and instead deal primarily with analytical cost curves, which are much more difficult to explain and to obtain statistically? The answer is that analysis of real policy problems—such as the desirability of having a single supplier of telephone services—leaves no choice in the matter. Rational decisions require analytical cost curves. Let us see why.

Resolving the Economies-of-Scale Puzzle

Since the 1940s there has been great technical progress in the telephone industry.

From ordinary open wire, the industry has gone to microwave systems, to telecommunications satellites and coaxial cables of enormous capacity, and new techniques using laser beams are on the way. Innovations in switching techniques and in the use of computers to send messages along uncrowded routes are equally impressive. All of this means that the *entire* analytical cost curve of telecommunications must have shifted downward quite dramatically from year to year. Innovation must have reduced not only the cost of large-scale operations *but also the cost of smaller-scale operations.*

Now, if we are to determine whether in 1985 a single supplier can provide telephone service more cheaply than can a number of smaller firms, we must compare the costs of *both* large- and small-scale production in 1985. It does no good to compare the cost of a large supplier in 1985 with its own costs as a smaller firm back in 1942, because that cannot possibly give us the information we need. The cost situation in 1942 is irrelevant for today's decision between large and small suppliers because no small firm today would use the obsolete techniques of 1942. Until we compare the costs of the large and small supplier *today* we cannot make a rational choice between single-firm and multi-firm production. It is the analytical cost curve, all of whose points refer to the same period, that, by definition, supplies this information.

Figures 22–9 and 22–10 show two extreme hypothetical cases, one in which economies of scale are present and one in which they are not. Yet both of them are based on the same historical cost data (in black) with their very sharply declining costs. (This curve is reproduced from Figure 22–1.) They also show (in colour) two possible average-cost curves, one for 1942 and one for 1985. In Figure 22–9 the

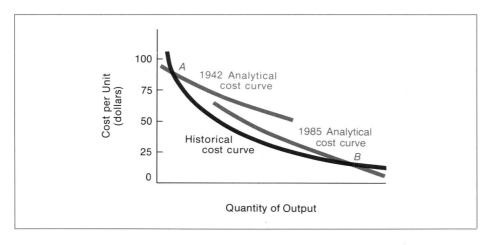

Figure 22-9
DECLINING HISTORICAL COST CURVE WITH THE ANALYTICAL AVERAGE– COST CURVE ALSO DECLINING IN EACH YEAR
The two analytical cost curves shown indicate how the corresponding points (*A* and *B*) on the historical cost diagram are generated by that year's analytical curve. Because the analytical cost curves are declining, we know that there are economies of scale in the production activity whose costs are shown.

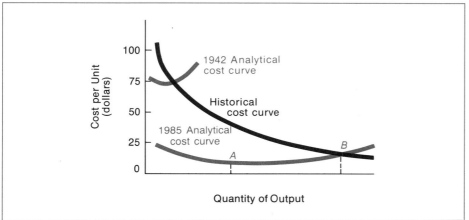

Figure 22-10
DECLINING HISTORICAL COST CURVE WITH U-SHAPED ANALYTICAL COST CURVES IN EACH YEAR
Here the shape of the average-cost curve does not show economies of scale.

analytical AC curve (in blue) has shifted downward very sharply from 1942 to 1985, as technological change reduced all costs. Moreover, both of the AC curves slope downward to the right, meaning that, in either year, the larger the firm the lower its average costs. Thus, the situation shown in Figure 22–9 really does represent a case in which there are economies of large-scale production so that one firm can produce at lower cost than many.

But now look at Figure 22–10, which shows exactly the same historical costs as Figure 22–9. Here, both analytical AC curves are U-shaped. In particular, we note that the 1985 AC curve has its minimum point at an output level, *A*, that is less than one-half the current output, *B*, of the large supplier. This means that in the situation shown in Figure 22–10, despite the sharp downward trend of historical costs, a smaller company can produce more cheaply than a large one can. In this case, one cannot justify domination of the market by a single large firm on the grounds that its costs are lower. In sum, the behaviour of historical costs tells us nothing about the cost advantages or disadvantages of a single large firm. More generally:

Because a diagram of historical costs does not compare the costs of large and small firms at the same point in time, it cannot be used to determine whether there are economies of large-scale production. Only the analytical cost curve can supply this information.

Cost Minimization in Theory and Practice

Lest you be tempted to run out and open a business, confident that you now understand how to minimize costs, we should point out that decision-making in business is a good deal harder than we have indicated here. Rare is the business executive who knows for sure what his production function looks like, or the exact shapes of his marginal revenue product schedules, or the precise nature of his cost curves. No one can provide a cookbook for instant success in business. What we have presented here is a set of principles that constitutes a guide to good decision-making.

Business management has been described as the art of making critical decisions on the basis of inadequate information, and in our complex and ever-changing world there is often no alternative to an educated guess. Actual business decisions will at best approximate the cost-minimizing ideal outlined in this chapter. Certainly, there will be mistakes. But when management does its job well and the market system functions smoothly, the approximation may prove amazingly good. While no system is perfect, inducing firms to produce at the lowest possible cost is undoubtedly one of the jobs the market system does best.

Summary

1. A firm's total-cost curve shows the lowest possible cost for producing any given level of output. It is derived from the input combination used to produce any given output and the prices of the inputs.
2. A firm's average-cost (AC) curve shows the lowest possible cost per unit at which it is possible to produce any given level of output. It is derived from the total-cost (TC) curve by simple arithmetic: AC = TC/Q.
3. A firm's marginal-cost (MC) curve shows for each output level the increase in total cost resulting from a one-unit increase in output.

4. The long run is a period sufficiently long for the firm's plant to require replacement and for all its current contractual commitments to expire. The short run is any period briefer than that.
5. Fixed costs are costs whose total amounts do not vary when output increases. All other costs are called *variable*.
6. At all outputs greater than one unit, the total-fixed-cost (TFC) curve is horizontal, the average-fixed-cost (AFC) curve declines toward the horizontal axis but never crosses it, and the marginal-fixed-cost (MFC) curve coincides with the horizontal axis.

7. TC = TFC + TVC; AC = AFC + AVC; MC = MFC + MVC.

8. It is normally possible to produce the same quantity of output in a variety of ways by substituting more of one input for less of another. Firms normally seek the least costly way to produce any output.

9. The marginal physical product of an input is the increase in total output resulting from a one-unit increase in the use of that input, holding the quantities of all other inputs constant.

10. The "law" of diminishing marginal returns states that if we increase the amount of one input (holding all other input quantities constant), the marginal physical product of the expanding input will eventually begin to decline.

11. The marginal revenue product of an input is the additional revenue the firm earns from the increased sales resulting from the use of one more unit of the input.

12. A firm that wants to minimize costs will use each input up to the point where its marginal revenue

product (MRP) is equal to its price (P).

13. The production function shows the relationship between inputs and output. It indicates the maximum quantity of output obtainable from any given combination of inputs.

14. If a doubling of all the firm's inputs *just* permits it to double its output, the firm is said to have constant returns to scale. If with doubled inputs it can *more than* double its output, it has increasing returns to scale (or economies of scale). If a doubling of inputs produces *less than* double the output, the firm has decreasing returns to scale.

15. With increasing returns to scale, the firm's long-run average costs are decreasing; constant returns to scale are associated with constant long-run average costs.

16. We cannot tell if there are economies of scale (increasing returns to scale) simply by inspecting a diagram of historical cost data. Only the underlying analytical cost curve can supply this information.

Concepts for Review

Total physical product	Fixed costs	Production function
Average physical product (APP)	Variable costs	Economies of scale (increasing
Marginal physical product (MPP)	Short and long runs	returns to scale)
"Law" of diminishing marginal	Substitutability of inputs	Constant returns to scale
returns	Cost minimization	Decreasing returns to scale
Total-cost curve	Marginal revenue product (MRP)	Historical versus analytical cost
Average-cost curve	Rule for optimal input use (MRP =	relationships
Marginal-cost curve	P of input)	

Questions for Discussion

1. A firm's total fixed cost is $36,000. Construct a table of total, average, and marginal fixed costs for this firm for output levels varying from 0 to 6 units. Draw the corresponding TFC, AFC, and MFC curves.

2. With the following data, calculate the firm's AVC and MVC and draw the graphs for TVC, AVC, and MVC.

QUANTITY	TOTAL VARIABLE COSTS (thousands of dollars)
1	10
2	20
3	30
4	44
5	60
6	90

3. From the figures in Questions 1 and 2, calculate TC, AC, and MC for each of the output levels from 1 to 6, and draw the three graphs.

4. If a firm's commitments in 1985 include machinery that will need replacement in five years, a factory building rented for ten years, and a two-year union contract specifying how many workers it must employ, when, from its point of view in 1985, does the firm's long run begin?

5. If the marginal revenue product of a kilowatt hour of electric power is 8 cents and the cost of a kilowatt hour is 12 cents, what can a firm do to increase its profits?

6. A firm hires two workers and rents 15 hectares of land for a season. It produces 100,000 bushels of crop. If it had doubled its land and labour, production would have been 300,000 bushels. Does it have constant, diminishing, or increasing returns to scale?

7. Suppose wages are $10,000 per season and land rent per hectare is $3000. Calculate the average cost of 100,000 bushels and the average cost of 300,000 bushels, using the figures in Question 6 above. (Note that average costs diminish when output increases.) What connection do these figures have with the firm's returns to scale?

8. Farmer Pfister has bought a great deal of fertilizer. Suppose he now buys more *land*, but not more fertilizer, and spreads the fertilizer evenly over all his land. What may happen to the marginal physical product of fertilizer? What, therefore, is the role of input proportions in the determination of marginal physical product?

9. Labour costs $10 per hour. Nine workers produce $180 of product per hour. Ten workers produce $196 of product; 11 workers produce $208, and 12 workers produce $215. Draw up a table of the marginal revenue products of 9, 10, 11, and 12 workers. What is the optimal amount of labour for the firm to hire?

10. (More difficult.) A firm finds there is a sudden increase in the demand for its product. In the short run, it must operate longer hours and pay higher overtime wage rates. In the long run, however, it will pay the firm to install more machines and not operate them for longer hours. Which do you think will be lower, the short-run or the long-run average cost of the increased output? How is your answer affected by the fact that the long-run average cost includes the new machines the firm buys, while the short-run average cost includes no machine purchases?

Appendix
Production-Indifference Curves

To describe a production function—that is, the relationship between input combinations and size of total output—we can use a graphic device called the **production-indifference curve** instead of the sort of numerical information described in Table 22–7 in the chapter.

A **production-indifference curve** (sometimes called an *isoquant*) is a curve in a graph showing quantities of *inputs* on its axes. Each indifference curve indicates *all* combinations of input quantities capable of producing a *given* quantity of output; thus, there must be a separate indifference curve for each quantity of output.

If you have read the appendix on indifference curves in Chapter 20 (on consumer choice), you will recognize a close analogy in logic (and in geometric shape) between consumers' and producers' indifference curves. Figure 22–11 represents different quantities of labour and land capable of producing given amounts of wheat. The indifference curve labelled 220,000 bushels indicates that an output of 220,000 bushels of wheat can be obtained with the aid of *any one* of the combinations of inputs represented by points on the curve. For example, it can be produced by 10 years of labour and 200 hectares of land (point *A*) or, instead, it can be produced by the labour–land combination shown by point *B* on the same curve. Because it lies considerably below and to the right of point *B*, point *A* represents a productive process that uses more labour and less land than shown at point *B*.

Points *A* and *B* can be considered *technologically* indifferent because each represents a bundle of inputs capable of yielding the same quantity of finished goods. However, "indifference" in this sense does not mean that the producer will be unable to make up his mind between input combinations *A* and *B*. Input prices will permit him to arrive at that decision, because the two input choices are not *economically* indifferent.

The production-indifference curves in a diagram such as Figure 22–11 constitute a complete description of the production function. For each combination of inputs, they show how much output can be produced. Since it is drawn in two dimensions, the diagram can deal only with two inputs at a time. In more realistic situations, there may be more than two

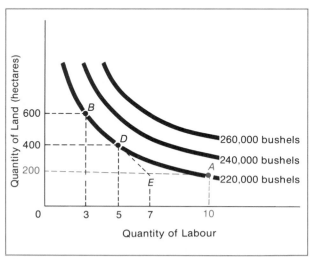

Figure 22-11

A PRODUCTION-INDIFFERENCE MAP

The figure shows three indifference curves, one for the production of 220,000 bushels of wheat, one for 240,000 bushels, and one for 260,000 bushels. For example, the lowest curve shows all combinations of land and labour capable of producing 220,000 bushels of wheat. Point *A* on that curve shows that 10 years of labour and 200 hectares of land are enough to do the job.

inputs, and an algebraic analysis must be used. But all the principles we need to analyse such a situation can be derived from the two-variable case.

Characteristics of Production-Indifference Curves

Before discussing input pricing and quantity decisions, we first examine what is known about the shapes of production-indifference curves. The main characteristics are straightforward and entirely analogous to the properties of consumer-indifference curves discussed in the appendix to Chapter 20.

Characteristic 1: Higher curves correspond to larger outputs.   Points on a higher indifference curve represent larger quantities of *both* inputs than the corresponding points on a lower curve. Thus, the higher the curve, the larger the output it represents.

Characteristic 2: The indifference curve will generally have a negative slope.   It goes downhill as we move toward the right. This means that if we reduce the quantity of one input used, and we do not want to cut production, we must use more of another input. For example, if we want to use less land to produce 220,000 bushels of wheat, we will have to hire more labour to make up for the reduced land input.

Characteristic 3: The curves are typically assumed to curve inward toward the origin near their "middle."   This is a reflection of the "law" of diminishing returns to a single input. For example, in Figure 22–11, points B, D, and A represent three different input combinations capable of producing the same quantity of output. At point B a large amount of land and relatively little labour is used, while the opposite is true at point A. Point D is intermediate between the two. Indeed, point D is chosen so that its use of land is exactly halfway between the amounts of land used at A and at B.

Now consider the choice among these input combinations. As the farmer considers first the input combination at B, and then the one at D, and finally the one at A, he is considering the use of less and less land, making up for it by the use of more and more labour so that he can continue to produce the same output. But the trade-off does not proceed at a constant rate because of diminishing returns in the substitution of labour for land.

When the farmer considers moving from point B to point D, he gives up 200 hectares of land and instead hires two additional years of labour. Similarly, the move from D to A involves giving up another 200 hectares of land. But this time, hiring an additional

two years of labour does not make up for the reduced use of land. Diminishing returns to labour as he hires more and more workers to replace more and more land means that now a much larger quantity of additional labour, five years rather than two, is needed to make up for the reduction in the use of land. If there had been no such diminishing returns, the indifference curve would have been a straight line, DE. The curvature of the indifference curve through points D and A reflects diminishing returns to substitution of inputs.

The Choice of Input Combinations

A production indifference curve only describes what input combinations *can* produce a given output; it indicates the technological possibilities. A business cannot decide which of the available options suits its purposes best without the corresponding cost information; that is, the relative prices of the inputs.

Just as we did for the consumer in the appendix to Chapter 20, we can construct a **budget line**—a representation of equally costly input combinations—for the firm. For example, if farmhands are paid $9000 a year and land rents for $1000 per hectare a year, then a farmer who spends $360,000 can hire 40 farmhands but rent no land (point K in Figure 22–12), or he can rent 360 hectares but have no money left for farmhands (point J). But it is undoubtedly more sensible for him to pick some intermediate point on his budget line, JK, at which he divides the $360,000 between the two inputs.

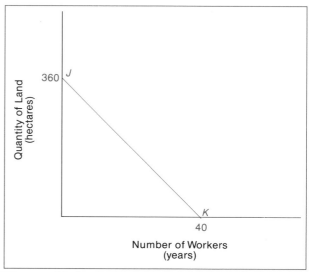

Figure 22–12
A BUDGET LINE
The firm's budget line, JK, shows all the combinations of inputs it can purchase with a fixed amount of money—in this case $360,000.

There is an important difference, however, in how this budget line is used. The consumer had a fixed budget and sought the highest indifference curve attainable with these limited funds. The firm's problem in minimizing costs is just the reverse. Its budget is not fixed. Instead, it wants to produce a given quantity of output (say, 240,000 bushels) with the *smallest possible budget*.

A way to find the minimum budget capable of producing 240,000 bushels of wheat is illustrated in Figure 22–13, which combines the indifference curve for 240,000 bushels from Figure 22–11 with a variety of budget lines similar to *JK* in Figure 22–12. The firm's problem is to find the lowest budget line that will allow it to reach the 240,000-bushel indifference curve. Clearly, an expenditure of $270,000 is too little; there is no point on budget line *AB* that permits production of 240,000 bushels. Similarly, an expenditure of $450,000 is too much, because the firm can produce its target level of output more cheaply. The solution is at point *T*, meaning that 15 workers and 225 hectares of land are used to produce the 240,000 bushels of wheat. In general:

The least costly way to produce any given level of output is indicated by the point of tangency between a budget line and the production-indifference curve corresponding to that level of output.

Cost Minimization, Expansion Path, and Cost Curves

Figure 22–13 shows how to determine the input combination that minimizes the cost of producing 240,000 bushels of output. We can repeat this procedure exactly for any other output quantity, such as 200,000 bushels or 300,000 bushels. In each case, we draw the corresponding production-indifference curve and find the lowest budget line that permits it to be produced. For example, in Figure 22–14 budget line *BB* is tangent to the indifference curve for 200,000 units of output and budget line *B'B'* is tangent to the indifference curve for 300,000 units of output. In this way, we obtain three tangency points: *S*, which gives us the input combination that produces a 200,000-bushel output at lowest cost; *T*, which gives the same information for a 240,000-bushel output; and *S'*, which indicates the cost-minimizing input combination for the production of 300,000 bushels.

This process can be repeated for as many other levels of output as we like. For each such output we draw the corresponding production-indifference curve and find its point of tangency with a budget line. That tangency point will show the input combination that produces the output in question at lowest cost.

Curve *EE* in Figure 22–14 connects all these cost-minimizing points; that is, it is the locus of *S*, *T*, and *S'*, and all the other points of tangency between a

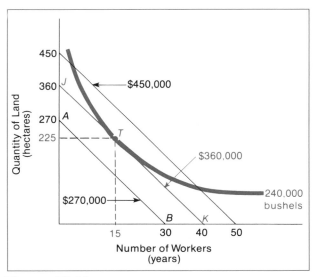

Figure 22-13
COST MINIMIZATION
The least costly way to produce 240,000 bushels of wheat is shown by point *T*, where the production-indifference curve is tangent to budget line *JK*. Here the farmer is employing 15 workers and using 225 hectares of land. It is not possible to produce 240,000 bushels on a smaller budget, and any larger budget would be wasteful.

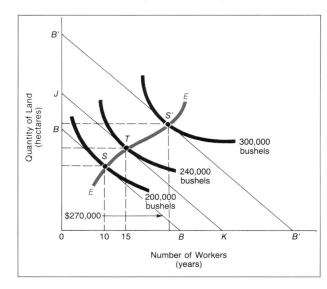

Figure 22-14
THE FIRM'S EXPANSION PATH
Each point of tangency, such as *S*, between a production-indifference curve and a budget line shows the combination of inputs that can produce the output corresponding to that indifference curve at lowest cost. The locus of all such tangency points is *EE*, the firm's expansion path.

production-indifference curve and a budget line. Curve EE is called the firm's **expansion path**, which is defined as the locus of the firm's cost-minimizing input combinations for all relevant output levels.

In Figure 22–13 we were able to determine for tangency point T the quantity of output (from the production-indifference curve through that point) and the total cost (from the tangent budget line). Similarly, we can determine the output and total cost for every other point on the expansion path, EE, in Figure 22–14. For example, at point S we see that output is 200,000 units and total cost is $270,000.

This is precisely the sort of information we need to find the firm's total-cost curve; that is, it is just the sort of information contained in Table 22–4 from which we first calculated the total-cost curve and then the average-and marginal-cost curves in Figure 22–4. Thus we see that:

The points of tangency between a firm's production-indifference curves and its budget lines yield its expansion path. The expansion path shows the firm's cost-minimizing input combination for each pertinent output level. This information also yields the output and total cost for each point on the expansion path, which is just what we need to draw the firm's cost curves.

Effects of Changes in Input Prices

Suppose now that the cost of renting land increases and the wage rate of labour decreases. This means that the budget lines will differ from those depicted in Figure 22–13. Specifically, with land now more expensive, any given sum of money will rent fewer hectares, so the intercept of each budget line on the vertical (land) axis will shift *downward*. Conversely, with labour cheaper, any given sum of money will buy more labour, so the intercept of the budget line on the horizontal (labour) axis will shift to the *right*. A series of budget lines corresponding to a $1500 per hectare rental rate for land and a $6000 annual wage for labour is depicted in Figure 22–15. We see that these budget lines are less steep than those shown in Figure 22–13 and that the least costly way to produce 240,000 bushels of wheat is now given by point E.

To assist you in seeing how things change, Figure 22–16 combines in a single graph budget line JK and tangency point T from Figure 22–13 and budget line WV and tangency point E from Figure 22–15. Notice that point E lies below and to the right of T, meaning that as wages decrease and rents increase the firm will hire more labour and rent less land. As common sense suggests, when the price of one input rises in comparison with that of others, it will pay the firm to hire less of this input and more of other inputs to make up for its reduced use of the more expensive input.

In addition to this substitution of one input for another, a change in the price of an input may induce the firm to alter the level of output that it decides to produce. But this is the subject of the next chapter.

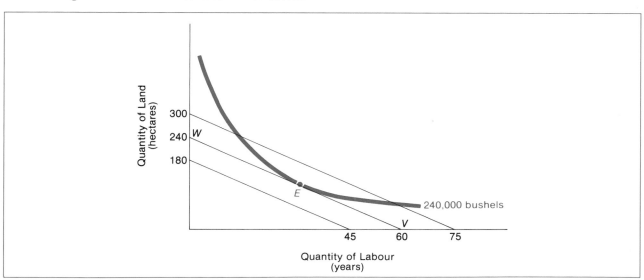

Figure 22–15

OPTIMAL INPUT CHOICE AT A DIFFERENT SET OF INPUT PRICES

If input prices change, the combination of inputs that minimizes costs will normally change, too. In this diagram, land rents for $1500 per hectare (more than in Figure 22–13) while labour costs $6000 per year (less than in Figure 22–13). As a result, the least costly way to produce 240,000 bushels of wheat shifts from point T in Figure 22–13 to point E here.

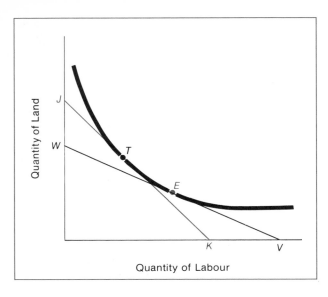

Figure 22-16
HOW CHANGES IN INPUT PRICES AFFECT INPUT PROPORTIONS
When land becomes more expensive and labour becomes cheaper, the budget lines (such as *JK*) become less steep than they were previously (see *WV*). As a result, the least costly way to produce 240,000 bushels shifts from point *T* to point *E*. The firm uses more labour and less land.

Summary

1. A production function can be fully described by a family of production-indifference curves, each of which shows all the input combinations capable of producing a specified amount of output.

2. As long as each input has a positive marginal physical product, production-indifference curves will have a negative slope and the higher curves will represent larger amounts of output than the lower curves. Because of diminishing returns, these curves characteristically bend toward the origin near their middle.

3. The optimal input combination for any given level of output is indicated by the point of tangency between a budget line and the appropriate production-indifference curve.

4. The firm's expansion path shows, for each of the firm's possible output levels, the combination of input quantities that minimizes the cost of producing that output.

5. From the production-indifference curves and the budget lines tangent to them along the expansion path, one can find the total cost for each output level. From these figures one can determine the firm's total-cost, average-cost, and marginal-cost curves.

6. When input prices change, firms will normally use more of the input that becomes relatively less expensive and less of the input that becomes relatively more expensive.

Concepts for Review

Production-indifference curve
Budget line
Expansion path

Point of tangency between the budget line and the corresponding production-indifference curve

Questions for Discussion

1. Typical Manufacturing Corporation (TMC) produces gadgets with the aid of two inputs: labour and glue. If labour costs $5 per hour and glue costs $5 per litre, draw TMC's budget line for a total expenditure of $100,000. In this same diagram, sketch a production-indifference curve indicating that TMC can produce no more than 1000 gadgets with this expenditure.

2. With respect to Question 1, suppose that wages rise to $10 per hour and glue prices rise to $6 per litre. How are TMC's optimal input proportions likely to change? (Use a diagram to explain your answer.)

3. What happens to the expansion path of the firm in Question 2?

The Common Sense of Business Decisions: Outputs and Prices

23

Annual income twenty
pounds, annual expenditure
nineteen pounds, nineteen
and six, result happiness.
Annual income twenty
pounds, annual expenditure
twenty pounds ought and six,
result misery.
CHARLES DICKENS

When Apple introduced its new Macintosh computer in 1984, it had to decide on the price at which each model would be offered and the number of each to produce. These were clearly among the most crucial decisions the firm ever made. They had a vital influence on Apple's labour requirements, on the reception given the product by consumers, and, indeed, on the very survival of the company.

This chapter describes the tools that firms like Apple can use to make decisions on outputs and prices—tools that are equally useful to government agencies and non-profit organizations in making analogous decisions. We begin the chapter by examining the relationship between the firm's price decisions and the quantity of product it sells. We then discuss the assumption of profit maximization before turning to the techniques firms can use to achieve the largest possible profit. We will explore, in words, with numerical examples, and with graphs, several methods of finding the level of output that maximizes profits. Each of these methods teaches us something else about the nature of the firm's decision-making process and provides some general lessons about the use of marginal analysis. The analysis will also yield two conclusions that may be somewhat surprising and show that unaided common sense can sometimes be misleading in business decisions. Specifically, it will be shown that a change in fixed costs does not change the levels of price and output that maximize a firm's profits, and that it may be possible for a firm to make a profit by increasing the amount it sells at a price that is below cost.

Two Illustrative Cases*

Price and output decisions can perplex even the most experienced business people, as the following real-life illustrations show.

CASE 1: PRICING A SIX-PACK
The managers of one of North America's largest manufacturers of soft drinks became concerned when a rival company introduced a cheaper substitute for one

*The figures in these examples are doctored to help preserve the confidentiality of the information and to simplify the calculations. The cases, however, are real.

of their leading products. As a result, some of the firm's managers advocated a reduction in the price of a six-pack from $1.50 to $1.35. This stimulated a heated debate. It was agreed that the price should be cut if it was not likely to reduce the company's profits. Although some of the managers maintained that the cut made sense because of the demand it would stimulate, others held that the price cut would hurt the company by cutting profit per unit of output. The company had reliable information about costs, but knew rather little about their consumers' responsiveness to price changes. At this point a group of consultants was called in to offer their suggestions. We will see how economic analysis enabled them to solve the problem even though the vital demand elasticity figures were unavailable.

CASE 2: SAVING THE COMPANY BY SELLING BELOW COSTS
A supplier of a canned meat product was selling 10 million units per year at a wholesale price of $11 per unit. It found that rising wages and raw material prices had increased its costs to $13 per unit, which was clearly a losing proposition. Yet the availability of competing canned meats convinced the firm's managers that they could not get away with a price increase. At this point a purchasing agent for a foreign government approached the firm and offered to buy an additional 10 million units, but at a price of only $7 per unit. At first, management considered the offer ludicrous, since the $7 price came nowhere near covering the unit cost of $13. But after some analysis, management was able to show that the firm could actually clear up its financial problem by agreeing to the proposed sale even though it was "below cost." At the end of the chapter we will explain just how this was possible.

Price and Quantity: One Decision, Not Two

This chapter is about how firms, like those in the preceding cases, select a *price* and a *quantity* of output that best serve their financial interests. While it would seem that firms must choose two numbers, in fact they can pick only one. Once they have selected the *price*, the *quantity* they will sell is up to consumers. Alternatively, firms may decide *how much* they want to sell, but then they must leave it to the market to determine the *price* at which this quantity can be sold.

Management gets its two numbers by making only one decision because the firm's demand curve tells it, for any quantity it may decide to market, the highest possible price its product can fetch. For purposes of illustration, consider a hypothetical firm, Computron, Inc., which produces giant computers. Computron's demand curve, *DD* in Figure 23–1, shows that if the company decides to charge the relatively high price of $15 million per computer (point *a* on the curve), then it can sell only one unit per year. On the other hand, if it wants to sell as many as six computers per year, it can do so only by offering its product at the low price of $8 million (point *f*). In summary:

Each point on the demand curve represents a price–quantity pair. The firm can pick any such pair. But it can never pick the price corresponding to one point on the demand curve and the quantity corresponding to another point, since such an output would never be sold at the selected price.

Throughout this chapter, then, we will not discuss price and output decisions separately, for they are merely two different aspects of the same decision. To analyse this decision, we will make a strong assumption about the behaviour of business firms, which, while not literally correct, seems to be a useful simplification of a much more complex reality—the assumption that firms strive for the largest possible total profit.

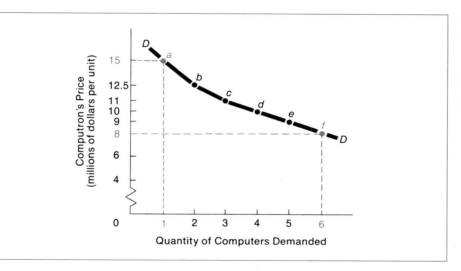

Figure 23-1
COMPUTRON'S DEMAND
CURVE
This graph shows the quantity of
product demanded at each price.
For example, the curve shows that
at a price of $8 million (point *f*), six
units will be demanded.

Do Firms Really Maximize Profits?

Naturally, many people have questioned whether firms really try to maximize profits, to the exclusion of all other goals. Business people are like other human beings: Their motives are varied and complex. Given the choice, many executives might prefer to control the largest firm rather than the most profitable one. Some may be influenced by envy, others by a desire to "do good." Different managers within the same firm may not always agree with one another. Thus, any attempt to summarize the objectives of management in terms of a single number (profit) is bound to be an oversimplification.

In addition, the exacting requirements for maximizing profits are tough to satisfy. In practice, the required calculations are rarely carried out fully. In deciding on how much to invest, on what price to set for a product, or on how much to allocate to the advertising budget, the range of available alternatives is enormous. And information about each alternative is often expensive and difficult to acquire. As a result, when a firm's management decides on an $18 million construction budget it rarely compares the consequences of that decision in any detail with the consequences of all the possible alternatives—such as budgets of $17 million or $19 million. But unless all the available possibilities are compared, there is no way management can be sure it has chosen the one that brings in the highest possible profits.

Often management studies with care only the likely effects of the proposed decision itself: What sort of plant will it obtain for the money? How costly will it be to operate the plant? How much revenue is it likely to obtain from the sale of the plant's output? Management's concern is *whether the decision will produce results that satisfy the firm's standards of acceptability*—whether its risks will not be unacceptably great, whether its profits will not be unacceptably low, and so on. Such analysis does not necessarily lead to the maximum possible profit, because, though the decision may be good, some of the alternatives that have *not* been investigated may be better.

Decision-making that seeks only acceptable solutions has been called **satisficing** to contrast with optimizing. Some analysts, such as Carnegie-Mellon University's Nobel Prize winner Herbert Simon, have concluded that decision-making in industry and government is often of the satisficing variety.

But even if this is true, it does not necessarily make profit maximization a bad assumption. Recall our discussion of abstraction and model-building in Chapter 1. A map of Vancouver that omits thousands of roads is no doubt "wrong" if interpreted as a literal description of the city. None the less, by capturing the most important elements of reality, it may help us understand the city better than a map that is cluttered with too much detail. Similarly, we can learn much about the behaviour of business firms by assuming that they try to maximize profits, even though we know that *all* of them do not act this way *all* of the time.

We will therefore assume throughout this and the next few chapters that the firm has only one objective: It wants to make its total profit as large as possible. Our analytic strategy will be to determine what output level (or price) achieves this goal.

Total Profit: The Important Difference

A firm's **total profit** is, by definition, the difference between what it earns in the form of sales revenue and what it pays out in the form of costs:

$$\text{Total profit} = \text{Total revenue} - \text{Total costs.}$$

Total profit defined in this way is called **economic profit**, to distinguish it from the accountant's definition of profit. The two concepts of profit differ because total cost, in the economist's definition, includes the opportunity cost of any capital, labour, or other inputs supplied by the owner of the firm.

To analyse how total profit depends on output, we must study its two components, total revenue (TR) and total cost (TC). We know from preceding chapters that both **total revenue** and **total cost** depend on the output–price combination the firm selects.

Total revenue can be calculated directly from the demand curve, since by definition it is the product of price times the quantity that will be bought at that price:

$$\text{TR} = P \times Q.$$

Table 23-1 shows how the total revenue schedule is derived from the demand schedule for our illustrative firm, Computron. The first two columns simply express the demand curve of Figure 23-1 in tabular form. The third column gives, for each quantity, the product of price times quantity. For example, if Computron markets three computers per year at a price of $11 million per computer, its annual sales revenue will be $3 \times \$11$ million = $33 million.

Figure 23-2 displays Computron's total revenue schedule in graphical form as the black TR curve. This graph shows precisely the same information as the demand curve in Figure 23-1, but in a somewhat different form. For example, point d on the demand curve in Figure 23-1, which shows a price–quantity combination of $P = \$10$ million and $Q = 4$ computers, appears as point D in Figure 23-2 as a total

Table 23-1

DEMAND SCHEDULE AND TOTAL- AND MARGINAL-REVENUE SCHEDULES FOR COMPUTRON, INC.
(Data corresponding to Figure 23-1)

NUMBER OF COMPUTERS (per year)	PRICE = AVERAGE REVENUE (millions of dollars per computer)	TOTAL REVENUE (millions of dollars per year)	MARGINAL REVENUE (millions of dollars per computer)
0	—	0	—
1	15	15	15
2	12.5	25	10
3	11	33	8
4	10	40	7
5	9	45	5
6	8	48	3

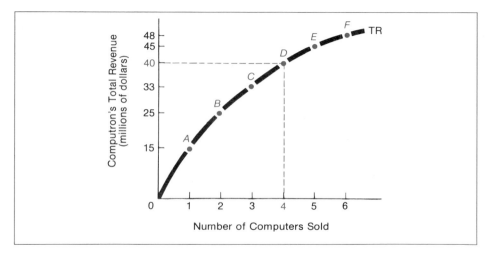

Figure 23-2

COMPUTRON'S TOTAL-
REVENUE CURVE

The total-revenue curve for
Computron, Inc., is derived directly
from the demand curve, since total
revenue is the product of price
times quantity. Points *A*, *B*, *C*, *D*, *E*,
and *F* in this diagram correspond
to points *a*, *b*, *c*, *d*, *e*, and *f*,
respectively, in Figure 23-1.

revenue of $40 million ($10 million price per unit times 4 units) corresponding to
a quantity of four computers. Similarly, each point on the TR curve in Figure 23–2
corresponds to the similarly labelled point in Figure 23–1.

The relationship between the demand curve and the TR curve can be
rephrased in a slightly different way. Since the price of the product is the revenue
per unit that the firm receives, we can view the demand curve as the curve of
average revenue. Average revenue (AR) and total revenue (TR) are related to
one another in the same way as average cost and total cost.[1] Specifically, since

$$AR = \frac{TR}{Q} = \frac{P \times Q}{Q} = P,$$

average revenue and price are two names for the same thing.

Finally, the last column of Table 23–1 shows the **marginal revenue** for
each level of output, that is, the *addition* to total revenue resulting from the
addition of one unit to total output. Its definition and calculation are precisely
analogous to those of marginal cost, which were described at length in Chapter 22
(pages 426–28). Thus, in Table 23–1 we see that when output rises from two to
three units, total revenue goes up from $25 million to $33 million, so that marginal
revenue is $33 million – $25 million = $8 million.

The revenue side is, of course, only one-half of the profit picture. We must
turn to the cost side for the other half. The last chapter explained how the total-
cost (TC), average-cost (AC), and marginal-cost (MC) schedules are determined by
the firm's production techniques and the prices of the inputs it buys. Rather than
repeat this analysis, we simply list the total-, average-, and marginal-cost schedules
for Computron in Table 23–2. Figure 23–3 depicts the total-cost curve as the blue
TC curve.

Notice that total costs at zero output are not zero, because Computron incurs
fixed costs of $2 million per year even if it produces nothing.[2] For example,
Computron will have to pay the rent for its factory and the salary of its president
whether it produces one computer, five computers, or ten.

To study how total profit depends on output, we bring together in Table 23–3
the total-revenue and total-cost schedules. The last column in Table 23–3, total
profit, is just the difference between total revenue and total cost for each level of
output. Remembering that Computron's assumed objective is to maximize its
profits, it is a simple matter to determine the level of production it will choose. By

Average revenue (AR) is
total revenue (TR) divided by
quantity.

Marginal revenue, often
abbreviated MR, is the
addition to total revenue
resulting from the addition
of one unit to total output.
Geometrically, marginal
revenue is the *slope* of the
total revenue curve.

---

[1]See the appendix to this chapter for a general discussion of the relationship between totals and
averages.

[2]For a review of the concept of fixed costs, see Chapter 22, pages 428–30.

Table 23-2

TOTAL, AVERAGE, AND MARGINAL COSTS FOR COMPUTRON, INC.

NUMBER OF UNITS (per year)	TOTAL COST (millions of dollars)	MARGINAL COST (millions of dollars per unit)	AVERAGE COST (millions of dollars per unit)
0	2		—
1	9	7	9
2	14	5	7
3	21	7	7
4	32	11	8
5	45	13	9
6	60	15	10

producing and selling three computers per year, Computron achieves the highest level of profits it is capable of achieving—some $12 million per year. Any higher or lower rate of production would lead to lower profits. For example, profits would drop to $8 million if output were expanded to four units.

Profit Maximization: A Graphical Interpretation

Precisely the same analysis can be presented graphically. In the upper portion of Figure 23-4 we bring together into a single diagram the total-revenue curve from Figure 23-2 and total-cost curve from Figure 23-3. Total profit, which is the difference between total revenue and total cost, appears in the diagram as the *vertical* distance between the TR and TC curves. For example, when output is four units, total revenue is $40 million (point *A*), total cost is $32 million (point *B*), and total profit is the distance between points *A* and *B*, or $8 million.

In this graphical view of the problem, Computron wants to maximize total profit, which is the vertical distance between the TR and TC curves. The curve of total profit is drawn in the lower portion of Figure 23-4. We see that it reaches its maximum value, $12 million, at an output level of three units per year. This is, naturally, the same conclusion we reached with the aid of Table 23-3.

The total-profit curve in Figure 23-4 is shaped like a hill. Though such a shape is not inevitable, we expect a hill shape to be typical for the following

Figure 23-3

COMPUTRON'S TOTAL-COST CURVE

The graph shows, for each possible level of output, Computron's total costs. Because Computron has some fixed costs, the level of total cost at zero output is $2 million, not zero.

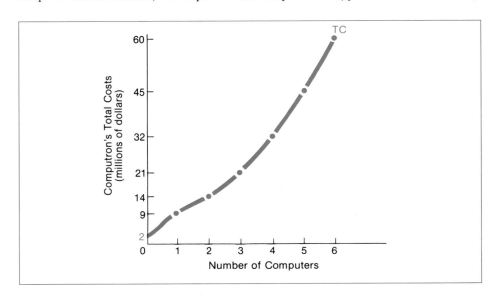

Table 23-3

TOTAL REVENUES, COSTS, AND PROFIT FOR COMPUTRON, INC.

NUMBER OF UNITS (per year)	TOTAL REVENUE	TOTAL COST	TOTAL PROFIT
		(millions of dollars per year)	
0	0	2	-2
1	15	9	6
2	25	14	11
3	33	21	12
4	40	32	8
5	45	45	0
6	48	60	-12

reason. If a firm produces nothing, it certainly earns no profit, and it will probably incur a loss if it has an idle factory on its hands and must spend money to guard it and keep it from deteriorating. At the other extreme, a firm can produce so much output that it swamps the market, forcing price down so low that it again loses money. Only at intermediate levels of output—something between zero and the amount that floods the market—will the company earn a positive profit. Consequently, the total-profit curve will rise from zero (or negative) levels at a very small output, to positive levels in between; and, finally, it will fall to negative levels when output gets too large. Thus, the total-profit curve will normally be a hill like the one shown in Figure 23-4.

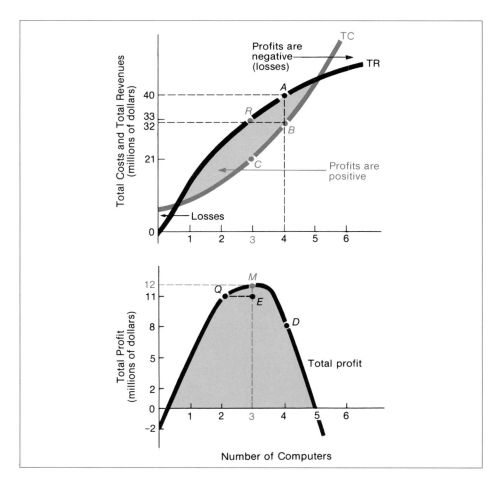

Figure 23-4

PROFIT MAXIMIZATION; A GRAPHICAL INTERPRETATION

Computron's profits are maximized when the vertical distance between its total-revenue curve, TR, and its total-cost curve, TC, is at its maximum. In the diagram, this occurs at an output of three units per year; total profits are CR, or $12 million. The total-profit curve is also shown in the figure. Naturally, it reaches its maximum value ($12 million) at three units (point M).

Marginal Analysis and Profit Maximization

If management really knew the exact shape of its profit hill, choosing the optimal level of output would be a simple task indeed. It would only have to locate a point like M in Figure 23-4, the top of its profit hill. However, management rarely if ever has so much information, so a different technique for finding the optimum is required. That technique is **marginal analysis**—the same set of tools that the consumer used to maximize utility in Chapter 20 and that the firm used to minimize costs in Chapter 22.

To see how marginal analysis helps solve Computron's problem, we introduce an expository concept: **marginal profit**. Referring back to Table 23-3, for example, we see that an increase in Computron's annual output from two to three computers would raise total profit from $11 million to $12 million. That is, it would generate $1 million in *additional* profits, which we call the *marginal profit* resulting from the addition of the third unit. Similarly, marginal profit from the fourth unit would be:

$$\frac{\text{Total profit}}{\text{from 4 units}} - \frac{\text{Total profit}}{\text{from 3 units}} = \$8 \text{ million} - \$12 \text{ million} = -\$4 \text{ million}.$$

The marginal rule for finding the optimal level of output is easy to understand:

If the marginal profit from increasing output by one unit is positive, then output should be increased. If the marginal profit from increasing output by one unit is negative, then output should be decreased. Thus, an output level can maximize profit only if at that output marginal profit equals zero.

In the Computron example, the marginal profit from the third unit is +$1 million, so it pays to produce the third unit. But marginal profit from the fourth unit is —$4 million, so the firm should not produce the fourth. Since Computron is dealing in whole numbers (for example, it cannot produce 3.12 computers) it cannot achieve a marginal profit of exactly zero. But by producing three units per year it comes quite close.

The profit hill in Figure 23-4 gives us a graphical interpretation of the "marginal profit equals zero" condition. Marginal profit is defined as the additional profit that accrues to the firm when output rises by one unit. So, when output is increased, say, from two units to three units (the distance QE in Figure 23-4), total profit rises by $1 million (the distance EM) and marginal profit is therefore EM/QE. This is precisely the definition of the *slope* of the total-profit curve between points Q and M. In general:

Marginal profit is the slope of the total-profit curve.

With this geometric interpretation in hand, we can easily understand the logic of the marginal-profit rule. At a point such as Q, where the total-profit curve is rising, marginal profit (= slope) is positive. Profits cannot be maximal at such a point, because we can increase profits by moving farther to the right. A firm that decided to stick to point Q would be wasting the opportunity to increase profits by increasing output. Similarly, the firm cannot be maximizing profits at a point like D, where the slope of the curve is negative, because there marginal profit (= slope) is negative. If it finds itself at a point like D, the firm can raise its profit by decreasing its output.

Only at a point such as M, where the total-profit curve is neither rising nor falling, can the firm possibly be at the top of the profit hill rather than on one of the sides of the hill. And point M is precisely where the slope of the curve—and hence the marginal profit—is zero. *An output decision cannot be optimal unless the corresponding marginal profit is zero.*

The firm is not interested in marginal profit for its own sake, but rather for what it implies about *total* profit. Marginal profit is like the needle on the pressure gauge of a boiler: The needle itself is of no concern to anyone, but if one fails to watch it the consequences may be quite dramatic.

One common misunderstanding that arises in discussions of the marginal criterion of optimality is the idea that it seems foolish to go to a point where marginal profit is zero. "Isn't it better to earn a positive marginal profit?" This notion springs from a confusion between the quantity one is seeking to maximize (*total* profit) and the gauge that indicates whether such a maximum has in fact been attained (*marginal* profit). Of course it is better to have a positive *total* profit than zero total profit. But a zero value on the *marginal* profit gauge merely indicates that all is apparently well, that *total* profit may be at its maximum.

Marginal Revenue and Marginal Cost: Guides to an Optimum

A more conventional version of the marginal analysis of profit maximization proceeds directly in terms of the cost and revenue components of profit. For this purpose refer back to Figure 23–4, where the profit hill was constructed from the total revenue (TR) and total cost (TC) curves. Observe that there is another way of finding the profit-maximizing solution. We want to maximize the vertical distance between the TR and TC curves. This distance, we see, is not maximal at an output level such as two units, because there the two curves are growing farther apart. If we move farther to the right, the vertical distance between them (which is total profit) will increase. Conversely, we have not maximized the vertical distance between TR and TC an an output level such as four units, because there the two curves are coming closer together. We can add to profits by moving farther to the left (reducing output).

The conclusion from the graph, then, is that total profit (the vertical distance between TR and TC) is maximized only when the two curves are neither growing farther apart nor coming closer together; that is, when their *slopes* are equal. While this conclusion is rather mechanical, we can breathe some life into it by interpreting the slopes of the two curves as **marginal revenue** and **marginal cost**. These concepts, which have already been defined and illustrated, permit us to restate the geometric conclusion we have just reached in an economically significant way:

Profit can be maximized only at an output level at which marginal revenue is (approximately) equal to marginal cost. In symbols:

$$MR = MC.$$

The logic of the MC = MR rule for profit maximization is straightforward.[3] When MR is *not* equal to MC, profits cannot possibly be maximized because the firm can increase its profits either by raising its output or by reducing it. For example if MR = $16 and MC = $12, the firm can increase its net profit by $4 by producing and selling one more unit. Similarly, if MC exceeds MR, say MR = $7 and MC = $10, then the firm loses $3 on its marginal unit, so it can add $3 to its profit by reducing output by one unit. Only when MR = MC is it impossible for the firm to add to its profit by changing its output level.

Table 23–4 reproduces marginal-revenue and marginal-cost data for Compu-tron Inc., from Tables 23–1 and 23–2. The table shows, as must be true, that the

[3]You may have surmised by now that just as total profit = total revenue – total cost, it must be true that marginal profit = marginal revenue – marginal cost. This is in fact correct. It also shows that when marginal profit = 0, we must have MR = MC.

Table 23-4

MARGINAL REVENUE AND MARGINAL COST FOR COMPUTRON, INC.

NUMBER OF UNITS (per year)	MARGINAL REVENUE (millions of dollars per year)	MARGINAL COST
0	—	—
1	15	7
2	10	5
3	8	7
4	7	11
5	5	13
6	3	15

MR = MC rule leads us to the same conclusion as Figure 23–4 and Table 23–3. Computron should produce and sell three computers per year.

The marginal revenue of the third computer is $8 million ($33 million from selling three computers less $25 million from selling two) while the marginal cost is only $7 million ($21 million minus $14 million). So the firm should produce the third unit. But the fourth computer brings in only $7 million in marginal revenue while its marginal cost is $11 million—clearly a losing proposition.

Because the graphs of marginal analysis will prove so useful in the following chapters, Figure 23–5(a) shows the MR = MC condition for profit maximization graphically. The black curve labelled MR in the figure is the marginal-revenue schedule from Table 23–4. The curve labelled MC is the marginal-cost schedule. They intersect at point E, which is therefore the point where marginal revenue and marginal cost are equal. The optimal output for Computron is three units.[4] Figures 23–5(b) and 23–5(c), respectively, are reproductions of the TR and TC curves from the upper part of Figure 23–4 and the total-profit curve from the lower portion of that figure. Note how MC and MR intersect at the same output at which the distance of TR above TC is greatest, which is the output at which the profit hill reaches its summit.

Application: Fixed Cost and the Profit-Maximizing Price

Our analytic apparatus can now be used to offer a surprising insight. Suppose there is a rise in the firm's fixed cost; say, the rent on the factory doubles. What will happen to the profit-maximizing price and output? Should price go up to cover the increased cost? Should the firm push for a larger output (even if that requires a fall in price)? The answer is: neither.

When a firm's fixed cost increases, its profit-maximizing price and output remain completely unchanged, so long as it pays the firm to stay in business.

In other words, there is nothing the firm's management can do to offset the effect of the rise in fixed cost. It must just lie back and take it.

Why is this so? Remember that, by definition, a fixed cost is a cost that does not change when output changes. Computron's rent increase is the same whether business is slow or booming, whether production is two or six computers. This is illustrated in Table 23–5, which also reproduces Computron's total profits from Table 23–3. The third column of the table shows that total fixed cost has risen by

[4]One important qualification must be entered. Sometimes marginal-revenue and marginal-cost curves do not have the nice shapes depicted in Figure 23–5(a), and they may intersect more than once. In such cases, while it remains true that MC = MR at the output level that maximizes profits, there may be other output levels at which MC is also equal to MR but at which profits are not maximized.

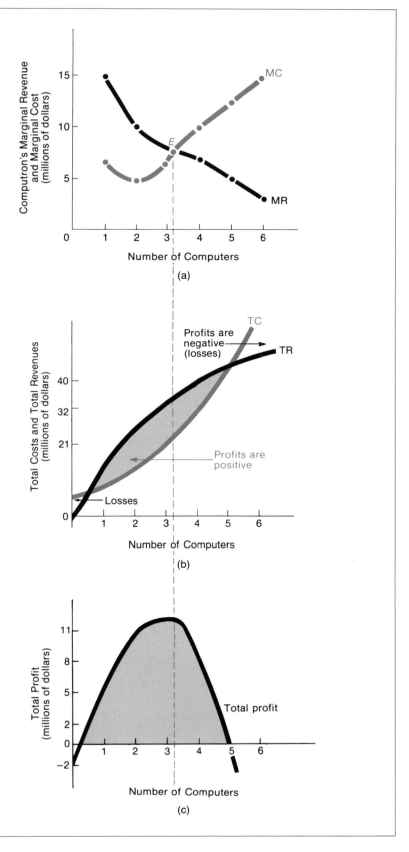

Figure 23-5

PROFIT MAXIMIZATION:
ANOTHER GRAPHICAL
INTERPRETATION

Profits are maximized where
marginal revenue (MR) is
(approximately) equal to marginal
cost (MC), for only at such a point
will *marginal profit* be zero. Part (a)
shows the MR = MC condition for
profit maximization graphically as
point *E*, where output is close to
three computers. Since
Computron does not produce
fractions of computers, the best it
can do is to produce three of
them. The diagram also
reproduces from Figure 23-4 the
TR and TC curves [part (b)] and
the total-profit curve [part (c)],
showing how all three agree that
the profit-maximizing output is a bit
larger than three units.

(a)

Computron's Marginal Revenue and Marginal Cost (millions of dollars)

MC

MR

E

Number of Computers

(b)

Total Costs and Total Revenues (millions of dollars)

TC

Profits are
negative
(losses)

TR

Profits are
positive

Losses

Number of Computers

(c)

Total Profit (millions of dollars)

Total profit

Number of Computers

Table 23-5

TOTAL PROFIT BEFORE AND AFTER A RISE IN FIXED COST

NUMBER OF UNITS (per year)	TOTAL PROFITS BEFORE RENT INCREASE	INCREASED RENT PAYMENT (millions of dollars per year)	TOTAL PROFIT AFTER RENT INCREASE
0	-2	2	-4
1	6	2	4
2	11	2	9
3	12	2	10
4	8	2	6
5	0	2	-2
6	-12	2	-14

$2 million per year, no matter what the firm's output. As a result, for each possible output of the firm, total profit is $2 million less than what it would have been otherwise. For example, when output is four units, we see the total profit must fall from $8 million (second column) to $6 million (last column).

Now, because profit is reduced by the same amount at each and every output level, the output level that was most profitable to the firm before the rent increase must still be the output that yields the highest profit. In Table 23-5 we see that $10 million is the largest entry in the last column showing profits after the rise in fixed cost. The highest profit is attained, as it was before, when output equals three units. Given the firm's demand curve (Figure 23-1) this, of course, means that the profit-maximizing price will remain $11 million—the price at which it sells three units (point c on the demand curve).

All of this is also shown in Figure 23-6, which shows the firm's total profit hill before and after the rise in fixed cost (reproducing Computron's initial profit hill from Figure 23-4). We see that the cost increase simply moves the profit hill straight downward by $2 million, so that the highest point on the hill is just lowered from point M to point N. But the top of the hill is shifted neither toward the left nor toward the right. It remains at the three-unit output level. Just as we saw before, the profit-maximizing output level remains unchanged when fixed costs rise.

Marginal Analysis in Real Decision Problems

We can now put the analysis of profit maximization to work to unravel the puzzles with which we began this chapter.

CASE 1: THE SODA-PRICING PROBLEM
Our first problem dealt with a firm's choice between keeping the price of a brand of soda at $1.50 per six-pack or reducing it to $1.35 when a competitor entered the market. The trouble was that to know what to do, the firm needed to know its demand curve (and hence its marginal-revenue curve). However, the firm did not have enough data to determine the shape of its demand curve. How, then, could a rational decision be made?

As we indicated, the debate among the firm's managers finally reached agreement on one point: The price should be cut if, as a result, profits were not likely to decline; that is, if *marginal profit* were not negative. Fortunately, the data needed to determine whether marginal profit was positive were obtainable. Initial annual sales were 10 million units, and the firm's engineers maintained emphatically that marginal costs were very close to constant at $1.20 per six-pack over the output range in question. Instead of trying to determine the *actual* increase in sales that would result from the price cut, the team of consultants decided to

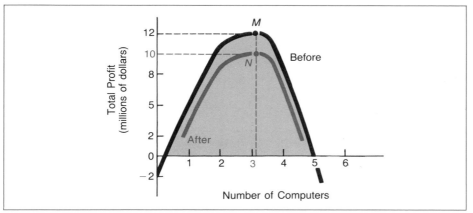

Figure 23-6
FIXED COST DOES NOT
AFFECT PROFIT-MAXIMIZING
OUTPUT
The graph reproduces
Computron's initial profit hill from
Figure 23-4 (the black curve
labelled "before"). A $2 million
increase in fixed cost shifts the
profit hill downward, to the curve
marked "after." But the original
point of maximum profit (point M)
and the new one (point N) are at
the same output level. This is so
because the cost increase pushes
the profit hill straight downward.

try to determine the *minimum necessary* increase in quantity demanded required to avoid a decrease in profits.

It was clear that the firm needed additional revenue at least as great as the additional cost of supplying the added volume, if profits were not to decline. The consultants knew that sales at the initial price of $1.50 per six-pack were $15 million ($1.50 per unit times 10 million units). Letting Q represent the (unknown) quantity of six-packs that would be sold at the proposed new price of $1.35, the economists compared the added revenue with the added cost of providing the Q new units. Since MC was constant at $1.20 per unit, the added cost amounted to:

$$\text{Added cost} = \$1.20 \times (Q - 10 \text{ million}).$$

This was to be compared with the added revenue:

$$\text{Added revenue} = \text{New revenue} - \text{Old revenue}$$
$$= \$1.35Q - \$15 \text{ million} .$$

No loss would result from the price change if the added revenue was greater than or equal to the added cost. The minimum Q necessary to avoid a loss therefore was that at which added revenue equalled added cost, or

$$1.35Q - 15 \text{ million} = 1.2Q - 12 \text{ million},$$

or

$$0.15Q = 3 \text{ million}.$$

This would be true if, and only if, Q, the quantity sold at the lower price, would be

$$Q = 20 \text{ million units}.$$

In other words, this calculation showed that the firm could break even from the 15-cent price reduction only if the quantity of its product demanded rose at least 100 percent (from 10 to 20 million units). Since past experience indicated that such a rise in quantity demanded was hardly possible, the price reduction proposal was quickly abandoned. Thus the logic of the MC = MR rule, plus a little ingenuity, enabled the consultants to deal with a problem that at first seemed baffling—even though they had no estimate of marginal revenue.

CASE 2: THE UNPROFITABLE CANNED MEAT PRODUCER
Our second case study concerned a firm that was losing money (because the price of its canned meat product was less than its average cost) and that was then offered the questionable opportunity to sell more of its product to a foreign buyer

Table 23-6

INITIAL COSTS AND REVENUES OF THE CANNED MEAT PRODUCER

UNITS SOLD (millions)	TOTAL COST (millions of dollars)	AVERAGE COST (dollars)	MARGINAL COST (dollars)	PRICE (dollars)	TOTAL REVENUE	TOTAL COST (millions of dollars)	PROFIT OR LOSS
10	130	13	3	11	110	130	– 20

Table 23-7

COSTS AND REVENUES OF THE SUPPLIER OF CANNED MEAT AFTER SALES "BELOW COST"

UNITS SOLD (millions)	TOTAL COST (millions of dollars)	AVERAGE COST (dollars)	MARGINAL COST (dollars)	TOTAL REVENUE	TOTAL COST (millions of dollars)	PROFIT OR LOSS
20	160	8	3	180	160	+ 20

at a price that was lower still. The relevant information is summarized in Table 23-6.

Obviously, this firm was in a bad way financially. Its average cost was $13, and yet the price it was charging for its product was only $11 per unit; so it was losing money on this product. Indeed, we see that it lost $20 million on the 10 million units of output it sold. Management might well have reasoned this way: It would be desirable to expand our volume, but we can't afford to do so. Instead, we must raise our price above our $13 average cost, even if it cuts down our sales.

While the managers were pondering their dilemma, a foreign purchasing group offered to buy an additional 10 million units of the company's canned meat product if the company would supply the units at a discount price of $7. On an average-cost calculation this arrangement seemed disastrous. After all, AC was $13 and the company was already losing money at a price of $11. How could it possibly afford to sell at an even lower price?

But was the proposition so ludicrous? With its marginal costs approximately constant at $3, by accepting the offer the company could change its situation from that shown in Table 23-6 to that shown in Table 23-7. We see that the total number of units sold will have doubled, from 10 million to 20 million. Total costs will have risen from $130 million to $160 million. That is, they will have gone up $30 million (the MC of $3 on each of the 10 million additional units). The arithmetic shows that, as a consequence, AC *must* have fallen from $13 = $130/10 to $8 = $160/20.

The last three columns report the resulting "miracle." The apparently ridiculous proposition that 10 million additional units of canned meat be sold at a price below either the old or the new average cost in fact succeeded in eliminating the deficit and actually put the company into the black, to the tune of $20 million in net profits. Just how was this "miracle" accomplished? The answer becomes clear when we apply the rules we have learned in this chapter. In Table 23-6, it can be seen that AC was indeed $13; but the corresponding MC figure was only $3. Therefore, every *additional* unit sold to the foreign buyer at a price of $7 brought in a marginal profit of $7 – $3 = $4. On such terms the more one sells the better off one is.

This case illustrates a point that is encountered frequently. The canned meat supplier was offered an opportunity to deal with a new class of customers at a price that appeared not to cover costs but really did. The same sort of issue frequently faces a firm considering the introduction of a new product or the opening of a new branch office. In many such cases the new operation may not cover *average* costs as measured by standard accounting methods. Yet to follow the apparent implications of those cost figures would amount to throwing away a valuable opportunity to add to the net earnings of the firm and, perhaps, to contribute to the welfare of the economy. Only *marginal* analysis can reveal whether the contemplated action is really worthwhile.

Conclusion: The Fundamental Role of Marginal Analysis

One of the most important conclusions that can be drawn from the last four chapters, a conclusion brought out vividly by the two examples we have just discussed, concerns:

The Importance of Marginal Analysis
In any decision about whether to expand an activity, it is always the *marginal* cost and *marginal* revenue that are the relevant factors. A calculation based on *average* figures is likely to lead the decision-maker to miss all sorts of opportunities, some of them critical.

More generally, if one wants to make *optimal* decisions, *marginal analysis* should be used in the planning calculations. This is true whether the decision applies to a business firm seeking to maximize profit or minimize cost, to a consumer trying to maximize utility, or to a less-developed country striving to maximize per capita output. It applies as much to decisions on input proportions and advertising as to decisions about output levels and prices. Indeed, this is such a general principle of economics that it is one of the **12 Ideas for Beyond the Final Exam**.

A real-life example far removed from profit maximization will illustrate the way in which marginal criteria are useful in decision-making. For some years before women were admitted to Princeton University (and to several other universities), the cost of the proposed change was frequently cited as a major obstacle. It had been decided in advance that any woman coming to the university would constitute a net addition to the student body because, for a variety of reasons involving relations with alumni and other groups, a reduction in the number of male students was not feasible. Presumably on the basis of a calculation of average cost, some critics spoke of figures as high as $80 million.

To economists it was clear, however, that the relevant figure was the *marginal cost*, the addition to total cost that would result from the introduction of the additional students. The women students would, of course, bring to Princeton additional tuition fees (marginal revenues). If these fees were just sufficient to cover the amount they would add to costs, the admission of the women would leave the university's financial picture unaffected.

A careful calculation showed that the admission of women would add far less to the university's financial problems than the *average cost* figures indicated. One reason was that (at that time) women's course preferences were characteristically different from men's and hence women frequently elected courses that were undersubscribed in exclusively male institutions. Therefore, the admission of one thousand women to a formerly all-male institution required fewer additional courses than if one thousand more men had been admitted.[5] More important, it was found that a number of classroom buildings were underutilized. The cost of operating these buildings was nearly fixed—their total utilization cost would be

[5]See Gardner Patterson, "The Education of Women at Princeton," *Princeton Alumni Weekly*, vol. 69, September 24, 1968.

changed only slightly by the influx of women. The corresponding marginal cost was therefore almost zero and certainly well below the average cost (cost per student).

For all these reasons, it turned out that the relevant marginal-cost figure was much smaller than the figures that had been bandied about earlier. Indeed, this cost was something like a third of the earlier estimates. There is little doubt that this careful marginal calculation played a critical role in the admission of women to Princeton and to some other institutions that made use of the calculations in the Princeton analysis. Subsequent data, incidentally, confirmed that the marginal calculations were amply justified.

A Look Back and a Look Forward

We have now completed four chapters describing how consumers and business managers can make optimal decisions. Will you find executives in head offices calculating marginal cost and marginal revenue in order to decide how much to produce? Hardly. Not any more than you will find consumers in stores computing their marginal utilities in order to decide what to buy. Like consumers, successful business people often rely heavily on intuition and "hunches" that cannot be described by any set of rules.

However, we have not sought a literal *description* of consumer and business behaviour, but rather a *model* to help us analyse and predict this behaviour. Just as astronomers construct models of the behaviour of objects that do not think at all, economists construct models of consumers and business people who do think, but whose thought processes may be rather different from those of economists. In the chapters that follow we will use these models to serve the purposes for which they were designed: to analyse the functioning of a market economy and to see what things it does well and what things it does poorly.

Summary

1. A firm can choose the quantity of its product it wants to sell or the price it wants to charge. But it cannot choose both because price affects the quantity demanded.

2. In economic theory, it is usually assumed that firms seek to maximize profits. This should not be taken literally, but rather interpreted as a useful simplification of reality.

3. Marginal revenue is the additional revenue earned by increasing sales by one unit. Marginal cost is the additional cost incurred by increasing production by one unit.

4. Maximum profit requires the firm to choose the level of output at which marginal revenue is equal to marginal cost.

5. Geometrically, the profit-maximizing output level occurs at the highest point of the total-profit curve. There the slope of the total-profit curve is zero, meaning that marginal profit is zero.

6. A change in fixed cost will not change the profit-maximizing level of output.

7. It may pay a firm to expand its output if it is selling at a price greater than marginal cost, even if that price happens to be below average cost.

8. Optimal decisions must be made on the basis of marginal-cost and marginal-revenue figures, not average-cost and average-revenue figures. This is one of the **12 Ideas for Beyond the Final Exam**.

Concepts for Review

Profit maximization	Total revenue and cost	Marginal analysis
Satisficing	Average revenue and cost	Marginal profit
Total profit	Marginal revenue and cost	
Economic profit	Fixed cost	

Questions for Discussion

1. "It may be rational for a firm not to try to maximize profits." Discuss the circumstances under which this statement may be true.

2. Suppose the firm's demand curve indicates that at a price of $7 per unit, customers will demand two million units of its product. Suppose management decides to pick *both* price and output, produces three million units of its product, and prices it at $9. What will happen?

3. Suppose a firm's management would be pleased to increase its share of the market, but if it expands its production the price of its product will fall and so its profits will decline somewhat. What choices are available to this firm? What would you do if you were president of this company?

4. Why does it make sense for a firm to seek to maximize *total* profit, rather than to maximize *marginal* profit?

5. A firm's marginal revenue is $15 and its marginal cost is $9. What amount of profit does the firm fail to pick up by refusing to increase output by one unit?

6. Calculate average revenue (AR) and average cost (AC) in Table 23–3. How much profit does the firm earn at the output at which AC = AR? Why?

7. A firm's total cost is $250 if it produces one unit, $350 if it produces two units, and $400 if it produces three units of output. Draw up a table of total, average, and marginal costs for this firm.

8. Draw average- and marginal-cost curves for the firm in Question 7. Describe the relationship between the two curves.

9. A firm with no fixed costs has the demand and total-cost schedules given in the table below. If it wants to maximize profits, how much output should it produce?

QUANTITY	PRICE (dollars)	TOTAL COST (dollars)
1	6	1
2	5	2.5
3	4	4
4	3	7
5	2	11

10. Review the concept of fixed cost in Chapter 22. Suppose Computron's total costs are increased by $10 million per year. Show in Table 23–2 how this affects Computron's total, average, and marginal costs.

11. Show with the aid of the marginal figures of Table 23–4 that the $10 million increase in fixed costs will not change Computron's profit-maximizing output level.

12. Why does it make sense for a change in a firm's fixed cost not to change the output level that maximizes its profit?

Appendix
The Relationships Among Total, Average, and Marginal Data

You may have surmised that there is a close connection between the average-revenue and average-cost curves and the corresponding marginal-revenue and marginal-cost curves. After all, we deduced our total-revenue figures from the average revenue and then calculated our marginal-revenue figures from the total revenues; and a similar chain of deduction applied to costs. In fact:

Marginal, average, and total figures are inextricably bound together. From any one of the three, the other two can be calculated. Total, average, and marginal figures bear relationships to one another that hold for *any* variable—such as revenue, cost, or profit—that is affected by the number of units in question.

To illustrate and emphasize the wide applicability

of marginal analysis, we switch our example from profits, revenues, and costs to a non-economic variable, human body weights. We do so because calculation of weights is more familiar to most people than calculation of profits, revenues, or costs, and we can use this example to illustrate several fundamental relationships between average and marginal figures. The necessary data are in Table 23–8[6]. We begin with an empty room (total weight of occupants is equal to zero). A person weighing 100 pounds enters; marginal and average weight are both 100 pounds. If the person is followed by a person weighing 140 pounds (marginal

---

[6]Note that in this illustration, "persons in room" is analogous to units of output, "total weight" to total revenue or cost, and so on.

weight equals 140 pounds), the average weight rises to 120 pounds (240 ÷ 2), and so on

The way to calculate average weight from total weight is quite clear. When, for example, there are four persons in the room with a total weight of 500 pounds, the average weight must be 500 ÷ 4 = 125 pounds, as shown in the corresponding entry of the third column. In general, the rule for converting totals to averages, and vice versa, is:

Table 23-8
WEIGHTS OF PERSONS IN A ROOM

NUMBER OF PERSONS IN ROOM	TOTAL WEIGHT (pounds)	AVERAGE WEIGHT (pounds)	MARGINAL WEIGHT (pounds)
0	0	—	—
1	100	100	100
2	240	120	140
3	375	125	135
4	500	125	125
5	600	120	100
6	660	110	60

Rule 1a. Average weight equals total weight divided by number of persons.

Rule 1b. Total weight equals average weight times number of persons.

And this rule naturally applies equally well to cost, revenue, profit, or any other variable of interest.

Calculation of *marginal* weight from *total* weight follows the *subtraction* process we have already encountered in the calculation of marginal utility, marginal cost, and marginal revenue. Specifically:

Rule 2a. The marginal weight of, say, the third person equals the total weight of three people minus the total weight of two people.

For example, when the fourth person enters the room, *total* weight rises from 375 pounds to 500 pounds, and hence the corresponding marginal weight is 500 – 375 = 125 pounds, as is shown in the last column of Table 23-8. We can also go in the opposite direction—from marginal to total—by the reverse, *addition*, process.

Rule 2b. The total weight of, say, three people equals the marginal weight of the first person plus the marginal weight of the second person plus the marginal weight of the third person.

Rule 2b can be checked by referring to Table 23-8. There it can be seen that the total weight of three persons, 375 pounds, is indeed equal to 100 + 140 + 135 pounds, the sum of the preceding marginal

weights. A similar relation holds for any other total weight figure in the table, as the reader should verify.[7]

In addition to these familiar arithmetic relationships, there are two other useful relationships. The first of these may be stated as:

Rule 3. In the absence of fixed weight (costs), the marginal, average, and total figures for the first person must all be equal.

This rule holds because when there is only one person in the room, whose weight is X pounds, the average weight will obviously be X, the total weight must be X, and the marginal weight must also be X (since the total must have risen from 0 to X pounds). Put another way, when the marginal person is alone, he or she is obviously also the average person, and also represents the totality of all relevant persons.

Now for the final and very important relationship:

Rule 4. If marginal weight is lower than average weight, then average weight must fall when the number of persons increases. If marginal weight exceeds average weight, average weight must rise when the number of persons increases; and if marginal and average weight are equal, the average weight must remain constant when the number of persons increases.

These three possibilities are all illustrated in Table 23-8. Notice, for example, that when the third person enters the room, the average weight rises from 120 to 125 pounds. That is because this person's (marginal) weight is 135 pounds, which is above the average, as Rule 4 requires. Similarly, when the sixth person—who is a 60-pound child—enters the room, the average falls from 120 to 110 pounds because marginal weight, 60 pounds, is below average weight.

The reason Rule 4 works is easily explained with the aid of our example. When the third person enters, we see that the average rises. At once we know that this person must be above average weight, for otherwise his arrival would not have pulled up the average. Similarly, the average will be pulled down by the arrival of a person whose weight is below the average (marginal weight is less than average weight). And the arrival of a person of average weight (marginal equals average weight) will leave the old average figure unchanged. That is all there is to the matter.

It is essential to avoid a common misunderstanding of this rule: It does *not* state, for example, that if the average figure is rising, the marginal figure must

---

[7]There is an exception in the case of costs. Summing up marginal-cost figures as in Rule 2b leads to total *variable* cost. If there are *fixed* costs, these must be added in to arrive at total (variable plus fixed) costs.

be rising. When the average rises, the marginal figure may rise, fall, or remain unchanged. The arrival of two persons both well above average will push the average up in two successive steps even if the second new arrival is lighter than the first. We see such a case in Table 23-8, where the arithmetic shows that while average weight rises successively from 100 to 120 to 125, the marginal weight falls from 140 to 135 to 125.

Graphic Representation of Marginal and Average Curves

We have shown how, from a curve of total profit (or total cost or total anything else), one can determine the corresponding marginal figure. We noted several times in the chapter that the marginal value at any particular point is equal to the *slope* of the corresponding total curve at that point. But for some purposes it is convenient to use a graph that records marginal and average values directly rather than deriving them from the curve of totals.

We can obtain such a graph by plotting the data in a table of average and marginal figures, such as Table 23-8. The result looks like the graph shown in Figure 23-7. Here we have indicated the number of persons in the room on the horizontal axis and the corresponding average and marginal figures on the vertical axis. The solid dots represent average weights; the small circles represent marginal weights. Thus, for example, point *A* shows that when two persons are in the room, their average weight is 120 pounds, as was reported on the third line of Table 23-8. Similarly, point *B* on the graph represents information provided in the next column of the table; that is, that the marginal weight of the third person who enters the room is 135 pounds. For visual convenience these points have been connected into a marginal curve and an average curve, represented respectively by the solid and the broken curves in the diagram. This is the representation of marginal and average values that economists most frequently use.

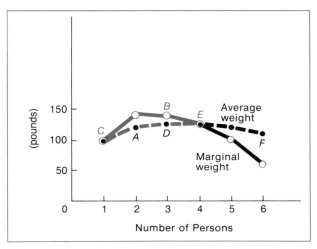

Figure 23-7
THE RELATIONSHIP BETWEEN MARGINAL AND AVERAGE CURVES
If the marginal curve is above the average curve, the average curve will be pulled upward. Thus, wherever the marginal curve is above the average curve, the average curve must be going upward (blue segment of curves). The opposite is true where the marginal curve is below the average curve.

Figure 23-7 illustrates two of our rules. Rule 3 says that, for the first unit, the marginal and average values will be the same. And that is precisely why the two curves start out together at point *C*. When there is only one person in the room, marginal and average weight *must* be the same. The graph also obeys Rule 4: Between points *C* and *E*, where the average curve is *rising*, the marginal curve lies *above* the average. (Notice, however, that over part of this range the marginal curve *falls* even though the average curve is rising—Rule 4 says nothing about the rise or fall of the marginal curve.) We see also that over range *EF*, where the average curve is falling, the marginal curve is below the average curve, again in accord with Rule 4. Finally, at point *E*, where the average curve is neither rising nor falling, the marginal curve meets the average curve: Average and marginal weights are equal at that point.

Questions for Discussion

1. Suppose the following is your record of exam grades in Principles of Economics:

EXAM DATE	GRADE	COMMENT
September 30	60	A slow start.
October 28	80	A big improvement.
December 13	91	Congratulations!
January 30	85	Slipped a little.
March 1	99	Well done!

Use these data to make up a table of total, average, and marginal grades for the five exams.
2. From the data in your table, illustrate each of the rules mentioned in this appendix. Be sure to point out an instance where marginal grade falls but average grade rises.

V

The Market System:
Virtues and Vices

Firms in Reality: The Corporation and the Stock Market

24

> The action of the stock market must necessarily be puzzling at times since otherwise everyone who studies it only a little bit would be able to make money in it.
> B. GRAHAM, D. L. DODD, AND S. COTTLE

The two preceding chapters have provided a theoretical analysis of the decisions of business firms. But a business firm does more than just select inputs, outputs, and prices. In this chapter, we look at some additional features of firms as they exist in reality. We will encounter small firms operated by individual owners, partnerships, and corporations of all sizes. We will also learn something about the ways in which firms acquire the resources they need for investment. In particular, we will look at the markets where stocks and bonds are sold and to which many individuals bring their money, hoping to make that money grow.

The stock market is really something of an enigma. No other economic activity is reported in such detail in so many newspapers and followed with such concern by so many people; yet no activity seems to have been so successful in eluding those who devote themselves to predicting its future. There is no shortage of "experts" who are prepared to evaluate the future of one stock versus that of another. And usually they are paid well for their efforts. But there are real questions about what these experts deliver. For example, Burton G. Malkiel of Yale University reported the following results from a study of leading analysts' predictions of company earnings, on which they based their price forecasts for the companies:

We wrote to nineteen major Wall Street firms ... among the most respected names in the investment business.

We requested—and received—past earnings predictions on how these firms felt earnings for specific companies would behave over both a one-year and a five-year period. These estimates ... were ... compared with actual results to see how well the analysts forecast short-run and long-run earnings changes.

Bluntly stated, the careful estimates of security analysts (based on industry studies, plant visits, etc.) do little, if any, better than those that would be obtained by simple extrapolation of past trends.

For example ... the analysts' estimates were compared [with] the assumption that every company in the economy would enjoy a growth in earnings of about 4 percent over the next year (approximately the long-run rate of growth of the national income). It turned out that ... this naïve forecasting model ... would make smaller errors in forecasting long-run earnings growth than ... [did] the forecasts of the analysts.

When confronted with the poor record of their five-year growth estimates, the security analysts honestly, if sheepishly, admitted that five years ahead is really too far in advance to make reliable projections. They protested that while long-term projections are admittedly important, they really ought to be judged on their ability to project earnings changes one year ahead.

Believe it or not, it turned out that their one-year forecasts were even worse than their five-year projections.[1]

Later in this chapter we will be in a position to give the explanation many economists offer for this poor performance record.

Firms in Canada

It is customary to divide firms into three groups: *corporations, partnerships,* and *individual proprietorships* (businesses having a single owner). Over three-quarters of the firms in the manufacturing sector are corporations, and these firms account for an even higher proportion of sales. Within the manufacturing sector, the one hundred largest firms own half of the manufacturing assets.

But while economic power resides in the corporations, this form of business organization actually constitutes a *minority* of Canadian business firms, measured in terms of the total number of enterprises, beyond manufacturing. The reason is that most firms are small. There are almost half a million firms in Canada.

Most industries in which the giant firms are found are *oligopolies,* a market form we will analyse in Chapter 28. A few are *monopolies,* the market form discussed in Chapter 27.

At the other end of the spectrum, the nation's small business firms have a disproportionately small share of Canadian business. These small firms have earnings that are not only relatively low but also very risky in the sense that bankruptcies frequently occur. When making economic decisions, the buyer is not the only one who has to beware!

Just what are the three basic forms of organization of business firms, and what induces organizers of a firm to choose one form rather than another?

Proprietorships

A proprietorship is a business firm owned by a single person.

The **proprietorship** is the form of business organization involving the fewest legal complications. Most small retail firms, farms, and many small factories are run as proprietorships. To start a proprietorship, an individual simply decides to go into business and opens up a new firm or takes over an existing firm. Aside from special regulations, such as health requirements for a restaurant or zoning restrictions that limit business activity to particular geographical areas, the individual does not need anyone's permission to go into business. This is one of the main advantages of the proprietorship form of organization. But probably its main attraction is that the owner can be his or her own boss and the firm's sole decision-maker. No partners or shareholders have to be consulted when the proprietor wants to expand or change the company's product line or modify the firm's advertising policy.

Unlimited liability is a legal obligation of a firm's owner(s) to pay back company debts with whatever resources he or she owns.

There are, on the other hand, two basic disadvantages of a proprietorship, difficulties that make it almost impossible to organize large-scale enterprises as proprietorships. First, the owner has **unlimited liability** for the debts of the

[1]Burton G. Malkiel, *A Random Walk Down Wall Street* (New York: W. W. Norton & Company, Inc., 1973), pages 140–41.

firm. If the company goes out of business leaving unpaid bills, the former owner can be forced to pay them out of personal savings. The owner can be made to sell the family home, private collections of stamps or paintings, or any other personal assets, no matter how unrelated to the business, so that the proceeds can be used to pay off the company's obligations. Often proprietors guard themselves against this danger by signing away all their property to other members of their families or to others whom they feel they can trust. But, there are many tales of tragedy that begin with the signing away of all of one's possessions—King Lear's betrayal by his daughters might well serve as the classic warning to those proprietors who are apt to be too trusting.

A second and equally basic shortcoming of the proprietorship is that it inhibits expansion of the firm by making it difficult to raise money. People outside the company are reluctant to put money into a firm over which they exercise no control. This means that the proprietorship's capital is usually no greater than the amount its owner is willing and able to put into it, plus the amount that banks or other commercial lenders are willing to provide.

SUMMARY
The two main advantages of the individual proprietorship are:

1. It leaves full control in the hands of the owner.
2. It involves little legal complication.

Its two main disadvantages are:

1. The unlimited liability of the owner for the obligations of the company.
2. The difficulty of increasing the amount of funds that can be raised for the firm.

Partnerships

Measured in terms of the amount of their capital, **partnerships** tend to be larger than proprietorships but smaller than corporations. However, the largest partnerships greatly exceed the smallest corporations in terms of both their financing and their influence. For example, some of the most prestigious law firms are partnerships. When you call a law firm and are greeted by "Smith, Jones, La Roche and Cohen, Good Morning," you are almost certainly being treated to a partial listing of the company's current or past senior partners (the partners who own the largest share of the firm or who founded the firm).

A **partnership** is a firm whose ownership is shared by a fixed number of proprietors.

The advantage of the partnership over the proprietorship is that it brings together the funds and expertise of a number of people and permits them to be combined to form a company larger than any one of the owners could have financed or managed alone. If one cannot hope to run a particular type of firm with an inventory of less than $2 million, a person who is not rich may be unable to get into the business without the aid of a partner. A partnership may also bring together a variety of specialists, as often happens in a medical practice.

But the partnership has disadvantages, some of them substantial. Decision-making in a partnership may be harder than in any other type of firm. The sole proprietor need consult no one before acting; the corporation appoints officers who are authorized to decide things for the company. But in a partnership it may be necessary for every partner to agree before any steps are taken by the firm, and this is the primary bane of this form of enterprise. A partnership has been compared to two people in a horse costume, each supplying two of the legs, each prepared to go in a different direction, and each unable to move without the other.

Furthermore, in a partnership, as in a proprietorship, the individual partners have unlimited liability, meaning that they can conceivably be in danger of losing their personal possessions to pay off company debts. Finally, the partnership suffers from unique legal complications. A partnership agreement is like a marriage contract entered into solely for the financial advantage of the participants, and so there is likely to be considerable haggling about the terms. And under the law, if a partner dies, or decides to leave the firm, or the others decide to buy that person's share in the enterprise, the partnership may have to be dissolved and haggling about the contract may start all over again.

SUMMARY
The benefits of the partnership to the owners of the firm are:

1. Access to larger quantities of capital.
2. Opportunity to combine expertise.

Its disadvantages are:

1. The need to obtain the agreement of many if not all partners to all major decisions.
2. Unlimited liability of the partners for the obligations of the company.
3. The legal complications, including possible dissolution of the partnership, when there is *any* change in ownership.

Corporations

A **corporation** is a firm that has the legal status of a fictional person. This fictional person is owned by a number of persons, called its shareholders, and is run by a set of elected officers (usually headed by a president) and a board of directors, whose chairman is often also in a powerful position to influence the affairs of the firm.

Limited liability is a legal obligation of a firm's owners to pay back company debts only with the money they have already invested in the firm.

Most big firms are **corporations**, a form of business that has quite a different legal status from a proprietorship or a partnership. Because a corporation is a person in the eyes of the law, its earnings, like those of other persons, are taxed. If a corporation pays some of its earnings to its shareholders as dividends, those dividends are also taxable.

But this disadvantage is counterbalanced by an important advantage: Any debt of the corporation is regarded as an obligation of that fictitious person, not as a liability of any shareholder. This means that the shareholders benefit from the protection of **limited liability**—they can lose no more than the money they have put into the firm. Creditors cannot force them to sell their personal possessions to help repay any outstanding debts incurred by the firm.

Limited liability is the main secret of the success of the corporate form of organization. Thanks to that provision, individuals from every part of the world are willing to put money into firms whose operations they do not understand and whose managements they do not know. A giant firm may produce computers, locomotives, and electrical generators; it may have, as subsidiaries, publishing houses and shoe factories. Few of its shareholders will know or care about all the firm's activities. Yet each investor knows that by providing money to the firm in return for a share of its ownership, no more is risked than the amount of money provided. This has permitted corporations to obtain financing from literally millions of shareholders, each of whom receives in return a claim on the firm's profits, and, at least in principle, a portion of the company's ownership.

As indicated, the profits of a corporation are subject to taxation. Smaller and privately held corporations get taxed at special low rates, but the larger firms with high profits pay tax at a rate of about 50 percent of income (varying somewhat depending on the nature of the company's business and the province where it is located). Were an individual to invest in stock of a corporation paying tax at a 50 percent rate, any earnings of the corporation passed on to the individual in dividends would first have been cut in half by corporate taxes, then subject to taxation as income to the individual.

SUMMARY
The main advantage of the corporate form of organization is *limited liability*, which enables such a firm to raise vast amounts of money from many shareholders. Its main disadvantage is the tax that must be paid on its profits.

Financing Corporate Activity

Our discussion of the earnings of an investor in corporate securities introduces a subject of interest to millions of Canadians—*stocks* and *bonds*, the financial instruments that provide funds to the corporate sector of the economy. When a corporation needs money to add to its plant or equipment or to finance other types of real investment, it can get it by printing new stocks and new bonds and selling them to people who are looking for something in which to invest their money. What enables the firm to get money in exchange for printed paper? Doesn't the process seem a bit like counterfeiting? If done improperly, there are grounds for this suspicion. But, carried out appropriately, it is a perfectly rational economic process.

As long as the funds derived from a new issue of stocks and bonds are used effectively to increase the firm's capacity to produce and earn a profit, then these funds will automatically yield the means for any required repayment and for the payment of appropriate amounts of interest and dividends to the purchasers of the new bonds and stocks. But there have been times when this did not happen. It is alleged that one of the favourite practices of the more notorious nineteenth-century manipulators of the market was "watering" of company stocks—the issue of stocks with little or nothing to back them up. The term is derived from the practice of some cattle dealers who would force their animals to drink large quantities of water just before bringing them to be weighed for sale.

Another major source of funds is **ploughback** or **retained earnings**. For example, if a company earns $30 million after taxes and decides to pay out only $10 million in dividends and invest the remaining $20 million back into the firm, that $20 million is called ploughback.

When business is profitable so that management has the funds to reinvest in the company, it will often prefer ploughback to other sources of funding. One reason for this preference is that it is less risky to management. This source of funds does not require prior approval by the appropriate provincial securities commission, as do other sources. Moreover, ploughback does not depend on the availability of eager customers for new company stocks and bonds, for an issue of such new securities turns into a disappointment if there is little demand for them when they are offered to the public. Above all, a ploughback decision generally does not lead anyone to re-examine the efficiency of management's operation in the way that a new stock issue invariably does. In these instances, the provincial securities commission, potential buyers of the stock, and their professional advisers all scrutinize the company carefully.

A second reason for the attractiveness of ploughback is that issuing new stocks and bonds is usually an expensive and lengthy process. The company is required by the provincial securities commission to gather data in its prospectus—a document describing the financial condition of the company—before the new issue is approved. Not only is this costly, but the many months of delay that are involved require the firm to wait for the funds when it needs them quickly. This delay also subjects the firm to the risk of a change in stock-market conditions (during the period of delay a brisk demand for new stocks and bonds may conceivably dwindle or even evaporate).

A final way for a company to obtain money is by borrowing it from banks, insurance companies, or other private firms with money to lend. It may also sometimes borrow from a government agency, either directly or with the agency's help (the agency serves as guarantor in this instance, promising to make sure the loan is repaid).

Ploughback is by far the most important source of corporate financing.

Ploughback or retained earnings is the portion of a corporation's profits that management decides to keep and invest back into the firm's operations rather than to pay out directly to shareholders in the form of dividends.

Stocks and Bonds

A **common stock** of a corporation is a piece of paper that gives the holder of the stock a share of the ownership of the company.

A **bond** is simply an IOU by a corporation that promises to pay the holder of the piece of paper a fixed sum of money at the specified *maturity* date, and some other fixed amount of money (the *coupon* or the *interest payment*) every year up to the date of maturity.

We turn now to the other major sources of corporate financing besides plough-back and direct borrowing—the corporate securities, like **common stocks** and **bonds**. Stocks represent ownership of part of the corporation. For example, if a company issues 100,000 shares, then a person who owns 1000 shares actually owns 1 percent of the company and is entitled to 1 percent of the company's *dividends*, which are the corporation's annual payments to shareholders. The shareholder's vote counts for 1 percent of the total votes in an election of corporate officers or in a referendum on corporate policy.

Bonds differ from stocks in several ways. First, whereas the purchaser of a corporation's stock *buys* a share of its ownership and receives some control over its affairs, the purchaser of a bond simply *lends* money to the firm. Second, whereas shareholders have no idea how much they will receive for their stocks when they sell them, or how much they will receive in dividends each year while they own them, bondholders know with a high degree of certainty how much money they will be paid if they hold their bonds to maturity. For instance, a bond with a face value of $1000, and an $80 coupon that matures in 1990, will provide to its owner $80 per year every year until 1990, and in addition it will repay the $1000 to the bondholder in 1990. Unless the company goes bankrupt, there is no doubt about this repayment schedule. Third, bondholders have a *legally prior claim* on company earnings, which means that nothing can be paid by the company to its shareholders until interest payments to the company's bondholders have been met. For all these reasons, bonds are considered less risky than stocks.

In reality, however, some of the differences between stocks and bonds are not as clear-cut as have just been described. Two such misconceptions are particularly worth noting. First, the ownership of the company represented by the holding of a few shares of its stock may be more apparent than real. A holder of 0.002 percent of the stocks of General Motors—which is a *very large* investment—exercises no real control over GM's operations. In fact, many economists believe that the ownership of large corporations is so diffuse that no shareholder or shareholder group has *any* effective control over management. In this view, the management of a corporation is a largely independent decision-making body; as long as it keeps enough cash flowing to shareholders to prevent discontent and rebellion, management can do anything it wants within the law. Looked at in another way, this last conclusion really says that shareholders are merely another class of persons who provide loans to the company. The only real difference between shareholders and bondholders, according to this interpretation, is that shareholders' loans are riskier and therefore entitled to higher payments.

Second, bonds *can* be quite risky to the bondholder. Persons who try to sell their bonds before maturity may find that the market price for bonds happens to be low, so that if they need to raise cash in a hurry, they may have to sell at a substantial loss. Also, bondholders may be exposed to losses from inflation. Whether the $1000 promised the bondholder at the 1990 maturity date represents substantial purchasing power or only a little depends on what happens to the general price level in the meantime. And no one can predict the price level this far in advance with any accuracy.

Bond Prices and Interest Rates

Why is investment in bonds risky? That is, what makes their price go up and down? The main element in the answer is that changes in interest rates cause bond prices to change. There is a straightforward relationship between bond prices and interest rates. Whenever one goes up, the other must go down. For example, suppose that the Hudson's Bay Company had issued some 15-year bonds when interest rates were comparatively low, so that the company had to offer to pay only 6 percent to find buyers for these bonds. People who invested $1000 in new Hudson's Bay bonds received in return a contract that promised them $60 per year for 15 years plus the return of their $1000 at the end of that period. Suppose further that two years later interest rates in the economy rise so that new 15-year bonds of companies of similar quality pay 12 percent. Now for $1000 one can buy a contract that offers $120 per year. Obviously, no one will any longer pay as much as $1000 for a bond that promises only $60 per year. Consequently, the market price of the two-year-old Hudson's Bay bonds must fall. There are many bonds in existence now that were issued years ago at interest rates of 6 percent and even less. In today's markets, with much higher interest rates, such bonds sell for a price well below their original value.

When interest rates in the economy rise, there must be a fall in the prices of previously issued bonds with their lower interest earnings. For the same reason, when interest rates in the economy fall, the prices of previously issued bonds must rise.

It follows that as interest rates in the economy change because of changes in monetary policy or for other reasons, bond prices will also fluctuate. That is one reason why investment in bonds can be risky.

Corporate Choice Between Stocks and Bonds

We have seen why a corporation may prefer to finance its real investment, such as construction of factories and equipment, through ploughback or retained earnings rather than the issue of new stocks or bonds. But suppose it has decided to do the latter. How does it determine whether bonds or stocks suit its purposes better?

Two considerations are of prime importance. Although issuing bonds generally causes more risk to the firm than issuing stocks, the corporation usually expects to pay more money to shareholders over the long run than to bondholders. In other words, to the firm that issues them, bonds are cheaper but riskier. The decision about which is better for the firm therefore involves a trade-off between the two considerations.

Why are bonds risky to the corporation? When it issues $20 million in new bonds at 10 percent, the company commits itself to pay out $2 million every year for the life of the bond. It is obligated to pay that amount each year, whether that year happens to be one in which business is booming or one in which the firm is losing money. That is a big risk. If the firm is unable to meet its obligation to bondholders in some year, it faces bankruptcy.

The issue of new stock does not burden the company with any such risk since the company does not promise to pay the shareholders *any* fixed amount. Shareholders simply receive whatever is left of the company's net earnings after payments to bondholders. If nothing is left to pay the new shareholders in some years, legally speaking, that is just their bad luck.

Why, then, do shareholders normally obtain higher average expected payments from the company than bondholders? The answer is obtained by looking at the risk–return trade-off from the investor's point of view. In the case of bonds, the company assumes as much risk as possible by guaranteeing a specified payment to the bondholder. In the case of stock, however, the company assumes little or no risk, leaving it all to the shareholder.

The situation is reversed for the individual who provides the money: Bonds are safer than stocks. Since this is true, no investor will want to buy stocks rather than bonds unless she can expect a sufficiently higher return on the stock to make up for their added risk. So if a company offers both stocks and bonds, their prices and prospective returns must offer a higher (but riskier) average rate of return to shareholders than to bondholders.

To the firm that issues them, bonds are riskier than stocks because they commit the firm to make a fixed annual payment even in years when it is losing money. For the same reason, stocks are riskier than bonds to the buyers of securities. That is why shareholders expect to be paid more money than bondholders.

Are there any rules for a firm to follow when it decides on the trade-off between risk and cost in choosing whether to issue stocks or bonds? There is no general rule, but some principles do hold. For example, new, relatively risky firms find it hard to raise money by issuing stocks because investors want protection from the perils of investing in an unproven company. For similar reasons, very safe companies prefer stock- to bond-financing because the safety of the firm means that shareholders will not have to be paid much more than bondholders.

Buying Stocks and Bonds

Although stocks and bonds can be purchased through any brokerage firm, not all brokers charge the same fees. Until recent years, the charges to small investors were fixed by collusive agreement and did not vary from broker to broker. The Toronto Stock Exchange was deregulated in 1983, and as a result, some bargain brokerage facilities are available. For example, the Toronto-Dominion Bank's Green Line Service merely buys and sells what the customers want them to, offering no advice, research, or other frills.

Many investors are not aware of the various ways in which stocks can be purchased (or sold). The following are some of the possibilities: (a) *Round* or *Board lot* purchases: Purchases of 100 shares or 200 shares or any number of shares in multiples of 100. (b) *Odd lot* purchases: The purchase of some number of shares that is not a multiple of 100. The brokerage fee per dollar of investment is normally higher on an odd lot than on a round lot. (c) A *market order* purchase: This simply tells the broker to buy a specified quantity of stock (either a round lot or an odd lot) at the best price the market currently offers. (d) A *limit order*: An agreement to buy a given amount of a stock when its price falls to a specified level. If the investor offers to buy at $18, then shares will be purchased by the broker if and when the market price falls to $18 per share or less.

There are many investment-information services that supply subscribers with a variety of information on performance of stocks, bonds, and other securities. These firms offer analyses of particular companies, forecasts, and advice.

Portfolio Diversification

Rational planning by an individual of what stocks, bonds, and other financial investments to hold requires more than just careful examination of the merits and demerits of individual securities. It is important to select a combination of securities that meet one's needs effectively. Such a combination of holdings is called the individual's **portfolio** of investments. For example, an individual who is saving to send children to university in ten years does not need securities that pay money out regularly in the meantime, while a retired person who depends on periodic payments from her security holdings will want securities that provide such a stream of payouts conveniently.

Diversification refers to an increase in the number and variety of stocks, bonds and other such items held by the owner of a portfolio. If the individual owns airline shares, diversification requires the purchase of stocks or bonds in a very different industry, such as a hydro-electric power company.

A far more important consideration in deciding what to include in a portfolio is the fact that the risks of the portfolio are affected by the combination of securities it includes, and the portfolio may well be far less risky than any of the individual securities it contains. The secret is **diversification**, meaning not putting all one's eggs in one basket. If Joe Jones holds only shares of company A and the company goes bankrupt, then all may be lost. However, if Joe Jones divides up his holdings among companies A, B, and C, the portfolio may perform satisfactorily even if company A goes broke. Moreover, suppose company A specializes in producing luxury items, which do well in prosperous periods but very badly during recessions, while company B sells cheap clothing, whose cyclical demand pattern differs greatly from that of company A. If Jones holds stock in both companies, the overall risk is smaller than if he owned stock in only one of the companies.

All other things being equal, a portfolio containing many different types of securities tends to be less risky than a portfolio with fewer types of securities.

Following a Portfolio's Performance

Newspapers carry daily information on stock and bond prices. Figure 24–1 is an excerpt from a stock-market report in *The Globe and Mail*. In the first two columns, before the company name, the report gives the stock's highest and lowest price in the current year. In the highlighted example, the price of Interprovincial Pipeline Co. is reported to have ranged between $33.50 and $25.50. Next, after the name of the stock, there appears the annual dividend per share ($1.80). The next four figures indicate that day's highest price ($31⅝), lowest price ($31⅜), the price at which the last transaction of the day took place ($31⅝), and the change in that price from the previous day (up ¼). The final column shows the number of shares traded that day (3610).

Figure 24–2, also from *The Globe and Mail*, gives similar information about bonds. The first thing to notice here is that a company may have several different bonds—differing in maturity dates and coupon (annual interest payment). For example, Bell Canada has two different bonds shown. The one that is highlighted is labelled Bell 11 Oct 15–04, meaning that these are bonds that pay an annual interest of 11 percent on their face value (this is called the "coupon"), and that their maturity (redemption) date is October 15, 2004. Since other bonds are available that earn yields in excess of 11 percent, it is not surprising that no one is prepared to pay the face value of $100 to acquire one of these bonds. The price quoted for this bond is $91.00, which is about what investors did pay for the bond on the day shown in the table. Anyone paying $91.00 for this bond, holding it until October 15, 2004, collecting $11 interest each year, then redeeming the bond for

1984 High	Low	Stock	Div	High	Low	Days Close	Ch'ge	Vol
16¼	7½	H Bay Mn s	y.27¾	$8⅝	8½	8½	− ¼	18718
340	75	H Bay Mn w		87	87	87		z400
24½	19	H Bay Co	.60	$19⅝	19⅝	19⅝		836
18⅞	15⅝	HBC A p	1.80	$17⅞	16⅞	16⅞	− ¼	1123
35⅛	25¾	HBC B p	2.25	$26⅝	26½	26⅝	− ⅛	1000
13⅛	9⅝	Husky Oil	.15	$12⅞	12⅝	12¾	− ⅛	35589
52½	42	Husky 13 p	3.25	$52	51⅜	51½	− ½	5150
31¾	20⅞	IU Intl	a1.20	$21½	21⅜	21½	+ ¼	600
41¼	31⅞	Imasco	1.24	$40⅝	40¼	40⅜		4506
28⅝	26⅛	Imp Life p	3.06	$27⅝	27	27	− ⅝	1500
44⅛	33⅝	Imp Oil A	1.40	$44	43¾	43¾	− ⅛	36533
7½	385	Inca o		450	440	445	−10	3200
19	11⅜	Inco	a.20	$14¾	14½	14⅝		6435
19½	16¾	Inco 7.85	1.96	$18½	18½	18½		400
25⅞	25¼	Inco 10	2.50	$25¾	25⅝	25⅝		2450
8	175	Inco wt		265	253	255	− 5	23300
13¾	10	Indal	.60	$11½	11¼	11¼	− ¼	400
17	13⅜	Inland Gas	1.10	$14⅝	14⅝	14⅝		200
10⅜	8¼	Innopac	.20	$9⅝	9½	9⅝	+ ⅛	600
11⅞	8⅞	Inter-City	.40	$10	10	10		5650
278	135	I Atlantis o		$155	155	155	− 5	1250
168½	129⅞	IBM	a4.40	$161	161	161	+1⅛	288
8⅝	6½	Intl Thom	a.14½	$8⅛	8	8		27100
33½	25½	Intpr Pipe	1.80	$31⅝	31⅜	31⅝	+ ¼	3610
8	475	Inverness		$6⅛	6	6	− ¼	1450
15¼	11¾	Ipsco	.48	$12¼	12⅛	12⅛	− ¼	26919
46	32	Ipsco rt						z17720
8½	5¾	Irwin Toy	.26	$7⅜	7⅜	7⅜	+ ⅞	206
28½	23½	Ivaco E p	2.00	$25¼	25	25¼		300
27¾	24	Ivaco F p	2.00	$25⅛	24¾	24¾	− ½	700
7⅜	375	Ivaco w		390	390	390		z20

Figure 24–1
EXCERPT FROM A STOCK-MARKET PAGE
This table from *The Globe and Mail* gives the highest and lowest price in the current year, the current dividend rate, the highest, lowest, and final price of the stock on that day, the change in price from the day before, and the number of shares traded on that day.
SOURCE: From "Toronto Quotations for Oct. 5, 1984 prepared by the Toronto Stock Exchange," *The Globe and Mail*, Toronto, October 6, 1984, page B7.

Figure 24-2
EXCERPT FROM A BOND PRICE TABLE
This table from *The Globe and Mail* shows the issuing company (or branch of government), the annual interest payment, the date on which the bond will be redeemed at face value, its approximate current price, the effective yield (that is, the average amount earned per year on the bond if held to its redemption date, expressed as a percent of the current price), and the change in the price from the previous day.
SOURCE: From "Bond Prices," *The Globe and Mail*, Toronto, October 6, 1984, page B9.

	Price	Yld	Ch'ge
GOVERNMENT OF CANADA			
Canada 13 May 1-85-90	102.62	12.33	+ 1/8
Canada 15 Mar 15-87	105.25	12.42	- -
Canada 10½ Mar 15-88	95.00	12.33	+ 1/8
Canada 11¼ Feb 1-93	92.75	12.68	+ ¼
Canada 13 May 1-01	101.25	12.82	+ ¾
Canada 9½ Oct 1-01	80.00	12.34	+ ¾
Canada 11¼ Dec. 15-02	84.12	12.80	+ ½
Canada 11¾ Feb. 1-03	92.75	12.78	+ 5/8
Canada 10¼ Feb 1-04	83.75	12.49	+ 5/8
Canada 12 Mar 1-05	94.00	12.83	+ ½
PROVINCIALS AND GUARANTEED			
Alta Mun 12¼ Dec 15-02	94.62	13.02	+ ½
BC Hyd 13½ Jan 15-11	101.75	13.25	+ ½
Man 11¾ Mar 15-93	94.50	12.83	+ 3/8
NB Ele 11¾ Feb 8-93	94.00	12.94	+ 3/8
Nfld 12 7/8 Apr 6-03	97.25	13.28	+ ½
NS Pow 13½ Dec 1-02	102.00	13.20	+ ½
Ont Hyd 10½ Feb 8-88	94.87	12.42	+ ¼
Ont Hyd 12½ Nov 30-02	96.75	12.96	+ ½
Ont Hyd 13 Jan 29-11	99.75	13.03	+ ½
Quebec 12 Apr 7-93	94.75	13.04	+ 3/8
Quebec 13 Apr 7-03	98.75	13.18	+ ½
Sask 12¼ Mar 30-03	94.50	13.04	+ ½
CORPORATES			
Bell 10½ Jul 15-85	98.50	12.57	- -
Bell 11 Oct 15-04	91.00	12.21	+ 1/8
Cdn Util 12 Jul 15-00	92.75	13.09	+ 3/8
IMO 12 Mar 31-93	95.62	12.87	+ ¼
Shell 11 3/8 Jan 15-88	97.50	12.69	- -
Transalta 13 Dec 16-97	99.25	13.11	+ 3/8
Westcoast 12½ Apr 1-93	96.62	13.18	+ ¼

$100, would have made an investment that yielded an average 12.21 percent per year, which is shown as "yield" in the table.

Stock Exchanges and Their Functions

Stock exchanges have existed in Europe since the thirteenth century. In North America the first trading of company shares took place in the early eighteenth century when merchants met at the foot of Wall Street in New York City. This early trading market was not restricted to shares. Wheat, tobacco, and slaves were also involved. The Montreal Stock Exchange is Canada's oldest, with records of trading dating back to 1832, followed by Toronto (1852), Vancouver (1907), and Alberta (1913). There is also a commodities exchange in Winnipeg.

The Toronto Stock Exchange, located near Bay Street in Toronto, is the largest in Canada, and it ranks fifth in the world by size (after the New York and American Stock Exchanges in New York City, and those in Tokyo and London). This is where the expression "power of Bay Street" comes from. The leading brokerage firms hold "seats" on the stock exchange, which enable them to trade directly on the floor of the exchange. The Toronto Stock Exchange has about 80 member organizations. Seats are traded on the open market, and today a seat can be purchased for about $90,000.

Someone who wants to buy a stock on the Toronto Stock Exchange must use a broker who will deal with a firm that has a seat on the Exchange. Suppose you live in New Brunswick and want to buy 200 shares of the Royal Bank. The broker you approach may be employed by a firm that holds a seat on the Exchange, or she may work through another firm that holds one. The broker who is to fill your order sends a trader to the area on the floor of the Exchange where Royal Bank stock is traded. The trader's responsibility is to buy the stock for you at the lowest possible price. Other traders will be trying to sell Royal Bank stock at the highest possible price for their clients. The traders shout their willingness to buy (bids) or their willingness to sell (offers or "asks") specified amounts of stock at specified prices until two traders agree on a price at which to do business with each other, at which time the sale is completed. This process is sometimes called the "auction-market" process.

About 10 percent of shares are traded through brokers on a basis known as "over the counter." This method of trade does not involve a public market at all. It is not a place where many buyers and sellers meet to make exchanges simultaneously. Rather, it is run by a number of firms, each operating more or less independently of the others. When a buyer brings an order to such a firm, the broker simply shops around by telephone, seeking to find someone to match the purchase demand with a corresponding supply offer, or the broker may buy or sell for his own account the stocks supplied or demanded by the order. Thus, each broker does the job that is done by a trader on one of the exchanges. Obviously, over-the-counter trading is a much less structured and less organized affair than it is on the exchanges.

With the advent of computers and improved electronic means of communication, it is now possible to automate the over-the-counter market via an electronic network through which every buy or sell order would be announced to brokers simultaneously across the country, as would the price and quantity of every completed transaction. In the United States, such a network exists on which thousands of stocks, including stocks of many Canadian companies, are traded. In Canada, a similar system is used through the stock exchanges for the trading of some of the less active stocks.

Stock Exchanges and Corporate Capital Needs

While corporations often raise the funds they need by selling stocks, they do not normally do so through any of the stock exchanges. When new stocks are offered by a company in Canada, the new issue is usually handled through a trust company. In contrast, the stock markets trade almost exclusively in "secondhand securities"—stocks in the hands of individuals and others who had bought them earlier and who now wish to sell them.

Thus the stock market does not provide funds to corporations that need the financing to expand their productive activities. The markets only provide money to persons who already hold stocks previously issued by the corporations.

Yet stock exchanges have two functions that are of critical importance for the financing of corporations. First, by providing a secondhand market for stocks, they make it much less risky for an individual to invest in a company. Investors know that their money is not locked in—if they need the money, they can always sell their stocks to other investors at the price the market currently offers. This reduction in risk makes it far easier for corporations to issue new stocks. Second, the stock market determines the current price of the company's stocks. That, in turn, determines whether it will be hard or easy for a corporation to raise money by selling new stocks. For example, suppose a company initially has one million shares and wants to raise $10 million. If the price is $40 per share, an issue of 250,000 shares can bring in the required funds, leaving the original shareholders with four-fifths of the company's ownership. But if the price of the stock is only $20, then 500,000 new shares will have to be issued, cutting the original shareholders back to two-thirds of the ownership of the company. This is a less attractive proposition.

Some people believe that the price of a company's stock is closely tied to the efficiency with which its productive activities are conducted, the effectiveness with which it matches its product to consumer demands, and the diligence with which it goes after profitable innovation. In this view, those firms that can make effective use of funds because of their efficiency are precisely the corporations whose stock prices will usually be comparatively high. In this way the stock market tends to channel the economy's investment funds to those firms that can make best use of the money. In sum:

If a firm has a promising future, its stock will tend to command a high price on the stock exchanges. The high price of its stock will make it easier for it to raise capital by permitting it to amass a large amount of money through the sale of a comparatively small number of new shares of stock. Thus, *the stock market helps to allocate the economy's resources to those firms that can make the best use of those resources.*

The Issue of Speculation

Dealings in securities are often viewed with hostility and suspicion because they are thought to be an instrument of **speculation**. When something goes wrong in the market, say, when there is a sudden fall in prices, *speculators* are often blamed. The word "speculators" is used by editorial writers as a term of strong disapproval, implying that those who engage in the activity are parasites who produce no benefits for society and often do it considerable harm.

Individuals who engage in **speculation** deliberately invest in risky assets, hoping to obtain a profit from the expected changes in the prices of these assets.

Economists disagree vehemently with this judgment. They say that speculators perform two vital economic functions:

1. They sell *protection from risk* to other people, much as a fire insurance policy affords protection from risk to a homeowner.

2. They help to smooth out price fluctuations by purchasing items when they are abundant (and cheap) and holding them and reselling them when they are scarce (and expensive). In that way, they play a vital economic role in helping to alleviate and even prevent shortages.

Some examples from outside the securities markets will make the role of speculators clear.

Speculators enable farmers or producers of metals and other commodities whose future price is uncertain to get rid of their risk. A farmer who has planted a large crop but who fears its price may fall before harvest time can protect himself by signing a *contract for future delivery* at an agreed-upon price at which the speculator will purchase the crop when it comes in. In that case, if the price happens to fall, it is the speculator and not the farmer who will suffer the loss. Of course, if the price happens to rise, the speculator will reap the gain—that is the nature of risk bearing. The speculator who has agreed to buy the crop at the preset price, regardless of market conditions at the time the sale takes place, has, in effect, sold an insurance policy to the farmer. Surely this is a useful function.

The second role of speculators is perhaps even more important; in effect, they accumulate and store goods in periods of abundance, making them available in periods of scarcity. Suppose the speculator has reason to suspect that next year's crop of a storable commodity will not be nearly as abundant as this year's. He will buy some now, when it is cheap, for resale when it becomes scarce and expensive. In the process, he will smooth out the swing in prices by adding his purchases to the total market demand in the period of low prices (which tends to bring the price up), and bringing in his supplies during the period of high prices (which tends to push the price down).[2]

Thus, the successful speculator will help to relieve matters during periods of extreme shortage. There are cases in which he literally helps to relieve famine by releasing the supplies he has deliberately hoarded for such an occasion. Of course, he is cursed for the high prices he charges on such occasions. But those who curse him do not understand that prices might have been even higher if the speculator's foresight and avid pursuit of profit had not provided for the emergency. On the securities market, famine and severe shortages are not an issue, but the fact

[2]For a diagrammatic analysis of this function, see Discussion Question 7 at the end of this chapter.

remains that successful speculators tend to reduce price fluctuations by increasing demand for stocks when prices are low and contributing to supply when prices are high.

Far from aggravating instability and fluctuations, speculators work as hard as they can to iron out fluctuations, for that is how they make their profits.

Even among government officials, journalists, and other thoughtful individuals, it is widely believed that speculators perform no real service for the economy; that their activity generally aggravates high prices and increases scarcity in times of shortages; and that they add to the instability of the economy in other ways. These impressions are virtually the reverse of the truth. Whether or not speculators are personally virtuous is not the point. The fact is that in earning their profits they make several vital contributions to the workings of the economy: (1) They take over risks from individuals seeking protection from risk; (2) They tend to add to supplies in periods of shortages; and (3) They work to depress prices when prices are unusually high and to raise prices when prices are unusually low—*for that is how speculators earn profits—by buying things when they are cheap in anticipation of their resale when they become expensive.*

Stock Prices as Random Walks

The beginning of this chapter cited evidence that the best professional securities analysts have a forecasting record so miserable that investors may do as well predicting earnings by hunch, superstition, or any purely random process as they would by following the advice of a professional. Similarly, it has been said that an investor is well advised to pick stocks by throwing darts at the stock-market page—since it is far cheaper to buy a set of darts than to obtain the apparently useless advice of a professional analyst. Indeed, there have been at least two experiments, one by a U.S. senator and one by *Forbes* magazine, in which stocks picked by dart throwing actually outperformed the mutual funds, whose stocks are selected by the experts. Does this mean that analysts are incompetent people who do not know what they are doing? Not at all. Rather, there is overwhelming evidence that their poor forecasting performance is attributable to the fact that the task they have undertaken is basically impossible.

How can this be so? The answer is that to make a good forecast of any variable—GNP, population, or fuel use—there must be something in the past whose behaviour is closely related to the future behaviour of the variable whose path we wish to predict. If a 10 percent rise in this year's consumption always produces a 5 percent rise in next year's GNP, this fact can help us predict future GNP on the basis of current observations. But if we want to forecast the future of a variable whose behaviour is completely unrelated to the behaviour of *any* current variable, there is no objective evidence that can help us make that forecast. Throwing darts or gazing into a crystal ball is no less effective than analysts' calculations.

There is a mass of statistical evidence that the behaviour of stock prices is in fact unpredictable. In other words, the behaviour of stock prices is essentially random; the paths they follow are what statisticians call **random walks**. A random walk is like the path followed by a drunk. All we know about his position after his next step is that it will be given by his current position plus whatever random direction his next haphazard step will carry him. The relevant feature of randomness, for our purposes, is that it is by nature unpredictable, which is just what the word *random* means.

If the evidence that stock prices follow a random walk stands up to research in the future as it has so far, it is easy enough to understand why the stock-market

The time path of a variable, such as the price of a stock, is said to constitute a **random walk** if its magnitude in one period (say, May 2, 1985) is equal to its value in the preceding period (May 1, 1985) plus a completely random number. That is:

Price on May 2, 1985 =
Price on May 1, 1985
+ Random number

where the random number (positive or negative) might be obtained by a roll of dice or some such procedure.

predictions are as poor as they are. The analysts are trying to forecast behaviour that is basically random; in effect, they are trying to predict the unpredictable.

Two questions remain. First, does the evidence that stock prices follow a random walk mean that investment in stocks is a pure gamble and never worthwhile? And, second, how does one explain the random behaviour of stock prices?

To answer the first question, it is false to conclude that investment in stocks is generally not worthwhile. The statistical evidence is that, over the long run, stock prices *as a whole* have had a marked upward trend, perhaps reflecting the long-term growth of the economy. Evidence *does* indicate that stock prices are likely to rise if one waits long enough for them to do so. Thus, the random walk does not proceed in just any direction—rather, it represents a set of erratic movements *around the basic trend in stock prices.*

Moreover, it is not in the *overall* level of stock prices that the most pertinent random walk occurs, but in the performance of one company's stock compared with another's. For this reason professional advice may be able to predict that investment in the stock market is likely to be a good thing over the long haul. But, if the random walk evidence is valid, there is no way professionals can tell us *which* of the available stocks is most likely to go up—that is, which combination of stocks is best for the investor to buy.

The only appropriate answer to the second question is that no one is sure of the explanation. There are two widely offered hypotheses—each virtually the opposite of the other. The first asserts that stock prices are random because clever professional speculators are able to foresee almost perfectly every influence that is *not* random. For example, suppose a change occurs that makes the probable earnings of some company higher than had previously been expected. Then, according to this view, the professionals will instantly become aware of this change and immediately buy enough to raise the price of the stock accordingly. Then, by the time investment "advice" is widely distributed, the only thing for the stock price to do between this year and next is wander randomly, because the professionals cannot predict random movements, and hence cannot force current stock prices to anticipate them.

The other explanation of random behaviour of stock prices is at the opposite pole from the view that all non-random movements are wiped out by supersmart professionals. This view holds that people who buy and sell stocks have learned that they cannot predict future stock prices. As a result they react to any signal, however irrational and irrelevant it appears. If the president catches cold, stock prices fall. If an astronaut's venture is successful, prices go up. For, according to this view, investors are, in the last analysis, trying to predict, not the prospects of the economy or of the company whose shares they buy, but the supply and demand behaviour of other investors, which will ultimately determine the course of stock prices. Since all investors are equally in the dark, their groping can only result in the randomness that we observe. The classic statement of this view of stock-market behaviour was provided by Lord Keynes, a successful professional speculator himself:

Professional investment may be likened to those newspaper competitions in which the competitors have to pick out the six prettiest faces from a hundred photographs, the prize being awarded to the competitor whose choice most nearly corresponds to the average preferences of the competitors as a whole; so that each competitor has to pick not those faces which he himself finds prettiest, but those which he thinks likeliest to catch the fancy of the other competitors, all of whom are looking at the problem from the same point of view. It is not a case of choosing those which, to the best of one's judgment, are really the prettiest, nor even those which average opinion genuinely thinks the prettiest. We have reached the third degree where we devote our intelligences to anticipating what average opinion expects the average opinion to be. And there are some, I believe, who practice the fourth, fifth and higher degrees.[3]

[3]John Maynard Keynes, *The General Theory of Employment, Interest, and Money* (New York: Harcourt Brace Jovanovich, 1936), page 156.

Summary

1. The three basic types of firms are corporations, partnerships, and individual proprietorships. Most Canadian firms are individual proprietorships, but most Canadian manufactured goods are produced by corporations.

2. Corporate investors have greater protection from risk than individual proprietorships or partnerships because they have *limited liability*—they cannot be asked to pay more than they have invested in the firm.

3. Corporations finance their activities mostly by ploughback (that is, by retaining part of their earnings and putting it back into the company) or by the sale of stocks and bonds.

4. A stock is a share in the ownership of the company. A bond is an IOU by a company for money lent to it by the bondholder. Many observers argue that the purchase of a stock also really amounts to a loan to the company—a loan that is riskier than the purchase of a bond.

5. If interest rates rise, bond prices will fall. In other words, if some bond amounts to a contract to pay 8 percent and the market interest rate goes up to 10 percent, people will no longer be willing to pay the old price for that bond.

6. If stock prices correctly reflect the future prospects of different companies, promising firms are helped to raise money because they are able to sell each stock they issue at favourable prices.

7. Bonds are relatively risky for the firms that issue them, but they are fairly safe for their buyers, because they are a commitment by the firm to pay a fixed annual amount to the bondholder whether or not the company made money that year. But stocks, which do not promise any fixed payment, are relatively safe for the company and risky for their owner.

8. A portfolio is a collection of stocks, bonds, and other assets with a single owner. The greater the number and variety of securities and other assets it contains the less risky it is.

9. Speculation affects stock market prices, but (contrary to what is widely assumed) there is reason to believe that speculation actually *reduces* the frequency and size of price fluctuations.

10. Speculators are also useful to the economy because they undertake risks that others wish to avoid, thereby, in effect, providing others with insurance against risk.

11. Statistical evidence indicates that *individual* stock prices behave randomly.

Concepts for Review

Proprietorship	Limited liability	Portfolio diversification
Unlimited liability	Ploughback or retained earnings	Stock exchanges
Partnership	Common stock	Speculation
Corporation	Bond	Random walk

Questions for Discussion

1. Why would it be difficult to run General Motors as a partnership or an individual proprietorship?

2. Do you think it is fair to tax a corporation more than a partnership doing the same amount of business? Why or why not?

3. If you hold shares in a corporation and management decides to plough back the company's earnings some year instead of paying dividends, what are the advantages and disadvantages to you?

4. Suppose interest rates are 12 percent in the economy and a safe bond promises to pay $12 a year in interest forever. What do think the price of the bond will be? Why?

5. Suppose in the economy in the previous example,

interest rates suddenly rise to 18 percent. What will happen to the price of the bond that pays $12 per year?

6. If you want to buy a stock, when might it be to your advantage to buy it using a market order? When will it pay to use a limit order?

7. Show in diagrams that if a speculator were to buy when price is high and sell when price is low he would increase price fluctuations. Why would it be in his best interest *not* to do so? (*Hint:* Draw two supply–demand diagrams, one for the high-price period and one for the low-price period. How would the speculator's activities affect these diagrams?)

8. If stock prices really are a random walk, can you nevertheless think of good reasons for getting professional advice before investing?

The Firm in the Marketplace: Perfect Competition

In Chapter 22 we analysed how a firm's input decisions determine its cost curves and in Chapter 23 we saw that cost and demand curves together lead to a decision about how much to produce. It may seem, therefore, that we have completed the analysis of the supply side of the market. This is not so, however, because firms do not operate in a vacuum. A single firm is but one component of a market, and what one firm does may affect the others. Thus, our discussion of supply is not complete until we have analysed how *all* the firms in an industry interact in the marketplace.

Industries differ dramatically in how populated they are and in the size of a typical firm. Some industries, like fishing, have a great many very small firms; others, like autos, are composed of a few industrial giants. This chapter deals with a very particular type of market structure—called *perfect competition*—in which firms are numerous and small. The chapter begins by comparing alternative market forms and defining perfect competition precisely. We then use the tools acquired in Chapter 23 to analyse the behaviour of the perfectly competitive firm and derive its supply curve. Next, we consider the supply curve of *all* the firms in an industry—the *industry supply curve*—and we investigate how developments in the industry affect the individual firms.

A Puzzle: Can Good Weather Be Bad for Farmers?

If you do your own gardening, you no doubt hope for the best possible weather—a nice mixture of sunshine and rain to help the plants grow. Drought and frost are your mortal enemies. For farmers, however, ideal weather sometimes spells disaster. After a bumper crop comes in, farmers often pressure Ottawa, complaining about the low prices that result. Legislators are urged to "protect" the farmer from these low prices, which is to say, to protect them from the consequences of good weather. On the other hand, adverse weather often leaves farmers *as a whole* rather well off. Even though bad weather ruins some particular farmers (to whom help *is* sometimes given), broad-based political action does not typically appear after droughts, floods, and premature frosts. What accounts for this strange behaviour? The tools we are about to describe—the analysis of competitive supply—will permit us to answer this question at the end of the chapter.

Varieties of Market Structure: A Sneak Preview

A **market** refers to the set of all sale and purchase transactions that affect the price of some commodity.

It will be helpful to open our discussion by explaining clearly what is meant by the word **market**. Economists do not reserve the term to denote only an organized exchange operating in a well-defined physical location. The more general and abstract notion of a market refers to a set of sellers and buyers whose activities affect the price at which a *particular commodity* is sold. For example, two separate sales of Canadian Pacific shares in different parts of the country may be considered as taking place on the same market, while the sale of bread and carrots in neighbouring stalls of a market square may, in our sense, occur on totally different markets.

Economists distinguish among different markets according to (1) how many firms there are, (2) whether the products of the different firms are identical or somewhat different, and (3) how easy it is for new firms to enter the market. Table 25–1 summarizes the main features of the four market structures we will study in this and subsequent chapters. It is provided here as a kind of road map of where we are going. *Perfect competition* is obviously at one extreme (many small firms selling an identical product) while *pure monopoly* (a single firm) is at the other. In between are hybrid forms—called *monopolistic competition* and *oligopoly*—that share some of the characteristics of perfect competition and some of the characteristics of monopoly.

Perfect competition is far from the typical market form in the Canadian economy. Indeed, it is quite rare. Some farming and fishing industries approximate perfect competition, as do some financial markets. Pure monopoly—literally *one* firm—is also infrequently encountered. Most of the products you buy are no doubt supplied by oligopolies or monopolistic competitors—terms we will be defining precisely in Chapter 28.

Table 25–1
VARIETIES OF MARKET STRUCTURE

TYPE OF MARKET STRUCTURE	DEFINITION			WHERE TO FIND IT	
	NUMBER OF SELLERS	NATURE OF THE PRODUCT	BARRIERS TO ENTRY	IN THE CANADIAN ECONOMY	IN THIS TEXTBOOK
Perfect competition	Many	All firms produce identical products (example: wheat)	None	Some agricultural markets and parts of retailing come close	Chapter 25
Monopolistic competition	Many	Different firms produce somewhat different products (example: restaurant meals)	Minor	Most of the retailing sector, textiles, and restaurants	Chapter 28
Oligopoly	Few	Firms may produce identical or differentiated products (example: brands of toothpaste)	May be considerable	Much of the manufacturing sector, especially autos, steel, and cigarettes	Chapter 28
Pure monopoly	One	Unique product	May be considerable	Public utilities	Chapter 27

Perfect Competition Defined

You can appreciate just how special perfect competition is once we provide a comprehensive definition. A market is said to operate under **perfect competition** when the following four conditions are satisfied:

1. *Numerous participants*.   Each seller and purchaser constitutes so small a portion of the market that their decisions have no effect on the price. This requirement rules out trade associations or other collusive arrangements strong enough to affect price.

2. *Homogeneity of product*.   The product offered by any seller is identical to that supplied by any other seller. (Example: Wheat of a given grade is a homogeneous product; different brands of toothpaste are not.) Because the product is homogeneous, consumers do not care from which firm they buy.

3. *Freedom of entry and exit*.   New firms desiring to enter the market face no special impediments that the existing firms can avoid. Similarly, if production and sale of the good proves unprofitable, there are no barriers preventing firms from leaving the market.

4. *Perfect information*.   Each firm and each customer is well informed about the available products and their prices. They know whether one supplier is selling at a price lower than another is.

These are obviously exacting requirements that are met infrequently in practice. One example might be a market for common shares: There are literally thousands of buyers and sellers of Bell Canada stock; all of the shares are exactly alike; anyone who wishes can enter the market easily; and most of the relevant information is readily available in the daily newspaper. But other examples are hard to find. Our interest in perfect competition is surely not for its descriptive realism.

Why, then, do we spend time studying perfect competition? The answer takes us back to the central theme of this book. It is under perfect competition that the market mechanism performs best. So, if we want to learn what markets do well, we can put the market's best foot forward by beginning with perfect competition.

As Adam Smith suggested some two centuries ago, perfectly competitive firms use society's scarce resources with maximum efficiency. And as Friedrich Engels suggested in the opening quotation of this chapter, perfectly competitive firms serve consumers' tastes effectively. So by studying perfect competition, we can learn just how much an *ideally functioning* market system might accomplish. This is the topic of the present chapter and the next one. Then, in Chapters 27 and 28 we will consider other market forms and see how they deviate from the perfectly competitive ideal. Still later chapters (especially Chapter 29 and Parts Six and Seven) will examine many important tasks that the market does not perform at all well, even under perfect competition. These chapters combined should provide a balanced assessment of the virtues and vices of the market mechanism.

The Competitive Firm and Its Demand Curve

To discover what happens in a market in which perfect competition prevails, we must deal separately with the behaviour of the *firm* and the behaviour of the *industry*. One basic difference between the firm and the industry under competition relates to *pricing*. We say that:

Under perfect competition, the firm is a *price taker*. It has no choice but to accept the price that has been determined in the market.

The fact that a firm in a perfectly competitive market has no control over the price it charges follows from the definition of perfect competition. The presence of a vast number of competitors, each offering identical products, forces each firm to meet but not exceed the price charged by the others. Like a shareholder with 100 shares of Bell Canada, the firm simply finds out the prevailing price on the market and either accepts that price or refuses to sell. But while the individual firm has no influence over price under perfect competition, the industry does. This influence is not conscious or planned—it happens spontaneously through the impersonal forces of supply and demand, as we observed in Chapter 4.

With two important exceptions, the analysis of the behaviour of the firm under perfect competition is exactly the same as that pertaining to any other firm, so the tools developed in Chapters 22 and 23 can be applied directly. The two exceptions are the special shape of the competitive firm's demand curve and the effects on the firm's profits of freedom of entry and exit. We will consider them in turn, beginning with the demand curve.

In Chapter 23, we always assumed that the firm's demand curve sloped downward; if a firm wished to sell more (without increasing its advertising or changing its product specifications), it had to reduce the price of its product. The competitive firm is an exception to this general principle.

A perfectly competitive firm has a **horizontal demand curve**. This means it can double or triple its sales without any reduction in the price of its product.

How is this possible? The answer is that the competitive firm is so insignificant relative to the market as a whole that it has absolutely no influence over price. The farmer who sells his barley through the exchange in Winnipeg must accept the current quotation his broker reports to him. Because there are thousands of farmers, the Winnipeg price per tonne will not budge because Farmer Jones decides he doesn't like the price and holds back a truckload for storage. Thus, the demand curve for Farmer Jones's barley is as shown in Figure 25-1; the price he is paid in Winnipeg will be $80 per tonne whether he sells one truckload (point *A*) or two (point *B*) or three (point *C*).

Short-Run Equilibrium of the Competitive Firm

We now have sufficient background to analyse how the competitive firm decides how much to produce. To begin, recall from Chapter 23 that profit maximization requires the firm to pick an output level that makes its *marginal cost equal to its marginal revenue*: MC = MR. The only feature that distinguishes the profit-

Figure 25-1

DEMAND CURVE FOR A FIRM UNDER PERFECT COMPETITION

Under perfect competition, the size of the output of a firm is so small a portion of the total industry output that it cannot affect the market price of the product. Even if the firm's output increases many times, market price remains $80.

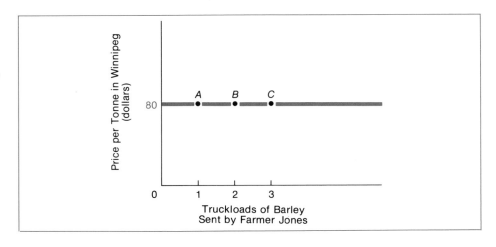

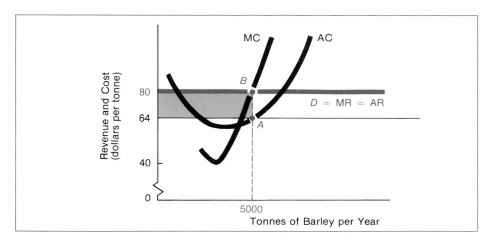

Figure 25-2
SHORT-RUN EQUILIBRIUM
OF THE COMPETITIVE FIRM
The profit-maximizing firm will
select the output (5000 tonnes per
year) at which marginal cost
equals marginal revenue (point B).
The demand curve, D, is horizontal
because the firm's output is too
small to affect market price; thus it
is also the marginal-revenue
curve. In the short run, demand
may be either high or low in
relation to cost. Therefore each
unit it sells may return a profit (AB)
or a loss.

maximizing equilibrium of the competitive firm from that of any other type of
firm is its horizontal demand curve.

Because the demand curve is horizontal, the competitive firm's marginal-
revenue curve is a horizontal straight line that coincides with its demand curve;
hence, MR = price (P). It is easy to see why this is so. If the price does not depend
on how much the firm sells (which is what a horizontal demand curve means),
then each *additional* unit sold brings in an amount of revenue (the *marginal
revenue*) exactly equal to the market price. So marginal revenue always equals
price under perfect competition; the demand curve and the MR curve coincide
because the firm is a price taker.

Once we know the shape and position of a firm's marginal-revenue curve, we
can use this information and the marginal-cost curve to determine its optimal
output and profit, as shown in Figure 25–2. As usual, the profit-maximizing output
is that at which MC = MR (point B). This competitive firm produces 5000 tonnes
per year—the output level at which MC and MR are equal to the market price,
$80. Thus:

Because it is a price taker, the *equilibrium* of a profit-maximizing firm in a perfectly
competitive market must occur at an output level at which marginal cost is equal
to price, or in symbols:

$$MC = P.$$

The same information is shown in Table 25–2, which gives the firm's total
revenue, total cost, and profit for different output quantities. We see from the last

Table 25-2
REVENUES, COSTS, AND PROFITS OF A COMPETITIVE FIRM

QUANTITY (thousands of tonnes)	TOTAL REVENUE	MARGINAL REVENUE	TOTAL COST	MARGINAL COST	TOTAL PROFIT
		(thousands of dollars)			
0	0				
1	80	80	· 80		0
2	160	80	140	60	20
3	240	80	180	40	60
4	320	80	240	60	80
5	400	80	320	80	80
6	480	80	440	120	40
7	560	80	640	200	-80

column that total profit is maximized at an output of either 4000 or 5000 tonnes, where total profit is $80,000. Table 25-2 also gives marginal costs and marginal revenues. We see that an increase in output from 4000 tonnes to 5000 tonnes incurs a marginal cost ($80,000) that is equal to the corresponding marginal revenue ($80,000), confirming that 5000 tonnes is the profit-maximizing level of output.[1]

Short-Run Profit: Graphic Representation

Let us see how the firm's profit is shown in Figure 25-2. By definition, profit per unit of output is revenue per unit minus cost per unit. To enable us to represent profit per unit graphically we have included in Figure 25-2 the firm's *average-cost* (AC) curve, which was explained in Chapter 22. We see in the figure that average cost at 5000 tonnes per year is only $64 per tonne (point *A*). Since the price, or average revenue (AR), is $80 per tonne (point *B*), the firm is making a profit of AR − AC = $16 per tonne. This profit margin appears in the graph as the vertical distance between points *A* and *B*.

Notice that in addition to showing the *profit per unit*, the graph can be used to show the firm's *total profit*. Total profit is the profit per unit ($16 in this example) times the number of units (5000 per year). Therefore, total profit is represented as the *area* of the shaded rectangle whose height is the profit per unit ($16) and whose width is the number of units (5000).[2] That is, total profit at any output is the area of the rectangle whose base equals the level of output and whose height equals AR − AC. Thus, in this case, profits are $80,000 per year.

The Case of Short-Term Losses

The market is obviously treating this farmer rather nicely. But what if the market were not so generous in its rewards? What if, for example, the market price were only $40 per tonne instead of $80? Figure 25-3 shows the equilibrium of the firm under these circumstances. The firm still maximizes profits by producing the level of output at which marginal cost is equal to price—point *B* in the diagram. But this time "maximizing" profits really means keeping the loss as small as possible.

At the optimal level of output (3000 tonnes per year) average cost is $60 per tonne (point *A*), which exceeds the $40 per tonne price (point *B*). The firm is therefore running a loss of $20 per tonne times 3000 tonnes, or $60,000 per year. This loss, which is represented by the area of the shaded rectangle in Figure 25-3, is the best the firm can do. If it selected any other output level, its loss would be even greater.

The price-taking firm will always equate MC and *P*, but in the short run it may wind up with either a profit or a loss.

Shut-Down and Break-Even Analysis

There is, however, a limit to the amount of loss the firm can be forced to accept. If losses get too big, the firm can simply go out of business. To understand the logic of the decision between shutting down and remaining in operation, we must return to the distinction between fixed costs and variable costs.

[1]The MC = MR rule yields the conclusion that the firm should produce exactly 5000 tonnes, while the profits column in Table 25-2 suggests that the firm should be indifferent between operating at 4000 and 5000 tonnes. This slight inconsistency is essentially a measurement error. To calculate marginal costs and marginal revenues accurately we should increase output one tonne at a time, instead of proceeding in leaps of 1000 tonnes. But that would require too much space!

[2]Recall that the formula for the area of a rectangle is area = height × width.

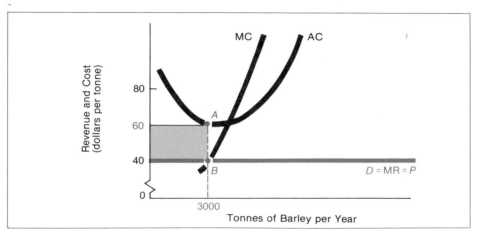

Figure 25-3

SHORT-RUN EQUILIBRIUM OF THE COMPETITIVE FIRM WITH A LOWER PRICE
In this diagram, the cost curves are the same as in Figure 25-2, but the demand curve (D) has shifted down to a market price of $40 per tonne. The firm still does the best it can by setting MC = P (point B). But since its average cost at 3000 tonnes per year is $60 per tonne, it runs a loss (shown by the shaded rectangle).

If the firm stops producing, its revenue will fall to zero. Its *variable* costs will also fall to zero. But its fixed costs—such as rent—will remain to plague it. If the firm is losing money, sometimes it will be better off continuing to operate until its obligations to pay fixed costs expire; but sometimes it will do better by shutting down. Two rules govern the decision:

Rule 1. The firm will not lose money if total revenue (TR) exceeds total cost (TC).

Rule 2. The firm should not shut down in the short run if TR exceeds total *variable* cost (TVC).

The first rule is obvious. If the firm's revenues cover its total costs, then it does not lose money.

The second rule is a bit more subtle. Suppose TR is less than TC. If our unfortunate firm continues in operation, how much will it lose? Clearly it will lose the difference between total cost and total revenue; that is:

$$\text{Loss if the firm stays in business} = \text{TC} - \text{TR}.$$

However, if the firm shuts down, both its revenues and *variable* costs become zero, leaving only the total *fixed* costs (TFC) to be paid:

$$\text{Loss if the firm shuts down} = \text{TFC}.$$

The firm will then find it advisable to shut down if it is better to lose TFC than to lose TC – TR. In other words, it will shut down if TC – TR > TFC or TC – TFC > TR. Remembering that TC = TVC + TFC, we can express this condition as if TVC > TR, which is Rule 2.

This rule is illustrated by the two cases in Table 25-3. Case A deals with a firm which loses money but is better off staying in business in the short run. If it closes down, it will lose its $60,000 fixed cost. But if it continues in operation, it will lose only $40,000 because TR ($100,000) exceeds TVC ($80,000) by $20,000, so that its operation contributes $20,000 toward meeting its fixed costs. In case B, on the other hand, it pays the firm to shut down because TVC ($130,000) exceeds TR ($100,000). In this case, continued operation only adds to the firm's losses.

The shut-down decision can also be analysed graphically. In Figure 25-4, the firm will run a loss whether the price is P_1, P_2, or P_3, because none of these prices is high enough to reach the minimum level of average cost (AC). The *lowest* price that keeps the firm from shutting down can be shown in the graph by introducing one more curve: the **average variable cost (AVC)** curve mentioned in

Table 25-3

THE SHUT-DOWN DECISION

	CASE A	CASE B
	(thousands of dollars)	
TR	100	100
TVC	80	130
TFC	60	60
TC	140	190
Loss if firm shuts down (TFC)	60	60
Loss if firm does not shut down (TC − TR)	40	90

Chapter 22. Why is this curve relevant? Because, as we have just seen, it pays the firm to remain in operation if its total revenue (TR) exceeds its total variable cost (TVC). If we divide both TR and TVC by quantity (Q), we get $TR/Q = P$ and $TVC/Q = AVC$, so this condition may be stated equivalently as the requirement that price exceed AVC. The conclusion, then, is:

The firm will produce nothing unless price lies above the minimum point on the AVC curve.

Figure 25–4 illustrates this principle by showing an MC curve, an AVC curve, and several alternative demand curves corresponding to different possible prices. Price P_1 is below the minimum average variable cost. With this price, the firm cannot even cover its variable costs and is better off shutting down (producing zero output). Price P_3 is higher. While the firm still runs a loss if it sets $MC = P$ at point A (because AC exceeds P_3), it is at least covering its *variable* costs, and so it pays to keep operating in the short run. Price P_2 is the borderline case. If the price is P_2, the firm is indifferent between shutting down and staying in business and producing at a level where $MC = P$ (point B). P_2 is thus the *lowest* price at which the firm will produce anything. As we see from the graph, P_2 corresponds to the minimum point on the AVC curve.

The Supply Curve of the Competitive Firm

Without realizing it, we have now derived the **supply curve of the competitive firm** in the short run. Why? Recall that a supply curve summarizes the

Figure 25-4

SHUT-DOWN ANALYSIS

At a price as low as P_1, the firm cannot even cover its average variable costs; it is better off shutting down entirely. At a price as high as P_3, the firm selects point A but operates at a loss (because P_3 is below AC). However, it is more than covering its average variable costs (since P_3 exceeds AVC), so it pays to keep producing. Price P_2 is the borderline case. With this price, the firm selects point B and is indifferent between shutting down and staying open.

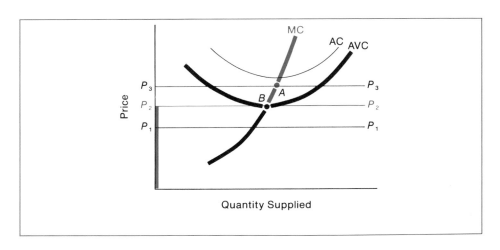

answers to such questions as, If the price is so and so, how much will the firm produce? We have now discovered that there are two possibilities, as indicated by the thick coloured line in Figure 25–4.

1. If the price exceeds the minimum AVC, in the short run it pays a competitive firm to produce the level of output that equates MC and *P*. Thus, for any price above point *B*, we can read the corresponding quantity supplied from the firm's MC curve.

2. If the price falls below the minimum AVC, then it pays the firm to produce nothing. Quantity supplied falls to zero.

Putting these two observations together, we conclude that:

The short-run supply curve of the perfectly competitive firm is its marginal-cost curve above the point where it intersects the average variable-cost curve; that is, above the minimum level of AVC. If price falls below this level, the firm's quantity supplied drops to zero.

The firm's long-run supply curve differs only slightly. Remember that the long run for a firm is defined as a period of time long enough so that *every* input becomes variable. This means that *all* costs become *variable* costs, so the distinction between average cost (AC) and average variable cost (AVC) disappears. As a consequence:

The long-run supply curve of the competitive firm is its MC curve above the point where it intersects its long-run AC (=AVC) curve.[3]

The Short-Run Supply Curve of the Competitive Industry

Having completed the analysis of the competitive firm's supply decision, we turn our attention next to the competitive *industry*. Again we need to distinguish between the short run and long run, but the distinction is different here. The short run for the *industry* is defined as a period of time too brief for new firms to enter the industry or for old firms to leave, so the number of firms is fixed. By contrast, the long run for the industry is a period of time long enough for any firm that so desires to enter (or leave). We begin our analysis of industry equilibrium in the short run.

With the number of firms fixed, it is a simple matter to derive the **supply curve of the competitive industry** from those of the individual firms. At any given price, we simply *add up* the quantities supplied by each of the firms to arrive at the industry-wide quantity supplied. For example, if each of 1000 identical firms in the barley industry supplies 4000 tonnes when the price is $60 per tonne, then the quantity supplied by the industry at a $60 price will be 4000 tonnes per firm × 1000 firms = 4 million tonnes.

This process of deriving the *market* supply curve from the *individual* supply curves of firms is perfectly analogous to the way we derive the *market* demand curve from the *individual* demand curves of consumers in Chapter 21. Graphically, what we are doing is *summing the individual supply curves horizontally*, as illustrated in Figure 25–5. At a price of $60, each of the 1000 firms in the industry supplies 4000 tonnes [point *c* in part (a)], so the industry supplies 4 million tonnes [point *C* in part (b)]. At a price of $80 each firm supplies 5000 tonnes [point *e* in

[3]The relationship between short-run and long-run average-cost curves was discussed in Chapter 22, pages 432–33.

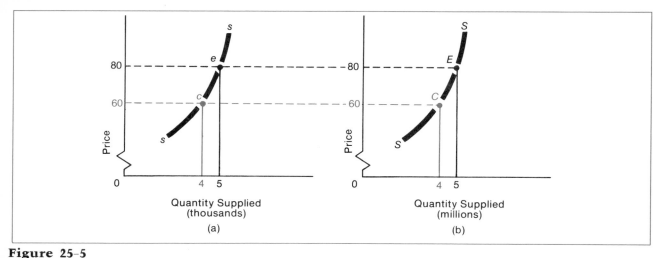

Figure 25-5

DERIVATION OF THE INDUSTRY SUPPLY CURVE FROM THE SUPPLY CURVES OF THE INDIVIDUAL FIRMS

In this hypothetical industry of 1000 identical firms, each individual firm has the supply curve *ss* in part (a). For example, quantity supplied is 4000 tonnes when the price is $60 per unit (point *c*). By *adding up* the quantities supplied by each firm at each possible price, we arrive at the industry supply curve *SS* in part (b). For example, at a unit price of $60, total quantity supplied by the industry is 4 million units (point *C*).

part (a)], and so the industry supplies 5 million tonnes [point *E* in part (b)]. Similar calculations can be done for any other price.

The supply curve of the competitive industry in the short run is derived by summing the supply curves of all the firms in the industry horizontally.

Notice that if the supply curves of individual firms are upward sloping, then the supply curve of the competitive industry will be upward sloping, too. We have seen that the firm's supply curve is its marginal-cost curve (above the level of minimum average variable cost), so it follows that rising marginal costs lead to an upward sloping *industry* supply curve.

Industry Equilibrium in the Short Run

Now that we have derived the industry supply curve, we need only add a market demand curve to determine the price and quantity that will emerge. This is done for our illustrative barley industry in Figure 25–6, where the industry supply curve [carried over from Figure 25–5 (b)] is *SS* and the demand curve is *DD*. Note that for the competitive industry, unlike the competitive firm, the demand curve is normally downward sloping. Why? Each firm by itself is so small that if it alone were to double its output the effect would hardly be noticeable. But if *every* firm in the industry were to expand its output, that would make a substantial difference. Customers can be induced to buy the additional quantities arriving at the market only if the price of the good falls.

Point *E* is the equilibrium point for the competitive industry, because only at the combination of price, $80, and quantity, 5 million tonnes, are neither purchasers nor sellers motivated to upset matters. At a price of $80, sellers are willing to offer exactly the amount consumers want to purchase.

Should we expect price actually to reach, or at least to approximate, this equilibrium level? The answer is yes. To see why, we must consider what happens when price is not at its equilibrium level. Suppose it takes a lower value, such as $60. The low price will stimulate customers to buy more; and it will also lead firms to produce less than at a price of $80. Our diagram confirms that at a price of $60, quantity supplied (4 million tonnes) is lower than quantity demanded (9.4

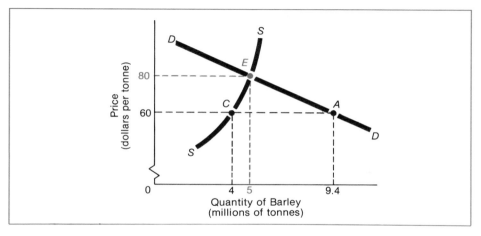

Figure 25-6

SUPPLY-DEMAND
EQUILIBRIUM OF A
COMPETITIVE INDUSTRY
The only equilibrium combination
of price and quantity is a price of
$80 and a quantity of 5 million
tonnes at which the supply curve
SS and the demand curve DD
intersect (point E). At a lower price,
such as $60, quantity demanded
(9.4 million tonnes as shown by
point A on the demand curve) will
be higher than the 4 million
tonne quantity supplied (point C).
Thus the price will be driven back
up toward the $80 equilibrium. The
opposite will happen at a price
such as $100, which is above
equilibrium.

million tonnes). Thus, unsatisfied buyers will probably offer to pay higher prices, which will force price *upward* in the direction of its equilibrium value, $80.

Similarly, if we begin with a price higher than the equilibrium price, we may readily verify that quantity supplied will exceed quantity demanded. Under these circumstances, frustrated sellers are likely to reduce their prices, so price will be forced downward. In the circumstances depicted in Figure 25-6, then, there is in effect a magnet at the equilibrium price of $80 that will pull the actual price in its direction if for some reason the actual price starts out at some other level.

In practice, there are few cases in which competitive markets, over a long period of time, seem not to have moved toward equilibrium prices. Matters eventually seem to work out as depicted in Figure 25-6. Of course, numerous transitory influences can jolt any real-world market away from its equilibrium point—a strike that cuts production, a sudden change in consumer tastes, and so on. And there also have been periods, sometimes of distressingly long duration, when the "bottom has dropped out" of some nearly competitive markets, such as stock exchanges. During such market "crashes," it certainly did not seem that prices were moving toward equilibrium.

Yet, as we have just seen, there are powerful forces that do push prices back toward equilibrium—toward the level at which the supply and demand curves intersect. These forces are of fundamental importance for economic analysis, for if there were no such forces, prices in the real world would bear little resemblance to equilibrium prices, and there would be little reason to study supply-demand analysis. Fortunately, the required equilibrating forces do exist.

Industry and Firm Equilibrium in the Long Run

The equilibrium of a competitive industry in the long run may differ from the short-run equilibrium that we have just studied. The reason is that in the long run, the number of firms in the industry (1000 in our example) is not fixed.

What will lure new firms into the industry or repel old ones? Profits. Remember that when a firm selects its optimal level of output by setting MC = P it may wind up with either a profit or a loss. Such profits or losses must be *temporary* for a competitive firm, because the freedom of new firms to enter the industry or of old firms to leave it will, in the long run, eliminate them.

Suppose very high profits accrue to firms in the industry. Then new companies will find it attractive to enter the business, and expanded production will force the market price to fall from its initial level. Why? Recall that the industry supply curve is the horizontal sum of the supply curves of individual firms. Under perfect

competition, new firms can enter the industry on *the same terms as existing firms.*
This means that new entrants will have the *same* individual supply curves as old
firms. If the market price did not fall, entry of new firms would lead to an increased
number of firms with no change in output *per firm.* Consequently, the total
quantity supplied on the market would be higher and would exceed quantity
demanded. But, of course, this means that in a free market entry of new firms *must*
push the price down.

Figure 25-7 shows how the entry process works. In this diagram, the demand
curve *DD* and the original (short-run) supply curve S_0S_0 are carried over from
Figure 25-6. The entry of new firms seeking high profits *shifts the short-run
supply curve outward to the right,* to S_1S_1. The new market equilibrium is at point
A (rather than at point *E*), where price is $70 per tonne and 7.2 million tonnes are
produced and consumed. Entry of new firms reduces price and raises total output.
(Had the price not fallen, quantity supplied after entry would have been 8 million
tonnes—point *F*.) Why must the price fall? Because the demand curve for the
industry is downward sloping—an increase in output will be purchased by
consumers only if the price is reduced.

To see where the entry process stops, we must consider how the entry of new
firms affects the behaviour of old firms. At first, this may seem to contradict the
notion of perfect competition; perfectly competitive firms are not supposed to care
what their competitors are doing. Indeed, these barley farmers do not care. But
they do care very much about the market price of barley, and, as we have just seen,
the entry of new firms into the barley-farming industry lowers the price of barley.

In Figure 25-8 we have juxtaposed the diagram of the equilibrium of the
competitive firm (Figure 25-2 on page 493) and the diagram of the equilibrium of
the competitive industry (Figure 25-7). Before entry, the market price was $80
[point *E* in Figure 25-8(b)] and each of the 1000 firms was producing 5000 tonnes—
the point where marginal cost and price were equal [point *e* in Figure 25-8(a)]. The
demand curve facing each firm was the horizontal line D_0 in Figure 25-8(a). There
were profits because average costs (AC) at 5000 tonnes per firm were less than
price.

Now suppose 600 new firms are attracted by these high profits and enter the
industry. Each has the cost structure indicated by the AC and MC curves in Figure
25-8(a). As we have noted, the industry supply curve in Figure 25-8(b) shifts to the
right, and price falls to $70 per tonne. Firms in the industry cannot fail to notice
this lower price. As we see in Figure 25-8(a), each firm reduces its output to 4500
tonnes in reaction to the lower price (point *a*). But now there are 1600 firms, so

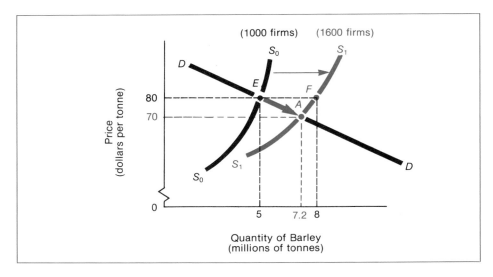

Figure 25-7

A SHIFT IN THE INDUSTRY
SUPPLY CURVE CAUSED BY
THE ENTRY OF NEW FIRMS
This diagram shows what happens
to the industry equilibrium when
new firms enter the industry.
Quantity supplied at any given
price increases; that is, the supply
curve shifts to the right, from S_0S_0
to S_1S_1 in the figure. As a result,
the market price falls (from $80 to
$70 and the quantity increases
(from 5 million tonnes to 7.2 million
tonnes).

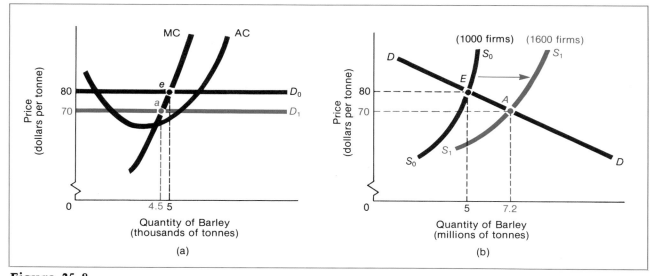

Figure 25-8

THE COMPETITIVE FIRM AND THE COMPETITIVE INDUSTRY

Here we show the interaction between developments at the industry level [in part (b)] and developments at the firm level [in part (a)]. An outward shift in the industry supply curve from S_0S_0 to S_1S_1 in part (b) lowers the market price from $80 to $70. In part (a), we see that a profit-maximizing competitive firm reacts to this decline in price by curtailing output. When the demand curve of the firm is D_0 ($80), it produces 5000 tonnes (point e). When the firm's demand curve falls to D_1 ($70), its output declines to 4500 tonnes (point a). However, there are now 1600 firms rather than 1000, so total industry output has expanded from 5 million tonnes to 7.2 million tonnes [part (b)]. Entry has reduced profits. But since P still exceeds AC at an output of 4500 tonnes per firm in part (a), some profits remain.

total industry output is $4500 \times 1600 = 7.2$ million tonnes [point A in Figure 25-8(b)].

At point a in Figure 25-8(a), there are still profits to be made because the $70 price exceeds average cost. Thus the entry process is not yet complete. When will it end? Only when all profits have been competed away. Only when entry shifts the industry supply curve so far to the right [S_2S_2 in Figure 25-9 (b)] that the demand curve facing individual firms falls to the level of minimum average cost

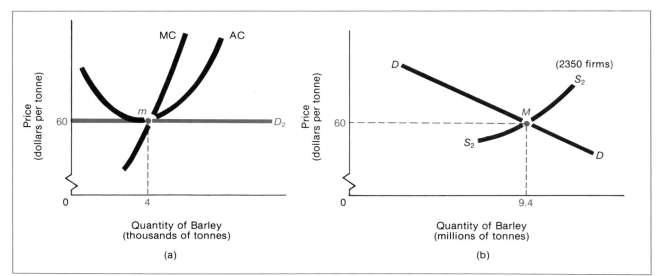

Figure 25-9

LONG-RUN EQUILIBRIUM OF THE COMPETITIVE FIRM AND INDUSTRY

By the time 2350 firms have entered the industry, the industry supply curve is S_2S_2 and the market price is $60 per tonne. At this price, the horizontal demand curve facing each firm is D_2 in part (a), so the profit-maximizing level of output is 4000 tonnes (point m). Here, since average cost and price are equal, there is no economic profit.

[point *m* in Figure 25–9 (a)] will all profits be eradicated and entry cease.

The two panels of Figure 25–9 show the competitive firm and the competitive industry in long-run equilibrium.[4] Notice that at the equilibrium point [*m* in part (a)], each firm picks its own output level so as to maximize its profit. This means that for each firm *P* = MC. But free entry forces AC to be equal to *P* in the long run [point *M* in part (b)], for if *P* were not equal to AC, firms would either earn profits or suffer losses. Thus:

When a perfectly competitive industry is in long-run equilibrium, firms maximize profits so that *P* = MC and entry forces the price down until it is tangent to the average-cost curve (*P* = AC). As a result, in competitive equilibrium it is always true that:

$$P = MC = AC.$$

Zero Economic Profit: The Opportunity Cost of Capital

At this point, something may be troubling you. Why would there be any firms in the industry *at all* if there were no profits to be made? What sense does it make to call a position of zero profit a "long-run equilibrium"? The answer is that the zero profit concept used in economics does not mean the same thing that it does in ordinary usage.

As has been noted repeatedly, when economists measure average cost, they include the cost of *all* the firm's inputs, *including the opportunity cost of the capital provided by the firm's owners.* Since the firm may not make explicit payments to those who provide it with capital, this element of cost may not be picked up by the firm's accountants. So what economists call *zero economic profit* may correspond to some positive amount of profit as measured by conventional accounting techniques. For example, if investors can earn 15 percent by lending their funds elsewhere, then the firm must earn a 15 percent rate of return to cover its opportunity cost of capital.

Because economists consider this 15 percent opportunity cost to be the *cost of the firm's capital,* they include it in the AC curve. If the firm cannot earn at least 15 percent on its capital, funds will not be made available to it, because investors can earn greater returns elsewhere. So, in the economist's language, in order to break even—earn zero **economic profit**—a firm must earn enough not only to cover the cost of labour, fuel, and raw materials, but also the cost of its funds, including the opportunity cost of any funds supplied by the owners of the firm.

Economic profit equals net earnings, in the accountant's sense, minus the firm's opportunity cost of capital.

To illustrate the difference between economic profits and accounting profits, suppose Canadian government bonds pay 15 percent, and the owner of a small shop earns 10 percent on her business investment. The shopkeeper might say she is making a 10 percent profit, but an economist would say she is *losing* 5 percent on every dollar she has invested in her business. The reason is that by keeping her money tied up in the firm, she gives up the chance to buy government bonds and receive a 15 percent return. With this explanation of the meaning of economic profit we can now understand the logic behind the zero-profit condition for the long-run industry equilibrium.

Zero profit in the economic sense simply means that firms are earning the normal economy-wide rate of profit in the accounting sense. This condition is guaranteed by freedom of entry and exit.

[4]If the original short-run equilibrium had involved losses instead of profits, firms would have exited from the industry, shifting the industry supply curve inward, until all losses were eradicated and we would end up in a position exactly like Figure 25–9. Exercise: To test your understanding, draw the version of Figure 25–8 that corresponds to this case.

Freedom of entry guarantees that those who invest in a competitive industry will receive a rate of return on their capital *no greater than* the return that capital could earn elsewhere in the economy. If economic profits were being earned in some industry, capital would be attracted. The new capital would shift the industry supply curve to the right, which would drive down prices and profits. This process would continue until the return on capital in this industry was reduced to the return that capital could earn elsewhere—its opportunity cost.

Similarly, freedom of exit of capital guarantees that in the long run, once capital has had a chance to move, no industry will provide a rate of return *lower than* the opportunity cost of capital. For if returns in one industry were particularly low, resources would flow out of it. Plant and equipment would not be replaced as it wore out. As a result, the industry supply curve would shift to the left, and prices and profits would rise toward their opportunity cost level.

Perfect Competition and Economic Efficiency

Economists have long admired perfect competition as a thing of beauty, like one of King Tut's funerary masks (and just as rare!). Adam Smith's invisible hand produces results that are considered *efficient* in a variety of senses that we will examine carefully in the next chapter. But one aspect of the great efficiency of perfect competition follows immediately from the analysis we have just completed.

In long-run competitive equilibrium, every firm produces at the minimum point on its average-cost curve. Thus, the outputs of competitive industries are produced at the lowest possible cost to society.

Why is it always most efficient if each firm in a competitive industry produces at the point where AC is as small as possible? Our example will bring out the point. Suppose the industry is in long-run equilibrium with 9.4 million tonnes of barley being produced by the 2350 farms (each producing 4000 tonnes). This total amount can also be produced by 4700 farms each producing 2000 or by 1880 farms each producing 5000 tonnes. This is so since $2000 \times 4700 = 4000 \times 2350 = 5000 \times 1880 = 9.4$ million. (Of course the job can be done by other numbers of farms, but for simplicity let us consider only these three possibilities.) The AC figures for the farms are as shown in Table 25–4. An output of 4000 tonnes corresponds to the lowest point on the AC curve, with an AC of 60 dollars per tonne. Which is the cheapest way for the industry to produce its 9.4 million tonne output? That is, what is the cost-minimizing number of firms for the job? Looking at the last column of Table 25–4, we see that the 9.4 million tonne output is produced at the least total cost if it is done by 2350 firms each producing the cost-minimizing output of 4000 tonnes.

Why is this so? The answer is not difficult to see. For a given industry output, it is obvious that total industry cost will be as small as possible if and only if AC for each firm is as small as possible, that is, if the number of firms doing the job is

Table 25–4
AVERAGE COST FOR THE FIRM AND TOTAL COST FOR THE INDUSTRY

FIRM'S OUTPUT (thousands of tonnes)	FIRM'S AVERAGE COST (thousands of dollars)	NUMBER OF FIRMS	INDUSTRY OUTPUT (millions of tonnes)	TOTAL INDUSTRY COST (millions of dollars)
2	70	4700	9.4	658
4	60	2350	9.4	564
5	64	1880	9.4	601.6

such that each is producing the output at which AC is as low as possible.

That this kind of cost efficiency characterizes perfect competition in the long run can be seen in Figures 25-8 and 25-9. Before full long-run equilibrium is reached (Figure 25-8), firms may not be producing in the least costly way. For example, the 5 million tonnes being produced by 1000 firms at points *e* and *E* in Figures 25-8(a) and (b) could be produced more cheaply by more firms, each producing a smaller volume, because the point of minimum average cost lies to the left of point *e* in Figure 25-8(a). This problem is rectified, however, in the long run by entry of new firms seeking profit. We see in Figure 25-9 that after the entry process is complete, every firm is producing at its most efficient (lowest AC) level—4000 tonnes. As Adam Smith might have put it, even though each farmer cares only about his own profits, the barley farming industry as a whole is guided *by an invisible hand* to produce the amount of barley that society wants at the lowest possible cost.

Why Good Weather Can Be Bad for Farmers

The interactions between the competitive firm and the competitive industry that we have just studied permit us to resolve the puzzle with which we began the chapter: Why is it that farm incomes often decline when the harvest is good and increase when the harvest is bad?

First, we should clarify the point. The statement is not that *every* farmer benefits from a drought or a flood. Obviously, these calamities can ruin the particular farmers who are Mother Nature's victims. The claim is that farmers who are not severely affected by bad weather come out ahead, and the reason is not hard to understand.

Once crops are planted, the supply curve of the farming industry is very nearly vertical. The harvest will be almost the same whether the price is high or low. A bumper crop means that the supply curve is far to the right, like S_1S_1 in Figure 25-10, instead of in its "normal" position (which is indicated by S_0S_0 in the figure). Consequently, a bumper crop leads to low prices—equilibrium will be at price P_1 instead of price P_0. As the graph indicates, the drop in price is often quite severe because the demand curves for most farm products are rather *inelastic* (food being a necessity). Each farmer's quantity produced may be increased by the good weather. But because the market price falls *by an even greater percentage*, the

Figure 25-10

THE PROBLEM WITH FARM INCOMES

The demand curve for most farm products is quite inelastic. Thus if good weather conditions lead to a bumper crop (the supply curve shifts outward from S_0S_0 to S_1S_1), the market price typically falls so much that farm income (the product of price times quantity sold) actually declines. Conversely, farm income often rises when the weather is bad and farm prices are high.

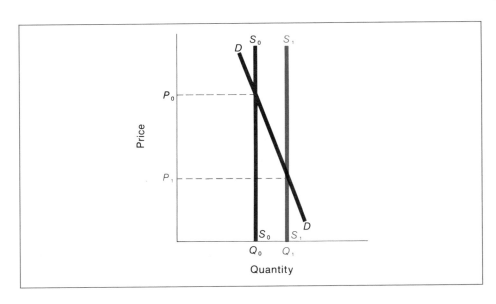

farmer's total income declines.[5] As noted at the outset of this chapter, this often sends farmers scurrying off to Ottawa crying "Foul!"

On the other hand, suppose bad weather damages the crop but that Farmer Jones escapes relatively unscathed. Because of the inelastic market-demand curve, the market price shoots up. (To see this, just use Figure 25–10 in reverse: Suppose S_1S_1 is the supply curve under normal weather conditions and S_0S_0 is the supply curve when the weather is bad.) Farmer Jones's harvest falls slightly, but the price he gets for each unit rises smartly, and Jones comes out ahead of the game.

[5]This is a consequence of the inelasticity of the demand curve. Recall that in Chapter 21 (pages 408–409) we showed that a reduction in price *lowers* total revenue if the demand curve is inelastic. This is the result we are using here.

Summary

1. Markets are classified into several types depending on the number of firms in the industry, the degree of similarity of their products, and the possibility of impediments to entry.
2. The four main market structures are monopoly (single-firm production), oligopoly (production by a few firms), monopolistic competition (production by many firms with somewhat different products), and perfect competition (production by many firms with identical products and free entry and exit).
3. Few industries satisfy the conditions of perfect competition exactly, although some come close. Perfect competition is studied because it is easy to analyse and because it is useful as a yardstick to measure the performance of other market forms.
4. The demand curve of the perfectly competitive firm is horizontal because its output is so small a share of the industry's production that it cannot affect price. With a horizontal demand curve, price, average revenue, and marginal revenue are all equal.
5. The short-run equilibrium of the perfectly competitive firm is at the level of output that maximizes profits; that is, where MC equals MR equals price. This equilibrium may involve either a profit or a loss.
6. The short-run supply curve of the perfectly competitive firm is the portion of its marginal-cost curve that lies above its average variable-cost curve.
7. The industry's short-run supply curve under perfect competition is the horizontal sum of the supply curves of all its firms.
8. In the long run, freedom of entry forces the perfectly competitive firm to earn zero economic profit; that is, no more than the firm's capital could earn elsewhere (the opportunity cost of the capital).
9. Industry equilibrium under perfect competition is at the point of intersection of the industry supply-and-demand curves.
10. In long-run equilibrium under perfect competition, the firm's output is chosen so that average cost, marginal cost, and price are all equal. Output is at the point of minimum average cost, and the firm's demand curve is tangent to its average-cost curve at its minimum point.

Concepts for Review

Market	Price taker	Supply curve of the firm
Perfect competition	Horizontal demand curve	Supply curve of the industry
Pure monopoly	Short-run equilibrium	Long-run equilibrium
Monopolistic competition	Average variable cost	Opportunity cost
Oligopoly	Total variable cost	Economic profit

Questions for Discussion

1. Explain why a perfectly competitive firm does not expand its sales without limit if its horizontal demand curve means that it can sell as much as it wants to at the current market price.
2. Explain why a demand curve is also a curve of average revenue. Recalling that when an average-

revenue curve is neither rising nor falling, marginal revenue must equal average revenue, explain why it is always true that $P = MR = AR$ for the perfectly competitive firm.

3. Explain why in the short-run equilibrium of the perfectly competitive firm $P = MC$, while in long-run equilibrium $P = MC = AC$.

4. Which of the four attributes of perfect competition (many small firms, freedom of entry, standardized product, perfect information) are primarily responsible for the fact that the demand curve of a perfectly competitive firm is horizontal?

5. Which of the four attributes of perfect competition is primarily responsible for the firm's zero economic profits in long-run equilibrium?

6. It is indicated in the text (page 497) that the MC curve cuts the AVC curve at the *minimum* point of the latter. Explain why this must be so. (*Hint:* Since marginal costs are by definition, all variable costs, the MC curve can be considered the curve of *marginal variable* costs. Apply the general relationships between marginals and averages explained in Chapter 23).

7. Explain why it is not sensible to close a business firm if it earns zero economic profits.

8. If the firm's lowest average cost is $7 and the corresponding average variable cost is $4, what does it pay a perfectly competitive firm to do if:
   a. The market price is $8?
   b. The price is $6?
   c. The price is $3?

9. If the market price in a competitive industry is above its equilibrium level, what would you expect to happen?

10. (More difficult.) A few years ago when oil prices were very high, it was proposed to mix alcohol distilled from grain with gasoline to make "gasohol." This obviously would have caused an upward shift in the demand for grain. Use Figure 25–9 to analyse the effects on barley-growing profit and output
    a. in the short run.
    b. in the long run.

The Price System and the Case for Laissez Faire

26

If there existed the universal mind that ... would register simultaneously all the processes of nature and of society, that could forecast the results of their inter-reactions, such a mind ... could ... draw up a faultless and an exhaustive economic plan. ... In truth, the bureaucracy often conceives that just such a mind is at its disposal; that is why it so easily frees itself from the control of the market.

LEON TROTSKY (a leader of the Russian Revolution)

E arly in the book, we posed a question that provides an organizing framework for our study of microeconomics: What does the market do well, and what does it do poorly? Given what we have learned about demand in Chapters 20 and 21 and about supply in Chapters 22–25, we are now in a position to offer a fairly comprehensive answer to the first part of this question: What does the market do well?

We begin by returning to two important themes raised in Chapters 3 and 4: First, that because all resources are scarce, it is critical to utilize them *efficiently*; second, that an economy must have some way to *co-ordinate* the actions of many individual consumers and producers. Specifically, we emphasize that society must somehow choose *how much* of each good to produce, *what input quantities* to use in the production process, and *how to distribute* the resulting outputs among consumers.

As the opening quotation suggests, these tasks are exceedingly difficult for central planners to accomplish effectively. But they are rather simple for a market system, which is why observers with philosophies as diverse as those of Adam Smith and Leon Trotsky have been admirers of the market. But the chapter should not be misinterpreted as a piece of salesmanship, for that is not its purpose.

The version of the price system we shall study here is an idealized one in which every good is produced under the exacting conditions of perfect competition. While, as we have seen, a few industries are reasonable approximations to perfect competition, other industries in our economy are as different from this idealized world as the physical world is from a frictionless vacuum tube. But just as the physicist uses the vacuum tube to illustrate the laws of gravity with a clarity that is otherwise unattainable, the economist uses the theoretical concept of a perfectly competitive economy to illustrate the virtues of the market. There will be plenty of time in later chapters to study its vices.

Efficient Resource Allocation: The Concept

The fundamental fact of scarcity limits the volume of goods and services that any economic system can produce. In Chapter 3 we illustrated the concept of scarcity with a graphical device called a *production possibilities frontier*, which we repeat here for convenience as Figure 26-1. The frontier, curve *BC*, depicts all combinations of manufactured goods and clean air that this society can produce given the limited resources at its disposal. For example, if it decides to use pollution control devices to maintain an air quality level of 20 on the pollution index, it will have enough resources left over to produce *no more than* $500 billion of manufactured goods (point *D*). Of course, it is always possible to produce fewer than $500 billion of manufactured goods—at a point, such as *G*, below the production possibilities frontier. But if society does this, it is wasting some of its productive potential; that is, it is not operating *efficiently*.

In Chapter 3 we defined efficiency rather loosely as the absence of waste. Since the main subject of this chapter is how a competitive market economy allocates resources efficiently, we now need a more precise definition. It is easiest to define an **efficient allocation of resources** by saying what it is *not*. Suppose it were possible to rearrange things so that some people would have more of the things they want and no one would have to give up anything. Then failure to change the allocation of resources to take advantage of this opportunity would surely be wasteful—that is, *inefficient*. When there are no such possibilities for reallocating resources to make some people better off without making anyone else worse off, we say that the allocation of resources is *efficient*.

Figure 26-1 illustrates the idea. Points below the frontier, like *G*, are inefficient because, if we start at *G*, we can make *both* clean-air lovers *and* material-consumption lovers better off by moving to a point *on* the frontier, like *E*. Thus *no point below the frontier* can represent an efficient allocation of resources. By contrast, *every point on the frontier* is efficient because, no matter where on the frontier we start, it is impossible to get more of one good without giving up some of the other.

> An **efficient allocation of resources** is one that takes advantage of every opportunity to make some individuals better off in their own estimation while not worsening the lot of anyone else.

Figure 26-1

THE PRODUCTION POSSIBILITIES FRONTIER AND EFFICIENCY

Every point on the production possibilities frontier, *BC*, represents an efficient allocation of resources, because it is impossible to get more of one item without giving up some of the other. Points below the frontier, like *G*, are inefficient, since it is possible to obtain more of both goods.

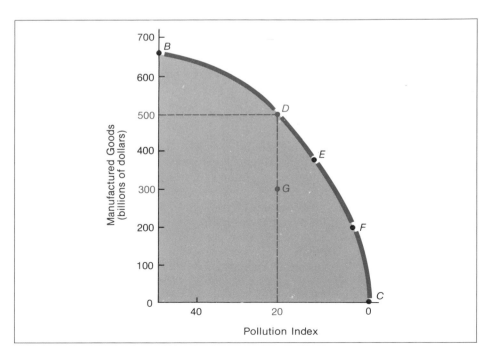

This example brings out two important features of the concept of efficiency. First, it is strictly a technical concept; there are no value judgments stated or implied, and tastes are not questioned. An economy is judged efficient if it is good at producing *whatever* people want. Thus the economy in the example is just as efficient when it produces only manufactured goods at point *B* as when it produces only pollution control devices at point *C*.

Second, there are normally *many* efficient allocations of resources; in the example, *every* point on frontier *BC* is efficient. As a rule, the concept of efficiency does not permit us to tell which allocation is "best" for society. In fact, the most amazing thing about the concept of efficiency is that it gets us anywhere at all. At first blush, the criterion seems vacuous. It seems to assert, in effect, that anything agreed to unanimously is desirable. If some people are made better off *in their own estimation*, and none are harmed, then society is certainly better off by anyone's definition. Yet, as we shall see in this chapter, the concept of efficiency can be used to formulate surprisingly detailed rules to steer us away from situations in which resources are being wasted.

Scarcity and the Need to Co-ordinate Economic Decisions

An economy may be thought of as a complex machine with literally millions of component parts. If this machine is to function efficiently, some way must be found to make the parts work in harmony.

A consumer in Calgary may decide to purchase two dozen eggs, and on the same day similar decisions are made by thousands of shoppers throughout the country. None of these purchasers knows or cares about the decisions of the others. Yet, scarcity requires that these demands must somehow be co-ordinated with the production process so that the total quantity of eggs demanded does not exceed the total quantity supplied. The supermarkets, wholesalers, shippers, and chicken farmers must somehow arrive at consistent decisions, for otherwise the economic process will deteriorate into chaos. And there are many other such decisions that must be co-ordinated. One cannot run machines that are completed except for a few parts that have not been delivered. Refrigerators and cars cannot be used unless there is an adequate supply of fuel.

In an economy that is planned and centrally directed, it is easy to imagine how such co-ordination takes place—though the implementation turns out to be far more difficult than the idea. Central planners set production targets for firms and may even tell firms how to meet these targets. In extreme cases, consumers may even be told, rather than asked, what they want to consume.

In a market system, prices are used to co-ordinate economic activity instead. High prices discourage consumption of the resources that are most scarce while low prices encourage consumption of the resources that are comparatively abundant. For example, if supplies of oil begin to run out while enormous reserves of coal remain, the price of oil can be expected to rise in comparison with the price of coal. As the price of oil rises, only those for whom oil offers the greatest benefits will continue to buy it. Firms or individuals that can get along almost equally well with coal or gas will switch to these more economical fuels. Some business firms will transform their equipment, and new homes will be built with heating systems that use gas. Only those who find alternative fuels a poor or unacceptable substitute for oil will continue to use oil despite its higher price. In this way, prices are the instrument used by Adam Smith's invisible hand to organize the economy's production.

The invisible hand has an astonishing capacity to handle a co-ordination problem of truly enormous proportions—one that will remain beyond the capabilities of computers at least for the foreseeable future. It is true that like any mechanism this one has its imperfections, some of them rather serious. But without understanding the nature of the overall task performed by the market system, it is all too easy to lose sight of the tremendously demanding task that it constantly accomplishes—unnoticed, undirected, and at least in some respects, amazingly well. Let us, then, examine in more detail just what this co-ordination problem is like.

Three Co-ordination Tasks in the Economy

We noted in Chapter 3 that any economic system, whether planned or unplanned, must find answers to three basic questions of resource allocation:

1. **Output Selection**: How much of each commodity should be produced?
2. **Production Planning**: What quantities of each of the available inputs should be used to produce each good?
3. **Distribution**: How should the resulting products be divided among the consumers?

Let us look at how each of these questions is answered by a system of free and unfettered markets, the method of economic organization that the eighteenth-century French economists named **laissez faire**. Under laissez faire, the government would prevent crime, enforce contracts, and build roads and other types of public works, but it would not set prices and would interfere as little as possible with the operation of free markets. How does such an unmanaged economy solve the three co-ordination problems?

Laissez faire refers to a program of minimal interference with the workings of the market system. The term means that people should be left alone in carrying out their economic affairs.

Output Selection

In a free-market system, the price mechanism decides what to produce via what we have called the "law" of supply and demand. Where there is a *shortage*—that is, where quantity demanded exceeds quantity supplied—the market mechanism pushes the price up, thereby encouraging more production and less consumption of the commodity in short supply. Where there is a *surplus*—that is, where quantity supplied exceeds quantity demanded—the same mechanism works in reverse: The price falls, which discourages production and stimulates consumption.

We can make these abstract ideas more concrete by looking at a particular example. Suppose millions of people wake up one morning with a craving for omelettes. For the moment, the quantity of eggs demanded exceeds the quantity supplied. But within days the market mechanism swings into action to meet this sudden change in demand. The price of eggs rises, which stimulates the production of eggs. In the first instance, farmers simply bring more eggs to market by taking them out of storage. Over a somewhat longer period of time, chickens that otherwise would have been sold for meat are kept in the chicken coops laying eggs. Finally, if the high price of eggs persists, farmers begin to increase their flocks, build more cages, and so on. Thus, a shift in consumer demand leads to a shift in society's resources; more eggs are wanted, and so the market mechanism sees to it that more of society's resources are devoted to the production of eggs.

Similar reactions follow if a technological breakthrough reduces the input quantities needed to produce some item. Electronic calculators are a marvellous example. Only 15 years ago, calculators were so expensive that they could be found only in business firms and scientific laboratories. Then advances in science and engineering reduced their cost dramatically, and the market went to work. With costs sharply reduced, prices fell dramatically and the quantity demanded skyrocketed. Electronics firms flocked into the industry to meet this demand, which is to say that more of society's resources were devoted to producing the calculators that were suddenly in such great demand. These examples lead us to conclude that:

Under laissez faire, the allocation of society's resources among different products depends on two basic influences: consumer preferences and the relative difficulty of producing the goods, that is, their production costs. Prices vary so as to bring the quantity of each commodity produced into line with the quantity demanded.

Notice that no bureaucrat or central planner arranges the allocation of resources. Instead, allocation is guided by an unseen force—the lure of profits, which is the invisible hand that guides chicken farmers to increase their flocks when eggs are in greater demand and guides electronics firms to build new factories when the cost of electronic products falls.

Production Planning

Once the composition of output has been decided, the next co-ordination task is to determine just how those goods are going to be produced. The production-planning problem includes, among other things, the assignment of inputs to enterprises—that is, which farm or factory will get how much of which materials. These decisions can be crucial. If a factory runs short of an essential input, the entire production process may grind to a halt.

As a matter of fact, inputs and outputs cannot be selected separately. The inputs assigned to the growing of coffee rather than to bananas determine the quantities of coffee and bananas that can be obtained. However, it is simpler to think of these decisions as if they occurred one at a time.

Once again, under laissez faire it is the price system that apportions fuels and other raw materials among the different industries in accord with those industries' requirements. The firm that needs a piece of equipment most urgently will be the last to drop out of the market for that product when prices rise. If more grain is demanded by millers than is currently available, the price will rise and bring quantity demanded back into line with quantity supplied, always giving priority to those users who are willing to pay the most for grain. Thus:

In a free market, inputs are assigned to the firms that can make the most productive (most profitable) use of them. Firms that cannot make a sufficiently productive use of some input will be priced out of the market for that item.

This task, which sounds so simple, is actually almost unimaginably complex. It is also one on which many centrally planned systems have floundered. We will return to it shortly, as an illustration of how difficult it is to replace the market by a central planning bureau. But first let us consider the third of our three co-ordination problems.

Distribution of Products Among Consumers

The third task of any economy is to decide which consumer gets each of the goods that have been produced. The objective is to distribute the available supplies so as to match the differing preferences of consumers as well as possible. Coffee lovers must not be flooded with tea while tea drinkers are showered with coffee.

The price mechanism solves this problem by assigning the highest prices to the goods in greatest demand and then letting individual consumers pursue their own self-interests. Consider our example of the rising price of eggs. As the price of eggs rises, those whose craving for omelettes is not terribly strong will begin to buy fewer eggs. In effect, the price acts as a rationing device, which apportions the available eggs among the consumers who are willing to pay the most for them.

But the price mechanism has one important advantage over other rationing devices: It is able to pay attention to consumer preferences. If eggs are rationed by the most obvious and usual means (say, two to a person), everyone ends up with the same quantity—whether he thinks eggs the more unpleasant component of his breakfast or the ingredients of his evening's soufflé, for which he pines all day

In this cartoon from a Soviet humour magazine, one construction worker comments to another, "A slight mistake in the plans, perhaps."

long. The price system, on the other hand, permits each consumer to set his own priorities. If you just barely tolerate eggs, a rise in their price quickly induces you to get your protein from some other source. But the egg lover is not induced to switch so readily. Thus:

The price system carries out the distribution process by rationing goods on the basis of preferences *and relative incomes.*

Notice the last three words. This rationing process *does* favour the rich, and this is a problem that market economies must confront. However, we may still want to think twice before declaring ourselves opposed to the price system. If equality is our goal, might not a more reasonable solution be to use the tax system to equalize incomes, and *then* let the market mechanism distribute goods in accord with preferences?

We have just seen, in broad outline, how a laissez-faire economy addresses the three basic issues of resource allocation: what to produce, how to produce it, and how to distribute the resulting products. Since it performs these tasks quietly, without central direction and with no apparent concern for the public interest, many radical critics have predicted that such an unplanned system must degenerate into chaos. Yet that does not seem to be the way things work out. Unplanned the market may be, but its results are far from chaotic. In fact, quite ironically, it is the centrally planned economies that often find themselves in economic chaos. Perhaps the best way to appreciate the accomplishments of the market is to consider how a centrally planned system copes with the three co-ordination problems we have just outlined. For this purpose, we will concentrate on just one of them: production planning.

Input–Output Analysis: The Near Impossibility of Perfect Central Planning

Of the three co-ordination tasks of any economy, the assignment of inputs to specific industries and firms has claimed the most attention of central planners. The reason is this: Because the production processes of the various industries are *interdependent*, the whole economy can grind to a halt if the production-planning problem is not solved satisfactorily.

Let's take a simple example. Gasoline is used both by consumers to run cars and by the trucking industry. Unless the planners allocate enough gasoline to trucking, products will not get to market, and unless they allocate enough trucks to haul the gasoline to gas stations, consumers will not be able to get to the market to buy the products. Thus, trucking activity depends on gasoline production but gasoline production depends on trucking activity. We seem to be caught in a circle. Although it turns out not to be a vicious circle, both problems must be dealt with together, not separately.

Because the output required from any one industry depends on the output desired from every other industry, planners can be sure that the production of the various outputs is sufficient to meet both consumer and industrial demands only by taking explicit account of the interdependencies among industries. If they change the output target for one industry, every other industry's output target also must be adjusted.

For example, if planners decide to provide consumers with more electricity, then more steel must be produced for more electric generators. But an increase in steel output requires more coal to be mined. More mining in turn means that still more electricity is needed to light the mines, to run the elevators, and perhaps even to run some of the trains that carry the coal, and so on and so on. Any single change in production sets off a chain of adjustments throughout the economy that require still further adjustments.

To decide how much of each output an economy must produce, the planner must use statistics to form a set of equations, one equation for each product, and then solve those equations *simultaneously*. (The simultaneous solution process prevents the circularity of the analysis—electricity output depends on steel production but steel output depends on electricity production—from becoming a vicious circle.) The technique used to solve these complicated equations—**input-output analysis**—was invented by economist Wassily Leontief, and it won him the Nobel Prize in 1973.

The equations of input-output analysis, which are illustrated in the boxed insert on page 514, take account of the interdependence among industries by describing precisely how each industry's target output depends on every other industry's target. Only by solving these equations *simultaneously* for the required outputs of electricity, steel, coal, and so on, can one be sure of a consistent solution that produces the required amounts of each product—including the amount of each product needed to produce every other product.

The example of input-output analysis that appears in the box is not provided so that you can learn how to apply the technique yourself. Its real purpose is to illustrate the *very complicated* nature of the problem that faces a central planner. For the problem faced by a real planner, while analogous to the one in the box, is enormously more complex. In any real economy, the number of commodities is far greater than the three outputs in the example. In Canada, some large manufacturing companies individually deal in hundreds of items, and keep thousands of different items in inventory. In planning, it is ultimately necessary to make calculations for each such item. It is not enough to plan the right number of bolts *in total*; we must make sure that the required number *of each size* is produced. (Try to put five million large bolts into five million small nuts.) So, to be sure our plans will really work, we need a separate equation for every size of bolt and one for every size and type of nut. But then, to replicate the analysis described in the boxed insert, we will have to solve simultaneously several *million* equations! Unfortunately, there is as yet no computer capable of doing this.

Worse still is the data problem. Each of our three equations requires *three* pieces of statistical information, making 3×3, or 9, numbers in total. This is because the equation for electricity must indicate on the basis of statistical information how much electricity is needed in steel production, how much in coal

Input–Output Equations: An Example

Imagine an economy with only three outputs: electricity, steel, and coal; and let E, S, and C represent the dollar value of their respective outputs. Suppose that for every dollar's worth of steel, $0.20 worth of electricity is used up, so that the total electricity demand of steel manufacturers is $0.2S$. Similarly, assume the coal manufacturers use up $0.30 of electricity in producing $1 worth of coal, or a total of $0.3C$ units of electricity. Since E dollars of electricity are produced in total, the amount left over for consumers, after subtraction of industrial demands for fuel, will be

$$E \quad - \quad 0.2S \quad - \quad 0.3C$$

(available   (use in steel   (use in coal
electricity)   production)   production)

Suppose further that the central planners have decided to supply $15 million worth of electricity to consumers.

We end up with the electricity output equation

$$E - 0.2S - 0.3C = 15.$$

The planner will also need such an equation for each of the two other industries, specifying for each of them the net amounts intended to be left for consumers after the industrial uses of these products. The full set of equations might then be:

$$E - 0.2S - 0.3C = 15$$
$$S - 0.1E - 0.06C = 7$$
$$C - 0.15E - 0.4S = 10.$$

These are typical equations in an input–output analysis. Only, in practice, a typical analysis has dozens and sometimes hundreds of equations with similar numbers of unknowns. This, then, is the logic of input–output analysis.

production, and how much is demanded by consumers. Therefore, in a five-industry analysis, 5×5, or 25, pieces of data are needed, a 100-industry analysis requires 100^2, or 10,000 numbers, and a million-item input–output study might need one *trillion* pieces of information. The data-gathering problems are therefore no easy task, to put it mildly. There are still other complications, but we have seen enough to conclude that:

A full, rigorous central-planning solution to the production problem is a tremendous task, requiring an overwhelming quantity of information and some incredibly difficult calculations. Yet this very difficult job is carried out automatically and unobtrusively by the price mechanism in a free-market economy.

Can Price Increases Ever Serve the Public Interest?

This last discussion raises a point that people untrained in economics always find difficult to accept: *low prices may not always be in the public interest.* The reason is clear enough. If a price is set "too low" (for example, the price of using a crowded airport or the price of oil), then consumers will receive the "wrong" signals. They will be encouraged to crowd the airport even more (at the congested times) or to consume more oil, thereby squandering society's precious resources. A historic illustration is perhaps the most striking way to bring out the point. In 1834, some ten years before the great potato famine caused unspeakable misery and death by starvation and brought so many people from Ireland to North America, a professor of economics named Mountifort Longfield lectured at the University of Dublin about the price system. He offered the following remarkable illustration of his point:

Suppose the crop of potatoes in Ireland was to fall short in some year one-sixth of the usual consumption. If [there were no] increase of price, the whole ... supply of the year would be exhausted in ten months, and for the remaining two months a scene of misery and famine beyond description would ensue. ... But when prices [increase] the sufferers [often believe] that it is not caused by scarcity. ... They suppose that there are provisions enough, but that the distress is caused by the

Pricing to Promote Efficiency: An Example

So far, we have only indicated in a general way how the market mechanism under perfect competition leads to economic efficiency. Let us now give an intuitive picture of the connection between pricing and efficiency, using a real-life example—the prices that are charged to use Canada's airports.

Congested airports have caused some of the most bitter squabbles about resource use. For example, Montreal's Dorval airport has long been congested *at peak times* (such as 5:00 P.M. on Fridays) but not at other times (such as the middle of Thursday afternoons). Because of the crowding that sometimes occurred, the federal government built the extremely underutilized Mirabel airport. It is fair to say that essentially no one denies the dramatic wastage of resources that was involved. A similar scenario developed in Toronto. Congestion at certain peak times at the Pearson airport led to a federal government decision to build a second airport at Pickering. All the required land was expropriated, but in the end, the Ontario government refused to provide certain necessary services to allow the second airport to go ahead. There was much bitterness between the governments and among the many individuals involved.

Most of this frustration and wastage has followed from the presumption that airport congestion must be approached from a purely technical point of view. Officials simply do not question the assumption that more runways, more parking and terminal facilities, and more efficient methods of refuelling and loading are the answers.

The problem is that *all* of these aspects of the issue involve resources that are not currently priced on any market. Transport Canada issues a complete book to airport administrations entitled "Air Service Fee Regulations." In it, the charges for landings, take-offs, plane parking, bridges (the structures used for passengers to enter the planes), and various aspects of terminal use are listed. These charges depend on all kinds of things, such as: whether the flight is domestic, trans-border, or transocean; the type of engine on the airplane; and the gross take-off weight of the aircraft. However, *none* of the fees depends at all on the economic value of the use of the airport. Consequently, a very few passengers in a small private aircraft can pay the current (1984) landing fee (at Toronto's Pearson airport) of $5.00 and significantly add to congestion at peak times. This is quite a general problem. At the 60 airports in Canada that have Transport-Canada-operated control towers, 55 percent of the take-offs and landings involve planes weighing less than 2 tons. Less than 4 percent of the take-offs and landings involve the larger aircraft like 747s and DC-10s.

To an economist, the problem of peak load congestion at airports is an obvious outcome of improper pricing. Airport charges for services should differ among airports and among times of the week and year. There should be low prices during hours when space is abundant and higher prices during rush hours when space is scarce. Such a variable price structure would provide the incentive for those who can conveniently change times or location (for example, use the airport at Hamilton instead of Toronto) to do so. As a result, use of the airport could be switched away from the congested periods with the least total sacrifice. This flexibility is precluded by the current rigid price structure. The result is much wastage, including airport lands that could have been (or were) used for farms, homes, parks, productive industries, or simply open space near the cities.

insatiable rapacity of the possessors ... [and] they have generally succeeded in obtaining laws against [the price increases] ... which alone can prevent the provisions from being entirely consumed long before a new supply can be obtained.[1]

Longfield's reasoning can usefully be rephrased. If the crop fails, potatoes become scarcer. If society is to use its very scarce resources efficiently, it must cut back on the consumption of potatoes—which is just what rising prices would do *automatically* if the market mechanism were left to its own devices. However, if the price is held artificially low, then consumers will be using society's resources

[1]Mountifort Longfield, *Lectures on Political Economy* (Dublin, 1834), pages 53–56.

inefficiently. In this case, the inefficiency shows up in the form of famine and suffering when the year's crop is consumed months before the next crop arrives.

It is not easy to accept the notion that higher prices can serve the public interest better than lower ones. Politicians who voice this view are put in the position of the proverbial father who, before spanking his child, announces, "This is going to hurt me much more than it hurts you!" Since advocacy of higher prices courts political disaster, the political system often rejects the market solution when resources suddenly become more scarce.

The pricing of oil in Canada in the 1970s provided an excellent example. For years after OPEC drastically increased the price of oil in 1973, legislation in Canada held domestic oil prices below free-market levels. The consequence, as economists were quick to point out, was that Canadian consumers faced a market price for oil that was below the true marginal cost of oil to society. Consumers were therefore encouraged to use too much oil, and our dependence on imported oil increased. Suggestions to end the price controls were rebuffed by lawmakers who feared the political consequences. John Crosbie's Budget during Joe Clark's brief government was an exception, since it involved a dramatic increase in domestic oil prices. Ontario voters in particular registered their disapproval and the government was replaced.

Prevention of a rise in prices where a rise is appropriate can have serious consequences indeed. We have seen from Longfield's example that it can contribute to famine. We know that it caused nationwide chaos in gasoline distribution in the United States after the sudden fall in Iranian oil exports in 1979. It has contributed to the surrender of cities under military siege when effective price ceilings discouraged the efforts of those who were taking the risk of smuggling food supplies through enemy lines. And it has discouraged the construction of housing in cities, when rent controls made building a losing proposition.

 Recall from Chapter 4 that one of the **12 Ideas for Beyond the Final Exam** states that interfering with free markets by preventing price increases can sometimes serve the public very badly. In extreme cases it can even produce havoc—undermining production and causing extreme shortages of vitally needed products. The reason is that prohibiting price increases in situations of true scarcity prevents the market mechanism from reallocating resources to help cut down the shortage efficiently. The invisible hand is not permitted to do its work.

Of course there are cases in which it is appropriate to resist price increases—where unrestrained monopoly would otherwise succeed in gouging the public; where taxes are imposed on products capriciously and inappropriately; and where rising prices fall so heavily on the poor that rationing becomes the more acceptable option. But it is important to recognize that artificial restrictions on prices can produce serious and even tragic consequences—consequences that should be taken into account before a decision is made to tamper with the market mechanism.

Perfect Competition and Efficiency: What to Produce

Earlier in the chapter we indicated how the market mechanism solves the three basic co-ordination problems of any economy—what to produce, how to produce, and how to distribute the goods to consumers. And we suggested that these same tasks pose almost insurmountable difficulties for central planners. One critical question remains. Is the allocation of resources that the market mechanism selects *efficient*, according to the precise definition of efficiency presented earlier in this chapter? The answer is that, under the idealized circumstances of perfect competition, it is. Since a detailed proof of this assertion for all three co-ordination tasks would be long and time-consuming, we will present the proof only for the first of the three tasks—output selection. The corresponding analyses for the production planning and distribution problems are quite similar and are reserved for the appendix.

Our question is this: Given the output combination selected by the market mechanism, is it possible to improve matters by producing more of one good and less of another? Might it be "better," for example, if society produced more beef and less lamb? We shall answer this question in the negative, thus showing that, at least in theory, perfect competition does guarantee efficiency in production.

We will do this in two steps. First, we will derive a criterion for efficient output selection, that is, a test which tells us whether or not production is being carried out efficiently. Second, we will examine why that test is *automatically* passed by the prices that emerge from the market mechanism under perfect competition.

Step 1: Rule for Efficient Output Selection

We begin by stating the rule for efficient output selection:

Efficiency in the choice of output quantities requires that, for each of the economy's outputs, the marginal cost (MC) of the last unit produced be equal to the marginal utility (MU) of the last unit consumed.[2] In symbols:

$$MC = MU.$$

Let us use an example to see why this rule *must* be satisfied for the allocation of resources to be efficient. Suppose the marginal utility of an additional pound of beef to consumers is $8, while its marginal cost is only $5. Then the value of the resources that would have to be used up to produce one more pound of beef (its MC) would be $3 less than the money value of that additional pound to consumers (its MU). In a sense, society could get more (the MU) out of the economic production process than it was putting in (the MC) by increasing the output of beef by one pound. Because an increase in output must be an improvement for society, the initial output cannot be optimal.

The opposite is true if the MC of beef exceeds the MU of beef. In that case, the last pound of beef must have used up more value (MC) than it produced (MU). It would therefore be better to have less beef and more of something else.

We have therefore shown that, if there is *any* product for which MU is not equal to MC, the economy must be wasting an opportunity to produce a net improvement in consumers' welfare. This is exactly what we mean by using resources *inefficiently*. Just as was true at point G in Figure 26–1, if MC ≠ MU for any commodity, it is possible to rearrange things so as to make some people better off while harming no one. It follows that efficiency in the choice of outputs is achieved only when MC = MU for *every* good.

Step 2: The Critical Role of the Price System

The next step in the argument is to show that under perfect competition the price system *automatically* leads buyers and sellers to behave in a way that makes MU and MC equal. To see this, recall from the last chapter that under perfect competition it is most profitable for each beef-producing firm to produce the quantity of beef at which the marginal cost of the beef is equal to the price of beef:

$$MC = P.$$

---

[2]It will be recalled from Chapter 20 that we measure marginal utility in money terms, that is, as the amount of money that a consumer is willing to give up for an additional unit of the commodity. Economists usually call this the marginal rate of substitution between the commodity and money.

This must be so because, if the marginal cost of beef were less than the price, the farmer could add to his profits by increasing the size of his herd (or the amount of grain that he feeds his animals); and the reverse would be true if the marginal cost of beef were greater than its price. Thus, under perfect competition, the lure of profits leads each producer of beef (and of every other product) to supply the quantity that makes MC = P.

We also learned, in Chapter 20, that it is in the interest of each consumer to purchase the quantity of beef at which the marginal utility of beef in terms of money is equal to the price of beef:

$$MU = P.$$

If he did not do this, we saw, either an increase or a decrease in his purchase of beef would leave him better off.

Putting these last two equations together, we see that the invisible hand enforces the following string of equalities:

$$MC = P = MU.$$

But if both the MC of beef and the MU of beef are equal to the same price, P, then they must surely be equal to each other. That is, it must be true that the quantity of beef produced and consumed in a perfectly competitive market satisfies the equation:

$$MC = MU,$$

which is precisely our rule for efficient output selection. Since the same must be true of every other product supplied by a competitive industry:

Under perfect competition, the unco-ordinated decisions of producers and consumers can be expected *automatically* to produce a quantity of each good that satisfies the MC = MU rule for efficiency in deciding what to produce. That is, under the idealized conditions of perfect competition, the market mechanism, *without any government intervention*, is capable of allocating society's scarce resources efficiently.

The Invisible Hand at Work

This is truly a remarkable result. How can the price mechanism automatically satisfy all the exacting requirements for efficiency—requirements that no central planner can hope to handle because of the masses of statistics and the enormous calculations they require? The conclusion seems analogous to the rabbit suddenly pulled from the magician's hat. But, as always, rabbits come out of hats only if they were hidden there in the first place. What really is the machinery by which our act of magic works?

The secret is that the price system lets consumers and producers pursue their own best interests—something they are probably very good at doing. Prices are the dollar costs of commodities to consumers. So, in pursuing their own best interests, consumers will buy the commodities that give them the most satisfaction *per dollar*. As we learned in Chapter 20, this means that each consumer will continue to buy beef until the marginal utility of beef is equal to the market price. And since every consumer pays the same price in a perfectly competitive market, the market mechanism ensures that *every* consumer's MU will be equal to this common price.

Turning next to the producers, we know from Chapter 25 that competition equates prices with marginal costs. And, once again, since every producer faces the same market price, the force of competition will bring the MC of *every* producer into equality with this common price. Since MC measures the resource cost (in every firm) of producing one more unit of the good and MU measures the money value (to every consumer) of consuming one more unit, then when MC = MU *the cost of the good to society is exactly equal to the value that consumers place on it.* Therefore:

When all prices are set equal to marginal costs, the price system is giving the correct cost signals to consumers. It has set prices at levels that induce consumers to use the resources of society with the same care they devote to watching their own money.

This is the magic of the invisible hand. Unlike central planners, consumers need not know how difficult it is to manufacture a certain product, nor how scarce are the inputs required by the production process. Everything the consumer needs to know to make his or her decision is embodied in the market price, which, under perfect competition, accurately reflects marginal costs.

Other Roles of Prices: Income Distribution and Fairness

So far we have stressed the role of prices most emphasized by economists: Prices guide the allocation of resources. But a different role of prices often commands the spotlight in public discussions: Prices influence the distribution of income between buyers and sellers. For example, high rents often make tenants poorer and landlords richer.

This rather obvious role of prices draws the most attention from the public, politicians, and regulators, and is one we should not lose sight of.[3] Markets only serve demands that are backed up by consumers' desire *and ability* to pay. Though the market system may do well in serving a poor family, giving that family more food and clothing than a less efficient economy would provide, it offers far more to the family of a millionaire. Many observers object that such an arrangement represents a great injustice, however efficient it may be.

Often, recommendations made by economists for improving the economy's efficiency are opposed on the grounds that they are unfair. For example, economists frequently advocate higher prices for transportation facilities at the time of day when they are most crowded. They propose a pricing arrangement called *peak, off-peak pricing* under which prices for public transportation are higher during rush hours than during other hours.

The rationale for this proposal should be clear from our discussion of efficiency, and the Pearson Airport example discussed earlier in this chapter (page 515). A seat on a train is a much scarcer resource during rush hours than during other times of the day when the trains run fairly empty. Thus, according to the principles of efficiency outlined in this chapter, seats should be more expensive during rush hours to discourage consumers from using the trains during peak periods. The same notion applies to other services. Charges for nighttime long-distance telephone calls are lower than those in the daytime and, in some places, electricity is sold more cheaply at night, when demand does not strain the supplier's generating capacity.

Yet the proposal that higher fares should be charged for public transportation during peak hours—say, from 8:00 A.M. to 9:30 A.M., and from 4:30 P.M. to 6 P.M.—often runs into stiff opposition on the grounds that most of the burden will fall on lower-income working people who have no choice about the timing of their trips. For example, a survey in Great Britain of members of Parliament and of economists found that while high peak-period fares were favored by 88 percent of the economists, only 35 percent of the Conservative Party M.P.'s and just 19 percent of

[3]Income distribution is the subject of Part Seven.

Table 26-1

REPLIES TO A QUESTIONNAIRE

QUESTION: In order to make the most efficient use of a city's resources, how should subway and bus fares vary during the day?	Economists (percent)	Conservative Party M.P.'s (percent)	Labour Party M.P.'s (percent)
a. They should be relatively low during rush hour to transport as many people as possible at lower costs.	1	—	40
b. They should be the same at all times to avoid making travellers alter their schedules because of price differences.	4	60	39
c. They should be relatively high during rush hour to minimize the amount of equipment needed to transport the daily travellers.	88	35	19
d. Impossible to answer on the data and alternatives given.	7	5	2

SOURCE: Adapted from Samuel Brittan, *Is There an Economic Consensus?* (London: Macmillan, 1973), page 93.

the Labour Party M.P.'s approved of this arrangement (see Table 26-1). We may surmise that the M.P.'s reflected the views of the public more accurately than did the economists. In this case, people simply find the efficient solution unfair, and so refuse to adopt it.

Economics alone cannot decide the appropriate trade-off between fairness and efficiency. It cannot even pretend to judge which pricing arrangements are fair and which are unfair. But it can and should indicate whether a particular pricing decision, proposed because it is considered fair, will impose heavy inefficiency costs upon the community. Economic analysis also can and should indicate how to evaluate these costs, so that the issues can be decided on the basis of an understanding of the facts.

Toward Assessment of the Price Mechanism

Our analysis of the case for laissez faire is not meant to imply that the free-enterprise system is an ideal of perfection, without flaw or room for improvement. In fact, it has a number of serious shortcomings that we will explore in subsequent chapters. But recognition of these imperfections should not conceal the enormous accomplishments of the price mechanism.

We have shown that, given the proper circumstances, it is capable of meeting the most exacting requirements of allocative efficiency, requirements that go well beyond the capacity of any central planning bureau. The market mechanism has provided an abundance of goods unprecedented in human history. Even centrally planned economies use the price mechanism to carry out considerable portions of the task of allocation, most notably the distribution of goods among consumers. No one has invented an instrument for directing the economy that can replace the price mechanism, which no one ever designed or planned for, but that simply grew by itself, a child of the processes of history.

Summary

1. An allocation of resources is considered *inefficient* if it wastes opportunities to change the use of the economy's resources in any way that makes consumers better off. Resource allocation is called *efficient* if there are no such wasted opportunities.

2. Resource allocation involves three basic co-ordination tasks: (a) How much of each good to produce, (b) What quantities of the available inputs to use in producing the different goods, and (c) How to distribute the goods among different consumers.

3. Under perfect competition, the free-market mechanism adjusts prices so that the resulting resource allocation is efficient. It induces firms to buy and use inputs in ways that yield the most valuable outputs per unit of input; it distributes products among consumers in ways that match individual preferences; and it produces commodities whose value to consumers exceeds the cost of producing them.

4. Efficient decisions about what goods to produce require that the marginal cost (MC) of producing each good be equated to its marginal utility (MU) to consumers. If the MC of any good differs from its MU, then society can improve resource allocation by changing the level of production.

5. Because the market system induces firms to set MC equal to price, and induces consumers to set MU equal to price, it automatically guarantees that the MC = MU condition is satisfied.

6. Sometimes improvements in efficiency require some prices to increase in order to stimulate supply or to prevent waste in consumption. This is why price increases can sometimes be beneficial to consumers.

7. In addition to allocating resources, prices also influence the distribution of income between buyers and sellers.

8. The workings of the price mechanism can be criticized on the grounds that it is unfair because of the preferential treatment it accords wealthy consumers. The most direct answer to this criticism is to redistribute income rather than to restrict the workings of the price mechanism.

Concepts for Review

Efficient allocation of resources
Co-ordination tasks: output
    selection, production planning,
    distribution of goods

Laissez faire
Input–output analysis
MC = P requirement of perfect
    competition

MC = MU efficiency requirement

Questions for Discussion

1. What are the possible social advantages of price rises in each of the two following cases?
   a. Charging higher prices for electrical power on very hot days when many people use air conditioners.
   b. Raising water prices in drought-stricken areas.
2. Discuss the fairness of the two preceding proposals.
3. Discuss the nature of the inefficiency in each of the following cases:
   a. An arrangement whereby relatively little coffee and much tea is made available to people who prefer coffee and that accomplishes the reverse for tea lovers.
   b. An arrangement in which watchmakers are assigned to ditch-digging and unskilled labourers to repairing watches.
   c. An arrangement that produces a large quantity of trucks and few cars, assuming both cost about the same to produce and to run but that most people in the community prefer cars to trucks.
4. In reality, which of the following circumstances might give rise to each of the preceding problem situations?
   a. Regulation of output quantities by a government.
   b. Rationing of commodities.
   c. Assignment of soldiers to different jobs in an army.
5. In a free market, how will the price mechanism deal with each inefficiency described in Question 3?
6. Suppose a given set of resources can be used to make either one handbag or two wallets, and the MC of a handbag is $14 while the MC of a wallet is $7. If the MU of a wallet is $7 and the MU of a handbag is $18, what can be done to improve resource allocation? What can you say about the gain to consumers?

Appendix

The Invisible Hand in the Distribution of Goods and in Production Planning

On pages 516–519 we offered a glimpse of the way economists analyse the workings of the invisible hand by showing how the market handles the problem of efficiency in one of the three tasks of resource allocation: the selection of outputs. We explained the MC = MU rule that must be followed for a set of outputs to be efficient, and showed how a free market can induce people to act in a way that satisfies that rule. In this appendix we complete the story, examining how the price mechanism handles the two other tasks of resource allocation: the distribution of goods among consumers and the planning of production.

Efficient Distribution of Commodities: Who Gets What?

While decisions about distribution among consumers depend critically on value judgments, a surprising amount can be said purely on grounds of efficiency. For example, consumers' desires are not being served efficiently if large quantities of milk are given to someone whose preference is for apple cider, while numerous litres of cider are assigned to a milk lover. Deciding how much of which commodity goes to whom is a matter that requires delicate calculation. It causes great difficulties during wartime when planners must ration goods. They generally end up utilizing a crude egalitarianism: the same amount of butter to everyone, the same amount of coffee to everyone, and so on. This may be justified, to paraphrase the statement of a high official in another country, by an "unwillingness to pander to acquired tastes," but it is easy to see that such fixed rations are unlikely to produce an efficient result.

The analysis of the efficient distribution of the economy's different products among its many consumers turns out to be quite similar to our previous analysis of efficient output selection. Suppose there are two individuals, Mr. Steaker and Ms. Chop, and that Steaker wants lots of beef and little lamb, while the opposite is true of Chop. Suppose each is getting one kilogram of lamb and one kilogram of beef per week. It is then possible to make *both* people better off without increasing their total consumption of two kilograms of beef and two kilograms of lamb if Mr. Steaker trades some of his lamb to Ms. Chop in return

for some beef. The initial distribution of goods was not efficient because it left room for trades that yield *mutual* gains.

It is easy enough to think of allocations of commodities among consumers that are *inefficient*—simply assign to each person only what he does not like. But how does one recognize an allocation that *is* efficient? After all, there are many of us whose preferences have much in common. If two individuals both like beef and lamb, how shall the available amounts of the two commodities be divided between them? We will now show that, as in the analysis of efficient output selection, there is a simple rule that must be satisfied by *any* efficient distribution of products among consumers. Consider any two commodities in the economy, such as beef and lamb, and any two consumers, like Steaker and Chop, each of whom likes to eat some of each type of meat. Then:

The basic rules for the efficient distribution of beef and lamb between Steaker and Chop are that

Steaker's MU of beef = Chop's MU of beef

and

Steaker's MU of lamb = Chop's MU of lamb.

Analogous equations must be satisfied for every other pair of individuals, and for every other pair of products.

Why are these equalities required for efficiency? Recall that a distribution of commodities among consumers can be efficient only if it has taken advantage of every potential gain from trade. That is, if two people can trade in a way that makes them *both* better off, then the distribution cannot be efficient. We can show that if *either* of the previous equations is not satisfied, then such trades are possible.

Suppose, for example, that the following are the relevant marginal utilities:

Steaker's MU of beef = $40
Chop's MU of beef = $20

Steaker's MU of lamb = $10
Chop's MU of lamb = $10.

In such a case a mutually beneficial exchange of beef

and lamb can be arranged. For example, if Steaker gives Chop three kilograms of lamb in return for one kilogram of beef, they will both be better off. Steaker loses three kilograms of lamb, which are worth $30 to him, and gets a kilogram of beef, which is worth $40 to him. So he winds up $10 ahead. Similarly, Chop gives up one kilogram of beef, which is worth $20 to her, and gets in return three kilograms of lamb, worth $30 to her. So she also gains $10. Such a mutually beneficial exchange is possible here because the two consumers have different marginal utilities for beef. Each can benefit by giving up what he or she considers less valuable in exchange for something valued more highly. The initial position in which the two equations were not both satisfied was therefore not efficient because *without any increase in the total amounts of beef and lamb available to them, both could be made better off.* The lesson of this example is quite general:

Any time that two persons have unequal MU's for any commodity, the welfare of both parties can be increased by an exchange of commodities. Efficiency requires that any two individuals have the same MU's for any pair of goods.

The great virtue of the price system is that it induces people to carry out *voluntarily* all opportunities for mutually beneficial swaps. Without the price system, Steaker and Chop might not make the trade because they do not know each other. But the price system enables them to trade with each other by trading with the market. Remember from our discussion of consumer choice in Chapter 20 that it pays any consumer to buy any commodity up to the point where the good's money marginal utility is just equal to its price. In other words, in equilibrium:

Mr. Steaker's MU of beef = Price of beef
= Ms. Chop's MU of beef.

This is so because, if, say, Mr. Steaker's MU of beef were greater than the price of beef, he could improve his lot by exchanging more of his money for beef. And the reverse could be true if Steaker's MU of beef fell short of the price of beef. For the same reason, since the price of lamb is the same to both individuals, each will choose voluntarily to buy quantities of lamb at which:

Mr. Steaker's MU of lamb = Price of lamb
= Ms. Chop's MU of lamb.

Thus, we see that as long as both consumers face the same prices for lamb and beef, their independent decisions *must* satisfy our criterion for efficient distribution of beef and lamb between them:

Steaker's MU of beef = Chop's MU of beef
Steaker's MU of lamb = Chop's MU of lamb.

Given any prices for two commodities, each consumer, acting only in accord with his or her preferences and with no necessary consideration of the effects on the other person, will automatically make out the purchase behaviour that efficiently serves the mutual interests of both purchasers.

This time, where have we sneaked the rabbit into our price system argument? The answer is that the market acts as an intermediary between any pair of consumers. Given the prices offered by the market, each consumer will use his or her dollars in a way that exhausts all opportunities for gains from trade *with the market.* Mr. Steaker and Ms. Chop each take advantage of every such opportunity to gain by trading with the market, and in the process they automatically take advantage of every opportunity for advantageous trades between themselves.

Efficient Production Planning: Allocation of Inputs

Finally, we note briefly that a similar analysis shows how the price system leads to an efficient allocation of inputs among the different production processes—the third of our allocative issues. For precisely the same reasons as in the case of the distribution of products among consumers:

Efficient use of two inputs (say, labour and fertilizer) in the production of two goods (say, wheat and corn) requires that

Marginal revenue product (MRP) of fertilizer in wheat production = MRP of fertilizer in corn production

MRP of labour in wheat production = MRP of labour in corn production.

By the same logic as before, it can be shown that if these equations do not hold, it is possible to produce more corn and more wheat using no more labour and fertilizer than before but merely by redistributing the quantities of the two inputs between the two crops.[4]

Similarly, since we learned in Chapter 22 that maximum profits require each farmer to hire each input until the input's marginal revenue product equals its price, and since the price of a tonne of

[4]See Discussion Question 2 at the end of this appendix.

fertilizer is the same for both wheat farmers and corn growers, it follows that we must have:

MRP of fertilizer in wheat production
= Price of fertilizer
= MRP of fertilizer in corn production.

The same relationship must be true for labour inputs:

MRP of labour in wheat production
= Price of labour
= MRP of labour in corn production.

Thus, we conclude that by making the independent choices that maximize their own profits, and without necessarily considering the effects on anyone else, each farmer (firm) will *automatically* act in a way that satisfies the efficiency conditions for the allocation of inputs among different products.

Summary

1. The condition for efficient distribution of commodities among consumers is that every consumer have the same marginal utility (MU) for every product. If this condition is not met, then two consumers can arrange a swap that makes both of them better off.
2. In a free market, all consumers pay the same prices. So, if they pursue their own self-interest by setting MU = P, they automatically satisfy the condition for efficient distribution of commodities.
3. The condition for efficient allocation of inputs to the various production processes is that the marginal revenue product (MRP) of any input be the same in every industry.
4. Since all producers pay the same prices for inputs under perfect competition, if each firm pursues its own self-interest by setting its MRP of any input equal to that input's market price, the condition for efficient production planning will be satisfied automatically.

Questions for Discussion

1. Show that commodities are not being distributed efficiently if Mr. Olson's marginal utilities of a kilogram of tomatoes and a kilogram of potatoes are, respectively, 50 cents and 25 cents while Mr. Johnson's are, respectively, 40 cents and 30 cents.
2. Suppose the marginal revenue product of a litre of petroleum in the trucking industry is 50 cents while the marginal revenue product of petroleum in the auto-racing industry is 28 cents. Show that petroleum inputs are being allocated inefficiently. Why would a market system tend to prevent this situation from occurring?

Pure Monopoly and the Market Mechanism

27

The price of monopoly is
upon every occasion the
highest which can be got.
ADAM SMITH*

In Chapters 25 and 26 we described an idealized market system in which all
industries are perfectly competitive, and we extolled the beauty of that system.
In this chapter, we turn to one of the blemishes—the possibility that some
industries may be monopolized, and the consequences of such monopolization.

We begin by defining *monopoly* precisely and investigating some of the
reasons for its existence. Then, using the tools of Chapter 23, we consider the
monopolist's choice of an optimal price–output combination. As we shall see,
while it is possible to analyse how much a monopolist will choose to produce, a
monopolist has no "supply curve" in the usual sense. This fact requires certain
modifications in our supply–demand analysis of the market mechanism, modifications that lead us to the central message of this chapter: that monopolized markets
do not match the ideal performance of perfectly competitive ones. In particular,
we will see that in the presence of monopoly the market mechanism no longer
allocates society's resources efficiently. This observation opens up the possibility
that government actions to curb the abuses of monopoly might actually improve
the workings of the market—a possibility we will study in detail in Chapters 30
and 31.

Application: Monopoly and Pollution Charges

We begin, as usual, with a real-life problem. Chapter 1 noted that most economists
want to control pollution by charging the polluter heavily, making him pay more
money the more pollution he emits. Making it sufficiently expensive for firms to
pollute, it is said, will force them to cut their emissions.[1]

A common objection to this proposal is that it simply will not work when the
polluter is a monopolist: "The monopolist can just raise the price of his product,
pass the pollution charge on to his customers, and go on polluting as before, with
total impunity." After all, if a firm is a monopoly, what is to stop it from raising its
price when it is hit by a pollution charge?

Yet observation of the behaviour of firms threatened with pollution charges
suggests that there is something wrong with this objection. If the polluter could
escape the penalty completely, we would expect him to acquiesce or to put up

*But Adam Smith's statement is incorrect! See Discussion Question 7 at the end of the chapter.
[1]Details on this method of pollution control are provided in Chapter 34.

only token opposition. Yet wherever it has been proposed to levy a charge on the emission of pollutants, the outcries have been enormous, even among firms with no important rivals. Lobbyists are dispatched at once to do their best to stop the legislation. In fact, rather than agree to being charged for their emissions, firms usually indicate a preference for direct controls that *force* them to adopt specific processes that are less polluting than the ones they are now using.

In this chapter we will see why monopolies cannot make their customers pay the pollution charge—or at least not all of it. We will see how the monopolist's downward-sloping demand curve keeps him from passing on all of a pollution tax or any other increase in his costs (any upward shift in his cost curves).

Monopoly Defined

A **pure monopoly** is an industry in which there is only one supplier of a product for which there are no close substitutes, and in which it is very hard or impossible for another firm to coexist.

Pure monopoly was defined in Table 25-1 on page 490; the definition is quite stringent. First, there must be only one firm in the industry—the monopolist must be "the only supplier in town." Second, there must be no close substitute for the monopolist's product. Thus, even the sole provider of natural gas in a city would not be considered a pure monopoly, since other firms offer close substitutes like heating oil and coal. Third, there must be some reason why survival of a potential competitor is extremely unlikely, for otherwise monopoly could not persist.

These rigid requirements make pure monopoly a rarity in the real world. The local telephone company and the post office are good examples of one-firm industries that face little or no effective competition. But most firms face competition from substitute products. Even if only one railway serves a particular town, it must compete with bus lines, trucking companies, and airlines. Similarly, the producer of a particular brand of beer may be the only supplier of that specific product but is not a monopolist by our definition. Since many other beers are close substitutes for its product, the company will lose much of its business if it tries to raise its price much above the prices of other brands.

And there is one further reason why the unrestrained pure monopoly of economic theory is rarely encountered in practice. We will learn in this chapter that pure monopoly can have a number of undesirable features. As a consequence, in markets where pure monopoly might otherwise prevail, the government has intervened to prevent monopolization or to limit the discretion of the monopolist to set its price.

If we do not study pure monopoly for its descriptive realism, why do we study it? Because, like perfect competition, pure monopoly is a market form that is easier to analyse than the more common market structures that we will consider in the next chapter. Thus, pure monopoly is a stepping stone toward models of greater reality. Also, the "evils of monopoly" stand out most clearly when we consider monopoly in its purest form, and this greater clarity will help us understand why governments have rarely allowed unfettered monopoly to exist.

Causes of Monopoly: Barriers to Entry and Cost Advantages

The key element in preserving a monopoly is keeping potential rivals out of the market. One possibility is that some specific impediment prevents the establishment of a new firm in the industry. Economists call such impediments **barriers to entry**. Some examples are:

1. *Legal restrictions.* Canada Post has a monopoly position because Parliament has given it one. Private companies that might want to compete with the post office are prohibited from doing so by law. Local monopolies of various kinds are sometimes established either because government grants some special

privilege to a single firm (for example, the right to operate a food concession in a municipal stadium) or prevents other firms from entering the industry (for instance, by licensing only a single local radio station).

2. *Patents.* A special, but very important, legal impediment to entry is the **patent**. To encourage inventiveness, the government gives exclusive production rights for a period of time to the inventor of certain products. As long as the patent is in effect, the firm has a protected position and is a monopoly. For example, Xerox had for many years (but no longer has) a monopoly in plain-paper copying.

3. *Control of a scarce resource or input.* If a certain commodity can be produced only by using a rare input, a company that gains control of the source of that input can establish a monopoly position for itself. For example, the DeBeers syndicate in South Africa owns almost the only land on earth on which diamonds can be mined.

Obviously, such barriers can keep rivals out and ensure that an industry is monopolized, but monopoly can also occur in the absence of barriers to entry if a single firm has important cost advantages over its potential rivals. Two examples of this are:

4. *Technical superiority.* A firm whose technological expertise vastly exceeds that of potential competitors can, for a period of time, maintain a monopoly position. For example, IBM for many years had very little competition in the computer business mainly because of its technological virtuosity. Eventually, however, competitors caught up.

5. *Economies of scale.* If mere size gives a large firm a cost advantage over a smaller rival, it is likely to be impossible for anyone to compete with the largest firm in the industry.

Natural Monopoly

This last type of cost advantage is important enough to merit special attention. In some industries, economies of large-scale production or economies from simultaneous production of a large number of items (for example, car motors and bodies, truck parts, and so on) are so extreme that the industry's output can be produced at far lower cost by a single firm than by a number of smaller firms. In such cases, we say there is a **natural monopoly**, because once a firm gets large enough relative to the size of the market for its product, its natural cost advantage will enable it to drive the competition out of business.

A natural monopoly need not be a large firm if the market is small enough. *What matters is the size of a single firm relative to the total market demand for the product.* Thus, a small bank in a rural town or a gasoline station at a lightly travelled intersection may both be natural monopolies even though they are very small firms.

Figure 27–1 shows the sort of average-cost (AC) curve that leads to natural monopoly. Suppose that any firm producing widgets would have this AC curve and that, initially, there are two firms in the industry. Suppose also that the large firm is producing two million widgets at an average cost of $2.50, and the small firm is producing one million widgets at an average cost of $3. Clearly, the large firm can drive the small firm out of business by offering its output for sale at a price below $3 (so the small firm can match the price only by running a loss) but above $2.50 (so it can still make a profit). The managers of the large firm will no doubt be smart enough to realize this possibility, and hence a monopoly will arise "naturally" even in the absence of barriers to entry. Once the monopoly is established (producing, say, 2.5 million widgets) the economies of scale act as a very effective deterrent to

A **natural monopoly** is an industry in which advantages of large-scale production make it possible for a single firm to produce the entire output of the market at lower average cost than a number of firms each producing a smaller quantity.

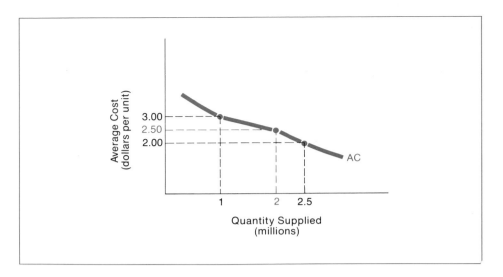

Figure 27-1

NATURAL MONOPOLY
When the average-cost curve of a firm is declining, as depicted here, natural monopoly may result. A firm producing two million widgets will have average costs of $2.50, which are well below those of a smaller competitor producing one million widgets (average cost = $3). The larger firm can cut its price to a level (lower than $3) that its competitor cannot match, and thereby drive the competitor out of business.

entry because no new entrant can hope to match the low average cost ($2) of the existing monopoly firm.

Many public utilities are permitted to operate as monopoly suppliers for exactly this reason. It is believed that the technology of producing or distributing their output enables them to achieve substantial cost reductions when they produce large quantities. It is therefore often considered desirable to permit these firms to obtain the lower costs they achieve by having the entire market to themselves, and to subject them to regulatory supervision rather than break them up into a number of competing firms. The issue of regulating natural monopolies will be examined in detail in Chapter 30. To summarize this discussion:

There are two basic reasons why a monopoly may exist: barriers to entry, such as legal restrictions and patents, and cost advantages of large-scale operation, such as those that lead to natural monopoly.

The rest of this chapter will analyse how such a monopoly may be expected to behave if its freedom of action is not limited by the government.

The Monopolist's Supply Decision

A monopolist does not have a "supply curve," as we usually define the term. He does not say to himself: "The price of my product is $6. How much should I produce?" For, unlike the case of a perfect competitor, a monopolist is not at the mercy of the market; he does not have to take the market price as given and react to it. Instead, the monopolist has the power to set the price, or rather to select the price–quantity combination on his demand curve that he prefers. For any price that the monopolist might choose, the demand curve for his product tells him how much consumers will buy.

Unlike the perfectly competitive firm, the monopolist's demand curve is normally downward sloping, not horizontal. That is, the monopolist is not a *price taker* who must simply adapt to whatever price the forces of supply and demand decree. Rather, the monopolist is a *price maker* who can, if he wishes, raise his price. Unlike the case of perfect competition, such a price rise will not cause him to lose all his customers. But it will cause him to lose *some* business. The higher his price, the less he can expect to sell.

It is because of the downward-sloping demand curve that the sky is not the limit in pricing by a monopolist. Some price increases are not profitable. In deciding what price best serves his interests, the monopolist must consider whether his

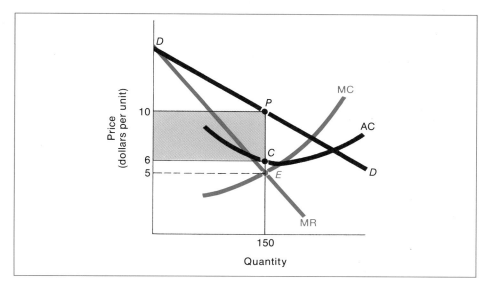

Figure 27-2
PROFIT-MAXIMIZING EQUILIBRIUM FOR A MONOPOLIST
This monopolist has the cost structure indicated by the black average-cost (AC) curve and the blue marginal-cost (MC) curve. His demand curve is the black line labelled *DD*, and his marginal-revenue curve is the blue line labelled MR. He maximizes profits by producing 150 units, because at this level of production MC= MR (point *E*). The price he charges is $10 per unit (as given by point *P* on the demand curve). Since his average cost per unit ($6) is given by point *C* on the AC curve, his total profit is indicated by the shaded rectangle.

profits can be increased by raising or lowering his price.

In our analysis, we shall assume that the monopolist wants to maximize his profits. In that case, the methods of Chapter 23 can be used to determine which price the monopolist will prefer. To maximize his profits, he must compare his marginal revenue (the addition to total revenue resulting from a one-unit rise in output) with his marginal cost (the addition to total cost resulting from that additional unit). For this purpose, a marginal-cost (MC) curve and a marginal-revenue (MR) curve for a typical monopolist are drawn in Figure 27-2, which also contains the monopolist's demand curve (*DD*).

The Monopolist's Price and Marginal Revenue

Notice that the marginal-revenue curve is always *below* the demand curve, meaning that MR is always less than price (*P*). This is an important fact, and is easy to explain. A monopolist normally must charge the same price to all his customers. So, if he wants to raise his sales by one unit, he must lower his price somewhat to *all* his customers. When he cuts his price to attract new sales, all his previous customers also benefit from the price reduction. Thus, the *additional* revenue that he takes in when he increases sales by one unit (his *marginal revenue*) is the price he collects from his new customer *minus the revenue he loses by cutting the price paid by all his old customers*. This means that MR is necessarily *less* than price; graphically, it implies that the MR curve is *below* the demand curve, as in Figure 27-2.

Figure 27-3 illustrates the relationship between price and marginal revenue in a specific example. Suppose a monopolist is initially selling 15 units at a price of $2.10 per unit (point *A*), and he wishes to increase sales by one unit. The demand curve tells him that in order to sell the 16th unit, he will have to reduce his price to $2 (point *B*). How much revenue will he gain from this increase in sales; that is, how large is his marginal revenue?

As we know, *total revenue* at point *A* is the area of the rectangle whose upper right-hand corner is point *A*, or $2.10 × 15 = $31.50. Similarly, total revenue at point *B* is the area of the rectangle whose upper right-hand corner is point *B*, or $2 × 16 = $32. The *marginal revenue* of the 16th unit is, by definition, total revenue when 16 units are sold minus total revenue when 15 units are sold, or $32 – $31.50 = $0.50.

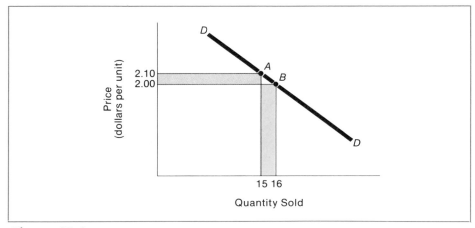

Figure 27-3

THE RELATIONSHIP BETWEEN MARGINAL REVENUE AND PRICE

Line *DD* is the demand curve of a monopolist. In order to raise his sales from 15 to 16 units, he must cut his price from $2.10 (point *A*) to $2 (point *B*). If he does this, his revenues *go up* by the $2 price he charges the buyer of the 16th unit (the area of the tall blue rectangle), but *go down* by the 10-cent price reduction he offers to his previous customers (the area of the flat grey rectangle). His marginal revenue, therefore, is the difference between these two areas. Since the price is the area of the blue rectangle, it follows that marginal revenue is less than price for a monopolist.

In Figure 27-3, marginal revenue appears as the area of the tall blue rectangle ($2) *minus* the area of the flat grey rectangle ($1.50). We can see that MR is less than price by observing that the price is shown in the diagram by the area of the blue rectangle.[2] Clearly, the price (area of the blue rectangle) must exceed the marginal revenue (area of the blue rectangle *minus* area of the grey rectangle), as was claimed.[3]

Determining the Profit-Maximizing Output

We return now to the supply decision of the monopolist depicted in Figure 27-2. Like any other firm, the monopoly maximizes its profits by setting marginal revenue (MR) equal to marginal cost (MC). It selects point *E* in the diagram, where output is 150 units. But point *E* does not tell us the monopoly price because, as we have just seen, price exceeds MR for a monopolist. To learn what price the monopolist charges, we must use the demand curve to find the price at which consumers are willing to purchase 150 units. The answer, we see, is given by point *P*. The monopoly price is $10 per unit, which naturally exceeds both MR and MC (which are equal at $5).

The monopolist depicted in Figure 27-2 is earning a tidy profit. This profit is shown in the graph by the shaded rectangle whose height is the difference between price (point *P*) and average cost (point *C*) and whose width is the quantity produced (150 units). In the example, profits are $4 per unit, or $600. The monopolist has the power to raise price above $10 per unit, but he chooses not to, since profits would be lower.

A monopolist's profit-maximization calculation can also be shown numerically. In Table 27-1, the first two columns show the price and quantity figures that

---

[2]Because the width of this rectangle is one unit, its area is height × width = ($2 per unit) × (1 unit) = $2.

[3]There is another way to arrive at this conclusion. Recall that the demand curve is the curve of *average revenue*. Since the average revenue is declining as we move to the right, it follows from one of the rules relating marginals and averages (see the appendix to Chapter 23) that the marginal-revenue curve must always be below the average.

Table 27-1

A PROFIT-MAXIMIZING MONOPOLIST'S PRICE-OUTPUT DECISION

DEMAND CURVE		REVENUE		COST		TOTAL PROFIT
(1)	(2)	(3)	(4)	(5)	(6)	(7)
Q	P	TR = P × Q	MR	TC	MC	TR − TC
0	—	$ 0		$ 10		$-10
1	$140	140	$140	70	$60	70
2	107	214	74	120	50	94
3	92	276	62	166	46	110
4	80	320	44	210	44	110
5	66	330	10	253	43	77
6	50	300	-30	298	45	2

constitute a monopolist's demand curve. Column 3 shows total revenue (TR) for each output, which is the product of price and quantity. Thus, for three units of output we have TR = $92 × 3 = $276. Column 4 shows marginal revenue (MR). For example, when output rises from 3 to 4 units, TR increases from $276 to $320 so MR is $320 − $276 = $44. Column 5 gives the monopolist's total costs for each level of output. Column 6 derives marginal cost (MC) from total cost (TC) in the usual way. Finally, by subtracting TC from TR for each level of output, we derive total profit in column 7.

This table brings out a number of important points. We note first (columns 2 and 3) that a cut in price sometimes raises total revenue. For example, when output rises from 1 to 2, P falls from $140 to $107 and TR rises from $140 to $214. But sometimes a fall in P reduces TR; when (between 5 and 6 units of output) P falls from $66 to $50, TR falls from $330 to $300. Next, by comparing columns 2 and 4, we observe that, after the first unit, price always exceeds marginal revenue. Finally, from columns 4 and 6, we see that MC = MR = $44 when Q is 4 units, indicating that this is the level of output that maximizes the monopolist's total profit. That is confirmed in the last column of the table, which shows that at that output profit reaches its highest level, $110, for any of the output quantities considered in the table.

Comparison of Monopoly and Perfect Competition

This completes our analysis of the monopolist's price–output decision. At this point it is natural to wonder whether there is anything distinctive about monopoly, and whether its consequences are desirable or undesirable. For the purpose of finding out, we need a standard of comparison. Perfect competition provides this standard because, as we learned in Chapters 25 and 26, it is a benchmark of ideal performance against which other market structures can be judged. By comparing the results of monopoly with those of perfect competition, we will see why economists since Adam Smith have condemned monopoly as inefficient.

The first difference between competition and monopoly is a direct consequence of the absence of barriers to entry in the former. Profits such as those shown in Figure 27-2 would be competed away by free entry in a competitive market. In the long run, a competitive firm must earn zero economic profit; that is, it can earn only enough to cover its costs, including the opportunity cost of the owner's capital and labour. But higher profits can persist under monopoly—if the monopoly is protected by barriers to entry. The fates can be kind to a monopolist and allow him to grow wealthy at the expense of the consumer. Because people find such accumulations of wealth objectionable, monopoly is widely condemned and, when monopolies are regulated by government, limitations are usually placed on the profits monopolists can earn.

Figure 27-4

COMPARISON OF A
MONOPOLY AND A
COMPETITIVE INDUSTRY

The monopoly output is point *E* at
which MC = MR. The short-run
competitive output is point *A*, at
which MC = *P*, and so is greater
than the monopoly output. The
long-run competitive output is
even greater (point *B*) because it
must be sufficiently large to yield
zero profit (*P* = AC).

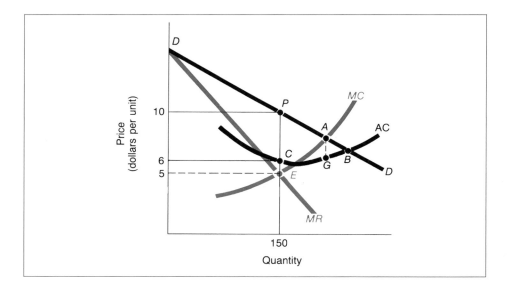

Excess monopoly profits may be a problem, but the second difference between competition and monopoly is even more worrisome in the opinion of economists:

As compared with the perfectly competitive ideal, the monopolist restricts his output and charges a higher price.

To see that this is so, let us conduct the following thought experiment. Imagine that a court order breaks up the monopoly firm depicted in Figure 27–2 (reproduced here as Figure 27–4) into a large number of competitive firms. Suppose further that the industry demand curve is unchanged by this event and that the MC curve in Figure 27–4 is also the (horizontal) sum of the MC curves of all the newly competitive firms. Under these assumptions, we can easily compare the output–price combinations that would emerge in the short run under monopoly and perfect competition.

Since the short-run supply curve of the competitive industry is the sum of the MC curves of all the individual firms (above minimum average variable costs), the MC curve in Figure 27–4 would constitute the supply curve of the competitive industry. Equilibrium under perfect competition would occur at point *A*, where quantity demanded (which we read from the demand curve) and quantity supplied (which we read from the MC = supply curve) are equal.

By comparing point *A* with the monopolist's equilibrium (point *E*), we can see that the monopolist produces fewer units of output than would a competitive industry with the same demand and cost conditions. Since the demand curve slopes downward, producing less output means charging a higher price. The monopolist's price, indicated by point *P*, exceeds the price that would result from perfect competition, point *A*. This is the essence of the truth behind the popular view that monopolists "gouge the public."

In fact, the reduction in output and increase in price may be even greater than we have indicated. Our analysis so far is correct, but only for the short run. In the short run, monopoly output is determined by MC = MR (point *E*) while competitive output is determined by MC = *P* (point *A*). But in the long run, as we learned in Chapter 25, the lure of profits will attract more firms into a perfectly competitive industry. In Figure 27–4, we can see that there *are* profits to be made. When the industry produces at point *A*, the market price (point *A*) clearly exceeds the average cost of production (point *G*). Each competitive firm will then be earning profits in excess of the opportunity cost of capital.

But, as we know, such a situation cannot persist if there is free entry. New firms will enter the industry, thereby pushing the supply (= MC) curve outward to the right. (The AC curve will also shift rightward as total industry capacity expands.) Long-run competitive equilibrium will eventually be established at a point similar to *B*, where price and average cost are equal (and hence economic profits are zero). Comparing point *B* with point *A*, we see that competitive output is *even higher* and competitive price is *even lower* than we indicated at first.

We conclude, then, that a monopoly will charge a higher price and produce a smaller output than will a competitive industry with the same demand and cost conditions. Why do economists find this situation so objectionable? Because, as you will recall from Chapter 26, a competitive industry devotes "just the right amount" of society's scarce resources to the production of its particular commodity. Therefore, if a monopolist produces less than a competitive industry, it must be producing too little.

Remember from Chapter 26 that efficiency in resource allocation requires that the marginal utility (MU) of each commodity be equal to its marginal cost, and that perfect competition guarantees that:

$$MU = P \text{ and } MC = P, \text{ so } MU = MC.$$

Under the monopoly, consumers continue to maximize their own welfare by setting MU equal to *P*. But the monopoly producer, we have just learned, sets MC equal to MR. Since MR is *below* the market price, *P*, we conclude that in a monopolized industry:

$$MU = P \text{ and } MC = MR < P, \text{ so } MU > MC.$$

Because MU exceeds MC, too few of society's resources are being used to produce the monopolized commodity. Adam Smith's invisible hand is sending out the wrong signals. Consumers are willing to pay an amount for an additional unit of the good (its MU) that exceeds what it costs to produce that unit (its MC). But the monopolist refuses to increase his production, for if he raises output by one unit, the revenue he will collect (the MR) will be less than the price the consumer will pay for the additional unit (*P*). So the monopolist does not increase his production and resources are allocated inefficiently. To summarize this discussion of the consequences of monopoly:

Because it is protected from entry, a monopoly firm earns profits in excess of the opportunity cost of capital. At the same time, monopoly breeds inefficiency in resource allocation by producing too little output and charging too high a price. For these reasons, some of the virtues of laissez faire evaporate if an industry becomes monopolized.

Can Anything Good Be Said About Monopoly?

Except for the case of natural monopoly—where a single firm offers important cost advantages—it is not easy to find arguments in favour of monopoly. But the comparison between monopoly and perfect competition in the real world is not quite as clean as it is in our example. For one thing, we have assumed that the market-demand curve is the same whether the industry is competitive or monopolized. But is this necessarily so? The demand curve will be the same if the monopolist does nothing about his demand, but that hardly seems likely.

Under perfect competition, purchasers consider the products of all suppliers in an industry to be identical, and so no supplier has any reason to advertise. A farmer who sells apples through one of the major markets has absolutely no motivation to spend money on advertising because he can sell all the apples he wants to at the going price.

When the monopolist takes over, however, it may very well pay him to advertise. If he believes that advertising can make consumers' hearts beat faster as they rush to the market to purchase the apples whose virtues have been extolled on television, the monopolist will allocate a substantial sum of money to accomplish this feat. This should shift his demand curve outward; after all, that is the purpose of these expenditures. The monopolist's demand curve and that of the competitive industry will then no longer be the same. The higher demand curve for the monopolist's product will perhaps induce him to expand his volume of production and to reduce the difference between the competitive and the monopolistic output levels indicated in Figure 27–4. It will also, however, induce him to charge even higher prices.

Similarly, the advent of a monopoly may produce shifts in the average- and marginal-cost curves. One reason for higher costs is the advertising we have just been discussing. Another is that the sheer size of the monopolist's organization may lead to bureaucratic inefficiencies, co-ordination problems, and the like. On the other hand, the monopolist may be able to eliminate certain types of duplication that are unavoidable for a number of small independent firms: One purchasing agent may do the job where many buyers were needed before; and a few large machines may replace many small items of equipment in the hands of the competitive firms. In addition, the large scale of his input purchases may permit the monopolist to avail himself of quantity discounts not available to small competitive firms.

If the unification achieved by monopoly does succeed in producing a downward shift in the marginal-cost curve, monopoly output will thereby tend to move up closer to the competitive level, and the monopoly price will tend to move down closer to the competitive price.

In addition to this, some economists, most notably Joseph Schumpeter, have argued that it is potentially misleading to compare the cost curves of a monopoly and a competitive industry *at a single point in time*. Because it is protected from rivals, and therefore sure to capture the benefits from any cost savings it can devise, a monopoly has a particularly strong motivation to invest in research, they argue. If this research bears fruit, then the monopolist's costs will be lower than those of a competitive industry in the long run, even if they are higher in the short run. Monopoly, according to this view, may be the hand-maiden of innovation. While the argument is an old one, it remains controversial. The statistical evidence is decidedly mixed.

Finally, we must remember that the monopoly depicted in Figure 27–2 is not a natural monopoly. But some of the monopolies you find in the real world are. Where the monopoly is natural, costs of production would, by definition, be higher and possibly much higher if the single large firm were broken up into many smaller firms. (Refer back to Figure 27–1 on page 528.) In such cases, it may be in society's best interest to allow the monopoly to exist so that consumers can benefit from the economies of large-scale production. But then it may be appropriate to place legal limitations on the monopolist's ability to set a price; that is, to *regulate* the monopoly. Regulation of business is an issue that will occupy our attention in Chapter 30.

Monopoly and the Shifting of Pollution Charges

We conclude our discussion of monopoly by returning to the application that began this chapter—the effectiveness of pollution charges as a means to reduce emissions. Recall that the question is whether a monopoly can raise its price enough to cover any pollution fees, thus shifting these charges entirely to its customers and evading them altogether.

The answer is that any firm or industry can, usually, shift *part* of the pollution charge to its customers. Economists argue that this shifting is a proper part of a pollution-control program since it induces consumers to redirect their purchases from goods that are highly polluting to goods that are not. For example, a significant increase in taxes on leaded gasoline with, perhaps, a simultaneous decrease in the tax on unleaded gasoline will send more motorists to the unleaded-gas pumps, and that will reduce dangerous lead emissions into the atmosphere.

But more important for our discussion here is the other side of the matter. While some part of a pollution charge is usually paid by the consumer, *the seller will usually be stuck with some part of the charge, even if he is a monopolist.* Why? Because of the negative slope of his demand curve. If he raises his price he will lose customers, and that will eat into his profits. He will then always be better off if he absorbs *some* of the charge himself rather than try to pass all of it on to his customers.

This is illustrated in Figure 27–5. In part (a) we show the monopolist's demand, marginal-revenue, and marginal-cost curves. As in Figure 27–2, equilibrium output is 150 units—the point at which marginal revenue (MR) equals marginal cost (MC). And price is again $10—the point on the demand curve corresponding to 150 units of output (point A).

Now, let a charge of $5 per unit be put on the firm's polluting output, shifting the marginal-cost curve up uniformly to the curve labelled "MC plus fee" in Figure 27–5(b). Then the profit-maximizing output falls to 100 units (point F), for here MR = MC + pollution fee. The new output, 100 units, is lower than the precharge output, 150 units. Thus, the charge leads the monopolist to restrict his polluting output. The price of his product rises to $12 (point B), the point on the demand curve corresponding to 100 units of output. But the rise in price from $10 to $12 is less than half the $5 pollution charge per unit. Thus:

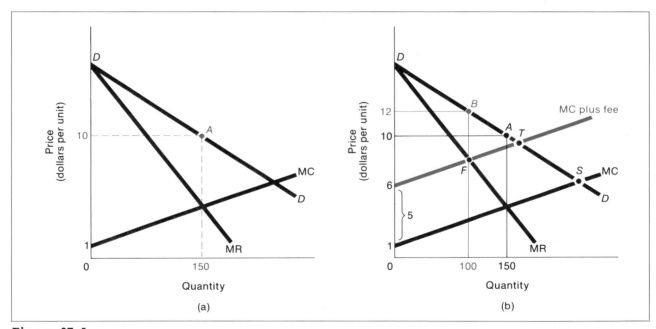

Figure 27-5
MONOPOLY PRICE AND OUTPUT WITH AND WITHOUT A POLLUTION CHARGE
Part (a) shows the monopoly equilibrium without a pollution charge, with price equal to $10 and quantity equal to 150 units. In part (b) a $5 fee is levied on each unit of polluting output. This raises the marginal-cost curve by the amount of the fee, from the black to the blue line. As a result, the output at which MC = MR falls from 150 to 100 units. Price rises from $10 to $12. Note that this $2 price rise is less than the $5 pollution fee, so the monopolist will be stuck with the remaining $3 of the charge.

The pollution charge *does* hurt the polluter even if he is a profit-maximizing monopolist, and it *does* force him to cut his polluting outputs.

No wonder the polluters' lobbyists fight so vehemently! Polluters realize that they often will be far better off with direct controls that impose a financial penalty *only* if they are caught in a violation, prosecuted, and convicted—and even then the fines are often negligible, as we will see in Chapter 34.[4]

We may note, finally, that *any* rise in a monopolist's costs will hurt him and reduce his profits. The reason is exactly the same as in the case of a pollution charge. Even though he is a monopolist, he cannot simply raise his price and make up for any cost increase. For consumers can and will respond by buying less of the monopolist's commodity—after all, that is what the negative slope of the demand curve means.

If a monopoly already charges the price that maximizes its profits, a rise in cost will always hurt because any attempt to offset it by a price rise must reduce profit. The monopolist cannot pass the entire burden of the cost increase to consumers.

---

[4]It is interesting to compare the reaction of the monopolist to the pollution fee, to that of a competitive industry in the short run. Using Figure 27–5(b) to represent a situation of perfect competition with the same demand and cost conditions, we see that the industry outcome point moves from point *S* before the fee to point *T* after the fee. By comparing the gap between points *S* and *T*, and the gap between points *A* and *B*, we see that the pollution fee can cut back output more in the competitive case, since *more* of the tax is passed on through higher prices in the competitive case.

Summary

1. A pure monopoly is a one-firm industry producing a product for which there are no close substitutes.
2. Monopoly can persist only if there are important cost advantages to single-firm operation or barriers to free entry. These barriers may be legal impediments (patents, licensing) or some unique advantage the monopolist acquires for himself (control of a scarce resource).
3. One important case of cost advantages is natural monopoly: instances where only one firm can survive because of important economies of large-scale production.
4. A monopoly has no supply curve. It maximizes its profit by producing an output at which its marginal revenue equals its marginal cost. Its price is given by the point on its demand curve corresponding to that output.
5. In a monopolistic industry, if demand and cost curves

are the same as those of a competitive industry, and if the demand curve has a negative slope and the supply curve a positive slope, output will be lower and monopoly price will be higher than those of the competitive industry.

6. Advertising may enable the monopolist to shift his demand curve above that of a comparable competitive industry's, and through economies such as large-scale input purchases, he may be able to shift his cost curves below those of a competitive industry.
7. If a pollution charge is imposed on the product of a profit-maximizing monopoly, that monopoly will raise its price, but normally not by the full amount of the charge. That is, the monopolist will end up paying part of the pollution fee.
8. Any rise in his costs generally hurts a monopolist. Because of his negatively sloping demand curve, he cannot simply pass them on to consumers.

Concepts for Review

Pure monopoly	Natural monopoly	Shifting of pollution charges
Barriers to entry	Monopoly profits	
Patents	Inefficiency of monopoly	

Questions for Discussion

1. Which of the following industries are pure monopolies?
   a. The only supplier of water in an isolated desert town.
   b. The only supplier of Esso gas in town.
   c. The only supplier of fuel oil in town.
2. Suppose a monopoly industry produces less output than a similar competitive industry. Discuss why this may be considered "socially undesirable."
3. If a competitive firm earns zero economic profits, explain why anyone would invest money in it. (*Hint:* What is the role of the opportunity cost of capital in economic profit?)
4. The following are the demand and *total*-cost schedules for Company Town Water Company, a local monopoly.

OUTPUT (litres)	PRICE (dollars per litre)	TOTAL COST (dollars)
50,000	0.10	2,000
100,000	0.09	5,500
150,000	0.08	10,000
200,000	0.07	15,000
250,000	0.06	22,000
300,000	0.04	31,000

How much output will Company Town produce, and what price will it charge? Will it earn a profit? How much? (*Hint:* You will first have to compute its MR and MC schedules.)

5. Show from the preceding table that for the water company, marginal revenue (per 50,000-litre unit) is always less than price.
6. Suppose a tax of $5 is levied on each item sold by a monopolist, and as a result he decides to raise his price by exactly $5. Why may this decision be against his own best interest?
7. Use Figure 27–2 to show that Adam Smith was wrong when he claimed that the price a monopoly would charge is always "the highest price which can be got."

Between Competition and Monopoly

I was grateful to be able to
answer promptly, and I did. I
said I didn't know.
MARK TWAIN

Most productive activity in Canada, as in any advanced industrial society, can be found between the two theoretical poles considered so far: perfect competition and pure monopoly. Thus, if we want to understand the workings of the market mechanism in a real, modern economy, we must look between competition and monopoly, at the hybrid market structures first mentioned in Chapter 25: *monopolistic competition* and *oligopoly*.

This chapter begins with a precise definition of monopolistic competition, a market structure characterized by many small firms selling somewhat different products. Monopolistic competition is quite prevalent in the retail sector of our economy; shoe stores, restaurants, and gasoline stations are some good examples. We will use the theory of the firm described in Chapter 23 to analyse the price–output decision of a monopolistically competitive firm, and then consider industrywide adjustments, as we did in Chapter 25.

Then we turn to oligopoly, a market structure in which a few large firms dominate the market. Industries like steel, automobiles, and tobacco are good examples of oligopoly in our economy. The critical feature distinguishing an oligopolist from either a monopolist or a perfect competitor is that the oligopolist cares very much about what other firms in that industry do. And the resulting interdependence of decisions, we will see, makes oligopoly very hard to analyse. Consequently, economic theory contains not one but many models of oligopoly (some of which will be reviewed in this chapter), and it is often hard to know which model to apply in any particular situation.

At several points in this chapter we will raise the following critical question: How good is the market mechanism at allocating resources when a commodity is produced under monopolistic competition or under oligopoly? A definitive answer is not usually possible, but we shall see that the case for laissez faire is seriously compromised by the existence of either monopolistic competition or oligopoly.

Some Puzzling Observations

It is easy to see that we need to study the hybrid market structures considered in this chapter, for many things we observe in the real world defy understanding within the framework of either perfect competition or pure monopoly. Here are some examples:

1. *Advertising.* While some advertising is primarily informative (for example, help-wanted ads), much of the advertising that bombards us on TV and in magazines is part of a competitive struggle for our business. Many big companies use advertising as the principal weapon in their battle for customers, and advertising budgets can constitute a very large share of their expenditures. Yet oligopolistic industries containing a few giant firms are often accused of being "uncompetitive" while farming is considered as close to perfect competition as any industry in our economy, even though most individual farmers spend nothing at all on advertising.[1] Why do the allegedly "uncompetitive" oligopolists make such heavy use of advertising while very competitive farmers do not?

2. *Oversupply.* We have all seen intersections with three or four gasoline stations in close proximity. Often, two or three of them may have no cars waiting to be served and the attendants are unoccupied. There seem to be more gas stations than the available amount of traffic warrants, with a corresponding waste of labour time, equipment, and other resources. Why do they all stay in business?

3. *Sticky prices.* Many prices in the economy change from minute to minute. Every day the latest prices of such items as soybeans, cocoa, and copper are published. But if you want to buy one of these at 11:45 A.M. some day, you cannot use yesterday's price because it has probably changed since then. Yet prices of other products, such as cars and refrigerators, generally change at most several times a year, even when inflation is proceeding at a double-digit pace. The firms that sell cars and refrigerators know that market conditions change all the time. Why don't they adjust their prices more often?

This chapter will offer explanations of each of these three phenomena.

Monopolistic Competition

For years, most economic theorists dealt with only two workable models of the behaviour of firms: the monopoly model and the perfectly competitive model. This gap was partially filled, and the realism of economic theory was thereby greatly increased, by the work of Edward Chamberlin of Harvard University and Joan Robinson of Cambridge University during the 1930s. The market structure they first analysed is called **monopolistic competition**.

A market is said to operate under conditions of *monopolistic competition* if it satisfies four conditions, three of which are the same as under perfect competition: (1) *Numerous participants*—that is, many buyers and sellers, all of whom are small; (2) *heterogeneity of products*—as far as the buyer is concerned, each seller's product is at least somewhat different from every other's; (3) *freedom of exit and entry*; and (4) *perfect information*.

Monopolistic competition is a market form that we encounter frequently in our economy. It is particularly characteristic of retailing, where the small shopkeeper still plays a significant role, and of many of the economy's services, such as medical and legal, which are provided under similar conditions. Gas stations and restaurants are other good examples.

Notice that monopolistic competition differs from perfect competition in only one respect (item 2 in the definition). While all products are identical under perfect competition, under monopolistic competition products differ from seller to seller—in quality, in packaging, or in supplementary services offered (for

---

[1]But farmers' associations and agricultural marketing boards do spend money on advertising. Furthermore, where marketing boards and similar agencies exist and impose price controls or production quotas, competition among farmers is reduced.

example, length of the guarantee, car-window washing by a gas station, and so on). The factors that serve to differentiate products need not be "real" in any objective or scientific sense. For example, differences in packaging or in associated services can and do distinguish products that are otherwise identical. On the other hand, two products may perform quite differently in quality tests, but if consumers know nothing about this difference, it is irrelevant for the market outcome.

Since products under monopolistic competition are not identical, there is no reason to expect the price of any firm's product to remain unchanged when the quantity supplied varies. Each seller, in effect, deals in a market slightly separated from the others and caters to a set of customers who vary in their "loyalty" to his product. If he raises his price somewhat, he may expect to drive some but not all of his customers into the arms of his competitors. If he lowers his price, he may expect to attract some trade from his rivals. But since his product is not a perfect substitute for theirs, if he undercuts them slightly he will not attract away *all* their business as he would in the perfectly competitive case.

Thus, if Harry's Hot Dog House reduces its price slightly, it will attract those customers of Sam's Sausage Shop who were nearly indifferent between the two. A bigger price cut by Harry will bring in some customers who have a slightly greater preference for Sam's product. But even a big cut in Harry's price will not bring him the hard-core sausage lovers who hate hot dogs. So the monopolistic competitor's demand curve is negatively sloped, like that of a monopolist, rather than horizontal, like that of a perfect competitor.

Since his product is distinguished from all others, a monopolistic competitor has something akin to a small monopoly. Can we therefore expect him to earn more profit than a perfect competitor? In the short run, perhaps he will. But in the long run, high economic profits will attract new entrants into a monopolistically competitive market—not entrants with products *identical* to an existing firm's, but with products sufficiently similar to hurt.

If one ice-cream parlour's location enables it to do a thriving business, it can confidently expect another, selling a *different* brand, to open nearby. When one seller adopts a new, attractive package, he can be sure that his rivals will soon follow suit, with a slightly different design and colour of their own. In this way freedom of entry ensures that the monopolistically competitive firm earns no higher return on its capital in the long run than it could earn elsewhere. Just as under perfect competition, price will be driven to the level of average cost, including the opportunity cost of capital.

Let us now examine the process that assures that economic profits will be driven to zero in the long run, even under monopolistic competition.

Price and Output Determination Under Monopolistic Competition

The short-run equilibrium of the firm under monopolistic competition differs little from the case of monopoly. Since the firm faces a downward-sloping demand curve (labelled D in Figure 28–1), its marginal-revenue (MR) curve will lie below its demand curve. Profits are maximized at the output level at which marginal revenue and marginal cost (MC) are equal. In Figure 28–1, the profit-maximizing output for a hypothetical gasoline station is 20,000 litres per week, and it sells this output at a price of 50 cents per litre (point P on the demand curve).

This diagram, you will note, looks much like Figure 27–2 (page 529) for a monopoly. The only difference is that the demand curve of a monopolistic competitor is likely to be much more flat than the pure monopolist's because there are many close substitutes for the monopolistic competitor's product. If our gas station raises its price to 60 cents per litre, most of its customers will go across the street. If it lowers its price to 40 cents per litre, it will have long lines at its pumps.

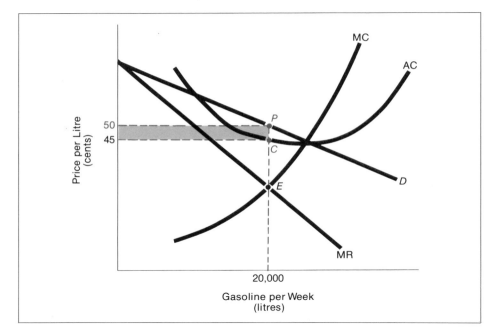

The gas station depicted in Figure 28-1 is making economic profits. Since average cost at 20,000 litres per week is only 45 cents per litre (point C), the station is making a profit on gasoline sales of 5 cents per litre, or $1000 per week in total (the shaded rectangle). Under monopoly, such profits can persist. But under monopolistic competition they cannot, because new firms will be attracted into the market. While the new stations will not offer the identical product, they will offer products that are close enough to take away some business from our firm (for example, they may sell Sunoco or Shell gasoline instead of Texaco).

When more firms share the market, the demand curve facing any individual firm must fall. But how far? The answer is basically the same as it was under perfect competition: until the best that can be done by maximizing profits is to achieve zero economic profits, for only then will entry cease.

Figure 28-2 depicts the same monopolistically competitive firm as in Figure 28-1 *after* the adjustment to the long run is complete. The demand curve has been pushed down so far that when the firm equates MC and MR in order to maximize profits (point E), it simultaneously equates price (P) and average cost (AC) so that profits are zero (point P). As compared with the short-run equilibrium depicted in Figure 28-1, price in long-run equilibrium is *lower* (47 cents per litre versus 50 cents per litre), there are *more firms* in the industry, and each firm is producing a *smaller* output (15,625 litres versus 20,000 litres) at a *higher* average cost per litre (47 cents versus 45 cents).[2] In general:

Long-run equilibrium under monopolistic competition requires that the firm's demand curve be tangent to its average-cost curve.

Why? Because if the two curves intersected, there would be output levels at which price exceeded average cost, which means that economic profits could be earned and there would be an influx of new substitute products. Similarly, if the average-cost curve failed to touch the demand curve altogether, the firm would be unable to obtain returns equal to those that its capital can get elsewhere, and firms would leave the industry.

[2]*Exercise*: Show that if the demand curve fell still further, the firm would incur a loss. What would then happen in the long run?

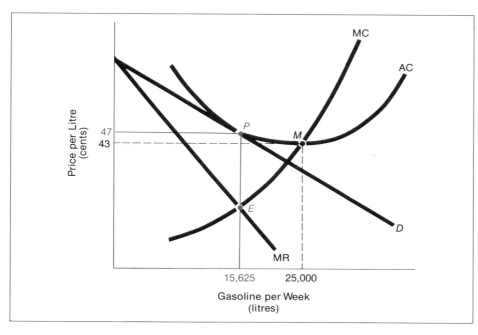

Figure 28-2
LONG-RUN EQUILIBRIUM OF
THE FIRM UNDER
MONOPOLISTIC
COMPETITION
In this diagram the cost curves are
identical to those of Figure 28-1,
but the demand curve (and hence
also the MR curve) has been
depressed by the entry of new
competitors. When the firm
maximizes profits by equating
marginal revenue and marginal
cost (point *E*), its average cost is
equal to its price (47 cents), so
economic profits are zero. For this
reason, the diagram depicts a
long-run equilibrium position.

This analysis of entry is quite similar to the perfectly competitive case. Moreover, the notion that firms under monopolistic competition earn exactly zero economic profits seems to correspond fairly well to what we see in the real world. Filling-station operators, whose market has the characteristics of monopolistic competition, do not earn notably higher profits than do small farmers, who operate under conditions closer to perfect competition.

The Excess-Capacity Theorem and Resource Allocation

But there is one important difference between perfect and monopolistic competition. Look at Figure 28-2 again. The tangency point between the average-cost and demand curves, point *P*, occurs along the *negatively sloping portion* of the average-cost curve, since only there does the AC curve have the same (negative) slope as the demand curve. If the AC curve is U-shaped, the tangency point must therefore lie above and to the left of the *minimum point* on the average-cost curve, point *M*. By contrast, under perfect competition the firm's demand curve is horizontal, so tangency must take place at the minimum point on the average-cost curve, as is easily confirmed by referring back to Figure 25-9(a) on page 501. This observation leads to the following important conclusion:

Under monopolistic competition, the firm in the long run will tend to produce an output lower than that which minimizes its unit costs, and hence unit costs of the monopolistic competitor will be higher than is necessary. Since the level of output corresponding to minimum average cost is naturally considered to be the firm's optimal capacity, this result has been called the **excess-capacity theorem of monopolistic competition**.

It follows that if every firm under monopolistic competition were to expand its output, cost per unit of output would be reduced. But we must be careful about jumping to policy conclusions from that observation. It does *not* follow that *every* monopolistically competitive firm *should* produce more. After all, such an overall increase in industry output means that a smaller portion of the economy's resources will be available for other uses; and from the information at hand we have no way of knowing whether that leaves us ahead or behind in terms of social benefits.

Yet the situation represented in Figure 28–2 can still be interpreted to represent a substantial *inefficiency*. While it is not clear that society would gain if *every* firm were to achieve lower costs by expanding its production, society *can* save resources if firms combine into a smaller number of larger companies that produce the same total output. For example, suppose that in the situation shown in Figure 28–2 there are 32 monopolistically competitive firms each selling 15,625 litres of gas per week. The total cost of this output, according to the figures given in the diagram, would be

$$\text{(Number of firms)} \times \text{(Output per firm)} \times \text{(Cost per unit)}$$
$$= 32 \times 15{,}625 \times \$0.47 = \$235{,}000.$$

If, instead, the number of stations were cut to 20, and each sold 25,000 litres, total production would be unchanged. But total costs would fall to $20 \times 25{,}000 \times \$0.43 = \$215{,}000$, a net saving of \$20,000 *for the same total output.*

This result is not dependent on the particular numbers used in our illustration. It follows directly from the observation that lowering the cost per unit must always reduce the total cost of producing any *given* industry output. The excess-capacity theorem explains one of the puzzles mentioned at the start of this chapter. The intersection with four filling stations, where two could serve the available customers with little increase in delays and at lower costs, is a practical example of excess capacity.

The excess-capacity theorem seems to imply that there are too many sellers in monopolistically competitive markets and that society would benefit from a reduction in their numbers. However, such a conclusion would be a bit hasty. Even if a smaller number of larger firms could reduce costs, society may not benefit from the change because it would leave consumers a smaller range of choice. Since all products are at least slightly different under monopolistic competition, a reduction in the number of firms means that the number of different products falls as well. We achieve greater efficiency at the cost of greater standardization. In some cases consumers may agree that this trade-off represents a net gain, particularly where the variety of products available was initially so great that it only served to confuse them. But for other products, many consumers might argue that the diversity of choice is worth the extra cost involved.

Oligopoly

An **oligopoly** is a market dominated by a few sellers, at least several of which are large enough relative to the total market to be able to influence the market price.

In terms of the dollar value of all manufactured goods produced in our economy, there seems little doubt that first place must be assigned to our final market form—**oligopoly**. An *oligopoly* is a market dominated by a few sellers, at least several of which are large enough relative to the total market to be able to influence the market price.

In highly developed economies, it is not monopoly, but oligopoly, that is virtually synonymous with "big business." Any oligopolistic industry includes a group of giant firms, each of which keeps a watchful eye on the actions of the others.[3] It is under oligopoly that rivalry among firms takes its most direct and active form. Here one encounters such actions and reactions as the frequent introduction of new products, free samples, and aggressive—if not downright nasty—advertising campaigns. One firm's price decision is likely to elicit a cry of pain from its rivals, and firms are engaged in a continuing battle in which strategies

---

[3]Notice that nothing is said in the definition about the degree of product differentiation. Some oligopolies sell products that are essentially identical (such as steel plate from steelmakers) while others sell products that are quite different in the eyes of consumers (for example, Chevrolets, Fords, and Plymouths).

are planned day by day and each major decision can be expected to induce a direct response.

The manager of a large oligopolistic firm who has occasion to study economics is somewhat taken aback by the notion of perfect competition, because it is devoid of all harsh competitive activity as he knows it. Remember that under perfect competition the managers of firms make no price decisions—they simply accept the price dictated by market forces and adjust their output accordingly. As we observed at the beginning of the chapter, a competitive firm does not advertise; it adopts no sales gimmicks; it does not even know who most of its competitors are. But since oligopolists are not as dependent on market forces, they do not enjoy such luxuries. They worry about prices, spend fortunes on advertising, and try to understand their rivals' behaviour patterns.

The reasons for such divergent behaviour should be clear. First, a perfectly competitive firm can sell all it wants at the current market price. So why should it waste money on advertising? By contrast, Ford and Chrysler cannot sell all the cars they want at the current price. Since their demand curves are negatively sloped, if they want to sell more they must either reduce prices or advertise more (to shift their demand curves outward).

Second, since the public believes that the products supplied by firms in a perfectly competitive industry are identical, if seller A advertises his product, the advertisement is just as likely to bring customers to seller B. Under oligopoly, however, products are usually not identical. Ford advertises to try to convince consumers that its automobiles are better than GM's or Toyota's. And if the advertising campaign succeeds, GM and Toyota will be hurt and probably will respond by more advertising of their own. Thus, it is the firm in an oligopoly with differentiated products that is forced to compete via advertising, while the perfectly competitive firm gains little or nothing by doing so.

Why Oligopolistic Behaviour Is So Hard to Analyse

The relative freedom of choice in pricing of at least the largest firms in an oligopolistic industry, and the necessity for them to take direct account of their rivals' responses, are potentially troublesome. Producers that are able to influence the market price may find it expedient to adjust their outputs so as to secure more favourable prices. Just as in the case of monopoly, such actions are likely to be at the expense of the consumer and detrimental to the economy's efficient use of resources.

It is not easy to reach definite conclusions about resource allocation under oligopoly, however. The reason is that oligopoly is much more difficult to analyse than the other forms of economic organization. The difficulty arises from the interdependent nature of oligopolistic decisions. For example, Ford's management knows that its actions will probably lead to reactions by General Motors, which in turn may require a readjustment in Ford's plans, thereby producing a modification in GM's response, and so on. Where such a sequence of moves and countermoves may lead is difficult enough to ascertain. But the fact that Ford executives know all this in advance, and may try to take it into account in making their initial decision, makes even that first step difficult, if not impossible, to analyse and predict.

The truth is that almost anything can happen under oligopoly, and sometimes does. Early American railroad kings went so far as to employ gangs of hoodlums who engaged in pitched battles to try to prevent the operation of a rival line. At the other extreme, overt or more subtle forms of collusion have been employed to avoid rivalry altogether—to transform an oligopolistic industry, at least temporarily, into a monopolistic one. Arrangements designed to make it possible for the firms to live and let live have also been utilized: Price leadership (see below) is one example; an agreement allocating geographic areas among the different firms is another.

Because of this rich variety of behaviour patterns it is not surprising that economists have been unable to agree on a single, widely accepted model of oligopoly behaviour. Nor should they. Since oligopolies in the real world are so diverse, oligopoly models in the theoretical world should also come in various shapes and sizes. The theory of oligopoly contains some really remarkable pieces of economic analysis, some of which we will review in the following sections.

A Shopping List

An introductory course cannot hope to explain all the different models of oligopoly; nor would that serve any purpose but to confuse you. Since economists differ in their opinions about which approaches to oligopoly theory are the most interesting and promising, we offer in this section a quick catalogue of some models of oligopoly behaviour. Then, in the remainder of the chapter, we will describe in greater detail a few other models.

Ignore Interdependence

One simple approach to the problem of oligopolistic interdependence is to assume that the oligopolists themselves ignore it; that they behave as if their actions will not elicit reactions from their rivals. It *is* possible that an oligopolist, finding the "if he thinks that I think that he thinks . . ." chain of reasoning just too complex, will decide to ignore his rivals' behaviour. He may then just maximize profits on the assumption that his decisions will not affect those of his rivals. In this case, the analysis of oligopoly is identical to the analysis of monopoly in the previous chapter.

While it is possible that *some* oligopolies ignore interdependence *some* of the time, it is very unlikely that such models offer a general explanation for the behaviour of *most* oligopoly behaviour *most* of the time. The reason is quite simple. Because they operate in the same market, the price and output decisions of the makers of Brand X and Brand Y soap suds *really are* interdependent. Suppose, for example, that the management of Brand X, Inc., decides to cut its price to $1.05 per box (on the assumption that Brand Y, Inc., will continue to charge $1.12 per box), to manufacture five million boxes per year, and to spend $1 million per year on advertising. It may find itself surprised when Brand Y, Inc., cuts its price to $1 per box, raises production to eight million boxes per year, and sponsors the Stanley Cup. If so, Brand X's profits will suffer, and the company will wish it had not cut its price. Most important for our purposes, it will learn not to ignore interdependence in the future. Thus it seems imperative to consider models that deal explicitly with oligopolistic interdependence.

Cartels

The opposite end of the spectrum from ignoring interdependence is for all the firms in an oligopoly to collude overtly with one another, thereby transforming the industry into a giant monopoly—a **cartel**.

A **cartel** is a group of sellers of a product who have joined together to control its production, sale, and price in the hope of obtaining the advantages of monopoly.

A notable example of the formation of a cartel is the Organization of Petroleum Exporting Countries (OPEC), which first began to make decisions in unison in 1973. OPEC is one of the most spectacularly successful cartels in history. By restricting output, the member nations managed to quadruple the price of oil in 1973-74. Then, unlike most cartels, which come apart in internal bickering or for other reasons, OPEC held together through two worldwide recessions and a variety of unsettling political events, and struck again with huge price increases in 1979-80.[4]

But the story of OPEC is not the norm. Cartels are not easy to organize and are even more difficult to preserve. Firms find it hard to agree on such things as the

[4]For further discussion of OPEC, see Chapter 35.

---

amount by which each will reduce its output in order to help push up the price. And once price is driven up and profitability increased, it becomes tempting for each seller to offer secret discounts in order to lure some of the profitable business away from other members of the cartel. (Indeed, some of this happened to OPEC in the period of limited oil demand in the early 1980s.) When this happens, or is even suspected by cartel members, it is often the beginning of the end of the collusive arrangement. Each member begins suspecting the others and is tempted to cut price first, before the others beat him to the punch.

Many economists consider cartels to be one of the least desirable forms of market organization. If a cartel is successful, it may end up charging the monopoly price and obtaining monopoly profits. But because the firms do not actually combine their operations but continue to produce separately, the cartel offers the public no offsetting benefits in the form of economies of large-scale production. For these and other reasons, open collusion among firms is illegal in Canada, as we will see in Chapter 31, and outright cartel arrangements are rarely found. (However, in many other countries cartels are common.)

Price Leadership

Though overt collusion is quite rare, some observers think that *tacit collusion* is quite common among oligopolists in our economy. Oligopolists who do not want to rock what amounts to a very profitable boat may seek to develop some indirect way of communicating with one another and signalling their intentions.

One common example of tacit collusion is **price leadership**, an arrangement in which one firm in the industry is, in effect, assigned the task of making pricing decisions for the entire group. It is expected that other firms will adopt the prices set by the price leader, even though there is no explicit agreement, only tacit consent. Typically, the price leader will be the dominant firm in the industry. But in some price-leadership arrangements the role of leader may rotate from one firm to another. For example, it has been suggested that the American steel industry for many years conformed to the price leadership model with U.S. Steel and Bethlehem Steel assuming the role of leader at different times.

Price leadership *does* overcome the problem of oligopolistic interdependence, though it is not the only possible way of doing so. If Brand X, Inc., is the price leader for the soap suds industry, it can predict how Brand Y, Inc., will react to any price increases it announces. (Brand Y will match the increases.) Similarly, Brand Z executives will be able to predict Brand Y's behaviour as long as the price-leadership arrangement holds up.

But one problem besetting price leadership is that, while the oligopolists as a group may benefit by avoiding a damaging price war, one of them may benefit more than the others. The firm that is the price leader is clearly in a better position to maximize its own profits than are any of the rival firms, which must simply fall in line. It is thus the responsibility of the price leader to take into account its rivals' welfare when making its price decision—or else it may find itself dethroned! For this reason, a price-leadership arrangement, if effective, can lead to the same sort of price and production decisions as would a cartel. Alternatively, leadership can break down entirely.

Sales Maximization*

Early in our analysis of the theory of the firm, we discussed the hypothesis that firms try to maximize profits and noted that other objectives are possible (see pages 453–54). Among these alternative goals, the one that has achieved the most attention is **sales maximization**.

Under **price leadership**, one firm sets the price for the industry and the others follow.

*The three sections that follow may be read in any combination, and in any order, without loss of continuity.

Modern industrial firms are managed and owned by entirely different groups of people. The managers are paid executives who work for the company on a full-time basis and may grow to identify their own welfare with that of the company. The owners may be a large and diffuse group of shareholders, most of whom own only a tiny fraction of the outstanding stock, take little interest in the operations of the company, and do not feel that the company is "theirs" in any real sense. In such a situation, it is not entirely implausible that the company's decisions will be influenced more heavily by management's goals than by the goal of the owners (which is, presumably, to maximize profit).

It has been suggested, for example, that management's salary and prestige may be tied more directly to the company's *size*, as measured by its dollar sales volume, rather than to its *profits*. Therefore, the firm's managers may select a price–output combination that maximizes sales rather than profits. But does sales-revenue maximization lead to different decisions than does profit maximization? We shall see now that the answer is yes.

Figure 28–3 is a diagram that should be familiar by now. It shows the marginal-cost (MC) and average-cost (AC) curves for a firm—in this case Brand X, Inc.—along with its demand and marginal-revenue (MR) curves. We have used such diagrams before and know that if the company wants to maximize profits, it will select point *A*, where MC = MR. This means that it will produce 2.5 million boxes of soap suds per year and sell them at a price of $1 each (point *E*). Since average cost at this level of output is only 80 cents per box, profit per unit is 20 cents. Total profits are therefore $0.20 × 2,500,000 = $500,000 per year. This is the highest attainable profit level for Brand X, Inc.

Now what if Brand X wants to maximize sales revenue instead? In this case, it will want to keep producing until MR is depressed to *zero*; that is, it will select point *B*. Why? By definition, MR is the *additional* revenue obtained by raising output by one unit. If the firm wishes to maximize revenue, then any time it finds that MR is positive it will want to increase output further, and any time it finds that MR is negative it will want to decrease output. Only when MR = 0 can the

Figure 28–3

SALES-MAXIMIZATION EQUILIBRIUM

A firm that wishes to maximize sales revenue will expand output until marginal revenue (MR) is zero—point *B* in the diagram, where output is 3.75 million boxes per year. This is a greater output level than it would choose if it were interested in maximizing profits. In that case, it would select point *A*, where MC = MR, and produce only 2.5 million boxes. Since the demand curve is downward sloping, the price corresponding to point *B* (75 cents) must be less than the price corresponding to point *A* ($1).

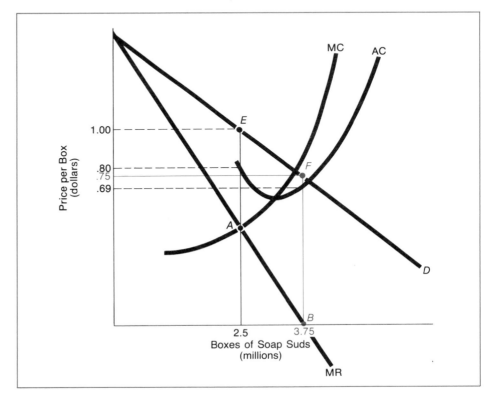

maximum sales revenue have possibly been achieved.[5]

Thus if Brand X, Inc. is a sales maximizer, it will produce 3.75 million boxes of soap suds per year (point B), and charge 75 cents per box (point F). Since average costs at this level of production are only 69 cents per box, profit per unit is 6 cents and, with 3.75 million units sold, total profit is $225,000. Naturally, this level of profit is less than what the firm can achieve if it reduces output to the profit-maximizing level. But this is not the firm's goal. Its sales revenue at point B is 75 cents per unit times 3.75 million units, or $2,812,500, whereas at point A it was only $2,500,000 (2.5 million units at $1 each). What we conclude, then, is that:

If a firm is maximizing sales revenue, it will produce more output and charge a lower price than it would if it were maximizing profits.

We see clearly in Figure 28–3 that this result holds for Brand X, Inc. But does it always hold? The answer is yes. Look again at Figure 28–3, but ignore the numbers on the axes. At point A, where MR = MC, marginal revenue must be positive because it is equal to marginal cost (which, we may assume is *always* positive). At point B, MR is equal to zero. Since the marginal-revenue curve is negatively sloped, the point where it reaches zero (point B) must necessarily correspond to a higher level of output than the point where it cuts the marginal-cost curve (point A). Thus, sales-maximizing firms always produce more than profit-maximizing firms and, to sell this greater volume of output, they must charge a lower price.

The Game-Theory Approach

Game theory, contributed in 1944 by mathematician John von Neumann (1903–1957) and economist Oskar Morgenstern (1902–1977), adopts a more imaginative approach than any other analysis of oligopoly. It attacks the issue of interdependence directly by assuming that each firm's managers proceed on the assumption *that their rivals are extremely ingenious decision-makers*. In this model, each oligopolist is seen as a competing player in a game of strategy. Since managers believe their opponents will always adopt the most profitable countermove to any move they make, they seek the optimal defensive strategy.

Two fundamental concepts of game theory are the *strategy* and the *payoff matrix*. A strategy represents an operational plan for one of the participants. In its simplest form it may refer to just one of a participant's possible decisions. For example, "I will add to my product line a car with a TV set that the driver can watch," or "I will cut the price of my car to $5500." Since much of the game-theory analysis of oligopoly has focused on an oligopoly of two firms—a *duopoly*—we illustrate the payoff matrix for a two-person game in Table 28–1.

This matrix is a table of numbers reporting the payoffs that our firm will receive for each possible pair of its own and its rival's strategies. It is read like a mileage chart. For example, if our firm selects strategy B (cut price to $5500) and its rival chooses W (offer diesel engine), we see that our company will end up with 70 percent of the market (third column, second row). The special case of pure rivalry, in which every gain for our firm means an *exactly* equal loss for its competitor, and vice versa, is referred to as a *zero-sum game*. In the zero-sum case, the payoff matrix has the convenient property of telling us all we need to know about our competitor's payoff matrix as well as our own. Given the market share of one firm, we can immediately deduce the other firm's market share by subtraction. For example, if the matrix tells us that our firm's market share will be 70 percent, we know that the rival's market share must be 30 percent.

---

[5] The logic here is exactly the same as the logic that led to the conclusion that a firm maximized *profits* by setting *marginal profit* equal to zero. If you need review, consult Chapter 23, especially pages 458–59.

Table 28-1

A PAYOFF MATRIX

		Rival's Strategy		
		U: Set Price at $6000	V: Set Price at $5000	W: Offer Diesel Engine
Our Strategy	A: Install TV Set	80	35	30
	B: Cut Price to $5500	45	28	70
	C: Offer Three-year Loan	60	50	90

The entries represent the share of market our firm will receive under any combination of strategies offered by itself and its competitor.

The **maximin criterion** means selecting the strategy that yields the maximum payoff, on the assumption that your opponent does as much damage to you as he can.

We can now begin to discuss optimal strategy choices for the two firms. Since our firm is in direct conflict with the other firm, we know that our rival will try to keep our market share as low as possible, and vice versa. Thus, in evaluating its strategies, the management of our firm may reason as follows: "If I select strategy A, the worst that can happen to me is that my adversary will select counterstrategy W, which would cut my market share to its minimum level, 30 percent (the coloured number in the first row of the payoff matrix). Similarly, if I utilize strategy B, the outcome I must be prepared for is 28 percent, which is the (coloured) minimum payoff to that strategy. Finally, if I use strategy C, my rival can damage me most by using strategy V, which gives me 50 percent."

What, if anything, can the management of our firm do to maximize its chances for success? Game theory suggests that it should select the strategy whose *minimum* payoff is higher than the minimum payoff for any other strategy. This is called the **maximin criterion**—one seeks the *max*imum of the *min*imum payoffs to the various strategies, the highest of the blue entries. In this case, the maximin payoff is 50 percent and leads to the choice of strategy C by our firm (and V by its adversary).

There is, of course, a great deal more to game theory than we have been able to suggest in a few paragraphs. We have only sought to suggest a little of its flavour. Game theory provides, for example, an illuminating analysis of coalitions, indicating, for cases involving more than two firms, which firms would do well to align themselves together against which others. The theory of games has also been used to analyse a variety of complicated problems outside the realm of oligopoly theory. It has been employed in management-training programs and by a number of government agencies. It is used in political science and in formulating military strategy. It has been presented here to offer the reader a glimpse of the type of work that is taking place on the frontiers of economic analysis and to suggest how economists think about complex analytical problems.

The Kinked Demand Curve Model*

As our final example of oligopoly analysis, we describe a model designed to account for the alleged stickiness in oligopolistic pricing, meaning that prices in oligopolistic markets change far less frequently than do prices in competitive markets. It will be recalled that this is one of the puzzling phenomena with which we began this chapter. The prices of corn, soybeans, cocoa, and silver, all of which are sold in

*Variants of this model were constructed by Hall and Hitch in England and by Sweezy in the United States. See R.L. Hall and C.J. Hitch, "Price Theory and Business Behavior," *Oxford Economic Papers.* No. 2, May 1939, and P.M. Sweezy, "Demand Under Conditions of Oligopoly," *Journal of Political Economy,* vol. 47, August 1939.

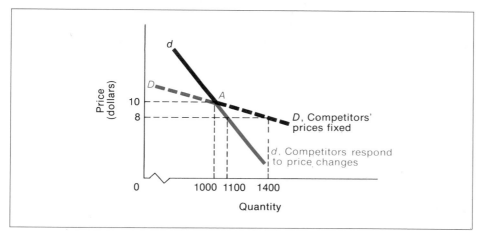

Figure 28-4
THE KINKED DEMAND
CURVE

It has been suggested that oligopolists are deterred from changing prices frequently because they fear the reactions of their rivals. If they raise prices, they will lose many customers to competitors because the competitors will not match the price increase. (Elastic demand curve *DD* therefore applies to price increases.) But if they cut prices, competitors will be forced to match the price cut, so that price cut will not bring many new customers. (The inelastic demand curve *dd* applies to price cuts.) Thus, the demand curve facing the firm is the kinked, blue curve *DAd*.

markets with large numbers of buyers and sellers, change minute by minute. But prices of such items as cars, TV sets, and dishwashers, all of which are supplied by oligopolists, may change only every few months. These prices seem to resist frequent change even in periods of inflation.

One reason may be that, when an oligopolist cuts his price, he is never sure how his rivals will react. One extreme possibility is that Firm Y will ignore the price cut of Firm X, that is, Y's price will not change. Alternatively, Y may reduce its price, precisely matching that of Firm X. Accordingly, the model makes use of two different demand curves: One curve represents the quantities a given oligopolistic firm can sell at different prices if *competitors match its price moves*, and the other demand curve represents what happens when competitors stubbornly *stick to their initial price levels*.

Point *A* in Figure 28-4 represents the initial price and output of our firm: 1000 units at $10 each. Through that point pass two demand curves: *DD*, which represents our company's demand if competitors keep their prices fixed, and *dd*, the curve indicating what happens when competitors match our firm's price changes.

The *DD* curve is the more elastic (flatter) of the two, and a moment's thought indicates why this should be so. If our firm cuts its price from its initial level of $10 to, say, $8, and if competitors do not match this cut, we would expect our firm to get a large number of new customers—perhaps its quantity demanded will jump to 1400. However, if its competitors respond by also reducing their prices, its quantity demanded will rise by less—perhaps only to 1100. Conversely, when it raises its price, our firm may expect a larger loss of sales if its rivals fail to match its increase, which the reader may readily verify by observing the relative steepness (inelasticity) of the curve *dd* in Figure 28-4.

How does this relate to sticky oligopolistic prices? Here our firm's fears and expectations must be brought into the matter. The hypothesis of those who designed this model was that a typical oligopolistic firm has good reason to fear the worst. If it lowers its prices and its rivals do not, its sales will seriously cut into its competitor's volume, and so the rivals will *have* to match the price cut in order to protect themselves. The inelastic demand curve, *dd*, will therefore apply if our firm decides on a price reduction (points below and to the right of point *A*).

On the other hand, if our company chooses to *increase* its price, management will fear that its rivals will continue to sit at their old price levels, calmly collecting the customers that have been driven to them. Thus, the relevant demand curve for price increases will be *DD*.

In sum, our firm will figure that it will face a segment of the elastic demand curve *DD* if it raises its price and a segment of the inelastic demand curve *dd* if it decreases its price. Its true demand curve will then be given by the heavy coloured

Figure 28-5

THE KINKED DEMAND
CURVE AND STICKY PRICES

The kinked demand curve *DAd*
that we derived in the previous
diagram leads to a marginal-
revenue curve that follows MR
down to point *B*, then drops
directly down to point *C*, and finally
follows mr thereafter.
Consequently, marginal-cost
curves a little higher or a little
lower than the MC curve shown in
the diagram will lead to the same
price–output decision. Oligopoly
prices are "sticky," then, in the
sense that they do not respond to
minor changes in costs. Only cost
changes large enough to push the
MC curve out of the range *BC* will
lead to a change in price.

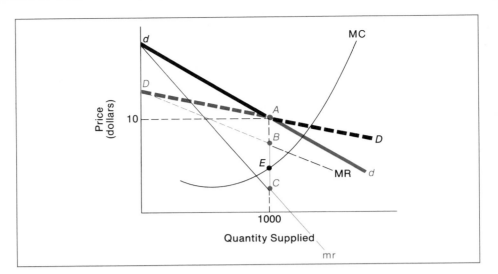

line. For obvious reasons, this is called a **kinked demand curve**.

In these circumstances, it will pay management to vary its price only under
extreme provocation; that is, only if there is an enormous change in costs. For the
kinked demand curve represents a "heads you lose, tails you lose" proposition in
terms of any potential price change. If it raises its price, the firm will lose many
customers (demand is elastic); if it lowers its price, the increase in volume will be
comparatively small (demand is inelastic).

Figure 28–5 illustrates this conclusion graphically. The two demand curves,
dd and *DD*, are carried over precisely from the previous diagram. The dashed
curve, labelled MR, is the marginal-revenue curve associated with *DD*, while the
solid curve, labelled mr, is the marginal-revenue curve associated with *dd*. Since
the marginal-revenue curve relevant to the firm's decision-making is MR for any
output level *below* 1000 units but mr for any ouput level *above* 1000 units, the
composite marginal-revenue curve facing the firm is shown by the thin coloured
line.

The marginal-cost curve drawn in the diagram cuts this composite marginal-
revenue curve at point *E*, which indicates the profit-maximizing combination of
output and price for this oligopolist. Specifically, the quantity supplied at point *E*
is 1000 units, and the price is $10, which we read from curve *DAd*.

The unique aspect of this diagram is that the kinked demand curve leads to a
marginal-revenue curve that takes a sharp plunge between points *B* and *C*.
Consequently, moderate upward or downward shifts of the MC curve will still
leave it intersecting the marginal-revenue curve somewhere between *B* and *C*, and
thus will *not* lead the firm to change its price–output decision. (Try this for
yourself in Figure 28–5.) This is the sense in which the kinked demand curve
makes prices "sticky."

If this is in fact the way oligopolists feel about their competitors' behaviour, it
is easy to see why they may be reluctant to make frequent price changes. We can
also understand why a system of price leadership might arise. The price leader can,
in times of inflation for instance, raise prices when he thinks it appropriate,
confident that he will not be left out on a limb (a kink?) by others' unwillingness to
follow.

Monopolistic Competition, Oligopoly, and Public Welfare

How good or bad, from the viewpoint of the general welfare, is the performance of
firms that are monopolistically competitive or oligopolistic?

The New Theory of Contestable Markets

Perfect competition has long been used as a standard for the structure and behaviour of an industry, though it is widely recognized to be unattainable in reality. Recently, some economists have tried to supplement this concept with the aid of a generalized criterion, called a *perfectly contestable market*. Some markets that contain a few relatively large firms are highly contestable, though they are certainly not perfectly competitive. Because perfect competition requires a large number of firms, all of them negligible in size relative to the size of the industry, no industry with economies of large-scale production can be perfectly competitive.

A market is defined as perfectly contestable if firms can enter it and, if they choose, exit without losing the money they invested. Note that the crucial issue is not the amount of capital that is required to enter the industry, but whether or not an entrant can get his investment out if he wishes. For example, if entry involves investing in highly mobile capital—such as airplanes, barges, or cars—the entrant may be able to exit quickly and cheaply. If a car-rental agency enters the Vancouver market and finds business disappointing, it can easily transfer its cars to, say, Winnipeg.

A profitable market that is contestable is therefore attractive to *potential* entrants. Because of the absence of barriers to entry or exit, firms undertake little risk by going into such a market. If their entry turns out to have been a mistake, they can move to another market without significant loss.

Performance of Contestable Markets

The constant threat of entry elicits good performance by oligopolists, or even by monopolists, in a contestable market. In particular, highly contestable markets have at least two desirable characteristics.

First, profits exceeding the opportunity cost of capital are eliminated in the long run by freedom of entry, just as they are in a perfectly competitive market. If the current opportunity cost of capital is 12 percent while the firms in a contestable market are earning a return of 18 percent, new firms will enter the market, expand the industry's outputs, and drive down the prices of its products to the point where all excess profit has been removed. To avoid this outcome, established firms must expand to a level that precludes excess profit.

Second, inefficient enterprises cannot survive in a perfectly contestable industry because cost inefficiencies invite replacement of the incumbents by entrants who can provide the same outputs at lower cost and lower prices. Only firms operating at the lowest possible cost, using the most efficient techniques, can survive.

In sum, firms in a perfectly contestable market will be forced to operate as efficiently as possible and to charge prices as low as long-run financial survival permits. Though first published only a few years ago these ideas are already widely used by courts and government agencies concerned with the performance of business firms. For they provide workable guidelines for improved or acceptable behaviour in industries in which economies of scale mean that only a small number of firms can or should operate.

The concept is particularly relevant for Canada, if considered in the context of tariff policy. The government can ensure that many markets within Canada become contestable if they lower existing tariffs. Indeed, if the government established a record of behaviour along these lines, even the *threat* of tariff reduction might make other markets contestable.

We have seen that their performance *can* leave much to be desired. For example, the excess-capacity theorem showed us that monopolistic competition can lead to inefficiently high production costs. Similarly, because market forces may not be sufficiently powerful to restrain their behaviour, oligopolists' prices and outputs may differ substantially from those that are socially optimal. Moreover, there are those who believe that misleading advertising by corporate giants often distorts the judgments of consumers, leading them to buy things they do not need and would otherwise not want. Others argue that much advertising simply cancels out advertising by rival brands. Thus, even if consumer choices are not significantly distorted, many resources may simply be wasted. It is also said that such corporate giants wield political power, economic power, and power over the minds of consumers—and that all of these undermine the beneficent workings of Smith's invisible hand. Finally, because many large firms in Canada are foreign owned, it is sometimes feared that the way in which they operate is even more likely to ignore the general welfare of this country.

But because oligopoly behaviour is so varied, we cannot generalize with confidence. Because one oligopolist decides on price, output, and advertising in a

A market is **perfectly contestable** if entry and exit are costless and unimpeded.

manner very different from another, the implications for social welfare vary from case to case.

Yet, recent analysis has provided one case in which both the behaviour and the quality of performance of an oligopolistic or monopolistically competitive firm can be predicted and judged. This is the case in which entry into or exit from the market is costless and unimpeded. In such a case, called a **perfectly contestable market** (see the boxed insert on the preceding page), the constant threat of entry forces even the largest firm to behave well—to produce efficiently and never to overcharge. For if that firm is inefficient or sets its prices too high, it will be threatened with replacement by an entrant.

Of course, many industries are not perfectly contestable or even nearly so. But in those industries that are highly contestable—that is, in which entry and exit costs are negligible—market forces can do a good job of forcing business to behave in the manner that most effectively promotes the public interest. And where an industry is not very contestable, but there are ways to reduce entry and exit costs, the new theory of contestable markets suggests that this may sometimes be a more promising approach than any attempt by government to interfere with the behaviour of the oligopolistic firms in order to improve their performance.

Summary

1. Under monopolistic competition, there are numerous small buyers and sellers; each firm's product is at least somewhat different from every other firm's product—that is, each firm has a partial "monopoly" of some product characteristics, and thus a downward-sloping demand curve; there is freedom of entry and exit; and there is perfect information.

2. In long-run equilibrium under monopolistic competition, free entry eliminates economic profits by forcing the firm's demand curve into a position of tangency with its average-cost curve. Therefore, output will be below the point at which average cost is lowest. This is why monopolistic competitors are said to have "excess capacity."

3. An oligopolistic industry is composed of a few large firms selling similar products in the same market.

4. Under oligopoly, each firm carefully watches the major decisions of its rivals and will often plan counterstrategies. As a result, rivalry is often vigorous and direct, and the outcome is difficult to predict.

5. One model of oligopoly behaviour assumes that the oligopolists ignore interdependence and simply maximize profits or sales. Another assumes that they join together to form a cartel and thus act like a

monopoly. A third possibility is price leadership, where one firm sets prices and the others follow suit. A fourth is that each firm might assume that its rivals will adopt the optimal countermove to any move it makes.

6. A firm that maximizes sales revenue will continue producing up to the point where marginal revenue is driven down to zero. Consequently, a sales maximizer will produce more than a profit maximizer and will charge a lower price.

7. Game theory provides new tools for analysing business strategies under conditions of oligopoly.

8. If a firm thinks that its rivals will match any price cut but fail to match any price increase, its demand curve becomes "kinked" and its price will be sticky—that is, it will be adjusted less frequently than would be the case under either perfect competition or pure monopoly.

9. Monopolistic competition and oligopoly can be harmful to the general welfare. But if the market is perfectly contestable, that is, if entry and exit are easy and costless, the threat of entry will lead to optimal performance.

Concepts for Review

Monopolistic competition	Cartel	Maximin criterion
Excess-capacity theorem	Price leadership	Kinked demand curve
Oligopoly	Sales maximization	Sticky price
Oligopolistic interdependence	Game theory	Perfectly contestable markets

Questions for Discussion

1. How many real industries can you name that are oligopolies? How many that operate under monopolistic competition? Perfect competition? Which of these is hardest to find in reality? Why do you think this is so?

2. Consider some of the products that are widely advertised on TV. By what kind of firm is each produced—a perfectly competitive firm, an oligopolistic firm, or what? How many major products can you think of that are *not* advertised on TV?

3. In what ways may the small retail sellers of the following products differentiate their goods from those of their rivals to make themselves monopolistic competitors: hamburgers, gasoline, aspirin, facial tissues?

4. Pricing of securities on the stock market is said to be done under conditions in many respects similar to perfect competition. The auto industry is an oligopoly. How often do you think the price of a share of Ford Motor Company's common stock changes? How about the price of a Ford Mustang? How would you explain the difference?

5. Suppose Chrysler hires a popular singer to advertise its compact automobiles. The campaign is very successful and the company increases its share of the compact-car market substantially. What is Ford likely to do?

6. Using game theory, set up a payoff matrix similar to one Chrysler's management might employ in analysing the problem presented in Question 5.

7. Discussion Question 4 at the end of Chapter 27 presented cost and demand data for a monopolist, and asked you to find the profit-maximizing solution. Use these same data to find the sales-maximizing solution. Are the answers different? Explain.

8. Can you think of any aspects of the behaviour of some particular oligopolistic firm that in your view is not in the public interest?

9. Do all oligopoly firms behave in the ways described in your answer to Question 8?

10. A new entrant, Bargain Airways, cuts air fares between Eastwich and Westwich by 30 percent. Biggie Airlines, which has been operating on this route, responds by cutting fares by 50 percent. What does Biggie hope to achieve?

11. If air transportation is perfectly contestable, why will Biggie fail to achieve the ultimate goal of its price cut?

12. Which of the following industries are most likely to be contestable?
    a. Steel production.
    b. Barge transportation.
    c. Airplane manufacturing.
    d. Air transportation.
    Explain your answers.

Shortcomings of the Market Mechanism and Government Attempts to Remedy Them

29

When she was good
She was very, very good.
But when she was bad
she was horrid.
HENRY WADSWORTH
LONGFELLOW

What does the market do well, and what does it do poorly? These questions constitute the central theme of our study of microeconomics, and we are by now well on our way toward getting some answers. We began in Chapters 25 and 26 by explaining and extolling the workings of Adam Smith's invisible hand—the mechanism by which a perfectly competitive economy allocates resources efficiently without any guidance from government. While the theoretical model studied there was an idealized one, observation of the real world confirms the accomplishments of the market mechanism. Free-market economies have achieved levels of output, productive efficiency, variety in available consumer goods, and general prosperity that are unprecedented in history.

Yet the market mechanism also displays some glaring weaknesses. One of these—the fact that large and powerful business firms can interfere with the invisible hand and lead both to concentrations of wealth and to misallocation of resources—was the subject of Chapters 27 and 28. Now we take a more comprehensive view of the failures of the market and some of the things that can be done to remedy these failures.

That the market cannot do everything we would like it to do is quite apparent. Amid the outpouring of goods and services, we find areas of depressing poverty, cities choked with traffic and pollution, and educational institutions and artistic organizations in serious financial trouble. Our economy, although capable of yielding an overwhelming abundance of material wealth, seems far less capable of eradicating social ills and controlling environmental damage. In this chapter, we will examine the reasons for the market's failings in these areas and indicate specifically why the price system *by itself* may be incapable of dealing with them.

What Does the Market Do Poorly?

While it is probably impossible to come up with an exhaustive list of the imperfections of the market mechanism, we can identify seven major areas in which the market has been accused of failing:

1. Market economies suffer from severe business fluctuations.
2. The market distributes income quite unequally.

3. Where markets are monopolized, they allocate resources inefficiently.
4. The market cannot deal properly with the incidental side effects of many economic activities.
5. The market cannot provide public goods, such as national defense.
6. The market mechanism makes public and personal services increasingly expensive.
7. The market does a poor job of allocating resources between the present and the future.

The first three of these issues—business fluctuations, income inequality, and monopoly—have already been discussed or will be discussed in detail later. The remaining four items on our list constitute the subject matter of this chapter. Each of these, like monopoly, is an instance in which the efficiency of the market mechanism is compromised. Therefore, to help us analyse these problems, we offer next a brief review of the concept of efficient resource allocation, which was discussed in detail in Chapter 26.

Efficient Resource Allocation: A Review

The basic problem of resource allocation is deciding how much of each commodity the economy should produce. At first glance, it may seem that the solution is simple: the more the better; so we should produce as much of each good as we can. But careful thinking tells us that this is not necessarily the right decision.

Outputs are not created out of thin air. They are produced from the available supplies of labour, fuel, raw materials, and machinery. And if we use these resources to produce, say, more handkerchiefs, we must take them away from some other products, such as linens. So, to decide whether increasing the production of handkerchiefs is a good idea, we must compare the utility of that increase with the loss of utility caused by having to produce less hospital linen. The increased output will be a good thing only if society considers the additional handkerchiefs more valuable than the forgone hospital linen.

Opportunity Cost and Resource Allocation

Here it is worth remembering the concept of *opportunity cost*, one of our **12 Ideas for Beyond the Final Exam**. The opportunity cost of an increase in the output of some product is the value of the other goods and services that must be forgone when inputs (resources) are taken away from their production in order to increase the output of the product in question. In our example, the opportunity cost of the increased handkerchief output is the decrease in output of hospital linen that results when resources are reallocated from the latter to the former. The general principle is that an increase in some output represents a *misallocation* of resources if the utility of that increased output is less than its opportunity cost.

To illustrate this idea, we repeat a graph encountered several times in earlier chapters—a *production possibilities frontier*—but we put it to a somewhat different use. Curve *ABC* in Figure 29-1 is a production possibilities frontier showing the alternative combinations of handkerchiefs and hospital linens the economy can produce by reallocating its resources between the production of the two goods. For example, point *A* amounts to allocation of all the resources to handkerchief production, so that 100 million of these items and no hospital linens are produced. Point *C* represents the reverse situation, with all resources allocated to hospital linens and none to handkerchiefs. Point *B* represents an intermediate allocation, resulting in the production of eight million metres of linen and 60 million handkerchiefs.

Suppose now that point *B* represents the *optimal* resource allocation—that is,

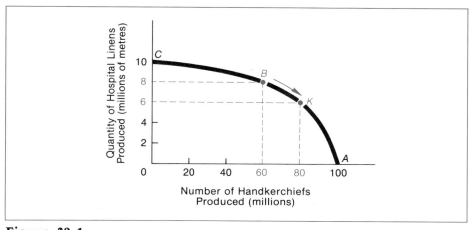

Figure 29-1

THE ECONOMY'S PRODUCTION POSSIBILITIES FRONTIER FOR THE PRODUCTION
OF TWO GOODS

This graph shows all combinations of outputs of the two goods that the resources available to the
economy enable it to produce. If *B* is the most desired output combination among those that are
possible, it will correspond to a market equilibrium in which each good's price is equal to its marginal
cost. If the price of linen is above its marginal cost, or the price of a handkerchief is below its marginal
cost, then linen output will be inefficiently small and handkerchief output inefficiently large (point *K*).

the only combination of outputs that best satisfies the wants of society among all
the possibilities that are *attainable* (given the technology and resources as
represented by the production frontier). Two questions are pertinent to our
discussion of the price system:

1. What prices will get the economy to select point *B*; that is, what prices will
   yield an *efficient* allocation of resources?
2. How can the wrong set of prices lead to a misallocation of resources?

The first question was discussed extensively in Chapter 26. There we saw
that:

An efficient allocation of resources requires that each product's price be equal to
its marginal cost; that is:

$$P = \text{MC}.$$

The reasoning, in brief, is as follows. In a free market, the price of any good
reflects the money value to consumers of an additional unit; that is, its *marginal
utility* (MU). Similarly, if the market mechanism is working well, the *marginal
cost* (MC) measures the value (the opportunity cost) of the resources needed to
produce an additional unit of the good. Hence, if prices are set equal to marginal
costs, then consumers, by using *their own money* in the most effective way to
maximize *their own* satisfaction, will automatically be using *society's resources* in
the most effective way. That is, as long as it sets prices equal to marginal costs, the
market mechanism automatically satisfies the MC = MU rule for efficient resource
allocation that we studied in Chapter 26.[1] In terms of Figure 29–1, this means that
if *P* = MC for both goods, the economy will automatically gravitate to point *B*,
which we assumed to be the optimal point.

This chapter is devoted mainly to the second question: How can the "wrong"

[1]If you need review, consult pages 517–18.

prices cause a misallocation of resources? The answer to this question is not too difficult, and we can use the case of monopoly as an illustration.

The "law" of demand tells us that a rise in the price of a commodity normally will reduce the quantity demanded. Suppose, now, that the linen industry is a monopoly, so the price of linens exceeds their marginal cost.[2] This will decrease the quantity of linens demanded below the eight million metres that we have assumed to be socially optimal (point *B* in Figure 29–1). So the economy will move from point *B* to a point like *K*, where too few linens and too many handkerchiefs are being produced for maximal consumer satisfaction. By setting the "wrong" prices, then, the market fails to achieve the most efficient use of the economy's resources. With the prices being "wrong," the market is sending the wrong signals to individual consumers. Thus, while they still maximize their own individual satisfaction, this does not lead to the society's optimum.

In sum, if the price of a commodity is above its marginal cost, the economy will tend to produce less of that item than maximizes consumer benefits. The opposite will occur if an item's price is below its marginal cost.

In the remainder of this chapter, we will encounter several other instances in which the market mechanism may set the "wrong" prices.

Externalities

We come now to the fourth item on our list of market failures—one of the least obvious yet one of the most consequential of the imperfections of the price system. Many economic activities provide incidental benefits to others for whom they are not specifically intended. For example, a homeowner who plants a beautiful garden in front of her house, incidentally and unintentionally provides pleasure to her neighbours and to those who pass by—people from whom she receives no payment. We say then that her activity generates a **beneficial externality**.

Similarly, there are activities that indiscriminately impose costs on others. For example, the operator of a motorcycle repair shop, from which all sorts of noise besieges the neighbourhood and for which he pays no compensation to others, is said to produce a **detrimental externality**. Pollution constitutes the classic illustration of a detrimental externality.

To see why the presence of externalities causes the price system to misallocate resources, we need only recall that the system achieves efficiency by rewarding producers who serve consumers well—that is, at as low a cost as possible. This argument breaks down, however, as soon as some of the costs and benefits of economic activities are left out of the profit calculation.

When a firm pollutes a river, it uses up some of society's resources just as surely as when it burns coal. However, if it pays for coal but not for the use of water, it is natural for management to be economical in its use of coal and wasteful in its use of water. Similarly, a firm that provides benefits to others for which it receives no payment is unlikely to be generous in allocating resources to the activity, no matter how socially desirable it may be.

In an important sense, the source of the difficulty is to be found in the definition of "property rights." Coal mines are *private property;* their owners will not let anyone take coal without paying for it. Thus, coal is costly and so is not used wastefully. But waterways are not private property. Since they belong to everyone in general, they belong to no one in particular. They therefore can be used free of charge as dumping grounds for wastes by anyone who chooses to do so.

An activity is said to generate a **beneficial** or **detrimental externality** if that activity causes incidental benefits or damages to others, and no corresponding compensation is provided to or paid by those who generate the externality.

[2]To review why price under monopoly may be expected to exceed marginal cost, you may want to reread pages 531–33.

Because no one pays for the use of the oxygen in a public waterway, that oxygen will be used wastefully. That is the source of detrimental externalities.

Externalities and Inefficiency

Using these concepts, we can see precisely why an externality has undesirable effects on the allocation of resources. In discussing externalities, it is crucial to distinguish between *social* and *private* marginal cost. We define **marginal social cost** (MSC) as the sum of two components: (1) **marginal private cost** (MPC), which is the share of marginal cost caused by an activity that is paid for by the persons who carry out the activity; and (2) *incidental cost*, which is the share borne by others.

If increased output by a firm increases the smoke it emits, then, in addition to its direct private costs as recorded in the company accounts, expansion of its production imposes incidental costs on others in the form of increased laundry bills, medical expenditures, outlays for air conditioning and electricity, as well as the unpleasantness of living in a cloud of noxious fumes. These are all part of the activity's marginal *social* cost.

Where the firm's activities generate detrimental externalities, its marginal social cost will be greater than its marginal private cost. In symbols, MSC > MPC. In equilibrium, that firm will choose an output for which its marginal benefits (MB) are equal to its marginal private cost (MB = MPC); and in competitive equilibrium, the consumer's marginal utility equals price (which is the firm's MB = MPC). It follows that marginal utility is *smaller* than marginal social cost. Society would then necessarily benefit if output of that product were *reduced*. It would lose the marginal benefit, but save the marginal social cost; and since MSC > MB, society would come out ahead. We conclude that:

Where the firm's activity causes detrimental externalities, free markets will leave us in a situation where marginal benefits are less than marginal social costs. Smaller outputs than those that maximize private profits will be socially desirable.

We have already indicated why this is so. Private enterprise has no motivation to take into account costs that it causes to others but for which it does not have to pay. So goods that cause such externalities will be produced in undesirably large amounts by private firms. For precisely analogous reasons:

Where the firm's activity generates beneficial externalities, free markets will produce too little output. Society would be better off with larger output levels.

These principles can be illustrated with the aid of Figure 29–2. This diagram repeats the two basic curves needed for the analysis of the equilibrium of the firm: a marginal-revenue curve and a marginal-cost curve (see Chapter 23). These represent the *private* costs and revenues accruing to a particular firm (in this case, a paper mill). The mill's maximum profit is attained with 100,000 tonnes of output corresponding to the intersection between the marginal-cost and marginal-revenue curves (point *A*).

Now suppose that the factory's wastes pollute a nearby waterway, so that its production creates a detrimental externality whose cost the owner does not himself pay. Then marginal social cost must be higher than marginal private cost, as shown in the diagram, and the socially desirable level of output (70,000 tonnes) is at point *B* rather than point *A*.

Notice that if instead of being able to impose the external costs on others the mill's owner were forced to pay them himself, his own private marginal-cost curve would correspond to the higher of the two curves shown. His output of the polluting commodity would then fall to 70,000 tonnes, corresponding to point *B*, the intersection between the marginal-revenue curve and the marginal-*social*-cost

Figure 29-2

EQUILIBRIUM OF A FIRM
WHOSE OUTPUT PRODUCES
DETRIMENTAL
EXTERNALITIES
(POLLUTION)

The firm's profit-maximizing output,
at which its marginal private cost
and its marginal private revenue
are equal, is 100,000 tonnes. But if
the firm paid all the social costs of
its output instead of shifting some
of them to others, its marginal-cost
curve would be the curve labelled
"marginal social cost." Then it
would pay the firm to reduce its
output to 70,000 tonnes, thereby
reducing the pollution it causes.

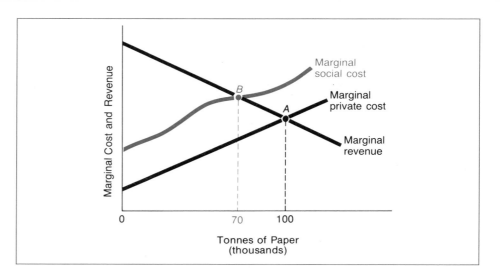

curve. But because the firm does not in fact pay for the pollution damage its
output causes, it produces an output (100,000 tonnes) that is larger than the
output it would produce if the cost imposed on the community were instead borne
by the firm (70,000 tonnes).

The same sort of diagram can be used to show that the opposite relationship
will hold when the firm's activity produces beneficial externalities. The firm will
produce less of its beneficial output than it would if it were rewarded fully for the
benefits that its activities yield.

But these results can perhaps be seen more clearly with the help of a
production possibilities frontier diagram similar to that in Figure 29-1. In Figure
29-3 we see the frontier for two industries: electricity generation, which causes air
pollution (a detrimental externality), and tulip growing, which makes an area more
attractive (a beneficial externality). We have just seen that detrimental externalities make marginal social cost greater than marginal private cost. Hence, if the
electric company charges a price equal to its own marginal (private) cost, that
price will be less than the true marginal (social) cost. Similarly, in tulip growing, a
price equal to marginal private cost will be above the true marginal cost to society.

We saw earlier in the chapter that an industry that charges a price above
marginal cost will reduce quantity demanded through this high price, and so it

Figure 29-3

EXTERNALITIES, MARKET
EQUILIBRIUM, AND
EFFICIENT RESOURCE
ALLOCATION

Because electricity producers emit
smoke (a detrimental externality),
they do not bear the true marginal
social cost of their output. So
electricity price will be below
marginal social cost, and
electricity output will be
inefficiently large (point K, not point
B). The opposite is true of tulip
production. Because they
generate beneficial externalities,
tulips will be priced above the
marginal social cost and tulip
output will be inefficiently small.

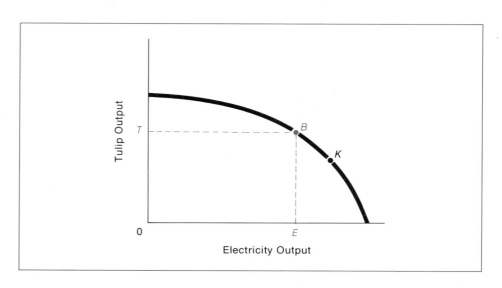

will produce an output too small for an efficient allocation of resources. The opposite will be true for an industry whose price is below marginal social cost. In terms of Figure 29–3, suppose point *B* again represents the efficient allocation of resources, involving the production of *E* kilowatt hours of electricity and *T* dozen tulips.

Because the polluting electric company charges a price below marginal social cost, it will produce more than *E* kilowatt hours of electricity. Similarly, because tulip growers generate external benefits, and so charge a price above marginal social cost, they will produce less than *T* dozen tulips. The economy will end up with the resource allocation represented by point *K* rather than that represented by point *B*. There will be too much smoky electricity production and too little attractive tulip growing. More generally:

An industry that generates detrimental externalities will have a marginal social cost higher than its marginal private cost. If its price is equal to its own marginal private cost, it will therefore be below the true marginal cost to society. The market mechanism thereby tends to encourage inefficiently large outputs of products that cause detrimental externalities. The opposite is true of products that cause beneficial externalities—private industry will provide inefficiently small quantities of these products.

The Universality of Externalities

Externalities occur throughout the economy. Many are beneficial. A factory that hires unskilled or semiskilled labourers gives them on-the-job training and provides the external benefit of better workers to future employers. Benefits to others are also generated when firms produce useful but unpatentable products, or even patentable products that can be imitated by others to some degree.

Detrimental externalities are also widespread. The emission of air and water pollutants by factories, cars, and airplanes is the source of some of our most pressing environmental problems. The abandonment of buildings causes the quality of a neighbourhood to deteriorate, and is the source of serious externalities in some cities. Externality represents a common form of market failure simply because there are so many areas in which property rights are not clearly established.

Externalities

Externalities lie at the heart of some of society's most pressing problems: the problems of the environment, research policy, and a variety of other critical issues. For this reason, the concept of externalities is one of our **12 Ideas for Beyond the Final Exam**. It is a subject that will recur again and again in this book as we discuss some of these problems in greater detail.

Government Policy and Externalities

Because of the market's inability to cope with externalities, governments have found it appropriate to support activities that are felt to generate external benefits. Education is subsidized not only because it helps promote equal opportunity for all citizens, but also because it is believed to generate beneficial externalities. For example, educated people normally commit fewer crimes than uneducated people, so the more we educate people, the less we will need to spend on crime prevention. Also, academic research that has been provided partly as a byproduct of the educational system often benefits the entire population and has, indeed, been judged to be a major contributor to the nation's economic growth. We have consequently come to believe that if education were offered only by profit-making institutions, the output of these beneficial services would be provided at less than the optimal level.

Similarly, governments have recently begun to impose fines on companies that contribute heavily to air and water pollution. This approach to policy is in fact suggested by the economist's standard analysis of the effects of externalities on resource allocation. The basic problem is that, in the presence of externalities, the price system fails to allocate resources efficiently. Resources are used for which no price is charged, and benefits are offered without financial compensation. As a result, with detrimental externalities, for example, the price does not cover the entire marginal social cost. Consequently:

One effective way to deal with externalities may be through the use of taxes and subsidies, making polluters pay for the costs they impose on society, and paying the generators of beneficial externalities for the positive incidental costs of their activities.

For example, firms that generate beneficial externalities should be given a subsidy per unit of their output equal to the difference between their marginal social costs and their marginal private costs. Similarly, those that generate detrimental externalities should be taxed so that the firm that creates such externalities will have to pay the entire marginal social cost. In terms of Figure 29–2, after paying the tax, the firm's marginal-private-cost curve will be shifted up until it coincides with its marginal-social-cost curve, and the market price will be set in a manner consistent with an efficient resource allocation.

While there is much to be said for this approach in principle, it often is not easy to implement in practice. Social costs are rarely easy to estimate, partly because they are so widely diffused throughout the community (everyone in the area is affected by pollution) and partly because many of the costs and benefits (effects on health, unpleasantness of living in smog) are not readily assessed in monetary terms. The pros and cons of this approach and the alternative policies available for the control of externalities will be discussed in greater detail in Chapter 34 on environmental problems.

Public Goods

Another area in which the market fails to perform adequately is in the provision of **public goods**. These are commodities that are valuable socially but whose provision, for reasons we will now explain, cannot be financed by private enterprise. Thus, government must pay for the public goods if they are to be provided at all. Standard examples range from national defense to the services of lighthouses.

It is easiest to explain the nature of public goods by contrasting them with the sort of commodities called **private goods**, which are at the opposite end of the spectrum. *Private goods are characterized by two important attributes.* One can be called **depletability**. If you eat a steak or use a litre of gasoline, there is that much less beef or fuel in the world available for others to use. Your consumption depletes the supply available for other people, either temporarily or permanently.

But a pure public good is like the legendary widow's jar of oil, which always remained full no matter how many people used it. Once the snow has been removed from a street, the improved driving conditions are available to every driver who uses the street, whether 10 or 1000 cars pass that way. One passing car does not make the road less snow-free for another. The same is true of the spraying of swamps near a town to kill disease-bearing mosquitoes. The cost of the spraying is the same whether the town contains 10,000 or 20,000 persons. A resident of the town who benefits from this service does not deplete its advantages to others.

The other property that characterizes private goods but not public goods is **excludability**, meaning that anyone who does not pay for the good can be excluded from enjoying its benefits. If you do not buy a ticket, you are excluded

A **public good** is a commodity or service whose benefits are *not depleted* by an additional user and for which it is generally difficult or *impossible to exclude* people from its benefits, even if they are unwilling to pay for them. In contrast, a **private good** is characterized by both excludability and depletability.

A commodity is **depletable** if it is used up when someone consumes it.

A commodity is **excludable** if someone who does not pay for it can be kept from enjoying it.

from the ball game. If you do not pay for an electric guitar, the storekeeper will not give it to you.

But some goods or services are such that, if they are provided to anyone, they automatically become available to many other persons whom it is difficult, if not impossible, to exclude from the benefits. If a street is cleared of snow, everyone who uses the street benefits, regardless of who paid for the snowplough. If a country provides a strong military establishment, everyone receives its protection, even persons who do not happen to want it.

A public good is defined as a good that lacks depletability. Very often, it also lacks excludability. Notice two important implications.

First, since non-paying users usually cannot be excluded from enjoying a public good, suppliers of such goods will find it *difficult or impossible to collect fees* for the benefits they provide. This is the so-called "free rider" problem. How many people, for example, will *voluntarily* cough up $2000 a year to support our national defense establishment? Yet this is roughly what it costs per Canadian family. Services like national defense and public health, which are not depletable and where excludability is simply impossible, *cannot* be provided by private enterprise because no one will pay for what he can get free. Since private firms are not in the business of giving services away, the supply of public goods must be left to government authorities and non-profit institutions.

The second thing we notice is that, since the supply of a public good is not depleted by an additional user, *the marginal cost of serving an additional user is zero.* With zero marginal cost, the basic principle of optimal resource allocation calls for provision of public goods and services to anyone who wants them *at no charge.* In a word, not only is it often *impossible* to charge a market price for a public good, it is often *undesirable* as well. Any non-zero price would discourage some users from enjoying the public good; but this would be inefficient, since one more person's enjoyment of the good costs society nothing. To summarize:

It is usually not *possible* to charge a price for a pure public good because people cannot be excluded from enjoying its benefits. It may also be *undesirable* to charge a price for it because that would discourage some people from using it even though using it does not deplete its supply. For both these reasons we find government supplying many public goods. Without government intervention, public goods simply would not be provided.

Referring back to our example in Figure 29–1, if hospital linens were a public good and their production were left to private enterprise, the economy would end up at point *A* on the graph, with zero production of hospital linens and far more output of handkerchiefs than is called for by efficient allocation (point *B*). Usually, communities have not been content to let that happen; and today a quite substantial proportion of government expenditure, indeed the bulk of municipal budgets, is devoted to the financing of public goods or to services believed to generate substantial external benefits. National defense, public health, police and fire protection, and research are among the services provided by governments because they offer beneficial externalities or because they are public goods.

The Cost Disease of the Service Sector

Our next problem may or may not be considered a failure of the market mechanism. While private standards of living have increased and material possessions have grown, the community has simultaneously been forced to cope with deterioration in a variety of services, both public and private.

Throughout the world, streets and subways have grown increasingly dirty. Public safety has declined as crimes of violence have become more commonplace in almost every major city. Bus and train service has been reduced. In the middle of the nineteenth century in suburban London, there were twelve mail deliveries per day on weekdays and one on Sundays. We all know what has happened to postal services since then.

There have been parallel cutbacks in the quality of private services. Doctors have become increasingly reluctant to visit patients at home; in many areas, the house call, which thirty years ago was a commonplace event, has now become something that occurs only in a life-and-death emergency, if even then. Another example, though undoubtedly a matter for less general concern, is what has happened to restaurants. Although they are reluctant to publicize the fact, a great number of restaurants, including some of the most elegant and expensive, serve preprepared, frozen, and reheated meals. They charge high prices for what amount to little more than TV dinners.

There is no single explanation for all these matters. It would be naïve to offer any cut-and-dried hypothesis purporting to account for phenomena as diverse as the rise in crime and violence throughout Western society and the deterioration in postal services. Yet at least one common influence underlies all these problems of deterioration in service quality—an influence that is economic in character and that may be expected to grow more serious with the passage of time. The issue has been called the **cost disease of the personal services**.

Consider these facts. During the inflationary 1970s, virtually all costs in the economy rose; but the costs of services rose even faster than most. During earlier periods, when the nation's price level was nearly constant, service costs nevertheless rose at a significant rate. One typical example will illustrate the point. Between 1945 and 1965, the cost of public education per pupil day in the United States rose, on the average, 4 percent a year *more rapidly* than the general price level. This means that every year—even when other prices in the economy were not increasing—the cost of education was rising. These cost differentials were cumulative and compounded so that over the two decades as a whole the cost of education per pupil rose more than 200 percent relative to the cost of manufactured goods. By the end of the period, the cost of an education was therefore equivalent to twice as many cars or refrigerators as it was at the beginning. A similar pattern has been followed by the costs of other services, such as health care, libraries, doctor's fees, and theatre tickets, throughout Western society.

One serious consequence of this phenomenon is that a terrible financial burden has been placed on municipal budgets by the soaring costs of education and police and fire protection. But what accounts for these ever-increasing costs? Are they attributable to inefficiencies in government management or to political corruption? Perhaps, in part, to both. But there is another reason—one that could not be avoided by any municipal administration no matter what its integrity and efficiency—and one that affects private industry just as severely as it does the public sector.

The problem stems from the basic nature of services. Most services require direct contact between those who consume the service and those who provide it. Firefighters, teachers, and librarians are all engaged in activities that require direct person-to-person contact. Moreover, the quality of the service deteriorates if less time is provided by firefighters, teachers, and librarians to each user of their services.

In contrast, the buyer of an automobile usually has no idea who worked on it, and, provided it operates well, could not care less how much labour time went into its production. A labour-saving innovation in auto production need not imply a reduction in product quality. As a result, it has proved far easier for technological change to save labour in manufacturing than in providing services. While output per hour of labour in manufacturing and agriculture went up in the period after World War II at an average rate of close to 3 percent a year, the number of teacher hours per pupil actually *increased* because classes became smaller.

These disparate performances in productivity have grave consequences for prices. When wages in manufacturing rise 3 percent, the cost of manufactured products is not affected because increased productivity makes up for the rise in wages. But the nature of services makes it very difficult to introduce labour-saving devices in the service sector. So a 3 percent rise in the wages of teachers or police officers is not offset by higher productivity, and must lead to an equivalent rise in municipal budgets. Similarly, a 3 percent rise in the wages of hairdressers must lead beauty salons to raise their prices.

The Cost Disease of the Personal Services

In the long run, wages and salaries throughout the economy tend to go up and down together, for otherwise the activity whose wage rate falls seriously behind will tend to lose its labour force. Thus, auto workers and police officers will see their wages rise at roughly the same rate in the long run. But if productivity on the assembly line advances while productivity in the patrol car does not, then police protection must grow ever more expensive as time goes on.

This phenomenon is another of our **12 Ideas for Beyond the Final Exam**. Because productivity improvements are very difficult for most services, their cost can be expected to rise faster, year in, year out, than the cost of manufactured goods. Over a period of several decades, this difference in the growth rate in costs of the two sectors can add up, making services enormously more expensive compared with manufactured goods.

If services continue to grow ever more expensive in comparison to goods, the implications for life in the future are profound indeed. This analysis portends a world in which the typical home contains luxuries and furnishings that we can hardly imagine; but it is a home surrounded by garbage and perhaps by violence. It portends a future in which the services of doctors, teachers, and police officers are increasingly mass-produced and impersonal, and in which the arts and crafts are increasingly supplied only by amateurs because the cost of professional work in these fields is too high.

If this is the shape of the economy a hundred years from now, it will be significantly different from our own, and some persons will undoubtedly question whether the quality of life has increased commensurately with the increased material prosperity. Some may even ask whether it has increased at all.

Is this future inevitable? Is there anything that can be done to escape it? The answer is that it is by no means inevitable. To see why, we must first recognize that the source of the problem, paradoxically, is the growth in productivity of our economy—or rather, the *unevenness* of that growth. Trash-removal costs go up not because garbage collectors become less efficient but because labour in car manufacturing becomes *more* efficient, thus enhancing the sanitation worker's value as a potential employee on the automotive assembly line. His wages must go up to keep him at his job of garbage removal.

But increasing productivity can never make a nation poorer. It can never make it unable to afford things it was able to afford in the past. Increasing productivity means that we can afford more of *all* things—medical care and education as well as TV sets and electric toothbrushes.

The role of services in our future depends on how we order our priorities. If we value services sufficiently, we can have more and better services— at *some* sacrifice in the rate of growth of manufactured goods. Whether that is a good choice for society is not for economists to say. But it is important to recognize that society *does* have a choice, and that if it fails to exercise it, matters are very likely to proceed relentlessly in the direction they are now headed—toward a world in which there is an enormous abundance of material goods and a great scarcity of many of the things that most people now consider primary requisites for a high quality of life.

Allocation of Resources Between Present and Future

When a society invests, more resources are devoted to building capacity to produce consumers' goods in the future. But the inputs that go into building new plant and equipment are unavailable for consumption now. Fuel used to make steel for a factory cannot be used to heat homes or drive cars. Thus, the allocation of inputs between current consumption and investment—that is, their allocation between present and future—determines how fast the economy grows.

In principle, the market mechanism should be as efficient in allocating resources between present and future uses as it is in allocating resources among different outputs at any one time. If future demands for a particular commodity, say computers for the home, are expected to be higher than they are today, it will pay manufacturers to plan now to build the necessary plant and equipment so they will be ready to turn out the computers when the expanded market materializes. More resources are thereby allocated to future consumption.

The allocation of resources between present and future can be analysed with the aid of a production possibilities frontier diagram, such as that in Figure 29-1. Suppose the issue is how much labour and capital to devote to producing consumer goods and how much to devote to construction of factories to produce output in the future. Then, instead of handkerchiefs and linens, the graph will show consumer goods and number of factories on its axes, but otherwise it will be exactly the same as Figure 29-1. Such a graph appears in Figure 29-4.

The profit motive directs the flow of resources between one time period and another just as it handles resource allocation among different industries in a given period. The lure of profits directs resources to those products *and those time periods* in which high prices promise to make output most profitable. But one feature of the process of allocation of resources among different time periods distinguishes it from the process of allocation among industries. This is the special role that the *interest rate* plays in allocation among the periods.

If the receipt of a given amount of money is delayed until some time in the future, the recipient suffers an *opportunity cost*—the interest that the money could have earned if it had been received earlier and invested. For example, if the rate of interest is 9 percent and you can persuade someone who owes you money to make a $100 payment one year earlier than originally planned, you come out $9 ahead. Put the other way, if the rate of interest is 9 percent and the payment of $100 is postponed one year, you lose the opportunity to earn $9. Thus, the rate of

Figure 29-4

PRODUCTION POSSIBILITIES FRONTIER BETWEEN PRESENT AND FUTURE

With a given quantity of resources, the economy can produce one million cars for immediate use and build no factories for the future (point *A*). Alternatively, at the opposite extreme (point *B*), it can build 10 factories where products will become available in the future, while no cars are produced for current consumption. At points in between on the frontier, such as *C*, the economy will produce a combination of some cars for present consumption and some factories for future use.

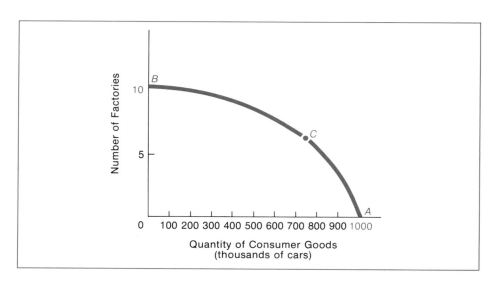

interest determines the size of the opportunity cost to a recipient who gets money at some date in the future instead of now. For this reason, as we saw in Chapter 8:

Low interest rates will persuade people to invest more now, since investments yield many of their benefits in the future. Thus, more resources will be devoted to the future if interest rates are low. Similarly, high interest rates make investment, with its benefits in the future less attractive. And so high interest rates will tend to increase the use of resources for current output at the expense of reduced future outputs.

On the surface, it seems that the price system can allocate resources among different time periods in the way consumers prefer. For the supply of and demand for loans, which determine the interest rate, reflects the public's preferences between present and future. Suppose, for example, that the public suddenly became more interested in future consumption (say, people wanted to save more for their old age). The supply of funds available for borrowing would increase and interest rates would tend to fall. This would stimulate investment and add to the future output of goods at the expense of current consumption.

But several questions have been raised about the effectiveness, in practice, with which the market mechanism allocates resources among different time periods.

One thing that makes economists uneasy is that the rate of interest, which is the price that controls allocation over time, is also used for a variety of other purposes. As we saw in Chapter 14, the interest rate is manipulated by fiscal and monetary policy in an attempt to control business fluctuations in large countries like the United States. In so doing, policy-makers seem to give little thought to the effects on the allocation of resources between present and future, and so one may well worry whether the resulting interest rates are the most appropriate ones. Also, for countries like Canada, whose bonds must compete in international financial markets to be sold, the level of interest rates is essentially predetermined by conditions in the rest of the world. Obviously this precludes the interest rate's serving as a flexible signal to allocate resources optimally between present and future in Canada, unless our rate of time preference is the same as that of the Americans.

Second, it has been suggested that even in the absence of government manipulation of the interest rate, the market may devote too many resources to immediate consumption. One British economist, A. C. Pigou, argued simply that people suffer from "a defective telescopic faculty"—that they are too short-sighted to give adequate weight to the future. A "bird in the hand" point of view leads people to care so much about the present that they sacrifice the legitimate interests of the future. As a result, too much goes into today's consumption and too little into investment for tomorrow.

A third reason why the free market may not invest enough for the future is that investment projects, like the construction of a new factory, are much greater risks to the investor than to the community. Even if a factory falls into someone else's hands through bankruptcy, it will probably go on turning out goods. But the profits will not to go the investor or his heirs. Therefore, the loss to the individual investor will be far greater than the loss to society. For this reason individual investment for the future may fall short of the amounts that are socially optimal. Investments too risky to be worthwhile to any group of private individuals may nevertheless be advantageous to society as a whole.

Fourth, our economy shortchanges the future when it despoils irreplaceable natural resources, exterminates whole species of plants and animals, floods canyons, "develops" attractive areas into acres of potential slums, and so on. Worst of all, industry, the government, and individuals bequeath a ticking time bomb to the future when they leave behind lethal and slow-acting residues, such as nuclear wastes, which may remain dangerous for hundreds or even thousands of years and whose disposal containers are likely to fall apart long before their contents lose their lethal qualities.

Such actions are essentially *irreversible*. If a factory is not built this year, the deficiency in facilities provided for the future can be remedied by building it next year. But a canyon, once destroyed, can never be replaced. For this reason:

Many economists believe that **irreversible decisions** have a very special significance and must *not* be left entirely in the hands of private firms and individuals.

Recently, however, several writers have questioned the general conclusion that the free market will not tend to invest enough for the future. They have pointed out that the prosperity of our economy has grown fairly steadily from one decade to the next, and that there is every reason to expect future generations to have real incomes and an abundance of consumer goods far greater than our own. Pressures to increase investment for the future then may be like taking from the poor to give to the rich—a sort of backward Robin Hood redistribution of income.

Some Other Sources of Market Failure

We have now completed our survey of the most important imperfections of the market mechanism. But that list is not complete, and it can never be. In this imperfect world nothing ever works out ideally, and by examining anything with a sufficiently powerful microscope one can always detect some more blemishes. However, some of the items we have omitted from our list are also important. Let us therefore conclude with a brief description of three of them.

Imperfect Information

The analysis of the virtues of the market mechanism in Chapter 26 assumed that consumers and producers have all the information they need for their decisions. But in reality things are very different. When buying a house or a second-hand car, or selecting a doctor, consumers are vividly reminded of how little they know about what they are purchasing. The old motto "Let the buyer beware" applies. Obviously, if participants in the market are ill-informed, they will not always make the optimal decisions described in our theoretical models.

Yet, not all economists agree that imperfect information is really a failure of the market mechanism. They point out that information, too, is a commodity that costs money to produce. Neither firms nor consumers have complete information because it would be irrational for them to spend the enormous amounts needed to get it. As always, the optimum is a compromise. One should, ideally, stop buying information at the point where the marginal benefit of further information is no greater than its marginal cost. With this amount of information, the business executive or the consumer is able to make what have been referred to as "optimally imperfect" decisions.

Rent Seeking

An army of lawyers, expert witnesses, and business executives crowd our courtrooms and pile up enormous costs. Business firms seem to sue each other at the slightest provocation, wasting vast resources and delaying business decisions. Why? Because it is possible to make money by such unproductive activities—by legal battles over profit-making opportunities.

For example, suppose a provincial government awards a contract to produce a highway to Firm A, offering $20 million in profit. It may pay Firm B to spend $5 million in a lawsuit against the province and Firm A, hoping the courts will award it the contract (and thus the $20 million profit) instead.

In general, any source of unusual profit, such as a monopoly, is a temptation for firms to waste economic resources in an effort to obtain control of the source of profits. This process, called **rent seeking** by economists (meaning that the firms hope to obtain earnings without contributing to production), has been judged by some observers to be a major source of inefficiency in our economy.

Rent seeking refers to unproductive activity in the pursuit of economic profit; that is, profit in excess of competitive earnings.

Moral Hazard

Another widely discussed problem for the market mechanism is associated with insurance. Insurance—the provision of protection against risk—is viewed by economists as a useful commodity like shoes or the provision of information. But it also creates a problem by encouraging the very risks against which it provides protection. For example, if an individual has jewellery that is fully insured against theft, she has little motivation to take steps to protect it against burglars. She may, for example, fail to lock it up in a safety deposit box, and this failure makes burglary a more attractive and lucrative profession. This problem—the tendency of insurance to encourage the source of risk—is called **moral hazard**, and it makes a free market in insurance hard to operate.

Moral hazard refers to the tendency of insurance to discourage policy-holders from protecting themselves from risk.

Market Failure and Government Failure

This chapter has pointed out some of the most noteworthy failures of the invisible hand. We seem forced to the conclusion that a market economy, if left entirely to itself, is likely to produce results that are, at least in some respects, far from ideal. In our discussion we have noted either directly or by implication some of the things government can do to correct these deficiencies. But the fact that government often *can* intervene in the operation of the economy in a constructive way does not always mean that it actually *will* succeed in doing so. The fact is that governments cannot be relied upon to behave ideally any more than business firms can be expected to do so.

It is apparently hard to make this point in a way that is suitably balanced. Commentators too often stake out one extreme position or the other. Those who think the market mechanism is inherently unfair and biased by the greed of those who run its enterprises seem to think of government as the savior that can cure all economic ills. Those who deplore government intervention are prone to consider the public sector as the home of every sort of inefficiency, graft, and bureaucratic stultification. The truth, as usual, lies in between.

Governments are inherently imperfect, like the humans who compose them. The political process leads to compromises that sometimes bear little resemblance to rational decisions, for example, the prolonged use of rent controls (see Chapter 4). Yet, often the problems engendered by an unfettered economy are too serious to be left to the free market. The problems of dealing with inflation, environmental decay, and the provision of public goods are cases in point. In such instances, government intervention is likely to yield substantial benefits to the general public.

But in other areas the market mechanism is likely to work reasonably well, and the small imperfections that are present do not constitute adequate justification for intervention. In any event, *even where government intervention is appropriate, it is essential to consider marketlike instruments as the means to correct the deficiencies in the workings of the market mechanism.* The tax incentives described in our discussion of externalities are an outstanding example of what we have in mind.

Evaluative Comments

This chapter, like Chapter 26, has offered a rather unbalanced assessment of the market mechanism. We spent Chapter 26 extolling the market's virtues and spent this chapter cataloguing its vices. We come out, as in the nursery rhyme, concluding that the market is either very, very good or it is horrid.

There seems to be nothing moderate about the performance of a market system. As a means of achieving efficiency in the production of ordinary consumer goods and of responding to changes in consumer preferences, it is unparalleled. It is, in fact, difficult to overstate the accomplishments of the price system in these areas.

On the other hand, it has proven itself unable to cope with business fluctuations, income inequality, or the consequences of monopoly. It has proved to be a very poor allocator of resources among outputs that generate external costs and external benefits, and it has shown itself completely incapable of arranging for the provision of public goods. Some of the most urgent problems that plague our society—the deterioration of services in the cities, the despoliation of our atmosphere, the social unrest attributable to poverty—can be ascribed in part to one or another of these shortcomings of the market system.

Most economists conclude from these observations that while the market mechanism is virtually irreplaceable, considerable modifications in the way it works are required. Proposals designed to deal directly with the problems of poverty, monopoly, and resource allocation over time abound in the economic literature. All of them call for the government to intervene in the economy, either by supplying directly those goods and services that, it is believed, private enterprise does not supply in adequate amounts, or by seeking to influence the workings of the economy more indirectly through regulation. Many of these programs have been discussed in earlier chapters; others will be encountered in chapters yet to come.

Summary

1. There are at least seven major imperfections in the workings of the market mechanism: inequality of income distribution, fluctuations in economic activity (inflation and unemployment), monopolistic output restrictions, beneficial and detrimental externalities, inadequate provision of public goods, deteriorating quality and rising costs of services, and finally, misallocation of resources between present and future.

2. Efficient resource allocation is basically a matter of balancing the benefits of producing more of one good against the benefits of devoting the required inputs to the production of some other good.

3. A detrimental externality occurs when an economic activity incidentally does harm to others; a beneficial externality occurs when an economic activity incidentally creates benefits for others.

4. When an activity causes a detrimental externality, the marginal social cost of the activity (including the harm it does to others) must be greater than the marginal private cost to those who carry on the activity. The opposite will be true when a beneficial externality occurs.

5. If manufacture of a product causes detrimental externalities, its price will generally not include all the marginal social cost it causes, since part of the cost will be borne by others. The opposite is true for beneficial externalities.

6. The market will therefore tend to overallocate resources to the production of goods that cause detrimental externalities and underallocate resources to the production of goods that create beneficial externalities. This is one of the **12 Ideas for Beyond the Final Exam**.

7. A public good is defined by economists as a commodity that (like clean air) is not depleted by additional users and from whose use it is difficult to exclude anyone, even those who refuse to pay for it. A private good, in contrast, is characterized by both excludability and depletability.

8. Free-enterprise firms generally will not produce a public good even if it is extremely useful to the community, because they cannot charge money for the use of the good.

9. Because personal services—such as education, medical care, and police protection—are not amenable to labour-saving innovations, they suffer from a cost disease whose symptom is that their costs tend to rise considerably faster than costs in the economy as a whole. This cost disease of the service sector is another of our **12 Ideas for Beyond the Final Exam.**

10. Many observers feel that the market often short-changes the future, particularly when it makes irreversible decisions that destroy natural resources.

Concepts for Review

Opportunity cost

Resource misallocation

Production possibilities frontier

Price above or below marginal cost

Externalities (detrimental and beneficial)

Marginal social cost and marginal private cost

Public goods

Private goods

Depletability

Excludability

Cost disease of the personal services

Irreversible decisions

Rent seeking

Moral hazard

Questions for Discussion

1. Specifically, what is the opportunity cost to society of a pair of shoes? Why may the price of those shoes not adequately represent that opportunity cost?

2. Suppose that because of a new disease that attacks coffee plants, far more labour and other inputs are required to raise a pound of coffee than before. How might that affect the efficient allocation of resources between tea and coffee? Why? How would the prices of coffee and tea react in a free market?

3. Give some examples of goods whose production causes detrimental externalities and some examples of goods that create beneficial externalities.

4. Compare cleaning an office building with cleaning the atmosphere of a city. Which is a public good and which is a private good? Why?

5. Give some other examples of public goods, and discuss in each case why additional users do not deplete them and why it is difficult to exclude people from using them.

6. Think about the goods and services that your local government provides. Which of these are "public goods" as economists use the term?

7. Explain why the services of a lighthouse are considered an example of a public good.

8. Explain why education is not a very satisfactory example of a public good.

9. In recent decades, university tuition costs have risen faster than the general price level even though the wages of professors have failed to keep pace with the price level. Can you explain why?

10. A firm holds a patent that is estimated to be worth $20 million. The patent is repeatedly challenged in the courts by a large number of (rent seeking) firms, each hoping to grab away the patent. In what sense may the rent seekers be "competing perfectly" for the patent? If so, how much will end up being spent in the legal battles? (*Hint*: Under perfect competition should firms expect to earn any economic profit?)

VI

The Government
and the Economy

Limiting Market Power: Regulation of Industry

30

The free enterprise system is
absolutely too important to be
left to the voluntary action
of the marketplace.
A U.S. CONGRESSMAN (1979)

Because the market system may not function ideally in monopolistic or
oligopolistic industries, governments have frequently intervened in these
areas. In Canada, such intervention has followed two basic patterns. The
Combines Investigation Act, which will be studied in detail in the next chapter,
has sought to prohibit the acquisition of monopoly power and to ban certain
monopolistic practices. Alternatively, some firms have been subjected to regulatory
supervision, which seeks to influence their pricing policies and other decisions.

In this chapter, we will describe the functioning of some of the principal
regulatory agencies. We will then offer a more detailed account of the reasons for
regulation, discuss the evidence on the effects and the effectiveness of regulation,
consider the reasons why regulatory agencies have devoted a great deal of attention
to limitation of price cuts, and examine both some of the criticisms of the
regulatory process and some of the suggestions that have been made to improve it.
We will also discuss some recent moves toward deregulation; that is, toward
reducing the number of regulations and the powers of the regulatory agencies.
This deregulation process is really just starting and it is too soon to say how it will
all end up. However, we will provide some preliminary evaluation of its likely
consequences. Finally, we will conclude the chapter with a few comments on the
nationalization of industries.

A Puzzle: Industry Opposition to Deregulation

An observer who knew nothing about regulated industries might expect that
deregulation would be welcomed by the firms affected. After all, regulations curb
their freedom of decision-making in many ways.

Yet when deregulation is considered, most companies—and their unions—
bitterly fight against the proposal. Later, we will discuss some of the reasons for
this opposition. But already we may surmise from this observation that regulation
may, inadvertently or deliberately, have been serving the interests of some of the
regulated firms rather than making life harder for them.

Practical Problem: Price Floors Versus Price Ceilings

In a famous passage in *The Wealth of Nations*, Adam Smith tells us:

It always is and must be the interest of the great body of the people to buy whatever they want of those who sell it cheapest. The proposition is so very manifest, that it seems ridiculous to take any pains to prove it; nor could it ever have been called into question had not the interested sophistry of merchants and manufacturers confounded the common sense of mankind.[1]

Since regulation of industry has presumably been instituted to protect "the interest of the great body of the people," it is quite natural to surmise that the bulk of the work of the regulatory agencies would have been devoted to the imposition of price reductions. Thus, one would think that the typical case before a regulatory agency would be based on the complaint that a firm with monopoly power was charging prices that were excessively high, and that a typical decision of the regulatory agency would require such prices to be reduced.

In fact, this seems to be virtually the reverse of what has happened. Although in some cases regulation *has* kept prices below the levels they might have reached in a free market, the bulk of cases devoted to price regulation have dealt with complaints that prices charged by the regulated firm are *too low!* Often the outcome in such cases has been a requirement on the part of regulators that the firms raise their prices higher than they wanted to. Where buyers have had a choice among several suppliers—for example, shippers of freight who have had a choice among trucks, railways, and barges—the regulatory agency has effectively prevented the consumer from purchasing from "those who sell cheapest."

How did regulation get itself into this curious pattern? What just reason is there for a regulatory agency to devote itself primarily to the imposition of *price floors* rather than *price ceilings*? Later in this chapter, through our analysis of the regulatory process, we will be able to indicate just how and why this has happened.

Monopoly, Regulation, and Nationalization

Throughout the Western economies a number of industries are traditionally run as monopolies. These include postal services, electricity generation, transportation, and gas supply. Since there are no competitive pressures to protect the interests of consumers from monopolistic exploitation in these cases, it is generally agreed that some substitute form of protection from excessive prices and restricted outputs should be found.

Most of Western Europe has adopted **nationalization** as its solution, which means that the state owns and operates certain monopolistic industries. In Canada, we seem more reluctant to have government involved in the running of businesses. Yet it has happened to some degree. Most cities now run their own public transport systems. Also, the post office and much of the passenger railway system are run by Crown corporations.

In Canada, the main instrument of control of public utility industries has generally been the regulatory agency. The federal and provincial governments have created a large number of agencies that regulate prices, standards of service, provisions for safety, and a variety of other aspects of the operations of telephone companies, radio and television stations, electric utilities, airlines, trucking companies, and firms in many other industries. Many of these industries are not pure monopolies, but include firms that nevertheless are suspected of possessing so much market power that their regulation is considered to be in the public interest.

[1]Adam Smith, *The Wealth of Nations* (New York: Modern Library, Random House, Inc., 1937), page 461.

The Development of Regulation in Canada*

The regulatory role of the state in Canada has been shaped by both economic and political pressures. Traditionally, in Canada, the federal government has played an interventionist role, particularly in what might be termed "key" industries. Thus we find the state present in transport (CNR, Air Canada), communications (Telesat Canada, CBC), and resources (Eldorado Uranium, Petro-Canada). These strategic involvements have often been carried out in response to the possibility of domination by U.S. interests (a policy known as defensive expansion).

Moreover, the desire of the provinces to retain economic power and thus political clout and credibility has led them to become involved in the operation of firms in areas that other countries might deem to be the realm of the "private" sector. Thus, we see today the majority interest of the Government of Ontario in Suncor, a petroleum refinery company purchased with the announced aim of maintaining a "window into the petroleum industry."

Governments at both the federal and provincial levels have become active participants in the marketplace, as well as regulators of what would otherwise be private economic activity. On the federal level, we see major sectors of the economy being regulated by bodies such as the National Energy Board, the Canadian Transport Commission, and the Canadian Radio–Television and Telecommunications Commission (CRTC). Overall, it has been estimated that those involved in economic activity in Canada are subject to the restrictions imposed by 97 federal statutes.[2]

At the provincial level, intervention and regulation are even more pervasive. For example, a study carried out in the late 1970s found that in Ontario there were 57 regulatory bodies, 35 licensing and appeal boards, 30 professional bodies, 14 compensation boards, and 20 arbitration bodies. These organizations included the Ontario Municipal Board, the Public Service Grievance Board (an arbitration body), the Ontario Securities Commission, the Ontario Energy Board, and the Pregnant Mare Urine Licence Review Board.[3]

Not all of the organizations were of a dynamic nature. For example, when surveyed, one chairman of a board stated that "since I have been chairman there has been no occasion for the committee to meet." Another replied, "We were never used so we have never received any money or pay for the job. I have requested a copy of the act but at this date have not received it."[4]

Even at the municipal level regulation is pervasive, carried out under the authority of "by-laws." Thus, we see limitation on store opening hours and even the activities of our pets (for example, poop-and-scoop laws).

The extensive regulation of our economy has spawned a new growth industry—the study of regulation. The Ontario Economic Council carried out a far-reaching analysis of regulation in 1978. In its study, *Government Regulation*, it not only analysed the rationale for regulation in general, but also published the results of sponsored studies on telecommunications, trucking, and milk marketing. In 1981, the Economic Council of Canada published a major study, *Reforming Regulation*, in which it summarized the results of studies on such diverse regulated areas as taxicabs, airlines, tidal fisheries, environmental pollution, and occupational health and safety.

Not all governmental activity has supported regulation. In 1980, the Bureau of Competition Policy in the federal department of Consumer and Corporate Affairs established a Regulated Sector Branch. The staff of this branch appear before federal and provincial regulatory bodies to argue on behalf of greater competition.

---

*This section follows closely the thoughts put forward by R. Schultz in "The Development of Regulation in Canada," Centre for the Study of Regulated Industries, McGill University, 1980.
[2]C.L. Brown-John, *Canadian Regulatory Agencies* (Toronto: Butterworths, 1981), page 29.
[3]Ontario Economic Council, *Government Regulation*, 1978.
[4]*Ibid.*, page 208.

Regulations Affecting Agriculture

The Crow Rate

In 1897, the Government of Canada contracted with the Canadian Pacific Railway to provide a subsidy to enable the railway to build a line through the Crow's Nest Pass from Alberta to British Columbia. In recompense, the railway agreed to reduce the freight rates on (among other things) the movement of grain to lake or ocean ports. In 1925, a statute was passed fixing the level of these rates. The "Crow Rate" remained unchanged for nearly six decades, until it was substantially increased in 1984.

It was estimated that, had the old Crow Rate remained in force, by 1986 the revenues received by the railway would have accounted for only 18 percent of the variable cost of moving the grain. Arguments for the abolition of the fixed rates were based on various consequences of this anomalous situation. Three stand out:

1. It did not pay the railway to maintain its branch lines, particularly those intended for wheat transportation. These were becoming degraded despite federal subsidies for branch "renewal."

2. In many cases, the most efficient mode of transportation was not being selected to move grain. The

railway was still being used, because of its subsidized cost, instead of trucks.

3. Wheat farmers in the west were receiving a "subsidy" in that they were competing in world markets at a world price for a relatively homogeneous product, and yet their costs of transporting this product were subsidized.

It is no wonder that analysts viewed the old Crow Rate as a classic example of inefficiency in the regulation process, while at the same time western farmers resisted a revision in these arrangements.

Broilers and Eggs: Producer Versus Consumer Welfare

A recent estimate indicates that the Canadian broiler-chicken and egg industries produce an annual output valued at approximately $1.4 billion. Since the early 1970s, the output of these industries has been controlled by the Canadian Egg Marketing Agency (CEMA) and the Canadian Chicken Marketing Agency (CCMA).

Output is controlled by issuing production quotas to farmers. These quotas give the holders monopoly power, which provides them with extra income. A conservative estimate by the Economic Council of Canada in 1981 put the size of this extra income at about $15,000 annually for the average quota-holding egg producer, and $23,000 annually for the broiler producer in the same position. These amounts could be three times as large for large-scale producers.*

Output restriction naturally raises price to a level higher than would exist if these products were sold in competitive markets. Thus, the consumer pays a higher than competitive price for eggs and broilers. The council estimates that in 1981 the extra annual payments made by each family in Canada totalled $10 in the case of broilers and $7 in the case of eggs. As the council notes, "while the additional food costs for Canadians are relatively small, the disproportionate flow of additional benefits to large producers warrants pause for thought."†

*Economic Council of Canada, *Reforming Regulation*, 1981, Ottawa, 1981, page 64.

†*Ibid.*, page 64.

It has been particularly effective in its dealings with the Canadian Radio–Television and Telecommunications Commission, the Air Transport Board of the Canadian Transport Commission, and, at the provincial level, the Ontario Securities Commission.

One newsworthy example of these activities was the hearings conducted by the CRTC from 1980 to 1982 on whether consumers should be able to *buy* telephones for their own use, or whether they must rent them from the telephone company, in this case, Bell Canada. Although Bell argued that its revenues, costs, and rates would be affected if customer ownership were allowed, evidence from other areas such as New York State indicated that this was not the case. In its decision, the CRTC allowed customers to buy their own phones. The competition

Table 30-1

AGRICULTURAL MARKETING BOARDS IN CANADA, 1978

	NUMBER OF BOARDS	PRODUCTS	NUMBER OF PRODUCERS	SHARE OF FARM RECEIPTS OBTAINED THROUGH MARKETING BOARDS (percent)
Federal boards:				
Canadian Wheat Board	1	Wheat	153,747	—*
Canadian Dairy Commission	1	Milk and dairy products	66,776	—*
Provincial boards:				
British Columbia	10	Grains, tree fruits, cranberries, grapes for processing, mushrooms, vegetables, sheep and wool, dairy products, broilers, turkeys, and eggs	4,575	58
Alberta	7	Grains, potatoes, vegetables (fresh and for processing), cattle, sheep and wool, hogs, dairy products, broilers, turkeys, eggs, and fowl	25,725	42
Saskatchewan	7	Grains, hogs, sheep and wool, dairy products, broilers, turkeys, and eggs	12,037	67
Manitoba	8	Grains, feed grains, potatoes, root crops, hogs, dairy products, broilers, turkeys, pullets and eggs, and honey	9,431	53
Ontario	22	Winter wheat, soybeans, seed corn, apples, fresh fruit, tender fruit for processing, grapes, (fresh and for processing), asparagus, white and yellow eye beans, tomato seedling plants, greenhouse vegetables, potatoes for processing, vegetables for processing, burley and flue-cured tobacco, hogs, dairy products, broilers, turkeys, and eggs	80,840	60
Quebec	23	Tomatoes, tobacco (cigar, pipe, and flue-cured), dairy products, broilers and turkeys, eggs, maple products, and wood	51,180	62
New Brunswick	11	Apples, bedding plants, hogs, dairy products, broilers, turkeys, eggs, and wood	4,686	53
Nova Scotia	8	Wheat, tobacco, hogs, dairy products, broilers, turkeys, pullets and eggs, and wool	2,056	62
Prince Edward Island	5	Potatoes, tobacco, pedigreed seed, hogs, dairy products, and eggs	1,522	42
Newfoundland	1	Eggs	38	—
Total	104		412,613	57

*Canadian Wheat Board and Canadian Dairy Commission receipts are allocated among provinces.
SOURCE: Economic Council of Canada, *Reforming Regulation*, 1981, page 56.

that this decision permitted led to a dramatic fall in the price of telephones.

The Regulated Sector Branch in the federal government has also been very active in the area dominated by agricultural marketing boards. It has consistently argued for greater recognition of the costs these boards impose on the consumer.

Agricultural marketing boards are pervasive in Canada (see Table 30-1). Some are the creatures of federal legislation and others of provincial legislation. The products affected include chickens, turkeys, tobacco, and well over a hundred other products. The boards, depending on their mandate, can carry out a number of different programs, including:

1. advertising (for example, the "Get Cracking" campaign for eggs);

2. bargaining with buyers;

3. carrying out price discrimination (milk used for industrial purposes, such as making cheese and butter, is priced lower than the milk we drink at home);

4. controlling production through the use of quotas (as is the case with flue-cured tobacco).

If it were not for the existence of the provincial marketing boards, which set quotas for individual suppliers, these agricultural industries would be competitive. Hence, in these cases, the whole point of regulation is to *create* monopoly power, so that total market supply can be managed. The purpose of this policy is to create higher and more stable incomes for farmers. While consumers lose from this policy, and there are often calls to do away with agricultural marketing boards, these boards seem destined to survive until more efficient and equitable methods of maintaining farm incomes are broadly understood to be available.

We do not further discuss agricultural boards in this chapter, since we wish to concentrate on government regulation that is at least *intended* to *reduce* monopoly practices.

A rough minimum estimate of the degree of regulation in the overall Canadian economy can be gleaned from Table 30–2. The figures indicate that almost 11 percent of Canadian GNP is accounted for by industries in which price and/or entry are regulated. It is noteworthy that this table does not include those industries regulated for the safety of their products or for protection of the environment. Nor does it include financial institutions or the agricultural sector. Finally, it does not record the share in GNP of the industries that, through government caveat, are "self-regulated." That is, the elected bodies (in most cases provincial legislatures) have given *carte blanche* to the practitioners to set their own rules of practice, and in many cases, charges. Industries that are self-regulated include medicine, law, and dentistry.

Why Regulation?

As we learned in Chapter 27, one main reason for regulation of industry is the phenomenon of *natural monopoly*. In some industries it is apparently far cheaper to have production carried out by one firm rather than by a number of different firms.

Table 30-2
1980 SHARE IN GNP OF SOME PRINCIPAL REGULATED CANADIAN INDUSTRIES

INDUSTRY	PERCENTAGE OF GNP
Air carriers	1.37
For-hire trucking	1.14
Railways	1.79
Gas	1.24
Electricity	2.79
Radio and TV	0.37
Telephone	2.00
Total	10.70

SOURCE: Statistics Canada.

One reason why this may occur is because of economies of large-scale production. An example of such **economies of scale** might be a milk-processing plant to which individual farmers send their product daily to be pasteurized by giant machinery rather than perform that crucial process at home. Use of the more elaborate equipment, which only becomes economical when it is employed by many farmers, reduces significantly the cost per litre of pasteurization. Here is a case in which savings are made possible by expanding the volume of an activity—a case of economies of scale.

Another reason why a single large firm may have a cost advantage over a group of small firms is that it is sometimes cheaper to produce a number of *different commodities together* rather than turn them out separately, each by a different firm. The saving made possible by simultaneous production of many different products is called **economies of scope**. An example of economies of scope is the manufacture of both cars and trucks by the same producer. The techniques employed in producing both commodities are sufficiently similar to make specialized production by different firms impractical.

In industries where there are great economies of scale *and* scope, society will obviously incur a significant cost penalty if it insists on maintaining a large number of firms. Supply by a number of smaller competing firms will be far more costly and use up far larger quantities of resources than if the good were supplied by a monopoly. Moreover, in the presence of strong economies of scale and economies of scope, society *will not be able to preserve free competition, even if it wants to.* The large, multiproduct firm will have so great an advantage over its rivals that the small firms simply will be unable to survive. We say in such a case that free competition is *not sustainable.*

Where monopoly production is cheapest, and where free competition is not sustainable, the industry is a natural monopoly. Because monopoly is cheaper, society may not want to have competition; and if free competition is not sustainable, it will not even have a choice in the matter.

But even if society reconciles itself to monopoly, it will generally not want to let the monopoly firm do whatever it wants to with its market power. Therefore, it will consider either regulation or nationalization of these firms.

A second reason for regulation is the desire for "universal service," that is, the availability of service at "reasonable prices" even to small communities where the small scale of operation makes costs extremely high. In such cases, regulators have sometimes encouraged a public utility to supply services to some consumers at a financial loss. But a loss on some sales is financially feasible only when the firm is permitted to make up for it by obtaining higher profits on its other sales.

This "averaging" of gains and losses, also referred to as **cross subsidization**, is possible only if the firm is protected from price competition and free entry of new competitors in its more profitable markets. If no such protection is provided by a regulatory agency, potential competitors will sniff out the profit opportunities in the markets where service is supplied at a price well above cost. Many new firms will enter the business and cause prices to be driven down in those markets. This practice is referred to as "cream skimming." The entrants choose to enter only into the profitable markets and skim away the cream of the profits for themselves, leaving the unprofitable markets (the skimmed milk) to the supplier who had attempted to provide universal service. This phenomenon is one reason why regulatory rules, until recently, made it very difficult or impossible for new firms to enter when and where they saw fit.

Airlines and telecommunications are two industries in which these issues have arisen. In both cases, fears have been expressed that without regulation of entry and rates, or the granting of special subsidies, less populous communities would effectively be isolated, losing their airline services and obtaining telephone

Economies of scale are savings that are acquired through increases in quantities produced.

Economies of scope are savings that are acquired through simultaneous production of many different products.

Cross subsidization means selling one product at a loss, which is balanced by higher profits on another product.

service only at cripplingly high rates. Many economists question the validity of this argument for regulation, which, they say, calls for hidden subsidy of rural consumers by all other consumers. In the United States, the airline deregulation act provided for government subsidies to help small communities attract airline service. In fact, what has happened is that this market has been taken over to a considerable extent by specialized "commuter" airlines flying much smaller aircraft than the major airlines, which have withdrawn from many such routes.

A third reason for regulation is to help prevent **self-destructive competition**, which, for example, economies of scale make possible. In an industry such as rail transportation, equipment—including roadbeds, tracks, switching facilities, locomotives, and cars—is extremely expensive. Suppose that two railways, having been built and equipped, are competing for some limited business that happens to be insufficient to use their total facilities to anything near capacity. That is, to meet this level of consumer demand, each railway may only have to run 40 percent as many trains over the track as can conveniently be scheduled over that route. The management of each railway will feel that, with its unused capacity, any business will be worthwhile, provided that it covers more than its short-run marginal costs—fuel, labour, and expenses other than plant and equipment. If the short-run marginal cost of shipping an additional tonne of, say, coal is $5, then either railway will be happy to lure coal-shipping customers away from the other at a price of, say, $7 per tonne, even though that price may not cover the entire cost of track and equipment. Each tonne of business that pays $7 when marginal cost is $5 will put the railway $2 ahead of where it would have been without the business. The new business does not add to the cost of the tracks or locomotives or other equipment, which must be paid for whether that business is acquired or not. Thus, even if the new business only pays for its own marginal cost and a little more, it seems financially desirable.

But the temptation to accept business on such terms will drive both firms' prices down toward their marginal costs, and, in the process, both railways are likely to go broke. If no customer pays for the track, the roadbed, and the equipment, the railway simply will be unable to go on. Thus there are those who believe that regulation of rates can be sensible, even in industries subject to competitive pressures, simply to protect the industries from themselves. Without this regulation, self-destructive competition could end up sinking those industries financially, and the public would thereby be deprived of vital services.

A fourth reason often given for public regulation is that some industries base their operations on a public resource of limited capacity, so that a public agency must intervene to ration out that resource "fairly." The most notable example of the need for this type of rationing is radio and television broadcasting. The frequency spectrum that is presently used for broadcasting is rather limited, and so it must be divided up among the users. If it were not divided up, and entry were not limited, the airwaves might become crowded and interference of broadcasters with one another's transmissions would undermine the quality of reception and perhaps even make the airwaves totally useless.

Many economists have argued that government has no business allocating scarce resources like the radio and TV spectrum among commercial users who employ such public resources for a profit. These economists argue that government rationing of the airwaves is a giveaway of public resources to favoured individuals who then grow rich at the public's expense—even though the CRTC, in return, does retain some right to regulate the content of broadcasts. Rather, it is proposed that firms be required to bid against one another for licences to run radio and TV stations. In that way the licences would go to those who can make the best use of them—an ability that would be determined by their bids. The profits would then go into the public treasury rather than private pockets, and they could be used to finance non-profit public-interest activities, such as public broadcasting.

A final reason for regulation is the danger that consumers will be misinformed or cheated, that the consumers or employees of the firm, or the environment, will be threatened by unscrupulous sellers, or that even conscientious sellers will be forced to keep up with the questionable practices of less scrupulous rivals. This sort of protection is the province of the second type of regulatory agency described earlier. Because some of the issues will be illustrated and examined in detail in Chapter 34 on environmental protection, the subject will not be discussed further in this chapter.

SUMMARY

There are five basic reasons for the activities of regulatory agencies:

1. Prevention of excess profits and other undesirable practices in an industry that is considered to be a natural monopoly.

2. The desire for universal service—that is, the desire to provide service at relatively low rates to customers whom it is particularly expensive to serve, and to do so without government subsidy.

3. The desire to prevent self-destructive price competition in multifirm industries with large capital costs and low marginal costs.

4. The desire to allocate fairly public facilities of limited capacity.

5. The desire to protect customers, employees, and the environment from damage resulting from inappropriate behaviour by firms.

Has Rate Regulation Made a Difference?

An obvious question is whether rate regulation has worked. In particular, has it made any difference in the rates paid by consumers? Would, for example, unregulated public utilities end up charging prices significantly higher than they are permitted to charge under regulation? The answer is by no means obvious. As a matter of fact, some analysts suggest that regulation may indeed make little or no difference in prices.

In one careful study comparing rates charged for electric power by regulated and unregulated utility firms over the period 1912 to 1937, a period when there were a substantial number of firms in both categories, the authors concluded that there was no significant difference between the average rates charged in the two categories.[5] The interpretation of the figures found in the study has been disputed, and the factual issue is by no means settled. But if further research should support the conclusion that regulation has not had any significant effects on *average* prices, it would severely undercut the case of those who advocate the regulatory approach.

Several explanations are possible for a conclusion that regulation has not reduced average prices. The first is that the regulatory procedure is simply a sloppy process that is inherently incapable of making much difference, one way or another.

A second explanation that is often proposed is that the regulatory agencies are simply captives of the firms they are intended to regulate. Owing to the great political clout of these big firms (so the argument goes), and because of the skillful lawyers and consultants they are able to afford, the regulated firm can overwhelm the regulatory agency, which has only a small staff and a limited budget. In this way the firm can get virtually anything it wants out of the agency. There is, however, some evidence against this argument. For example, in 1984, Bell Canada was not given the right to increase its rates for telephone service when it appeared

[5]See George Stigler and Clair Friedland, "What Can Regulation Regulate?—The Case of Electricity," *Journal of Law and Economics*, October 1962, pages 1–16.

before the body regulating these rates, the Canadian Radio–Television and Telecommunications Commission.

A third argument for the conjecture that regulation does not significantly affect *average* prices is the fact that regulators, for reasons we will discuss just below, often impose on the regulated firms prices *higher* than they would like to charge.

Whatever the overall effect of regulation on average prices, there is no doubt that in many individual cases it has significant effects on *particular* prices charged by regulated firms. One of the most widely publicized examples in the United States was the difference in airplane fares between San Francisco and Los Angeles and those between Washington, D.C., and New York City before the airlines were deregulated. The former fare was never regulated by the Civil Aeronautics Board (since the flight is entirely within the state of California), whereas the board did control the interstate flight between New York and Washington, D.C. The distance of the California trip is nearly twice as great as the East Coast trip, and neither is sparsely travelled nor beset by any other noteworthy features that would make for substantial differences in cost. Yet at the time of deregulation, fares were a little over $40 for the long California trip and a little over $50 for the short Washington to New York trip.

Why Regulators Sometimes Raise Prices

Why should regulators ever push for higher prices? The answer is that typically they do so when they want to introduce or preserve competitors in an industry. We saw earlier that where there are strong economies of scale and scope it simply may be impossible for a number of firms to survive. The largest of the firms in the industry will have such cost advantages over its competitors that it will be able to drive them out of the market while still operating at prices that are profitable. Most observers applaud low prices and price cuts that reflect such cost advantages. However, a firm that wants the market for itself may conceivably engage in price cutting even when such cuts are not justifiable in terms of cost.

The reason such price cutting may not reduce the overall profits of a regulated firm is that regulation often imposes an upper limit on the amount of profit a firm is permitted to earn. To see the connection, consider a regulated firm that produces two commodities, A and B, and which is setting each price below its profit-maximizing level in order to limit profits to the allowable ceilings. The firm may be able, without loss of profit, to cut the price of A even below its marginal cost, and make up for any resulting decrease in profit by a sufficient rise in the price of B. In this case, we say that the firm has instituted a *cross subsidy* from the consumers of product B to the consumers of product A. That is, consumers of B are paying an excessive amount for their purchase in order to make up for the deficit in the sale of product A.

Why would any firm want to do this? Suppose A is threatened by competition while B has no competitors on the horizon. Then a cross subsidy from B to A may be a way of preventing the entry of the potential competitors of A or even of driving some current competitors out of the field. An example of these possibilities has occurred recently. The fear on the part of the Department of Consumer and Corporate Affairs that Bell Canada might subsidize the production of telecommunications equipment produced by its subsidiary, Northern Telecom, led to the major hearings before the Restrictive Trade Practices Commission.

But regulation sometimes goes beyond the prevention of cross subsidy. Firms that feel they are hurt by competitive pressures will complain to regulatory commissions that the prices charged by their rivals are "unfairly" low. The commission, afraid that unrestrained pricing will reduce the number of firms in the industry, then attempts to "equalize" matters by imposing price floors that permit all the firms in the industry to operate profitably.

Many economists maintain that this approach to pricing is a perversion of the idea of competition. The virtue of competition is that, where it occurs, firms force one another to supply consumers with products of high quality at *low* prices. Any firm that cannot do this is driven out of business by the market forces. If competition does not do this, it loses its purpose because to the economist it is a means to an end, not an end in itself. An arrangement under which firms are enabled to coexist only by *preventing* them from competing with one another preserves the appearance of competition but destroys its substance.

Marginal Versus Full-Cost Rate Floors

The issue of price floors has raged over hundreds of thousands of pages of records of regulatory hearings and has involved millions of dollars of expenditures in fees for lawyers, expert witnesses, and research in preparation of the cases. The question has been not whether all floors on the prices of regulated utilities are improper, for virtually everyone agrees that some sort of lower boundary on prices is required in order to prevent cross subsidies, but rather what constitutes the proper *nature* of the rate floors.

The use of prices as a means to induce an efficient allocation of resources, the function of prices that most concerns the economist (see Chapter 26), is not the main concern of the regulatory hearings. Rather, the two primary concerns of price regulation are: (1) whether the prices under dispute are in some sense *unfair to competitors;* and (2) whether the prices are *unfair to customers of other products* produced by the same firm. In other words, is that supplier cross subsidizing products for which he has substantial competition while overcharging for products for which competition is negligible? The issues are questions of equity and justice rather than efficiency in the use of resources. Two alternative criteria have been proposed to determine appropriate floors for prices.

Criterion 1.   The price of a commodity should never be less than its *long-run marginal cost.*

Criterion 2.   The price should not be less than that commodity's *fully distributed cost*—that is, its "fair share" of the firm's total cost as determined by some accounting calculation.

To calculate the **fully distributed costs** of the various products of the firm, one simply takes the firm's total costs and divides them up in some way among its various products. First, one allocates to each product the costs for which it is obviously directly responsible. For example, a railway allocates to coal transportation the cost of hauling all cars that were devoted exclusively to carrying coal, plus the cost of operating locomotives on runs in which they carried only coal cars, and so on.

Then, one takes all costs that are incurred *in common* for several or all of the outputs of the company (such as the cost of constructing the roadbed and tracks) and divides them on the basis of some rule of thumb (generally conceded to be arbitrary) among the firm's various products. Usually, the basis of this allocation is some measure on the relative use of the common facilities by the different products. But even "relative use" is an ambiguous term. How does one divide up the cost of the track of a railway among its shipments of lead, lumber, and gold? If relative use is defined by the weight of the shipments, then the accountants will assign a high proportion of the costs to lead shipments. If prices are then required to exceed full cost, under this definition of "relative use" the railway will be placed at a disadvantage in competing for lead traffic. If, instead, relative use is defined in terms of bulk, the railway's lumber business will be harmed; if relative use is defined in terms of market value, it will lose out in competing for gold shipments.

Those who advocate the use of *marginal cost* rather than fully distributed cost

The **long-run marginal cost** of an output is the *addition* to the supplier's total cost resulting from the supply of that output *including whatever additional plant and equipment* is needed in the long run to provide that output. The inclusion of this marginal capital cost (the cost of the necessary additions to plant and equipment) is the crucial feature that distinguishes *long-run* marginal cost from *short-run* marginal cost.

as the appropriate basis for any floor on prices argue that **long-run marginal cost** is the relevant measure of the cost that any shipment actually incurs. For, by definition, marginal cost is the difference that an additional shipment makes to the firm's total cost—it is the difference between the cost to the firm if that shipment takes place and the cost to the firm if the shipment is carried by some other means of transportation. The advocates of marginal cost criteria argue that customers of *every* product of the supplier may benefit if the company is permitted to charge a price based on long-run marginal cost, particularly if, as is usual under regulation, there is a legal ceiling on the firm's total profits.

Suppose that a railway considers taking on some new business whose marginal cost is $7 and whose fully distributed cost is figured at $12. Suppose also that at any price over $10 the railway will lose the business to truckers. If the railway charges $10 and gets the business, the price does not cover the fully distributed cost, but it still adds $3 to the company's net earnings for every unit it sells to the new customers. If it was already earning as much profit as the law allows, the company would normally have to reduce its prices on other products. Thus every group of customers can gain—the new customers because they get the product more cheaply than it can be supplied by competitors, and the old customers because the prices on their products must be cut in order to satisfy the firm's profit ceiling. Everyone gains except the company's competitors, who will, of course, complain that the price is unfair because it does not cover fully distributed cost.

A Problem with Marginal Cost Pricing

Setting price equal to marginal cost is a solution generally favoured by most economists, *where it is feasible*. However, a serious problem prevents the use of the principle of marginal cost pricing in many regulated industries and marginal cost pricing in regulated industries is, consequently, not very common in practice. The problem is easily stated:

In many regulated industries, if prices were set equal to marginal cost, the firms would go bankrupt.

This seems a startling conclusion, but its explanation is really quite simple. The conclusion follows inescapably from three simple facts:

Fact 1: In many regulated industries, there are significant economies of large-scale production. As we pointed out earlier, economies of scale are one of the main reasons why certain industries were regulated in the first place.

Fact 2: In an industry with economies of scale, the long-run average-cost curve is downward sloping. This means that long-run average cost falls as the quantity produced rises, as illustrated by the AC curve in Figure 30–1. Fact 2 is something we learned back in Chapter 22 (pages 430, 440–41). The reason, to review briefly, is that total costs must double if all input quantities are doubled. But, where there are economies of scale, output will *more* than double if all input quantities are doubled. Since average cost (AC) is simply total cost (TC) divided by quantity (Q), AC = TC/Q must decline when all input quantities are doubled.

Fact 3: If average cost is declining, then marginal cost must be below average cost. This fact follows directly from one of the general rules relating marginal and average data that were explained in the appendix to Chapter 23. Once again, the logic is simple enough to review briefly. If, for example, your average quiz score is 90 percent but the next quiz pulls your average down to 87 percent, the grade on this most recent test (the marginal grade) must be below both

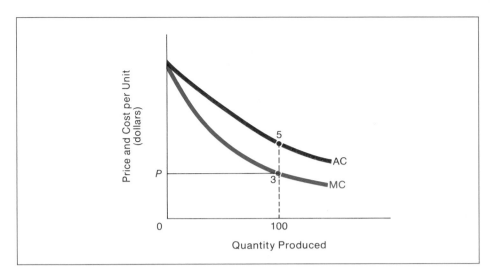

Figure 30-1

MARGINAL COST PRICING UNDER ECONOMIES OF SCALE

Economies of scale imply that the average-cost (AC) curve is declining, and therefore that the marginal-cost (MC) curve is below the average-cost curve. If, for example, the regulator forces the firm to produce 100 units and charge a price equal to its marginal cost ($3 per unit), then the firm will take in $300 in revenues. But, since its average cost at 100 units is $5 per unit, its total cost will be $500, and the firm will lose money.

the old and the new average quiz scores. That is, it takes a marginal grade (or cost) that is below the average to pull the average down.

Putting these three facts together, we conclude that in many regulated industries marginal cost (MC) will be below average cost, as depicted in Figure 30-1. Now suppose regulators set the price at the level of marginal cost. Since P = MC, P must be below AC. But $P < AC$ (price per unit less than cost per unit) means that the firm must be losing money, which is the conclusion we set out to demonstrate.

In industries where there are economies of scale, therefore, a regulation that requires P = MC is simply not an acceptable option. What, then, should be done? One possibility is to nationalize the industry, set price equal to marginal cost, and make up for the deficit out of public funds. (More is said about nationalization at the very end of the chapter.)

A second option, which is quite popular among regulators, is to (try to) set price equal to *average cost*. In practice, this principle leads to pricing at *fully distributed cost*. But, as explained in the previous section, this method of pricing is neither desirable nor possible to carry out except on the basis of arbitrary decisions.

The problem is that almost no firm produces only a single commodity. Almost every company produces a number of different varieties and qualities of some product, and often they produce thousands of different products, each with its own price. Even General Motors, a fairly specialized firm, produces many makes and sizes of cars and trucks in addition to refrigerators, washing machines, and quite a few other things. In a multiproduct firm we cannot even define AC = TC/Q, since to calculate Q (total output) we would have to add up all the apples and oranges (and all the other different items) the firm produces. But we know that one cannot add up apples and oranges. So, since we cannot calculate AC for a multiproduct firm, it is hardly possible for the regulator to require P = AC for each of the firm's products, though regulators sometimes *think* they can do so.

The Ramsey Pricing Rule

In recent years economists have been attracted to a very imaginative third approach to the problem of pricing in regulated industries that produce a multiplicity of products. This approach derives its name from its discoverer, Frank

Ramsey, a brilliant English mathematician who died in 1930 at the age of 26 after making several enduring contributions to both mathematics and economics.

The basic idea of Ramsey's pricing principle can be explained in a fairly straightforward manner. We know that prices must be set *above* marginal costs if a firm with increasing returns to scale is to break even. But how much above? In effect, Ramsey argued as follows: The reason we do not like prices to be above marginal costs is that such high prices distort the choices made by consumers, leading them to buy "too little" of the goods whose prices are set way above MC. Yet, it is necessary to set prices somewhat above marginal costs to allow the firm to survive. Therefore it makes sense to raise prices *most* above marginal cost where consumers will respond the *least* to such price increases; that is, where the *elasticity of demand* is the lowest so that price rises will create the least distortion of demand. This line of argument led Ramsey to formulate the following rule:

Ramsey Pricing Rule: Where prices must exceed marginal cost in order to permit the regulated firm to break even, the ratios of *P* to MC should be largest for those products whose elasticities of demand are the smallest.

Many economists accept this pricing rule as the correct conclusion on theoretical grounds. It has even been proposed for postal and telephone pricing.

Regulation and Efficiency of Operation

Many opponents of regulation maintain that it seriously impairs the efficiency of Canadian industry. Government regulation, these critics argue, interferes with the operation of Adam Smith's invisible hand. One source of inefficiency—the seemingly endless paperwork and complex legal proceedings that impede the firm's ability to respond quickly to changing market conditions—is obvious enough. (Though what to do about this administrative problem is far from obvious.)

But there is another source of inefficiency that may be even more important. It stems from the problem regulators have of trying to prevent the regulated firm from earning excessive profits, while at the same time (a) offering it financial incentives for maximum efficiency of operation, and (b) allowing it enough profit to attract the capital it needs when growing markets justify expansion. From this point of view, it would be ideal if the regulator would just permit the firm to take in that amount of revenue that covers its costs, including the cost of its capital. That is, the firm should earn exactly enough to pay for its ordinary costs plus the normal profit that potential investors could get elsewhere for the same money. Thus, if the prevailing rate of return is 10 percent, the regulated firm should recover its expenditures plus 10 percent on its investment and not a penny more or less.

The trouble with such an arrangement is that it removes all incentive for efficiency, responsiveness to consumer demand, and innovation. For under such an arrangement the firm is in effect *guaranteed* just *one standard rate* of profit, no more and no less. This is so whether its management is totally incompetent or extremely talented and hard working.

Competitive markets do *not* work in this way. While under perfect competition the *average* firm will earn just the opportunity cost of capital, a firm with an especially ingenious and efficient management will do better, and a firm with an incompetent management is likely to go broke. It is the possibility of great rewards and harsh punishments that gives the market mechanism its power to cause firms to strive for high efficiency and productivity growth.

We have strong evidence that where firms are guaranteed a fixed return, no matter how well or poorly they perform, gross inefficiencies are likely to result. For example, many contracts for purchases of military equipment have offered prices calculated on a *cost-plus* basis, meaning that the supplier was guaranteed that his costs would be covered and that, in addition, he would receive some prespecified amount as a contribution to profit. Studies of the resulting performance of cost-plus arrangements have confirmed that the suppliers' inefficiencies have been enormous.

A regulatory arrangement that in effect guarantees a firm its cost plus a "fair rate of return" on its investment is virtually the same as a cost-plus contract. Fortunately, under regulation, matters do not work out in exactly the same way. For one thing, when a regulated industry is in financial trouble, as is true of the railways, there is nothing the regulator can do to guarantee a "fair rate of return." If the current return on capital is 10 percent, but market demand for rail transportation is only sufficient to give it 3 percent at most, the regulatory agency cannot help matters by any act of magic. Even if it grants higher prices to the railway (or forces the railway to raise its prices) the result will be to drive even more business away and therefore cause the firm to earn still lower profits.

There is a second reason why profit regulation does not work in the same way as does a cost-plus arrangement. Curiously, this is a result of the much-criticized delays that characterize many regulatory procedures. In a number of regulated industries, a proposed change in rates is likely to take a minimum of several months before it gets through the regulatory machinery. This phenomenon, known as **regulatory lag**, is perhaps the main reason that profit regulation has not eliminated all rewards for efficiency and all penalties for inefficiency.

Suppose, for example, the regulatory commission approves a set of prices calculated to yield exactly the "fair rate of return" to the company, say 10 percent. If management then invests successfully in new processes, which reduce its costs sharply, the rate of return under the old prices may rise to, say, 12 percent. If it takes two years for the regulators to review the prices they previously approved, and adjust them to the new cost levels, the company will earn a 2 percent bonus reward for its efficiency during the two years of regulatory lag. Similarly, if management makes a series of bad decisions, which reduces the company's return to 7 percent, the firm may well apply to the regulator for some adjustments in prices to permit it to recoup its losses. If the regulator takes 18 months to act, the firm suffers a penalty for its inefficiency. It may be added that where mismanagement is *clearly* the cause of losses, regulators will be reluctant to permit the regulated firm to make up for such losses by rate adjustments. But in most cases it is difficult to pinpoint responsibility for a firm's losses.

All in all, those who have studied regulated industries have come away deeply concerned about the effects of regulation upon economic efficiency. Although some regulated firms seem to operate very efficiently, others seem to behave in quite the opposite way.

While regulatory lag does permit some penalty for inefficiency and some reward for superior performance by the regulated firm, the arrangement only works in a rough and ready manner. It still leaves the provision of incentives for efficiency as one of the fundamental problems of regulation. How can one prevent regulated firms from earning excessive profits, but also permit them to earn enough to attract the capital they need while still allowing rewards for superior performance and penalties for poor performance?

Modifications in Regulatory Arrangements to Preserve Efficiency

The problems of regulation just mentioned, along with some other criticisms, have in recent years produced a number of proposals for changes in the regulatory process. Three such proposals are discussed below.

Deregulation Plus Increased Competition

One of the most widely advocated proposals is for regulators to get out of the business of regulating, leaving much more (if not all) of the task of looking after consumer interests to the natural forces of competition. This approach is promising in areas of the economy in which competition can be expected to survive without government intervention—for example, in freight transportation, airlines, and pipelines. As a consequence, a number of economists representing a broad range of political views have been advocating at least some deregulation in these fields. Of course, deregulation will not work in industries where self-destructive competition would result without government regulation.

Performance Criteria for Permitted Rate of Return

The argument for deregulation addresses itself to all of the problems discussed in the previous section, but there are other proposals that are concerned with only one or another of these problems. We turn now to proposals designed to prevent profit controls from discouraging efficiency.

Some observers have advocated that the legally permitted rate of return not be set at a fixed number, say 10 percent, but that it be varied from firm to firm depending on the firm's record of efficiency and performance. That is, if some measure of quality of performance can be agreed upon (a measure that should take account of cost efficiency as well as product and service quality), then the better the performance score of the regulated firm the more it would be permitted to earn. A firm that performed well in a given year might be permitted 12 percent profits for that year, whereas a firm that did badly might be allowed only 8 percent, and a firm that performed abominably might be permitted only 4 percent.

However, financial incentives cannot easily be built into rate of return formulas that contain no good objective criteria of performance (such as number of minutes behind schedule for a train). Moreover, it is difficult to balance incentives for different aspects of performance. For example, if the formula assigns too high a weight to product quality and too low a weight to low cost, the firm will be encouraged to incur costs that are unjustifiably high from the point of view of public welfare in order to turn out products of slightly higher quality.

Institutionalized Regulatory Lag

It has been proposed that instead of the regulatory lag working haphazardly as it does now, regulation should consciously take advantage of the incentive for efficiency made possible by the lag. Under such a program, the regulators would assign product prices to the firms they oversee, decreeing that, *aside from automatic adjustments for inflation*, these prices are unchangeable until the next regulatory review, to occur at a time *selected by the agency*. The regulated firm would be told that the next review will occur, say, sometime between two and six years in the future, depending on what events occur in the economy. But in the meantime, any firm that can manage cost savings by economy or innovation, or that can attract more customers by improving its product without increasing its costs, will be permitted to keep the higher profits that this superior performance elicits. Of course, for the regulated firm there is a catch. If the firm proves able to reduce costs by, say, 30 percent during a period between regulatory reviews, it can, at the next review, expect to have its prices reduced correspondingly. Thus, in order to earn profits, management would constantly be forced to look for ever more economical ways of doing things.

This approach, too, has its problems. For one thing, in a period of inflation, when costs go up no matter how efficient management is, it is not clear how regulated prices should be adjusted to make up for inflation *between* review periods.

Some Effects of Deregulation

Deregulation of industries is much more advanced in the United States than it is in Canada, although, even there, it is too early to reach final evaluations of its consequences. Yet, several conclusions are becoming clear from the American experience, and these should be borne in mind when considering the pros and cons of deregulation in Canada.

1. ***Effects on prices***.   There seems little doubt that deregulation has generally led to lower prices. According to *Business Week*: "Long-distance airline fares, adjusted for inflation, have declined almost 50% in the past seven years. Many trucking rates have skidded down 30% in real terms since 1980. The costs of standard telephones in 1983 have fallen by one-third, compared with last year."[6]

2. ***Effects on local service***.   During the debates on deregulation in the United States, it was widely feared, even by supporters of deregulation, that smaller and more isolated communities would be deprived of service because the small number of customers would make service unprofitable. It was said that airlines, railways, and telephone companies would withdraw from such communities once they were no longer forced to stay there by the regulators.

    So far, these worries seem largely to be proving groundless. True, the larger airlines have left the smaller communities, as predicted. But they have usually been replaced by smaller commuter airlines that have provided, on the average, more frequent service than their regulated predecessors. Of course, a few communities have been left without service or with service of poorer quality, but other locations have benefited considerably.

3. ***Effects on entry***.   As a result of deregulation, older airlines have invaded one another's routes and a number of new airlines have sprung up, offering a variety of special features. (People's Express specializes in low fares; Metro Air specializes in luxury service.) Altogether some 14 new airlines and about 10,000 new truck operators have entered the markets since deregulation in the United States.

4. ***Effects on profits***.   Just as deregulation of airlines and trucking went into effect, a severe recession hit the U.S. economy. The profits of the older firms in the industry fell sharply and in many cases turned into losses. Whether deregulation or recession or both are responsible is very much disputed. Some experienced observers argue that without deregulation, losses would have been even worse, but no one can be sure.

    What was surprising was that deregulation turned out, even during the recession, to be profitable to many new entrants. A number of new airlines, trucking companies, and telephone companies either showed a profit almost at once or showed promise of becoming profitable very soon.

    Indeed, in airlines, trucking, and bus transportation it turned out that the new entrants, instead of suffering from a cost handicap, often had a substantial cost advantage over the older firms. The reason was that the older firms had agreed to costly union contracts under regulation. The entrants often entered business using a good deal of non-union labour, and paying much lower wages.

5. ***Effects on the unions***.   Deregulation has badly hurt unions such as the Teamsters (of the trucking industry) and the Airline Pilots Association. These organizations have spearheaded efforts to get the U.S. Congress to reimpose regulation. The article excerpted in the box on page 594 indicates that the same pressures can certainly be expected in Canada.

[6]"Deregulating America," *Business Week*, November 28, 1983, page 80.

Canadian Unions and Deregulation

Not all interests support the concept of deregulation, as the following excerpt from a recent newspaper item illustrates.

CLC says deregulation will 'wreck our very lifestyle'

MONTREAL—The movement toward deregulating transportation, communications and other commerce will cost thousands of jobs and affect public service, says the president of the Canadian Labor Congress.

"It's going to wreck our very lifestyle, even reach to our culture," said Dennis McDermott....

Yesterday several speakers from the airline and transportation industries condemned the deregulation move, saying it has costs thousands of jobs in the U.S.

"Deregulation is the sleeziest form of union-busting I have seen in a long time," says Dennis Lee, of the Canadian Airline Employees Association.

"It reaches into the question of all of labor legislation," said Bob White, Canadian director of the United Auto Workers.

"It gets to the question of Canadian content in our broadcasting, it gets to the question of the whole corporate control of our society."...

A paper prepared for the CLC constitutional convention said deregulation was "the new buzzword" for returning to the operation of private enterprise in "an unfettered, free market".

In the U.S., deregulation has led to loss of jobs, wage rollbacks, threats to public safety and inequalities in prices and services, says the paper.

Contrary to the move away from regulations, says the CLC paper, the country needs tougher rules. Otherwise, the public interest will suffer when business cuts costs and inefficient options, the paper concludes....

SOURCE: *The Spectator*, Hamilton, May 31, 1984, page A14.

---

6. ***Why regulated industries opposed deregulation***. It should be clear now why many airlines, trucking firms, and bus lines, as well as their unions, strongly opposed deregulation. They realized that regulation protected them from entry and competition. Rather than serving as an instrument to foster competition, regulation had become a means to forestall it. Of course, there were other reasons why regulated firms were unhappy about the offer of increased freedom provided by deregulation, but fear of competition was surely a major reason.

Some Final Comments on the Regulatory Process

The problems we have described here and the proposals that have been made to deal with them are by no means all of the criticisms that have been raised or all of the proposals that have been offered. We have attempted only to provide some feeling for the complexity of the regulatory process and to show the difficulty of finding workable alternatives. It is too easy simply to seek villains and lay blame on them for all that has gone wrong—as many observers of regulation tend to do.

For instance, it is often argued that what is wrong with the regulatory process is that the commissions have become captives of the firms they are supposed to regulate, doing whatever those companies want them to do. And perhaps there are some cases where the charge has some validity. But most of the time, matters are much more complicated. The regulated firms are often just as convinced that the regulators are "out to get them" and that the best they can hope for from a set of hearings is to delay a decision for as long as possible.

In truth, under the current process of regulation, virtually everyone may be dissatisfied by the decisions that emerge. The tendency of regulatory agencies to prevent low rather than high prices is one source of this general dissatisfaction. The regulator does not enjoy the role of defender of high prices; the regulated firm that is prevented from charging proposed lower prices feels deprived of vital business; and customers certainly are not pleased by having to pay prices higher than the company wants to offer. On all these counts it is clear that the regulation of prices does not work out as one might have wished. But solutions to these problems are not to be found by identifying a villain to take the blame.

A Word on Nationalization

As we indicated at the beginning of the chapter, in industries in which monopoly or near monopoly offers clear advantages to society over competition, there is an alternative to regulation. This alternative is government ownership and operation of the firms in that industry, or *nationalization*. A number of cities operate their own public transport facilities, collect their own garbage, and offer other services that elsewhere are provided by private enterprise.

It is almost an instinctive reaction by people in Canada to consider such public enterprises as being prone to extreme mismanagement and waste. And the near-legendary problems of the Post Office do seem to support this supposition. However, here too, one should be careful not to jump to conclusions. It is true that for many years visitors found the nationalized French telephone system a model of chaos and mismanagement. But at the same time, the Swedish telephone system, which is also nationalized, has consistently been smooth-working and efficient. And the French government-supplied electricity system has set world standards in its use of the most modern analytic techniques of economics and engineering, and has adopted innovative pricing policies that promote efficiency.

Despite these accomplishments, no one has yet found a systematic incentive mechanism for efficiency that can do for nationalized industries what the profit motive does for private enterprise. Where the market is unsparing in its rewards for accomplishments and in its penalties for poor performance, one can be quite sure that a firm's inefficiency will not readily be tolerated. But nationalized industries have no such automatic mechanism handing out rewards and penalties dependably and impartially. We have seen, however, that there are analogous problems under regulation; where profits are controlled by the regulator, the rewards for efficiency are also far from automatic. Hence, the relative efficiency of nationalized and regulated private firms is far from clear.

Summary

1. Regulation has three primary purposes: to put brakes on the decisions of industries with monopoly power; to contribute to public health and safety; or to manage market supply so that producer incomes (for example, those of farmers) can be raised and stabilized.
2. Railways, trucking, telecommunications, and gas and electricity supply are among the industries that are regulated in Canada.
3. In recent years there has been a major push toward reduction of regulation, except in agriculture and self-regulated areas such as law and medicine.
4. Among the major reasons given for regulation are: (a) economies of scale and scope, which make industries into natural monopolies; (b) the danger of self-destructive competition in industries with low (short-run) marginal costs; (c) the desire to provide service to isolated areas where supply is expensive and un-profitable; (d) the desire for fair allocation of scarce resources (such as radio and television air space); and (e) the protection of consumers, employees, and the environment.
5. Some economists believe that regulation has had very little effect on regulated industries, but this conclusion is not accepted by everyone.
6. Regulators often reject proposals by regulated firms to cut their prices, and sometimes the regulators even force firms to raise their prices. The purpose of such action is to prevent "unfair competition," and to protect customers of some of the firm's products from being forced to cross-subsidize customers of other products. Many economists disagree with such actions and argue that the result is usually to stifle competition and make all customers pay more than they otherwise would.

7. Economists generally argue that a firm should be permitted to cuts its price as long as it covers its long-run marginal cost. However, others (usually non-economists) argue that fully distributed cost is a better criterion. A fully distributed cost criterion, in this sense, usually means that price will be higher than it will be if marginal cost is used as the standard.

8. Regulation is often criticized for providing little or no incentive for efficiency, for tending to push prices upward, and for forcing the regulated parties to engage in an expensive and time-consuming adversary process.

9. Nationalized (government-run) industries are frequently suspected of being wasteful and inefficient, but the evidence is not uniform and there are cases in which nationalized firms seem more efficient than similar regulated firms.

Concepts for Review

Nationalization	Economies of scope	Marginal cost pricing
Price floor	Cross subsidy	Ramsey Pricing Rule
Price ceiling	Self-destructive competition	Regulatory lag
Natural monopoly	Fully distributed cost	
Economies of scale	Short- and long-run marginal cost	

Questions for Discussion

1. Why is a hydro-electric company in a city usually considered to be a natural monopoly? What would happen if two competing hydro-electric companies were established? How about telephone companies?

2. Suppose a 20 percent cut in the price of freight transportation brings in so much new business that it permits a railway to cut its passenger fares by 2 percent. In your opinion, is this equitable? Is it a good idea or a bad one?

3. In some regulated industries, prices are prevented from falling by the regulatory agency and as a result many firms open up business in that industry. In your opinion, is this competitive or anticompetitive? Is it a good idea or a bad one?

4. List some industries with regulated rates whose services you have bought. What do you think of the quality of their service?

5. In which if any of the regulated industries mentioned in your previous answer is there competitive rivalry? Why is regulation appropriate in these cases? (Or is it inappropriate in your opinion, and if so, why?)

6. Do you think it is fair or unfair for local users of telephone service to be cross subsidized by other telephone services?

7. A regulated industry is prohibited from earning profits higher than it now is getting. It begins to sell a new product at a price above its long-run marginal cost. Explain why the prices of other company products will, very likely, have to be reduced.

Limiting Market Power: Competition Policy

31

There is enough for the needy,
but not for the greedy.
MAHATMA M. K. GANDHI

The preceding chapter described the process of regulation, one of the two traditional instruments used by the Canadian government in an attempt to offset the undesirable effects that unrestrained monopoly and oligopoly would have on the market mechanism. This chapter analyses the second of these instruments, *competition policy*. **Competition policy** attempts to control the growth of monopoly and to prevent firms from engaging in "undesirable" practices through the use of legislation and various programs. Firms violating competition laws risk a lawsuit from the federal government, which will seek a ruling that both prevents the practice from recurring and punishes the offender by fines or even prison terms.

Competition cases are likely to be well-publicized because the accused firms are often household names. Prominent cases have involved Canadian General Electric, Atlantic Sugar, Canadian Breweries, Canada Safeway, K. C. Irving, and the T. Eaton Company. The magnitude of a suit for violation of a competition law is difficult to envision. After the charges have been filed, it is not unusual for several years to elapse before the case even comes up for trial. The parties spend this period preparing their cases: assembling witnesses, gathering evidence, and drawing up numerous documents. Dozens of lawyers, scores of witnesses, and many researchers are likely to be involved in the process of preparation. The trial itself may run for many months, with each day's proceedings producing a fat volume of transcript. An example of this process is the government prosecution of five major moving companies for price fixing. The combines investigation began in 1966 but a guilty plea *without trial* was only entered on December 14, 1983.

When the Attorney General of Canada decides to bring suit against a company, the cost of fighting the suit automatically imposes a financial penalty upon that company whether or not it is subsequently found to have violated the law—or even if the case is thrown out of court before it comes to trial. This is an awesome power and a great responsibility. What justifies the investment of so much power in a government agency? What are the purposes of the competition laws? And how well has the program succeeded? These questions are the main concerns of this chapter. Starting with a little history, we describe how competition policy has fared over the nine decades since its inception. We outline the activities that are currently prohibited by law, and then examine the role of monopoly in the economy and the pros and cons of the competition policy program from the viewpoint of economic analysis.

The Origin and Development of Competition Policy

In 1888, a Select Committee of the House of Commons investigating alleged combinations in the manufacturing, trade, and insurance industries, reported that combines existed in thirteen commodities or industries in Canada (for example, sugar, groceries, coal, and stoves). As a result, in 1889, the Parliament of Canada passed into law **An Act for the Prevention and Suppression of Combinations in Restraint of Trade**. Thus a formal competition policy in Canada predated that in the United States (the Sherman Act) by one year.

The Canadian act was part of the criminal code and provided that:

Every person who conspires, combines, agrees or arranges with any other person ...unlawfully...to restrain or injure trade or commerce in relation to any...article or commodity; to unduly prevent...[its] manufacture or production..., to unreasonably enhance [its] price...or to unduly prevent or lessen competition in [its] production, manufacture, purchase, barter, sale, transportation or supply...is guilty of a misdemeanor and liable on conviction to a penalty not exceeding $4,000 and not less than $200, or to imprisonment for any term not exceeding 2 years. And if a corporation, it is liable on conviction to a penalty not exceeding $10,000 and not less than $1,000.

Note the words "unduly" and "unreasonably." They still exist in important sections of current legislation and have been the cause of great concern because in criminal law it is necessary to prove guilt beyond a reasonable doubt, a difficult task considering the amorphous nature of the words.

In any case, the original act was not effective because no machinery was set up to secure evidence. Not until 1910, at the peak of a merger movement in Canada, was a formal process of investigation enacted. Under the terms of the legislation, six citizens could apply to a judge to appoint a board of investigation. This board, if approved, would submit a report and could recommend fines. However, the mere publication of a report was considered to be the main punishment. For example, in 1923 Mackenzie King asked the House of Commons:

What is the power of the criminal code to prosecute some particular person or group of persons in comparison with the power of spreading broadcast throughout the land accurate and true information with regard to a situation which is inimical to the public interest, and which the people themselves are certain to be concerned in remedying.[1]

Over the next forty years some changes were made in legislation, but the most important occurred in 1952. These changes were a result of the report of the MacQuarrie Committee, which was set up in 1950 to study combines legislation. Upon the advice of the committee, the government established two entities that remain today as the administrators of competition policy in Canada. One is the **Director of Investigation and Research** and the second is the **Restrictive Trade Practices Commission**. The function of each in the administration of competition policy will be described in detail later in the chapter.

Between 1952 and 1976 a number of amendments were made to the existing legislation, which was now called the **Combines Investigation Act**. However the government remained dissatisfied with the legislation because the rules relied on criminal, rather than civil, law. As a result, the government was losing *all* of its major cases. In 1971, in an attempt to rectify this and a number of other

---

[1] *House of Commons Debate, Second Session*, 1923, page 262S.

weaknesses, the government introduced a **Competition Act**, which would facilitate the prosecution of major forms of anti-competitive behaviour. The introduction of the new act sparked one of the largest lobbying efforts in Canadian history. The business community, in particular, opposed any strengthening of the law and in the end was at least partially successful. After more than three years the government split the act into two parts (Stage 1 and Stage 2) and passed only the first (less controversial) stage into law on January 1, 1976. Stage 2 was re-introduced in 1984, and it will be discussed later in this chapter.

Current Legislation

The Combines Investigation Act deals with events that change the **structure** of the economy, such as mergers or monopolization, and with **conduct** in business that is considered not to be to the benefit of the economy as a whole. Examples of such conduct include agreements to restrict competition and certain problematic pricing, distribution, and sales practices.

Monopoly

Section 2 of the Combines Investigation Act defines a *monopoly* as:

A situation where one or more persons either substantially or completely control ...the class or species of business in which they are engaged and have operated such business or are likely to operate it to the detriment or against the interest of the public....

Public policy concerns with monopoly are basically twofold. First, a firm possessing a monopoly will probably reduce output from levels which would exist in a competitive market, and raise prices. Second, there may be a tendency for the monopolist not to seek lowest cost methods of production because of the lack of competitive pressure in the marketplace.

Only *one* conviction has been obtained, after trial, under this section of the act. In 1952, the Eddy Match company was found guilty of monopolizing the market for wooden matches over a twenty-year period. It had maintained its monopoly by buying up rivals and carrying out industrial spying, among other things.

Nine other cases have been brought to trial and in five of these cases the companies were acquitted. In one of the remaining four, the company, Electric Reduction Company of Canada Ltd., pleaded guilty without trial. In the other three, the companies involved agreed to the terms of *prohibition order* (an order issued forbidding the repetition or continuation of an offence) without admitting guilt. One of the prohibition orders prevented the grocery chain, Safeway, from acquiring existing stores from competitors for a five-year period.

Generally, prosecutions have failed because, while the government can often show that monopoly exists, it has not been able to *prove* that monopolies were operating *to the detriment of the public*. As a result, in the K. C. Irving case, the company was found innocent even though, from 1944 to 1971, it had acquired all five of the English-language daily newspapers in New Brunswick.

Mergers

Mergers have long been a subject of suspicion by the competition-policy authorities. Particularly when a merger is **horizontal**, it is often feared that because the number of competing firms in the industry is reduced (that is, concentration is increased), competition will decline.

The authorities do not wish to impede mergers that seem likely to increase efficiency by improving the co-ordination of production activities, permitting economies of scale, getting one of the firms out of financial difficulties, or

A **merger** occurs when two previously independent firms are combined under a single owner or group of owners. A **horizontal merger** is the merger of two firms producing similar products, as when one toothpaste manufacturing firm purchases another.

A **vertical merger** involves the joining of two firms, one of which supplies an ingredient of the other's product, as when an auto maker acquires a tire manufacturing firm. A **conglomerate merger** is the union of two unrelated firms, as when a defence industry firm joins a firm that produces phonograph records.

facilitating operations in a variety of other ways. But the authorities do want to prevent mergers that threaten to reduce competition.

Though by no means unanimous on the subject, most economists agree that mergers *sometimes* reduce competition, particularly in a market that is not contestable,[2] so that threats of entry do not prevent the merged firm from raising prices above competitive levels. This danger is particularly acute if the number of firms is sufficiently small to make collusion a real possibility.

On the other hand, where there is reason to believe that the merger will not reduce competition, many economists oppose impediments to merger. They believe that mergers that are not undertaken to reduce competition have only one purpose—to achieve greater efficiency. For example, the larger firm that results from the merger may enjoy substantial economies of scale not available to smaller firms. The two merging companies may learn special skills from one another, or they may offset one another's risks. Mergers have sometimes proved disappointing and have brought little cost saving. But economists who defend freedom to merge when there is no demonstrated threat to competition pose a challenging question: Who can judge better than the firms involved whether their marriage is likely to make their activities more efficient?

In Canada, because of our relatively small market size, government policy has long been favourable to the existence of large firms and a reflection of this general policy can be seen in the results of attempts to prosecute certain mergers under the terms of the Combines Investigation Act.

In the years up to 1984, only six merger prosecutions have been undertaken. One prosecution resulted in a guilty plea before trial while the remainder resulted in acquittals. The insignificance of these numbers becomes apparent when we note the number of mergers that have taken place in Canada between 1960 and 1982, which are presented in Table 31-1.

The reason for the lack of success in prosecutions and for the apparent unwillingness of the government to initiate new cases can be found in the courts' interpretation of the existing law. Just as in the case of monopoly, a finding of guilty under the Canadian law requires proof that because of a merger, competition is or is likely to be lessened *to the detriment of the public*. The courts have interpreted the latter phrase to mean the existence of a virtual monopoly. Thus, in the British Columbia Sugar case, even though it was shown that the company through merger had a near monopoly of sugar in the four western provinces, the presiding judge decided that the eastern sugar companies presented a viable source of potential competition.

Agreements to Restrict Competition

Section 32 of the Combines Investigation Act provides that:

Everyone who conspires, combines, agrees or arranges with another person ... to ... restrain or injure competition unduly ... is guilty of an indictable offence and is liable to imprisonment for five years or a fine of one million dollars or to both.

Since the inception of the act, the government has been successful in approximately 75 percent of the nearly 100 cases brought under this section. However, two recent cases, Aetna and Atlantic Sugar, have produced judgments that have made successful prosecution virtually impossible. The problem arises in the newly required *proof of double intent*. Prior to these recent cases, it was sufficient for the government to prove that the parties in the conspiracy *intended to enter an agreement*. It was not necessary to show that they *intended to limit competition*. Since these cases, both conditions are required for a conviction. As a result of this interpretation, the presiding judge in the Atlantic Sugar case held

[2]See Chapter 28, page 554 for a definition and discussion of this concept.

Table 31-1

MERGERS IN CANADA, 1960–1982

YEAR	FOREIGN*	DOMESTIC**	TOTAL
1960	93	110	203
1961	86	152	238
1962	79	106	185
1963	41	88	129
1964	80	124	204
1965	78	157	235
1966	80	123	203
1967	85	143	228
1968	163	239	402
1969	168	336	504
1970	162	265	427
1971	143	245	388
1972	127	302	429
1973	100	252	352
1974	78	218	296
1975	109	155	264
1976	124	189	313
1977	192	203	395
1978	271	178	449
1979	307	204	511
1980	234	180	414
1981	200	291	491
1982	371	205	576

*Acquisitions involving a foreign-owned or foreign-controlled acquiring company (the nationality of the controlling interest in the acquired company prior to the merger could have been foreign or Canadian).

**Acquisitions involving an acquiring company not known to be foreign-owned or foreign-controlled (the nationality of the controlling interest in the acquired company prior to the merger could have been foreign or Canadian).

SOURCE: *Annual Report, Director of Investigation and Research, Combines Investigation Act*, March 31, 1984, page 57.

that although the companies shared virtually the entire market (each having a constant market share for a quarter of a century), they should be acquitted of conspiracy charges because: "The reason for maintaining traditional market shares was to avoid a price war which would have resulted had the accused taken the only method of increasing them by price cutting through excessive discounts".[3] Notice that there is no mention of consumer interest.

Pricing Practices

The Combines Investigation Act deals with three different practices that are assumed to reduce competition in an economy. These practices are price discrimination, resale price maintenance, and predatory pricing.

Price discrimination. The intent of this section of the act is to ensure that a seller does not sell products of like quality to competing buyers at different prices. Such a practice would naturally confer an undue advantage to the buyer paying the lower price. This section is not utilized to a great extent because of difficulties in dealing with matters such as whether the buyers are competitors (which involves defining relevant markets). In fact only two cases have been brought to trial, with one conviction and one acquittal being recorded.

Price discrimination is charging different prices, relative to costs, to different buyers of the same product.

[3]See G. Kaiser, *World Law of Competition, Vol. 3A Canada*, Mathew Brender, 1982 for an account of this and other relevant cases.

Resale price maintenance is forcing retailers to keep the price of a product at or above that specified by the wholesaler.

Predatory pricing refers to price cuts that take place only to keep other firms from entering the industry.

Resale price maintenance. This pricing practice typically involves the manufacturer forcing a retailer to maintain the price of a product at, or at least not below, some specified price. If a retailer refuses to carry out the manufacturer's wishes, the manufacturer normally cuts off the supply of the product. This practice has been illegal in Canada since 1951, although allowance is made in the law for some exemptions, such as a case in which the retailer is using the product as a "loss leader."

In contrast to the other sections of the Combines Investigation Act discussed above, prosecutions against resale price maintenance have generally been successful. Fines are usually assessed, and prohibition orders are often issued.

Predatory pricing. This term refers to price cuts by existing firms, which are effected in an attempt to keep other firms from entering the industry. Unfortunately, a crucial element in this section of the act states that prices cannot be "unreasonably low." In addition, to obtain a conviction it must be proved that the predatory-pricing practice was part of a policy and that a competitor or competition was or could be threatened or extinguished.

Two major cases dealing with this section of the act have reached full trial. In the Hoffman–La Roche case, the company was found guilty because for a six-month period it had adopted a policy of giving away one of its products (Valium) to hospitals in order to build up a consumer preference. It was noted at trial that a zero price was certainly a large drop from regular prices. In the second case, R. V. Consumers Glass Company, a producer of cup lids, was charged with lowering prices unreasonably in order to drive out a competitor. However, the company successfully argued that due to excess capacity in the industry it was merely lowering it prices to make the maximum possible recovery of its fixed costs. That is, given the market situation, it was "loss minimizing" by charging a price greater than average variable cost, but less than what was called average total cost.

Distribution Practices

Since the passing of the latest (1976) version of the Combines Investigation Act, the following distribution practices are subject to review by the Restrictive Trade Practices Commission: tied selling, exclusive dealing, consignment selling, refusal to supply, and market restriction. Being "reviewable" means these practices are not considered to be offences under the act. There is basically no appeal from a decision by the commission, and the commission may only issue remedial orders.

These practices deal generally with **vertical marketing** arrangements, which are considered harmful to competition in that through such practices the wholesaler or retailer might be given a local monopoly on the sale of a product, or the supplier itself might be abusing a monopoly position.

Two cases will illustrate the nature of these practices. In the case of Bombardier Ltée., the company's exclusive dealing practices in snowmobiles were brought under review. The company admitted that it had supplied dealers with their snowmobiles under the explicit condition that dealers would not handle any other brand of snowmobiles. Eight dealers had their franchises terminated for breaching this contract. Although the Restrictive Trade Practices Commission agreed that Bombardier controlled a substantial share of the snowmobile market (50 percent in Quebec, Ontario, and Atlantic Canada), it found that this fact had not produced a substantial lessening of competition. Accordingly, the case was dismissed.

In a case dealing with tied selling, the results were different. The BBM Bureau of Measurement was a major supplier of television rating services and the sole supplier of radio rating services in Canada. The company had a requirement that anyone desiring its radio ratings, over which it had a monopoly, would also have to purchase its television ratings. The commission held that this practice was unfair to an existing competitor and would impede entry into or expansion within the ratings market. It therefore issued a prohibition order in this matter.

Unfair Sales Practices

Other sections of the Combines Investigation Act contain provisions dealing with misleading advertising and deceptive marketing practices. It is important that any violations in these areas be prosecuted if our economic system is to operate under the assumption of the "knowledgeable buyer."

These sections have spawned by far the largest number of prosecutions and convictions since 1976. For example, in his annual report for the year ended March 31, 1983, the Director of Investigation and Research of the Combines Investigation Act reports that 169 cases were completed dealing with misleading advertising and deceptive marketing practices, while only 16 were completed dealing with *all* other sections (resale price maintenance accounted for nine of these).

A small sample of unfair sales practices dealt with over the years includes: (a) making free offers that are not genuine; (b) advertising goods that are not in fact available: (c) misstatements as to the origin of goods; and (d) statements misrepresenting the fuel consumption of an automobile.

In recent years, convictions have brought increasing levels of fines as well as prohibition orders. The largest fine to date was levied on Simpsons–Sears in 1983. The amount of the fine was $1 million and the offence was misleading product advertising during the firm's campaign to sell diamond rings.

It should be noted that many federal and provincial agencies are involved in activities dealing with unfair sales practices. At the federal level, aspects are covered by the Hazardous Products Act, the Textile Labelling Act, and the Food and Drugs Act, among others. Provincially, areas of concern include warranties, insurance, lotteries, and securities.

Penalties and Exemptions

When guilty verdicts are obtained, competition policy is enforced by one or more of the following penalties, which are provided for in various sections of the Combines Investigation Act:

1. Fines—the limit varies with the section of the act and is unlimited in some sections of the act.
2. Divestiture—forcing convicted companies to sell some of their assets.
3. Prohibition orders—the order prohibits the repetition or continuation of an offence.
4. Restitution—payment of a sum to certain persons identified by the court.
5. Interim injunctions—prevent certain activities pending a trial.
6. Post conviction reporting.
7. Declaring invalid patents or trademarks.
8. Imprisonment to a maximum of five years.

In addition, private damage actions can be based on a breach of the Combines Act. However, class actions, which are available in the United States, are not provided for in the Canadian act.

While this list of penalties sounds imposing, it must be remembered that the government has achieved *very few* prosecutions, except under the resale price maintenance and unfair trade practices sections of the Combines Investigation Act. In addition to this, many activities are currently exempt from the act, including:

1. The formation of labour unions.
2. Any association between fishermen and fish processors.
3. Agreements between banks and bank mergers.
4. The operation of shipping conferences (cartels of ship owners who collude on prices).

5. Competition-reducing agreements in the professions (for example, the ban on price advertising imposed by law societies in Canada).
6. The conduct of firms that are effectively regulated.
7. Monopoly behaviour of firms holding a valid patent or trademark.
8. With some exceptions, agreements among exporters.
9. With some exceptions, the activities of crown agencies.

The Administration of Competition Policy

The federal minister charged with the responsibility of administering competition policy in Canada is the Minister of Consumer and Corporate Affairs. The day-to-day administration of this program is carried out by the Director of Investigation and Research, under the auspices of the Bureau of Competition Policy (one of the three bureaus in Consumer and Corporate Affairs Canada). The bureau had an authorized strength of 241 person-years in 1982–83. The majority of these personnel (192) were situated in headquarters in Hull, Quebec, while the remainder comprised the field staff of the Marketing Practices Branch.

An inquiry into any alleged violation of the Combines Investigation Act can be initiated in one of three ways: upon the direction of the minister, upon a formal request from six Canadian residents, or by the director. In fact, the vast majority of inquiries are initiated by the director, often in response to complaints by companies or individuals regarding alleged violations.

In general, a preliminary inquiry into a complaint is carried out by the staff of the bureau, and if the preliminary evidence gives the director reason to believe that a violation has in fact been committed, he initiates a formal inquiry. Once an inquiry has become formal, evidence can be obtained by searching premises, formally requesting data, or holding hearings under the auspices of the Restrictive Trade Practices Commission.

If the formal investigation finds sufficient evidence of wrongdoing, the director can either refer the case to the commission for formal hearings or to the Attorney General of Canada, to be considered for the laying of criminal charges. In recent years, the latter has been the route most often taken.

The Attorney General reviews the case (a most time-consuming process ranging from months to years), and decides either to drop the case or lay formal charges. (Note that it is the Attorney General and *not* the Director of Investigation and Research who lays charges and formally prosecutes the cases.) Once charges are laid, cases travel along the normal route of criminal justice in Canada.

The director also has authority under the act to undertake independent research on topics he considers to be of general economic interest. His aim in carrying out this task is to present his findings to the Restrictive Trade Practices Commission as a basis for a general inquiry. One recent inquiry that has followed this route in Canada concerned the effects of the vertical integration between Bell Canada and Northern Telecom. Here, the director argued that the relationship between these companies precluded other producers of telecommunications equipment from the lucrative Bell market. In another case, the so-called Petroleum Inquiry, the director questioned the economic benefits to the general Canadian economy of a number of practices carried on by the major petroleum refineries and distributors in Canada.

New Directions

It has long been recognized that the Competition Act of 1976 solved only some of the ongoing problems of competition policy, and that more changes—in the areas of merger, monopoly, and conspiracy—are required to enhance competition.

After a long gestation period, the Minister of Consumer and Corporate Affairs tabled in Parliament further proposed revisions to the Combines Investigation Act in early 1984. The main amendments proposed included the following:

1. Mergers would be dealt with under civil law instead of criminal law. When the Director of Investigation and Research challenged mergers, he would do so on the basis that they "are likely to lessen competition significantly," and "are not likely to bring about gains in efficiency which result in a substantial real net savings of resources for the Canadian economy."[4]

2. Monopoly would be dealt with under civil law. The civil law proposed concerns the abuse by a firm or group of firms of their dominant position. For a court to make an order against a firm or a group of firms it must be satisfied that three conditions exist:

   i) The firm or firms substantially control the relevant market.

   ii) The firm or firms are engaging in anti-competitive acts (examples are given in the draft act).

   iii) The practices noted in the charge are "having or likely to have the effect of lessening competition substantially."[5]

3. A new civil provision proposed would exempt certain specialization agreements from charges of conspiracy and exclusive dealing. Such agreements would allow each of the parties involved to discontinue production of one or more articles so that all producers involved could achieve cost reductions through economies of scale.

4. The Combines Investigation Act would be made binding on federal and provincial crown corporations with respect to commercial activities which they carry out in competition with other firms. This would avoid a repetition of the situation created in December 1983 when the Supreme Court of Canada ruled that Eldorado Nuclear Limited and Uranium Canada Limited were not subject to the act, while four private firms, alleged to be part of a cartel which included the crown corporations, were.

5. It was proposed that agreements among banks be subject to the Combines Investigation Act.

6. All reviewable matters that are presently adjudicated by the Restrictive Trade Practices Commission would be adjudicated by the regular courts. This change would reduce the workload of the commission, limiting its main tasks to the assessment of specialization agreements and the holding of general inquiries, such as those concerning Bell–Northern and the petroleum industry noted on page 604.

The fate of these amendments is by no means certain because of the vagaries of the parliamentary timetable and the opposition of interest groups. In an attempt to reduce the latter problem, the minister carried out an intensive three-year consultation process with interested parties before bringing forth the proposed amendments. Following the change in government in 1984, the new minister indicated that there was political consensus on the general approach to be taken to amending the Combines Investigation Act.

Issues in Concentration of Industry

Having reviewed competition policy and its interpretation by the courts, the next logical question is: Does it work? One very rough way to measure the success of combines legislation, especially on the merger–monopoly front, is to look at what has happened to the share of Canadian business in the hands of the largest firms.

First, we can compare the degree of domination by large firms in the Canadian

[4]Minister of Consumer and Corporate Affairs, *Combines Investigation Act Amendments 1984 Background Information and Explanatory Notes*, Ottawa, 1984, page 7.
[5]Ibid.

Two Current Competition Policy Issues

Buying Groups

For decades, groups of firms (usually retailers) have banded together to buy products from wholesalers. These buying groups exist in a number of fields such as hardware (Home Hardware), and automobile parts and accessories (Canadian Tire). Recently, however, the creation of large buying groups in the grocery industry has focused the attention of officials administering Canadian competition on the costs and benefits of buying groups. For example, Dominion and Steinbergs recently formed a buying group called Volume 1 Inc.

Briefly, what are some of the pros and cons to the existence of buying groups? On the plus side, buying groups:

- Can obtain volume discounts because of their large size.
- Can carry out more balanced negotiations with large sellers.
- Reduce costs by allowing deliveries to be made at one point and by facilitating inventory planning.
- Allow retailers to consolidate their advertising efforts.

All of these factors will reduce costs, an effect that will benefit the ultimate consumer if the cost reductions are passed on.

On the minus side, buying groups:

- Might have undue monopoly power, particularly if they are dealing with a number of relatively small sellers.
- Can be detrimental to other buyers by tying suppliers to long-term exclusive contracts.
- Can use strong-arm tactics, such as the threat of blacklisting, to keep purchase prices down.
- Might force sellers to boycott other buyers.
- Might reduce consumer choice because volume rebates penalize stores that prefer to carry a wide variety of merchandise.

Resale Price Maintenance

Since 1951, it has been considered illegal in Canada for suppliers to dictate to retailers the price at which their products must be sold. However, certain exemptions are allowed. In the United States, where no exemptions have been allowed, the Department of Justice recently asked the courts to overturn the universality of this prohibition, letting such issues be decided case by case, depending on the facts involved.

In the United States, discounting and discount houses flourish as in no other country and provide unique opportunities for bargain shopping. Manufacturers who want to dictate resale prices seek to prevent discounters from carrying their products. The manufacturers claim that discounters cut corners in customer service, offering little help in product selection, installation, or repair. But the discounters make it difficult for full-service retailers to survive. Potential customers go to a full-service department store for product information, then buy the item from a discounter. The final result, it is claimed, can be a decrease in competition, as the full-service retailer is forced out of that business.

economy with that in other countries. Canadian programs designed to limit monopoly power go back further than do comparable programs in virtually any other major free-market economy. Indeed, in some European and Far Eastern countries, monopoly is not really discouraged. Thus, one way to evaluate the effectiveness of competition policy is to compare the status of the larger firms in Canada with that of their counterparts abroad.

A second method of evaluation involves observations of firms over a long period of time. Some observers, particularly Marxist economists, have predicted that capitalism will have a basic tendency towards **concentration of industry**. They argue that because small firms are increasingly driven out of business, especially during economic crises, large firms consequently acquire ever-larger shares of the market. One can therefore investigate whether such a tendency has been observed in Canada. If, in fact, concentration has not increased, someone who holds these views might be led to surmise that competition policy has had a hand in preventing the growth of monopoly. But first, we should consider what might have been expected to happen to concentration in Canada in the absence of any countermeasures by government. Is there good reason to expect an inexorable trend toward bigness, as the Marxists suggest?

There are two basic reasons why the larger firms in an industry may triumph over the small. First, larger firms may obtain monopoly power, which they can use to their advantage. They can force sellers of equipment, raw materials, and other inputs to give them better terms than are available to small competitors; and they can also force retailers to give preference to their products. These are, of course, the sorts of advantages to bigness that the combines laws are intended to eliminate.

The second reason why an industry's output may tend to be divided among fewer and larger firms with the passage of time has to do with technology. In some industries, fairly small firms can produce as cheaply or more cheaply than large ones, while in other industries only rather large firms can achieve minimum costs. By and large, the difference in the number of firms from one industry to another has tended to correspond to the size of firm that is least costly. Automobile, steel, and airplane manufacturing are all industries in which tiny companies cannot hope to produce economically, and indeed, these are all industries made up of a relatively few large firms. In clothing production and farming, matters go the other way.

Frequently, innovation seems to have increased the plant size that minimizes costs. Such examples as automated processes or assembly lines suggest that new techniques always call for gigantic equipment; but this is not always true. For example, the introduction of truck transportation took much of the freight-shipping market away from the giant railroads and gave it to much smaller trucking firms. Technological change also seems to have favoured the establishment of small electronics firms. Similarly, the continued development of cheaper and smaller computers is likely to provide a competitive advantage to smaller firms in many other industries. Furthermore:

If innovation provides increased cost advantages to larger firms, the growth of firms will be stimulated. But a fall in the number of firms in the industry need not inevitably result. If demand for the industry's output grows faster than the optimal size of the firm, we may end up with a larger number of firms, each of them bigger than before, but each having a smaller share of an expanded market.

For example, suppose in some industry a new process is invented that requires a far larger scale of operation than currently is typical. Specifically, suppose that the least costly plant size becomes twice as large. If demand for the industry's product increases only a little, we can expect a decrease in the number of firms. But if demand for the industry's product happens to triple at the same time, then the optimal number of firms will in fact increase to one and a half times the original number—each firm will be twice as big as before, so that together they serve three times the volume. In such a case, each firm's share of industry output will in fact have declined.

In the twentieth century, technological developments do seem to call for larger firms, which are best adapted to take advantage of the resulting economies of scale. Perhaps this has somewhat outstripped the rate of growth in output—that is, the growth of GNP. If so, we should expect some fall in the number of firms in a typical industry, somewhat as many Marxists expect. However, as was just noted, not all technological change has worked in this direction. For example, many firms in the electronics industry are relatively small, and there are observers who argue that new techniques will permit smaller firms to supply some telecommunications services without incurring high costs. We must turn to the evidence to judge whether or not Canadian industry has grown more concentrated.

Evidence on Concentration in Industry

There have been many statistical studies of concentration in Canadian industry. One common way of measuring concentration is to calculate the share of the industry's output produced by the four largest firms in an industry, the so-called

Table 31-2

1980 CONCENTRATION RATIOS FOR REPRESENTATIVE INDUSTRIES

INDUSTRY	4-FIRM RATIO	INDUSTRY	4-FIRM RATIO
Tobacco products manufacturers	99.6	Toys and games	48.6
Breweries	99.0	Coffins and caskets	41.5
Motor vehicle manufacturers	93.7	Bakeries	33.5
Iron mines	86.7	Sand pits	29.6
Iron and steel mills	77.9	Hosiery mills	29.2
Major appliances	77.0	Logging	21.4
Petroleum refining	61.7	Machine shops	6.4
Agricultural implements	61.0	Women's clothing factories	6.4

SOURCE: *Industrial Organization and Concentration in the Manufacturing, Mining and Logging Industries, 1980*, Statistics Canada, Catalogue Number 31–402, October 1983.

A **concentration ratio** is the percentage of an industry's output produced by its *four* largest firms. It is intended to measure the degree to which the industry is dominated by large firms; that is, how closely it approximates a monopoly.

concentration ratio. Of course, there is no theoretical reason why the three or five or ten largest firms could not be used for the purpose, but conventionally four firms are used as the standard. In Canada, the use of four firms is also dictated by the Statistics Act, which, for reasons of confidentiality, does not permit more detailed information regarding individual companies to be published.

Table 31-2 shows concentration ratios in a number of industries in Canada. We see that concentration varies greatly from industry to industry: Automobiles, beer, and tobacco products are produced by highly concentrated industries, while machine shops and women's clothing factories show very little concentration. But only comparisons over time and by geographic area can reveal the most significant implications of these figures. Here, the available evidence suggests that concentration in Canadian industry is somewhat higher than it is in the United States and the United Kingdom. The relatively small size of the Canadian market (which is separated from world markets by tariffs and quotas), and the virtual absence of an effective Canadian merger policy have been put forward as two major explanations for this fact. However, some of the differences are also likely to be the result of different methods of measurement.

In Canada there seems to have been little trend in concentration ratios between 1970 and 1980, and indeed between earlier periods and later. Data for the 1970–80 period are presented in Table 31-3.

In a frequently quoted statement, M. A. Adelman, a noted American authority on the subject, concluded, "Any tendency either way, if it does exist, must be at the pace of a glacial drift."[6] Or, as a more recent report interprets similar findings for the United States, "Almost all observers of the industrial scene…agree that…the evidence fails to support a claim that competition has declined. While concentration has increased in some areas, decreases have occurred elsewhere, leaving the overall structure unaffected."[7]

Since concentration is intended as a measure of the "bigness" of the firms in an industry, from such information one can perhaps surmise that competition policy has been effective to some degree in inhibiting whatever trend toward bigness may in fact exist. But even this very cautious conclusion has been questioned by some observers. In fact, some economists and other observers have expressed the view that these laws have made virtually no difference in the size and the behaviour of Canadian business. Whether it is even desirable for competition policy or for some other program to limit concentration or the size of firms is the issue to which we now turn.

[6]M.A. Adelman, "The Measurement of Industrial Concentration," *Review of Economics and Statistics*, Vol. 33 (Nov. 1951), pages 295–96.

[7]P.W. McCracken and T.G. Moore, "Competition and Market Concentration in the American Economy," Subcommittee on Antitrust and Monopoly, U.S. Senate, March 29, 1973.

Table 31–3

THE TREND IN CONCENTRATION RATIOS

	YEAR					
	1970	1972	1974	1976	1978	1980
Average 4-firm concentration ratio	50.6	50.7	50.5	50.7	50.1	49.8

SOURCE: As for Table 31–2.

The Pros and Cons of Bigness

Why has competition policy become so accepted a part of government policy? Are the effects of bigness or monopoly always undesirable? We do know that monopoly power can be abused. And even when businesses are not particularly swashbuckling in their operations, unrestrained monopoly and bigness give rise to a number of problems:

1. ***Distribution of income.*** The flow of wealth to firms with market power—and thus to those who are able to influence prices in their favour—is widely considered to be unfair and socially unacceptable.

2. ***Restriction of output.*** We learned in Chapter 27 that if an unrestrained monopoly is to maximize its profits, it must restrict its output to below the amount that would be provided by an equivalent competitive industry. This means that unregulated monopolized industries are likely to produce smaller outputs than the quantities that serve society's interests.

3. ***Lack of inducement for innovation.*** It is sometimes argued that firms in industries with little or no competition are under less pressure to introduce new production methods and new products than are firms in industries in which each is constantly trying to beat out the others. Without competition, the management of a firm may choose the quiet life, taking no chances on risky investments in research and development. But a firm that operates in constant fear that its rivals will come up with a better idea, and come up with it first, can afford no such luxury.

So far we have presented only one side of the picture. In fact, bigness in industry need not be advantageous only to the firm. It can also, at least *sometimes*, work to the advantage of the general public. Again, there are several reasons:

1. ***Economies of large size.*** Probably the most important advantage of bigness is to be found in those industries in which technology dictates that small-scale operation is inefficient. One can hardly imagine the costs if automobiles were produced in little workshops rather than giant factories. The notion of a small firm operating a long-distance railway does not even make sense, and a multiplicity of firms replicating the same rail service would clearly be incredibly wasteful.

    On these grounds, most policy-makers have never even considered an attempt to eliminate bigness. Their objective, rather, is to curb its potential abuses and to try at the same time to help the public benefit from its advantages. Of course, it does not follow that every industry in which firms happen to be big is one in which big firms are best. There are observers who argue that many firms in fact exceed the size required for cost minimization.

2. ***Required scale for innovation.*** Some economists have argued that only large firms have the resources and the motivation for really significant

innovation. While many inventions are still contributed by individuals, to put a new invention into commercial production is often an expensive, complex venture that can only be carried out on a large scale. And only large firms can afford the funds and bear the risks that such an effort demands. In addition, according to this view, only large firms have the motivation to lay out the funds required for the innovation process, because only large firms will get to keep a considerable share of the benefits. A small company, on the other hand, will find that its innovative idea is soon likely to be followed by close imitations, which enable competitors to profit from its research outlays.

There have been studies of the relationship between firm size, competitiveness of the industry, and the level of expenditure on research and development (R & D). While the evidence is far from conclusive, it does indicate that highly competitive industries comprising very small firms tend not to spend a great deal on research. Up to a point, R & D outlays and innovation seem to increase with size of firm and concentration of industry. However, some of the most significant innovations introduced in the twentieth century have been contributed by smaller firms. Examples include the electric light, alternating current, the photocopier, FM radio, and the electronic calculator.

Other Government Programs Related to Bigness

Because the issues raised by bigness and concentration are complex, they would appear to call for a variety of policy measures. Certainly competition policy programs alone cannot do everything that the public interest requires. For example, in cases where large firms are far more efficient than small ones, it does not seem reasonable to break up industrial giants. In fact, it is often considered most desirable, on grounds of economy, to permit a market to be served by only a single firm—such as a supplier of hydro-electricity, local transportation, or local telecommunications services.

Where one firm offers considerable savings in comparison to a multiplicity of suppliers—that is, where the industry is a natural monopoly—it is usually agreed that it would not serve the public interest to subdivide the supplying firm into a number of rival companies. Instead, one of two policies is usually adopted. Either the monopoly firm is *nationalized* and run as a government enterprise (telephone service in England and electricity generation in France are good examples), or, as is typical in Canada, the natural monopoly is left as a private firm (for example, Bell Canada), but its operations are *regulated* in one of the ways described in the previous chapter.

The possibility of inhibition of innovation by competition is another important issue that, as we have seen, affects policy toward bigness and concentration. The main instrument government has employed in this area is the **patent** system, which rewards the innovator by the grant of a temporary monopoly. The patent restricts imitation and is designed to offer small-firm innovators the same advantages from their research activities as are enjoyed by innovators in industries that contain no competitors ready to erode profits by imitation. Thus, somewhat ironically, while government prohibits monopolies, it also guarantees monopoly power to protect small firms in competitive industries. Of course, sometimes the protected firms themselves grow big with the help of the protection. Once-small firms like Polaroid and Xerox grew into industrial giants with the help of government protection through the patent laws.

Questions have been raised about the effectiveness of patents in inducing expenditure on R & D, and the evidence certainly does not provide overwhelming support for the view that patents constitute a strong stimulus for innovation. Questions have also been raised about the desirability of granting an innovator an

A **patent** is a temporary grant of monopoly rights over an innovation.

unrestricted monopoly for seventeen years, as the patent program now does in Canada. Similar issues have been raised about copyright laws, which restrict reproduction of written works, trademarks, and registered industrial designs.

Finally, government has provided special help to small business in a variety of ways. For example, there are programs designed to make it easier for small firms to raise capital, and special government agencies have been set up for the purpose. There is also some degree of *progressivity* in business taxation, meaning that smaller firms are subject to taxes lower than those paid by larger firms.

Issues in Competition Policy

In recent years there has been a searching re-examination of government policy toward business. For example, there have been calls for a decrease in the overall power of the regulatory agencies, and competition policy has not been ignored. Some voices call for abolition of the combines laws altogether, while others advocate their strengthening and expansion. But even if one grants the desirability of a competition policy with "teeth," there still remain questions about whom or what to "bite."

Structure Versus Conduct

A major issue is the relative weights that should be assigned to *structure* and *conduct* in deciding which firms it is in the social interest to prosecute. Most people accept the basic notion that socially damaging conduct, such as price fixing or threats of physical violence, should be discouraged; though there is often disagreement over what types of conduct are undesirable.

But many more questions are raised about the use of structural criteria in competition policy. Is bigness always undesirable per se? What if the large firm is more efficient and has engaged in no practices that can reasonably be considered to constitute predatory competition? Many economists have reservations about the prosecution of such a firm, fearing that it will only serve to grant protection to inefficient competitors and do so at the expense of consumers. They also point out the danger that successful firms will be singled out for attention under the combines laws simply because their success makes them noticeable and their efficiency enables them to outstrip their competitors. The fear is that such an orientation will discourage efficiency and entrepreneurship and reduce competition.

Another Look at Price Discrimination

An example of lack of agreement between economists and lawmakers about the sorts of conduct that the law should proscribe concerns the issue of *price discrimination*, which, we learned earlier in the chapter, is the sale of the same item to two different customers at different prices. To economists, this legal definition is misleading. Suppose, for instance, that one person lives on a mountaintop far from the place where a good is produced, and another customer is located in an area that enjoys easy access to the good in question. Economists would say that it is not discriminatory to charge each a different price. *On the contrary, economists hold that in such cases it is discriminatory to charge both customers the same price, because it does not account for the substantial difference in the two delivery costs.*

Even more important than this definitional argument, though, is the issue of the desirability or undesirability of discrimination. The word *discrimination* is what has been called a "persuasive term"—in this case, a word that automatically implies gross misconduct. *But, in fact, price discrimination can sometimes be beneficial to all parties to a transaction.*

Suppose, for example, a commodity is available to the poor only if it is sold at a relatively low price, though one that still more than covers the good's marginal cost (the cost incurred in expanding into the lower-income market). In this case, the contribution from the lower-income market may permit *some* reduction in price to the rich, since the firm might not be able to cover its total cost if it were to charge the rich the *same* low price necessary for entry into the low-income market. The result is that everyone—the poor, the wealthy, and the selling firm—will benefit from this discriminatory pricing.

Another example may be seen in the pricing practices of doctors before the existence of universal medicare. At that time, doctors were known to charge higher fees to their wealthy patients than to their poor ones. The reduced fees presumably permitted more poor patients to visit them, and doctors may thus have been able to earn an even better income than they could by charging a uniformly high fee to everyone. Even the fee to the rich may have gone down in the process because of the doctors' increased earnings from their enlarged pool of poor patients. Again, discrimination led to lower fees for everyone, and all parties were made better off—the wealthy patients, the poor ones, and the doctors. Are such acts of discrimination really so unjust?

Concentration and Market Power

Why should anyone care about concentration ratios? One should care about them if they are a good measure of market power. **Market power** is the ability of a firm to raise its price significantly above the competitive price level and to maintain this high price profitably for a considerable period. The question, then, is this: If an industry becomes more concentrated, will the firms necessarily increase their ability to institute a profitable rise in price above the competitive level?

Many economists have concluded that this does not necessarily happen. Specifically, the following three conclusions are now widely accepted:

Market power is the ability of a firm to raise its price significantly above the competitive price level and to maintain this high price profitably for a considerable period.

1. If, after an increase in concentration, an industry still has a very low concentration ratio, then its firms are very unlikely to have any market power either before or after the rise in concentration.

2. If circumstances in the industry are in other respects favourable for successful price collusion (tacit or explicit agreement on price), then a rise in concentration will facilitate market power. It will do so by reducing the number of firms that need to be consulted in arriving at an agreement and by decreasing the number of firms that have to be watched to make sure they do not betray the collusive agreement.

3. Where entry into and exit from the industry are easy and costless, that is, where the market is highly *contestable*, then even when concentration increases, market power will not be enhanced. This is because an excessive price will attract new entrants who will soon force the price down.

As long as barriers to foreign trade do not preclude foreign firms entering Canadian markets, the openness of the economy should permit many of our markets to be contestable. Tariffs and quotas limit this process, however, and so they raise the likelihood that high concentration truly does represent significant market power. Thus, tariff cuts can be used as a substitute for the traditional, legal approach to competition policy that we have considered in this chapter. This is why tariffs are examined in the next chapter.

Summary

1. Competition policy refers to programs designed to control the growth of monopoly and to prevent big business from engaging in "undesirable" practices.
2. Recent proposals to amend the Combines Investigation Act have stressed:
   a. Changing the laws to civil rather than criminal provisions.
   b. Changing the legal interpretation of monopoly so that "complete elimination" of competition is not a requirement for prosecution.
   c. Extending the law to cover crown corporations and banks.
3. The evidence indicates that there has been no significant increase in the concentration of individual Canadian industries into larger firms during the twentieth century. Direct evidence as to whether competition policy has been effective in preventing monopoly is inconclusive, but it is generally agreed that Canada has not had an effective merger policy.
4. The arguments *against* unregulated monopoly are that it is likely to distribute income unfairly, produce undesirably small quantities of output, and provide inadequate motivation for innovation.
5. Defenders of big business argue that only large firms have funds sufficient for effective research, development, and innovation, and that where economies of scale are available, large firms can serve customers more cheaply than can small ones.
6. Contrary to popular thinking, price discrimination is not necessarily undesirable per se. Discriminatory pricing in some instances can be beneficial to all parties to a transaction.

Concepts for Review

Competition policy
Combines Investigation Act
Price discrimination
Resale price maintenance
Predatory pricing

Structure versus conduct
Vertical merger
Horizontal merger
Conglomerate merger
Concentration of industry

Concentration ratio
Patent
Market power

Questions for Discussion

1. Suppose Sam lives in the central city while Fran's home is far away, so that it requires much more gas to deliver newspapers to Fran than to Sam. Yet the newspaper charges them exactly the same amount. Would the courts consider this to be price discrimination? Would an economist? Would you? Why?
2. A shopkeeper sells his store and signs a contract that restrains him from opening another store in competition with the new owner. The courts have decided that this contract is a *reasonable* restraint of trade. Can you think of any other types of restraint of trade that seem reasonable? Any that seem unreasonable?
3. Why do you think some industries are highly concentrated?
4. Do you think structure or conduct is the more reasonable basis for competition policy? Give reasons for your answer.
5. Do you think it is in the public interest to launch a combines suit that costs a billion dollars? What leads you to your conclusions?

Limiting Market Power: Tariff Policy

No nation was ever ruined
by trade.
BENJAMIN FRANKLIN

S ince the attempts to control powerful corporations by direct *regulation* and by competition *laws* have met with only limited success, many economists argue that we should rely instead on the discipline of the *market*. This discipline could be enforced by exposing firms that operate in Canada to more competition with firms already existing elsewhere in the world. This competition is currently limited by a series of import taxes known as tariffs and by import quota regulations. Canada's average tariff rate on industrial products is just under 13 percent, while the comparable figure for the United States is 6 percent; for Japan, 5 percent; and for the European Economic Community, 6.5 percent.

As a result of Canada's tariff barriers, and those imposed by other countries against our manufactured goods, Canadian producers have largely concentrated on the small domestic market. This has meant operating at relatively low volume, with higher unit costs and higher industrial concentration. Tariff cuts by Canada would force our producers to expand operations (to reduce unit costs) and sell a significant part of their output on world markets, or to get out of business.

The *benefits* of this policy are rather obvious: Canadian consumers would be able to buy a host of products at reduced prices, since the increased competition would force producers to more closely approximate the efficiency gains that exist in a perfectly competitive economy. To many people, the *costs* of this policy are equally obvious. They fear that our producers would not be able to compete with those employing "cheap foreign labour." These opponents of tariff cuts think that many business failures and a large increase in unemployment would follow any cut in tariffs. Thus they argue that we simply cannot afford to lower our trade barriers unilaterally. Many economists disagree, and we explain why in this chapter.

To be complete, our investigation into the cost of tariff cuts must take a rather circuitous route. First, we will explain the purposes of foreign trade and the ways in which governments have sought to influence or limit it. Second, we will study the crucial *law of comparative advantage*, which determines what commodities a country finds advantageous to export and what commodities it finds advantageous to import. This principle shows that *even* if there are *no* economies of large-scale production, both trading countries benefit from increased international exchange. Third, we will see how the prices of goods traded between countries are determined by supply and demand. And, finally, we will examine the pros and cons of tariffs and other devices designed to protect a country's industries from foreign competition. By the end of the chapter, we will have exposed the fallacy behind the view that "cheap foreign labour" necessitates tariff barriers.

Issue: The Competition of "Cheap Foreign Labour"

When analysing the issues of international trade, common sense can be extremely valuable; indeed, there is no substitute for it. Yet sometimes conclusions based on common sense without factual confirmation and careful analysis can be very misleading.

One example of a foreign trade issue that has been misunderstood for lack of factual analysis is the argument that buying products made by cheap foreign labour is unfair and destructive to domestic interests. Some Canadian business people and union leaders argue that such purchases take bread out of the mouths of Canadian workers and depress standards of living in this country. According to this view, cheap imports cause job losses and put pressure on Canadian businesses to lower wages.

Yet the facts are not consistent with this scenario. Many of Canada's imports come from Western Europe and Japan. Since the early 1960s, wages have risen far more dramatically in these other countries than here. Yet we keep importing such items as Volkswagens, Volvos, and Datsuns in greater numbers. More important, the rise in these foreign wages, compared with those in Canada, has not brought an increasing strength in the Canadian position in the international marketplace.

In the 1950s, when European and Japanese wages were far below those in Canada, we had no trouble marketing our products abroad. It was far easier then than now to sell the amount of exports needed to pay for the amount of goods that were imported. Then, in the 1960s and 1970s, as wages in Europe and Japan rose closer to—and in some cases surpassed—those in Canada, we ran into serious trouble selling goods abroad. We were, and still are, often unable to export enough to pay for our imports. Clearly, cheap foreign labour does not always serve as a crucial obstacle to Canadian sales abroad, as a "common sense" view of the matter suggests. In this chapter we will see what is wrong with that view.

Why Trade?

The main reason that countries trade with one another rather than try to run completely independent economies is that the earth's resources are not equally distributed across its surface. Canada has an abundant supply of forests and fresh water, resources that are quite scarce in most of the rest of the world. Saudi Arabia has very little land that is suitable for farming, but it sits atop a huge pool of oil. Because of this seemingly whimsical distribution of vital resources, every nation must trade with others to acquire what it lacks. In general, the more varied the endowment of a particular country, the less it will have to depend on others to make up for its deficiencies.

Even if countries had all the resources they needed, other differences in natural endowments—such as climate, terrain, and so on—would lead them to engage in trade. Canadians *could*, with great difficulty, grow their own banana trees and coffee shrubs in hothouses; but these items are much more efficiently grown in such places as Honduras and Brazil, where the climate is appropriate. On the other hand, wheat grows in Canada with little difficulty, while mountainous Switzerland is not good at growing either bananas or wheat.

The skills of a country's labour force also play a role. If New Zealand has a large group of efficient farmers and few workers with industrial experience while the opposite is true in Great Britain, it makes sense for New Zealand to specialize in agriculture and let Great Britain concentrate on manufacturing.

This last point suggests one other important reason why countries trade—the advantage of **specialization**. If one country were to try to produce everything, it would end up with a number of industries whose scale of operation was too small to permit the use of mass-production techniques, specialized training facilities, and other arrangements that give a cost advantage to large-scale operations. Even now, despite the considerable volume of world trade, this problem seems to arise for some countries whose operation of their own international airlines or their own steel mills, for example, seems explainable only in political rather than economic terms. Inevitably, small nations that insist on operating in industries that are economical only when their scale of operation is large find that these enterprises can survive only with the aid of large government subsidies.

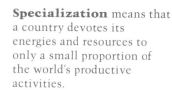

Specialization means that a country devotes its energies and resources to only a small proportion of the world's productive activities.

To summarize: International trade is essential for the prosperity of the trading nations for at least three reasons: (1) every country lacks some vital resources that it can get only by trading with others; (2) each country's climate, labour force, and other endowments make it a relatively efficient producer of some goods and an inefficient producer of other goods; and (3) specialization permits larger outputs and can therefore offer economies of large-scale production.

Mutual Gains from Trade

Some of the early writers on international trade implied that one nation could gain from an exchange only at the expense of another. It was pointed out that since nothing is produced by the act of trading, the total collection of goods in the hands of the two parties at the end of an exchange is no greater than before the exchange took place. Therefore, it was argued (fallaciously), if one country gains from a swap, the other country must necessarily lose.

One of the consequences of this mistaken view was a policy prescription calling for each country, in the interests of its citizens, to do its best to act to the disadvantage of its trading partners—in Adam Smith's terms, to "beggar its neighbours." The idea that one nation's gain must be another's loss means that a country can promote its own welfare only by harming others.

Yet, as Adam Smith and others after him emphasized, in any *voluntary exchange*, unless there is misunderstanding of the facts, both parties *must* gain (or at least expect to gain) something from the transaction. Otherwise why would both parties agree to the exchange?

But how can mere exchange, in which no production takes place, actually leave both parties better off? The answer is that while there can be no gain in the *physical quantities* of the products exchanged, the holdings of both parties can end up much better suited to the needs of each. Suppose Brian has four sandwiches and nothing to drink, while David has four cartons of milk and nothing to eat. A trade of two of Brian's sandwiches for two of David's cartons of milk does not increase the total supply of either food or beverages, but it clearly produces a net increase in the welfare of both boys.

Mutual Gains from Voluntary Exchange

Any *voluntary exchange* must promise to make *both* parties better off. Trade can bring about mutual gains by redistributing products in such a way that both participants end up holding a combination of goods that is better adapted to their preferences than the goods they held before. This principle, which is one of our **12 Ideas for Beyond the Final Exam**, applies to nations just as it does to individuals.

International Versus Intranational Trade

The logic of international trade is essentially no different from that underlying trade among different provinces; the basic reasons for trade are equally applicable *within* a country or *among* countries. If we can learn about trade from strictly domestic exchanges why study international trade as a special subject? There are at least three reasons.

First, domestic trade takes place under a single government, while foreign trade must involve at least two governments. At least in theory, the government of a nation is concerned with the welfare of all its citizens. But governments are usually much less deeply concerned with the welfare of citizens of other countries. As we have already seen, a major issue in the economic analysis of international trade is the use and misuse of impediments to free international trade. Later in the chapter such trade barriers will be discussed in greater detail.

Second, all trade within Canadian borders is carried out in a single currency—dollars. But trade across national borders must involve at least two currencies. Rates of exchange between different currencies can and do change. This variability in exchange rates brings with it the host of complications and policy problems that we discussed in Chapter 16.

Third, it is usually much easier for labour and capital to move within a country than to move from one country to another. If there are jobs in Alberta but none in Ontario, workers can move freely to follow the job opportunities. Of course, there are personal costs—not only the dollar cost of moving, but also the psychological cost of giving up friends and familiar surroundings. But such moves are not inhibited by immigration quotas or by laws restricting the employment of foreigners, as are moves from one country to another.

There are also more impediments to the transfer of capital from one country to another than to its movement within a country. The shipment of plant and equipment between countries can be expensive. Such investment abroad is also subject to special risks, such as the danger of outright expropriation if, say, after a political revolution the new government decides to take over all foreign properties without compensation. But even if nothing so extreme occurs, capital invested abroad faces risks from possible variations in exchange rates. An investment in the U.K. yielding a million pounds a year will be worth $2 million to Canadian investors if the pound is worth $2 but only $1 million if the pound should fall to $1.

While labour, capital, and other factors of production do move from country to country when offered an opportunity to increase their earnings abroad, they are less likely to do so than to move from one region of a country to another to gain similar increases.

Comparative Advantage: The Fundamental Principle of Specialization

We have seen that trade can be beneficial to both parties. Some of the reasons are obvious. But now we turn to an important source of mutual benefit that is far from obvious.

One country is said to have an **absolute advantage** over another in the production of a particular good if it can produce that good using smaller quantities of resources than can the other country.

We know that coffee can be produced in Colombia using less labour and smaller quantities of other inputs than would be needed to grow it in Canada. And we know that Canada can produce passenger aircraft at a lower resource cost than can Colombia. We say then that Colombia has an **absolute advantage** over Canada in coffee production, and Canada has an absolute advantage over Colombia in aircraft production.

A numerical example will illustrate the idea. According to Table 32–1, one year of labour time in Canada can produce either 50 kilograms of coffee or 1/20 of

Table 32-1

ALTERNATIVE OUTPUTS FROM ONE YEAR OF LABOUR INPUT

	IN CANADA	IN COLOMBIA
Coffee (kilograms)	50	300
Airplanes	1/20	1/100

an airplane. By contrast, one year of labour time in Colombia can produce 300 kilograms of coffee or 1/100 of an airplane. Thus, six years of labour input would be required to produce 300 kilograms of coffee in Canada, whereas Colombia could do the job with only one year's worth of labour. On the other hand, it would take Colombia 100 years of labour to produce an airplane, a job Canada could do in only 20 years.

Obviously, if Canada wants coffee and Colombia wants airplanes, both can save resources by trading—each exporting to the other the good in which it has an absolute advantage.

Suppose, however, that one country is more efficient than another in producing *every* item. Can they still gain by trading? The surprising answer is *definitely yes*, and a simple parable will help explain why.

The work of a highly-paid business consultant frequently requires computer analysis. Suppose the consultant began her career as a computer operator doing her own data entry, and was extremely good at it. In her current position she may grow impatient with the slow, sloppy work of some of the low-paid support staff who work for her, and at times be tempted to do all the work herself. Good judgment, however, tells her that though she is better *both* at giving business advice *and* at data entry than are her employees, it is foolish to devote any of her valuable time to the low-skilled job. That is because the opportunity cost of an hour devoted to data entry is an hour less devoted to business consulting—a far more lucrative activity.

This is an example of the principle of **comparative advantage** at work. The consultant specializes in business advice despite her absolute advantage in data entry because she has a still greater absolute advantage in her role as a business consultant. She suffers some direct loss by not doing her own data entry. But that loss is more than compensated for by the earnings she makes selling her consulting services to clients.

This example brings out the fundamental principle that underlies the bulk of economic analysis of patterns of specialization and exchange among different nations. This principle is called the *law of comparative advantage*, and it is one of our **12 Ideas for Beyond the Final Exam**. It was discovered by David Ricardo, one of the giants in the history of economic analysis.

> One country is said to have a **comparative advantage** over another in the production of a particular good relative to other goods it can produce if it produces that good least inefficiently as compared with the other country.

The Law of Comparative Advantage

Even if one country is at an absolute *disadvantage* relative to another country in the production of *every* good, it is said to have a *comparative advantage* in making the good in whose production it is *least inefficient* in comparison with the other country.

Ricardo's basic finding was that two countries can still gain by trading even if one country is more efficient than another in the production of *every* commodity (that is, it has an absolute advantage in every commodity).

In determining the most efficient patterns of production, what matters is *comparative* advantage, not *absolute* advantage. Thus, one country will often gain by importing a certain good even if that good can be produced at home more efficiently than it can be produced abroad. Such imports will be profitable if the country is even more efficient at producing the goods that it exports in exchange.

The Arithmetic of Comparative Advantage

Let's see precisely how this works using numbers based on Ricardo's own example. Suppose labour is the only input used in producing wine and cloth in two countries, England and Portugal. Suppose further that Portugal has an absolute advantage in both goods, as indicated in Table 32–2. In this example, a week's worth of labour can produce either 12 metres of cloth or 6 barrels of wine in Portugal, but only 10 metres of cloth or 1 barrel of wine in England. So Portugal is the more efficient producer of both goods. None the less, as our multitalented-consultant example suggests, it pays for Portugal to specialize in wine production and get its cloth from England. We will now demonstrate this conclusion.

Table 32–2
ALTERNATIVE OUTPUTS FROM ONE WEEK OF LABOUR INPUT

	IN ENGLAND	IN PORTUGAL
Cloth (metres)	10	12
Wine (barrels)	1	6

The numbers in Table 32–2 indicate that Portugal is 20 percent more efficient than England in producing cloth: It can produce 12 metres with a week's labour, whereas England can produce only 10 metres. However, Portugal is six times as efficient as England in producing wine: It produces 6 barrels per week rather than 1. So we say that Portugal has a *comparative advantage in wine* while England has a *comparative advantage in cloth*. According to Ricardo's law of comparative advantage, both countries can gain if Portugal specializes in producing wine, England specializes in producing cloth, and the two countries trade with one another.

Suppose that Portugal transfers a million weeks of labour out of the textile industry and into winemaking. According to the figures in Table 32–2, its cloth output falls by 12 million metres while its wine output rises by 6 million barrels. (See Table 32–3.) Suppose, at the same time, England transfers 2 million weeks of labour out of winemaking (thereby losing 2 million barrels of wine) and into clothmaking (thereby gaining 20 million metres of cloth). Table 32–3 shows us that these transfers of resources in the two countries increase the world's production of both outputs!

Together, the two countries now have 4 million additional barrels of wine and 8 million additional metres of cloth—surely a nice outcome. But there seems to be some sleight-of-hand here. All that has taken place is an exchange; yet, somehow Portugal and England gain both cloth and wine. How can such gains in physical output be possible?

The explanation is that the trade process we have just described involves more than just a swap of a fixed bundle of commodities. It is also a *change in the production arrangements*, with some of England's wine production taken over by the more efficient producers of Portuguese wine, and with some of Portugal's cloth production taken over by English weavers who are *less in*efficient at producing cloth than English vintners are at producing wine.

Table 32–3
EXAMPLE OF THE GAINS FROM TRADE

	ENGLAND	PORTUGAL	TOTAL
Cloth (millions of metres)	+20	–12	+8
Wine (millions of barrels)	– 2	+ 6	+4

Biographical Note: David Ricardo (1772–1823)

David Ricardo was born four years before publication of Adam Smith's *Wealth of Nations*. Descended from a family of well-to-do stockbrokers of the Jewish faith who migrated to London from Amsterdam and were, in turn, descended from Portuguese Jews, he had about twenty brothers and sisters. At a school in Amsterdam, Ricardo's formal education ended at the age of 13, and so he was largely self-educated. He began his career by working in his father's brokerage firm. At age 21, Ricardo married a Quaker woman and decided to become a Unitarian, a sect then considered "little better than atheist." By Jewish custom, Ricardo's father broke with him, though apparently they remained friendly.

Ricardo then decided to go into the brokerage business on his own and was enormously successful. During the Napoleonic Wars he regularly scored business coups over leading British and foreign financiers, including the Rothschilds. After gaining a huge profit on government securities that he had bought just before the Battle of Waterloo, Ricardo decided to retire from business when he was just over 40 years old.

He purchased a country estate, Gatcomb (now owned by the royal family), where a brilliant group of intellectuals met regularly. Particularly remarkable for the period was the number of women included in the circle, among them Maria Edgeworth, the novelist (who wrote extravagant praise of Ricardo's mind), and Jane Marcet, an author of textbooks, one of which was probably the first text in economics. Ricardo's close friends included the economists T.R. Malthus and James Mill, father of John Stuart Mill, the noted philosopher–economist. Malthus remained a close friend of Ricardo even though they disagreed on many subjects and continued their arguments in personal correspondence and in their published works.

James Mill persuaded Ricardo to go into Parliament. As was then customary, Ricardo purchased his seat by buying a piece of land that entitled its owner to a seat in Parliament. There he proved to be a noteworthy liberal,

strongly supporting many causes that were against his personal interests.

James Mill also helped persuade Ricardo to write his masterpiece, *The Principles of Political Economy and Taxation*, which may have been the first book of pure economic theory. It was noteworthy that Ricardo, the most practical of practical men, had little patience with empirical economics and preferred instead to rest his analysis explicitly and exclusively on theory. His book made considerable contributions to the analysis of pricing, wage determination, and the effects of various types of taxes, among many other subjects. It also gave us the law of comparative advantage. In addition, the book described what has come to be called the Ricardian rent theory—even though Ricardo did not discover the analysis and explicitly denied having done so.

Ricardo died in 1823 at the age of 51. He seems to have been a wholly admirable person—honest, charming, witty, conscientious, brilliant—altogether too good to be true.

When every country does what it can do best, all countries can benefit because more of every commodity can be produced without increasing the given quantity of labour.

If this result still seems a bit mysterious, the concept of *opportunity cost* will help remove the remaining mystery. If the two countries do not trade, Table 32–2 shows that England can acquire a barrel of wine only by giving up 10 metres of cloth. Thus, the opportunity cost of a barrel of wine in England is 10 metres of cloth. But in Portugal the opportunity cost of a barrel of wine is only 2 metres of cloth (again, see Table 32–2). Thus, in terms of real resources forgone, it is cheaper—for either country—to acquire wine in Portugal. By a similar line of reasoning, it can be shown that the opportunity cost of cloth is higher in Portugal than in England, so it makes sense for both countries to acquire their cloth in England.[1]

The Graphics of Comparative Advantage

The gains from trade can also be displayed graphically, and doing so helps us to understand how these gains arise.

The lines *EF* and *PQ* in Figure 32–1 are the *production possibilities frontiers* of the two countries, drawn on the assumption that each country has 6 million weeks of labour available.[2] For example, with 6 million weeks of labour, Table 32–2 tells us that England can produce 6 million barrels of wine and no cloth (point *E*), 60 million metres of cloth and no wine (point *F*), or any combination in between (the line *EF*). Similar reasoning shows that *PQ* is Portugal's production possibilities frontier.

Note that Portugal's production possibilities frontier lies above England's throughout the diagram. That is because Portugal is the more efficient producer of both commodities. With the same amount of labour, it can obtain more wine and more cloth than England. Thus, the higher position of Portugal's frontier is the graph's way of showing Portugal's *absolute* advantage.

Portugal's comparative advantage in wine production and England's comparative advantage in cloth production are shown in a different way—by the relative *slopes* of the two production possibilities frontiers. Portugal's frontier is not only higher than England's, it is also flatter. What does this mean economically? One way of looking at the difference is to remember that while Portugal can produce six times as much wine as England (compare points *P* and *E*), it can produce only 20 percent more cloth than England (points *Q* and *F*). England is, relatively speaking, much better at cloth production than at wine production. That is what is meant when we say it has a *comparative* advantage in the former.

We may express this difference more directly in terms of the slopes of the two lines. The slope of Portugal's production possibilities frontier is $OQ/OP = 72/36 = 2$. This means that if Portugal reduces its wine production by one barrel it will obtain two metres of cloth. Thus, the *opportunity cost* of a barrel of wine in Portugal is two metres of cloth, as we observed earlier.

In the case of England, the slope of the production possibilities frontier is

---

[1]As an exercise, provide this line of reasoning.

[2]To review the concept of the production possibilities frontier, see Chapter 3.

Figure 32–1

ABSOLUTE AND COMPARATIVE ADVANTAGE SHOWN BY TWO COUNTRIES' PRODUCTION POSSIBILITIES FRONTIERS

Portugal's absolute advantage is shown by its ability to produce more of every commodity using the same quantity of labour as does England. Therefore, Portugal's production possibilities frontier, *PQ*, is higher than England's *EF*. But Portugal has a comparative advantage in wine production in which it is six times as productive as England. It can produce 36 million barrels (point *P*), compared with England's 6 million barrels (point *E*). On the other hand, Portugal is only 20 percent more productive in cloth production (point *Q*) than England (point *F*). Thus, England is less inefficient in producing cloth, where it consequently has a comparative advantage.

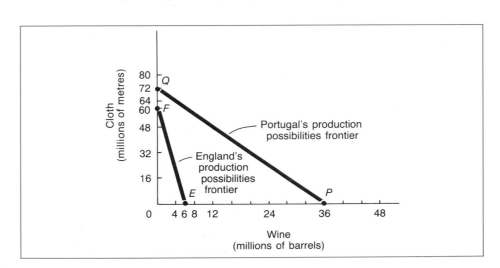

$OF/OE = 60/6 = 10$. That is, if England reduces wine production by one barrel, it gets 10 additional metres of cloth. So in England, the *opportunity cost* of a barrel of wine is 10 metres of cloth.

A country's absolute advantage in production over another country is shown by its having a higher production possibilities frontier. The difference in the comparative advantages of the two countries is shown by the difference in the slopes of their frontiers.

Because opportunity costs differ in the two countries, gains from trade are possible. How these gains are divided between the two countries depends on the prices for wine and cloth that emerge from world trade, which is the subject of the next section. But we already know enough to see that world prices must make a barrel of wine cost less than 10 metres of cloth and more than 2 metres. Why? Because, if a barrel of wine cost more than 10 metres of cloth (its opportunity cost in England), England would be better off producing its own wine rather than trading with Portugal. Similarly, if a barrel of wine fetched less than two metres of cloth (its opportunity cost in Portugal), Portugal would prefer to produce its own cloth rather than trade with England.

We conclude, therefore, that if both countries are to benefit from trade, the rate of exchange between cloth and wine must be somewhere between 10 to 1 and 2 to 1. To illustrate the gains from trade in a concrete example, suppose the world price ratio settles at 4 to 1; that is, one barrel of wine costs 4 metres of cloth. How much, precisely, do England and Portugal gain from world trade?

Figure 32–2 is designed to help us see the answer. Production possibilities

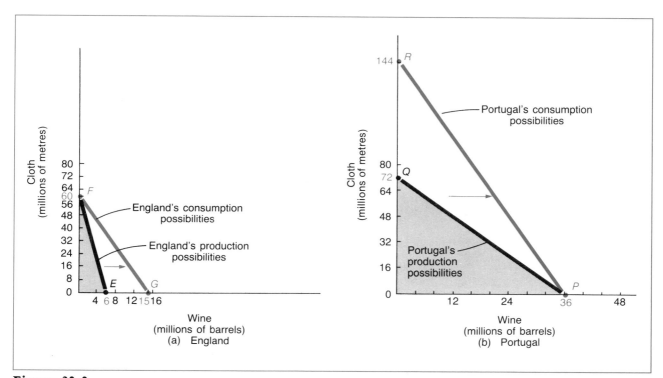

Figure 32-2

THE GAINS FROM TRADE

In this diagram, we suppose that trade opens up between England and Portugal and that the world price of wine is four times the world price of cloth. Now England's consumption possibilities are all the points on line *FG* (which starts at *F* and has a slope of 4), rather than just the points on its own production possibilities frontier, *EF*. Similarly, Portugal can choose any point on line *PR* (which begins at *P* and has a slope of 4), rather than just points on *QP*. Thus both nations gain from trade.

frontiers EF in part (a) and PQ in part (b) are the same as in Figure 32–1. But England can do better than EF. Specifically, with a world price ratio of 4 to 1, England can buy a barrel of wine by giving up only 4 metres of cloth rather than 10 metres (which is the opportunity cost of wine in England). Hence, if England produces only cloth [point F in Figure 32–2(a)] and buys its wine from Portugal, England's *consumption possibilities* will be as indicated by the blue line that begins at point F and has a slope of 4—indicating that each additional barrel of wine costs England 4 metres of cloth. Since trade allows England to choose a point on FG rather than on FE, trade opens up consumption possibilities that were simply not available before.

The story is similar for Portugal. If the Portuguese produce only wine [point P in Figure 32–2(b)], they can acquire 4 metres of cloth from England for each barrel of wine they give up as they move along the blue line PR (whose slope is 4). This is better than they can do on their own, since a sacrifice of one barrel of wine yields only 2 metres of cloth in Portugal. Hence world trade enlarges Portugal's consumption possibilities from PQ to PR.

Figure 32–2 shows graphically that gains from trade arise to the extent that world prices (4 to 1 in our example) differ from domestic opportunity costs (10 to 1 and 2 to 1 in our example). So it is a matter of some importance to understand how prices in international trade are established. Supply and demand is a natural place to start.

Supply–Demand Equilibrium and Pricing in Foreign Trade

In the context of international trade, the supply–demand model runs into several complications we have not encountered before. First, it involves at least two demand curves: that of the exporting country and that of the importing country. Second, it may also involve two supply curves, since the importing country may produce some part of the amount it uses. The third and final complication is that equilibrium does not take place at the intersection point of *either* pair of supply–demand curves. Why? Because if there is any trade, the exporting country's quantity supplied must be *greater* than its quantity demanded, while the quantity supplied by the importing country must be *less* than its quantity demanded.

These complications are illustrated in Figure 32–3, where we show the supply and demand curves of a country that exports wine, in part (a), and the supply and demand curves of a country that imports wine, in part (b). For simplicity, we assume that these countries do not deal in wine with anyone else.

Where will the two-country wine market reach equilibrium? The equilibrium price in a free market must satisfy two requirements:

1. The price of wine must be the same in both countries.
2. The quantity of wine exported (the excess of the exporting country's quantity supplied over its quantity demanded) must equal the quantity of wine imported (the excess of the importing country's quantity demanded over its quantity supplied).

In Figure 32–3, this happens at a price of $100 per barrel. At that price, the distance AB between what the exporting country produces (point B) and what it consumes (point A) equals the distance CD between the quantity demanded of the importing country (point D) and its quantity supplied (point C). At a price of $100 per barrel, the amount the exporting country has available to sell abroad is exactly equal to the amount the importer wants to buy, and matters are in balance. So $100 per barrel is the market price.

At a price higher than $100, we can expect producers in both countries to

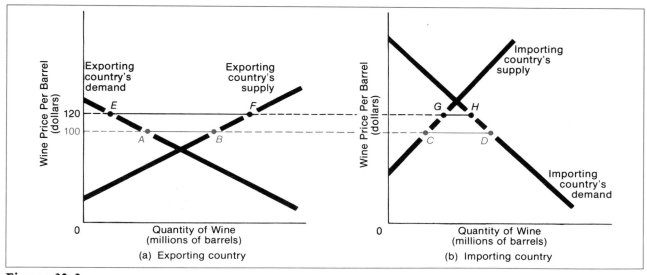

Figure 32-3

SUPPLY-DEMAND EQUILIBRIUM IN THE INTERNATIONAL WINE TRADE

Equilibrium requires that the net exports, *AB* (that is, the exporting country's quantity supplied, *B*, minus the exporter's quantity demanded, *A*), exactly balance imports, *CD*, by the importing country. At $100 per barrel of wine, there is equilibrium. But at a higher price, say $120, there is disequilibrium because net export supply, *EF*, exceeds net import demand, *GH*.

want to sell more and consumers in both countries to want to buy less. For example, if the price rises to $120 per barrel, the exporter's quantity supplied will rise from *B* to *F*, and the exporter's quantity demanded will fall from *A* to *E*, as shown in Figure 32-3(a). As a result, there will be a rise in the amount available for export, from *AB* to *EF*. For exactly the same reason, the price increase will cause higher production and lower sales in the importing country, leading to a shrinkage in the amount the importing country wants to import—from *CD* to *GH* in part (b). This means that the new price, $120 per barrel, cannot be sustained if the international market is free and competitive. With export supply *EF* far greater than import demand *GH*, there must be a downward pressure on price and a move back toward the $100 equilibrium price. Similar reasoning shows that prices below $100 also cannot be sustained.

We can now see the straightforward role of supply–demand equilibrium in international trade:

In international trade, the equilibrium price must be at a level at which the excess of the exporter's quantity supplied over its domestic quantity demanded is exactly equal to the excess of the importer's quantity demanded over its quantity supplied. Equilibrium will occur at a price at which the horizontal distance *AB* in Figure 32-3(a) (the excess of the exporter's quantity supplied over its quantity demanded) is equal to the horizontal distance *CD* in Figure 32-3(b) (the excess of the importer's quantity demanded over its quantity supplied). At this price, the *world's* quantity demanded is equal to the *world's* quantity supplied.

Comparative Advantage and Competition of "Cheap Foreign Labour"

The principle of comparative advantage takes us a good part of the way toward an explanation of the fallacy in the "cheap foreign labour" argument described earlier in the chapter. Given the assumed productive efficiency of Portuguese labour and the inefficiency of British labour in Ricardo's example, we would expect wages to be much higher in Portugal than in England. Indeed, if workers receive all of the nation's output, and wine and cloth are produced in the same proportions in both countries, then this *must* be so, because output per person in Portugal is so much higher.

In these circumstances, one can expect Portuguese workers to be apprehensive about an agreement to permit trade between the countries—"How can we hope to meet the unfair competition of those underpaid British workers?" And British labourers are also likely to be concerned—"How can we hope to meet the competition of those Portuguese, who are so efficient in producing everything?"

The principle of comparative advantage shows us that both fears are unjustified. As we have just seen, when trade is opened up between Portugal and England *workers in both countries will be able to earn higher real wages than before* because of the increased productivity that comes about through specialization.

Figure 32-2 (page 623) shows this fact quite directly. We have seen from our illustration that, with trade, England can end up with more wine and more cloth than it had before, and so the living standards of its workers can rise even though they have been left vulnerable to the competition of the superefficient Portuguese. Portugal also can end up with more wine and with more cloth, so the living standards of its workers can rise even though they have been exposed to the competition of cheap British labour.

The lesson to be learned here is that nothing helps raise standards of living more than does a greater abundance of goods.

Tariffs, Quotas, and Other Interferences with Trade

Despite the mutual gains obtained, international trade has historically been subjected to unrelenting pressure for government interference. In fact, until the rise of a free-trade movement in England at the end of the eighteenth and the beginning of the nineteenth centuries (with such economists as Adam Smith and David Ricardo at its vanguard), it was taken for granted that one of the essential tasks of government was the imposition of regulations to impede trade, presumably in the national interest.

There were many who argued then (and some who still argue today) that a nation's wealth consists of the amount of gold or other monies at its command. Consequently, the proper aim of government policy is to do everything it can to promote exports (in order to increase the amount foreigners owe to it) and to discourage imports (in order to decrease the amount the country owes to foreigners).

Obviously, there are limits to which this policy can be carried out. A country *must* import vital foodstuffs or critical raw materials that it cannot supply for itself; for if it does not, it must suffer a severe fall in living standards. Moreover, it is mathematically impossible for *every* country to sell more than it buys—one country's exports *must* be some other country's imports. If everyone competes in this game and cuts imports to the bone, then obviously exports must go the same way. The result will be that everyone is deprived of the mutual gains that trade can provide.

In more recent times, notably in the United States during the first three decades of the twentieth century, there was a return to an active policy designed to reduce competition from foreign imports. Since then, Western countries have attempted to promote freedom of trade, and barriers have gradually been reduced, though, very recently, there have been moves back the other way.

Three main devices have been used by modern governments to control trade: tariffs, quotas, and export subsidies.

A **tariff** is a tax on imports.

A **tariff** is simply a tax on imports. An importer of wine, for example, may be charged $10 for each barrel of wine he brings into the country. As noted at the

Non-Tariff Barriers to Trade

Many Western countries have committed themselves to tariff reductions by signing the General Agreement on Tariffs and Trade (GATT). By 1987 these commitments will reduce tariffs in the United States and the EEC to less than five percent, and those in Japan and Canada to less than three percent and eight percent, respectively. But non-tariff barriers to trade such as quotas are not covered by GATT regulations, and these have grown noticeably in recent years. The following excerpt from the 1983 Annual Review of the Economic Council of Canada discusses this problem.

Non-tariff barriers ... to trade take a variety of forms: quotas, voluntary export restraints,... administrative delays ... and export subsidies.... Canada has been ... guilty, having used administrative delays in Vancouver to pressure the Japanese into lowering their "voluntary" export quotas....

Except for quotas, in many cases non-tariff barriers are not readily amenable to trade liberalization because they are frequently qualitative aspects of a nation's domestic policy arrangements.... In many respects non-tariff barriers are now a greater threat than tariffs to world trade.... It has been estimated... that by 1982... non-tariff barriers... covered 34 percent of the market for American manufacturers. In Japan, the comparable figure was 7 percent; in Canada, 10 percent; in West Germany, 20 percent; in France, 32 percent. This does not include... subsidies.

Non-tariff barriers are now coming under the scrutiny of GATT.... The GATT discussions on non-tariff barriers, which will, to some extent, take negotiators inside the economic decision-making processes of member countries, may raise the whole issue of the legitimacy of "industrial policy"—a generic term covering all kinds of governmental interventions designed to affect the structure of industry. There are considerable ideological differences on this subject, turning on such questions as "picking the winners," "aiding the adjustment of workers and firms out of unviable industries", and "letting the market decide." In some European countries, industrial policy is seen as a crucial part of building a just and equitable society; in Japan, it has been described as a way of unifying the people in a crusade to maximize the nation's economic potential; in Canada, so far, no consensus is in sight about whether industrial policy is even desirable, although a pot-pourri of government aids to industry has been allowed to develop in the pursuit of various ends. Given these diverse attitudes on the subject, the discussion about industrial policy and non-tariff barriers is unlikely to be rapidly concluded.

SOURCE: Economic Council of Canada, *On the Mend*, Annual Review, 1983, pp. 27–29.

---

beginning of this chapter, Canada is a relatively high-tariff country, although there are some countries that rely far more heavily on tariffs to protect their industries. Tariff rates of 100 percent or more are not unheard of. Also, other countries rely more heavily on quotas and export subsidies.

A **quota** is a legal limit on the amount of a good that may be imported. For example, the government might allow no more than 5 million barrels of wine to be imported in a year. In some cases, governments ban the importation of certain goods outright—a quota of zero. In recent years, the combination of high unemployment rates and a deterioration in Canada's competitive position in world trade has led to political pressures for increased use of quotas. One of the more visible quotas in Canada in recent times has been that on Japanese cars.

An **export subsidy** is a payment by the government to an exporter. By reducing the exporter's costs, such subsidies permit exporters to lower their selling prices and compete more effectively in world trade. Export subsidies are used extensively by some foreign governments to assist their industries—a practice that provokes bitter complaints from Canadian manufacturers about "unfair competition."

A **quota** specifies the maximum amount of a good that is permitted into the country from abroad per unit of time.

An **export subsidy** is a payment by the government to exporters to permit them to reduce the selling price of their goods so they can compete more effectively in foreign markets.

How Tariffs and Quotas Work

Both tariffs and quotas restrict supplies coming from abroad and drive up prices. The tariff works by raising prices and hence cutting the demand for imports, while the sequence associated with a quota goes the other way—restriction in supply forces prices up.

Let us use our international trade diagrams (Figure 32–3) to see what a quota does. The supply and demand curves in Figure 32–4 are like those of Figure 32–3. Just as in Figure 32–3, equilibrium in a free international market occurs at a price of $100 per barrel of wine (in both countries). At this price, the exporting country produces 10 million barrels [point *B* in part (a)] and consumes 5 million barrels (point *A*), so that exports are 5 million barrels—the distance *AB*. Similarly, the importing country consumes 8 million barrels [point *D* in part (b)] and produces only 3 million (point *C*), so that imports are also 5 million barrels (the distance *CD*).

Now suppose the government of the importing nation imposes an import quota of (no more than) 3 million barrels. The free-trade equilibrium is no longer possible. Instead, the market must reach equilibrium at a point where both exports and imports are 3 million barrels. As Figure 32–4 indicates, this requires different prices in the two countries.

Imports in part (b) will be 3 million—the distance *QT*—only when the price of wine in the importing nation is $110 per barrel, because only at this price will quantity demanded exceed quantity supplied by 3 million barrels. Similarly, exports in part (a) will be 3 million barrels—the distance *RS* only when the price in the exporting country is $95 per barrel. At this price, quantity supplied exceeds quantity demanded by 3 million barrels in the exporting country. Thus, the quota raises the price in the importing country to $110 and lowers the price in the exporting country to $95. In general:

An import quota on a product normally will reduce the volume of that product

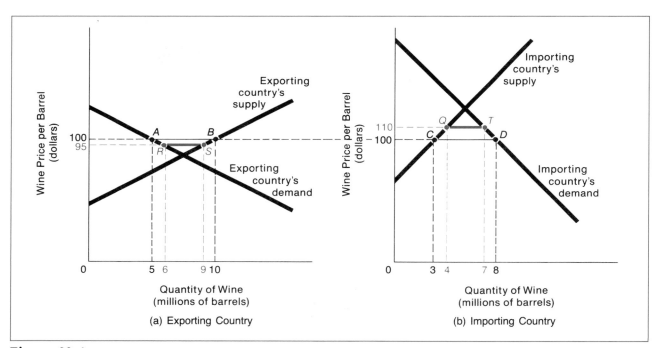

Figure 32–4

QUOTAS AND TARIFFS IN INTERNATIONAL TRADE

Under free trade, the equilibrium price of wine is $100 per barrel. The exporting country, in part (a), sends *AB*, or 5 million barrels, to the importing country (distance *CD*). If a quota of 3 million barrels is imposed by the importing country, these two distances must shrink to 3 million barrels. The solution is shown by distance *RS* for exports and distance *QT* for imports. Exports and imports are equal, as must be the case, but the quota forces prices to be unequal in the two countries. Wine sells for $110 per barrel in the importing country but only $95 per barrel in the exporting country. A tariff achieves the same result differently. It *requires* that the prices in the two countries be $15 apart. And this, as the graph shows, dictates that exports (= imports) will be equal at 3 million barrels.

traded, raise the price in the importing country, and reduce the price in the exporting country.

The same restriction of trade can be accomplished through a tariff. In the example we have just completed, a quota of 3 million barrels resulted in a price that was $15 higher in the importing country than in the exporting country ($110 – $95). Suppose, then, that instead of a quota the importing nation posts a $15 per barrel tariff. International trade equilibrium then must satisfy the following two requirements:

1. The price that consumers in the importing country pay for wine must exceed the price that suppliers in the exporting country receive by $15 (the amount of the tariff).

2. The quantity of wine exported must equal the quantity of wine imported.

By consulting the graphs in Figure 32–4, you can see exactly where these two requirements are satisfied. If the exporter produces at S and consumes at R, while the importer produces at Q and consumes at T, then exports and imports are equal (at 3 million barrels) and the two domestic prices differ by exactly $15. (They are $110 and $95.) What we have just discovered is a very general result of international trade theory:

Any restriction of international trade (exports and imports) that is accomplished by a quota normally can also be accomplished by a tariff.

In this case, the tariff corresponding to an import quota of 3 million barrels is $15 per barrel.

Tariffs versus Quotas

But while tariffs and quotas can accomplish the same reduction in international trade and lead to the same domestic prices in the two countries, there *are* some important differences between the two types of restrictions.

First, under a quota, profits from the price increases in the importing country usually go into the pockets of the foreign and domestic sellers of the product. Because supplies are limited by quotas, customers in the importing country must pay more for the product. So the suppliers, be they foreign or domestic, receive more for every unit they sell. For example, the Canadian quota on imports of Japanese automobiles raises the profit margins of both Canadian and Japanese automakers.

On the other hand, when trade is restricted by a tariff, the profits go as tax revenues to the *government* of the importing country. In effect, the government increases its tax revenues partly at the expense of its citizens and partly at the expense of foreign exporters, who must accept a reduced price because of the resulting decrease in quantity demanded in the importing country. (Domestic producers again benefit, because they are exempt from the tariff.) In this respect, a tariff is certainly a better proposition than a quota from the viewpoint of the country that enacts it.

Another important distinction between the two measures is the difference in their implications for productive efficiency and long-run prices. A tariff handicaps all exporters equally. It still awards sales to the importers who are most efficient and can therefore supply the goods most cheaply.

A quota, on the other hand, necessarily awards its import licences more or less capriciously—perhaps on a first-come, first-served basis or in proportion to past sales or by some other arbitrary standard or even on some political criteria. There is not the slightest reason to expect the most efficient and least costly suppliers to get the import permits. In the long run, the population of the importing country is likely to end up with significantly higher prices, poorer products, or both.

The Canadian quota on Japanese cars illustrates all of these effects. Japanese automakers responded to the limit on the number of small cars by shipping bigger models equipped with more "optional" equipment, and many more Japanese trucks. And the newer, smaller Japanese automakers—like Subaru—found it difficult to compete in the Canadian market because their quotas were so much smaller than those of Toyota, Datsun, and Honda.

If a country must inhibit imports, there are two important reasons for it to give preference to tariffs over quotas: (1) some of the resulting financial gains from tariffs go to the government of the importing country rather than to foreign and domestic producers; and (2) unlike quotas, tariffs offer no special benefits to inefficient exporters.

Why Inhibit Trade?

To state that tariffs are a better way to inhibit international trade than quotas leaves open a far more basic question: Why limit trade in the first place? There are two primary reasons for adopting measures that restrict trade: First, they may help the importing country get more advantageous prices for its goods, and second, they protect particular industries from foreign competition.

Shifting Prices in Your Favour

How can a tariff make prices more advantageous for the importing country if it raises consumer prices there? The answer is that it forces foreign exporters to sell more cheaply. Because their market is restricted by the tariff, they will be left with unsold goods unless they cut their prices. Suppose, as in Figure 32-4(b), that a $15 tariff on wine raises the price of wine in the importing country from $100 to $110 a barrel. This rise in price drives down imports from an amount represented by the length of the black line CD to the smaller amount represented by the blue line QT. And to the exporting country, this means an equal reduction in exports [see the change from AB to RS in Figure 32-4(a)].

As a result, the price at which the exporting country can sell its wine is driven down (from $100 to $95 in the example) while producers in the importing country—being exempt from the tariff—can charge $110 per barrel. In effect, such a tariff amounts to government intervention to rig prices in favour of domestic producers and to exploit foreign sellers by forcing them to sell more cheaply than they otherwise would.

However, this technique works only as long as foreigners accept tariff exploitation passively. And they rarely do. Instead, they retaliate, usually by imposing tariffs or quotas of their own on their imports from the country that first began the tariff game. This can easily lead to a trade war in which no one gains in terms of more favourable prices and everyone loses in terms of the resulting reductions in overall trade. Something like this happened to the world economy in the 1930s and helped prolong the worldwide depression. At present, it is threatening to happen again. Tariffs or quotas can benefit a country that is able to impose them without fear of retaliation. But when every country uses them, everyone is likely to lose in the long run.

Even if there is no retaliation, the tariff or quota can only rig prices in favour of domestic producers if the country imposing the tariff is a significant part of the world demand for that commodity. This requirement is not satisfied in Canada's case. Indeed, we often represent an insignificant portion of world demand for many of our imports. As a result, Canada is essentially in the same position as an individual firm in a perfectly competitive industry. We are a price taker on the world market for our imports.

With this realistic simplification, our analysis of tariffs can be accomplished without the two-part diagram used above. In Figure 32–5, the demand curve and supply curve of the importing country are shown precisely as they were in Figure 32–4(b). Also, the world supply curve of this commodity (wine) to the small economy is shown as the horizontal line at the price of $100 per barrel. The world supply curve is perfectly elastic at the going world price, since a small country can purchase whatever quantity it desires and have no effect on the world price.

In our example, before any tariff is levied, the country produces 3 million barrels of wine, consumes 8 million barrels and imports 5 million barrels (as indicated by distance *CD* in Figure 32–5). If world suppliers must pay a $15 per barrel tariff to sell within this economy, the world supply curve shifts up to the $115 point on the price axis. Just as before, equilibrium requires a $15 per barrel gap between the going world price and the price of wine in the country that levies the tariff. However, when the importing country is small, its price rises by the *full amount of the tariff*, and the world price is not forced down at all. This is shown in Figure 32–5, since, after the tariff, domestic production increases to 4.5 million barrels, purchases fall to 6.5 million barrels and imports fall to 2 million barrels (given by distance *VW* in the diagram). Our analysis simply verifies the common-sense notion that a small country cannot rig world prices in its favour.

We conclude that Canada is too small to shift world prices of imports in her favour. Thus, even without considering retaliation, this is an illegitimate argument for tariffs and quotas in Canada.

Protecting Particular Industries

The second, and probably more frequent, reason why countries restrict trade is to protect particular industries from foreign competition. If foreigners can produce

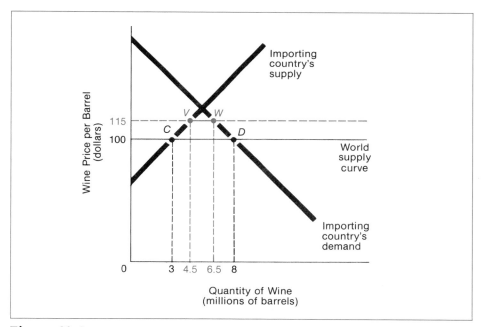

Figure 32–5
QUOTAS AND TARIFFS WHEN THE IMPORTING COUNTRY IS SMALL
Canada is too small to affect the world price of wine, which is $100 per barrel in this example. Under free trade, Canada produces 3 million barrels, consumes 8 million barrels and imports 8 – 3 = 5 million barrels (distance *CD*). This amount is an insignificant portion of world production. If a tariff of $15 per barrel is imposed in Canada, our price rises by the full amount from $100 to $115 per barrel. Price is unaffected in the rest of the world. Domestic production increases to 4.5 million barrels, consumption falls to 6.5 million barrels, and imports fall to 6.5 – 4.5 = 2 million barrels (distance *VW*).

steel or watches or shoes more cheaply, domestic businesses and unions in these industries are quick to demand protection; and their government is often reluctant to deny it to them. It is here that the cheap foreign labour argument is most likely to be invoked.

But the fact is that the firms that are unable to compete in the market are the ones whose relative inefficiency does not permit them to beat foreign exporters at their own game. In Ricardo's example of comparative advantage, one can well imagine the complaints from Portuguese clothmakers as the opening of trade led to increased importation of English cloth. At the same time, the English grape growers would, very likely, have expressed equal concern over the flood of imported wine from Portugal. Protective tariffs and quotas are designed to undercut harsh competition coming from abroad; but it is precisely this competition that gives consumers the benefits of international specialization.

Usually, when an industry feels itself threatened by foreign competition, it is argued that some form of protection against imports is needed to prevent loss of jobs. But we know from our discussion of macroeconomics in Part Three that there are better ways to stimulate employment. Yet it must be admitted that any program that limits foreign competition will, in the short run, preserve jobs in the protected industry. It will work, but often at a very considerable cost to consumers, in the form of higher prices, and to the economy, in the form of inefficient use of resources. For example, several recent American studies have estimated that various tariffs and import quotas *cost consumers in the United States about $80,000 for every job they preserve.*

Nevertheless, union complaints over proposals to reduce a tariff or a quota are well justified unless something is done to ease the cost to the individual workers of switching to those lines of production that trade has now made profitable.

The argument for free trade between countries cannot be considered airtight if there is no adequate program to assist the minority of citizens in each country who will be harmed whenever patterns of production change drastically, as would happen, for example, if tariff and quota barriers were suddenly brought down.

Owners of wineries in Britain and of textile mills in Portugal may see heavy investments suddenly rendered unprofitable, as would workers whose investments in acquiring special skills and training are no longer marketable. Nor are the costs to displaced workers only monetary. Often they will have to move to new locations as well as to new industries, uprooting their families, losing old friends and neighbours, and so on. That the *majority* of citizens undoubtedly will gain from free trade will be no consolation to those who are its victims. To help alleviate this problem, it is often argued that Canada should expand its programs to assist workers who have lost jobs because of the changing patterns of world trade. Some **trade adjustment assistance** is provided. For instance, the federal government's Industry and Labour Adjustment Program (ILAP) pays two-thirds of workers' former wages (after unemployment insurance has expired for workers over age 45) if they have been released by declining, low-productivity industries.

Trade adjustment assistance provides special unemployment benefits, loans, retraining programs, or other aid to workers and firms that are harmed by foreign competition.

Other Arguments for Protection

National Defence and Other Non-economic Considerations

There are times when a tariff or some other measure to interfere with trade may be justified on non-economic grounds. If a country considers itself vulnerable to military attack, it may be perfectly rational to keep alive industries whose outputs can be obtained more cheaply abroad but whose supplies might dry up during an emergency. For example, airplane production by small countries makes sense only in such circumstances.

The danger is that every industry, even those with the most peripheral defence relationship, is likely to invoke this argument on its behalf. For instance, the U.S. watch-making industry claimed protection for itself for many years on the grounds that it trained skilled workers whose craftsmanship would be invaluable in wartime. Perhaps so, but a technicians' training program probably could have done the job more cheaply and even more effectively by teaching exactly the skills needed for military purposes.

Non-economic reasons also explain the recent European quotas on seal skins. These quotas may be a competitive boon to the European countries' domestic leather and fur industries, but protection of endangered species rather than protection of industries is their justification.

The Infant-Industry Argument

It is often suggested that temporary protection of a newly established industry can serve the national interest. Until that industry can expand to a point at which it is able to compete unaided with established foreign firms, it may be essential to prevent its strangulation by foreign competition.

The argument, while valid in certain instances, is less defensible than it may at first appear. It makes sense only if the industry's prospective future gains are sufficient to repay the social losses incurred while it is being protected. But if the industry is likely to be so profitable in the future, why doesn't private capital rush in to take advantage of the prospective net profits? The annals of business are full of cases in which a new product or a new firm lost money at first but profited handsomely later. Only where funds are not available to a particular industry for some reason, despite its glowing profit prospects, does the infant-industry argument for protection stand up to scrutiny.

It is hard to think of examples, but even if such a case were found one would have to be careful that the industry not remain in diapers forever. There are too many cases in which new industries were awarded protection when they were being established and, somehow, the time to withdraw the protection never arrived. One must beware of infant industries that never grow up.

Strategic Trade Policy

A new argument for protectionism has become popular in recent years. Advocates of this argument agree that free trade for all is the best system. But they point out that we live in an imperfect world in which some nations refuse to live by the rules of the free-trade game. And they fear that a nation that pursues free trade in a protectionist world is likely to lose out. It therefore makes sense, they argue, to threaten to protect your markets unless other nations agree to open theirs.

This is a hard argument for economists to deal with. While it accepts the superiority of free trade, it argues that threatening protectionism is the best way to establish free trade. Such a strategy might work, but it clearly involves great risks. If threats that Canada will turn protectionist induce other countries to scrap existing protectionist policies, then the gamble will have succeeded. But, if the gamble fails, the world ends up with even more protection than it started with. Probably there would be little effect in other countries from such threats made by Canada, so this is not a compelling argument for Canadian tariffs. For the United States, however, it could be a worthwhile strategy.

The analogy to recent arms negotiations is pretty obvious—and a little frightening. The Americans threaten to install new missiles unless the Russians agree to dismantle some of theirs. If they do, the world is a safer place and everyone is better off. But, if they do not, the arms race accelerates and everyone is worse off. Is the American threat to build new missiles therefore a wise or a foolish policy? There is no agreement on this question, and so we should not expect agreement on the advisability of using protectionist measures in a strategic way.

What Import Price Levels Benefit a Country?

Dumping means selling goods in a foreign market at lower prices than those charged in the home market.

One of the most curious features of the protectionist position is the fear of low prices charged by foreign sellers. Countries that subsidize exports are accused of **dumping**—of getting rid of their goods at unconscionably low prices. For example, in the last few years Japan has frequently been accused of dumping various goods on the Canadian and American markets, and Europe has been accused of dumping its agricultural goods.

A moment's thought should indicate why this fear must be considered curious. As a nation of consumers, we should be indignant when the prices of our imports are *high*, not when they are *low*. That is the common-sense rule that guides every consumer, and the consumers of imported commodities should be no exception. Only from the topsy-turvy viewpoint of an industry seeking protection from competition are high prices seen as being in the public interest.

Ultimately, it is always in the interest of a country to get its imports as cheaply as possible. It would be ideal for Canada if the rest of the world were willing to provide its exports to us free or virtually so. We could then live in luxury at the expense of the rest of the world.

The notion that low import prices are bad for a country is a fitting companion to the idea—so often heard—that it is good for a country to export much more than it imports. True, this means that foreigners will end up owing us a good deal of money. But it also means that we will have given them large quantities of our products and have gotten relatively little in foreign products in return. That surely is not an ideal way for a country to benefit from its foreign transactions.

Our gains from trade do not consist of accumulations of gold or of heavy debts owed us by foreigners. Rather, our gains are composed of the goods and services that others provide minus the goods and services we must provide them in return.

Conclusion

The preceding discussion should indicate the fundamental fallacy in the argument that Canadian workers have to fear "cheap foreign labour." If workers in other countries are willing to supply their products to us with little compensation, this must ultimately *raise* the standard of living of the average Canadian worker. As long as the government's monetary and fiscal policies succeed in maintaining high levels of employment at home, how can we possibly lose by getting the products of the world at little cost to ourselves?

It must be admitted that there are two dangers to this prognosis. First, our employment policy may not be effective. If workers who are displaced by foreign competition cannot find jobs in other industries, then Canadian workers will indeed suffer from international trade. But that is a shortcoming of the government's employment program, not of its international trade policies.

Second, we have noted that an abrupt stiffening of foreign competition resulting from a major innovation in another country, or from a discovery of a new and better source of raw materials, or from a sharp increase in export subsidies by a foreign country, *can* hurt Canadian workers by not giving them an adequate chance to adapt gradually to the new conditions. The more rapid the change, the more painful it will be. If it occurs fairly gradually, workers can retrain and move on to the industries that now require their services. If the change is even more gradual, no one may have to move. People who retire or leave the threatened industry for other reasons simply need not be replaced. But competition that inflicts its damage overnight is certain to impose very real costs upon the affected workers, costs that are no less painful for being temporary.

But these are, after all, minor qualifications to an overwhelming argument. They call for intelligent monetary and fiscal policies and for transitional assistance

Unfair Foreign Competition

Satire and ridicule are often more persuasive than logic and statistics. Exasperated by the spread of protectionism to so many industries under the prevailing Mercantilist philosophy, French economist Frédéric Bastiat decided to take the protectionist argument to its illogical conclusion. The fictitious petition of the French candlemakers to the Chamber of Deputies, written in 1845 and excerpted below, has become a classic in the battle for free trade.

We are subject to the intolerable competition of a foreign rival, who enjoys, it would seem, such superior facilities for the production of light, that he is enabled to *inundate* our *national market* at so exceedingly reduced a price, that, the moment he makes his appearance, he draws off all custom for us; and thus an important branch of French industry, with all its innumerable ramifications, is suddenly reduced to a state of complete stagnation. This rival is no other than the sun.

Our petition is, that it would please your honorable body to pass a law whereby shall be directed the shutting up of all windows, dormers, skylights, shutters, curtains, in a word, all openings, holes, chinks, and fissures through which the light of the sun is used to penetrate our dwellings, to the prejudice of the profitable manufactures which we flatter ourselves we have been enabled to bestow upon the country....

We foresee your objections, gentlemen; but there is not one that you can oppose to us ... which is not equally opposed to your own practice and the principle which guides your policy....

Labor and nature concur in different proportions, according to country and climate, in every article of production.... If a Lisbon orange can be sold at half the price of a Parisian one, it is because a natural and gratuitous heat does for the one what the other only obtains from an artificial and consequently expensive one....

Does it not argue the greatest inconsistency to check as you do the importation of coal, iron, cheese, and goods of foreign manufacture, merely because and even in proportion as their price approaches *zero*, while at the same time you freely admit, and without limitation, the light of the sun, whose price is during the whole day at *zero*?

SOURCE: F. Bastiat, *Economic Sophisms* (New York: G. P. Putnam's Sons, 1922).

to unemployed workers, not for abandonment of free trade and permission for monopoly power to flourish behind protection.

In the long run, labour will be "cheap" only where it is not very productive. Wages will tend to be highest in those countries in which high labour productivity keeps costs down and permits exporters to compete effectively despite high wages.

We note that in this matter it is absolute advantage, not comparative advantage, that counts. The country that is most efficient in every output can pay its workers more in every industry.

We started this chapter by noting that tariff cuts involve both benefits and costs. The benefits are that consumers acquire goods at lower prices, and that the anti-competitive behaviour of firms can be limited without relying on regulations and attempted prosecutions. The costs of tariff cuts are the jobs that many expect would be lost to "cheap foreign labour." This chapter has shown that these costs are very much exaggerated in popular discussion. This is because the principle of comparative advantage is not generally appreciated and because the problems associated with increased competition can be better solved by appropriate monetary, fiscal, and adjustment assistance policies. The two chapters preceding this one have shown that the other approaches to competition policy—regulation and attempted prosecution—have met with only limited success. Taken together, then, these three chapters suggest that trade liberalization should constitute a significant element in our competition policy.

Summary

1. Countries trade because differences in their natural resources and other inputs create discrepancies in the efficiency with which they can produce different goods, and because specialization may offer them greater economies of large-scale production.

2. Voluntary trade will generally be advantageous to both parties in an exchange. This is one of our **12 Ideas for Beyond the Final Exam**.

3. International trade is more complicated than trade within a nation because of political factors, different national currencies, and impediments to the movement of labour and capital across national borders.

4. Both countries will gain from trade with one another if each exports goods in whose production it has a comparative advantage. That is, even a country that is generally inefficient will benefit by exporting the goods in whose production it is least inefficient. This is another of the **12 Ideas for Beyond the Final Exam**.

5. When countries specialize and trade, each can enjoy consumption possibilities that exceed its production possibilities.

6. The prices of goods traded between countries are determined by supply and demand, but one must consider explicitly the demand curve and the supply curve of *each* country involved. Thus, in international trade, the equilibrium price must be where the excess of the exporter's quantity supplied over its domestic quantity demanded is equal to the excess of the importer's quantity demanded over its quantity supplied.

7. The "cheap foreign labour" argument ignores the principle of comparative advantage, which shows that real wages can rise in both the importing and exporting countries as a result of specialization and, thus, increased productivity.

8. Tariffs and quotas are designed to protect a country's industries from foreign competition. Such protection may sometimes be advantageous to that country, but not if foreign countries adopt tariffs and quotas of their own as a means of retaliation, and not if the country constitutes a small share of the world market.

9. While the same restriction of trade can be accomplished by either a tariff or a quota, tariffs offer at least two advantages to the country that imposes them: (1) some of the gains go to the government rather than to foreign producers, and (2) there is greater incentive for efficient production.

10. When a nation shifts from protection to free trade, some industries and their workers will lose out. Equity then demands that these people and firms be compensated in some way. The Canadian government has begun experimenting with adjustment assistance to do this.

11. Several arguments for protectionism can, under the right circumstances, have validity. These include the national defence argument, the infant-industry argument, and the use of trade restrictions for strategic purposes. But each of these arguments is frequently abused.

12. Dumping may hurt domestic producers, but it always benefits consumers.

13. Since tariff cuts are beneficial even if domestic industries are competitive (as illustrated by the principle of comparative advantage), they are doubly appealing if domestic industries are non-competitive. Thus, tariff cuts represent a significant element in a country's competition policy.

Concepts for Review

Imports
Exports
Specialization
Mutual gains from trade
Absolute advantage

Comparative advantage
"Cheap foreign labour" argument
Tariff
Non-tariff barriers
Quota

Export subsidy
Trade adjustment assistance
Infant-industry argument
Dumping

Questions for Discussion

1. You have a dozen eggs worth $1.50 and your neighbour has 500 grams of bacon worth about the same. You decide to swap six eggs for 250 grams of bacon. In financial terms, neither of you gains anything. Explain why you are nevertheless both likely to be better off.

2. In the eighteenth century, some writers argued that one person in a trade could be made better off only by gaining at the expense of the other. Explain the fallacy in the argument.

3. A brilliant chemist is also a master glass blower. In what circumstances does it pay him to hire a glass blower for his lab? When does it make sense for him to do some glass blowing for himself?

4. Country A has lots of hydroelectric power, a cold

climate, and a highly skilled labour force. What sorts of products do you think it is likely to produce? What are the characteristics of countries with which you would expect it to trade?

5. Upon removal of a tariff on shoes, a Canadian shoe-making firm goes bankrupt. Discuss the pros and cons of the tariff removal in the short run and long run.

6. Country A's government believes that it is best always to export more (in money terms) than the value of its imports. As a consequence, it exports more to country B every year than it imports from country B. After 100 years of this arrangement, both countries are destroyed in an earthquake. What were the advantages and disadvantages of the surplus to country A? To country B?

7. The table below describes the number of red socks and white socks that can be produced with an hour of labour in two different cities:

	IN BOSTON	IN CHICAGO
Red socks (pairs)	3	1
White socks (pairs)	3	2

a. If there is no trade, what is the price of white socks relative to red socks in Boston?
b. If there is no trade, what is the price of white socks relative to red socks in Chicago?
c. Suppose each city has 1000 hours of labour available per year. Draw the production possibilities frontier for each city.
d. Which city has an absolute advantage in the production of which good(s)? Which city has a comparative advantage in the production of which good(s)?

e. If the cities start trading with each other, which city will specialize and export which good?
f. What can be said about the price at which trade will take place?

8. Suppose that Canada and Mexico are the only two countries in the world. In Canada a worker can produce 12 bushels of wheat *or* 1 barrel of oil a day. In Mexico, a worker can produce 2 bushels of wheat or 2 barrels of oil.
a. What will be the price ratio between the two commodities (i.e., the price of oil in terms of wheat) in each country if there is no trade?
b. If free trade is allowed and there are no transportation costs, what commodity would Canada import? What about Mexico?
c. In what range will the price ratio have to fall under free trade? Why?
d. Picking one possible post-trade price ratio, show clearly how it is possible for both countries to benefit from free trade.

9. (More difficult.) The table below presents the demand and supply curves for cars in Germany and Canada.
a. Draw the demand and supply curves for Canada on one diagram and those for Germany on another one.
b. If there is no trade between Canada and Germany, what are the equilibrium price and quantity in the car market in Canada? In Germany?
c. Now suppose trade is opened up between the two countries. What will be the equilibrium price of cars in the world market? What has happened to the price of cars in Canada? In Germany?
d. What has happened to the quantity of cars produced, and therefore to employment, in the car industry in Canada? In Germany? Who benefits and who loses *initially* from free trade?

PRICE PER CAR IN BOTH COUNTRIES (thousands of dollars)	QUANTITY DEMANDED IN CANADA (hundreds of cars)	QUANTITY SUPPLIED IN CANADA (hundreds of cars)	QUANTITY DEMANDED IN GERMANY (hundreds of cars)	QUANTITY SUPPLIED IN GERMANY (hundreds of cars)
0	100	0	100	0
1	90	10	90	25
2	80	20	80	50
3	70	30	70	70
4	60	40	60	80
5	50	50	50	90
6	40	60	40	100
7	30	70	30	110
8	20	80	20	120
9	10	90	10	130
10	0	100	0	140

Taxation, Government Spending, and Resource Allocation

The hardest thing in the
world to understand is
income tax.
ALBERT EINSTEIN

Chapter 29 examined several reasons why the government might want to interfere with the workings of the market mechanism. Some of these interferences involve levying taxes; for example, we noted that taxes may be useful in correcting misallocations of resources caused by externalities. Other interferences involve direct spending by government—provision of national defence is a good example—and this spending, in turn, requires that taxes be levied to raise the necessary revenue. These, then, are the two main reasons for taxes: to improve resource allocation and to raise revenue to pay for government expenditures. Of the two, it is clear that the revenue-raising function is by far the more important in practice. So this chapter opens with a brief look at the things on which governments in Canada spend money; that is, the reasons why government needs revenue. We then turn to the types of taxes that are used to raise this revenue, the effects these taxes have on the allocation of resources and the distribution of income, and the principles that distinguish "good" from "bad" taxes.

Government Spending: An Overview

During the fiscal year ending in 1983, the federal government spent over $90 billion. Perhaps the best way to understand this sum is to note that federal spending amounted to over $3700 for every man, woman, and child in Canada. Figure 33–1 shows where that money went. More than half, or 52 percent, of these funds were spent on *transfer payments*: the Canada Pension Plan, Old Age Security, unemployment insurance payments, interest on the public debt, and revenue grants to provincial governments. Health, education, and national defence expenditures accounted for another 15 percent of federal government funds. The remaining one-third of the budget went for expenditures on natural resources, agriculture, the environment, communications, transportation, industrial development, protection of persons and property, foreign affairs and international assistance, recreation and culture, research assistance, housing, and other general services.

The distribution of expenditures by provincial and municipal governments is also shown in Figure 33–1. Fifty-five percent of their funds went for health, welfare, and education.

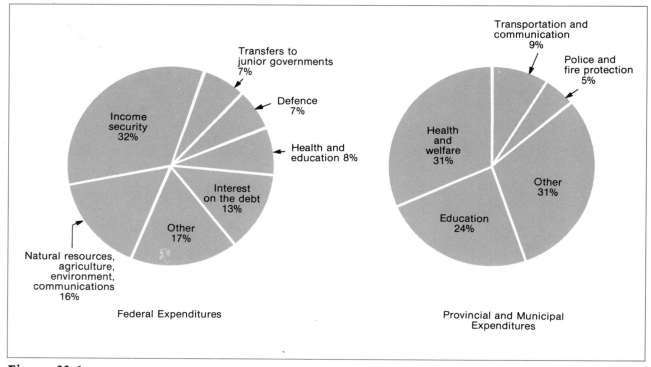

Figure 33-1

THE ALLOCATION OF GOVERNMENT EXPENDITURES

These graphs show how the government dollar is spent. Slightly over one-half of the federal government's funds are spent on transfer payments: either to lower level governments, to retirees, the poor, the unemployed, or to the holders of government bonds as interest. Over one-half of the provincial and municipal expenditures are for health, welfare, and education.

SOURCE: Canadian Tax Foundation, *The National Finances.*

It is interesting to relate these spending programs to the discussion in Chapter 29 of the reasons for government intervention in the marketplace. Many income security and welfare programs are designed to *redistribute income*: from the young to the old (pension plans), from the nonpoor to the poor (welfare programs), from the employed to the unemployed (unemployment insurance), and so on. National defence is the classic example of a **public good**. Some of the other spending programs can be rationalized on the grounds that they provide **beneficial externalities** (education, support of research), though critics of "big government" question how strong these externalities really are. A variety of other public services (various transportation programs, for example) are difficult to rationalize on any of the grounds enumerated in Chapter 29; but, for one reason or another, governments have not left provision of these services to the free market. We should not lose sight of the fact that political, not economic, considerations often dictate what services the government will provide.

Taxes in Canada

To finance this array of goods and services, taxes are required. Sometimes it seems that the tax collector is everywhere. We have income and payroll taxes withheld from our paycheques, sales taxes added to our purchases, property taxes levied on our homes; we pay gasoline taxes, liquor taxes, and so on and on. According to the old saying, nothing is certain but death and taxes. And, if there is one thing that many Canadians seem to agree on it is that there are too many taxes and that they are too high.

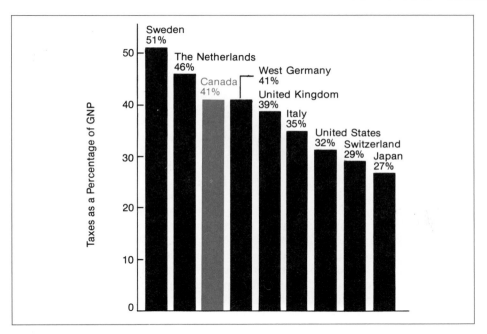

Figure 33-2
THE BURDEN OF TAXATION
IN SELECTED COUNTRIES,
1981
Canadians are not heavily taxed in
comparison with the citizens of the
Netherlands and Sweden, but we
do pay more tax than the Italians,
Swiss, Americans, and Japanese.
SOURCE: *National Accounts of OECD
Countries. 1964-1981*, Volume II.

By international standards, Canadians are taxed to about the same extent as
the citizens of West Germany and the United Kingdom. Figure 33–2 compares the
fraction of income paid in taxes in Canada with that paid by residents of other
industrialized nations. Canadians are not heavily taxed in comparison with the
Swedes or the Dutch, but we do pay more taxes than the Italians, Swiss, Americans,
and Japanese.

Another way to put the burden of taxation into perspective is to study how it
has changed over time. Figure 33–3 helps you to do this by charting the behaviour

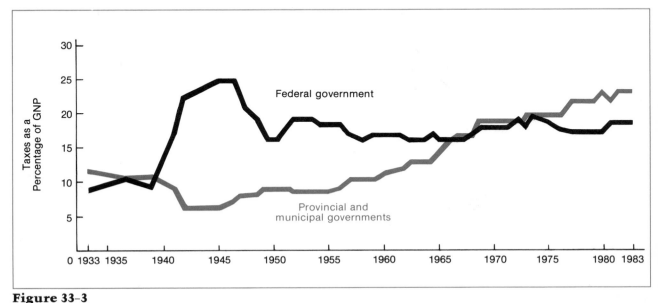

Figure 33-3
TAXES AS A PERCENTAGE OF GROSS NATIONAL PRODUCT
Federal taxes have accounted for a fairly constant fraction of GNP since the late 1940s. Provincial and municipal taxes, however, have
absorbed an ever-increasing portion from the 1940s until the 1980s.
SOURCE: Historical Statistics of Canada (Series H-74, H-91) and Department of Finance, *Annual Review*.

of both federal and provincial/municipal taxes *as a percentage of GNP* since 1933. The figure shows that the share of federal taxes in GNP has been rather steady for almost 40 years. It climbed from less than 10 percent in 1933 to 25 percent during World War II, fell back to 16 percent in the immediate postwar period, and has generally fluctuated in the 17 percent to 19 percent range ever since. The share of GNP taken in taxes by the federal government has not increased since World War II. It simply is not true that the federal government has been thrusting its hand deeper and deeper into our pockets each year. But the same cannot be said of provincial and municipal governments. There was an unmistakable upward trend in the fraction of GNP taken in provincial and municipal taxes until the 1980s. This fraction climbed from 6 percent in 1945 to 19 percent in 1970. In 1983, it was 23 percent.

This trend has worried many tax reformers, who, for reasons to be explained in this chapter, view the income tax as superior to other taxes. Since the federal government relies more heavily on the income tax than do the junior-level governments, the growth in provincial and municipal government operations means an increased reliance on relatively inferior taxes.

The main reason for the faster growth of provincial and municipal taxes than of federal taxes seems to be the differing expenditure patterns of the various levels of government. Apart from national defence, the federal government spends very little on direct purchases of goods and services; but direct provision of public services accounts for the preponderant share of provincial and municipal budgets. It seems that citizens demand more and better schools, hospitals, parks, and other public services as the economy gets richer. And—for reasons explained in Chapter 29—these services become more and more expensive each year. The resulting strain on provincial and municipal budgets has forced these units of government into tax increases that the federal government has, by and large, managed to avoid.

Progressive, Proportional, and Regressive Taxes

Economists like to classify taxes according to whether they are *progressive*, *proportional*, or *regressive*. Under a **progressive tax**, the fraction of income paid in taxes *rises* as a person's income increases. Under a **proportional tax**, this fraction is constant. And under a **regressive tax**, the fraction of income paid to the tax collector *declines* as income rises. Since the fraction of income paid in taxes is called the **average tax rate**, these definitions can be formulated as they are in the margin.

Often, however, the *average* tax rate is less interesting than the **marginal tax rate**, which is the fraction of each *additional* dollar that must be paid to the tax collector. The reason, as we will see, is that the *marginal* tax rate, not the *average* tax rate, most directly affects economic incentives.

Direct Versus Indirect Taxes

Another way to classify taxes is to divide them into two broad categories: **direct taxes** and **indirect taxes**. Direct taxes are levied directly on *people*. Primary examples are *income taxes* and *inheritance taxes*, though the notoriously regressive *head tax*—which charges every person the same amount—is also a direct tax. In contrast, indirect taxes are levied on goods and services, such as buying gasoline, using the telephone, owning a home, and so on. *Sales taxes* and *property taxes* are the most important indirect taxes in Canada, although many other countries rely heavily on the *value-added tax*, a tax that has never been adopted in Canada.[1] In fact, as a broad generalization, the Canadian and U.S. governments rely more heavily on direct taxation than do the governments of most other countries.

A **progressive tax** is one in which the average tax rate paid by an individual rises as his income rises. A **proportional tax** is one in which the average tax rate is the same at all income levels. A **regressive tax** is one in which the average tax rate falls as income rises.

The **average tax rate** is the ratio of taxes to income.

The **marginal tax rate** is the fraction of each *additional* dollar of income that is paid in taxes.

Direct taxes are taxes levied directly on people. **Indirect taxes** are taxes levied on specific economic activities.

---

[1] The concept of value added was defined and explained in an appendix to Chapter 7. The value-added tax simply taxes each firm on the basis of its value added.

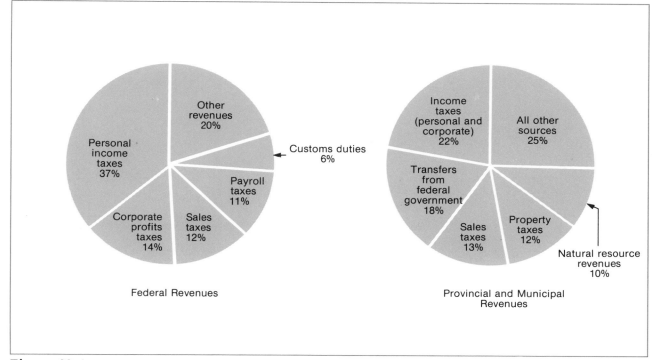

Figure 33-4

THE SOURCES OF GOVERNMENT REVENUE

These diagrams give the share of each of the major sources of government revenue. Personal income and payroll taxes account for almost one-half of federal revenues. Transfer payments from the federal government and sales and property taxes account for almost one-half of provincial and municipal revenues.

SOURCE: Canadian Tax Foundation, *The National Finances*.

The federal government relies heavily on direct taxes, while, in comparison, the provincial and municipal governments depend more on indirect taxes. The three big direct taxes used by the federal government are the personal income tax, the corporate profit tax, and the payroll tax. Together these taxes represent nearly two-thirds of the federal government's revenue. Nearly one-fifth of the provincial and municipal government revenues come from direct transfers from the federal government. Nearly one-third of the remaining junior-level government revenue comes from sales and property taxes. The provincial governments rely largely on sales taxes and related sources, such as natural resource revenues and profits from liquor sales. The municipal governments depend on property taxes and grants from the provinces. A more complete breakdown of these revenue sources is given in Figure 33-4. Let us now look at the major taxes in more detail.

The Personal Income Tax

The tax on individual incomes began during the First World War, and it is now the biggest revenue raiser. Roughly 10 million individuals have filed tax returns in recent years. It is well known that the personal income tax is progressive. Table 33-1 contains an abbreviated version of the tax table that applied to Ontario residents during 1983.[2] The progressivity is shown by the way average tax rates rise as income rises.

---

[2]The provincial income-tax rates vary. Nine provinces allow the federal government to collect their income tax revenue for them. Quebec continues to levy and collect its own tax, and does not participate in the intergovernmental tax-collection agreements.

Table 33-1

PERSONAL INCOME-TAX RATES FOR THE 1983 TAX YEAR

INCOME BEFORE PERSONAL EXEMPTIONS* (dollars)	TAXABLE INCOME (dollars)	LEGISLATED AVERAGE TAX RATE (percent)	MARGINAL TAX RATE (percent)	ACTUAL AVERAGE TAX RATE† (percent)
10,000	1,410	9	24	9
15,000	6,410	22	27	13
20,000	11,410	25	28	16
25,000	16,410	26	30	18
30,000	21,410	28	37	19
45,000	36,410	32	44	23
70,000	61,410	38	50	26

*This example involves a family of four, with two young children and only one parent working outside the home, that live in Ontario.

†The legislated tax rate is taken from the tax form. The actual rate is calculated by dividing total taxes paid by total taxable-income earned by all income-tax filers at that income level. (Source: Canadian Tax Foundation, *The National Finances*). The actual tax rate is lower, since individuals can use various tax shelters.

A **tax shelter** is a special provision in the Income Tax Act that reduces or defers taxation if certain conditions are met.

A **capital gain** is the profit made from the sale of an asset at a higher price than was paid for it.

The last column of the table shows that the personal income tax is not as progressive as the legislated rate structure suggests. These actual average tax rates are calculated by dividing all income-tax filers into a set of income classes. Then, for each income class, the total tax actually paid by this group is divided by the group's total taxable income. The actual tax rates are lower than the legislated ones, since individuals can use various **tax shelters**. The table shows that low-income earners are not able to take advantage of these tax shelters as effectively as high-income earners. Let us see what some of the major tax shelters are.

Lenient taxation of capital gains.   Our laws tax a **capital gain** at one-half the rates at which other sources of income are taxed. Since such gains accrue almost exclusively to upper-income groups, this tax shelter is the reserve of the rich. Why did the government create such a thing? One reason is to encourage people to save and invest in risky ventures. Another is that extremely high taxes might have to be paid on large capital gains if they were treated like ordinary income.

For example, Jane Doe earns $40,000 a year and owns $100,000 worth of stock that she bought 10 years ago for $20,000. If she sells her stock this year, she will enjoy an $80,000 capital gain, which will push her income for the year up to $120,000. The tax bill on such an income is quite substantial. In particular, because of progressive rates, it could be much larger than the tax she would have paid if the $80,000 capital gain had been earned evenly at the rate of $8000 a year over 10 years. To reduce this burden, the government decided to tax only 50 percent of capital gains, so that Jane's taxable income is only $40,000 + $40,000 = $80,000. But, tax reformers point out, there are many other ways to ease the tax burden on such gains. The simplest way perhaps is to charge individuals the tax they would have paid if the gain really had occurred gradually; that is, to tax Jane Doe as if her income had been $40,000 + $8000 = $48,000 a year for 10 years. Even without this reform, the Canadian tax system now involves forward-averaging provisions that solve some of these problems.

Tax-exempt status of some interest income.   When individuals calculate taxable income, they can exclude up to $1000 of interest income, dividends received from Canadian companies, and capital gains made on Canadian shares. Also, individuals can lend funds to other family members (at a zero interest rate), so the other family members earn the interest, and the family's total interest

Table 33-2

OWNING VERSUS RENTING A HOME

ITEM	MUTT (owner)	JEFF (renter)
Income	$25,000	$25,000
Interest income	—	7,000
Property tax	2,000	—
Rent	—	9,000
Taxable income	$25,000	$32,000

exemption can be extended to several thousand dollars.

Tax benefits for homeowners.   Many individuals think that our income tax system should allow homeowners to deduct their payments of mortgage interest and property tax, when calculating taxable income. After all, it is argued, such deductions are allowed in the United States and certain European countries, and it seems fair to treat homeowners in a similar way to shopkeepers. But the fault in this reasoning is that unlike shopkeepers, homeowners already receive a tax shelter by *not* having to declare the income they earn by incurring these expenses. This is because the "income" from owning a home accrues not in cash, but in the form of living without paying rent.

Once again, an example will make things clear. Mutt and Jeff are neighbours. Each earns $25,000 a year, and each has just won a lottery and received $70,000 in cash. Mutt uses his winnings to buy a $70,000 house for cash. Thus, he has no mortgage or rent payments, but must pay $2000 per year in property tax. Jeff uses his winnings to buy a bond that yields 10 percent interest. Thus, his interest income is $7000 (in this example we ignore the $1000 interest income exemption). Jeff rents the house next door to Mutt's, which is exactly the same and which rents for $9000 per year. Most observers would agree that Mutt and Jeff *should* pay the same income tax. But, ignoring other deductions and exemptions, Mutt's taxable income is $25,000, while Jeff's is $32,000 (see Table 33–2).

How can this disparity be rectified? One way is to allow *both* homeowners *and* renters to deduct their expenses. This would make Mutt's taxable income fall by $2000 to $23,000, and it would allow Jeff's taxable income to fall by $9000 to $23,000. Another way is to force homeowners to add their "imputed rent" to their income. In this example, Mutt would have to add the implicit rental income of $9000 (that he is receiving from himself), but he would be allowed to deduct his expenses involved (the property tax of $2000). Thus, his taxable income would be $32,000, just like Jeff's. The fact that the implicit rental income of homeowners is not taxed represents a major tax shelter that favours the well-to-do. Homeowners get a further break since no taxes are levied on the capital gains obtained from the sale of one's principal residence.

We could go on and on listing more tax shelters, but enough has been said to illustrate the point:

Our personal income tax offers many opportunities to avoid payment of tax through tax shelters. Since most shelters are mainly beneficial to rich people, they erode the progressivity of the income tax quite seriously.

Other Taxes

Corporate Profits Tax

The tax on corporate profits is also considered to be a "direct" tax, because corporations are considered to be fictitious "people" in the eyes of the law. Smaller and privately held corporations get taxed at special low rates, but the larger firms pay a tax rate of about 50 percent of income. The specific rate depends on the nature of the company's business and on the province in which it is located. In 1984, the Department of Finance estimated that 181,000 of the 455,000 Canadian-controlled private corporations benefited from the tax breaks that are offered to small businesses.

But many tax shelters permit large corporations to reduce tax obligations. For example, some companies set up subsidiaries in other countries with low corporate-tax rates. Then these companies adjust the prices charged for services rendered between its various affiliates, to ensure that most of their profits are officially earned in the countries having the lowest tax rates. We discuss the difficulties in taxing profits more fully later in this chapter (pages 654–55).

Sales and Excise Taxes

An **excise tax** is a tax levied on a particular commodity or service, as a fixed amount of money per unit of product sold or as a fixed percentage of the purchase price.

Most provincial governments levy a broad-based sales tax on the purchase of goods and services. There are exceptions, such as food, children's clothing, services, and housing rents, so that just under 50 percent of consumer expenditure is exempt. Overall sales-tax rates are in the region of 7 percent. In addition, there are special **excise taxes** in most provinces on such things as tobacco products, liquor, gasoline, and luxury items. The federal government levies a general manufacturer's-level sales tax. It also imposes excise taxes on a hodgepodge of miscellaneous goods and services including cigarettes, oil and gasoline, liquor, and on many imported products (in the form of tariffs and duties).

Property Taxes

Municipalities raise revenue by taxing the values of properties, such as houses and office buildings, again with certain exemptions (educational institutions, church property, and so on. For some of these, the province makes grants to municipalities instead.) The procedure is generally to assign each taxable property an *assessed value*, which was originally intended to be an estimate of its market value, and then to place a tax rate on the community's total assessed value that yields enough revenue to cover expenditures on local services. Because properties are *reassessed* much less frequently than market values change, and since market values are usually estimated by crude rules of thumb, certain inequities arise. For example, one person's house may be assessed at almost 100 percent of its true market value while another's may be assessed at little more than 50 percent of its value.

The property tax is among the most controversial in the entire tax system. Some economists view it as a tax on one particular type of wealth—real estate. In this view, since families with higher incomes generally own much more real estate than do families with low incomes, the property tax is *progressive* relative to income; that is, the ratio of property tax to income rises as we move up the income scale. However, other economists view the property tax as an excise tax on rents; and since expenditures on rent generally account for a larger fraction of the incomes of the poor than of the rich, this makes it seem *regressive* relative to income.

There is also political controversy over the property tax. Municipal property-tax revenues and provincial grants have been the traditional source of financing for public schools. As a result, wealthy communities with a lot of expensive real estate have been able to afford higher-quality schools than have poor communities. The reason is made clear with a simple arithmetical example. Suppose that real estate holdings in a wealthy municipality average $100,000 per family, while in a poor municipality real estate holdings average only $40,000 per family. If both municipalities levy a 2 percent property tax to pay for their schools, the wealthy municipality will generate $2000 per family in tax receipts, while the poor one will generate only $800.

Payroll Taxes and Social Benefits

There are two important payroll taxes in Canada: contributions to the Canada (or Quebec) Pension Plan, and contributions to the unemployment insurance program. The unemployment insurance account typically runs a surplus during years of reasonable economic growth, and it runs a deficit during years of recession. The recession during the early 1980s was so severe and protracted that the government made some changes in the regulations concerning contributions (payroll taxes on both employers and employees), and benefits to the unemployed. The government considers that these changes are necessary, since any deficit that occurs in the unemployment insurance fund must be covered by general federal government revenues, and the government wants to reduce its general deficit.

The other major payroll tax—employer and employee contributions to the Canada Pension Plan—is paid into another fund. This fund does not operate exactly like the trust funds involved in most private pension plans. In the private plans, you pay in money while you are working, it accumulates at compound interest, and then you withdraw it bit by bit in your retirement years. The solvency of such a plan is never in doubt, since it never involves a commitment to pay out more to the individual than he or she has put in, plus the accumulated interest.

However, with the Canada Pension Plan, people who are now retired are receiving funds from the contributions of those that are presently working. So the solvency of the system depends on changes in the patterns of economic and population growth. The proportion of the Canadian population that is over 65 years of age has risen from 6½ percent in the 1940s, to 9½ percent in the 1980s. This proportion will rise to over 11 percent in the 1990s. Unless economic growth occurs at a rapid rate, payroll taxes will need to be raised, or pension levels will need to be cut, if the Canada Pension Plan is to remain solvent. This is *not* an immediate problem, since the surplus in the pension plan account is still increasing, as the interest earned on the loans to provincial governments compounds. However, few economists expect sufficient economic growth to counteract the underlying demographic trends.

The other federal government programs for retirement are the Old Age Security and Guaranteed Income Supplement schemes. These are not financed by payroll-tax contributions to trust funds, but are paid for out of the federal government's current general revenues. There are some provincially levied payroll taxes: Workers Compensation in all provinces, and health-insurance premiums in Ontario, British Columbia and Alberta.

Fiscal Federalism

Figure 33–4 pointed out that grants from the federal government are a major source of revenue to provincial and municipal governments. In addition, grants from the provinces are vital to municipal governments. This system of transfers from one level of government to the next is referred to as **fiscal federalism**, and has a long history.

> **Fiscal federalism** refers to the system of transfer payments from one level of government to the next.

Under the British North America Act, most of the areas for which government programs have been demanded are the jurisdiction of the junior levels of government. Health care, education, and welfare programs are the most notable. As a result, the junior-level governments have faced an on-going squeeze between the growth in their expenditure requirements and available revenues. The federal government has relieved this squeeze in several ways: by reducing federal government income-tax rates (to "make room" for provincial tax-rate increases), by making transfer payments to the provincial governments, and by directly undertaking income-security programs (such as the Canada Pension Plan and the unemployment insurance program).

While the provinces have welcomed these revenues, they have often resented the loss of provincial discretion that is involved. Before 1977, there was a complicated set of transfer payments called **conditional grants**. Under these schemes, the federal government matched provincial government spending, according to various formulae, *if* the provinces spent their money in specified ways. The provinces often argued that the funds should have "no strings attached." The federal government discontinued conditional grants, because it disliked the fact that these grants gave the provinces the power to decide how large the grants were. The provinces received more **unconditional grants**, and an increased share of the personal income tax in return.

As the name implies, unconditional grants involve transfers from the federal government to the provinces, with "no strings attached." The grants are paid out of general federal revenues, and most grants only go to provinces that would have to levy very high tax rates in order to raise per capita revenues equal to the national average. Many different taxes are involved in these schemes, and the arrangements are revised every few years. The negotiations associated with revising these "equalization payments" are often the major source of dispute at federal–provincial conferences.

The Concept of Equity in Taxation

Taxes are judged on two criteria: *equity* (Is the tax fair?) and *efficiency* (Does the tax interfere unduly with the workings of the market economy?). It is curious that economists have been mostly concerned with the latter, while public discussions about tax proposals almost always focus on the former. Let us, therefore, begin our discussion by investigating the concept of equitable taxation.

Horizontal Equity

Horizontal equity is the notion that equally situated individuals should be taxed equally.

There are three distinct concepts of tax equity. The first is **horizontal equity**, which simply asserts that equally situated individuals should be taxed equally. Stated in this way, there are few who would quarrel with the principle. But it is often quite difficult to apply in practice, and violations of horizontal equity can be found throughout the tax act.

Consider, for example, the personal income tax. Horizontal equity calls for two families with the same income to pay the same tax. But what if one family has eight children and the other has one child? Well, you answer, we must define "equally situated" to include equal family sizes, so only families with the same number of children can be compared on grounds of horizontal equity. But what if one family has unusually high medical expenses, while the other has none? Are they still "equally situated"? By now the point should be clear: Determining when two families are "equally situated" is no simple task. In fact, the Canadian tax provisions involve many requirements that must be met before two families are construed to be "equal."

Vertical Equity

Vertical equity is the notion that differently situated individuals should be taxed differently in a way that society deems to be fair.

The **ability-to-pay principle** is the idea that people with greater ability to pay taxes should pay higher taxes.

The second concept of fair taxation seems to flow naturally from the first. If equals are to be treated equally, it appears that unequals should be treated unequally. This precept is known as **vertical equity**.

Just saying this, of course, does not get us very far. For the most part, vertical equity has been translated into the **ability-to-pay principle**, according to which those most able to pay should pay the highest taxes. But this still leaves a definitional problem similar to the problem of defining "equally situated": How do we measure ability to pay? The nature of each tax often provides a straightforward answer. In income taxation, we measure ability to pay by income; in property taxation, we measure it by property value; and so on.

A thornier problem arises when we try to translate the notion into concrete terms. Consider the three alternative income-tax plans listed in Table 33–3. Under

Table 33-3

THREE ALTERNATIVE INCOME-TAX PLANS

	TAX PAYMENTS (dollars)			AVERAGE TAX RATES (percent)		
INCOME	PLAN 1	PLAN 2	PLAN 3	PLAN 1	PLAN 2	PLAN 3
1,000	100	100	100	10	10	10
10,000	2,000	1,000	500	20	10	5
100,000	40,000	10,000	2,500	40	10	2½

all three plans, families with higher incomes pay higher income taxes. So all three plans could be said to operate on the ability-to-pay concept of vertical equity. Yet the three are quite different in their distributive consequences. Plan 1 is a progressive tax, something like the individual income tax in Canada: The average tax rate is higher for richer families. Plan 2 is a proportional tax: Every family pays 10 percent of its income. Plan 3 is quite regressive: Since tax payments rise more slowly than income, the tax rate for richer families is lower than that for poor families.

Which plan comes closest to the ideal notion of vertical equity? Many people find that Plan 3 offends their sense of "fairness," but there is much less agreement over the relative merits of Plan 1 (progressive taxation) and Plan 2 (proportional taxation). Very often, in fact, the notion of vertical equity is taken to be synonymous with progressivity. Other things being equal, progressive taxes are seen as "good" taxes in some ethical sense while regressive taxes are seen as "bad." On these grounds, advocates of greater equality of incomes support progressive income taxes and oppose sales taxes.

The Benefits Principle

Whereas the principles of horizontal and vertical equity, for all their ambiguities and practical problems, at least do not conflict with one another, the third principle of fair taxation may often violate commonly accepted notions of vertical equity. According to the **benefits principle of taxation**, which is often applied when the proceeds from certain taxes are earmarked for specific public services, those who reap the benefits from government services should pay the taxes.

One clear example is admission fees to national parks. Most people seem to find the use of the benefits principle in such cases fair. But in other contexts— such as public schools, hospitals, and libraries—the body politic has been loathe to apply the benefits principle because it clashes so dramatically with common notions of fairness. So these services are normally financed out of general tax revenues rather than by direct charges for their use.

> The **benefits principle of taxation** holds that people who derive the benefits from the service should pay the taxes that finance it.

The Concept of Efficiency in Taxation

The concept of economic *efficiency* is the central notion of Parts Four through Six of this book. The economy is said to be *efficient* if it has used every available opportunity to make someone better off without making someone else worse off. In this sense, taxes almost always introduce *inefficiencies*. That is, if the tax were removed, some people could be made better off without anyone being harmed.

However, a comparison of a world with taxes to a world without taxes is not terribly pertinent. The government does, after all, need to raise revenues to pay for the goods and services it provides. For this reason, when economists discuss notions of "efficient" taxation, they are usually looking for the taxes that cause the *least* amount of inefficiency.

To explain the concept of efficient taxation, we need to introduce one new term. Economists define the **burden of a tax** as the amount of money the

> The **burden of a tax** to an individual is the amount of money he would have to be given to make him just as well off with the tax as he was without it.

taxpayer would have to be given to make him just as well off in the presence of the tax as he is in its absence. An example will clarify this notion and also make clear why *the burden of a tax normally exceeds the revenues raised by the tax.*

Suppose the government, in the interest of energy conservation, levies a high tax on the biggest gas-guzzling cars, with progressively lower taxes on smaller cars.[3] For example, a simple tax schedule might be the following:

CAR TYPE	TAX
Cadillac	$1000
Dodge	$ 500
Escort	0

Harry has a taste for big cars, and has always bought Cadillacs. (Harry is clearly no pauper.) Once the new tax takes effect, he has three options. He can still buy a Cadillac and pay $1000 in tax, he can switch to a Dodge and avoid half the tax, or he can switch to an Escort and avoid the entire tax.

If Harry chooses the first option, we have a case in which the burden of the tax is exactly equal to the amount of tax the person pays. Why? Because if Harry's rich uncle gives him $1000, Harry winds up exactly as well off as he was before the tax was enacted. In general:

When a tax induces no change in economic behaviour, the burden of the tax can be measured accurately by the revenue collected.

However, this is not what we normally expect to happen. And it is certainly not what the government intends by levying a tax on big cars. Normally, we expect taxes to induce some people to alter their behaviour in ways that reduce or avoid tax payments. So let us look into Harry's other two options.

If he decides to purchase a Dodge, Harry pays only $500 in tax. But this is an inadequate measure of the burden of the new tax because Harry is greatly chagrined by the fact that he no longer drives a Cadillac. How much money would it take to make Harry just as well off as he was before the tax? Only Harry knows for sure. But we do know that it is more than the $500 tax that he pays. Why? Because, even if someone were to give Harry the $500 needed to pay his tax bill, he would still be less happy than he was before the tax was introduced, owing to his switch from a Cadillac to a Dodge. Whatever the (unknown) burden of the tax is, the amount by which it exceeds the $500 tax bill is called the **excess burden** of the tax.

> The **excess burden** of a tax to an individual is the amount by which the burden of the tax exceeds the tax that is paid.

Harry's final option makes the importance of understanding excess burden even more clear. If he switches to buying an Escort, Harry will pay no tax. Are we therefore to say he has suffered no burden? Clearly not, for he longs for the Cadillac that he no longer has. The general principle is:

Whenever a tax induces people to change their behaviour—that is, whenever it "distorts" their choices—the tax has an excess burden. This means that the revenue collected by the tax systematically understates the true burden of the tax.

The excess burdens that arise from tax-induced changes in economic behaviour are precisely the inefficiencies we referred to at the outset of this discussion. And the basic precept of efficient taxation is to try to devise a tax system that minimizes these inefficiencies. In particular:

In comparing two taxes that raise the same total revenue, the one that produces less excess burden is the more efficient.

[3]Some provinces differentiate automobile licence fees in this way.

Notice the proviso that the two taxes being compared must yield the *same* revenue. We are really interested in the *total* burden of each tax. Since:

Total burden = Tax collections + Excess burden,

only when tax collections are equal can we unambiguously state that the tax with less *excess* burden is more efficient. Since excess burdens arise when consumers and firms alter their behaviour on account of taxation, this precept of sound tax policy can be restated in the following way:

In devising a tax system to raise revenue, try to raise any given amount of revenue through taxes that induce the smallest changes in behaviour.[4]

Shifting the Burden of Taxation: Tax Incidence

When economists speak of the **incidence of a tax**, they are referring to who actually bears the burden of the tax. In discussing the tax on gas-guzzling autos, we have adhered, so far, to what has been called the **flypaper theory of tax incidence**: that the burden of any tax sticks where the government puts it. In this case, the theory holds that the burden stays on Harry. But often things do not work out this way.

The **incidence of a tax** is an allocation of the burden of the tax to specific individuals or groups.

Consider, for example, what will happen if the government levies a $1000 tax on luxury cars like Cadillacs. Figure 33–5 shows this tax as a $1000 vertical shift of the supply curve. If the demand curve does not shift, the market equilibrium moves from point *A* to point *B*. The quantity of luxury cars declines as Harrys all over Canada react to the higher price by buying fewer luxury cars. Notice that the price rises from $18,000 to $18,500, an increase of $500. So people who continue buying luxury cars bear a burden of only $500—just half the tax that they pay!

Does this mean that the tax imposes a *negative* excess burden? Certainly not. What it means is that consumers who refrain from buying the taxed commodity have managed to *shift* part of the burden of the tax away from consumers as a whole, including those who continue to buy luxury cars. Who are the victims of this **tax shifting**? In our example, there are two main candidates. First are the

Tax shifting occurs when the economic reactions to a tax cause prices and outputs in the economy to change, thereby shifting part of the burden of the tax onto others.

[4]Sometimes a tax is levied not primarily as a revenue-raiser, but as a way of inducing individuals or firms to alter their behaviour. This possibility will be discussed in a later section.

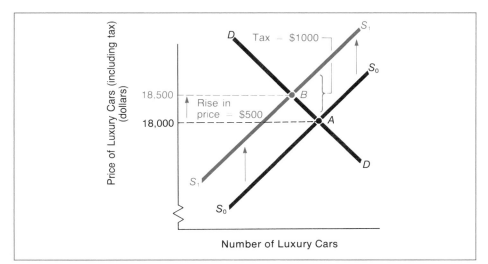

Figure 33–5
THE INCIDENCE OF AN EXCISE TAX
When the government imposes a $1000 tax on luxury cars, the supply curve relating quantity supplied to the price *inclusive of tax* shifts upward from $S_0 S_0$ to $S_1 S_1$. The equilibrium price in this example rises from $18,000 to $18,500, so the burden of the tax is shared equally between car sellers (who receive $500 less) and car buyers (who pay $500 more, including the tax). In general, how the burden is shared depends on the elasticities of demand and supply.

automakers, or, more precisely, their shareholders. Shareholders bear the burden to the extent that the tax, by reducing auto sales, cuts into their profits. The other principal candidates are auto workers. To the extent their reduced production leads to layoffs, or to lower wages, the automobile workers bear part of the burden of the tax.

People who have never studied economics almost always believe in the flypaper theory of tax incidence, which holds that sales taxes are borne by consumers, property taxes are borne by homeowners, and taxes on corporations are borne by shareholders. Perhaps the most important lesson of this chapter is that:

The flypaper theory of tax incidence is often wrong.

Failure to grasp this basic point has led to all sorts of misguided tax legislation in which governments, *thinking* they were placing a tax burden on one group of people, inadvertently placed it squarely on another. Of course, there are cases where the flypaper theory of tax incidence comes very close to being correct. So let us consider some specific examples of tax incidence.

The Incidence of Excise Taxes

Excise taxes have already been covered by our automobile example, because Figure 33-5 could represent any commodity that is taxed.[5] The basic finding is that *part* of the burden will fall on consumers of the taxed commodity (including those who stop buying it because of the tax), and part will be shifted to the firms and the workers who produce the commodity.

The amount that is shifted depends on the slopes of the demand and supply curves. We can understand intuitively how this works. If consumers are very loyal to the taxed commodity, so that they will continue to buy almost the same quantity no matter what the price, then it is clear that they will be stuck with most of the tax bill because they have left themselves vulnerable to it. Thus, we would expect that:

The more inelastic the demand for the product, the larger is the share of the tax that consumers will pay.

Similarly, if suppliers are determined to supply the same amount of the product no matter how low the price, then most of the tax will be borne by suppliers. That is:

The more inelastic the supply curve, the larger is the share of the tax that suppliers will pay.

One extreme case arises if no one stops buying luxury cars when their prices rise. The demand curve becomes vertical, like the demand curve *DD* in Figure 33-6. Then there can be no tax shifting. The price of a luxury car (inclusive of tax) rises by the full amount of the tax—from $18,000 to $19,000. So consumers bear the entire burden.

The other extreme case arises when the supply curve is totally inelastic (see Figure 33-7). Since the number of luxury cars supplied is the same at any price, the supply curve will not shift when a tax is imposed. Consequently, automakers must bear the full burden of any tax that is placed on their product. Figure 33-7 shows that the tax does not change the market price (including tax), which, of course, means that the price received by sellers must fall by the full amount of the tax.

[5]Although we did not use the term "incidence," excise taxes were analysed in detail in Chapter 21. If you need a review, see pages 401–404.

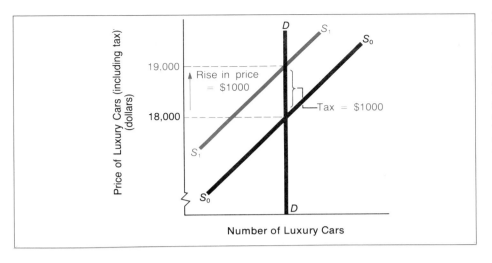

Figure 33-6

AN EXTREME CASE OF TAX INCIDENCE

If the quantity demanded is totally insensitive to price (completely *inelastic*), then the demand curve will be vertical. As the diagram shows, the price inclusive of tax rises to $19,000, so buyers bear the entire burden. Since price exclusive of tax remains at $18,000, none of the burden falls on the sellers.

Demand and supply schedules for most goods and services are not as extreme as those depicted in Figures 33-6 and 33-7, so the burden is shared. Precisely how it is shared depends on the elasticities of the supply and demand curves.

The Incidence of the Payroll Tax

The payroll tax may be thought of as an excise tax on the employment of labour. As we mentioned earlier, the Canadian payroll tax comes in two parts: Some of it is levied on the employees (payroll deductions) and the rest on employers. A fundamental point, which people who have never studied economics often fail to grasp, is that:

The incidence of a payroll tax is the same whether it is levied on employers or employees.

A simple numerical example can illustrate why this is so. Consider an employee earning $100 a day with a 14 percent payroll tax that is "shared" equally between the employer and the employee. How much does it cost the firm to hire

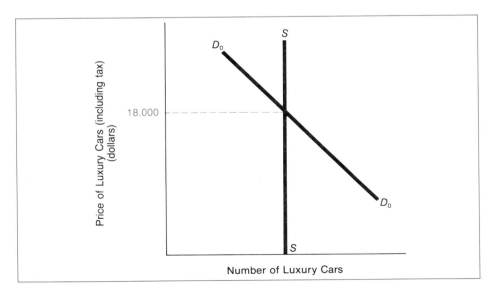

Figure 33-7

ANOTHER EXTREME CASE OF TAX INCIDENCE

If the quantity supplied is totally insensitive to price, then the supply curve *SS* will be vertical and will not shift when a tax is imposed. The seller will bear the entire burden, because the price that he receives ($17,000) will fall by the full amount of the tax.

this worker? It costs $100 in wages paid to the worker plus $7 in taxes paid to the government, for a total of $107 a day. How much does the worker receive? He gets $100 in wages paid by the employer less $7 deducted and sent to the government, or $93 a day. The difference between wages paid and wages received is $107 - $93 = $14.

Now suppose the government tries to "shift" the burden of the tax entirely onto firms, by raising the employer's tax to $14 while lowering the employee's tax to zero. At first, the daily wage is fixed at $100, so firms' total labour costs (including tax) rise to $114 per day and workers' net incomes rise to $100 per day. The government seems to have achieved its goal.

But this is not an equilibrium situation. With the daily wage at $114 for firms and $100 for workers, the quantity of labour *demanded* by firms will be *less* and the quantity of labour *supplied* by the workers will be *more* than when the two wages were $107 and $93. There will, therefore, be a *surplus of labour* on the market (an excess of quantity supplied over quantity demanded), and this surplus will put downward pressure on wages.

How far will wages have to fall? It is easy to see that a wage of $93 will restore equilibrium. If the daily wage is $93, labour will cost firms $107 per day, just as it did before the tax change. So firms will demand the same quantity as they did when the payroll tax was shared. Similarly, workers will receive the same $93 net wage as they did previously; so quantity supplied will be the same as it was before the tax change. Thus, in the end, the market will completely frustrate the intent of the government.

The payroll tax is an excellent example of a case in which the government, misled by the flypaper theory of tax incidence, thinks it is "taxing firms" when it raises the employer's share and that it is "taxing workers" when it raises the employee's share. In truth, who is really paying depends on the incidence of the tax. But no difference results from a change in the employee's and the employer's shares.

Who, then, really bears the burden of the payroll tax? Like any excise tax, the incidence of the payroll tax depends on the elasticities of the supply and demand schedules. In the case of labour supply, there is a large body of empirical evidence pointing to the conclusion that the quantity of labour supplied is not very responsive to price for most population groups. The supply curve is almost vertical, like that shown in Figure 33–7. The result is that workers as a group are able to shift very little of the burden of the payroll tax.

But employers *can* shift it in most cases. Firms view their share of the payroll tax as an additional cost of using labour. So when payroll taxes go up, firms try to substitute cheaper factors of production (capital) for labour wherever they can. This reduces the quantity of labour demanded, lowering the wage received by workers. And this is how market forces shift part of the tax burden from firms to workers.

To the extent that the supply curve of labour has some positive slope, the quantity of labour supplied will fall when the wage goes down, and in this way workers can shift some of the burden back onto firms. But the firms, in turn, can shift that burden onto consumers by raising their prices. As we know from Part Five, prices in competitive markets generally rise when costs (like labour costs) increase. It is doubtful, therefore, that firms bear any of the burden of the payroll tax. Here, the flypaper theory of tax incidence could not be further from the truth. Even though the tax is collected by the firm, it is really borne by workers and consumers.

The Incidence of the Tax on Capital

The corporate profit tax is difficult to analyse since it is partly a tax on pure economic profit and partly an excise tax on the employment of capital equipment.

Also, as we noted in Chapter 11 (page 217), the Canadian profits tax can have no effect on profits or the earnings of capital when it is levied on multinationals that receive a tax credit in their home country equal to the taxes paid in Canada. In the case of the multinationals, the burden of any unsheltered Canadian profits tax is squarely on the government (and therefore on the citizens) of the foreign country where the company is based. Our corporate tax simply lowers the tax revenue of the company's home country, dollar for dollar, as long as the company does not avoid paying the taxes to both governments. Large corporations can avoid paying taxes by transferring portions of profits out of both Canada and the United States (which is usually the relevant home country) to affiliates in third countries where corporate tax rates are low.

Even for purely domestic firms that cannot escape taxes in this way, the flypaper theory of tax incidence is again far from the truth.

In the case of domestic firms, much about the incidence of the profits tax can be learned by treating it as a tax on the earnings of capital. The supply of capital to the Canadian economy is very elastic. If Canadian owners of capital cannot obtain an after-tax return in Canada equal to what is available elsewhere, they will invest elsewhere. Capital is far more mobile internationally than is labour, and for a country as small as Canada, the minimum acceptable rate of return for capital is determined from outside. Thus, we investigate the incidence of the tax on capital on the assumption that the supply is perfectly elastic, as shown in Figure 33–8.

Before the domestic tax is imposed, the supply of capital is perfectly elastic at a 10 percent rate of return (the return that we assume for this discussion is available in the rest of the world). Equilibrium in the capital market is initially at point A. If a 50 percent tax is imposed in Canada, capital owners require a 20 percent before-tax return to continue to employ their capital in Canada. Thus, the supply curve shifts upward from S_0S_0 to S_1S_1, and the equilibrium position after the tax is levied is given by point B. Since the before-tax rate of return rises by the full amount of the tax, the owners of capital completely escape the tax. The burden falls entirely on consumers and on the labour employed by the firms.

The conclusion is that it is difficult to impose a tax that sticks on the owners of capital.

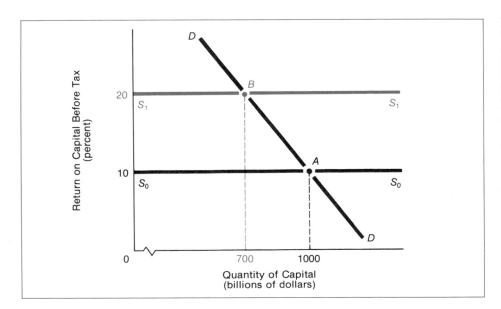

Figure 33–8
THE INCIDENCE OF A TAX ON MOBILE CAPITAL
Before the domestic tax is imposed, the supply of capital is perfectly elastic at a 10 percent rate of return, the assumed return that is available in the rest of the world. If a 50 percent tax is imposed in Canada, capital owners require a 20 percent return before tax, so the supply curve shifts from S_0S_0 to S_1S_1, and the owners of capital bear none of the tax.

When Taxation Can Improve Efficiency

We have spent much of this chapter discussing the kinds of inefficiencies and excess burdens that arise from taxation. But, before we finish this discussion, two things must be pointed out.

First, economic efficiency is not society's only goal. For example, the tax on gas-guzzling cars causes inefficiencies if it changes people's behaviour patterns. But this, presumably, was exactly what the government sought to accomplish. The government wanted to reduce the number of big cars on the road to conserve energy, and it was willing to tolerate some economic inefficiency to accomplish this end. We can, of course, argue whether this was a good idea—whether the conservation achieved was worth the efficiency loss. But the general point is that:

Some taxes are a good idea even though they introduce economic inefficiencies, because they help achieve some other goal.

A second, and more fundamental, point is that:

Some taxes that change economic behaviour may lead to efficiency *gains* rather than to efficiency *losses*.

As you might guess, this can happen only when there is an inefficiency in the system prior to the tax. Then an appropriate tax may help set things right. A very clear-cut example of this will occupy much of the next chapter. There we will see that because firms and individuals who despoil clean air and clean water often do so without paying any price, these precious resources are used inefficiently. A corrective tax on pollution can remedy this problem.

Equity, Efficiency, and the Optimal Tax

In a perfect world, the ideal tax would reflect society's views on equity in taxation, and it would induce no changes in economic behaviour and so would have no excess burden. Unfortunately, there is no such tax.

Sometimes, in fact, the taxes with the smallest excess burdens are the most regressive. For instance, a head tax, which charges every person the same number of dollars, is very regressive. But it is also quite efficient. Since there is no change in economic behaviour that will enable anyone to avoid it, there is no reason for anyone to change his or her behaviour. As we have noted, the regressive payroll tax also seems to have small excess burdens.

Fortunately, however, there is a tax that, while not ideal, still scores very high on both the equity and efficiency criteria: a comprehensive personal income tax.

While it is true that income taxes can be avoided by earning less income, we have already observed that in reality the supply of labour is changed little by taxation. Investing in relatively safe assets (like government bonds) rather than risky ones (like common stocks) is another possible reaction that would reduce tax bills, since less risky assets pay lower rates of return. But it is not clear that the income tax actually induces such behaviour because, while it taxes away some of the profits when investments turn out well, it also offers a tax deduction when investments turn sour. Finally, because an income tax reduces the return on saving, many economists have worried that it would discourage saving, and thus retard economic growth. This is the reason that many tax analysts in Canada favour schemes such as extending the limits for tax-deductible contributions to registered retirement savings plans. However, the empirical evidence does not suggest that the amount of saving is affected to any great extent by such changes.

On balance then, while there are still unresolved questions and research is continuing:

Possible Tax Reforms

A Simplified Income Tax?

As the personal income tax has become more complex, dissatisfaction with both the equity and the efficiency aspects of the tax has grown.

Critics cite at least three major problems: (1) rates are too high; (2) there are numerous tax shelters that enable much income to escape taxation; and (3) the tax law is complex, and preparing a tax return can be a major burden. These problems have attracted a number of politicians and economists to the idea of a "flat tax."

Under a pure flat tax, there are no deductions or tax preferences. Families simply pay tax—at a low flat rate like 20 percent—on all income above a certain exempt amount. With the tax rate low, and equal on all types of income, most of the efficiency problems mentioned in the text would disappear. Further, our tax return could be limited to a single page, so the flat tax is an attractive idea.

There is, however, at least one *severe* problem: It is hard to make a flat tax as progressive as our current tax system. While the progressivity of a flat tax can be increased by raising the exemption, this necessitates a higher tax rate (to make up for the lost revenue). And no flat tax places as heavy a burden on the richest families as does the present system. Most specific proposals along these lines have involved significant tax *increases* for those earning between $5000 and $15,000, and tax *reductions* for those earning in excess of $50,000.

As a result, most economists believe that a tax system with many fewer shelters (though not zero) and fewer bracket rates (though not just one) than we have now is what is required. Whether we will get such a tax remains to be seen.

A Move Toward the Benefits Principle?

Immediately following its election in 1984, the government of Prime Minister Brian Mulroney commenced a review of Canada's social assistance programs, to see whether the principle of universal access should be reconsidered. All but our public health-care programs are being examined, to see whether access should be restricted. The universality of health care is to remain a "sacred trust" (as were all programs, according to election campaign remarks).

The government's indecision in this area illustrates the fundamental trade-off between equity and efficiency. Even for health care, a strong case can be made on efficiency grounds for an increased use of the benefits principle. To an economist, the dramatic increase in health-care costs that we have observed is a predictable result of there being no service charge involved in the public health-care program.

The key feature of our current programs is that the *private marginal* cost of medical care is *zero* for *all* users, while the *true social* marginal cost is high. As a result, there is no mechanism to encourage people to economize on the use of medical services, and therefore no mechanism to induce doctors to consider more cost-effective techniques. Some sort of user charge (that is, application of the benefit principle of taxation) is necessary if the runaway increase in medical costs is to be controlled without a deterioration in service.

To protect the poor, the government would still have to pay the user charges for those with insufficient income. It seems that many people find it objectionable to have free medical care available only for those on lower income. They feel it should be a "right" for everyone, so that those on lower incomes should not face a demoralizing means-test, just to have basic health. The sad truth, however, is that *noticeable inefficiency* costs appear to be necessary to maintain this *equity* principle. Economists *cannot* say whether we should pay these costs, but it *is* their job to ensure that policy-makers and voters are informed about the terms of the equity–efficiency trade-off.

Most of the studies that have been conducted to date suggest that a comprehensive personal income tax with no unintended tax shelters induces few of the behavioural reactions that would reduce consumer well-being, and thus has a rather small excess burden.

On the equity criterion, we know that personal income taxes can be made as progressive as society deems desirable, though if marginal tax rates on rich people get extremely high, some of the potential efficiency losses might get more serious than they now seem to be. On both grounds, then, many economists—including both liberals and conservatives—view a comprehensive personal income tax as one of the best ways for a government to raise revenue.

The Real Versus the Ideal

That seems to be a cheerful conclusion, because the personal income tax is the biggest tax in the Canadian revenue system. Unfortunately, however, our actual tax system does not much resemble an ideal, comprehensive income tax. In this chapter, we have mentioned just a few tax shelters (pages 644–45), but there are so many that legal tax avoidance has become a major industry.

We have already noted that shelters make the income tax much less progressive than it seems to be. But they also make it far less efficient than it could be. The reason follows directly from our analysis of the incidence of taxation.

When different income-earning activities are taxed at different marginal rates, economic choices are distorted by tax considerations; and this impairs economic efficiency.

Our present tax system encourages people to devote more time and energy to lightly taxed sources of income (like capital gains and tax shelters) and less to heavily taxed activities (like earning wages). Consequently, economic activity is distorted in many ways. The result is that the personal income tax, which could *in principle* raise a lot of revenue with very little excess burden, *in fact* imposes large excess burdens on society. As a result, there are always proposals for tax reform being debated, as the boxed insert on the preceding page indicates.

Summary

1. Spending patterns differ across the various levels of government. The federal government spends money on income-security programs and such items as resources and communication. Provincial and municipal governments spend more on education, health, and public welfare.

2. Taxes in Canada are lower than they are in Sweden and the Netherlands, but they are higher than the taxes levied in most other industrial countries. While federal taxes as a percentage of gross national product have been quite constant over the last 30 years, provincial and municipal taxes have increased substantially.

3. The federal government raises most of its revenue by direct taxes, such as the personal and corporate income taxes and payroll taxes.

4. While the personal income tax is not as progressive as its might be because of its many tax shelters, it undoubtedly is a progressive tax. Many other taxes, by contrast, are regressive.

5. Provincial and municipal governments rely more on indirect taxes. Municipalities are dependent upon property taxes.

6. There is controversy over whether the property tax is progressive or regressive, and over whether local property taxes are an equitable way to finance public education.

7. In our multilevel system of government, the federal government makes grants to provincial governments, and provinces in turn make grants to municipalities. This system of intergovernmental transfers is called fiscal federalism.

8. There are three concepts of fair or "equitable" taxation that occasionally conflict. Horizontal equity simply calls for equals to be treated equally. Vertical equity, which calls for unequals to be treated unequally, has often been translated into the ability-to-pay principle—that people who are more able to pay taxes should be taxed more heavily. The benefits principle of tax equity ignores ability to pay and seeks to tax people according to the benefits they receive.

9. The burden of a tax is the amount of money an individual would have to be given to make her as well-off with the tax as she was without it. This burden normally exceeds the taxes that are paid, and

the difference between the two is called the excess burden of the tax.

10. Excess burden arises when a tax induces some people or firms to change their behaviour. Excess burdens represent economic inefficiencies, so the basic principle of efficient taxation is to utilize taxes that have small excess burdens.

11. When people change their behaviour on account of a tax, they often shift the burden of the tax onto someone else. This is why the "flypaper theory of tax incidence"—the belief that the burden of any tax always stays where government puts it—is often incorrect.

12. The burden of sales or excise tax normally is shared between the suppliers and the consumers. The manner in which it is shared depends on the elasticities of supply and demand.

13. A payroll tax is like an excise tax on labour services. Since the supply of labour is much less elastic than the demand for labour, workers bear most of the burden of the payroll tax. This includes both the employer's and the employee's share of the tax.

14. The corporate profits tax can be treated like an excise tax on capital's services. Since the supply of capital is much more elastic than the demand for capital, buyers of the products produced by capital bear most of the burden of the tax.

15. Sometimes, "inefficient" taxes—that is, taxes that cause a good deal of excess burden—are none the less desirable because the changes in behaviour they induce further some other social goal.

16. When there are inefficiencies in the system for reasons other than the tax system (for example, externalities), taxation can conceivably improve efficiency.

17. When both equity and efficiency are considered, many economists feel that a personal income tax is one of the best ways to raise revenue.

18. Unfortunately, the actual personal income tax in Canada falls short of the ideal. Scores of tax shelters lessen both equity and efficiency aspects of the tax.

Concepts for Review

Progressive, proportional, and regressive taxes	Average and marginal tax rates	Benefits principle of taxation
Corporate profits tax	Tax shelters	Burden of a tax
Excise tax	Capital gain	Excess burden
Direct and indirect taxes	Property tax	Incidence of a tax
Personal income tax	Fiscal federalism	Flypaper theory of tax incidence
Payroll tax	Horizontal and vertical equity	Tax shifting
	Ability-to-pay principle	

Questions for Discussion

1. "If the federal government continues to raise taxes as it has been doing, it will ruin the country." Comment.

2. Why have provincial and municipal taxes been increasing so much faster than federal taxes? Is this trend likely to continue?

3. Using the adjacent hypothetical income-tax table, compute the marginal and average tax rates. Is the tax progressive, proportional, or regressive?

INCOME (dollars)	TAX (dollars)
2000	300
4000	360
6000	450
8000	480

4. Which concept of tax equity, if any, seems to be served by each of the following:
   a. The progressive income tax.
   b. The federal tax on gasoline.
   c. The property tax.

5. Think of some tax that you personally pay. What steps have you taken or could you take to reduce your tax payments? Is there an excess burden on you? Why or why not?

6. Suppose the supply and demand schedules for cigarettes are as follows:

PRICE PER CARTON (dollars)	QUANTITY DEMANDED (millions of cartons per year)	QUANTITY SUPPLIED (millions of cartons per year)
3.00	360	160
3.25	330	180
3.50	300	200
3.75	270	220
4.00	240	240
4.25	210	260
4.50	180	280
4.75	150	300
5.00	120	320

   a. What is the equilibrium price and equilibrium quantity?

b. Now the government levies a $1.25 per carton excise tax on cigarettes. What is the equilibrium price paid by consumers, price received by producers, and quantity now?

c. Explain why it makes no difference whether the government levies the $1.25 tax on the consumer or the producer. (Relate your answer to the discussion of the payroll tax on page 647 of the text.)

d. Suppose the tax is levied on the producers. How much of the tax are producers able to shift onto consumers? Explain how they manage to do this.

e. Will there be any excess burden from this tax? Why? Who bears this excess burden?

f. By how much has cigarette consumption declined on account of the tax? Why might the government be happy about this outcome, despite the excess burden?

7. The country of Taxmania produces only two commodities: bread and mink coats. The poor spend all their income on bread, while the rich purchase both goods. Both demand for and supply of bread are quite inelastic. In the mink coat market, both supply and demand are quite elastic. Which good would be heavily taxed if Taxmanians cared most about efficiency? What if they cared most about vertical equity?

The Economics of Environmental Protection

34

Everything's a trade-off. If
you want a high standard
of living, you have to settle
for a low quality of life.

Overheard conversation reported
at a meeting of the
American Philosophical Society

We learned in Chapter 29 that *externalities* (or the incidental benefits or damages imposed upon people not directly involved in an economic activity) can cause the market mechanism to malfunction. This chapter takes up a particularly important application of the analysis of externalities—the problem of environmental deterioration.

Environmental problems are by no means new. What *is* new and different is the amount of attention the community is now prepared to give them. Perhaps much of this increased interest can be attributed to rising incomes, which have freed people from the more urgent concerns about food, clothing, and shelter, and thus have allowed them the luxury of concentrating on the next level of needs— the *quality* of their lives.

Economic thought on the environment preceded the outburst of public concern with the subject by nearly half a century. In 1911, a noted British economist, A. C. Pigou, wrote a remarkable book called *The Economics of Welfare*, which offered an explanation of the market economy's poor environmental performance that is still generally accepted by economists today. What is more, that same book outlined an approach to environmental policy that is still favoured by most economists and that is beginning to win over lawmakers and bureaucrats as well. Pigou's analysis of how the tax system can be used to protect the environment will be explained here in some detail. In particular, we will learn that a system of charges on emissions may be an effective and efficient means of controlling pollution. In this way, the price mechanism can remedy one of its own shortcomings.

How *Not* to Clean Up a River

The most common method for controlling water pollution in Canada is for the provincial governments to issue specific discharge limits for each individual firm. This same approach is used in the United States, and a study of the clean-up of the Delaware River illustrates both the nature of this standard approach to environmental policy and some of the ways that economists believe it can be improved.[1]

---

[1] The following discussion is based primarily on Bruce A. Ackerman, Susan Rose Ackerman, James W. Sawyer, Jr., and Dale W. Henderson, *The Uncertain Search for Environmental Quality* (New York: The Free Press, 1974).

A major rehabilitation program was planned for this river, which flows through four eastern states and past a number of industrial cities. The authorities decided that the best way to improve the quality of the river was to require everyone who had been discharging pollution into it to reduce the amount of discharge (measured in terms of its expected oxygen use) by approximately the same percentage—a reduction of between 85 and 90 percent. While this approach may seem both fair and effective, it turned out to have neither of these virtues. In fact, when a team of economists assessed the cost of achieving the stated goals in this way, they estimated that the proposed technique would be between 100 and 150 percent more expensive than the use of pollution charges.[2] In addition, after the haggling and negotiations had been completed, it turned out that the required reductions in emissions were far from uniform. For example, petroleum refineries of rather similar output capacity were assigned quotas for reductions in emissions of wastes that ranged between 1300 and 6500 kilograms per day.

The analysis presented in this chapter will enable us to see why assignment of equal percentage reductions, the method often favoured by environmental authorities, is, in general, both inefficient and grossly inequitable.

The Environment in Perspective: Is Everything Getting Steadily Worse?

Much of the discussion of environmental problems in the popular press leaves the reader with the impression that matters have been growing steadily worse, and that pollution is largely a product of the profit system and modern industrialization. As we will see, there are environmental problems today that are both enormous and pressing, but in fact pollution is nothing new. Medieval cities were pestholes—the streets and rivers were littered with garbage and the air stank of rotting wastes. At the beginning of the eighteenth century, a German traveller reported that to get a view of London from the tower of St. Paul's, one had to get there very early in the morning "before the air was full of coal smoke." And early in the twentieth century the automobile was hailed as a source of major improvement in the cleanliness of city streets, which until then had fought a losing battle against the proliferation of horse dung.

Since 1960 there has been marked progress in solving a number of pollution problems, much of it the result of concerted efforts to protect the environment. The quality of the air in most Canadian cities has improved. In Toronto, for example, the concentration of suspended particulates, or soot, in the air has fallen dramatically since the Grey Cup "Smog Bowl" of 1962. On that weekend, the air pollution index rose to 155. To put this in perspective, it should be noted that the current health advisory level for the index is 32. At the level of 58, people with chronic respiratory diseases may be affected. At 100, even healthy people may be affected by prolonged conditions and those with cardiac and respiratory diseases could suffer severe effects. Depending on weather conditions, readings in excess of 50 can trigger a first alert and cause industrial operations to be curtailed. At 100, the air pollution threat is considered serious and the province can order all operations not essential to public health and safety to cease.

In 1982 in Toronto, there were only three days in which the index exceeded 32, and on none of these days did it exceed 50. Similar improvements have occurred elsewhere. In Hamilton in 1982, the air pollution index exceeded 32 only eight times, for a total of 118 hours. The index never reached 50.

Even the famous, or rather infamous, "fogs" of London are almost a thing of the past. There have been two high readings of particular note in the British capital: in

---

[2]For details see A. Kneese, S. Rolfe, and J. Harned, editors, *Managing the Environment: International Economic Cooperation for Pollution Control* (New York: Praeger Publishers, 1971), Appendix C, pages 225–74.

1959 (when the index rose to 275 and there was a 10 percent increase over the normal number of deaths) and in 1962 (when the index rose to 575 and there was a 20 percent increase in mortality). But today, London's cleaner air has resulted in an astounding 50 percent increase in the number of hours of winter sunshine. In short, pollution problems are not a uniquely modern phenomenon, nor is every part of the environment deteriorating relentlessly.

Environmental problems do not occur exclusively in capitalist economies. For example, in the People's Republic of China, coal soot from factory smokestacks in Peking envelops the city in a thick black haze reminiscent of Pittsburgh in the old days of unbridled industrial activity. And the Soviet Union has all sorts of serious environmental troubles, which it has publicized widely in its own newspapers and magazines.[3] For example, because of smoke in the air, the number of clear daylight hours is 40 percent lower in Leningrad than in Pavlovsk—a town only 32 kilometres away. The Iset and the Volga rivers are so filled with chemicals that they have actually caught fire! The number of dams, canals, and reservoirs along the waterways leading into the Aral and Caspian seas have caused so much evaporation that both seas have fallen rapidly. In fact, some claim that by the end of the century, the Aral Sea may have deteriorated into a salt marsh.

In the preceding discussion we have tried to put matters into perspective, but we do not mean to suggest that all is well with our environment, nor that there is nothing more to do. While there have been improvements, problems remain. Montreal still dumps raw sewage into the St. Lawrence, and even the Yukon has problems (see the newspaper excerpt in the box on page 664). More important, our world is now subject to a number of new pollutants, most of which are far more dangerous than those we have reduced, even though they may be less visible and less malodorous.

A variety of highly toxic substances—PCBs (polychlorinated biphenyls), chlorinated hydrocarbons, dioxin, heavy metals, and radioactive materials—are dumped carelessly, left to cause cancer and threaten life and health in other ways. Some of these substances linger in the environment so long that they are likely to constitute a threat for many thousands of years. The accumulation of these and other by-products of modern technology may well cause damage that is all but irreversible. Two of the boxes in this chapter describe particularly important environmental issues: acid rain (pages 668–69), and the problem of carbon dioxide buildup in the earth's atmosphere (and the resulting increase in global temperatures that some scientists predict will occur within the next two decades) (page 665).

While environmental problems are neither new nor confined only to capitalist, industrialized economies, these facts are not legitimate grounds for complacency. The potential damage that we may be inflicting on ourselves, as well as on our surroundings, is very real and very substantial.

The Law of Conservation of Matter and Energy

It is impossible to describe completely all the ways in which we damage our environment. Our very existence creates pollution problems. We exhale "used" air and excrete food wastes; we cut down trees for housing and clear fields to plant crops; the examples can go on and on. Nevertheless, three major sources of environmental damage have continued to play a major role in these difficulties. They are: (1) the law of conservation of matter and energy, which tells us that all produced goods that are not recycled must ultimately constitute disposal problems;

[3]For an excellent nontechnical discussion see Marshall Goldman, *The Spoils of Progress* (Cambridge, Mass.: M.I.T. Press, 1972).

Going Northward for the Air? Maybe You Should Think Twice

WHITEHORSE—You'd expect it in Los Angeles, San Francisco, Tokyo—any big city. But in the great white north? In the land to which people come to find fresh air, clean water, wildlife, the great outdoors?

Smog in this northern town of only 15,000 is so bad that the federal Government is spending between $50,000 and $100,000 this winter to monitor the air.

Ottawa's well-intentioned plan of offering subsidies to wean people from oil and hydro-electric heating appears to have aggravated the problem.

...[When] monitoring of the town's air quality began in 1974 carbon monoxide levels were found to be un- usually high during the winter. That was the result of people leaving their vehicles idling to keep them warm in the frigid northern temperatures.

During the frequent temperature inversions caused by extreme cold, little wind and the fact that Whitehorse sits in a river valley, these levels sometimes exceeded national safety levels ...

In recent years, wood smoke has added to the problem—especially in Riverdale, a suburb of about 5,000 where nearly every second house has a wood stove and the surrounding bluffs block breezes that could disperse the noxious compounds. (The national average is a wood stove in every seventh home.)

More than 100 chemicals and compounds make up wood smoke, with carbon monoxide topping the list. A wood stove produces more than 300 times the carbon monoxide exhaled by an oil furnace and more than any other combustion system.

The concern ... is mainly over the polynuclear aeromatic hydrocarbons, some of which are carcinogenic. Emphysema, cancer, nausea, headaches, dizziness and respiratory problems can all be caused by the pollutants from exhaust fumes and wood stoves....

SOURCE: Ian Mulgrew, "Going Northward for the Air?", *The Globe and Mail*, January 15, 1983.

(2) the "edifice complex," which is the notion that anything that can be done by the bulldozer and the crane necessarily constitutes progress—and the bigger the project the better; and (3) the problem of externalities, the fact that under current economic arrangements the harm done by the polluter predominantly affects people other than himself, so that he has no economic motivation to bring under control the damage he does to the environment. We will discuss each of these issues in turn.

The physical law of conservation of matter and energy tells us there is no way that objects can be made to disappear—at most they can be changed into something else. Oil, for instance, can be transformed into heat (and smoke) or into plastic—but it will never vanish. This means that after a raw material has been used, either it must be used again (recycled) or it becomes a waste product that must somehow be disposed of.

If it is not recycled, any input used in the production process *must* ultimately become a waste product. It may end up on the garbage heap of some municipal dump. It may literally go up in smoke, contributing its bit to the pollution of the atmosphere. Or it may even be transformed into heat, warming up adjacent waterways and killing aquatic life in the process. The laws of physics tell us there is nothing we can do to make used inputs disappear altogether from the earth.

In fact, only a small proportion of the economy's inputs are made up of recycled materials, and recycling activities have in many cases been declining despite the large amount of volunteer effort and publicity that has been devoted to

Atmospheric Carbon Dioxide and the "Greenhouse Effect"

Recently there has been increasing concern about an environmental problem that scientists have warned about for a long time—the steadily rising, and essentially irreversible, concentration of carbon dioxide (CO_2) in the earth's atmosphere and its consequences for global climatic conditions. Estimated to have increased some 15 to 25 percent since the beginning of the Industrial Age, the major source of this buildup of CO_2 is the burning of fossil fuels such as coal and oil. CO_2 in the atmosphere causes a "greenhouse" effect by allowing incoming sunlight to pass through to the earth while partially trapping outgoing heat radiated by the planet. The higher the concentration of CO_2, the more heat is trapped. Thus, scientists say that a general global warming trend is inevitable and imminent.

Although there is considerable uncertainty about the exact size and speed of the temperature change, and some reports differ in their degree of urgency, it appears that average global temperatures will increase 2° Celsius by the year 2040 and 5° C by 2100.* Significant climatological effects could occur as early as the 1990s.

The consequences of these temperature increases will be dramatic. It is predicted, among other things, that the world will have to deal with major upheavals in agricultural patterns, increased desertification in many parts of the globe, disrupted food production, and significantly higher coastal waters (as the polar icecaps begin to melt). While there are some benefits to be expected from the predicted temperature rises (like longer growing seasons, improved photosynthesis, and more pleasant weather in northern areas), many of the possible changes will affect the earth's populations adversely. The consequences for the poorer countries of the world may be particularly harsh, because they are less able to deal with the necessary adjustments. Here in Canada, the Prairies would be parched and the even more severe drought predicted for the United States could produce heavy pressure to share the remaining North American waters.

Observers have suggested that appropriate responses to the threat of the CO_2 problem may include: a slowing of the use of fossil fuels, wherever possible, and replacing

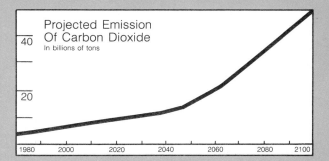

Projected Emission Of Carbon Dioxide
In billions of tons

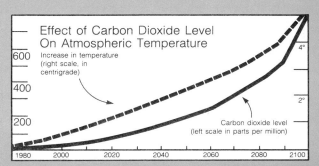

Effect of Carbon Dioxide Level On Atmospheric Temperature
Increase in temperature (right scale, in centigrade)

Carbon dioxide level (left scale in parts per million)

them with non-CO_2-producing and/or renewable energy sources like solar power; the use of fossil fuels that produce relatively little CO_2 (like natural gas instead of coal); reforesting areas where trees have been cleared (since forests "eat up" CO_2); and finally learning to live with a warmer climate now so as to be able to move more easily and gracefully into the warmer era when it occurs.

*Based on the most likely (mid-range) scenario.

SOURCES: U.S. Council on Environmental Quality, *Environmental Quality, 1980*, and *Environmental Quality, 1981* (Washington, D.C. 1980 and 1981); "E.P.A. Report Says Earth Will Heat Up Beginning in 1990's," *New York Times*, October 18, 1983; "Haste on Global Warming Trend Is Opposed," *New York Times*, October 21, 1983; *Resources*, No. 68, October 1981 (Washington, D.C.: Resources for the Future, 1981); Inquiry on Federal Water Policy, *Water is a Mainstream Issue* (Ottawa: Supply and Services Canada, 1984).

them in recent years. The recycling of waste paper declined relative to the use of raw-material paper during the 1960s. And during recessions some voluntary collection centres have been forced to close their doors because they simply could find no takers for the recyclable products that had previously enabled them to meet their expenses. Even optimistic projections predict that the amount of waste recycled will rise only to 10 percent of the total waste generated by the late 1980s.[4]

The upshot is that in an economy whose output is growing and whose input

[4]*Environmental Quality, The Tenth Annual Report of the Council on Environmental Quality*, pages 256–61.

use is consequently increasing, waste disposal and pollution are virtually certain to be growing problems. There are only three ways to ameliorate these difficulties: (1) increased recycling, (2) increased durability or reuse of the products (that is, the use of returnable bottles instead of throwaway containers), and (3) increased efficiency in the use of raw materials so that smaller quantities are utilized in a given quantity of output. In fact, this last remedy has already been used to some extent in our economy, in which nearly two-thirds of our output growth has been achieved without an increased use of raw materials.

The Edifice Complex

Many think of industry as the primary villain in environmental damage. But:

While private firms have done their share in harming the environment, private individuals and government have also been prime contributors.

The emissions of private passenger cars play an important role in the air pollution problems of most major cities. Wastes from flush toilets and residential washing machines also cause significant harm. Governments, too, add to the problem. The wastes of municipal treatment plants are a major source of water pollution. Nuclear facilities such as power plants produce nuclear materials that are among the most dangerous of all wastes, and the problem of their disposal is far from solved.

There is at least one type of environmental damage that, in particular, has been closely associated with government activity. Government agencies, presumably in an attempt to maximize their influence, have undertaken the construction of giant dams and reservoirs that flood farmlands and destroy canyons, that render surrounding soil unusable because of seepage of salts into the earth, and that change the water table (the level of water under the ground) by evaporation and seepage. Often, the drainage of swamps has subsequently altered local ecology irrevocably; the building of canals has diverted the flow of rivers; and the construction of dams has flooded and destroyed irreplaceable areas of natural beauty.

Evidence of the "edifice complex" is not lacking in Canada. It has been estimated that if our sixty major water diversions were combined, they would create the third largest river in Canada after the St. Lawrence and Mackenzie. Most are for power production: megaprojects like the Churchill River diversion in Manitoba, the Lagrande Project in Quebec's James Bay region, and the Churchill Falls project in Labrador.[5]

Environmental Damage as an Externality

We have already indicated that our very existence means that some environmental damage is inevitable. Products of the earth must be used up, and wastes must be generated in the process of creating the means of subsistence.

There is no question of reducing environmental damage to zero. As long as the human race survives, complete elimination of such damage is literally impossible. *It is not even desirable to get as close as possible to zero damage.* Some pollutants in small quantities are quickly dispersed and rendered harmless by natural processes, and it is not worth the opportunity cost to eliminate others whose damage is slight. Use of a large quantity of resources for this purpose may so limit their supply that there will not be materials available for the construction of

[5]Michael Keating, "Diversions would equal huge river," *The Globe and Mail*, Toronto, January 25, 1984.

hospitals, schools, and other things more important to society than the elimination of some pollutants.

The real issue then is not whether pollution should exist at all, but whether environmental damage in an unregulated market economy tends to be more serious and widespread than the public interest can tolerate. This issue immediately raises three key questions. First, why do economists believe that environmental damage is unacceptably severe *in terms of the public interest*? And how do they measure "the public interest"? Second, why does the market mechanism, which is so good at providing about the right number of toasters and trucks, generate too much pollution? What goes wrong with the system? And, third, what can we do about it? We will consider these questions in order.

Economists do not claim any special ability to judge what is good for the public interest. They normally prefer to accept the wishes of the members of the public as adequate indicators of "the public interest." When the economy reflects these wishes as closely as it can, given the resources and technology available, economists conclude that it is working effectively. When it operates in a way that frustrates the desires of the people, they conclude that the economy is functioning improperly. Why, then, do economists believe that the market mechanism generates "too much" pollution?

To answer this, we must deal with the fundamental analysis of A. C. Pigou that we referred to at the beginning of this chapter. In Chapter 29 we discussed some of the failures of the market mechanism and singled out externalities as a primary cause of market failure. An *externality*, it will be recalled, is an incidental consequence of some economic activity that can be either beneficial or detrimental to someone who neither controls the activity nor is intentionally served by it. The emission of pollutants constitutes one of the most clear-cut and standard examples of a detrimental externality. The smoke from a chemical plant affects persons other than the management of the plant or its customers. Because the damage done by the smoke to parties incidentally involved does not enter the financial accounts of the firm whose plant produces the emissions, the owners of the firm have no financial incentive to restrain those emissions, particularly since emission control costs money. Instead, they will find it profitable to produce their chemical product and to emit their smoke as though it caused no external damage to the community.

One way to look at the matter is as a failure of the pricing system. Through the smoke externality, the business firm is able to use up some of the community's clean air without paying for the privilege. Just as the firm would undoubtedly use oil and electricity wastefully if they were obtainable at no charge, the firm will also use the community's air wastefully, despoiling it with smoke far beyond the level that the public interest can justify. Rather than being at the (low) socially desirable level, the quantity of smoke will be at whatever (usually high) level is necessary to save as much money as possible for the firm that emits it, because the external damage caused by the smoke costs the firm nothing.

The achievement of any solution to this externality problem is particularly difficult when the smoke crosses political boundaries. This represents a very large problem for Canada, as the boxed insert on pages 668-69 indicates.

Externalities

Externalities play a crucial role affecting the quality of life. They show why the market mechanism, which is so efficient in supplying consumers' goods, has a much poorer record in terms of its effects on the environment. The problem of pollution illustrates the importance of externalities for public policy and indicates why their analysis is one of our **12 Ideas for Beyond the Final Exam**.

The Gathering Storm of Acid Rain

Acid rain is the latest, and probably the ultimate, example of the pollution truism: what goes up must come down somewhere. But in this case, south-central Ontario is where much of North America's air pollution is coming down.

Acid rain is the result of air pollution. It is created by almost 20 million tons of sulphur dioxide and nitrogen oxides . . . annually spewed out of eastern North American smokestacks from fossil-fueled power plants, smelters, and automobile exhausts. The oxides mix with water vapour in the air and gradually turn to weak sulphuric and nitric acid, which eventually falls as acid rain.

The taller the smokestack, the higher the oxides are pushed into the atmosphere, and the further they are blown by the wind. There are more than 400 tall stacks in eastern North America. Acid-laden air masses have been tracked from St. Louis to Toronto, and from Sudbury (site of the world's-tallest Inco Ltd. smelter stack) to Rochester.

But because of prevailing weather patterns, almost half of the eastern United States' annual output of 17 million tons of sulphur-nitrogen oxides drifts north to Canada, particularly Ontario, and falls as acid rain. . . .

Rain normally measures an acidity of about 5.6 on the pH scale.

On that scale, 7 is neutral and every downward drop of one unit is a 10 times increase in acidity. The rain falling on central Ontario, loaded with man-made pollutants, averages pH 4— 40 times more acidic than normal rain. Specific snowfalls . . . have been so acidified they have approached the acidity of vinegar (pH 2.4). . . .

Ontario has two particularly large sources of sulphur dioxide pollution (the dominant component of acid rain): the somewhat less than 1.3 million tons annually from Inco's giant Sudbury smelter, and 500,000 tons from Ontario Hydro's fossil-fueled power plants.

Largely because of Inco's estimated cost of installing pollution controls at Sudbury (between $500 million and $1 billion for a 50% reduction), and—according to Inco—because of continuing uncertainty about appropriate and feasible emission levels, the Ontario government [in 1979] reversed a previous order and allowed Inco to

Supply–Demand Analysis of Environmental Problems

Basic supply–demand analysis can be used to explain both how externalities lead to environmental problems and how these problems can be cured. As an illustration, let us deal with the problem of solid wastes—and the damage that the massive generation of garbage is doing to our environment.

In Figure 34–1 we see a demand curve, DE, for garbage removal. As usual, this curve has a negative slope, meaning that if the price of garbage removal is set sufficiently high, people will become more sparing in the amount of garbage removal they order. They may more often bring papers, bottles, and cans to recycling centres and public dumps; they may repair broken items rather than throwing them out; and so on. In short, a higher price of garbage removal can be expected to reduce the quantity demanded of garbage removal services.

The graph also shows the supply curve, SS, which we can expect to prevail in an ideal market for garbage removal. Garbage disposal is expensive to society—it requires people and trucks to haul it away; garbage dumps occupy valuable land; and the use of fire or other means to get rid of the garbage creates pollution that, as we have seen, has a high real cost to the community. As we saw in our analysis of competitive industries (Chapter 25), the position of the market's supply curve

continue its pollution. Inco, after all, is the key employer in Sudbury, and the company argues such costs would cripple the smelter's financial stability (and jobs).

Hydro has no "clean" smokestacks and adamantly refuses to spend hundreds of millions of dollars on installing pollution scrubbers at the new Atikokan plant now under construction....

It is worthy of mention that sulphur dioxide emissions in Ontario have been abated by close to 25% since 1972. The tragedy is that this is not enough. Inco, Hydro and the Ontario government also argue that cleaning up Ontario sources is a useless and costly gesture without an even more rapid abatement south of the border. The air-borne pollution from Ohio, Pennsylvania and Tennessee coal-fired plants will still blow north to Ontario....

In the U.S. acid rain is simply a question of priorities and money; the priority now is more coal-fired power plants, and no expensive cut-backs on the several hundred which already exist—very dirty plants....

The Americans have argued that they will better understand the Canadian concern about acid rain when they see some action taken in Canada. They point to the continuing operations of Inco and Ontario Hydro. (Although Inco at least has cut its emissions by 40% since 1972.)

SOURCE: Excerpts from Ross Howard, "The Gathering Storm of Acid Rain," *The Cottager Magazine* (March, 1980).

This article was published in March 1980. A major step toward solving transboundary pollution problems was taken in August 1980, when representatives of the Canadian and American governments signed a memorandum of intent to curb acid rain. However, in 1981, the United States failed to match Canada's unilateral decision to reduce sulphur dioxide emissions by 25 percent by 1990, and then rejected our 1982 offer of a further 25 percent reduction. Unfortunately, our unwillingness to practise what we preach limits our ability to pressure the Americans. Forty percent of the sulphur dioxide emissions are produced in Ontario, and here scrubbers that capture emissions from smokestacks have been rejected in favour of a gradual switch to nuclear power. In the United States, 80 coal-burning plants have installed scrubbers, at a cost of $250 million apiece.

U.S.–Canada relations on environmental policy were particularly strained in 1983, after the U.S. government registered Canadian documentary films on acid rain and nuclear war as "propaganda" under their Foreign Agents Registration Act.

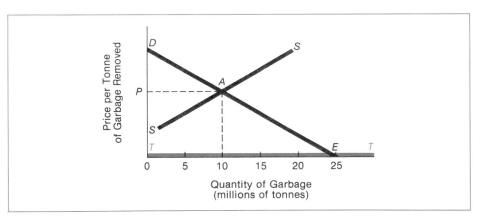

Figure 34-1

FREE DUMPING OF POLLUTANTS AS AN INDUCEMENT TO ENVIRONMENTAL DAMAGE

Whether wastes are solid, liquid, or gaseous, they impose costs upon the community. If the emitter is not charged for the damage, it is as though the resulting wastes were removed with zero charges to the polluter (blue removal supply curve *TT*). The polluter is then induced to pollute a great deal (25 million tonnes in the figure). If the charges to him reflect the true cost of the community (supply curve *SS* of waste removal), it would pay to emit a much smaller amount (10 million tonnes in the figure).

depends on the marginal cost of garbage removal. If suppliers had to pay the full costs of garbage removal, the supply curve would be comparably high (as drawn in the graph) and have a positive slope, meaning that the marginal cost of garbage disposal rises as the quantity rises. We see that, for the community depicted in the graph, the price of garbage removal will be P dollars per tonne, and at that price 10 million tonnes will be generated (point A).

But what if the community's government decides to remove garbage "free"? Of course, that means the government is really charging the consumer for the service in the form of taxes, but not in a way that makes each consumer pay an amount that reflects the quantity of garbage that he produces. The result is that the supply curve is no longer SS; rather, it becomes the blue line TT, which lies along the horizontal axis. What this says is that any one household can increase the garbage it throws away as much as it wishes and still pay a zero price for the additional amount. Now the intersection of the supply and demand curve is no longer point A. Rather it is point E, at which the price is zero and the quantity of garbage generated is 25 million tonnes—an amount substantially greater than would be produced if those who made the garbage had to pay the cost of getting rid of it.

Similar problems occur if the community offers the oxygen of its waterways and the purity of its atmosphere at a zero price to all who choose to utilize them, however wastefully and however great the quantities they decide to use up. The amount that will be wasted and otherwise used up is likely to be enormously greater than it would be if users had to pay for the cost of their actions to society. And that, in the view of economists, is one major reason for the severity of our environmental problems. Several conclusions follow:

1. The magnitude of our pollution problem is attributable in large part to the fact that the community lets individuals, firms, and government agencies deplete such resources as oxygen in the water and pure air without financial charge.

2. One way of dealing with pollution problems is to charge those who emit pollution, and who despoil the environment in other ways, a price commensurate with the costs they impose on the community.

3. This is another instance in which higher prices—on environmentally damaging activities—can be beneficial to the community.

Basic Approaches to Environmental Policy

In broad terms, three general methods have been proposed for the control of activities that damage the environment.

1. *Voluntary programs*, such as non-mandatory investment in pollution control equipment by firms that decide to act in a manner that meets their social responsibilities, or voluntary separation of solid wastes by consumers who deliver them to collection centres for recycling.

2. *Direct controls*, which either (a) impose legal ceilings on the amount any polluter is permitted to emit (as in the Delaware River program); or (b) specify how particular activities must be carried on—for example, they may prohibit backyard incinerators, or the use of high-sulphur coal, or require smokestack "scrubbers" to capture emissions of electric-generating installations.

3. *Taxes on emissions*, or the use of other monetary incentives or penalties to make it unattractive financially for emitters of pollutants to continue to pollute as usual.

Each of these methods has its place. If used appropriately, together they can constitute an effective and efficient environmental program. Let us consider each of them in turn.

Voluntarism

We can deal very briefly with voluntary programs. Voluntary control of pollution has usually proved to be weak and unreliable. Voluntary programs for the collection and separation of garbage into different and easily recyclable materials have rarely managed to reroute more than a small fraction of a community's wastes from the garbage dump to the recycling plants. Some business people with strong consciences have manifested good intentions and made sincere attempts to improve the practices of their companies. Yet competition has usually prevented them from spending more than token amounts for this purpose. No business, whatever its virtues, can long afford to have the prices of its products undercut by rival suppliers. As a result, voluntary business programs have often been more helpful to the companies' public relations activities than to the environment, and those with a real interest in environmental protection have called for legislation that *requires* all firms, including competitors, to undertake the same measures, thereby subjecting all firms in the industry to similar handicaps.

Yet voluntary measures do have their place. They are appropriate where alternative measures are not readily available. Where surveillance and, consequently, enforcement are impractical, as in the prevention of littering by campers in isolated areas, there is no choice but an appeal to people's consciences. And in brief but serious emergencies, in which there is no time to plan and enact a systematic program, there may also be no good substitute for voluntary compliance. Several major cities have, for example, experienced episodes in which there were temporary but dangerous concentrations of pollutants and the authorities were forced to appeal to the public to avoid activities that would have aggrevated the problem. One can easily cite cases in which experience shows that public response to appeals requiring cooperation for short periods has been enthusiastic and gratifying. To summarize:

Voluntary programs are not dependable ways to protect the environment. However, in brief, unexpected emergencies or where effective surveillance is impossible, the policy-maker may have no other choice. Sometimes in these cases voluntary programs even work.

Direct Controls

Direct controls have been the chief instrument of environmental policy in Canada. According to the Constitution, legislative authority for the environment is shared between the provincial and federal governments. The job of enforcing federal standards often falls to the provinces. Probably the best known of these are automobile emissions standards. The federal government establishes emissions standards for new vehicles being sold in Canada, but the provincial governments are responsible for the control of pollution after the vehicles have been sold.

Controls in provincial legislation such as Ontario's Environmental Protection Act include control orders, stop orders, and program approvals. These restrictions focus on the *results* of pollution. Such was the case on October 13, 1970, when the Ontario government ordered 48 firms and institutions in Toronto and Hamilton to reduce operations because the air pollution index exceeded 50.

Since then, major operations such as Ontario Hydro, Inco, and Falconbridge have co-operated with provincial authorities by changing their fuels and reducing their activities whenever readings go above 32.

Taxes on Emissions

Most economists agree that a nearly exclusive reliance on direct controls is a mistake and that, in most cases, financial penalties on polluters can do the same job more dependably, more effectively, and more economically. The most common suggestion is that firms be permitted to pollute all they want but be forced to pay a tax for the privilege to make them *want* to pollute less. A tax on emissions requires the polluter to install a meter that records his emissions in the same way his electric meter records his use of electricity. At the end of the month the government automatically sends him a bill charging him a stipulated amount for each litre of wastes (the amount must also vary with the quality of the wastes—a higher tax rate being imposed on wastes that are more dangerous or unpleasant). Thus, the more damage the polluter does the more he must pay. This tax is deliberately designed to *encourage* the use of its glaring loophole—the polluter *can* reduce the tax he pays by decreasing the amount he emits. In terms of Figure 34-1, if the tax is used to increase the payment for waste emissions from zero (blue supply line TT) and instead forces the polluter to pay its true cost to society, emissions will automatically be reduced from 25 down to 10 million tonnes.

People do respond to such taxes. The most widely publicized example is the Ruhr River basin in West Germany, where emissions taxes have been used for more than three decades. Though the Ruhr is one of the world's most concentrated industrial centres, those of its rivers that are protected by taxes are sufficiently clean to be usable for fishing and other recreational purposes. Firms have also found it profitable to avoid the taxes by extracting pollutants from their liquid discharges and recycling them. For example, almost 40 percent of the industrial acids used in the Ruhr have been recovered in this way.

Emissions Taxes Versus Direct Controls

It is important to see why taxes on emissions may prove more effective and reliable than direct controls. Direct controls essentially rely on the enforcement mechanism of the criminal justice system. Rules are set up that the polluter must obey. If the polluter violates those rules, he must first be caught. Then the regulatory agency must decide whether it has enough evidence to prosecute. Next, it must win its case before the courts. And, finally, the courts must impose a penalty that is more than just a token gesture. If any one of these steps does not occur, then the polluter gets away with his damaging activities.

Enforcing Direct Controls

The enforcement of direct controls requires vigilance and enthusiasm by the regulatory agency, which must assign the resources and persons needed to carry out the task of enforcement. Yet experience indicates that regulatory vigour is far from universal and often evaporates as time passes and public concern recedes. In many cases the resources devoted to enforcement are pitifully small.

The effectiveness of direct controls also depends upon the speed and rigour of the courts. Yet the courts are often slow and lenient. An example is the notorious case of the Reserve Mining Company, which was involved in one of the longest environmental and public health lawsuits in the United States. Starting in September 1969, several Minnesota communities, environmentalists, federal agencies, and officials from three states attempted to stop this company from pouring its wastes (which contain asbestos-like fibres believed to cause cancer) into Lake Superior, the source of the communities' drinking water. In 1980, after more than a decade of litigation and 16 judicial decisions, the courts finally ordered Reserve to curb this discharge (which totalled 61,000 tonnes over nearly a quarter of a century); the company was also ordered to pay $1.84 million to the city of Duluth and three other communities for water filtration systems.

Lags are common in Canada as well. In 1973, a CPR freight train was derailed near Dowling, a small town just northwest of Sudbury, Ontario, spilling almost 4000 litres of battery transformer fluid that was 70 percent polychlorinated biphenyls—PCBs. Soil samples taken after the initial cleanup showed more contamination in the soil. Nearly two years later the highly toxic chemicals had emigrated to a point where massive excavation and encapsulation of the soil was required. By the time the provincial environment ministry had worked out a control program in 1977, a serious situation had become catastrophic.[6]

Finally, direct controls can work only if the legislation imposes sizable penalties for violators. But the following is not atypical: Between 1968 and 1976 only twelve convictions under the Ontario Water Resource Act and five under the Environmental Protection Act were obtained against pulp and paper companies in Ontario. The average fine for water pollution was $812.[7] One can cite many cases in which large firms have been convicted of polluting and fined less than $5000— an amount beneath the notice of even a relatively small corporation.

Where more drastic penalties are available, their very magnitude may make the authorities reluctant to impose them. (See the newspaper excerpt in the box on the next page.) In an extreme case, in which the only legal remedy is to force the closing of an offending plant, the government agency is likely to back down under local pressure to preserve the community's source of jobs and income.

Enforcing Taxes

In contrast, pollution taxes are automatic and certain. No one need be caught, prosecuted, convicted, and punished. The tax bills are just sent out automatically by the untiring tax collector. The only sure way for the polluter to work his way out of paying pollution charges is to cut down his emissions.

A second difference between direct controls and taxes is worth noting. Suppose there is a ruling under a program of direct controls that Filth, Inc., must cut its emissions by 50 percent. Then that firm has absolutely no motivation to go one drop further. Why should it cut its emissions by 55 or even 52 percent when the law offers it neither reward nor encouragement for going beyond the selected quota? Under a system of emission taxes, however, the more the firm cuts back on its pollution, the more it saves in tax payments.

A third important difference between direct controls and taxes on emissions is the greater efficiency of the latter in the use of resources. It is claimed that the tax approach can do the job far more cheaply, saving labour, fuel, and raw materials, which can instead be used to build schools, hospitals, and housing for low-income groups. Statistical estimates for several pollution control programs suggest that the cost of doing the job through direct controls can easily be twice as high as under the tax alternative.

Why should there be such a difference? The answer is that under direct controls the job of cutting back emissions is apportioned among the various polluters on some principle (usually intended to approximate some standard of fairness) that is selected by the regulators. This rarely assigns the task in accord with ability to carry it out cheaply and efficiently. Suppose it costs firm A only 2 cents a litre to reduce emissions while firm B must spend 10 cents a litre to do the same job. If both firms spew out 2000 litres of pollution a day, a 50 percent reduction in pollution can be achieved by ordering both firms to limit emissions to 1000 litres a day. This may or may not be fair, but it is certainly not efficient. The social cost will be 1000 times 2 cents, or $20, to firm A and 1000 times 10 cents, or $100, to firm B, a total of $120.

If, instead, a tax of 5 cents a litre had been imposed, all the work would have been done by firm A—which can do it more cheaply. Firm A would have cut its emissions out altogether, paying the 2 cents a litre this requires, to avoid the 5 cents a litre tax. Firm B would probably go on polluting as before, because it is cheaper to pay the tax than the 10 cents a litre it costs to control its pollution. In this way, under the tax, *total daily emissions will still be cut by 2000 litres a day.*

[6]Canadian Environmental Law Research Foundation, *Environment on Trial* (Toronto: 1978), page 191.

[7]"Pollution pays for pulp mills, report says," *The Globe and Mail*, Toronto, November 20, 1976, page 2, cited in *Environment on Trial*, Canadian Environmental Law Research Foundation (Toronto: 1978).

Watchdog Won't Seek Mop Up of Big N-Spill

OTTAWA—The country's nuclear watchdog says it sees no need to mop up the 87 million litres . . . of radioactive water spilled at the Key Lake uranium mine in northern Saskatchewan last month.

The Atomic Energy Control Board, which is expected to be overruled when the Saskatchewan government releases its own report next month, also appears willing to let the Key Lake Mining Corporation's violations of federal regulations pass without comment or prosecution.

[The] manager of the board's waste-management division said . . . "We feel the company has violated their operating licence. . .but we haven't sat down to discuss regulatory action. We don't see it as a high priority."

The Atomic Energy Control Act says any individual or firm that violates AECB regulations can be fined $5000 or two years upon summary conviction or up to $10,000 or five years in jail, if charged by federal or provincial attorneys general.

The Key Lake mine, called the world's largest and most efficient uranium mine, went into operation 1000 kilometres (600 miles) north of Saskatoon in October. In early January, water in a huge reservoir outside the mine overflowed and its radioactive contents drained into nearby Gerald Lake—the biggest spill at a Canadian uranium mine in 20 years.

It was later learned the mine had been breaching the terms of both its legally binding agreement with the Saskatchewan government and its AECB operating licence. Earlier radioactive spills were not reported to AECB, and the reservoir held more water than the federal licence allowed.

Government authorities ignored the violations until the reservoir burst and grabbed national attention. . . .

SOURCE: Southam News story appearing in the Hamilton *Spectator*, February 22, 1984.

But the entire job will be done by the polluter who can do it more cheaply, and the total daily cost of the program will therefore be $40 (2 cents × 2000 litres) instead of the $120 it would cost under direct controls.

The secret of the efficiency induced by a tax on pollution is straightforward. Only polluters who can reduce emissions cheaply and efficiently can afford to take advantage of the built-in loophole—the opportunity to save on taxes by reducing emissions. The tax approach simply assigns the job to those who can do it most effectively.

Advantages and Disadvantages

Given all these advantages of the tax approach, why would anyone want to use direct controls?

There are three general and important situations in which direct controls have a clear advantage:

1. *Where an emission is so dangerous that it is decided to prohibit it altogether. Here there is obviously nothing to be gained by installing complicated procedures for the collection of taxes that will never be paid because there will be no emissions for which payment is required.*

2. *Where a sudden change in circumstances—for example, a dangerous air quality crisis—calls for prompt and substantial changes in conduct, such as temporary*

reductions in use of cars or incinerators. It is difficult and clumsy to change tax rules, and direct controls will usually do a better job here.

3. *Where effective and dependable metering devices have not been invented or are prohibitively costly to install and operate.* In such cases there is no way to operate an effective tax program because the amount of wastes the polluter has emitted cannot be determined and so his tax bill cannot be calculated. In that case the only effective option may be to *require* him to use "clean" fuel, or install emissions-purification equipment.

In reality there is often no device analogous to a gas or water meter that can be used to measure pollution emissions cheaply and effectively. For example, to evaluate emissions in waterways, the standard procedure is to take samples, bring them to a laboratory, and subject them to a series of complicated tests that often take weeks to carry out, to determine the chemical contents of the emissions. For a polluter whose emissions are very large, this may be worth doing. But for the emitter who only spews out a few litres of pollutants a day, the cost of such a complex process is likely to exceed the benefits. Whatever their other inefficiencies, direct controls are still likely to do the job of controlling such sources of pollution more cheaply. On the other side of the argument, however, the widespread adoption of emissions charges and the resulting rise in demand for metering devices may lead to research and development that produces cheaper and more effective meters.

Other Financial Devices to Protect the Environment

The basic idea underlying the emissions-tax approach to environmental protection is that it provides financial incentives that induce the polluter to reduce the damage he does to the environment. But emissions taxes are not the only form of financial inducement that have been proposed. There are at least two others that deserve consideration: *subsidies for reduced emissions* and the requirement of *emissions permits* for polluters, each permit authorizing the emission of a specified quantity of pollutant. Such permits would be offered for sale in limited quantities fixed by the authorities at prices set by demand and supply.

Subsidies

Subsidies are already in use. Their advocates say that financial inducements can be just as effective when they take the form of a reward for good behaviour as when they are composed of penalties (taxes) on behaviour that is considered harmful. A donkey can be induced to move forward just as surely (and with much less unpleasantness) by dangling a carrot in front of his noise as by applying a stick to his rump. Environmental subsidies usually take one of two forms:

1. Partial payment of the cost of installation of some sort of pollution-control equipment.

2. The offer of a fixed reward for every reduction in emissions from some base level, usually some amount that the polluter used to emit in the past.

A subsidy to help defray the cost of control equipment can be effective when the purchaser of the equipment was considering doing it anyhow but did not because of the high cost. This may be the case for a municipality that wants to treat its wastes more thoroughly but has not found a way to afford the cost. It may also be the case in private industry, where collection of the wastes that would otherwise be emitted can yield products that are valuable and reusable but where the equipment required for the process is too costly. But where the polluter gains nothing from such control, a partial subsidy for the purchase of control equipment is not likely to be very effective. It simply reduces the cost of something he does not want to do in any event.

The second type of subsidy—a reward based on quantity of reduced emissions—does indeed have the same sort of incentive effects as a tax for the *individual* polluter. In both cases the more he emits, the worse off he is financially, either because he receives a smaller subsidy payment or because his tax bill is higher. But as far as the *industry* is concerned, there is a world of difference between the effect of a tax and the effect of a subsidy. *A tax discourages the output of commodities whose production causes pollution, whereas a subsidy encourages such output to expand.* Consider the difference between the tax and subsidy approaches in the case of automotive emissions. A tax will increase the cost of operating cars, thereby encouraging the use of public transportation (which produces far lower quantities of emissions per passenger-kilometre travelled than does the automobile). On the other hand, a subsidy for the installation of emissions-control devices will tend to encourage the use of autos at the expense of public transportation by keeping down the price of cars.

It is a paradox that a subsidy intended to induce an industry to reduce its emissions can actually *increase* the size of the industry's output and consequently *increase* its total emissions.

This paradox is readily illustrated with the help of a standard supply–demand diagram for a competitive industry. We see in Figure 34–2 that a tax on polluting output will raise the costs of the industry and hence raise the price of whatever quantity it supplies. Thus, the supply curve will be shifted upward by a tax to the curve labelled "supply after tax." Similarly, the subsidy will reduce dollar costs to the industry and so will shift the supply curve downward to the curve labeled "supply after subsidy." So, under a tax on emissions, the equilibrium point will move from point E to point T, reducing the output of the polluting product from e to t. But the subsidy, which moves the supply-demand equilibrium point from E to S, will actually increase the output of the polluting industry from e to s! How does this happen? While the pollution-reduction subsidy will induce firms to decrease their emissions somewhat, it will attract new polluting firms into the industry, and as the graph shows, the net result may be that the subsidy will backfire, and

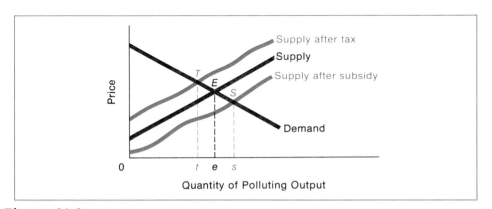

Figure 34-2
SUPPLY-DEMAND EQUILIBRIUM IN A POLLUTING COMPETITIVE INDUSTRY
A tax on pollution raises costs and so shifts the supply curve upward; that is, a higher price is needed to elicit a given quantity supplied. This causes equilibrium output to fall from *e* to *t* and succeeds in its purpose—reducing pollution. But a subsidy to those who decrease their polluting output reduces costs and shifts the supply curve downward. By reducing costs, it attracts more firms into the industry. Paradoxically, output of the polluting product actually must increase from *e* to *s*.

instead of reducing pollution, as it is intended to do, it will actually increase it.

The main advantage of subsidies over taxes as a financial inducement to decrease pollution is that subsidies attract less opposition and are therefore more easily adopted through the political process. Obviously, industry always prefers a subsidy to a tax. But the rest of the community may well be worse off if a subsidy is selected instead of an emissions tax.

Emissions Permits

A third type of financial inducement strongly advocated by some economists, but so far not adopted directly by any government, is the sale of *emissions permits*. Under this arrangement, the environmental agency decides what quantity of emissions per unit of time (say, per month) is tolerable and then issues a batch of permits authorizing (altogether) just that amount of pollution. The permits are offered for sale to the highest bidders. Their price is therefore determined by demand and supply. It will be high if the number of permits offered for sale is small and there is a large amount of industrial activity that must use the permits. Similarly, the price of a permit will be low if many permits are issued but the quantity of pollution for which they are demanded is small.

The emissions permit in many ways works like a tax—it simply makes it too expensive for the polluter to continue emitting as much as he would have without it. In addition, the permit offers two clear advantages over the tax approach. First, it reduces uncertainty about the quantity that will be emitted into the community. Under a tax we cannot be sure about this in advance, since that depends on the extent to which polluters respond to the tax rate that is selected. In the case of permits, the ceiling on emissions is decided in advance by the environmental authorities, who enforce the ceiling simply by issuing permits authorizing a specific total quantity of emissions.

Second, a given tax on emissions can be made ineffective by inflation. For example, a tax of X dollars may become insignificant as inflation erodes the value of the dollar, even though it may have been effective when it was first enacted and the price level was much lower. However, as long as there is no change in quantity of emissions authorized by licence, inflation will obviously have no effect on the amount of pollution. It will simply raise the price of a licence along with the prices of other commodities.

A shortcoming of the pollution-licence idea is its apparent political unattractiveness: Many people react indignantly to the notion of "licences to pollute." Yet the Environmental Protection Agency in the United States has recently introduced some compromise measures that are approximations to a market in emissions permits. It is too soon to judge the effectiveness of these new programs, but they do illustrate how much can be achieved by intelligent compromise in policymaking.

On the Equity and Cost of Some Current Programs

This chapter began with a discussion of some shortcomings in the plans for the protection of the Delaware River. We are now in a position to identify the sources of those shortcomings and to note why the same difficulties are likely to be encountered in other environmental programs. It will be recalled that the two issues that were raised were the unnecessarily high costs of the plans for the Delaware and the inequities that appeared to beset the emissions quotas assigned under the program.

The source of the inefficiencies should be clear from the discussion of the last section. The Delaware program was one of direct controls, and consequently it did not have any procedures to apportion the task of emissions reduction in accord with the relative efficiency with which different emitters could carry it out.

Because much of the job is assigned to those for whom the cost of controlling discharges is high, the entire program becomes unnecessarily costly. This is just a particular example of the cost of using direct controls rather than a tax on emissions, a cost to which, economists believe, policy-makers have given inadequate attention.

Under direct controls the authorities usually aim at an *equitable* assignment of emissions quotas. For example, they may require all polluters to reduce their discharges by the same percentage. How, then, did it happen that one large firm was assigned a quota five times as large as another, similar enterprise? The answer is that equal percentage reductions turn out to be far less equitable than they sound at first. As a result, any attempt to put them into practice almost always results in complaints, political pressures, renegotiation of quotas, and a consequent set of assignments that seem to have been designed with the aid of a roulette wheel rather than a deliberate decision-making process.

Why are equal percentage reductions in emissions not generally equitable? We have already seen one reason: Costs of reduction are not the same for all industries or all plants in an industry. For example, the cost for a typical beet sugar plant to reduce its emissions (as measured in terms of the oxygen these wastes use up) is only about one-sixth as large as an equivalent reduction for a petroleum refinery. A modern paper plant can usually decrease its discharges at much less cost than can an antiquated plant in the same industry. Is it really *fair* to require all these firms to cut back their emissions by the same amounts when, through no fault of their own, the resulting financial burden and the resulting loss of jobs is so different?

There are even clearer examples of the potential inequity in equal percentage reductions. Consider two companies, one run by a conscientious environmentalist who has voluntarily installed substantial amounts of equipment to cleanse and reduce his emissions, and the other run by an irresponsible management, which has continued to allow as much garbage to pour into the public waterways as maximum profitability requires. Is it really fair for both these firms to be told to cut back equally?

Once such problems and others like them are recognized, and an attempt made to reassign emissions quotas accordingly, it will become clear that each emitter is a special case requiring special treatment. The regulator is almost forced to proceed case by case, and the resulting quotas end up following complex patterns that are at best difficult to defend in terms of equity or efficiency.

Two Cheers for the Market

The lesson of this chapter is a very general one. The focus of Parts Three through Five has been to learn which tasks the market mechanism performs well and which it performs poorly. We have seen in this chapter that protecting the environment is one task that cannot be left to the free market: because of the important externalities involved, the market will systematically allocate too few resources to the job. This problem is particularly difficult to solve politically, when the pollution extends beyond political boundaries, as is the case with acid rain and the greenhouse effect. However, if pollution is localized, the market failure does not imply that the price mechanism must be discarded. On the contrary, we have seen that a legislated market solution—based on pollution charges—may well be the best way to protect the environment. At least in this case, the power of the market mechanism can be harnessed to correct its own failings.

Summary

1. Pollution is as old as human history; and contrary to some popular notions, some forms of pollution were actually decreasing even before recent programs were initiated to protect the environment.
2. Both planned and market economies suffer from substantial environmental problems.
3. The production of commodities *must* cause waste disposal problems unless everything is recycled, but even recycling processes cause pollution (and use up energy).
4. Industrial activity causes environmental damage, but so does the activity of private individuals (as when they drive cars that emit pollutants). Government agencies also damage the environment (as when military airplanes emit noise and exhaust, or a hydroelectric project floods large areas).
5. Pollution is an externality—when a factory emits smoke, it dirties laundry and may damage the health of persons who neither work for the smoking factory nor buy its products. Hence, pollution control cannot be left to the free market. This is another of our **12 Ideas for Beyond the Final Exam**.
6. Pollution can be controlled by voluntary programs, direct controls, taxes on emissions, or other monetary incentives for the reduction of emissions.
7. Most economists believe that the tax approach is the most efficient and effective way to control detrimental externalities.
8. Subsidies for reduced pollution by the individual firm may actually backfire by making it profitable for more polluting firms to go into business.

Concepts for Review

Externality	Pollution charges (taxes on	Subsidies for reduced emissions
Direct controls	emissions)	Emissions permits

Questions for Discussion

1. What sorts of pollution problems would you expect in a small African village? In a city in India? In communist China? In Toronto?
2. Economists maintain that while *some reduction* in pollution is usually desirable, it is not desirable to reduce most pollutants to zero. Why may this be a reasonable view?
3. Suppose you are assigned the task of drafting a law to impose a tax on the emission of smoke. What provisions would you put into the law?
   a. How would you decide the size of the tax?
   b. What would you do about smoke emitted by a municipal electricity plant?
   c. Would you use the same tax rate on densely and sparsely settled areas?
   What information will you need to collect before determining what you would do about each of the preceding provisions?
4. Production of commodity X creates 10 kilograms of emissions for every unit of X produced. The demand and supply curves for X are described by the following table:

Price (dollars)	10	9	8	7	6	5
Quantity demanded	80	85	90	95	100	105
Quantity supplied	100	95	90	85	80	75

   What is the equilibrium price and quantity, and how much pollution will be emitted?
5. If the price of X to consumers is $9, and the government imposes a tax of $2 per unit, show that because suppliers get only $7 they will produce only 85 units of output, not the 95 units of output they would produce if they received the full $9 per unit.
6. Show that, with this tax, the equilibrium price is $9 and the equilibrium quantity demanded is 85. How much pollution will not be emitted?
7. Compare your answers to Questions 4 and 6 and show how large a reduction in pollution emissions occurs because of the $2 tax on the polluting output.

The Economics of Energy and Natural Resources

Since Fuel is become so expensive
and will of course grow scarcer
and dearer, any new Proposal for
saving the [fuel] ... may at least
be thought worth Consideration.
BENJAMIN FRANKLIN (1744)

The 1970s witnessed a marked dampening of the buoyant optimism that previously was held to characterize Canadian attitudes. The energy situation probably contributed significantly to this change. The old attitude that unlimited stocks of resources promise unlimited growth was proven wrong in a very rude way. In the 1970s and early 1980s, we suddenly found ourselves facing shortages of a great variety of commodities—coffee, paper products, and, above all, energy. People were led to wonder, as one magazine headline put it, "Are we running out of everything?"

This chapter will try to put matters into perspective. It will show that neither the optimism of the era preceding the "energy crisis" nor the more recent panic is quite justified by the facts. Natural resources have always been scarce, and one may argue with good reason that they have been used wastefully. On the other hand, we are *not* about to run out of most vital resources, there is reason to be optimistic about the availability of substitutes, and many of the shortages of the 1970s can with some justice be ascribed as much to the folly of government programs and misunderstanding by the general public as to any signs of imminent exhaustion of petroleum and other natural resources.

This chapter begins by reviewing the facts and allegations about the available stocks of natural resources. It then describes what economic theory tells us will happen in a free market to the prices and usage of finite resources as time passes and the available quantities decline. Then the history of the energy crisis will be examined. Finally, several important policy issues—such as energy independence, rationing, and protection of the environment—will be discussed.

A Puzzle: Those Resilient Resource Supplies

It is a plain fact that the earth is endowed with only finite quantities of such vital resources as oil, copper, lead, coal, and many others. This fact has fascinated pessimists through the years. In 1972, extreme pessimism assumed its most scientific guise in a publication by the Club of Rome called *The Limits to Growth*. Using computers to project future world conditions, the authors concluded "with some confidence" that if there is "no major change in the present system ... industrial growth will certainly stop within the next century, at the latest." As they describe the process, "The behaviour mode of the system is one of

Table 35-1

EXPECTED LIFE (IN YEARS) OF SOME WORLD MINERAL RESERVES, 1980

ZINC	NICKEL	LEAD	COPPER
42	71	47	59

Table 35-2

EXPECTED LIFE (IN YEARS) OF SOME WORLD MINERAL RESERVES, ESTIMATES FOR 1960 AND 1980

	ZINC	NICKEL	LEAD	COPPER
1960	24	43	19	37
1980	42	71	47	59

Note: We had more years' supply of each of these depletable resources in 1980 than in 1960, despite 20 years of consumption!

SOURCE: Bureau of Mines, U.S. Department of the Interior, *The Domestic Supply of Critical Minerals*, 1983, page 21.

overshoot and collapse.... Growth ... depletes a large fraction of the resource reserves available ... the industrial base collapses, taking with it the services and agricultural systems ... [and] population finally decreases when the death rate is driven upward by lack of food and health services."[1]

Table 35-1 shows the sort of data that are frequently used to support such doomsday forecasts. Roughly speaking, it shows for four minerals the number of years of consumption (assuming unchanged rates of use) that could be met by known reserves of these resources as of 1980. Reading this table without knowing what lies behind it can indeed be alarming. It seems to say that we will run out of all of these vital minerals in less than 75 years. For example, according to this table, by 2000 we should have only 39 years of copper reserves, 27 years of lead reserves, 51 years of nickel reserves, and only 22 years of zinc reserves remaining. What happens after that?

But now look at Table 35-2, which compares the 1980 figures with similar data for 1960. Surely something mysterious is going on! We see that in 1960 only about a 24-year supply of zinc was apparently left to mankind. Yet 20 years later, despite all the zinc that had been used in the meantime, the reserves of zinc were estimated to last 42 years! Each of the other resources also had *larger* reserves in 1980 than in 1960, even though rates of consumption had risen in the interim. This does indeed seem like a funny way to keep score.

In part, this puzzle is ascribable to the misleading nature of figures on "known reserves," though these are the sorts of statistics commonly cited by pessimists on resource depletion. But economic principles also help a great deal in clearing up the mystery, as we will see at the end of the chapter.

The Free Market and Pricing of Depletable Resources

If figures on known reserves behave as peculiarly as those we have just seen, one begins to doubt their ability to indicate whether we are really coming uncomfortably close to running out of certain resources. Is there some other indicator of growing scarcity that seems more reliable? Most economists agree that there is—that the *price of the resource* serves this function well.

As a resource becomes scarcer, we expect its price to rise for several reasons.

[1]Donella H. Meadows, et al, *The Limits to Growth* (New York: Universe Books, 1972), pages 125–26.

One is that for most resources the process of depletion is not simply a matter of gradually using up the supply of a homogeneous product, every unit of which is equally available. Rather, the most accessible and highest quality deposits of the resource are generally used up first, then industry turns to less accessible locations and/or deposits of lower purity or quality, and then finally to deposits that are still harder or more costly to extract or of still poorer quality. Oil is a clear example of this. First, Canadians relied primarily on the most easily found domestic oil wells. Then they turned to imports from South America and elsewhere, with their higher transport costs. At that point it was not yet profitable to embark on the dangerous and extremely costly process of bringing up oil from the ocean floor off Newfoundland. (See the box on page 684 for an illustration of what sort of investment it takes to extract oil from sea beds.) We know that Canada still possesses tremendous stocks of petroleum embedded in the Alberta tar sands, and in the Arctic, but until recently this has been too difficult and, therefore, too costly to get at.

Increasing scarcity of a resource such as oil is not usually a matter of imminent and total disappearance. Rather, it takes the form of exhaustion of the most accessible and cheapest sources so that new supplies become more costly.

A second reason for rising resource prices is hidden in the operation of the supply–demand mechanism. To see how it works, let us consider the simpler (if less realistic) case in which extraction of a resource does not grow increasingly difficult as its reserves dwindle. That is, we envision the earth's supply of a mythical mineral, Zipthon, all of identical quality, which can be extracted and delivered to market with negligible extraction and transportation costs. How quickly will the reserves of Zipthon be used up, and what will happen to its price with the passage of time?

If the market for Zipthon is perfectly competitive, we can provide a remarkably concrete answer about the behaviour of prices. The answer, which was discovered by the American economist Harold Hotelling, tells us that as long as the supply of Zipthon lasts, its price must rise at a rate equal to the rate of interest. That is, if in 1985 the price of Zipthon is $100 per tonne and the rate of interest is 10 percent, then its price in 1986 must be $110.

Under perfect competition the price of a depletable resource whose costs of transportation and extraction are negligible must rise at the rate of interest. If the rate of interest is 10 percent, the price of the resource must rise 10 percent every year.

Why is this so? The answer is simple. People who have money tied up in inventories of Zipthon must earn exactly as much per dollar of investment as they would by putting their money into, say, a government bond. Suppose that $100 invested in bonds would next year rise in value to $112, while $100 in Zipthon would grow only to $110, and suppose the two were equally risky. What would happen? People who owned Zipthon would obviously find it profitable to sell the Zipthon and put their money into bonds instead.

But as more Zipthon was dumped on the market it would become increasingly abundant today and increasingly scarce tomorrow. So its expected *future* price would rise while its actual *current* price would fall. This and other associated changes in Zipthon prices and bond prices would continue until there was no further advantage in the one investment as against the other—that is, until both offered the same rate of return per dollar of investment.

The same process, working in reverse, would apply if Zipthon prices were rising faster than the rate of interest. Investors would switch from bonds to Zipthon, and with more Zipthon held for investment rather than released for current consumption, current prices of Zipthon would rise. At the same time the

The Search at Sea

Imagine a tower nearly as tall as the Empire State Building set on the ocean bottom in 455 feet of water 120 miles from shore—a tower that weighs 715,000 tons, whose platform covers six acres, houses 200 workers, and generates enough electricity for a city of 33,000.

That giant structure is the Mobil-operated Statfjord A drilling and production platform. Constructed at a cost of $1.3 billion, Statfjord A will eventually produce 300,000 barrels of oil a day from the turbulent North Sea, where winds can howl at 120 miles per hour and waves reach a height of 100 feet. The tower's enormous size and cost reflect the increasingly huge projects required to get oil out of almost inaccessible pockets of the earth.

The problem—and the challenge—is how to get at this undersea resource. Most offshore drilling takes place in waters less than 600 feet deep. In depths greater than 1000 feet, costs and technological problems multiply. In fact, even a Statfjord-type tower is unsuited for such deep water. For this reason, engineers have had to devise other solutions.

One such solution, still in the planning stage, is a Mobil-pioneered, deep-sea production system that would eliminate the conventional platform altogether. Well-head, terminal, and pipelines would be placed on the

seabed by remote-controlled mechanisms, making it possible to produce in depths of up to 2500 feet—far deeper than divers can work.

SOURCE: From a Mobil Oil Corporation Advertisement, *The New York Times*, August 14, 1980, page A23. Copyright ©1981 by Mobil Corporation.

---

abundance of future stocks would be increased and thus expected future prices would fall.

Following this fundamental principle about the pricing of a scarce resource with fixed extraction costs, let us see what will happen to the price of $100 worth of Zipthon over the course of, say, four years. We have the following pattern of Zipthon prices:

INITIAL DATE	ONE YEAR LATER	TWO YEARS LATER	THREE YEARS LATER	FOUR YEARS LATER
$100	$110	$121	$133.10	$146.41

These prices follow from the fact that $110 is 10 percent higher than $100, $121 is 10 percent higher than $110, and so on. What is to be noted is that because of the compounding effect, the dollar amount of the price increase is greater and greater each year. Zipthon rises in value by $10 in the first year, $11 in the second year, $12.10 in the third, $13.31 in the fourth, and so on indefinitely. Thus we conclude:

The basic law of pricing of a depletable resource tells us that as its stocks are used up its price in a perfectly competitive market will rise every year by greater and greater dollar amounts.

Notice that we have been able to make these predictions about the price of Zipthon without any knowledge about the supply of Zipthon or consumer demand for it. This is really remarkable. But if we want to go on to determine

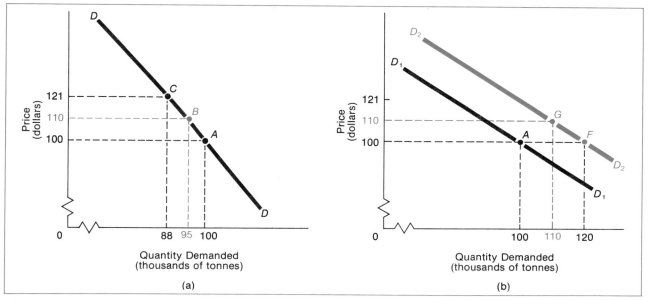

Figure 35-1

CONSUMPTION OVER TIME OF A DEPLETABLE RESOURCE

The price of the resource must rise, year after year (from $100 to $110 to $121, and so on). If the demand curve does not shift [part (a)], quantity demanded will be reduced every year. Even if the demand curve does shift outward [as in part (b)], the increasing price will keep any rise in quantity demanded lower than it would otherwise have been.

what will happen to the consumption of Zipthon—the rate at which its inventory will be used up—we need to know something about supply and demand.

In Figure 35-1(a) there is a demand curve for Zipthon, *DD*, which shows the amount people want to use up *per year* at various price levels. On the vertical axis we show how the price must rise from year to year in the pattern we have just calculated—from $100 per tonne in the initial year to $110 in the next year, and so on. Because of the negative slope of the demand curve it follows that each year consumption of Zipthon will fall. That is, *if there is no shift in the demand curve*, consumption will fall from 100,000 tonnes initially, to 95,000 tonnes in the next year, and so on.

But in reality such demand curves rarely do stay still. As the economy grows and population and per-capita incomes increase, demand curves can be expected to shift outward. And there is every reason to believe that this has been true of the demands for most scarce resources. Shifts in the demand curve will naturally tend to increase consumption, thereby offsetting at least part of the reduction in quantity demanded that results from rising prices. Nevertheless, it remains true that rising prices do help to cut back consumption growth relative to what it would have been if price had remained constant. In Figure 35-1(b) we depict an outward shift in demand from curve D_1D_1 in the initial period to curve D_2D_2 a year later. If price had remained constant at the initial value, $100 per tonne, quantity consumed per year would have risen from 100,000 tonnes to 120,000 tonnes. But since, in accord with the basic principle, price must rise to $110, quantity demanded will only increase to 110,000 tonnes—which is smaller than 120,000 tonnes. Thus, whether or not the demand curve shifts, we conclude:

The ever-rising prices that accompany increasing scarcity of a depletable resource discourage consumption (encourage conservation). Even if quantity demanded is growing, it will grow less rapidly than if prices were not rising.

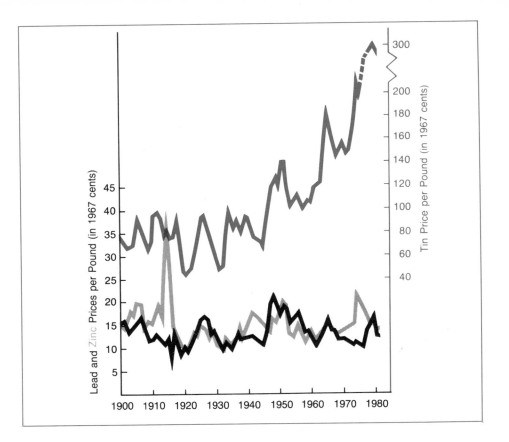

Figure 35-2

PRICES OF LEAD, ZINC, AND TIN 1900-1981, IN 1967 CENTS*

Note that these prices have not been rising steadily even though all three minerals are gradually being used up.

SOURCE: *Historical Statistics of the U.S.* and *Metal Statistics*, 1981, American Metal Market, Fairchild Publications.

*As deflated by the producer price index (all commodities).

Resource Prices in the Twentieth Century

How do the facts match up with this theoretical analysis? As we will see now, their correspondence is very poor indeed. Figure 35–2 shows the behaviour of the prices of three critical metals: lead, zinc, and tin, since the beginning of the twentieth century. These figures are all expressed in real terms; that is, they have all been recalculated in terms of dollars of constant purchasing power to eliminate the effects of inflation or deflation.

What we find is that instead of rising steadily, as the theory might have led us to expect, two of them actually remained amazingly constant. Between 1900 and 1940, lead and zinc prices actually rose more slowly than the general price level, while tin prices just about kept pace with general inflation between 1900 and 1945. More recently, the price of tin has gone up substantially faster than other prices—in 1980 its relative price was nearly twice as high as it was in 1970. But even during the 1970s, zinc and lead prices rose only slightly faster than prices in general.

Figure 35–3 shows similar figures for the relative price of crude oil in the United States since 1947. It gives price at the wellhead (that is, at the point of production) with no transportation cost included. The data show that in 1973 the price of oil was actually about eight percent lower, relative to other prices, than it was in 1948. Only from 1973 to 1981 did it rise faster than prices in general. There are even more peculiar cases. From 1923 (the earliest date for which figures are available) to 1980, the price of magnesium actually fell relative to other prices by nearly 84 percent.

How does one explain this strange behaviour of the prices of finite resources, which surely are being used up, even if only gradually? Have the laws of supply

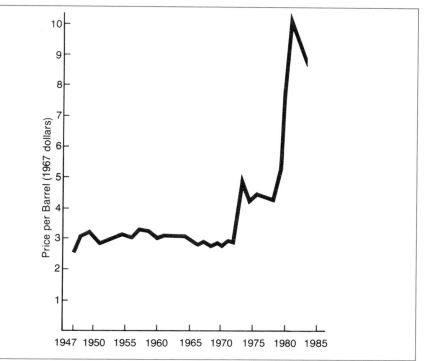

Figure 35–3
PRICE OF U.S. DOMESTIC
OIL AT THE WELLHEAD
1947–1983, IN 1967 DOLLARS*
Note the long period of near
constancy in real oil prices.

SOURCE: *Historical Statistics of the
U.S., Monthly Energy Review, Minerals
Year Book*, U.S. Energy Information
Administration, and U.S. Department of
Labor, Bureau of Labor Statistics.

*As deflated by the producer price
index (all commodities).

and demand somehow broken down? Actually, what these figures indicate is that reality is much more complicated than our simple analytic model, and that sometimes the complications grow so extreme that prices behave very differently from what the simple theory predicts. While many things can interfere with the price patterns that the theory led us to expect, we mention only four:

1. **Unexpected discoveries of reserves whose existence was previously not suspected.** If we were to stumble upon a huge and easily accessible reserve of Zipthon, which came as a complete surprise to the market, the price of Zipthon would obviously fall. This is illustrated in Figure 35–4, where we see that people originally believed the available supply curve to be that represented by curve S_1S_1. The discovery of the new Zipthon reserves leads

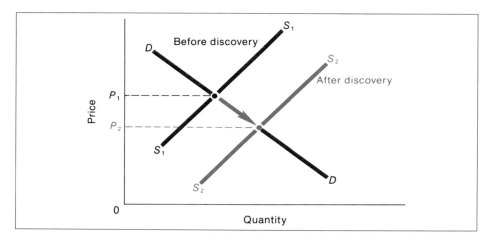

Figure 35–4
PRICE EFFECTS OF A
DISCOVERY OF ADDITIONAL
RESERVES
A discovery causes a rightward
shift in the supply curve of the
resource. That is so because the
cost to suppliers of any given
quantity of the resource is
reduced by the discovery, so it will
pay them to supply a larger
quantity at any given price. This
must lead to a price fall (from P_1 to
P_2).

them to recognize that the supply is much larger than they had thought (curve S_2S_2). Like any outward shift in a supply curve, this can be expected to cause a fall in price. A clear historical example was the discovery of gold and silver in Central and South America by the Spaniards in the sixteenth century. This led to sharp and substantial drops in the prices of these precious metals in Europe, and was a source of major economic problems for the Tudor monarchs.

2. ***The invention of new methods of mining or refining that may significantly reduce extraction costs.*** This, too, can lead to a rightward shift in the supply curve as it becomes profitable for suppliers to deliver a larger quantity at any given price. The situation is therefore again represented by a diagram like Figure 35-4, only it is now a reduction in cost, not a new discovery of reserves, that shifts the supply curve to the right.

3. ***A government subsidy.*** From the point of view of the supplier, a government subsidy is exactly the same as a reduction in mining or processing costs—either technological improvement or a handout from the government will decrease the cost per tonne of supplying the resource. Thus the supply curve will shift to the right (from S_1S_1 to S_2S_2 in Figure 35-4) and the price will fall.

4. ***Price controls that hold prices down or decrease them.*** The government can pass a law prohibiting the sale of the resource at a price higher than P^* (see Figure 35-5). Sometimes this works, though not always, for in many cases an illegal black market emerges, where very high prices are charged more or less secretly. But even where it does work it causes problems. Since the objective is to make the legal ceiling price, P^*, lower than the market equilibrium price, P, at price P^* quantity demanded (five million tonnes in the figure) will be higher than the free-market level (four million tonnes). Similarly, we may expect that now quantity supplied (two million tonnes in the figure) will be less than its free-market level. Thus, as always happens in these cases, the quantity supplied is insufficient to match the quantity demanded—a shortage emerges.

Many economists believe that this is exactly what happened after 1971 in the United States when price controls were imposed for a time. It was just at this time that the economy experienced a sudden plague of shortages and the Americans seemed to be "running out of nearly everything." But the shortages apparently were attributable to the controls, not to anything happening to

Figure 35-5
CONTROLS ON THE PRICE OF A RESOURCE

By law, price is kept to P^* which is below the equilibrium price, P. This reduces quantity supplied from four million to two million tonnes and raises quantity demanded from four million to five million tonnes. A shortage measured by length AB, or three million tonnes, is the result.

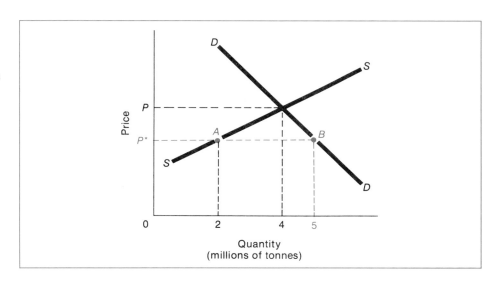

resource supplies or the productive process. And after price controls ended in 1974, most of the "shortages" disappeared.

Each of the examples of minerals whose prices did not rise can be explained by one or more of these factors. For example, both zinc and magnesium have benefited from technological changes that lowered extraction costs. In the case of the latter, the process that turns the mineral into ingots has grown far more efficient than it was in the 1920s. The case of lead is quite different. There, some new mines in Missouri turned out to hold abundant quantities of ore that was much easier to extract and much cheaper to refine than what had been available before. This was apparently enough to keep the price of lead from rising quickly. Obviously, events in reality are more complex than a naïve reading of theoretical models might lead us to believe.

Yet, despite these influences, which have postponed the price rises in depletable resources predicted by the theory, both logic and evidence indicate that in the long run supply and demand must win out. As a resource really becomes scarce and costly to obtain, its free-market price must ultimately rise, and so must its actual price, unless government interferes.

The Messy Story of Oil Prices

The case of oil must be singled out both because of its critical importance for our economy and because it illustrates how different the real world can be from the pure supply–demand model of perfect competition. Yet we will see that even with almost constant government interference and control by a powerful cartel (that is, a monopolistic association of suppliers), the forces of supply and demand continue to play a crucial role. Indeed, we will see that the cartel succeeded not *in spite of* the supply–demand mechanism, but *because* it was able to use that mechanism. Traditionally, the oil industry was virtually controlled by seven large companies, which made price and production decisions, negotiated terms separately with each of the oil-producing countries, and extracted the oil from the ground. In 1951, when Mohammed Mossadegh, Prime Minister of Iran, tried to seize the assets of British Petroleum, the "seven sisters" simply acted together to increase production in more docile areas, refused to buy Iranian oil, and waited for his government to be overthrown.

Throughout the 1950s, the world market price of oil remained low, enabling oil to drive out many competing energy sources. Both the world's output and energy consumption tripled during this decade, and oil became very nearly the unchallenged source of power. During the 1960s, it apparently became increasingly difficult for production to keep up with the burgeoning demand, a sure sign that prices were being kept artificially low.

The oil-producing countries sought to overcome the oil companies' domination. After some earlier abortive attempts, Iran, Iraq, Kuwait, Saudi Arabia, and Venezuela formed the Organization of Petroleum Exporting Countries (OPEC) in Baghdad on September 14, 1960. OPEC was quiet until 1970, when Muammar al-Qaddafi, President of Libya, opened an offensive to gain control of oil resources in his country. He applied pressure by the use of production cutbacks and threatened shutdowns against individual companies, beginning with the weaker independents. Working in Libya's favour were the growing costs of finding and extracting non-Middle East oil, particularly of the low-sulphur variety found in Libya, and the growing aversion on the part of the governments of oil-producing countries to political interference. Unlike the Mossadegh incident, no British cruiser appeared in the Persian Gulf. Qaddafi achieved a price rise of 30 cents a barrel, and increased the tax rate from 50 percent to 55 percent. The other oil-producing countries, having remained on the sidelines throughout the confrontation, demanded and won similar concessions.

By 1973, partly through extensive expropriation by the OPEC countries, the role of the oil companies had been reduced to that of technical contractors. The OPEC countries now imposed massive price increases. The price of crude oil rose 12 percent in June 1973, 66 percent in October 1973, and doubled in January 1974.

The immediate cause of these price increases was the attempt by 11 oil-producing countries to punish the United States and Holland for their support of Israel in October 1973. The Arab countries announced a production cutback of five percent, and an embargo of sales to those countries, thus causing an inward shift of the supply curve and a sharp price rise.

For a while thereafter, OPEC price increases became more moderate, roughly keeping pace with world inflation. Then suddenly, in January 1979, the government of the Shah of Iran toppled and was replaced by the Islamic Republic. Oil exports dropped sharply, again shifting the supply curve inward. Predictably, the price of oil shot up, rising from $12 a barrel in the beginning of 1979 to more than $25 at the end of that year; by mid-1982 the world price was about $33 a barrel. (Throughout this period, the Canadian government kept domestic oil prices from rising anything like these increases in the rest of the world. We examine specific details of the Canadian policy later in this chapter.)

But, even in the presence of the OPEC cartel, forces of supply and demand beyond its control played a part. In 1981 and 1982, widespread recession in the industrialized world together with measures to induce conservation shifted the demand curve for oil inward. The world price actually dropped and world oil production in 1981 declined by a record year-to-year amount: six percent. By mid-1981 oil consumption outside the communist countries had fallen to 46 million barrels per day from 49.5 million a year earlier. Global oil surpluses are now expected to continue until the late 1980s. But ultimately the fact that oil is a finite resource means that its continued depletion is likely to cause its price to begin to rise once more.

The Free Market and Resource Depletion

Popular views of the process of depletion of a vital resource envision a scenario in which consumption grows year after year and stocks of the item dwindle as a result until, one day, quantity supplied can no longer keep up with quantity demanded. From then on, the nation faces a history of steady shortfalls, with rationing or chaos the inevitable result. Economists pay little attention to such scenarios. Though it seems implausible to anyone who has not studied economics, it is nevertheless true that:

In a free market, quantity demanded can never exceed quantity supplied, even if a finite resource is undergoing rapid depletion. The reason is simple: In any free market, quantity demanded must always equal quantity supplied, for price will automatically adjust to eliminate any difference between them.

In fact, there have been cases of real shortages in the past. For example, twice during the 1970s the quantities of gasoline supplied were, in many parts of the United States, lower than the quantities demanded, and chaos did indeed result. There were long lines of cars at those gas stations that remained open, and huge amounts of petroleum and time were wasted in the process as the cars inched forward (sometimes for hours) toward the gas pumps. During World War II, meat, sugar, and other commodities were in short supply, and there was a period in the 1970s when supplies of paper, copper, and other commodities were inadequate to meet demand. But in every such case there were regulations or laws that prohibited full adjustment of prices. In a sense, then, it was these price regulations, and not any disappearance of resources, that were responsible for the shortages.

In theory, any shortage—any excess of quantity demanded over quantity supplied—must be artificial; that is, it must be ascribed to a decision to prevent the price mechanism from doing its job.

To say that the cause is artificial, of course, does not settle the basic issue—whether freedom of price adjustments is desirable when resource depletion is underway, or whether interference with the pricing process is justified. We will see that there are, in fact, valid grounds on which to question the desirability of completely unrestricted freedom of pricing in such circumstances.

However, there are many economists who believe that this is another of those cases in which the disease—shortages and the resulting dislocations in the economy—is far worse than the cure—deregulation of prices. They hold that the general public is misguided in its clamour against the rising prices that must ultimately accompany depletion of a resource, and that people are mistaken in regarding these price rises as the problem, when in fact they are part of the cure.

It is, of course, easy to understand why no consumer loves a price rise. And it is also easy to understand why many consumers ascribe any such price rise to a plot—to a conspiracy by greedy suppliers who somehow deliberately arrange shortages in order to force prices upward. Sometimes, this view is even correct. For example, the members of OPEC have openly and frankly undertaken to influence the flow of oil in order to increase the price they receive for it. But it is important to recognize from the principles of supply and demand that when a resource grows scarce its price will tend to rise automatically, even without any conspiracies or plots.

Let us first see how economists can possibly say that rising prices for scarce resources are good for the economy. Then we will consider some valid reservations about the desirability of an unfettered market solution as we discuss the controversy over Canadian energy policy.

On the Virtues of Rising Prices

Rising prices help control the process of resource depletion in three basic ways:

1. They discourage consumption and waste and provide an inducement for conservation.

2. They stimulate more efficient use of the resource by industry, providing incentives for the employment of processes that are more sparing in their use of the resource or that use substitute resources.

3. They encourage innovation—the discovery of other, more abundant resources that can do the job and of new techniques that permit these other resources to be used economically.

Let us examine each of these a bit more carefully.

It used to be said that consumer demand for oil was highly *inelastic*—that prices would never make a significant dent in consumption of petroleum. Recent events seem to have proved otherwise. With rising fuel prices people have begun to insulate their homes, to keep home temperatures lower, to take fewer shopping trips, and to buy smaller automobiles. Moreover, in the long run, we can expect even more demand adjustment—that is, the long-run demand curve for oil is probably more elastic than the short-run curve. As the nation's fleet of cars wears out, they will gradually be replaced by vehicles that economize on fuel. New homes will be built more snugly to save on heat, and they will be located closer to the workplace to save on fuel in transportation.

Evidence indicating how much difference price can make is provided by the pattern of fuel consumption in Europe. There, fuel taxes have long habituated the public to high gasoline prices, and fuel consumption per capita is over 45 percent less than it is in the United States, even in countries like Sweden, with its harsh climate and its relatively substantial driving distances.

The second way in which a price increase helps to conserve a scarce resource is through its effect on industrial usage. Like a final consumer, a business firm can economize on its use of a resource. It can use more fuel-efficient means of transportation and more insulation. It can locate its new plants in ways that reduce the need for transportation. And it can substitute labour and other inputs for scarce resources. The use of a pick and shovel involves the employment of more labour to save the fuel that might have been used by a bulldozer. Farmers who gather manure save the fuel necessary to produce chemical fertilizers.

There is evidence that such substitutions are already occurring. Warehouses that used to have open loading bays have installed doors to keep in heat, hiring people to open and close them. Because of rising gas prices, ranchers reportedly are hiring additional cowhands to drive cattle on foot instead of carrying them on trucks. The examples can be multiplied indefinitely.

Finally, rising prices help to slow the disappearance of a resource by stimulating the production of substitutes and even by inducing more production of the resource itself. The last statement is paradoxical—If a resource is finite how can more be produced? Certainly it can be extracted and sold faster, but that only hastens the process of depletion. How can we get *more* of a *finite* resource? Of course, we cannot. But rising prices will make it feasible to use repositories of the resource that otherwise would have been considered too inaccessible and simply not worth the effort. It has recently become economically feasible, for example, to extract oil from Canada's tar sands—formations that it was formerly too expensive to exploit. Similarly, piping natural gas from the Arctic has long been talked about, but only higher prices will make it feasible.

And higher prices of the vanishing resource also stimulate research and development which lead to the emergence of substitute products. It is high oil prices that will transform solar energy, wind energy, and biomass energy from romantic notions, which cynics can deride as impractical, into effective sources of fuel which may some day make substantial contributions to the economy's energy flows. At the oil prices in effect during the 1960s these sources simply could not compete.

A final word on the price mechanism and resource conservation is in order. One often hears about the rape of our natural resources by greedy owners who rush to exchange them for profits without any thought for the needs of the future. But the price mechanism has built-in incentives to prevent this from happening. We have seen how a resource's price can be expected to rise automatically as its stocks dwindle. Obviously, when the price rise is sufficiently rapid it becomes more profitable to leave more of it underground for future extraction rather than to sell it now at today's lower prices. That, indeed, is one of the things some of the OPEC countries may now be doing and one of the reasons oil prices have risen so rapidly. One may legitimately object to this for many reasons, but surely *not* on the grounds that oil supplies are being squandered by excessive and irresponsible rates of extraction.

Freedom of pricing of a dwindling resource induces conservation by consumers and by industry; it encourages the introduction of substitute products; and it induces moderation in rates of extraction by the owners of their sources.

The Controversy Over Canadian Energy Policy

In Canada, the 1974–84 controversy over oil prices stemmed from four basic facts. First, many Canadian consumers of oil felt that the high world price was *artificial*.

It had been caused by a monopolistic cartel in foreign lands. Since Canada has the resources to be self-sufficient in oil, many felt that we should not be "held to ransom" by such monopoly practices. After all, the only reason we import oil in the East and export it in the West is that we lack sufficient pipeline facilities. It was argued that if we could solve this problem, our self-sufficiency in oil would permit a lower, "made in Canada" price.

The second major influence in the oil price debate was the *fear of unemployment* expressed by many workers in manufacturing firms in central Canada. Their concern was that large increases in energy prices would force firms to lay off some of their workers. We learned in Chapter 10 that this reasoning is correct: Rising costs of energy cause an inward shift of the aggregate-supply curve, leading simultaneously to a rise in the overall price level and to a fall in real GNP (review Figure 10-2 and pages 173–77 if necessary). But the decrease in output for the country as a whole would be much smaller than that which would occur in central Canada. This is because of the large number of Canadian workers employed in the energy industry in the West. These workers feared that low producer prices for energy in Canada would eliminate the profit incentive for their employers, so that exploration and other activities would diminish, with a consequent loss of jobs in the West. We learned earlier in this chapter that this reasoning is also correct. Thus, fear of unemployment and lower incomes boiled down to a *distribution problem*: Whose incomes should the governments protect—those of Canadians in the East or those in the West?

The third major issue in the oil price discussions was the fight between the federal and provincial (mainly Alberta) governments concerning tax revenue. *Both levels of government wanted the tax revenue* that could stem from higher oil prices. Natural resources are owned by the provinces, which can impose various taxes (known as royalties) on producers operating on provincial lands. But the federal government has jurisdiction over international and interprovincial trade, so it can levy export and import taxes and subsidies as oil crosses provincial and international borders. The two levels of government were forced to negotiate, because there is a limit to the total amount of tax that can be imposed. If taxes are very high, consumer prices must also skyrocket to provide some operating revenue to the producer. So the total tax is bounded by concern for both consumers and producers.

The fourth important factor in the oil price issue was the high degree of *foreign ownership* in the energy industry. Approximately 70 percent of the shares of oil companies operating in Canada were foreign-owned. The federal government thought a low oil price was a good idea because it would limit the profits of these companies, and so preclude a large transfer of income from Canadians to foreigners.

How did the federal government's energy policy accommodate these four concerns? The Canadian price of oil was allowed to increase, but only very *gradually*, so that by 1981 it was still at only half the level of world oil prices. This pricing policy followed from two considerations: (1) the federal government's sympathy with the view that Canadian resource endowments give us the right and ability to ignore world prices, and (2) its view that potential unemployment in manufacturing operations in Ontario is more important, on political grounds, than potential unemployment in the energy industries in the West. The government's attempt to overcome the problem of there being no pipeline to Atlantic Canada involved imposing export taxes on oil and gas from the West to pay for an import subsidy for foreign oil purchased in the East.

Concerning the distribution of energy tax revenues between Ottawa and the provinces, the federal government simply saw the world price developments as an opportunity to tap a lucrative new tax source. It imposed the Petroleum and Natural Gas Revenue Tax at such a level that producer returns became *negative*.[2]

---

[2]See Brian L. Scarfe, "The National Energy Program After Three Years: An Economic Perspective," *Western Economic Review*, 1984.

This forced provincial governments (principally Alberta) to reduce their taxes, just to try to stimulate economic activity within their own regions.

Two components of the federal National Energy Program were directed at the issue of foreign profits. One involved direct purchases of oil operations from foreigners (this included such measures as the creation of Petro-Canada), and the other involved levying a tax on producing firms that was designed to avoid limiting the return on *new* exploration and development. The idea in this case was to tax oil discovered before 1981 much more heavily than that found later. The "old" oil is produced at much lower cost than that from recent operations. Thus, economic rents exist on these older operations, since the going market price is sufficient to make viable the more recent, expensive extractions. From a microeconomic point of view, the attempt to tax only rents makes sense, as long as the tax is not set too high.

How did the federal government's decisions turn out? Were they consistent with sound economic analysis? Again, let us consider each part of the problem in turn. Of course, our energy supplies made it *possible* for Canadians to pay a price below world levels. Nevertheless, the option of selling at the world price was available, so it represented the true opportunity cost of Canadians using energy. A lower price simply precluded the "correct" signals of relative scarcities from reaching individual Canadian decision-makers. Only if the high world price could have been viewed as temporary (based, for example, on an expectation that OPEC would collapse as a result of internal struggles over production quotas for member countries), would it have made sense to insulate our economy from a needless series of adjustments. However, the Canadian government resisted the move to world prices long after any hope that the world situation was temporary could be sustained.

The federal government's views concerning unemployment in central Canada versus unemployment in the West appear to have been somewhat short-sighted. Job prospects are not enhanced in Canadian manufacturing if artificially low energy prices encourage the perpetuation of production techniques that are inefficient by international comparison. Finally, unemployment in central Canada was increased when the depressed energy industry in the West sent fewer orders back East for industrial equipment and job-seekers ceased their migration to the West.

The federal government soon amended the details of its tax arrangements (for example, the export tax on natural gas was removed), so that producer returns were no longer negative. These moves suggest that the government admitted taking too large a share of taxes. Given their policy of precluding a sufficient rise in the consumer price for energy, producer prices fell too much.

Some "Canadianization" of the energy industry has followed from the National Energy Program, but any contribution this might have made to establishing "security of supply" was certainly nullified in the short run by the cutbacks in exploration and development that stemmed from low producer prices and high taxes. Unfortunately, the retroactive taxing of the oil industry's most profitable operations (the "old" oil), and the nationalization program, came at a most inopportune time—just as deregulation was occurring in the United States. When combined with the negative returns, it was enough to cause a significant shift in economic activity to the United States.

In summary, with the passage of time, any validity of the "made in Canada" oil price diminished. By late 1984, Canadian prices were roughly in line with world prices, but the lag was too long. Among the problems that have resulted from this lag are the cutback in oil development, the delay in moving toward less energy-intensive production methods, and the deterioration of federal–provincial dialogue within the country.

Environmental Considerations

The energy issue is further complicated by the environmental problems with which it is associated. Virtually every major energy source causes some environmental damage. The dangers of nuclear power have been publicized widely by its opponents, as has the damage done by strip mining (that is, the mining of coal from the surface rather than from underground). Even a form of energy like wind harnessed by turbines and windmills, which is widely favoured by those who oppose nuclear sources, generates some damage. If used extensively, it would be a source of significant noise pollution and a serious threat to birds.

Attempts to deal with such environmental problems have contributed to the rise in the cost of energy. By requiring the installation of devices that limit the emissions of electricity-generating stations, automobiles, and other major sources of pollution, fuel efficiency has been decreased. Many (but by no means all) observers believe that the additional use of fuel is well worth it, but it is important to recognize that there is a cost and that it is real and substantial. For example, it has been estimated by the U.S. Council on Environmental Quality that pollution controls can raise the cost of generating a given quantity of electricity from coal by about 25 percent.[3]

Environmental issues also have other implications for fuel policy. For example, they inhibit the substitution of coal for oil in electricity generation. The United States has enormous reserves of coal, at least enough to meet U.S. fuel demands for 1000 years at current rates of consumption. But coal is also a treacherous energy source. Its extraction regularly kills many miners and seriously damages the health of others. Its use releases sulphur dioxide and particulate pollution into the atmosphere, both of which endanger the health of the population and, generally, make for dirtier communities whose buildings deteriorate more rapidly. Also, this use of coal is a major contributor to the acid rain problem throughout North America. And strip mining leaves behind it scars that turn beautiful countryside into unsightly ditches.

In Chapter 34 we described what may be potentially the most serious environmental problem of all: Burning fossil fuels raises the concentration of carbon dioxide in the earth's atmosphere, thereby increasing global temperatures (the "greenhouse effect"). As we noted, many observers now predict that by the end of this century, gradually increasing temperatures may well have disastrous effects on crops, will begin to melt the polar icecaps (causing massive flooding along coastlines), and will cause other calamitous consequences.

Growing Reserves of Exhaustible Resources: Our Puzzle Revisited

We began this chapter with a brief discussion of the more pessimistic views about future resource supplies, including an estimate made in 1960 that by 1985 we would have only 18 years of nickel reserves and 12 years of copper reserves, and would have run out of zinc and lead. Yet in Table 35–2 (page 682) we saw, strangely enough, that between 1960 and 1980 the reserves of all of these finite resources actually increased!

This paradox has a straightforward economic explanation: Rising reserves are a tribute to the success of exploration activity that took place in the meantime. Minerals are not discovered by accident. They are discovered by difficult and costly work requiring the services of geologists and engineers and the use of extremely expensive machinery. Exploration requires an enormous expenditure which industry does not find worth making when reserves are high and when mineral prices are low.

[3]Council on Environmental Quality, *Environmental Quality*, 1966, page 160, and 1979, page 439.

Consequently, over the course of the twentieth century proven reserves have not changed very much. Every time some mineral's known reserves fell, particularly if its price therefore tended to rise, exploration increased until the decline was offset. The law of supply and demand worked. Falling reserves or rising prices of a mineral caused an upsurge in exploration, just as we expect from supply–demand analysis. In the 1970s, for example, the rising price of oil led to very substantial increases in oil exploration, which helped to build up reserves.

A Few Words on Future Prospects

We close this chapter with a few words about the future. Despite the current oil glut there seems to be a good reason to fear that for the next decade or two fuel problems will continue to be serious. OPEC is not the only cause of the problems by any means. Easily accessible sources of oil *are* growing scarcer, and this means that the cost of oil must rise.

But for the longer run there is reason for optimism about the availability of energy. Past history and research already under way suggest that new techniques will become feasible as higher prices encourage the development of alternative energy sources. Already solar heating has become economically viable in certain cases (especially for private homes in sunny climates) and can be expected to spread. Also, Canada has additional sources of hydro-electric energy. Finally, scientists are studying the use of geothermal energy, and nuclear fusion promises a virtually unlimited supply of energy if we can learn to harness it.

In all these ways, then, higher prices will lead to a lower quantity demanded and a greater quantity supplied of energy, thus helping to avert an "energy crisis." Calculations that show when current demand will exhaust the current supply are simply beside the point.

Yet we certainly do not want to paint too rosy a picture. Adjustment to higher relative prices can be painful, as owners of gas-guzzling cars and fuel-inefficient homes have already found out. In peering into the crystal ball, we can see that goods and services that rely either directly or indirectly on fossil fuels are likely to remain relatively expensive. This can hardly be considered good news. But the point to emphasize is that we *can* see an end to this process. And this end is not a cataclysmic one where we run out of energy, industrial activity ceases, and we all freeze. Instead, it is one where new technology based on non-depletable energy resources like the sun and the atom takes over the business of powering vehicles, heating homes, and turning the wheels of industry. Energy then will probably be more expensive than it is today, but it *will* be available.

Summary

1. The quantity demanded of a scarce resource can exceed the quantity supplied only if something prevents the market mechanism from operating freely.

2. As a resource grows scarce on a free market, its price will rise, inducing increased conservation by consumers, increased exploration for new reserves, and increased substitution of other items that can serve the same purpose.

3. In fact, in the twentieth century the relative prices of many resources have remained roughly constant, largely because of the discovery of new reserves and because of cost-saving innovations.

4. The price mechanism and rationing are the only known alternatives to chaos in the allocation of scarce resources.

5. In the 1970s, OPEC succeeded in raising the relative price of petroleum, but the rise in price led to a substantial decline in world demand as well as to an increase in production in countries outside OPEC.

6. Canada's energy policy during the late 1970s and early 1980s kept domestic energy prices below world levels, while producers were heavily taxed. Energy consumers obtained a short-term benefit, but longer-run costs include: a cut-back in exploration and development

and reduced investment in energy-efficient production techniques in Canadian manufacturing.

7. Many programs for the reduction of oil consumption have undesirable environmental consequences.
8. Known reserves for depletable scarce resources have not tended to fall with the passage of time because as the price of the resource rises with increasing scarcity, increased exploration for new reserves becomes profitable.

Concepts for Review

Known reserves
Organization of Petroleum
    Exporting Countries (OPEC)

Rationing
Paradox of growing reserves of
    finite resources

Questions for Discussion

1. Discuss some valid and some invalid objections against letting rising prices eliminate shortages of supplies of scarce resources.
2. Describe what must be done by a government agency that is given the job of rationing a scarce resource.
3. Some observers believe that a program of rationing may work fairly satisfactorily for a few months or for one or two years, particularly during an emergency period when patriotic spirit is strong. However, they believe that over longer periods and when there is no upsurge of patriotism it is likely to prove far less satisfactory. Do you agree or disagree? Why?
4. Try to describe the various ways that fuel is used up in the production of gasohol, including that used up making the required equipment; that used in transporting the fuel inputs; and so on.
5. Why may a rise in the price of fuel lead to more conservation after several years have passed than it does in the months following the price increase? What does your answer imply about the relative size of the long-run elasticity of demand for fuel and its short-run elasticity?

VII

The Distribution and Growth of Income

Input Prices: Interest, Rent, and Profits

36

The most common and durable
source of factions has been
the various and unequal
distribution of property.

JAMES MADISON

Parts Four, Five, and Six have been devoted to examining the things the free-market system does well and the things it does poorly. We mentioned in Chapter 29 that the market mechanism cannot be counted on to distribute income in accord with ethical notions of "fairness" or "justice," and we listed this failing as one of the market's shortcomings. But there is much more to be said about how income is distributed in a market economy and about how governments interfere with and alter this distribution process. These are the subjects of Part Seven.

The broad outlines of how the market mechanism distributes income are familiar to all of us. Each person owns some **factors of production**—the inputs used in the production process. Many of us have only our own labour; but some of us also have funds that we can lend, land that we can rent, or natural resources that we can sell. These factors are sold on markets at prices determined by supply and demand. So the distribution of income in a market economy is determined by the level of employment of the factors of production and by their prices. For example, if wages are rather high and are fairly equal among workers, and if unemployment is low, then few people will be poor. But if wages are low and unequal, and unemployment is high, then many people will be poor.

For purposes of discussion, the factors of production may be grouped into five broad categories: land, labour, capital, exhaustible natural resources, and a rather mysterious input called **entrepreneurship**. Exhaustible natural resources were studied in Chapter 35. In this chapter, we will study the payments made for the use of three factors: the interest paid to capital, the rent of land, and the profits earned by entrepreneurs.

Since this chapter focuses on the *theories* of interest, rents, and profits, it may be useful first to have a brief look at how much these factors earn in *reality*. According to Canadian data for 1983, interest payments accounted for about 10.1 percent of national income, land rents and non-corporate profits for a mere 5.5 percent, and corporate profits for about 10.7 percent. In total, the returns to all the factors of production dealt with in this chapter amounted to about one-quarter of national income. Where did the rest of it go? The answer is that almost three-quarters of national income was composed of employee compensation—wages and salaries. The huge share of labour in national income is one of the reasons why the next chapter is devoted entirely to this subject.

Entrepreneurship is the act of starting new firms, introducing new products and technological innovations, and, in general, taking the risks that are necessary in seeking out business opportunities.

The distribution of income is perhaps the one area in economics in which any one individual's interests almost inevitably conflict with someone else's. By definition, if a larger share of the total income is distributed to me, a smaller share will be left for you. It is also a topic about which emotions run high and the facts or the logic of the issues are often ignored. In this chapter, we will encounter several examples of serious misunderstandings about the facts: misapprehensions about the true magnitudes of interest rates and profits, people's unwillingness to face up to the consequences of rent controls, and so forth.

The Principle of Marginal Productivity

By now it will not surprise you to learn that factor prices are analysed in terms of supply and demand. The supply sides of the markets for the various factors differ enormously from one another, which is why each factor market must be considered separately. But one basic principle, the **principle of marginal productivity**, has been used to explain the demand for every input. Before restating the principle, it will be useful to recall two concepts that were introduced in Chapter 22: **marginal physical product** (MPP) and **marginal revenue product** (MRP).[1]

Table 36–1, which repeats Table 22–6 (page 434), helps us review these two concepts by recalling the example of Farmer Pfister, who had to decide how much fertilizer to apply to his fixed plot of land. The marginal *physical* product (MPP) column tells us how many additional bushels of corn each additional tonne of fertilizer yields. For example, according to the table, the fourth tonne increases the crop by 300 bushels. The marginal *revenue* product (MRP) column tells us how many dollars this marginal physical product is worth. In the example in the table, corn is assumed always to sell at $2 per bushel, so the marginal revenue product of the fourth tonne of fertilizer is $2 per bushel times 300 bushels, or $600. We can now state the marginal productivity principle formally:

The marginal productivity principle states that when factor markets are competitive it always pays a profit-maximizing firm to hire that quantity of any input at which the marginal revenue product is equal to the price of the input.

The basic logic behind the principle is both simple and powerful. If the input's marginal revenue product is, for example, greater than its price, it will pay the firm to hire more and more of it until diminishing returns reduce the MRP to the level

[1]To review these concepts see Chapter 22, pages 424 and 434.

> The **marginal physical product** (MPP) of an input is the increase in output that results from a one-unit increase in the use of the input, holding the amounts of all other inputs constant.
>
> The **marginal revenue product** (MRP) of an input is the additional sales revenue the firm takes in by selling the marginal physical product of that input.

Table 36–1
MARGINAL PHYSICAL PRODUCTS AND MARGINAL REVENUE PRODUCTS OF FARMER PFISTER'S FERTILIZER

FERTILIZER (tonnes)	MARGINAL PHYSICAL PRODUCT (bushels)	MARGINAL REVENUE PRODUCT (dollars)
1	250	500
2	300	600
3	350	700
4	300	600
5	250	500
6	150	300
7	50	100
8	0	0
9	−50	−100

of the input's price. Conversely, if MRP is less than price, the firm is using too much of the input. Let us use Table 36-1 to demonstrate how the marginal productivity principle works.

Suppose the firm were using four tonnes of fertilizer at a cost of $350 per tonne. Since the table tells us that a fifth tonne has a marginal revenue product of $500, the firm could obviously add $150 to its profit by buying a fifth tonne. Only when the firm has used so much fertilizer that (because of diminishing returns) the MRP of still another tonne is less than $350 does it pay to stop expanding the use of fertilizer. In this example, five tonnes is the optimal amount to use.

One corollary of the principle of marginal productivity is obvious: The quantity of the input demanded depends on its price. The lower the price of fertilizer, the more it pays a firm to hire. In the example of the previous paragraph, it pays the firm to use five tonnes when the price of fertilizer is $350 per tonne. But if fertilizer were more expensive, say $550 per tonne, that price would exceed the value of the marginal product of the fifth tonne. It would, therefore, pay the firm to stop after the fourth tonne. Thus, *marginal productivity analysis shows that the quantity demanded of an input normally will decline as the price of the input rises.* The "law" of demand applies to inputs just as it applies to consumer goods.

The Derived Demand Curve for an Input

We can, in fact, be much more specific than this, for the marginal productivity principle tells us precisely how the demand curve for any input is derived from its marginal revenue product (MRP) curve.

Figure 36-1 presents graphically the MRP schedule from Table 36-1. Recall that, according to the marginal productivity principle, the quantity demanded of the input is determined by setting MRP equal to the input's price. Figure 36-1 considers three different possible prices for a tonne of fertilizer: $600, $500, and $300. At a price of $600 per tonne, we see that the quantity demanded is four tonnes (point *A*) because at that point MRP equals price. Similarly, if the price of fertilizer drops to $500 per tonne, quantity demanded rises to five tonnes (point *B*). Finally, should the price fall all the way to $300 per tonne, the quantity demanded would be six tonnes (point *C*). Points *A*, *B*, and *C* are therefore three points on the demand curve for fertilizer. Thus:

The demand curve for any input is the downward-sloping portion of its marginal revenue product curve.

Note that we restrict ourselves to the *downward-sloping* portion of the MRP

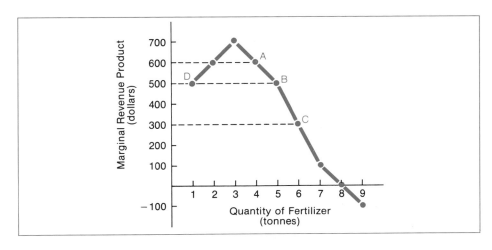

Figure 36-1
A MARGINAL REVENUE PRODUCT SCHEDULE
This diagram depicts the data in Table 36-1, which show how the marginal revenue product (MRP) of fertilizer first rises and then declines as more and more fertilizer is used. Since the optimal purchase rule is to keep applying fertilizer until MRP is reduced to the price of fertilizer, the *downward-sloping portion* of the MRP curve is Farmer Pfister's demand curve for fertilizer.

curve. The logic of the marginal productivity principle dictates this. For example, if the price of fertilizer is $500 per tonne, there are two input quantities for which MRP is $500: one tonne (point D) and five tonnes (point B). But point D cannot be the optimal stopping point because the MRP of a second tonne ($600) is greater than the cost of the second tonne ($500). The marginal productivity principle applies only in the range where returns are diminishing.

The demand for fertilizer (or for any other input) is called a **derived demand** because it is derived from the underlying demand for the final product (corn in this case). For example, suppose that a surge in demand drove the price of corn to $4 per bushel. Then, at each level of fertilizer usage, the MRP would be twice as large as when corn fetched $2 per bushel. This is shown in Figure 36–2 as an *upward* shift of the (derived) demand curve for fertilizer, from $D_0 D_0$ to $D_1 D_1$.[2] We conclude that, in general:

> An outward shift in the demand curve for any commodity causes an outward shift of the derived demand curve for all factors utilized in the production of that commodity.

Conversely, an inward shift in the demand curve for a commodity leads to inward shifts in the demand curves for factors used in producing that commodity.

This completes our discussion of the marginal productivity principle as a general explanation of the *demand* for any and all inputs. Now we will deal with the main factors of production individually, and see how their earnings are determined by the interaction of demand *and* supply. We begin with *interest payments*, the return to financial capital.

[2]To make the diagram easier to read, the (irrelevant) upward-sloping portion of each curve has been omitted.

Figure 36–2

A SHIFT IN THE DEMAND CURVE FOR FERTILIZER

If the price of corn goes up, the marginal *revenue* product curve shifts upward—from $D_0 D_0$ to $D_1 D_1$ in the diagram—even though the marginal *physical* product curve has not changed. In this sense, a greater demand for corn leads to a greater *derived* demand for fertilizer.

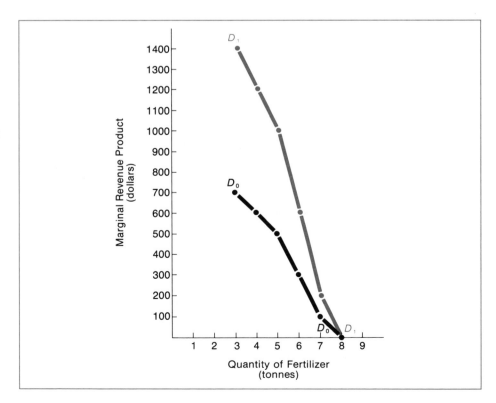

The Issue of Usury Laws: Are Interest Rates Too High?

The rate of interest is the price at which funds can be rented (borrowed). And, like other factor prices, the rate of interest is determined by supply and demand. However, this is one area in which many people have been dissatisfied with the outcome of the market process. Fears that interest rates, if left unregulated, would climb to exorbitant levels have made usury laws quite popular in many times and places. However, usury laws, when they are effective, interfere with the operation of supply and demand and are often harmful to economic efficiency.[3]

Whether a usury ceiling will or will not be effective depends on what the equilibrium rate of interest would have been in a free market. For example, a ceiling of 18 percent annual interest on consumer loans is quite irrelevant if the free-market equilibrium is 15 percent, but it can have important effects if the free-market rate is 25 percent. To see why this is so, we turn to the market determination of interest rates through the forces of supply and demand.

Investment, Capital, and Interest

There are many ways in which funds are loaned (meaning that they are rented to users): home mortgages, corporation or government bonds, consumer credit, and so on. On the demand side of these credit markets are borrowers—people or institutions that, for one reason or another, wish to spend more than they currently have.

In business, loans are used primarily to finance investment. To the business executive who "rents" (borrows) funds in order to finance an **investment** and pays interest in return, the funds really represent an intermediate step toward the acquisition of the machines, buildings, inventories, and other forms of physical **capital** that the firm will purchase.

Though the words "investment" and "capital" are often used interchangeably in everyday parlance, it is important to keep the distinction in mind. The relation between investment and capital has an analogy in the filling of a bathtub: The accumulated water in the tub is analogous to the stock of capital, while the flow of water from the tap (which adds to the tub's water) is like the investment. Just as the tap must be turned on in order for more water to accumulate, the capital stock increases only when there is investment. If investment ceases, the capital stock stops growing. Notice that when investment is *zero*, the capital stock *remains constant*; it does not fall to zero any more than a bathtub suddenly becomes empty when you turn off the tap.

The process of building up capital by investing, and then using this capital in production can be divided into five steps, which are listed below and summed up in Figure 36–3.

Step 1. The firm decides to enlarge its stock of capital.

Step 2. It raises the funds with which to finance its expansion.

Step 3. It uses these funds to hire the inputs, which are put to work building factories, warehouses, and the like. This step is the act of *investment*.

Step 4. After the investment is completed, the firm ends up with a larger stock of *capital*.

Step 5. The capital is used (along with other inputs) either to expand production or to reduce costs. At this point the firm starts earning *returns* on its investment.

Investment is the *flow* of resources into the production of new capital. It is the labour, steel, and other inputs devoted to the *construction* of factories, warehouses, railways, and other pieces of capital during some period of time.

Capital refers to an inventory (a stock) of plant, equipment, and other productive resources held by a business firm, an individual, or some other organization.

[3]For example, usury laws caused particularly severe problems for housing during periods of rapid inflation in the United States and hence many of them were abolished.

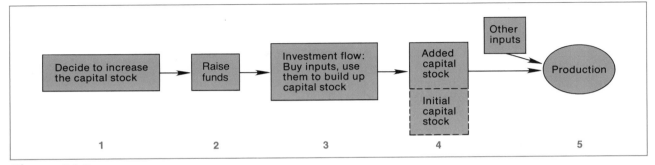

Figure 36-3

THE INVESTMENT-PRODUCTION PROCESS

The investor (1) decides to increase the capital stock; (2) raises funds; (3) uses the funds to buy inputs that produce capital stock (this step is called *investment*); (4) now holds more capital than before; and (5) uses this capital and other inputs to produce goods and services.

Interest is the payment for the use of funds employed in the production of capital; it is measured as a percent per year of the value of the funds tied up in the capital.

Notice that what the investor puts into the investment process is *money*, either his own or funds that he has borrowed from others. The funds are then transformed, in a series of steps, into a physical input suitable for use in production. If the funds were borrowed, the investor will someday return them to the lender with some payment for their use. This payment is called **interest**, and it is calculated as a percentage per year of the amount borrowed. For example, if the *interest rate* is 12 percent per year and $1000 is borrowed, the annual interest payment is $120.

The marginal productivity principle governs the quantity of funds demanded just as it governs the quantity of fertilizer demanded:

Firms will demand the quantity of borrowed funds that makes the marginal revenue product of the investment financed by the funds just equal to the interest rate charged for borrowing.

There is one noteworthy feature of capital that distinguishes it from other inputs, like fertilizer, however. The fertilizer applied by Farmer Pfister is used once and then it is gone; but a blast furnace, which is part of a steel company's capital, normally lasts many years. The furnace is a *durable* good; and because it is durable it contributes not only to today's production, but also to future production. This fact makes calculating the marginal revenue product more complex for a capital good than for other inputs.

To determine whether the MRP of a capital good is greater than the cost of financing it (that is, to decide whether an investment is profitable), we need a way to compare money values received at different times. To make such comparisons, economists and business people use a calculation procedure called **discounting**. Discounting is explained in detail in Appendix A to this chapter, but it is not important that you master this technique in an introductory course. There are really only two important points to learn:

1. A sum of money received at a future date is worth less than a sum of money received today.
2. This difference in values between money today and money in the future is greater when the rate of interest is higher.

It is not difficult to understand why this is so. Consider what you could do with a dollar that you received today rather than a year from today. If the annual rate of interest were 10 percent, you could lend it out (for example, by putting it in a bank account), and receive $1.10 in a year's time—your original $1 plus 10 cents interest. For this reason, money received today is worth more than the same number of dollars received later. Specifically, at a rate of interest of 10 percent per year, $1.10 to be received a year from today is equivalent to $1 of today's money. This illustrates the first of our two points.

Now suppose the annual rate of interest was 15 percent instead. In this case $1 invested today would grow to $1.15 (rather than $1.10) in a year's time, which means that $1.15 (not $1.10) received a year from today would be equivalent to $1 received today. This illustrates the second point.

The Market Determination of Interest Rates

The Downward-Sloping Demand Curve for Funds

These two points are all we need to explain why the quantity of funds demanded declines when the interest rate rises, or why the demand curve for funds has a negative slope.

Remember that the demand for borrowed funds is a *derived demand*, derived from the desire to invest in capital goods. But part, and perhaps all, of the marginal revenue product of a machine or a factory is received in the future. Hence, the value of this MRP *in terms of today's money* shrinks as the rate of interest rises. The consequence of this shrinkage is that a machine that appears to be a good investment when the rate of interest is 10 percent may look like a terrible investment when the rate of interest is 15 percent.

Here is a simple example that is easy to work out. Suppose a particular machine costs $1000 and its MRP is $1140, all of which is received one year from today. Should the machine be bought? If the rate of interest is 10 percent, $1000 in today's money is worth the same as $1100 in money a year from today. Since the machine will return $1140, the machine is worth more than its $1000 price. It is therefore a good investment. But what if the rate of interest were 15 percent instead? Then the $1000 that it takes to buy the machine would grow to $1150 after a year. Since this sum ($1150) is more than the machine will yield ($1140), it would be unwise for the firm to purchase the machine. While this example is quite contrived, the basic principle is valid:

As the rate of interest on borrowing rises, more and more investments that previously looked profitable start to look unprofitable. The demand for borrowing for investment purposes, therefore, is lower at higher rates of interest.

An example of a derived demand schedule for borrowing is given in Figure 36–4. Its

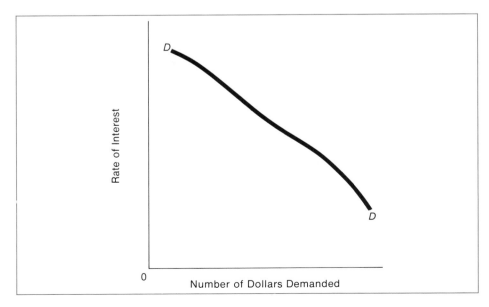

Figure 36-4
THE DERIVED DEMAND CURVE FOR LOANS
The rate of interest is the cost of a loan to the borrower. The lower the rate of interest, the more it will pay a business firm to borrow in order to finance new plant and equipment. That is why this demand curve has a negative slope.

negative slope illustrates the conclusion we have just stated—the higher the interest rate, the less money people and firms will want to borrow to finance their investments.

The Supply of Funds

Similar principles apply on the supply side of the market for funds—where the *lenders* are consumers, banks, and other types of business firms. Funds lent out are usually returned to the owner (with interest) only over a period of time. Loans will look better to lenders when they bear higher interest rates, so it is natural to think of the supply schedule for loans as being upward sloping—at higher rates of interest, lenders supply more funds. Such a supply schedule is shown by the curve *SS* in Figure 36–5, where we also reproduce the demand curve, *DD*, from Figure 36–4.

It is interesting to note, incidentally, that some lenders may have supply curves that do not slope uphill to the right like curve *SS*. Suppose, for example, that Jones is saving to buy a $10,000 boat in three years, and that if he lends money out at interest in the interim, at current interest rates he must save $3000 a year to reach his goal. If interest rates were higher, he could save less than $3000 each year and still reach his $10,000 goal. (The higher interest payments would, of course, contribute the difference.) So his saving (and lending) might decline. But this argument applies only to savers, like Jones, with a fixed accumulation goal.

Generally, we do expect that the quantity of loans supplied from domestic sources rises when the interest reward rises, so the domestic-supply curve has a positive slope, like *SS* in Figure 36–5. The equilibrium rate of interest is at point *E*, where quantity supplied and quantity demanded are equal. Thus, if our loan market operated in isolation from the rest of the world, we conclude that the equilibrium interest rate on loans is 17 percent.

Ceilings on Interest Rates

Let us now assume that Figure 36–5 refers to the supply of loans by banks to consumers. Consider what happens if there is a usury law that prohibits interest of more than 12 percent per annum on consumer loans. At this interest rate, the quantity supplied (point *A*) falls short of the quantity demanded (point *B*). This means that many applicants for consumer loans are being turned down even though the banks consider them to be creditworthy.

Figure 36-5
EQUILIBRIUM IN THE MARKET FOR LOANS
If there is no foreign lending, the free-market interest rate is 17 percent. At this interest rate, the quantity of loans supplied is equal to the quantity demanded. However, if an interest-rate ceiling is imposed, say, at 12 percent, the quantity of funds supplied (point *A*) will be smaller than the quantity demanded (point *B*).

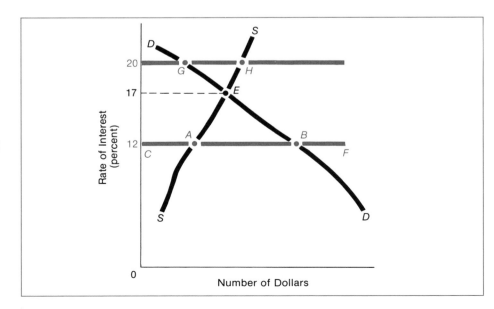

Who generally gains and who loses from this usury law? The gainers are easiest to identify: Those lucky consumers who are able to get loans at 12 percent even though they would have been willing to pay 17 percent. The law represents a windfall gain for them. The losers come on both the supply side and the demand side. First, there are the consumers who would have been willing and able to get credit at 17 percent but who are not lucky enough to get it at 12 percent. Then there are the banks (or, more accurately, bank shareholders) who could have made profitable loans at rates of up to 17 percent if there were no interest-rate ceiling.

This analysis helps explain the political popularity of usury laws. Few people sympathize with bank shareholders; indeed, it is the feeling that banks are "gouging" their borrowers that provides much of the impetus for usury laws. The consumers who get loans at lower rates will, naturally, be quite pleased with the result of the law. The others, who would like to borrow at 12 percent but cannot because quantity supplied is less than quantity demanded, are quite likely to blame the bank for refusing to lend, rather than blaming the government for outlawing mutually beneficial transactions.

This analysis has little good to say about usury ceilings, and economists generally oppose them. However, as is the case for minimum-wage laws (see the next chapter), interest-rate ceilings can play a constructive role when there is a monopoly over credit. If there is a monopoly lender, the analysis of Chapter 27 leads us to expect him to restrict his "output" (the volume of loans) by raising his "price" (the interest rate). Under such circumstances, an interest-rate ceiling may conceivably make sense.[4] But *may* is not *will*. Most economists believe that, except for isolated instances, the credit market is far closer to the competitive model than it is to the monopoly model.

The Importance of Foreign Lending for Interest-Rate Determination

The existence of foreign lending makes the supply curve of loans horizontal at the height given by existing foreign interest rates. This case is most relevant for Canada, since our financial markets are so integrated with those in the rest of the Western world. In particular, Canadians regularly borrow in the United States, and the total of our borrowing is very small relative to the overall size of their loan market. This makes Canadian sellers of bonds like perfectly competitive sellers on the world bond market—they can sell whatever quantity they wish at the going price (that is, interest rate). Thus, the world demand curve for our bonds (which is the same thing as the foreign supply curve of loan funds to Canada) is horizontal at the interest-rate value observed in the United States.

Suppose the American interest rate is 12 percent. Since Canadian savers have the option of lending their funds in the United States at 12 percent, the Canadian supply of funds in Figure 36–5 is no longer SS. Only the part above 12 percent is relevant, so the supply curve becomes CAE. The foreign supply curve is CF. Given this foreign supply, domestic borrowers can obtain all the funds they want at 12 percent, and so choose point B. In this case, point A simply indicates what proportion of loans come from domestic sources, and what quantity of foreign borrowing takes place (amount AB).

This analysis shows that a tax on foreign interest earnings in Canada and an increase in U.S. interest rates have exactly the same effects on Canadian interest rates. Either event would raise the horizontal line indicating the foreign willingness to lend in Canada. Suppose the tax or U.S. interest-rate hike raised the line to GH in Figure 36–5. Canadian borrowing (demand for funds) would drop to that indicated by point G, and Canadian savers would lend abroad an amount given by the distance GH. Canadian interest rates would rise along with American rates, to 20

---

[4]As we will see in the appendix to the next chapter, in such a case a usury ceiling might actually increase the volume of loans.

percent in this example. We can now appreciate why U.S. interest-rate increases are so unpopular in Canada, except among Canadians with money to lend. The analysis shows that our interest rates must rise along with theirs, with the result that many of our firms' investment projects become unprofitable. The end result is lower employment in Canada. Perhaps the more surprising conclusion to follow from the analysis is that a tax on foreign interest income in Canada has the same result. Often, the politicians who express the most concern over high interest rates are the ones who most favour increased taxes on foreigners who earn income in Canada.

The Determination of Rent: Simple Version

In dealing with interest, the special feature is that both the demand curve and the supply curve depend on the evaluation of flows of money received at different dates. When we turn our attention to the market for land—the second main factor of production—the special feature occurs on the supply side: Land is one factor of production whose quantity supplied is the same at every possible price. Indeed, the classical economists used this notion as the working definition of land. And the definition seems to fit, at least approximately. Although people may clear land, drain its swamps, fertilize it, build on it, or convert it from one use (a farm) to another (a housing development), it is very difficult to change the total supply of land by human effort.

What does this fact tell us about the determination of land rents? Figure 36–6 helps to provide an answer. The vertical supply curve *SS* represents the fact that no matter what the level of rents there are still 1000 hectares of land in a small hamlet called Littletown. The demand curve *DD* is a typical marginal revenue product curve, predicated on the notion that the use of land, like everything else, is subject to diminishing returns. The free-market price is determined, as usual, by the intersection of the supply and demand curves. In this example, each hectare of land in Littletown rents for $2000 per year. The interesting feature of this diagram is that, because quantity supplied is rigidly fixed at 1000 hectares whatever the price:

The market level of rent is entirely determined by the demand side of the market.

If, for example, the relocation of a major university in Littletown attracts more people who want to live there, the *DD* curve will shift outward, as depicted in

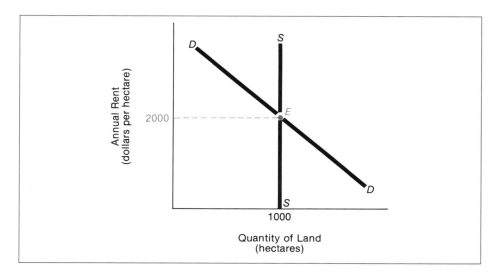

Figure 36-6

DETERMINATION OF LAND RENT IN LITTLETOWN
The supply curve of land, *SS*, is vertical, meaning that 1000 hectares are available in Littletown regardless of the level of rent. The demand curve for land slopes downward for the usual reasons. Equilibrium is established at point *E*, where the annual rental rate is $2000 per hectare.

Figure 36–7. Equilibrium in the market will shift from point E to point A; there will still be only 1000 hectares of land, but now each hectare will command a rent of $2500. The landlords will collect more rent, though they themselves have done nothing productive.

The same process also works in reverse, however. Should the university shut its doors and the demand for land decline as a result, the landlords will suffer even though they in no way have contributed to the decline in the demand for land. (To see this, simply reverse the logic of Figure 36–7. The demand curve begins at D_1D_1 and shifts to D_0D_0.)

The Rent of Land: Some Complications

If every parcel of land were of identical quality, this would be all there is to the theory of land rent. But, of course, plots of land do differ—in quality of soil, in topography, in access to sun and water, in proximity to marketplaces, and in other ways. The classical economists realized this, of course, and took it into account in their analysis of rent determination—a remarkable piece of economic logic formulated late in the eighteenth century and still considered valid today.

The basic notion is that capital invested on any piece of land must yield the same return as capital invested on any other piece that is actually used. Why? If it were not so, capitalists would bid against one another for the more profitable pieces of land until the rents of these parcels were driven up to a point where their advantages over other parcels had been eliminated.

Suppose that on one piece of land a given crop is produced for $160,000 per year in labour, fertilizer, fuel, and other non-land costs, while the same crop is produced for $120,000 on a second piece of land. The rent on the second parcel must be *exactly* $40,000 per year higher than the rent on the first, because otherwise production on one plot would be cheaper than on the other. If, for example, the rent difference were only $30,000 per year, it would be $10,000 cheaper to produce on the second plot of land. No one would want to rent the first plot and every grower would instead bid for the second plot. Obviously, rent on the first plot would be forced down by a lack of customers, and rent on the second would be driven up by eager bidders. These pressures would come to an end only when the rent difference reached $40,000, so that both plots became equally profitable.

At any given time, there are some pieces of land of such low quality that it does not pay to use them at all—remote deserts are a prime example. Any land

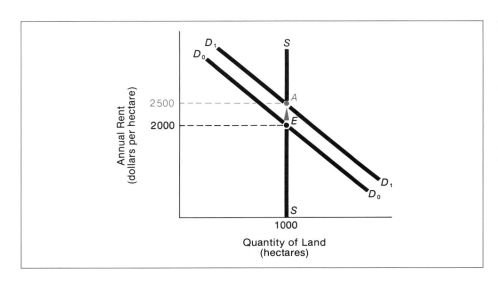

Figure 36-7
A SHIFT IN DEMAND WITH A VERTICAL SUPPLY CURVE
Now imagine that something happens to increase the demand for land—that is, to shift the demand curve from D_0D_0 to D_1D_1. Quantity supplied cannot change, but the rental rate can, and does. In this example, the annual rental for a hectare of land increases from $2000 to $2500.

that is exactly on the borderline of being used is called **marginal land**. By definition, marginal land earns no rent because if any rent were charged for it, there would be no takers.

We now combine these two observations—that the difference between the costs of producing on any two pieces of land must equal the difference between their rents, and that zero rent is charged on marginal land—to conclude that:

Rent on any piece of land will equal the difference between the costs of producing the output on that land and the cost of producing it on marginal land.

That is, competition for the superior plots of land will permit the landlords to charge prices that capture the full advantages of their superior parcels.

A useful feature of this analysis is that it helps us to understand more completely the effects of an outward shift in the demand curve for land. Suppose there is an increase in the demand for land because of a rise in population. Naturally, rents will rise. But we can be more specific than this. In response to an outward shift in the demand curve, two things will happen:

1. *It will now pay to employ some land whose use was formerly unprofitable*. The land that was previously on the zero-rent margin will no longer be on the borderline, and some land that is so poor that it was formerly not even worth considering will now just reach the borderline of profitability. The settling of the West illustrates this process quite forcefully. Land that once could not be given away is now quite valuable.

2. *People will begin more intensive use of the land that was already in use*. Farmers will use more labour and fertilizer to squeeze larger crops out of their land, as has happened in recent decades. Urban real estate on which two-story buildings previously made most sense will now be used for high-rise buildings.

Rents will be increased in a predictable way by these two developments. Since the land that is marginal *after* the change must be inferior to the land that was marginal previously, rents must rise by the difference in yields between the old and new marginal lands. Table 36–2 illustrates this point. We deal with three pieces of land: A, a very productive piece; B, a piece that was initially marginal; and C, a piece that is inferior to B but nevertheless becomes marginal when the upward shift in the demand curve for land occurs.

The crop costs $80,000 more when produced on B than on A, and $12,000 more when produced on C than on B. Suppose, initially, that demand for the crop is so low that C is unused and B is just on the margin between being used and left idle. Since B is marginal, it will yield no rent. We know that the rent on A will be

Table 36–2

NON-RENT COSTS AND RENT ON THREE PIECES OF LAND

TYPE OF LAND	NON-LAND COST OF PRODUCING A GIVEN CROP	TOTAL RENT Before	After
A. A tract that was better than marginal before and after	$120,000	$80,000	$92,000
B. A tract that was marginal before but is not any more	200,000	0	12,000
C. A tract that was previously not worth using but is now marginal	212,000	0	0

equal to the $80,000 cost advantage of A over B. Now suppose demand for the crop increases enough so that plot C is just brought into use. Plot C is now marginal land, and B acquires a rent of $12,000, the cost advantage of B over C.

But there is a second factor pushing up land rents—the increased intensity of use of land that was already in cultivation. As farmers apply more fertilizer and labour to their land, the marginal productivity of land increases, just as factory workers become more productive when they are given better equipment. Once again, the landowner is able to capture this increase in productivity in the form of higher rents. (If you do not understand why, refer back to Figure 36–7 and remember that the demand curves are marginal revenue product curves.) Thus, we can summarize the classical theory of rent as follows:

As the use of land increases, landlords receive higher payments from two sources:

1. Increased demand leads the community to employ land previously not good enough to use; the advantage of previously used land over the new marginal land increases, and rents go up correspondingly.
2. Land is used more intensively; the marginal revenue product of land rises, thus increasing the ability of the producer who uses the land to pay rent.

As late as the end of the nineteenth century, this analysis still exerted a powerful influence beyond technical economic writings. An American journalist, Henry George, was nearly elected mayor of New York in 1886, running on the platform that all government should be financed by "a single tax"—a tax on landlords who, he said, are the only ones who earn incomes while contributing nothing to the productive process and who reap the fruits of economic growth without contributing to economic progress.

Generalization: What Determines Wayne Gretzky's Salary?

Land is not the only scarce input whose supply is fixed, at least in the short run. Toward the beginning of this century some economists realized that the economic analysis of rent can be applied to inputs other than land. As we will see, this extension yielded some noteworthy insights.

Consider as an example the earnings of Wayne Gretzky of the Edmonton Oilers. Performers such as Gretzky seem to have little in common with plots of land in downtown Toronto. Yet, to an economist, the same analysis—the theory of rent—explains the incomes of these two factors of production. To understand why, we first note that there is only one Wayne Gretzky. That is, he is a scarce input whose supply is fixed just like the supply of land. Because he is in fixed supply, the price of his services must be determined in a way that is similar to the determination of land rents. Hence, economists have arrived at a more general definition of **economic rent** as *any payment made to a factor that is not necessary to keep that factor on the market.*

To understand the concept of economic rent, it is useful to divide the payment for any input into two parts. The first part is simply the minimum payment needed to acquire the input: the cost of equipment or the compensation for the unpleasantness, hard work, and loss of leisure involved in performing labour. The second part of the payment is a bonus that does not go to every input, but only to those that are of particularly high quality. Payments to workers with exceptional natural skills are a good example. These bonuses are like the extra payment for a better piece of land, and so are called *economic rents*.

Notice that only the first part of the factor payment is essential to induce the owner to supply the input. If a worker is not paid at least this first part, he will not supply his labour. But the additional payment—the economic rent—is pure gravy.

Economic rent is said to be earned whenever a factor of production receives a reward that exceeds the minimum amount necessary to keep the factor in its present employment.

The skillful worker is happy to have it as an extra. But it is not a deciding consideration in the choice of whether or not to work.

A moment's thought shows how this general notion of rent applies both to land and to Wayne Gretzky. The total quantity of land available for use is the same whether rent is high, low, or zero; no payments to landlords are necessary to induce land to be supplied to the market. So, by definition, the payments to landholders for their land are entirely economic rent—payments that are not necessary to induce the provision of the land to the economy. Wayne Gretzky is (almost) similar to land in this respect. He has hockey talents that are rare and cannot be reproduced. What determines the income of such a factor? Since the quantity supplied of such a unique, nonreproducible factor is absolutely fixed, and therefore unresponsive to price, the analysis of rent determination summarized in Figure 36–6 applies. *The position of the demand curve determines the price.*

Figure 36–8 summarizes the "Wayne Gretzky market." Vertical supply curve *SS* represents the fact that no matter what wage he is paid there is only one Wayne Gretzky. Demand curve *DD* is a marginal-productivity curve of sorts, but not quite the kind we encountered earlier in the chapter. Since the question, "What would be the value of a second unit of Wayne Gretzky?" is nonsensical, the demand curve is constructed by considering only the *portion* of his time demanded at various wage levels. The curve indicates that at an annual salary of $4 million, no employer can afford even a little bit of Wayne Gretzky. At a lower salary of, say, 2 million per year, however, there are enough profitable uses to absorb two-thirds of his time. At $1 million per year, Gretzky's full time is demanded; and at lower wage rates, the demand for Gretzky's time exceeds the amount of it that is for sale.[5]

Equilibrium is at point *E* in the diagram, where the supply of and demand for his time are equal. His annual salary here is $1 million. Now we can ask: How much of Wayne Gretzky's salary is economic rent? According to the economic definition of rent, his entire $1 million salary is rent. Since, according to the

---

[5]These numbers are not entirely hypothetical. At the time this book was written, this equilibrium price corresponded with Gretzky's actual annual salary, as it was reported in the news media.

Figure 36–8

HYPOTHETICAL MARKET FOR WAYNE GRETZKY'S SERVICES

At an annual wage of $4 million or more, no one is willing to bid for his time. At a somewhat lower wage, $2 million, two-thirds of his time will be demanded (point G). Only at an annual wage no higher than $1 million will all of Gretzky's available time be demanded (point E).

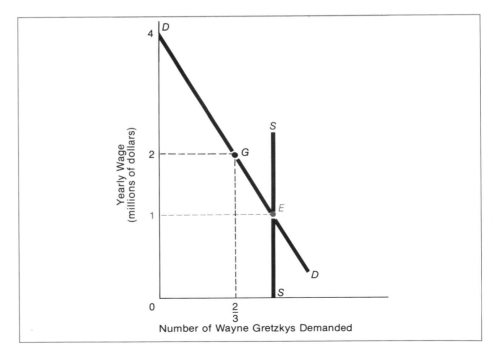

vertical supply schedule, Gretzky's financial reward is unnecessary to get him to supply his services, every penny he earns is rent.

This is why we said that stars like Gretzky are *almost* good examples of pure rent. For, in fact, if his salary were low enough, Gretzky might well prefer to stay home rather than work. Suppose, for example, that $50,000 per year is the lowest salary at which Gretzky will offer even one minute of his services, and that his labour supply then increases with his wage up to an annual salary of $200,000, at which point he is willing to work full time. Then, while his equilibrium salary will still be $1 million per year, not all of it will be rent, because some of it, at least $50,000, is required to get him to supply any services at all.

This same analysis applies to any factor of production whose supply curve is not horizontal, that is, whose *elasticity of supply* is less than infinite. Any such factor earns some rent—or gets paid more than the minimum amount that would induce it to work. Almost all employees earn some rent. What sorts of factors earn no rent? Those that can be exactly reproduced by a number of producers at constant cost. No supplier of ball bearings will ever receive any rent on a ball bearing, at least in the long run, because any desired number of them can be produced at (roughly) constant cost. If one supplier tried to charge a price that included rent, someone else would undercut him and take his customers away.

Rent Controls: The Misplaced Analogy

Why is the analysis of economic rent important? Because only economic rent can be taxed away without reducing the quantity of the input supplied. And here common English gets in the way of sound reasoning. Many people feel that the *rent* that they pay to their landlord is economic rent. After all, their apartments will still be there if they pay $500 per month, or $300, or $100. This view, while true in the short run, is quite myopic.

Like the ball-bearing producer, the owner of a building cannot expect to earn *economic* rent because there are too many other potential owners whose costs of construction are roughly the same as his own. If he tried to charge a price that included some economic rent—that is, a price that exceeded his production costs plus the opportunity cost of his capital—other builders would undercut him. Thus, far from being in perfectly *inelastic* (vertical) supply, like raw land, buildings come rather close to being in perfectly *elastic* (horizontal) supply, like ball bearings. As we have learned from the theory of rent, this means that builders and owners of buildings cannot collect economic rent in the long run. Since apartment owners collect very little economic rent, the payments that tenants make in a free market must be just enough to keep those apartments on the market. (This is the definition of zero economic rent.) If rent controls push these prices down, the apartments will start disappearing from the market.[6]

Issue: Are Profits Too High or Too Low?

This completes our analysis of rent. We turn next to business profits, a subject whose discussion seems to elicit more passion than logic. With the exception of some economists, almost no one thinks that the rate of profit is at about the right level. Critics on the left point accusingly at the billion-dollar profits of some giant corporations and argue that they are unconscionably high. They call for much

---

[6]None of this is meant to imply that temporary rent controls in certain locations cannot have salutory effects in the short run. In the short run, the supply of apartments and houses really is fixed, and large shifts in demand would hand windfall gains to landlords—gains that are true economic rents. Controls that eliminate such windfalls should not cause serious problems. But knowing when the "short run" fades into the "long run" can be a tricky matter. "Temporary" rent-control laws have a way of becoming rather permanent as we saw in Chapter 4, pages 64–66.

stiffer profits taxes. On the other hand, the Chambers of Commerce, Canadian Manufacturers' Association, and other business groups complain that regulations and "ruinous" competition keep profits too low, and they are constantly petitioning the government for tax relief.

The public has many misconceptions about the nature of the economy, but probably none is more severe than the popular view of the amount of profit that corporations earn. We suggest to you the following experiment. Ask five of your friends who have never had an economics course what fraction of our national income they imagine is accounted for by profits. While the correct answer varies from year to year, in 1983 only 10.1 percent of national income was corporate profits. A comparable percent of the prices you pay represents before-tax profit. Most people think this figure is much, much higher. (See the boxed insert at the top of the next page.)

As you have no doubt noticed by now, economists are reluctant to brand factor prices as "too low" or "too high" in some moral or ethical sense. Rather, they are likely to ask, first: What is the market equilibrium price? And then they will ask whether there are any good reasons to interfere with the market solution. This analysis, however, is not so easy to apply to the case of profits, since it is hard to use supply and demand analysis when you do not know what factor of production earns profit.

In both a bookkeeping and an economic sense, *profits are the residual*: They are what remains from the selling price after all other factors have been paid.

But what factor of production receives this reward? What factor's marginal productivity constitutes the profit rate?

What Accounts for Profits?

Economic profit, it will be recalled from Chapter 25, is the amount a firm earns *over and above* the payments for all other inputs, including the interest payments for the capital it uses and the opportunity cost of any capital provided by the owners of the firm. The profit rate and the interest rate are closely related. In an imaginary (and uninteresting) world in which everything was certain and unchanging, capitalists who invested money in firms would simply earn the market rate of interest on their funds. Profits beyond this level would be competed away. Profits below this level could not persist, because capitalists would withdraw their funds from the firms and deposit them in banks. Capitalists in such a world would be mere money-lenders.

But the real world is not at all like this. Some capitalists are much more than money lenders and the amounts they earn often exceed the interest rate by a considerable margin. Those activist capitalists who seek out or even create earnings opportunities are called **entrepreneurs**. They are the ones who are responsible for the constant change that characterizes business firms and who prevent the operations of the firms from stagnating. Since they are always trying to do something new, it is difficult to provide a general description of their activities. However, we can list three primary ways in which entrepreneurs are able to drive profits above the level of interest rates.

Exercise of Monopoly Power.   If the entrepreneur can establish a monopoly over some or all of his products, even for a short while, he can use the monopoly power of his firm to earn monopoly profits. The nature of these monopoly earnings was analysed in Chapter 27.

Risk Bearing.   The entrepreneur may engage in risky activities. For example, when a firm prospects for oil it will drill an exploratory shaft hoping to find a pool

Public Opinion on Profits

Most people think corporate profits are much higher than they actually are. A recent public-opinion poll, for example, found that the average citizen thought that corporate profits *after* tax amounted to 37 percent of sales for the typical manufacturing company. The actual profit rate at the time was only 3.8 percent! Interestingly, when a previous poll asked how much profit was "reasonable," the response was 26 cents on every dollar of sales—over six times as large as profits actually were.

SOURCE: "Public Attitudes Toward Corporate Profits," Opinion Research Corporation *Public Opinion Index*, Princeton, N.J., August 1983.

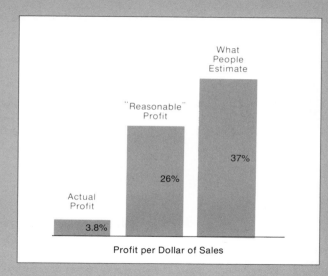

of petroleum at the bottom. But a high proportion of such attempts produce only dry holes, and the cost of the operation is wasted. Of course, if the investor is lucky and does find oil, he may be rewarded handsomely. The income he obtains is a payment for bearing risk.

Obviously, a few lucky individuals make out well in this process, while most suffer heavy losses. How well can we expect risk takers to do on the average? If, on the average, one exploratory drilling out of ten pays off, do we expect its return to be exactly ten times as high as the interest rate, so that the *average* firm will earn exactly the normal rate of interest? The answer is that the payoff will be *more* than ten times the interest rate if investors dislike gambling; that is, if they prefer to avoid risk. Why? Because investors who dislike risk will be unwilling to put their money into a business in which nine firms out of ten lose out unless there is some compensation for the financial peril to which they expose themselves.

In reality, however, there is no certainty that things always work out this way. Some people love to gamble, and these people tend to be overoptimistic about their chances of coming out ahead. They may plunge into projects to a degree unjustified by the odds. If there are enough such gamblers, the average payoff to risky undertakings may end up below the interest rate. The successful investor will still make a good profit, just like the lucky winner in Las Vegas. But the average participant will have to pay for the privilege of bearing risk.

Returns to Innovation. The third major source of profits is perhaps the most important of all from the point of view of social welfare. The entrepreneur who is first to market a desirable new product, or to employ a new cost-saving machine, or to innovate in some other way will receive a special profit as his reward. **Innovation** is different from **invention**. Invention is the act of generating a new idea; innovation is the next step, the act of putting the new idea into practical use. Business people are rarely inventors, but they are often innovators.

When an entrepreneur innovates, even if his new product or his new process is not protected by patents, he will be one step ahead of his competitors. He will be able to capture much of the market either by offering customers a better product or by supplying the product more cheaply. In either case he will temporarily find himself with some monopoly power left by the weakening of his competitors, and monopoly profit will be the reward for his initiative.

Invention is the act of generating a new idea.
Innovation, the next step, is the act of putting the new idea into practical use.

However, this monopoly profit, the reward for innovation, will only be temporary. As soon as the success of the idea has demonstrated itself to the world, other firms will find ways of imitating it. Even if they cannot turn out precisely the same product or use precisely the same process, they will have to find ways to supply close substitutes if they are to survive. In this way, new ideas are spread through the economy. And in the process the special profits of the innovator are brought to an end. The innovator can only resume earning special profits by finding still another promising idea.

Entrepreneurs are forced to keep searching for new ideas, to keep instituting innovations, and to keep imitating those that they have not been the first to put into operation. This process is at the heart of the growth of the capitalist system. It is one of the secrets of its extraordinary dynamism.

The Issue of Profits Taxation

So profits in excess of the market rate of interest can be considered as the return on entrepreneurial talent. But this is not really very helpful, since no one can say exactly what entrepreneurial talent is. Certainly we cannot measure it; nor can we teach it in a college course (though business schools try!). Therefore, we do not know how the observed profit rate relates to the minimum reward necessary to attract entrepreneurial talent into the market—a relationship that is crucial for the contentious issue of profits taxation.

Consider a windfall profits tax on oil companies as an example. If oil company profit rates are well above this minimum, they contain a large element of economic rent. In that case, we could tax away these excess profits (rents) without fear of reducing oil production. On the other hand, if the profits being earned by oil companies do not contain much economic rent, then the windfall profits tax might seriously curtail exploration and production of oil.

This example illustrates the general problem of deciding how heavily profits should be taxed. Critics of big business who call for high, if not confiscatory, profits taxes believe that profits are mostly economic rent. But if they are wrong, if most of the observed profits are necessary to attract people into entrepreneurial roles, then a high profits tax can be dangerous. It can threaten the very lifeblood of the capitalist system. Business lobbying groups predictably claim that this is the case. Unfortunately, neither group has offered much evidence for its conclusion.

Criticisms of Marginal Productivity Theory

The theory of factor pricing described in this chapter is another example of supply–demand analysis. Its special feature is its heavy reliance on the principle of marginal productivity to derive the shape and position of the demand curve. For this reason, the analysis is often rather misleadingly called *the marginal productivity theory of distribution*.

Over the years this analysis has been subject to attack on many grounds. One frequent accusation, which is largely (but not entirely) groundless, is the assertion that marginal productivity theory is merely an attempt to justify the distribution of income that the capitalist system yields—that it is a piece of pro-capitalist propaganda. According to this argument, when marginal productivity theory claims that each factor is paid exactly its marginal revenue product (MRP), this is only a sneaky way of asserting that each factor is paid exactly what it deserves. These critics claim that the theory legitimizes the gross inequities of the system—the poverty of many and the great wealth of the few.

The argument is straightforward but wrong. Payments are made not to *factors of production* but to the people who happen to own them. If land earns $2000 because that is its MRP, this does not mean the payment is *deserved* by the landlord, who may even have acquired it by fraud.

Second, an input's MRP does not depend only on "how hard it works" but also on how much of it happens to be employed—for, according to the "law" of diminishing returns, the more that is employed the lower its MRP. Thus, that factor's MRP is not (and cannot legitimately be interpreted as) a measure of the intensity of its "productive effort." In any event, what an input deserves may be taken to depend on more than what it does in the factory. A worker may be held to deserve funds because he is sick, because he has many children, and for many reasons other than his productivity. On these and other grounds, no economist today claims that marginal productivity analysis shows that distribution under capitalism is either just or unjust. It is simply wrong to claim that marginal productivity theory is pro-capitalist propaganda.[7] The marginal productivity principle is just as relevant to organizing production in a socialist society as it is in a capitalist one.

Others have attacked marginal productivity theory for using rather complicated reasoning to tell us very little about the really urgent problems of income distribution. In this view, it is all very well to say that everything depends on supply and demand to express this in terms of many complicated equations (as is done in more advanced books and articles). But these equations do not tell us what to do about such serious distribution problems as malnutrition or poverty.

Though it does exaggerate somewhat, there is certainly truth to this criticism. We have seen in this chapter that the theory does provide some insights on real policy matters, though perhaps not as many as the obsolete Ricardian model described in Appendix B to this chapter, and certainly not as many as we would like. In Chapters 38 and 40 we will see that economists do have things to say about the problems of poverty and underdevelopment. But much of this does not flow from marginal productivity analysis.

Perhaps, in the end, what should be said for marginal productivity theory is that it is the best model we have at the moment, that it offers us *some* valuable insights into the way the economy works, and that until a more powerful model is found we are better off hanging on to what we have.

---

[7]For more on this criticism of marginal-productivity theory, see Chapter 42, especially pages 850–51.

Summary

1. A profit-maximizing firm purchases the quantity of any input at which the price of the input equals its marginal revenue product.

2. Interest rates are determined by the supply of and demand for funds. The demand for funds is a derived demand, since these funds are used to finance business investment. Thus the demand for funds depends on the marginal productivity of capital.

3. A dollar obtainable sooner is worth more than a dollar obtainable later because of the interest that can be earned in the interim.

4. Increased demand for a good that needs land to produce it will drive up the prices of land either because inferior land will be brought into use or because land will be used more intensively.

5. Rent controls do not significantly affect the supply of land, but they do tend to reduce the supply of buildings.

6. Economic rent is any payment to the supplier of a factor of production that is greater than the minimum amount needed to induce the desired quantity of the factor to be supplied.

7. Factors of production that are unique in quality and difficult or impossible to reproduce will tend to be paid relatively high economic rents because of their scarcity.

8. Factors of production that are easy to produce at a constant cost and that are provided by many suppliers will earn little or no economic rent.

9. Economic profits over and above the cost of capital are earned (a) by exercise of monopoly power, (b) as a payment for bearing risk, and (c) as the earnings of successful innovation.

10. The desirability of increased taxation of profits depends on its effects on the supply of entrepreneurial talent. If most profits are economic rents, then higher profits taxes will have few detrimental effects. But if most profits are necessary to attract entrepreneurs into the market, then higher profit taxes can threaten the capitalist system.

Concepts for Review

Factors of production
Entrepreneurship
Marginal productivity principle
Marginal physical product
Marginal revenue product

Derived demand
Investment
Capital
Interest
Discounting

Marginal land
Economic rent
Entrepreneurs
Risk bearing
Invention versus innovation

Questions for Discussion

1. A profit-maximizing firm expands its purchase of any input up to the point where diminishing returns has reduced the marginal revenue product so that it equals the input price. Why does it not pay the firm to "quit while it is ahead," buying so small a quantity of the input that diminishing returns do not set in?

2. Which of the following inputs do you think include a relatively large economic rent in their earnings?
   a. Nails.
   b. Coal.
   c. A champion racehorse.
   Use supply–demand analysis to explain your answer.

3. Three machines are employed in an isolated area. They each produce 1000 units of output per month, the first requiring $17,000 in raw materials, the second $21,000, and the third $23,000. What would you expect to be the monthly charge for the first and second machines if the services of the third machine can be hired at a price of $9000 a month? What part of the charges for the first two machines is economic rent?

4. Economists conclude that a tax on the profits of firms will be shifted in part to consumers of the products of those firms, in the form of higher product prices. However, they believe that a tax on the rent of land usually cannot be shifted. What explains the difference?

5. Many economists argue that a tax on apartment houses is likely to reduce the supply of apartments but that a tax on all land, including the land on which apartment houses stand, will not reduce the supply of apartments. Can you explain the difference? What is the relation of this answer to the answer to Question 4?

6. Distinguish between investment and capital.

7. If you have a contract under which you will be paid $10,000 two years from now, why do you become richer if the rate of interest falls?

8. What is the difference between interest and profit? Who earns interest in return for what contribution to production? Who earns economic profit, in return for what contribution to production?

9. Do you know any entrepreneurs? What do they do for a living? How do they differ from managers?

10. Explain the difference between an invention and an innovation. Give an example of each.

11. "Marginal productivity does not determine how much a worker will earn—it only determines how many workers will be hired at a given wage. Therefore, marginal productivity analysis is a theory of demand for labour, not a theory of distribution." What, then, do you think determines wages? Does marginal productivity affect their level? If so, how?

Appendix A
Discounting and Present Value

Frequently, in business and economic problems, it is necessary to compare sums of money received (or paid) at different dates. Consider, for example, the purchase of a machine that costs $11,000 and will yield a marginal revenue product of $14,520 two years from today. If the machine can be financed by a two-year loan bearing 10 percent interest, it will cost the firm $1100 in principal repayment at the end of the second year (see table). Is the machine a good investment?

COSTS AND BENEFITS OF INVESTING IN A MACHINE

	End of Year 1	End of Year 2
Benefits		
Marginal revenue product of the machine	0	$14,520
Costs		
Interest	$1100	1100
Repayment of principal on loan	0	11,000
Total	$1100	$12,100

The total costs of owning the machine over the two-year period ($1100 + $12,100 = $13,200) are less than the total benefits ($14,520). But this is clearly an invalid comparison, because the $14,520 in future benefits are not worth $14,520 in terms of today's money. Adding up dollars received (or paid) at different dates is a bit like adding apples and oranges. The process that has been invented for making these magnitudes comparable is called **discounting**, or **computing the present value** of a future sum of money.

To illustrate the concept of present value, let us ask how much $1 received a year from today is worth *in terms of today's money*. If the rate of interest is 10 percent, the answer is about 91 cents. Why? Because if we invest 91 cents today at 10 percent interest, it will grow to 91 cents plus 9.1 cents in interest = 100.1 cents in a year. Similar considerations apply to any rate of interest. In general:

If the rate of interest is i, the present value of $1 to be received in a year is: $\dfrac{\$1}{(1 + i)}$.

This is so, because in a year $\dfrac{\$1}{(1 + i)}$ will grow to $\dfrac{\$1}{(1 + i)} (1 + i) = \$1$.

What about money to be received two years from today? Using the same reasoning, $1 invested today will grow to $1 × (1.1) = $1.10 after one year and to $1 × (1.1) × (1.1) = $1 × (1.1)² = $1.21 after two years. Consequently, the present value of $1 to be received two years from today is:

$$\frac{\$1}{(1.1)^2} = \frac{\$1}{1.21} = 82.64 \text{ cents.}$$

A similar analysis applies to money received three years from today, four years from today, and so on.

The general formula for the present value of $1 to be received N years from today when the rate of interest is i is: $\dfrac{\$1}{(1 + i)^N}$.

The present value formula highlights the two variables that determine the present value of any future flow of money: the rate of interest (i) and how long you have to wait before you get it (N).

Let us now apply this analysis to our example. The present value of the revenue is easy to calculate since it all comes two years from today. Since the rate of interest is assumed to be 10 percent ($i = 0.1$) we have:

$$\text{Present value of revenues} = \frac{\$14,520}{(1.1)^2}$$

$$= \frac{\$14,520}{1.21}$$

$$= \$12,000.$$

The present value of the costs is a bit trickier in this example since costs occur at two different dates.

The present value of the first interest payment is $1100/(1 + i) = $1100/1.1 = $1000. And the present value of the final payment of interest plus principal is:

$$\frac{\$12,100}{(1 + i)^2} = \frac{\$12,100}{(1.1)^2} = \frac{\$12,100}{1.21} = \$10,000.$$

Now that we have expressed each sum in terms of its present value, it is permissible to add them up. So the present value of all costs is:

$$\text{Present value of costs} = \$1000 + \$10,000$$
$$= \$11,000.$$

Comparing this to the $12,000 present value of the revenues clearly shows that the machine is really a good investment. This same calculation procedure is applicable to all investment decisions.

Summary

To determine whether a loss or a gain will result from a decision whose costs and returns will come at several different periods of time, the figures represented by these gains and losses must all be discounted to obtain their present value. For this, one uses the present value formula for X dollars receivable N years from now.

$$\text{Present value} = \frac{X}{(1 + i)^N}.$$

One then adds together the present values of all the returns and all the costs. If the sum of the present values of the returns is greater than the sum of the present values of the costs, then the decision to invest will promise a net gain.

Concepts for Review

Discounting
Present value

Questions for Discussion

1. Compute the present value of $1000 to be received in four years if the rate of interest is 15 percent.
2. A government bond pays $100 in interest each year for three years and also returns the principal of $1000 in the third year. How much is it worth in terms of today's money if the rate of interest is 10 percent? If the rate of interest is 15 percent?

Appendix B
David Ricardo's Theory of Income Distribution

Theories of the supply and demand for each factor of production enable us to determine both the price and employment of each factor, and thus that factor's income. Once this sort of analysis is applied to all factors of production, we have a complete *theory of income distribution*, because the entire national income is accounted for. That is, we are in a position to analyse the share of an economy's output that goes to workers, to capitalists, and to landlords.

The first such complete theory of income distribution was worked out in the early part of the nineteenth century by the British stockbroker-turned-economist David Ricardo. Though much of Ricardo's work has been rendered obsolete by the passage of almost 200 years, it is in many ways still a model of what an economic theory of income distribution should be. It shows clearly the role of land-holders, capitalists, and workers, and seeks to bring out explicitly the extent to which their interests conflict or are held in common. It also attempts to account directly for the relative wealth or poverty of the different economic classes. And it relates directly to issues of policy, suggesting measures that can be used to increase equality, stimulate economic growth,

and so forth. Ricardo's analysis rests on five major premises:

1. That land rents are determined in the way described in this chapter (see pages 710–12).

2. That, after landlords are paid, the remainder of the product is divided between labour and capital, with the wage of labour determined by the law of supply and demand.

3. That an increase in wages above what constitutes the normal standard of living for workers in the economy ("the subsistence level of wages") simply enables workers to enlarge their families, thus leading to expansion of the population. (This is discussed in more detail in Chapter 40.)

4. That an increased population working with a fixed quantity of land will run into diminishing returns to increased quantities or labour input.

5. That the basic objective of capitalists is to accumulate wealth, and that they reinvest whatever profits they do not consume in order to expand their earning power.

These five assumptions lead to a simple scenario. Capitalists accumulate and invest their money. The resulting expansion of business activity increases the demand for labour and raises wages. Workers respond by increasing the size of their families. Ultimately, the rise in population affects distribution in three ways:

1. It lowers wages back toward subsistence as the supply of labour grows.

2. It increases the use of land and raises rents in the way described in this chapter.

3. It ultimately must reduce profits because wages cannot be pushed below subsistence, because rents are increasing, and because (as a result of diminishing returns) production does not keep up with population size.

This last and crucial conclusion follows as a matter of simple arithmetic. Subsistence wage payments must increase in proportion to the labour force, but diminishing returns cause production to expand less rapidly than the labour force. With landlords increasing their share of the pie, less must be left over for profits.

Figure 36-9 summarizes the story. As we move from left to right in the diagram, we see what happens as the population and the size of the labour force increase. The top curve represents total production of the economy. Because of diminishing returns it flattens out as the size of the labour force increases. The lower curve shows what remains of production after

rent is deducted from it. Since rents increase as population grows, this curve must flatten out even faster than the total product curve. However, since the subsistence wage is a fixed amount per worker, total subsistence wages must increase *proportionately* with the size of the labour force. That is why *total* subsistence wages are represented by an upward-sloping straight line.

At a particular size of labour force, L, total wage payments are represented by LW, the distance to the subsistence wage line. Total profit is represented by WP, the distance between the subsistence wage line and the curve of total product minus rent. Total rent is therefore shown by PR, the amount of total product that has gone neither to wages nor to profits.

We see that as population increases—that is, as we move to the right in the graph—both rent and total wage payments increase, but total profits are squeezed lower and lower. That is, there is less and less distance between the subsistence wage line and the curve of production minus rent. The two finally meet at point S when population reaches M, and there profits are eliminated altogether. The classical economists called this point *the stationary state* in which all growth ceases and stagnation is the normal state of affairs.

It would seem that only capitalists are hurt by this process. But, in fact, the workers suffer too. For, as we saw, it is only capital accumulation that raises wages above subsistence. Once profits are eliminated, there is no further motive to save and invest, so wages are permanently limited to the subsistence level. This is in marked contrast with a period of growth and high profits when rapid accumulation will generally make the forces of supply and demand work more favourably for labour. Ricardo drew several main conclusions from his analysis.

1. Only landlords benefit from population growth. Capitalists are hurt by it directly, and workers suffer indirectly because it reduces the reward for investment, which decreases the demand for labour and drives wages toward subsistence.

2. Unrestricted trade with foreign countries, by indirectly increasing the supply of land used by the economy, retards the speed with which diminishing returns set in and therefore makes the whole process less painful.

3. There are two ways in which workers' standards of living can be raised. First, incentives for capital accumulation increase the demand for labour and lead wages to be bid up by the forces of supply and demand. Second, by getting workers to insist on higher living standards before they are ready to have children, the rate of population growth can be

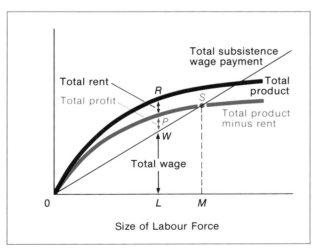

Figure 36-9
THE RICARDIAN DISTRIBUTION MODEL
This diagram illustrates the division of total product into wages, profit, and rent. Rent is determined by differences in quality of the lands that are in use and by diminishing returns to other inputs. If wages approximate subsistence, then profit is what is left over. As population increases, profits are squeezed by diminishing returns to labour and rising rents. When the labour force reaches M, profit vanishes (point S), and accumulation of capital ceases.

retarded and therefore the downward pressure on wages can be reduced. If people were unwilling to marry and have children until their earnings were high enough to support their families in a "decent" style of living, that, in Ricardo's judgment, would be the best thing that could happen from the point of view of workers' welfare. For that is the way to hold back the growth of population that subjects the labour market to oversupply and the economy to diminishing returns.

Nowadays, when workers' wages are bargained for by powerful unions, when continued innovations have held off the workings of diminishing returns for two centuries, and when population growth in the industrialized Western world has declined in some places almost to zero, the Ricardian model of income distribution seems more than a little out of date. But its relevance to the agricultural economies of its day was more immediate, as was its impact on policy. And, as we will see in Chapter 40, there are many places in the Third World today where its message is still all too relevant.

The Labour Market and Wages

37

Masters are always and every where in a sort of tacit, but constant and uniform combination, not to raise the wages of labour . . .
ADAM SMITH

One man's pay rise is another man's price increase.
SIR HAROLD WILSON

Labour is by far the most important factor of production. As noted in the previous chapter, the earnings of labour amount to about 75 percent of national income. Wages and employment are important because they represent the primary source of income to the vast majority of Canadians and because they are related to a variety of important social and political issues.

The chapter is divided into two main parts. In the first part we deal with the determination of wages and employment in *competitive labour markets*; that is, labour markets in which there are many buyers and many sellers, none of whom is large enough to have any appreciable influence on wages. We consider why some types of workers are paid far more than others and explore a number of important issues, including the effects of education on wages and of minimum-wage legislation. In the second part of the chapter we consider labour markets that are monopolized on the selling side by trade unions. First, the development of the labour movement in Canada is summarized. Then we consider alternative goals for a union and how these goals might be pursued. Finally, we turn to situations in which a single seller of labour (a union) confronts a single buyer of labour (a monopsony firm), and examine some of the analytical and practical difficulties that arise under collective bargaining.

Issue: The Minimum Wage and Unemployment

Unemployment among the young is always higher than it is in the labour force as a whole. Figure 37-1 shows the record. It indicates that whenever unemployment rates went down in the economy as a whole, they almost always decreased for the young. However young workers have always suffered more from unemployment than the average worker. When things are generally bad, things are much, much worse for them. Despite numerous "opportunities for youth" programs, there has been no improvement in youth unemployment in recent years.

Many economists feel less surprised than other concerned persons about the intractability of this problem. They maintain that despite all the legislation that has been adopted to improve the position of the young and inexperienced, there is a law on the books, which, though apparently designed to protect low-skilled workers, is actually an impediment to any attempt to improve job opportunities for the young. As long as this law remains effective, the young, the inexperienced,

Figure 37-1
THE YOUTH
UNEMPLOYMENT PROBLEM
Youth unemployment rates have
consistently been much higher
than the overall unemployment
rate.
SOURCE: Statistics Canada

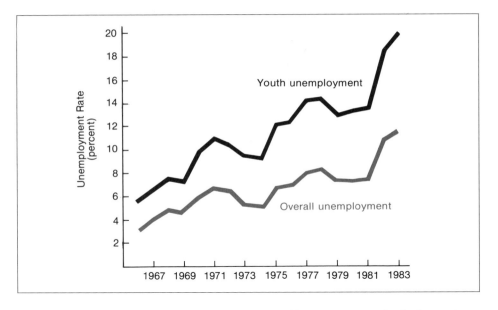

and those with educational disadvantages will continue to find themselves handicapped on the job market; and attempts to eliminate their more serious unemployment problems will stand only a limited chance of success.

What is the law? None other than the **minimum-wage law**. Later in this chapter we will explain the grounds on which many observers believe that this law has such pernicious—and presumably unintended—effects.

Competitive Labour Markets

The minimum-wage law interferes with the operation of a free labour market. But to understand how, we must first understand how the labour market would operate in its absence. We approach this in three steps. First we consider the determinants of the supply of labour, then the determinants of demand, and finally the market equilibrium, in which both wages and employment levels are established.

The Supply of Labour

The economic analysis of labour supply is based on the following simple observation: Given the fixed amount of time in a week, a person's decision to *supply labour* to firms is simultaneously a decision to *demand leisure* time for oneself. Assuming that after necessary time for eating and sleeping is deducted a worker has 90 usable hours in a week, a decision to spend 40 of those hours working is simultaneously a decision to demand 50 of them for other purposes.

This suggests that we can analyse the *supply* of this particular input— labour—with the same tools we used in Chapter 20 to analyse the *demand* for commodities. In this case, the commodity is leisure. A consumer "buys" her own leisure time, just as she buys bananas, or back scratchers, or pizzas. In Chapter 20 we observed that any price change has two distinct effects on quantity demanded: an income effect and a substitution effect. Let us review these two effects and see how they operate in the context of the demand for leisure (that is, the supply of labour).

1. *Income effect*. Higher wages make consumers richer. We expect this increased wealth to raise the demand for most goods, leisure included.

The income effect of higher wages probably leads most workers to want to work less.

2. Substitution effect. Consumers "purchase" their own leisure time by giving up their hourly wage, so the wage rate is the "price" of leisure. When the wage rate rises, leisure becomes more expensive relative to other commodities that consumers might buy. Thus, we expect a wage increase to induce them to buy *less* leisure time and *more* goods.

The substitution effect of higher wages probably leads most workers to want to work more.

Putting these two effects together, we are led to conclude that some workers may react to an increase in their wage rate by working more, while others may react by working less. Still others will have little or no discretion over their hours of work. In terms of the market as a whole, therefore, higher wages could lead to either a larger or a smaller quantity of labour supplied.

Statistical studies of this issue have reached the conclusions that (a) the response of labour supply to wage changes is not very strong for most workers; (b) for low-wage workers the substitution effect seems clearly dominant, so they work more when wages rise; and (c) for high-wage workers the income effect just about offsets the substitution effect, so they do not work more when wages rise. Figure 37–2 depicts these approximate "facts." It shows labour supply rising (slightly) as wages rise up to point A. Thereafter, labour supply is roughly constant as wages rise.

It is even possible that when wages are raised sufficiently high, further increases in wages will lead workers to purchase more leisure and therefore to work less. The supply curve of labour is then said to be "backward bending," as illustrated by the broken portion of the curve above point B.

Does the theory of labour supply apply to university students? A study of the hours of work performed by students at Princeton University found that it does.[1]

[1]Mary P. Hurley, "An Investigation of Employment among Princeton Undergraduates During the Academic Year," Senior thesis submitted to the Department of Economics, May 1975.

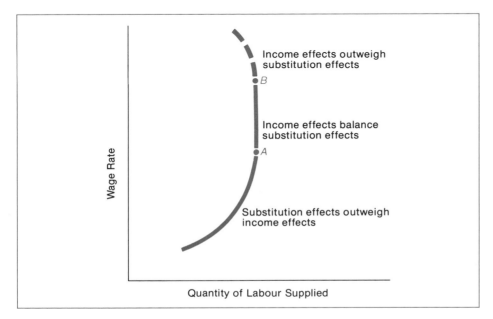

Figure 37–2

A TYPICAL LABOUR SUPPLY SCHEDULE

The labour supply schedule depicted here has a positive slope up to point A, as substitution effects outweigh income effects. At higher wages, however, income effects become just as important as substitution effects, and the curve becomes roughly vertical. At still higher wages (above point B), income effects might overwhelm substitution effects.

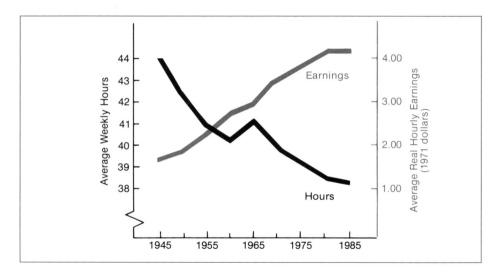

Figure 37-3

TRENDS IN REAL WAGES
AND HOURS WORKED

This graph shows how real wages
(measured in dollars of 1971
purchasing power) have been
rising, while hours worked per
week have been declining, despite
the higher rewards for each hour
of work.

SOURCE: Historical Statistics of
Canada, Series E-31, E-90, K-8, and
CANSIM Series 4677.

Estimated substitution effects of higher wages on the labour supply of Princeton students were positive and income effects were negative, just as the theory predicts. Apparently, substitution effects outweighed income effects by a slim margin, so that higher wages attracted a somewhat greater supply of labour. Specifically, a 10 percent rise in wages was estimated to increase the hours of work of the Princeton student body by about 3 percent.

An Application: The Labour-Supply Paradox

Labour-supply analysis helps explain the following puzzling observation. Throughout the twentieth century, wages have generally been rising, both in number of dollars paid per hour and in the quantity of goods those dollars can buy, as is clearly shown by the data depicted in Figure 37–3. Yet labour has asked for and received *reductions* in the length of the workday and workweek. At the beginning of the century, a workweek of 5½ days and a workday of 10 or more hours was standard, making a workweek of 50 to 60 hours. Since then, labour hours have generally declined. Today the standard workweek is down to 35 to 40 hours. Where has the common-sense view of the matter gone wrong? Why, as hourly wages have risen, have workers not sold more of the hours they have available instead of pressing for a shorter and shorter workweek?

Part of the answer becomes clear when one recalls that any wage increase sets in motion *both* a substitution effect *and* an income effect. If only the substitution effect operated, then rising wages would indeed cause people to work longer hours because the high price of leisure makes leisure less attractive. But this reasoning leaves out the income effect. As higher wages make workers richer, they will want to buy more of most commodities, including vacations and other leisuretime activities. Thus, the income effect of increasing wages induces workers to work fewer hours.

It is the strong income effect of rising wages that may account for the fact that labour supply has responded in the "wrong" direction, with workers working ever-shorter hours despite their rising real wages. If so, the long-run supply curve of labour is indeed backward bending.

The Demand for Labour and the Determination of Wages

There is not much to be said about the demand for labour that has not already been said about the demand for other inputs. Like any factor of production, labour

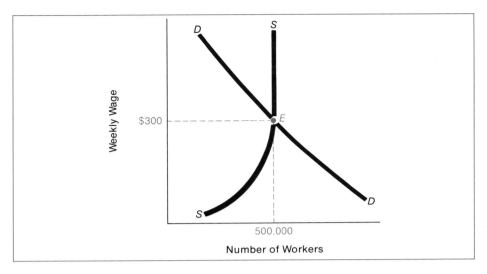

Figure 37–4
EQUILIBRIUM IN A
COMPETITIVE LABOUR
MARKET
In a competitive labour market,
equilibrium will be established at
the wage that equates the quantity
supplied with the quantity
demanded. In this example,
equilibrium is at point E, where
demand curve DD crosses supply
curve SS. The equilibrium wage is
$300 per week and equilibrium
employment is 500,000 workers.

has a marginal-revenue product curve from which a downward-sloping demand
curve for labour can be derived. This demand curve is shown in Figure 37–4 as
curve *DD*. The figure also includes a supply curve, labelled *SS*, much like the one
depicted in Figure 37–2.

If there are no interferences with the operation of a free market in labour
(such as minimum wages or unions—which we will consider later), equilibrium
will be at point *E*, where the supply and demand curves intersect. In this example,
500,000 workers will be employed at a wage of $300 per week.

Why Wages Differ

But, of course, there is not one labour market but many—each with its own supply
and demand curves and its own equilibrium wage. We all know that certain groups
in our society (the young, the uneducated) earn relatively low wages, and that
some of our most severe social ills (poverty, crime, drug addiction) are related to
this fact. But why are some wages so low while others are so high?

Supply and demand analysis at once tells us everything and nothing about
this question. It implies that wages are relatively high in markets where demand is
great and supply is small [see Figure 37–5(a)], while wages are comparatively low in
markets where demand is weak and supply is high [see Figure 37–5(b)]. This can
hardly be considered startling news. But to make the analysis useful, we need to
breathe some life into the supply and demand curves.

We begin our discussion on the demand side. Why is the demand for labour
greater in some markets than in others? The marginal productivity principle
teaches us that there are two types of influences to be considered. Since a worker's
marginal revenue product depends both on his *marginal physical product* and on
the *price of the product* that he produces, variables that influence either of these
will influence his wage.

The determinants of the prices of commodities were discussed at some length
in earlier chapters, and there is no need to repeat the analysis here. It is sufficient
to remember that because the demand for labour is a *derived demand*, anything
that raises or lowers the demand for a particular product will tend to raise or lower
the wages of the workers that produce that product.

A worker's marginal physical product depends on several things, including, of
course, his own *abilities* and *degree of effort* on the job. But sometimes these
characteristics are less important than the *other factors of production* that he has
to work with. Workers in Canadian industry are more productive than workers in

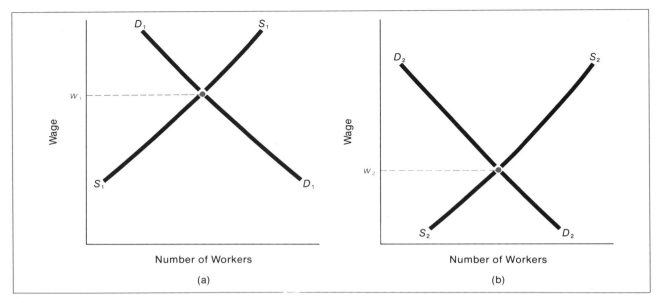

Figure 37-5

WAGE DIFFERENTIALS

(a) The market depicted here has a high equilibrium wage, w_1, because demand is high relative to supply. This can occur if qualified workers are scarce, or if productivity on the job is high, or if the demand for the product is great. (b) By contrast, the equilibrium wage, w_2, is low here, where supply is high relative to demand. This can result from an abundant supply of qualified workers, or low productivity, or weak demand for the product.

many other countries because they have generous supplies of machinery, natural resources, and technical know-how to work with. As a consequence, they earn high wages.

Turning next to the supply of labour, it is clear that the *size of the available working population* relative to the magnitude of industrial activity in a given area is of major importance. This helps explain why wages rose so high in the sparsely populated North when exploration for Arctic oil created many new jobs, and why wages have been and remain so low in the Maritimes where industry is relatively dormant.

Second, it is clear that the *non-monetary attractiveness* of any job will also influence the supply of workers to it. (The monetary attractiveness is the wage itself, which governs movements *along* the supply curve.) Jobs that people find pleasant and satisfying will attract a large supply of labour and will consequently pay a relatively low wage. In contrast, a premium will have to be paid to attract workers to jobs that are onerous, disagreeable, or dangerous—such as washing the windows of skyscrapers.

Finally, the amount of ability and training needed to enter a particular job or profession is relevant to its supply of labour. Brain surgeons and professional football quarterbacks earn generous incomes because there are few people as highly skilled as they, and because it is time consuming and expensive to acquire these skills even for those who have the ability.

Ability and Earnings

In considering the effects of ability on earnings, it is useful to distinguish between skills that can be duplicated easily and skills that cannot. If Jones has an ability that Smith cannot acquire, even if he undergoes extensive training, then the wages that Jones earns will contain an element of *economic rent*, just as in the case of Wayne Gretzky.[2]

[2]See the previous chapter, pages 713–15.

Virtually anyone with moderate athletic ability can be taught to shoot a hockey puck at a net. But in most cases, no amount of training will teach the player to play hockey like Gretzky. His high salary is a reward for his unique ability.

But many of the abilities that the market rewards generously—such as the skills of doctors and lawyers—clearly are duplicable. Here the theory of rent does not apply, and we need a different explanation of the high wages that these skilled professionals earn. Once again, however, part of our analysis from Chapter 36 finds an immediate application because the acquisition of skills, through formal education and other forms of training, has much in common with business investment decisions. Why? Because the decision to undertake more education in the hope of increasing future earnings involves a sacrifice of *current* income for the sake of *future* gain—precisely the hallmark of an investment decision.

Investment in Human Capital

That education is an investment is a concept familiar to most university students. You made a conscious decision to go to university rather than to enter the labour market, and you are probably acutely aware that this decision is now costing you money—lots of money. Your tuition payments may be only a minor part of the total cost of going to university. Think of a highschool friend who chose not to go to university and is now working. The salary that he or she is earning could, perhaps, have been yours. You are deliberately giving up this possible income in order to acquire more education.

In this sense, your education can be thought of as an *investment* in yourself—a *human investment*. Like a firm that devotes some of its money to building a plant that will yield profits at some future date, you are investing in your own future, hoping that your university education will help you earn more than your highschool-educated friend or enable you to find a more pleasant or prestigious job when you graduate. Economists call activities like going to university **investments in human capital** because such activities give the human being many of the attributes of a capital investment.

Doctors and lawyers earn such high salaries partly because of their many years of training. That is, part of their wages can be construed as a *return on their (educational) investments*, rather than as economic rent. Unlike the case of Wayne Gretzky, there are a number of people who conceivably *could* become surgeons if they found the job sufficiently attractive to endure the long years of training that are required. Few, however, are willing to make such a large investment of their own time, money, and energy. Consequently, the few who do become surgeons earn very generous incomes.

Economists have devoted quite a bit of attention to the acquisition of skills through human investment. There is an entire branch of economic theory—called **human capital theory**—which analyses an individual's decisions about education, training, and so on in exactly the same way as we analysed a firm's decision to buy a machine or build a factory in the previous chapter. Though educational decisions can be influenced by love of learning, desire for prestige, and a variety of other preferences and emotions, human-capital theorists find it useful to analyse a schooling decision as if it were made purely as a business plan. The optimal length of education, from this point of view, is to stay in school until the marginal revenue (in the form of increased future income) of an additional year of schooling is exactly equal to the marginal cost.

One implication of human capital theory is that university graduates should earn enough more than highschool graduates to compensate them for their extra investments in schooling. Do they? Will your university investment pay off? Many generations of university students have supposed that it would, and for years studies of the incomes earned by university students indicated that they were right. These studies showed that the income differentials earned by university graduates provided a good "return" on the tuition payments and sacrificed earnings that they "invested" while in school. But university investments turned a bit sour in the 1970s. The reason was the obvious one: Relative to highschool graduates, the supply of university graduates expanded much more rapidly than the demand.

This, of course, does not mean that only fools go to university. What it does mean is that the financial incentive *alone* is not what it used to be. If you simply enjoy the experience, or want to acquire knowledge for its own sake or attend because you think it will help to get you a more pleasant job, attending university can still be a perfectly rational decision. It does not, however, offer quite the financial bonanza it once did.

Human-capital theory stresses that jobs that require more education *must* pay higher wages if they are to attract enough workers, because people insist on a financial return on their human investments. But the theory does not address the other side of the question: What is it about more-educated people that makes firms willing to pay them higher wages?

Put differently, the theory explains why the quantity of educated people *supplied* is limited but does not explain why the quantity *demanded* is substantial even at high wages.

Most human-capital theorists complete their analyses by assuming that students in highschools and universities are acquiring particular skills that are productive in the marketplace. In this view, educational institutions are factories that take less-productive workers as their raw materials, apply doses of training, and produce more-productive workers as outputs. It is a view of what happens in schools that makes educators happy and accords well with common sense. However, a number of social scientists doubt that this is how schooling raises earning power.

Education and Earnings: Dissenting Views

Just why is it that jobs with stiffer educational requirements typically offer higher wages? The common-sense view that educating people makes them more productive is not universally accepted.

Education as a Sorting Mechanism   One alternative view denies that the educational process teaches students anything directly relevant to their subsequent performance on jobs. On this view, people differ in ability when they enter the school system and differ in more or less the same way when they leave. What the educational system does, according to this theory, is to *sort* individuals by ability. Skills like intelligence and self-discipline that lead to success in schools, it is argued, are closely related to the skills that lead to success in jobs. As a result, more able individuals stay in school longer and perform better. Prospective employers know this, and consequently seek to hire those whom the school system has suggested will be the most productive workers.

The Radical View of Education[3]   Many radical economists question whether the educational system really sorts people according to ability. The rich, they note, are better situated to buy the best education and to keep their children in school regardless of ability. Thus, education may be one of the instruments by which a more privileged family passes its economic position on to its heirs while making it appear that there is a legitimate reason for firms to give them higher earnings. As radicals see it, education sorts people according to their social class, not according to their ability.

Radicals also hold a different idea about what happens inside schools to make workers more "productive." On this view, instead of serving primarily as instruments

---

[3]Radical economics is considered in greater depth in Chapter 42, especially pages 847–54.

for the acquisition of knowledge and improved ability to think, what schools do primarily is teach people discipline—how to show up five days a week at 9:00 A.M., how to speak in turn and respectfully, and so on. These characteristics, radicals claim, are what business firms prefer and what causes them to seek more educated workers. They also suggest that the schools teach docility and acceptance of the capitalist status quo, and that this, too, makes schooling attractive to business.

The Dual Labour Market Theory   A third view of the linkages among education, ability and earnings is part of a much broader theory of how the labour market operates—the theory of **dual labour markets**. Proponents of this theory suggest that there are two very different types of labour markets, with relatively little mobility between them.

The "primary labour market" is where most of the economy's "good jobs" are—jobs like computer programming, business management, and skilled crafts that are interesting and offer considerable possibilities for career advancement. The educational system helps decide which individuals get assigned to the primary labour market and, for those who make it, greater educational achievement does indeed offer financial rewards.

The privileged workers who wind up in the primary labour market are offered opportunities for additional training on the job; they augment their skills by experience, and by learning from their fellow workers; and they progress in successive steps to more responsible, better-paying positions. Where jobs in the primary labour market are concerned, dual labour market theorists agree with human-capital theorists that education really is productive. But they agree with the radicals that admission to the primary labour market depends in part on social position, and that firms probably care more about steady work habits and punctuality than about reading, writing, and arithmetic.

Everything is quite different in the "secondary labour market"—where we find all the "bad jobs." Jobs like domestic service and fast-food service offer low rates of pay, few fringe benefits, and virtually no training to improve the workers' skills. They are dead-end jobs with little or no hope for promotion or advancement. As a result, lateness, absenteeism, and thievery are expected as a matter of course, so that workers in the secondary labour market tend to develop the bad work habits that confirm the prejudices of those who assigned them to inferior jobs in the first place.

In the secondary labour market, increased education leads neither to higher wages nor to increased protection from unemployment—benefits that increased schooling generally offers elsewhere in the labour market. For this reason, workers in the secondary market have little incentive to invest in education.

In sum, we have a well-established fact—that people with more education generally earn higher wages—but very little agreement on the theory that accounts for this fact.

The Effects of Minimum-Wage Legislation

As we have observed, the "labour market" is really composed of many sub-markets for labour of different types, each with its own supply and demand curves. To understand the possible effects of minimum-wage legislation, it suffices to consider two such markets, which we call for convenience "skilled" and "unskilled" labour and portray in the two parts of Figure 37-6. As drawn, the demand curve for skilled workers is higher than that for unskilled workers. The reason is obvious: Skilled workers have higher productivity. Conversely, we have drawn the supply curve of skilled workers farther to the left than the supply curve of unskilled workers to reflect the greater scarcity of skilled workers. The consequence, as we can see in Figure 37-6, is that the equilibrium wage is much higher for skilled workers. In the

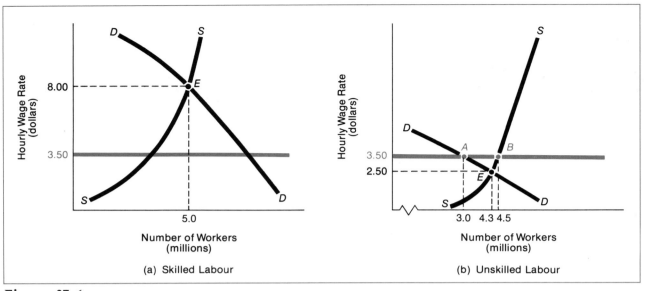

Figure 37-6

POSSIBLE EFFECTS OF MINIMUM-WAGE LEGISLATION

(a) Imposing a minimum wage of $3.50 per hour does not affect the market for skilled labour because the equilibrium wage there ($8 per hour) is well above the legal minimum. (b) However, the minimum-wage legislation does have important effects in the market for unskilled labour. There the equilibrium wage ($2.50 per hour) is below the minimum, so the minimum wage makes the quantity supplied (4.5 million workers) exceed the quantity demanded (3.0 million workers). The result is unemployment of unskilled labour.

example, the equilibrium wages are $8 per hour for skilled workers and $2.50 per hour for unskilled workers.

Now suppose the government, seeking to protect unskilled workers, imposes a legal minimum wage of $3.50 per hour (the heavy coloured line in both parts of Figure 37-6). Turning first to part (a), we see that the minimum wage has no effect in the markets for skilled workers like carpenters and electricians. Since their wages are well above $3.50 per hour, a law prohibiting the payment of wage rates below $3.50 cannot possibly matter.

But the effects of the minimum wage may be pronounced in the markets for unskilled labour—and presumably quite different from those that the government intended. Figure 37-6(b) indicates that at the $3.50 minimum wage, firms want to employ only 3 million unskilled workers (point *A*) whereas employment of unskilled workers would have been 4.3 million (point *E*) in a free market. Although the 3 million unskilled workers lucky enough to retain their jobs do indeed earn a higher wage ($3.50 instead of $2.50 per hour) in this hypothetical example, 1.3 million of their compatriots earn no wage at all because they have been laid off. The job-losers will clearly be those workers with the lowest productivity, since the minimum wage effectively bans the employment of workers whose marginal revenue product is less than $3.50 per hour.

Although the minimum wage does lead to higher wages for those unskilled workers who retain their jobs, it also restricts employment opportunities for unskilled workers.

In addition, minimum wages may have particularly pernicious effects on those who are the victims of discrimination. Because of the minimum wage, as Figure 37-6(b) shows, employers of unskilled labour have more applicants than job openings. Consequently, they will be able to pick and choose among the available applicants and may, for example, discriminate against races who have been

Minimum Wages in Zimbabwe

Minimum-wage laws have proven to be politically popular in many countries. The following news item suggests that their effects in Africa are quite similar to their effects in Canada.

Zimbabwe Minimum Wage Spurs Many Dismissals

SALISBURY, Zimbabwe, July 6 (Reuters)—A Government decision to set a minimum wage for workers has backfired for thousands with dismissals reported throughout the country.

Officials of the ruling party of Prime Minister Robert Mugabe said today that in the Salisbury area alone more than 5,000 workers were dismissed before the minimum wage bill went into effect last Tuesday.

Worst hit, according to the officials, were domestic servants and farm workers for whom the minimum has been set at $45 a month. Employees in the commercial and industrial sectors, where the minimum has been fixed at $105 a month have also been dismissed. The officials said that every party office in the country was dealing with hundreds of workers each day complaining of unfair dismissal.

SOURCE: *The New York Times*, July 7, 1980. Copyright ©1980 by The New York Times Company. Reprinted by permission.

---

prevented by past discrimination from acquiring the skills required for admission to the higher-paid portion of the labour force.

For these reasons, many economists feel that the youth unemployment problem, and especially the unemployment problem of minority groups, will be very difficult to solve as long as the minimum wage remains effective. Obviously, the minimum wage is not the only culprit; the data strongly suggest that there is more to the story. Yet it is hard to dismiss the analytic conclusion that forced overpricing of unskilled labour contributes significantly to unemployment.

Unions and Collective Bargaining

Our analysis of competitive labour markets has ignored one rather important fact: The supply of labour is not at all competitive in many labour markets; instead it is controlled by a labour monopoly, a **union**.

While unions are important, fewer than 40 percent of Canadian workers belong to unions (see Figure 37–7). Union membership seems much more significant than this to the public because unions are large, and therefore newsworthy, institutions.

Unions are less prevalent in the United States, where only 24 percent of the workers are unionized, but they are more prevalent in some other industrialized countries. For example, about 50 percent of British workers and about 80 percent of Swedish workers belong to unions.

The Development of Unionism in Canada

There is no doubt that industrial working conditions were terrible before unions were formed, and that these conditions created widespread support among workers for the labour movement. Even just forty years ago, working conditions remained poor, and significant resistance to the organization of unions existed (see the boxed insert on page 737).

The original unions in Canada, which appeared in the early 1800s, were formed by workers in a particular craft or skill. These **craft unions** appeared first for two reasons: The relatively small numbers of members meant that organization costs were small, and there were few substitutes for the services offered by these skilled workers (so the threat of a strike represented a much bigger problem for

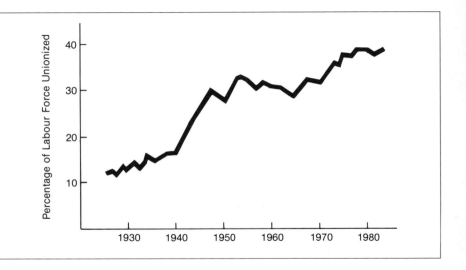

Figure 37-7

UNIONIZATION IN CANADA, 1926–1983

After important legislation and legal precedents in 1939 and 1945, union membership grew rapidly. It peaked in the 1970s. SOURCE: Statistics Canada, and Historical Statistics of Canada, Series E-176.

employers than would have been the case with easily replaced unskilled workers).

Early union history included a number of ugly incidents. Sometimes employers would hire men to intimidate union leaders or strike organizers, and often violent incidents were arranged to cast the labour leaders as the trouble-makers. Another problem that limited union growth was the treatment of unions in the courts. Initially the courts interpreted the withholding of services for higher wages as a form of restraint of trade.

In the late 1800s, an attempt was made to organize the less-skilled workers by the Knights of Labour, an American union with a Canadian affiliate that tried to organize all workers within a particular industry (no matter which crafts were involved). The Knights of Labour stressed the broader political issues concerning the role of labour in society. It turned out that workers cared more about what they saw as bread-and-butter issues, and since the approach of the Knights of Labour was more general, its membership began falling after 1886. The Knights of Labour and some smaller Marxist-oriented unions in British Columbia continued to exert some influence until about 1930.

The first widely successful confederation of labour in Canada was the Trades and Labour Council of Canada (TLC), founded in 1883, which became the Canadian affiliate of the American Federation of Labor (AFL). Those involved reverted to an emphasis on skilled workers, organizing them on a country-wide basis by craft. They devoted full time to the day-to-day issues of pay, work week, working and safety conditions, and related problems.

Another attempt to include unskilled workers took place with the formation of the Canadian Congress of Labour (CCL) in 1940. This organization was the Canadian affiliate of the Congress of Industrial Organizations (CIO) in the United States. It resembled the Knights of Labour in that its aim was to organize all workers by plant and industry groups, rather than by crafts. However, the CCL, like the TLC, avoided the broad political emphasis that characterized the Knights of Labour, and the two main wings of the labour movement merged in 1956, forming the Canadian Labour Congress (CLC). A similar merger took place in the United States, creating the AFL–CIO.

It is interesting to compare union growth in Canada with that in the United States. Big membership growth occurred earlier in the United States, mainly because of legal differences. By 1935, American workers acquired the legal right to strike, and in the same year it became illegal for employers to fire pro-union employees. In Canada, such firings were not illegal until 1939, and it was only later, during the war, that there was an official recognition of the workers' right to organize. As a result, union membership grew rapidly from 1935 to 1945 in the

Working Conditions Forty Years Ago: An Individual's Account

I started work for Stelco in 1940, and one of the jobs we had will give you an idea of conditions.

When the brick lining on the big open hearths would go down, all the labour gangs from all over the plant were called over to tear them down and to rebuild them. I was on the labour gang at the slag dump, and the foreman would come along about 4:00 in the afternoon and say: "You go home now and be back here at 6:00 and report over to open hearth." They didn't give you a chance to object at all. The inference was there—if you're not there at 6:00, don't bother to come back at all.

These furnaces had just been shut down, and they were still hot—I mean red hot, not white hot. The company didn't want to waste time. They didn't make any money when the furnaces were down.

You wore big wooden clogs on your feet, because your boots would start to burn if you didn't wear these clogs, and you wrapped a scarf around your ears and your ears would start to burn. You'd stand outside the door, and spot a brick. You'd spot the brick, because if you got in there and started to fish around, you started to burn. You couldn't stay in there any longer than 30 seconds or your clothes would start to smoulder. So you made up your mind—that's the brick right there! You had a big pair of tongs, and you made a lunge, and grabbed that brick, and ran right out. I've seen big, strong husky men—the heat would make them drop like flies. But there was a job that had to be done.

SOURCE: From *Baptism of a Union: Stelco Strike of 1946*, W. Roberts (ed.), Department of Labour Studies, McMaster University.

United States and from 1940 to 1950 in Canada.

The favourable public attitude toward unions in the United States soured somewhat after World War II, perhaps because of the rash of strikes that took place in 1946. One result of these strikes was the **Taft-Hartley Act** of 1947, which specified and outlawed certain "unfair labour practices" by unions. Specifically, the act severely limited the extent of the **closed shop**, under which only union members can be hired, and permitted state governments, at their discretion, to ban the **union shop**, an arrangement that requires employees to join the union. These so-called right-to-work laws have been adopted by quite a number of states.

A rather different legal decision took place in Canada. In 1945 there was a long strike involving the workers of the Ford Motor Company of Canada over the issue of union security. The dispute was finally resolved by an arbitration decision within the Supreme Court. The resulting rules have become known as the **Rand Formula** (named after the Supreme Court judge). These rules made it illegal for workers to be forced to join a union, but it became compulsory for workers to pay union dues, whether or not they were members. This court decision had the effect of solidifying union rights. Various versions of the Rand Formula have been adopted in many collective agreements, and it has recently become a part of Ontario's labour law.

The net result of the different laws and legal precedents is that only 20 percent of American workers are union members, a much lower proportion than in Canada. The other difference between the labour movements is that Canadian unions maintained their historical involvement with general political reforms in a more direct way than their American counterparts.

The major membership growth since 1960 has been in the public sector. But this growth has just compensated for declining membership in other areas. Membership has fallen because there is now a lower percentage of workers in the heavy industries (where unions have been popular) and also because a larger percentage of the work force is young and female, and a growing number want part-time employment. These groups seem less attracted to unions. Finally, the deep recession of the 1980s, and the widespread public frustration with visible public-sector unions such as the Canadian Union of Postal Workers have made unions less popular. Some of the problems faced by unions are illustrated in the

A **closed shop** is an arrangement that permits only union members to be hired.

A **union shop** is an arrangement under which non-union workers may be hired, but then must join the union within a specified period of time.

Wages and Unions Under Pressure

Until recently it was widely believed that, partly because of the power of the unions, wages tend to rise when they receive the slightest stimulus, but that they fall only under the severest economic pressures. Perhaps recent events in the United States may be interpreted as severe pressures: the recession of 1981–82, the process of deregulation, the decline in union membership, and the growing strength of foreign competition in many industries. In any event, they have brought a decline in demands for wage increases and even a number of wage cuts in the United States, as the following news story describes:

When the Greyhound Corporation demanded huge roll-backs from workers at its bus lines, the strike that ensued seemed tailor-made for a union victory.

The strikers started out solidly against concessions. In light of the large profits of the entire corporation, they were angered by the company's assertion that it needed wage cuts. Competitors scrambled to capture Greyhound's ridership during the strike. What is more, many Greyhound passengers were blue-collar workers likely to honor the picket lines.

Nevertheless, the Amalgamated Transit Union, facing a management intent upon concessions in an era when the labor-management balance has tipped more in favor of management than at any time since World War

II, was routed. Fearing the strike would be broken and the union destroyed, the union caved in, agreeing to a 7.8 percent pay cut.

Thus, the Greyhound workers joined the steel, auto, meat and rubber workers in swallowing "givebacks.". . .

Indeed, so successful has management been in its push for concessions that in contracts negotiated in the first nine months of 1983, first-year wage increases averaged just 1.7 percent, down from 9.1 percent the last time those contracts were negotiated.

In many industries, with profits decimated by recession, deregulation and foreign competition and with the breaking of the air controllers' strike still fresh in memory, managements feel the time is ripe to take back some of what they once granted.

Management knows it can bargain more aggressively because of the declining power of unions, workers' fears of more plant closings and bankruptcies and the large pool of labor ready to replace strikers, as was the case at Greyhound. . . . [A] new, tougher attitude pervades management, with even highly profitable companies pushing for givebacks.

And unions today certainly have reason to feel weak. They now represent under one-fifth of the work force.

Many unions may follow the lead of workers at Eastern Airlines. They granted wage concessions after examining the books and received in return a quarter of Eastern's stock, several seats on the airline's board and some say in management. . . .

SOURCE: From Steven Greenhouse, "Unions Pressed on 'Give-backs,'" *The New York Times*, January 11, 1984, D2.

---

accompanying box. While these problems are naturally somewhat more severe for American unions, the pressures are very real in Canada, too.

Unions as a Labour Monopoly

Unions require that we alter our economic analysis of the labour market in much the same way that monopolies required us to alter our analysis of the goods market (see Chapter 27). You will recall that in a monopolized product market the firm selects the point on its demand curve that maximizes its profits. Much the same idea applies to unions, which are, after all, monopoly sellers of labour. They too face a demand curve—derived this time from the marginal productivity schedules of firms—and can choose the point on it that suits them best.

The problem for the economist trying to analyse union behaviour—and perhaps also for the union leader trying to select a course of action—is how to decide which point on the demand curve is "best." Unlike the case of the business firm, there is no obvious goal analogous to profit maximization that clearly delineates what the union should do. Instead there are a number of *alternative* goals that sound plausible.

Alternative Union Goals

These goals can be illustrated with the aid of Figure 37-8, which depicts a demand curve for labour, labelled *DD*. The union leadership must decide which point on the curve is best. One possibility is to treat the size of the union as fixed and force employers to pay the highest wage they will pay and still employ all the union members. If, for example, the union has 4000 members, this would be point *A*, with a wage of $12 per hour. But this is a high-risk strategy for a union. Firms forced to pay such high wages will be at competitive disadvantage compared with firms that have non-union labour, and may even be forced to shut down.

Alternatively, union leaders may be interested in increasing the size of their unions. As an extreme case of this, they might try to make employment as large as possible without pushing the wage below the competitive level. If the competitive wage were $6 per hour in the absence of the union, this strategy would correspond to selecting point *C*, with employment for 8000 workers. In this case the existence of the union has no effect on wages or on employment.

An intermediate strategy that has often been suggested is that the union maximize the total income of all workers. This would dictate choosing point *B*, with a wage of $9 per hour and jobs for 6000 workers (since point *B* is where the demand elasticity is unity in this numerical example). Other possible strategies can also be imagined, but these suffice to make the basic point clear.

Unions, as monopoly sellers of labour, have the power to push wages above the competitive levels. However, since the demand curve for labour is downward sloping, such increases in wages normally can be achieved only by reducing the number of jobs. Just as the monopolist must limit his output to push up his price, so the union must restrict employment to push up the wage.

This can be seen clearly by comparing points *B* and *A* with point *C* (the competitive

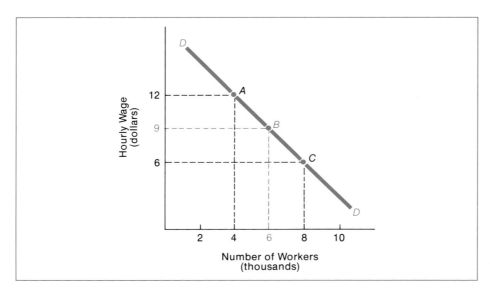

Figure 37-8
ALTERNATIVE GOALS FOR A UNION
Line *DD* is the demand curve for labour in a market that becomes unionized. Point *C* is the equilibrium point before the union, when wages were $6 per hour. If the union wants to push wages higher, it normally will have to sacrifice some jobs. Points *A* and *B* show two of its many alternatives.

solution). If it selects point B, the union raises wages by $3 per hour, but at the cost of 2000 jobs. If it goes all the way to point A, wages are raised to twice the competitive level, but employment is cut in half.

What do unions actually try to do? There are probably as many different choices as there are unions. Some seem to pursue a maximum-employment goal much like point C, raising wages very little. Others seem to push for the highest possible wages, much like point A. Most probably select an intermediate route. This implies, of course, that the effects of unionization on wage rates and employment will differ markedly among industries.

Alternative Union Strategies

How would a union that has decided to push wages above the competitive level accomplish this task? Two principal ways are illustrated in Figure 37–9, where we suppose that point U on demand curve DD is the union's choice, and point C is the competitive equilibrium.

In Figure 37–9(a), we suppose that the union pursues its goal by *restricting supply*. By keeping out some workers who would like to enter the industry or occupation, it shifts the supply curve of labour inward from S_0S_0 to S_1S_1. This sort of behaviour is often encountered in craft unions, which may require a long period of apprenticeship. Such unions sometimes offer only a small number of new memberships each year, largely to replace members who have died or retired. Membership in such a union is very valuable and is sometimes offered primarily to children of current members. Restricting supply is also practised within the medical profession (whose association operates like a union), by limiting enrolment in medical schools. Many other professional associations exist, which perform the functions of unions for their members.

In Figure 37–9(b), instead of restricting supply, the union simply *sets a high wage rate*, W in the example. In this case, it is the employers who will restrict entry into the job, because with wages so high they will not want to employ many workers. This second strategy is more typically employed by industrial unions

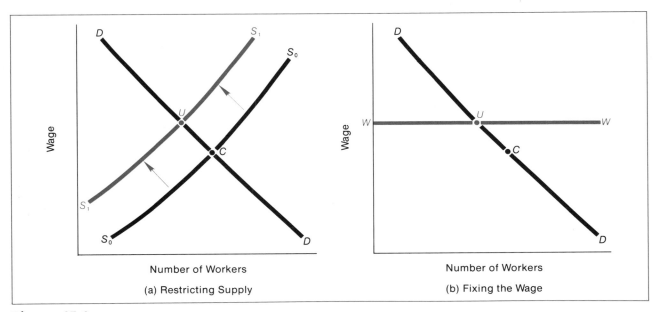

Figure 37-9

TWO UNION STRATEGIES

The two parts indicate two alternative ways for the union to move from point C to point U. In part (a), it keeps some workers out of the industry, thereby moving the supply curve to the left from S_0S_0 to S_1S_1. As a consequence, wages rise. In part (b), it fixes a high wage (W), and provides labour only at this wage. As a consequence, firms reduce employment. The effects are the same under both strategies.

like those representing automobile or mine workers. As the figure makes clear, the two wage-raising strategies achieve the same result (point U in either case) by what turns out to be the same means. Wages are raised only by reducing employment in either case.

In some exceptional cases, however, a union may be able to achieve wage gains without sacrificing employment. To do this, the union must be able to exercise effective control over the demand curve for labour. Figure 37–10 illustrates such a possibility. Union actions push the demand curve outward from D_0D_0 to D_1D_1, simultaneously raising both wages and employment. Typically, this is difficult to do. One way to do it is by *featherbedding*—forcing management to employ more workers than they really need.[4] Quite the opposite technique is to institute a campaign to raise worker productivity, which some unions seem to have been able to do. Alternatively, the union can try to raise the demand for the company's product either by flexing its political muscle (for example, by obtaining legislation to reduce foreign competition) or by appealing to the public to buy union products.

Have Unions Really Raised Wages?

The theory of unions as monopoly sellers of labour certainly suggests that unions have some ability to raise wages, but it also shows that they may be hesitant to use this ability for fear of reducing employment. To what extent do union members actually earn higher wages than non-members?

The consensus that has emerged from economic research on this question would probably surprise most people. It seems that most union members earn wages 10 percent to 15 percent above those of non-members who are otherwise identical (in skill, geographical location, and so on). While certainly not negligible, this can hardly be considered a huge differential. Perhaps the differential is not

---

[4]The best-known example of featherbedding involved the railway unions, which for years forced management to keep "firemen" in the cabs of diesel engines, in which there were no burning fires. Similarly, the musicians' union requires the O'Keefe Centre in Toronto to hire a "house minimum" of 22 musicians each night, even if fewer musicians are needed for the performance. Of course, it is not only labour that has tried to create an artificial demand for its services. Lawyers, doctors, and business firms, among others, have sought ways to induce consumers to buy more of their products and services. *EXERCISE:* Can you think of ways in which they have done this?

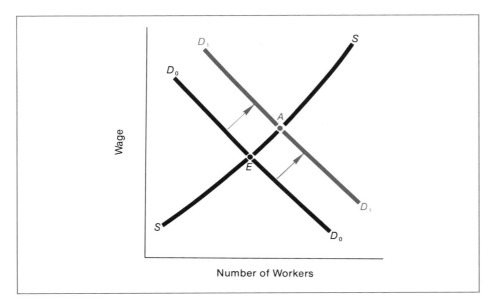

Figure 37–10
UNION CONTROL OVER THE DEMAND CURVE
This diagram indicates yet a third way in which unions may affect the labour market—a pleasant alternative for workers in that wages can be raised while adding to employment. Strong unions may succeed in raising the demand curve from D_0D_0 to D_1D_1 by (a) featherbedding, (b) raising worker productivity, or (c) using their influence to increase demand for the product. Equilibrium then shifts from point E to point A.

larger because employers of non-unionized workers adjust their wages to keep the gap small enough to avoid unionization of their shops.

Monopsony and Bilateral Monopoly

While the analysis we have just presented has its applications, it oversimplifies matters in several important respects. For one thing, it envisions a market situation in which one powerful union is dealing with many powerless employers: The labour market is assumed to be monopolized on the selling side but competitive on the buying side. There are industries that more or less fit this model. The giant Teamsters' union negotiates with a trucking industry that comprises thousands of firms, most of them quite small and powerless. Similarly, most of the unions within the construction industry are much larger than the firms with which they bargain.

But there are many cases that simply do not fit the model. The "Big Four" automakers do not stand idly by while the UAW picks its favourite point on the demand curve for auto workers. Nor does the Steelworkers' union sit across the bargaining table from representatives of a perfectly competitive industry. In these and other industries, while the union certainly has a good deal of monopoly power over labour supply, the firms also have some **monopsony** power over the labour demand. Just as a monopoly union on the selling side of the labour market does not passively sell labour at the going wage, a monopsony firm on the buying side does not passively purchase labour at the going wage, nor at the wage suggested by the labour union. Analysts find it very difficult to predict the wage and employment decisions that will emerge when both the buying and selling side of a market are monopolized—a situation called **bilateral monopoly**.

The difficulties here are quite similar to those we encountered in considering the behaviour of oligopolistic industries in Chapter 28. Just as one oligopolist, in planning his strategy, is acutely aware that his rivals are likely to react to anything he does, a union dealing with a monopsony employer knows that any move it makes will elicit a countermove by the firm. And this knowledge makes the first decision that much more complicated. An economic analysis of monopsony is given in the appendix of this chapter. In practice, the outcome of bilateral monopoly will depend partly on economic logic, partly on the relative power of the union and management, partly on the skill and preparation of the negotiators, and partly on luck.

Monopsony refers to a market situation in which there is only one buyer.

Bilateral monopoly is a market situation in which there is both a monopoly on the selling side and a monopsony on the buying side.

Collective Bargaining and Strikes

The process by which unions and management settle upon the terms of a labour contract is called **collective bargaining**. Unfortunately, there is nothing as straightforward as a supply–demand diagram to tell us what wage level will emerge from a collective-bargaining session. Furthermore, actual collective-bargaining sessions range over many more issues than wages. For example, fringe benefits—such as pensions, health and life insurance, paid holidays, and the like—may be just as important as wages to both labour and management. Wage premiums for overtime work and seniority privileges will also be negotiated. Work conditions, such as the speed with which the assembly line should move, are often crucial issues. Many labour contracts specify in great detail the rights of labour and management to set work conditions—and also provide elaborate procedures for resolving grievances and disputes. This list could go on and on. The final contract that emerges from collective bargaining may well run to many pages of fine print.

With the issues so varied and complex, and with the stakes so high, it is no wonder that both labour and management employ skilled professionals who specialize in preparing for and carrying out these negotiations, and that each side enters a collective-bargaining session armed with reams of evidence supporting its positions.

The bargaining in these sessions is often heated, with outcomes riding as much on personalities and skills of the negotiators as on cool-headed logic and economic facts. Negotiations may last well into the night, with each side seeming to try to wear the other out. Each side may threaten the other with grave consequences if it does not accept its own terms. Unions, for their part, generally threaten to strike or to carry out a work slow-down. Firms counter with the threat that they would rather face a strike than give in, or may even close the plant without a strike. (This is called a "lock-out.")

Mediation and Arbitration

Where the public interest is seriously affected, or when the union and firm reach an impasse, government agencies may well send in a **mediator**, whose job is to try to speed up the negotiation process. This impartial observer will sit down with both sides separately to discuss their problems, and will try to persuade each side to yield a bit to the other. At some stage, when an agreement looks possible, he may call them back together for another bargaining session in his presence.

A mediator, however, has no power to force a settlement. His success hinges on his ability to smooth ruffled feathers and to find common ground for agreement. Sometimes, in cases where unions and firms simply cannot agree, and where neither wants a strike, differences are finally settled by **arbitration**—the appointment of an impartial individual empowered to settle the issues that negotiation could not resolve. In fact, in some vital sectors where a strike is too injurious to the public interest, the labour contract or the law may stipulate that there must be *compulsory arbitration* if the two parties cannot agree. However, both labour and management are normally reluctant to accept this procedure.

Strikes

Most collective-bargaining situations do not lead to strikes. But the right to strike and to take a strike remain fundamentally important for the bargaining process. Imagine, for example, a firm bargaining with a union that was prohibited from striking. It seems likely that the union's bargaining position would be quite weak. On the other hand, a firm that always capitulated rather than suffer a strike would be virtually at the mercy of the union. So strikes, or more precisely, the possibility of strikes, serve an important economic purpose.

Figure 37–11 reports both the actual length of strikes and the percentage of total work time lost as a result of strikes. For the families involved, the work stoppages clearly represent major dislocations. Despite this, and the headline-grabbing nature of major national strikes, however, the total amount of work time lost to strikes is small—far less, for example, than the time lost to coffee breaks! It is noteworthy, though, that Canada's record of time lost from strikes is not good, when compared with that of other countries (see Figure 37–12).

Collective Bargaining in the Public Sector

We have argued that strikes serve an important function in private-sector bargaining, as a way of dividing the fruits of economic activity between big labour and big business. But does the same rationale for strikes apply to the public sector, where strikes or work stoppages have become increasingly common among postal workers, garbage collectors, teachers, and others?

It is not clear that it does. In most private-sector strikes, labour and management are inflicting harm upon one another in a kind of battle of "survival of the fittest." Consumers normally suffer only mild inconveniences. When General Motors is on strike, many potential car buyers will be disappointed, but they can turn to Ford, Chrysler, or many imports. Similarly, when other private

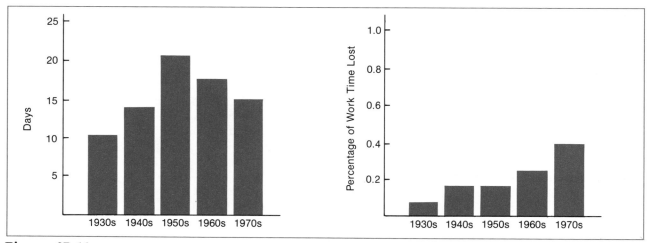

Figure 37–11

(a) AVERAGE STRIKE LENGTH
This chart shows the average days on strike per worker involved.
SOURCE: Historical Statistics of Canada, Series E-196

(b) PERCENTAGE OF WORK TIME LOST BECAUSE OF STRIKES
This chart shows the average annual work time lost to work stoppages.
SOURCE: Historical Statistics of Canada, Series E-197

products disappear from the shelves because of strikes, the consumer can easily replace them with close substitutes. Thus, in many cases we can think of consumers as being relatively innocent and unharmed spectators when large unions and large private firms slug it out.

But public-sector bargaining is different. Here, management does not represent the interests of capital against those of labour; rather, it represents the public. And there is no pool of profits to be divided between the union and the shareholders. Instead, what management agrees to give the union comes out of the pockets of the taxpayers.

Finally, it is quite clear that the public is not just a spectator in such strikes, but is the primary victim. When police or fire-protection services are reduced, when mail delivery ceases, when public schools or airports shut down, consumers cannot find substitutes for these services. In a very real sense, then, strikes in the public sector are strikes against citizens, not strikes against management. They pit representatives of a particular group of workers against representatives of taxpayers as a whole.

For these reasons, the right of public employees to strike was traditionally more severely limited than the corresponding right of private-sector workers. Nevertheless, federal government employees were given the right to strike in the late 1960s. Partly as a result of this, the biggest growth in union membership has been in the public sector. Today, six of the largest ten unions in Canada are those representing "white-collar" government employees.

Unfortunately, our system of labour relations for public employees is showing significant signs of strain. The most visible indication of this has been the series of inconvenient postal strikes. Even when Parliament acts to order public-sector employees back to work, only limited legal action is taken against those who continue with illegal strike action. One reaction to these developments occurred in British Columbia in 1983 when Premier Bennett's government took steps to dramatically remove job security within the B.C. public service.

Corporatism and Industrial Democracy

Our discussion of public-sector unions raises the more general issue of sectional interests. Trade unions are not the only institutions trying to acquire market

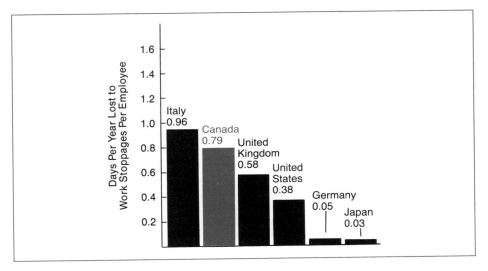

Figure 37–12
THE INCIDENCE OF STRIKES
IN INDUSTRIAL COUNTRIES
Contrary to popular impressions,
Canada loses more work time to
strikes than does the United
Kingdom. And although strikes
here are less common than they
are in Italy, they are much more
common here than in Japan or
Germany. (*Note*: Data are
averages for the five-year period
1974–78.)
SOURCE: U.S. Department of Labor,
Handbook of Labor Statistics,
December 1980.

power for the benefit of their restricted membership. Professional associations (such as those for doctors and lawyers) have the same purpose, as do firms that engage in take-overs and mergers to increase market share. All these institutions attempt to increase the general support for their actions by claiming that they act in the public interest. For example, firms are simply "trying to achieve the economies of large-scale operations," and the unions are "fighting a general battle for the working class."

The market mechanism limits the power of these institutions, since it facilitates the introduction of cheaper substitutes, such as goods from abroad, or labour-saving production inputs. It is perfectly rational for self-seeking institutions to use the political process to limit the market's ability to undermine their market power. This is why both firms and unions call for increased protection through foreign tariffs and quotas, and why unions support minimum-wage legislation. If market power exists, and the political process is used to maintain it, what is the prognosis for the price system?

One suggested solution is corporatism or tripartism. It was tried in England by Prime Minister Edward Heath when he asked employers and unions to "share fully with the government the benefits and obligations involved in running the national economy." The idea was to blunt the forces of special interest by making big business and big labour truly responsible for the public interest. For instance, it was hoped that this co-operative approach would reduce the competitive wage increases of *particular* labour groups, *all* of which had been justified by reference to the public interest. Margaret Thatcher's government discarded this approach, since it was felt that tripartism simply enables private groups to strengthen their ability to use the political process for their own purpose.

Industrial democracy is another suggested institutional change that might solve these problems. It is based on the assumption that it is simply not feasible to dismantle the power of large firms and unions. Instead, workers should be allowed fuller participation in management decisions. The reasoning behind this suggestion is that only under such a system involving worker self-management will workers be forced to appreciate and accept the constraints of the market faced by employers. There is a successful example of this arrangement at a Shell chemical plant in Sarnia, involving the Energy and Chemical Workers Union.

Critics of industrial democracy fear that it lacks any incentive for the worker-managed firm with monopoly power to charge competitive product prices. Also, they worry that entrepreneurial drive would not be rewarded, and therefore would decrease. The current state of Canadian labour relations suggests that these issues will continue to be actively debated.

Summary

1. The supply of labour is determined by free choices made by individuals. Because of conflicting income and substitution effects, the quantity of labour supplied may rise or fall as a result of an increase in wages.

2. Historical data show that hours of work per week have fallen as wages have risen, suggesting that income effects may be dominant, in the long run.

3. The demand curve for labour, like the demand curve for any factor of production, is derived from the marginal-revenue product curve. It slopes downward because of the "law" of diminishing marginal returns.

4. In a free market, the wage rate and the level of employment are determined by the interaction of supply and demand. Workers in great demand or short supply will command high wages and, conversely, low wages will be assigned to workers in abundant supply or with skills that are not in great demand.

5. Some valuable skills are virtually impossible to duplicate. People who possess such skills will earn economic rents as part of their wages.

6. But most skills can be acquired by "investments in human capital," such as education. The financial rate of return on university education, while still positive, is not as high as it was in the 1960s.

7. Human-capital theory assumes that people make educational decisions in much the same way as businesses make investment decisions and tacitly assumes that people learn things in schools that increase their productivity on jobs.

8. Other theories of the effects of education on earnings deny that schooling actually raises productivity. One view is that the educational system primarily sorts people according to their abilities. Another view holds that schools sort people according to their social class and teach them discipline and obedience.

9. According to the theory of dual labour markets, there are two distinct types of labour markets with very little mobility between them. The primary labour market contains the "good" jobs, where wages are high, prospects for advancement are good, and higher education pays off. The secondary labour market contains the "bad" jobs, with low wages, little opportunity for promotion, and little return to education.

10. One reason that teen-agers suffer from such high unemployment rates is that minimum-wage laws prevent the employment of low-productivity workers.

11. About one-third of all Canadian workers belong to unions, which can be thought of as monopoly sellers of labour.

12. Analysis of union behaviour is complicated by the fact that a union can have many goals. For the most part, unions probably force wages to be higher and employment to be lower than they would be in a competitive labour market. However, there are exceptions.

13. Collective-bargaining agreements between labour and management are complex documents covering much more than employment and wage rates.

14. Strikes (or at least threats of strikes) play an important role in collective bargaining as a way of dividing the fruits of economic activity between big business and big labour.

15. Strikes in the public sector, however, take on a different character because the adversaries are no longer "labour" versus "capital" but rather a particular group of labourers versus the general public.

Concepts for Review

Minimum-wage law	Dual labour markets	Bilateral monopoly
Income and substitution effects	Union	Collective bargaining
Backward-bending supply curve	Industrial and craft unions	Mediation
Economic rent	Closed shop	Arbitration
Investments in human capital	Union shop	Public-sector bargaining
Human-capital theory	Monopsony	

Questions for Discussion

1. Universities are known to pay rather low wages for student labour. Can this be explained by the operation of supply and demand in the local labour market? Is the concept of monopsony of any use? How might things differ if students formed a union?

2. University professors are highly skilled (or at least highly educated!) labour. Yet their wages are not very high. Is this a refutation of the marginal productivity theory?

3. The following table shows the number of pizzas that can be produced by a large pizza parlour employing various numbers of pizza chefs.

NUMBER OF CHEFS	NUMBER OF PIZZAS PER DAY
1	80
2	150
3	205
4	240
5	250
6	230

a. Find the marginal physical product schedule of chefs.

b. Assuming a price of $3 per pizza, find the marginal revenue product schedule.

c. If chefs are paid $30 per day, how many will this pizza parlour employ? How would your answer change if chefs' wages rose to $40 per day?

d. Suppose the price of pizza rises from $3 to $4. Show what happens to the derived demand curve for chefs.

4. Discuss the concept of the financial rate of return to a university education. If this return is less than the return on a bank account, does that mean you should quit university? Why might you wish to stay in school anyway? Are there circumstances under which it might be rational not to go to university, even when the financial returns to university are very high?

5. It seems to be a well-established fact that workers with more years of education typically receive higher wages. What are some possible reasons for this?

6. Explain why many economists blame the minimum-wage law for much of the employment problems of youth.

7. Approximately what fraction of the Canadian labour force belongs to unions? (Try asking this question of a person who has never studied economics.) Why do you think this fraction is as low as it is?

8. What are some reasonable goals for a union? Use the tools of supply and demand to explain how a union might pursue its goals, whatever they are. Consider a union that has been in the news recently. What was it trying to accomplish?

9. "Strikes are simply intolerable and should be outlawed." Comment.

10. "Public employees should have the same right to strike as private employees." Comment.

Appendix
The Effects of Unions and Minimum Wages Under Monopsony

We have argued in this chapter that if a union or a minimum-wage law raises wages, it must necessarily reduce employment. In this appendix we examine a possible exception to this rule.

When there is a monopsony on the buying side of the labour market, a union or a minimum-wage law might succeed in raising wages without reducing employment. It might even be able to increase employment.

The Hiring Decisions of a Monopsonist

To establish these results, we begin by considering the hiring decision of a single firm operating in a labour market that is competitive on the supply side. (Later we will bring unions into the picture.) In such a market structure, there is a competitive *supply* curve for labour as usual, but there is a rather different sort of *demand* curve. In Figure 37–13, the supply curve is labelled *SS* and the firm's marginal revenue product (MRP) schedule is labelled *RR*. In this context, however, the MRP schedule is *not* the demand curve. The diagram has one additional curve, which will be explained presently.

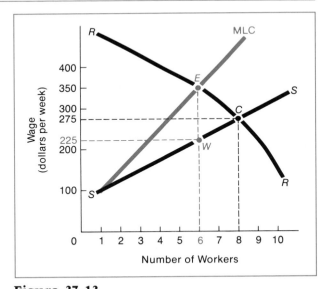

Figure 37–13
LABOUR-MARKET EQUILIBRIUM UNDER MONOPSONY
Under monopsony, labour-market equilibrium occurs at the employment level that equates marginal labour cost (curve MLC in the diagram) to the marginal revenue product (curve RR). In this case, equilibrium is at point E, where six workers are employed. The corresponding wage is $225 per week. By contrast, if this were a competitive market, equilibrium would be at point C, with a wage of $275 and employment of eight workers.

How many workers will the monopsonist wish to hire? Table 37–1 helps us answer this question by displaying the monopsonist's cost and revenue calculations. What does he gain by hiring an additional worker? He gains that worker's marginal revenue product, which is given in column 5 of the table. What does he lose? Not just the wage he pays to the new worker. Because he is the only employer, and because the labour supply schedule is upward sloping, he can attract an additional worker only by *raising the wage rate*. And this higher wage must be paid to *all his employees*, not just the new one. For this reason, the cost of hiring an additional worker—what we call **marginal labour costs**—exceeds the wage rate. By how much? Table 37–1 provides the answer. The first two columns are just the labour supply schedule, curve *SS* of Figure 37–13. By multiplying the wage rate by the number of workers, we can compute the *total labour cost*, which is shown in column 3. For example, the total labour cost of hiring five workers is five times the weekly wage of $200, or $1000. From these data, *marginal labour costs* are computed in the usual way—as the changes in successive total labour costs—and the results are displayed in column 4. This is the information the monopsonist wants, for it tells him that the first worker costs him $100, the next $150, and so on. The numbers in column 4 are displayed on the graph by the blue curve labelled MLC (marginal labour cost).

What employment level maximizes the monopsonist's profits? The usual marginal analysis applies. As he hires more workers, his profits rise if the marginal revenue product exceeds the marginal labour cost. For example, when he expands from one worker to two, he receives $450 more in revenue and pays out only an additional $150 to labour; so profits rise by $300. This continues up to the point where marginal labour costs and the marginal revenue product are equal—at six workers in the example. Pushing beyond this point would reduce profits. For example, hiring the seventh worker would cost $400 and bring in only $325 in increased revenues—clearly a losing proposition. We therefore conclude:

A monopsonist maximizes profits by hiring workers up to the point where marginal labour costs are equal to the marginal revenue product.

In the example, it is optimal for the firm to hire six workers, and it does this by offering a wage of $225 per week. This solution is shown in Figure 37–13 by points *E* and *W*. Point *E* is the equilibrium of the firm, where marginal labour costs and marginal revenue product are equal. To find the corresponding wage rate, we move vertically downward from *E* until we reach the supply curve at point *W*.

Let us compare this result with what would have emerged in a competitive labour market. As we know, equilibrium would be established where the supply curve of labour intersects the marginal-revenue-product curve because the marginal-revenue-product curve *is* the demand curve of a competitive industry. Figure 37–13 shows that this competitive equilibrium (point *C*) would have been at a wage of $275 and employment of eight workers.[5] In contrast, the monopsonist hires fewer workers (only six) and pays each a lower wage (only $225 per week). This finding is quite a general result:

As long as the supply curve of labour is upward sloping and the marginal revenue product schedule is downward sloping, a monopsonist will hire fewer

[5]This conclusion can also be seen in Table 37–1 where, in a competitive market, columns 1 and 2 give the supply curve, while columns 1 and 5 give the demand curve. Quantity supplied equals quantity demanded when the wage is $275.

Table 37–1
LABOUR COSTS AND MARGINAL REVENUE PRODUCT OF A MONOPSONIST

(1) NUMBER OF WORKERS	(2) WAGE RATE (dollars)	(3) TOTAL LABOUR COST (dollars)	(4) MARGINAL LABOUR COST (dollars)	(5) MARGINAL REVENUE PRODUCT (dollars)
1	100	100	100	475
2	125	250	150	450
3	150	450	200	425
4	175	700	250	400
5	200	1000	300	375
6	225	1350	350	350
7	250	1750	400	325
8	275	2200	450	275
9	300	2700	500	225
10	325	3250	550	150

workers and pay lower wages than would a competitive industry.

Unions Under Monopsony

Where monopsony firms exist, their workers are very likely to be unionized. Let us therefore consider what would happen if the workers organized into a union and demanded a wage of no less than $250 per week. This action would change the supply curve, and hence the MLC curve, that the monopsonist faces in a straightforward way. No labour could be hired at wages below $250 per week. At that wage, the monopsonist could attract up to seven workers (see column 2 of Table 37–1). At higher wages, he could attract still more labour according to the supply curve. Thus, his new effective supply curve would be *horizontal* at the wage of $250 up to the employment level of seven workers, and then would follow the old supply curve. This is given numerically in column 2 of Table 37–2 and is shown graphically by the kinked supply curve SWS in Figure 37–14.

From this information, we can compute the revised marginal labour cost (MLC) schedule just as we did before. Column 3 in Table 37–2 gives us total labour costs at each employment level, and column 4 shows the corresponding marginal cost. The heavy blue curve labelled MLC in Figure 37–14 depicts this information graphically. Notice that the marginal labour cost schedule has become *horizontal* up to the point where seven workers are hired. This is a result of the union's behaviour, which tells the monopsonist that he must pay the *same* wage per worker whether he hires one or seven employees. Beyond seven workers, the schedule returns to its previous level since the union minimum is irrelevant.

The condition for profit maximization is unchanged, so the monopsonist seeks the employment

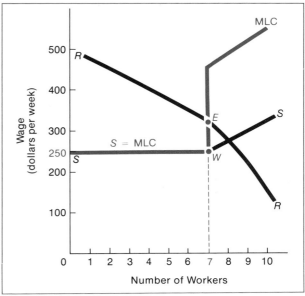

Figure 37-14
THE EFFECTS OF A UNION UNDER MONOPSONY
A union can change the character of the MLC schedule facing a monopsonist. In this example, MLC is horizontal up to seven workers, and then jumps as indicated by the heavy blue line. Consequently, equilibrium employment is determined by point E, where seven workers are employed at a wage of $250. Comparing this with Figure 37-13, we see that the union can raise both wages and employment.

level at which marginal labour costs and marginal revenue product are equal. Since MLC jumps abruptly from $250 for the seventh worker to $450 for the eighth, this cannot be achieved exactly. But Table 37–2 makes it quite clear that it is now profitable to employ the seventh worker (marginal labour cost equals $250, marginal revenue product equals $325),

Table 37-2
LABOUR COSTS AND MARGINAL REVENUE PRODUCT OF A MONOPSONIST FACING A UNION

(1) NUMBER OF WORKERS	(2) WAGE RATE (dollars)	(3) TOTAL LABOUR COST (dollars)	(4) MARGINAL LABOUR COST (dollars)	(5) MARGINAL REVENUE PRODUCT (dollars)
1	250	250	250	475
2	250	500	250	450
3	250	750	250	425
4	250	1000	250	400
5	250	1250	250	375
6	250	1500	250	350
7	250	1750	250	325
8	275	2200	450	275
9	300	2700	500	225
10	325	3250	550	150

but unprofitable to employ the eighth (marginal labour cost equals $450, marginal revenue product equals $275). Points E and W in Figure 37–14 show, once again, the monopsonist's equilibrium point and the wage he must pay.

Comparing Figures 37–13 and 37–14 (or Tables 37–1 and 37–2), we see that the union has raised wages from $225 to $250 per week, and at the same time has *increased* employment from six to seven workers. As was claimed, the union can raise both wages and employment in the presence of monopsony.

Minimum-Wage Laws Under Monopsony

Virtually the same kind of result as the one just discussed *can* be achieved by a minimum-wage law under monopsony. That is, *if* the government selects the right minimum wage, it might succeed in raising both wages and employment.

Refer back to Figure 37–13, in which we depicted the equilibrium wage ($225 per week) and employ-

ment level (six workers) in a monopsonized labour market with no minimum wage. Just like a union, a minimum-wage law creates a horizontal supply curve at the minimum wage. The effects will be just the same as the effects of the union. In both cases, the differences between wages and marginal labour costs are eliminated. As an exercise, use Figure 37–13 to convince yourself that a minimum wage can succeed in raising *both* wages *and* employment by imposing a horizontal supply curve of labour at a wage between $225 and $350 per week. (*Hint*: What will be the monopsonist's MLC under the minimum wage?)

We caution you against reading strong policy conclusions into this finding, however. Examples of actual monopsony (one buyer) in labour markets are quite hard to find. Certainly the types of service establishments that tend to hire the lowest-paid workers— restaurants and snack bars, amusement parks, car washes, and so on—have no monopsony power whatever. While minimum-wage laws *can* conceivably raise employment, few economists believe that they actually have this pleasant effect except in some exceptional cases.

Summary

1. A profit-maximizing monopsonist hires labour up to the point where the marginal revenue product equals the marginal labour cost.
2. Because marginal labour cost exceeds the wage rate, this results in less employment and lower wages than would emerge from a competitive labour market.

3. By eliminating the difference between marginal labour costs and wages, it is possible that a union could raise both wages and employment under monopsony.
4. For the same reason, a minimum-wage law can conceivably raise wages without sacrificing jobs if the employer is a monopsonist.

Concept for Review

Marginal labour costs

Questions for Discussion

1. Consider the pizza chef example of Question 3 on page 746 and suppose that pizzas sell for $3 each. Let the supply curve of chefs be as follows:

NUMBER OF CHEFS	WAGES PER DAY
1	$10
2	15
3	20
4	25
5	30
6	40

   a. How many chefs will be employed, and at what

   wage, if the market is competitive?
   b. How many chefs will be employed, and at what wage, if the market has a monopsony pizza parlour? (*Hint*: First figure out the schedule of marginal labour cost.)
   c. Compare your answers to a. and b. What do you conclude?
   d. Now suppose that a union is organized to fight the monopsonist. If it insists on a wage of $30 per day, what will the monopsonist do?
2. Given what you have learned about minimum-wage laws in the chapter and in the appendix, do you think they are a good or a bad idea?

Poverty and Inequality

38

From each according to his ability, to each according to his needs.
KARL MARX

Τ he last two chapters analysed the principles by which factor prices—wages, rentals, and interest rates—are determined in a market economy. One reason for concern with this issue is that these factor payments determine the *incomes* of the people to whom the factors belong. The study of factor pricing is, therefore, an indirect way to learn about the *distribution of income* among individuals.

In this chapter we turn to the problem of income distribution more directly. Specifically, we seek answers to the following questions: How much income inequality is there in Canada, and why? How can society decide rationally on how much equality it wants? And, once this decision is made, what policies are available to pursue this goal? In trying to answer these questions, we must necessarily consider the related problems of poverty and discrimination, and so these issues, too, receive attention in this chapter.

We will also offer a full explanation of one of the **12 Ideas for Beyond the Final Exam**: *the fundamental trade-off between economic equality and economic efficiency*. Taking it for granted that equality and efficiency are both important social goals, we shall learn why policies that promote greater income equality (or less poverty or less discrimination) often threaten to interfere with economic efficiency. In this chapter we explain *why* this is so and *what* can be done about it.

The Politics and Economics of Inequality

It is apparent that the trade-off between equality and efficiency is not widely understood. Social reformers often argue that society should adopt even the most outlandish programs to increase income equality or eradicate poverty, regardless of the potential side effects these policies might have. Defenders of the status quo, for their part, often seem so obsessed with these undesirable side effects—whether imagined or actual—that they ignore the benefits of redistribution programs.

The continuing debate over supply-side economics is a good illustration.[1] Many of the tax incentives advocated by supply-siders, such as reducing or eliminating taxes on dividends and capital gains, clearly would be of greatest

---

[1]This debate is considered in greater detail in Chapter 11, pages 211–18.

benefit to the wealthy. The poor, after all, do not own much corporate stock. On the other hand, these measures are designed to increase the incentives to save and invest; and, if they are successful, the whole nation will benefit from the resulting increase in productivity. The more zealous advocates of supply-side initiatives trumpet the hoped-for gains in productivity and show little appreciation of the harmful effects on income equality. Some of their opponents vocally decry the widening of income differentials and show little concern for increasing the nation's productivity. Each side claims to have virtue in its corner.

Economists try not to paint these issues in black and white. They prefer to phrase things in terms of trade-offs—to reap gains on one front, you often must make sacrifices on another. A policy is not necessarily ill conceived simply because it has some undesirable side effects, *if* it makes an important enough contribution to one of society's basic goals. But, on the other hand, some policies have such severe side effects that they deserve to be rejected, even if they serve a laudable goal.

Admitting that there is a trade-off between equality and efficiency—that while supply-side tax cuts may help solve the productivity problem, they may also increase inequality—may not be the best way to win votes; but it does face the facts. And in that way it helps us make the inherently political decisions about what should be done. If we are to understand these complex issues, a good place to start is, as always, with the facts.

The Facts: Poverty

In 1962, Michael Harrington published a little book called *The Other America*, which was to have a profound effect on North American society. The "other Americans" of whom Harrington wrote were the poor who lived in the land of plenty. Ill clothed in the richest country on earth, inadequately nourished in a nation where obesity was a problem, infirm in a country with some of the world's highest health standards, these people lived an almost unknown existence in their dilapidated hovels, according to Harrington. And, to make matters worse, their inadequate nutrition, lack of education, and generally demoralized state often condemned the children of the "other Americans" to repeat the lives of their parents. There was, Harrington argued, a "cycle of poverty"—a cycle that could be broken only by government action.

The work of Harrington and others touched the hearts of many in both the United States and Canada who, it seemed, really had no idea of the abominable living conditions of the less fortunate. Within a few years, the growing concern over the plight of the poor led to a special Senate committee to investigate poverty in Canada, and official definitions of poverty were adopted. The dividing line between the poor and non-poor was called the **poverty line**. The definition of the poverty line was subsequently refined to account for differences in family size and the size of one's community, and it is adjusted each year to reflect changes in the cost of living.

The **poverty line** is an amount of income below which a family is considered "poor."

The basic poverty line is set at the level of income at which the average person spends 59 percent of that income on the essentials of life (food, clothing, and shelter). The average Canadian family spends 39 percent of income on these essentials. For 1983, this definition meant that the poverty line was an income of $7000 per year in the country, and $9500 per year in a large city, for an individual. For a family of four, the corresponding low-income cut-offs were $14,000 and $19,000 in 1983. Using these National Council of Welfare definitions, about 13.5 percent of Canadian families were poor in 1983. Other definitions have been proposed, such as those of the special Senate committee and the Canadian Council on Social Development. Both these alternative definitions involve higher poverty lines.

Substantial progress toward eliminating poverty was made during the 1970s;

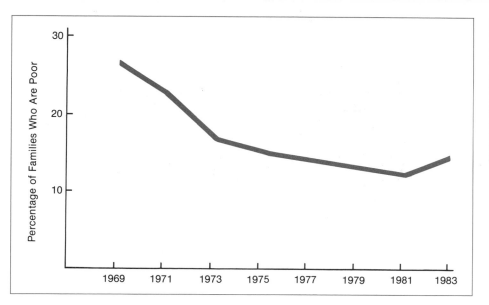

Figure 38-1
PROGRESS IN THE
REDUCTION OF POVERTY
This figure charts the decline in
the percentage of Canadian
families classified as "poor" by
official definitions. While
substantial progress has been
made, more than 13 percent of
Canadian families remain below
the poverty line.
SOURCE: Statistics Canada 13-207.

the percentage of families in Canada living below the poverty line fell from 26 percent to 13 percent (see Figure 38–1). However, the severe recession in the early 1980s has meant that the poverty rate in 1983 was no better than it was in 1977. This fact has worried a number of people. But some critics have argued that the official data may overstate the incidence of poverty, since the official definition is based only on cash income. A number of goods are received by the poor in kind: for example, public education, public housing, and health care. The Census Bureau in the United States has developed an experimental measure of poverty that includes the value of goods given in kind. These figures suggest that the number of poor people in the United States is roughly one-third fewer than what is indicated by the official figures. The figures also show an increase in poverty in the United States since 1979.

This debate raises the fundamental question of how we define "the poor." Continuing economic growth will eventually pull almost everyone above any arbitrarily established poverty line. Does this event mark the end of poverty? Some would say, "Yes." But others would insist that the biblical injunction is right: "The poor ye have always with you."

There are two ways to define poverty. The more optimistic definition uses an *absolute concept of poverty*: If you fall short of a certain minimum standard of living, you are poor; once you pass this standard, you are no longer poor. The second definition is based on a *relative concept of poverty*: The poor are those who fall too far behind the average income.

Each definition has its pros and cons. The basic problem with the absolute-poverty concept is that it is arbitrary. Who sets the line? Most of the people of Bangladesh would be delighted to live a bit below the Canadian poverty line and would consider themselves quite prosperous. Similarly, the standard of living that we now call "poor" would probably not have been considered so in Canada in 1780, and certainly not in Europe during the Middle Ages. (See the boxed insert on page 755.) Different times and different places apparently call for different poverty lines.

The fact that the concept of poverty is culturally, not physiologically, determined suggests that it must be a relative concept. For example, one suggestion is to define the poverty line as one-half of the national average income. In this way, the poverty line would automatically rise as the nation grows richer.

"There is a perfect example of what is wrong with this country today."

"There is a perfect example of what is wrong with this country today."

Once we start moving away from an absolute concept of poverty toward a relative concept, the sharp distinction between the poor and the non-poor starts to evaporate. Instead, we begin to think of a parade of people from the poorest soul to the richest millionaire. The "poverty problem," then, seems to be that the disparities in income are "too large" in some sense. The poor are so poor because the rich are so rich. If we follow this line of thought far enough, we are led away from the narrow problem of *poverty* toward the broader problem of *inequality of income*.

The Facts: Inequality

There is nothing in the market mechanism that works to prevent large differences in incomes. On the contrary, it tends to breed inequality, for the basic source of the great efficiency of the market mechanism is its system of rewards and penalties. The market is generous to those who are successful in operating efficient enterprises that are responsive to consumer demands, and it is ruthless in penalizing those who are unable or unwilling to satisfy consumer demands efficiently. Its financial punishment of those who try and fail can be particularly severe. At times it even brings down the great and powerful.

Most people have a pretty good idea that the income distribution is quite spread out—that the gulf between the rich and the poor is a wide one. But few have any concept of where they stand in the distribution. In the next paragraph, you will find some statistics on the 1982 income distribution in Canada (the most recent data that was available when this book was written). But before looking at these, try the following experiment. First, write down what you think your family's income before tax was in 1982. (If you do not know, take a guess.) Next, try to guess what percentage of Canadian families had incomes *lower* than this. Finally, if we divide Canada into three broad income classes—rich, middle class, and poor—to which group do you think your family belongs?

Now that you have written down answers to these three questions, look at the income distribution data for 1982 in Table 38–1. If you are like most university students, these figures will contain a few surprises for you. First, if we adopt the tentative definitions that the lowest 20 percent are the "poor," the highest 20 percent are the "rich," and the middle 60 percent are the "middle class," many fewer of you belong to the celebrated "middle class" than thought so. In fact, the cut-off

Life in a Slum and in a Castle

There can be little doubt that the unfortunate souls who inhabit today's worst urban slums are "poor" by any reasonable definition. Yet there are striking parallels between the standard of living of these people and that of the powerful but vermin-covered barons of the Middle Ages, as the following two passages show. Together these passages graphically point out the need for a relative concept of poverty.

A Twentieth Century Slum

We were living in deplorable conditions. We would cook a pot of oatmeal in the morning, then reheat it up on the radiator in the afternoon.... Whenever the sewer would back up, all that filth would come up under our floor and run around all over the floor.... One time this went on for four days. My wife had to keep the kids up on the bed. All that stuff floating around through the apartment until they got the Roto-Rooter man there.

In the wintertime ... we go to bed with all our clothes on....

When it's real cold, we close off the two bedrooms completely and burn the oven and then we all sleep in here together....

One of my babies has been in the hospital twice for lead poisoning. She'd pick plaster and paint and stuff off the walls....

SOURCE: Herb Goro, *The Block* (New York: Random House, 1970), pages 82–86.

A Medieval Castle

The knight's castle was extremely simple and must have been most uncomfortable. There were usually two rooms: the hall and the chamber. In the hall the knight did his business.... The chamber was the private room of the

lord and his family. There he entertained guests of high rank. At night the lord, his lady, and their children slept in beds, while their personal servants slept on the chamber floor.... The castles were cold and drafty. The windows were covered by boards, or open. If the castle was of wood—as most were before the thirteenth century—the knight could not have a fire. In a stone castle one could have fire, but as chimneys did not appear until the late twelfth century, the smoke must have been almost unbearable. It seems likely that if one of us were offered the choice between spending a winter night with the lord or his serf, he would choose the comparatively tight mud hut with the nice warm pigs on the floor.

SOURCE: Sydney Painter, *A History of the Middle Ages 284–1500* (New York: Alfred A. Knopf, 1953), page 122.

---

point that defined membership in the "rich" class in 1982 was just over $46,000 before taxes, an income level exceeded by the parents of many university students. (Your parents may be shocked to learn that they are rich!)

Next, use Table 38–1 to estimate the fraction of Canadian families that have incomes lower than your family's. Most students who come from households of moderate prosperity have an instinctive feeling that they stand somewhere near the middle of the income distribution; so they estimate about half, or perhaps a little more. In fact, if your parents earned a pre-tax income of $50,000 in 1982, over 80 percent of Canadian families are poorer than yours!

This exercise has perhaps brought us down to earth. Let us now look past the average level of income and see how the pie is divided. Table 38–2 shows the shares of income accruing to each fifth of the population in 1982 and several earlier years. In a perfectly equal society, all the numbers in this table would be "20 percent" since each fifth of the population would receive one-fifth of the income. In fact, as the table shows, this is certainly not the case. In 1982, for

Table 38-1

DISTRIBUTION OF FAMILY INCOME IN CANADA, 1982

INCOME RANGE (dollars)	PERCENTAGE OF ALL FAMILIES IN THIS RANGE	PERCENTAGE OF FAMILIES IN THIS AND LOWER RANGES
Under 5,000	1.6	1.6
5,000 to 6,999	1.8	3.4
7,000 to 9,999	4.1	7.5
10,000 to 11,999	4.1	11.6
12,000 to 14,999	6.7	18.3
15,000 to 16,999	4.1	22.4
17,000 to 19,999	5.8	28.2
20,000 to 21,999	4.0	32.2
22,000 to 24,999	6.9	39.1
25,000 to 29,999	11.4	50.5
30,000 to 34,999	10.6	61.1
35,000 to 39,999	9.5	70.6
40,000 to 44,999	7.7	78.3
45,000 and over	21.7	100.0

If your family's income falls close to one of the end points of the ranges indicated here, you can approximate the fraction of families with income *lower* than yours just by looking at the last column.
SOURCE: Statistics Canada 13-207.

Table 38-2

INCOME SHARES IN SELECTED YEARS

INCOME GROUP	1982	1979	1973	1965
Lowest fifth	6.3	6.1	6.1	6.2
Second fifth	12.6	13.0	12.9	13.1
Middle fifth	18.0	18.4	18.1	18.0
Fourth fifth	24.1	24.3	23.9	23.6
Highest fifth	38.9	38.3	38.9	39.0

SOURCE: Statistics Canada 13-207.

example, the poorest fifth of all families had only just over 6 percent of the total income, while the richest fifth had 39 percent—six and one-half times as much.

Depicting Income Distributions: The Lorenz Curve

Statisticians and economists use a convenient tool to portray data like these graphically. The device, called a **Lorenz curve**, is shown in Figure 38–2. To construct a Lorenz curve, we first draw a square whose vertical and horizontal dimensions both represent 100 percent. Then we record the percentage of families (or persons) on the horizontal axis and the percentage of income that these families (or persons) receive on the vertical axis, using all the data that we have. For example, point C in Figure 38–2 depicts the fact (known from Table 38–2) that the bottom 60 percent (the three lowest fifths) of Canadian families in 1982 received 36.9 percent of the total income. Similarly, points A, B, and D represent the other information contained in Table 38–2. We can list four important properties of a Lorenz curve:

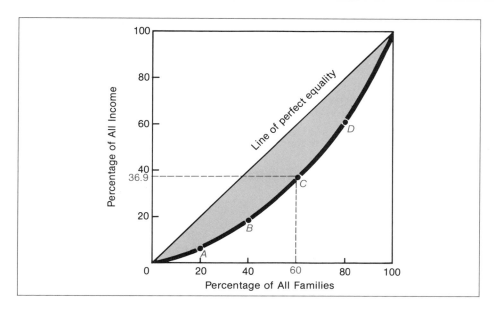

Figure 38-2

A LORENZ CURVE FOR CANADA

This Lorenz curve for Canada is based on the 1982 distribution of income given in Table 38-2. The percentage of families is measured along the horizontal axis, and the percentage of income that these families receive is measured along the vertical axis. Thus, for example, point *C* indicates that the bottom 60 percent of Canadian families received 36.9 percent of the total income in 1982.

1. It begins at the origin, where zero families of course have zero income.

2. It always ends at the upper-right corner of the square, since 100 percent of the nation's families must necessarily receive all the nation's income.

3. If income were distributed equally, the Lorenz curve would be a straight line connecting these two points (the thin solid line in Figure 38–2). This is because, with everybody equal, the bottom 20 percent of the families would receive 20 percent of the income, the bottom 40 percent would receive 40 percent, and so on.

4. In a real economy, with significant income differences, the Lorenz curve will "sag" downward from this line of perfect equality. It is easy to see why this is so. If there is any inequality at all, the poorest 20 percent of families must get less than 20 percent of all the income. This corresponds to a point below the equality line, such as point *A*. Similarly, the bottom 40 percent of families must receive less than 40 percent of the income (point *B*), and so on.

In fact, the size of the area between the line of perfect equality and the Lorenz curve (the shaded area in Figure 38–2) is often used as a handy measure of inequality. The larger this area, the more unequal is the income distribution. For Canadian family incomes, this so-called area of inequality usually fills up about one-third of the total area underneath the equality line.

Standing by itself, the Lorenz curve tells us rather little. To interpret it, we must know what it looked like in earlier years or what it looks like in other countries. The historical data in Table 38–2 show that *the Canadian Lorenz curve has not moved much in the last two decades*. To some, this remarkable stability in the income distribution is deplorable. To others, it suggests some immutable law of the capitalist system. In fact, neither view is correct. The apparent stability in the income distribution is the result of a standoff between certain demographic forces that were pushing the Lorenz curve outward, such as more young and old people and more families headed by women, and other forces that were pulling it inward, such as government anti-poverty programs.

Comparing Canada with other countries is much harder, since no two countries use precisely the same definition of income distribution. In 1976, the Organization for Economic Cooperation and Development (OECD) made a heroic effort to standardize the income distribution data of its member countries so they could be compared.[2] In this analysis, Japan stood out as the industrialized country with the most equal income distribution, with Australia, West Germany, the Netherlands, and Sweden bunched rather closely in second place. Canada placed between this group and France and the United States, which seemed to have the most inequality. Before extrapolating from these findings, it should be pointed out that only 12 industrial countries were compared. Israel, which is often thought to have the most equal income distribution in the non-communist world, is not in the OECD. Nor are any of the less developed countries, which are generally found to have much more inequality than the developed ones.

Some Reasons for Unequal Incomes

Let us now begin to formulate a list of the causes of income inequality. Here are some that come to mind.

1. ***Differences in ability***.   Everyone knows that people have different capabilities. Some can run faster, ski better, do calculations more quickly, type more accurately, and so on. Hence it should not be surprising that some people are more adept at earning income. Precisely what sort of ability is relevant to earning income is a matter of intense debate among economists, sociologists, and psychologists. The kind of talents that make for success in school seem to have some effect, but hardly an overwhelming one. The same is true of innate intelligence. It is clear that some types of inventiveness are richly rewarded by the market, and the same is true of that elusive characteristic called "entrepreneurial ability."

2. ***Differences in intensity of work***.   Some people work longer hours than others, or labour more intensely when they are on the job. This results in certain income differences that are largely voluntary.

3. ***Risk taking***.   Most people who have acquired large sums of money have done so by taking risks—by investing their money in some uncertain venture. Those who gamble and succeed become wealthy. Those who try and fail go broke. Most others prefer not to take such chances and wind up somewhere in between. This is another way in which income differences arise voluntarily.

4. ***Compensating wage differentials***.   Some jobs are more arduous than others, or more dangerous, or more unpleasant for other reasons. To induce people to take these jobs, some sort of financial incentive normally must be offered. For example, factory workers who work the night shift normally receive higher wages than those who work during the day.

5. ***Schooling and other types of training***.   In Chapter 37 we spoke of schooling and other types of training as "investments in human capital." We meant by this that workers can sacrifice *current* income in order to improve their skills so that their *future* incomes will be higher. When this is done, income differentials naturally rise. Consider a high school friend who did not go on to university. Even if you are working at a part-time job, your earnings are probably much below his or hers. Once you graduate from university, however, the statistics suggest that your earnings will rise and soon overtake your friend's earnings.

   It is generally agreed that differences in schooling are an important cause of income differentials. But this particular cause has both voluntary and involuntary aspects. Young men or young women who *choose* not to go to university have made voluntary decisions that affect their incomes. But many

[2]Malcolm Sawyer, "Income Distribution in OECD Countries," *OECD Occasional Studies* (July 1976), pages 3–36.

never get the choice: Their parents simply cannot afford to send them. For them, the resulting income differential is not voluntary.

6. **Inherited wealth**. Not all income is derived from work. Some is the return on invested wealth, and part of this wealth is inherited. While this cause of inequality does not apply to very many people, a great number of Canada's super-rich got that way through inheritance. And financial wealth is not the only type of capital than can be inherited; so can human capital. In part this happens naturally through genetics: Parents of high ability tend to have children of high ability, although the link is an imperfect one. But it also happens partly for economic reasons: Well-to-do parents send their children to the best schools, thereby transforming their own *financial* wealth into *human* wealth for their children. This type of inheritance may be much more important than the financial type.

7. **Luck**. No observer of our society can fail to notice the role of chance. Some of the rich and some of the poor got there largely by good or bad fortune. A farmer digging for water discovers oil instead. An investor strikes it rich on the stock market. A student trains herself for a high-paying occupation only to find that the opportunity has disappeared while she was in university. A construction worker is unemployed for a whole year because of a recession that he had no part in creating. The list could go on and on. Many of the large income differentials among people arise purely by chance.

Discrimination

Some of the factors we have just listed lead to income differentials that are widely accepted as "just." For example, few quarrel with the idea that it is fair for people who work longer hours to receive higher incomes. Other factors on our list ignite heated debates. For example, some people view income differentials that arise purely by chance as perfectly acceptable. Others find these same differentials intolerable. However, almost no one is willing to condone income inequalities that arise strictly because of discrimination.

The facts about discrimination are not easy to come by. **Economic discrimination** is defined as occurring when equivalent factors of production receive different payments for equal contributions to output. But this definition is hard to apply in practice because we cannot always tell when two factors of production are "equivalent."

Probably no one would call it "discrimination" if a woman with only a high school diploma receives a lower salary than a man with a university degree (though one might legitimately ask whether discrimination helps to explain the difference in their educational attainments). Even if they have the same education, the man may have 10 more years of work experience than the woman. If they receive different wages for this reason, are we to call that "discrimination"?

Similar ambiguities plague discussions on racial discrimination. For example, if a Native Indian receives less pay than a white when working in a "same job," it may be that the white has had more education and training, which makes him more productive. Thus, it is not clear that the employer is discriminating. It may be that discrimination exists at the schooling level, and that this is what caused the skill differential assumed in our example. But discrimination within the educational system is not the fault of an individual employer.

Ideally, we would compare men and women, or natives and whites, whose *productivities* are equal. In this case, if women receive lower wages than men, or if natives receive lower wages than whites, we would clearly call it discrimination. But, very often, discrimination takes much more subtle forms than paying unequal wages for equal work. For instance, employers can simply keep women or natives relegated to inferior jobs, thus justifying the lower salaries they pay them.

Economic discrimination is defined as occuring when equivalent factors of production receive different payments for equal contributions to output.

One clearly *incorrect* way to measure discrimination is to compare the typical incomes of different groups. For example, in 1983, the average earnings of women were about 60 percent of average male earnings. Virtually everyone agrees that the amount of discrimination is less than these differentials suggest, but far greater than zero. Precisely how much is a topic of continuing economic research. Several studies in the United States suggest that about one-third of the observed wage differential between white women and white men is caused by discrimination in the labour market (though more might be due to discrimination in education, and so on). Other studies have reached somewhat different conclusions. While no one denies the existence of discrimination, its quantitative importance is a matter of ongoing controversy and research.

The Economic Theory of Discrimination*

Let us see what economic theory tells us about discrimination. In particular, consider the following two questions:

1. Must the existence of *prejudice*, which we define as arising when one group dislikes associating with another group, always lead to *discrimination* (unequal pay for equal work)?

2. Are there "natural" economic forces that tend either to erode or to exacerbate discrimination over time?

As we shall see now, the analysis we have provided in previous chapters sheds light on both these issues.

Discrimination by Employers

Most attention seems to focus on discrimination by employers, so let us start there. What happens if, for instance, some firms refuse to hire women for certain positions? Figure 38–3 will help us find the answer. Part (a) pertains to firms that

*This section may be omitted in shorter courses.

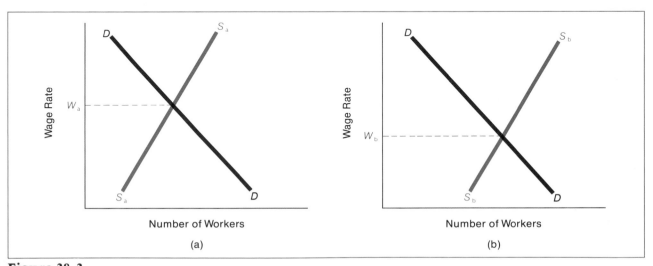

Figure 38–3
WAGE DISCRIMINATION
Part (a) depicts supply and demand curves for labour among discriminatory firms; part (b) shows the same for non-discriminatory firms. Since only men can work in part (a), while both sexes can work in part (b), the supply curve in part (b) is farther to the right than the supply curve in part (a). Consequently, the wage rate in part (b), W_b, winds up below the wage rate in part (a), W_a. Workers in part (b) are discriminated against.

discriminate; part (b) pertains to firms that do not. There are supply and demand curves for labour in each part based on the analysis of Chapter 37. We suppose the two demand curves to be identical. However, the supply curve in part (b) must be farther to the right than the supply curve in part (a) because men *and* women can work in part (b) whereas *only* men can work in part (a). The result is that wages will be lower in part (b) than in part (a). Since all the women are forced into part (b), we therefore conclude that there is discrimination against women.

But now consider the situation from the point of view of the employers. Firms in part (a) of Figure 38–3 are paying more for labour; they are paying for the privilege of discriminating against women. The non-discriminatory firms in part (b) have a cost advantage. As we learned in earlier chapters, if there is effective competition, these non-discriminatory firms will tend to capture more and more of the market. The discriminators will gradually be driven out of business. If, on the other hand, many of the firms in part (a) have protected monopolies, they will be able to remain in business. But they will pay for the privilege of discriminating by earning lower monopoly profits than they otherwise could (because they pay higher wages than they have to).

Discrimination by Fellow Workers

We have just seen that if employers are the source of discrimination, then competitive forces will tend to reduce discrimination over time. Such optimistic conclusions cannot necessarily be reached, however, if it is workers who are prejudiced. Consider what happens if, for example, men do not like to have women as their supervisors. If men do not give their full co-operation, female supervisors will be less effective than male supervisors and, hence, will earn lower wages. Here prejudice does lead to discrimination, even in the long run.

However, there is a possible way out: Non-discriminatory employers may start firms that hire *only* women. If women are in fact just as productive as men, the all-female firms will be just as efficient as the all-male firms, and female workers will earn just as much as male workers. In this case, prejudice by workers may lead to *segregation* in the workplace without discrimination in wages.

Statistical Discrimination

A final type of discrimination, called **statistical discrimination**, may be the most stubborn of all, and may survive even in the absence of prejudice. Here is an important example. It is, of course, a fact that only women can have babies. It is also a fact that many, though certainly not all, working women who have babies quit their jobs (at least for a while) to care for their newborns. Employers know this. What they cannot know, however, is *which* women of child-bearing age are likely to drop out of the labour force for this reason.

Suppose three candidates apply for a job that requires a long-term commitment. Susan plans to quit after a few years to raise a family. Jane does not plan to have any children. Jack is a man. If he knew all the facts, the employer would prefer either Jane or Jack to Susan, but would be indifferent between Jane and Jack. But the employer cannot tell Susan and Jane apart. He therefore presumes that both Jane and Susan, being young women, are more likely to quit to raise a family than Jack is; so he hires Jack, even though Jane is just as good a prospect. Jane is discriminated against.[3]

In terms of the two questions with which we began this section, we conclude that different types of *discrimination* lead to different answers. Some types of prejudice lead to economic discrimination but other types lead to *segregation* instead. And

Statistical discrimination is said to occur when the productivity of a particular worker is estimated to be low just because that worker belongs to a particular group (such as women).

---

[3]Lest it be thought that this example justifies discrimination against women, it should be pointed out that women generally have less absenteeism and job turnover for non-pregnancy health reasons than men do.

discrimination may occur even in the absence of prejudice. Finally, the forces of competition will tend to erode some, but not all, of the inequities caused by discrimination. Most observers feel that much more must be done to combat the effects of discrimination; the market will not do the job by itself.

The Optimal Amount of Inequality

We have seen that substantial income inequality exists in Canada and have noted some reasons for it. Let us now ask a question that is loaded with value judgments, but to which economic analysis has something to contribute none the less: *How much inequality is the ideal amount?* We shall not, of course, be able to give a definitive answer to this question. Nobody can do that. Our objective is rather to see the type of analysis that is relevant to answering the question. We begin our analysis in a simple setting in which the answer is easily obtained. Then we shall see how the real world differs from this simple model.

Consider a world in which there are two people, Smith and Jones, and suppose that we want to divide $100 between them in the way that yields the most *total utility*. Suppose further that Smith and Jones are alike in their ability to enjoy money; technically, we say that their *marginal-utility* schedules are identical.[4] This identical marginal-utility schedule is depicted in Figure 38-4. We can prove the following result: *The optimal distribution of income is to give $50 to Smith and $50 to Jones*, which is point E in Figure 38-4.

To prove it, we show that if the income distribution is unequal, we can improve things by moving closer to equality. So suppose that Smith has $75 (point S in the figure) and Jones has $25 (point J). Then, as we can see, because of the law of diminishing marginal utility, Smith's *marginal* utility (which is s) must be *less* than Jones's (which is j). If we take $1 away from Smith, Smith *loses* the low marginal utility, s, of a dollar to him. Then, when we give it to Jones, Jones *gains* the high marginal utility, j, that a dollar gives him. On balance, then, society's total utility must rise by j – s because Jones's gain exceeds Smith's loss. Therefore, a distribution with Smith getting only $74 is better than one in which he gets $75. Since the same argument can be used to show that a $73–$27 distribution is better

---

[4]If you need to refresh your memory about marginal utility, see Chapter 20, especially pages 382–84.

Figure 38-4

THE OPTIMAL DISTRIBUTION OF INCOME

If Smith and Jones have the identical marginal-utility schedule (the curve *MU*) then the optimal way to distribute $100 between them is to give $50 to each (point *E*). If income is not distributed this way, then their marginal utilities will be unequal, so that a redistribution of income can make society better off. This is illustrated by points *J* and *S*, representing an income distribution in which Jones gets $25 (and hence has marginal utility *j*), while Smith gets $75 (and hence has marginal utility *s*).

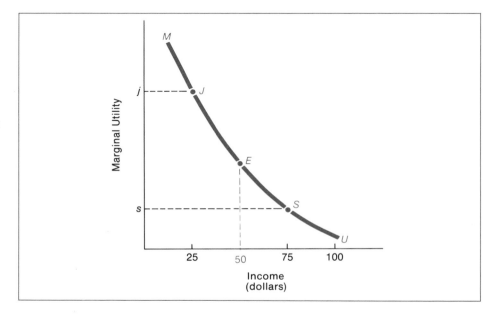

than $74–$26, and so on, we have established our result that a $50–$50 distribution—point *E*—is best.

Now in this argument there is nothing special about the fact that we assumed only two people or that exactly $100 was available. Any number of people and dollars would do as well. What really *is* crucial is our assumption that the same amount of money would be available no matter how we chose to distribute it. Thus we have proved the following general result:

To maximize total utility, the best way to distribute any fixed amount of money among people with identical marginal-utility schedules is to divide it equally.

The Trade-Off Between Equality and Efficiency

If we seek to apply this analysis to the real world, two major difficulties arise. First, people are different and have different marginal-utility schedules. Thus *some* inequality can probably be justified.[5] The second problem is much more formidable.

The total amount of income in society is *not* independent of how we try to distribute it.

To see this in an extreme form, ask yourself the following question: What would happen if we tried to achieve perfect equality by putting a 100 percent income tax on all workers and then dividing the tax receipts equally among the population? No one would have any incentive to work, to invest, to take risks, or to do anything else to earn money, because the rewards for all such activities would disappear. The gross national product (GNP) would fall drastically, perhaps even vanish. While the example is extreme, the same principle applies to more moderate policies to equalize incomes; indeed, it is the basic idea behind supply-side economics.

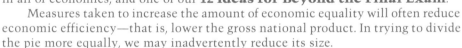

The Trade-Off Between Equality and Efficiency
Policies that redistribute income reduce the rewards of high-income earners while raising the rewards of low-income earners. Hence they reduce the incentive to earn high income. This gives rise to a trade-off that is one of the most fundamental in all of economics, and one of our **12 Ideas for Beyond the Final Exam**.

Measures taken to increase the amount of economic equality will often reduce economic efficiency—that is, lower the gross national product. In trying to divide the pie more equally, we may inadvertently reduce its size.

Because of this trade-off, the result that equal incomes are always optimal cannot be applied to the real world. On the contrary:

The optimal distribution of income will always involve *some* inequality.

But this does not mean that attempts to reduce inequality are always misguided. What we should learn from this analysis are two things:

1. There are better and worse ways to promote equality. In pursuing further income equality (or fighting poverty), we should seek policies that do the least possible harm to the nation's productivity.

---

[5] It can be shown that if we know that people differ, but cannot tell who has the higher marginal-utility schedule, then the best way to distribute income is still in equal shares.

2. Equality is bought at a price. Thus, like any commodity, we must decide rationally how much to purchase. We will probably want to spend some of our potential income on equality, but not all of it.

Figure 38–5 illustrates both these lessons. The curve *abcde* represents possible combinations of GNP and income equality that are obtainable under the present system of taxes and transfers. If, for example, point *c* is the current position of the economy, raising taxes on the rich to finance more transfers to the poor might move us downward to the right, toward point *d*. Equality increases, but GNP falls as the rich react to higher marginal tax rates by producing less. Similarly, reducing both taxes and social-welfare programs might move us upward to the left, toward point *b*. The curve *ABCDE* represents possible combinations of GNP and equality under some new, more efficient, redistributive policy.

The first lesson is that we should stick to the higher of the two curves. Any point chosen on curve *abcde* can be improved upon by moving to the corresponding point on curve *ABCDE*. By picking the more efficient redistributive policy, we can have more equality *and* more GNP. In the rest of this chapter we discuss alternative policies and try to indicate which ones are more efficient.

The second lesson is that neither point *B* nor point *E* would normally be society's optimal choice. At point *B* we are seeking the highest possible GNP with utter disregard for whatever inequality might accompany it. At point *E* we are forcing complete equality, even if a minuscule GNP is the result.

It is astonishing how much confusion is caused by a failure to understand these two lessons. Proponents of measures that further economic equality often feel obligated to deny that their programs will have any harmful effects on economic efficiency. At times these vehement denials are so obviously unrealistic that they undermine the very case that the egalitarians are trying to defend. Conservatives who oppose these policies also undercut the strength of their case by making outlandish claims about the efficiency losses that are likely to arise from greater equality. Neither side, it seems, is willing or able to acknowledge the basic trade-off between equality and efficiency depicted in Figure 38–5. And hence the debate generates more heat than light. Since these debates are sure to continue for the next 10 or 20 years, and probably for the rest of your lives, we hope that some understanding of this trade-off stays with you well **Beyond the Final Exam**.

Figure 38-5

THE TRADE-OFF BETWEEN EQUALITY AND EFFICIENCY

This diagram represents the fundamental trade-off between equality and efficiency. If the economy is initially at point *c*, then movements toward greater equality (to the right) normally can be achieved only by reducing economic efficiency, and thus reducing the gross national product. The movements from points *C* and *c* toward points *D* and *d* represent two alternative policies for equalizing the income distribution. The policy that leads to *D* is preferred since it is more efficient.

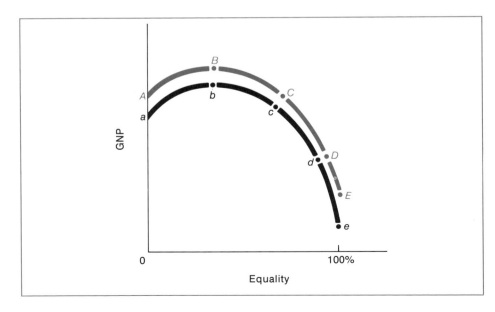

But just understanding the terms of the trade-off will not tell you what the right answer is. By looking at Figure 38–5, we know that the optimal amount of equality lies between points B and E, but we do not know what it actually is. Is it something like point D, with more equality and less GNP than we now have? Or is it a movement back toward point B? Everyone will have a different answer to this question, because it is basically one of value judgment. Just how much is more equality worth to you?

The late Arthur Okun, an influential American economist, put the issue graphically. Imagine that money is liquid, and that you have a bucket that you can use to transport some money from the rich to the poor. The problem, however, is that the bucket is leaky. As you move the money, some gets lost. Will you use the bucket if only one cent is lost for each one dollar you move? Probably everyone would say yes. But what if each dollar taken from the rich results in only 10 cents for the poor? Only the most extreme egalitarians will still say yes. Now try the hard questions. What if 20 cents to 40 cents is lost for each dollar that you move? If you can answer questions like these, you can decide how far down the hill from point B you think society should travel, for you will have expressed your value judgments in quantitative terms.

Policies to Combat Poverty

Let us take it for granted that the nation has a commitment to reduce the amount of poverty. What are some policies that can promote this goal? Which of these is most efficient? The traditional approach to poverty fighting in Canada has utilized a variety of programs collectively known as *social assistance*. The best-known of these is the welfare system administered by the municipalities.

Our welfare system has been attacked as a classic example of an inefficient redistributive program. Why? One reason is that it provides little incentive for a welfare recipient to get a job and earn income. Only by acquiring skills on the job can welfare recipients ever break out of the unemployment–poverty circle. The following example for Ontario families in 1979 was used by the Economic Council of Canada in its 1983 *Annual Review*: If a single mother with two dependent children works regularly as a sales clerk at half the average industrial wage, the family would still likely qualify for some welfare. However, for each dollar earned, welfare is reduced by 75 cents. Also, the family would likely have its Ontario Tax Credit reduced, and the mother would have to make contributions to unemployment insurance and to the Canada Pension Plan. Furthermore, her taxable income would have increased enough to cross the income-tax threshold. When all these reductions in transfer payments and increases in taxes and contributions are added up, the effective tax rate on the women's earnings from the job are 110 percent! The family's income position is actually reduced by working. This sort of disincentive effect makes it essentially impossible for many individuals to escape the poverty trap.

Some attempts have been made to ease this transition from welfare to paid employment. For example, late in 1979, Ontario initiated the Work Incentive Program (WIN), but only about 5000 persons have participated in the program during its first three years of existence. A recent international study ranked countries according to how generous were their social programs for helping the needs of families with children. Canada ranked sixth out of the eight countries studied.[6]

It should also be noted that many of the poor are provided with a number of important goods and services, either at no charge or at prices that are well below market levels. Medical care, free prescription drugs, and subsidized public housing

---

[6]The countries were: Australia, Canada, West Germany, France, Israel, Sweden, the United Kingdom, and the United States.

are some notable examples. These programs significantly enhance the living standards of the poor. However, most of them offer benefits that decline as family income rises. As a result, these anti-poverty programs accentuate the basic problem—that many poor families are *worse* off if their earnings *rise*. With an effective tax rate of more than 100 percent, there is a powerful incentive not to work.

The Negative Income Tax

These problems, and others like them, have contributed to the "welfare mess" and have led to frequent calls to scrap the whole system and replace it with a simple structure designed to get income into the hands of the poor without providing such adverse incentives. The solution suggested most frequently, at least by economists, is the so-called **negative income tax (NIT)**.

The name "negative income tax" derives from its similarity to the regular (positive) income tax. Let us illustrate how NIT would work. To describe a particular NIT plan we require two numbers: A minimum income level below which no family is allowed to fall (the "guaranteed annual income") and a rate at which benefits are "taxed away" as income rises. Consider a plan with a $4000 guaranteed income (for a family of four) and a 50 percent tax rate. A family with no earnings would then receive a $4000 payment (a "negative tax") from the government. A family earning $1000 would have the basic benefit reduced by 50 percent of its earnings. Thus, since half its earnings is $500, it would receive $3500 from the government plus the $1000 earned income for a total income of $4500 (see Table 38–3).

Notice in Table 38–3 that the increase in total income as earnings rise is always half of the increase in earnings. With a 50 percent tax rate, there is always *some* incentive to work under an NIT system. Notice also that there is a "break-even" level of income at which benefits cease. In this case, the break-even level is $8000. This is not another number that policy-makers can arbitrarily select in the way they select the guarantee level and the tax rate. Rather, it is dictated by the choice of the guarantee level and the tax rate. This is easy to explain. In our example, since $4000 is the maximum possible benefit, and since benefits are reduced by 50 cents for each $1 of earnings, then benefits will be reduced to zero when 50 percent of earnings is equal to $4000. This occurs when earnings are $8000 in our example. The general relation is:

Guarantee = Tax rate × Break-even level.

Table 38–3
ILLUSTRATION OF A NEGATIVE INCOME TAX PLAN

EARNINGS (dollars)	BENEFITS PAID (dollars)	TOTAL INCOME (dollars)
0	4000	4000
1000	3500	4500
2000	3000	5000
3000	2500	5500
4000	2000	6000
5000	1500	6500
6000	1000	7000
7000	500	7500
8000	0	8000
Above 8000	0	Same as earnings

The fact that the break-even level is completely determined by the guarantee and the tax rate creates an annoying problem. If we are truly to make a dent in the poverty population through an NIT system, the guarantee will have to come fairly close to the poverty line. But then, if we are to keep the tax rate moderate, the break-even level will have to be much above the poverty line. This means that families who are not considered "poor" (though they are certainly not very rich) will also receive benefits. For example, a low tax rate of 33⅓ percent means that some benefits are paid to families whose income is as high as three times the guarantee level.

But if we raise the tax rate to bring the guarantee and break-even level closer together, the incentive to work shrinks, and with it the principal rationale for the NIT in the first place. So the NIT is no magic cure-all. Difficult choices must be made.

The Negative Income Tax and Work Incentives

For people now covered by welfare programs, the NIT would increase the incentive to work. However, we have just seen that it is virtually inevitable that a number of families who are now too well-off to collect welfare would become eligible for NIT payments. For these people, the NIT imposes work disincentives, both because it provides them with more income and because it subjects them to the relatively high NIT tax rate, which reduces their after-tax wage rate.[7]

These possible disincentive effects have worried both social reformers and legislators, so in the late 1960s the government initiated a series of social experiments to estimate the effect of the NIT on the supply of labour. Families in several communities in Manitoba were offered negative income-tax payments in return for allowing social scientists to monitor their behaviour. A matched set of "control" families, who were not given NIT payments, were also observed. The idea was to measure how the behaviour of the families receiving NIT payments differed from that of the families that did not receive them. The experiments lasted about a decade and showed pretty clearly that the net effects of the NIT on labour supply were quite small. Apparently, the fears of those who claimed that NIT payments would induce people to stop working were unfounded.

In terms of Figure 38–5, economists believe that it is more efficient to redistribute income through an NIT system than through the existing welfare system. The NIT is curve *ABCDE*, while the present system is curve *abcde*. If this view is correct, then by replacing the current welfare system with NIT, we can have more equality *and* more efficiency at the same time. But this does not mean that equalization would become costless. The curve *ABCDE* still slopes downward—by increasing equality, we still diminish the GNP.

The Personal Income Tax

If we take the broader view that society's objective is not just to eliminate poverty, but to reduce income disparities, then the fact that many non-poor families would receive benefits from the NIT is perhaps not a serious drawback. After all, unless the plan is outlandishly generous, these families will still be well below the average income. Still, in popular discussions the NIT is largely thought of as an anti-poverty program, not as a tool for general income equalization.

By contrast, the personal income tax *is* thought to be a means of promoting equality. Indeed, it is probably given more credit for this than it actually deserves. The reason is that the income tax is widely known to be *progressive*.[8] The fact that the tax is progressive means that incomes *after* tax are distributed more

---

[7]For a review of income and substitution effects in labour-supply analysis, refer to Chapter 37, pages 726–28.

[8]For definitions of progressive, proportional, and regressive taxes, see Chapter 33, page 642.

equally than incomes *before* tax because the rich turn over a larger share of their incomes to the tax collector. This is illustrated by the two Lorenz curves in Figure 38–6. These curves, however, are not drawn accurately to scale. If they were, they would lie almost on top of each other because the degree of equalization that can be attributed to the tax is very modest.

Why such modest equalizing effects from a tax whose marginal tax rates escalate upward from zero to a maximum of 50 percent? There are two principal reasons.

Incentive Effects

First, firms and individuals, acting in their own best interests, often take steps that frustrate the equalizing intent of a progressive income tax. An example from each end of the income distribution will illustrate how this might work.

Looking first at the rich, it is clear that a steeply progressive tax tries to place a heavy tax burden on a corporate executive. In order to preserve his incentive to work, his company may react by raising his before-tax salary, or by giving him fringe benefits (such as a company car, use of a yacht, expense accounts, and so on) that often escape taxation.[9] At the other end of the income scale, welfare programs that give payments to the poor may lead the beneficiaries to "spend" some of their newly found income on "leisure"; that is, to work less, and therefore to earn less.

Thus, a redistributive tax system might induce the *before-tax* incomes of the rich to rise, and those of the poor to fall. Ironically, efforts to *equalize* the *after-tax* distribution of income may lead to more *inequality* in the *before-tax* distribution. In terms of Figure 38–6, this means that even the small distance between the two Lorenz curves *overstates* the equalizing effects of the income tax. The income distribution that we would have *if there were no income tax* is probably somewhere in between these two curves.

Tax Shelters

The other principal reason why the personal income tax does not redistribute income as much as many people think is that the wealthy have learned, with the aid of legal and financial advisers, to take advantage of a variety of **tax shelters**,

[9]The progressivity of the income-tax system has recently been enhanced somewhat, since some of these fringe benefits must now be included in taxable income.

Figure 38-6

THE EFFECT OF PROGRESSIVE INCOME TAXATION ON THE LORENZ CURVE

Since a progressive income tax takes proportionately more income from the rich than from the poor, it reduces income inequality. Graphically, this means that society's Lorenz curve shifts in the manner shown here. The magnitude of the shift, however, is exaggerated to make the graph more readable. In reality, the income tax has only a very small effect on the Lorenz curve.

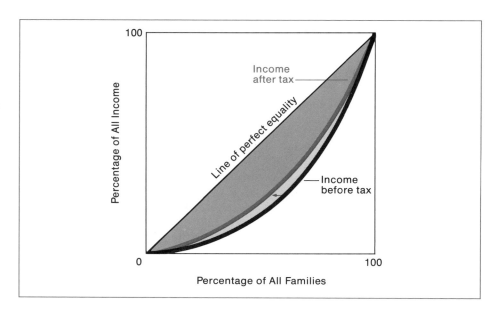

and have managed to pare their tax payments significantly. There is nothing sinister about this tax avoidance; it is all legal. But because shelters mainly benefit the rich, they seriously reduce the progressivity of the income tax.[10]

Other Taxes and Expenditure Programs

There are many other taxes in the Canadian system and most experts agree that the remaining taxes as a group are decidedly regressive. Since low-income earners spend a higher proportion of their incomes, and spend an especially high proportion on their housing, the sales and property taxes can be quite regressive. On balance, the evidence suggests that when the effects of these taxes are combined with those of the income tax, the tax system as a whole is only slightly progressive.

It is more difficult to measure the income-distribution effects of government expenditure programs. Nevertheless, studies have been done to estimate which income classes benefit more from each individual expenditure scheme, such as highways, university education, the protection of private property, and so on. These studies show that those with higher incomes benefit to such an extent that government expenditures as a whole are regressive. In fact, they are so regressive that they outweigh the mildly progressive effect of total taxes, and the income-distribution effect of the entire government sector is estimated to be slightly regressive.

Regional Transfer Payments

One set of government transfer policies redistributes funds from the "have provinces" to the "have-not provinces." The most important is the equalization scheme that involves grant payments from federal government revenues to all provincial governments except Ontario, British Columbia, Alberta, and Saskatchewan. While federal revenues are collected in all provinces, this scheme involves very significant redistribution.

The federal government also distributes a set of lump-sum transfers to provincial governments; these payments are designed to make it possible for the provincial governments to provide an acceptable level of public services (on a per-capita basis) without imposing tax rates above the national average. This scheme helps provinces that have a small tax base, either because of small populations or because of a small industrial base.

Finally, there are numerous regional incentives offered to companies who locate or expand in the so-called depressed regions.

Unfortunately there is a dearth of research on the effectiveness of these regional policies. Some economists have argued that transfers to the have-not regions have significantly reduced out-migration from these areas. This leaves the depressed regions with an excess supply of labour, with low wages, and with the slow growth that is usually associated with a state of dependency on the federal government. Other economists argue that the regional redistribution payments have stimulated much local economic activity, thereby lessening the general poverty problem. Further research is very much needed in this area.

Policies to Combat Discrimination

The policies that we have considered so far for combating poverty or reducing income inequality are all based on taxes and transfer payments—on moving dollars from one set of hands to another. This has not been the approach used to fight discrimination. Instead, governments have decided to make it *illegal* to discriminate.

[10]Some tax shelters were discussed in Chapter 33, pages 644–45.

Originally, it was thought that the problem could best be attacked by outlawing discrimination in rates of pay and in hiring standards—and by devoting resources to enforcement of these provisions. While progress toward the elimination of discrimination according to race and sex was made during the 1960s and 1970s, and will undoubtedly continue in the context of the new Canadian Charter of Rights and Freedoms, some people have felt the pace has been too slow. One reason is that discrimination in the labour market proved to be more subtle than was first thought. Officials rarely could find proof that unequal pay was being given for equal work because determining when work was "equal" turned out to be a formidable task. And, as noted early in this chapter, discrimination often takes the form of paying the *same* wages to (say) men and women who perform the same job, but segregating the women into inferior jobs.

So, in the early 1970s in the United States, a new wrinkle was added. Firms and other organizations with suspiciously small representation of minority groups or women in their work forces were required not just to end discriminatory practices, but also to demonstrate that they were taking **affirmative action** to remedy this imbalance. That is, they had to *prove* that they were making efforts to locate members of minority groups and females and to hire them if they proved to be qualified. The possibility of affirmative action legislation is currently a much-debated issue in Canada.

Affirmative action refers to active efforts to locate and hire members of minority groups.

This new approach to fighting discrimination is highly controversial. Critics claim that affirmative action really means hiring quotas and compulsory hiring of unqualified workers simply because they are female or members of a minority group. Proponents counter that without affirmative action discriminatory employers would simply claim they could not find qualified minority or female employees. The difficulty revolves around the impossibility of deciding on *purely objective criteria* who is "qualified" and who is not. What one person sees as government coercion to hire an unqualified applicant to fill a quota, another sees as a discriminatory employer being forced to mend his ways. Nothing in this book—or anywhere else—will teach you which view is correct in any particular instance.

This controversy provides yet another example of the trade-off between equality and efficiency. Without a doubt, giving more high-paying jobs to members of minority groups and to women would move society's Lorenz curve in the direction of greater equality. Supporters of affirmative action seek this result. But if it is done by disrupting industry and requiring firms to replace "qualified" white males by other "less qualified" workers, economic efficiency may suffer. Opponents of affirmative action are greatly troubled by these potential losses. How far should affirmative action be pushed? A good question, but one without a good answer.

A more definite analysis can be given concerning other policies aimed at women's rights on the job market. Paternity leave should be as available as maternity leave. With only the institution of maternity leave, the demand for female labour is reduced because the relative cost of employing women is increased. For similar reasons, part-time job opportunities should be encouraged for men, not just for women.

Postscript on the Distribution of Income

Now that we have completed our analysis of the distribution of income, it may be useful to see how it all relates to our central theme: What does the market do well, and what does it do poorly?

We have learned that a market economy uses the marginal productivity principle to assign an income to each individual. In so doing, the market attaches high prices to scarce factors and low prices to abundant ones, and therefore guides firms to make *efficient* use of society's resources. This is one of the market's great strengths. However, by attaching high prices to some factors and low prices to others, the market mechanism often creates a distribution of income that is quite unequal; some people wind up fabulously rich while others wind up miserably poor. For this reason, the market has been widely criticized for centuries for doing a rather poor job of distributing income in accord with commonly held notions of *fairness* and *equity*.

On balance, most observers feel that the criticism is justified: The market mechanism is extraordinarily good at promoting efficiency but rather bad at promoting equality. As we said at the outset, the market has both virtues and vices.

Summary

1. Substantial progress toward eliminating poverty was made during the 1970s; the percentage of families living below the poverty line fell from 26 percent to 13 percent. However, the severe recession in the early 1980s has increased the poverty rate.

2. The difficulty in agreeing on a sharp dividing line between the poor and the non-poor leads one to broaden the problem of poverty into the problem of inequality in incomes.

3. In Canada today, the richest 20 percent of families receive 39 percent of the income, while the poorest 20 percent of families receive just above 6 percent. These numbers have changed little over the past 20 years and represent an average level of inequality when compared with other advanced industrial nations.

4. Individual incomes differ for many reasons. Discrimination, differences in native ability, in the desire to work hard and to take risks, in schooling, and in inherited wealth all account for income disparities. All of these factors, however, explain only part of the inequality that we observe. A portion of the rest is due simply to good or bad luck, and the balance is unexplained.

5. Prejudice against a minority group or against women may lead to discrimination in rates of pay, or to segregation in the workplace, or to both. However, discrimination may also arise even when there is no prejudice (this is called statistical discrimination).

6. There is a trade-off between the goals of reducing inequality and enhancing economic efficiency: Policies that help on the equality front normally harm efficiency, and vice versa. This is one of the **12 Ideas for Beyond the Final Exam**.

7. Because of this trade-off, there is an optimal degree of inequality for any society. Society finds this optimum in the same way that a consumer decides how much to buy of different commodities: The trade-off tells us how costly it is to "purchase" more equality, and preferences then determine how much should be "bought." However, since people differ in their value judgments about the importance of equality, there will inevitably be disagreement over the ideal amount of equality.

8. There may, however, be some hope of reaching agreement over the policies to use in pursuit of whatever goal for equality is selected. This is because the more efficient redistributive policies let us buy any amount of equality at a lower price in terms of lost output. Economists claim, for example, that a negative income tax is preferable to our current welfare system on these grounds.

9. Even the negative income tax, though, is no magical cure. Its primary virtue lies in the way it preserves incentives to work. But if this is done by keeping the tax rate low, then either the minimum guaranteed level of income will have to be very low or many non-poor families will become eligible to receive benefits.

10. The goal of income equality is also pursued through the tax system, especially through the progressive income tax. However, the equalization achieved by this tax is much less than is commonly believed because of tax shelters and because people who are heavily burdened by the tax often can take steps to relieve themselves of these burdens. In addition, taxes other than income taxes are typically regressive, as are many government expenditure programs, so the government sector as a whole is slightly regressive.

11. Many regional transfer payments augment the revenues of the provincial governments in the "have-not" areas of the country. However, some economists argue that these policies have reduced out-migration from these areas, so that an excess supply of labour and a low-wage problem remains.

12. The problem of economic discrimination has been attacked by making it illegal, not through the tax and transfer system. But simply declaring discrimination to be illegal is much easier than actually ending discrimination. The trade-off between equality and efficiency applies once again: Strict enforcement of affirmative action will certainly reduce discrimination and increase income equality, but it may do so at a serious cost in terms of economic efficiency.

Concepts for Review

Poverty line
Absolute and relative concepts of
    poverty
Lorenz curve
Economic discrimination

Statistical discrimination
Optimal amount of inequality
Trade-off between equality and
    efficiency
Negative income tax (NIT)

Tax shelters
Provincial Equalization Grants
Affirmative action

Questions for Discussion

1. Discuss the "leaky bucket" analogy (page 765) with your classmates. What maximum amount of income would you personally allow to leak from the bucket in transferring money from the rich to the poor? Explain why people differ in their answers to this question.

2. Continuing the leaky bucket example, explain why economists believe that replacing the present welfare system with a negative income tax would help reduce the leak.

3. Suppose you were to design a negative income tax system for Canada. Pick a guaranteed income level and a tax rate that seem reasonable to you. What break-even level of income is implied by these choices? For the plan you have just devised, construct a corresponding version of Table 38–3 (page 766).

4. Following is a complete list of the distribution of income in Canada's Wonderland. From these data, construct a Lorenz curve for Canada's Wonderland.

NAME	INCOME
Fred Flintstone	$ 75,000
Barney Rubble	120,000
Yogi Bear	54,000
Boo-Boo	36,000
Ticket taker	15,000

How different is this from the Lorenz curve for Canada (Figure 38–2 on page 757)?

5. Suppose you were assigned the task of defining the poor. Would you choose an absolute or a relative concept of poverty? Why? What would be your specific definition of poverty?

6. Discuss the concept of the "optimal amount of inequality." What are some of the practical problems in determining how much inequality really is optimal?

Productivity Problems

Japan commercially, I regret to say, does
not bear the best reputation for executing
business. Inferior goods, irregularity and
indifferent shipments have caused no end
of worry . . . you are a very satisfied easy-
going race who reckon time is no object.
When I spoke to some managers they
informed me that it was impossible to
change the habits of national heritage.
(FROM A REPORT OF AN AUSTRALIAN EXPERT
FOR THE JAPANESE GOVERNMENT, 1915)

Productivity is a measure of the amount of output obtained from a given amount of input. So productivity grows if innovation, improved education, or other influences increase the number of cars or the number of watches produced by an hour of work.

Only rising productivity can raise standards of living in the long run. Indeed, as we pointed out in our list of **12 Ideas for Beyond the Final Exam:**

It is hardly an exaggeration to say that, in the long run, almost nothing counts for the determination of a nation's standard of living but its *rate of productivity growth.*

Over long periods of time, small differences in rates of productivity growth compound, like interest in a bank account, and can make an enormous difference to a society's prosperity. Nothing contributes more to reduction of poverty, to increases in leisure, and to the country's ability to finance education, public health, environmental protection, and the arts.

To take a rather exaggerated example, let us assume that productivity data for the year 1800 were available for Canada. If productivity had increased at a rate of 1 percent per year between then and now, the average Canadian today would command about six times as many goods and services as his forebears did in 1800. If productivity growth had been 3 percent, the average living standard would be an incredible *137* times as high as it was in 1800.

Consequently, productivity growth can make an enormous difference for a nation's standing in the hierarchy of the world's economies. It has been remarked that the success of the United States in keeping its annual productivity growth about one percent ahead of England's for about a century transformed America from a minor, developing country into a superpower and transformed the United Kingdom from the world's pre-eminent power into a second-rate economy.

Unfortunately, productivity growth in Canada in recent years has been very slow, in comparison with both its earlier record and that of many other countries. This chapter reviews the recent record of Canadian productivity performance and summarizes some of the explanations that have been offered for our productivity problems, though the evidence is very unclear. Much of the chapter is devoted to productivity policy—what is being done and what other measures are possible.

A Puzzle: Productivity Growth Lags, Foreign Competition, and Employment

A common view of the dangers of the lag in Canadian productivity growth is that as foreign producers become more efficient in comparison with ours, they will capture more of our industries' markets at home and abroad. First our steel industry, then our telecommunications industry, and, perhaps, our automobile industry will fall victim to the growing productivity of the Japanese. This conjures up the vision of Canada's industries being driven out of almost all their export markets, and Japanese exports taking over an increasing share of Canadian consumer purchases of manufactured goods. The result, it would seem, will be growing unemployment and an increasing Canadian debt to foreigners.

Yet British history suggests that this will not happen. Despite a century of lag in productivity growth, Britain has shown no long-term trend toward increasing unemployment, and its foreign debt, while sometimes large, certainly has not shown an extraordinarily rising trend. In the 1960s and 1970s, British unemployment was extremely low, and in a number of recent years the value of the goods and services Britain sold to foreigners was greater than the value of the items imported. Why did the steady decline in British efficiency compared to many other countries not cause it to lose its export markets and its demand for employment? What does this mean for Canada? We will return to this subject later in the chapter.

Measuring Productivity

Labour productivity is a measure of total output divided by the amount of labour that was used to produce it. It is a measure of output per unit of labour employed.

Most productivity statistics report **labour productivity**; that is, output per worker. One can measure the labour productivity of a single factory, an industry, or an entire economy. Since output consists of a mixture of very different items—automobiles, shoes, computers, and telephone calls—one runs into the problem of adding apples and oranges in measuring its total amount. Statistics that weight outputs by relative prices, such as GNP or national income, are usually used as the output data in measuring the labour productivity of a country. Analogous price-weighted sums are used for industries or individual factories that turn out more than one output. It is also generally agreed that quantity of labour is best measured as number of hours worked rather than number of persons employed.

Dimensions of the Canadian Productivity Problem

Canada actually has not one, but two, different productivity problems. First, our own productivity growth has slowed substantially since the 1960s. Second, for nearly twenty years, our productivity growth rate has been much lower than that of most industrialized and industrializing countries in Europe and the Far East. We will refer to the second of these problems as the Canadian **productivity growth gap**. The two problems probably have somewhat different explanations, almost certainly have different consequences for the welfare of our country, and may require somewhat different policy responses.

What are the magnitudes of these problems? From 1946 to 1982, labour productivity in Canadian manufacturing grew at about 4 percent per year, on the average. But the performance of recent years has been pulling this average down, since the average annual rate of change for the 1979–82 period was approximately *minus* one percent. Indeed, the rate of growth figure for 1982 alone—*minus* 2.7 percent—represents the largest decrease that has been recorded since the series on the growth in manufacturing output per man hour began in 1946.[1]

---

[1]Statistics Canada, *Aggregate Productivity Measures 1982* (Catalogue 14-201), page 8.

It should be noted that throughout most of this period the *level* of productivity continued to improve. In almost every year, it was higher than the last. But the *rate* of improvement has steadily slowed from a gallop to a walk, and finally to a crawl.

The second Canadian productivity problem—the gap in Canadian productivity growth relative to other industrial countries—should be analysed in two steps. First, our performance must be compared to that of our major trading partner, the United States, then it must be compared to that of other industrialized countries.

For the 1946–82 period as a whole, productivity growth in Canadian manufacturing exceeded that in the United States: 4 percent per year in Canada versus 2.5 percent in the United States. But for the years since 1970, we are tied with U.S. manufacturing—both countries have averaged 2 percent annually for this later period. However, the 1982 productivity growth rate of minus 2.7 percent in Canadian manufacturing was well below the United States' rate of minus 1 percent. Thus, while Canada might be considered the overall "winner" in the productivity race in the past, a concern for our current competitiveness is indeed warranted. This is especially true since increases in compensation per man hour in Canada have typically exceeded those in the United States.

At the broader international level, Figure 39-1 presents data comparing overall productivity growth for various countries for the period 1973–79. Note that Canada and the United States trail the pack.

Clearly, Canadian productivity growth has been in trouble in comparison with both its own record and that of other countries.

The Canadian productivity growth rate has fallen drastically from where it was right after World War II, and it is far behind productivity growth rates in a number of other countries.

The analogy between recent Canadian productivity statistics and those relating to Great Britain during the period when it lost its economic pre-eminence is disturbing. Historians date the British decline between 1870 and 1914. By no coincidence, British labour productivity growth in industry fell fairly steadily from 1.2 percent per year between 1870 and 1880 to 0.2 percent between 1890 and

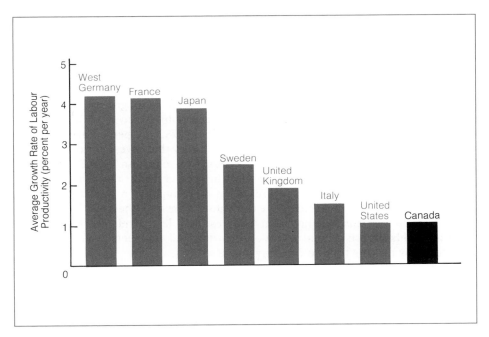

Figure 39-1
AVERAGE LABOUR PRODUCTIVITY GROWTH RATES, 1973–1979, FOR EIGHT COUNTRIES
Each country's productivity growth has fallen relative to earlier periods. Nevertheless, Canada is at the bottom.
SOURCE: New York Stock Exchange

1913.[2] During this same period, British productivity growth lagged slightly behind that of France and well behind the American and German performances.[3] What happened in Britain can happen here.

Why Did Canadian Productivity Growth Slow Down?

Many statisticians and economists have worked very hard to determine why Canadian productivity growth has fallen so much since the mid-1960s. But because so many things have changed at once, no clear and easy answers have emerged. But several culprits have been identified.

Low Investment

Probably most widely cited as a cause of the slowdown is what many regard as insufficient investment in plant and equipment. The more a society invests, the more plant and equipment an average member of the labour force has available to work with. More and better equipment enables her to turn out more output per hour, so productivity grows. Also, new machines usually incorporate the latest designs; conversely, obsolete equipment tends to be kept longer when investment lags. Thus investment and the savings that make investment possible are crucial for productivity growth.

After World War II, business investment in Canada actually rose faster than GNP for a while. However, investment was not large enough to keep pace with the rapidly expanding labour force. Consequently, the amount of capital each worker had to work with fell. Because of differences in measurement procedures, there is some disagreement about the actual magnitude of this decline, but analysts agree that lagging investment played a definite role in the general decline in Canadian productivity growth.

Low Research and Development Expenditure

Another prime suspect in the slowing of Canadian productivity growth is expenditure on applied research. Innovation is one of the main sources of productivity growth. New and more efficient productive procedures—from the steam engine to robotics—have multiplied the output a worker is capable of producing. However, innovation requires more than a new idea. It usually needs careful research to get out the "bugs" and to make the new procedures operational. This work is called **research and development (R & D)**. About half of Canada's R & D expenditures are made by businesses, and the other half by government and non-profit institutions. Because R & D is a critical step between the original invention and its final adoption by business enterprise, a big drop in R & D expenditures can do substantial damage to productivity growth.

The ratio of R & D outlays to GNP has been rising since 1977. In that year, they accounted for 0.98 percent of GNP while in 1982 the percentage was 1.29. However, published data indicate that Canada has the lowest ratio of R & D outlays in relation to GNP of eight OECD countries. In fact, in 1979 Canada's was only 67 percent of that in the country with the second lowest ratio, France.

Why haven't R & D expenditures risen more rapidly in Canada? Why has innovation seemed to slow? No one really knows. One hypothesis is that a decade of stagflation just made innovation and research less attractive to business. Another holds that rising real wages of scientists and engineers discouraged R & D activity by making it more expensive.

[2]Derek H. Aldcroft and Harry W. Richardson, *The British Economy 1870–1939* (London: Macmillan, 1969), page 126.
[3]Trevor May, *The Economy 1815–1914* (London: Collins, 1972), page 163.

Government Regulation

Government regulation is also sometimes blamed for the slowdown. In the 1960s and 1970s, regulations for protection of the health and safety of workers and for defence of the environment were strengthened. These absorbed some of the investment outlays of business and increased the costs of production. Some business leaders believe that this has been a substantial impediment to productivity growth.

Shift to the Service Industries

Another possible culprit is the fact that the share of the nation's labour force employed in **service industries** has more than doubled since 1951. Historically, growth of productivity in many (but by no means all) of the services has been far lower than in manufacturing. This is so in part because for many services quality depends, or is believed to depend, directly on the amount of time the supplier devotes to the activity (for example, the time devoted by a doctor to an average patient, or the amount of faculty time per student). Also, many services (such as diagnosis and treatment of a sick person) cannot be standardized and put on an assembly line. When workers leave manufacturing, with its relatively rapid productivity growth, and go into those services whose productivity growth is slow, overall productivity growth slows down. How serious is this phenomenon? Unfortunately, statistical estimates vary enormously. We really are not sure.

In any event, the shift of the labour force toward the services cannot be considered an example of poor performance by our economy. Unlike lack of innovation, it is not something we must "cure."

A **service** is an industry that does not turn out any physical products. Telecommunications, medical care, teaching, police protection, and the work of lawyers are examples of service industries. Some, like telecommunications, use highly sophisticated equipment, and their productivity has grown rapidly. In many other services, such growth has been very slow.

Rising Energy Prices

Probably part of the slowdown in productivity growth resulted from the sharply rising price of energy, which led to many economic changes. The building insulation business grew. The demand for large, gas-guzzling cars plunged. Much plant and equipment had to be changed to adapt them to the new patterns of consumer and business demands induced by rising energy prices and to substitute fuel-efficient equipment for items that had been installed when energy was cheap.

Because energy constitutes a small proportion of the nation's total expenditure on inputs, most statistical studies suggest that higher energy prices did not contribute much to the slowdown. A typical estimate is that they account for about 15 percent of the total decline in productivity growth. Yet there are many, including the authors of this book, who suspect that energy may be responsible for more than that. The equipment that had to be replaced or modified to save on fuel probably used up a far from negligible portion of the country's investment.

Macroeconomic Conditions

Finally, some portion of the slowdown is probably attributable to the fact that the 1970s and early 1980s were not generally characterized by healthy business conditions. Several recessions and inflation of unprecedented severity and duration are not conditions that encourage business investment and innovation. There is no clear statistical evidence on the importance of this influence, but it is not hard to believe that it was important.

The causes of the slowdown in Canadian productivity growth are far from certain. Lagging investment, modest growth in R & D, government regulation, the shift to service industries, rising energy prices, and repeated recessions and protracted inflation probably all played a part.

Causes of the Canadian Productivity Growth Gap

As already indicated, Canada has two productivity problems: first, the slowdown from its previous growth performance (a problem we share with other countries) and, second, the productivity gap—the fact that our growth rate has been poorer than those of our main foreign competitors.

Five explanations have been offered for the gap in Canadian productivity growth: higher rates of saving and investment in some of the other countries than in Canada; a decline in Canadian entrepreneurship; special foreign institutions and cultural characteristics, such as an alleged superiority in the standards of workmanship in Japan; government programs to assist industrial growth in other countries; and the existence in Canada of plants operating at less than the most efficient level of production.

Investment and Saving

During the 1960s, capital investment in manufacturing as a percentage of output was 30 percent in Japan, 16 percent in West Germany, 14.4 percent in Canada, and 9 percent in the United States. One would expect the Canadian productivity growth gap to emerge, if this ranking of investment rates was maintained, and this is what has occurred. During the late 1970s and early 1980s, the average annual growth in capital formation was 4.7 percent in Japan, 5.2 percent in Germany, 2.3 percent in Canada, and 3.3 percent in the United States.[4]

While investment can be financed by borrowing from foreigners in the short run, the supply of domestic savings represents the ultimate constraint on what is available for firms to invest. Thus, it is not surprising that the ranking of countries by growth in investment is mirrored reasonably well in their ranking by savings rates. Total savings as a percentage of national income was 30.7 percent in Japan, 23.1 percent in Germany, 21.5 percent in Canada, and 18.3 percent in the United States in 1980 (the last year for which comparable international data were available when this book was written).

The differences in investment and saving rates means that workers in Japan and Germany (and in some other countries) have been supplied with increasing amounts of equipment relative to Canadian workers. Their equipment, having been acquired more recently, is generally more modern and more efficient than our own. According to one study, the Ford Motor Company turns out two car engines per day per employee, while Toyota produces nine. A U.S. colour TV set requires 3.5 to 4.5 labour hours while in Japan only 1.8 labour hours are required. It is hardly surprising, therefore, that studies have attributed as much as 80 percent of the superior Japanese growth record (compared to the United States) to Japan's persistently higher saving and investment.[5]

Entrepreneurial Activity

Entrepreneurship is also widely cited as a reason for the gap in productivity growth. No one knows how to measure **entrepreneurship**, and there is not even agreement on its definition. Roughly speaking, it refers to the imagination, daring, alertness, and skillful intuition of the men and women who innovate, take advantage of opportunities to enter fields where incumbent managements have performed badly, and generally keep bringing changes to the economy.

The prevailing legend (which, like many legends, may have a great deal of truth to it) is that, perhaps until the Great Depression of 1929, American entrepreneurship was unbeatable, setting an example of accomplishment that was

---

[4]Organization for Economic Cooperation and Development, *Economic Surveys 1982–83.*
[5]See, for example, J.R. Norsworthy, testimony before the U.S. Senate Subcommittee on Employment and Productivity (97th Congress, 2nd Session, April 2, 1982).

envied by the rest of the world. Because of our close connections with the American economy, Canadian business reflected the same drive.

Then, in the period after World War II, something happened. Some say entrepreneurs were gradually replaced by products of business schools who knew how to manage firms well, but whose style encouraged good organization and good routine rather than the constant upheaval that characterizes entrepreneurship. Others say businesses turned ever more toward the courts and regulators to protect them from the pressures of competition, relying on lawyers rather than engineers for their prosperity. Still others claim that the alleged decline in entrepreneurship reflects a general change in the attitudes of our society, involving a lower valuation of business success and less widespread appreciation of material rewards.

Whatever the explanation, the conclusion is that business leadership no longer resides in North America, but has been seized by the Far East: Japan, Hong Kong, Taiwan, Singapore, and South Korea. Historically, this would not be the first time such an event has occurred. In the seventeenth century, Holland was the economic and cultural leader of the world until Britain took over that position in the eighteenth century, only to be succeeded by the United States and Germany in the nineteenth century.

How valid is this view of declining entrepreneurship in North America? We simply do not know.

Institutional and Cultural Differences

The third factor widely blamed for the productivity gap is the difference in cultural characteristics. It has been said that Japanese culture, for example, tends to make workers very loyal to their firms and to lead to an emphasis on product quality. This may be true. But the organization of production in large Japanese and Canadian firms differs in ways designed to promote such attitudes.

Japanese workers change jobs from one company to another far less frequently than do Canadian workers. Perhaps one-third to half of the labour force is granted **lifetime employment** and is promoted steadily. At about age 55 these workers are automatically transferred to less responsible positions. Some observers believe that this lifetime employment system has made Japanese workers more willing than their North American and European counterparts to accept labour-saving innovations such as robotics.

The salaries of workers and management in Japan are closer to one another than those in Canada, and management is less likely to dine by itself in a separate, elegant dining room. Workers often organize themselves into small groups called **quality circles**, designed to improve productivity and product quality. Special rewards are given to such groups for outstanding achievements. (See the boxed insert on the next page.)

Emulating Japanese management techniques has recently become fashionable in North America. Delegations of North American executives stream to Japan to see for themselves how quality circles and other such things are run. Imitations have appeared in Canadian factories, and plants run by Japanese managers in the United States using American workers claim to be matching Japanese productivity standards.

Yet there are voices of caution. First, some people who have studied the issue question whether the methods that work in Japan can be transferred successfully to North America, with its different traditions and institutions. Moreover, the statistical evidence suggests that no more than 10 to 20 percent of the superior Japanese growth performance can be attributed to the Japanese management style. So this alone will not enable us to catch up.

Government Assistance

The fourth explanation for the gap in Canadian productivity growth is government assistance programs in other countries. In France and Japan, the government has

The Quality of Japanese Products

Before World War II the label "made in Japan" was generally taken to mean that the item was a shoddy product of poor workmanship and design. Clearly that is no longer true.

This issue has been studied in some detail by Peter G. Peterson, chairman of the National Commission on Productivity in the United States. According to Peterson, "One study found that 96 percent of [Japan's] automobiles leave the production line in fit shape for delivery, versus 75 percent of ours. American rent-a-car companies report that cars made in the United States require two to three times more servicing than comparable Japanese cars."

The accompanying figure shows the frequency of service calls for U.S. and Japanese television sets. According to the data, in 1973 about 3 percent of the Japanese sets required service calls during their warranty period, compared with about 20 percent of American sets. Since then, U.S. performance has improved substantially, and that of the Japanese has deteriorated slightly. By 1979, the most recent year for which figures are available, the U.S. servicing requirements were a bit less than twice as high as the Japanese, but the trend seems to be encouraging for the Americans.

Even more dramatic are the figures reported by Hewlett-Packard summarizing the differences in quality between integrated circuit chips from the United States and those from Japan. Three different manufacturers from each country were represented in the sample. On arrival, 0.16 percent of the American chips failed the acceptance test, but none of the Japanese chips did. When the chips

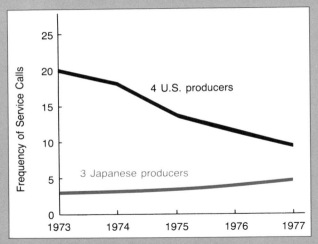

PERCENTAGE OF THE POPULATION OF COLOUR TV SETS REQUIRING SERVICE CALLS DURING THE WARRANTY STAGE, 1973-1977. (DATA ARE WEIGHTED EQUALLY AND REPRESENT THE AVERAGE FOR THE FIRST AND SECOND QUARTERS.)

were used in the field for 1000 hours, the Japanese failure rate was 0.014 percent; the U.S. failure rate was almost ten times as high.

SOURCE: The data are taken from Peter G. Peterson, "The U.S. Competitive Position in the 1980s—And Some Things We Might Do About It," speech presented to the Center for International Business, March 1981.

---

also taken on the task of guiding private investment toward fields that are judged promising for future growth. Thus, particular industries are singled out for assistance in obtaining capital, choice locations, and tax advantages. While much of the co-operation of private firms has been voluntary, the planning agencies have incentives that make it easier to persuade businesses to participate. There is a great deal of controversy about the effectiveness and the wisdom of these programs, and we will return to this issue later in the chapter, when we discuss "industrial strategy" proposals that call for similar programs in Canada.

Short Production Runs

Finally, productivity differentials between Canada and other countries have been linked to the fact that the Canadian tariff has protected some domestic industries from competitive pressures. Since some producers are insulated from these competitive pressures, there is nothing to force them to adjust the scale of plant so that the average cost of production is pushed down to its minimum possible point. Fixed costs are relatively important for firms operating for the small market in Canada. Furthermore, most technological improvements reduce variable costs more than fixed costs. Thus, technological improvements reduce average costs more for firms that are not in existence solely to service a small domestic market.

The Economic Council of Canada has emphasized this point in a recent study.

The study compared many industries in Canada to their counterparts in the United States, and the conclusion was that much of the lower productivity levels in Canada were due to the protected nature of the small Canadian markets.[6]

Several factors are responsible for the Canadian productivity gap. Our saving and investment rates are below those of many other countries. Canadian growth is also handicapped by relatively poor management–labour relations, by decline in the quality and quantity of entrepreneurship, and by the tariff. Labour's resistance to labour-saving innovation may also be greater in Canada than in the Far East, but it may be less than in Europe.

Why Encourage Productivity Growth?

The two different productivity problems have very different consequences for public welfare in Canada. Thus, the reasons for Canada to try to resume its past growth record are different from the reasons for trying to catch up with growth rates in other countries.

Consequences of the Decline in Canadian Productivity

The slowdown in Canadian productivity growth has had at least three unfortunate consequences, each of which can be ameliorated by increased productivity growth:

1. It has kept living standards from rising as rapidly.
2. It has impeded the expansion of social expenditures on, for example, public health, education, and protection of the environment.
3. It has contributed to inflation.

The first of the three consequences is the most obvious. Without rising output per worker, it is very difficult to increase the quantity of goods and services available to each consumer.

Besides holding down living standards, a decline in productivity growth makes it difficult politically and psychologically to finance a variety of social programs that many Canadians consider important. Improvements in health care, education, the arts, environmental protection, attempts to reduce poverty, and many other such activities generally require higher expenditures and therefore higher taxes. If productivity is growing rapidly, these taxes are not too painful because there is enough left over so that workers' take-home pay can still rise. But if productivity growth is slow, any substantial increase in expenditure for social purposes is likely to cut into workers' real incomes. So it was no accident that the slowdown in productivity created pressures to reduce spending on social programs.

Productivity also affects inflation in the long run. The arithmetic here is simple. Inflation rises if the growth of aggregate demand speeds up or if the growth of aggregate supply slows down. Aggregate supply, by definition, is the product of the number of labour hours available times productivity (the amount of output produced by each hour of labour). Thus, if productivity growth slows down, the growth rate of aggregate supply slows down and inflation is likely to rise.

The slowdown in Canadian productivity growth has aggravated inflation. It has made it harder to finance social programs such as public health, anti-poverty schemes, and environmental protection. Above all, it has held living standards almost level.

[6]J.R. Baldwin and P.K. Gorecki (with J. McVoy and J. Crysdale), "Trade, Tariffs and Relative Plant Scale in Canadian Manufacturing Industries: 1970–1979," Discussion Paper No. 232, Economic Council of Canada, Ottawa, May, 1983.

Consequences of the Gap in Canadian Productivity Growth

The relatively slow growth in Canadian productivity compared to that of many other countries has consequences that are different from those of the slowdown from earlier Canadian performance:

1. It causes painful shifts in the jobs done by Canadian workers, requiring retraining and geographic relocation, replacement of specialized plant and equipment, and other substantial readjustment costs using resources that might be better employed for other purposes;

2. While it does *not* threaten to drive Canadian products from the markets of the world or to create ever-growing unemployment rates, it can avoid this only by constant (and costly) restructuring of the composition of Canadian industry, and by driving the real wages of Canadian workers lower and lower relative to those of other countries.

The lag in Canadian productivity growth can be expected to cause continuous shifts in the products that Canada can turn out most profitably. For example, we have observed a decline in marketability of Canadian clothing, footware, steel, and automobiles relative to the products of other countries. Meanwhile, the demand for Canadian agricultural products, telecommunications equipment, energy, and other items has risen. In the long run, the decline of one industry, if accompanied by the rise of another, is not a bad thing. But in the shorter run it may be very costly and painful to the community. A young steelworker may be retrained if he loses his job, but it may involve months of unemployment. An older worker may find himself in far more serious trouble. Factories in dying industries must be abandoned and replaced by new plants to house the growing industries. Families must be uprooted, leaving friends and relatives, to follow the geographic movement of job opportunities. Flourishing communities sometimes are transformed into ghost towns. Thus, even if in the long run a new job arises for every one that was lost, the transition is a costly and painful process.

The Lag in Living Standards (The Puzzle Resolved)

A widespread but mistaken belief about the lag in Canadian productivity growth behind other countries is that it will enable foreigners to outcompete Canadian industries, causing catastrophic Canadian unemployment. This seems plausible enough, but neither history nor economic analysis provides any confirmation for this view. This is the puzzle that we encountered earlier in this chapter. If the Germans, the Japanese, and the Americans are growing ever more productive and efficient in comparison with Canada, why will they not eventually take all our markets away?

An answer is to be found in the laws of supply and demand, which tell us that if the productivity gap reduces foreign demand for Canadian products, the derived demand curve for Canadian labour will also shift downward. That, in turn, will reduce wages in Canada below what they would otherwise have been, until costs have been cut to the point where Canadian products again become competitive.

It should be clear that if the gap in Canadian productivity growth raises the relative cost of Canadian products to the point where its exports fall materially and widespread unemployment results, then real wages in Canada will indeed be forced to lag behind those in other countries that are encountering no difficulty in selling their products. That is precisely why real wages in Great Britain, though they have risen in the postwar period, have lagged far behind those in a number of other countries.

To complete the story, that is, to explain how Canadian products as a group will regain their export market despite the productivity gap, it only remains to confirm that lagging wages are an effective substitute for productivity growth as a

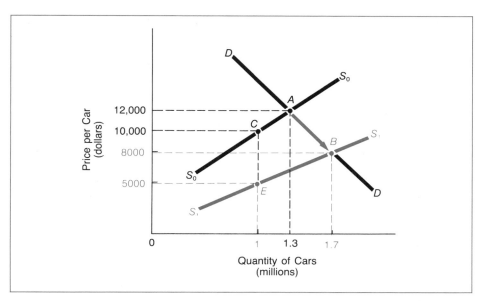

Figure 39-2
SUPPLY, PRODUCTIVITY
AND REAL WAGES
The supply curve of a product can
be shifted to the right, and product
price can be decreased, either by
a rise in productivity or by a fall in
wages. Thus, a country that suffers
from a productivity gap must
compete by providing cheap
labour.

means to preserve international competitiveness. That is, one country may retain the market for its exports through rapid productivity increases while another can keep its market by means of lagging real wages.

Figure 39-2 explains how this works. First, consider the case of a hypothetical Japanese industry whose productivity is assumed to double over a ten-year period. For simplicity we also assume that Japanese real wages remain unchanged over the decade in question. Let S_0S_0 be Japan's supply curve of the product, call it cars, at the beginning of the decade. We see (point C) that to induce the industry to produce one million cars, it must receive $10,000 per car. But as productivity doubles, it takes half the quantity of inputs to produce a given quantity of cars that it required ten years earlier. Thus, to get Japan to produce one million cars at the end of the decade, a price of only $5,000 is required (point E). This means that the Japanese supply curve will have shifted downward from S_0S_0 to S_1S_1. With the demand curve DD unchanged, the equilibrium point will move from A to B. The number of cars produced by Japan will rise from 1.3 million to 1.7 million and the market price per car will fall from $12,000 to $8,000.

Can Canada match this performance despite the gap in its productivity growth? It can if its wages and other input prices fall sufficiently. If productivity growth in Canada is zero, but input prices fall 50 percent over the same period, it can match the Japanese cost performance precisely. If it started out with the same supply and demand curves as Japan, it too will be able to cut the cost per car (when producing one million cars) from $10,000 to $5,000. That is, the corresponding point on its supply curve will move from C to E. Consequently, the Canadian supply curve will also shift from S_0S_0 to S_1S_1, just as Japan's did. The Canadian equilibrium will also move from point A to point B, and its prices and outputs will change just like Japan's.

That may sound easy and painless, but it is really a disaster for Canada. It is a mechanism for the impoverishment of Canadian workers. In effect, it enables the country to compete through low real wages rather than efficiency. By giving Canadian workers smaller and smaller quantities of goods for their efforts, it brings on the day when the rest of the world becomes afraid of the "unfair competition of cheap Canadian labour"—precisely the danger many Canadians once feared from competition with Japan and other countries in the Far East.

In practice, the process will, however, not affect all Canadian export industries similarly. Some traditional export industries will become unprofitable while others will arise to take their place. There are two reasons: First, productivity growth inevitably lags more severely in some industries than in others. Canadian investment will then move away from those industries in which the Canadian lag is greatest, toward industries in which it is smallest relative to other countries. Second, the fall in relative Canadian wages will not reduce the costs of all Canadian industry equally. Cheaper labour will reduce costs most heavily in handicraft activities in which other inputs play a comparatively minor role, and the wage lag will provide less of a cost advantage to high-tech industries with heavy capital–labour ratios. Both of these forces will depress some industries and benefit others, bringing about the painful transition problems of moving labour from one industry to another that were discussed earlier.

Falling real wages is not the only mechanism involved in preserving the markets for Canadian exports. Chapter 16, on the international monetary system, shows how the value of the dollar in relation to other currencies will always adjust in the long run to restore the foreign market for Canadian exports. Moreover, the law of comparative advantage described in Chapter 32 tells us that as Canada loses its competitiveness in some industries there must necessarily be other industries in which its *comparative* advantage increases; that is, in which it becomes comparatively less *in*efficient. It is industries in the latter category that will then produce Canada's exports.

The lag in Canadian productivity behind other countries does not threaten to cause cumulatively growing unemployment or to drive all Canadian industries from world markets. But the cost is nevertheless very high. It can lead to lower relative incomes for Canadians, transforming Canada into a cheap labour country. It can also cause shifts among industries, with some declining or dying and others rising to take their place, causing costly and painful transition problems.

Toward Remedies

No one has yet devised a foolproof set of prescriptions to raise productivity growth. However, a number of policy changes can be helpful. We will first discuss more or less obvious approaches designed primarily to encourage investment and innovation. Then we will turn to two highly publicized approaches with some political overtones—*supply-side economics* and *industrial strategy*. Each of these has a kernel of truth, but each has been badly oversold and suffers from serious practical shortcomings.

Encouragement of Saving and Investment

No one is sure exactly why Canadians save and invest so much less of their incomes than the Japanese. But some Canadian laws clearly discourage industrial investment; and others encourage investment in non-industrial items such as housing. Obviously, if one wants to increase the growth of labour productivity by stimulating industrial investment, these disincentives should be reversed. Here are two noteworthy proposals.

A **capital gain** is the difference between the price at which a piece of capital is sold and the price for which it was bought earlier. The **nominal capital gain** is calculated in current dollars without adjustment for inflation. The **real capital gain** is obtained after the price is adjusted for inflation; it is calculated in dollars of constant purchasing power.

1. Tax real capital gains. If a firm invested $100,000 in a machine in 1970 and sold it ten years later for $140,000, it would seem to have earned a **capital gain** of 40 percent. However, because the price level roughly doubled during this period, the $140,000 received in 1980 had the purchasing power of only $70,000 in 1970 dollars. In other words, the firm had spent 100,000 1970 dollars and received only 70,000 1970 dollars in return—an actual capital loss of 30 percent. We say that the firm earned a **nominal** capital gain of 40 percent but suffered a **real** capital loss of 30 percent.

   It is the real capital loss that matters to the investor. But, in Canada, taxes on investments are based on *nominal* capital gains instead. The firm in our example would be taxed on its 40 percent paper profit, even though it suffered a 30 percent real loss.

Such a tax provision means that even if an investor loses out on an investment in terms of purchasing power, she may nevertheless have to pay a tax besides—just as if she had made a profit. Obviously, this can discourage investment during an inflationary period. Many observers believe that a switch from taxation of nominal capital gains to taxation of real capital gains can make a major contribution to investment, encouraging construction of plant and equipment. However, as we noted in Chapter 11 (page 217), it is difficult for Canada to act alone in the corporate tax area. For branch companies of multi-nationals, tax reductions here often just mean taxes transferred to the government where the parent company is based.

2. Eliminate tax subsidies to housing. Homebuilding clearly takes resources that could be used to build factories instead. Investment in housing has for many years been accorded preferential tax treatments, such as the RHOSP program, the government allowance for first-time home buyers, and the exemption from any tax on the implicit rents received by house owners living in their own homes (see Chapter 33, page 645). Many economists believe that elimination of some of these tax subsidies to housing can contribute to business investment by redirecting resources from home construction to industrial investment.

Savings and investment can be encouraged by policies such as reduced subsidies for private housing construction and taxation of real rather than nominal capital gains.

Encouragement of Innovation

Besides stimulating investment, one can seek to increase productivity by facilitating innovation through more government financing of basic research. Basic research is one of the mainstays of innovation and long-term productivity growth. Electronics, computers, and a variety of other technological innovations would not have been possible without **basic research**.

Basic research is research carried out to increase knowledge, without any particular practical use in mind. For example, what is the structure of the atom?

Most basic research is already financed by government, and only a little by private industry. The reason is that, while basic research generally has large payoffs, the researcher may not benefit from his or her ideas. Basic research in mathematics made modern automation possible many decades later. Basic research in physics made nuclear energy possible much later. But there was no practical way for the pioneering researchers to receive payment from the then unidentified future entrepreneurs who would profit from their work.

Thus, basic research is said to suffer from the **free-rider problem**—that is, those who benefit obtain their benefits free. Basic research is therefore unprofitable; and so private industry cannot be expected to invest a great deal in it. Consequently, basic research is usually financed by governments. It has been suggested that government funding of basic research should be increased.

The **free-rider problem** arises whenever provision of a service to one individual or group automatically benefits others (the free riders) whether or not the others make any contribution to the costs. For example, if individual A on a private street builds drains to reduce flooding, all others who live on the street will automatically benefit.

Supply-Side Economics

We come, finally, to two controversial packages of proposals that have been widely advertised by their advocates as means to stimulate productivity.

Since **supply-side economics** has already been discussed in Chapter 11, we can deal with it rather briefly here. In a sense, any plan for the encouragement of productivity must be a supply-side measure in that it seeks to raise output primarily through its effect on supply rather than through any effects on demand. But serious questions have been raised about whether the measures advocated by supply-siders (many of which were described in Chapter 11) can really be expected to make an appreciable difference to productivity.

Careful examination of the bundle of measures that the United States Congress passed in the early 1980s under the supply-side banner gives a somewhat mixed picture. There were a number of targetted incentives of the sort discussed in this chapter; for example, tax breaks for increased investment and for retirement savings. But the mainstay of the program was simply a set of reductions in the taxes paid by individuals and business firms, in the hope that tax cuts will induce individuals to work harder and firms to pursue profits through growth.

Critics of Reaganomics question whether the tax cuts will make much difference. An analogy will illustrate the issue: Consider two firms which want to increase their sales. Firm A simply raises each salesperson's base wages by a flat 25 percent, no matter how much or how little she sells. Firm B, instead, increases the commission it pays on each item that an individual sells by 25 percent. At firm B, but not firm A, the more a salesperson manages to sell, the higher will be the rise in that individual's take-home pay. Which of the two companies do you think will end up with the larger increase in sales? The point is that a general tax reduction is very much like the approach taken by firm A in our example. The benefits are not, in general, contingent on the amount the firm or the individual does to increase productivity.

Industrial Strategy

Over the past decade, a very different approach to productivity stimulation has been advocated by a number of university researchers and embraced by many politicians. Called **industrial strategy**, the idea is to follow the example of the Japanese and the French by setting up a government planning agency to encourage the particular industries that, in the judgment of the agency, can make the largest contribution to the nation's productivity growth. If it judged that industry C has poor growth prospects while industry D promises the possibility of extraordinary growth, the agency could use means such as tax breaks, loans, and informal pressure to induce a flow of capital and labour out of industry C and into industry D. This, together with some industry-by-industry advice and other attempts to influence business decisions, would, it is hoped, make a major contribution to productivity growth in Canada.

Many economists object that no government agency can do as well as the forces of the market in picking probable future winners and losers. The profit motive already spurs investors to identify the winners and back them with their resources, while withdrawing funds from the likely losers. Private investors do make mistakes. But, in the view of many observers, the mistakes of government agencies are likely to be far more frequent, more serious, and more difficult to reverse, since the individual decision-makers involved do not stand to gain or lose to the same extent as private entrepreneurs.

For this and other reasons, critics of industrial strategy worry that an avowed policy of "picking winners" might degenerate into a habit of "backing losers." This seems to have happened in countries like Britain and Sweden. And recently, some leaders of troubled industries in the United States have proclaimed their support for industrial strategy—interpreting it as a call for trade barriers against imports and for help to sick and dying industries. This is, of course, a perversion of the basic logic of the industrial strategy idea, providing encouragement to the industries with the least promising future rather than to those whose prospects are brightest.

Market Mechanism Industrial Policy

Perhaps more in line with the way economists think is a proposal that might be described as market mechanism industrial policy or "real supply-side economics." This proposal seeks to apply to the economy the approach of our illustrative firm B, which sought to stimulate sales by paying salespersons according to results.

Market mechanism industrial policy would provide reductions in business taxes, but not uniformly for all firms. Rather, firms would be given a rebate based on the rate of increase in their productivity.[7] The faster a firm increases its productivity, all other things being equal, the lower the tax bill it will have to pay at the end of the year. Such a plan would increase the profitability of industries in which it is easy to raise productivity, and reduce the profitability of investment in industries in which it is hard to raise productivity. In this way, the program could induce businesspeople to make the type of decisions that a government agency under an industrial strategy would strive for. But, by avoiding government intervention on an industry-by-industry basis—with its mixture of subsidies, tax breaks, and special stimuli—a market-based approach might achieve the same end at lower economic cost and with less government interference in individual decisions.

The Cost of Productivity Growth

These are but some examples of policies that have been advocated to stimulate productivity growth. What is clear is that there is a large menu of ideas from which to choose. But, if there is to be any hope of making a big improvement in the Canadian rate of productivity growth, small doses of just a few of these remedies will not suffice. As usual, large effects cannot be expected to follow from small measures.

According to some business persons, all that is needed to raise productivity growth significantly is an end to inflation, a sharp reduction in business taxes, and a great decrease in the severity of regulation. It is easy to understand why they advocate such changes. But we can hardly be confident that these changes alone will bring about a great rise in the Canadian productivity growth rate. In this connection, it is suggestive to recall that in the period 1870–1914, when Great Britain lost its lead in productivity, it had no inflation, virtually no business taxes, and virtually no regulation of business.

Effective action to increase productivity growth also cannot be completely painless. At a minimum, it will require an increase in investment relative to GNP, which must entail a painful sacrifice of current consumption, at least in the short run. To use one of the economist's favourite clichés, here, as everywhere, there is no such thing as a free lunch.

---

[7]This is not the place to discuss how productivity would be measured for this purpose or to examine some other difficulties entailed in carrying out the proposal. It is described here merely to indicate a general approach through which the market mechanism might be enlisted to achieve the goals of an industrial strategy.

Summary

1. Productivity growth is the primary determinant of real income per capita, that is, of standards of living.
2. Over long periods, a small increase in annual productivity growth compounds into an enormous rise in living standards. This is one of our **12 Ideas for Beyond the Final Exam**.
3. In recent decades, Canada has suffered from two different productivity problems: (1) our rate of productivity growth has fallen from about four percent per year to almost zero percent per year; and (2) our rate of annual productivity growth has been less than those of many industrial economies.
4. No one is sure about what has caused productivity growth in Canada (and in other countries) to slow down. Probably, the main causes are a lag in growth of investment in plant and equipment, the rise in energy prices in the 1970s, and some lag in innovation, which may be attributable to the protracted period of simultaneous inflation and unemployment.
5. The decline in Canadian productivity growth from its earlier rates has held back the growth of per capita income, made it harder to finance social programs such as health care and environmental protection, and contributed to inflation.

6. The lag in Canadian productivity growth behind other countries is partly explained by the fact that Canadians save and invest a lower proportion of their incomes than people in some other countries do. In addition, it may be explained in part by a decline in entrepreneurship; by special foreign labour relations practices such as quality circles and lifetime employment (which encourage workers to accept labour-saving innovations); by other countries' government programs to encourage growth; and by the combination of our tariffs and small domestic markets, which keep average costs high.

7. The lag of Canadian productivity growth relative to other countries has reduced relative real wages in Canada and caused heavy adjustment costs by changing the mix of viable Canadian industries. In the long run, however, it will not cause growing Canadian unemployment or loss of all export markets to Canadian industry.

8. Canadian productivity growth can be encouraged by measures such as taxation of real rather than nominal capital gains to encourage investment, by reduced taxation of savings, and by greater government support for basic research.

9. An effective productivity program requires some short-term sacrifices in consumption to make more investment possible, and may entail other costs as well.

10. Supply-side economics is a program to encourage investment and harder work primarily through tax reductions. However, the U.S. program that was tried by President Reagan has been criticized as a tax giveaway, because it did not base the size of an individual's or a firm's tax break to any appreciable degree on what the recipient of the tax advantage has done for productivity growth.

11. Industrial strategy is a proposed program involving a government agency that would select industries whose productivity growth is most promising, and would provide special assistance to those industries. It has been criticized as a source of all the inefficiencies that usually accompany case-by-case government intervention.

Concepts for Review

Compounding of productivity gains
Labour productivity
Productivity growth
Research and Development (R & D)
Service industries

Lifetime employment
Quality circles
Entrepreneurship
Capital gain
Real capital gain

Nominal capital gain
Basic and applied research
Free-rider problem
Supply-side economics
Industrial strategy

Questions for Discussion

1. With a one percent productivity growth rate, productivity will quadruple in about 140 years. With a two percent growth rate it will increase 16 times in about the same period. Can you account for the disproportionate difference?

2. Are there ways to increase income per capita other than raising productivity? Can you give examples? How much can they help a country's living standard in the short run? In the long run? (Hint: Can a country benefit by borrowing from abroad?)

3. Why do you think productivity growth in most industrialized countries fell at about the same time—between the end of the 1960s and the beginning of the 1970s?

4. What do *you* suspect are the main causes of the slowdown in Canadian productivity growth?

5. What do *you* think are the main causes of the lag in Canadian productivity growth behind other countries?

6. If Canadian productivity growth continues to lag behind that of other countries for another 50 years, which industries do you think will be hurt most severely? Which industries will benefit? Why? (Hint: Which industries will benefit most from relatively low real wages?)

7. Besides requiring a reduction in consumption, what other sacrifices may be entailed by an increase in productivity growth? (Hint: Do people enjoy working harder? What will be the effects on the environment? May there be any benefits for the environment?)

8. How would you design an effective supply-side program?

9. Discuss the pros and cons of industrial strategy.

10. Suppose that an average annual three percent growth rate of labour productivity is adopted as a target by the Canadian government for the next decade. Discuss what combination of measures offers any hope of achieving such a major increase in productivity growth. (No one is sure of the correct answer to this, or even whether an answer is possible.)

Growth in Developed and Developing Countries

40

The development of capitalist production ... compels [the capitalist] to keep constantly extending his capital ... by means of progressive accumulation.... Fanatically bent on making value expand itself, he ... forces the development of the productive powers of society, and creates those material conditions, which alone can form the real basis of a higher form of society.

KARL MARX

I n this chapter we discuss the factors that determine the rate at which an economy grows and examine the desirability of rapid growth. We begin by considering how growth can be measured and go on to examine the effects of population growth on prospects for rising incomes per capita. Next, we examine the views of those who have argued that in wealthier countries economic growth is a mixed blessing that may do more harm than good. Then, in the second part of the chapter, we turn to the special problems of the less developed countries (LDCs) and look at the measures that have been proposed to increase their rate of growth. We show that although in recent years standards of living in the LDCs have begun to rise significantly, their rapid population growth and their vulnerability to such external shocks as the rise in oil prices and other similar perils mean that many problems still threaten their economies. Next, we examine the problems that impede growth in the LDCs, including scarcity of capital, lack of education, and unemployment. While doing this we consider what the LDCs can do to help themselves and what the rest of the world can do to help them.

Growth in General

How to Measure Growth: Total Output or Output per Capita?

Adam Smith, like many of his successors, took it for granted that expansion of productive capacity is inherently desirable. But he also took it for granted, apparently without examining the matter very closely, that growth in the size of population is to be wished for. His reason was that a larger population provides a larger work force, and a larger work force makes a larger national output possible. Few economists since Smith's time have argued in this way. Nowadays we usually measure a nation's prosperity not in terms of its total output but in terms of its output *per person*. India has a GNP more than twice as large as Sweden's. But with a population more than 80 times as large as Sweden's, India remains a poor country while Sweden is highly prosperous. The point is that:

If the objective of growth is the material welfare *of the individuals* who make up a country, then the proper measure of the success of a program of economic development is how much it adds to output per person. The relevant index is not total output. It is total output *divided by total population*; that is, *output per capita.*

From this point of view, the appropriate objective of growth is not, as the old cliché puts it, "the greatest good for the *greatest number*"—it is the greatest good *per person* in the economy. Per-capita figures tell this story well. To make the appropriate comparison of well-being in Sweden and India, we note that per-capita GNP in Sweden is about $14,000 a year; whereas in India, even after a generous adjustment to correct for lower prices in that country, the figure is $260 a year.

Only where the objective of the government is grandeur or military strength may the number of inhabitants alone seem an appropriate part of its goal. A small country like Finland, for instance, cannot hope to overwhelm a giant neighbour like the Soviet Union, even if Finland has a much higher per-capita GNP than that of the Soviet Union.[1] But where the goal of the government is not national power but the elimination of poverty, illiteracy, and inadequate medical care, sheer increase in population becomes a questionable pursuit.

On Growth in Population: Is Less Really More?

In 1798, the Reverend Thomas R. Malthus (who was to become England's first professor of political economy) published *An Essay on the Principle of Population.* This book was to have a profound effect on people's attitudes toward population growth. Malthus argued that sexual drives and other influences induce people to reproduce themselves as rapidly as their means permit. Unfortunately, he said, when the number of humans increases, the production of food and other consumption goods generally cannot keep up.

As the earth becomes more crowded, people must work each piece of farmland more intensively than before, and they must look for new land to farm. But neither of these ways to increase production will help enough to meet the increased need. There are limits to what a given piece of land can produce. Moreover, as people put soil under cultivation, they will naturally tend to pick the best lots first. Thus, as they extend the area that is cultivated, people will be forced to make use of increasingly inferior farmland.

Together, these two phenomena lead to the noted *law of diminishing returns* to additional labour used with a fixed supply of land, a relationship we encountered before (in Chapter 22). This hypothesis states that if we use more and more labour to cultivate a fixed stock of land we will eventually reach a point at which each additional labourer will contribute less additional output than the previous labourer. Ultimately, as the labour force increases, output per worker will decline.

Malthus and his followers concluded that the tendency of humankind to reproduce itself must constantly exert pressure on the economy to keep living standards from rising. Wages will gravitate toward some minimal subsistence level—the lowest income on which people are willing to marry and raise a family. If wages are above subsistence, the population can and will grow. But, as we have seen, rising population without any rise in available land must reduce output per worker because of the law of diminishing returns. Thus, a wage that is above subsistence will set forces into motion that will drive wages down toward subsistence.

[1]Even where military power is the primary objective, a large but impoverished population may not be a very effective means to that end. China has long had an enormous population, but in the modern era its military presence is certainly quite recent.

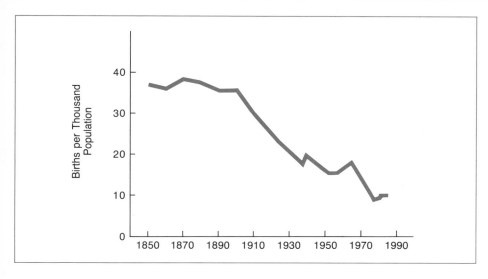

Figure 40-1
GERMAN BIRTHRATES,
1850–1982
This chart shows that birthrates in
Germany have generally been
declining since 1870.
SOURCE: Statistisches Bundesamt,
Statistisches Jahrbuch (Weisbaden,
Germany).

Sometimes, according to Malthus, the population will grow beyond the capability of the economy to support it. Then the number of people will be brought back into line by means that are far more unpleasant than a decrease in wages—by starvation and disease or by wars that produce the required number of casualties.

Later in the nineteenth century and during the first half of the twentieth century, the gloomy Malthusian vision seemed to lose credibility. New technology and improved agricultural practices generally enabled the output of food and other agricultural products to increase faster than the population (at least in the wealthier industrialized nations). In addition, it turned out that as living standards rose, people became less anxious to reproduce, and so the expansion of population slowed substantially. Figure 40-1 illustrates this trend in Germany over a 133-year period. All in all, it began to look as though population growth constituted no significant threat—it was something with which human technological skills and ingenuity could cope.

More recently, however, there has been renewed concern over population. With improvements in medicine—notably improved hygiene in hospitals, the use of such public-health measures as swamp drainage, and the discovery of anti-biotics—death rates have plunged in the developing countries, especially for infants. At the same time, birth-control programs in most of these countries have, at least until quite recently, not been very successful. As a result, the populations of developing countries have continued to expand dramatically, eating up a good proportion of any output increases obtained through their governments' economic-development programs.

It has been widely concluded that significant improvement in living standards in the developing areas is impossible without a substantial reduction in their population growth. But the neo-Malthusians, as one dedicated group is sometimes called, go further than this, arguing that a rapid approach to birthrates so low that populations cease expanding—that is, to *zero population growth*—is virtually a matter of life and death even for the most prosperous nations. It is illuminating to consider the logic of their argument.

The Crowded Planet: Exponential Population Growth

In advocating his position, Malthus adopted a line of argument that has caught many imaginations ever since:

Figure 40-2

PROJECTED GROWTH OF
THE WORLD'S POPULATION
IN 175 YEARS AT CURRENT
RATE OF GROWTH

This figure shows the sensational
acceleration of population growth
if population expands
exponentially.

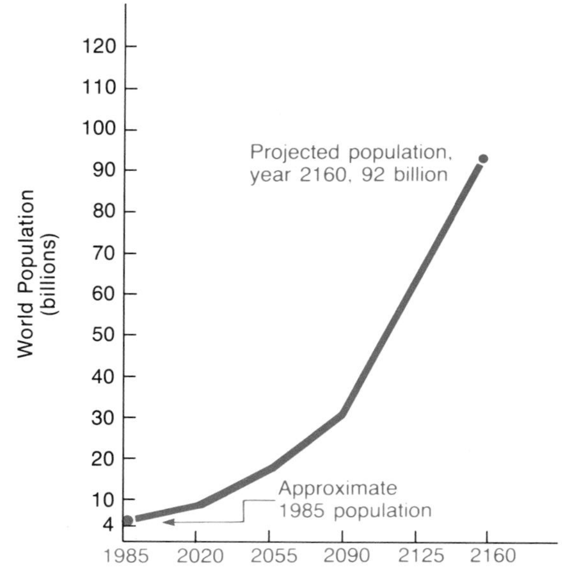

Population, when unchecked, increases in a geometrical ratio. Subsistence increases only in an arithmetical ratio. A slight acquaintance with numbers will shew the immensity of the first power in comparison of the second.[2]

Exponential growth is
growth at a constant
percentage rate.

In modern discussions, such a "geometric" growth pattern is referred to as **exponential growth**, or "compounded growth" or "snowballing." Exponential growth is growth at a constant *percentage* rate. For example, at a 10 percent growth rate, a population of 100 persons will increase by 10 persons a year; but a population of a million persons will increase by 100,000 persons a year. Thus, although the *rate* of growth is the same for large and small populations, the *numbers* are dramatically different. The bigger the population, the more it will add annually. And each year's growth implies still faster growth in the following year. It is like a snowball rolling downhill, accumulating more snow the bigger it gets and so expanding faster and faster all the time.

If the population doubles (grows 100 percent) in 35 years, it will quadruple (grow another 100 percent) in 70 years, increase 8-fold in 105 years, 16-fold in 140 years, and so on indefinitely. The doubling sequence 2, 4, 8, 16, 32, 64, and so on, is the basic pattern of exponential growth. Figure 40–2 shows how astronomical such a growth sequence can be. By projecting the world's population 175 years into the future on the assumption that population will grow exponentially at about its current rate, it shows that by the year 2160 the population will have grown to about 92 billion, with almost 20 times as many inhabitants on the earth as there are today.

It turns out that in his assumptions about exponential growth, Malthus was being conservative. He did not begin to spell out the wonders and the horrors that his premise implied. Consider some calculations by one leading authority on population (who has derived his conclusions simply by carrying through the arithmetic of exponential growth rates):

• *If population were to grow at today's rates for another 600–700 years, every square foot of the surface of the earth would contain a human being;*

[2]Malthus, *An Essay on the Principle of Population* (London, 1798), page 20.

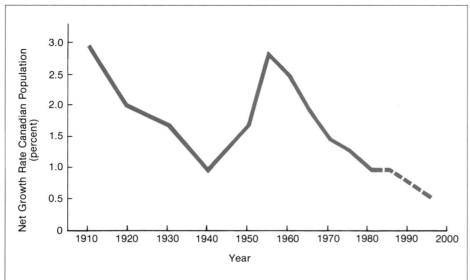

Figure 40-3
ANNUAL PERCENTAGE
GROWTH RATE OF THE
CANADIAN POPULATION
Note how rapidly the rate has
fallen in recent years. It has just
about returned to the low level that
was observed at the end of the
Great Depression.
SOURCE: Canada Year Book.

- *If it were to expand at the same rate for 1200 years, the combined weight of the human population would exceed that of the earth itself;*
- *If that growth rate were to go on for 6000 years (a very short period of time in terms of biological history), the globe would constitute a sphere whose diameter was growing with the speed of light.*[3]

And none of this is conjecture. It is *sure* to come about *if* the present (exponential) rate of growth on the earth's population continues unabated.

Of course, none of this can really happen. Our finite earth just does not have room for that sort of expansion. The fate of humanity is not determined by the rules of arithmetic—it depends on the course of nature and on the behaviour of the human race. It is true that if the number of humans continues to swell until it presses upon the earth's capacity, the process will ultimately be brought to a halt in a Malthusian apocalypse. Disease, famine, and war must finally put a stop to the expansion process.

But there is a better alternative. People can choose to stop raising large families. There is no inevitability about the family of six or ten children. As we have just noted, there has in fact been a decline in the rate of expansion in the wealthier societies—so much so that in North American in the last few years the rate of reproduction has reached what can ultimately give us zero population growth (see Figure 40–3). Even in the developing nations, as we will see later in this chapter, the birthrate has recently been declining.

A more balanced view of the matter recognizes the serious difficulties that rapid population growth can lead to, and suggests that its encouragement will not serve the interests of society. Yet, it does *not* imply that a great catastrophe is necessarily at hand or that the appropriate reaction is panic.

Requirements for Increased Growth

What can be done to increase the growth rate of an economy? Unfortunately, no one has a handy list of sure-fire recipes.

---

[3]Ansley J. Coale, "Man and His Environment," *Science*, vol. 179 (October 9, 1970), pages 132–36. Copyright 1970 by the American Association for the Advancement of Science.

Growth can be attributed to a number of factors that no one knows how to explain: (1) *inventiveness*, which produces the new technology and other innovations that have contributed so much to economic expansion; (2) *entrepreneurship*, the leadership that recognizes no obstacles and undertakes the daring industrial ventures needed to move the economy ahead; and (3) *the work ethic* that leads a work force to high levels of productivity. No one really knows what features of economic organization and social psychology actually lead a community to adopt these goals, as Great Britain is said to have done at the beginning of the nineteenth century, as the United States is reputed to have done in the first half of the twentieth century, and as Japan is apparently doing today. We do know, however, that:

Growth requires two things that people can influence directly:

1. A large expenditure on *capital equipment*: factories, machinery, transportation, and telecommunications equipment.
2. The devotion of considerable effort to research and development from which innovations are derived.

Both these types of expenditures help to increase the economy's ability to *supply* goods, which brings us back to the analyses of Parts Two and Three of this book. There we stressed that the level (and, consequently, the growth) of national income is determined by the interaction of aggregate supply and aggregate demand. It is the need for capital equipment in any growth process that provides a vital link between aggregate demand and aggregate supply, for an economy acquires a larger capital stock by investing. Recall that aggregate demand is the sum of consumption, investment, government spending, and net exports, $Y = C + I + G + X - IM$. But I is the only part of Y that creates more capital for the future.

The *composition* of aggregate demand is a major determinant of the rate of economic growth. If a larger fraction of total spending goes toward investment rather than toward consumption, government purchases, or exports, the capital stock will grow faster and the aggregate-supply schedule will shift more quickly to the right.

Accumulating Capital by Sacrificing Consumption: The Case of the Soviet Union

The importance of the *composition* of demand stands out sharply if we turn away from Canada and consider a *centrally planned* economy, such as that of the Soviet Union.

When the Soviet Union undertook to expand its industrial output very rapidly, it was clear from the earliest stage of planning that a tremendous amount of capital equipment would be required to carry out the expansion. Not only did the Soviets have to build modern factories and acquire sophisticated machinery, they also needed a **social infrastructure**—a transportation network to bring raw materials to the factories and take finished products to the markets, an efficient telecommunications system, and schools in which to train the population sufficiently to be an effective labour force. All this and much more was needed, and all of it required labour, raw material, and fuel for its construction.

Obviously, such a use of resources has its *opportunity cost*. Fuel and steel that are employed to build a train become unavailable for the production of refrigerators and washing machines. The real price of accumulating plant, equipment, and infrastructure is paid in the form of consumer goods that must be given up in order to build that capital equipment. In other words:

Through saving, the public gives up some consumption, which is the price it must pay for the accumulation of plant, equipment, and infrastructure. Without this sacrifice, growth generally cannot occur.

This is the hard lesson that the inhabitants of the Soviet Union have been living with for over half a century. Ever since the Russian Revolution in 1917, the Soviet leadership has been determined to promote rapid economic growth and has imposed on the general public whatever sacrifices of current consumption were deemed necessary for the purpose. Only in the most recent decades has an increase in the supply of consumer goods been assigned any priority. As a result, Soviet living standards have been rising very slowly, particularly because the demands of the military forces have joined those of the growth planners in competing for the resources that might otherwise go into consumption.

The reason for this harsh trade-off is clear enough. If the economy is producing at its full potential—and the Soviet economy generally has been—then real output Y cannot be increased further. Since $Y = C + I + G + X - IM$, and since exports are needed to finance imports, a decision to devote more resources to the production of heavy machinery (which is in I) or armaments (which are in G) is simultaneously a decision to forgo some consumption. Where resources are already fully employed, it is simply not possible to have both more guns and more butter.

The Payoff to Growth: Higher Consumption in the Future

We may seem to be painting a rather grim picture of growth, and indeed, the process has often been harsh in the U.S.S.R. and in other nations that have enforced a high rate of economic growth. But it is also true that if the growth process is successful, the sacrifice of consumption that it requires is only a temporary loss. Consumers give up goods and services now in order to make possible the construction of a productive capacity that will permit them to consume even more goods and services at a later date. After all, from the consumers' point of view, that is what growth is all about. It is not an end in itself, but a means to an end—a standard of living higher than they could have attained without the process of economic expansion.

At least in a consumer-oriented economy, the decision to save in order to promote economic growth is simply an *exchange between present and future consumption*. Consumers sacrifice consumption now in order to be able to increase consumption in the future by more than they gave up in the past.

Of course, the payoff may never come if something goes wrong. An earthquake may destroy factories and roads, or a government with military ambitions may divert the increased productive capacity into the manufacture of armaments. So there is a risk in the decision to give up consumption now for increased consumption later. The growth process is a gamble—it means trading in a relatively sure thing (present consumption) for a risky future return (increased future consumption).

But betting on the future is not necessarily foolhardy. Economies would remain stagnant if people were unwilling to take chances. And some of the risk of investment plans can be reduced if decision-makers understand fully the terms of the trade-off.

Growth Without Sacrificing Consumption: Something for Nothing?

Of course, some growth can be achieved without much sacrifice of present consumption. For at least one of the main engines of growth can be powered with relatively small increases in the nation's stock of factories, equipment, and infrastructure. Research and development can teach society new and more efficient ways of using the nation's productive resources. Thus, *innovation*—the process of putting inventions into operation—can permit an economy to get more output from the same inputs rather than by *expansion* of capital stock.

Everyone knows that this has in fact occurred. From the invention of the steam engine to that of the modern computer, our economy has benefitted from a stream of inventions—some sensational, some more routine—that together have increased enormously the productivity of the nation's resources. Another way of describing this process is to say that while a substantial proportion of growth is *embodied* in increased quantities of plant, equipment, and infrastructure, a very large proportion of the economy's growth is *disembodied*. That is, it is attributable to better ideas—to improved methods of finding and using the same quantities of resources.

Typically, though, growth involves a combination of the two: the new ideas and the commitment of capital to put them into effect. The widespread use of computers could not have happened without the electronic gear from which they are composed and the flow of electricity by which they are operated. Computers are worthwhile because they reduce the quantities of resources necessary to do a given job, but originally some accumulation of resources was required in order to make possible the resulting savings.

For the long run, society has a considerable stake in the relative role of embodied and disembodied growth. Embodied growth has two serious costs that disembodied growth avoids. First, embodied growth necessarily speeds up the use of society's depletable resources: its iron ore, its petroleum supplies, and its stocks of other minerals and fuels. This means that smaller quantities of those resources will be available to future generations.

The second cost of embodied growth is of comparable importance. The resources that are used up in a process of embodied growth must ultimately end up on society's garbage heap. The physical laws of conservation of matter and energy tell us that no raw material can ever disappear. It can be transformed into smoke or solid waste, but unless it is recycled *entirely* (something that is both beyond the capability of our technology and impractical for other reasons), the greater the quantity of resources used in the productive process, the greater the quantity of wastes that must ultimately result.

Economist Kenneth Boulding has likened our planet to a spaceship hurtling through the solar system but constrained by terrestrial littering laws to keep its garbage on board. In spaceship Earth, we can transform waste materials into other forms—as by melting old bottles for reuse or converting them into energy, or by burning combustible garbage for heat—but we cannot simply toss them overboard.

Both of these environmental concerns—resource depletion and waste disposal—lead us to favour disembodied over embodied growth. To the extent that we can succeed in increasing the productivity of our resources, we can reduce both the rate at which they are depleted and the severity of the community's waste-disposal problems.

One final remark on disembodied growth is in order. Economists are fond or pointing out that there is no such thing as a free lunch. Except in rare instances, improvements in technology are not "manna from heaven." They result, instead, from the work of scientists and technicians in government and industrial laboratories, from the labour of inventors in their basements or garages, and from the effort of management specialists studying the organization of factories and assembly lines. This means that labour (along with other resources) is diverted from other activities into the production of knowledge. *In a fully employed economy, the opportunity costs of investing in the discovery of new knowledge are the consumption of and physical investment in goods that would otherwise have been produced.* So even here, we cannot get something for nothing.

Is More Growth Really Better?

A number of writers have raised questions about the desirability of faster economic growth as an end in itself, at least in the wealthier industrialized countries. Yet faster growth does mean more wealth, and to most people the desirability of wealth is beyond question. "I've been rich and I've been poor—and I can tell you, rich is better," a noted stage personality is said to have told an interviewer, and most people seem to have the same attitude about the economy as a whole. To those who hold this belief, a healthy economy is one that is capable of turning out vast quantities of shoes, food, cars, and TV sets. An economy whose capacity to provide all these things is not expanding is said to have succumbed to the disease of *stagnation.*

Economists from Adam Smith to Karl Marx saw great virtue in economic growth. Marx argued that capitalism, at least in its earlier historical stages, was a vital form of economic organization by which society got out of the rut in which the medieval stage of history had trapped it. As we saw in the opening quotation of this chapter, Marx believed that "the development of the productive powers of society... alone can form the real basis of a higher form of society...." Marx went on to tell us that only where such great productive powers have been unleashed can one have "a society in which the full and free development of every individual forms the ruling principle."[4] In other words, only a wealthy economy can afford to give all individuals the opportunity for full personal satisfaction through the use of their special abilities in their jobs and through increased leisure activities.

Yet the desirability of further economic growth for a society that is already wealthy has been questioned on grounds that undoubtedly have a good deal of validity. It is pointed out that the sheer increase in quantity of products has imposed an enormous cost on society in the form of pollution, crowding, proliferation of wastes that need disposal, and debilitating psychological and social effects. It is said that industry has transformed the satisfying and creative tasks of the artisan into the mechanical and dehumanizing routine of the assembly line. It has dotted our roadsides with junkyards, filled our air with smoke, and poisoned our food with dangerous chemicals. The question is whether the outpouring of frozen foods, talking dolls, CB radios, and headache remedies is worth its high cost to society. As one well-known economist put it:

The continued pursuit of economic growth by Western Societies is more likely on balance to reduce rather than increase social welfare....Technological innovations may offer to add to men's material opportunities. But by increasing the risks of their obsolescence it adds also to their anxiety. Swifter means of communications have the paradoxical effect of isolating people; increased mobility has led to more hours commuting; increased automobilization to increased separation; more television to less communication. In consequence, people know less of their neighbors than ever before in history.[5]

Virtually every economist agrees that these concerns are valid, though many question whether economic growth is their major cause. Nevertheless, they all emphasize that pollution of air and water, noise and congestion, and the

---

[4]Marx, *Capital*, vol. I (Chicago: Charles H. Kerr Publishing Co., 1906), page 649.

[5]E. J. Mishan, *The Costs of Economic Growth* (New York: Frederick A. Praeger Publishers, 1967), pages 171, 175.

mechanization of the work process are very real and very serious problems. There is every reason for society to undertake programs that grapple with these problems. Chapter 34, which dealt with problems of the environment, examined these issues more closely and described some policies to deal with them.

Economists agree also that growth in human well-being is measured very poorly by statistics such as GNP, which indicates only the growth rate of the production of *material* goods and services and takes no account of the effects of growth on the quality of life. Two economists at Yale University, William Nordhaus and James Tobin, have attempted to calculate a better set of figures for the purpose. Their index, the *measure of economic welfare* (MEW), attempts to take into account such items as pollution and congestion as well as the more tangible products of the economy.[6] Thus, for example, if the output of goods and services were to go up slightly some year but there was also a huge increase in pollution, the statistics would report that GNP had risen but that MEW, or the quality of life, had decreased. In fact, the calculations show that throughout most of the post-World War II period, both GNP per capita and MEW per capita have been growing but that growth in the latter has been very much slower.

Despite the costs of growth in terms of human and environmental damage, there is strong evidence that if the economy's total output were kept at its present level, the community would pay a high price over and above the loss of additional goods and services.

First, it is not easy to carry out a decision to prevent further economic growth. Mandatory controls are abhorrent to most Canadians. We cannot *order* people to stop inventing means to expand productivity. Nor does it make any sense to order every firm and industry to freeze its output level, since changing tastes and needs require some industries to expand their outputs at the same time that others are contracting. But who is to decide which should grow and which should contract, and how shall such decisions be made? *The achievement of zero economic growth may very well require government intervention on a scale that becomes expensive and even repressive.*

Second, zero economic growth may seriously hamper efforts to eliminate poverty both within our economy and throughout the world. Much of the earth's population today lives in a state of extreme want. And though wealthier nations have been reluctant to provide more than token amounts of help to the underdeveloped countries, less wealth means there would be even less to share. So perhaps the only hope for improved living standards in the impoverished countries of Africa, Asia, and Latin America lies in continued increases in output.

Finally, without continued growth, it will be no easy matter to finance effective programs of environmental protection. To improve the purity of our air and water and to clean up urban neighbourhoods, billions of dollars must be made available every year. Continued growth would enable the required resources to be provided without any reduction in the availability of consumer goods. But without such growth, we may actually be forced to cut back on our programs to protect the environment. Society could thus end up with less goods and a worse environment.

Problems of the Less Developed Countries

While for wealthier countries the desirability of increased growth may not be completely obvious, for the poorer, **less developed countries (LDCs)** there is less question about the matter. In these nations, increasing the level of per-capita income is a top priority.

[6]W. Nordhaus and J. Tobin, "Is Growth Obsolete?" *Fiftieth Anniversary Colloquium*, V, National Bureau of Economic Research (New York: Columbia University Press, 1972).

Living in the LDCs

Three-quarters of the world's population lives in areas whose average per-capita GNP is $750 or less per year, evaluated (as well as it is possible to do) in terms of today's prices in Canada. Table 40-1 shows that there are countries in which annual per-capita income is under $200. Even after adjustment for differences in measurement of GNP in Canada and the poorer countries, this probably comes to an annual income figure under $700.

To us in Canada, residents of an economy that offers an average GNP almost 20 times as high, such a figure is not only likely to seem incredible, it is all but incomprehensible. Few of us can *really* imagine what life would be like it our family income were reduced to, say, $2000 per year. It is even hard to envision survival on such amounts. It must be emphasized that these figures do *not* represent the living standards of a small group of outcasts from their own societies. Rather, they are *typical* of perhaps a majority of those who live in Asia, Africa, and Latin America.

What can life be like in such circumstances? No brief description can really bridge the gulf between our range of experience and theirs. Yet it can offer us a glimpse into a way of life that few of us will want to share.

Inhabitants of many of the less developed countries live with their large families in one-room shanties or apartments, their water supplies are scanty, polluted, and often miles from home, their only source of energy is that of man and beast, and their sparse harvests are wrung from miserable soil in goods years, with starvation threatened perhaps every five years when the rains do not come and the crops fail.[7] With no surplus in production, no good can be put into reserves, and the old, the infirm, and the very young are likely to perish.

The life of a male in an LDC is hard enough, with its low nutritional level, its lack of equipment to help in work, and its frequency of debilitating diseases. But his life is luxurious compared with that of his wife. She is usually married by the

---

[7]It has been estimated that in some famine years in the 1970s, half a million people died as a result in Bangladesh; 200,000 in Ethiopia; 100,000–250,000 in the Sahelian zone of Africa; and more than 800,000 in just three of the states of India (*The New York Times*, October 27, 1976). In 1984, the famine in Ethiopia resulted in another disaster on this same scale.

Table 40-1

PER-CAPITA GNP IN DEVELOPED AND LESS DEVELOPED COUNTRIES, 1982–1983

	(measured in U.S. dollars)
Developed Countries	
United States	13,160
West Germany	12,460
Sweden	14,040
Canada	12,323
Less Developed Countries	
Egypt	690
Bolivia	570
China	310
Haiti	300
Bangladesh	140
Chad	80

SOURCE: Population Reference Bureau.

Table 40-2

INFANT MORTALITY AND LIFE EXPECTANCY IN DEVELOPED AND LESS DEVELOPED COUNTRIES, 1982–1983

	INFANT MORTALITY (deaths per 1000 live births)	LIFE EXPECTANCY AT BIRTH (years)
Developed Countries		
United States	11	74
West Germany	11	73
Sweden	7	76
Canada	13	74
Less Developed Countries		
Egypt	80	56
Bolivia	130	50
China	35	65
Haiti	113	52
Bangladesh	148	47
Chad	147	40

SOURCE: Population Reference Bureau.

age of 14 and bears 8 or 10 children. If (as is true of some 80 percent of the population) she inhabits a rural area, she may have to trudge miles every day to fetch water for the family. She sews all the family's clothes by hand and cooks its meals. There is not enough money for pre-ground flour, so part of the woman's daily work is to pound the grain by hand for food for the family—perhaps an additional two hours of hard labour. She also tends the gardens that produce food for the family, although, except in Moslem countries where women are sequestered, she is also expected to put in a full day in the fields during the six months of the agricultural season.

Another duty of the woman in an LDC is to bring produce, wood, or whatever she has to trade to market a couple of times a week, and she must often walk as many as 10 miles each way with bundles as heavy as she can carry on her back or on her head. She has no respite in the raising of her children, since they are likely not to have a school to attend when they are well or a hospital to go to when they are sick.

Table 40-2 gives the percentage of infant deaths for each 1000 live births and the average life expectancy of a newborn child in some countries ranging from the most underdeveloped to the most affluent. The contrasts are dramatic. In Bolivia, 130 babies die of every 1000 that are born, while the comparable figure in Sweden is only seven. In many countries people survive only until their late 40s, while in Scandinavia they live to be 76. There is little question about the quality of life in less developed lands.

Most of the inhabitants of many LDCs are shockingly poor. Malnutrition and disease are widespread. The sheer process of living and surviving taxes the people to the utmost and makes them old before their time.

Recent Trends

Do recent trends offer hope of improvement? Here there is both good news and bad. The good news is perhaps the most remarkable. In the 1970s, real GNP in the LDCs grew, on average, more than 5 percent a year (see Table 40-3 for examples).

Table 40-3
AVERAGE ANNUAL GROWTH RATES OF REAL GROSS DOMESTIC PRODUCT IN DEVELOPED AND LESS DEVELOPED COUNTRIES, APPROXIMATELY 1960-1979

	APPROXIMATELY 1960-70 (percent)	APPROXIMATELY 1970-79 (percent)
Developed Countries		
United States	4.4	3.2
West Germany	4.4	2.6
Sweden	4.4	2.0
Canada	5.3	3.4
Less Developed Countries		
Columbia	5.1	5.8
Haiti	0.7	4.1
Iran	10.6	8.8
Pakistan	5.2	4.8
Cuba	3.7	2.5
Zimbabwe	6.1	2.3
Zambia	1.8	1.0

SOURCE: United Nations.

Table 40-4
BIRTHRATE MINUS DEATH RATE IN DEVELOPED AND LESS DEVELOPED COUNTRIES, 1983 (ESTIMATED)

	(births minus deaths as percent of population)
Developed Countries	
United States	0.7
West Germany	-0.2
Sweden	0.0
Canada	0.8
Less Developed Countries	
Bolivia	2.7
Burma	2.4
Egypt	2.7
Ethiopia	2.4
Haiti	2.2
India	2.0

SOURCE: Population Reference Bureau.

Even more important, income per capita grew at an annual rate greater than 2½ percent. The world recession of the early 1980s hit some LDCs very hard and enmeshed them in a serious debt burden (see pages 802, 804). Nevertheless, for some LDCs the long-term outlook continues to be promising. This means that:

Despite population increases, some LDCs have succeeded in breaking out of the stagnation trap. If growth continues as it has recently, an average family in an underdeveloped area can look forward to a doubling of its living standards in less than 30 years. Or put another way, standards of living will be increasing faster than they did in Canada in the nineteenth century!

Clearly, the experience of the 1970s offered hope for a major reduction in absolute poverty for many of the LDCs.

Thus, there was good news in the 1970s, though the beginning of the 1980s was not quite so favourable for the LDCs. Aside from their debt problems, which will be discussed a bit later, there are several developments that can be considered either as merely unfortunate or as thoroughly ominous.

First, while the percentage rates of growth of per-capita incomes in the LDCs have been very impressive, the industrialized countries, with their initially high incomes, have not exactly been standing still. Indeed, largely because their population growth has been slower, the percentage growth rate in per-capita incomes has been higher in the developed countries. But even if the *percentage* increases in their per-capita incomes had been very similar, *absolute* incomes would have continued to rise more quickly in the richer lands. Where per-capita income is $100 a year, a 2½ percent growth rate translates into a $2.50 annual improvement; however, where per-capita income is $5000 a year, the same 2½ percent rate of growth adds $125 a year to the income of the average person. As a result:

The purchasing power of the average family in an LDC is falling further behind that of a typical family in a wealthy economy.

Second, many critics emphasize that the 2½ percent growth rate has been accompanied by a worsening distribution of income in some of the LDCs. The rise in population has worsened the living standards of people on marginal lands with inadequate rain (about 40 percent of Indian farmers and a large proportion of Africans). Add the massive explosion of urban unemployment, and one gets several hundred million people who are no better off and possibly worse off.

Third, a continuing problem within the LDCs is the high growth rate of their populations.

While in Canada, the United States, and some countries of Western Europe, net population growth has fallen almost to zero, the population explosion continues in some of the LDCs, particularly in Africa.

Table 40–4 tells the story: For the sample of LDCs shown, the annual growth rate of population continues perhaps ten times as high as it is in the industrialized countries. Clearly, the more closely the growth in population approximates the growth in national income, the more slowly standards of living will rise, since there will be that many more persons among whom the additional product must be divided. If population growth is exactly equal to the growth rate of national income, obviously the average standard of living must be at an absolute standstill. A recent estimate indicates that the rise in population in LDCs is in fact consuming nearly half the increase in their GNP.

Fourth, the relatively high growth rate in per-capita incomes has not been uniform throughout the LDCs. In some countries, such as Sri Lanka, Ghana, Chad, and Cuba, growth rates have been extremely low. Yet in others, notably the Ivory

Coast, Singapore, South Korea, and Taiwan, growth has been so spectacular that some of them are no longer considered LDCs, despite oil shocks, increasing restrictions against their exports, and lack of mineral resources.

Finally, the LDCs have shown themselves highly vulnerable to such events as the oil crisis in 1979 and the high real interest rates of the 1980s. Much as the fall in Iranian oil exports and rise in oil prices affected the industrialized economies, it undoubtedly damaged the LDCs even more, leading to enormous deficits and foreign debts for the countries least able to afford them. (See the boxed insert on page 804.) In other words, the new growth trends in the LDCs may be quite fragile, and their continuation cannot simply be taken for granted.

It is ironic that the levelling off of oil prices at the beginning of the 1980s not only left many oil-importing LDCs with their crippling debts, but caused similar problems for some of the oil exporters. As a result, Mexico and Venezuela joined Brazil in the group of countries whose economies are severely constrained by huge indebtedness to the rest of the world.

Before leaving the issue of recent growth in the LDCs, it may be helpful to offer a little perspective on the entire matter. First, it should be recognized that sustained growth is a very recent invention, dating from the Industrial Revolution—the beginning of the eighteenth century. It has been estimated that per-capita income in England in 1800 was no higher than in third-century Rome. Before the Industrial Revolution, real wages in England may have reached their peak in the fifteenth century—the end of the Middle Ages—from which they fell to their lowest level ever reached after the Middle Ages in the reign of Queen Elizabeth, more than a century later.

On the other hand, growth in the LDCs is not an innovation of recent decades. In the three decades before World War I, exports from the tropical countries grew faster than national income in the wealthier countries, and, no doubt, in these LDCs output per capita was also growing. Since income data for that period are not available, we do not know by how much, but we do know that the earlier growth was vulnerable to disruption—World War I, the Great Depression, and other catastrophic events all but ended growth in the LDCs for nearly 40 years. Thus, recent high growth rates cannot just be taken for granted and extrapolated into the future.

Impediments to Development in the LDCs

No one has produced a definitive list of causes of the poverty of the LDCs, just as no one can pretend to have produced a foolproof prescription for its cure. Yet there is general agreement on the main conditions contributing to the economic problems of LDCs. These include lack of physical capital, rapid growth of populations, lack of education, unemployment, and social and political impediments to business activity. Let us examine each of these in turn.

Scarcity of Physical Capital

The LDCs are obviously handicapped by their lack of modern factories and machinery. In addition, they lack infrastructure—good roads, railways, port facilities, and so on. But capital is not easy to acquire. If it is to be provided by the populations of the LDCs themselves they must save the required resources—that is, as we saw earlier in this chapter, they must give up consumption in order to free the resources needed to build plants, equipment, and roads. That is fairly easy in a rich community, where substantial saving still leaves the public well off in terms of current consumption. But in an LDC, where malnutrition is a constant threat, the bulk of the inhabitants cannot save except at enormous sacrifice to their families. Moreover, in many of the LDCs, tradition imputes little virtue to investment in business, so that even the wealthy are not terribly eager to put their savings into productive equipment. Thus:

Because of poverty, which makes saving difficult, if not impossible, and because of traditions that do not encourage investment, the LDCs' growth rates of domestically financed capital are lower than those in the developed countries.

One way to help matters is to obtain the funds for investment from abroad. There is a long tradition of foreign investment in developing countries. For example, throughout much of Canadian history, we drew capital from abroad, to finance such projects as the national railway. In recent decades a considerable share of the resources going to the LDCs from abroad has come from foreign governments as part of their aid programs. While some of the resources provided in this way have been used wastefully, informed observers generally agree that the waste incurred under these programs has not been spectacularly great, and they conclude that these capital transfers from the rich countries to the poor have at least worked in the right direction.

Capital can also be transferred to an LDC when a private firm chooses to invest money in such a country to build a factory or to explore for oil in order to increase its own profits. This too seems to have been helpful to the LDCs. In earlier days, it sometimes gave an unacceptable degree of political influence to the foreign firms, particularly when the LDC was a colony of an industrial country. In recent years this difficulty may have become rarer. Nowadays, it is more often the outside firm that is afraid of the government of the LDC rather than vice versa, with foreign proprietors frequently fearful of rigid control by the government of the LDC in which it invests. Sometimes it even fears outright expropriation—that the government will simply take over its property in the LDC with, or even without, compensation because of the hostile attitudes that residents of many LDCs hold toward large foreign companies.

It is difficult for a resident of an industrialized country like Canada to realize how much hatred and resentment is felt in less developed countries toward the "northern imperialist powers." This resentment is focused in particular on **multinational corporations**—companies like IBM, Royal Dutch Shell, Volkswagen, and Unilever—which have their headquarters in an industrialized country and their operations in a variety of less developed countries. Multinationals may first process their own raw materials in one country, ship them to another to make them into parts, and assemble them in still a third. Some of these corporations, among them the oil companies, specialize in the extraction and/or marketing of raw materials, while others, like IBM and Volkswagen, specialize in manufacturing. Many LDCs regard these and other giant foreign corporations as instruments of imperialist exploitation, not as firms that happen to carry on their activities wherever the dictates of efficiency require, contributing benefits to each of the countries in which they operate.

It is true that foreign firms hope to make more money out of an LDC than they put into it, but that is only natural, since otherwise their investment would not have been expected to be profitable, and the funds would therefore not have been invested in the first place. But there are usually *mutual gains* from trade. Investment will be useful to the LDCs if in the process of earning these profits foreign firms build factories, infrastructure, and provide jobs that leave the community wealthier than it would otherwise have been. The evidence is that this is in fact what foreign private investment has typically accomplished in recent decades.

A problem with foreign business investment that is more serious is the danger that foreign firms will fail to train native personnel in the skills necessary to run the factories built by those companies. Often the foreigner brings with him his own managers, engineers, and technicians, and the work force from the LDCs is kept in menial jobs in which on-the-job training is minimal. In recent years the

The Debt Crisis of the Developing Countries

Although there had been previous isolated cracks in the international debt terrain, it was not until 1982 that the problem erupted in dramatic proportions. In August of that year, Mexico announced that it was unable to meet its debt obligations to foreign creditors, although it was taking steps to rectify the situation. In response, the U.S. Government mounted a rescue operation, involving the creditor banks, the International Monetary Fund (IMF), and other creditor governments. The package included a strict program of adjustment for the Mexican economy and a rescheduling of much of the debt. Nervous banks began to cut back lending to other countries that appeared to be heavily indebted, with Brazil the most obvious target. As long as the banks had been willing to continue lending, the debtor countries had had the foreign exchange necessary to continue servicing their accumulated debt, i.e., making scheduled payments of interest and amortization of principal. As the banks cut back, the debtors found debt-service obligations increasingly difficult to meet. One by one, Brazil, Argentina, and many other debtor countries found it necessary to seek debt relief from their creditors, while implementing programs of economic adjustment monitored by the IMF.

(From the *Economic Report of the President*, February 1984, page 71)

The debt problem threatens to undermine growth in much of Latin America, particularly Mexico, Brazil, Argentina, and African countries such as Nigeria. It was caused by overborrowing and overspending during the 1970s when prosperity and growth seemed easy to sustain; by the high oil prices of the 1970s, which hurt the oil-importing LDCs; by the fall in oil prices in the early 1980s, which hurt the oil-exporting LDCs; and by high interest rates, which hurt them all.

The debt crisis is forcing widespread adoption of austerity policies—reducing already low consumption levels so that less has to be imported and more goods are left over for export. It prevents any ambitious investment programs for the same reason, thus impeding future growth. It is indeed a major problem for the LDCs and, incidentally, for the shareholders of large banks in the industrialized countries to whom the money is owed and who fear the loss of their loans.

LDCs have begun to deal with this problem by restricting immigration of foreign personnel, giving them work permits only for limited periods and requiring at least some minimum employment of native personnel in key positions.

Another danger posed by foreign investment is that it may prevent future financial independence. Profits are a major source of the funds used for investment. If foreign investment takes over the LDCs' most profitable industries, then newly formed capital—new plants and equipment—will also be owned predominantly by foreigners.

Population Growth

Population growth is often described as the primary villain in the LDCs. We have already noted that their populations grow far more rapidly than those in the wealthier countries. And though the growth rate has recently been declining in many of the less developed countries, overall the population of the LDCs is expanding at a rate that will double in less than 30 years, requiring a doubling of housing, schools, hospitals, and so on—a heavy real cost for an LDC.

The growth in population has been stimulated by improvements in medical care, which have reduced death rates spectacularly. Today, in some areas, death rates (ratio of deaths to population) are only one-quarter or one-fifth as high as birthrates. While formerly it was not unusual for half a nation's children to die before the age of 20, today in many countries this is true of only some 4 percent of those populations. This dramatic decline can be attributed primarily to inexpensive public health measures—reduction in stomach diseases through purer water supplies, reduction in the incidence of malaria by the draining of swamps, insecticide spraying of the breeding grounds of infectious mosquitoes, eradication of smallpox by vaccination, and so forth. The more expensive treatment of illness, using modern medical techniques and miracle drugs, seems to have contributed far less.

But not all LDCs suffer from serious population problems. India, Indonesia, and Egypt are frequently cited examples of population pressures. On the other hand, many African countries and parts of Latin America still have populations so small that they are denied economies of large-scale communication and transportation. The economy of a sparsely settled country whose electric power and telecommunication lines must traverse great unpopulated areas is under a costly handicap.

Governments in a number of LDCs have been struggling to find workable ways to cut population growth. Programs set up to distribute contraceptives and propaganda against large families have achieved modest success; but in some countries with particularly severe population problems the governments have been dissatisfied with the results of these voluntary efforts. In India, a program making use of compulsory sterilization aroused the anger of the public and finally led to the downfall of the government.

Ironically enough, it was communist China that, along with Singapore, decided to employ strong financial incentives for the purpose. In China, government support is provided for a first child. For a second, the support is withdrawn and some financial penalties imposed; and for a third child, the penalties are really prohibitive for most people. Because this program has been launched only recently it is impossible to provide clear evidence of its success or failure. However, observers come away impressed with its initial impact. Everywhere in China one meets people who say they are determined to have only one child. If this proves to be reasonably accurate, it may produce one of the most dramatic decreases in birthrates the world has ever seen.

Educational and Technical Training

Everyone knows that educational levels in the LDCs are much lower than they are in the wealthier countries. There are fewer graduates of elementary schools, far fewer graduates of high schools, and enormously fewer university graduates. The percentage of the population that is literate is much lower than in industrialized nations. The issue is how much of a handicap this constitutes for economic growth.

If, by "education," we refer to general learning rather than technical (trade) schooling, the evidence is that it makes considerably less difference for economic growth than is often believed. For example, the number of jobs that clearly require secondary (high school) education rarely seems to exceed 10 percent of the labour force. Various studies that have investigated whether there is a statistical relationship between the economic growth of an economy and its typical educational level have failed to turn up any significant correlation between the two. Other suggestive evidence can easily be cited. For example, in 1840 when Great Britain ruled the markets of the world, only 59 percent of the British adult population was literate, while in the United States, Scandinavia, and Germany, then all relatively undeveloped, the figure was about 80 percent.

All of this is not meant to imply that education is worthless. On the contrary, it obviously offers many benefits in and of itself, which need not be discussed here. But it does suggest that if a government invests in education *purely as a means to stimulate economic growth*, only a very limited outlay is justifiable on these grounds.

Matters are quite different when we turn to technical training. There is clearly a high payoff to the training of electricians, machinists, draftsmen, construction workers, and the like. While the number of persons involved need not be very high in proportion to the population, the role played by such specialists is crucial. However, the LDCs would find it a very heavy drain upon their scarce foreign currency to send young people abroad to learn these skills in the numbers called for by the needs of the economy. One of the main inhibitions to adequate training in these areas is that in many countries such skills are held in low esteem and considered inferior to training in the liberal arts. Consequently, technical education is often handicapped by low budgets, low teacher salaries—which discourage good people from entering the field—and the prejudice of potential students against such fields.

Training in improved farming methods also has a great deal to contribute. In many of the LDCs, agricultural methods produce yields far lower than the best of the known techniques can offer. As one leading observer, Nobel Prize-winner Sir W. Arthur Lewis, has remarked:

If this gap could be closed, the economies of these countries would be unrecognizable. Indeed ... no impact can be made on mass living standards without revolutionizing agricultural performance.[8]

There seem to be no easy ways to provide the necessary education to the farmers who cannot spare the time to attend schools; and training their children also involves a number of critical obstacles. Religious beliefs often lead parents to object to schooling of their children, particularly of girls; in areas where literacy is low (where the problem is generally most serious), truly literate and knowledgeable teachers are almost impossible to find in any substantial numbers; and children who do complete schooling have a tendency to leave the farms and move to the cities.

Programs to provide help to the peasants on their own farms have had only limited success. Indeed, lack of training is only part of the problem. Many other things are needed to make modern farming methods possible—farms larger than the two hectares (or five acres) that are typical in a number of countries are required to permit the use of modern machinery where it is appropriate. Roads and storage facilities must be built. Credit must be made available to farmers. Financial arrangements must be changed so the farmer need no longer give up half his crop to landlords and tax collectors whom he can surely regard as little more than parasites and who undermine his incentives for improved productivity.

Unemployment

One of the most noteworthy features of the growth of the LDCs has been an increase in unemployment as population shifted out of agriculture into the cities. Increased schooling has stimulated the migration out of rural areas, as has unionization, which has often produced a huge gap between urban and rural wages. Government investment policies have also favoured construction of schools, hospitals, and other facilities in the cities, and as a result, large numbers of migrants have entered the cities to swell the ranks of the unemployed. The unemployment rate among young urban workers has been particularly high; indeed, rates as high as 50 percent are not unheard of.

These figures are compounded by the phenomenon of **disguised unemployment**. For example, ten persons may do a job for which only six are needed.

[8]W. A. Lewis, *Development Economics, An Outline* (Morristown, N.J.: General Learning Press, 1974), page 25.

The statistics would show no unemployment among the ten workers, even though four of them really contribute nothing to output. Some observers believe that this is such a widespread problem in rural areas that even a substantial reverse migration of the urban unemployed back to the farms would add very little to production, at least in some of the LDCs.

An important consequence of all this is that in many LDCs unemployment may not be accompanied by any substantial reduction in output, in contrast to the situation in industrialized economies. But this does not mean that unemployment in the LDCs is not a serious problem. What it does mean is that it may sometimes be desirable for those economies to avoid the use of labour-saving equipment, partly because it will result in better use of an abundant resource, and partly because it will contribute to the solution of a serious social problem. Thus, increased output is desirable perhaps primarily because it helps to sop up unemployed labour. This is in contrast to the usual situation in the developed countries in which increased employment is desirable perhaps primarily because it increases income and output.

Social Impediments to Entrepreneurship

As we saw earlier in this chapter, one of the magic ingredients of economic growth is **entrepreneurship**. It is clear that the LDCs need entrepreneurs if their economies are to grow rapidly. But in many of these economies, there are serious inhibitions to entrepreneurship. Traditional social values often accord relatively low status to business activity. Indeed, those traditional values even prevent businesses from seeking ways to attract and please their customers and their work force. In addition, high positions in business in many LDCs are often determined by family connections and inheritance, not by ability.

In the LDCs, growth will be inhibited until customs can be modified to increase the social status of economic activity, to make it respectable for private business people and managers of public enterprises to do their best to attract business and increase productivity, and to assign responsibility on the basis of ability rather than family connections.

Government Inhibition of Business Activity

In addition to social impediments to business, the political situation in the LDCs often is detrimental to business success. Business is not helped by unstable governments or by the uncertainty that accompanies such an environment, especially if there is a high likelihood of revolution. Foreign investment will be discouraged where there is fear of expropriation or of unstable currencies that may fall in value and wipe out hard-earned profits. And native business people may live in fear of nationalization or even imprisonment—possibilities that are not likely to encourage investment.

In addition, in the normal course of events, governments in the LDCs are often inclined to interfere with business activity in a variety of ways that seem relatively innocuous—but whose effects can be deadly. Price controls are often imposed at levels that make the controlled activity totally unprofitable and cause it to wither. Licences and other direct controls are frequently administered by incompetent bureaucrats, who tie up business activity in red tape. As a matter of prestige of the currency, exchange rates are often set so high that exports from the LDC cannot compete on the world market. The governments sometimes expropriate and seek to operate foreign firms before they have trained native personnel to run them. In short:

Poorly conceived economic policies can impede business activity and hence economic growth in the LDCs. But, then, it must be admitted that the LDCs have no monopoly on foolish economic policies!

Help from Industrialized Economies

We have just seen that two of the primary needs of the LDCs are technical skills and capital resources. Happily, these are precisely the things that the more prosperous nations are in a position to offer. We have the trained teachers, classrooms, laboratories, and equipment necessary to provide an education of the highest quality to students from the LDCs.

However, there is a danger here that has received a great deal of attention, the so-called **brain drain**. This refers to the temptation for students from LDCs to try to stay in the countries where they have studied and enjoy the higher living standard, rather than to return home where their abilities are needed so badly.

There are several ways to deal with this. For example, one can require students to return to their homelands for at least some given number of years after completion of the educational program, or offer higher wages for trained persons in the LDCs to make returning more attractive. Yet the problem is there, and the large number of doctors, teachers, and other skilled personnel from LDCs who are seeking jobs in the developed countries suggests that it is not negligible.

A second major contribution that the wealthier countries can make to the LDCs is to offer them trained technicians and technical advice from their own populations. Such counselling and personnel can be very helpful as a temporary measure, but in the long run they can prove detrimental if provision for the training of local personnel for the ultimate replacement of the foreign technicians and advisers is not built into the program.

A third, and very important, type of assistance from the developed to the less developed countries takes the form of money or physical resources provided either as loans made on favourable terms or as outright grants (gifts). In a moment we will consider some of the contributions that the industrial world has recently made in this area.

Fourth, the world can help the LDCs through research. One of the hardest problems for the developing world is what to do in the rural areas that suffer from inadequate rainfall, where several hundred million people live in both Asia and Africa. These people are badly in need of new dry-farming techniques. Until some are discovered, their poverty will increase as their numbers grow. An international research organization devoted to food production in problem areas in the LDCs would have much to contribute.

Finally, and perhaps most important, the developed countries can help by encouraging freedom of trade and investment. This will help those LDCs whose exports are readily expanded but that are now being held back by barriers to trade. Exports of sugar, meat, cotton, and other agricultural products are inhibited by tariffs and other restrictions. There are many discriminatory duties against processed, as distinct from crude, materials. A significant number of LDCs would also benefit substantially from a lifting of quotas and other restrictions upon the export of manufactured goods. Increased freedom of trade will also help those LDCs whose economies offer business prospects sufficiently bright to attract significant quantities of private capital from abroad. All in all, increased freedom of trade is a matter of highest priority for the LDCs.[9]

[9]Not everyone agrees with this conclusion. There are those who have argued that participation of LDCs in international trade is bad for them because it weakens their capacity to develop as self-reliant, mature economies. It is held that new manufacturing industries in the LDCs will not take off without protection from foreign competition. Development of primary product exports creates a rich and politically powerful vested interest that inhibits measures that would favour manufacturing. The extent to which foreign trade and production of exports are in foreign hands inhibits domestic saving and the development of local entrepreneurship.

In this view, LDCs are therefore held back by international trade and they would do better to integrate regionally and develop their own home markets without foreigners, who also bring unsuitable habits, unsuitable tastes, and unsuitable technology, and impart a crippling inferiority complex to the natives.

Loans and Grants to the LDCs

The Canadian International Development Agency (CIDA) is the government department that supervises Canada's aid programs for developing countries. Canada provides assistance to approximately 80 countries, and in 1981–82 this aid amounted to $1.46 billion. Just over one-third of our contributions to developing countries are made directly to the country (bilaterally), and the remainder is made through the U.N., development banks, and other agencies (multilaterally). The bilateral assistance takes the form of grants or low-interest-rate loans. The loans are used to purchase materials or services for industry or agriculture from Canada or to gain access to the Canadian market. Asia receives the largest share of our bilateral aid ($209 million in 1980–81), then Francophone Africa ($137 million), Commonwealth Africa ($110 million), Latin America ($29 million), and the Caribbean ($27 million). The multilateral assistance supports 65 programs, with a major portion going to the World Bank Group and regional development banks.

The World Bank was created after World War II, and has 144 member countries. Each member provides an amount of capital to the bank that is related to the member country's wealth; for instance, the United States has contributed approximately one-third of the total. The Bank makes loans that are financed by bonds that it issues and sells, and has acted as guarantor of repayment to encourage some private lending and has established agencies, that have played major roles in providing funds to the LDCs. The Bank has loaned almost $70 billion to LDCs and to countries that can be considered on the borderline. It has tended to emphasize loans for infrastructure, dams, communications and transportation, and, in addition, has provided technical assistance and planning advice.

The remainder of Canadian aid to the LDCs goes to U.N. programs, relief funds for disaster victims, food aid, business, labour, and academic exchanges, and technical assistance.

In the past few years, expenditures on foreign aid have become less popular politically, and the amounts provided by Canada have consequently gone down from 0.5 percent of GNP in the mid-1970s to 0.4 percent of GNP in 1982. Contributions have fallen more drastically in the U.S., from about half a percent of U.S. GNP in 1965 to well under 0.27 percent of GNP in 1982.

Aid has come from other industrialized countries, notably France, Great Britain, West Germany, and the Soviet Union. While the Soviet funds have obviously been distributed in a way intended to maximize its political advantage, it can hardly be claimed that Western aid programs have been free of political considerations.

Many economists have advocated greater generosity in our assistance to LDCs and have deplored cuts in our aid programs. Aside from any moral responsibility to help the impoverished countries, it is argued that an effective aid program that really helps the growth of LDCs will also serve our own interests. By making those countries more stable economically and politically, we can contribute to our own economic tranquility. By increasing the LDCs' power to buy and sell, we are in effect contributing to the prosperity of the entire world.

The "North–South" Controversy and Commodity Price Stabilization

The conflict of interests between the LDCs and the industrialized countries has come to be called, somewhat inaccurately, the "North–South confrontation," with the "North" referring to the wealthy nations and the "South" denoting the poor countries. The international trade arrangements, which the North considers to constitute a free market for the unhampered exchange of goods for the mutual benefit of all participants, are widely viewed in the South as a thinly disguised instrument of old-fashioned imperialism to be used to exploit the poorer economies.

A major cause of this discontent is the prices of the commodities, such as cocoa and sugar, which the South considers to be unfairly low and distressingly unstable. There has been considerable pressure for international agreements that will take steps to reduce the upswings and downswings of these prices. It has been proposed that a stabilization fund be organized and used to buy such commodities when their prices are falling and to sell them when their prices are rising. That is, by shifting demand outward when prices are relatively low, the fund would raise these prices; and by shifting demand downward when prices are comparatively high, it would force these prices downward.

But negotiations have stalled over at least two issues. First, the industrialized countries want much of the money for the stabilization fund to be supplied by the less developed countries themselves, while the latter want most of the fund to be financed by the industrialized countries who buy these products. So far, a tentative agreement has been reached for the creation of a modest fund with both North and South contributing to it. But the second issue is perhaps more serious. The North intends the stabilization fund to do only what its name implies: to iron out fluctuations in commodity prices, not to raise or lower those prices on the average. But to many southern countries "stabilization" actually is a diplomatic way of referring to their desire to *raise* commodity prices, something the North is predictably reluctant to do.

Can LDCs Break Away from Poverty?

It is easy to jump to the conclusion that the economic problems of the LDCs are staggering and that the prospects of their ever catching up with the industrialized countries are negligible. Certainly, some LDCs are in very bad straits. Yet a number of LDCs and former LDCs have made enormous progress. The African countries Kenya, Cameroon, and the Ivory Coast increased their GNPs during the 1970s at a rate of about 5 percent to 6 percent a year, which is considerably faster than their population growth. In the Americas, Costa Rica's performance has been comparable. Even more striking is the expansion of output in a number of places in the Far East—particularly Hong Kong, Taiwan, South Korea, and Singapore, where prosperity is unprecedented and economic activity is expanding at an astonishing rate. Here per-capita GNPs have been growing at a rate of 6.5 percent a year and more.

But the most impressive case is that of Japan. Many of your professors will remember clearly when North American businesses feared the flood of goods produced by cheap Japanese labour, and when the label "made in Japan" suggested inexpensive and shoddy merchandise. From one of the world's impoverished countries, Japan has risen to one of the world's richest. Its goods are now feared by manufacturers elsewhere not because they are produced and sold so cheaply, but because their quality is so high. Japanese cars and sophisticated electronic equipment find a ready market throughout the world. And as a result, per-capita income in Japan has surpassed that in Great Britain. A less developed country need not lag behind forever.

Summary

1. If growth is evaluated in terms of its effect upon the well-being of individuals, a country's economic growth should be measured in terms of *per-capita* income, not in terms of GNP or some other index of total output of the economy.

2. A rapidly rising population poses a threat to growth of per-capita incomes.

3. On our finite planet, exponential growth (growth at a constant percentage rate) is, in general, impossible except for relatively brief periods.

4. Increases in growth depend heavily on entrepreneurship, accumulation of capital equipment, and research and development.

5. Saving is necessary for the accumulation of resources with which to produce factories, machinery, and other capital equipment. Thus, saving is a critical requisite for growth, particularly in less developed countries.

6. Many observers argue that even if continued growth does not lead to catastrophically rapid depletion of resources (as some have predicted), its desirability is nevertheless questionable because it produces pollution, overcrowding, and many other undesirable consequences.

7. Those who favour growth argue that without it there is no chance of ridding the world of poverty.

8. Standards of living in many LDCs are extremely low; per-capita incomes that are equivalent to $600 a year are not uncommon. Life expectancy is low and daily living is very difficult, particularly for women.

9. GNP and per-capita incomes in many LDCs grew considerably in the 1970s.

10. Nevertheless, the gap between family incomes in the less developed and the industrialized countries has continued to widen.

11. In many LDCs population continues to grow much faster than that in the industrialized countries.

12. Growth in the LDCs is impeded by shortages of capital caused by poverty, traditions that do not encourage investment, rapid population growth, poor education, unemployment, lack of entrepreneurship, and government impediments to business.

13. Industrialized countries can help the LDCs by providing capital through loans and grants, by offering training and education to people from those lands, and by encouraging freedom of trade with the LDCs.

14. In the post-World War II period, many countries have provided money to the LDCs in the form of loans and grants, as does Canada through CIDA.

15. Several international organizations, most notably the World Bank, have been organized to provide economic assistance to the LDCs.

Concepts for Review

Output per capita
Exponential growth
Social infrastructure
Exchange between present and future consumption
Embodied growth

Disembodied growth
Less developed countries (LDCs)
Growth rate in GNP vs. per-capita income
Multinational corporations
Disguised unemployment

Entrepreneurship
Brain drain
World Bank
CIDA

Questions for Discussion

1. Which do you think has the higher total GNP, Pakistan or Luxembourg? Which has the higher per-capita GNP? In which do you think people are better off economically?

2. Suppose population grows at a constant exponential rate and doubles every 10 years. How many times will it have grown in 30 years? How many years does it require to expand to 16 times its initial level?

3. Can you think of any innovations that permit growth without proportionate increases in use of inputs?

4. Name as many undesirable consequences of growth as you can think of.

5. Are the undesirable consequences of growth more likely to be considered serious in a less developed country or in an industrialized country? Why?

6. To many families living in less developed countries, an income equivalent to $2000 per year is considered a high standard of living. Can you make up a budget for a Canadian family of four earning $2000 a year?

7. Explain how it is possible for the per-capita income of an LDC to grow at a faster rate than that in Canada and yet for the difference between the incomes of average families in both countries to increase. Can you give a numerical example showing how this happens?

8. Discuss the advantages and disadvantages to an LDC of a Canadian manufacturing company investing in that country.

9. If you were economic adviser to the president of an LDC, what might you suggest that he or she do to encourage increases in saving and investment?

10. No one knows what encourages or discourages the supply of entrepreneurs. Do you have any ideas about policies that may be capable of stimulating entrepreneurship?

11. Name some countries in which entrepreneurship seems to be abundant these days; some countries in which it seems to be scarce.

12. Discuss what you have read in the newspapers and heard from other sources about the Japanese "growth miracle." What does it portend for the future of the Japanese economy? For that of Canada?

VIII

Alternative
Economic Systems

Comparative Economic Systems: What Are the Choices?

Every generation regards as
natural the institutions to
which it is accustomed.
R. H. TAWNEY

These words of the British historian and economist R. H. Tawney are worth heeding as we near the end of this book, which has been geared very closely to the particular circumstances of contemporary Canada. Our current economic institutions are not eternal. Economic systems are not static; they grow, adapt, and evolve. Even in the relatively stable environment of Canada, the economy of the 1980s is far different from the economy of the 1880s, and by the year 2080 our economy will have changed even more.

Tawney's remark can be applied across geographical space as well as through time. The world today has a great diversity of economic systems, and this diversity seems likely to prevail in the future. There are, in fact, many ways to organize an economy other than the mixed capitalistic structure that we have focused on in this book. And no one form of economic organization is likely to be the right one for all countries for all time.

In this chapter, we examine some of these *alternative economic systems* and consider how a society might choose an appropriate form of economic organization. The first parts of the chapter sketch out the elements of the two major choices that must be made by every society: Should economic activity be organized through *markets*, or by government *plan*? And should industry be *privately* or *publicly* owned? As we shall see, there are arguments on both sides of each question; and, as you might expect, different countries in different times have made different choices.

In the last sections of the chapter, we therefore turn to some of the actual choices that have been made in the contemporary world. We examine, in turn, the economic structures of Sweden, France, Yugoslavia, the Soviet Union, and the People's Republic of China, looking in each case for similarities and differences among countries, and for areas in which one system has either succeeded admirably or failed miserably. Does Canada have much to learn from the experiences of these other countries? Read this chapter, and then decide.

The Challenge to Modern Capitalism

The question of choosing among economic systems is far from academic. Indeed, it has been of vital concern to people throughout the world for centuries, and it remains an issue today. For example, almost 30 years ago former Soviet leader Nikita Khrushchev made his famous promise to Americans that "we will bury you." This was not a military threat nor a prediction that capitalism would perish under the weight of its own garbage; rather it was a pledge that the great productivity and growth of the Soviet economy would enable it to surpass the productive capacity of the U.S. economy. So far, the Russians have not redeemed this pledge. (See the boxed insert on the next page.) But the economic competition between these two giant nations has captured the attention of the world for decades.

Many of the observers of this competition have a keen interest in its outcome. Nations of the Third World have watched attentively, wondering which economic system might be best for them. During the years since Khrushchev's declaration, a number of these nations seem to have made a choice. But many others are still teetering on the brink of indecision. Should they try to emulate the U.S. system of free markets, as, to a degree, Taiwan and Brazil have done? Should they follow the route of "democratic socialism" that is favoured by many Western European nations, a route approximately travelled by Israel and India? Should they enter the Soviet sphere and opt for a communist system with rigid state planning, as North Korea and Vietnam seem to have done? Or, finally, should they choose a more revolutionary brand of communism, following the model of Cuba?

The choices are many. And they are of the utmost importance because a nation's economic structure has a profound influence not only over its material well-being, but also over its political system, the individual rights of its citizens, its relations with other countries, and so on.

And the Third World is not the only place where the contest among alternative economic systems is going on. In recent years, several countries in Western Europe—including France, Spain, and Italy—have flirted with communism in a serious way. Most observers agree that the miserable failure of the capitalist world to perform satisfactorily during the 1970s gave Eurocommunism, as it is called, much of its momentum.

On the other side of the Iron Curtain, several nations are flirting with capitalism. Yugoslavia and Hungary, in particular, rely very heavily on markets and the price system to guide their "communist" economies, and China is moving in that direction.

Naturally, non-economic factors play major roles in any debate over the future of a nation's economic system. Internal political considerations, for example, are probably far more important than economic analyses. Yet, to a considerable extent, the proof of the pudding will be in the eating. Demonstrated success of either free markets or state planning in solving economic problems probably will do more to sway the undecided nations than all the ideological incantations in the world.

Economic Systems: Two Important Distinctions

Economic systems can be distinguished along many lines, but two seem most important. The first is, *How is economic activity co-ordinated—by the market or by the plan?* The question does not, of course, demand an "either, or" answer. Rather the choice extends over an entire range, running from laissez faire to rigid central planning, with many, many gradations in between. Society must decide to what extent it wants decisions made by individual businesses and consumers, each acting in their own self-interest, to determine their economic destiny, and to what extent it wants to persuade these businesses and consumers to act more "in the national interest." It is worth stressing that most types of planning involve some degree of *coercion*. This term is not necessarily pejorative, however; all societies, for example, coerce people into not stealing from their neighbours.

The second crucial distinction among economic systems concerns the

Will They Bury the American Economy?

In 1958, Soviet Premier Nikita Khrushchev made his boastful pledge about "burying" the United States economically. His optimistic mood was probably coloured both by Russia's successful launching of an earth satellite and by the outstanding performance of the Soviet economy that year: real growth of almost 11 percent over 1957. With the United States simultaneously slipping into a severe recession, the ratio of Soviet GNP to American GNP jumped from 39 percent in 1957 to 44 percent in 1958 (see the accompanying chart).

No sensible statistician would extrapolate the performance of one year very far into the future. But Khrushchev was a flamboyant political leader, not a sensible statistician. By 1965, the ratio was still stalled at 44 percent and, perhaps by coincidence, Khrushchev had been ousted and was living the quiet life. As the chart shows, the Soviet/U.S. GNP ratio resumed its upward climb in the late 1960s, and by 1975 had reached 53 percent—owing in part to another serious recession in the United States. The ratio was about the same in 1982.

It may be helpful to put these figures into historical perspective. According to one estimate, Russian and American GNPs were about equal on the eve of the American Civil War. But czarist Russia did not do well compared with capitalist America, and by 1913 Russian GNP had dwindled to only 39 percent of American GNP. With the enormous human and economic losses of World War I, the Russian Revolution, and the ensuing civil war, Soviet GNP fell still further—to only about 27 percent of U.S. GNP at the start of the First Five-Year Plan (1928).

Then came the beginnings of rapid economic growth in the U.S.S.R. and the Great Depression in the United States. Soviet GNP climbed swiftly to 42 percent of the U.S. level at the start of World War II, only to fall back to

29 percent after the wartime devastation. From that point, it climbed rather steadily and was still rising when Khrushchev made his famous boast.

What of the future? It is anyone's guess. A prudent long-run estimate for the U.S. growth rate might be 3 percent a year. As for the Soviet Union, only a few years ago experts were projecting a long-term annual growth rate of 5 to 5½ percent. However, the poor performance of the Soviet economy in recent years has led these estimates to be scaled down to the 2 to 3 percent range, or even lower.

If the Soviet economy does manage to grow 5 percent per year while the U.S. economy grows 3 percent per year, the Soviet Union will indeed "bury" the United States with a larger GNP by around the year 2015. (Remember, though, that the population of the U.S.S.R. is about 20 percent larger than that of the United States.) On the other hand, if current projections prove correct and the Russian economy grows no faster than that in the United States, the burial will never take place.

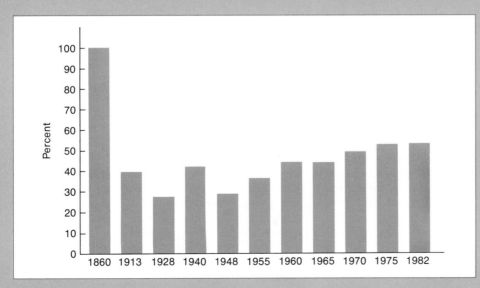

RATIO OF RUSSIAN REAL GNP TO U.S. REAL GNP

SOURCE: Herbert Block, "Soviet Economic Power Growth— Achievements under Handicaps," *Soviet Economy in a New Perspective. A Compendium of Papers Submitted to the Joint Economic Committee,* Congress of the United States, 94th Congress, 2nd Session, October 1976. Updated to 1982 by the authors.

question, *Who owns the means of production?* Specifically, are they privately owned by individuals or publicly owned by the state? Again, there is a wide range of choice and, to our knowledge, there are no examples of nations at either the **capitalist** extreme where all property is privately owned or at the **socialist** extreme where no private property whatever is permitted.

> **Capitalism** is a method of economic organization in which private individuals own the means of production, either directly or indirectly through corporations.

For example, while most industries are privately owned in Canada the owners face restrictions on what they can do with their capital. Owners of automobile companies must comply with environmental and safety regulations. Owners of communication and transportation companies, where these are privately owned, often have both their prices and the conditions of their services regulated by the government. And in communist Russia, where no one can own a factory, anyone who can afford it can own a car or hold a bank account. There is also a small "capitalist" sector in which, for example, peasant farmers can sell what they have grown on their small private plots of land.

> **Socialism** is a method of economic organization in which the state owns the means of production.

There is a tendency to merge the two distinctions between economic systems and think of capitalist economies as those that have both a great deal of privately owned property *and* rely heavily on free markets. By the same token, socialist economies typically are thought of as heavily planned. However:

While there is an undeniable association between the degree of socialism in a country and the degree to which it plans its economy, it would be a mistake to regard these two features as equivalent.

Modern Yugoslavia, for example, provides an important instance of a country in which the means of production are socially owned but economic activity is organized mainly by markets. Closer to home, there is a great deal of state ownership in the United Kingdom, which is most assuredly a market economy. Germany under Hitler provided an example of a capitalist economy with rigid central planning.

We are not suggesting that capitalist economies are typically as heavily planned as socialist ones. In fact, socialist states normally have more economic planning. However, in thinking about the society's *choice* among economic systems, it is best to keep the two distinctions separate.

The Market or the Plan? Some Issues

The choice between **planning** and reliance on **free markets** requires an understanding of just what the market accomplishes and where its strengths and weaknesses lie. Since these issues have been the focal point of much of this book, our review can be rather concise here.

What goods to produce and how much of each.   In a market economy, consumers, by registering their dollar votes, determine which goods and services shall be provided and in what quantities. Items that are not wanted, or that are overproduced, will suffer a fall in price, while items that are in short supply will rise in price. These price movements act as *signals* to profit-seeking firms, which then produce larger amounts of the goods whose prices rise and less of the goods whose prices fall. This mechanism is what we call **consumer sovereignty**.

> **Consumer sovereignty** means that consumer preferences determine what goods shall be produced, and in what amounts.

Of course, the doctrine of consumer sovereignty must be qualified in several ways when we deal with the real, rather than the ideal, world. For one thing, governments interfere with the price mechanism in many ways—taxing some goods and services while subsidizing others. These interferences certainly alter the bill of goods that the economy produces. For another, we have learned that in the presence of **externalities** the price system sends out false signals, leading to inappropriate levels of output for certain commodities.

How to produce each good.   In a market economy, firms decide on the production technique, guided once again by the price system. Inputs that are in short supply will be assigned high prices by the market. This will encourage producers to use them sparingly. Other inputs whose supply is more abundant will be priced lower, which will encourage firms to use them.

Once again, the same two qualifications apply: Government taxes and subsidies alter relative prices, and externalities may make the price system malfunction. But on the whole, the market system has yet to meet its match as an engine of productive efficiency.

How income is distributed.   The same price system that determines the levels of wages, interest rates, and profits also determines the distribution of income among individuals in a market economy. As we have stressed (especially in Chapter 38), there is no reason to expect the resulting income distribution to be "good" from an ethical point of view. And, in fact, the evidence shows that capitalist market economies produce a considerable degree of inequality.

This is certainly one of capitalism's weak points, though there are many ways for the government to alter the distribution of income without destroying either free markets or private property (for example, through progressive income taxation or a negative income tax, both of which were discussed in Chapter 38). It is also noteworthy that some planned economies have rather unequal income distributions.

Economic growth.   The rate of economic growth depends fundamentally upon how much society decides to save and invest. In a free-market economy, these decisions are left to private firms and individuals who determine how much of their current income they will consume today and how much they will invest for the future. Once again, however, government policies can influence these choices by, for example, making investment more or less attractive through tax policy.

Business fluctuations.   As we explained in Parts Two and Three a market economy is subject to business fluctuations—periods of boom and bust, inflation and unemployment. This holds not only in capitalist market economies like Canada's, but also in socialist market economies like that of Yugoslavia. Interestingly, the highly planned but mostly capitalist economy of France showed very little evidence of business-cycle problems from 1958 until the mid-1970s. Thus it seems that the business cycle, which Marx dubbed one of the fundamental flaws of *capitalism*, is really a problem for *market* economies, be they capitalist or socialist.

Let us now go over this list again, seeing how each question is resolved in a planned economy, and comparing this with a market economy.

What to produce and how much.   Under central planning, the bill of goods that society will produce normally is not selected by consumer sovereignty. Instead, the planners decide. Depending on their particular beliefs and on the political structure of the country, their decisions may or may not be strongly influenced by consumers' desires.

Whether this is a strength or weakness of central planning depends upon your point of view. On the one hand, there is the danger that society's resources will be devoted to producing items that nobody wants. In Soviet Russia, for example, there are clearly fewer cars and more copies of Marx's *Das Kapital* than consumers want to buy. On the other hand, consumer sovereignty can lead to some bizarre products, the kinds of things that social reformers find offensive: designer jeans, fast-food chains, low-quality television programming, and so on. But, on balance, most adherents to traditional Western values will find more to like than to dislike under consumer sovereignty. After all, who knows what is good for consumers better than consumers themselves?

How to produce.   Planned economies can allow plant managers to choose a production technique, or they can let central planners do it instead. Under Soviet-style planning, plant managers have rather little discretion, and this has led to such monumental inefficiencies as production curtailments due to lack of materials, poor quality, and high production costs. No incentive system has yet been designed that can match the profit motive of competitive firms for keeping costs down.

How income is distributed.   The distribution of income is always influenced by government to some extent. Even in basically market economies like ours, the government taxes different people at different rates and makes transfer payments to others, seeking thereby to mitigate the inequality that capitalism and free markets tend to generate. Planned economies do the same things, and more. For instance, they may try to tamper directly with the income distribution by having the planners, rather than the market, set relative wage rates. This, however, leads to troubles similar to those mentioned in the previous paragraph. Thus, even in the Soviet Union relative wages are established more or less by supply and demand.

Economic growth.   In general, planned economies have much more direct control over their growth rates than do unplanned ones, simply because the state can determine the volume of investment. They therefore can, if they choose to, engineer very high growth rates—an option they often have exercised. Whether such rapid growth is a good idea, however, is another question. In Stalin's Russia and Mao's China, for example, this goal was achieved at enormous cost—some of it paid for by sacrificing current consumption, some by sacrificing personal freedom, and some by bloodshed. Furthermore, as we have seen, the U.S.S.R. has not been very successful in achieving its growth goals recently, while some of the fastest growth rates in the post-war world have been achieved by countries with market economies, like Japan.

Business fluctuations.   We explained in Chapter 8 (page 155) that business fluctuations are not much of a problem for highly planned economies. This is because total spending in such economies is controlled tightly by the planners, and it is not permitted to get far out of line with the economy's capacity to produce. As we shall see later in this chapter, the U.S.S.R. has many serious economic problems, but the business cycle is not one of them.

The Market or the Plan? The Scoreboard

As we look back over this list, what do we find? Concerning *what to produce*, an adherent to Western values probably would give a clear edge to the market, though conceding the need to curb some of its more flagrant abuses. But, of course, much of the world does not prize individualism as dearly as we in the West do.

As to *productive efficiency*, the market mechanism is clearly superior. But when we consider the *distribution of income*, we find that all societies have decided to plan; they differ only in degree.

High growth, it seems, can be achieved with or without planning, though planned systems may have an easier time of it. Here an advanced nation will pause to question whether faster is always better, and often will conclude that it is not. But among the less developed countries, the goal of rapid development is typically of paramount importance. Many of these countries also lack the savings and the financial markets needed to channel funds into their most productive uses. If so, they may have little choice but to plan.

Finally, in managing *business fluctuations*, there is no question that planned economies can do much better. The results of our scoreboard are clearly mixed. Do we, therefore, score the contest a tie? Certainly not. What we do conclude is:

Different countries—with their different political systems, value judgments, traditions, and aspirations—will score the contest differently. Some will find the market more attractive, while others will opt for the plan. Most will divide their economies into two sectors—leaving some decisions to the market mechanism and others to conscious planning.

Capitalism or Socialism?

Although the choice between capitalism and socialism seems to excite more ideological fervour, it may be much less important than the choice between the market and the plan.

If it could design an appropriate incentive structure, a socialist market economy could do just as well as a capitalist market economy in terms of producing the right set of goods in the most efficient way. However, we have emphasized the word "if" to underscore the fact that designing such an incentive system may be quite difficult under socialism.

Lacking the profit motive, a socialist society must provide incentives, either material or otherwise, for its plant managers to behave in the optimal way. This has proved difficult enough. But a still deeper problem caused by the absence of the profit motive is the need to maintain inventiveness, innovation, and risk-taking in a system in which large accumulations of personal wealth are impossible. Socialist systems are noticeably low on "high rollers."

Income distribution under socialism seems naturally more equal than under capitalism simply because the profits of industry do not go to a small group of shareholders but instead are dispersed among the workers or among the populace as a whole. However, if supply and demand rules the labour market, a socialist nation may have just as much inequality in the distribution of labour income as a capitalist economy does—and for the same reasons: to attract workers into risky, or highly skilled, or difficult occupations. Indeed, students of the Soviet economy have concluded that wage differentials in the U.S.S.R. are comparable to those in the United States.

The capitalist–socialist cleavage is much more important in regard to the issue of economic growth. To oversimplify, under capitalism it is the capitalists who determine the growth rate, while under socialism it is the state. Still, government incentives can prod capitalists to invest more; and instances of both fast and slow growth can be found under both systems.

Finally, the persistence of business fluctuations in a country depends much more on whether its economy is planned or unplanned than on whether its industries are publicly or privately owned.

Socialism, Planning, and Freedom

There is, however, a *non-economic* criterion that is of the utmost importance in choosing between capitalism and socialism, or between the market and the plan— *individual freedom.*

Planning must by necessity involve some degree of coercion; if it does not, then the plan may degenerate into wishful thinking. In the extreme case of a command economy (the Soviet Union, Nazi Germany), the abridgement of personal freedom is painfully obvious. Less rigid forms of planning involve commensurately smaller infringements of individuals rights, infringements that most people find quite tolerable. Even within a basic framework of free markets, some activities may be banned—such as prostitution and selling liquor to minors. Other economic activities may be compelled by law—safety devices in automobiles and labelling requirements on foods and drugs are just two examples. Each of these can be considered a type of planning, and each limits the freedom of some people. Yet most of these restrictions command broad public support in Western countries. The doctrines of consumer sovereignty and freedom of enterprise are not absolutes.

Taxation is still a more subtle form of coercion. Most people do not view taxes as seriously impairing their personal freedom because, even though tax laws may make them pay for the privilege, they remain free to choose the courses of action that suit them best. Indeed, this is one major reason why most economists favour taxes over quotas and outright prohibitions in many instances. It is true, however, that taxation can be a very potent tool for changing individual behaviour.

Individual freedom is also involved in the choice between capitalism and socialism. After all, under socialism there are many more restrictions on what a person can do with his or her wealth than there are under capitalism. On the other hand, the poorest people in a capitalist society may find little solace in their "freedom" if they are homeless and hungry.

Once again, it would be a mistake to paint the issue in black and white. Under extremely rigid authoritarian planning, the restrictions on individual liberties are so severe that they are probably intolerable to most people with Western values. But more moderate and relaxed forms of planning—for example, the French system discussed later in this chapter—seem quite compatible with personal freedoms.

Similarly, a doctrinaire brand of socialism that bans all private property (even the clothes on your back?) would entail a major loss of liberty. But a country with a large socialized sector can be basically free; the British, for example, do not feel any less free than do Canadians. And citizens of some countries with largely capitalist economies, such as South Korea or the Philippines, do not enjoy much political freedom.

The real question is not *whether* we want to allow elements of socialism or planning to abridge our personal freedoms, but by *how much*.

Just as your freedom to swing your arm is limited by the proximity of your neighbour's chin, the freedom to build a factory need not extend to building it in the midst of a residential neighbourhood. Just as freedom of speech does not justify yelling "Fire!" in a crowded movie theatre when there is no fire, freedom of enterprise does not imply the right to monopolize trade or to pollute.

A Catalogue of Blueprints

Different societies have struck the balance between the market and the plan and between socialism and capitalism in different places. What follow in the rest of this chapter are rather brief descriptions of some of the alternative economic systems actually in existence today.

The catalogue is ordered from the least socialized economy to the most. Thus we start with Sweden, where public ownership of the means of production is only slightly more common than it is in the United States and Canada, and work our way toward the "communist" economies of Russia and the People's Republic of China, where state socialism is the dominant form of economic organization.

This sampling of countries brings home the point that socialism and planning are not identical. Had we ordered the countries from the least highly planned to the most, Yugoslavia might come before France (perhaps even before Sweden), and China might come before Russia (see Table 41–1).

Sweden's Welfare State

The Swedish economy is sometimes characterized as a happy marriage between capitalism and socialism. But, in fact, at least as we have defined the terms, Sweden is almost as capitalistic as Canada and the United States: More than 90 percent of Swedish industry is privately owned. A more accurate statement is that:

Sweden has a capitalist market economy very much like our own, but with much more extensive government interference to promote two social goals of overriding importance: full employment and an equal distribution of well-being.

Table 41-1

ECONOMIC SYSTEMS OF SELECTED COUNTRIES

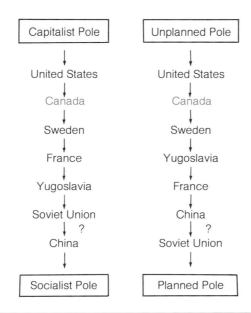

Economic systems may be ranked according to the extent of socialism or the extent of central planning. As this table shows, the rankings do not always correspond. There is some controversy over the relative rankings of China and the Soviet Union.

Full Employment Policy

Sweden has one of the longest and most active traditions of Keynesian macro-economic management in the world—a tradition that even predates Keynes's *General Theory of Employment, Interest, and Money* (1936). In addition to using the standard tools of monetary and fiscal policy more vigorously than we do in Canada, and inventing a few novel tools of their own, the Swedes limit unemployment by intervening directly in the labour market. For example, the Swedish government offers subsidies to private firms that maintain employment when production falls, allows early retirement for workers who lose their jobs, sponsors retraining programs, and, when necessary, hires workers directly into government jobs. As a result of all this, unemployment does not rise very much even when GNP falls.

Judging by the results, the Swedish full-employment policy seems to have borne fruit. Figure 41-1 compares the unemployment rates in Sweden and in Canada from 1960 to 1983. It is clear not only that the average rate of unemployment has been kept quite low (always below three percent until quite recently), but also that the fluctuations have been quite restrained. However, the Swedes have not been able to avoid recessions, and industrial production in Sweden has increased rather little in the last decade. In addition, as our discussion of the trade-off between inflation and unemployment suggests, the Swedes have paid the price for their low unemployment by making sacrifices on the inflation front (see Figure 41-2). Their inflation rate has typically been higher than ours.

Income-Distribution Policy

Sweden, as is well known, has one of the world's most comprehensive **welfare states**, with social programs that extend, quite literally, from the cradle to the grave. These include financial allowances for children, municipal day-care centres,

The term **welfare state** refers to a variety of government programs aimed at assisting the poor and unfortunate and protecting individuals from the rigours of the marketplace.

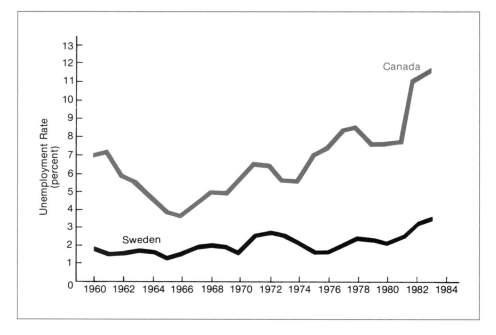

Figure 41-1

UNEMPLOYMENT IN SWEDEN AND CANADA

As this figure indicates, Sweden's unemployment rate has been consistently lower than ours, and its fluctuations have also been less severe.

SOURCE: Statistics Canada, *Statistical Abstract of Sweden*, and International Labour Office.

free education at all levels, a national health service, extensive benefits for the unemployed, retirement pensions that are more generous than our own Canada Pension Plan, and more social-assistance programs.

Naturally, the heavy burden of financing these programs leads to commensurately high taxes, and in recent years some of the disadvantages of a comprehensive welfare state have become more apparent. Critics argue, for example, that the steeply progressive Swedish income tax is destroying incentives to work.

None the less, Sweden's social-welfare programs have been effective in

Figure 41-2

INFLATION IN SWEDEN AND CANADA

As might be expected, Sweden has paid the price for lower unemployment by having more inflation than Canada. This figure shows that inflation in Sweden has normally been higher than inflation in Canada.

SOURCE: Organization for Economic Cooperation and Development.

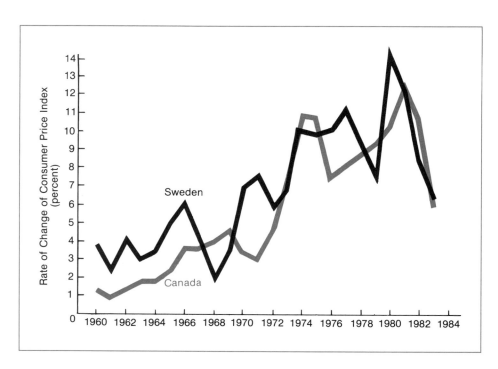

accomplishing their goals. It is really difficult to find the tell-tale signs of poverty, such as slums and shabby clothing, in Sweden. And it is widely agreed that Sweden has one of the most equal income distributions anywhere—a feat it has managed to accomplish while also becoming one of the richest nations in the world. Yet, here too there are problems. Absenteeism has been rising, demands for greater worker control over industry are being heard, and class antagonisms have arisen in this "classless" society.

In many ways, the Swedish and Canadian economic systems seem quite similar, and the apparent success of Swedish economic policy has raised the question of whether their principles can be applied here. Yet some fundamental differences exist, differences that may make it impossible to import Swedish economic policy to Canada.

First, Sweden is a very small country whose labour unions and industries are both highly concentrated. This facilitates "consensus building" and also makes co-ordination easy to accomplish without formal planning. Second, Sweden is a homogeneous country, so the linguistic and regional difficulties that underlie some of our problems are absent. Third, the Swedes care much more about full employment and much less about inflation than most Canadians do. They are proud of their strong record on employment and less concerned with their inability to maintain price stability. Canadians might react differently to this same record.

France: Planning by Consensus

The basically capitalist economy of France has developed a unique method of organizing economic activity that one expert has called "the most elaborate and detailed planning system among the advanced Western nations."[1] The system is called **indicative planning**, a name meant to suggest planning by voluntary compliance and agreement rather than by government coercion.

Under the French system, a national economic plan is hammered out and agreed to by representatives of government, industry, and labour, along with other technical experts. The aim is to achieve a good degree of *co-ordination* of economic activity without the need for *coercion* simply by passing both information and ideas back and forth among all the parties.

For example, if it turned out that the production plan of the automobile industry required the use of more steel than the steel industry was expecting to sell, the participants in the plan could sit down and reconcile the differences. Was one forecast too optimistic or too pessimistic? Would government actions (such as tariffs and import quotas) render these two forecasts consistent or inconsistent? Through negotiations like these, French planners hope that individual industries can discover potential shortages and surpluses before they arise, and thereby adjust their own plans to conform with a broad overall plan for the nation.

They further hope that *participation* in the plan will lead to *voluntary compliance*. Often this is so. But when it fails, the French government does not hesitate to use a wide variety of tools—including taxes, subsidies, and price controls—to persuade businesses to abide by the plan. It has been said that "French planning may be indicative, but it is not permissive or passive."[2]

The government exercises particularly strong control over both the volume and direction of investment spending: It directly controls about half of national investment and strongly influences the rest by regulating access to the credit market.

How well has the system performed? Until recently, very well indeed. Except

Indicative planning
means government *guidance*, rather than direct *control*, of economic activity.

[1]Gregory Grossman, *Economic Systems*, Second Edition (Englewood Cliffs, N.J.: Prentice-Hall, 1974), page 87.

[2]Egon Neuberger and William Duffy, *Comparative Economic Systems* (Boston: Allyn and Bacon, 1976), page 235.

Figure 41-3
FRENCH ECONOMIC
GROWTH SINCE 1958
This chart of real gross national
product in France shows a
remarkable absence of business
fluctuations. Only the severe
worldwide recession of 1974–1975
broke the upward march of real
GNP in France. But growth slowed
substantially in the early 1980s.
SOURCE: Organization for Economic
Cooperation and Development.

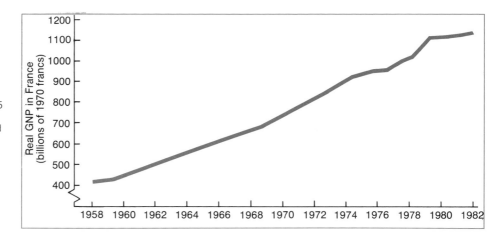

for the worldwide recessions of the mid-1970s and early 1980s, the French record is one of full employment and rapid growth (see Figure 41–3). Of course, this does not prove that indicative planning has been the key to France's success; West Germany, for example, grew even faster without planning. But it does suggest that something has gone right.

Indicative Planning for Canada?

While recent years have not been the best ones for the French economy, many countries envied the French growth record in the 1950s and 1960s, and some tried to emulate it. Can indicative planning be practised successfully in Canada? There are several reasons to think that it would not work as well here. First, the Canadian government controls a much smaller fraction of total investment than does the French government.

A second difference is that Canada does not have the French tradition of a close marriage between government and industry. The "old-boy" network is particularly strong in France, and many of the government officials and industrialists who work together on the plan are old friends from their days as students at France's elite *écoles*. State intervention in business has long been the norm in France; here it would be a major departure. Third, planning along French lines would run afoul of Canada's competition policy. With firms sharing common forecasts and production plans, and with the government parcelling our investment allotments to industries that then divide them among their constituent firms, collusion among firms is almost inevitable. This sort of cozy arrangement is widely accepted in France, where government tolerance of and even support for monopolies and cartels is traditional. It is only partly accepted in Canada; this sort of co-ordination is only permitted for export agreements.

Workers' Management in Yugoslavia

Yugoslavia was forced by events to become the clearest illustration in the contemporary world of the fact that "socialism" need not be synonymous with "planning." A serious political rift between Tito and Stalin in the 1940s kept Yugoslavia out of the Soviet economic sphere, and forced the Yugoslavs to go it alone.

Searching for a way out of their economic plight, the Yugoslavs embarked on a great economic experiment by passing the *Law on Worker Management of Enterprises* in 1950. This law and subsequent legislation gave to the workers of each firm the authority to make most of the decisions that are normally reserved for management. The world has watched this experiment with great interest.

Nowadays there is even talk that nations as far apart ideologically as Great Britain and China may have something to learn from the Yugoslav system, and experiments with **workers' management** have been made in the United States and Canada.

While Yugoslav industry is almost wholly socialistic, enterprises are *not* run by state-appointed managers following a national plan. Instead, Yugoslav managers are chosen by the workers and are expected to seek high profits.

While firms in Yugoslavia are subject to more regulations than firms in Canada, each Yugoslav firm can decide within limits *what* to produce, *how much* to produce, and by *what technique* to produce. Though there are a number of price controls, taxes, and subsidies, most commodity prices are established in free markets, and consumer sovereignty calls the tune. Firms flourish if they produce what consumers want and produce it efficiently. After paying for its non-labour inputs, each enterprise can decide how much of its net income to invest in expansion and how much to pay out in wages to its workers.

Under workers' management, Yugoslavia has achieved a record of very good growth in total output, but a number of problems have surfaced.

For one, like other market economies, Yugoslavia is subject to the ups and downs that we call the *business cycle*. This country has had periodic bouts with stagnation and seems plagued with both chronically high inflation and unemployment. The persistent inflation has led to greater reliance on price controls—a movement away from free markets that has been motivated not by ideology, but by desperation.

Income distribution has posed another problem. Since what is called *wages* in Yugoslavia includes a share of what is called *profits* in a capitalist system, equal work in different firms is not rewarded equally. Instead, workers in the most efficient enterprises earn a bonus, and the resulting wage disparities among different firms and different regions in the country have caused social friction.

Related to this are the twin problems of inadequate labour mobility and sluggish employment growth. In a capitalist system, the most efficient firms would expand, hiring more workers, and thus driving down their marginal productivity. Under Yugoslavia's system of worker control, this may not happen because workers in a highly profitable firm may care more about maximizing *profits per worker* than about *total* profits. Since profits per worker may well *fall* if more labour is allowed to join the enterprise, new employment opportunities may not arise very often.

While there is virtually no central planning of the Soviet variety, we would not want to leave the impression that the Yugoslav economy is totally unmanaged. This is not the case. But what planning there is, is of the French *indicative* style. As in France, the government exercises its control, often quite rigorously, through the credit market. There it influences both the overall volume of credit for investment purposes and the allocation of these funds among regions and industries.

The Soviet Economy: Historical Background

In November 1917, a determined group of Bolsheviks led by V.I. Lenin overthrew the democratic provisional government that Kerensky had established after the fall of the Czar just eight months earlier, and Russia became the first country in the world to establish a communist government. There is a great irony here in that this first triumph of communism contradicted one of the tenets of Marxian theory. Marx had prophesied that socialism would be the inevitable outgrowth of a decaying, advanced capitalist system. Instead, it came first to a land that had barely emerged from feudalism.

The Russian Revolution both surprised and dismayed the Western world, the more so since Lenin was an outspoken apostle of worldwide communist revolution. Outside support for the anticommunists helped prolong a bloody civil war between "Red" and "White" Russians, a war that Lenin's army finally won. It was out of the dire circumstances of a wartime economy that the Soviet system of state planning as we know it today emerged.

When the war was won, a pragmatic Lenin reacted to the chaotic legacy of the war by permitting substantial amounts of both capitalist ownership and market organization under his New Economic Policy (NEP). The NEP was a great success, especially among the peasants who were very hostile to the Communist regime, and it helped rebuild the badly battered Russian economy. After Lenin's death, there was both a fierce struggle for power within the Communist party and a vigorous policy debate over basic economic strategy. Joseph Stalin won both contests and ruthlessly set the Soviet Union on a course that it has followed, more or less, to this day.

Stalin's strategy called for single-minded application of Soviet resources to the goal of rapid *industrial* development with emphasis on *heavy* industry, particularly *armaments*.

To achieve such rapid growth and industrialization, it was necessary to limit consumption severely; so the Soviet consumer was asked—or rather forced—to make sacrifices. To feed the urban labourers needed for industrial expansion, the Soviet Union's backward agricultural peasants were forced—at an extremely high human and economic cost—onto collective farms, where they were required to sell their food at very low prices and to work for pitifully low wages.

The events of the early Stalinist years left their mark on Soviet economic life. To this day, the Soviet economy is characterized by:

- A high degree of centralization, with basic economic goals set by planners, particularly by the leaders of the Communist party. Lower levels of the hierarchy are expected to follow orders, though the methods of guaranteeing compliance are far less Draconian than in Stalin's day.

- A stress on growth, industrialization, and military power, with corresponding downgrading of consumption. While the Soviet GNP has grown quite rapidly since 1928, the Soviet consumer shared few of the fruits of this growth until quite recently.

- Continuing problems in the agricultural sector, where productivity is very low and the rural peasants remain quite poor.

- A planning system based on quantity targets and quotas, which makes very little use of the price system.

In surveying almost fifty years of Soviet economic development, one expert commented that "the surprising thing about the Soviet planning system is not how much it has changed since its inception, but how little."[3]

Central Planning in the Command Economy

The structure of the Soviet economic system is in many ways similar to the hierarchy of a giant corporation.

[3]Neuberger and Duffy, *Comparative Economic Systems*, page 168.

At the top may be a single strongman or a ruling clique. The political leadership plays the role of chairman of the board, setting overall policy objectives, but has much more absolute authority than that of the chairman of any corporation.

Given the overall goals and priorities established by the top echelons of the Communist party, the State Planning Commission (Gosplan, in Russian) has responsibility for the preparation of the national economic plans (discussed below). Beneath the Gosplan are a number of ministries, which direct each industrial sector, and the various regional authorities. These bureaus oversee the day-to-day management of the individual industries or regions within their purview.

Several other layers of the hierarchy intervene as we move down the organizational pyramid. Finally, we reach the level of the enterprise. Enterprise managers in the U.S.S.R. have far less authority than do their counterparts in Canada. They are expected to carry out directives handed down from above, fill their quotas, and send information back up the hierarchical ladder. They are bureaucrats rather than entrepreneurs.

Communications within the hierarchy are predominantly vertical. Orders flow down from top to bottom, while data flow up from bottom to top. Since the data requirements are so immense, and the number of layers within the bureaucracy so large, the problems of accurate data transmission and processing are monumental.[4] A detailed study of the operation of a large Soviet enterprise in the 1960s found that compliance with the plan required that 44 *million* characters of information be passed up to the next highest level in a single year, and that this was only about 12 to 15 percent of the total information gathered by the enterprise. This situation led one Soviet cyberneticist, in one of those wild extrapolations, to observe that preservation of the same planning apparatus until 1980 would require the employment of every Soviet adult.[5] As far as we know, the prophecy has not been fulfilled.

Markets and Prices in Soviet Economic Life

Although central planning is certainly dominant in Soviet economic life, the Soviets do rely on the market mechanism for some purposes.

For instance, *given* the production target for each consumer good as set down in the plan, Soviet planners try to set prices to ration the quantity demanded down to the available quantity supplied. The result is that consumer prices often are set far above production costs, with the difference made up by the so-called *turnover tax*, the main source of government revenue. But the planners often do not succeed in equating the quantities supplied and demanded, and any visitor to the Soviet Union is struck by the frequency with which long lines appear in front of many stores. Conversely, large stocks of unwanted goods sit waiting for customers at other establishments. Consumers do exercise free choice among the available goods, but they are certainly not sovereign.

The price system is used even more extensively in the labour market. Given the plan for industrial output, Soviet planners try to set wages to attract workers to the right industries and the right regions. With some exceptions, Soviet workers now have considerable freedom to work where they please—a far cry from the situation in Stalin's day. Partly as a result of the strong desire to direct labour to the areas assigned top priority by the plan, wage differentials among Soviet blue-collar workers are quite large. According to most observers, they are at least as large as those in the United States, and they lead to considerable inequality in the distribution of labour income. Of course, income from property is negligible in the

---

[4]Giant corporations have a similar problem of handling and transmitting data. However, not even the largest corporation approaches the size and scope of the Soviet economy.

[5]Neuberger and Duffy, *Comparative Economic Systems*, pages 179–80.

U.S.S.R., and the gap between blue-collar and white-collar incomes is far smaller than in Canada. Thus, the overall distribution of income is much more equal than ours.

The Five-Year and One-Year Plans

The Soviet Union's celebrated Five-Year Plans lay down the basic strategies and growth targets for Soviet economic development, but in many ways they are not as important as the less well known One-Year Plans.

Both of these documents are the responsibility of the Gosplan.

The **Five-Year Plans** set the nation's basic strategy for resource allocation: How much for investment? How much for consumption? How much for military procurement and for scientific research? They also provide guidelines for the distribution of these totals among the various industries (Will there be more cars or more refrigerators?), and they may include specific large construction projects, such as hydroelectric power plants.

Much attention is paid, both in the West and in the U.S.S.R., to the numerical goals posted by these plans. Table 41–2 lists a few of the goals and actual achievements of the Tenth Five-Year Plan (1976–80) and the Ninth Five-Year Plan (1971–75). It is clear that the goals set out in recent plans have not been attained. And it appears that the Soviet economy will also fail to meet the goals of the Eleventh Five-Year Plan (1981–85).

The Five-Year Plans are not detailed enough to serve as blueprints for action. This job is left to the **One-Year Plans**—enormous sets of documents covering almost every facet of Soviet economic life. In fact, One-Year Plans are so detailed and complex that any one of them is normally not completed until well into the year to which it applies. Sometimes these plans are never completed at all.

The planning procedure starts with a set of broad national goals (and some rather specific ones) handed down from the political leadership to the Gosplan. The planners then attempt to translate these goals—which are partly reflections of the current Five-Year Plan—into a set of specific directives for subordinate ministries and agencies. As the plan is passed down from one level of the hierarchy to the next, the lower level is constantly supplying the higher level with both data and suggestions for changes—changes in specific tactics, not in basic goals (which are never questioned).

One perennial problem of Soviet planning is that enterprises strive to obtain low production quotas that they will find easy to meet and surpass, because their success is measured by their ability to meet the quotas. To this end, they may deliberately mislead their superiors and understate their productive capacity.

Table 41–2
THE NINTH AND TENTH SOVIET FIVE-YEAR PLANS

ITEM	TENTH FIVE-YEAR PLAN (1976–80)		NINTH-FIVE YEAR PLAN (1971–75)	
	TARGET GROWTH RATE (percent per year)	ACTUAL GROWTH RATE (percent per year)	TARGET GROWTH RATE (percent per year)	ACTUAL GROWTH RATE (percent per year)
GNP	5.0	2.7	6.7	5.1
Industrial output	6.3	3.6*	8.0	7.4
Agricultural output	4.9	2.3*	4.0	2.5

*Pertains to 1976–79.
SOURCE: *The Soviet Economy in 1978–1979 and Prospects for 1980.* National Foreign Assessment Center, Central Intelligence Agency, June 1980, updated by authors.

The process of give-and-take up and down the hierarchy eventually leads to a complete One-Year Plan that, the planners hope, is *internally consistent*. Consistency, however, is not often achieved. To see why, let us briefly consider one of the major problems of Soviet planning—achieving what they call **material balance**. This phrase means nothing more than equating quantity supplied and quantity demanded for each type of input—a manageable task for a market economy, but an overwhelming one for Soviet planners.

To take a simple example, suppose three industries (called A, B, and C) use ball bearings. The output targets for industries A, B, and C will then imply a corresponding need for inputs of ball bearings. This quantity (the quantity of ball bearings demanded) must, then, be equal to the output target of the ball-bearing industry (the quantity of ball bearings supplied). This seems simple enough. But the complications become apparent once it is realized that the ball-bearing industry needs inputs, too, and that some of these inputs may be the outputs of industries A, B, and C. So if, for example, the production of ball bearings is to be increased, more steel and machinery may be required; and these additional outputs will require more ball bearings as inputs; and so on and so on.

To see the complexity of the task facing Soviet planners, try your hand at the following simple problem. Suppose there are only three goods—ball bearings, steel, and automobiles—and that the national plan calls for individual consumers to get no ball bearings, $\frac{1}{2}$ unit of steel, and 1 unit of automobiles. How much must each of the three industries produce to achieve material balance?

To try to answer this, you must know the input requirements of each industry. Suppose the inputs required *per unit of output* of each industry are as follows:

OUTPUT	NECESSARY INPUTS
Ball bearings (one unit)	$\frac{1}{2}$ unit of steel *plus* $\frac{1}{4}$ unit of automobiles
Steel (one unit)	$\frac{1}{4}$ unit of ball bearings *plus* $\frac{1}{4}$ unit of steel *plus* $\frac{1}{4}$ unit of automobiles
Automobiles (one unit)	$\frac{1}{3}$ unit of ball bearings *plus* $\frac{1}{2}$ unit of steel *plus* $\frac{1}{6}$ unit of automobiles

Use trial and error to figure out the necessary production levels for each industry. It will not take long to convince yourself that the problem is quite difficult.[6]

The mathematical technique devised to cope with problems like this is called *input–output analysis*,[7] and the preceding little problem is easily solved using this method. But the Soviet planners face a problem of this character with, literally, tens of thousands of commodities. Not even the most sophisticated high-speed computer is capable of carrying out the necessary calculations—even if all the data were available. In short, a perfectly correct solution to the problem of material balance is currently impossible.

What, then, do the Soviets do? In practice, input–output analysis is of little

[6]The answer is: 2 units of ball bearings, 4 units of steel, and 3 units of automobiles.
[7]Input–output analysis was discussed in Chapter 26, pages 512–14.

use in formulating One-Year Plans. Trial and error is the only viable approach, and planners seek to avoid as many material imbalances as they can in the time allotted to them. They concentrate particularly on avoiding any bottlenecks in those industries that are accorded highest priority by the political leadership. If necessary, Soviet planners will redirect scarce inputs to the high-priority sectors to make sure that production there is not interrupted. Thus, Soviet spacecraft factories are unlikely to close down for lack of steel, but factories producing toasters are quite likely to.

Performance and Problems of Soviet Planning

Most observers rate the Soviet performance as quite good on growth, at least until recently, but quite poor on economic efficiency.

Rigorous economic planning brought the backward Soviet economy of the 1920s into the modern age very quickly. Post-war economic growth averaged about 7 percent in the 1950s and somewhat more than 5 percent in the 1960s. However, like the Western economies, the Soviet economy has experienced a growth retardation in recent years. The Soviet growth rate slipped into the 3 to 4 percent range—about the same as the U.S. growth rate—during the 1970s and seems to have been only about 2 percent per year in the early 1980s.

There are several reasons for this slowdown in Soviet economic growth. For one thing, part of the rapid early growth was achieved by borrowing advanced technology from the West; this obviously could not last forever.

For another, the Soviet Union (like the Western countries) achieved part of its industrial growth through the migration of peasants to the cities—which also could not last forever.

A third factor was the increasing outcry of the Soviet citizenry for more and better consumer goods. Only in recent years was the regime willing to accommodate these demands, and this required cutting back on investment.

Finally, the plain fact is that the Soviet economic mechanism does not function very smoothly and seems to be growing increasingly arthritic. The rigorous system of central planning that worked in Stalin's day, when the economic goals were simple and well defined, seems ill-suited to the more sophisticated modern Soviet economy, with its complex and diverse goals.

Both Western and Soviet observers agree that the Soviet Union's economic problems are manifold:

- Concern with quotas and targets *stifles innovation*, despite rewards for plant managers who innovate. Innovation carries risks, and Soviet managers worry about not fulfilling their plan. They also realize that a brilliant production performance this year will bring with it a much tougher quota next year.

- We have already mentioned the tremendous *burden of information transmission*. The result is that planners are often misinformed and make correspondingly incorrect decisions. The fact that firms seeking easy quotas have an incentive to falsify information compounds this problem.

- The system of production targets based on physical quantities rather than on profits or sales often leads to *huge stockpiles of unwanted and inferior goods and equally huge waiting lines for other goods*. For example, since automobile factories generally have quotas stated in terms of cars, there is an almost legendary shortage of spare parts in the Soviet Union. Manufacturers simply do not want to produce things that do not help fulfill their quotas. Similarly, a manufacturer ordered to produce 10,000 pairs of shoes, but faced with a shortage of leather, may produce 10,000 pairs of children's shoes. Selling them is not his concern.

The Visible Absence of the Invisible Hand

Since we live in a consumer-oriented society, it is hard to imagine what everyday life is like in a society where the consumer is not king. No one disputes the fact that the consumer has not yet ascended to the throne in the Soviet Union. In the following excerpt from an article in *Time* magazine, we get a glimpse of the problems that plague the Russian consumer.

The workingman, and particularly the working woman, ... spends an inordinate amount of time tracking down scarce consumer goods.... Although the capital is by far the best-supplied city in the Soviet Union, TIME Moscow Bureau Chief Marsh Clark reports that "soap, toothpaste, perfumes, detergents, toilet paper, hairpins and matches are either of inferior quality or not available at all. The soaps don't clean, the mint-flavoured toothpaste is harsh and repugnant, and the perfumes smell like overripe raspberries." The shortages are so common that people join any queue they see, then ask what it is for. In Moscow recently, Clark spotted a crowd jostling about a man selling something at a table. As the eager buyers got nearer, they saw the choice item on sale was an English-language textbook entitled *Animal Physiology*.

Along with shortages, there are bizarre examples of superabundance. Because of poorly coordinated planning and lack of inventory control, goods may suddenly appear in disproportionate profusion. Tiny commissaries on collective farms that carry only the barest necessities may suddenly receive shipments of silk neckties or Italian vermouth. A decade ago there was a glut of condoms, which Russians casually used as bottle caps and garters; today, there is a rubber shortage, and prophylactics can scarcely be found in Moscow....

Letters and editorials in the Soviet press often

complain about the inferior quality of Soviet-made merchandise.... According to Moscow's *Literary Gazette*, the seal of quality, which indicates that an item conforms to international standards, was awarded in 1974 to only .6% of all Soviet footwear and less than 1% of clothes. *Krokodil* [a Soviet humour magazine] recently published a satirical sketch about a couple seeking to buy furniture. The sofas were all big, clumsy and "of a shade combining the colors of a country backroad in autumn and of a World War I dreadnought destroyer." The author recommended against buying these dreadnought sofas because "one mustn't scare the children with furniture."

SOURCE: "Inside Russia: A Nation of Parallel Lives," TIME, March 8, 1976, pages 7–8. Copyright 1976 Time Inc. All rights reserved. Reprinted by permission from TIME.

- Because government policy has generally led to shortages of most consumer goods, managers of enterprises producing these goods have been able to turn out *low-quality merchandise*, knowing that eager consumers will buy up almost anything. (See the boxed insert above.)

- Worries about the future unavailability of materials have led some Soviet enterprises to maintain *inventories of crucial materials at levels that would be considered ludicrous in North America*, and sometimes even to hide this fact from the authorities.

- The Soviet Union has never been able to develop a satisfactory agricultural system.

Widely publicized reforms in 1965, following suggestions made by the Soviet economist E. Liberman (and hence dubbed "Libermanism"), attempted to deal with some of these problems by introducing the profit motive into Soviet enterprise. With managerial bonuses based on *sales* or *profits*, it was hoped that some of the adverse incentives of the quantity-oriented planning system could be avoided. The reforms scored some measure of success, but most observers feel that they were too limited to change the basic character of Soviet industry. For many enterprises, the quantity of output is still the most important indicator of success. Furthermore, the profit motive may not produce desirable results when market prices indicate neither production costs nor values to consumers.

China Under Mao: Revolutionary Communism

A brief look at the economy of the People's Republic of China is an excellent way to conclude this chapter because the Chinese have spent much of the last 35 years groping to find an economic model that suits them. In the process, they have vividly confronted the fundamental questions of this chapter—socialism or capitalism? market or plan?—and have come up with different answers at different times.

Immediately after the communist takeover in 1949, the Chinese economy was patterned on the Soviet model and developed with Soviet economic aid and technical expertise. In particular, China's was very much a command economy, perhaps even more so than the Soviet economy. Also, China's emphasis on rapid economic growth, particularly industrial growth, was quite similar to that of the U.S.S.R. Finally China, like the U.S.S.R., accorded high priority to the goal of economic self-sufficiency. Until the mid-1970s, China's foreign trade was negligible.

But there were also important differences stemming in part from ideology and in part from the fact that the Soviet model was not quite suitable to China. Probably the most important of these differences was the decision by Mao Tse-tung *not* to rely on **material incentives** to motivate the work force. Mao and the Chinese leadership looked with disdain at this "bourgeois" practice and preferred to motivate Chinese workers by exhortation, patriotism, and, where necessary, force. The U.S.S.R. bent its socialist doctrine somewhat in order to accommodate human nature. But Chinese communism for many years seemed determined to bend human nature to accommodate Maoist doctrine—to create "the new man in the new China," an effort that has now been abandoned.

A second, less important, difference is that Chinese planning has always been rather less centralized than Soviet planning. Local and industrial authorities have more power and discretion than they do in the U.S.S.R. This decentralization probably was dictated by China's immense size and economic backwardness in 1949. Without modern communications equipment (and perhaps even *with* it), there was no way for planners in Peking to hope to control economic activity in the outlying provinces.

Chinese economic growth under the communist regime has proceeded in fits and starts.

The immediate problem after the Maoist takeover was to lift China from the devastation of World War II, and to establish communist institutions and values in a vast and semi-literate country. With Soviet assistance, the plan was apparently quite successful at first. But when the Soviet model ran into problems, Mao changed course.

China's next step, the **Great Leap Forward** (1958–60), turned out to be a giant step backward. Why did the Great Leap Forward fail so miserably? First, the Great Leap's production goals were unrealistically ambitious from the start. Second, because the ideologically pure "Reds" were in Mao's favour while the technocratic "experts" were not, the means selected for carrying out the Great Leap were more romantic than rational. China's vast economic structure was supposed to be decentralized, though tightly controlled by the communist party; massive applica-

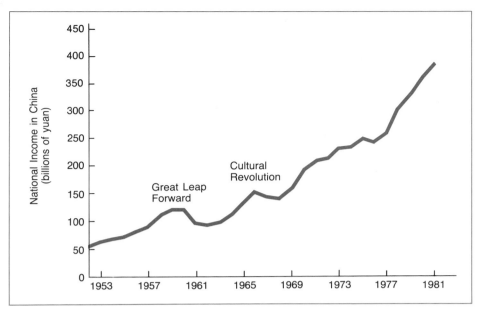

Figure 41-4
NATIONAL INCOME IN THE PEOPLE'S REPUBLIC OF CHINA
While Chinese economic statistics are notoriously inaccurate, the official data are portrayed here. The data are in current prices, with no correction for inflation. However, inflation in China has been quite low. The Great Leap Forward and the Cultural Revolution stand out as major blemishes on the record of Chinese economic growth.
SOURCE: Statistical Yearbook of China.

tions of brute labour were supposed to make up for China's shortages of machinery and advanced technology; and material incentives were de-emphasized.

In retrospect, the Great Leap Forward seems to have achieved several things—most of them not very good for China. First, China's gross national product fell substantially (see Figure 41-4), particularly in the agricultural sector. It took years to make up for the losses of 1958-60. Second, the ideological excesses of the period accelerated the growing schism between the U.S.S.R. and China. Third, it persuaded the Chinese leadership to throw out the "Reds" and bring back the "experts," signalling a return to rational economic calculation.

In large measure, China's Five-Year Plan covering 1961 to 1965 moved this giant nation back toward the Soviet model, though some elements of decentralization from the Great Leap were retained. One departure both from Soviet practice and from China's first Five-Year Plan (1953-57), however, was the greater emphasis on agricultural development—no doubt a wise decision given China's resources. As a result, economic growth resumed.

Then, inexplicably, Mao changed China's course once again with the **Great Proletarian Cultural Revolution** (1966-69). The "Reds" were in and the "experts" were out as never before. The infamous Red Guards (later assisted by the army) were sent out to purge rightist elements from Chinese society, organize revolutionary cadres, and spread the teachings of Chairman Mao. If anyone worried about economic productivity in this environment, it did not show. By the summer of 1967, both the Chinese economy and other elements of Chinese society were in utter disarray. Output fell again, but recovered much more quickly than it had from the Great Leap (see Figure 41-4).

Things began to change in the 1970s. The period until Mao's death in 1976 was one of consolidation and economic growth. The Chinese revolutionary fever receded and, once again, the "experts" were rehabilitated. There was a restoration of material incentives and of rational economic calculation—both of which had been considered reactionary during the Cultural Revolution. In general, there was less politics and ideology and more economic growth.

China Since Mao

Since the death of Mao, the Chinese economic system has once again been changing rapidly. The leaders who succeeded Mao have shown themselves to be far less interested in doctrine and far more interested in results.

The technicians and scientists who fell into disgrace under Mao's Cultural Revolution were rehabilitated and put into positions of influence. In a startling reversal of roles, it was Mao and the revolutionaries whose wisdom was questioned.

Late in the 1970s, the Chinese began a series of reforms that eventually amounted to the virtual abandonment of the Soviet model and the adoption of important features of the market economy in its place. China, long closed to the West, began to welcome Western tourism, trade, and technology. Chinese managers, engineers, and economists visited Western nations to study modern business techniques.

Perhaps most important, material incentives were restored, and the Chinese showed themselves willing to experiment with a wide variety of different models of economic organization. The Yugoslav system of worker management was studied carefully. Even capitalism was allowed back on the Chinese mainland.

These trends have accelerated in the 1980s, as market forces have been allowed to supplement central planning more and more. Farmers have been given land to do with as they please—after they pay a fixed amount of produce to the state. Markets, and even limited amounts of local entrepreneurship, have been allowed to flourish. Foreign companies have been invited to set up operations in China, and the Chinese seem eager to learn the ways of Western business. Late in 1984, the Chinese government announced its intention to allow more elements of free enterprise into its economy.

Given China's volatile past, no one really knows how far these trends will go or how long they will last. As of this writing, China remains a firmly communist and highly planned economy—but one that is moving further and further away from the Soviet model.

Summary

1. Economic systems differ in the amount of planning they do and in the extent to which they permit private ownership of property. However, socialism (state ownership of the means of production) need not go hand in hand with central planning, and capitalism need not rely on free markets. The two choices are distinct, at least conceptually.

2. Free markets seem to do a good job of selecting the bill of goods and services to be produced and at choosing the most efficient techniques for producing these goods and services. Planned systems have difficulties with both these choices.

3. Market economies, however, do not guarantee an equitable distribution of income and are often plagued by business fluctuations. In these two areas, planning seems to have clear advantages.

4. A major problem for socialism is how to motivate management to achieve maximal efficiency and to maintain inventiveness in the absence of the profit motive.

5. Individual freedom is a non-economic goal that is of major importance in the choice among economic systems. Any elements of planning or of socialism will infringe upon the personal freedoms of some individuals. Yet complete freedom does not exist anywhere, and certain limitations on individual freedom command wide popular support.

6. The Swedish economy is almost entirely capitalistic, and there is little planning. The chief departures from the Canadian economic system are in the comprehensive ways the Swedish government intervenes to maintain full employment and in its extensive "welfare state."

7. Much more planning is done in France, which also has a somewhat larger socialist sector than Sweden. But French planning differs from coercive Soviet-style planning in that it is "indicative," that is, it relies on consensus-building and on voluntary compliance.

8. Yugoslavia has a unique type of economic system called workers' management in which the managers of a firm are actually employed by the workers, who make all major decisions for themselves. While it is almost entirely socialist, the Yugoslav economy relies mainly on free markets and does very little planning.

9. Since the days of Stalin, the Soviet Union has followed a rather rigid system of central planning in which heavy industry and armaments are emphasized and consumer needs are de-emphasized.

10. The U.S.S.R.'s planning system is very bureaucratic and hierarchical; it has encountered monumental difficulties in transmitting accurate information. Goals and methods are set forth in Five-Year Plans and in even more detailed One-Year Plans.

11. While Soviet consumers are free to spend their money on what they please, there is no consumer sovereignty. Instead, it is the planners, not the consumers, who decide what will be produced. The labour market, however, operates much like it does in North America—using wage rates to equate supply and demand.

12. With central planning replacing the price system, even tasks that are rather simple for a market economy can become inordinately complex. The Soviet Union's difficulties in achieving material balance—that is, in equating supply and demand for the various inputs—illustrate this complexity.

13. The Chinese economic system has changed several times since the Communist takeover in 1949, passing through several periods of intense revolutionary fervour and little economic progress. Planning there appears now to be similar to that in the U.S.S.R., although somewhat less centralized.

14. Recently, the Chinese have been introducing more and more aspects of the market economy—and even bits of capitalism—into their economic system.

Concepts for Review

Capitalism
Socialism
Planning
Free markets
Consumer sovereignty

Welfare state
Indicative planning
Workers' management
Soviet Five-Year and One-Year
   Plans

Material balance
Material incentives
Great Leap Forward
Great Proletarian Cultural
   Revolution

Questions for Discussion

1. Explain why the choice between capitalism and socialism is not the same as the choice between markets and central planning. Cite an example of a socialist market economy and of a planned capitalist economy.

2. If you were the leader of a small, developing country, what are some of the factors that would weigh heavily in your choice of an economic system?

3. Which type of economic system generally has the most trouble achieving each of the following goals? In each case, explain why.
   a. An equal distribution of income.
   b. Adequate incentives for industrial managers.
   c. Eliminating business fluctuations.
   d. Balancing supply and demand for inputs.

4. What are some of the advantages and disadvantages of the system of workers' management of industry as it is practised in Yugoslavia?

5. "Both the goals and the techniques of Soviet economic planning have changed dramatically since Stalin's day." Comment.

6. If you were a Soviet plant manager, what are some of the things you might do to make your life easier and more successful? (Use your imagination. Soviet plant managers do!)

7. At the beginning of the chapter, we posed the question, "Does Canada have much to learn from the experiences of these other countries?" Given what you now know about Sweden, France, Yugoslavia, the U.S.S.R., and the People's Republic of China, what do you think?

Dissenting Opinions: Conservative, Moderate, and Radical

42

Let a hundred flowers
blossom. . .
Let a hundred schools of
thought contend.
MAO TSE-TUNG

The principles that have been expounded in this book represent the mainstream view of modern economics. While they command the assent of a large majority of Canadian economists, there are dissenters. And these dissenters are not all fanatics and polemicists. Many of them are serious thinkers who are disturbed in one way or another by some aspects either of the Canadian economy or the state of economic science, or both.

The dissent comes both from the left and the right of the mainstream of economics. On the right are the *libertarians*, who, while they agree with the portrayal of the virtues of the capitalist market economy given in this book, would no doubt insist that we have vastly overstated its vices and limited the realm of the market much too severely. To libertarians, the market rather than the state is the ultimate guarantor of freedom, and, consequently, they argue that the realm of the market should be expanded at the expense of the state. These are economic Jeffersonians who believe "that government is best that governs least."

Toward the left, the celebrated Canadian-born liberal economist and author, John Kenneth Galbraith, has been arguing for thirty years that most of the economics profession has been using the wrong model of the economy and, as a predictable result, has been generating policy prescriptions that look more and more absurd. Still farther to the left, a new group of *radical economists*, claiming to be the intellectual heirs of Marx, has attracted increasing numbers of adherents since its beginnings in the late 1960s. These critics claim that mainstream economists not only are asking all the wrong questions and seeking answers in all the wrong ways, but are little more than apologists for the interests of the capitalist ruling class.

The reader who has come this far will no doubt realize that the authors of this book generally ascribe to the mainstream view. But since that perspective has had a sufficiently long airing in this book, we believe it is useful now to take a brief look at the views of the dissenters. For one thing, history may yet prove that at least some of the dissenters have been right after all! In any event, it is certain that each of the critiques carries valuable lessons for mainstream economic analysis. Indeed, as we shall see, parts of each dissenting view have already been integrated into the body of standard economic analysis.

The Libertarian Credo

Libertarianism is a school of thought that emphasizes the importance of individual freedom.

Libertarianism is really a philosophy rather than a system of economic thought. Libertarians prize individual freedom above all other social goals—way above them. They are willing to tolerate restrictions on individual freedom in only a very few cases; so few, in fact, that most observers find the more extreme variants of libertarian doctrine totally outlandish. Would you, for example, permit unhappy 10-year-olds to run away from home *legally*, provided only that they could support themselves? Would you sell city streets and highways to private businesses to operate for a profit? Would you permit drug companies to sell anything they want, without labelling requirements (but with legal liability for any harm done by their products)? There are libertarians who would advocate all of these measures, and many, many more.[1]

On economic matters, libertarians are usually associated with the political right wing as staunch defenders of laissez faire. But in issues concerning civil rights, legislation of morality, and protection of citizens against government coercion, their views coincide more with the political left wing. There can be no question that they fervently support civil liberties. As one outspoken libertarian put it:

The central idea of libertarianism is that people should be permitted to run their own lives as they wish. We totally reject the idea that people must be forcibly protected from themselves. A libertarian society would have no laws against drugs, gambling, pornography—and no compulsory seat belts in cars. We also reject the idea that people have an enforceable claim on others, for anything more than being left alone.[2]

The Libertarian Economics of Milton Friedman

The hallmark of libertarian economics is a belief—we might call it a *devout* belief—in the ability of free markets not only to do the tasks normally assigned to them by economists (efficient production of goods, utilization of scarce resources, and so on), but to do *almost everything.*

There is no question that the leading apostle of libertarian economics is Milton Friedman. So unquestioned is his pre-eminence that the libertarian school is often referred to by economists as the "Chicago School," a name acquired during the many years that Friedman taught at the University of Chicago.[3] While he is a sufficiently brilliant technical economist to have earned the Nobel Prize, he is also an irrepressible public advocate of his libertarian views. In fact, it is in this latter role (frequently voiced in newspaper and magazine articles) that Friedman has received the most notice, or notoriety. We might as well treat Friedman as the spokesman for all libertarian economists, for that is more or less what he is. According to Friedman:

The kind of economic organization that provides economic freedom directly, namely, competitive capitalism, also promotes political freedom because it separates economic power from political power and in this way enables the one to offset the other.

Historical evidence speaks with one voice on the relation between political

---

[1]See, for example, David Friedman, *The Machinery of Freedom* (New York: Harper & Row, 1973), where each of these is advocated.

[2]Friedman, *The Machinery of Freedom*, page xiii.

[3]He is now retired and a resident scholar at the Hoover Institution in Stanford, California. In fairness, we should note that the University of Chicago has had several other great libertarian economists on its faculty.

---

freedom and a free market. I know of no example in time or place of a society that has been marked by a large measure of political freedom, and that has not also used something comparable to a free market to organize the bulk of economic activity.[4]

We have spent many pages in this book detailing the appropriate role of government in a modern mixed capitalist society (see especially Chapters 26 and 29). Friedman would make this role much smaller, limiting it essentially to the following three tasks.

1. *The government as umpire*. Friedman is surely no anarchist, although some libertarians are. He recognizes that any society needs laws, and that legislation and enforcement of the laws are proper roles for government in a free society. The government must, for example, enforce private contracts and adjudicate disputes.[5]

2. *Control of natural monopoly*. As we have noted in earlier chapters (see especially Chapters 27 and 30), some industries have such strong economies of large-scale production that it is inevitable, for technical reasons, that only one firm can survive. Telephone service, for example, probably comes close to fitting this model. Some have suggested (though others have disputed the claim) that the post office also is a good example. In such cases, *competitive* capitalism is simply impossible, so society has only three choices:

- Allow an unregulated private monopoly to exist.
- Make the industry a public monopoly (as in the case of Canada Post).
- Allow private monopoly to exist, but regulate it carefully "in the public interest" (as we do, for example, with telephone companies).

To Friedman, "all three are bad, so we must choose among evils." While Friedman is willing to decide which of the three alternatives is least bad on a case-by-case basis, he is skeptical that the choice that is often made (regulated monopoly) is the best one.

3. *Externalities*. For reasons we have elaborated at some length in this book (see especially Chapters 31 and 34), the government must intervene to promote or protect the public welfare wherever there are beneficial or detrimental externalities. If it does not, the competitive price system will send out false signals and, as a result, will misallocate resources.

Friedman accepts this analysis but cautions against applying it too freely. The externalities argument, he notes, often is just an excuse for allocating to the public sector something that could be done better by the private sector. And even in such cases as the control of pollution, where government intervention in the market can *in principle* improve the allocation of resources, the government may not have the knowledge it needs to correct the externality.

...the very factors that produce the market failure also make it difficult for government to achieve a satisfactory solution. Generally, it is no easier for government to identify the specific persons who are hurt and benefited than for market participants, no easier for government to assess the amount of harm or benefit to each. Attempts to use government to correct market failure have often simply substituted government failure for market failure....The imperfect market may ... do as well or better than the imperfect government.[6]

---

[4]Reprinted from *Capitalism and Freedom* by Milton Friedman by permission of the University of Chicago Press (Chicago: University of Chicago Press, 1962), page 9.

[5]More extreme libertarians will suggest that even police protection could be a private enterprise. See, for example, Robert Nozick, *Anarchy, State, and Utopia* (New York: Basic Books, 1974), in which the state *arises from* a private system of police protection.

[6]Milton and Rose Friedman, *Free to Choose* (New York: Harcourt Brace Jovanovich, Inc., 1979), pages 214–18.

An Application of Libertarian Economics: The Licensing of Doctors

Your family doctor has a licence to practise medicine in your province. He probably displays it prominently on his wall. You probably would be worried if he did not have one. Yet libertarians like Professor Friedman think that licensing of doctors is a bad idea. He explains why in this excerpt from his celebrated book *Capitalism and Freedom.**

Offhand, the question, "Ought we to let incompetent physicians practice?" seems to admit of only a negative answer. But I want to urge that second thought may give pause.

Licensure is the key to the control that the medical profession can exercise over the number of physicians. . . .The American Medical Association is perhaps the strongest trade union in the United States. The essence of the power of a trade union is its power to restrict the number who may engage in a particular occupation. . . .

Control over admission to medical school and later licensure enables the profession to limit entry in two ways. The obvious one is simply by turning down many applicants. The less obvious, but probably far more important one, is by establishing standards for admission and licensure that make entry so difficult as to discourage young people from ever trying to get admission.

To avoid misunderstanding, let me emphasize that I am not saying that individual members of the medical profession . . . deliberately go out of their way to limit entry in order to raise their own incomes . . . the rationalization for restriction is that the members of the medical profession want to raise what they regard as the standards of "quality" of the profession. . . .

It is easy to demonstrate that quality is only a rationalization and not the underlying reason for restriction. The power of the . . . American Medical Association has been used to limit numbers in ways that cannot possibly have any connection whatsoever with quality.

The simplest example is their recommendation . . . that citizenship be made a requirement for the practice of medicine. I find it inconceivable to see how this is relevant to medical performance.

It is clear that licensure has been at the core of the restriction of entry and that this involves a heavy social cost. . . . Does licensure have the good effects that it is said to have?

It is by no means clear that it does raise the standards of competence in the actual practice of the profession. . . .The rise of the professions of osteopathy and of chiropractic is not unrelated to the restriction of entry into medicine. . . .These alternatives may well be of lower quality than medical practice would have been without the restrictions on entry into medicine.

More generally, if the number of physicians is less than it otherwise would be, and if they are fully occupied, as they generally are, this means that there is a smaller total of medical practice by trained physicians.

When these effects are taken into account, I am myself persuaded that licensure has reduced both the quantity and quality of medical practice. . . . I conclude that licensure should be eliminated as a requirement for the practice of medicine.

*For further discussion of this issue, see Discussion Question 3 at the end of this chapter (page 854).

SOURCE: *Capitalism and Freedom* by Milton Friedman by permission of the University of Chicago Press (Chicago: University of Chicago Press, 1962), pages 149–59.

Beyond this short list, Friedman believes, there is little else for government to do in a free society.

Libertarian Economics and Public Policy

We began this discussion of libertarianism by giving some examples of rather extreme policy proposals made by some libertarians (though not necessarily by Milton Friedman). Yet some of Friedman's suggestions, which many people considered absurd when they were first made, have since been incorporated into the mainstream of economic thought or have become the law of the land, or both.

For example, Friedman's was one of the first voices arguing that the system of fixed exchange rates among currencies was potentially dangerous and should be replaced by a system of floating rates, set not by governments but by supply and demand. We now have such a system. Friedman was also among the earliest advocates of the all-volunteer army in the United States. This piece of "insanity" became fact in 1973. His proposal for a negative income tax as a means to help poor people (see Chapter 38) is now supported by almost all economists—be they of the left, the centre, or the right. The hostility toward the many government regulatory agencies that is now so much in vogue was present in Friedman's speeches and writings long before it became fashionable.

Yet there are many, many other issues about which the majority of economists and society as a whole continue to believe that Friedman is wrong. (See the boxed insert on the preceding page.) His voice continues to be one of dissent, and one that is every bit as radical as those on the far left. But that voice is irrepressible. As a *Wall Street Journal* columnist put it:

Mr. Friedman, it appears, has grown convinced that his ideas can be made to work here on earth just as marvelously as they already do in heaven.[7]

John Kenneth Galbraith: The Economist as Iconoclast

Milton Friedman is barely over five feet tall; John Kenneth Galbraith is about six and one-half feet tall. There the similarity ends. Friedman's reverence for the market is countered by Galbraith's irreverence about almost everything. Friedman's proposals for laissez faire are opposed by Galbraith's proposals to control almost everything.

John Kenneth Galbraith is a phenomenon in modern economics. This perpetual maverick, who has been blasting (often in ascerbic tones) what he calls "the conventional wisdom" for thirty years, was a member of the Department of Economics at Harvard University—the bastion of the "establishment"—until his retirement in 1975. Without a doubt the most widely read economist in the world, he is perhaps more highly regarded outside the profession than within it. Yet his fellow economists elected him president of the prestigious American Economic Association in 1972. In addition to his achievements in economics, he has been an adviser to presidents, the U.S. ambassador to India, leader of the Americans for Democratic Action, novelist, and TV personality. As one prominent economist put it:

Galbraith is ... something special. His books are not only widely read, but actually enjoyed. He is a public figure of some significance; he shares ... the power to shake stock prices by simply uttering nonsense. He is known and attended to all over the world. He mingles with the Beautiful People; for all I know, he may actually be a Beautiful Person himself.[8]

Galbraith began to move away from his successful career as a mainstream economist—which included a stint as a price-controller during World War II—with the publication of his book *American Capitalism* in 1952. There he argued that economists, in focusing on the interplay between supply and demand in impersonal markets, ignored the pervasiveness of **economic power** and thereby blinded

A buyer or seller is said to have **economic power** if, by his own actions, he can influence the market price.

[7]Alfred L. Malabre, Jr., "The Milton Friedman Show," *The Wall Street Journal*, January 11, 1980. Reprinted by permission of *The Wall Street Journal*© Dow Jones & Company, Inc. 1978. All rights reserved.

[8]Robert M. Solow, "The New Industrial State or Son of Affluence," *The Public Interest*, no. 9 (Fall 1967), page 100. Copyright© 1967 by National Affairs, Inc.

themselves to some of the most important things that were going on in the economy. He added further wrinkles to his developing view of the modern capitalist economy in his best-selling book *The Affluent Society* (1958), in which he argued that modern corporations, far from being the servants of consumer sovereignty they are supposed to be, actually *create* demand for their products through advertising.

These and other strands of Galbraithean thought were brought together in *The New Industrial State* (1967), which remains perhaps the most comprehensive statement of his views on modern capitalist enterprise. The book was, and is, quite controversial.

The Galbraithean Critique of Conventional Economic Theory

Galbraith maintains that conventional economists have squirreled themselves away in a dream world of their own creation, a world that has less and less to do with the real modern economy. In this hypothetical framework:

The best society is the one that best serves the economic needs of the individual. Wants are original with the individual; the more of these that are supplied the greater the general good. Generally speaking, the wants to be supplied are effectively translated by the market to firms maximizing profits therein. If firms maximize profits they respond to the market and ultimately to the sovereign choices of the consumer.[9]

The crucial omission from this picture, in Galbraith's view, is *power*, especially the power of the giant corporation, but also the power of big labour, government bureaucracies, and so on. Rather than being controlled by the market, he believes, the modern corporation controls, or even supplants, the market.

By ignoring these phenomena, Galbraith claims, economists have been led into increasingly ridiculous policy positions. For example, the theory of monopoly (outlined in Chapters 27 and 30) stresses the *inefficiency* caused by its *restriction of output* in order to raise prices. Yet, as Galbraith sees the world, it is precisely the giant corporations that are most *efficient* and who produce *excessive amounts* of output. They do this by advertising campaigns that create the demand for the goods they are so adept at supplying.

As another example, the focus on markets has led the vast majority of economists to oppose wage and price controls and therefore to accept the disagreeable trade-off between inflation and unemployment (see Chapter 18). Galbraith's is one of the few voices that refuses to accept this trade-off, putting his faith instead in a *permanent* system of wage–price controls.

What does the Galbraithean model of our economy look like? In the first place, according to Galbraith, our economy involves a great deal of *planning*.

In place of the market system, we must now assume that for approximately half of all economic output, there is a power or planning system ... I cannot think that the power of the modern corporation, the purposes for which it is used or the associated power of the modern union would seem implausible or even very novel were they not in conflict with the vested doctrine.[10]

[9] J. K. Galbraith, "A Review of a Review," *The Public Interest* (Fall 1967), page 117.
[10] J. K. Galbraith, "Power and the Useful Economist," *American Economic Review* (March 1973), page 4.

This *planning system* is run by *technocrats*: managers, engineers, accountants, lawyers, cyberneticists, even economists! The kinds of work they do, and the kinds of hierarchical structures they create, are more or less similar in corporations, non-profit institutions, government bureaus, and even (to a limited extent) labour unions. The nature of their work is also basically the same under capitalism as it is under socialism, in market economies, or in planned economies. It is dictated not by ideology, but by the overwhelming complexity of modern technology. "The enemy of the market is not ideology but the engineer."[11]

These technocrats, whom Galbraith calls the **technostructure**, manipulate consumer demand through advertising. They also manipulate costs to a considerable degree, or else render them quite predictable through long-term contracts with labour unions and suppliers of other inputs (which are also giant corporations). And since the industrial giants can finance their own investment through retained earnings, they need not rely on the capital market. Thus, the market is bypassed.

The firm must take every feasible step to see that what it decides to produce is wanted by the consumer at a remunerative price. And it must see that the labour, materials, and equipment that it needs will be available at a cost consistent with the price it will receive. It must exercise control over what is sold. It must exercise control over what is supplied. It must replace the market with planning.[12]

The technocrats are guided by their own self-interest, not by the interests of their shareholders. In particular, they are certainly *not* interested in maximizing profits.

Instead, their primary interest is growth and expansion.

If the technostructure ... maximizes profits, it maximizes them ... for the owners. If it maximizes growth, it maximizes opportunity for ... advancement, promotion and pecuniary return for itself. That people should so pursue their own interest is not implausible.[13]

The Galbraithean Critique of the Modern Economy

What are the results of this system for organizing economic activity? Not very good, according to Galbraith. First, North American society is deluged with a dazzling array of private consumption goods of dubious merit:

What is called a high standard of living consists, in considerable measure, in arrangements for avoiding muscular energy, increasing sensual pleasure and for enhancing caloric intake above any conceivable nutritional requirement.[14]

Second, the nature of the system of want-creation effected by the planning system dictates that the outputs of the giant corporations will be produced in abundance while the outputs of what might be considered "competitive" industries (home building, for example) will remain puny:

That the present system should lead to an excessive output of automobiles, an improbable effort to cover the economically developed sections of the planet with

[11]J. K. Galbraith, *The New Industrial State* (Boston: Houghton Mifflin, 1967, and London: André Deutsch, Ltd., 1967), page 33.
[12]Galbraith, *The New Industrial State*, page 24.
[13]Galbraith, "A Review of a Review," page 113.
[14]Galbraith, as quoted by R. M. Solow, "The New Industrial State or Son of Affluence," page 107.

asphalt, a lunar preoccupation with moon exploration, a fantastically expensive and potentially suicidal investment in missiles, submarines, bombers, and aircraft carriers, is as one would expect. These are the industries with power.[15]

Third, there is a shocking disparity between the abundant supplies of private consumption goods and the pitiful supplies of public consumption goods. The reason? The advertising industry does not whet consumers' appetites for public goods. "The engines of mass communication, in their highest state of development, assail the eyes and ears of the community on behalf of more beer but not of more schools."[16]

Fourth, and finally, the system shows a shocking disregard for the environment, or what may be termed more generally "the quality of life":

The family which takes its mauve and cerise, air-conditioned, power-steered, and power-braked automobile out for a tour passes through cities that are badly paved, made hideous by litter, blighted buildings, billboards, and posts for wires that should long since have been put underground. They pass on to a countryside that has been rendered largely invisible by commercial art....They picnic on exquisitely packaged food from a portable icebox by a polluted stream and...spend the night at a park which is a menace to the public health and morals. Just before dozing off on an air mattress, beneath a nylon tent, amid the stench of decaying refuse, they may reflect vaguely on the curious unevenness of their blessings. Is this, indeed, the American genius?[17]

A Critique of the Critique

The typical mainstream economist's reaction to Galbraith is to ignore him. However, on occasion, the Galbraithean challenge has been met head-on.

Undoubtedly, the best of these occasions was when a prominent mainstream economist, Professor Robert Solow of M.I.T., published a scathing review of *The New Industrial State* in 1967. Solow's basic contentions were, first, that while the Galbraithean view of the economy no doubt contains some important insights (for example, modern economics pays too little attention to the giant corporation), the things that Galbraith appeals to as "facts" are really not facts at all; and second, that the Galbraithean model as a whole lacks structure and coherence. Our guess is that Solow's review of Galbraith represents the views of many economists. And since Solow is one of the few economists who can match Galbraith's wit and verbal dexterity, their debate is both lively and informative.

Has the modern corporation really pre-empted the market mechanism? Solow thinks not:

It is unlikely that the economic system can usefully be described either as General Motors writ larger or as the family farm writ everywhere ... it will behave like neither extreme.... Galbraith's story that the industrial firm has "planned" itself into complete insulation from the vagaries of the market is an exaggeration, so much an exaggeration that it smacks of the put-on.[18]

Has advertising really robbed the consumer of his sovereignty and made him a puppet of the corporation? Solow finds the claim vaguely implausible, and wants to see evidence:

[15]Galbraith, "Power and the Useful Economist," page 7.
[16]J. K. Galbraith, *The Affluent Society* (Boston: Houghton Mifflin Company, 1958, and London: André Deutsch, Ltd., 1958), page 205.
[17]Galbraith, *The Affluent Society*, pages 199–200.
[18]Solow, "The New Industrial State or Son of Affluence," pages 103–104.

Professor Galbraith offers none; perhaps that is why he states his conclusion so confidently and so often.... I should think a case could be made that much advertising serves only to cancel other advertising.

If Hertz and Avis were each to reduce their advertising expenditures by half ... what would happen to the total car rental business? Galbraith presumably believes it would shrink. People would walk more, and spend their money instead on the still-advertised deodorants. But suppose ... that all advertising were reduced ... Galbraith believes that in the absence of persuasion ... total consumer spending would fall. Pending some evidence, I am not inclined to take this popular doctrine very seriously.[19]

Is the model of profit maximization, so beloved by mainstream economists, really irrelevant to modern forms of business organization? While recognizing that profit maximization cannot be a *literal* description of corporate behaviour ("Most large corporations are free enough from competitive pressure to afford a donation to the Community Chest"), Solow suggests that it is still a workable *approximation*. There is, for example, an *opportunity cost* of funds even when those funds are generated by internal financing. Furthermore, managements that stray too far from profit maximization in the pursuit of other goals, thereby depressing the value of their common stock, may find their jobs threatened by a takeover bid.

Are the outputs of the system really that bad? As Solow notes, it is hard to disagree with Galbraith's disparaging remarks about chrome-plated automobiles, pungent deodorants, and ostentatiously useless gadgets "without appearing boorish." Yet these are not the wasteful expenditures of the idle rich. It must be remembered that the median family income in the United States is not excessively high—it is currently about $27,000 per year. And by definition, fully *half* of American families earn less than this. Are they squandering their money on frivolities, or are these the things that the American people really want?

His [Galbraith's] attitudes toward ordinary consumption remind one of the Duchess who, upon acquiring a full appreciation of sex, asked the Duke if it were perhaps too good for the common people.[20]

In sum, Solow views *The New Industrial State* as strong on style and wit, but weak on substance: "A book for the dinner table not for the desk."

Not surprisingly, Galbraith was unmoved by this and other attacks, viewing them as the predictable reactions of conventional economists who see their vested interests threatened:

Neoclassical economics is not without its instinct for survival. It rightly sees the unmanaged consumer, the ultimate sovereignty of the citizen and the maximization of profits and resulting subordination of the firm to the market as the three legs of a tripod on which it stands. These are what exclude the role of power in the system. All three propositions tax the capacity for belief.[21]

The Radical Economics of the New Left

The newest of the three major challenges to mainstream economics comes from the far left. Spawned by the radical student movement of the 1960s, the "New Left" is highly critical both of contemporary capitalism and of contemporary economic analysis as practised by most economists. Radical economics has grown and matured. Its views are no longer circulated in leaflets handed out on street corners.

[19]Solow, "The New Industrial State or Son of Affluence," page 105.
[20]Solow, "The New Industrial State or Son of Affluence," page 108.
[21]Galbraith, "Power and the Useful Economist," page 5.

Biographical Note: Karl Marx (1818–1883)

Karl Marx was born in Trier, Germany, the son of a successful Jewish lawyer who later converted to Christianity. Marx's acquaintances considered him brilliant, but he was also stubborn and quarrelsome. Throughout his life he broke with one associate after another, with the only exception being Friedrich Engels, his lifelong friend, collaborator, and benefactor.

Marx studied at the universities of Bonn and Berlin, hoping first to become a poet. After a resounding failure at poetry, he entered a circle of young philosophers in Berlin, all devoted followers of Hegel, whose ideas about the crucial role of history in understanding current events, art, and science had recently swept German universities. The young Hegelians, however, were radical in their opposition to Hegel's religious views, and this attitude may have influenced Marx's later attacks against religion. Marx received his doctorate of philosophy at the age of 23, meanwhile having married ("above his station") Jenny von Westphalen, the daughter of his father's closest friend. Jenny's family opposed the marriage, and, as it turned out, their reasons were justified, since Marx was never able to support her. Much of their lives was spent in great poverty, and the deaths of three of their six children were probably the result of privation.

After a brief stint as a newspaper editor, Marx's troubles with the authorities propelled him first out of Germany and then Paris and Belgium. It was in Paris that Marx first met Engels, and in Brussels they together wrote the *Communist Manifesto*, a revolutionary pamphlet that was the only writing of Marx's to achieve wide circulation during his lifetime. After the demise of the revolutions that shook all of Europe in 1848, but in which Marx played little part, he fled finally to London, where he spent the rest of his life. There Marx helped form revolutionary groups, and otherwise spent most of his time cloistered in the British Museum studying the history of economic thought and writing *Das Kapital*. Aside from some meager earnings as correspondent for *The New York Tribune*, a job he held for about ten years, Marx lived entirely on money given to him by Engels (who, although an anti-capitalist, nevertheless owned factories in Manchester and Germany) and by other admirers.

Marx was never very successful in organizing revolutionary groups, and he finally engineered the breakup of The First International, the revolutionary organization that he had helped found and develop but which seemed about to fall into the hands of opponent radicals. Marx finished writing volume I of *Capital* and saw it published in 1867. He had previously written most of volumes II and III, but never completed them in the 15 years that remained to him. It was left to Engels to edit and publish these volumes after Marx's death. Marx died in 1883, two years after the death of his wife, Jenny, and only several months after the unexpected death of his eldest daughter, Jenny Longuet.

Throughout his life Marx attracted and fascinated many people by his brilliance and through the force of his personality and ideas. And though most of his associates eventually became estranged from Marx the man, almost all retained their allegiance to his ideas.

They appear in the most prestigious scholarly journals. While the movement is too diverse to define concisely, it behooves us to take a close look at some of what the New Left has been saying.

New Left economists view themselves as the inheritors of Marxism, both of its intellectual traditions and its political activism.

Like Marx, the New Left economists stress the pervasive importance of the *mode of production*, including not only its influence on economic activity, but also its effects on personal attitudes and social institutions. They write much about the *class struggle* and leave no doubt about where they line up. Like Marx, they seek to uncover the inner *contradictions* in modern capitalism, contradictions that, they believe, will contribute to its ultimate demise. And, also like Marx, their writings are replete with stinging criticisms of both contemporary economic analysis and contemporary economic institutions. There is also much of Galbraith in the writings of the New Left economists: They share his emphasis on power rather than on markets, his critique of the giant corporation, his belief that consumers are manipulated by producers, and his dismay over the outputs of the industrial system. But Galbraith is surely no radical economist, and the radical economists are not Galbraithean. They find his propensity to turn to the government to solve problems hopelessly naïve. In their view, the government is part and parcel of the corporate state—a contributor to the problem, not an instrument toward a solution.

The Shortcomings of Mainstream Economics: Point and Counterpoint

In brief, New Left economists hold that mainstream economists are asking all the wrong questions and using the wrong set of tools (economic models) to provide the answers. Let us examine their criticisms one by one.[22]

Narrowness of Focus
Radicals argue that economists typically narrow their field of inquiry so much that they are incapable of addressing the important questions.

For one thing, in contrast to Marx's teachings, modern economics is *ahistorical*. It is very much based on the here and how, with scant attention paid to the origins of the current system or the directions in which it may be headed. Perhaps as a consequence of this narrow scope, mainstream economics *accepts institutions as given and (tacitly) as immutable*. Little attention is paid to how institutions change.

Orthodox economics takes the existing social system for granted, much as though it were part of the natural order of things.[23]

Amplifying the attack, the New Left chides conventional economists for their preoccupation with analysis of *marginal* changes, using the celebrated tools of marginal analysis that we have described in earlier chapters. This, they argue, makes economics incapable of dealing with the really big issues: the institution of private property, poverty and discrimination, unemployment, and alienation. For example, Professor John Gurley of Stanford University, who converted from conventional to radical economics many years ago, scoffed at a prominent economist who expressed the belief that reducing unemployment would do more good things for the distribution of income than any measure he could imagine.

Well, any radical economist can imagine a direct measure that would do even better things—expropriation of the capitalist class and turning over of ownership of capital goods and land to all the people. That, of course, sounds wild— unimaginable—to anyone who does not question the existing system.[24]

The consequence of this disciplinary narrowness, radicals contend, is that economists become, whether deliberately or unwittingly, apologists for the present system, supporters of the propertied class, and defenders of the status quo.

Most economists are prepared to plead guilty to the charge of disciplinary narrowness. As Yale's Nobel Prize winner, James Tobin, put it:

[22]Another attempt to draw up a list of key tenets of the New Left, similar in spirit to what we do here, appears in Assar Lindbeck's *The Political Economy of the New Left: An Outsider's View*, 2nd ed. (New York: Harper & Row, 1977).

[23]Paul Sweezy, "Toward a Critique of Economics," *Monthly Review*, vol. 21, no. 8 (January 1970), page 1. Copyright© 1970 by Monthly Review, Inc. Reprinted by permission of Monthly Review Press.

[24]J. G. Gurley, "The State of Political Economics," *American Economic Review* (May 1971), page 59.

Most contemporary economists feel ill at ease with respect to big topics—national economic organization, interpretation of economic history, relations of economic and political power, origins and functions of economic institutions. The terrain is unsuitable for our tools. We find it hard even to frame meaningful questions, much less to answer them.[25]

But mainstream economists tend to view their inadequacy in this area as a misdemeanor, not a felony. They point out, in their defence, that a narrow focus is imperative if progress in analysis is to be made. And they are quite proud of the achievements of economic science compared with those of the more diffuse social sciences, such as sociology and political science. They counter that radicals try to paint with such broad strokes that everything becomes necessarily superficial and imprecise. And they argue that the radicals, with their very clear political biases, are hardly in a position to question the objectivity of other economists.

Acceptance of Tastes and Motivation as Given

Just as they do with institutions, conventional economists accept the tastes of consumers and the motivations of workers and managers as given and unchangeable: "just human nature."

Radicals, on the other hand, agree with Galbraith that the consumer is manipulated; and they go on to widen the charge. Not only is the consumer bombarded by advertising, he is brainwashed in the school system, influenced by politicians, and subtly molded by other social institutions.

These institutions, furthermore, are set up for the convenience of the ruling (capitalist) class.

Economics . . . takes preferences as being exogenously determined and then shifts the burden of studying their formation and change onto "other disciplines." The New Left rejects this compartmentalization and takes the Marxian view . . . that new needs are created by the same process by which their means of satisfaction are produced.[26]

This argument is broadened further by the assertion that the need for material incentives to motivate both workers and managers is culturally acquired rather than innate, a product of capitalism rather than a cause of it.

Naturally, mainstream economists do not really believe that tastes are God-given. Everyone realizes that they are acquired, and influenced by many things. The question is: What are we to do about this? Lacking a theory of taste formation, basic economic analysis proceeds on the assumption that consumer tastes are to be respected *regardless* of how they got to be what they are. If we forsake this principle we find ourselves on some dangerous ground: If consumers do not know what's good for them, who does? Still, most economists would willingly concede that more research into taste formation is desirable; and some have worked on this. The radicals have no doubt pushed the profession in a healthy direction.

Obsession with Efficiency Rather Than Equality

Earlier in this book we described in some detail the fundamental trade-off between efficiency and equality. All mainstream economists appreciate and understand this principle, and a great many—in their role as private citizens—advocate greater equality. However, the New Left is quite right to complain that:

[25]J. Tobin, book review of Lindbeck's *The Political Economy of the New Left, Journal of Economic Literature* (December 1972), page 1216.

[26]S. Hymer and F. Roosevelt, "Comment," *Quarterly Journal of Economics* (November 1972), page 649.

The preponderant majority of economic analysis and research is concerned with efficiency, not with equality.

Many conventional economists agree with this criticism.[27]

But New Left economists do not ask simply for a change in emphasis; they also want a change in the economist's tool kit. The marginal-productivity theory of income distribution, they argue, is irrelevant. They maintain that to understand the distribution of income in contemporary market economies, we must first understand the distribution of *power*, which is largely determined by who controls the means of production.

According to marginal-productivity theory, workers receive the marginal product of labor and capitalists receive the marginal product of capital. This conservative theory tries to justify the present distribution of income. Critics ... claim that it explains nothing, is unrealistic and refers to nothing measurable, and confuses the product of capital with the product of the capitalist.

According to radical theory, workers produce the whole product but capitalists expropriate part of it in profits (by means of their control of all the resources and productive facilities).[28]

As a radical economist sees it, the shares of national income going to workers and to property owners are largely determined by the relative power of the two groups.[29]

Here the conventional and the radical economists part company. The conventional economist wants to know just how this "power" is measured. Are there statistical studies showing that "power" influences the distribution of income? In short, mainstream economics treats this approach to distribution theory as rhetoric, not as science.

Myopic Concentration on Quantity Rather Than Quality

Much like Galbraith, the New Left is critical of mainstream economists' preoccupation with policies designed to increase the gross national product. They argue that a great deal of this output is no more than junk, and using society's resources to produce such things is patently irrational. They also point to the spoliation of the environment caused by modern industrial production, though at least some radicals concede that conventional economics has some solutions to these problems (see Chapter 34). And they echo Galbraith's dismay that a system that is so good at producing private consumer goods should be so pathetically bad at feeding the hungry, housing and clothing the poor, and providing public services of all kinds.

The New Left adds one further element to Galbraith's indictment. In addition to ruining the quality of the environment, capitalist production ruins human beings.

It makes them aggressive, competitive, even dehumanized, by forcing them into a rat race for material gain. In Marxian terms, workers have little voice in determining the nature of their productive activities and so become *alienated* from their work rather than being proud of their accomplishments.

[27] Alice M. Rivlin, "Income Distribution—Can Economists Help?" *American Economic Review* (May 1975), pages 1–15; R. A. Gordon, "Rigor and Relevance in a Changing Institutional Setting," *American Economic Review* (March 1976), pages 1–14.

[28] E. K. Hunt and Howard J. Sherman, *Economics: An Introduction to Traditional and Radical Views*, 2nd ed. (New York: Harper & Row, 1975), pages 249–50.

[29] Gurley, "The State of Political Economics," page 59.

The answers that conventional economists have to most of these charges have already been noted in connection with our discussion of Galbraith (refer back to pages 843–47). The new charges are those of alienation and the dehumanizing effects of capitalism. We think it is safe to say that conventional economists have never known what to make of the notion of alienation. They scratch their heads about it, but that is about all. If this is an important way in which capitalism has damaged the quality of life, then conventional economics surely has been blind to it. Like "power," however, no one has yet figured out a way to measure alienation. As to the alleged dehumanization of the labour force, this seems to be a side effect of modern industrial activity—whether that activity is conducted under capitalism or under socialism.

Naïve Conception of the State

New Left economists maintain that both mainstream economists and Galbraith hold a naïve and sentimental view of the state. In this view, government is available to set things right when the market system fails (as in the case of externalities, for example), and in so doing, government decisions are dictated by the broad public interest. By contrast:

The State, in the radical view, operates ultimately to serve the interest of the controlling class in a class society. Since the "capitalist" class fundamentally controls capitalist societies, the state functions in capitalist societies to serve that class. It does so either directly, by providing services only to members of that class, or indirectly, and probably more frequently, by helping preserve and support the system of basic institutions which support and maintain the power of that class.[30]

This *subservience of the state to the capitalists* manifests itself in several ways. First, since capitalists are driven by competition to accumulate capital continually and to expand production, more and bigger markets are necessary on which to sell this bountiful output. As a result, capitalist nations turn to *imperialist ventures* to secure new markets. Second, in order to maintain domestic demand at high levels, the military–industrial complex promotes a *war economy*, which, if not actually at war, is continually spending inordinate sums on armaments. Third, even reforms that appear to be pro-labour, such as social-welfare programs, unemployment insurance, and the like, are really intended to *"buy off" the working class* so that they will not rise up in revolt, as they imply Marx had predicted. In this view, for example, the New Deal was not motivated by a desire to help the working class, but rather by a desire to forestall the coming revolution.

Mainstream economists admit to a certain political naïvete. Yet most economists are unimpressed by the radicals' view of the state. Without denying that corporations often curry political favour, and often succeed, mainstream economists wonder how the radical model can explain progressive income taxation, inheritance taxes, competition policy, equal-opportunity laws, affirmative-action regulations, and many, many more acts that the preponderance of the wealthy opposed bitterly at the time they were enacted. Furthermore, they point out, the policy prescriptions that conventional economists offer to improve the functioning of markets are intended as just that—as prescriptions for improvement, not as predictions about what government will actually do. Economists are not *that* naïve.

What is the Radical Alternative?

Much of the New Left's criticism of modern industrial capitalism has already been mentioned in connection with its criticism of modern economics. Radicals dislike

[30]D. M. Gordon, *Theories of Poverty and Underemployment* (Lexington, Mass.: D. C. Heath & Company, 1972), page 61.

the great disparities in income and wealth that the system produces; they despise the discrimination that, they argue, capitalism promotes; they blame the system for alienating its labour force and dehumanizing people in other ways (as in the schools); they cite the irrational use of resources to produce too much private junk and too few public services; they abhor what they see as its imperialist and militaristic tendencies; and they claim that the system is unable to cope with the problem of macroeconomic instability.

Taken as a whole, this is a powerful indictment. But almost all these problems have been raised many times before by non-radical economists.

What distinguishes the radical attack from the attitudes of liberal reformers is that the radicals have a unified view of it all.

Liberals see each of these ... problems as separate and distinct. The problems, they believe, are the results of past mistakes, inabilities, and ineptitudes or the results of random cases of individual perversity ... liberals generally favor government-sponsored reforms designed to mitigate the many evils of capitalism. These reforms never threaten the two most important features of capitalism: private ownership of the means of production, and the free market.

Radicals, however, see each of the ... problems ... as the direct consequence of *private ownership of capital and the process of social decision making within the impersonal cash nexus of the market. The problems cannot be solved until their underlying causes are eliminated, but this means a fundamental, radical economic reorganization.*[31]

What would the radicals put in place of our system of market capitalism? There are many answers, but none commands anything like universal support among members of the New Left.

Few prefer a system of rigid state planning along Soviet lines. Most radicals see oppression by bureaucrats of the Soviet type as little better than (and little different from) oppression by capitalists, and they deplore the losses of human rights that accompany totalitarianism. Some advocate a system of market socialism, along Yugoslav lines. But this runs counter to the argument that the institution of markets is one of the root causes of the difficulties of capitalism. Others see the Israeli kibbutz system, perhaps the purest form of communism ever practised, as a model.

In fact, the radicals' hostile attitude both toward markets *and* central planning has put them in an awkward position. As one thoughtful critic of the New Left put it:

It may be possible to make a strong case against either markets or administrative systems, but if we are against both *we are in trouble; there is hardly a third method for allocating resources and coordinating economic decisions, if we eliminate physical force.*[32]

If both the market and the plan are discarded, how is the economy to be organized? The radical viewpoint is perhaps vague, but two characteristics stand out quite clearly. First, the New Left wants a *decentralized* system, not one in which power is concentrated (either in the hands of capitalists or of commissars). Second, it wants a *participatory* system in which workers have some real control over what they do and how they do it, not one in which orders only flow from the top down. These changes, they believe, would make workers both happier and more productive.

[31]Hunt and Sherman, *Economics*, page 186.
[32]Lindbeck, *The Political Economy of the New Left: An Outsider's View*, page 32.

In the radical view, therefore, the trade-off between efficiency and equality can be defeated. By reforming the basic structure of society, they contend, we can achieve a more egalitarian economy which is also more productive.

Summary

1. Mainstream economic analysis is not without its dissenters—conservative, moderate, and radical.

2. The libertarian philosophy translates, in economic matters, to a defence of laissez faire and to a devout belief in the workings of the markets. This is because libertarians see free markets as the best guarantor of individual freedom.

3. Libertarian economists like Milton Friedman would limit government to three basic roles: enforcement of the law, regulation of natural monopolies, and control of externalities. Some libertarians would give government even less scope than this.

4. John Kenneth Galbraith has argued for years that conventional economic analysis has accorded insufficient attention to large and powerful organizations like the modern corporation. In his view, this omission has made modern economics largely irrelevant to modern society.

5. According to Galbraith, large corporations have the power to control, or even supplant, market forces by creating the demand for their products through advertising, and by manipulating their own costs. This "planning system" is run by technocrats, who are more interested in growth and expansion than in maximizing profits.

6. Because the modern corporation controls the market, rather than vice versa, according to Galbraith, our economy turns out tonnes of consumer baubles of dubious merit but underproduces crucial goods like housing, keeps the public sector starved, and despoils the environment.

7. Mainstream economists feel that Galbraith overstates his case and substitutes assertion for fact. They doubt that the corporation can avoid the discipline of the market entirely, and they are skeptical of the view that the consumer is a puppet of the advertising media.

8. Radical economists are the economic and political heirs of Marx, though their analysis of twentieth-century capitalism bears the unmistakable stamp of Galbraith. However, they disdain Galbraith's "liberal" view of the state and view the government as an instrument of the capitalist class.

9. Radicals criticize mainstream economists for having an unduly narrow focus; for accepting consumer tastes and human nature as "givens" rather than treating them as the results of the economic system; for stressing efficiency rather than equality as an economic goal; and for concentrating on increasing the quantity of output rather than the quality of life.

10. While their critique of both economic theory and the modern economy is quite clear and forceful, radicals are much less clear about what type of system should be put in its place.

Concepts for Review

Libertarianism	New Left economics	Liberal versus radical views of the state
Economic power	Manipulation of the consumer	
Technostructure	Alienation	

Questions for Discussion

1. What might a libertarian think of:
   a. Laws prohibiting smoking cigarettes in public places?
   b. Laws prohibiting smoking marijuana in private?
   c. Compulsory seat belts in cars?
   d. Speed limits on highways?
   e. Censorship?

2. Explain why a libertarian would support the all-volunteer army. Explain why many who are not libertarians also support it. How are the concepts of *supply and demand* and *opportunity cost* relevant?

3. Friedman believes that the medical profession has kept doctors' fees high by making it difficult to get into medical school (see page 842). Explain his argument with a supply-and-demand diagram. What are the costs and benefits to society of licensing doctors? How would you go about deciding whether the benefits exceed the costs, or vice versa?

4. Friedman has advocated replacing the current system of public schools by a "voucher" plan in which the parents of each school-age child would get a voucher worth, say, $2000. These educational vouchers could be spent only on education, but could be spent in any accredited school, public or private, of the parents'

choosing.[33] What do you think of this idea? How might your own elementary and secondary schooling have differed if this plan had been in effect?

5. Galbraith says that about 50 percent of the American economy is in the "planning system" rather than in the competitive market. What are some industries that seem to fall under both headings?

6. Some years ago, sharp limitations were placed on cigarette advertising—including the banning of such ads from TV. Yet smoking did not decrease noticeably for many years. How does this experience bear on Galbraith's claim that the modern corporation creates demand through advertising? Would a libertarian support the ban on TV advertising? Would a radical economist? Would you?

7. According to Galbraith, modern economic analysis rests on three assumptions: consumer sovereignty, profit maximization, and the subordination of the firm to the market. Explain what he means.

8. Discuss the divergent views of the role of the state in the economy held by (a) libertarians, (b) Galbraith, and (c) radical economists. Which do you find most appealing?

9. Discuss the radical critique of conventional economics, point by point. Where do you find room for improvement in mainstream economics?

[33]For a full discussion of the proposal, see Milton and Rose Friedman, *Free to Choose*, Chapter 6.

Glossary

Numbers in parentheses indicate pages in the text where the terms are discussed.

Ability-to-pay principle The idea that persons with greater ability to pay taxes should pay higher taxes. (648)

Absolute advantage Of one country over another in the production of a particular good is said to occur if it can produce that good using smaller quantities of resources than can the other country. (618)

Abstraction Ignoring many details in order to focus on the most important factors in a problem. (11)

Affirmative action Active efforts to locate and hire members of minority groups. (770)

Aggregate demand The total amount that all consumers, business firms, government agencies, and foreigners are willing to spend on final goods and services. (114)

Aggregate-demand curve Graphic presentation of the quantity of national product that is demanded at each possible value of the price level. (75, 150)

Aggregate saving The difference between disposable income and consumer expenditure. (131)

Aggregate supply The total amount that all business firms are willing to produce. (174)

Aggregate-supply curve A graph that shows, for each possible price level, the quantity of goods and services that all the nation's businesses are willing to produce, holding all other determinants of aggregate quantity supplied constant. (75, 174)

Aggregation Combining many individual markets into one overall market. Economic aggregates are the focus of macroeconomics (74)

Appreciation (of a nation's currency) Is said to occur when exchange rates change so that a unit of its own currency can buy more units of foreign currency. (248)

Arbitration Process in which an outsider is authorized to dictate the terms of a settlement of a labour–management dispute if a voluntary agreement cannot be reached. (743)

Asset An item that an individual or a firm owns. (232)

Automatic stabilizer An arrangement that automatically supports aggregate demand when it would otherwise sag and holds down aggregate demand when it would otherwise surge ahead; thus reduces the sensitivity of the economy to shifts in demand. (372)

Autonomous increase in consumption An increase in consumer spending without any increase in incomes. Represented graphically as a shift of the entire consumption function. (167)

Average-cost curve Shows, for each output, the cost per unit, that is, total cost divided by output. (426)

Average physical product (APP) Total physical product (TPP) divided by the quantity of input utilized. (423)

Average revenue (AR) Total revenue (TR) divided by quantity. (455)

Balance sheet An account statement listing the values of all assets on the left-hand side and of all liabilities and net worth on the right-hand side. (232)

Bank of Canada Canada's central bank. (243)

Bank rate The rate of interest charged by the Bank of Canada when reserves are loaned to the chartered banks (advances from the central bank). It is used as a signal of the direction of monetary policy. (247)

Barter A system of exchange in which people directly trade one good for another, without using money as an intermediate step. (225)

Benefits principle of taxation The idea that people who derive benefits from a service should pay the taxes that finance it. (649)

Bilateral monopoly Market situation in which there is both a monopoly on the selling side and a monopsony on the buying side. (742)

Bond A corporation's promise to pay the holder a fixed sum of money at the specified *maturity* date and some other fixed amount of money (the *coupon* or *interest payment*) every year up to the date of maturity. (478)

Brain drain Occurs when the educated natives of a less developed country emigrate to wealthier nations. (808)

Budget deficit Amount by which the government's expenditures exceed its receipts during a specified period of time, usually one year. (318)

Budget line Represents graphically all the possible combinations of two commodities that a household can purchase, given the prices of the commodities and some fixed amount of money at its disposal. (391)

Burden of a tax The amount of money an individual would have to be given to make him just as well off with the tax as he was without it. (649)

Capital Inventory (stock) of plant, equipment, and other productive resources held by a business firm, an individual, or some other organization. (705)

Capitalism Method of economic organization in which private individuals own the means of production, either directly or indirectly through corporations. (818)

Capital gain An increase in the market value of a piece of property that occurs between the time it is bought and the time it is sold. (212, 644, 784)

Capital loss A decrease in the market value of a piece of property that occurs between the time it is bought and the time it is sold. (212)

Cartel Group of sellers of a product who have joined together to control its production, sale, and price in the hope of obtaining the advantages of monopoly. (546)

Central bank A bank for banks. The central bank of Canada is the Bank of Canada. (243)

Closed shop An arrangement that permits only union members to be hired. (737)

Collective bargaining Negotiations between union representatives of an industry's labour force and the employers of those workers. (742)

Commodity money An object used as a medium of exchange that also has a substantial value in alternative (non-monetary) uses. (226)

Common stock A piece of paper

that gives the holder a share in the ownership of a corporation. (478)

Comparative advantage Of one country over another in the production of a particular good relative to other goods it can produce is said to occur if it produces that good least inefficiently compared with the other country. (619)

Competition policy Government policy that attempts to control the growth of monopoly and to prevent firms from engaging in "undesirable" practices through the use of legislation and various programs. (597)

Complements Two goods are called complements if an increase in the price of one reduces the quantity demanded of the other, all other things remaining constant. (411)

Concentration of industry The share of the industry's total output (in money terms) supplied by some given number (usually four) of its largest firms. (606)

Concentration ratio Percentage of an industry's output produced by its *four* largest firms. It is intended to measure the degree to which the industry is dominated by large firms, that is, how closely it approximates a monopoly. (608)

Conditional grants Transfer payments from the federal government to provincial governments, matching provincial spending in areas specified by the federal government. Discontinued in 1977. (648)

Consumer expenditure (consumption) Symbolized by the letter C; the total amount spent by consumers on newly produced goods and services (excluding purchases of new homes, which are considered investment goods). (114)

Consumer Price Index The most popular index number for the price level. Its weights are based on the spending patterns of a typical urban household. (109)

Consumer sovereignty Consumer preferences determine what goods shall be produced, and in what amounts. (818)

Consumption function Relationship between total consumer expenditure and total disposable income in the economy, holding all other determinants of consumer spending constant. (123)

Corporation A firm with the legal status of a fictional individual. It is owned by shareholders and run by elected officers and a board of directors, whose chairman often influences the firm's affairs. (476)

Correlation A relationship between two variables such that they tend to

go up or down together. Correlation need not imply causation. (14)

Cost disease of personal services Tendency of the cost of services such as auto repair and legal counsel to rise faster than the economy's overall inflation rate because it is difficult to increase productivity (output per person hours) in these services. (566)

Craft union Represents a particular type of skilled worker regardless of the industry. (735)

Cross elasticity of demand For product X to a change in the price of another product, Y, is the ratio of the percentage change in quantity demanded of product X to the percentage change in the price of product Y that brings about the change in quantity demanded. (412)

Cross subsidization Selling one product at a loss, which is balanced by higher profits on another product. (583)

Crowding out Occurs when deficit spending by the government forces private investment spending or exports to contract. (330)

Cyclical unemployment The portion of unemployment that is attributable to a decline in the economy's total production. Cyclical unemployment rises during recessions and falls as prosperity is restored. (92)

Deficit, balance of payments Amount by which the quantity supplied of a country's currency (per year) exceeds the quantity demanded. Such deficits arise when the exchange rate is artificially high. (252)

Deflating (by a price index) Dividing some nominal magnitude by a price index in order to express that magnitude in dollars of constant purchasing power (110)

Deflation A sustained decrease in the general price level. (80)

Demand, law of States that a lower price generally increases the amount of a commodity that people in a market are willing to buy. Thus, for most goods, demand curves have a negative slope. (400)

Demand curve A graph showing how the quantity demanded of some product during a specified period of time will change as the price of that product changes, holding all other determinants of quantity demanded constant. (54)

Demand schedule A table showing how the quantity demanded of some product during a specified period of time changes as the price of that product changes, holding all other determinants of quantity demanded constant (54)

Depletability An attribute of

private goods, as opposed to public goods. A commodity is depletable if it is used up when someone consumes it. (564)

Deposit creation Process by which the banking system turns a dollar of reserves into several dollars of deposits. (233)

Deposit insurance A system that guarantees that depositors will not lose money even if their bank goes bankrupt. (231)

Depreciation (of capital goods) The value of the portion of the nation's capital equipment that is used up within the year. It indicates how much output is needed just to keep the economy's capital stock intact. (136)

Depreciation (of a nation's currency) Is said to occur when exchange rates change so that a unit of its own currency can buy fewer units of foreign currency. (248)

Depreciation allowances Tax deductions that businesses may claim when they spend money on investment goods. (143)

Devaluation Reduction in the official value of a currency. (249)

Direct taxes Taxes levied directly on the people. (642)

Discounting Process of determining the present worth of a quantity of money receivable or payable at some future date. (706)

Discouraged worker An unemployed person who gives up looking for work and is therefore no longer counted as part of the labour force. (90)

Discrimination, economic Occurs when equivalent factors of production receive different payments for equal contributions to output. (759)

Discrimination, statistical Occurs when the productivity of a particular worker is estimated to be low just because that worker belongs to a particular group. (761)

Disguised unemployment Occurs when tasks are carried out by a number of persons larger than the number that can complete them most efficiently. (806)

Disinflation The process of reducing inflation. (83)

Disposable income A measure of income derived by subtracting personal income taxes from personal income. (115, 138)

Diversification An increase in the number and *variety* of stocks, bonds, and other such items in an individual's portfolio of investments. (480)

Division of labour Breaking up a task into a number of smaller, more specialized tasks so that each worker can become more adept at his or her particular job. Division of labour creates efficiency and increases productivity. (44)

Dual labour market theory Asserts that workers generally work in one of two types of jobs—those which offer opportunities for acquisition of skills and promotions, and "dead end jobs" which offer little scope for improvement (733)

Dumping Selling goods in a foreign market at lower prices than those charged in the home market. (634)

Economic model A simplified, small-scale version of some aspect of the economy. Economic models are often expressed in equations, by graphs, or in words. (15)

Economic power A buyer or seller is said to have economic power if, by his own actions, he can influence the market price. (843)

Economic profit Net earnings minus the firm's opportunity cost of capital. (502)

Economic profit, total The total revenue a firm or an industry derives from the sale of its products minus the total cost of its inputs, including the opportunity cost of any inputs supplied by the proprietors. (454)

Economic rent Said to be earned whenever a factor of production receives a reward that exceeds the minimum amount necessary to keep the factor in its present employment. (713)

Economies of scale Savings acquired through increases in quantities produced. (440, 583)

Economies of scope Savings acquired through simultaneous production of many different products. (583)

Efficiency The absence of waste, achieved primarily by gains in productivity resulting from specialization, division of labour, and a system of exchange. (43)

Efficient allocation of resources One that takes advantage of every opportunity to make some individuals better off in their own estimation while not worsening the lot of anyone else. (508)

Elasticity of demand, price Ratio of the *percentage* change in quantity demanded to the *percentage* change in price that brings about the change in quantity demanded. (405)

Entrepreneurship The act of starting new firms, introducing new products and technological innovations, and, in general, taking the risks necessary in seeking out business opportunities. (701)

Equalization payments *See* Unconditional grants.

Equation of exchange States that

the money value of GNP transactions must be equal to the product of the average stock of money times velocity ($M \times V = P \times Y$). (272)

Equilibrium A situation in which there are no inherent forces that produce change. Changes away from an equilibrium position occur only as a result of "outside events" that disturb the status quo. (56, 144)

Equilibrium level of GNP (on the demand side) Level of GNP which makes aggregate demand equal to production. (145)

Equilibrium price Price at which quantity demanded and quantity supplied are equal. This common quantity is called the equilibrium quantity. (56)

Excess burden of a tax The amount by which the burden of the tax exceeds the tax that is paid. (650)

Excess capacity theorem Asserts that monopolistic competitive firms will tend to produce outputs lower than those that minimize average costs, that is, that they will tend to produce less than their capacity. (543)

Excess reserves Reserves held in excess of the legal minimum. (233)

Exchange A mechanism by which workers can trade the various products resulting from specialization and the division of labour. (44)

Exchange controls Laws restricting the exchange of one nation's currency for that of another. (309)

Exchange rate States the price, in terms of one currency, at which another currency can be bought. (67, 177)

Exchange rates, fixed Rates set by government decisions and maintained by central bank actions. (252)

Exchange rates, floating or flexible Rates determined in free markets by the law of supply and demand. (249)

Excise tax A tax levied on a particular commodity or service, as a fixed amount of money per unit of product sold or as a fixed percentage of the purchase price. (401)

Excludability An attribute of private goods, as opposed to public goods. A commodity is excludable if someone who does not pay for it can be kept from enjoying it. (564)

Expansion path The locus of a firm's cost-minimizing input combinations for all relevant output levels. (449)

Expected rate of inflation Forecasted rate of price change. Also, the difference between the

nominal interest rate and the real interest rate. (101)

Expenditure schedule Illustration of how total spending varies with the level of national income (GNP). (146)

Exponential growth Growth at a constant percentage rate. (792)

Export subsidy Payment by the government to exporters to permit them to reduce the selling price of their goods so they can compete more effectively in foreign markets. (627)

Externality, beneficial Result of an activity that causes incidental benefits to others with no corresponding compensation provided to or paid by those who generate the externality. (560)

Externality, detrimental Result of an activity that causes damages to others with no corresponding compensation provided or paid by those who generate the externality. (560)

Fiat money Money decreed as such by the government. It has little value as a commodity, but it maintains its value as a medium of exchange because people have faith that the issuer will stand behind the pieces of printed paper and limit their production. (226)

Final goods and services Those that are purchased by their ultimate users. (78)

Fiscal federalism The system of transfer payments from one level of government to the next. (647)

Fiscal policy The government's plan for spending and taxation, designed to steer aggregate demand in some desired direction. (196)

Fixed cost Cost of the indivisible inputs which the firm needs to produce any output at all. The total cost of these inputs does not change when output changes. (428)

A 45° line A ray through the origin with a slope of $+1$. It marks off points where the variables measured on each axis have equal values, assuming that both variables are measured in the same units. (24)

Fractional reserve banking A system under which bankers keep in their vaults as reserves only a fraction of the funds they hold on deposit. (230)

Free-rider problem Arises when provision of a service to one individual or group automatically benefits others (the free riders) whether or not the others contribute to the costs. (785)

Frictional unemployment Unemployment resulting from the normal workings of the labour market. Includes people who are temporarily between jobs because they are moving or changing occupations, or for similar reasons. (90)

Game theory Analyses the behaviour of competing firms mathematically, treating it as analogous to the strategies of rival players in a competitive game. (549)

Gold-exchange system (Bretton Woods system) International monetary system that prevailed from 1944 to 1971. Under this system, the United States fixed the value of the dollar in terms of gold, and other countries fixed the values of their currencies in terms of the U.S. dollar. (307)

Gold standard System in which exchange rates are set in terms of gold and pegged by buying or selling gold as necessary. (306)

Government purchases Symbolized by the letter G, all the goods and services purchased by all levels of government. Transfer payments to individuals (such as welfare benefits) and payments from one level of government to another are not included. (114)

Gross national product (GNP) The sum of the money values of all final goods and services produced by the economy during a specified period, usually one year. (76, 133)

Gross national product, nominal Calculated by valuing all outputs at current prices. (77)

Gross national product, real The sum of the real values of all final goods and services produced by the economy during a specified period, using the prices that prevailed in some agreed-upon year (1971 at the time of writing). (77)

Gross national product deflator Price index obtained by dividing nominal GNP by real GNP. (110)

Growth, disembodied Refers to increases in an economy's output which can occur without being accompanied by (embodied in) additional capital stock. (796)

Growth, embodied Refers to increases in an economy's output which are made possible by increased or improved plant, equipment, or other forms of capital. (796)

High-employment budget Hypothetical budget Canada *would have* if the economy were operating near full employment (324)

Horizontal equity The notion that equally situated persons should be taxed equally. (648)

Human capital theory Interprets education as an investment in a human being's earning power, just as an improvement in a factory is

an investment in the factory's earning capacity. (731)

Incidence of a tax An allocation of the burden of the tax to specific individuals or groups. (651)

Income effect A portion of the change in quantity of a good demanded when its price changes. A rise in price cuts the consumer's purchasing power (real income), which leads to a change in the quantity demanded of that commodity. That change is the income effect. (387)

Income-expenditure diagram (45° line diagram) A plotting of total real expenditure (on the vertical axis) against real income (on the horizontal axis). The 45° line marks off points where income and expenditure are equal (149)

Incomes policy Variety of measures to curb inflation *without* reducing aggregate demand. (363)

Incomes policy, tax-based Uses the tax system to provide incentives favouring non-inflationary behaviour. (368)

Increasing costs, principle of As the production of one good expands, the opportunity cost of producing another such unit generally increases. (39)

Indexing Provisions in a law or contract whereby monetary payments are automatically adjusted whenever a specified price index changes; sometimes called *escalator clauses*. (368)

Index number A number indicating the percentage change in some variable (such as the price level) between the base period and some other period. Typically, the value of the index number in the base period is arbitrarily set to 100. (108)

Indicative planning Government guidance rather than direct control of economic activity. (825)

Indifference curve Line connecting all combinations of commodities that are equally desirable to the consumer. (393)

Indirect taxes Taxes levied on specific economic activities. (642)

Induced increase in consumption An increase in consumer spending that stems from an increase in consumer incomes. Represented graphically as a movement along a fixed consumption function. (167)

Induced investment Investment that rises when GNP rises and falls when GNP falls. (146)

Industrial union Represents all types of workers in a single industry. (736)

Inferior good A commodity whose quantity demanded falls when the

purchaser's real income rises, all other things remaining equal. (387)

Inflation A sustained increase in the general price level. (76)

Inflation, creeping Inflation that proceeds for a long time at a moderate and fairly steady pace. (105)

Inflation, galloping Inflation that proceeds at an exceptionally high rate, perhaps for only a relatively brief period. This type of inflation is generally characterized by accelerating inflation rates, so that the inflation rate is higher this month than last month. (105)

Inflation accounting Adjusting standard accounting procedures for the fact that inflation lowers the purchasing power of money. (321)

Inflationary gap The amount by which equilibrium real GNP exceeds the full-employment level of GNP. (153)

Innovation The act of putting a new idea into practical use. (717)

Interest Payment for the use of funds employed in the production of capital; measured as a percent per year of the value of the funds tied up in the capital. (706)

Intermediate good One that is bought for resale or for use in producing another good. (78)

International Monetary Fund (IMF) International organization set up originally to police and manage the gold-exchange system. (307)

Invention The act of generating a new idea. (717)

Investment Flow of resources into the production of new capital. (705)

Investment, gross private domestic Sum of business investment expenditures on plant and equipment, residential construction expenditures, and inventory change. (134)

Investment good An item that is used to produce other goods and services in the future rather than being consumed today. (42)

Investment schedule Table or curve showing how investment spending depends on GNP. (157–58)

Investment spending Symbolized by the letter I, the sum of the expenditures of business firms on new plant and equipment, and inventories, plus the expenditures of households on new homes. Financial "investments" and resales of existing physical assets are not included. (114)

Jawboning Informal pressures on firms and unions to slow down the rates at which prices and wages are rising. (363)

Labour force The number of people employed or seeking employment. (88)

Labour productivity A measure of total output divided by the amount of labour used to produce it. It is a measure of output per unit of labour employed. (774)

Laissez faire A program of minimal interference with the workings of the market system. (510)

Less developed countries (LDCs) Countries whose share of output composed of agricultural products, mining, and the like is relatively high, which engage in relatively little industrial high-technology activity, and whose per capita incomes are generally comparatively low. (798)

Liability An item that an individual or a firm owes; collectively, liabilities are known as *debts*. (232)

Liability, limited Legal obligation of a firm's owners to pay back company debts only with the money they have already invested in the firm. (476)

Liability, unlimited Legal obligation of a firm's owners to repay company debts with whatever resources they own. (474)

Libertarianism School of thought that emphasizes the importance of individual freedom. (840)

Liquidity, of an asset The ease with which it can be converted into cash. (229)

Long run Period of time long enough for all the firm's commitments to come to an end. (431)

Lorenz curve Graph depicting the distribution of income. (756)

M1 The narrowly defined money supply, which is the sum of all coins and paper money in circulation, plus pure chequing deposits at chartered banks. (228)

M2 The broadly defined money supply, which is the sum of currency in public hands, plus chequing and all savings deposits at chartered banks. (229)

Macroeconomics The study of the behaviour of entire economies. (74)

Marginal cost, long-run *Addition* to the supplier's total cost resulting from the supply of the output *including whatever additional plant and equipment* is needed in the long run to provide that output. Inclusion of this marginal capital cost (of the necessary additions to plant and equipment) is the crucial distinction between *long-run* and *short-run* marginal cost. (588)

Marginal-cost curve Shows, for each output, the increase in the firm's total cost required if it increases its output by an additional unit. (426)

Marginal land Land that is just on the borderline of being used. (712)

Marginal physical product (MPP) Increase in total output that results from a one-unit increase in an input, holding the amounts of all other inputs constant. (424, 702)

Marginal propensity to consume (MPC) Ratio of the change in consumption to the change in disposable income that produces the change in consumption. On a graph, it appears as the slope of the consumption function. (123)

Marginal propensity to save (MPS) Graphically, the slope of the saving function, which indicates how much more consumers will save if disposable income rises by one unit. (132)

Marginal returns, law of diminishing Asserts that if the quantities of all other inputs are held constant, the employment of additional quantities of any one input by a firm or an industry will eventually yield smaller and smaller (marginal) increases in output. (424)

Marginal revenue (MR) The *addition* to total revenue resulting from the addition of one unit to total output. Geometrically, marginal revenue is the *slope* of the total revenue curve. (455)

Marginal revenue product (MRP) Additional revenue earned as a result of increased sales when an additional unit of an input is used. (434, 702)

Marginal social cost (MSC) The sum of *marginal private cost (MPC)*, which is the share of marginal cost caused by an activity that is paid for by the persons who carry out the activity, and *incidental cost*, which is the share borne by others. (561)

Marginal utility, law of diminishing Asserts that additional units of a commodity are worth less and less to a consumer in money terms. As the individual's consumption increases, the marginal utility of each additional unit declines. (383)

Market The set of all sale and purchase transactions that affect the price of some commodity. (490)

Market-demand curve Shows how the total quantity demanded of some product during a specified period of time changes as the price of the product changes, other things being constant. (400)

Market power The ability of a firm to raise its price significantly above the competitive price level and to maintain this high price profitably for a considerable period. (612)

Maximin criterion Selecting the strategy that yields the maximum payoff, on the assumption that your opponent does as much damage to

you as he can. (550)

Mediation Process in which an outsider is brought into a labour–management negotiation in the hope that this person can lead the two sides to a voluntary agreement through persuasion. (743)

Merger The combining of two previously independent firms under a single owner or group of owners. A **horizontal merger** involves two firms producing similar products. A **vertical merger** involves two firms, one of which supplies an ingredient of the other's product. A **conglomerate merger** is the union of two unrelated firms. (599–600)

Microeconomics The study of the behaviour of individual decision-making units, such as farmers or consumers. (73)

Minimum-wage law Requires all employees (with some specified exceptions) to be paid at least some fixed given dollar amount per hour. (726)

Monetarism Mode of analysis that uses the equation of exchange to organize macroeconomic data. (275)

Monetary policy Actions that the Bank of Canada takes to change the equilibrium of the money market; that is, to alter the money supply, move the exchange rate, or both. (257)

Monetizing the deficit The effect of the central bank's purchasing the bonds that the government issues. (328)

Money Medium of exchange; that is, the standard object used in exchanging goods and services. (225)

Money fixed asset Asset with a face value fixed in terms of dollars, such as money, government bonds, and corporate bonds. (126)

Monopolistic competition Competition among firms, each of which has products that are somewhat different from those of its rivals. (540)

Monopoly, pure Industry in which there is only one supplier of a product for which there are no close substitutes, and in which it is difficult or impossible for another firm to coexist. (526)

Monopsony Market situation in which there is only one buyer. (742)

Moral hazard Tendency of insurance to discourage policy-holders from protecting themselves from risk. (571)

Multinational corporations Corporations whose production activities occur in a number of different countries. (803)

The multiplier The ratio of the change in equilibrium GNP (*Y*) divided by the original change in spending that causes the change in GNP. (161)

National debt The federal government's total indebtedness, which has resulted from previous deficits. (318)

National income The sum of the incomes of all individuals in the economy earned in the forms of wages, interest, rents, and profits. It excludes transfer payments and is calculated before any deductions are taken for income taxes. (115)

National income accounting Bookkeeping and measurement system for national economic data. (133)

Nationalization Government ownership and operation of a business firm. (595)

National product The total production of a nation's economy. (74)

Natural monopoly Industry in which advantages of large-scale production make it possible for a single firm to produce the entire output of the market at lower average cost than a number of firms each producing a smaller quantity. (527)

Natural rate of unemployment Also referred to as the "full-employment" unemployment rate. The specific rate of unemployment toward which the economy's self-correcting mechanism tends to push the unemployment rate. (345)

Near moneys Liquid assets that are close substitutes for money. (229)

Negative income tax (NIT) Transfer program under which families with incomes below a certain threshold (the "breakeven level") would receive cash benefits from the government; these benefits would decline as income rose. (766)

Net exports Symbolized by $X - IM$, the excess of foreign expenditures on our products over our purchases of their goods (Canadian exports minus Canadian imports). (114)

Net national product (NNP) Gross national product minus depreciation. (136)

Net worth The value of all assets minus the value of all liabilities. (232)

Oligopoly Market dominated by a few sellers, at least several of which are large enough relative to the total market to be able to influence the market price. (544)

Open-market operations The Bank of Canada's purchase or sale of government securities through transactions in the open market. (245)

Opportunity cost The forgone

value of the next best alternative that is not chosen. (37)

Origin The lower left-hand corner of a graph where the two axes meet. In two-variable diagrams, both variables equal zero at the original. (20)

Paradox of thrift The fact that an effort by a nation to save more may simply reduce national income and fail to raise total saving. (169)

Partnership A firm whose ownership is shared by a fixed number of proprietors. (475)

Patent A temporary grant of monopoly rights over an innovation. (610)

Perfectly contestable market One in which entry and exit are costless and unimpeded. (554)

Personal income A measure of income derived by subtracting corporate profits, retained earnings, and payroll taxes from national income, then adding in transfer payments. Personal income measures the income that actually accrues to individuals. (138)

Phillips curve Graph depicting the rate of unemployment on the horizontal axis and either the rate of inflation or the rate of change of money wages on the vertical axis; normally downward sloping, indicating that higher inflation rates are associated with lower unemployment rates. (341)

Phillips curve, vertical (long run) Shows the menu of inflation/unemployment choices available to society in the long run; a vertical straight line at the natural rate of unemployment. (345)

Potential gross national product The real GNP the economy would produce if its labour and other resources were fully employed. (95)

Poverty line Amount of income below which a family is considered "poor." (752)

Predatory pricing Price cuts that take place only to keep other firms from entering the industry. (602)

Price ceiling Legal maximum price that can be charged. (64)

Price discrimination Charging different prices, relative to costs, to different buyers of the same product. (601)

Price floor Legal minimum price that can be charged. (66)

Price leadership One firm sets the price for the industry and the others follow. (547)

Private good Commodity or service whose benefits are depleted by an additional user and for which people are excluded from its benefits. (564)

Production function The *maximum* amount of product that

can be obtained from any specified *combination* of inputs, given the current state of knowledge. (435)

Production-indifference curve (sometimes called an *isoquant*) A curve in a graph showing quantities of *inputs* on its axes. Each indifference curve indicates *all* combinations of input quantities capable of producing *a given* quantity of output. (446)

Production possibilities frontier A graphical presentation of the different combinations of various goods that a producer can turn out, given the available resources and existing technology. (38)

Productivity The amount of output produced by a unit of input. (177)

Productivity of labour The amount of output produced per hour of labour input. (216)

Progressive tax One in which the average tax rate paid by an individual rises as his income rises. (642)

Property tax Tax on assessed value of real property. (646)

Proportional tax One in which the average tax rate is the same at all income levels. (642)

Proprietorship Business firm owned by a single person. (474)

Public good Commodity or service whose benefits are *not depleted* by an additional user and for which it is generally difficult or *impossible to exclude* people from its benefits, even if they are unwilling to pay for them. (564)

Purchasing power The purchasing power of a given sum of money is the volume of goods and services it will buy. (97)

Purchasing-power parity theory (of exchange rates) Theory that the exchange rate between any two national currencies adjusts to reflect differences in the price levels of the two nations. (299)

Quantity theory of money A simple theory of aggregate demand based on the idea that velocity is constant, so that nominal GNP is proportional to the money stock. (271)

Quota Specifies the maximum amount of a good that is permitted into the country from abroad per unit of time. (627)

Random walk The time path of a variable, such as the price of a stock, when its magnitude in one period equals its value in the preceding period plus a completely random number. (485)

Rate of interest, nominal The percentage by which the money the

borrower pays back exceeds the money that he borrowed, making no adjustment for any fall in the purchasing power of this money that results from inflation. (101)

Rate of interest, real The percentage increase in purchasing power that the borrower pays to the lender for the privilege of borrowing. It indicates the increased ability to purchase goods and services that the lender earns. (101)

Rational decision A decision that best serves the objective of the decision-maker, whatever the objective may be. The term "rational" connotes neither approval nor disapproval of the objective. (37)

Rational expectations Forecasts that, while not necessarily correct, are the best that can be made given the available data. If expectations are rational, forecasting errors are pure random numbers. (352)

Ray through the origin (or ray) A straight line emanating from the origin, or zero point on a graph. (24)

Recession A period during which the total output of the economy declines. (76)

Recessionary gap The amount by which the equilibrium level of real GNP falls short of potential GNP. (151)

Regressive tax One in which the average tax rate falls as income rises. (642)

Relative price The price of an item in terms of some other item rather than in terms of dollars. (98)

Rent seeking Unproductive activity in the pursuit of economic profit. (571)

Required reserves The minimum amount of reserves (in cash or the equivalent) required by law. Required reserves are usually proportional to the volume of deposits. (231)

Resale price maintenance Forcing retailers to keep the price of a product at or above that specified by the wholesaler. (602)

Research, basic Research conducted to increase knowledge, with no particular practical use in mind. (785)

Retained earnings (ploughback) The portion of a corporation's profits that management decides to keep and reinvest in the firm's operations rather than pay out directly to shareholders in the form of dividends. (477)

Revaluation Increase in the official value of a currency. (249)

Run on a bank An event that occurs when many depositors withdraw cash from their accounts simultaneously. (224)

Sales maximizing firm One whose objective is to sell as much of its outputs as possible (measured in terms of the revenue they bring in) rather than to maximize the company's product. (547)

Saving function The schedule relating total consumer saving to disposable income in the economy, holding other determinants of saving constant. (132)

Saving schedule Table or curve showing how saving depends on GNP. (158)

Scatter diagram Graph showing the relationship between two variables. Each year is represented by a point in the diagram. The co-ordinates of each year's point show the value of the two variables in that year. (120)

Self-correcting mechanism The economy's way of curing inflationary or recessionary gaps automatically via inflation or deflation. (186)

Service industry One that does not turn out physical products. (777)

Shortage An excess of quantity demanded over quantity suplied. When a shortage exists, buyers cannot purchase the quantities they desire. (56)

Short run A shorter period of time than the long run so that some, but not all, of the firm's commitments will have ended. (431)

Slope of a budget line Amount of one commodity the market requires an individual to give up in order to obtain one additional unit of another commodity without any change in the amount of money spent. (394)

Slope of a curved line At any particular point, the slope of the straight line that is tangent to the curved line at that point. (23)

Slope of an indifference curve Referred to as the marginal rate of substitution between the commodities involved, represents that maximum amount of one commodity the consumer is willing to give up in exchange for one more unit of another commodity. (394)

Slope of a straight line The ratio of the vertical change to the corresponding horizontal change as we move to the right along the line. The ratio of the "rise" over the "run." (21)

Socialism Method of economic organization in which the state owns the means of production. (818)

Specialization The process whereby a country devotes its energies and resources to only a small proportion of the world's productive activities. (617)

Speculation Investment in risky assets in the hope of obtaining a profit from expected changes in the prices of these assets. (484)

Stabilization policy The name given to government programs designed to prevent or shorten recessions and to counteract inflation (that is, to *stabilize* prices). (83)

Stagflation Inflation that occurs while the economy is growing slowly ("stagnating") or having a recession. (83)

Store of value An item used to store wealth from one point in time to another. (226)

Structural unemployment Refers to workers who have lost their jobs because they have been displaced by automation, because their skills are no longer in demand, or for similar reasons. (92)

Substitutes Two goods are called substitutes if an increase in the price of one raises the quantity demanded of the other, all other things remaining constant. (411)

Substitution effect Change in quantity demanded of a good resulting from a change in its relative price, exclusive of whatever change in quantity demanded may be attributable to the associated change in real income. (387)

Supply curve A graph showing how the quantity supplied of some product during a specified period of time will change as the price of that product changes, holding all other determinants of quantity supplied constant. (56)

Supply-demand diagram Diagram showing both a supply curve and a demand curve. (56)

Supply schedule A table showing how the quantity supplied of some product during a specified period of time changes as the price of that product changes, holding all other determinants of quantity supplied constant. (55)

Surplus An excess of quantity suplied over quantity demanded. When there is a surplus, sellers cannot sell the quantities they desire to supply. (56)

Surplus, balance of payments Amount by which the quantity demanded of a country's currency (per year) exceeds the quantity supplied. Such surpluses arise when the exchange rate is artificially low. (253)

Tariff Tax on imports. (207, 626)

Tax rate, average Ratio of taxes to income. (642)

Tax rate, marginal Fraction of each *additional* dollar of income that is paid in taxes. (642)

Tax shelter A special provision in the Income Tax Act that reduces or defers taxation if certain conditions are met. (644)

Tax shifting Occurs when the economic reactions to a tax cause prices and outputs in the economy to change, thereby shifting part of the burden of the tax onto others. (651)

Technostructure Professionals who, according to Galbraith, run most of the important economic institutions, including corporations, government bureaus, and large unions. (845)

Theory A deliberate simplification of factual relationships whose purpose is to explain how those relationships work. (14)

Time-series graph A type of two-variable diagram that depicts the change in a variable over time. The horizontal axis always represents time. (26)

Total-cost curve Shows, for each possible quantity of output, the total amount which the firm must spend for its inputs to produce that amount of output plus any opportunity cost incurred in the process. (426)

Trade adjustment assistance Provides special unemployment benefits, loans, retraining programs, and other aid to workers and firms that are harmed by foreign competition. (632)

Transfer payments Sums of money that certain individuals receive as grants from the government rather than as payments for services rendered to employers. (116)

Unconditional grants Transfer payments from the federal government to the provinces, with "no strings attached," paid to provinces that would have to levy very high taxes in order to raise per capita revenues equal to the national average. Also known as "equalization payments." (648, 769)

Unemployment insurance Government program under which some, but not all, unemployed workers receive transfer payments. (93)

Unemployment rate The number of unemployed people, expressed as a percentage of the labour force. (88)

Union shop An arrangement under which non-union workers may be hired but then must join the union within a specified period of time. (737)

Unit of account The standard unit for quoting prices. (226)

Utility, marginal Of a commodity to a consumer (measured in money terms), is the maximum amount of money he or she is willing to pay for *one more unit* of it. (382)

Utility, total Of a quantity of goods to a consumer (measured in money terms), is the maximum amount of money he or she is willing to give in exchange for it. (382)

Value added The value added by a company is its revenue from selling a product minus the amounts paid for goods and services purchased from other firms. (136)

Variable cost Any cost that is not a fixed cost. (428)

Velocity Number of times per year that an "average dollar" is spent on goods and services; the ratio of nominal GNP to the number of dollars in the money stock. (271)

Vertical equity The notion that differently situated persons should be taxed differently in a way that society deems fair. (648)

Wage-price controls Legal restrictions on the ability of industry and labour to raise wages and prices. (364)

Wage-price freeze An outright ban on wage or price increases. (366)

Wage-price guidelines Numerical standards for permissible wage and price increases. (364)

Welfare state A variety of government programs aimed at assisting the poor and protecting individuals from the rigours of the marketplace. (823)

Workers' management System under which employees of an enterprise make most of the decisions normally reserved for management. (827)

Index

Illustration Credits

Page 11: Greater Vancouver Convention and Visitors' Centre; p. 12: Allmaps Canada Ltd.; p. 15: London School of Economics and Political Science; p. 25: Surveys and Mapping Branch, Energy, Mines and Resources Canada; p. 46: Brown Brothers; p. 53: Historical Pictures Service, Chicago; p. 81: Public Archives Canada/PA 35132; p. 91: Brian Willer; p. 98: From *The Wall Street Journal*, permission Cartoon Features Syndicate; p. 106: Camera Press—PHOTO TRENDS; p. 152: Brown Brothers; p. 217: Reprinted with permission—The Toronto Star Syndicate; p. 225: By permission of Johnny Hart and News America Syndicate; p. 227: The University Museum, University of Pennsylvania; p. 261: The Bank of Canada; p. 301: MacDonald's Corporation; p. 305: © The Image Bank Canada; p. 310: *The New Yorker*; p. 376: Courtesy Canadian Conference of Catholic Bishops; p. 388: Harvard University; p. 413: Brian Willer; p. 439: Photo Centre/Phototheque; p. 512: Krokodil/Sovfoto; p. 515: Miller Services Ltd.; p. 580: Corporate Archives, Canadian Pacific; p. 621: Culver Pictures; p. 635: Culver Pictures; p. 664: Brian Willer; p. 665: EPA; p. 668: Miller Services Ltd.; p. 674: Key Lake Mining Corporation; p. 684: Mobil Oil; p. 714: Brian Willer; p. 738: UPI; p. 754: *The New Yorker*; p. 775: NY Urban Development Corporation; p. 804: HBJ; p. 817: UPI; p. 833: Sovfoto; p. 842: UPI; p. 844: UPI; p. 848: The Bettman Archive.

Every effort has been made to obtain permission for copyright material used in this book and to acknowledge all such indebtedness accurately. Any errors and omissions called to our attention will be corrected in future printings.

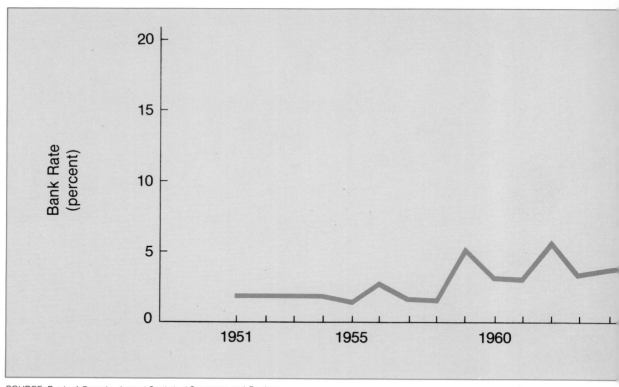

SOURCE: Bank of Canada, *Annual Statistical Summary* and *Review.*
Note: Bank Rate as of June 1 each year.

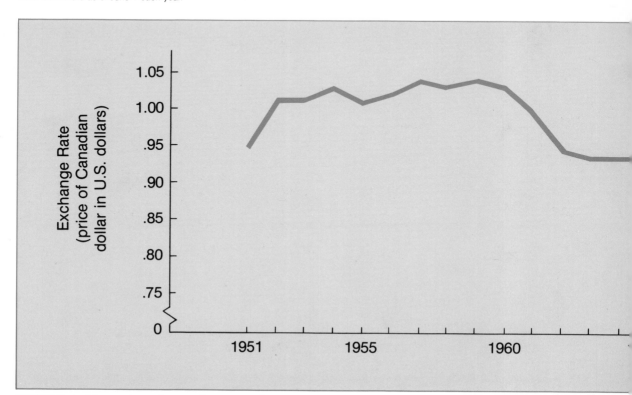

SOURCE: Bank of Canada, *Annual Statistical Summary* and *Review.*
Note: Yearly average noon rate.